Trees and Shrubs

HARDY IN THE BRITISH ISLES

Volume II

D – M

Trees and Shrubs

HARDY IN THE BRITISH ISLES

W. J. BEAN
C.V.O., I.S.O., V.M.H.

Eighth Edition fully revised

GENERAL EDITOR
SIR GEORGE TAYLOR
D.Sc., F.R.S., V.M.H.
Formerly Director of the Royal Botanic Gardens, Kew

Volume II

D – M

JOHN MURRAY

First Edition (Vols I & II) 1914
First Edition (Vol. III) 1933
Seventh Edition 1950

Eighth Edition fully revised (Vol. II) 1973
Published in collaboration with
The Royal Horticultural Society
Revisions and additions for Eighth Edition
© *M. Bean and John Murray (Publishers) Ltd 1973*

Printed in Great Britain by
Butler & Tanner Ltd, Frome and London

0 7195 2256 0

CONTENTS

PREFACE TO VOLUME II

With the publication of Volume II, the preparation of the Eighth Edition is well past half way. As in Volume I Mr Desmond Clarke has continued the most exacting task of coordinating the revision, preparing the final text and reading the proofs. The vital and supreme importance of his efforts cannot be exaggerated. Without his patient and untiring work the revision would long ago have been abandoned. Those of us who have been associated with him in this enterprise are greatly in his debt and were immensely gratified when his notable work for botany and horticulture was recognised by The Royal Horticultural Society in awarding him its highest distinction of the Victoria Medal of Honour in 1972.

Next, most grateful acknowledgement must be made to Mr J. Robert Sealy who has devoted much time and trouble to unravelling the many taxonomic and nomenclatural problems that have arisen. His dedication to the work stems from his memory of working with W. J. Bean and his involvement provides the most important continuity with the earlier editions of the work.

Sadly I have to record the death of Mr Sydney Pearce in 1972 shortly after he retired from Kew. It is a mark of his great courage and interest that only a few weeks before he died he was hoping to help by visiting gardens in the West Country to report on important specimens.

The work of revision has continued to attract much generous help. First, I must thank my friend, Professor J. Heslop Harrison, who is my successor as Director of the Royal Botanic Gardens, Kew, for allowing his staff to devote time to the revision and for permitting access to the facilities of the Kew Herbarium and Library: Mr P. S. Green and Mr C. Jeffrey have given valuable help to revision of the Oleacae and Compositae; Miss Mary Grierson has again provided many new drawings. I should like to take the opportunity of repeating our thanks to the staff of the Royal Horticultural Society; to Miss Margaret Bean; to Mr H. G. Hillier and his assistants, Mr Roy Lancaster and Mr P. H. Gardner; and to Mr Graham Thomas. For measurements of specimen trees we have again relied almost entirely on Mr Alan Mitchell's unique series of records; we are very grateful to him for making them available.

Many of those who were kind enough to give information for Volume I have also given help for Volume II, in particular Mr H. S. J. Crane, Mr T. H. Findlay, Mr Eliot Hodgkin, Captain Collingwood Ingram, Mr Will Ingwersen, Dr Brian Mulligan, Mr C. G. Nice, Mr Leslie Slinger, Mr Patrick Synge, Mr Donald Waterer and Mr David Wright.

Our thanks are due to the following for supplying information for Volume II:

Mr M. C. Bagshawe
Mr R. A. Banks
Dr F. Benčat
Mr H. P. Boddington
Sir Walter Burrell, Bt
Mr J. T. Caller
Mr George Catt
Mr A. Chater
Mr Gordon Clark
Mr F. Constable
Mrs A. Doncaster
Cmdr. T. M. Dorrien-Smith
Mr Maxwell Eley
Mr E. R. Elkin
Mr O. M. Ellis
Mr P. R. Ellis
Mr L. S. Fortescue

Mr Michael Glover
Miss E. Godman
Mr J. Grant
Mr M. Haworth-Booth
Mr P. Horder
Mr Rowland Jackman
Mr F. P. Knight
Mr E. Leyshon
Mr D. McClintock
Mr G. R. Muir
Mr R. Ransom
Mr T. H. Rivers
Mr B. P. Tompsett
Mrs Desmond Underwood
Mr E. J. Wills
Mr G. J. E. Yates

GEORGE TAYLOR

LIST OF DRAWINGS IN TEXT

Those marked with an asterisk were drawn by Miss E. Goldring; the remainder are by Miss Mary Grierson.

ix

APPROXIMATE METRIC EQUIVALENTS

INCHES TO MILLIMETRES

$\frac{1}{32}$ in	=	0·8 mm	$\frac{5}{8}$ in	= 15·9 mm	4 in	= 101 mm
$\frac{1}{16}$	=	1·6	$\frac{3}{4}$	= 19·1	5	= 127
$\frac{1}{8}$	=	3·2	$\frac{7}{8}$	= 22·2	6	= 152
$\frac{3}{16}$	=	4·8	1	= 25·4	7	= 178
$\frac{1}{4}$	=	6·4	$1\frac{1}{4}$	= 31·8	8	= 203
$\frac{5}{16}$	=	7·9	$1\frac{1}{2}$	= 38·1	9	= 229
$\frac{3}{8}$	=	9·5	$1\frac{3}{4}$	= 44·5	10	= 254
$\frac{7}{16}$	=	11·1	2	= 51	11	= 279
$\frac{1}{2}$	=	12·7	3	= 76	12	= 305

FEET TO METRES

2 ft	= 0·61 m	12 ft	= 3·66 m	60 ft	= 18·3 m
3	= 0·91	15	= 4·57	70	= 21·3
4	= 1·22	20	= 6·10	80	= 24·4
5	= 1·52	25	= 7·62	90	= 27·4
6	= 1·83	30	= 9·15	100	= 30·5
7	= 2·13	35	= 10·67	110	= 33·5
8	= 2·44	40	= 12·20	120	= 36·6
9	= 2·74	45	= 13·72	130	= 39·6
10	= 3·05	50	= 15·2	140	= 42·7
11	= 3·55			150	= 45·7

ALTITUDES TO METRES

500 ft	= 152 m	4,000 ft	= 1,219 m
1,000	= 305	5,000	= 1,524
1,500	= 457	10,000	= 3,048
3,000	= 914	15,000	= 4,572

TEMPERATURES: °F TO °C

0 °F	= −17·8 °C	45 °F	= 7·2 °C
10	= −12·2	50	= 10·0
20	= −6·7	55	= 12·8
32	= 0·0	60	= 15·6
40	= 4·4	65	= 18·3
		70	= 21·1

TREE MEASUREMENTS

All measurements of girth were taken at 5 ft (1·52 m) unless otherwise stated.

SOURCES OF PLATES

LIST OF PLATES

61 JASMINUM POLYANTHUM

62 JAMESIA AMERICANA

63 JUGLANS NIGRA

64 JUGLANS REGIA

65 JUNIPERUS RECURVA

66 JUNIPERUS HORIZONTALIS in Glacier National Park, USA

67 JUNIPERUS SQUAMATA 'MEYERI' at Wayford Manor, Somerset

68 KOELREUTERIA PANICULATA

69 KALMIA LATIFOLIA

70 LABURNUM ALPINUM

71 LARIX × EUROLEPIS

72 LARIX DECIDUA at Dunkeld Cathedral, Perthshire

73 LARIX OCCIDENTALIS near Mission Peak, Washington State, USA

74 LEPTOSPERMUM HUMIFUSUM

75 LEDUM GROENLANDICUM

76 LEYCESTERIA FORMOSA

77 LEPTODERMIS KUMAONENSIS

78 LIBOCEDRUS DECURRENS at Westonbirt, Glos.

79 LIGUSTRUM HENRYI

80 LINDERA CERCIDIFOLIA

81 LIRIODENDRON TULIPIFERA

82 LINNAEA BOREALIS

83 LONICERA SEMPERVIRENS

84 LYONIA MARIANA

85 LONICERA TRAGOPHYLLA

86 MAGNOLIA CAMPBELLII

87 MAGNOLIA DENUDATA

88 MAGNOLIA MACROPHYLLA

89 MAGNOLIA SARGENTIANA var. ROBUSTA

90 MAGNOLIA SINENSIS

91 MAGNOLIA × SOULANGIANA

92 MAGNOLIA STELLATA at Kew

1 DACRYDIUM CUPRESSINUM

2 DAPHNE BHOLUA growing in Bhutan

3 Daphne × burkwoodii

4 Daphne retusa

5 DAVIDIA INVOLUCRATA

6 DECAISNEA FARGESII

7 Dendromecon rigida

8 DESFONTAINIA SPINOSA

9 DEUTZIA SETCHUENENSIS

10 Deutzia × hybrida 'Mont Rose'

11 Dipelta floribunda

12 DRIMYS WINTERI

13 Dryas octopetala

14 Edgeworthia chrysantha

15 EHRETIA THYRSIFLORA at Kew

16 EMBOTHRIUM COCCINEUM. A long-leaved form

17 ENKIANTHUS DEFLEXUS in Bhutan, growing with *Clematis montana*

18 A view of the Heather Garden at Wisley

19 Escallonia 'Donard Seedling

20 Erinacea anthyllis

21 ESCALLONIA 'IVEYI'

22 Eucalyptus species at Mount Usher, Co. Wicklow

23 Eucommia ulmoides at Kew

24 EUCRYPHIA × NYMANSENSIS

25 EUODIA DANIELLII at Kew

26 Euonymus latifolius

27 Exochorda × macrantha

28 Fagus sylvatica 'Pendula'
at Kew

29 Fabiana imbricata

30 Fagus sylvatica 'Asplenifolia' at Kew

31 FATSIA JAPONICA

32 FOTHERGILLA MAJOR

33 Fraxinus angustifolia at Kew

34 Fraxinus ornus at Kew

35 Forsythia × intermedia
'Spectabilis'

36 Gaultheria cuneata

37 Gevuina avellana

38 Garrya elliptica

39 Ginkgo biloba at Kew

40 Genista aetnensis

41 Gleditsia sinensis

42 GENISTA LYDIA

43 GLOBULARIA CORDIFOLIA

44 Gordonia axillaris

45 Halesia monticola var. vestita

46 × HALIMIOCISTUS SAHUCII

47 HALIMIUM LASIANTHUM subsp.
FORMOSUM

48 Hamamelis mollis

49 Hoheria 'Glory of Amlwch'

50 Hebe 'Autumn Glory'

51 HYPERICUM 'ROWALLANE'

52 HIBISCUS SYRIACUS 'TOTUS ALBUS'

53 HYDRANGEA PETIOLARIS

54 HYDRANGEA PANICULATA
'FLORIBUNDA'

55 ILEX AQUIFOLIUM 'FEROX
ARGENTEA'

56 Clipped holly in the Rose
Garden at Kew

57 ITEA ILICIFOLIA

58 ILEX CRENATA

59 ITEA VIRGINICA

60 JASMINUM MESNYI

61 JASMINUM POLYANTHUM

62 Jamesia americana

63 Juglans nigra

64 Juglans regia

65 Juniperus recurva

66 Juniperus horizontalis in Glacier National Park, USA

67 Juniperus squamata 'Meyeri' at Wayford Manor, Somerset

68 KOELREUTERIA PANICULATA

69 KALMIA LATIFOLIA

70 Laburnum alpinum

71 Larix × eurolepis

72 LARIX DECIDUA at Dunkeld
Cathedral, Perthshire

73 LARIX OCCIDENTALIS near
Mission Peak, Washington
State, USA

74 Leptospermum humifusum

75 Ledum groenlandicum

76 Leycesteria formosa

77 Leptodermis kumaonensis

78 LIBOCEDRUS DECURRENS at Westonbirt, Glos.

79 LIGUSTRUM HENRYI

80 LINDERA CERCIDIFOLIA

81 Liriodendron tulipifera

82 Linnaea borealis

83 LONICERA SEMPERVIRENS

84 LYONIA MARIANA

85 LONICERA TRAGOPHYLLA

86 MAGNOLIA CAMPBELLII

87 Magnolia denudata

88 Magnolia macrophylla

89 Magnolia sargentiana var. robusta

90 Magnolia sinensis

91 MAGNOLIA × SOULANGIANA

92 MAGNOLIA STELLATA at Kew

93 Magnolia × soulangiana 'Rustica Rubra'

94 MAGNOLIA VIRGINIANA

95 MAHONIA LOMARIIFOLIA

96 Malus baccata at Kew

97 Malus prunifolia var. rinki

98 MELIOSMA VEITCHIORUM

99 MELIOSMA CUNEIFOLIA

100 MENZIESIA CILIICALYX
var. PURPUREA

101 Mespilus germanica

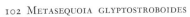

102 Metasequoia glyptostroboides

103 Morus nigra

104 Moltkia petraea

105 Mutisia oligodon

106 Myrtus nummularia

DABOECIA ERICACEAE

A genus of two species, one of Atlantic Europe from Ireland to Portugal, the other of the Azores. Although classed with the heaths (*Erica* and *Calluna*) in gardens, it is more closely allied to such genera as *Phyllodoce*. Among ericaceous genera of heath-like habit it is distinguished by the elongated, racemose inflorescence; deciduous, urn-shaped corollas, and by the septicidal capsules.

D. AZORICA Tutin & E. F. Warb.

An evergreen shrub of more or less procumbent habit, apparently usually under 1 ft high; young shoots very slender, glandular-hairy. Leaves linear-ovate, bluntish, averaging about ¼ in. long, made very narrow by the rolling back of the margins, dark green and sprinkled with glandular hairs above, covered with white down beneath; leaf-stalk glandular bristly. Flowers in an erect, very glandular raceme 2 to 3 in. long, carrying four to ten flowers. Corolla roundish egg-shaped, ¼ to ⅜ in. long, deep red, nodding, borne on a glandular stalk ⅜ in. long. *Bot. Mag.*, n.s., t. 46.

Native of the Azores, especially on the islands of Fayal and Pico. It was introduced from the latter in 1929 by E. F. Warburg, and was exhibited in flower from Sir Oscar Warburg's garden at Boidier, near Epsom, at Westminster, on 7th June 1932. It is nearly akin botanically to *D. cantabrica*, but the distinct colour of the flowers (which have no purple), the dwarf habit and small leaves distinguish it. It also comes into bloom rather earlier and is less hardy, being damaged or killed in any severe winter.

Spontaneous hybrids between this species and *D. cantabrica* arose around 1953 in the garden of W. Buchanan of Bearsden, Glasgow, and have been put into commerce by Jack Drake of Aviemore. Of the three clones propagated, No. 3 is considered by him to be the best, and the nearest to *D. azorica*, from which it differs, however, in its much greater hardiness; the habit is dwarf and the flowers 'garnet-red'. No. 1 is also distinct and after trial at Wisley was considered to be the better of the two. It has been named 'WILLIAM BUCHANAN'.

D. CANTABRICA (Huds.) K. Koch

Vaccinium cantabricum Huds.; *D. polifolia* D. Don; *Erica daboecia* L.

An evergreen shrub up to 2 ft high, with slender, erect stems, furnished with glandular hairs. Leaves alternate, ovate-oblong, ¼ to ⅜ in. long, $\frac{1}{10}$ to ¼ in. wide, tapering at both ends, very dark glossy green and with a few scattered hairs above, covered beneath with a close white wool; stalk scarcely evident. During the summer a cluster of two or three small leaves comes in the axil of each leaf. Flowers produced from June to November in erect, terminal, glandular racemes, ultimately 3 to 5 in. long. Corolla broadly egg-shaped, ⅜ to ½ in. long, contracted at the mouth, where are four tiny reflexed lobes, rosy purple. Calyx with four

B   1

glandular, hairy divisions, which are ⅛ in. long. Seed-vessel four-celled, hairy; flower-stalk ¼ in. long.

Native of W. Europe, including Ireland, where it is found in Connemara. This beautiful little shrub is one of the most valuable we possess, flowering as it does from late June until after the autumn frosts come. It makes a charming picture planted in large patches, either of one sort, or more mixed. It may be propagated by seed, and its varieties by cuttings. The plants are better if pruned over in early spring, so as to remove the old flower-spikes and part of the previous year's shoots. This tends to keep them closer in habit and more effective in blossom. It likes a peaty soil or a light, sandy loam, free from lime, with which leaf-mould has been mixed.

f. ALBA (D. Don) Dipp. *D. polifolia* var. *alba* D. Don—Flowers pure white; such plants are found wild with the type and said to produce white-flowered seedlings. The plant to which Don gave the name was found in Connemara *c.* 1832 (Sweet's *Brit. Flow. Gard.*, t. 276). As seen in cultivation, the white form is hardier than the type, with vividly green leaves that never burn or turn purple in the winter; it is also very floriferous and altogether one of the finest of dwarf ericaceous shrubs.

cv. 'ALBA GLOBOSA'.—The plant dwarfer and more spreading than the type; corolla larger, almost spherical, white.

f. ATROPURPUREA Dipp.—Flowers richer red-purple than in the type.

cv. 'BICOLOR'.—This variety has some of its flowers white, others purple, whilst others are partly white and partly purple; all on the same plant.

cv. 'PRAEGERAE'.—A less robust plant than the type, with flowers of a deep, pure pink. Discovered by Mrs Praeger in Connemara and put into commerce around 1948.

DACRYDIUM   PODOCARPACEAE

Evergreen unisexual trees chiefly natives of Australasia, but occurring also in Chile, Borneo, and the Malay Peninsula; the genus includes altogether about twenty species. They are related to *Podocarpus*, which they resemble in producing the seed in a fleshy, cup-shaped receptacle. The leaves vary from scale-like ones (such as are common in the cypresses) on old trees to linear or awl-shaped ones on young trees.

D. BIDWILLII Hook. f.

An evergreen shrub up to 10 ft high, closely branched; sometimes erect and pyramidal, sometimes prostrate with the lower branches taking root. Leaves of two kinds: those of young plants and of the lower branches of older ones flat, linear, abruptly pointed, ¼ to ⅓ in. long; on mature plants they become small, scale-like, closely pressed to the stem like those of a cypress, triangular, blunt and thick, but only 1/24 to 1/12 in. long. Male flowers solitary, stalkless, 1/10 to ⅛ in. long, terminal. Female flowers close to the tips of the branches ultimately developing one or two small compressed nuts about 1/12 in. long set in a fleshy white cup.

Native of the mountainous districts of the North Island of New Zealand; also of the South Island at from 2,000 to 4,500 ft altitude. This shrub is little known in cultivation but appears to be fairly hardy. There are small examples in the National Pinetum, Bedgebury; and at Wakehurst Place, Sussex.

D. CUPRESSINUM Lamb.   RIMU   [PLATE 1

An evergreen tree up to 100 (sometimes more) ft high, with a trunk 2 to 5 ft in diameter. When young, and as we know it in this country, it is of thinly furnished, slender habit, with long, thin, quite pendulous branches, but it is described as forming a comparatively round-topped head at maturity. The dark brown bark is shed in large flakes. Leaves of young trees awl-shaped, ⅛ to ¼ in. long, densely arranged all round the branchlets forty or more to the inch, their overlapping bases completely covering the stem. On old trees the leaves become much smaller, 1/12 to ⅛ in. long, blunter pointed and more appressed to the stem. The trees are unisexual and on female ones the flowers are borne singly at the recurved tips of the twigs, eventually developing an egg-shaped seed about ⅛ in. long, set in a cup-shaped, often (but not always) fleshy receptacle.

Native of both islands of New Zealand up to 2,500 ft altitude and known there as the 'Rimu' or 'red pine'; discovered during Capt. Cook's first expedition about 1770. Its timber is much used for furniture and house-building. It is one of the fine trees of the Dominion, and Cheeseman records that Sir David Hutchinson found two trees in the Westland forests that were 198 ft and 168 ft high respectively. As a young tree it is very distinct and graceful, its pale green branchlets (with the leaves) ¼ in. or so in diameter hanging undivided 1 to 2 ft in length. It is only hardy in the milder counties and even there does not really thrive. The best specimen recorded is one of 20 ft on Garinish Island (Illnacullin), Eire.

D. FRANKLINII Hook. f.   HUON PINE

An evergreen unisexual tree of straight pyramidal shape up to 100 ft high in Tasmania, with a trunk 3 to 6 ft in diameter. In a comparatively young state in cultivation it is a graceful plant with arching branches and pendulous twigs. Leaves about 1/24 in. long, blunt, closely pressed to the stem like those of a cypress, sharply keeled so as to give a rather quadrangular shape to the twig, sprinkled with stomata. The female cones are very small and are clustered at the recurved ends of the twigs.

Native of Tasmania, often on the banks of rivers; first collected by Allan Cunningham in 1810; cultivated at Kew in the forties of last century. It was named in honour of Sir John Franklin, the Arctic explorer, and is the most valuable timber tree of the island.

Like some other southern hemisphere conifers it has proved hardy enough in the milder parts of the country, but grows slowly and gives no promise of developing into more than a small bushy tree, though a very decorative one none the less. Of the examples mentioned in earlier editions, the tree at Cold-rennick, Cornwall, is now dead, after taking a century to reach a height of 22 ft; the specimen at Borde Hill, Sussex, 10 ft high in 1939, is only a little taller now (1971), but suffered no damage in recent hard winters; one of those planted in the National Pinetum, Bedgebury, in 1926 still survives and is 14 ft high (1971). The tallest known are at Castlewellan, Co. Down, and at Fota, Co. Cork, Eire, both 28 ft high (the latter planted in 1854). Other examples can be seen at Leonardslee and Sheffield Park, Sussex; and at Bodnant, Denbigh.

DANAË   LILIACEAE

A genus of one species, closely allied to *Ruscus*. It is, however, quite distinct in its terminal inflorescence, bisexual flowers, and unarmed 'leaves'. The so-called 'leaves', as in *Ruscus*, are really flattened branches (phylloclades), but perfectly resemble leaves and serve the same functions. The flowers have a small whitish perianth (receptacle) with six short lobes; there is a fleshy rim below the lobes, and below this the stamens arise, their filaments united to form a tube; the ovary is rounded, the style short and slender, with a capitate stigma; the fruit is a fleshy berry.

DANAË RACEMOSA

D. RACEMOSA (L.) Moench   ALEXANDRIAN LAUREL
Ruscus racemosus L.; *D. laurus* Med.

An elegant evergreen shrub 2 to 4 ft high, with green, slender, erect or spreading semi-woody stems, once-branched and quite glabrous. 'Leaves' alternate, oblong-lanceolate, $1\frac{1}{2}$ to 4 in. long, $\frac{1}{4}$ to $1\frac{1}{2}$ in. wide; bright green on both surfaces, taper-pointed, abruptly narrowed at the base but scarcely stalked. Flowers greenish yellow, small, bisexual, produced four to six together at the end of the branches each on a stalk, $\frac{1}{8}$ in. long. Fruit a berry, $\frac{1}{4}$ in. across, red, with a pale, saucer-shaped disk at the base.

Native of N. Persia and Asia Minor; introduced in 1713. It is a pretty evergreen with a rather bamboo-like habit. The sprays are valuable for winter cutting, and placed in vases in association with flowers, remain fresh a long time, and very pleasing in their cheerful, polished green. The plant thrives well in semi-shaded spots in moist soil. Its fruits are not borne regularly with us, but seeds can be purchased from seedsmen. Failing them, it is easily increased by division in spring.

DAPHNE   THYMELAEACEAE

A genus of small, beautiful, mostly fragrant-flowered shrubs, both evergreen and deciduous; with tough, flexible bark and young wood. Leaves alternate, except in *D. genkwa*, never toothed or divided, and with little or no stalk. Flowers very like those of a lilac, in having a tubular base, expanding at the mouth into four spreading lobes. (There is only one floral envelope, and it is usually called the 'calyx' or 'perianth'.) They are produced in terminal heads or axillary clusters. Stamens eight, in two rows of four. Fruit berry-like, one-seeded. The outside of the flower is frequently hairy, the inside frosted or glistening. Most of the cultivated daphnes are European, and are usually found on limestone. A few are Asiatic. None is found in N. America, but *Dirca palustris* of the eastern United States is a near ally.

Whilst some of the daphnes are easy to cultivate, others are found by many growers and in many places to be difficult to establish. Most of the European species prefer a neutral soil; they also like good drainage combined with abundant moisture. A soil of good sandy loam is likely to suit the majority. In places like the Thames Valley, where there are frequently hot dry spells during the summer, small pieces of stone are useful laid over the roots to conserve moisture. The majority like abundant sunshine whilst they abhor dryness at the root. *Daphne laureola* and *pontica* grow well in semi-shaded spots. The rock garden affords an admirable site for all the dwarfer species. All or nearly all transplant badly, and should be given permanent places early.

Most of the evergreen species can be increased by cuttings taken in June or early July; *D. blagayana* by layering; and *D. cneorum* by either method.

D. mezereum is propagated by seed, which should be harvested as soon as the fruits show colour and sown immediately; owing to the increasing prevalence of virus disease it is important that seed should only be taken from vigorous and healthy specimens. Any other species that produces fruit may be increased in the same way. Grafting is also resorted to, and generally *D. mezereum* seedlings for the deciduous ones and seedlings of *D. laureola* for the evergreen ones, though the former may be used for both. See further under *D. petraea*.

It has, however, to be admitted that many of the daphnes are still untamed wildings. In some places a few species find the conditions so suitable that they thrive without any special care. But I know of no place where the cultivation of all the daphnes, or even the hardier ones, has been satisfactorily achieved. It is quite possible also that, like many shrubs that flower with the same profusion, they are naturally short-lived.

There has been no botanical study of the genus since Keissler published his monograph on the section *Daphnanthes* (*Bot. Jahrb.*, Vol. 25, 1898, pp. 29–125). For an authoritative horticultural survey see: Eliot Hodgkin in *Journ. R.H.S.*, Vol. 86, 1961, pp. 481–488. Mr Hodgkin has provided us with useful comments and information during the preparation of this volume. An earlier study by A. M. Amsler will be found in Vol. 78, 1953, pp. 5–18.

D. ACUTILOBA Rehd.

An evergreen shrub 4 to 8 ft high, with an often bi-forked branching; young shoots covered with pale, forward-pointing bristles, becoming glabrous and purplish brown the second season. Leaves leathery, mostly oblanceolate or lanceolate, tapered to both ends, pointed, 2 to 4 in. long, ½ to 1 in. wide, glossy and quite glabrous on both surfaces; scarcely stalked. Flowers white, borne during July in stalked heads of six or more at, or near, the apex of the shoots; perianth tubular, ¾ in. long, ⅜ in. wide across the four narrowly ovate-oblong lobes, not downy; flower-stalks bristly. Fruit at first scarlet, then dark red.

Native of China; introduced by Wilson in 1907–8 from Hupeh and Szechwan. It is related closely to *D. odora* but is inferior to that species as regards its blossom, which has no fragrance (or only an intermittent one); the fruit, however, is handsome.

D. ALPINA L.

A dwarf, deciduous shrub 6 to 18 in. high, with short, erect, downy twigs. Leaves oblanceolate, ½ to 1¼ in. long, ⅛ to ⅓ in. wide, often crowded towards the end of the shoot, grey-green, downy on both sides. Flowers white, fragrant, produced during May and June in terminal clusters of six to ten, the cylindrical, slender tube ⅓ in. long, downy outside; the four lobes lanceolate, pointed; fruit yellowish red, rather downy.

Native of the European Alps; in cultivation 1759. Suitable for the rock garden, especially in association with limestone, on which formation it is always found. A neat plant of no great beauty, but pleasing for its fragrance.

D. ALTAICA Pall.

A low, deciduous shrub with glabrous shoots and leaves, the latter oblanceolate or narrowly oblong, pointed, $1\frac{1}{2}$ to $2\frac{1}{2}$ in. long, $\frac{3}{8}$ to $\frac{5}{8}$ in. wide, glabrous. Flowers only slightly scented, usually five to ten in a terminal cluster; white, $\frac{1}{2}$ in. in diameter, downy outside; perianth segments reflexed; ovary glabrous; fruit red.

Native of the Altai Mountains; discovered about 1780. It is closely allied to *D. caucasica*, but is considered to differ in having a looser, less silky down on the corolla-tube. As represented in cultivation, *D. altaica* has larger, more pointed leaves, fewer flowers on an average in the cluster, and does not produce a crowd of short flowering twigs from the previous year's shoot, as does *D. caucasica*. The two, however, are probably geographical forms of the one species, to which *D. sophia* (q.v.) also belongs. Another close ally is:

D. LONGILOBATA (Lecomte) Turrill *D. altaica* var. *longilobata* Lecomte—A southern relative of *D. altaica*, differing in its evergreen leaves, which, especially when young, bear a tuft of hairs near the apex. The perianth lobes are lanceolate and acute (ovate-lanceolate and obtuse in *D. altaica*). The plant at Kew figured in *Bot. Mag.*, n.s., t. 344, is of unknown origin, but the species has been introduced by Ludlow, Sherriff and Elliot from S.E. Tibet in 1947 under their No. 15803 and was in cultivation in 1928, probably from seeds collected by Forrest in Yunnan. The species is hardy in the south of England but of little worth as a decorative plant.

D. AURANTIACA Diels

An evergreen shrub up to 5 ft high in the wild; leaves, shoots and flowers free from down. Leaves oval to obovate or oblong, pointed, tapered at the base to a very short stalk, margins recurved, $\frac{1}{3}$ to $\frac{5}{8}$ in. long, $\frac{1}{8}$ to $\frac{3}{8}$ in. wide, dull green above, pale and rather glaucous beneath with the green midrib prominently raised there. Flowers bright orange-yellow, fragrant, slenderly tubular, $\frac{1}{2}$ in. long, expanding at the mouth into four broadly ovate lobes and there $\frac{3}{16}$ in. wide. They are produced in May at the end of the shoots in twos or threes from the leaf-axils, making altogether a leafy panicle 2 or 3 in. long and 1 in. wide. *Bot. Mag.*, t. 9313.

Native of S.W. China; discovered by Forrest in 1906 growing in crevices of limestone cliffs at 10,000 to 12,000 ft altitude on the eastern flank of the Lichiang Range. At Werrington Park in Cornwall it was successfully cultivated by being planted in small openings of a retaining wall where its roots had access to the soil behind. Grown thus it made plants up to 6 ft across. It was given a First Class Certificate when shown by A. K. Bulley at Chelsea in May 1927. It is tender.

D. BHOLUA Buch.-Ham.   [PLATE 2
D. cannabina Wall., in part

A sparsely branched evergreen or deciduous shrub up to 12 ft high. Leaves borne near the tips of the branchlets, on very short stalks, elliptic-lanceolate to oblanceolate, 2 to 4 in. long, pointed or bluntly acuminate at the apex, tapered at the base, thinly leathery. Flowers fragrant, borne from midwinter to spring in terminal and axillary clusters; perianth-tube slender, downy on the outside, about ½ in. long, purplish pink. Fruit ovoid, black. Native of the Himalaya; apparently first introduced in the thirties. It flowered with the late Fred Stoker in 1938 and was given an Award of Merit when shown by Mrs Stoker on 3rd Dec. 1946. It is also in cultivation from seeds sent by Dr Herklots from Nepal in 1962. Plants from this introduction may not prove hardy. In the same year, however, Major Spring Smyth collected and sent to England (under Field Number T.S.S. 132 A–C) three seedlings that he found growing at 10,000 ft on the Milke Banjyang ridge, Nepal, where severe frosts and snowstorms occur during winter. Of these plants, which are deciduous, one has flourished in the introducer's garden in Hampshire.

The colouring of the flowers in *D. bholua* is variable. They are said to be normally purplish pink on the outside, with a paler limb, but in some forms the colouring is diluted to almost white. The bark of *D. bholua* is used for making paper in the Himalaya. There are two related species whose bark is put to the same use, and might, with *D. bholua*, be known collectively as the 'paper-daphnes'. These are:

D. PAPYRACEA Wall. ex Steud., emend. W. W. Sm. & Cave *D. cannabina* Wall., in part—This differs from *D. bholua* in having the leaves bluntly acute (not acuminate), flowers white, not fragrant, and red fruits. Also the floral bud-scales are persistent, whereas in *D. bholua* they fall as the flower-buds open. It has a more western distribution, from around the Indus eastward to Nepal, whereas *D. bholua* ranges from Nepal eastward to Assam. Where the two species meet in Nepal is not certain.

D. SUREIL W. W. Sm. & Cave—This species occurs in the same area as *D. bholua* but at lower altitudes (up to about 6,000 ft). The flowers are white, fragrant, the bud-scales deciduous, and the fruits orange-red. The leaves are more slenderly pointed than in either of the two other species in this group. Certainly tender. *Bot. Mag.*, t. 9297.

D. BLAGAYANA Freyer

A dwarf, evergreen shrub of spreading habit, rarely more than 1 ft high. Leaves stalkless, aggregated in a tuft at the end of the twig, narrowly obovate, tapered towards the base, rounded at the apex, 1 to 1¾ in. long, ⅓ to ¾ in. wide, glabrous on both surfaces. Flowers creamy white, very fragrant, produced in March and April, crowded in a head of twenty to thirty blossoms at the end of the twig and about 2 in. across, consisting of several umbels, subtended by thin, greenish, silky bracts. Flowers ½ in. in diameter; the lobes broadly ovate, ¼ in.

long; the tube ⅝ to ¾ in. long, slenderly cylindrical, slightly silky. Fruit pinkish white, rarely seen in cultivation. *Bot. Mag.*, t. 7579.

Native of northern Greece, Yugoslavia, Bulgaria and Rumania; discovered by Count Blagay on his estate in Slovenia in 1837; introduced about 1875. This beautiful and sweet-scented daphne has perhaps nowhere been so successfully cultivated as in the Glasnevin Botanic Gardens. It was there planted on low mounds composed of stones and loam from a granite district. The secret of success appears to be in the continuous layering of the shoots. As soon as the young growths are an inch or so long, the previous summer's branches are weighed down to the ground by placing stones on them. A little soil may come between. By this system the whole plant is always renewing its root system at the younger parts. The late Sir Frederick Moore, then the Keeper of the garden, did not consider that this daphne needs lime. He recommended good loam or peat and leaf-soil, and partial shade.

D. blagayana no longer succeeds at Glasnevin, and there seems to be no plant in British gardens at the present time that can compare with the one mentioned above in health or vigour. Mr Hodgkin suggests as a possible reason that the stock has deteriorated, perhaps through virus infection.

D. × BURKWOODII Turrill [PLATE 3

A hybrid between *D. caucasica* and *D. cneorum*, raised by Albert Burkwood in his garden at Kingston-on-Thames, Surrey, the pollen parent being *D. caucasica*. Only three seeds resulted but all germinated. One plant was retained by Mr Burkwood and taken with him to Poole, to which he moved shortly afterwards, and was shown at Vincent Square on May 21, 1935, when it received an Award of Merit. The clone descended from this plant should be distinguished as 'ALBERT BURKWOOD'. The other two plants were the share of his brother, the late Arthur Burkwood; of these one died but the other survived and is the original plant of the clone 'SOMERSET', which received an Award of Merit in 1937 when shown by Messrs Scott of Merriott, who put it into commerce. For this information we are indebted to Mr Albert Burkwood.

The two clones are very similar and both are excellent garden plants. They take after *D. cneorum* in foliage and their sweetly scented flowers, which are pale pink in colour. The object of Mr Burkwood and his brother was to combine the floral characters of *D. cneorum* with the habit of the taller-growing *D. caucasica* and in this they succeeded. Both forms of the cross make vigorous bushes to at least 3 ft high, but of the two 'Somerset' is said to make the larger plant, attaining 4 ft in height and more across. The foliage in both is semi-evergreen and in this respect intermediate between the two parents.

D. × *burkwoodii* is figured in *Bot. Mag.*, n.s., t. 55, where the late Dr Turrill points out that the cross is an interesting one, combining as it does the sub-section *Alpinae*, to which *D. caucasica* belongs, with the subsection *Cneorum*.

D. CAUCASICA Pall.

A deciduous shrub up to 4 to 6 ft high, with flowering twigs downy; barren young twigs less so, or glabrous. Leaves produced along the entire shoot, oblanceolate, tapered at the base and oftener rounded than tapered at the apex, 1 to 1¾ in. long, ⅓ to ½ in. wide; glabrous, pale green above, somewhat glaucous beneath. Flowers glistening white, fragrant, produced during May and June in terminal heads of usually four to twenty blossoms; the perianth ⅓ in. across, with ovate lobes; tubes ⅓ in. long, cylindrical, silky outside; ovary slightly downy. *Bot. Mag.*, t. 7388.

Native of the Caucasus; many times introduced and lost. It is not outstanding, but is pleasing in its fragrance and for its abundant flower-clusters borne at the end of crowded, short, leafy shoots springing from the previous year's growth. It differs from *D. alpina* in its glabrous leaves.

D. CNEORUM L.   GARLAND FLOWER

An evergreen trailing shrub, producing a great number of long, slender, minutely downy branches, densely clothed with leaves, and forming a low, spreading mass under 1 ft high. Leaves oblanceolate, with a tapering base and broadly wedge-shaped apex, ending in a minute bristle-like tip, ¾ to 1 in. long, ⅛ to ⅕ in. wide, dark green above, greyish beneath, glabrous. Flowers crowded in a dense terminal cluster, numerous, scarcely stalked; they are fragrant and rich rosy pink, the tube ⅜ in. long, very downy outside, the expanded part ⅜ in. across, with ovate-oblong lobes. Blossoms in May. *Bot. Mag.*, t. 313.

Native of Europe from Spain to S.W. Russia; cultivated 1752. It is the best and most useful of the evergreen species, from all the rest of which grown in gardens it is distinguished by its lax, prostrate habit. It flowers with remarkable freedom, the leaves being almost entirely hidden by bloom. It likes a permanently moist root-run, and apparently thrives well in calcareous soil. Some of the healthiest plants I have seen in the London district were (some years ago) in one of the plots under the control of the London County Council on Plumstead Common, Kent. This place is on a limestone formation, and is perhaps 200 ft above the Thames. The plants had, apparently, treatment similar to that meted out to privets and such-like, but were in rude health. At the same time it succeeds splendidly in the R.H.S. Garden at Wisley, where the soil is a sandy peat. It is a good plan to layer the outer shoots by placing stones on them, as recommended for *D. blagayana*.

cv. 'ALBA'.—Flowers white. It received an Award of Merit when shown by Messrs Tucker in 1920. The plant now in commerce resembles the var. *pygmaea* in habit.

f. ARBUSCULOIDES Tuzson—Habit rather erect and leaf-margins revolute. This variant has been recorded from W. Hungary, S.E. Austria and N. Yugoslavia and is said to be confined to acid soils. For this information we are indebted to the revision of *Daphne* in *Flora Europaea*, Vol. 2 (1968), p. 258, where it is suggested that this variant may perhaps deserve recognition as a subspecies.

cv. 'EXIMIA'.—Flowers larger than in the type, deep pink; it is also somewhat larger in leaf. The parent of this clone was one of a number of collected plants supplied to the late A. T. Johnson by Stormonth's nursery, Carlisle. It was given an Award of Merit in 1938 and a First Class Certificate in 1967. What was apparently a similar form (at least in size of flower and leaf) was described by Dippel in the last century as var. *major*.

var. PYGMAEA Stoker—Smaller in all its parts than the type; perianth tube irregularly wrinkled on the outside. Described by the late Fred Stoker from plants found and collected by him in the Venetian Alps at 8,000 ft (*The New Flora and Sylva*, Vol. 7, p. 275). Dwarf forms of *D. cneorum* found in the calcareous pre-Alps of S.E. France are discussed by Ruffier-Lanche in the article referred to below under var. *verlotii* (for an important correction to the text of this article see op. cit., Vol. 27, p. 156). A dwarf form of diffuse habit, with deep pink flowers, was introduced from the Pyrenees.

var. VERLOTII (Gren. & Godr.) Meissn. *D. verlotii* Gren. & Godr.—A distinct variety. Leaves up to 1 in. long but rarely more than ⅛ in. wide. Lobes of perianth lanceolate-linear, three times longer than wide, rose-coloured inside and out; tube to ⅜ in. long. Found by Verlot at St-Eynard near Grenoble and described in 1856. The distribution of this variety is uncertain, but plants found in Bavaria, Switzerland, etc., are referred to it by Hegi (*Fl. Mitteleuropa*, Vol. 5, p. 717) and by Keissler (op. cit., p. 80). For a further discussion see Eliot Hodgkin in *Bull. A.G.S.*, Vol. 25, p. 319. Also R. Ruffier-Lanche, ibid., Vol. 26, p. 65, in which other variants of *D. cneorum* found wild in France are discussed.

D. JULIA Kozo-Polianski—Although recognised as a species in the Flora of the Soviet Union, this daphne is very near to *D. cneorum* and indeed less distinct from the normal form of that species than is var. *verlotii*. Of the characters by which Kozo-Polianski distinguished his species from *D. cneorum* the most marked would seem to be the narrower leaves and the more congested inflorescences, with up to twenty-five flowers in each. This daphne is, however, of great interest to plant geographers, being a local endemic found in a restricted area from north-west to south-west of Voronezh (commonest near Barkalovka) and forming part of the remarkable flora referred to under *D. sophia*. Its habitat is on open slopes at a few hundred feet above sea-level, where it grows in limestone rubble or lime-rich black-earth (chernozem) in a steppe-like vegetation which contains, however, many species which, like the daphne, are alien to the steppe.

D. julia was introduced to this country by Eliot Hodgkin, who received four plants from Moscow in 1960. One of these grew to be 3 ft across in the garden of the late E. B. Anderson.

D. COLLINA Smith

An evergreen bush 2 to 3 ft high, of bushy habit; young shoots silky-hairy. Leaves obovate, tapered at the base, mostly rounded or blunt at the apex; ¾ to 1¾ in. long, ¼ to ⅝ in. wide, dark glossy green above, pale and very hairy beneath. Flowers fragrant, purplish rose, produced in a terminal head of ten to fifteen blossoms; they are ½ in. across, and felted with silky hairs outside; lobes roundish ovate; ovary silky. *Bot. Mag.*, t. 428.

Native of the Mediterranean region, with two main areas of distribution, one on the west coast of Italy from Tuscany to the Naples area and the other in

Crete and southern Asia Minor; cultivated in 1752. In previous editions of this work it was stated that *D. collina* is 'not very hardy'. This may have been true of the form known to the author (the species has a wide range and may well vary in this respect). But the form current in gardens at the present time appears to be perfectly hardy, though, like most daphnes, not long-lived.

D. SERICEA Vahl is very closely allied to the preceding and the two might well be considered to be states of one species. Typically, *D. sericea* differs in its generally shorter and narrower leaves, which are thinly silky-hairy beneath, and by its fewer (six to eight) flowers; other points of difference are given by Keissler, but are not reliable. *D. sericea* appears to have much the same natural range as *D. collina*.

D. GENKWA Sieb. & Zucc.
D. fortuni Lindl.

A deciduous shrub probably 3 or 4 ft high, the erect, slender, sparsely branched shoots covered with silky hairs when young. Leaves oval to lanceolate, from 1 to 2 in. long, ⅓ to ⅝ in. wide; pointed, silky-hairy beneath, short-stalked; mostly opposite, occasionally alternate. Flowers lilac-coloured, produced during May at the joints of the naked wood of the previous year in stalked clusters, the stalks up to ½ in. long, silky. There are from three to seven flowers in each cluster, the tube ⅓ to ½ in. long, slender, silky-hairy outside, the expanded portion ½ in. across. Ovary usually silky-hairy, more rarely partly glabrous. *Bot. Mag.*, n.s., t. 360.

Introduced from China by Fortune in 1843, and later from Japan, where it has long been cultivated but is not native. Unfortunately it is short-lived in cultivation. The flower is very like that of a common lilac in form and colour, and when the shoots are well furnished with them the plant is a beautiful object. Shoots 1½ ft long are sometimes made in a season, the upper two-thirds of which will be covered with blossom. These long, slender wands of blossom, the comparatively long-stalked clusters, and especially the opposite leaves, make this daphne very distinct. It is said to require a soil devoid of chalky substances, but its treatment is little understood.

In the New York Botanic Garden there is a remarkable example of this species 10 ft in diameter, which has grown in the open there for more than thirty years and receives no winter protection. Plants from this source are now in cultivation in Britain but have not so far proved better adapted to our climate than the form previously grown. It is probable that *D. genkwa* is one of those species that fail in this country not through any inherent tenderness but from lack of summer heat and sun. The average July temperature in New York is 74°F, at Kew 63°F— a very significant difference. Mr B. N. Starling, in an interesting letter, suggests that abundant moisture during the growing season is also desirable, remarking that in China this daphne is often found growing at the margins of ricefields. It is also more than probable that it resents stagnant moisture at the root during the winter. A deep, rubbly, well-drained soil in a warm corner, artificially watered during the growing season, are perhaps the conditions that would best suit this beautiful species.

D. GIRALDII Nitsche

A deciduous shrub up to 2½ ft high, of bushy growth, free from down in all its parts. Leaves stalkless, oblanceolate, blunt or pointed, with a minute tip, tapered at the base, 1½ to 3 in. long, ¼ to ⅝ in. wide. Flowers rather fragrant, golden yellow, produced during May in clusters terminating leafy young shoots, four to eight in a cluster. The flower has a tubular base ¼ to ⅓ in. long, dividing at the top into four spreading lobes each ⅛ in. long; quite glabrous and scarcely stalked. Fruit egg-shaped, ¼ in. wide, red. *Bot. Mag.*, t. 8732.

Native of N. Shensi and Kansu, China; discovered by Père Giraldi in the former province in 1894; introduced from Kansu by W. Purdom in 1911. It is a beautiful daphne especially to be prized for its yellow flowers. (*D. aurantiaca*, also with rich yellow flowers, is very distinct from it in its evergreen much smaller foliage.) It was first raised from Purdom's seeds in Veitch's Coombe Wood nursery and first flowered in this country by Lord Wakehurst, in Sussex, in 1916, by which date it was 2½ ft high and 4 ft wide. It is quite hardy but difficult to cultivate successfully.

D. × HOUTTEANA Lindl.
D. laureola purpurea Hort.; *D. mezereum* var. *atropurpurea* Dipp.

There seems to be little doubt that this is a hybrid between *D. mezereum* and *D. laureola*. It was first described and figured by Louis Van Houtte, in the *Flore des Serres*, t. 592, in 1850, but he did not know its origin or even venture to give it a name. He alludes to it as "*D. mezereum foliis atropurpureis* of several gardens". It has since been mostly called *D. laureola purpurea*, but is distinct from both species.

A partially evergreen shrub, 2 to 4 ft high, with stiff, erect branches. Leaves usually crowded towards the tip of the shoot, and resembling those of *D. laureola* in size, shape, and texture, but of a dark purplish tinge. Flowers pale lilac, produced two to five together in short-stalked clusters. At the time of flowering (April) there usually remain a few purple leaves of the preceding summer's growth. It is from the axils of these and the buds beneath them that the flowers are borne. There is also a form with deep-purple flowers.

D. × HYBRIDA Sweet
D. dauphinii Hort.

This is an evergreen shrub with very much the aspect of *D. odora*, between which and *D. collina* it is supposed to be a hybrid. Its leaves are narrowly oval, 1 to 3 in. long, glossy green above, glabrous. Flowers in a terminal cluster, very fragrant, about the size of those of *odora* and of a similar colour (reddish purple), but readily distinguished from those of that species by the hairiness of the tube outside, also of the lobes. This character it inherits from *D. collina*. This hybrid daphne is somewhat hardier than *D. odora*, but is not really happy out-of-doors near London, needing at least winter shelter there. It is essentially a south and west country evergreen. Propagated by cuttings. *Bot. Mag.*, n.s., t. 320.

D. LAUREOLA L.   SPURGE LAUREL

An evergreen shrub of bushy habit 2 to 4 ft high, devoid of down in all its parts. Leaves oblanceolate, tapered gradually to the base, more abruptly to the point; from 1½ to 4½ in. long, ½ to 1½ in. wide, dark lustrous green, and of thick, firm texture. Flowers yellowish green, fragrant at times, opening in February and March; they are borne in clusters of three to eight blossoms, each cluster on a common stalk about ½ in. long, springing from the axils of the uppermost leaves of the preceding year's growth. Flowers ⅓ in. long, ¼ in. diameter. Fruit ovoid, bluish black when ripe, poisonous.

Native of S. and W. Europe, including England, and of N. Africa and the Azores. It prefers a moist soil and semi-shade, and is useful in woodland, chiefly for its shining evergreen foliage, for the flowers are only intermittently fragrant and have no bright colour to recommend them. *D. pontica* differs in having larger, mostly twin flowers produced at the base of the new shoots six or eight weeks later, and thinner leaves.

var. PHILIPPI (Gren. & Godr.) Meissn. *D. philippi* Gren. & Godr.—A dwarf, densely bushy shrub with sturdy, short shoots. Leaves closer and more densely arranged on the shoot than in the type; obovate, ¾ to 2 in. long, ⅓ to ¾ in. wide, dark glossy green. Flowers smaller than in the type, fragrant. Native of the Pyrenees.

D. (*laureola* var. *philippi* × *cneorum*) 'Rossetii'.—This daphne was found in the Pyrenees between the wars by M. Rosset, nursery manager to Henri Correvon, who put it into commerce. Leaves narrowly oblanceolate, acute and often apiculate at the apex, narrowly wedge-shaped at the base, ⅝ to 1⅛ in. long, densely set on the shoot, sessile to short stalked. The flowers, although rarely borne, have been observed in the nurseries both of Messrs Marchant and Messrs Hillier, and are small and greenish. It differs from *D. laureola* var. *philippi* in its smaller, relatively much narrower leaves and its more woody, pale brown stems (also, no doubt, in its flowers, but these have not been examined botanically).

D. MEZEREUM L.   MEZEREON

A deciduous, erect-branched shrub, ultimately 3 to 5 ft high and as much through, usually tapering to a naked base; young shoots covered with small flattened hairs. Leaves oblanceolate, tapering at the base to a short stalk, rounded or pointed at the apex, 1½ to 3½ in. long, ¼ to ¾ in. wide, dull rather grey-green, especially beneath, glabrous. Flowers purplish red, very fragrant, produced from the buds of the leafless twigs in February and March; clustered closely on the branches in twos and threes. Each flower is ½ in. across, the four segments of the perianth ovate; the tube ¼ in. long, slender, downy. Berries globose, ⅓ in. in diameter, red.

Native of Europe and Siberia; found apparently wild, though sparsely so in Britain. This is one of the earliest and most attractive of our spring-flowering shrubs, and a healthy specimen with its erect, cylindrical masses of blossom is precious for both its rich colour and its exquisite fragrance. It is also beautiful with fruit in autumn. In many places it is not easy to grow, and is apt to die off suddenly without any apparent cause. I think it loves cool, moist conditions, and is liable to exhaustion through excessive seed-bearing. In the summer of 1910 I saw it naturalised in a wood just above the Falls of Niagara, on the Canadian side, very damp, and traversed by a multitude of streams making their way to the river.

f. ALBA (West.) Schelle—Flowers dullish white; fruits yellow. This form comes true from seed and is found in the wild. There are, however, cultivated plants in which the flowers are pure white. Such is 'PAUL'S WHITE', which, according to E. A. Bowles, made the older form appear cream-coloured. This improved form is said to come true from seed, and no doubt the plant which received an Award of Merit when shown by Mr Bowles under the name 'BOWLES' WHITE' was a seedling of the Paul plant, for it is difficult to believe that he would have claimed credit for a plant he had not raised, especially as it was he who described 'Paul's White' in the first place (in *Garden* (1910), p. 255).

cv. 'AUTUMNALIS'.—It begins to flower in October and lasts until February. The flowers are rather larger than in the type and equally richly coloured and fragrant. As it does not bear fruit usually, it is grafted on the type. The epithet *grandiflora* is sometimes applied to this form and is also used, in a general sense, for plants with larger flowers than in the type.

Unfortunately, *D. mezereum* is subject to attack by a lethal virus. Imported plants with larger and deeper coloured flowers than usual seem to be particularly vulnerable.

D. × NEAPOLITANA Lodd.
D. collina var. *neapolitana* (Lodd.) Lindl.

A dense, erect-branched shrub 2 to 3 ft high, of bushy habit, and evergreen; shoots dark brown, with minute forward-pointing hairs. Leaves short-stalked, scattered along the branches, oblanceolate or narrowly obovate, rounded or obtusely angled at the apex, ¾ to 1¼ in. long, ⅛ to ⅓ in. wide; dark glossy green and glabrous above, glaucous and more or less hairy towards the base beneath. Flowers in one or more leafy clusters at the apex of the branches, from ten to fourteen flowers in a cluster, opening successively from March to May, and even later; at first they are rosy purple, but turn pale with age, sweetly scented, ⅓ in. long and wide, covered outside with minute whitish down. Fruit not seen.

This daphne, which is one of the most robust and easiest to cultivate of a difficult class of plants, would appear to be a hybrid of natural origin. Lindley, who gave an excellent figure of it in *Bot. Reg.*, t. 822, called it *D. collina neapolitana*. The general opinion now held is that it is a hybrid; its parentage is usually given as *collina × cneorum*, but I should rather judge it to be *oleoides × cneorum*. It is grown in gardens under a variety of names, often as *D. oleoides*. One of the most useful of daphnes, and fond of lime in the soil.

The status of this daphne remains as controversial at the present time (1971) as when the above words were written. Lindley's view, that it was no more than a variant of *D. collina*, was strongly upheld by Keissler in his monograph (*Bot.*

Jahrb., Vol. 25, p. 97) and in this he is followed by Rehder. However, the indumentum of the perianth suggests the influence of *D. cneorum*; the other parent is more likely to have been *D. collina* than *D. oleoides*.

The identity of the daphnes once grown under such names as *D. elisae*, *D. delahayana* and *D. fioniana* is not certain; they are said to resemble *D. × neapolitana* and may be of the same parentage.

DAPHNE × NEAPOLITANA

D. ODORA Thunb.

D. japonica Thunb.; *D. indica* Hort., not L.

An evergreen shrub 4 to 6 ft high, with glabrous, round, dark branches. Leaves narrowly oval, 1½ to 3½ in. long, ½ to 1 in. wide; pointed and tapered about equally at both ends, dark green, quite glabrous on both surfaces. Flowers red-purple, very fragrant, produced densely in a terminal head; each flower ½ in. long, ⅝ in. across; the tube not downy, rich purple; the four lobes paler, spreading, ovate. Flower-stalks very short, hairy.

Native of China, long cultivated in Japan; introduced from the latter country in 1771; hardy in the southern and western counties, but surviving only mild winters near London; 'Aureo-Marginata' is, however, hardier than the normal form. In Devon, Cornwall, and Isle of Wight there are beautiful bushes of this daphne in the open air, which begin to flower in midwinter and continue until spring. It is one of the most deliciously fragrant of evergreens.

This species does not need a calcareous soil, and can be increased by layers or cuttings, the latter made of moderately ripened shoots in July.

cv. 'ALBA'.—Flowers white.

cv. 'AUREO-MARGINATA'.—Flowers reddish purple on the outside, paler (often nearly white) within; leaves faintly margined with yellow. This form, once known erroneously as "*D. japonica*", is quite hardy in the R.H.S. Garden at Wisley, Surrey, and worthy of wider cultivation.

cv. 'MAZELII'.—Of the same size and aspect as the type. The foliage, too, is similar, and the flowers of the same shape, size and fragrance, but instead of being borne exclusively in terminal clusters the flowers are also produced on short-stalked clusters from the leaf-axils along the branches; they are pink outside, whitish within. This daphne is somewhat hardier than *D. odora*, but requires winter protection near London. It begins to bloom in November and lasts through the winter. Introduced from Japan to France by E.-A. Mazel of Montsauve around 1866 and figured in *Garden*, 16th Nov. 1878. It is now very rare. (*D. mazelii* Carr. in *Rev. Hort.*, 1872, p. 392; *D. japonica* Sieb. ex Hort.)

D. KIUSIANA Miq. *D. odora* var. *kiusiana* (Miq.) Keissler—This Japanese species is closely allied to the Chinese *D. odora*, but is smaller in all its parts; flowers white, perianth finely downy on the outside.

D. OLEOIDES Schreb.

D. glandulosa Bertol.; *D. buxifolia* Vahl; *D. oleoides* var. *glandulosa* (Bertol.) Keissler; *D. o.* var. *buxifolia* (Vahl) Keissler; *D. jasminea* sensu Griseb., not Sibth. & Sm.; *D. o.* var. *brachyloba* Meissn.; *D. o.* var. *jasminea* Meissn.

An evergreen shrub usually under 2 ft high; young shoots hairy, at least when young. Leaves varying in shape, being broadest at, above or below the middle, obtuse or acute at the apex, usually tapered at the base, $\frac{1}{2}$ to $1\frac{3}{4}$ in. long, $\frac{1}{8}$ to $\frac{1}{2}$ in. wide, more or less hairy on both sides when young, usually becoming glabrous and glossy above when mature, but sometimes permanently downy on both sides. Flowers usually white, cream or yellowish, sometimes tinged with pink, fragrant, borne in May and June in terminal clusters of three to eight; bracts none; tube of perianth hairy on the outside, $\frac{1}{4}$ to $\frac{1}{2}$ in. long, lobes lanceolate to ovate, acute or obtuse at the apex, varying in length from almost as long as the tube to one-third as long. Fruits red, enclosed in the perianth tube until almost ripe.

D. oleoides, originally described from Crete, has a wide distribution from Spain and N. Africa through southern Europe to Asia Minor. It is a very variable species, especially in degree of hairiness of the shoots and leaves and in the length and shape of the perianth-lobes, but it is impossible to subdivide it satisfactorily into varieties or subspecies.

D. oleoides was probably introduced early in the 19th century, though Keissler doubted whether the cultivated plant figured in *Bot. Mag.*, t. 1971 (1818) really was *D. oleoides*, as it was thought to be. It is not common in gardens and less attractive than either *D. collina* or *D.* × *neapolitana*.

D. KOSANINII (Stoyanov) Stoyanov *D. oleoides* var. *kosaninii* Stoyanov— Near to *D. oleoides* but taller, with reddish bark, smaller leaves, deep-pink flowers and shorter sepals. Either an extreme form of *D. oleoides* or possibly a hybrid between it and *D. cneorum* (*Fl. Europ.*, Vol. 2, p. 257). It was described from S.W. Bulgaria and has also been found nearby on Greek territory, in the mountains north of Serrai.

D. JASMINEA Sibth. & Sm.—This species has recently been introduced to cultivation. It is a gnarled shrublet inhabiting rock-faces and stony places in parts of S. Greece (W. Euboea and Mt Parnassus) and has nothing to do with the *D. jasminea* of Grisebach, nor with the *D. oleoides* var. *jasminea* of Meissner, both of which are forms merely of *D. oleoides*. For an account of *D. jasminea* by Brian Mathews see *Bull.A.G.S.*, Vol. 35, Sept. 1967, pp. 199–200.

D. GNIDIUM L.—An erect, bushy, evergreen shrub to 4 ft high. Branchlets densely clad with leaves throughout their length, downy when young. Leaves thick and brittle, glabrous, linear to lanceolate, terminated by a prickly point and up to $1\frac{3}{5}$ in. long. Flowers fragrant, borne in short racemes at the ends of the shoots and in the uppermost leaf-axils, forming all together a terminal, leafy panicle; perianth tube white. Native of the Mediterranean region and the Canary Islands; introduced in the 16th century. It is not so much cultivated today as formerly, but is said to be hardy.

D. PETRAEA Leybold
D. rupestris Facchini

A tiny evergreen shrub 3 to 5 in. high, forming a low tuft of gnarled twigs. Leaves crowded, hard and leathery, narrowly obovate or oblong, tapered towards the base, obtusely pointed or rounded at the tip, thickened at the margins, and triangular in section, $\frac{1}{4}$ to $\frac{1}{2}$ in. long, $\frac{1}{16}$ to $\frac{1}{12}$ in. wide, not stalked, dark green. Flowers rich glowing pink, fragrant, produced in June in terminal clusters of about four blossoms; the tube of the flower is slenderly cylindrical and covered with fine down; across the spreading oval lobes the flower is $\frac{1}{4}$ to $\frac{1}{3}$ in. in diameter.

Native of the mountains west of the northern end of Lake Garda, where it now inhabits inaccessible cliffs of dolomitic rock, safe from the depredations of greedy collectors, who have exterminated it in its more easily reached stations. When the first edition of this work was published the most successful cultivator of this lovely alpine shrub was Reginald Farrer, who used to show little bushes grown in pots at the Temple Show in London, almost covered with blossom. In recent years specimens equally fine have been exhibited at the R.H.S. Hall.

It was in the year that this work was first published, in 1914, that Dr Jenkin and Robert Tucker collected the parent of the clone 'GRANDIFLORA', which has larger flowers than the forms previously cultivated and has now almost displaced them in cultivation. (For a coloured illustration see *Journ. R.H.S.*, Vol. 91, fig. 117—of a fine potted specimen grown by Mrs Greenfield of Epsom.)

Propagation is usually achieved by grafting on to seedling stocks of *D. mezereum*, but evergreen species are also used as the stock and are perhaps preferable. Cuttings, though they strike readily enough, do not grow or flower so well as grafted plants. *D. petraea* is perfectly hardy and will grow well in the open ground if given a place in full sun with a deep and moist root-run in gritty soil with lime added. Its full beauty and delicious scent is, however, best enjoyed when it is grown as a pot-plant. For its cultivation the reader will find detailed guidance in an article by Will Ingwersen in *Bull.A.G.S.*, Vol. 20, pp. 71–73, and in Frank Barker, *The Cream of Alpines*.

D. × THAUMA Farrer—A hybrid, probably between *D. petraea* and *D. striata*, found by Farrer on the Cima Tombea. It is of little garden value, being reluctant to flower, and like the second parent, difficult to keep happy in cultivation. A similar plant, perhaps of the same parentage, was cultivated at Kew but proved impossible to propagate and has died.

D. ARBUSCULA Čelakovsky—A dense, evergreen bushlet usually not exceeding 8 in. in height; branchlets stout, slightly downy or glabrous, reddish when young. Leaves oblong, $\frac{2}{5}$ to 1 in. long, blunt at the apex, furrowed along the midrib, margins revolute; dark green and glabrous above, downy beneath when young, later more or less glabrous. Flowers pink, borne in terminal clusters of three to eight; tube about $\frac{3}{8}$ in. long.

A rare native of the Carpathians of E. Czechoslovakia, discovered by A. Richter in 1855, at which time its habitat lay in Hungarian territory. It is closely related to *D. petraea*, but differs in its foliage characters and reddish young stems, and prefers a lime-free soil. It is also easier to cultivate. See further in *Bull. A.G.S.*, Vol. 39, pp. 129–134.

D. PONTICA L.

An evergreen shrub 3 to 5 ft high, naked and tapering to a single stem at the base, spreading at the top; branchlets and leaves glabrous. Leaves obovate, 1 to 3 in. long, $\frac{1}{2}$ to $1\frac{1}{4}$ in. wide; stalkless, tapered to the base, more abruptly so to the pointed apex, glossy green. Flowers yellowish green, fragrant, borne during April in pairs from the axils of bracts at the base of the new shoots, the whole forming a dense mass of blossom crowned by the tips of the pushing young twigs. Perianth tube $\frac{1}{3}$ in. long, slender; lobes narrow, pointed, recurved. Flower-stalk about $\frac{1}{3}$ in. long, forking near the top. *Bot. Mag.*, t. 1282.

Native of Asia Minor; cultivated in 1752. Although the flowers of this daphne have no bright colour, they are fragrant and profuse, and the shrub is a cheerful evergreen. It likes a moist, loamy, or peaty soil in a sheltered, partially shaded spot. Useful for grouping near woodland walks.

D. GLOMERATA Lam.—This species, said to be one of the most beautiful of the daphnes, is difficult to grow and rare in cultivation. It is a low, suckering evergreen, allied to *D. pontica*, native of Asia Minor and the Caucasus region. Flowers very fragrant, creamy white, ageing to pink; they are borne in axillary clusters, but owing to the crowding of the leaves near the ends of the shoots,

appear to be borne in dense terminal heads—hence the specific epithet *glomerata*.
Young plants of this species are in cultivation, raised from seed collected in
Turkey by Cheese and Watson (seed number 2390) and by Mathew and Tomlin-
son (seed number 4356). Mr Eliot Hodgkin tells us that the late A. G. Weeks
cultivated this species successfully in a peat-bed.

DAPHNE PONTICA

D. PSEUDOMEZEREUM A. Gray

A deciduous shrub free from down in all its parts, very much resembling
D. mezereum in growth. Leaves oblanceolate, tapered at the base to a short stalk,
rounded or shortly pointed at the apex, 2 to 3 in. long, ⅜ to 1 in. wide, dark
dull green. Flowers shortly stalked and produced in lateral clusters with the
leaves, greenish yellow, nearly ½ in. wide; lobes ovate, rounded at the end. Fruit
red, oval, ⅓ in. long.

Native of Central and South Japan; named by Gray in 1858–9 from specimens
collected by Charles Wright. It was introduced around 1910 but had probably
been in cultivation before and lost. It is easily recognised by its similarity to the
mezereon in leaf and growth and by its yellowish flowers being produced when
the plant is leafy. The bark is tough and fibrous.

D. KAMTSCHATICA Maxim.—This species, in its typical state, is a native
of Korea, the Russian Far East, Sakhalin and the Kuriles. It is represented in
cultivation by the following variety:

var. JEZOENSIS (Maxim.) Ohwi *D. jezoensis* Maxim.—A native of Japan
in subalpine woodland, differing from *D. pseudomezereum* in its obovate-oblong
leaves, rounded at the apex, and its yellow, fragrant flowers. It was in flower

in the Alpine House at the R.H.S. Garden, Wisley, in March 1968. Typical *D. kamtschatica*, which is probably not in cultivation, differs from the variety in its narrower leaves and smaller flowers.

D. RETUSA Hemsl. [PLATE 4

A low, densely branched, evergreen shrub, of close, neat, sturdy habit; young shoots hairy. Leaves leathery, thick, densely arranged towards the end of the twig; oval inclined to obovate; 1 to 2 in. long, ½ to ¾ in. wide; stalkless, the base tapered, the apex rounded and notched, margin revolute; dark glossy green, glabrous. Flowers produced during early May in a crowded cluster 3 in. across terminating the branch, each flower borne on a short, conspicuously brown-felted stalk; perianth tube glabrous, ⅝ in. long; rosy purple outside; glistening white, tinged with purple inside; lobes ovate, ⅓ in. long. Fruit bright red. *Bot. Mag.*, t. 8430.

Native of W. China and the E. Himalaya; discovered by Pratt near Tatsien-lu (Kangting) at 13,500 ft elevation. Introduced from the same spot by Wilson in 1901 and more recently by Ludlow, Sherriff and Elliot from S.E. Tibet (LSE 15756). This delightful daphne makes a compact bush growing slowly to about 2 ft high; the flowers are fragrant, like lilac. It is very hardy and amenable to cultivation. See also *D. tangutica*.

D. × MANTENSIANA T. M. C. Taylor & F. Vrugtman—A hybrid between *D. × burkwoodii* and *D. retusa*, raised at Manten's nursery, British Columbia, and put into commerce in 1953. It is a bushy evergreen shrub with very fragrant flowers resembling those of *D. retusa* in their colouring. Leaves oblong or narrow-obovate, retuse at the apex. It is in cultivation at Wisley and other gardens. The original clone has been named 'MANTEN'.

D. SOPHIA Kalenichenko

A deciduous shrub of shapely form about 2 ft high. Leaves 2 to 3 in. long, oblong-ovate, blunt or pointed, dark green, of rather soft texture. Flowers pure white, borne in terminal clusters of six to fifteen, covered with appressed down, very fragrant; perianth-lobes oblong-ovate, pointed.

Native of S.W. Russia, described and named in 1847 and introduced to cultivation at Moscow in 1895, but not to England before 1939, in which year T. Hay, then of Hyde Park, obtained a pot-grown plant from Moscow which flowered with him in March 1940 under glass protection but was destroyed shortly after in an air-raid. In his article on this plant (*Journ. R.H.S.*, Vol. 65, p. 150) he described it as a 'lovely species'. Mr Eliot Hodgkin tells us (1971) that he has young plants of this species from Russia, which have flowered but so far do not justify Tom Hay's eulogy.

Daphne sophia is closely allied to *D. altaica*, though now separated from it by some two thousand miles of steppe and desert. Both species, and *D. caucasica*, probably derive from an ancestral stock of more continuous distribution that became fragmented during the Ice Age. *D. sophia* is also of note as one of an interesting contingent of plants found on limestone hills at the south-eastern end of the mid-Russian Plateau, in the region where the provinces of Voronezh, Kursk and Belgorod adjoin. They are believed to be relics of the late Tertiary, having persisted *in situ* throughout the Ice Age. Another member of this flora is a race of *Pinus sylvestris* to which Kalenichenko gave specific status as *P. cretacea*. The daphne grows in the now decimated stands of this pine and also in light oak woodland; it is intolerant of dense shade. See also *D. julia* (mentioned under *D. cneorum*).

D. STRIATA Tratt.

An evergreen shrub forming close, dense mats and rarely much more than 6 to 12 in. high, the lower branches semi-prostrate; young shoots glabrous. Leaves ½ to 1 in. long, oblanceolate, pointed, crowded at the end of the shoots, dullish green. Flowers in terminal heads of eight to twelve; perianth ½ in. long, the lobes giving it a diameter of about ¼ in., rosy pink, charmingly fragrant.

A native of the European Alps, which has been cultivated since 1827, but is very rare in gardens and hard to cultivate successfully. It is nearly related to *D. cneorum*, which is well distinguished, however, by its downy, plain perianth which in *D. striata* is glabrous and striated.

D. TANGUTICA Maxim.
D. wilsonii Rehd.

An evergreen shrub of sturdy, rounded shape 3 to 5 ft high; young shoots stout, greyish brown, at first clothed with pale grey bristles, finally quite glabrous. Leaves leathery in texture; narrowly oval, oblong or oblanceolate, notched at the apex, tapered at the base, margins slightly decurved, 1 to 3 in. long, ¼ to ¾ in. wide, dark rather bright green above, paler and dull beneath; stalk stout, ⅛ in. long. Flowers closely packed in a terminal umbel 1½ in. wide, opening in March or April from the axils of pointed oblong scales that are fringed with minute hairs. Each flower is about ½ in. wide, with a tube ⅝ in. long, the four spreading lobes ovate and blunt, white tinged with purple inside, two of the lobes more deeply stained than the others, all rosy purple outside. Ovary glabrous, egg-shaped, with a short style and a rounded glabrous stigma. Fruit roundish egg-shaped, red, ¼ in. wide. *Bot. Mag.*, t. 8855.

Native of W. China from Kansu to N. Yunnan; discovered by Przewalski, the Russian traveller, in 1873; introduced by Farrer (No. 271) in 1914 and also some four or six years earlier by Wilson from farther south (plants from this seed were originally known as *D. wilsonii*). It is closely related to *D. retusa* but is scarcely so ornamental a shrub, the umbels being smaller although the flowers are more brightly coloured. It is more free in growth and the leaves are longer and more tapered towards the end. Judging from specimens collected in the wild, *D. retusa* is more branched, with short branches, and the young stems are densely downy or hirsute. In contrast, wild specimens of *D. tangutica* are much less branched and the branches longer and straighter; the young stems are glabrous or soon become so.

Farrer also introduced, under his No. 585, a form with creamy-white flowers and paler green leaves. This is now rare in cultivation: according to Eliot Hodgkin (*Journ. R.H.S.*, Vol. 86, p. 48) all the present stock descends from one plant grown by the late Dr Jenkin of Hindhead, who increased it by grafting. He adds that it is semi-evergreen, straggling in habit, but a beautiful plant.

DAPHNIPHYLLUM DAPHNIPHYLLACEAE

The two shrubs cultivated in gardens belonging to this genus are handsome, robust evergreens, with alternate, stout-textured rhododendron-like leaves. Flowers unisexual, with the sexes on separate plants, of no beauty. The males have no petals, very small sepals, but curious, large, stout anthers. Fruit a roundish or oval drupe. The two following shrubs will grow in any good soil, and are useful for moist, shady positions. Both are lime-tolerant but perhaps not suitable for really chalky soils. Propagated by cuttings made of moderately ripened wood in July, and placed in gentle bottom heat.

D. HUMILE Maxim.

D. macropodum var. *humile* (Maxim.) Rosenth.; *D. jezoense* Hort. ex Bean

A low, much-branched, evergreen bush 6 to 7 ft high, but much more in width; quite glabrous in all its parts. Leaves oval or slightly obovate, 2 to 5 in. long, ¾ to 2 in. wide, tapered at both ends, dark shining green above, with a glaucous bloom beneath; vein-pairs twelve to fifteen; stalk ⅜ to ⅝ in. long. Flowers not seen. Fruit blue-black, according to wild specimens.

Native of Yezo (Hokkaido), Japan, where, according to Sargent, it is a common undershrub in the deciduous forests; also of the north-western part of the main island (Honshu), and of Korea; introduced by Maries for Messrs Veitch about 1879. It is very distinct in habit from *D. macropodum*; a plant at Kew, of uncertain age but more than twenty years old, is only 3 ft high and 3 ft in diameter. It does not dislike moderate shade, and would make a useful, low, evergreen cover where such is required without the annual cropping that shrubs like laurels and rhododendrons need. It has been known in gardens as *D. jezoense*, and also considered a variety of *D. macropodum*, but I am unable to distinguish it from Maximowicz's specimen of *D. humile* preserved at Kew; and that is the only species recorded from the Island of Yezo.

D. MACROPODUM Miq.

D. glaucescens Hort., not Bl.

An evergreen shrub of bushy, rounded form at present 8 to 20 ft high in this country, and as much or more in diameter; young shoots glabrous, glaucous, often reddish. Leaves rhododendron-like, 3 to 8 in. long, 1 to 3½ in. wide, oblong or narrowly oval, taper-pointed at the apex, wedge-shaped at the base, quite glabrous, dark green above, glaucous beneath; vein-pairs sixteen to nineteen; stalk 1 to 1½ in. long, stout, often red like the midrib. Flowers small and inconspicuous, pale green, with a strong pungent odour; produced during late spring from the leaf-axils of the previous year's growth in racemes 1 in. long; bracts and stamens pink. Fruit blue-black, pea-shaped.

Native of Japan; introduced by Maries for Messrs Veitch in 1879. A handsome and vigorous evergreen, becoming in Japan, and perhaps in this country, eventually a small tree. It is quite hardy, having withstood 30° of frost at Kew

DAPHNIPHYLLUM MACROPODUM

but nevertheless likes shelter. The red colouring of the leaf-stalks, midribs, and young wood adds to its beauty, but is not always present.

cv. 'VARIEGATUM'.—Leaves with a broad, irregular margin (sometimes reaching to the midrib) of creamy white; not so hardy as the type.

DAVIDIA   DAVIDIACEAE

A genus of a single species (two in some interpretations) native to W. China. It is thought to derive from the same ancestral stock as the Cornaceae, Nyssaceae and Araliaceae, but is sufficiently distinct from these to rank as a monotypic family.

D. INVOLUCRATA Baill.   DOVE OR HANDKERCHIEF TREE

D. laeta Dode, in part   [PLATE 5

A deciduous tree reaching a height of 40 to 65 ft in the wild, in habit
resembling a lime tree (*Tilia*); young branches glabrous, covered more or less
with a glaucous bloom, afterwards turning very dark. Leaves vivid green,
broadly ovate or roundish, 3 to 6 in. long, and about three-fourths as wide,
heart-shaped at the base, the apex drawn out into a long fine point; margins set
with coarse triangular teeth; upper surface furnished with silky hairs, the lower
one felted with a thick grey down; stalks slender, 1½ to 3 in. long. About eight
pairs of nearly parallel veins proceed from the midrib at an angle of 45°. Flowers
produced in May with the strongly scented young leaves from the buds of the
previous year's shoots; they are crowded in a rounded head about ¾ in. diameter,
borne at the end of a drooping stalk about 3 in. long; male flowers composed
of numerous long stamens with white filaments and reddish anthers, forming a

DAVIDIA INVOLUCRATA

brush-like mass; female flower reduced to an egg-shaped ovary, with a short six-
rayed style and a ring of abortive stamens at the top. It is not, however, in the
flowers themselves where the remarkable beauty of the davidia lies, but in two
(rarely three) enormous bracts by which each flower-head is subtended. These
bracts are white or creamy white, hooded, oblong, long-pointed, and of unequal

size, the lower one being the larger, and sometimes nearly 8 in. long and half as wide; the upper bract is about half the size, and stands above the flower-head like a canopy. Fruit a solitary drupe about 1½ in. long, green with a purplish bloom but becoming russet-coloured and speckled with red when completely ripe; it contains a single, hard, ridged nut with three to five seeds. For the shape of the fruit, see below.

Native of China in W. Szechwan and parts of W. Hupeh; first discovered near Mupin in 1869 by the Abbé David, after whom the genus is named. The first introduction of this species to Europe belonged to the var. *vilmoriniana* (see below). Seed of typical *D. involucrata* was first sent by Wilson in November 1903 and again in 1904, during his second expedition for Messrs Veitch. It is a curious fact that the young trees raised from this seed at Veitch's Coombe Wood nursery first showed very little of the hairy character of the parent but became conspicuously hairy later (when about seven years old).

The type seems to be rarer in garden than the glabrous-leaved trees (var. *vilmoriniana*). This scarcity is no doubt due in part to the relatively small number of plants that were raised and distributed ('several hundreds' only, according to Wilson) compared to the thirteen thousand raised from the seed of var. *vilmoriniana*. A further reason is that it seems in many gardens to have proved (in the form introduced) less easy to establish than the variety, less vigorous, and more subject to damage by late spring-frost. Wilson remarks (*Pl. Wilsonianae*, Vol. 2, p. 257) that in typical *D. involucrata* the shoots on young plants are dark red, but dull grey or slightly purplish in var. *vilmoriniana*.

var. VILMORINIANA (Dode) Wanger. *D. vilmoriniana* Dode; *D. laeta* Dode, in part.—Undersides of leaves yellowish green or somewhat glaucous, slightly downy on the veins at first but otherwise quite glabrous. According to Wilson this variety is common in N. W. Hupeh and also occurs, though more sparingly, in E. Szechwan; it is rare in W. Szechwan, where the type predominates, though the two are sometimes found growing commingled.

The var. *vilmoriniana* is commoner in cultivation than the type and introduced some years earlier. In 1897 a parcel of thirty-seven seeds was sent to Maurice de Vilmorin by the French missionary Farges. Of this sending only one seed germinated, and that not until June 1899. The plant grew and flourished, flowering for the first time at Les Barres in May 1906. This plant and a few cuttings from it were the only representatives of *Davidia* in Europe until Wilson's first journey in China for Messrs Veitch, 1899–1901, during which a large supply of seeds was sent home from which some thirteen thousand plants were raised. At about the same time Vilmorin received a further consignment of seeds from Père Farges which this time germinated successfully. Thus the abundant representation of *Davidia* in European gardens was assured. Wilson's introduction first flowered in Veitch's Coombe Wood nursery in 1911.

As seen in cultivation this variety is rather variable in the colouring and texture of the leaves. Some trees have them dark green, rather thick and somewhat glaucous beneath, while in others they are a lighter green, thinner, and yellowish green beneath. The second form agrees with Dode's *D. laeta* but Wilson observed that in nature both kinds of leaf are to be found on the same tree. This is true also of many cultivated trees which, if carefully examined, will be found to have the darker, glaucescent leaf on the outer part of the crown and the lighter green *laeta*-type leaf on the inside.* There are certainly no grounds, in our present state of knowledge, for distinguishing more than one variety of *D. involucrata*. It must be added that Dode's *D. laeta* is a thoroughly confused entity, based mainly on young nursery plants some of which were, in fact, typical *D. involucrata* raised from seed of Wilson's 1903 sending; in 1908, when Dode described *D. laeta*, these had not yet produced the adult, hairy leaf.

There remains the question whether the glabrous-leaved trees might not better be regarded as an independent species (*D. vilmoriniana*). The status of variety given them in the present revision is based on the assumption that the glabrous underside of the leaf is the only consistent and substantial difference between them and typical *D. involucrata*; this was Wilson's own conclusion from his study of the species in its natural habitat. However, if it could be shown that the two forms of *Davidia* also differ constantly in the shape of their fruits this judgement would have to be reconsidered. From a study of a number of samples from cultivated trees K. A. Beckett (*Journ. R.H.S.*, Vol. 87, 1962, p. 24) concluded that the fruit in *D. involucrata* is oblate, whereas in the glabrous-leaved trees it is broad- to long-ovoid. He tells us, however, that two samples received subsequently from Westonbirt suggest that the difference is not a constant one; these on their leaf-characters were referable to typical *D. involucrata* but bore ovoid, not oblate, fruits. Mr Beckett's observations are of great interest, but no definitive conclusion can be reached until the variations shown by wild trees have been more thoroughly studied. For further observations on *Davidia* fruits see H. Cocker in *Gard. Chron.*, Dec. 6, 1952, p. 226, and H. J. Ivens, ibid., Jan. 17, 1953, p. 22.

In the half-century that has passed since the first edition of this work was published the davidia has become one of the best known of all hardy exotic trees. Wilson considered it to be 'the most interesting and beautiful of all trees of the north-temperate flora' and likened the white bracts to 'huge butterflies hovering among the trees'. It thrives best in a moist soil and a sheltered situation. Although quite winter-hardy those forms which start into growth early are subject to damage by late spring-frosts, the typical, hairy-leaved form being, as already remarked, particularly vulnerable in this respect. Given favourable conditions it grows rapidly and reaches the flowering stage in ten years or even less. It is easily propagated by cuttings, or by the seed, which in most years is abundantly borne.

D. involucrata is represented in most of the larger tree collections, usually by the var. *vilmoriniana*. The largest are 45 to 57 ft high, 3½ to 5 ft in girth.

* It is, of course, possible that the garden trees with the predominantly darker green, glaucescent leaves are not from Wilson's seed but belong all to one clone descended from the original tree at Les Barres which Dode took as the type of his *D. vilmoriniana*. This tree is known to have been multiplied by cuttings and layers when still only a few years old (*Frut. Vilm.*, p. 146, 1904) and some of its vegetative progeny may well have been imported by British nurseries other than Veitch's and used as stock plants. A tree of the Les Barres clone was obtained for Kew around 1904 and grown in the Temperate House; this too was propagated vegetatively.

DECAISNEA   LARDIZABALACEAE

A genus of two Asiatic species, distinct from all other members of the Lardizabala family in their shrubby (not climbing) habit, in their pinnate (not palmately compound) leaves and their bisexual flowers. The name commemorates Joseph Decaisne (1807–82), at one time Director of the Jardin des Plantes, Paris.

D. FARGESII Franch.   [PLATE 6

A deciduous shrub reported to attain 15 ft in the wild state, but already higher in cultivation, consisting of a cluster of erect stems containing abundant pith and distinct in winter for their large, pointed buds; young shoots glabrous, thick. Leaves pinnate, from 2 to 3 ft long, consisting of from 6½ to 12½ pairs of leaflets. Leaflets ovate, slender-pointed, entire, 3 to 6 in. long, glaucous beneath, glabrous or nearly so; main-stalk often purplish brown. Flowers produced in a loose drooping panicle 12 to 18 in. long terminating the young growths. Each flower is borne on a slender stalk ¾ in. long, the six sepals (petals absent) being erect, narrow lanceolate, finely pointed, 1 to 1¼ in. long; yellowish green, the upper half curving outwards. Fruit dull blue, cylindrical, 3 to 4 in. long, ¾ in. wide, with numerous tiny warts on the surface. *Bot. Mag.*, t. 7848.

This interesting and striking shrub is a native of the mountains of W. China, where it was collected and sent to France by the missionary, Père Farges, in 1895. Two years later it was sent by Maurice de Vilmorin to Kew, where it has proved quite hardy, and where it flowers and produces fruit regularly, but is subject to injury by late spring frosts. It is a handsome foliage plant. It likes a rich loamy soil, and is propagated by seeds.

D. INSIGNIS (Griff.) Hook. f. & Thoms.

—In foliage and flower this species resembles the preceding but is quite distinct in its golden-yellow fruits. Native of the Himalaya and Yunnan. Probably not hardy. *Bot. Mag.*, t. 6731.

DECUMARIA   HYDRANGEACEAE

A genus of two species, one American the other Chinese, both climbers that cling to their supports by aerial roots. The name is derived from *decimus* and refers to the number of the various parts of the flower. Of the sepals, petals and cells of the ovary there are up to ten and of stamens twenty to thirty.

D. BARBARA L.

A climbing, deciduous shrub ascending the trunks of trees in the wild; stems round, slightly downy when young, forming aerial roots like an ivy; buds hairy. Leaves opposite, oval or ovate, tapering at both ends, short-pointed, 3 to 5 in. long, 1½ to 3 in. wide, quite glabrous on both surfaces, or slightly hairy beneath when young, shallowly toothed towards the apex, often entire; stalk 1 to 2 in. long. Flowers white, produced in June and July in an erect terminal corymb 2 to 3 in. long and wide. The individual flower is small, ¼ in. across, with seven to ten narrow oblong petals, alternating with a similar number of calyx teeth; stamens twenty to thirty. Fruit urn-shaped, ⅓ in. long, the lower part prettily striped with numerous whitish ridges, upper part glabrous, tapering.

Native of the south-eastern United States; introduced in 1785, but an uncommon plant in gardens owing to its tenderness. It thrives in the south-western counties of England and Ireland, but elsewhere should be grown on a sheltered wall. It can be increased by cuttings of firm shoots. Its nearest allies are the climbing hydrangeas and schizophragmas, from which it is quite distinct in the always perfect flowers and more numerous petals and stamens.

D. SINENSIS Oliver

An evergreen climber growing probably 10 to 15 ft high; young shoots slightly furnished with appressed hairs at first, becoming grey; winter buds downy. Leaves opposite, mostly narrowly obovate or oval, rounded and blunt at the apex, more or less tapered at the base, entire or slightly toothed, 1 to 3½ in. long, ½ to 1¾ in. wide, shining green and quite glabrous; stalk ¼ to ¾ in. long, often with appressed hairs near the base. Flowers yellowish white, produced in terminal, broadly pyramidal panicles 1½ to 3½ in. high and wide; petals seven to ten to each flower, oblong, up to $\frac{3}{16}$ in. long, blunt at the apex; stamens twenty to thirty, conspicuous; flower-stalks slender, sometimes downy. *Bot. Mag.*, t. 9429.

Native of Central China; discovered in the Ichang Gorge by Henry; introduced by Wilson in 1908. It is interesting as a Chinese representative of a genus only known previously by *D. barbara*, a native of eastern N. America. According to Wilson it is often found growing over rocks. The best plant I have seen was growing on a wall in the garden of the late Sir Stuart Samuel at Chelwood Vatchery, near Nutley, in Sussex. It clung to the wall with a close mat of branches and in late May was sprinkled with a few flower-panicles (this plant no longer exists). Henry described it as a 'creeper hanging down from the walls of cliffs with beautiful clusters of fragrant white flowers', which, judging by cultivated plants, is a flattering description. The blossoms are faintly scented. It succeeds well on a south wall at Kew and in the walled garden at Wakehurst Place, Sussex.

DENDROMECON   PAPAVERACEAE

A Californian genus of two species, though by the splintering of these the number has been inflated to twenty in one interpretation of the genus.

The generic name signifies 'Tree poppy'. It is allied to *Romneya*, but differs in the entire leaves and yellow flowers.

D. HARFORDII Kell.

D. *rigidum* var. *harfordii* (Kell.) K. Brandegee

An evergreen shrub 8 to 10 ft high with erect or arching branches. Leaves crowded on the stems, elliptic to oblong-ovate, 1 to 3 or 4 in. long and about half as wide, rounded at the apex. Flowers yellow, up to 3 in. across, borne singly on the ends of side-shoots as in *D. rigida* but on shorter pedicels.

Native of California, found there only on the islands of Santa Cruz and Santa Rosa; first described in 1873 but not introduced to cultivation in the U.S.A. until 1933, after which it gradually became known to Californian gardeners (E. K. Balls in *Gard. Chron.*, 7th May 1960). Not in cultivation in the British Isles, so far as is known.

var. RHAMNOIDES (Greene) Munz *D. rhamnoides* Greene; *D. arborea* Greene —Leaves pale glaucous-green, less crowded on the shoot than in the type, and up to 5 in. long, sharply tapered at the apex. This variety, like the type, is insular in distribution but found farther south, on Santa Catalina and San Clemente islands, which lie off the Californian coast south of Los Angeles. It was introduced to cultivation in Britain in 1963 by F. P. Knight, Director of the Royal Horticultural Society's Gardens at Wisley, who received seed from the Rancho Santa Ana Botanic Garden early that year (*Journ. R.H.S.*, Vol. 90, pp. 480–1).

It is too early to judge this new introduction. It has survived three mild winters out-of-doors on a wall at the Savill Gardens but Mr Findlay tells us that it has so far proved less free-flowering than *D. rigida*.

D. RIGIDA Benth. [PLATE 7]

A shrub up to 10 ft high in the wild; the branchlets half-woody, slender, glabrous, glaucous. Leaves thickish, ovate or narrow lanceolate, pointed, 1 to 3 in. long, glaucous, nearly or quite stalkless. Flowers poppy-like, bright yellow, 2 to 3 in. in diameter, borne singly on stalks 1½ to 3 in. long, fragrant. Petals four; calyx of two sepals; stamens numerous. *Bot. Mag.*, t. 5134.

Native of California, where it was discovered by David Douglas on dry rocky hills. First introduced by W. Lobb about 1854, this beautiful plant has from time to time disappeared and been reintroduced. It is undoubtedly tender, but thrives at Kew at the foot of a sunny wall until a winter like that of 1908–9 kills it. It needs the sunniest position available, and the soil should be of a loamy character, lightened by the addition of sand, and especially mortar rubble, well drained. Propagated by cuttings made of well-ripened, firm summer shoots; the cuttings should consist of three joints, and be placed singly in small 'thumb' pots in moderate heat in very sandy soil. A plant in the garden of Capt. Riall at Old Conna Hill, near Bray, in Ireland, covered a wall to the height of 12 ft. Its main stem was 6 in. thick, and the plant was always more or less in bloom. Against a hot-house wall it reached 16 ft with Major A. Pam in Hertfordshire.

DENDROPANAX ARALIACEAE

A genus of about thirty species in E. Asia and Central and S. America of which only the species described below can be grown out-of-doors in Britain.

D. JAPONICUM (Junghuhn) Seem.

Hedera japonica Junghuhn

An evergreen shrub 10 to 15 ft high or a small tree; free from down in all its parts. Leaves dark glossy green, of leathery texture, variable in shape and size, distinctly three- or five-veined from the base. In the adult stage of the tree they are mostly of oval, ovate or rhomboidal outline, broadly wedge-shaped at the base, not toothed; in young plants they are mostly more or less deeply three-lobed, and some similarly shaped leaves occur also in adult trees. The three-lobed leaves are much the larger and measure as much as 8 in. by 6 in.; the others vary from 2 to 5 in. long by 1 to 3 in. wide. Leaf-stalks usually long; in the case of the larger leaves as much as 5 in. Flowers inconspicuous, produced in August in solitary long-stalked umbels 1 in. or so wide at the end of the shoot, or in clusters of three to five. Fruit oval, black, ribbed, ¼ to ⅜ in. long.

Native of Japan, China, and Khasia. This araliad lives in the open air at Kew but is better suited in milder parts of the kingdom, where it makes a handsome evergreen useful for shady situations.

It is probable that the plant that Thunberg described under the name "*Acer trifidum*" was really this species, in which case its name would be *D. trifidum* (Thunb.) Makino.

DESFONTAINIA POTALIACEAE

A small genus of some five species, native of S. America, once placed in the family Loganiaceae but, with a few tropical and subtropical genera, now considered to constitute an independent family—the Potaliaceae—which differs from Loganiaceae in the fleshy fruits and in the flowers, the lobes of which are contorted in bud (convolute), each overlapping its neighbour along one edge only.

D. SPINOSA Ruiz & Pavon [PLATE 8

D. spinosa var. *hookeri* (Dun.) Reiche; *D. hookeri* Dun.; *D. spinosa* var. *chilensis* (C. Gay) Reiche

An evergreen shrub 10 ft or more high in favourable localities, branches covered with pale, glabrous, shining bark. Leaves very like those of a holly, but opposite, 1 to 2½ in. long, ¾ to 1½ in. wide, oval or ovate in the main, but armed at the edges with sharp triangular spines ⅛ to ⅓ in. long, shining dark green, glabrous; stalk ⅓ in. long. Flowers solitary on stalks ⅓ to ½ in. long, produced from July until late autumn. Corolla funnel-shaped, 1½ in. long, ½ in. wide at the mouth, crimson scarlet, with five rounded, yellow, shallow lobes; calyx green, with five oblong lobes ⅓ in. long, edged with hairs; anthers five, with scarcely any stalk, attached at the base of the corolla lobes. *Bot. Mag.*, t. 4781.

Native of the Andes from Colombia to the region of the straits of Magellan; described by Ruiz and Pavon in 1799 from plants collected by them in Peru; introduced by William Lobb from Chile in 1843 and again by Comber in 1925–6. In the northern part of its range in Chile this species grows in cool, mountain cloud-forests; farther south it descends to sea-level and ranges through the fiords and innumerable islands of the Pacific coast as far as the Magellan region, where the climate throughout is exceedingly moist and equable.

In cultivation it finds its most congenial conditions on or near the west coast of Scotland and in N. Ireland, where it grows to a great size. There are fine specimens at Stonefield, Argyll; Brodick, Isle of Arran; Inverewe, Wester Ross; and at Rowallane, Co. Down. The last is a remarkable plant 10 ft high, 32 ft across and 118 ft in circumference. In other parts of the country, wherever the climate is not too dry and continental, it grows and flowers quite well. It is, for example, hardy in an exposed position on the rock garden at Edinburgh. In the south there are two good specimens in the walled garden at Nymans in Sussex, raised from Comber's seed. One of these was given an Award of Merit when a flowering branch was shown at Vincent Square in 1955; the flower colour differs somewhat from that of the older introduction, being vermilion shading to Orient Red.

NOTE: A word should be added about the varieties of *D. spinosa* recognised in some works. The description of the species by Ruiz and Pavon is accompanied by a plate (*Fl. Peru. Chil.*, Vol. 2, t. 186) which shows a shoot with broad-oval leaf-blades 2⅗ to 3⅘ in. long, 1⅕ to ⅘ in. wide, with seven to nine teeth on each side. There is nothing to match this in the Kew Herbarium, where the species is well represented by material collected throughout the Andes from Colombia to Chile. In this material the leaf-blades are mostly 1⅗ to 2 in. long and ⅘ to 1 in. wide; very occasionally the odd leaf exceeds these dimensions and a few specimens have much smaller leaves. All have three to four teeth on each side, most often four, very rarely five. The calyx is variable; most often the segments are oblong-obtuse, but sometimes narrow and long-pointed as figured by Ruiz and Pavon.

D. spinosa var. *hookeri* (Dunal) Reiche rests on the figure and description of a plant collected by Bridges near the town of Valdivia, Chile (Hooker's *Icones Plantarum*, Vol. 1, t. 33, 1836). It was published as *D. spinosa* but Dunal, who seems to have worked solely from the published figures and description, treated it as a distinct species, *D. hookeri*. It is clear, however, the var. *hookeri* represents the normal form of the species as found throughout the Andes (it is not confined to Chile) and can only be maintained as a variety if there is, in fact, a typical variety (var. *spinosa*) such as the plant in Ruiz and Pavon's plate. *D. spinosa* was introduced by Lobb from Valdivia and this introduction would belong to var. *hookeri* if that variety were recognised.

D. spinosa var. *chilensis* (C. Gay) Reiche is a plant with relatively narrower, more oblong leaves and a smaller calyx, but the odd specimens with these characters are only part of the variation of the species and do not represent a distinct variety.

DESMODIUM   LEGUMINOSAE

A large genus of shrubs and herbs, widely spread chiefly in tropical and warm temperate regions; about 150 species are known, very few of which are hardy with us. They are nearly akin to *Lespedeza*, a genus with one-seeded pods, whereas they have a several-seeded, jointed pod.

D. PRAESTANS Forrest

A deciduous shrub to 15 ft high; young shoots downy. Leaves usually composed of a single leaflet, which is broad-ovate, rounded or obtuse at the apex rounded or truncate at the base, 4 to 9 in. long and 3½ to 6¾ in. wide; more rarely the leaves are trifoliolate, the terminal one of the same size and shape as the single leaflets, lateral ones smaller; pale green above, downy beneath. Flowers purplish pink in downy terminal panicles up to 16 in. long, which may be broad and lax or spike-like. *Bot. Mag.*, n.s., t. 407.

Native of S.W. China; discovered by Forrest and introduced by him in 1914; in nature it occupies dry, open places among rocks and in scrub at 7,000 to 10,000 ft. This species, which Forrest himself admired very much, has always been rare in gardens. It is rather tender and most of the cultivated plants seem to have been lost during the last war or in the winter of 1946-7. The flowering shoot figured in the *Botanical Magazine* was taken from a plant growing in the Moat Garden at Windsor Castle (for which see also *Journ. R.H.S.*, Vol. 68, fig. 36). It is probably best grown on a south wall.

D. SPICATUM Rehd.

A deciduous, laxly branched shrub up to 6 or 8 ft high; young shoots herbaceous, purplish, hairy, ribbed. Leaves trifoliolate, 3 to 6 in. long; main-stalk downy, grooved. Terminal leaflet the largest, up to 2 in. long, roundish obovate to rhomboid with a stalk up to ¾ in. long; lateral leaflets shortly stalked, obliquely ovate, smaller; all bluntish or minutely pointed, dark green and with short hairs above, covered with a grey, thick, soft down beneath. Inflorescence a terminal raceme up to 6 in. long, sometimes with a branch or two at the base, the pea-like flowers in whorls of six or eight. Corolla rosy-carmine, ⅝ in. long, standard petal heart-shaped with incurved margins, greenish at the base. Calyx funnel-shaped at the base, 1/10 in. long, downy, with five ovate pointed lobes. Pod curved, 2 in. long, 3/16 in. wide, downy, four- to six-jointed, flattened, scalloped or crenulated on the upper side as is common to this genus. *Bot. Mag.*, t. 8805.

Native of W. Szechwan, China; raised by Maurice de Vilmorin from Chinese seeds in 1896. By him it was sent to Kew, where it has proved quite hardy, flowering very freely in September and October provided it gets a sunny autumn. It was also found by Wilson in W. Szechwan and plants raised from his seeds are in gardens.

D. TILIIFOLIUM (D. Don) G. Don

Hedysarum tiliifolium D. Don

A semi-woody plant, which sends up annually from a woody root-stock a number of erect stems 2 to 4 ft high, more or less downy. Leaves trifoliolate, with a main-stalk 2 to 3 in. long. Leaflets nearly glabrous on both sides, or very downy beneath, the end one larger than the others, broadly obovate, 2 to 4 in. long, $1\frac{1}{2}$ to 3 in. wide; the side leaflets half to two-thirds as large, and broadly ovate. Panicles terminal, 8 to 12 in. high, the lower sections borne in the uppermost leaf-axils. Flowers $\frac{1}{2}$ in. long, varying from pale lilac to dark pink, borne on a slender stalk not quite so long as itself; calyx $\frac{1}{10}$ in. wide, hairy, with broad shallow teeth. Pod 2 to 3 in. long, $\frac{1}{8}$ in. wide; six- to nine-jointed, with the scalloping on the upper side characteristic of the genus.

Native of the Himalaya at 9,000 ft; the specimens now at Kew were raised from seed obtained from Kashmir in 1879. It flowers from August to October, but needs a hot summer to bring out its best qualities. In cold, wet seasons the flowers do not open at all. Propagated by division of the root-stock in spring. The late Sir Henry Collett called this a 'protean plant'; the form in cultivation is one whose leaves are not very downy.

DEUTZIA   PHILADELPHACEAE

An Asiatic group of deciduous shrubs allied to *Philadelphus*, but very distinct from that genus in having ten stamens with winged stalks, often toothed or forked at the top; in the starry hairs or scurf with which most parts of the plants are furnished; and in five (instead of four) petals and calyx-lobes. Leaves opposite. Flowers either in racemes, as in *D. gracilis* and *scabra*, or in corymbose panicles.

The deutzias are some of the most beautiful shrubs flowering in June. Nearly all the species mentioned in the following descriptive notes are quite winter-hardy; but, unfortunately, some deutzias are easily excited into growth by unseasonable warmth in the early spring months, and are often, especially in low-lying districts, injured and their crop of flowers ruined by late frosts. This is true in particular of *D. gracilis*. *D.* × *lemoinei* and *D. setchuenensis*. But *D. longifolia*, *D. discolor*, *D. purpurascens*, *D. scabra* and their hybrids give no trouble in this respect. Deutzias like a good loamy soil and plenty of moisture; most are lime-tolerant. The only pruning required is an occasional (say biennial) thinning out of the old worn-out branches. As they flower on the shoots made the previous year, no shortening back can be done except at the loss of bloom. They are very easily propagated by cuttings of half-ripened wood placed in gentle bottom-heat about the end of June or later.

The genus was named after Johann van der Deutz who lived at Amsterdam in the 18th century and was a friend and patron of Thunberg.

D. AMURENSIS (Reg.) Airy Shaw

D. parviflora var. *amurensis* Reg.; *D. parviflora* Hort., not Bge.

A shrub of erect habit up to 6 ft high; young wood nearly glabrous, pale brown; bark peeling the second year. Leaves ovate-lanceolate or ovate, with a usually short, slender point, tapered at the base, sharply toothed, 1½ to 4 in. long, ½ to 1¾ in. wide; dull green and sprinkled over with minute starry down above; paler, glossy green, and almost glabrous beneath. Flowers white, ½ in. across, produced in corymbs 2 or 3 in. across; petals imbricate in the bud. Wings of stamens variable, sometimes none, sometimes a proportion toothed.

Native of the Amur region and Korea, where it may be said to represent *D. corymbosa*, to which species it is most nearly allied in botanical characters, but distinct in its smaller leaves with more open teeth and fewer-rayed (four to nine) hairs. In low-lying districts it is of little value owing to its susceptibility to injury by late frosts, but pretty in continental gardens, where it is not excited so early into growth as with us.

D. amurensis differs from *D. parviflora*, with which it has been confused, by the leaves being more noticeably discolorous and lacking the simple hairs on the lower surface which are a feature of that species. There is also a difference in geographical distribution, *D. parviflora* being a native of Hopeh and Chengtu, while *D. amurensis* occurs farther to the north-east. Whether the true D. *parviflora* is in cultivation in Britain it is impossible to say, but the specimens from garden plants in the Kew Herbarium are *D. amurensis*. It should be added that the deutzia called *D. parviflora* which Lemoine used as the seed-parent of *D.* × *lemoinei* was probably *D. amurensis*.

D. COMPACTA Craib

A deciduous shrub whose young shoots are at first clothed with close stellate down, becoming glabrous and brown the second year. Leaves lanceolate to oval-lanceolate, mostly rounded at the base, the apex long and tapered, minutely toothed, up to 2½ in. long by 1 in. wide on the sterile shoots, much smaller on the short flowering ones; the upper surface dull dark green, furnished with appressed, stellate, mostly four- or five-rayed hairs; grey-green beneath, with more minute and more numerous stellate hairs (only visible with a lens); veins in five to seven pairs; leaf-stalks ⅛ to ⅙ in. long. Flowers borne numerously during July at the end of leafy twigs about 3 in. long, in compact corymbose panicles 2 in. across. Flowers white, ⅓ in. wide, closely packed; petals roundish, imbricate in the bud; calyx bell-shaped at the base, the lobes broadly ovate; flower-stalks stellately hairy. *Bot. Mag.*, t. 8795.

Native of China; introduced by Maurice de Vilmorin, and distributed by him under the number 4277. It flowered for the first time at Kew and Glasnevin in July 1913. It is distinct in its small, densely clustered blossoms.

D. CORYMBOSA R. Br.

A deciduous shrub up to 9 ft high, of vigorous habit; bark bright brown, peeling off in rolls; young shoots sprinkled when quite young with tiny stellate hairs, becoming glabrous. Leaves ovate, with a long tapered point and a rounded or broadly tapered base, finely toothed, 2 to 5 in. long, 1 to 2¼ in. wide, green on both sides. To all appearance glabrous, they are, especially when young, really furnished with minute starry scales, only visible under the lens. Flowers crowded in a corymb or broad panicle, 2 to 3 in. across; each flower ⅝ in. in diameter. Petals pure white, imbricate in the bud, roundish ovate, overlapping; styles rather longer than the stamens; anthers large and conspicuously yellow, wings of the stamens toothed. Calyx-lobes broadly triangular, glabrous except for embedded starry scales.

Introduced from the Himalaya in 1830. The flowers have a charming hawthorn-like scent, and form compact, full clusters. The anthers, through their size and colour, give a yellowish tinge to the inflorescence. A distinct and fine species, the year-old branches forming large pyramidal panicles in June and later.

D. HOOKERANA (Schneid.) Airy Shaw *D. corymbosa* var. *hookerana* Schneid. —A close ally of the preceding, differing chiefly in the leaves, of which the undersides are densely and conspicuously covered with starry scales. It ranges from Nepal to S.W. China, where Forrest collected it under F. 19646 and other numbers, while *D. corymbosa*, as now understood, is confined to the W. Himalaya.

The beautiful deutzia introduced by Kingdon Ward under seed-number 6393 is very near to *D. hookerana*, but the filaments of the stamens are not toothed. The leaves are lanceolate or elliptic-lanceolate, mostly 2 in. long, ¾ in. wide, densely coated beneath with white stellate hairs. Flowers white, about ½ in. wide, in fairly dense clusters 2 to 3 in. across. Kingdon Ward collected the seeds of this deutzia in December 1924 during his journey of exploration through Tsangpo Gorge, at the eastern end of the Himalaya.

D. DISCOLOR Hemsl.

A shrub 5 or 6 ft high, young shoots scurfy, ultimately pale greyish brown, glabrous, and with peeling bark. Leaves of thinnish texture, narrowly ovate-oblong, 1½ to 4½ in. long, ½ to 1½ in. wide, dull green, with starlike hairs above, grey beneath, and furnished with very minute, stellate scurf; rounded or broadly tapered at the base, slender-pointed or sometimes acute. Flowers in corymbs 3 in. across; each flower ½ to 1 in. wide, the best forms very showy, varying in colour from white to pink. Calyx and flower-stalks scurfy.

Native of Central and W. China. The best form of this species is 'MAJOR', which has white or faintly rose-tinted flowers 1 in. across, produced in long arching sprays. It was introduced by Wilson for Messrs Veitch in 1901. The distinctions between this species and *D. longifolia* are pointed out under the latter.

Although many of Lemoine's hybrids were sent out as varieties of *D. discolor*, this species, as understood here, had no part in their make-up, the parent or grandparent being in fact *D. purpurascens*, which Lemoine, following the French botanist Franchet, considered to be a variety of *D. discolor*. See *D.* × *elegantissima* and *D.* × *rosea*.

DEUTZIA DISCOLOR 'MAJOR'

D. × ELEGANTISSIMA (Lemoine) Rehd.

D. discolor elegantissima Lemoine

The hybrids of this group were distributed by Lemoine as 'varieties' of *D. discolor*, but there is little doubt that the parentage is *D. purpurascens* × *sieboldiana*. The typical form of the cross—'ELEGANTISSIMA'—is a shrub of erect habit that bears some resemblance to *D. purpurascens* but shows the influence of the second parent in the broader, sharply acuminate leaves. Flowers rosy pink in bud and on the reverse, white flushed with rose on the inside, in loose, erect corymbs, borne in June. Award of Garden Merit 1954. 'FASCICULATA', put out by Lemoine two years later, is similar. A newer hybrid of the *elegantissima* group is 'ROSEALIND', which was raised by the Slieve Donard Nursery Co. and received a Preliminary Commendation in 1962. It bears flowers of a deep carmine-pink and grows to 4 or 5 ft high.

D. GLOMERULIFLORA Franch.

A deciduous shrub up to 6 ft high, with arching branches; shoots clothed at first with pale, starry down, then turning brown and beginning to peel. Leaves lanceolate, long and slenderly pointed, finely toothed, tapered to a usually rounded base, $1\frac{1}{2}$ to 3 in. long, $\frac{3}{8}$ to 1 in. wide, starry-downy above, greyish and much more downy beneath with five- or six-rayed hairs; on the midrib and veins there are numerous simple hairs; stalk $\frac{1}{12}$ in. or less long. Flowers $\frac{4}{5}$ in. wide, white, produced in May and June in rounded clusters $1\frac{1}{2}$ in. high and 2 in. wide; petals oval; stamens about half as long as the petals, the stalks of the outer ones conspicuously winged. Calyx grey with starry down, the lobes awl-shaped and as long as the tube, purple. Seed-vessels urn-shaped, $\frac{3}{16}$ in. wide, the remains of the four or five styles adhering at the top.

Native of W. China; first discovered by the Abbé David in W. Szechwan in 1869; introduced by Wilson in 1908. There are two great divisions of the genus *Deutzia*, one in which the petals in the bud state of the flower overlap each other, the second in which they do not do so. *D. glomeruliflora* belongs to the latter and it is distinct amongst them by reason of its softly downy leaves. It is quite hardy.

D. GRACILIS Sieb. & Zucc.

A deciduous, erect-growing shrub up to 6 ft high; young shoots soon quite glabrous. Leaves lanceolate, tapered or rounded at the base, long and slenderly pointed, rather coarsely and unequally toothed, 1 to 3 in. long, $\frac{3}{4}$ to $\frac{7}{8}$ in. wide, deep green. Seen under the lens the upper surface shows numerous star-shaped depressions in which are embedded minute, star-shaped hairs. Flowers pure white, $\frac{5}{8}$ to $\frac{3}{4}$ in. across, produced in erect racemes or panicles $1\frac{1}{2}$ to 3 in. long. Petals obovate, rounded at the apex; styles distinctly longer than the stamens; calyx slightly scaly, with small, triangular, greenish-white lobes. Flower-stalks glabrous.

Native of Japan; introduced about 1840. Well known for forcing early into blossom for conservatory decoration, this species is also very handsome out-of-doors where the climate suits it. It is quite hardy, but in low-lying districts is very frequently injured by late frosts. When frosted in bud, *D. gracilis* has the peculiarity of producing minute but otherwise apparently quite normal flowers. This phenomenon has been observed in the R.H.S. Garden at Wisley and, judging from specimens sent in by Fellows of the Society, it is not uncommon.

cv. 'AUREA'.—Leaves yellow.

cv. 'MARMORATA'.—Leaves spotted with yellow.

Lemoine used *D. gracilis* as a parent of some of his finest hybrids. Two of the groups in which they have been classified—*D.* × *rosea* and *D.* × *lemoinei*—are described in their alphabetical position. A third of lesser importance may be mentioned here:

D. × CANDELABRA (Lemoine) Rehd.—These hybrids are the result of crossing *D. gracilis* with *D. sieboldiana*. The typical form of the cross— 'CANDELABRA'—was put out by Lemoine in 1909. It resembles *D. gracilis* in foliage and habit but is hardier and has larger and denser panicles. Other forms of the cross are 'ERECTA' and 'FASTUOSA'. All were originally distributed as 'varieties' of *D. gracilis*.

D. GRANDIFLORA Bunge

A deciduous shrub up to 6 ft high, young shoots at first grey with stellate down. Leaves ovate, toothed (the teeth rather outwardly set), pointed, usually broadly wedge-shaped, sometimes rounded at the base, 1 to 2½ in. long, ½ to 1½ in. wide, rough to the touch above, white beneath with a close, fine, starry down; stalk up to ⅛ in. long. Flowers white, 1 to 1¼ in. wide, produced in May one to three together at the end of short leafy twigs; petals oblong or broadening towards the rounded ends. The wings of the stamens spread outwards and are decurved at the ends.

Native of N. China; named as long ago as 1835; introduced in 1910. It is very distinct amongst cultivated deutzias in the large size of the flowers and in their being borne not more than three together. For one of its genus it flowers early in China, i.e., towards the end of April and in May. The wings of the stamens, curved back like the hooks of a halberd, are also distinctive.

D. × HYBRIDA Lemoine   [PLATE 10

An important group of hybrid deutzias raised by Lemoine and put into commerce 1925-36. One parent was *D. longifolia*; the other is usually given as *D. discolor* but it may be that *D. purpurascens* or *D. × elegantissima* were used. The type of the group is 'MONT ROSE', which was put into commerce in 1925 as *D. hybrida* Mont Rose. Leaves narrowly ovate, sharply toothed, to 3½ in. long. Flowers fuchsia purple, slightly crimped at the margins; anthers golden yellow. Others in this group are: 'CONTRASTE', with gracefully arching branches; flowers star-shaped, similar in colour to 'Mont Rose', but with a darker stripe on the reverse of the petals. 'MAGICIEN' is similar, but the petals are edged with white. In 'JOCONDE' the flowers are white, about 1¼ in. across, purple in bud and on the reverse of the petals. Finally, 'PERLE ROSE' has smaller flowers than in other members of the group, but freely borne. They are pale pink.

D. × LEMOINEI Bois

A small group of hybrids between *D. gracilis* and *D. parviflora* raised by Lemoine of Nancy. The typical form of the cross—'LEMOINEI'—was raised in 1891. It is an erect shrub up to 7 or 8 ft high, with glabrous young shoots, and lanceolate leaves, 1½ to 4 in. long, ½ to 1¼ in. wide, sharply toothed, long-pointed; the upper surface has minute star-like hairs, beneath it is almost glabrous. Flowers pure white, ⅝ in. across, produced in erect corymbs. For forcing into flower early this is a very valuable shrub, more beautiful and effective than *gracilis*, and in that state was very popular at spring flower shows.

Out-of-doors, at least in low-lying localities, it rarely has a chance to do itself justice, owing to the destruction of its flower-buds by unseasonable frosts. Its natural flowering time is May and June. See further under *D. amurensis*.

cv. 'AVALANCHE'.—Flowers white, very freely borne in small clusters on arching branches; leaves small, dark green. This is thought to be a back-cross between *D. gracilis* and 'Lemoinei' but the exact parentage is unknown. Rehder considers it to be a form of *D.* × *maliflora* (see below).

cv. 'BOULE DE NEIGE'.—Habit dwarf and compact; flowers large, pure white, in dense, rounded clusters.

D. × **MALIFLORA** Rehd.—This name is founded on the deutzia 'FLEUR DE POMMIER' raised by Lemoine by crossing *D.* × *lemoinei* with *D. purpurascens*. It is a small shrub bearing clusters of twenty to thirty flowers which are pink fading to white, with frilled margins.

D. LONGIFOLIA Franch.

A deciduous shrub 4 to 6 ft high; young shoots sparsely scurfy; afterwards glabrous, bright brown, peeling. Leaves narrowly oval-lanceolate, rounded or tapered at the base, slender-pointed, finely toothed, 1½ to 5 in. long, ½ to 1¼ in. wide, upper surface dull greyish green, sprinkled with pale, flat, usually five- or six-rayed, stellate hairs, under-surface greyish white, covered with a close felt-like layer of eight- to twelve-rayed stellate scales, the midrib and chief veins furnished on each side with few to many white simple hairs. Flowers in corymbose panicles, 2 to 3 in. long and wide, produced in June at the end of short two- to six-leaved twigs; each flower is about 1 in. across, pale purplish rose, paling at the margins of the petals. The wings of the inner stamens are deeply bilobed at the top, the anthers set in the notch; calyx-lobes linear-oblong, persistent, covered like the calyx-tube and flower-stalks with pale starry scurf. Fruit ¼ in. across. *Bot. Mag.*, t. 8493.

Native of W. China; introduced by Wilson in 1905. This is one of the finest of the Chinese deutzias, both in size of flower and beauty of tint. It is closely allied to *D. discolor*, but is distinguished by the longer, narrower leaves, more distinctly veined beneath, and especially, by the simple hairs along the midrib—absent in *discolor*; the wings of the inner stamens are deeply bilobed in *discolor*, but the lobes do not reach up to or above the anther as in *longifolia*.

var. FARRERI Airy Shaw—Flowers white, 1 in. wide, produced in early June in cymose clusters 2 to 3 in. long and wide. *Bot. Mag.*, t. 9532. A native of Kansu, China; introduced by Farrer during his journey of 1914–15. He described it as a noble shrub whitening, when in flower, the coppiced slopes on which it grows 'with a surf of snow'. A plant from the original seed is 7 ft high at Highdown, near Worthing, where it gives a beautiful display.

This deutzia was at first considered to be D. ALBIDA Batal., discovered by the Russian traveller Potanin in 1885, but in the text to the plate in the *Botanical Magazine*, Airy Shaw pointed out that it does not agree well with that species and is better placed under *D. longifolia* from which, indeed, it differs little save in the colour of the flowers. The true *D. albida*, which is probably not in cultivation, is also closely allied to *D. longifolia*.

cv. 'VEITCHII'.—A superior form with larger flowers, coloured deep lilac-pink.

D. longifolia is one parent of the important hybrid group *D.* × *hybrida* (q.v.).

D. × MAGNIFICA (Lemoine) Rehd.
D. crenata magnifica Lemoine

A group of hybrids between *D. scabra* and *D. vilmoriniae*, all raised by Lemoine of Nancy and put into commerce from 1909 onwards, mostly as 'varieties' of *D. crenata* (now known as *D. scabra*). In 'MAGNIFICA', the first and typical form of the group, the foliage resembles that of *D. scabra* but the flowers are borne in shorter, broader and denser panicles; they are white and double. A vigorous, erect shrub, flowering June–July, to about 8 ft high. Others in this group are:

cv. 'EBURNEA'.—Flowers single, white, bell-shaped, in loose trusses.

cv. 'ERECTA'.—Flowers single, white, in very large erect panicles. Award of Merit, 1931.

cv. 'LATIFLORA'.—Flowers white, single, more than 1 in. across, with widely spreading petals, borne very numerously in erect panicles. Award of Merit, 1925.

cv. 'LONGIPETALA'.—Flowers single, white, with long and narrow petals. The leaves, too, are smaller and narrower than in the other forms.

cv. 'STAPHYLEOIDES'.—Large, single white flowers, with reflexed petals, recalling those of a species of *Staphylea*.

D. MAXIMOWICZIANA Makino.*
D. discolor Maxim., not Hemsl.; *D. hypoleuca* Maxim.

A deciduous shrub 5 or 6 ft high, with brown slender branches furnished with starry down. Leaves narrowly oval-lanceolate, slenderly pointed, wedge-shaped at the base, inconspicuously toothed, 1½ to 3½ in. long, ½ to 1 in. wide, covered with a white, very close down beneath; stalk about ⅛ in. long. Flowers white, ¾ in. wide, borne in May on erect, slender panicles 2 to 3½ in. long, that terminate short lateral twigs carrying one or two pairs of leaves; petals oblong; calyx cup-shaped with short teeth.

Native of Japan; introduced in 1915. It is closely related botanically to

* In previous editions of this work, this species was named *D. hypoleuca*. It was described by Maximowicz in 1888 as *D. discolor*, evidently in ignorance of the fact that Hemsley had used that name for another species in the previous year. In 1892 Maximowicz renamed his own species as *D. hypoleuca*, but he was antedated by Makino, who, in the same year, but nine months earlier, had named the species in honour of its author.

D. scabra, differing from that well-known species in the long narrow leaves being white beneath (green in *scabra*) and in the more slender growths.

D. MOLLIS Duthie

A deciduous shrub 5 or 6 ft high, with reddish-brown, hairy young shoots. Leaves lanceolate, oval, or broadly ovate, 2 to $4\frac{1}{2}$ in. long, $\frac{5}{8}$ to $2\frac{1}{4}$ in. wide; shortly or slenderly pointed, rounded or tapered at the base, finely toothed, dull

DEUTZIA MOLLIS

green and rough with stellate hairs above, grey and thickly felted with soft down beneath. Flowers white, $\frac{1}{2}$ in. across, produced during June in dense corymbs 2 to 3 in. in diameter. Petals rounded, imbricate in the bud; wings of stamens tapered from the base to the top, and quite entire; calyx-lobes very short, broad, and reflexed. Flower-stalks and calyx densely covered with short hairs and starry scales. *Bot. Mag.*, t. 8559.

Native of Hupeh, China; discovered by Wilson, and introduced by him in
1901. It is very distinct from the older deutzias in the thick down beneath the
leaves, and in the tapering filaments. It flowers in June, but has not yet made
a great display.

D. MONBEIGII W. W. Sm.

A deciduous shrub 4 to 6 ft high; young shoots reddish brown, slender,
furnished with minute, grey, starry scales. Leaves ovate-lanceolate, pointed,
minutely toothed, ½ to 1 in. long, half or less than half as wide, white and
entirely covered beneath with twelve- to fourteen-rayed scales, much more
thinly above with five- or six-rayed ones; stalk $\frac{1}{16}$ in. long. Flowers in corymbs
of up to fifteen blossoms produced at the end of short twigs; petals white, $\frac{2}{5}$ in.
long, $\frac{1}{6}$ in. wide, broadening towards the apex; calyx scaly, with five triangular
lobes; stamens about $\frac{1}{5}$ in. long, notched where the anthers are attached. Seed-
vessel globose, $\frac{1}{8}$ in. wide. *Bot. Mag.*, n.s., t. 123.

Native of N.W. Yunnan, China; introduced by Forrest, who collected it first
in November 1917, and again in July 1921, at an altitude of 8,000 ft. It is
distinct on account of its small leaves and small fruits. It is quite hardy at Kew
and plants flower freely there in late May and June. An attractive shrub.

This species is rather variable in flowering time, but the form usually seen in
gardens is not in full blossom until July and all the more valuable on that
account. On strong shoots the leaves may be up to 1¾ in. long.

D. PULCHRA Vidal

A deciduous shrub 8 ft or more high; young shoots covered with minute
scales. Leaves lanceolate to narrowly ovate, slender-pointed, wedge-shaped to
nearly rounded at the base, remotely and minutely toothed, 1½ to 4 in. long,
¾ to 2 in. wide, furnished on the upper side with stellate hairs or scales having
five to eight rays, much more thickly beneath with many-rayed ones; stalk ¼ to
⅜ in. long. Flowers pendulous, produced in early May in slender panicles 2 to
4 in. long terminating short leafy twigs, often forming as a whole a compound
panicle 12 in. long by 6 in. wide. Petals narrowly oblong or linear, pointed,
nearly ½ in. long, ⅛ in. wide, rather erect but recurved towards the end, scaly,
white tinged with pink. Calyx bell-shaped, very scaly, with five short, broadly
triangular teeth; styles five; stamens with two spreading lobes or wings at the
top. *Bot. Mag.*, t. 8962.

Native of the Philippines (N. Luzon) and of Formosa, whence it was introduced in 1918 by Wilson (W. 10906). It first flowered with the late Marquess of
Headfort at Headfort House, Co. Meath, in 1922. It has been confused with
D. taiwanensis (q.v.) which is also a native of Formosa. It is a very beautiful
species, well worthy of a choice position. 'The long sprays of flowers are like
Lily of the Valley, and I have counted as many as thirty-five blossoms in a single
raceme. The closely clustered anthers are bright orange. The deep-green leaves
are perfectly shaped and the whole shrub has an aristocratic bearing' (H. G.

Hillier in *Ornamental Flowering Trees and Shrubs* (Conf. Rep.), 1938). The peeling orange-buff stems are an additional attraction. At Kew it is only hardy when grown against a wall.

D. PURPURASCENS (L. Henry) Rehd.

D. discolor var. *purpurascens* L. Henry

A shrub 6 or 7 ft high; shoots pale brown, rather scurfy when quite young. Leaves ovate or ovate-lanceolate, 2 to 3 in. long, ¾ to 1½ in. wide, broadly tapered or rounded at the base, slender-pointed, toothed, scurfy, with starry minute scales on both surfaces, especially above; stalk ⅛ to ⅜ in. long. Corymbs rounded, 1½ to 2 in. across, expanding in early June; flowers ¾ in. across, white suffused with purple on the outside; petals roundish ovate, scurfy outside except at the margins. The five longer stamens have the apex of the wings forked so that each fork stands above the anther, the five smaller ones have the apex undivided and the anther attached below it on the inner side; calyx with linear-lanceolate lobes, and, like the flower-stalk, covered with starry scurf. *Bot. Mag.*, t. 7708.

Native of Yunnan; discovered by the Abbé Delavay, and sent by him to Vilmorin in 1888. It is allied to *discolor*, but as indicated by Rehder is distinguished by the scales on the leaves being only five- to seven-rayed (half as many as in *D. discolor*), and by the wings of the filaments being extended above the anthers. A very handsome shrub and the parent of several beautiful hybrids, for which see *D.* × *elegantissima* and *D.* × *rosea*. Another less common in cultivation is:

D. × KALMIIFLORA Lemoine—This hybrid, of which the pollen parent is *D. parviflora*, was raised by Lemoine and distributed in 1900. Its flowers are pale rose inside, deeper outside, and about ⅘ in. across.

D. REFLEXA Duthie

A shrub 3 ft or more high; young shoots glabrous. Leaves oval-lanceolate, tapered at the base, slenderly pointed, 2 to 4 in. long, ½ to 1 in. wide, upper surface beset with rather scattered starry scales, the lower one grey, densely clothed with much smaller scales, and furnished with simple hairs along the chief veins. Flowers pure white, produced in May and early June in dense, rounded, corymbose panicles about 2 in. across. Petals ⅓ in. long, reflexed at the margins; wings of the stamens distinctly bilobed at the top; calyx-lobes narrow-oblong, persistent; calyx and flower-stalks scaly.

Native of Central China; discovered and introduced by Wilson in 1901. It is very pretty about the beginning of June, the previous year's stems being then loaded with the numerous flower-clusters. It is allied to *D. vilmoriniae*, and has the same fringe of simple hairs along the midrib and veins, but the flower-stalks are shorter, the inflorescence more crowded, the flowers smaller; the reflexed margins of the petals are also very distinctive.

D. REHDERANA Schneid.

D. dumicola W. W. Sm.

A deciduous shrub up to 6 ft high, of close bushy growth; young shoots slender, covered with starry down. Leaves ovate, mostly rounded at the base, pointed or bluntish at the apex, minutely, closely and sharply toothed, ½ to 1¼ in. long, half as much wide, both sides furnished with starry scales, those on the upper side four- to seven-rayed, those below five- to ten-rayed, dull green and rough to the touch; stalk $\frac{1}{16}$ in. long. Flowers white, about ½ in. wide, produced three to five together in the leaf-axils, or at the end of twiggy shoots in April and May; petals oblong; calyx ⅛ in. long with a cup-shaped base and five short triangular teeth, grey with starry scales; stamens deeply cleft at the top, the anthers partially embedded in the notch.

Native of Yunnan, China; discovered by Schneider and introduced by Forrest in 1913 as *D. dumicola*. In the smallness of its leaves it resembles *D. monbeigii*, but in that species they are more tapered at the base and are white beneath. *D. monbeigii* also has more flowers in each cluster.

D. × ROSEA (Lemoine) Rehd.

D. gracilis rosea Lemoine

A group of hybrids raised by Lemoine of Nancy around 1895–1900. All were put into commerce as 'varieties' of *D. gracilis*, which was one of the parents, the other being *D. purpurascens*. The first of the set ('ROSEA'), which Rehder took as the type, has ovate-lanceolate to ovate-oblong leaves about 2 in. long, which are more hairy than those of the first parent. Flowers in short broad panicles (not in elongated panicles as in the first parent, nor in cymes as in the second); petals pink on the outside, paler within. It makes a rather dense shrub, with arching branches and grows to about 3 ft high.

cv. 'CARMINEA'.—This is the best-known of the group and one of the most delightful of dwarf deciduous shrubs. The flowers are pale rosy pink within, darker on the reverse and in bud, about ¾ in. across, borne in May–June in large panicles. It makes a rather spreading plant, with arching branches, to about 3 ft high. Put into commerce in 1900.

Several other forms of the cross were distributed but are less common in gardens. 'CAMPANULATA' is an erect, bushy shrub with large, white, rather bell-shaped flowers, with purple stalks and calyces. 'EXIMEA' is near to *D. gracilis*; flowers white within, pink on the reverse and bright pink in bud; leaves dark, bronzy green.

The form of *D. × rosea* figured in *Bot. Mag.*, n.s., t. 189, is of uncertain identity, but near to 'Carminea'.

D. RUBENS Rehd.

D. hypoglauca Rehd.

A deciduous shrub of vigorous growth about 6 ft high, with erect, much-branched stems; young shoots glabrous, with reddish-brown bark that peels off the second year, leaving the branches grey. Leaves ovate to ovate-lanceolate, finely toothed, rounded or broadly wedge-shaped at the base, abruptly or slenderly pointed, 1½ to 3 in. long, ½ to 1¼ in. wide, green and sprinkled with mostly four-rayed (sometimes three-rayed) hairs above, undersurface often glaucous and covered very sparsely to fairly densely with three- to six-rayed hairs; chief veins four to six each side the midrib; stalk ⅛ in. long. Inflorescence a rounded cluster of white blossom 3 or 4 in. wide; petals obovate, imbricate in bud; calyx ⅛ in. long, sprinkled with minute starry down, cup-shaped at the base, with five triangular lobes; flower-stalks glabrous. The winged, petal-like stalks of the stamens are erect and form a kind of tube in the centre of the flower, the bright yellow anthers being set in a notch at the top. *Bot. Mag.* t. 9362.

Native of Hupeh and Shensi, China; discovered by Wilson in 1901; introduced by W. Purdom in 1910. It is a distinct and beautiful species and is perfectly hardy in this country. It blooms in June.

D. SCABRA Thunb.

D. crenata Sieb. & Zucc.

A deciduous shrub up to 10 ft high; branches erect, covered with brown peeling bark; young shoots glabrous or slightly rough. Leaves ovate to ovate-lanceolate, the larger ones of the barren shoots rounded or heart-shaped at the base, slender-pointed, up to 4 in. long by nearly 2 in. wide; the smaller ones and those of the flowering twigs tapered at the base, all stellately scurfy on both sides, the marginal teeth are small and fine, standing upwards rather than outwards from the margin. Panicles erect, cylindrical, 3 to 6 in. long, terminating short leafy lateral twigs. Flowers pure white or tinged with pink outside, ½ to ¾ in. long and wide; petals nearly erect, oblong, pointed; style about as long as the petals, calyx-lobes deciduous, covered with starlike scales; the lobes triangular; wings of stamens with two distinct shoulders below the anthers. Flowers in late June. *Bot. Mag.*, t. 3838.

Native of Japan and China; introduced in 1822. This is undoubtedly the best and most reliable of deutzias in this country. It usually escapes damage by late frosts, and produces its showy erect panicles in great profusion. Strong branches will, in their second year, become transformed into pyramidal masses of bloom 2 ft long. The double-flowered and rosy forms are excellent shrubs.

cv. 'CANDIDISSIMA'.—Flowers double, pure white. Put into commerce by Froebel around 1867.

cv. 'FLORE PLENO'.—Flowers double, white, tinged with rosy purple on the outside. Introduced by Fortune in 1861 and exhibited by Standish's nursery in 1863 as *D. crenata flore pleno*. Also known under such epithets as *plena* and *rosea plena*.

cv. 'PRIDE OF ROCHESTER'.—Similar to the preceding, but the rosy tinge is paler. Raised in the USA by Ellwanger and Barry.

cv. 'PUNCTATA'.—This variety has single, pure white flowers, but the leaves are strikingly marbled with white and two or three shades of green. It is a rather pretty variegated shrub, but apt to revert to the ordinary green state.

cv. 'WATERERI'.—Flowers 1 in. across, single; petals rosy outside.

Although this species is perfectly distinct from *D. sieboldiana* (q.v. for the points of difference), they were confused by Thunberg, and it has long been a matter of controversy for which of the two his name *D. scabra* should be used. In Ohwi's *Flora of Japan* (1965) the species described above is treated under the name *D. crenata* Sieb. & Zucc. (*D. scabra* Thunb., in part), and *D. sieboldiana* accepted as the true *D. scabra* Thunb.

D. SCHNEIDERANA Rehd.

A deciduous shrub 6 to 8 ft high, the quite young shoots sprinkled with tiny starry down, soon glabrous, the bark becoming brown, afterwards peeling. Leaves ovate to lanceolate, slender-pointed, rounded to wedge-shaped at the base, minutely but sharply toothed; 1½ to 4 in. long, ½ to 1¼ in. wide; upper surface sprinkled with five- or six-rayed hairs, the lower surface greyish white with many-rayed hairs, the midrib and chief veins; stalk ⅛ to ¼ in. long. Inflorescence a panicle 1½ to 2½ in. long, opening in June. Flowers white, ¾ in. wide, the petals narrowly oblong, rounded at the end, covered with stellate down outside; calyx bell-shaped at the base, ⅛ in. long, grey with stellate down, the five lobes triangular; stamens notched at the top where the anthers are attached; styles usually three.

Native of W. Hupeh, China; discovered by Henry, introduced in 1907. This is nearly akin to *D. scabra*, which differs in being much more thinly starry downy beneath the leaf and in having none of the simple hairs near the chief veins such as occur in this species. The inflorescence of *D. schneiderana* is not so cylindrical and the petals are also narrower and smaller.

var. LAXIFLORA Rehd.—A variety with laxer panicles and rather narrower leaves.

A beautiful deutzia at Nymans in Sussex is near to *D. schneiderana* and received an Award of Merit when shown under that name on 5 July 1938.

D. CHUNII Hu—A near ally of the preceding, differing in its narrower, willow-like leaves, ½ to ⅔ in. wide, only sparsely stellate-hairy above. The flowers are smaller (¼ in. wide) but borne with great freedom in numerous panicles up to 3 in. long. This is a beautiful species, with graceful foliage, flowering in July when most deutzias are over or past their best. It was introduced from E. China in 1935.

D. NINGPOENSIS Rehd.—This is allied to the two preceding species, from which it may be distinguished by the broader, ovate-oblong leaves with remotely dentate or entire margins and by the longer panicles (to almost 5 in. long). It was described in 1911 from a specimen collected by Faber in Chekiang.

D. SETCHUENENSIS Franch. [PLATE 9

This species is mainly represented in cultivation by the following variety, which is greatly superior to the type as a garden plant:

var. CORYMBIFLORA (Lemoine) Rehd. *D. corymbiflora* Lemoine—A shrub up to 6 ft high, of graceful habit; young shoots covered with loose hairs, rather rough, glossy the first year, brown the second year, finally peeling. Leaves oval-lanceolate, rounded at the base, taper-pointed, finely toothed, $1\frac{1}{2}$ to $4\frac{1}{2}$ in. long, $\frac{5}{8}$ to $1\frac{1}{2}$ in. wide, dull green and rough with minute starry hairs above, grey and more densely covered with similar hairs beneath; stalk $\frac{1}{4}$ to $\frac{3}{8}$ in. long. Flowers white, about $\frac{5}{8}$ in. across, produced in June and July in corymbs 3 or 4 in. across. Petals ovate, clothed with minute starry down outside; calyx-lobes triangular, persistent, they and the flower-stalks grey-felted. The wings of the longer stamens terminate at the top in two prominent teeth; the shorter stamens have several smaller teeth. *Bot. Mag.*, t. 8255.

A native of Szechwan and Hupeh, China; introduced to France in 1895 and put into commerce by Lemoine two years later as "*D. corymbiflora*". It is likely to be a failure in gardens subject to late spring frosts and may suffer winter-damage through inadequate ripening of the wood in the cooler and rainier parts of the country. But given the right conditions there are few more beautiful summer-flowering shrubs than this. The small, starlike flowers of a dazzling whiteness are borne one to three hundred together in branched clusters and open successively over a period of two months from June onward. It thrives in chalky soils.

Typical *D. setchuenensis* was introduced from the same area at the same time and distributed by Lemoine as "*D. corymbiflora erecta*". It is inferior to the var. *corymbiflora* as a garden plant owing to its smaller corymbs; botanically it differs from it in the smaller, narrower leaves and certain other minor characters.

D. × MYRIANTHA Lemoine, is a beautiful hybrid between *D. setchuenensis* and *D. parviflora*. Flowers pure white, very numerous in large corymbs, hardier than the first parent.

D. SIEBOLDIANA Maxim.

D. scabra Sieb. & Zucc., not Thunb.

A deciduous shrub of bushy, rather lax habit 4 to 6 ft high; young shoots covered with scurfy stellate down. Leaves ovate or oval, $1\frac{1}{2}$ to 3 in. long on the barren shoots, $\frac{5}{8}$ to $1\frac{1}{4}$ in. wide, rounded, heart-shaped, or tapered at the base, pointed, sharply and irregularly toothed, dull green, stellately hairy on both surfaces, the hairs with three to five rays; veins prominent beneath; stalk $\frac{1}{4}$ in. or less long. Leaves of the flowering twigs smaller and comparatively broader; often scarcely stalked. Flowers pure white, $\frac{1}{2}$ in. in diameter, produced during early June in corymbose-paniculate clusters 1 to $2\frac{1}{2}$ in. long, terminating short lateral twigs which carry one or two pairs of leaves. Petals ovate; style rather longer than the stamens, whose wings (at least of the longer ones) taper towards the anthers; calyx felted, the lobes broadly triangular, persistent. Flower-stalks rough with bristles and stellate down.

Native of Japan; and an elegant though not showy shrub. It is of dwarfer habit than *D. scabra*, to which it is allied, and differs botanically in having the leaves on the flowering wood almost sessile; and in the longer, tapered stamens (see also *D. scabra*). The flowers are mignonette-scented and the stamens orange-coloured.

DEUTZIA SIEBOLDIANA

D. STAMINEA R. Br.

A deciduous shrub 4 to 5 ft high; shoots rough when young with starlike scales. Leaves ovate, with long slender points, and a rounded or tapered base, unequally toothed, dull green and rough above, grey beneath, and thickly covered with minute starry scales, 1 to 2½ in. long, ½ to 1½ in. wide. Flowers in short racemes or corymbs 2 in. wide; petals ⅜ to ½ in. long, downy; wings of stamens toothed; calyx grey with stellate scales, its lobes narrow, pointed.

T S—C

Native of the Himalaya; tender in this country. At Kew it is cut down to the ground almost every year, and its flowers consequently are not often seen.

var. BRUNONIANA Hook. f. & Thoms. *D. brunoniana* Wall., nom. nud.; *D. corymbosa* Lindl., not R. Br.; *D. canescens* Hort.—This is the form usually seen in cultivation. It has more broadly ovate, longer-pointed leaves and larger flowers than are typical.

D. TAIWANENSIS (Maxim.) Schneid.

D. crenata var. *taiwanensis* Maxim.

A deciduous shrub up to 6 ft or more high; young shoots slender, starry downy. Leaves ovate-lanceolate to ovate, pointed, the larger ones rounded at the base, finely toothed, 2 to 4 in. long, ¾ to 1½ in. wide, upper surface furnished with three- or four-rayed scales, the lower surface with four- or five- (occasionally six-) rayed ones; stalk ⅛ to ¼ in. long. Flowers white, borne in slender panicles 3 to 5 in. long, terminating leafy twigs; petals ⅜ in. long, ⅛ in. wide; calyx cup-shaped, very scaly, with triangular short teeth; stamens with two triangular teeth below the anthers.

Native of Formosa, where it was originally collected by Richard Oldham in 1864. W. R. Price found it again in 1912 but the plants in cultivation were raised from seed gathered by E. H. Wilson in 1918. It occurs up to 12,000 ft altitude, so should be hardy in most parts of the kingdom. The description given above was made from Oldham's original specimen, but Price's and Wilson's dried specimens have much smaller stellate scales on the leaves. It has been confused with *D. pulchra* which has leaves greyer underneath, the scales many-rayed, and the leaf-margins often almost toothless. *D. pulchra* has also larger flowers, and is easily distinguished by the longer leaf-stalk and thicker leaves.

D. VILMORINIAE Lemoine

A vigorous shrub of erect habit up to 8 ft or perhaps more high; young shoots slightly rough with scurfy stellate hairs at first, becoming brown and shining. Leaves oblong-lanceolate, rounded or broadly tapered at the base, slenderly pointed, sharply toothed, 2 to 5½ in. long, ⅝ to 2 in. wide, dark dull green and rough with stellate hairs above, grey and covered with a close felt of starry down beneath; also with simple hairs at the sides of the midrib and veins; stalk ⅛ to ½ in. long. Flowers white, 1 in. across, in broad corymbose panicles up to 3 in. long. Petals ovate with the edges upturned; wings of stamens dilating upwards to about midway, then narrowing, awl-like, to the anthers. Calyx-lobes linear-lanceolate, reflexed, covered like the flower-stalk with grey scurf, persistent. Fruits hemispherical, 3/16 in. across.

Native of Szechwan, China; sent to Maurice de Vilmorin at Les Barres by the Abbé Farges in 1897; introduced to England in 1905. It is a rapid grower, and its fine flowers escape damage by late frosts better than those of most deutzias do, and usually make a good display. It was named after the late Madame de Vilmorin of Les Barres. Allied to *D. discolor*.

D. WILSONII Duthie

A shrub 4 to 6 ft high, whose young branches are slightly scurfy at first, soon becoming dark reddish brown; the bark peeling. Leaves 2 to 5 in. long, ⅝ to 1½ in. wide, ovate-oblong to oblong-lanceolate, tapered or rounded at the base, acute or acuminate, rough, with four- to ten-rayed stellate hairs above, dark dull green; grey beneath, and covered with minute stellate scurf, and furnished also with pale bristle-like simple hairs, especially along the midrib and veins. Flowers in corymbose panicles; each flower nearly 1 in. across, white; longer stamens with tapered wings, shorter ones toothed. *Bot. Mag.*, t. 8083.

Native of W. and Central China; discovered and introduced by Wilson about 1901. It is a handsome shrub allied to *D. discolor*, but distinct in the hairiness of the lower surface of the leaves, suggesting *D. mollis* when young. It has been suggested that it may be a hybrid between this species and *D. discolor*.

DICENTRA FUMARIACEAE

A small genus of herbaceous perennials in N. America and E. Asia. The species described is exceptional in forming a woody base, but it is perhaps straining a point to regard it as a shrub at all.

D. CHRYSANTHA (Hook. & Arn.) Walp.

Dielytra chrysantha Hook. & Arn.

A semi-herbaceous or sub-shrubby plant which becomes woody at the base, sending up annually stems and flowering branches 2 to 4 ft high. It is quite free from down in all its parts. Leaves of a pale glaucous hue, up to 12 in. long, bi-pinnately or tri-pinnately divided; the ultimate divisions lobed, ¼ to 1 in. long, ⅛ to ¼ in. wide, the lobes linear or wedge-shaped. Panicles 1 to 2 ft high, erect, slender, sparsely branched. Flowers erect, yellow, ½ to 1 in. long and wide, opening first in June or July and continuing for two or three months. There are four petals of two shapes: the two outer ones are baggy at the base, curving inwards halfway up and spreading outwards at the pointed, recurved apex; the two inner ones are erect and enclose the six stamens and stigma. *Bot. Mag.*, t. 7954.

Native of California, where it was first discovered by David Douglas. It was introduced to cultivation by William Lobb, who sent seeds to Messrs Veitch of Exeter, from which plants were raised that first flowered in 1852. Since then it has had an only intermittent existence in our gardens, where it does not appear to be long-lived, missing probably the heat and brilliant sunshine of its natural home. It is found wild on dry hills in S. California up to 5,000 ft. It should be grown in well-drained soil at the foot of a south wall in full sunshine, all the better if the wall is that of a hot-house. The whitish foliage and bright yellow blossom give a charming effect. The shape of the flowers recalls that of *D. specta-bilis*, the common border plant popularly known as 'Dutchman's Breeches', but in *D. chrysantha* they are erect.

DICHOTOMANTHES   ROSACEAE

A genus of one species in E. Asia related to *Cotoneaster*, but well distinguished by its peculiar fruit.

D. TRISTANIICARPA Kurz

An evergreen tree up to 20 ft high, or a shrub; young shoots densely clothed with white wool. Leaves alternate, oval, pointed, tapered towards the base, entire; 1 to 4 in. long, ½ to 1¼ in. wide; dark slightly lustrous green and glabrous above, clothed with pale silky hairs beneath; stalk $\frac{1}{12}$ in. long; stipules minute, thread-like, silky, soon falling away. Flowers white, each ¼ in. wide, produced during June in terminal corymbs about 2 in. wide. Petals five, rounded; stamens fifteen to twenty, glabrous; calyx five-lobed, woolly outside. The fruit is really a dry oblong capsule ¼ in. long, but is almost entirely enclosed by the calyx which remains, enlarges, and becomes fleshy.

Native of Yunnan, China, and found there by Henry and other collectors; introduced by Forrest in 1917. In outward appearance it much resembles a cotoneaster and the flowers also strongly suggest that genus. The fruit, however, is very distinct on account of the calyx persisting, enlarging and ultimately covering all except its tip. It does not appear to be very hardy at Kew in the open ground, at least when young, but succeeds quite well on a wall. A specimen in the R.H.S. Garden at Wisley, growing in the open in Seven Acres, was badly cut in the winter of 1962–3, though previously never more than slightly frosted. It has little garden value.

DICKSONIA   FILICES—CYATHEACEAE

The propriety of including a tree fern in this work is perhaps open to question, but *D. antarctica* provides in some gardens of the west an exotic feature of great beauty scarcely comparable with any other there. It is the only tree fern at all commonly seen in gardens and then only in the dampest and mildest parts. But *Cyathea dealbata*, the best known of the New Zealand tree ferns, thrives just as well as the dicksonia at Rossdohan in Co. Kerry, Eire. It is well distinguished by its fronds, which are vividly white to glaucous beneath.

Dicksonia has about twenty species in Australasia and the larger Pacific Islands. *Cyathea* is a much larger genus, distributed in the tropical and subtropical parts of both the New and the Old Worlds.

D. ANTARCTICA Labill.

The trunk of this fern has a black, woody core of bone-like texture covered with matted rootlets which by their increase keep adding to its diameter. According to Hooker the trunks are occasionally 30 to 50 ft high in the wild and as much as 4 ft in diameter. In the wild the fronds of large old trees are up to 12 ft long, tapering to a point at the end; in smaller, younger ones 4 to 6 ft long. They are twice pinnate, the primary divisions up to 18 in. long, thus giving the tronds a diameter of 3 ft. The ultimate divisions are 1 to 2 in. long, ¼ to ⅜ in. wide, pinnately lobed, upper surface dark bright green, lower one dull. The life of a frond is from one to two years, and when a new tier of the young, bishop's crozier-like fronds are uncurling in spring, those of the older tier start to droop downwards and fall against the stem, where they soon die but cling on for several years. There they serve a useful purpose in keeping the youngest rootlets of the trunk moist and growing, and although to many people somewhat unsightly, undoubtedly add to the vigour and rate of growth of the plant.

The dicksonia is a native of New South Wales, Victoria, S. Australia, and Queensland, as well as of Tasmania, where 10 to 20 ft is the usual height.

It thrives and reproduces itself freely at Caerhays Castle, Trewidden and Penjerrick, Cornwall; at Logan in Wigtownshire; and in Eire at Derreen and Rossdohan, Co. Kerry. At Penjerrick the tallest has a stem 14½ ft high and 4¾ ft in girth (1966). The colony at Derreen, Lady Mersey tells us, was planted around 1900. The tallest there have less luxuriant fronds than the younger ones and have put on little growth in the past twenty-five years.

A thriving colony of this fern might well serve as an indicator of the British climate in its mildest and dampest form. Apart from freedom from severe frost, shade, moisture and protection from wind are its chief necessities.

DIERVILLA CAPRIFOLIACEAE

As now understood, this is a small genus of deciduous shrubs native to N. America. Its Asiatic relatives, which are of far greater importance in gardens, are now placed in the genus *Weigela* and are described in Vol. IV. The two genera are well distinguished from each other: in *Diervilla* the flowers are two-lipped, invariably yellow and borne on the current season's growth; in *Weigela* the corolla is regular, yellow only in *W. mid-dendorfiana*, and the flowers are borne on short lateral twigs on the growth of the previous year.

D. LONICERA Mill.

D. canadensis Willd.; *D. humilis* Pers.

A spreading, suckering shrub 2 to 4 ft high; young wood glabrous. Leaves oval or ovate-oblong, taper-pointed, usually heart-shaped at the base on strong shoots, tapering on weak shoots, 2 to 5 in. long, 1 to 2½ in. wide, evenly toothed, quite glabrous on both surfaces, hairy on the margin when quite young; stalk ¼ in, or less long. Cymes few-flowered, axillary and terminal, produced in June and July on the current season's shoots, the terminal ones three- or five-flowered; axillary flowers often solitary. Corolla yellow, becoming deeper with age, funnel-shaped, the tube ½ in. long, wider across the five narrow lobes. Calyx glabrous, with five erect, awl-shaped lobes. Style and stamens hairy below. *Bot. Mag.* t. 1796.

Native of eastern N. America, from Newfoundland to the S. United States. First brought to Europe by Dr Dierville, a French surgeon, after whom the genus is named; cultivated by Miller in 1739. It is the least ornamental of cultivated diervillas, and rarely seen outside botanic gardens.

D. SESSILIFOLIA Buckl.

A deciduous shrub of somewhat tufted habit, 3 to 5 ft high, with four-angled young branches which are downy only on the corners. Leaves ovate-lanceolate, 2½ to 7 in. long, half as wide; sharp-toothed, rounded, or heart-shaped at the base, taper-pointed, glabrous except on the midrib above, stalkless. Flowers much crowded in terminal cymose clusters up to 3 in. across, or in smaller axillary ones, produced from June to August. Corolla sulphur-yellow, ½ in. long, a narrow tube with five narrow-oblong, blunt lobes. Calyx with five narrow, awl-shaped lobes. Seed-vessel ½ in. long.

Native of the south-eastern United States. This is much superior to its ally *D. lonicera*, producing large clusters of flowers on the current season's shoots. It should be pruned back in spring before growth commences, when it will send up a dense mass of shoots that will blossom during the summer.

D. × SPLENDENS (Carr.) Kirchn. *Weigela splendens* Carr.; *D. sessilifolia splendens* Hort.—A hybrid between the above and *D. lonicera*. It originated about 1850.

D. RIVULARIS Gatt.—This is closely allied to and very similar to *D. sessilifolia*, but the leaves are stalked, downy on both sides, especially beneath; the young shoots are downy all over; and the seed-vessel is only ¼ in. long. Flowers lemon-yellow. Native of the south-eastern United States; introduced in 1902 to Kew.

DIOSPYROS   EBENACEAE

Of this large and important genus (to which the ebony tree belongs) only three species are known to be really hardy in this country, although a fourth—*D. kaki*—will succeed in the warmer counties in the open, and in many places elsewhere against a wall. They are trees with alternate, entire leaves, and the shoots do not form terminal buds. The male and female flowers are on separate trees, and both are small and without beauty. The fruits are large, and beset at the base by the calyx, which continues to grow after the rest of the flower has fallen. These trees like a good loamy soil, and should be raised from seed, except the named varieties of *D. kaki*, which are grafted on seedlings.

D. ARMATA Hemsl.

A semi-evergreen tree of sturdy, rounded habit 20 ft high, much branched the branchlets clothed with a thick minute down, and occasionally terminated by a stout thorn. Leaves $\frac{1}{2}$ to $2\frac{1}{2}$ in. long, $\frac{1}{2}$ to $1\frac{1}{4}$ in. wide, entire, the smaller ones roundish, the larger ones oval, tapered about equally at both ends, blunt or rounded at the apex, dark shining green, the midrib minutely downy above, minutely hairy beneath; the blade is specked with minute transparent dots; stalk $\frac{1}{8}$ in. or less long. Flowers not seen. Fruit yellow, roundish, $\frac{3}{4}$ in. in diameter, furnished with appressed bristles; borne on a stalk about $\frac{1}{2}$ in. long and set in a persistent calyx, the four lobes of which are ovate, $\frac{1}{2}$ in. long.

Native of Central China; discovered by Henry, introduced by Wilson in 1904, and now growing in the open air at Kew apparently quite hardy, and forming a sturdy bush. In the original description the leaves are described as persistent, but cultivated plants are quite deciduous in hard winters.

D. KAKI L. f.   KAKI OR CHINESE PERSIMMON

A deciduous tree, ultimately 20 to 40 ft high, with more or less downy young shoots and winter buds. Leaves oval, 3 to 8 in. long, $1\frac{1}{2}$ to $3\frac{1}{2}$ in. wide, tapering at both ends, strongly veined, soon glabrous and glossy green above, more or less downy beneath. Fruit 3 in. wide, yellow, and of the shape of an average tomato, supported by the persistent calyx, 2 in. across. *Bot. Mag.*, t. 8127.

Native of China; long cultivated in Japan, where several scores of varieties have been raised, remarkably diverse in size of fruit. Kakees are now being extensively cultivated in the south of Europe, and the fruits sent from there are becoming well known in London shops as 'persimmons'. As regards the British Isles, it or some of its forms, for it is difficult now to distinguish the type, are perfectly hardy in the milder parts. Canon Ellacombe obtained fine crops in his garden at Bitton, from trees trained against a wall. At Kew, splendid crops are obtained in a cool greenhouse, and a tree on a south wall there bore many scores of fruits in 1935. This species is well distinguished from the other hardy ones by its large leaves and fruit and by its globose winter buds.

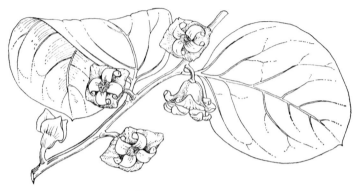

DIOSPYROS KAKI

D. LOTUS L.   DATE PLUM

A deciduous tree usually under 40 ft high in this country, but probably twice as high in warmer climates; young shoots more or less downy, often becoming quite glabrous. Leaves oval, 2 to 5 in. long, 1 to 2 in. wide, tapered at both ends, entire, dark polished green above, and glabrous except on the midrib, pale, somewhat glaucous, and with small scattered hairs beneath; stalk ¼ to ½ in. long, downy. Trees unisexual; male flowers produced on very short, downy stalks one to three together, in the leaf-axils of the shoots of the year in July; female flowers solitary. Calyx large in both sexes, remaining attached to the base of the fruit, and growing larger with it; corolla pitcher-shaped, green suffused with red, ¼ in. long. Fruit orange-shaped, ultimately ½ to ¾ in. across, purplish or yellowish.

Native of China, whence it has several times been introduced; of the Himalaya; possibly also of Asia Minor. It was cultivated early in the 17th century in England, but has never become very common in gardens, although perfectly hardy. Fruits develop freely, but remain very astringent, and unfit for food. The trees emit a curious heavy odour, especially on damp days in autumn. It is due apparently to some exhalation from the leaves.

It is as a specimen rather than as a fruiting tree that this species should be judged and as such it ranks high, owing to its dark but lustrous green leaves, which contrast with the more common greens of the garden landscape. It has reached a height of 35 ft at Kew and 40 ft at Westonbirt.

D. VIRGINIANA L.   PERSIMMON

A deciduous tree 40 to 65 ft high in this country, but occasionally over 100 ft high in the wild, with a trunk 2 ft in diameter; young shoots more or less downy. Leaves oval to ovate, tapering or more or less heart-shaped at the base, pointed at the apex, 1½ to 5 in. long, ¾ to 2 in. wide, glossy green above, pale beneath, glabrous except for a little down on both sides of the midrib; stalk downy, ⅓ to 1 in. long. Male flowers produced one to three together in the leaf-axils, on very short downy stalks. Corolla pitcher-shaped, ⅓ in. long, with four short recurved lobes. Female flowers solitary, larger, yellowish white. The fruit I have not seen in this country, but it is described as more or less orange-shaped, 1 to 1½ in. across, pale yellow with a red cheek.

Native of the eastern United States as far north as Connecticut, but most abundant in the Southern and Central States, where the fruit is eaten in large quantities. The tree is somewhat tender when very young, but perfectly hardy after a few years. The finest tree in the British Isles was one growing near the Sun Temple at Kew. It was a male tree 65 ft high, with a trunk 5 ft 6 in. in girth. The trunk was singularly picturesque because of the rugged bark, which was deeply cut into square or rectangular blocks. This tree was planted where it stood in 1762, being one of a large collection transferred from the Duke of Argyll's garden at Whitton to the then newly formed arboretum at Kew. In a young state the persimmon is rather like the date plum, but the leaves are longer-stalked, not of so polished a green, broader and more rounded at the base. A specimen in the Oxford Botanical Garden measures 55 × 5¾ ft (1970).

DIOSTEA   VERBENACEAE

A genus of three species in the Andes, related to *Verbena*.

D. JUNCEA (Gill. & Hook.) Miers

Verbena juncea Gill. & Hook.; *Baillonia juncea* (Gill. & Hook.) Briq.

A slender, tall, deciduous shrub of thin, erect habit, eventually a small tree 15 to 20 ft high; young branches long, slender, rush-like; with scattered down at first, then glabrous. Leaves opposite, few, the pairs often about 2 in. apart, stalkless, usually ⅓ to ¾ in. long, ⅛ to ¼ in. wide, ovate-oblong, triangular-toothed, thick, slightly downy. Flowers pale lilac, produced during June, crowded on spikes about 1 in. long, which terminate short lateral twigs. Corolla ¼ in. long, tubular, narrowed towards the base, with five small rounded lobes. Calyx cylindrical, downy. *Bot. Mag.*, t. 7695.

Native of the Andes of Chile and the Argentine; introduced to Kew about 1890. This shrub or small tree, which is perfectly hardy in the open, has some-what the aspect of *Spartium junceum*, but is, of course, quite dissimilar in flower; and even without flowers the opposite leaves show the absence of relationship. It is an interesting plant, pretty without being showy, and worth a place in a shrubbery where its naked base is hidden and its slender top can stand up above the other shrubs. It is quite well able to take care of itself in such a position. Increased by cuttings in July and August.

DIOSTEA JUNCEA

DIPELTA   CAPRIFOLIACEAE

Four species belonging to this genus are known, three of which are in cultivation. They are deciduous shrubs, exclusively Chinese, and are allied to *Diervilla* and *Weigela*, which they resemble in shape of corolla. The most distinctive feature of the dipeltas is the number of bracts at the base of the ovary, which persist, grow, and ultimately form dry disk-like wings to the fruit, similar in texture to the wings on elm seed. Two of them are much larger than the others, and being attached by their centres to the fruit have the shield-like appearance to which the generic name refers. Leaves opposite. The following species are promising garden shrubs, more especially *D. floribunda*. They like an open, moist, loamy soil, and can be increased by cuttings of half-ripened growths.

D. FLORIBUNDA Maxim.   [PLATE 11

A deciduous shrub, with peeling bark, ultimately (according to travellers) 10 to 15 ft high; young twigs downy (partially glandular-downy). Leaves ovate to oval-lanceolate, tapering at the base, long-pointed, not toothed, 2 to 4 in. long, ⅝ to 1½ in. wide, downy on both sides and at the margin, at least when young; stalks ¼ in. or less long. Flowers fragrant, produced in the axils of the leaves and at the end of short twigs, from one to six on a stalk. Corolla 1 to 1¼ in. long, funnel-shaped, 1 in. wide, with five rounded, spreading lobes, pale pink with yellow in the throat. Calyx persistent, with five linear, downy lobes scarcely ¼ in. long. Flower-stalk hairy, ½ in. long, with four unequal-sized bracts below the ovary, which continue to grow as the fruit ripens and hide it. The two largest bracts are ¾ in. long and ⅝ in. wide. *Bot. Mag.*, t. 8310.

Native of Central and W. China; discovered in 1875, but not introduced until 1902, when Wilson sent home living plants to Messrs Veitch. Seeds were sent two years later. The first flowers opened in the Coombe Wood nursery in 1907. This shrub bears its fragrant blossoms abundantly, the year-old shoots developing short side twigs on which they appear in May and June, thus forming sprays with the flowers in a double row of clusters. At Messrs Hilliers' nursery at Winchester, on chalky soil, this species has reached a height of 20 ft.

D. VENTRICOSA Hemsl.

A deciduous shrub up to 18 ft high; young shoots downy. Leaves oval or ovate-lanceolate, rounded at the base, the apex long and taper-pointed, edged with a few gland-tipped teeth, sometimes quite entire, 2 to 6 in. long, ¾ to

DIPELTA VENTRICOSA

1¾ in. wide, downy on the margins and slightly so on both surfaces; stalks ⅛ to ⅓ in. long. Flowers produced at the end and in the leaf-axils of short side shoots; usually they are solitary in the leaf-axil and in a terminal corymb of three. Corolla between tubular and pitcher-shaped, 1 to 1¼ in. long, and ¾ in. wide at the mouth; the tube protruded on one side near the base; five-lobed, the lobes rounded, and the two upper ones the smaller; deep rose outside, paler within, except in the throat, which is orange-coloured. Calyx with five awl-shaped lobes ⅓ in. long, fringed with short hairs. Flower-stalk slender, and furnished with several bracts at the base of each flower. These bracts (the largest ⅔ in. long, ⅓ in. wide), are persistent and become attached to the fruit, which is also covered by the persistent calyx. Distinct from *D. floribunda* in the smaller, bellied corolla. *Bot. Mag.*, t. 8294.

Native of W. China; discovered and introduced by Wilson in 1904, flowered in the Coombe Wood nursery in May 1908. It thrives very well, and makes an ornamental as well as an interesting shrub.

D. YUNNANENSIS Franch.

A deciduous shrub of spreading graceful habit 6 to 12 ft high in the wild; young shoots four-angled, minutely downy. Leaves opposite, ovate-lanceolate, slender-pointed, rounded to broadly wedge-shaped at the base, not toothed, 2½ to 5 in. long, 1 to 2 in. wide, slightly downy and dark glossy green above, more downy beneath especially on the midrib; stalk ⅛ to ¼ in. long. Flowers usually produced in May in short clusters terminating short leafy shoots that spring from the growths made the previous year. Corolla ¾ to 1 in. long, tubular at the base, expanding at the mouth into five short rounded lobes; the colour is creamy white, more or less stained with rose; throat orange. Calyx of five awl-shaped, downy lobes. Flower-stalks slender, downy, ½ to 1 in. long, carrying four heart-shaped, membranous bracts beneath the calyx, the two larger ones enlarging, persisting and enclosing the small dry fruit, at the apex of which the calyx also remains attached.

Native of Yunnan, China; discovered in 1886 by the Abbé Delavay; introduced by Forrest about 1910; it flowered at Glasnevin in May 1919. From *D. floribunda* it is distinguished by its longer flower-stalks and, on the average, larger flowers with deeper corolla lobes. *D. ventricosa* differs in its corolla being more bellied towards the base and more barrel-shaped. It is perfectly hardy in the Edinburgh Botanic Garden, where there are three plants over 5 ft in height. It is 10 ft high at Westonbirt, in Mitchell Drive.

DIPTERONIA   ACERACEAE

This small genus, with two species in C. and S. China, is the only member of the Maple family other than *Acer* itself. From the true maples it is very distinct in its fruit, in which each of the pair of nutlets is evenly winged all around; the leaflets, too, are more numerous than in any of the pinnate-leaved maples.

D. SINENSIS Oliver

A deciduous, small tree up to 30 ft high, with a trunk 6 in. or more in diameter, or sometimes merely a big bush. Leaves opposite, pinnate, 9 to 12 in. long, consisting usually of from seven to eleven leaflets, which are opposite, ovate or lanceolate, short-stalked; 1½ to 4 in. long, one-third as much wide, sharply, coarsely, and irregularly toothed, covered like the twigs when young with scattered hairs; there are small tufts in the vein axils. Panicles erect, pyramidal, 6 to 12 in. long. Flowers polygamous, very small, greenish white; stamens white, six to eight, ⅛ in. long. Fruits produced in large clusters, each one composed of two flat, winged carpels (like the fruits of wych-elm or *Ptelea*), obovate, ¾ to 1 in. long, soft red.

Native of Central China, at from 3,500 to 5,000 ft elevation. This interesting and handsome species was introduced by Wilson for Messrs Veitch about 1900. It is beautiful in foliage, and its fruits are very interesting; it flowered at Kew in June 1912, but the blossoms were in no way effective. It is evidently quite hardy, thriving well in good soil, and can be propagated by cuttings taken in July and put in gentle bottom heat; it also roots readily from layers.

There is an example measuring 37 × 3 ft at Hergest Croft, Heref. (1969).

DIRCA   THYMELAEACEAE

A genus of two species, both natives of N. America. *Dirca* is closely allied to the daphnes, from which it differs in the indistinctly lobed perianth-tube and the exserted stamens.

D. PALUSTRIS L.   LEATHERWOOD

A deciduous shrub 3 to 6 ft high, with flexible, jointed branches, and very tough, glabrous bark; buds downy. Leaves alternate, oval or obovate; 1½ to 3 in. long, about half as wide; tapered at both ends, not toothed, glabrous and pale green above, somewhat glaucous beneath; stalk ⅛ in. or less long. Flowers appearing in March at the joints of the naked wood, usually three together on very short stalks. Perianth-tube ⅓ in. long, narrowly funnel-shaped, faintly lobed, pale yellow; stamens eight, protruded. Fruit a pale, oval drupe, ⅓ in. long, rarely seen in Britain.

Native of eastern N. America; introduced in 1750. This is not a showy plant, and its yellow flowers are often injured by spring frost, but it is an interesting one. It is moisture-loving, and likes a deep soil to which some peat is added. A specimen in the Cambridge Botanic Garden attained a diameter of 9 ft. The remarkable toughness and flexibility of the shoots have been taken advantage of in several ways. In early times the American Indians used the bark for making ropes, and the twigs are still used in rural districts as tying material and for basket-making.

DISANTHUS   HAMAMELIDACEAE

A monotypic genus of the witch-hazel family, from all other members of which it is distinguished by the combination of palmately veined leaves, flowers borne in pairs (hence the generic name), and fruits with several seeds in each cell.

D. CERCIDIFOLIUS Maxim.

A deciduous shrub up to 8 or 10 ft high, with slender, spreading branches; young shoots perfectly glabrous, round, and marked with small whitish lenticels. Leaves alternate, firm, very broadly ovate to roundish, heart-shaped or truncate at the base, blunt and rounded at the apex, 2 to 4½ in. long, and almost or quite as broad, perfectly glabrous, glaucous green and entire; stalk 1 to 2 in. long. Flowers dark purple, two of them set back to back at the end of a stalk ¼ in. long, produced from the leaf-axils. Each flower is ½ in. across, with five narrow tapering petals, arranged starwise, its odour faint and unpleasant; calyx with five short recurved lobes; stamens five. Seed-vessel a nut-like capsule. *Bot. Mag.*, t. 8716.

Native of Japan; introduced in 1893 but even now, three-quarters of a century later, still rather uncommon in gardens. The flowers, borne in October, are not attractive. It does, however, possess one excellent quality: its foliage—handsome and Judas-tree-like in form—turns in autumn to lovely shades of claret-red and purple, sometimes suffused with orange. Few shrubs, indeed, are more beautiful in this respect. Except when young, it is quite hardy, but a rather difficult shrub to satisfy. At Kew it has not been a success and other gardeners too have reported failure. It appears to need a good, deep, moist and lime-free soil and is most at home in light woodland, where it is protected from wind and strong sun. In such conditions it thrives admirably and never fails to colour well every autumn. At the Winkworth Arboretum, Surrey, there is a group growing in full sun by the lake, but isolated plants might not thrive so well in such a position.

It resembles its ally the Virginian witch-hazel in flowering in October when the previous year's seeds are ripening.

DISCARIA RHAMNACEAE

A genus of small trees or shrubs closely allied to *Colletia*, and found chiefly in S. America. One almost hardy species is found in New Zealand, and the same or a nearly allied one in Tasmania and S. Australia. The leading characteristics of these plants are their large opposite spines, which are really reduced branches; their opposite or clustered leaves, and their numerous small, clustered, axillary flowers, of which a bell-shaped calyx is the most conspicuous part, the petals being often absent. Fruit a dry, three-lobed capsule.

The discarias like a sheltered, sunny position, ordinary garden soil, and they can be multiplied by means of cuttings taken in July and placed in a close frame.

D. CRENATA (Clos) Reg.
Colletia crenata Clos; *D. foliosa* Miers

A deciduous shrub or small tree with long, slender, pendulous, spiny branches. Leaves opposite, $\frac{1}{2}$ to 1 in. long, ovate-oblong, with shallow, rounded teeth; both surfaces glabrous and lustrous green, especially the upper one, which has an almost varnished appearance. The spines, stiff, sharp, and $\frac{3}{4}$ in. or more long, are produced in pairs at each joint. Flowers crowded in clusters on short twigs from the year-old shoots, each flower about $\frac{1}{5}$ in. across, with no petals, but a greenish-white calyx tubular at the base, divided at the top into five triangular lobes. Anthers exserted; ovary downy. *Bot. Mag.*, t. 9335.

Native of Chile from the central provinces to the Magellan region, and of bordering parts of Argentina; cultivated at Kew since 1842, and quite hardy. The example now in the collection is about 30 ft high. Although it has no colour-beauty to recommend it, its flowers are borne so abundantly in June as to render it quite pretty, and they are, besides, charmingly fragrant. It is well worth cultivating for these, as well as for its distinct and graceful appearance and glossy dark foliage.

D. crenata has been confused with:

D. SERRATIFOLIA (Vent.) Benth. & Hook. f. *Colletia serratifolia* Vent.— This species is closely allied to *D. crenata* but has less leafy branchlets, sharply serrated leaves and flowers with sessile anthers and glabrous ovaries. It is uncertain whether the true species is in cultivation; most plants grown under the name are *D. crenata*.

Another species in this group sometimes seen in cultivation is D. LONGI- SPINA Miers, a native of Uruguay. It has small obovate leaves, $\frac{1}{2}$ in. or less long, slender spines 2 in. or more long, and crowded clusters of small yellowish-white flowers. It requires the protection of a wall.

D. DISCOLOR (Hook.) Macloskie
Colletia discolor Hook.

A deciduous shrub 4 to 6 ft high and as much as 8 ft in diameter, with the main branches sometimes prostrate, nearly or quite glabrous in all its parts, the branchlets opposite and often ending in a spine. Leaves opposite, elliptic or elliptic-obovate, tapered at the base, rounded or notched at the apex, toothless or shallowly toothed; $\frac{1}{6}$ to $\frac{3}{4}$ in. long, $\frac{1}{4}$ in. wide; stalk very slender, $\frac{1}{12}$ in. or less long. Flowers produced in clusters of two or three at each leaf-axil, each on a slender stalk $\frac{1}{8}$ to $\frac{1}{6}$ in. long. Corolla absent; calyx white, bell-shaped, $\frac{3}{16}$ in. long, not so much wide, with four triangular lobes. Fruit consisting of three dry, globose lobes, each containing a seed.

Native of the Andes of Argentina and Chile, up to elevations of 2,700 ft. It was first called *Colletia* by the elder Hooker in 1843, from specimens collected by Capt. King at Port Famine (Fuerte Bulnes), on the Straits of Magellan. Introduced by H. F. Comber during his Andean travels, 1925–7, under three numbers, viz., 722, 766, and 794. The last he described as a 'good weeping form'; No. 766 as the best. It is a handsome shrub producing an amazing profusion of blossom, which is sweetly scented and borne in May and June. As it is found wild on hot, rocky sites it should be given a well-drained spot, as sunny as possible. It is quite hardy in mid-Sussex, but rarely seen outside those gardens in which it was raised from Comber's seed.

D. TOUMATOU Raoul   WILD IRISHMAN

A deciduous shrub, varying in New Zealand from a low, scrubby bush 2 ft high, to a small tree 25 ft high, with long, slender, flexuous and exceedingly spiny branches. Spines 1 to $1\frac{1}{2}$ in. or even more long, opposite, sharply pointed, stiff, standing out from the branchlets at almost right angles. Leaves opposite

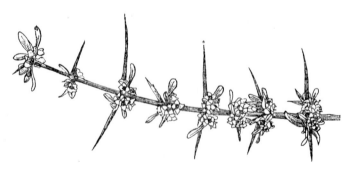

DISCARIA TOUMATOU

on the shoots of the year, or in clusters beneath the spines on the year-old shoots, from $\frac{1}{2}$ to $\frac{3}{4}$ in. long, varying in shape from narrow oblong to obovate. Flowers greenish white, $\frac{1}{6}$ in. across, produced very numerously in clusters along with the leaves; calyx with four or five lobes, petals absent. Fruit a round, three-valved capsule, ⅙ in. wide.

Native of New Zealand. This remarkable shrub is unfortunately too tender to thrive in the open at Kew, but succeeds very well against a south wall, where it flowers in great profusion every May. It is worth growing for its extraordinary spines, which are green and terete, and as thick as the shoot from which they spring. The leaves are sometimes absent on old plants. It is quite hardy in the Royal Horticultural Society's Gardens at Wisley, where there is a specimen in Seven Acres some 8 ft high and 10 ft across—possibly a hardier form than the one grown at Kew.

D. TRINERVIS (Poepp.) Reiche
Ochetophila trinervis Poepp.

A shrub with long, arching, usually spineless branchlets. Leaves elliptical to oblong-lanceolate, blunt and shortly mucronate at the apex, tapered at the base, about ½ to 1 in. long, three-veined from the base. Flowers borne singly or in threes; calyx with four or five teeth; petals spoon-shaped, four or five in number.

A native of the Andes of Chile and Argentina. A plant received from Bodnant in 1924 is quite hardy against a sheltered south wall in the Edinburgh Botanic Garden but is of no particular note as a garden plant. This species is distinct from *D. discolor* and its allies in having petals to the flower and in its three-veined leaves.

DISTYLIUM HAMAMELIDACEAE

A genus of about eight species of evergreen trees and shrubs in China, Japan and the Indo-Malaysian region. The species described below is one of three evergreen members of the witch-hazel family cultivated in the British Isles and the most common, though all are rare. The following combinations of characters distinguish them: flowers apetalous, in slender racemes—*D. racemosum*; flowers apetalous, in clusters—*Sycopsis sinensis* flowers with white petals—*Loropetalum chinense*.

D. RACEMOSUM Sieb. & Zucc.

An evergreen shrub with rigid, short branches or a tree up to 60 ft; young shoots minutely warted. Leaves alternate, leathery, entire, narrow-oblong or obovate, tapering at the base to a short stalk, often blunt at the apex, 1½ to 3 in. long, ½ to 1¼ in. wide, shining deep green, glabrous on both sides except when very young. Flowers sometimes unisexual, in small erect racemes about 1 to 1½ in. long. There are no petals, but a five-parted, red, downy calyx, and several lurid purple stamens; flower-stalks covered with rusty-coloured scurf. Fruit semi-woody, downy, surmounted by the two styles which remain attached at the top, and to which the generic name refers. *Bot. Mag.*, t. 9501.

Native of S. Japan, where it is an evergreen tree yielding, according to Sargent, an exceedingly hard, dark-coloured, valuable wood. In this country, however, it has never made more than a small, somewhat stiff shrub. It is hardy at Kew and grows well and flowers out-of-doors there in April and May. In the Edinburgh Botanic Garden there are several specimens, the tallest about 7 ft high. In the Glasnevin Botanic Garden, Dublin, the best example makes a spreading shrub 6 ft high and about 10 ft wide. It belongs to the curious rather than to the beautiful class of shrubs. Propagated by cuttings.

cv. 'VARIEGATUM'.—Leaves narrow, often deformed; blotched and margined irregularly with creamy white; once grown in cool greenhouses.

DOCYNIA   ROSACEAE

A genus of some five species of evergreen or partially evergreen trees or shrubs with alternate leaves. The generic name is an anagram of 'Cydonia' and the genus is indeed closely allied to the true quince, which differs from it by its free styles.

D. DELAVAYI (Franch.) Schneid.

Pyrus delavayi Franch.

An evergreen shrub or small tree up to 30 ft, of spreading habit; young shoots hairy, becoming chocolate-brown and glabrous, finally nearly black, often developing spine-tipped spurs. Leaves ovate-lanceolate, often narrowly so, 1½ to 3 in. long and up to 1 in. wide, almost entire, pointed, closely felted beneath at first; stalk ¼ to ½ in. long, downy. Flowers stalkless, apple-like, 1 to 1¼ in. across, white, pink-tinted in bud, produced in umbels of two to four, hawthorn-scented; calyx felted; styles united. Fruit oval, 1½ in. long, 1 in. wide, downy.

Native of Yunnan, China; introduced to France about 1890 and cultivated by Maurice de Vilmorin at Les Barres in 1901. Little was known of this species in Britain until a plant (probably from seed collected by Forrest in 1917–19) flowered at Wisley for the first time in 1938, when 14 ft high. An interesting account of this species by B. O. Mulligan will be found in *Journ. R.H.S.*, Vol. 65, pp. 120–1 (1940). It is of botanical interest but has little value as an ornamental plant.

D. INDICA Decne.—This species is a native of the E. Himalaya, Assam, Upper Burma, N.W. and S.E. Yunnan, and possibly of Szechwan also. It is closely allied to D. *delavayi* but distinguished mainly by its leaves, which are ovate or oblong-ovate, mostly 2⅕ to 3⅕ in. long, 1 to 1⅕ in. wide, acute or

acuminate at the apex, rounded at the base, woolly-tomentose at first, later glabrous, margins finely toothed, sometimes almost entire; juvenile leaves lobed and toothed, hawthorn-like. See further under *D. rufifolia*.

D. RUFIFOLIA (Lévl.) Rehd. *Pyrus rufifolia* Lévl.; *Malus docynioides* Schneid.; *Docynia docynioides* (Schneid.) Rehd.—This species is founded on a specimen collected in E. Yunnan, China, and to it Rehder referred Schneider 1349 (the type of *Malus docynioides*) from S. Szechwan, and certain specimens collected by Henry in S.E. Yunnan and by Wilson in Szechwan, the Wilson specimens are Veitch Expedition No. 3493 and Arnold Expedition No. 2998, and seeds may also have been sent under these numbers and distributed as *D. delavayi*. However, Rehder himself was doubtful about the distinctness of this species from *D. delavayi*, and material in the Kew Herbarium which would, by his criteria, belong to *D. rufifolia* has by other workers been assigned to either *D. indica* or *D. delavayi*, mostly to the latter. The specimen under Wilson 3493 seems, however, to be intermediate between these two species.

DORYCNIUM LEGUMINOSAE

Of the dozen or so species that make up this genus none is genuinely shrubby, for much of the growth they make during summer dies the following winter after bearing flowers and seeds. But the two here described (especially *D. suffruticosum*) form woody permanent bases. They belong to the pea-flowered section of Leguminosae and are distinguished by the capitate inflorescence and the thick, short seed-pods. The leaves are really trifoliolate, but are made to appear quinquefoliolate by having two leaf-like stipules similar to the real leaflets. Very easily cultivated in an open position in a light loamy soil.

D. HIRSUTUM (L.) Ser.

Lotus hirsutus L.

A semi-herbaceous plant, with erect, branching, annual stems, round, slightly ribbed and hairy, springing from a woody base; the leaflets with scarcely any stalk, obovate, ¾ to 1 in. long, ⅛ to ⅓ in. wide; hairy, especially beneath. Flower-heads 1½ in. across, produced on hairy stalks 1 to 2 in. long, from the leaf-axils and at the ends of the shoots. Flowers ¾ in. long, six to ten in a head, white; sometimes flushed with pink, calyx ⅓ in. long, five-lobed, very hairy. Pod ⅓ in. long, glabrous, oblong, containing about four seeds, the calyx persisting at the base.

Native of S. Europe; cultivated in England in 1683. When in bloom it has a resemblance to some brooms of the *Cytisus supinus* group, but is, of course, very distinct in the smooth pods and axillary inflorescence. It flowers from June to

September, and produces seed abundantly; these afford the best means of increase,
though the resulting plants will vary somewhat in habit. It is more attractive if
grown in a poor soil and hot situation.

D. SUFFRUTICOSUM Vill.
Lotus dorycnium L.

A deciduous sub-shrub 2 to 3 ft high, of thin, elegant habit. Stems very
slender, much-branched, slightly ribbed, furnished when quite young with grey
appressed down. Leaves of three (apparently five) leaflets, stalkless; leaflets
linear-obovate, ¼ to ¾ in. long, greyish, with silky hairs. Flowers produced in
numerous rounded heads, ½ in. or so across, from the leaf-axils near the top of
the branch, each head being borne on a slender stalk 1 to 2½ in. long. Flowers
pinkish white, ¼ in. long, ten to twelve in a head; calyx ⅛ in. long, with five
narrow, pointed lobes, silky grey. Pod rounded, about ⅛ in. long, containing
one seed.

Native of S. Europe, known in gardens since the middle of the seventeenth
century, but not much grown now. The base only of the plant is shrubby, the
upper part being semi-herbaceous, and dying back in winter. It is a graceful but
not showy plant, flowering from June to September. Occasionally it ripens a
good crop of seed, by which, and by soft wood-cuttings placed in bottom heat,
it can be propagated. The two 'apparent' leaflets on each leaf are really stipules.

DRIMYS   WINTERACEAE

A genus of about twenty species (fewer in some interpretations), natives
of Malaysia, E. Australia, New Caledonia and Central and S. America.
The family Winteraceae differs from Magnoliaceae (in which *Drimys* was
once placed) in the leaves without stipules; small, rarely solitary flowers;
carpels borne in a single whorl (not arranged spirally on a conical axis
as in Magnoliaceae). The family is also represented in gardens by the
New Zealand species *Pseudowintera colorata* and *P. axillaris*, described in
Vol. III.

D. LANCEOLATA (Poir.) Baill.   MOUNTAIN PEPPER
Winterania lanceolata Poir.; *D. aromatica* (R. Br.) F. v. Muell.;
Tasmannia aromatica R. Br.

A dense evergreen shrub or small tree attaining 15 ft high in the wild state.
Young stems rich crimson and remaining so for a year or more. Leaves elliptic
to oblanceolate, bluntly or sharply pointed, tapered at the base into a short stalk,
which is coloured like the stems; they are variable in size, from ⅗ to 3 in. or more

long, $\frac{2}{5}$ to $1\frac{3}{5}$ in. wide; medium green and glossy above, paler beneath, leathery.
Flowers dioecious, about $\frac{1}{2}$ in. wide, produced in April and May in fascicles at
the ends of the previous season's growths; sepals deciduous, $\frac{1}{5}$ in. long; petals
two to eight, whitish, linear or narrowly oblanceolate; female flowers with a
single carpel; male flowers with twenty to twenty-five buff-coloured stamens.
Fruit black.

Native of Tasmania, where it is very abundant, and of Victoria and New
South Wales; introduced in 1843. The leaves are aromatic and have a pungent,
peppery taste; the dried fruits have been used as a substitute for pepper. Although

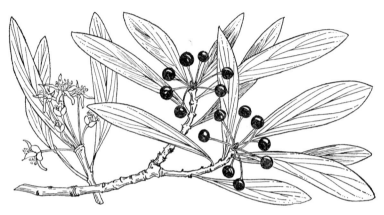

DRIMYS LANCEOLATA

reputed to be tender, this species seems to have survived the winters of 1961–3
in most of the few gardens where it is grown. The form introduced by Comber
in 1929 certainly appears to be quite hardy, given shelter from cold, drying
winds. It is of dense, broadly columnar habit and has leaves to about $1\frac{3}{4}$ in. long.

The mountain pepper is a handsome evergreen, very distinct in the deep red
tints that suffuse the stems, buds and petioles, and might well be tried as a hedge-
plant in sheltered gardens (it is already being used as such in Ireland). The
female flowers are inconspicuous, but the male, with their dense clusters of
pinkish-buff stamens, are quite pretty.

D. WINTERI J. R. & G. Forst.   WINTER'S BARK
Wintera aromatica Murr.   [PLATE 12

An evergreen tree to about 50 ft, or a large shrub, usually of rather conical
habit, with a greyish, highly aromatic bark. Leaves entire, oblong-elliptic to
oblanceolate, up to $7\frac{1}{2}$ in. long, $1\frac{1}{2}$ to $2\frac{3}{4}$ in. wide, acute to rounded at the apex,
light or dark green above, more or less glaucous beneath; stalks up to 1 in. long.
Inflorescence umbellate or fascicled; individual flowers on pedicels up to 1 in.
long, ivory-white, fragrant, to $1\frac{1}{2}$ in. across; petals oblong elliptic, variable in

number from about five to twenty; stamens numerous; carpels four to ten. Fruit compound, each fertilised carpel becoming fleshy and bearing up to about fifteen seeds.

If interpreted in a wide sense, *D. winteri* is a species of enormous range, from Tierra del Fuego to Mexico. But A. C. Smith, in his monograph on the American species of *Drimys* (*Journ. Arn. Arb.*, Vol. 24, pp. 1–33, 1943) recognises four species and restricts *D. winteri* to the region from Central Chile southward. He recognises two lowland varieties:

var. WINTERI *D. winteri* var. *punctata* (Lam.) DC.; *D. punctata* Lam.—This is the typical variety, found mainly south of 42°S. Leaves clustered at the ends of the branchlets. Inflorescence with one-flowered peduncles, more rarely umbellate; flowers with five to seven petals.

var. CHILENSIS (DC.) A. Gray *D. chilensis* DC.—This variety is of more northerly distribution, from 30° 30′ to about 44° 40′ S. Leaves distributed more evenly along the branchlets than in the preceding. Inflorescence compound, consisting of four to five simple umbels, each with four to seven flowers; petals six to fourteen. This variety appears to be what is commonly cultivated as *D. winteri* and is figured in *Bot. Mag.*, t. 4800, and n.s., t. 200. Unless the typical variety comes into cultivation the distinction is scarcely worth recognising in garden nomenclature. For the more distinct var. *andina*, see below.

D. winteri var. *latifolia* was described by Miers in 1858 from a specimen collected by Bridges near Valdivia. In this specimen, preserved in the Kew Herbarium, the leaves are oblanceolate, up to 5¾ in. long, 2⅝ in. wide, with a rather broad roundish or abruptly acuminate apex. It is part of the normal variation of the species and is given by Smith as a synonym of var. *chilensis* (see further below).

D. winteri first became known to science in 1578 when (to quote Don's account) 'Capt. William Winter, who went out with Sir Francis Drake, when he went round the world, at his return brought the bark of this tree with him from the Straits of Magellan. He had found it to be very useful to his ship's crew, both instead of other spices to their meat, and as a medicine very powerful against the scurvy.' It was described some two centuries later from a specimen collected on Cook's second voyage.

It is interesting that *D. winteri* is most tree-like and most prominent in the forest vegetation in the far south of the continent; in the northern part of its range, in spite of the warmer climate, it makes a small tree, preferring damp soils, where it forms colonies known as 'Canelares'. Although mainly a Chilean species, it also occurs in Argentina, mainly in Tierra del Fuego, but also on the eastern side of the Andes in Santa Cruz province and on the western shores of Lake Nahuel Huapi.

The form of *D. winteri* once commonest in gardens is of shrubby habit, with numerous stems from the base. The plant at Kilmacurragh in Eire is of this habit; it is a vast bush about 50 ft high, and one of its many stems is 8 ft in girth (1966). The leaves are oblong-elliptic to oblong-lanceolate, up to 6¼ in. long and 2 in. wide, bluntly acute to slightly acute at the apex, scarcely glaucous beneath. A plant at Trengwainton in Cornwall has similar foliage and habit and belongs, as probably does the Kilmacurragh plant, to the var. *chilensis*.

Plants are also in cultivation which are more slender and upright than is the form just mentioned, with definite leaders, in this respect resembling *D. winteri* as usually seen in the Andes. The origin of this form is not known, but according to the catalogue of the collection at Fota, Co. Cork, sent to Kew by the Hon. Mrs Bell, the two original trees there came in 1903 as seedlings from Wakehurst Place, Sussex, where they had been raised from seeds collected in South America. There is strong though not conclusive evidence that the seeds came from H. J. Elwes, who visited the Andes in the southern summer of 1901–2. There are two fruiting specimens in the Kew Herbarium collected by him during this visit. According to a note on these provided by Mr Philcox of Kew, one came from the Renaico Valley (in the Andes east of Temuco) and has leaves elliptic-oblong, slightly glaucous beneath. The other, from near Lake Llanquihue (at the southern end of the central valley of Chile), has leaves obovate to oblong-elliptic, glaucous beneath. Of the two originals at Fota one, which no longer exists, had narrower leaves than the other, which is listed as *D. winteri glauca latifolia* in the Fota catalogue. This is about 35 ft high. There is also a beautiful narrow-habited tree at Mount Usher in Co. Wicklow, about 40 ft high, with the leaves pale green above and silvery beneath.

The tree-like forms are often known in gardens as "var. *latifolia*", and a plant under this name received an Award of Merit when a flowering branch was exhibited by Gerald Loder from Wakehurst Place in 1930. The plant there no longer exists, but it most probably came from the same batch of seeds as the Fota plants. A tree at Trengwainton in Cornwall, also known as *D. winteri* "var. *latifolia*", certainly has leaves larger and relatively broader than in the old form, and is more slender in habit, with a definite leader. But in the Savill Gardens there is a tree of similar habit, propagated around 1950 from one growing at Lanarth in Cornwall, in which the leaves are slenderly oblanceolate and quite different from those of the Trengwainton plant or of the type-specimen of var. *latifolia* Miers. It has been said that the "var. *latifolia*" of gardens is hardier than the bushy form but this may not hold good generally. It should be added that there would seem to be no foundation for the belief that the "var. *latifolia*" always has green stems. The Trengwainton plant is shown as having green stems in the figure in the *Botanical Magazine*, but they were red in a specimen from the same plant seen in 1970. The plant in the Savill Gardens, which is "var. *latifolia*" of gardens in the sense that it is tree-like in habit, has the stems and petioles strongly tinged with red.

D. winteri is not reliably hardy outside the milder parts, where it thrives. In southern England it should survive most winters in a well-sheltered position but would be safer against a wall. It is certainly worth persevering with, for there are few more beautiful evergreens than *D. winteri* in its finest forms, with their soft-green leaves, silvery beneath, and spire-like habit. It has no objection to chalky soil, but being a moisture-lover it is not likely to thrive where the soil is dry or shallow. It can be propagated by cuttings of half-ripened wood, or by layers. Fertile seeds are often borne, but cannot be relied on to reproduce all the characters of the parent.

var. ANDINA Reiche—A very distinct variety of dwarf habit found in tree-line woodland in the Andes and the coastal range, where it grows to about 3 ft tall, but flowers freely when only a third of that size. Introduced by Comber in 1926 from near Llolli on the frontier between Chile and Argentina at 4,000 ft. A plant in the walled garden at Nymans in Sussex, raised from his seeds, is now, after forty years, about 5 ft high and 12 ft across.

DRYAS   ROSACEAE

A genus of four species (twenty in one interpretation), natives of the colder parts of the northern hemisphere. They are evergreen, creeping shrubs, whose closest allies (*Fallugia*, *Cowania* and *Chamaebatia*) are all warmth-loving shrubs of western N. America and Mexico. The most recent treatment is: E. Hulten, 'Studies in the Genus *Dryas*', *Svensk. Bot. Tidsk.*, Vol. 53, pp. 507–542 (1959).

D. OCTOPETALA L.   MOUNTAIN AVENS [PLATE 13

A prostrate evergreen plant 2 or 3 in. high, whose woody stems are covered with the persisting bases of fallen leaves and brown bark, which ultimately peels off. Leaves oval, oblong or ovate, usually heart-shaped at the base, blunt at the apex, with mostly four to eight large teeth or lobes along each margin, $\frac{1}{2}$ to $1\frac{1}{4}$ in. long, $\frac{1}{4}$ to $\frac{1}{2}$ in. wide, dark dull green with hairs along the midrib above, white with down beneath; stalk $\frac{1}{4}$ to $\frac{1}{2}$ in. long, very slender, downy. Flowers solitary on an erect downy stalk 1 to 3 in. high, lengthening at the fruiting stage; they are 1 to $1\frac{3}{4}$ in. wide, white; petals usually eight, oval-oblong, rounded at the end; sepals eight, linear, $\frac{3}{8}$ in. long, covered with pale wool outside. The fruit is somewhat like that of a clematis, each of the numerous seed-vessels being terminated by a tail 1 in. or more long, furnished over its whole length with silky hairs.

Native of the high latitudes and altitudes of the northern hemisphere; widely spread over the mountainous parts of the British Isles. Among other places I have seen it freely scattered over the rocky hills in the neighbourhood of Arncliffe in Yorkshire, flowering there in July and August. It is of easy cultivation but appears to prefer limestone rock and is excellently adapted for the rock garden.

f. ARGENTEA (Blytt) Hulten *D. o.* var. *argentea* Blytt; *D. o.* var. *vestita* Beck—Leaves silver-hairy on the upper surface as well as below. Found in Norway and in the Eastern Alps (Lower Engadine, Tyrol and Upper Styria), more rarely further west. This form belongs to the typical subspecies (subsp. *octopetala*), which is the only race of the mountain avens found in W. Europe.

D. INTEGRIFOLIA Vahl *D. o.* var. *integrifolia* (Vahl) Hook. f.—Leaves to $\frac{1}{2}$ in. or a little more long, $\frac{1}{4}$ in. or less wide, narrow-lanceolate to oblong, entire

or more rarely with a few teeth near the base. Native of Greenland, northern N. America and the Kolyma Peninsula.
More distinct is:

D. DRUMMONDII Hook.—This has the same habit and the leaves are similarly white beneath and lobed at the margin, but they are tapered at the base and longer stalked; the flowers differ in being pale yellow instead of white; the flower-stalk is usually taller (sometimes 9 in.) and more conspicuously downy. Filaments of anthers hairy (glabrous in *D. octopetala*). Native of the high latitudes of N. America; first discovered by Richardson, the botanist, who accompanied Sir John Franklin on his first voyage to the Polar Sea, 1819–22. It must soon after have been introduced as it was figured in the *Botanical Magazine* in 1830 (t. 2972).

D. × SUENDERMANNII Kellerer ex Suenderm.—A hybrid between the above and *D. octopetala*. Flowers (in the type) yellow in bud, afterwards white. Described from a cultivated plant, but such crosses occur in the wild where the two species are in contact.

ECCREMOCARPUS   BIGNONIACEAE

A genus of a few sub-shrubby evergreen tendril-climbers, natives of Chile and Peru. Flowers tubular, yellow or red, with four included stamens. Fruit a many-seeded capsule; seeds winged all around.

E. SCABER Ruiz & Pavon

A semi-woody climber with herbaceous shoots and the habit of a clematis; stems ribbed, not downy. Leaves opposite, doubly pinnate; leaflets three, five, or seven on each subdivision, ovate, oblique, irregularly and unequally lobed, ¼ to 1¼ in. long, often heart-shaped at the base, glabrous; the main-stalks end in a much-branched tendril which supports the plant by twisting round any available object. Flowers nodding, produced from June onwards in racemes 4 to 6 in. long, of usually seven to twelve blossoms. Corolla nearly 1 in. long, bright orange-red, tubular, bellied on one side, contracted at the mouth to a narrow orifice, where are five small, rounded lobes; stamens four. Calyx minutely glandular. Seeds flat, winged, numerous, in inflated pods 1½ in. long, ⅝ in. wide. *Bot. Mag. t.* 6408.

Native of Chile; introduced in 1824. This handsome climber is not reliably hardy and usually treated as an annual or biennial. The seed should be sown in February in heat and the seedlings planted out, after being once potted, in May; larger plants are obtained if the seed is sown in August and the seedlings over-wintered in a frost-free house or frame.

Usually classed with woody plants, it scarcely has a right to be considered as such out-of-doors, although in greenhouses it lives an indefinite time, and forms a stout woody base. Open-ground plants, if left through the winter, will not infrequently break into growth again from soil level. At Brodick in the Isle of Arran this species is counted as hardy and makes seasonal growths 8 to 10 ft long. It produces self-sown seedlings at Belhaven House, E. Lothian. Forms with yellow and with crimson flowers are available in the trade.

ECCREMOCARPUS SCABER

EDGEWORTHIA   THYMELAEACEAE

A genus of two Asiatic shrubs allied to *Daphne*, differing in the cylindric style with an elongated stigma (in *Daphne* the stigma is capitate and usually sessile).

E. CHRYSANTHA Lindl.   [PLATE 14

E. papyrifera Sieb. & Zucc.

A deciduous shrub up to 6 or 8 ft high; young shoots clothed at first with silky hairs, becoming glabrous and olive green, extraordinarily tough and supple. Leaves alternate, narrowly oval to narrowly ovate, pointed, wedge-shaped at the base, entire, 3 to 5½ in. long, ¾ to 2 in. wide, dark dull green and glabrous or with scattered hairs above, greyish green beneath and clothed with appressed silky hairs when young; stalk ¼ to ⅝ in. long. Flowers slightly fragrant, scarcely stalked, produced in February and March, forty to fifty packed together in a usually globose terminal head measuring 1 to 1½ or even 2 in. in width; main-stalk ½ in. long. As in *Daphne* the flower has only one floral envelope, which is called the calyx or perianth. This is tubular, ½ to ¾ in. long, slender, expanding

at the apex into four rounded lobes which are deep yellow. The outside of the
tube is entirely clothed with long, white silky hairs. Stamens eight, in two row
of four.

Native of China; introduced in 1845. It has long been cultivated in Japan for
the manufacture of a high-class paper used for currency but is not indigenous
there. It has not proved hardy at Kew, but can be grown outside in the milder
counties and in maritime districts. Although the flowers are mostly covered with
white silky hairs, the rich cowslip yellow of the lobes gives a pleasing touch of
colour, especially at the early season when they appear. The young twigs are
so remarkably supple that they can easily be tied into knots. A specimen in
Roath Park, Cardiff, planted in 1957–8, was over 7 ft high in 1966 and suffered
no damage in the winter of 1962–3 (*Gard. Chron.*, June 1, 1966, p. 558).

E. GARDNERI (Wall.) Meissn. *Daphne gardneri* Wall.—A native of the
Himalaya from Nepal and Sikkim. It is closely akin to E. *chrysantha* but is evergreen and the leaves are not, on the whole, so large. The flowers are yellow and
fragrant, but the hairs on the outside are shorter and less silky. It has long been
cultivated in the greenhouses at Kew, but is not so hardy as E. *chrysantha*. The
flowers turn black with drying. *Bot. Mag.*, t. 7180.

EHRETIA   EHRETIACEAE

A genus of about fifty species, mostly tropical or subtropical, formerly
placed in the family Boraginaceae. The generic name commemorates
G. D. Ehret, a German botanical artist who died in England in 1770.

E. THYRSIFLORA (Sieb. & Zucc.) Nakai   [PLATE 15

Cordia thyrsiflora Sieb. & Zucc.

A small deciduous tree 15 to 30 ft high in this country, of open, spreading
habit; young shoots soon glabrous, marked with pale spots. Leaves alternate,
oval, ovate, or slightly obovate, 3 to 7 in. long, $1\frac{1}{2}$ to 3 in. wide, smaller on
the flowering shoots, tapered or rounded at the base, short-pointed, toothed;
furnished above when young with small appressed hairs which soon fall away,
tufted in the vein-axils beneath; stalk $\frac{1}{2}$ to $\frac{3}{4}$ in. long. Flowers fragrant, white,
produced in August in terminal pyramidal panicles 3 to 8 in. long; the corolla
is $\frac{1}{4}$ in. across, deeply five-lobed; calyx with five rounded lobes. Fruit a globose
drupe $\frac{1}{6}$ in. wide, at first orange, finally black; rarely seen in this country. *Bot.
Mag.*, n.s., t. 440.

Native of China and Japan; rare in cultivation. The species is interesting
botanically but is not showy. It seems highly probable that it is the one to
which Hasskarl gave the name E. *ovalifolia* in 1844. If so, this name would have
priority over E. *thyrsiflora* but, as there is an element of doubt concerning the

identity of Hasskarl's plant, the name is not adopted here (see the note by Dr Turrill accompanying the figure in the *Botanical Magazine*).

Although tender when young, and liable to have its shoots winter-killed, *E. thyrsiflora* is perfectly hardy in the adult state at Kew, where there is a tree by King William's Temple, planted in 1904, which is 30 ft high and 5¼ ft in girth, with a deeply corrugated bark (1967). There is a specimen 37 ft high at Birr Castle, Co. Offaly, Eire (1966).

A nearly allied, or the same, plant was introduced in 1795 from the Himalaya, and grown in the early part of last century as *E. serrata* Roxb.

E. MACROPHYLLA Wall.—A handsome foliaged plant, not getting beyond the dimensions of a shrub with us, and more tender than *E. thyrsiflora*. It is frequently killed to the ground at Kew, but sends up stout, erect shoots several feet high during the ensuing summer. Leaves roundish, 4 to 6 in. long, two-thirds to nearly as much wide, rough with small bristles on both surfaces, especially above; young shoots similar. Native of the Himalaya.

A third species is E. DICKSONII Hance, a native of China, Formosa, etc., introduced by E. H. Wilson. It is a tree 30 to 35 ft high with slightly downy young shoots. Leaves elliptic, 4 to 8 in. long, rounded varying to slightly cordate or tapered at the base, shortly pointed, more or less downy on both surfaces. Flowers open in May and June in flattish panicles 2 to 4 in. long and broad; corolla white, ⅖ in. wide. Fruit subglobose, ½ in. wide, greenish yellow. It is over 20 ft high in Messrs Hillier's nursery at Winchester on chalky soil and grows well at Kew. It is apt to suffer in high winds, but otherwise is hardy.

ELAEAGNUS   OLEASTER   ELAEAGNACEAE

Of the three genera which form the natural order of scaly shrubs called Elaeagnaceae, *Elaeagnus* itself is distinguished from the other two—*Shepherdia* and *Hippophaë*—by its perfect (not one-sexed) flowers, and from *Shepherdia* further by its alternate leaves. It consists of about thirty species of evergreen or deciduous trees and shrubs, all the younger parts of which are covered with silvery or brownish scales. The flowers are in axillary clusters, and mostly fragrant; the perianth (there are no petals) has a cylindrical or bell-shaped tube expanding at the mouth into four lobes, resembling a miniature fuchsia. Stamens four, very shortly stalked, and attached at the top of the tube. Fruit a one-seeded drupe. Some of the scales as seen under the lens are beautifully fringed with silvery hairs; in fact, the whole aspect of the young parts of *Elaeagnus* under a sufficient magnifying power is remarkably beautiful.

The oleasters need a soil of only moderate quality, for the silvery-leaved deciduous ones develop a better colour on a light, sandy loam than on a rich one. The evergreen species are best increased by cuttings, the deciduous ones by seed. Grafting is sometimes recommended for the evergreen ones, but as the stocks have to be raised from deciduous species, plants so raised are not so healthy and long-lived as those on their own roots. The deciduous species need exposure to full sunlight.

E. ANGUSTIFOLIA L.

E. hortensis Bieb.; *E. argentea* Moench, not Pursh

A deciduous shrub or small tree up to 40 ft high, with occasionally spiny branches; young shoots covered with glistening silvery scales, becoming glabrous and dark the second year. Leaves narrow-oblong or lanceolate, 1 to 3½ in. long, ⅜ to ⅝ in. wide, dull green and scaly above, silvery scaly beneath. Flowers ⅜ in. long, fragrant, produced in early June, one to three in each leaf-axil of the young shoots. Each flower has a bell-shaped tube and four spreading lobes about as long as the tube; silvery outside like the under-surface of the leaves, yellow inside; stalk $\frac{1}{12}$ in. long. Fruit oval, ½ in. long, yellowish, silvery scaly; flesh mealy, sweet.

Native of W. Asia, naturalised in S. Europe, cultivated in England since the sixteenth century. It is a striking tree, especially when associated with dark-leaved evergreens, because of the whiteness of the twigs and under-surface of the leaves. In this respect, however, it is not so remarkable as *E. commutata*, whose leaves are silvery on both sides, but it is a larger, better-shaped tree. A kind of sherbet is made from the fruit in the Orient. In Central Europe especially in the parks and gardens of Germany and Austria, it is much planted, and as the foliage is much whiter under the continental sun than it is in Britain, it often makes a very telling feature in the landscape. There is a fine specimen at Hardwicke Court, Glos., 37 ft high and 50 ft in diameter of spread, with a trunk 8 ft in girth at ground level (c. 1966).

var. ORIENTALIS (L.) O. Kuntze *E. orientalis* L.—Leaves ovate, shorter than in the type (1½ to 3 in. long); they are not so glistening beneath and differ, too, in the presence of stellate down. Native of the Near East and Central Asia. Introduced in 1739. It does not flower so freely as the type and on the whole is not so desirable.

E. COMMUTATA Rehd. SILVER BERRY

E. argentea Pursh, not Moench

A deciduous shrub 6 to 12 ft high, of thin, erect habit, with rather slender branches; spreading by underground suckers; young shoots covered with reddish glistening scales. Leaves oval to narrowly ovate, 1½ to 3½ in. long, ¾ to 1½ in. wide, wedge-shaped at the base, rounded or pointed at the apex, both surfaces white and lustrous with silvery scales; stalk ⅛ in. long. Flowers produced during May in great profusion in the leaf-axils of the young twigs, often three in each axil; they are drooping, ½ in. long, with a stalk ⅛ in. long; narrow tubular, shining and silvery outside, yellow on the inside of the four pointed lobes; very fragrant. Fruit roundish, egg-shaped, silvery, ⅓ in. long, with a dry, mealy flesh, said to be edible. *Bot. Mag.*, t. 8369.

The only species native of N. America, reaching from the Hudson Bay Territory and British Columbia to the Central United States; introduced in 1813.

This shrub is one of the most striking of those with silvery foliage, and when laden with its yellow, delightfully fragrant flowers, few others are more pleasing. It is increased by taking off the sucker growths by which it spreads. There is a great confusion in gardens and nurseries between this plant and *Shepherdia*

ELAEAGNUS COMMUTATA

argentea, which seems to have existed in Loudon's time. Loudon does not seem to have known the true plant. There is one simple distinction between them: *Elaeagnus* has alternate leaves, *Shepherdia* opposite ones. The latter, moreover, is far from being as fine a shrub.

E. GLABRA Thunb.

There is much confusion in gardens between this species and *E. pungens*, but *E. glabra* differs in the following respects. It is not thorny, its longer-pointed leaves are of thinner texture, not undulate, their lower surface brown and shining with a metallic lustre (*E. pungens* is whitish and dull beneath); and it is of more rambling, even climbing habit. For the rest, *E. glabra* is a vigorous evergreen shrub, with us 15 to 20 ft high, but twice as much on trees and houses in the south of France. The flowers appear in October and November, and are funnel-shaped, white, clothed with brownish scales, fragrant. Young shoots slender, covered with brown, glossy scales.

Native of Japan and China. There appears to be no variegated form of *E. glabra* in cultivation.

E. MACROPHYLLA Thunb.

A robust evergreen shrub of rounded, spreading habit, reaching at present 8 to 12 ft in height in this country; usually wider than high; young shoots silvery white, with a dense coat of scales. Leaves ovate to broadly oval, rounded at the base, pointed; 2 to 4½ in. long, 1½ to 2¾ in. wide, silvery all over when young, but afterwards dark lustrous green and slightly scaly above, always of a beautiful silvery metallic lustre beneath; stalk ½ to ¾ in. long. Flowers produced during October and November, usually in clusters of four to six in the leaf-axils; they are about ½ in. long and wide, each on a stalk ¼ in. long; silvery scaly, shaped like a fuchsia, nodding, very fragrant, the four segments triangular. Fruit oval, ⅝ in. long, red, scaly, the perianth persisting at the top. *Bot. Mag.*, t. 7638.

Native of the Korean Archipelago and Japan, described by Thunberg in 1784; introduced by Maries for Messrs Veitch in 1879. It is perfectly hardy, and flowers annually at a time of year when few blossoms remain out-of-doors. It is the largest-leaved and handsomest of evergreen oleasters, and is very effective in spring before the young silvery leaves lose their sheen. Allied to *pungens* and *glabra*, it is very distinct from them in the broader silvery leaves and broader more bell-shaped flowers.

E. × EBBINGEI Hort.—This name has been given to a batch of six seedlings from *E. macrophylla* raised by S. G. A. Doorenbos in the municipal nursery at The Hague in 1929; the pollen parent was *E. pungens* or *E. × reflexa* (*E. pungens* var. *reflexa*). All six were propagated and distributed and two clones are still in commerce at the present time, one smaller-leaved and more compact than the other. Although not so handsome in foliage as the seed parent, they are more vigorous (G. S. Thomas in *Journ. R.H.S.*, Vol. 91, p. 37).

cv. 'GILT EDGE'.—Leaves margined with gold. Raised by Messrs Waterer, Sons and Crisp, this variety received an Award of Merit when shown by them on October 26, 1971.

E. SUBMACROPHYLLA Servett.—A putative hybrid between *E. macrophylla* and *E. pungens*. It is possible that *E. × ebbingei* belongs here in synonymy.

E. MULTIFLORA Thunb.
E. longipes A. Gray

A deciduous or semi-evergreen shrub 6 to 10 ft high, as much or more across; young branches covered with red-brown scales. Leaves oval, obovate, or ovate,

1½ to 2½ in. long, ¾ to 1½ in. wide, tapered at both ends, green, and furnished with scattered tufted hairs above, becoming glabrous later, silvery beneath, with a dense covering of tiny scales, intermingled with which are larger reddish-brown ones; stalk ¼ in. long. Flowers fragrant, produced in April and May along with, and in the leaf-axils of, the new shoots; often solitary, about ⅝ in. long, ⅜ in. wide; scaly like the under-surface of the leaf. Fruit ½ in. long, oblong, deep orange, scaly, with a very acid but agreeable flavour; stalk ¾ to 1 in. long. *Bot. Mag.*, t. 7341.

Native of Japan, whence it was introduced about 1862; also of China and probably Korea. It is cultivated in Japan for its fruit, and, according to Sargent, becomes a small tree 20 to 25 ft high, with a trunk 1 ft in diameter. The fruits

<small>ELAEAGNUS MULTIFLORA (in fruit)</small>

are very abundantly borne, and make the bush very handsome when ripe in July, hanging along the underside of the branches. Birds are fond of them.

E. multiflora is a rather variable species. The leaves may be narrower than in the tree described, and the fruit-stalks up to 2 in. long.

E. PUNGENS Thunb.

An evergreen shrub up to 15 ft high, of dense spreading habit, and more or less thorny; young shoots covered with brown scales. Leaves leathery, oval or oblong, 1½ to 4 in. long, ¼ to 1¾ in. wide, often blunt at the apex, rounded at the base, margins wavy, upper surface dark green and glossy, sprinkled with scales when young, afterwards glabrous, lower surface dull white dotted with large brownish scales; stalk ¼ to ½ in. long, brown like the young wood and midrib. Flowers pendulous, ½ in. long, the tubular portion widening abruptly above the ovary; silvery white, fragrant, clustered often in threes in the leaf-axils, and opening in October and November. Fruit ½ to ¾ in. long, at first brown-scaly with the perianth persisting, red when ripe; rarely seen in Britain.

Native of Japan; perfectly hardy near London. It is often grown as *E. glabra,* a distinct species (q.v. for the differences). The fragrance of the flower is like that of gardenias.

cv. 'AUREA'.—Leaves margined with rich yellow. *Rev. Hort. Belg.*, Vol. 14, p. 356 (1864), as *E. p. foliis aureo-marginatis.* In 'DICKSONII' the golden margin is broad, and some leaves are wholly golden in the upper third.

cv. 'FREDERICI'.—Leaves rather small and narrow, the cream-coloured or pale yellow centre bordered with a thin margin of glossy dark green. First described in 1888 as "*E. frederici variegata*" and probably introduced by Siebold. Also known as *E. p. aureo-picta.*

cv. 'MACULATA'.—A richly coloured form, whose large leaves are sometimes 4½ in. long and 2¼ in. wide, variously marked with deep yellow, much richer than the yellow of 'Frederici'. The coloured patch is always in the centre, but varies in size; often there is only a thin border of dark green, sometimes only one side of the midrib is coloured. Between the yellow and the green there are frequently patches of an intermediate yellowish shade. This shrub is probably the most ornamental and striking of all variegated evergreens. Its effect in midwinter is bright and pleasing. Like many variegated shrubs with the colouring in the centre of the leaf, it is liable to revert to the green type; shoots showing this disposition must be cut away. It was given a First Class Certificate when shown by Veitch in 1891, but its origin is uncertain. The name adopted here appears to be the correct one, but it is also known as *E. p. aureo-variegata.*

cv. 'SIMONII'.—Leaves larger than in the type, very silvery beneath, with few brownish scales. *Rev. Hort.*, 1869, p. 100, as "*E. simonii*".

cv. 'VARIEGATA'.—Leaves with a yellow border like 'Aurea', but of a paler shade. Origin unknown.

E. × REFLEXA Morr. & Decne. *E. pungens* var. *reflexa* (Morr. & Decne.) Schneid.—A hybrid between *E. pungens* and *E. glabra.* It is less thorny than *E. pungens*; leaves very brown-scaly beneath; margins not wavy. Like the second parent, it will climb when planted under trees.

E. UMBELLATA Thunb.

A large, wide-spreading, deciduous, often thorny shrub, sometimes 20 to 30 ft across, 12 to 18 ft high; twigs covered with brownish scales. The shoots sometimes retain a few leaves at the ends throughout the winter. Leaves narrowly oval, 2 to 4 in. long, ¾ to 1½ in. wide, tapered at the apex, tapered or rounded at the base, rather bright green above, shining and silvery beneath; stalk about ⅓ in. long. Flowers produced during May and June, when the young leaves are about one-third grown, in clusters of one to three; each flower ½ in. long, funnel-shaped, silvery outside, creamy white inside. Fruit globose, ¼ to ⅓ in. diameter, at first silvery, finally red; stalk ¼ in. long.

Native of the Himalaya, China, and Japan; varying considerably in several respects, one form coming into flower when another is almost past. The habit also varies, some forms being much wider-spreading than others. The largest plant at Kew is 30 ft across. A handsome species both in flower and fruit.

var. PARVIFOLIA (Royle) Schneid. *E. parvifolia* Royle—Shoots at first

T S—D

silvery; leaves covered with distinctly starry hair-tufts on the upper surface when young, becoming glabrous later; silvery and scaly beneath. There is a fine specimen of this variety at Dartington Hall, Devon, about 20 ft high and 25 ft across. *E. umbellata* differs from *E. multiflora* in its globose, short-stalked fruits; in the tube of the perianth being more slender; and in the leaves being paler, longer, and proportionately narrower. It also flowers later.

ELLIOTTIA   ERICACEAE

A monotypic genus rare in the wild, allied to *Tripetaleia*, *Botryostege*, *Cladothamnus* and *Ledum*. It resembles these in its free petals but is distinguished by the combination of: deciduous leaves; racemose inflorescence; corollas with four (rarely five) petals. It is named after the botanist Stephen Elliott (1771–1830), who discovered the one species described here.

E. RACEMOSA Elliott

A deciduous shrub 4 to 10 ft high, or occasionally a small tree twice as large; young shoots downy. Leaves narrowly oval or obovate, tapering towards both ends, 2 to 5 in. long, ¾ to 1¾ in. wide, dark dull green and glabrous above, paler and sparsely hairy beneath; stalk ¼ to ½ in. long, hairy. Flowers thinly arranged in a terminal raceme or panicle 4 to 10 in. high, pure white, slightly fragrant; petals four, oblong, rounded at the end, ⅝ in. long, reflexed, downy at the margins; calyx ⅛ in. diameter, with four rounded lobes; stamens eight, shorter than the petals, and with broad, flattened stalks; style as long as the petals. Flower-stalk white, slender, usually one- sometimes three-flowered, ½ to ¾ in. long, with a pair of tiny bracts midway. Fruit a flattened-globose capsule ⅜ in. wide; seeds winged. *Bot. Mag.*, t. 8413.

Native of Georgia and S. Carolina in the southern United States, and only found in a few isolated spots. It was introduced to England in 1894, when Mr Berckmans of Augusta, Georgia, sent a plant to Kew. It first flowered in July 1911. It was believed at one time that this beautiful and interesting shrub had become extinct in the wild, but about 1933 W. A. Knight of Biltmore, North Carolina, discovered the species growing in quantity in Georgia and reintroduced it to cultivation by means of seeds and young plants in 1937 (see *New Flora and Sylva*, Vol. 10, pp. 154–64, 1938). In 1958 arrangements were being made for the main area where the species grows to be carefully preserved.

ELLIOTTIA RACEMOSA

ELSHOLTZIA   LABIATAE

A genus of about thirty species of herbs and sub-shrubs, natives of Asia for the most part but also represented in Europe (though not by woody species) and in Abyssinia. The spelling of the generic name is sometimes confused with *Eschscholzia*, a genus of Californian plants allied to the poppies.

E. STAUNTONII Benth.

A semi-woody plant about 5 ft high, scarcely shrubby, the growths dying back considerably during winter, sending up each summer erect leafy growths, bearing the flowers in panicles at the top during September and October. Shoots cylindrical, clothed with a very fine down. Leaves opposite, lanceolate, slenderly tapered at both ends, coarsely triangular-toothed except at the ends, 2 to 6 in.

long, ½ to 1½ in. wide, dark green above, pale and covered with minute dots beneath, glabrous on both sides, minutely downy on the margins. When crushed the leaf emits an odour like mint. Flower-panicles narrow-cylindrical, grey, woolly, 4 to 8 in. long, about 1 in. wide, produced at the end of the main and axillary secondary shoots, forming a large branched inflorescence at the top. Flowers small, purplish pink, crowded in short-stalked umbels on the main axis of the panicle. *Bot. Mag.*, t. 8460.

Native of China; long known to botanists, but only introduced to cultivation in 1909. It is useful for flowering late in the season, but is of a rather weedy character. Propagated very easily by cuttings of youngish growths. Thrives in rich loamy soil and in full sunshine.

EMBOTHRIUM   PROTEACEAE

A genus of a few species in S. America, E. Australia and New Guinea. In Sleumer's interpretation, all these, with the sole exception of *E. coccineum* (the species described here), are referred to the genus *Oreocallis*. The group of Proteaceae to which *Embothrium* belongs is also represented in gardens by *Telopea truncata*, which is easily distinguished by its compact inflorescence surrounded by an involucre of coloured bracts; and by a few species of *Lomatia*, in which the flowers are white or cream-coloured.

E. COCCINEUM J. R. & G. Forst.   FIRE BUSH   [PLATE 16

E. lanceolatum Ruiz & Pavon; *E. coccineum* var. *lanceolatum* (Ruiz & Pavon) O. Kuntze; *E. longifolium* Hort., not Poir.; *E. valdivianum* Gandoger; *E. gilliesii* Meissn.

An evergreen (more rarely semi-deciduous) shrub or small tree, of suckering habit, glabrous in all its parts. Leaves entire, very variable in size and shape even on the same individual, obovate, oblong-elliptic or lanceolate, rounded or acute at the apex, up to 6 in. (rarely more) long, ⅗ to 1⅕ in. wide, dark glossy green above, paler and greyish green beneath; leaf-stalks ⅕ to ⅖ in. long. Flowers brilliant crimson-scarlet or orange-scarlet, borne in May–June in terminal and axillary racemes; pedicels slender, ½ to ¾ in. long; the floral envelope is not differentiated into calyx and corolla but consists of a perianth which is at first tubular through most of its length but ovoid at the apex, and splits during flowering into four strap-shaped, recurved segments; stamens four, sessile, borne in the cup-shaped tips of the segments; ovary narrow, with a long style. Fruit a follicle, woody when mature, crowned by the persistent style and containing numerous winged seeds.

Native of Chile and bordering parts of Argentina, from about 37° S. to Tierra del Fuego; first named from a specimen collected during Cook's second voyage; introduced by William Lobb in 1846 when collecting for Veitch. It inhabits open places, often forming extensive thickets, and ranges from the sea-coasts to the tree-line. At high altitudes and on exposed headlands it is reduced to a small bush; in favourable situations it makes a tree to about 30 ft high, attaining its largest dimensions in the island of Chiloé, but in cultivation (in Cornwall and Ireland) it has reached almost 50 ft in height. It yields a prettily marked timber which, owing to the scarcity of large specimens, is mostly used in turnery.

E. coccineum is very variable in shape and size of leaf. During their journey in S. America in 1777–88 Ruiz and Pavon collected in the coastal range near Concepcion a plant with long, narrow, pointed leaves, which they named *E. lanceolatum*, but this is linked by intermediates to the typical form with shorter, relatively broader leaves, rounded at the apex. South American botanists relegate this species to synonymy under *E. coccineum* and there is no reason to dissent from this judgement.

There have been many introductions of *E. coccineum*, of which only the best known are treated here.

1. The original introduction by William Lobb first flowered in Veitch's Exeter nursery in 1853 and is figured in *Bot. Mag.*, t. 4856. Leaves oblong-elliptic, 2½ to 3 in. long, rounded at the apex; axillary racemes not so freely produced as in the later introductions. The seed was probably collected near Valdivia, on the island of Chiloé, or the mainland facing it.

2. The Veitchian collector Richard Pearce sent seed in 1860–2 but little is known of this introduction except that the flowers were of a different colour from that of Lobb's plants. Thanks to the more settled conditions, Pearce was able to penetrate farther inland than Lobb did, but the origin of the seed is not known.

3. The long-leaved form generally known as "*E. longifolium*" or "*E. coccineum* var. *longifolium*" was apparently first cultivated at Rostrevor, Co. Down, at the beginning of this century and was first distributed in England by Messrs Marchant in the 1930s. It was given a First Class Certificate when shown by them in 1948. This is a vigorous and fast-growing form with orange-scarlet flowers produced freely all along the shoots. It agrees well with the *E. lanceolatum* of Ruiz and Pavon in having long, narrow leaves, pointed at the apex but very much shorter, relatively broader leaves on the spurs. It should be added that similar plants are reported from Cornwall which may be of independent origin.

4. Outside the older gardens of the west and south-west, *E. coccineum* is now mainly represented by the hardy forms introduced by H. F. Comber from the Andes in 1926–7. The seed was collected near the northern (equatorward) end of the range of this species, in the Argentine province of Neuquen, at 3,000 to 5,000 ft altitude. Here the climate is harsher and drier than it is on the Pacific Coast—a fact which helps to explain the hardiness of Comber's plants and their semi-deciduous habit. They are variable in foliage, but generally the leaves are rather small and narrow-lanceolate and the racemes are produced all along the branches. Seed under C.387 was collected near Pulmari (39° 10′ S., south of Lake Aluminé) and in the Norquinco Valley, west of that village. C.774 was collected a little farther south, in the area of San Martin de los Andes. A plant raised from C.387 was given an Award of Merit when a branch from it was shown from Bodnant in 1947 as *E. lanceolatum* 'Norquinco form'. In this plant

the racemes are set so close together on the branch 'that it looks as if the tree had donned a number of scarlet "Plus Fours" ' (*Journ. R.H.S.*, Vol. 73, p. 380 and fig. 139).

Perhaps no tree cultivated in the open air in the British Isles gives so striking and brilliant a display of colour as does E. *coccineum*. It needs a moist, not too heavy, lime-free soil and a position sheltered from cold, drying winds but not too crowded and shaded by neighbouring trees (it is not in nature a plant of the forest and needs abundant light if it is to flower freely). It is propagated by seeds or suckers.

No colour-variants have occurred in cultivation but according to Dr Carlos Muñoz (*Flores Silvestres de Chile*, Santiago, 1966) a white-flowered form is known and yellow-flowered plants occur in one locality in the Chilean province of Curacautin.

EMMENOPTERYS   RUBIACEAE

A genus of two species, natives of the temperate forests of China, Siam, and Burma. It is allied to *Luculia*.

E. HENRYI Oliver

A deciduous tree 30 to 80 ft high, with a trunk 6 to 9 ft in girth, clothed with grey, rough bark, scaly on young trees; young shoots glabrous, purplish the second year. Leaves opposite, oval or ovate, mostly tapered to the base, pointed, rather fleshy in texture; variable in size, the larger ones up to 8 or 9 in. long and 4 in. wide, dark dull green and glabrous above, pale and with down on the midrib and veins beneath; chief veins in five to eight pairs; leaf-stalk reddish, ½ to 2 in. long. Flowers in terminal, rounded or pyramidal panicles as much as 10 in. wide and 6 or 8 in. high, borne on leafy shoots. Corolla white, 1 in. wide and long, funnel-shaped at the base, opening at the top into five spreading rounded lobes, downy on both surfaces, especially inside. Calyx small, urn-shaped, ¼ in. long, with five rounded ciliate lobes; on a certain proportion of the flowers one lobe of the calyx becomes extraordinarily enlarged and develops into a large, white, stalked, more or less oval 'bract', the largest as much as 2 in. long by 1½ in. wide. Stamens five, about the length of the corolla tube. Fruit a spindle-shaped capsule 1 to 1½ in. long, ⅓ to ⅝ in. wide, ribbed. Seeds winged.

Native of central and south-western China; introduced by Wilson in 1907. He found it about Ichang up to 4,000 ft altitude and describes it as 'one of the most strikingly beautiful trees of Chinese forests'. It has been grown outside at Kew since 1913 and has never suffered from winter cold and only a few times from spring frosts. Wilson was rather surprised at its hardiness. The most remarkable feature of the inflorescence is the extraordinary development of an occasional calyx-lobe, which very much resembles what is seen in *Schizo-*

phragma. The largest plant at Kew is 36 ft high and perfectly healthy but, like the others in Britain, has never flowered (1971). The tallest specimens known grow at Caerhays Castle, Cornwall; they measure 53 × 3 ft and 48 × 3 ft (1966). Judging by dried specimens the combination of flowers and large white 'bracts' should be very beautiful. In China they open in June and July on leafy shoots of the current year. It succeeds in open loamy soil and can be increased by cuttings of moderately ripened wood taken in August. Forrest introduced a slightly differing form of this from Yunnan, which does not grow so well in Sussex as the Wilson introduction, but has attained a height of 37 ft at Trewithen in Cornwall.

E. *henryi* flowered, probably for the first time in Europe, in 1971, at the Villa Taranto, Pallanza, on Lake Maggiore (*Journ. R.H.S.*, Vol. 96 (1971), pp. 496–497 and fig. 220).

EMPETRUM   Crowberry   empetraceae

A small genus of low or procumbent evergreen shrubs, found in the colder regions of both the northern and the southern hemisphere. The number of species recognised by recent workers ranges from two (R. D. Good in *Journ. Linn. Soc.*, Vol. 47, pp. 489–523, 1927) to eighteen (V. N. Vasiliev, in a monograph published in Russia in 1961). The only allied genus in gardens is *Corema*. The affinities of these shrubs are doubtful, but the general opinion now is to regard them as nearest to the box family. The generic name derives from the Greek and means 'on rocks'. The introduced species are very hardy and easy to grow if planted in lime-free soil.

E. nigrum L.

A low, evergreen, heath-like shrub about 1 ft high in gardens, with spreading, wiry, procumbent stems, minutely downy when young. Leaves narrow-linear, ⅛ to ¼ in. long, sometimes arranged in fours, but usually arranged indiscriminately on the shoot, always crowded, blunt at the apex, dark green with a white line beneath, margins much decurved. Flowers unisexual, with the sexes on different plants, produced during March singly in the leaf-axils near the tips of the previous summer's shoots. They are very small, and the only conspicuous part is the stamens, of which there are three to each male flower; they are pinkish, and have long, very slender stalks holding the anthers slightly beyond the leaves. The fruit is an orange-shaped black berry, $\frac{3}{16}$ in. wide, borne in clusters near the end of the twigs, each containing six to nine seeds.

If interpreted in a broad sense, this species is widely distributed in high latitudes in the northern hemisphere and in the mountains of lower latitudes, but many of its reported locations would belong to E. *hermaphroditum* if that is recognised as an independent species. The crowberry is not common in gardens, but it thrives very well in the London district and makes a low, dense, neat mass of greenery, easily increased by cuttings. It is a moorland plant, and an associate of the heather, cranberry and whortleberry, and likes a sandy, peaty soil. The fruits are edible but not very desirable.

f. PURPUREUM (Raf.) Fern. *E. purpureum* Raf.—Berries reddish purple. Found in various parts of N. America.

E. HERMAPHRODITUM (Lange) Hagerup *E. nigrum* f. *hermaphroditum* Lange —Flowers hermaphrodite (not unisexual as in *E. nigrum*) habit denser and more erect. Young stems dull green. This species, only recently separated from *E. nigrum*, appears to have a fairly wide distribution including Scotland.

E. RUBRUM Willd.   SOUTH AMERICAN CROWBERRY

A low, evergreen, heath-like shrub 6 to 18 in. high, of spreading habit; young shoots furnished with greyish-white wool. Leaves arranged spirally on the branchlets or in whorls of three or four; linear, rounded at the end, $\frac{1}{8}$ to $\frac{1}{4}$ in. long, $\frac{1}{20}$ in. wide, dark dull green above with a thin white line beneath, margins densely covered with grey wool especially when the leaves are young, a little of it persisting on the year-old leaves. The flowers do not differ appreciably from those of *E. nigrum*. Fruit red.

Native of the southern latitudes of S. America, especially about the Straits of Magellan; if interpreted in a wide sense, it is also found on Tristan da Cunha and in the Falkland Islands. It was introduced from the last-named habitat to Kew in 1911, but does not grow so freely as our native species (*E. nigrum*). It is an interesting dwarf evergreen and is very distinct from *E. nigrum* in the woolly shoots and leaf margins. Since the flowers are normally unisexual and dioecious, fruit will not be borne unless plants of both sexes are grown. According to Lindley it was originally introduced from the south point of S. America, about 1832, by Low of Clapton; there it is associated with *Pernettya mucronata*. It prefers a peaty soil.

E. EAMESII Fern. & Wieg. *E. rubrum* subsp. *eamesii* (Fern. & Wieg.) Good —A close ally of the preceding. Leaves shorter, to $\frac{1}{6}$ in. long. Fruits smaller pink or pale red. Found in various localities in N. America.

ENKIANTHUS   ERICACEAE

A distinct group of about ten species of deciduous shrubs and small trees, native of N.E. Asia. In habit they are marked by the branches and leaves being in whorls, which give to some species a peculiar tabulated appearance. The flowers are in pendulous umbels or racemes; the corolla either bell-shaped or pitcher-shaped, with five small lobes. Calyx five-lobed, and persistent on the seed-vessel. Stamens ten, not so long as the corolla.

These shrubs like a moist soil, with which decayed leaves and some peat have been mixed. Like so many of their family, they dislike lime. Their general treatment is the same as for the hardy azaleas, and they have a similar dislike of heavy shade. In flower they are pretty and interesting, but their great beauty comes in autumn, when the leaves turn to various brilliant shades of red and yellow. They are best propagated from seed treated in the same way as recommended for rhododendrons. Cuttings may also be rooted.

E. CAMPANULATUS (Miq.) Nichols.

Andromeda campanulata Miq.

A deciduous shrub usually 4 to 12 ft high, occasionally a small tree, branches in whorls; young shoots glabrous, reddish. Leaves produced in a cluster at the the end of the twig, or alternate on strong growths; obovate to oval, tapered

ENKIANTHUS CAMPANULATUS

more gradually towards the base, finely toothed, 1 to 2½ in. long, ½ to 1¼ in. wide, hairy on the veins of both surfaces, dull green; stalk ⅛ to ⅝ in. long. Flowers produced during May from the terminal bud of the previous year's growth in a hairy raceme sometimes almost reduced to an umbel. Corolla bell-shaped, ⅓ in. long, pendulous, with five rounded lobes, pale creamy yellow, veined and tipped with red; calyx with five lanceolate, pointed divisions ⅙ in. long; stamens very short; flower-stalk downy, ½ to 1 in. long. Ovary and style glabrous. Seed-vessel egg-shaped, ¾ in. long.

Native of Japan; introduced in 1880, by Maries, for Messrs Veitch. This is the most satisfactory of the species of *Enkianthus* in our gardens, being quite hardy and flowering freely. It is sometimes cut by late frost. In the Arnold Arboretum, Mass., where the frosts are much more severe than ours, it succeeds remarkably well. The leaves turn golden and red in autumn.

f. ALBIFLORUS (Mak.) Mak.   E. *pallidiflorus* Craib—Flowers white or greenish white. *Bot. Mag.*, n.s., t. 512.

var. MATSUDAE (Komatsu) Mak.   E. *matsudae* Komatsu—Leaves broadly lanceolate to narrowly ovate, rather coarsely toothed. Flowers deep red.

var. PALIBINII Bean   E. *palibinii* (Bean) Craib; E. *rubicundus* Matsumura & Nakai—The plant figured in *Bot. Mag.*, t. 7059 is a distinct form, the flowers being almost wholly of a rich deep red, rather smaller than in the ordinary form, and produced in a distinct raceme. There is a conspicuous line of reddish down bordering the base of the midrib of the leaf beneath. Similar plants are found in the wild state.

E. *campanulatus* varies somewhat in the shape of its leaves, the length of the inflorescences, colour of flower, depth of lobing of the corolla and length of style. W. G. Craib (*Notes Bot. Gard. Edin.*, Vol. 11, Oct. 1919) made a number of species out of these variations, described from plants raised from Japanese seed (perhaps of garden origin) in the Edinburgh Botanic Garden. They are: E. *ferrugineus, latiflorus, pendulus, recurvus* and *tectus.*

E. CERNUUS (Sieb. & Zucc.) Makino

Meisteria cernua Sieb. & Zucc.

A deciduous shrub 5 to 10 ft high, with glabrous, bifurcating branches. Leaves obovate, ¾ to 1½ in. long, half to two-thirds as wide, finely round-toothed, glabrous, or with a few hairs at the base of the midrib beneath. Flowers in a nodding raceme of ten or twelve blossoms, produced in May, each on a downy stalk ¼ to ½ in. long. Corolla bell-shaped, ¼ in. long and broad, white, the margin cut up into numerous slender-pointed, unequal teeth; calyx-lobes ovate-lanceolate, fringed with short hairs; seed-vessel ⅙ to ¼ in. long.

Native of Japan. It is easily distinguished by the almost fringed mouth of the corolla.

var. RUBENS (Maxim.) Mak.—This is similar to the type, except that its leaves are usually shorter and broader (roundish obovate), often from ½ to ¾ in. long, and the flowers of a rich deep red. Very distinct and beautiful. Such red-flowered forms are found in the wild state but perhaps not invariably with this shape of leaf.

E. CHINENSIS Franch.

E. *himalaicus* var. *chinensis* (Franch.) Diels; E. *sinohimalaicus* Craib

A shrub 8 to 12 ft high; young shoots glabrous. Leaves lanceolate to oblong or oval, 2 to 3 in. long, ¾ to 1¼ in. wide, tapered to both ends, pointed, shallowly bluntly toothed, downy along the midrib above, bright green above, rather glaucous and glabrous beneath; stalk slender, up to 1 in. long. Flowers in pendulous racemes of one to two dozen, 3 to 5 in. long. Corolla bell-shaped, ⅜ in. long and a little wider at the mouth, yellowish striated conspicuously with rose; lobes rose-coloured, recurved. *Bot. Mag.*, t. 9413. Native of W. China and N.E. Upper Burma. Judging by descriptions made by collectors and the plate in the *Botanical Magazine*, the colour of its flowers would appear to be somewhat variable although rose is usually dominant. The species is closely akin to *E. deflexus* (*himalaicus*), but that species is well distinguished by its pubescent leaves. *E. chinensis* was introduced in 1900.

E. DEFLEXUS (Griff.) Schneid. [PLATE 17
Rhodora deflexa Griff.; *E. himalaicus* Hook. f. & Thoms.

A shrub or small tree from 6 to over 20 ft high; young branches bright red, glabrous or hairy. Leaves produced in a cluster at the end of the shoot, 1 to 3 in. long, ½ to 1¾ in. wide, oval, obovate or lanceolate, tapering to both ends, with scattered hairs on both sides, but especially on the midrib beneath. Flowers produced in June along with the young shoots in a terminal, umbellate or racemose cluster, each of the eight to twenty blossoms borne on a drooping, downy stalk ¾ to 1¼ in. long. Corolla broadly bell-shaped, ⅝ in. broad, of various shades of yellowish red with darker lines; lobes triangular, deeper-coloured. Calyx-lobes 1/12 in. long, triangular and long-pointed; ovary and style downy. Seed-vessel almost globose, downy. *Bot. Mag.*, t. 6460.

Native of the Himalaya up to 11,000 ft altitude, and of W. China. The Himalayan plant is not very hardy and is usually wintered indoors, but the Chinese plants introduced for Messrs Veitch by Wilson in 1908 are hardier. This Chinese form is not quite identical with the Himalayan one figured in the *Botanical Magazine*, having usually more distinctly racemose flowers and glabrous young shoots. *E. deflexus* has the largest flowers in the genus, and Wilson described it as one of the most beautiful shrubs of the Western Chinese mountains.

E. PERULATUS (Miq.) Schneid.
Andromeda perulata Miq.; *E. japonicus* Hook. f.

A deciduous shrub 3 to 6 ft high; branches bifurcated or arranged in tiers; glabrous, reddish. Leaves clustered at the end of the twigs, 1 to 2 in. long, scarcely half as much wide, narrowly oval to obovate, fine-pointed, tapering at the base to a short stalk, minutely toothed, downy only at the base of the midrib. Flowers in a terminal cluster of three to ten, each one on a perfectly glabrous, slender, drooping stalk about ½ in. long. Corolla white, pitcher-shaped, ¼ to ⅓ in. long, much contracted at the mouth where are five shallow, rounded, reflexed lobes, and five swellings at the base. Calyx of five awl-shaped, glabrous lobes 1/12 in. long. Seed-vessel ⅓ in. long, cylindrical. *Bot. Mag.*, t. 5822.

Native of Japan; discovered in 1859 in the neighbourhood of Nagasaki by Sir Rutherford Alcock, and introduced some ten years later by Messrs Standish.

It is easily distinguished by its white flowers on glabrous stalks. It blossoms in April, and its leaves turn a beautiful golden yellow or red in autumn.

ENKIANTHUS PERULATUS

E. QUINQUEFLORUS Lour.

A deciduous or semi-evergreen bush 3 to 6 ft high (occasionally in a wild state a small tree); young shoots and leaves quite glabrous. Leaves of stout leathery texture, narrowly oval or obovate, entire, sharply pointed, tapered at the base, 2 to 4 in. long, ¾ to 1½ in. wide, reddish when unfolding, changing to dark bright green, and very much net-veined; stalk ¼ to ¾ in. long. Flowers nodding, produced (often in clusters of five) in the axils of large pink bracts in spring, each on a pink stalk ½ to 1 in. long. Corolla bell-shaped, pink, ⅜ to ½ in. long, with five reflexed shallow lobes of paler hue and five nectaries at the base. Calyx-lobes varying from shallowly to slenderly triangular, minutely ciliate. Fruit a dry capsule, erect, egg-shaped, ⅜ in. long, strongly ribbed. *Bot. Mag.*, t. 1649.

Native of China, including Hong Kong; first flowered in Knight's Royal Exotic Nursery at Chelsea (afterwards Veitch's) in 1814. It is too tender for any but the mildest parts of the British Isles and requires the protection of a cool greenhouse at Kew. It is unsurpassed among enkianthuses in the size and beauty of the individual flowers and the clusters with their attendant pink bracts give a charming effect.

E. SERRULATUS (Wils.) Schneid.
E. quinqueflorus var. *serrulatus* Wils.

This is closely related to *E. quinqueflorus* and was at first considered by E. H. Wilson to be a variety of it. It is a native of Central and W. China and was introduced in 1900. A shrub or small tree up to 20 ft high, differing from *quinqueflorus* in being quite deciduous; young shoots glabrous; bud-scales minutely ciliate. Leaves narrowly oval or obovate, slender-pointed, tapered at the base; 1½ to 3 in. long, about half as wide; quite glabrous. They differ from those of *quinqueflorus* in being very finely toothed and not so leathery. Flowers in clusters of up to six, each on a stalk ¾ to 1 in. long, bell-shaped, ½ in. long, with small reflexed lobes. They differ from the flowers of *quinqueflorus* in being pure white.

E. SUBSESSILIS (Miq.) Makino

Andromeda subsessilis Miq.; *A. nikoensis* Maxim.

A deciduous shrub of bushy habit 3 to 8 ft high; branchlets bifurcated or in whorls, glabrous. Leaves produced in a rosette at the end of the twig, oval to obovate, ¾ to 1½ in. long, about half as wide, tapering to a very short stalk; abruptly pointed, finely toothed; dark dull green above, with white hairs on the midrib, paler beneath, and with darker, longer hairs along the midrib. Flowers produced in late May in slender, nodding, downy racemes, 1½ to 2 in. long, carrying six to twelve blossoms. Corolla pitcher-shaped, white, $\frac{3}{16}$ in. long, much contracted at the mouth, where are five short recurved lobes; calyx-lobes ovate, pointed, $\frac{1}{16}$ in. long, edged with hairs; flower-stalks slender, ¾ in. long, glabrous except at the base; seed-vessel egg-shaped, $\frac{1}{6}$ in. long.

Native of Japan; collected in the Central Province by Maries in 1878; introduced to cultivation by Prof. Sargent in 1892, from the Nikko Mountains. It is hardy at Kew, but slow-growing. It has not much beauty of flower, but its foliage turns bright red in autumn. To some extent it resembles *E. perulatus*, having the same white pitcher-shaped corolla, but it is smaller and has not the five rounded protuberances at the base as in *perulatus*; the inflorescence too is racemose instead of fasciculate; and finally the fruits are pendulous (not held erect on a stiff, straight pedicel as in *perulatus*).

E. NUDIPES (Honda) Ohwi—A closely related species, differing chiefly in its glabrous racemes. Native of Central Japan.

EPHEDRA EPHEDRACEAE

A group of curious shrubs, sometimes climbing, with a mode of growth and branching resembling that of horse-tail (*Equisetum*). They have little garden value, and are rarely seen except in scientific collections. The older parts of the plants are truly woody, the younger parts very pithy; the branchlets slenderly cylindrical, rush-like, dark or greyish green, minutely ribbed, opposite or borne in whorls, very tough and flexible, but snapping at the joints. The joints (nodes) are clasped by small membranous sheaths which sometimes develop a pair of leaf-like blades, usually $\frac{1}{8}$ to $\frac{1}{4}$ in. long. The flowers are unisexual, the sexes usually on separate plants, the males being borne on short spikes from the joints, each flower consisting of two opposite membranous sepals and two to eight anthers, which are borne at the top of one central stalk formed by the union of their stalks. The female flower is composed of a naked ovule prolonged at the top into a style-like tube and enclosed in a bag-like calyx or bract, which in the fruiting stage becomes fleshy, red and often sweet and edible.

In cultivation out-of-doors, so far as I have seen, they do not flower profusely or regularly in this country; still less frequently do they bear fruit. The best crop of blossom I have seen was in the early summer of 1912, this being due presumably to the ripening influences of the unusually hot summer of 1911. The flowers are yellow, but have little beauty.

The ephedras, which in the vegetable kingdom make a connecting link between ordinary flowering plants and conifers, usually inhabit dry, inhospitable regions. Under cultivation they need a well-drained, loamy soil and a sunny spot. They are propagated by seeds and layers and by division. Such species as *E. distachya*, *E. gerardiana*, and *E. major* make evergreen patches, interesting in the garden as being absolutely distinct from any other hardy shrubs. The identification of the species is a difficult botanical study, and a brief general description of a few of the commoner species only can be given here.

E. ANDINA C. A. Mey. *E. americana* var. *andina* (C. A. Mey.) Stapf—A more or less prostrate, much-branched shrub. Branchlets slender, clustered, with the internodes $\frac{1}{4}$ to $1\frac{1}{4}$ in. long. Male flower-spikes solitary or grouped, on short side-branchlets, to $\frac{3}{5}$ in. long. Fruits broadly egg-shaped, about $\frac{3}{5}$ in. long, bright red. Native of the Andes; it is in cultivation from Comber's seed, collected in 1926, but the plant figured in *Bot. Mag.*, n.s., t. 142, was introduced to the Cambridge Botanic Garden in 1899.

E. DISTACHYA L.—A shrub variable in height up to 3 or 4 ft, the branchlets rather rigid, with the joints $\frac{1}{2}$ to 2 in. apart. Leaves $\frac{1}{12}$ in. long. Male flower-spike usually solitary; female flowers in pairs. Fruit globose, $\frac{1}{4}$ in. long, red. Native of S. and E. Europe; cultivated in the sixteenth century. Var. MONOSTACHYA (L.) Stapf has solitary female flowers.

E. GERARDIANA Stapf—A densely furnished shrub, often very dwarf (2 or 3 in. high) in a wild state, but up to 2 ft high in cultivation, forming a spreading close mass. Branchlets slender, erect, with the joints $\frac{3}{4}$ to 1 in. apart. Male flowers yellow, in a globose or ovate spike $\frac{1}{6}$ in. long. Fruit globose, $\frac{1}{4}$ in. long, red. Native of the Himalaya, the Pamirs, Yarkand, Tibet, etc.

E. INTERMEDIA C. A. Mey.—An erect shrub about 3 ft high, branchlets roughish, with the joints $1\frac{1}{2}$ to $2\frac{1}{2}$ in. apart. Flowers of both sexes often on the same plant. Fruit red, globose, $\frac{1}{4}$ in. long. Native of Central Asia. Distinguished from the others here mentioned by the stouter branchlets and longer internodes.

E. MAJOR Host *E. nebrodensis* Tineo—A shrub sometimes 3 ft or more high, the lower branches prostrate; branchlets with the slightly thickened joints $\frac{1}{2}$ to

1 in. apart. Male flower-spikes solitary, or two or three together; female solitary. Fruit red, rarely yellow, globose, ¼ in. long. Native of the Mediterranean region, N. Africa, and Canary Islands. It occurs along the coast of Dalmatia, and I have seen it making very charming evergreen patches at Spalato (Split), on the walls of Diocletian's palace, also in the vicinity of Ragusa (Dubrovnik).

EPIGAEA ERICACEAE

A genus of two species, one Asiatic, the other N.E. American. The generic name is from the Greek *epi*, on, and *gaea*, earth, referring to the creeping habit of both species. The monotypic genus *Orphanidesia* is closely allied to *Epigaea* and included in it by some botanists. The name of *Orphanidesia gaultherioides*, if this species is considered to belong to *Epigaea*, would be *E. gaultherioides* (Boiss. and Bal.) Takht.

E. ASIATICA Maxim.

A low, creeping evergreen shrub a few inches high; young shoots clothed with outstanding, bristle-like, often gland-tipped hairs. Leaves strongly veined, ovate, with a heart-shaped base and an abruptly pointed apex, 1½ to 3 in. long, ¾ to 1¾ in. wide, leathery and harsh to the touch, dark dull green above and sprinkled with short stiff bristles when young, paler beneath and bristly on the midrib, margins edged with gland-tipped hairs; stalk ⅙ to ⅓ in. long, hairy like the young shoots. Flowers produced in April in terminal or axillary racemes of three to six blossoms, with hairy bracts at the base. Corolla rose-coloured, ½ in. long, tubular to urn-shaped with five shallow, recurved, rounded lobes at the mouth where it measures ¼ to ⅓ in. wide; downy only near the base inside. Calyx segments ovate, membranous, pointed, glabrous or minutely downy, ¼ in. long. Stamens short, hairy at the base; style stout, shorter than the stamens; flower-stalk hairy; seed-vessel orange-shaped. *Bot. Mag.*, t. 9222.

Native of Japan, in Honshu and Hokkaido (Yezo); described by Maximowicz in 1867 but introduced to cultivation about 1929. In general appearance it is like its American congener, *E. repens*, which is the only other species known, but is distinct in its more uniformly sharply pointed, longer-stalked leaves. The corolla of *E. repens* is more downy inside. It is shade-loving and requires the same moist, peaty soil as *E. repens*, but is apparently no more amenable to cultivation.

E. × INTERTEXTA Mulligan

This cross between *E. repens* and *E. asiatica* was made by Messrs Marchant in 1928 and described by B. O. Mulligan in *Journ. R.H.S.*, Vol. 64, pp. 507–510

(1939). Of the many seedlings raised, one, named 'APPLE BLOSSOM', is more satisfactory as a garden plant than *E. repens*, which it resembles in general character but from which it differs in its larger and more numerous flowers, of a deeper pink. Later the raisers back-crossed 'Apple Blossom' on to *E. asiatica* and one seedling from this cross was put into commerce in 1938 as 'AURORA'. This is closer to the second parent, which it resembles in its thick, dark green leaves. The flowers are fewer in each truss (three to nine), but larger and better displayed, with spreading lobes.

E. REPENS L.   TRAILING ARBUTUS

A creeping, evergreen shrub reaching only 4 to 6 in. above the ground, the slender hairy stems rooting at intervals. Leaves leathery, alternate, ovate-oblong, with a heart-shaped base and a round or short-pointed apex, 1 to 3 in. long, $\frac{3}{4}$ to 2 in. wide, of a rather dark glossy green, rough and sprinkled with short bristles on both surfaces and at the margin; leaf-stalk $\frac{1}{2}$ to $\frac{3}{4}$ in. long, hairy. Flowers produced in April, four to six together in a dense terminal head about 1 in. across, furnished at the base with green, hairy, lanceolate bracts. Corolla tubular, $\frac{5}{8}$ in. long, with five spreading, roundish ovate lobes, making it about $\frac{1}{2}$ in. across at the mouth, woolly within; white or rosy tinted; calyx-lobes lanceolate, glabrous, half as long as the corolla, green.

Native of eastern N. America, from Canada to Georgia. It is abundant near Plymouth, in Massachusetts, where the Pilgrim Fathers landed in 1620. By them, tradition says, it was named after their own famous vessel. It is said to have been introduced to Britain in 1736, but, owing to the difficulty experienced in cultivating it, has never become common. Although capable of withstanding any frost experienced in this country, it misses its native covering of snow, and is excited into premature growth by our mild winters only to be cut off by later frost. It likes a peaty soil; in the Knap Hill nursery it throve admirably on the shady side of a clump of rhododendrons but died out during the war years. On the other hand, I have seen it equally good in the botanic garden at Dresden in full sun; but there the climate is not dissimilar to that of its native home. The best success in Britain has been attained by giving it the shelter of a handlight in late winter, and during frosty nights in spring. Propagated by layers.

ERCILLA   PHYTOLACCACEAE

A genus containing the species described and another in Peru. The name commemorates Alonso de Ercilla (1533–94), author of a famous epic poem on a campaign waged by the Spanish forces in Chile against the Araucanians.

E. VOLUBILIS A. Juss.

Galvezia spicata Bert. (nomen); *Bridgesia spicata* (Bert.) Hook. & Arn.; *E. spicata* (Bert.)
Moquin

An evergreen climber producing a dense mass of slender, sparsely branched, very leafy stems, ultimately 15 to 20 ft high, attaching themselves to walls or tree-trunks by means of aerial roots; young wood glabrous. Leaves alternate, ½ in. or less apart; ovate or oblong, ¾ to 1½ in. long, ½ to 1 in. wide; tapered or rounded at the base, blunt at the apex, wavy at the margin; glabrous, stout, fleshy, dark shining green; stalk ⅛ to ¼ in. long. Flowers produced in March and April in dense spikes which are 1 to 1½ in. long, ½ in. through, cylindrical. Calyx ⅓ in. across, with five dull white, ovate sepals; stamens white, about eight, ¼ in. long, much protruded. Corolla none.

Native of Chile; introduced in 1840 by Thomas Bridges, a very industrious collector of South American plants. The genus was named after him by Hooker but the name had to give way to an earlier one. It lives outside at Kew, and flowers regularly, but succeeds better against a wall, where, if the leading shoots are securely nailed, it will form a heavy tangle. Its natural means of attachment appear to be scarcely efficient enough to enable the plant to bear its own weight on a vertical surface.

ERICA   HEATH   ERICACEAE

Of the several hundreds of known species of heath, the vast majority are native of the Cape of Good Hope; the only hardy ones are of European origin. Of the species described in the following notes, six are natives of the British Isles. These heaths are all evergreen, and are distinct among hardy shrubs for the smallness and the great number of their leaves, which are linear and usually have the margins recurved so as to form a groove at the back; they are arranged in whorls of three or four, sometimes five or six. In stature these hardy heaths range from small trees over 20 ft high, to dwarf semi-prostrate shrubs 2 in. high. The corolla varies from globular to cylindrical, and has usually four small teeth at the contracted opening; it does not fall in the ordinary way, but withers and remains long on the stalk encasing the seed-vessel. Calyx four-parted; stamens eight; fruit a many-seeded capsule.

The best way to use heaths in gardens is to plant them in broad masses. Fine colour effects can be produced in that way by both the early- and late-flowering sorts. But near London, or in places with a similar climate, it would not be wise to plant masses of *E. lusitanica, australis, arborea,* and the hybrid × *veitchii,* which are likely to suffer damage in severe winters, nor of *E. scoparia,* which is scarcely worth it. They thrive in almost any soil that is not calcareous; *E. carnea, mediterranea,* × *darleyensis* and *terminalis* can be grown even in such soils but only the last named is really tolerant of pure chalk. The soil may have decayed leaves mixed with it, but it should not be enriched by manure. The ideal soil is one of light sandy peat, but that is by no means essential.   [PLATE 18

In most gardens the soil is too rich for the dwarf heaths, and, in consequence, they grow too fast and soft and become lanky, very different from the dense sturdy plants one sees wild. To correct this, especially in those that flower late, it is advisable occasionally to prune over the plants in spring before they start growth. This makes them break into growth lower down, and tends to keep them dwarfer and more compact. Whilst this annual pruning is more especially needed by *E. cinerea*, *multiflora*, *vagans*, *ciliaris*, and *tetralix*, the early-flowering *E. carnea* and ×*darleyensis* are also improved if treated the same way as soon as the flowers begin to fade; but with them it is not so necessary.

Heaths can be propagated by seeds and by cuttings. The former should be sown in very sandy peat in spring, and kept in a cool frame until germinated; when large enough to handle they should be pricked off into shallow boxes of similar soil, and when 2 or 3 in. high planted out in nursery beds or even in permanent places. But cuttings perhaps are preferable and, of course essential for the propagation of the cultivars. They should be made in July and August, of moderately ripened twigs about 1 in. long; side twigs of that length springing direct from older branches are best. The leaves should be carefully removed from the lower half, and for this work a very sharp knife is essential, so that the leaves are cut cleanly away without tearing the bark of the cuttings. These are then put in pots of very sandy peat, surfaced with silver sand when finished, and placed in slight bottom heat with a bell-glass over them. They will take root in a few weeks, but need not be disturbed until the following spring, when they can be treated as advised for seedlings.

We are grateful to Mr David McClintock for reading the text of *Erica* and making many helpful comments.

E. ARBOREA L.   TREE HEATH

A shrub of bushy habit, or in favourable localities a tree over 20 ft high, with a distinct trunk; young wood very hairy, the hairs branched. Leaves very densely packed in whorls of threes, ⅛ to ¼ in. long, glabrous, linear, grooved beneath. Flowers very fragrant, borne in great profusion in March and April, and usually clustered near the end of short twigs that clothe the shoots of the preceding year, the whole making a slender panicle up to 1½ ft in length. Corolla globular, ⅛ in. long, almost white; sepals ovate, not half as long as the corolla; stigma much flattened, white; flower-stalk ⅛ in. long, smooth.

Native of S. Europe, N. Africa and northern Asia Minor as far as Lazistan and the foothills of the W. Caucasus; also in Abyssinia and on many of the higher mountains of eastern and central Africa (including Mt Kilimanjaro); introduced in 1658. This fine heath is not seen at its best near London, although it grows 8 to 10 ft high there. Ultimately, however, there comes a frost that kills it. In the Isle of Wight there is, or used to be, a tree in the gardens of Steephill Castle,

Ventnor, over 20 ft high, with a trunk $2\frac{1}{2}$ ft in girth near the ground. Even on the Dalmatian islands, where I have seen this heath wild, these dimensions are not exceeded. It appears to be able to withstand about 20° of frost with impunity, if it be of only one or two nights' duration. The stems are very brittle and easily broken by heavy snow. In former times the wood was largely used at Cannes for turning and making into 'briar-root' tobacco pipes—a corruption of the French 'bruyère'. It was once abundant along the coast from Marseilles to Genoa. The flowers, whose odour is like that of honey, remain, after fading, on the plants till June.

var. ALPINA Dieck—A very distinct and valuable form of tree heath. It was introduced to Kew in 1899, and has proved to be a very hardy and handsome evergreen, and has never suffered in the least by any frost experienced since that date. In the trying winter of 1908–9 even the smallest twigs were uninjured, preserving a peculiarly fresh and vivid green all the time. In more recent cold winters it has again proved to be somewhat more hardy than the type. It is a sturdy bush, stiffer and more erect in its growth than *E. arborea*. The young wood has the same mossy apperanace, due to the abundance of branched hairs. The flowers are not freely borne whilst the plant is young, but afterwards they appear crowded in stiff, pyramidal panicles 1 ft or more long. They are rather dull white, but the beauty of the plant is as much in the rich cheerful green of the plumose branches all through the winter. It is now 8 to 10 ft high and 24 ft across at Kew. It was found in the mountains near Cuenca, in Spain, at over 4,500 ft.

Precisely where Dieck found the plants it is impossible to say, but according to his account it was in a wild and inaccessible part of the interior of Cuenca province, at the headwaters of the rivers Tagus and Jucar (hence probably in the mountains immediately to the north or north-east of the town of Cuenca). They grew in immense quantities at the tree-line. At the time of his visit (1892), the region where the plants were found was dominated by the all-powerful bandit Don Antonio de Torriz, and only by his favour was Dieck able to enter it.

E. AUSTRALIS L.   SPANISH HEATH

A shrub of rather open, ungainly habit, usually 3 or 4 ft high, occasionally to 8 ft or more; young shoots erect, covered with a short thick down. Leaves linear, $\frac{1}{4}$ in. long, glandular on the margins when quite young, arranged in whorls of fours; dark green above, channelled beneath. Flowers borne on the previous year's growth in clusters of four or eight at the end of the shoot. Corolla cylindrical, $\frac{1}{3}$ in. long, bright purplish red, with four rounded lobes at the mouth; calyx less than half as long as the corolla, slightly downy; anthers slightly exposed; flower-stalk $\frac{1}{12}$ in. long. *Bot. Mag.*, t. 8045.

Native of Spain and Portugal, introduced according to Aiton by the then Earl of Coventry in 1769. In the richness and brightness of its colouring it is the best of the taller heaths, and flowers from April to June. Unfortunately it is not absolutely hardy, and very severe winters almost clear the country of it, for which reason it has often been rare. It has lived in the open at Kew since 1896, although sometimes hard hit by frost. It will thrive permanently in the

Isle of Wight, Cornwall, etc. In gardens, E. *mediterranea* is often confused with
it and flowers at the same time, but is readily distinguished by its cylindrical
clusters of blossom, the individual flowers coming in the leaf-axils along the
shoot—not terminal as in *australis*. The flower arrangement of E. *australis* is
similar to that of E. *terminalis*, but the latter only starts to bloom when *australis*
is over, and it does so on the shoots of the current year.

cv. 'MR ROBERT'.—A form of E. *australis* with pure white flowers of the
same size and shape as in the type and clustered at the end of the twigs in the

ERICA AUSTRALIS

same way. It was first found wild in 1912 by the late Lieut. Robert Williams, of
Caerhays, in the mountains of southern Spain near Algeciras, and by him was
introduced to cultivation. At Caerhays in 1930 it was 9 ft high. It flowers very
freely in spring, its pure white blossom making it a very charming addition to
the hardy heaths. Lieut. Williams belonged to the 3rd Grenadier Guards and
fell on one of the battlefields near Loos on 8th October 1915. As a young man
at home he was known as 'Mr Robert', and this heath has been named after him

to perpetuate his memory and his enthusiasm, for it cost him ten days' hard searching to find it. It seems to be a little hardier than E. *australis*.

E. CANALICULATA Andrews
E. *melanthera* Lodd., not L.

An evergreen bush up to 18 ft high, elegant in branching and often somewhat columnar in outline; young shoots greyish owing to a dense covering of whitish, branched hairs. Leaves of the typical heath shape, mostly in whorls of three, $\frac{3}{16}$ to $\frac{1}{4}$ in. long, the thickness of a stout thread, dark green, the margins much recurved. Flowers lilac-pink in the open, white or pale rose under glass, $\frac{1}{8}$ in. wide; corolla cup-shaped with wide shallow lobes; calyx-lobes white, ovate, pointed; anthers brown, exposed; style white, standing out $\frac{1}{8}$ in. above the anthers; flower-stalk downy, $\frac{1}{8}$ in. long. The flowers are mostly crowded towards the end of short twigs, making the older shoots from which they spring cylindrical panicles of blossom. *Bot. Mag.*, n.s., t. 339.

Native of S. Africa; introduced about 1802. This heath was once well known throughout the country, under the name "*melanthera*", as a greenhouse plant grown in pots, and not infrequently hawked in the streets. But it is hardier than is generally believed and is not sufficiently planted out-of-doors in the milder parts of the country. It is seen at its best in the Cornish gardens, and there was a singularly fine form in the garden at Ludgvan, near Penzance. It should, however, be tried more frequently in the southern parts of Sussex, Hampshire, and Dorset. Even at Kew, at the foot of a wall, with a shelter of canvas in cold weather, it survived three winters and flowered outside, although the winter of 1928–9 proved too much for it. It begins to bloom early in the year and continues one of the most beautiful of flowering shrubs for three months.

E. CARNEA *see* E. HERBACEA

E. CILIARIS L.   DORSET HEATH

A straggling shrub 6 to 12 in. high, with long prostrate stems from which the flowering branches spring erect in dense masses; young stems thickly covered with hairs. Leaves in whorls of threes, ovate, about $\frac{1}{8}$ in. long, green above, whitish beneath, glabrous on both surfaces, but the edges furnished with long gland-tipped hairs; stalk scarcely perceptible. Flowers arranged in whorls of threes on erect terminal racemes, 2 to 5 in. long, and opening from late June to October. Corolla rosy red, pitcher-shaped, $\frac{3}{8}$ in. long, suddenly and obliquely contracted towards the mouth, where are four rounded, shallow teeth. Sepals very similar to the smallest leaves, but more densely hairy on the margin; flower-stalk $\frac{1}{10}$ in. long; seed-vessel quite glabrous.

Native of S.W. Europe, also of Cornwall, Devon, Dorset, and W. Ireland. Among hardy heaths it is only likely to be confused with E. *tetralix*, but that species has its leaves in fours, and its flowers are arranged in short terminal umbels—not on an elongated axis as in *E. ciliaris*. The latter is charming for planting in broad masses for late summer and autumnal flowering.

cv. 'MAWEANA'.—A very distinct and superior form of *E. ciliaris* found in 1872 in Portugal by George Maw. It differs from the ordinary *ciliaris* in its stiffer, sturdier habit, and is less inclined to develop long trailing branches. The flower is larger, being ½ in. long, and the foliage stouter and darker green. It flowers from July to November, and is a most attractive plant. The cultivar name 'Maweana' belongs only to the original clone, figured in *Bot. Mag.*, t. 8443 (*E.c.* var. *maweana* (Backhouse) Bean; *E. maweana* Backhouse).

Another clone of wild origin, discovered in Dorset, is 'STOBOROUGH', tall-growing, with large white flowers. Others (among many now in commerce) are: 'MRS C. H. GILL', of compact growth, with clear red flowers and dark green foliage; and 'GLOBOSA', with grey-green foliage and pink flowers. The flowering time of all these is July to October.

E. × WATSONII (Benth.) Bean—This is the collective name for hybrids between *E. ciliaris* and *E. tetralix*, which occur quite commonly in the wild and are rather variable. The type was found by H. C. Watson on a heath near Truro and described by Bentham in 1839 as *E. ciliaris* var. *watsonii*. Its flowers are arranged much after the fashion of *E. ciliaris*, and they have the obliquely pitcher-shaped form of that species, but the raceme is not so elongated. The leaves are mostly in whorls of four, as in *E. tetralix*, and have the narrower shape of that species. The original clone has been named 'TRURO'.

Other cultivars that belong to this group include 'GWEN', 'DAWN' and 'H. MAXWELL'.

E. mackaiana, once thought to be a hybrid of *E. ciliaris* and *tetralix*, is now accepted as a species (q.v.).

E. CINEREA L.   BELL-HEATHER

A low shrub from 6 in. to 1½ ft high, with rather stiff, much-divided branches; young shoots downy. Leaves normally three in a whorl, linear, ⅛ to ¼ in. long, flat above, convex beneath, pointed, deep green and glabrous. Flowers produced from June to September in terminal umbels of four to eight flowers, or in racemes 1 to 3 in. long; corolla egg-shaped, ¼ in. long, bright purple, with four teeth at the opening. Calyx-lobes narrow-lanceolate, one-third the length of the corolla, semi-transparent, glabrous; flower-stalk ⅛ to ⅙ in. long, downy.

Native of W. Europe from Norway to Spain and N. Italy, and very generally distributed over the moors of Britain. It is, perhaps, the most beautiful of the dwarf summer- and autumn-flowering heaths, and produces an enormous profusion of blossom. In cultivated ground in the Thames Valley it is apt to be short-lived, growing too fast in the early summer and often scorched by excessive heat in July and August. It is improved by cutting over in the early spring before growth starts. It has varied much in the colour of the flowers, and the dozen or so clones in commerce when the first edition of this work was published has now risen to one hundred. For the following short selection we are indebted to the Royal Horticultural Society:

'ALBA MAJOR'.—White flowers in clusters at the ends of the stems. June–August.

'ALBA MINOR'.—White compact growth, light green foliage. June–October.

'ATRORUBENS'.—Long sprays of ruby-red flowers. June–August.

'C. D. EASON'.—Rich rosy-red flowers, deep green foliage. June–September.

'CEVENNES'.—Upright growth with lavender-rose flowers. June–Aug.

'EDEN VALLEY'.—Rosy-lilac flowers fading to white at the base. June–September.

'GOLDEN DROP'.—Golden-copper foliage in summer, changing to red in the winter. Flowers pinkish purple but sparsely produced.

'KNAP HILL PINK'.—Bright pink flowers, deep green foliage. June–September.

'P. S. PATRICK'.—Very rich purple flowers in long spikes. July–September.

'ROSEA'.—Bright pink. June–September.

These and the type are worth planting freely for producing broad masses of colour at a season when comparatively few shrubs are in bloom.

A form of *E. cinerea* was named by Boulger var. SCHIZOPETALA; in it the corollas, normally egg- or pitcher-shaped, are divided to the base into four lanceolate lobes. This abnormality has been noted several times among wild plants and is also seen in the cultivars *E. cinerea* 'W. G. NOTLEY' and 'WINIFRED WHITLEY'. It is difficult to agree with G. Krüssmann's view that these plants are intergeneric hybrids between the bell-heather and *Calluna vulgaris* (*Deutsche Baumschule*, 1960, p. 154, and *Handbuch der Laubgehölze*, Vol. 1, p. 419, where the three clones mentioned are referred to x *Ericalluna bealeana* Krüssmann). A similar polypetalous malformation is noted under *Kalmia latifolia* and is to be found in other ericaceous species.

E. x DARLEYENSIS Bean

E. mediterranea hybrida Hort.; *E. hybrida* Hort.

This heath appeared about 1890 in the heath nursery of Messrs James Smith & Son, at Darley Dale, in Derbyshire, and showed characters intermediate between those of *E. herbacea* and *E. erigena*. They named it "*E. mediterranea hybrida*", but as it shows as much, or more, affinity with *E. carnea*, I have adopted another name for it. The name "*hybrida*" has been given to it, but that is already in use for a S. African heath. In the characters of its leaves, young wood, and flowers it is identical with those two species, which themselves scarcely differ; but planted in groups it eventually forms dense masses 2 ft high—at least twice as high as *herbacea*, yet never showing any disposition to grow erect and form a single stem like *erigena*. Quite young plants are scarcely distinguishable from *E. herbacea*, but soon show they are not the same by their stronger growth. A valuable character of *E. x darleyensis* is its habit of commencing to flower as early as November and continuing until May. It ought to be in every garden.

The heath described above is the type ('DARLEY DALE') of the hybrid group
E. × *darleyensis*, to which the following also belong:

cv. 'ARTHUR JOHNSON'.—A spontaneous hybrid between, it is thought,
E. *erigena* "var. *hibernica*" and E. *herbacea* 'Ruby Glow', raised by the late
A. T. Johnson and given an Award of Merit in 1952. Flowers rose, foliage light
green. A compact bush to about 2 ft high and 3 ft or more across.

cv. 'GEORGE RENDALL'.—Flowers of a deeper hue than in 'Darley Dale'
and habit more compact.

cv. 'SILBERSCHMELZE'.—A white-flowered sport of 'Darley Dale' raised in
Germany.

E. ERIGENA R. Ross

E. *mediterranea* of most authors, not L.; E. *hibernica* (Hook. & Arn.) Syme; E. *mediterranea*
var. *hibernica* Hook. & Arn.

A shrub 6 to 10 ft high, of dense bushy form; branches erect and glabrous.
Leaves linear, $\frac{1}{6}$ to $\frac{1}{3}$ in. long, dark green, produced in whorls of four. Flowers
borne singly or in pairs at each of the leaf-axils at the ends of the twigs of the
previous year, the buds being formed the previous summer. They make dense
leafy racemes 1 to 2 in. long. Corolla cylindrical, $\frac{1}{4}$ in. long, of a rich rosy red;
calyx-lobes narrow-oblong, rather more than half as long as the corolla; anthers
dark red, exposed; flower-stalk $\frac{1}{8}$ in. or less long.

Native of S.W. France, Portugal, Spain, and of Co. Galway and Co. Mayo in
Ireland, but not of the Mediterranean region. It was in cultivation, according
to Aiton, in 1648. Of the spring-flowering heaths it is the finest and best for a
climate like that of London. It is quite hardy at Kew except in the severest of all
winters, and planted there in large masses provides a continuous feast of colour
and fragrance from March (or even earlier) to May. Its fragrance is like that of
honey.

cv. 'ALBA'.—Flowers white; plant not so large and robust as the type,
growing to about 2 ft high. 'W. T. RACKLIFF' is similar, with larger flowers.

cv. 'BRIGHTNESS'.—This grows to about 2 ft high; foliage dark green.
Flowers pink, from bronzy-red buds. Of Irish origin, before 1925.

cv. 'NANA'.—A dwarf plant forming a rounded tuft 1 to $1\frac{1}{2}$ ft high. Not so
free-flowering as the type.

cv. 'SUPERBA'.—A vigorous form growing to 6 ft or more high. Flowers
clearer pink than in the type.

In his paper in *Journ. Linn. Soc.*, Vol. 60 (1967), pp. 61–71, Ross showed
conclusively that the name E. *mediterranea* had been misapplied and he was
forced to find another name for the plants generally known as E. *mediterranea*.
He first took up E. *hibernica* (Hook. & Arn.) Syme but subsequently found that
this was antedated by E. *hibernica* Utinet, so a new name was necessary. Hence
E. *erigena*.

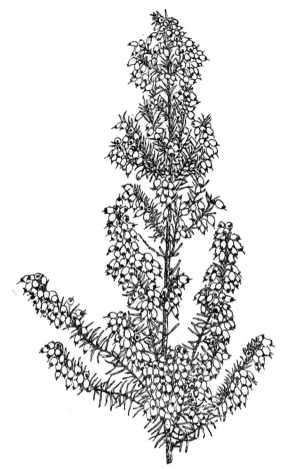

ERICA ERIGENA

E. HERBACEA L.   WINTER OR SNOW HEATH

E. carnea L.; *E. mediterranea* L. (but *not* of gardens)

A low shrub of tufted habit from 6 to 10 in. high, the branches becoming prostrate and spreading on old plants; young twigs glabrous. Leaves linear, $\frac{1}{6}$ to $\frac{1}{3}$ in. long, dark glossy green above, channelled beneath; arranged mostly in whorls of fours, the whorls $\frac{1}{12}$ to $\frac{1}{8}$ in. apart. Flowers borne singly or in pairs in the leaf-axils at the end of the previous summer's growth, making cylindrical racemes 1 to 2 in. long. Corolla deep rosy red, scarcely $\frac{1}{4}$ in. long, cylindrical; calyx-lobes narrowly oblong, more than half the length of the corolla, anthers protruded, dark red; flower-stalk about as long as the calyx.

Native of the Alps, the Apennines and some of the mountains of E. Europe; introduced by the Earl of Coventry in 1763. One of the most delightful of all dwarf shrubs, this heath is especially valuable for its early flowering. Soon after New Year's Day (or even earlier) the blossoms begin to open, and often by February the plants are transformed into masses of rosy red, all the more pleasing because the prevailing tints of the plants then in flower are yellow, white, and blue. In a young state the plants form dainty little tufts, but with age the branches spread over the ground, and one plant will in time cover 2 ft or more of space, always keeping its surface well clothed with the dark green leafy twigs. Plants can be kept particularly neat, thick, and dwarf, by cutting them over in early April or as soon as the flowers lose colour. This heath is admirable for furnishing the shelves of the rock garden, and for forming broad patches of colour wherever a dwarf evergreen is suitable. By some authors it and E. erigena are regarded as forms of the same species. In botanical characteristics the two are similar, but E. herbacea is, of course, very distinct in its dwarf or semi-prostrate habit, in its more conspicuously exposed anthers, and in flowering earlier. It is also much hardier.

It is regrettable that the familiar name E. carnea has to give way to E. herbacea, for reasons explained by R. Ross in Jour. Linn. Soc. (Bot.), Vol. 60 (1967), pp. 61–68.

f. ALBA (Dipp.) Schneid.—Plants with white flowers occur quite commonly in the wild. The form once cultivated as alba has been superseded by 'Springwood White' (see below).

Many named clones of E. herbacea are in commerce, of which the following is only a selection:

'KING GEORGE'.—Flowers clear, rosy crimson; dark green foliage. December–February. Often wrongly called 'Winter Beauty'.

'RUBY GLOW'.—Flowers deep carmine-red; foliage bronzy green; spreading habit. March–April.

'SPRINGWOOD PINK'.—Flowers light pink; vigorous trailing habit. January–March.

'SPRINGWOOD WHITE'.—Of a similar habit to 'Springwood Pink'; flowers white, with prominent brown anthers, in long spikes. January–March.

'VIVELLII'.—Flowers deep carmine-red; foliage dark green in summer, bronzy in winter. February–March.

E. LUSITANICA Rudolph
E. codonodes Lindl.

An erect, elegant shrub, eventually 10 to 12 ft high, forming large plumose branches; young shoots clothed with simple hairs. Leaves about $\frac{1}{4}$ in. long, linear, slightly grooved beneath, irregularly arranged. Flowers slightly fragrant, produced in great profusion during March and April, or even in January and February in mild seasons and warm districts; they are borne in clusters towards the end of small lateral twigs. Corolla cylindrical, $\frac{3}{16}$ in. long, white; calyx and flower-stalk glabrous, the former with triangular teeth; stamens and style deep pink. Bot. Mag., t. 8018.

Native of S.W. Europe; introduced early in the nineteenth century. The only other species with which this is likely to be confused is *E. arborea*. From it *E. lusitanica* differs in the paler foliage, in the more plumose erect branching, in the hairs on the young shoots being unbranched, and in the longer, larger, but less fragrant flowers with a small red stigma. Seen together they are quite distinct. *E. lusitanica* is, if anything, more tender than *E. arborea*, but thrives well in the south and south-west counties. In the wild garden at Lytchett Heath, near Poole, the progeny of a single plant have naturalised themselves in thousands, and now cover 1½ acres of ground. Near London, it will not survive any lengthened exposure to much more than 20° of frost. This heath flowers with extraordinary profusion, the whole plant with its pyramidal branches 1 to 2 ft long, being covered with blossoms which last long in beauty.

E. MACKAIANA Bab.
E. mackaii Hook.

This heath has been regarded by many authorities as a variety of *E. tetralix* or a hybrid between it and *E. ciliaris*, but is now accepted as an authentic species. It is about 1 ft high, with its leaves in whorls of four, ovate-oblong, the margins less recurved than in *E. tetralix*, and thus apparently broader; usually glabrous above. The flowers are in terminal umbels as in *E. tetralix*; the corolla of a deeper rosy red, shorter and broader. Seed-vessel comparatively glabrous (it is downy in *E. tetralix*). The only homes of this heath in the British Isles are near Roundstone (Co. Galway), where it was discovered by W. M'Alla in 1833, and in W. Donegal. It is also found in N.W. Spain, where it is equally rare and local. A pretty dwarf heath, useful for planting in broad patches as recommended for its allies.

cv. 'PLENA'.—A double-flowered form discovered in W. Galway. The urn-shaped corolla is rather wider at the mouth than in the type, and encloses several small, closely packed petals which have replaced the stamens. Superior to the type in lasting longer in flower (*E. m. flore pleno*; *E. crawfurdii*).

E. × PRAEGERI Ostenfeld—This is the group-name for hybrids between *E. mackaiana* and *E. tetralix*. These occur where the two species are in contact in the wild and have tended to obscure the distinctiveness of the former. A form of this hybrid is usually listed as a cultivar of *E. tetralix*. It is a dwarf plant with pink flowers.

E. 'STUARTII'.—This heath, collected in W. Galway in 1890, is regarded by some authorities as a hybrid between *E. mackaiana* and *E. mediterranea* but this attribution is unlikely (*Heather Soc. Y.B.*, 1965, pp. 12–13).

E. MEDITERRANEA *see* E. ERIGENA

E. MULTIFLORA L.

A low shrub 1 to 2½ ft high; young shoots glabrous. Leaves ¼ to ½ in. long, linear, almost cylindrical, slightly downy at the base, arranged in fours or fives.

Flowers clustered in the leaf-axils as in *E. vagans*, forming an erect, cylindrical, terminal raceme, 2 or 3 in. long. Corolla pale rose, pitcher-shaped, $\frac{3}{16}$ in. long; anthers oblong, protruding, each anther with its two cells (loculi) separated only slightly at the top; sepals lance-shaped, not quite half as long as the corolla; flower-stalk $\frac{1}{2}$ in. long, holding the flower clear of the leaves.

Native of S. Europe; introduced in 1731. This heath is very rare in gardens, a form of *E. vagans* being usually made to do duty for it. The two have been much confused by botanists, but *E. multiflora* is easily distinguished by the anthers being only slightly notched at the top, whereas in *E. vagans* the anther-cells are free from one another right to the base; the sepals also are longer and narrower than in *E. vagans*.

E. PAGEANA L. Bolus

E. campanulata Guthrie & Bolus, not Andr.

It is, perhaps, stretching the limits of this work somewhat unduly to include in it this heath—a native of the Cape of Good Hope—but there seems a likelihood that it may succeed in Cornwall where *E. canaliculata* (formerly known as "*E. melanthera*") thrives so well. If that should prove to be the case, it will make a notable addition even to the Cornish garden flora. Its great charm is in bearing yellow flowers, a colour comparatively rare among heaths. I saw it at Caerhays in April 1930, where, growing in a sheltered sunny nook, a small plant gave a patch of colour as bright as a bit of double gorse. It seems first to have been noticed in Cape Town in 1904 when it was being offered for sale in the streets by a native flower-seller. Twenty years later it was exhibited at the British Empire Exhibition at Wembley amongst the wonderful S. African plants brought there in cold storage. Latterly it has been found to be a native of Caledon, the great heath country of S. Africa. It was raised about 1921 at Kew from seed obtained from the National Botanic Garden at Kirstenbosch. At first thought to be a form of *E. campanulata*, it was made a species by Mrs L. Bolus, and its name perpetuates the memory of the late Miss Mary Page, botanical artist at Cape Town University.

An evergreen shrub probably 3 or 4 ft (perhaps more) high; young twigs downy. Leaves densely arranged in fours, linear, $\frac{1}{6}$ to $\frac{1}{4}$ in. long, faintly grooved with a thin sunken line beneath and generally of the ordinary heath type of plant. Flowers bell-shaped $\frac{1}{4}$ to $\frac{3}{8}$ in. long, $\frac{1}{4}$ in. wide at the mouth, rich yellow, forming cylindrical clusters towards the ends of the branches; stamens included in the corolla; anthers dark brown. There are several membranous, ovate, ciliate bracts on the short flower-stalk. *Bot. Mag.*, t. 9133.

E. SCOPARIA L.

A shrub of loose, uneven habit, as much as 9 or 10 ft high, its branches erect and, like the leaves, free from down. Leaves in whorls of threes (sometimes fours), $\frac{1}{4}$ in. long, linear, pointed, glossy dark green. Flowers produced in May and June, in clusters of two to five, in the leaf-axils, over almost the whole of the preceding year's growth. Corolla greenish, $\frac{1}{8}$ in. long, globular. Calyx and flower-stalk quite glabrous. Stigma included or slightly exserted.

Native of S.W. Europe, N. Africa and Madeira, and much used there for making besoms. It is hardy; and, though loose and irregular in habit, it is decidedly elegant. It blossoms with great freedom, but the blossoms are small and of no great beauty, and it is only for its beauty of habit that it is desirable.

cv. 'PUMILA'.—A dwarf form, growing to about 2 ft high. This, or a similar clone, was in cultivation at Woburn in 1825 as *E. scoparia minima*.

E. TERMINALIS Salisb.

E. corsica DC.; *E. stricta* Willd.

An erect shrub up to 8 or 9 ft high, the branches covered with scarcely perceptible down. Leaves arranged in whorls usually of fours, sometimes fives or sixes; linear, $\frac{1}{4}$ to $\frac{1}{3}$ in. long, dark glossy green. Flowers in terminal umbels carrying four to eight blossoms, and in beauty from June to September. Corolla cylindrical, narrowing towards the mouth, where are four recurved teeth; pale rose, $\frac{1}{4}$ in. long; calyx with four lanceolate lobes, glabrous. *Bot. Mag.*, t. 8063.

Native of S. Spain, Italy, Corsica and Sardinia; introduced, according to Aiton, in 1765. Although one of the tallest of the heaths, it is perfectly hardy at Kew. It passed through the winter of 1962–3 without serious injury. It strikes freely from cuttings, and flowers well when 12 in. high. Its pleasing habit, erect, clustered twigs, and deep green, healthy-looking foliage; its bright rosy blossoms; and the fact that it flowers in late summer, make it a most desirable shrub. Yet it is almost neglected in gardens. It seems to be more tolerant of chalk than any other heath.

E. TETRALIX L.   CROSS-LEAVED HEATH

A low shrub 6 to 18 in. high, with the older stems spreading or prostrate, the young flower-bearing ones erect; young shoots downy. Leaves arranged in whorls of four, forming a cross, narrower than in *E. ciliaris*, and averaging $\frac{1}{8}$ in. long; dark green above, white beneath, edged with glandular hairs, and downy. Flowers in a dense head of from four to twelve or more blossoms. Corolla cylindrical, $\frac{1}{4}$ in. long, rose-coloured, contracted at the mouth, where are four shallow recurved lobes. Sepals like the leaves, but more hairy; flower-stalk and seed-vessel downy.

Native of N. and W. Europe, and common throughout the British Isles, where it is abundant in wet heaths and moors. It blossoms from June to October, and although so common in a wild state is well worth planting in masses in the garden. It is sometimes confused with *E. ciliaris*, under which the distinctions between the two are pointed out.

f. ALBA (Ait.) Braun-Blanquet—Flowers white; not uncommon in the wild state.

cv. 'ALBA MOLLIS'.—Flowers white; foliage distinctly greyish, due to the abundant whitish down on the leaves and stems. The whole plant has a frosted appearance.

cv. 'CON UNDERWOOD'.—Large crimson flowers; foliage silvery.

E. UMBELLATA L.

An evergreen shrub to about 2 ft high of erect or semi-prostrate habit; young shoots downy. Leaves linear, about $\frac{1}{6}$ in. long, of a soft greyish green. Inflorescence an umbel or two to eight flowers; corollas egg-shaped to globose, sharply contracted at the mouth, about $\frac{1}{6}$ in. long and clear rosy pink in colour, with dark, exserted anthers; calyx-lobes linear-oblong. Main flowering time May–June.

Native of Spain, Portugal and Morocco; probably first introduced late in the eighteenth century but little known in gardens until W. E. Th. Ingwersen introduced it from the Sierra de Estrella, Portugal, in the early twenties. Another form was introduced by Dr Giuseppi at about the same time. Although not completely hardy, it is certainly not so tender as was once supposed and should come through most winters unharmed in southern and western gardens. It is said to be tolerant of lime in the soil. It is one of the prettiest of the European heaths and valuable for having its main season of blossom when few other heaths are in flower.

E. VAGANS L.   CORNISH HEATH

A low, spreading shrub from 1 to $2\frac{1}{2}$ ft high, becoming ultimately 5 ft or more wide, and rather sprawling; branchlets glabrous. Leaves arranged four or five in a whorl; the whorls $\frac{1}{4}$ in. or less apart on the stems; linear, $\frac{1}{8}$ to $\frac{1}{2}$ in. long, channelled beneath, dark green and glabrous. Flowers produced usually in pairs from the leaf-axils, each on a glabrous stalk $\frac{1}{3}$ in. long, the whole forming an erect, leafy, cylindrical raceme 4 to 7 in. long, the flowers opening from below upwards from July to October. Corolla almost globular, about $\frac{1}{8}$ in. long, pinkish purple, the four lobes but little recurved; sepals ovate; anther-cells free from one another to the base, pink, rarely yellow.

Native of Cornwall and S.W. Europe. A showy and very attractive shrub in late summer and autumn, useful for planting on sunny slopes, and in broad masses. It is easily raised from cuttings, and thrives well in almost any soil not heavy or limy. Like the other late-flowering heaths it should be cut over occasionally in spring before growth recommences, removing all that part of the shoot that has borne flowers. This keeps the plants neater and causes them to flower more profusely, but done too often reduces the size of raceme.

cv. 'GRANDIFLORA'.—Of tall, loose-growing habit, with long tapering spikes of pink flowers.

cv. 'HOLDEN PINK'.—Flowers pale pinkish white, flushed with mallow-purple.

cv. 'LYONESSE'.—Flowers white, with distinctive brown anthers. It is superior to the older 'Alba' in purity of shade.

cv. 'M rs D. F. M axwell'.—Flowers warm rosy pink with no trace of purple.

cv. 'St Keverne'.—This form of the Cornish heath differs from the type in the corolla being more broadly bell-shaped, in its lobes being more recurved, and in its colour being pure rosy pink with no suggestion of purple in it. The other parts of the plant do not seem to differ. It was originally discovered on some moorland on Trelanvean farm, St Keverne, Cornwall, by P. D. Williams, who struck cuttings of it and established it in his garden at Lanarth. It was fortunate that he did so as the original plant was trodden out of existence by cattle the year following its discovery. It is now well established in gardens, where its clear rosy-pink flowers cause it to be preferred to the type with purplish ones.

E. × veitchii Bean

A hybrid raised in the Exeter nurseries of Messrs R. Veitch & Sons, and first exhibited by them at the Royal Horticultural Hall on 14th February 1905. It appears to have been of accidental origin, but there is no doubt that *E. arborea* and *E. lusitanica* are its parents. It is intermediate in many respects between them. In the colour of its foliage it resembles *E. lusitanica*, but the habit is rather that of *E. arborea*. The flowers are intermediate in shape, and white. They show their hybrid origin in the shape and colour of the stigma, the flattened shape being that of *E. arborea*, the pinkish colour that of *E. lusitanica*; stamens pink. A further indication of hybridity is in the hairs on the young shoots, which are partly branched like those of *E. arborea*, and partly simple like those of *E. lusitanica*.

E. × veitchii is quite as beautiful a heath as its parents, and of more vigorous growth.

E. × williamsii Druce

This heath was found on moorland near St Keverne, Cornwall. It is considered to be a hybrid between *E. vagans* and *E. tetralix*. It grows to 30 in. high and is of dense close habit, the young shoots slightly downy. Leaves closely set in whorls of four, linear, $\frac{1}{8}$ in. long, furrowed beneath and with very short glandular hairs on the margin. Flowers produced in the leaf-axils towards the end of the shoot so as to form a leafy raceme 1 to $1\frac{1}{2}$ in. long with the shoot protruding through it, or sometimes clustered so as to resemble an umbel at the end. Corolla bell-shaped, $\frac{1}{10}$ in. wide, rose-pink, with the four lobes erect; anthers brown, included in the corolla; style protruding $\frac{1}{12}$ in.

The plant grows well in light loamy or peaty soil and in gardens often puts on and can be recognised by a pale green or yellowish (but not unhealthy) tinge. It appears first to have been found about 1860 by Richard Davey, one-time Member of Parliament for West Cornwall, but lost sight of until found again in October 1910 by his nephew, P. D. Williams, after whom it is named and to whom its establishment in gardens is due.

E. × *williamsii* is a botanical collective name for hybrids between *E. vagans* and *E. tetralix* and therefore cannot be restricted to the original clone described above, which should be distinguished as 'P. D. WILLIAMS'. Another member of the *E.* × *williamsii* group is 'GWAVAS', which is dwarfer than 'P. D. Williams' and considered to be a better garden plant.

ERINACEA   LEGUMINOSAE

A monotypic genus of the Pea family, belonging to the tribe Genisteae, but very distinct from its other European representatives in the colouring of its flowers.

E. ANTHYLLIS Link   HEDGEHOG BROOM

E. pungens Boiss.; *Anthyllis erinacea* L.   [PLATE 20

A dwarf, much-branched, stiff, spiny shrub under 1 ft high in this country. The branches are erect, sharp-pointed, and in shape like small bodkins. They have very few leaves, and these are scarcely noticeable, being ¼ to ½ in. long, very narrow. Flowers borne two to four together on a short stalk just below the apex of the branchlet; they are ½ to ¾ in. long, with purplish-blue petals, and a peculiarly large, membranous, silky calyx two-thirds the length of the flower. Pod oblong, ¾ in. long, glandular-hairy, usually two- or three-, sometimes four- to six-seeded. Flowers in April and May.

Native of Spain and N. Africa. It was in gardens by 1759, but still remains one of the rarer of hardy plants. The distinct colour of its flowers, more blue than those of any other hardy leguminous shrub, should have gained it more notice. It is, however, very slow-growing, and misses the sunlight of its native mountains. In the vicarage garden at Bitton it formed low dense tufts of spiny stems, occasionally perfecting seed. At the foot of a sunny wall in the Cambridge Botanic Garden it also flowers admirably and it is, perhaps, in gardens with a similar soil and climate that it is most likely to thrive. It can be propagated by cuttings or layers, occasionally by seed. It is said to grow so plentifully on some of the mountains of Spain that horses can scarcely make their way through it. Suitable for a sunny nook in the rock garden. It thrives and seeds itself at Belhaven House, E. Lothian.

ERIOBOTRYA   ROSACEAE

A genus of about ten species of evergreen trees, natives of E. Asia. It is allied to *Photinia*, but differs in the larger, three- to five-celled fruit.

E. JAPONICA (Thunb.) Lindl.   LOQUAT

Mespilus japonica Thunb.; *Photinia japonica* (Thunb.) Franch. & Sav.

An evergreen tree up to 20 or 30 ft high, of rounded, bushy form; young branches thick and woolly. Leaves varying in size according to the vigour of the plant, sometimes 1 ft. long by 5 in. wide; ordinarily 6 to 9 in. long and 3 to 4 in. wide; wrinkled, coarsely but not deeply toothed, strongly set with parallel ribs ¼ to ½ in. apart; stalk very short and woolly. The lower surface is covered with a brownish wool, whilst the upper is dark glossy green and glabrous, except when young, being then covered with a loose white floss. Flowers ¾ in. across, fragrant like hawthorn, closely packed on a stiff, terminal, pyramidal panicle, 3 to 6 in. high, the stalks and calyx covered with a dense brown wool; petals yellowish white. Fruit pear-shaped or oblong, 1½ in. long, yellow; sometimes formed but rarely ripened in England. Blossoms in autumn.

Native of China and Japan; introduced to England in 1787 by Sir Joseph Banks, but not hardy enough to have ever become widely cultivated. It can only be grown against a south wall at Kew, where a plant has grown well for over thirty years, and makes a handsome and striking display of foliage, but rarely flowers. But at Maidwell Hall, Northamptonshire, in the heart of the Midlands, there is a specimen on a wall which is not only quite hardy there but bears fruit in most years; it has narrower leaves than the form commonly seen in cultivation. In the Mediterranean region this species is cultivated for its fruits, which ripen in spring and are known as 'nespole' or 'néfliers'—names which belong properly to the medlar (*Mespilus germanica*). It is best raised from seeds obtained from Southern Europe, where there are several named varieties, or by vegetative propagation from a tree of proved hardiness. Its leaves are amongst the handsomest in all evergreens that can be grown out-of-doors.

cv. 'VARIEGATA'.—Leaves variegated with white. It was awarded first prize amongst new plants at the Ghent Exhibition of 1913.

ESCALLONIA   ESCALLONIACEAE

A well-marked genus of hardy or half-hardy shrubs, of which all the species in cultivation except *E. virgata* are evergreen. The leading characters of the genus are: leaves alternate, simple, without stipules, often arranged in clusters on the twigs, each cluster in the axil of a larger leaf, and really representing a short branch; flowers white or red, mostly arranged in terminal racemes or panicles; petals five, long-clawed, free, but forming an imitation tube (except in *E. virgata*). Ovary inferior, enclosed in a top- or bell-shaped receptacle (hypanthium). This part of the flower is often referred to as the 'calyx-tube', but Dr Sleumer in his monograph on *Escallonia* uses this term for the basal part of the true calyx, which forms a rim above the receptacle and is divided into five lobes. The ovary is surmounted by a so-called disk, the shape and depth

T S—E

of which is useful for identification. It is narrowly conic or cylindric-conic in *E. alpina, E. revoluta, E. rosea,* and *E. rubra*; flat and truly disk-like in *E. virgata*; broadly conic or cushion-shaped in the other species described here. Fruit a capsule, with numerous small seeds. Many escallonias are furnished with resin glands on the leaves and branchlets, but these are far from being as abundant in cultivated plants as they are in wild ones. All of them are natives of S. America and are most abundant in Chile. The genus was named in honour of Escallon by the Spanish botanist Mutis, his companion and teacher.

As garden shrubs the escallonias are nearly all too tender to thrive well, except in the milder counties, without some protection. This protection is best afforded by a wall, and few evergreens make more effective and beautiful wall-coverings. For such as can be grown in the open a sunny position should be selected, and the soil should not be very rich—an ordinary sandy loam suffices, without manure or other fertilising material. They are easily increased by cuttings of half-ripened wood placed in pots of sandy soil in gentle heat. The wood is in proper condition in August.

The Chilean species of *Escallonia* are revised by E. Kausel in *Darwinia*, Vol. 10, pp. 169–225, 1951. More recently the whole genus has been revised by H. Sleumer in: *Die Gattung Escallonia* (1968), and this excellent monograph has been followed in the present revision.

E. ALPINA DC.

E. fonckii Phil. ("*fonkii*"); *E. glaberrima* Phil.

An evergreen shrub of dense habit 2 to 5 ft high in exposed places and often considerably more in width than in height, but up to 12 ft high in forests. It is glabrous in all its parts or with the young stems, leaves, inflorescence axes, and calyx clad with erect hairs of variable length. Leaves mostly obovate to spatulate-obovate, pointed or bluntish at the apex, cuneate at the base, finely toothed in the upper part, ½ to 1⅛ in. long, ⅛ to ½ in. wide, glossy green on both sides but rather paler beneath. Flowers produced towards the end of June at the ends of side-growths, the lower ones in the axils of leaves, the upper subtended by bracts, the inflorescence being in effect a raceme which becomes progressively less leafy from base to apex and consists of four to twelve flowers. Calyx-lobes triangular, contracted to a slender apex. Petals about ½ in. long, with the linear-spatulate shape and erect pose so common in this genus.

Native of Chile and Argentina, where it ranges from about 35° S. to the Magellan region and ascends above the tree-line in the Andes. The type, collected by Poeppig in Antuco province, was a downy state of the species, while the name *E. fonckii*, by which the species has hitherto been known in gardens, is founded on a glabrous specimen. But intermediate forms occur and only one species is involved, for which *E. alpina* is the earlier name. It was introduced by Harold Comber during his expedition to the Andes 1925–7 under his seed-numbers 955 and 1178. On an east-facing wall of the Laboratory at Wisley, *E. alpina* has attained a height of 15 ft. At Kew, where it is grown fully in the open, the habit is low and bushy, as it usually is in wild plants.

E. BIFIDA Link & Otto

E. montevidensis (Cham. & Schlecht.) DC.; *E. floribunda* var. *montevidensis* Cham. & Schlecht.; *E. floribunda* Hort., not H. B. K.

An evergreen shrub up to 10 ft or more high when grown on walls in this country, but occasionally attaining the dimensions of a small tree in S. America; branchlets glabrous and usually slightly viscid. Leaves 1½ to 3 in. long, narrowly oval to obovate or spathulate, tapering at the base, rounded or often conspicuously notched at the apex, minutely toothed, glabrous and bright green above, furnished with small resinous dots beneath. Flowers pure white, ½ to ¾ in. across, produced in September in rounded terminal panicles, the largest of which are as much as 9 in. long, and 5 in. wide, but usually much smaller; petals spreading; calyx with pointed, triangular lobes, which are furnished with minute, glandular teeth; style as long as the calyx-lobes, with a large capitate stigma.

Native of eastern S. America, in S. Brazil and in Uruguay near Montevideo; probably introduced in 1827. This is the handsomest of white-flowered escallonias in cultivation, but is best grown on a wall except in the mildest parts, though it is fairly hardy in the open in the R.H.S. Garden, Wisley, in a sunny, sheltered position. It is better known under the synonym *E. montevidensis*.

This species has been much confused with *E. paniculata* var. *floribunda* (H. B. K.) McBride (*E. floribunda* H. B. K.), a native of the Andes of Ecuador and Peru, which is distinguished from *E. bifida* (*montevidensis*) by its pointed leaves, smaller flowers, shorter and blunter calyx-lobes and shorter style.

E. × EXONIENSIS Veitch

An evergreen shrub or small tree up to 15 or 20 ft high, of quick growth and open, graceful habit; branches ribbed, downy, and slightly glandular. Leaves variable in size, from ½ to 1½ in. long, half or less than half as wide; doubly toothed, glossy green above, paler beneath, glabrous on both sides except for a line of down along the midrib above. Flowers white or rose-tinted, produced from June to October in terminal panicles 1½ to 3 in. long, petals nearly ½ in. long, the bases forming a tube, the ends expanded. Calyx and flower-stalks downy and glandular.

A hybrid between *E. rosea* and *E. rubra* raised in the nurseries of Messrs Veitch of Exeter. It is a most attractive evergreen, flowering more or less continuously from June until the frosts come, and quite as hardy as *E. rubra*.

Dr Sleumer suggests that the second parent of *E.* × *exoniensis* may have been *E. rubra* var. *macrantha*. Hybrids between *E. rosea* and *E. rubra* also occur in the wild and it may be that the escallonia distributed by Veitch of Exeter under the name *E. montana* Phil. was a hybrid of this parentage. It was raised from seeds collected by Pearce in Valdivia province.

cv. 'BALFOURII'.—Raised by Sir Isaac Bailey Balfour at the Edinburgh Botanic Garden by crossing 'a particularly fine form of *E. rubra*' with *E. rosea*.

It is a graceful evergreen 10 ft or more high, with drooping twigs, the flowers blush-tinted white, resembling those of *E. rosea* in their columnar shape and the short limb of each petal.

E. ILLINITA Presl

E. glandulosa Lodd., not Sm.; *E. grahamiana* Hook. & Arn.

An open, loose-habited, evergreen shrub up to 10 (perhaps more) ft high; branchlets not downy, but furnished with stalked glands, and resinous when young. Leaves obovate or oval, from ¾ in. to 2½ in. long, nearly to quite half as wide; tapered at the base, rounded or abruptly pointed at the apex, finely toothed, not downy on either surface, but glossy green above and more or less clammy with a resinous secretion when young; stalk ⅛ to ¼ in. long. Panicle 3 or 4 in. long, 1½ in. diameter, cylindrical, thinly hairy and glandular; each branch of the panicle one- to five-, more often three-flowered and springing from the axil of a leaf-like bract. Flowers white, ⅓ in. wide at the top, the claws of the petals forming a tube ½ in. long. Calyx green, bell-shaped, with five linear lobes.

Native of Chile; introduced early in the nineteenth century. This plant has an odour distinctly suggestive of the pigsty, but by no means so offensive as that comparison would suggest. *E. illinita* is one of the hardiest of the genus. It has for many years been grown in the open at Kew, and survives even severe winters although sometimes badly cut.

var. PUBICALYCINA Briq.—Young stems and the veins on underside of leaf sparsely to densely clad with short hairs. Calyx-tube downy and minutely glandular. Such plants, which are known to have been in cultivation, are perhaps back-crosses of typical *E. illinita* with the natural hybrid *E. illinita* × *revoluta* (Sleumer, op. cit., p. 81).

A notably viscid escallonia was in cultivation as long ago as 1825 as *E. viscosa* Forbes (*Hort. Woburn*, p. 231), a name which was not properly validated until 1900, when an illustration and description were provided by de Wildeman (*Ic. Select. Hort. Thenensis*, p. 65 and t. 16). In his monograph, Dr Sleumer has sunk this species in *E. illinita*, and there is no doubt that this judgement is botanically correct. But, as noted in previous editions, the plant grown as *E. viscosa* at Kew differed from the common run of *E. illinita* in the following respects: 'It is laxer in habit; the panicles are longer, one-sided (instead of cylindrical); and the leaves and young shoots are much more sticky and resinous, especially in autumn, and much more scented. The most impressive peculiarity of this shrub, indeed, is its odour, even more suggestive of the pigsty than that of *illinita*, but intermingled with a resinous smell . . . So strongly are the shoots imbued with it that herbarium specimens, years after drying, still retain it. On living plants it is strongest on damp, still days.'

E. ILLINITA × E. RUBRA.—Hybrids of this parentage are fairly frequent in Chile where the two species are in contact and were introduced to cultivation in the 1830s. They have been grown under various erroneous names such as "*E. resinosa*" (correctly the name of an escallonia native to central S. America), "*E. grahamiana*" (a synonym of *E. illinita*), or "*E. glandulosa*" (a synonym of

E. illinita and of *E. rubra*). To this hybrid group also belongs *E. rubra* var. *albiflora* Hook. & Arn. (though one specimen cited by these authors in their original description is *E. leucantha*). An escallonia cultivated in California and named *E.* × *franciscana* by Miss Eastwood is *E. illinita* × *E. rubra* var. *macrantha*. These hybrids have the resin-glands and odour of *E. illinita* but the stalked glands on the receptacle show the influence of *E. rubra* (the above is based on Sleumer, op. cit., pp. 139–140).

E. 'IVEYI' [PLATE 21

Originally found at Caerhays Castle at the foot of plants of *E. bifida* and *E.* × *exoniensis* growing together, this evergreen shrub is assumed to be a hybrid between them, the cross fertilisation having been done by a bee or other insect. It was noticed first by Mr Ivey, a gardener at Caerhays. As a garden shrub it is one of the finest of escallonias. The young shoots are angled and furnished with scattered dark hairs. Leaves mostly oval, tapered at the base, rounded at the apex, finely toothed, 1 to 2¾ in. long, ¾ to 1½ in. wide, quite glabrous and of a glittering dark green above, paler and lustrous beneath; stalk ⅛ to ¼ in. long. The flowers are white, ½ in. across, with the terminal part of each petal rounded and recurved; they are produced during late summer and autumn in terminal pyramidal panicles 5 to 6 in. high and about 4 in. wide at the base.

Quite hardy in the south-west, this escallonia has been grown on a west wall at Kew for many years, and although slightly injured in severe winters can be counted as hardy there. Even away from a wall it survived the winters of 1961–3 in many gardens in southern England. Its very dark green, burnished leaves, vigorous growth and fine panicles of white flowers opening in July and August make it one of the finest evergreens.

E. LAEVIS (Vell.) Sleum.
Vigiera laevis Vell.; *E. organensis* Gardn.

An evergreen shrub of robust habit 4 to 6 ft high, with stout, angled, very leafy branchlets; not downy but slightly glandular-resinous. Leaves narrowly obovate or oval, stiff, the largest 3 in. long by 1 in. wide; toothed except towards the tapering base, rather blunt at the apex, glabrous; stalk very short, reddish. Flowers clear rosy red, ⅓ to ½ in. across, produced late in the year in short, densely flowered, terminal panicles; petals forming a tube at the base, upper part spreading; flower-stalks and calyx quite glabrous or minutely glandular, the latter with five narrow, awl-shaped lobes. *Bot. Mag.*, t. 4274.

Discovered in ravines near the summit of the Organ Mountains of Brazil by Gardner in 1841, and introduced to England by W. Lobb very soon after. Gardner named it *E. organensis*, but the species had been described some years earlier by the Portuguese botanist Vellozo under the name *Vigiera laevis*. It is not hardy except in Cornwall, etc., but worth growing on a wall for its beautiful rosy flowers.

E. 'LANGLEYENSIS'

An elegant evergreen, or in hard winters, semi-evergreen, shrub, becoming eventually 8 ft or more high, and producing long, slender, arching shoots in one season; branchlets copiously furnished with stalked glands. Leaves ½ to 1 in. long, about half as wide; obovate or narrowly oval, toothed, stalkless; glabrous and glossy green above, specked beneath with minute resin-glands. Flowers of a charming bright rosy carmine, ½ in. across, produced during June and July (a few later) in short racemes of about half a dozen blossoms terminating short leafy twigs; calyx and flower-stalk slightly glandular. Petals with a distinct but short claw, which is slightly more than half as long as the limb.

This very attractive shrub was raised in Messrs. Veitch's nursery at Langley about 1893, by crossing *E. virgata* with a selection from *E. rubra* raised by the same firm and called "*E. macrantha sanguinea*". Although not quite so hardy as the first of these, it is hardy enough to stand all but the severest of frosts, and even then will break up again from the ground.

This hybrid is usually given botanical status as *E.* × *langleyensis* Veitch (1897), but the correct botanical name for *E. rubra* × *E. virgata* would be E. × RIGIDA Phil., given in 1894 to a wild plant of this parentage.

'Langleyensis' is the original member of an important group of garden hybrids all deriving (through back-crossing and inter-crossing) from *E. virgata* and *E. rubra* (or its var. *macrantha*). Some resemble 'Langleyensis' in shape of flower (limb of petals spreading, much longer than the claw); others are nearer to *E. rubra* or its var. *macrantha* in having flowers with a longish "tube" and the limbs of the petals relatively shorter than in 'Langleyensis'; while 'Apple Blossom' and similar clones (q.v.) have flowers of a shape unlike that of any cultivated species. All the hybrids in this group (except 'Gwendolyn Anley') have flowers with a cushion-shaped disk, which helps to distinguish them even after flowering from the cultivars of *E. rubra* (in which the disk is narrowly conical). All the hybrids described below were raised by the Slieve Donard Nursery Company, Newry, Co. Down, with the exception of 'Edinensis', 'Gwendolyn Anley', and 'William Watson'.

'APPLE BLOSSOM'.—Flowers apple-blossom pink, shading paler on the outside of the claws and at the centre of the limbs. Petals about ½ in. long, more or less upright; limb slightly longer than the claw, not spreading. The unusual posture of the petals gives to the flower a form described by the raiser as 'chalice-shaped'. Leaves mostly elliptic, finely toothed. Height and width about 5 ft. This beautiful escallonia received an Award of Merit in 1946 and an Award of Garden Merit five years later. Two hybrids deriving from this and with flowers of a similar shape are: 'PEACH BLOSSOM', with petals of a deeper pink; and 'PRIDE OF DONARD', in which the petals are of a clear red. The latter flowers somewhat earlier than the others in this section, from early June.

'DONARD BEAUTY'.—Flowers similar to those of 'Langleyensis', very freely borne. This hybrid resembles 'Edinensis' in having the receptacle of the flower almost eglandular, but the leaves are mostly under 1 in. long and roundish obovate. Semi-pendulous habit. Height 5 to 7 ft. A.M. 1930.

'DONARD GEM'.—Flowers light pink, inclining to *E. virgata* in shape, sweetly scented. Leaves with coarse spreading teeth, densely gland-dotted beneath. A.M. 1927.

'DONARD RADIANCE'.—Flowers chalice-shaped, rich pink; petals with a distinct claw about ¼ in. long, abruptly widened into a roundish, erect, or spreading limb. Leaves obovate, coarsely toothed in the upper part, rounded or truncate at the apex. Similar in habit to 'Apple Blossom'. A.M. 1954.

'DONARD ROSE'.—Flowers deep rosy-pink from richly coloured buds, shaped as in 'Donard Star' but smaller. Habit semi-pendulous. Leaves with deeply impressed veins.

'DONARD SEEDLING'.—Buds pink opening white flushed with pale rose. Flowers about ⅝ in. wide, shaped as in 'Langleyensis' but with shorter-clawed petals. Leaves obovate, ½ to 1 in. long. A very hardy hybrid which received an

ESCALLONIA 'LANGLEYENSIS'

Award of Merit in 1916 and is still common in gardens. Said to be a backcross of 'Langleyensis' onto *E. virgata*. Ultimate height 8 ft or even more. [PLATE 19

'DONARD STAR'.—Flowers deep rosy-pink, about 1 in. wide across the top; claw of petals about ⅜ in. long, limb spreading, about the same length. Leaves dark glossy green. Compact habit. Height 5 to 6 ft.

'DONARD WHITE'.—Flowers pure white, about ½ in. wide, from pink buds. Petals with a very short claw. Anthers rather large and conspicuous, golden yellow. Compact, 5 to 6 ft high. Fairly hardy.

'EDINENSIS'.—This hybrid was raised at the Edinburgh Botanic Garden, before 1914. It bears some resemblance to 'Langleyensis' but the habit is not so pendulous and the flowers somewhat paler. A reliable botanical distinction is that the receptacle of the flower is completely devoid of stalked glands. Hardy.

'GWENDOLYN ANLEY'.—Flowers pink in the bud, opening white slightly pink-flushed, ⅜ to ¾ in. wide, with spreading almost clawless petals; disk flat, as in E. *virgata*. A completely hardy deciduous shrub 3 to 4 ft high, 10 ft or more wide, with small finely toothed leaves. Near to E. *virgata* but with larger flowers.

'SLIEVE DONARD'.—Flowers shaped as in 'Langleyensis', with a paler ground-colour but deeper, carmine-pink markings. Receptacle of flower rather densely clad with stalked glands. Arching habit, 5 to 7 ft high.

'WILLIAM WATSON'.—Flowers shaped as in 'Langleyensis' but deep pink and with relatively longer-clawed petals. Receptacle without glands. Leaves broad-obovate or broad elliptic. Dense habit. Height 5 to 6 ft in the milder parts, but fairly dwarf at Kew.

E. LEUCANTHA Rémy

E. *bellidifolia* Phil.

An evergreen shrub to about 15 ft high in cultivation (taller in the wild state); branchlets downy when young. Leaves obovate to oblanceolate, ½ to 1 in. long, blunt or pointed at the apex, tapered at the base, glabrous except for the downy and prominent midrib beneath; margins finely toothed. Flowers small, white, in short racemes at the end of the laterals, together forming in effect a panicle 1 ft long and 3 to 7 in. wide; flower-stalks short and slender, downy; calyx downy, tube top-shaped, with short triangular teeth; petals about ⅕ in. long.

Native of Chile, common in Valdivia and Llanquihue provinces; introduced by H. F. Comber in 1927 under his No. 988. But some plants raised from these seeds, and from No. 989, are natural hybrids between E. *leucantha* and E. *virgata*, which grew nearby (Comber 981). These hybrids were originally identified as E. *bellidifolia* Phil., but according to Dr Sleumer this is synonymous with E. *leucantha*. The correct name for the cross E. *leucantha* × E. *virgata* is E. × STRICTA Remy *emend.* Sleumer (op. cit., pp. 127-9).

E. MACRANTHA *see* E. RUBRA var. MACRANTHA

E. MONTEVIDENSIS *see* E. BIFIDA

E. ORGANENSIS *see* E. LAEVIS

E. PTEROCLADON *see* E. ROSEA

E. PULVERULENTA (Ruiz & Pavon) Pers.

Stereoxylon pulverulentum Ruiz & Pavon

An evergreen shrub 10 to 12 ft high, with downy, viscid, varnished branchlets. Leaves very viscid, oblong, with a rounded end and tapering base; 2 to

4 in. long, ¾ to 1½ in. wide; finely toothed, bristly hairy on both surfaces, the upper one with a varnished appearance. Flowers white, densely crowded on slender, cylindrical racemes 4 to 9 in. long, ¾ to 1 in. through; sometimes branched at the base.

Native of Chile; introduced early in the nineteenth century, but now uncommon. It is not hardy in any but our warmest districts, although in colder ones it may live and thrive for many years on a wall. From all the other white-flowered escallonias in cultivation this is readily distinguished by its long slender racemes. (*E. revoluta* is sometimes grown in gardens under the name, but is well distinguished by its thick grey down.)

E. REVOLUTA (Ruiz & Pavon) Pers.

Stereoxylon revolutum Ruiz & Pavon

An evergreen shrub up to 20 ft high; branchlets thickly covered with a grey felt, angled. Leaves ¾ to 2 in. long, from ½ to 1¼ in. wide; obovate, pointed or rounded at the apex, tapering at the base, unevenly toothed; both surfaces covered with a thick grey down. Flowers white, produced in racemes or panicles 1½ to 3 in. long, at the end of leafy twigs; petals ⅝ in. long, the bases forming a slender tube; calyx and flower-stalks covered with grey hairs. Blossoms in September and October. *Bot. Mag.*, t. 6949.

Native of Chile from 31° to 41° S. It succeeds admirably in the south-western counties, but needs wall protection in colder localities. The name refers to the rolling inwards of the leaf-margins, which is usually more or less noticeable but is a character by no means confined to this species. Its most noticeable characteristic is the grey down which covers the entire plant, but varies in density.

E. × MOLLIS Phil. *E. rubra* var. *pubescens* Hook. & Arn.—Here belong hybrids between *E. revoluta* and *E. rubra*, which occur fairly frequently in the coastal parts of Chile from Valparaiso to Valdivia. An escallonia grown at Wakehurst Place, Sussex, probably belongs here, though it is very near to *E. revoluta*. The flowers are, however, a definite shade of pink and the leaves differ from those of *E. revoluta* in being regularly saw-toothed. Similar plants are, or have been, in cultivation as "*E. rubra* var. *pubescens*" and "*E. revoluta rosea*", and also as *E. mollis*.

E. ROSEA Griseb.

E. pterocladon Hook.; *E. montana* Phil.

An evergreen, bushy shrub usually 4 to 8 ft high, but twice as high when trained against a wall, or grown in very mild localities; branchlets downy and distinctly angled. Leaves narrowly obovate, ⅓ to 1 in. long, ⅛ to ¼ in. wide; tapering at the base to a very short stalk, toothed; dark shining green above, paler beneath and glabrous on both surfaces except for a line of down on the midrib above. Flowers in slender racemes 1½ to 3 in. long, terminating short, rigid, leafy twigs, the lower flowers solitary in the axils of small leaves. Petals white, ⅓ in. long, spreading at the ends, but erect at the base, and so close together as to form a tube; receptacle glabrous, top-shaped. Flowers fragrant, appearing from June to August. *Bot. Mag.*, t. 4827.

Native of Chile from 39° 30′ southward; introduced by Lobb in 1847. It is perhaps safer on a wall in the London district, but in the south and west counties it thrives excellently as a bush in the open. It has proved hardy in the open in the R.H.S. Garden at Wisley, where there are two examples about 6 ft high in Seven Acres. In Co. Wicklow, Ireland, it reached a height of 15 ft.

E. 'NEWRYENSIS'.—A hybrid between *E. rosea* (*pterocladon*) and *E.* 'Langleyensis', raised at the Daisy Hill Nursery, Newry, Co. Down. It is said to be fast-growing and to make a good shelter-plant in milder parts.

E. RUBRA (Ruiz & Pavon) Pers.

Stereoxylon rubrum Ruiz & Pavon; *E. punctata* DC.; *E. rubra* var. *punctata* (DC.) Hook. f.; *E. duplicato-serrata* Rémy

An evergreen shrub up to 15 ft high, with a peeling bark; young stems downy or hairy and often somewhat viscid and glandular. Leaves very variable in shape, even on the same plant, being broadest at, above, or below the middle, mostly 1 to 2 in. long, ⅜ to 1 in. wide, acute or short-acuminate at the apex, tapered at the base onto a short petiole, simply or doubly toothed in the upper part, glabrous and glossy above, undersides speckled with resin-glands, often densely so, but glabrous except for the sometimes hairy midrib, veins impressed above, prominent beneath. Flowers pink to deep crimson, produced in loose terminal panicles, few- to many-flowered, 1 to 4 in. long, often leafy at the base; pedicels ⅛ to ⅜ in. long, clad with erect hairs and usually glandular also. Calyx normally glabrous, at least on wild plants, the glands more or less stalked and usually mixed with short erect hairs; calyx-lobes triangular, tapered at the apex. Claws of petals erect, forming a tube ½ in. or slightly less long, the limbs spreading. Disk narrowly conical, enclosing the base of the style. Capsules obovoid, about ⅛ in. long.

Native of Chile and bordering parts of Argentina, ranging in the former country from the central provinces to the Straits of Magellan. It is a very variable species, perhaps the result (as Kausel suggests) of the merging through hybridisation of several once independent species. Hooker remarked that no two specimens are exactly alike. The original garden stock of *E. rubra* derives from an introduction to the University of Liverpool in 1827 and is hardy. This form is only slightly glandular, and more or less glabrous, except for the downy young shoots; flowers red. It is figured in *Bot. Mag.*, t. 2890. A later introduction, with deeper-coloured flowers and with much more abundant glands, was figured in *Bot. Mag.*, t. 6599 (1881), under the name *E. rubra* var. *punctata*. The origin of the plant figured was not stated, but it appears to have been grown previously under the horticultural name "*E. sanguinea*". The escallonia introduced by Comber under No. 1023 belongs to *E. rubra*, though his field specimen under this number resembles the var. *macrantha* in size of leaf.

var. GLUTINOSA (Phil.) Reiche *E. glutinosa* Phil.—A low-growing shrub with lanceolate or elliptic leaves, densely dotted with resin glands beneath.

Flowers red, rather small (less than ½ in. long), in few-flowered inflorescences. Calyx-tube glandular but devoid of down; calyx-lobes about 3/16 in. long. A variety of local distribution in the Chilean Andes, mainly east of Chillan.

var. MACRANTHA (Hook. & Arn.) Reiche *E. macrantha* Hook. & Arn.—A shrub 6 to 10 ft high, forming a dense bush of luxuriant habit, the glutinous branchlets covered with down, intermingled with which are numerous erect glands. Leaves broadly oval or obovate, tapering at the base; 1 to 3 in. long, ½ to 1¾ in. wide, deeply toothed, glabrous, and of a dark shining green above, dotted beneath with numerous resinous glands; stalkless. Racemes terminal, sometimes branched and forming a panicle, 2 to 4 in. long. Flowers bright rosy-red, about ⅝ in. long and wide; receptacle covered with sticky glands intermixed with hairs; flower-stalk downy. *Bot. Mag.*, t. 4473.

Introduced from the Island of Chiloe by Wm. Lobb, about 1846, and now one of the commonest evergreen shrubs in the south-western maritime districts, where it is frequently used to make hedges. In the London district and farther north it needs in most places the protection of a wall, making indeed one of the handsomest of evergreen wall-coverings. It thrives admirably in most of the southern seaside resorts, flowering during June and the succeeding months.

At the Rosewarne Experimental Station at Camborne, Cornwall, this variety has been found to make the most reliable screen against the Atlantic winds. Two new cultivars raised by Messrs Treseder—'CRIMSON SPIRE' and 'RED HEDGER' —have proved almost as wind- and spray-resistant and are of faster growth. The former is of stiffer habit than the other and will make a hedge 6 to 7 ft high in four years; it also has smaller leaves than in 'Red Hedger', very dark and glossy, and better flowers. Both arose in the nursery as self-sown seedlings.

var. UNIFLORA Poepp. & Endl.—This name is available for states of *E. rubra* with few-flowered inflorescences (sometimes reduced to a single flower) but these are really part of the normal variation of the species. Some plants grown as "*E. montana*" may belong here. *E. montana* Phil. is a synonym of *E. rosea*, however.

cv. 'WOODSIDE'.—This shrub originated in Ireland from a witch's broom growth found on ordinary *E. rubra*. It is a dwarf evergreen of dense compact habit and rounded form and promises to keep 1 to 2 ft high. But it has a tendency to revert to the typical form and would no doubt do so completely if left alone. It is necessary, therefore, to remove the strong-growing shoots of typical *E. rubra* as soon as their character becomes evident. The rosy crimson flowers commence to appear in summer and continue until autumn. Suitable for the rock garden.

This escallonia is more commonly known as 'Pygmaea', but the plants usually seen under this name are not true to type; either they have reverted, or they have been propagated from reverted stock-plants. The true variety seems to be rare, but a sample of it was sent by Mr Leslie Slinger from the Slieve Donard Nursery, and there is a dried specimen in the Kew Herbarium from the Rosewarne Experimental Station, both very dense and twiggy. For the name 'Woodside' see *Ornamental Trees and Shrubs* (R.H.S. 1938 Conference Report), p. 134.

The following escallonias have *E. rubra* or its var. *macrantha* as one parent:

E. 'C. F. BALL'.—A very vigorous, free-flowering and beautiful hybrid, with large, rich-red flowers. It was raised at Glasnevin about 1912 by Mr Ball, after whom it was named and who, a few years later, was killed in the Gallipoli campaign. It is possibly not a hybrid but a colour-form of *E. rubra* var. *macrantha*. It attains 7 or 8 ft in height in the milder parts.

E. 'COMPACTA'.—Flowers rose-red; claw about ¼ in. long, abruptly widened into the limb, which is slightly more than half as long as the claw. Receptacle downy, not glandular. Leaves glossy, without resin-dots beneath. Stems distinctly winged. Of compact, columnar habit. It probably derives partly from *E. rosea*.

E. 'GLASNEVIN HYBRID'.—Flowers resembling those of 'C. F. Ball' but slightly more rosy in colour. Leaves dull above, undersides densely resin-dotted and rough to the touch.

E. 'INGRAMII'.—Flowers of a similar colour to those of the commonly cultivated form of *E. rubra* var. *macrantha* but scarcely so large. Leaves smaller and proportionately narrower. Possibly a hybrid or intermediate between *E. rubra* and the var. *macrantha*.

E. TUCUMANENSIS Hosseus

A shrub or small tree reported to attain a height of 15 ft in the wild, occasionally 20 ft; young growths reddish, minutely downy or almost glabrous. Leaves oblong or elliptic, rather oblique, shortly acuminate or rounded and mucronate at the apex, tapered at the base into a short petiole, 2 to 3 in. long, ⅝ to ¾ in. wide, glossy above, dotted with blackish glandular pits beneath. Flowers white, borne July and early August in slender panicles, which are leafy at the base, becoming bracteate towards the apex. Calyx-lobes awl-shaped, ⅛ to ³⁄₁₆ in. long. Corollas about ½ in. long, ½ in. wide at the mouth. Disk thin, rising at the centre around the base of the style. Capsule roundish, about ¼ in. long. *Bot. Mag.*, n.s., t. 565.

A native of N.W. Argentina at 2,500 to 6,700 ft altitude; introduced to Kew in 1961 by means of seeds collected by Dr F. Vervoorst in Tucuman province. Two examples on the Temperate House Terrace, planted in 1963, have so far suffered no winter-damage apart from some scorching of the foliage, and the species is also cultivated at Wakehurst Place in Sussex, in a sheltered position. It is quite a handsome escallonia but the flowers, although remarkably large for the genus, do not make much display. It is unlikely to be tolerant of salt-laden winds.

E. VIRGATA (Ruiz & Pavon) Pers.

Stereoxylon virgatum Ruiz & Pavon; *E. philippiana* (A. Engl.) Mast.

A deciduous shrub of robust habit and graceful form 6 to 8 ft high, the branches very leafy, often arching. Leaves obovate, ½ to ¾ in. long, ⅙ to ¼ in. wide, tapering at the base, toothed; quite glabrous on both surfaces. Flowers pure white, ⅓ to ½ in. across, produced during June and July in the uppermost leaf-axils and at the end of short twigs, the whole forming a leafy raceme ¾ to 1½ in. long; calyx top-shaped, with five triangular lobes.

Native of Chile from 37° S. to the end of the continent, and of neighbouring parts of Argentina; introduced by Pearce for Messrs Veitch, between 1860 and 1866, and first flowered in their nursery in 1873. This is undoubtedly the hardiest of all known escallonias; it has survived without any injury 32° of frost at Kew, quite unprotected. It is also very distinct; besides being deciduous, its petals do not, as in so many species, form a kind of tube. Both in leaf and flower it bears a considerable resemblance to the New Zealand shrub *Leptospermum scoparium*—

ESCALLONIA VIRGATA

an ally, however, of the myrtle. It is undoubtedly one of the most pleasing of later-flowering shrubs. It is rather variable in habit in the wild state. Near the tree-line it forms a spreading procumbent shrub, while in the Magellan region it is sometimes seen as a small fastigiate bush.

EUCALYPTUS MYRTACEAE

No other single genus of trees dominates so vast and climatically so diverse an area as do the eucalypts in Australia. By far the greater part of the natural vegetation of the sub-continent outside the deserts and semi-deserts consists of communities of woody plants in which the eucalypts play a predominant or leading role. Only in those parts of eastern Australia and Tasmania where the rainfall is high enough to support tropical to temperate rain-forest do they recede in importance.

Some 500 species are recognised, all in Australia and Tasmania save a few found in the larger islands of the S.W. Pacific. The genus is absent from New Zealand in the wild state. In life-form the eucalypts range from tall trees—in *E. regnans* attaining a height of over 300 ft—to shrubs and small, stunted trees. A peculiar form—the mallee—is assumed by many species in the dry regions of southern Australia; in these the most permanent part of the plant is a large, woody root-stock bearing numerous slender stems and containing a supply of dormant buds which quickly develop if the stems are killed by fire or drought.

The bark is very varied and serves as a useful character for identification in the field. In many species it is persistent and in mature trees becomes thick, hard and deeply furrowed (as in the Ironbarks) or fibrous (as in the Stringybarks and so-called Ashes). In the Gumbarks—and here belong nearly all the species cultivated outdoors in this country—the bark is smooth and deciduous, the outer (older) layers being regularly shed in flakes or ribbons. The freshly exposed bark is white or distinctly coloured, and contrasts with the darker colouring of the older layers.

The eucalypts have the peculiarity, not uncommon among Australasian plants, of having a juvenile phase during which the leaves produced are strikingly different from those of the adult plant. In *Eucalyptus* these are usually shorter and broader than the adult ones, sessile or short-stalked and, at least at the base of the shoot, opposite. The duration of this phase varies with the species and usually gives way, through an intermediate phase, to the production of adult leaves, which are alternate, stalked, mostly lanceolate or sickle-shaped, with entire margins. The blades are usually identical in appearance on the two surfaces (isobilateral). In some species (e.g. *E. cordata*) there is little difference between the juvenile and adult leaves. The juvenile phase can be prolonged by regular pruning and there is always a reversion to it on stump shoots.

Flowers in most species are borne in axillary umbels (rarely solitary). The buds are formed in summer on the young shoots and open about a year later. The most conspicuous feature of the flower is the numerous stamens, which are creamy white in the species described here but in the beautiful but tender *E. ficifolia* (and other species from W. Australia) they are in some shade of red. They are inserted on the rim of the calyx-tube (receptacle) and in bud are enclosed in a cap known as the 'operculum', made up of the united sepals and petals, which fall off as the stamens develop. The ovary is embedded in the calyx-tube and develops into a capsule opening by valves to release the numerous small seeds; the calyx-tube itself becomes enlarged and woody, and is the most conspicuous feature of the fruit. The top of the capsule may be more or less level with the rim of the tube, with the valves exserted; or it may be sunk within the tube, with the valves wholly or partly concealed. The nectar-secreting disk of the flower may become woody and enlarged in fruit, partly covering the top of the capsule. The capsules need at least one year to ripen and may remain closed for several years. The seeds are small and usually, at least on cultivated trees, only a few are formed in each capsule, most of the ovules remaining unfertilised and turning into chaff.

Eucalyptus is, for the taxonomist, a genus full of complexities. A species of wide range may be subdivided into numerous geographical and ecological races which have in common the broader characters by which the species is defined but may differ quite considerably in minuter details. Intercrossing between species is also quite common in nature: this further increases the difficulty of identification and necessitates the proviso that some of the cultivated specimens mentioned in the following account might prove not to be true to type were they to be examined by an experienced eucalyptologist. It should also be added that there are few woody genera in which more complete material is needed if a specimen is to be accurately identified. In addition to adult foliage, flower and fruit, the sample should include juvenile foliage and a description of the bark.

These taxonomic complexities may not be of much concern to the grower, but the variability in hardiness shown by many species when brought into cultivation is of the greatest importance. All but the very hardiest species will have their more tender forms and equally the reputed tenderness of a certain species may be due simply to its having hitherto been represented in cultivation by a tender provenance. Seed from Australia, and plants raised from it, should therefore be treated with some circumspection, unless it is known that the seed was collected with frost-resistance in mind.

The eucalypts must be raised from seed, which should be sown thinly in deep containers and the seedlings potted-off, when the second pair of seed-leaves has developed, into paper, fibre, or polythene pots (or sleeves) $3\frac{1}{2}$ in. deep or longer. Ideally, the seed should be germinated in February–March with artificial heat, the plants grown on under cool-house conditions and put into their final positions during the summer of the same year. By autumn they will have become well established and can face the dangers of the ensuing winter with as good a chance of survival as potted plants overwintered in an unheated house or frame. Despite the obvious risks, this early planting out is to be recommended, as the eucalypts resent any restrictions at the roots and will develop quicker and need artificial support for a much shorter time if allowed to grow freely from an early age. If it is intended that the young plants should be planted out in their second year, the seed should be sown later, in late spring or early summer and potted-off by August. For further details, see the article by R. C. Barnard cited below.

Eucalypts have been so infrequently planted on the chalklands of south-eastern England that nothing can be said for certain about their suitability for such soils. But *E. parvifolia* lived for many years in chalk at Messrs Hilliers Winchester nursery and it has been reported that *E. dalrympleana* will tolerate a similar soil.

The most recent work on the taxonomy of the genus is: W. F. Blakely, *A Key to the Eucalypts*, 2nd Ed., Canberra, 1955. Emendations to this, with references to recent literature, will be found in: R. D. Johnston and R. Marryatt, *Taxonomy and Nomenclature of Eucalypts*, Canberra, 1965. For British growers the most useful works are 'An Introduction to some Garden Eucalypts', by R. C. Barnard, published in *Journ. R.H.S.*, Vol.

91 (1966), pp. 209–216, 250–261, 293–303; and the section on *Eucalyptus* in *Dictionary of Gardening*, Supplement 1969, pp. 282–288. Mr Barnard has kindly read through the following pages in proof and made some valuable suggestions.

E. COCCIFERA Hook. f. MOUNT WELLINGTON PEPPERMINT, TASMANIAN SNOW GUM

A tree to 70 ft or over in favoured situations, but reduced to a shrub or small stunted tree at high altitudes; bark white when freshly exposed, darkening to grey, shed in longitudinal strips; twigs yellowish or red-brown, covered (in some forms) with a bluish bloom. Juvenile leaves opposite, stalkless, broadly elliptical to heart-shaped, 1 to 2 in. long and $\frac{3}{5}$ to $1\frac{3}{5}$ in. wide, pale green or glaucous, thin in texture. Adult leaves alternate, stalked, lanceolate, 2 to $2\frac{1}{2}$ in. long and $\frac{2}{5}$ to $\frac{4}{5}$ in. wide, terminated by a fine, hooked point and varying in colour from green to glaucous; they smell of peppermint when crushed. Flowers in axillary umbels of four to seven (but only three in the form found in the Mt Wellington range); common-stalk angular in cross-section; buds stalkless or almost so, club-shaped, angled or ridged, operculum short, wrinkled; anthers reniform. Fruit funnel-shaped to hemispherical, often strongly two-ribbed; disk broad, valves small.

Native of Tasmania, where it is widespread in the mountains from 2,500 ft to the tree-line at about 4,500 ft; discovered by Gunn in 1840 and introduced to Britain in the same year. In its high-level stands this species has to withstand a quite severe climate, with 100 to 150 frosts a year and frequent snow. Seed from such stands yields hardy, bushy trees, but so far the taller forms from lower altitudes have not proved reliably hardy, the older specimens being nearly all in the milder parts.

At Inverewe on the coast of Ross-shire, now the property of the National Trust for Scotland, there are several trees planted by Osgood Mackenzie about seventy years ago and now standing at 75 to 80 ft; one has a girth of $9\frac{1}{2}$ ft at breast-height, where it forks into several stems; another with a clean bole is $7\frac{3}{4}$ ft in girth. In giving us these measurements, Mr G. E. Collins remarks that the only damage that can be recalled was severe browning of the leaves in the winter of 1961–2, probably due to an exceptionally salty gale rather than to frost. This species has recently been planted as a street tree at Ullapool, on the coast some fifty miles north of Inverewe. At Kinlock Hourn, Inverness-shire, there are several notable survivors from the collection made by Robert Birkbeck from about 1880 onwards, up to 90 ft high and $11\frac{3}{4}$ ft in girth. At Crarae, Argyll, the best specimen, *pl.* 1939, measures 51 × $3\frac{1}{2}$ ft (1969). In Devon there grew until recently at Powderham a tree believed to be from the original introduction. It measured 80 × 13 ft in 1907 and 85 × $20\frac{1}{2}$ ft in 1963, the year before its death. A tree at Holkham, Norfolk, measures 63 × $2\frac{3}{4}$ ft (1969).

E. LINEARIS Dehnhardt WHITE PEPPERMINT.—An elegant, slender tree to about 50 ft high with a smooth, white, deciduous bark. Juvenile leaves opposite for five to six pairs, similar to, but smaller than, the adult leaves, which are green or slightly glaucous, linear, 2 to 4 in. long but only $\frac{1}{5}$ in. or so wide. Umbels with five to twelve flowers; buds club-shaped. Fruit varying from pear-shaped with a truncate base to ovoid or almost hemispherical. A native of Tasmania, found locally in the south-east and around Hobart, from 500 to 2,500 ft. It is definitely tender but is represented in Ireland by the following specimens: Rowallane, Co. Down, 45 × 6 ft, and Mount Usher, Co. Wicklow

EUCALYPTUS COCCIFERA

Eire, 50 × 2¾ ft (both measured 1966). A most ornamental species, remarkable for its very narrow leaves.

E. SIMMONDSII Maiden SMITHTON PEPPERMINT.—A tree to 65 ft high; bark on trunk persistent, dark grey and fibrous, but smooth and peeling on the branches. Juvenile leaves opposite, sessile or almost so, ovate to broadly lanceolate, pointed at the apex, dark green or glaucous and often with crimson margins and midrib. Adult leaves stalked, narrowly elliptic, to 6 in. long but less than 1 in. wide. Flowers seven to twenty-three in dense umbels; buds club-shaped. Fruit in dense, globose clusters which remain on the branches for several years. Native of W. Tasmania from sea-level to about 1,500 ft. There is an example of this species in the Edinburgh Botanic Garden raised from seed received in 1949; it measures 55 × 3 ft (1970). It is still growing quickly and very wind-firm. In other Scottish gardens too it is proving satisfactory.

E. CORDATA Labill.   SILVER GUM

A tree to about 50 ft high; bark smooth, white or greenish white; young shoots warted. Juvenile and adult leaves similar; they are opposite, stalkless, vividly blue-white, orbicular to ovate or broader than long, rounded or short-pointed at the apex, heart-shaped at the base with the basal lobes of each leaf overlapping those of the opposite one; 1½ to 3½ in. long, 1 to 2¼ in. wide; margins with distant, rounded teeth. Flowers produced in November and December, usually three in a cluster in each leaf axil; common-stalk $\frac{1}{5}$ to $\frac{2}{5}$ in. long; buds ovate; operculum conical to hemispherical, shorter than the calyx-tube, and usually with a rounded knob at the top. Fruit glaucous, hemispherical to top-shaped, about $\frac{2}{5}$ in. long; capsule deeply enclosed in the calyx-tube.

Native of Tasmania, confined to the south-eastern part of the island at 500 to 2,000 ft; introduced before 1850. It is a rather tender species, best suited to Cornwall, Ireland and the west coast of Scotland. There is a specimen some 60 ft high at Castlewellan, Co. Down, and smaller ones at Fota and Ashbourne House, Co. Cork, Eire. Near London it has lived long enough to flower in the open but this is owing to its reaching the flowering state very early. Its leaves do not change in colour or shape as the tree grows older, a character that well distinguishes it from the other eucalypts treated here, with the exception of those mentioned below. In the small state it is used in summer bedding for the sake of its brilliantly glaucous foliage.

E. PULVERULENTA Sims *E. cordata* Lodd., not Labill.—This species, found locally in New South Wales, is closely allied to the preceding but may be distinguished by the entire leaves, which are smaller than in *E. cordata* (usually less than 2 in. long); and by the top-shaped buds with a conical operculum about as long as the calyx-tube. *E. pulverulenta* was introduced in 1819. The following specimens were recorded in Eire in 1966: Kilmacurragh, Co. Wicklow, 90 × 7$\frac{3}{4}$ ft; Mount Usher, Co. Wicklow, 70 × 6$\frac{1}{2}$ and 59 × 4$\frac{3}{4}$ ft; Fota, Co. Cork, *pl.* 1935, 59 × 3$\frac{3}{4}$ ft.

E. CINEREA Benth. *E. pulverulenta* var. *lanceolata* Howitt—This species closely resembles *E. pulverulenta* in juvenile foliage and other characters but differs markedly in its bark, which on the trunk and main branches is rough, fibrous and red-brown. Also the adult leaves, though often similar to the juvenile ones, sometimes become lanceolate and up to 4 in. long. Native of New South Wales and Victoria and known as the Argyle apple. Of recent introduction.

E. DALRYMPLEANA Maiden BROAD-LEAVED KINDLING BARK

A tree up to 120 ft in the wild; bark smooth, shed in large patches, pale cream at first, ageing through salmon-pink to light brown. Juvenile leaves green or glaucous, opposite, sessile, broadly ovate to orbicular, more or less cordate, and sometimes stem-clasping, at the base, 1$\frac{3}{4}$ to 2$\frac{1}{4}$ in. long. Adult leaves stalked, lanceolate or sickle-shaped, 4 to 7 in. long, $\frac{1}{2}$ to 1$\frac{3}{8}$ in. wide. Umbels three-flowered on a slightly flattened common-stalk $\frac{1}{8}$ to $\frac{1}{4}$ in. long; buds almost stalkless, ovoid or cylindrical, the operculum about equal in length to the calyx-tube. Capsules hemispherical or truncate-ovoid, about $\frac{1}{3}$ in. wide; disk usually convex and prominent; valves exserted.

Native of Tasmania, Victoria, and New South Wales. This beautiful and fast-growing eucalyptus is unfortunately less hardy than *E. gunnii*, but since it ascends to 4,500 ft on the mainland it is possible that a more reliably hardy form might be found. The tree planted by R. C. Barnard at Brimley in Devon in 1956 lost all its leaves in the winter of 1962–3 but quickly recovered and in 1966 was 44 ft high. Seeds received from Australia under the name *E. dalrympleana* sometimes produce *E. viminalis* (q.v.), but that species has such different juvenile foliage that the mistake is apparent at an early stage.

E. DELEGATENSIS R. T. Baker   ALPINE ASH

E. gigantea Hook. f., not Dehnhardt

A tall tree, reaching 200 ft or more in the wild, with a straight, clean trunk and open crown; bark on lower part of trunk rough and fibrous, but smooth and deciduous in the upper part, where it is whitish or bluish grey and shed in thin, longitudinal strips; branchlets glaucous or dark red. Juvenile leaves opposite for three or four pairs only, then alternate; they are broadly lanceolate, stalked, thick and rather glaucous; fully adult leaves alternate, stalked, lanceolate, 3 to 7 in. long and up to 2 in. wide, often curved; dull green or slightly glaucous, with conspicuous venation. Flowers in umbels of seven to fifteen on a stout common-stalk $\frac{2}{5}$ to $\frac{4}{5}$ in. long; buds club-shaped, with a hemispherical or conical operculum shorter than the calyx-tube, which is glaucous on the outside; anthers reniform. Fruit stalked, top- or pear-shaped, about $\frac{3}{8}$ in. long; valves level with the rim of the tube or enclosed.

Native of the mountains of Tasmania and the south-eastern parts of the mainland, found at 3,000 to 4,500 ft in Victoria and 1,000 to 3,000 ft in Tasmania; the date of introduction is uncertain, but before 1907. It yields a good timber, marketed as Australian or Tasmanian oak. There are two large specimens at Mount Usher, Co. Wicklow, Eire, planted in 1905 and measuring 98 × 6$\frac{3}{4}$ and 96 × 9$\frac{3}{4}$ ft (1966). It is growing well at Crarae on Loch Fyne, Argyll, where a specimen planted in 1946 measures 62 × 3$\frac{1}{4}$ ft (1969). Young plants came through the winter of 1962–3 at Glendoick, E. Perthshire, and Malahide Castle, near Dublin.

E. GLOBULUS Labill.   TASMANIAN BLUE GUM

A tree to 180 ft in the wild state; bark, except near the base, shed in long, thin ribbons which expose a smooth, grey or bluish surface. Juvenile leaves opposite, stalkless and often stem-clasping, oblong-ovate to oblong-lanceolate, 2$\frac{1}{2}$ to 6 in. long, vividly silver-glaucous. Adult leaves alternate, lanceolate or sickle-shaped, 4 to 12 in. long and 1 to 1$\frac{3}{5}$ in. wide, green and glossy, leathery. Flowers usually solitary in the leaf-axils, more rarely in twos or threes; buds glaucous, up to 1 in. or more long, top-shaped, ridged and wrinkled. Fruit hemispherical to top-shaped, up to $\frac{3}{4}$ in. long and 1$\frac{1}{4}$ in. wide, with a wide, thick disk.

Native of Tasmania, also found in one small area on the mainland; discovered in 1792 and introduced to Europe soon after. The first large-scale plantings outside Australia were made in the fifties and sixties of the last century and since then the blue gum has become one of the most widely planted of all trees in warm temperate and subtropical climates. In our climate it is definitely tender, but thanks to its rapid growth it is able to attain a remarkable size before succumbing, as it usually does, to a severe winter. Elwes and Henry record that a tree in

Jersey, planted in 1862, attained in thirty years the dimensions of 110 × 10¾ ft, but was killed in the great frosts of 1894–5. A similar fate has more recently befallen many large trees, both here and in the Mediterranean region, after abnormally hard winters. The cost—and often the damage to other trees—entailed in removing such bulky corpses needs no emphasising.

At the present time the largest specimens on record are all in Eire. These are (all measured 1966): Powerscourt, Co. Wicklow, 115 × 8¾ + 7 ft and 95 × 9½ ft; Killiney Hill Road, Shankhill, Co. Dublin, 102 × 9¼ and 96 × 7 ft; Ashbourne House, Co. Cork, 100 × 12 ft; Derreen, Co. Kerry, three of about the same size, the largest 98 × 14½ ft.

E. BICOSTATA Maiden & Simmonds EURABBIE.—A close ally of *E. globulus* from the mainland of S.E. Australia, where it ascends to 3,500 ft. It is likely to be hardier than the blue gum but is at present little known in cultivation. There is an example at Mount Usher, Co. Wicklow, measuring 42 × 2½ ft (1966).

E. GUNNII Hook. f. CIDER GUM

E. archeri Maiden and Blakely; *E. divaricata* McAulay & Brett

A tree to about 100 ft in the wild and as much or more in cultivation, but in unfavourable habitats it is found as a small, stunted tree; bark smooth, shed in large flakes, pale green or creamy white when freshly exposed, ageing to dark grey or greyish brown; branchlets glaucous or green, smooth or somewhat wrinkled. Juvenile leaves opposite, stalkless, broadly elliptical to orbicular, 1 to 1¾ in. long, glaucous or green; adult leaves alternate, stalked, lanceolate to ovate, 1⅗ to 3 in. long, ⅗ to 1⅖ in. wide, glaucous or green. Flowers borne in autumn in usually three-flowered umbels; buds stalkless or almost so; calyx-tube cylindrical or slightly urn-shaped, operculum shorter than the calyx-tube and hemispherical or conical. Fruits green or glaucous, cylindrical to campanulate, ovoid or slightly urn-shaped, with the valves usually enclosed.

Native of Tasmania, found in marshy situations on the central plateau, where it forms subalpine woodland, often in association with *Athrotaxis selaginoides*; discovered in 1840 and introduced not long after. It is a variable species in such characters as the colouring of the leaves and fruit, which may be green or glaucous, and in the shape of the latter. There is also some variability in hardiness, as might be expected of a species that grows in a broken mountain terrain from 2,000 to 3,500 ft. But of all the arborescent eucalypts that have been widely enough planted for any firm judgement to be made, *E. gunnii* has so far proved to be the hardiest.

Many of the trees cultivated in this country descend from the famous tree (blown down a few years ago) that grew at Whittingehame in East Lothian, a few miles from the North Sea. It was probably planted in 1853 and measured 96 × 19¾ ft in 1957. Its seed and seedlings were widely distributed and seem to have proved uniformly hardy. It has been suggested that it was a hybrid with *E. urnigera*, but Maiden—in his day the foremost authority on the genus—considered it to be typical *E. gunnii*. Another important source of seed is the planting at Brightlingsea, Essex, near the Colne estuary; this was made by

Thomas Bateman around 1887 and probably raised from seed received from the Estancia Negrete in S. Argentina. Many trees of this planting still exist at Brightlingsea, and an account of them will be found in *Gard. Chron.*, Nov. 23, 1963.

The following are the largest specimens of *E. gunnii* recorded in recent years: Trebah, Cornwall, 110 × 11¾ ft (1959); Sidbury, Devon, *pl.* 1890, 75 × 13½ ft (1959); Sheffield Park, Sussex, *pl.* 1912, 90 × 10½ ft (1968); Wakehurst Place, Sussex, 77 × 12 ft (1965); Castle Kennedy, Wigtown, 90 × 11½ ft (1967). A tree at Kew near the Pagoda, raised from Whittingehame seed and planted in 1896, blew down in 1963. There is another by the Unicorn Gate, probably from the same source and planted at the same time, which measures 60 × 5 ft (*c.* 1965).

E. GLAUCESCENS Maiden & Blakely *E. gunnii* var. *glauca* Deane & Maiden
TINGIRINGI GUM.—This species, of recent introduction, makes a mallee or small tree to about 40 ft high; bark white when first exposed, darkening to grey; young stems reddish brown, covered with a silvery bloom. Juvenile foliage brilliantly silver-glaucous. Adult leaves glaucous, rather thick and leathery, up to 5 in. long and ⅘ in. wide. Buds and fruit both glaucous, the latter barrel-shaped, with a truncate base. It is a native of New South Wales and Victoria at high altitudes. Only recently introduced, it promises to make a hardy and very ornamental tree of moderate size.

E. PERRINIANA Rodway *E. gunnii* var. *montana* Hook. f. SPINNING GUM.
—A small tree of the mallee type growing to about 20 ft high in the wild state, with a deciduous brownish and grey bark. Juvenile leaves glaucous, but less so in some forms than in others. They are opposite for an indefinite number of pairs, semi-circular, but each pair united into an apparently single, perfoliate leaf. These connate leaves eventually become detached from the stem and spin around in the wind—hence the popular name. Adult leaves lanceolate or sickle-shaped, 3 to 4½ in. long and up to 1 in. wide, usually glaucous. Fruits small (⅕ in. long), borne in threes on a short, stout common stalk.

A native of Tasmania from 1,000 to 2,000 ft, and of the mountains of Victoria and New South Wales, where it ascends to 5,000 ft. It once had the reputation for tenderness but provenances of recent introduction have proved hardy. At Goudhurst in Kent V. R. Waldron has a very glaucous and hardy strain deriving from seeds sent by Dr Martin from Tasmania in 1957.

E. JOHNSTONII Maiden

E. subcrenulata Maiden & Blakely; *E. muelleri* T. B. Moore,
not Miq., nor Naudin

A tree to 200 ft in favourable situations, with a clean, straight bole, but dwarf and stunted at high altitudes; bark deciduous, orange-red to brownish green, scaly at the base of the trunk on mature trees. Juvenile leaves glossy green, opposite, orbicular to ovate, stalkless, 1¼ to 2¼ in. long, margins with shallow, rounded teeth. Adult leaves alternate, stalked, ovate to lanceolate, 2 to 5 in. long (but smaller and more rounded in the dwarfer, high-mountain forms), dark, lustrous green, leathery; margins with faint, rounded teeth. Inflorescence a three-flowered umbel on a short, stout, flattened stalk; buds stalkless, calyx-tube wrinkled; operculum conical or hemispherical, with a boss at the apex. Fruit hemispherical to bell- or top-shaped, wrinkled; disk prominent; valves exserted. Native of Tasmania from 2,000 to 4,500 ft; described in 1886 (as *E. muelleri*) but probably introduced to Britain some years earlier. The dwarfer, smaller-leaved form is maintained as a distinct species by some authorities under the name *E. subcrenulata*. It promises to be hardy. The arborescent form (*E. johnstonii* in the narrow sense) is probably not hardy enough for general planting but has reached a good size in the milder parts. The following were recorded in Eire in 1966: Mount Usher, Co. Wicklow, 118 × 8¾, 90 × 5¼ and 87 × 6¼ ft; Fota, Co. Cork, *pl.* 1948, 80 × 3½ ft. There is a fine specimen at Kinloch Hourn in Inverness-shire. In his large collection of eucalypts at Casa di Sole, Salcombe, Devon, Dr Barker has a specimen measuring 59 × 3¾ ft (1970), planted in 1955.

Allied to *E. johnstonii* is the shrubby or mallee-like E. VERNICOSA Hook. f., native of the mountains of Tasmania at high altitudes. It is a hardy species with glossy, leathery, broadly elliptical to oblong leaves in both the juvenile and the adult state; they are about 2 in. long. One of the least effective of the eucalypts, though pretty in flower.

Another species in the same group is E. NEGLECTA Maiden, a small, compact tree with dense, dark green foliage. It grows taller than *E. vernicosa* and the adult leaves are longer (3 to 4 in.). Found in one locality in Victoria.

E. OVATA Labili.   SWAMP GUM

E. acervula Miq., not Sieber;
E. stuartiana F. v. Muell. ex Miq. (1859), not F. v. Muell. (1866)

A tree to about 100 ft high (sometimes attaining 200 ft); bark deciduous, creamy, pinkish or bronze when first exposed, later grey, shed in long, thick ribbons; usually it is persistent and furrowed at the base of the trunk. Juvenile leaves ovate to orbicular, 1⅗ to 3 in. long or even more, on short stalks. Adult leaves ovate to lanceolate, up to 5 in. or more long, acute at the apex, tapered at the base, leathery in texture and usually glossy. Umbels on slender common-stalks up to about ½ in. long, with four to seven flowers; buds elliptical to diamond-shaped, operculum conical and about as long as the calyx-tube. Fruits obconical or hemispherical; disk flat; valves level or slightly exserted.

Native of Tasmania and S.E. Australia from sea-level to 2,000 ft; commonly found in swampy ground and valley bottoms, but not invariably so; introduced before 1894. It has so far proved tender in the British Isles but Lord Talbot has a young tree at Malahide Castle near Dublin which came through the winter of 1962–3 unharmed.

E. AGGREGATA Deane & Maiden BLACK GUM.—A tree to about 70 ft high, differing from *E. ovata* in its rough, flaking, dark-grey bark; in the smaller, more rounded juvenile leaves and smaller fruit. Native of New South Wales in swampy ground. It ascends higher in the mountains than *E. ovata* and is likely therefore to prove hardier. Of recent introduction.

EUCALYPTUS 135

E. CAMPHORA R. T. Baker BROAD-LEAVED SALLY.—A tree to about 65 ft high with a dark, deciduous bark shed in broad ribbons. A native of Victoria and New South Wales, introduced recently by R. C. Barnard. Growing as it does in damp frost-hollows, it is likely to be very hardy but is scarcely tried as yet. *E. ovata* var. *aquatica* Blakely, said to form thickets in shallow water, is now included in *E. camphora*.

E. PARVIFOLIA Cambage   SMALL-LEAVED GUM

A small, densely crowned tree to about 30 ft high, with a smooth, greyish bark. Juvenile leaves opposite, sessile or shortly stalked, ovate to ovate-lanceolate, about 1¼ in. long, dark green or somewhat glaucous. Adult leaves stalked, alternate or opposite, linear-lanceolate to ovate-lanceolate, up to 2½ in. long but less than ½ in. wide. Flowers in umbels of four to seven on a short common-stalk; buds elliptical, about ⅕ in. long. Fruits hemispherical, slightly contracted at the apex.

Native of New South Wales, confined to one locality, where it grows at 3,500 to 5,000 ft. It is one of the hardiest species and makes an elegant small tree. Mr Barnard records that of over three hundred plants of a high-altitude provenance raised by him in S. Devon only three were killed in the winter of 1962–3. A specimen thrived for many years in the chalky soil of Messrs Hilliers' West Hill nursery.

E. NICHOLII Maiden & Blakely —This species is certainly tender but few eucalypts are more beautiful in the young state. The juvenile leaves are very narrow (¼ in. or less wide) and about 2 in. long and coated, like the young stems, with a purple bloom. It makes an elegant tree to 100 ft high, easily distinguished from *E. parvifolia* by the persistent, fibrous bark. Native of New South Wales.

E. PAUCIFLORA Sieber   CABBAGE GUM
E. coriacea Schauer

A tree usually seen under 60 ft high in the wild state, with several crooked stems produced from near ground-level; trunk smooth with a deciduous bark, white when freshly exposed, darkening to grey; young growths dark red and lustrous. Juvenile leaves opposite for three to five pairs, sessile or short-stalked, ovate to almost orbicular, 1 to 2½ in. long, ¾ to 2 in. wide, grey-green, rather thick and leathery. Adult leaves alternate, stalked, broadly lanceolate to sickle-shaped, 2½ to 6 in. long, ½ to 1¼ in. wide, thick and leathery and bright, glossy green on both surfaces. Inflorescence an axillary umbel of seven to twelve flowers on a stout common-stalk; buds club-shaped with a smooth and lustrous calyx-tube; anthers reniform. Fruit globose to pear-shaped; disk flat and thick; valves enclosed.

Native of Tasmania, Victoria and New South Wales; it is mainly a species of the mountains, found on the mainland from 2,500 to 5,500 ft, but from sea-level to 2,000 ft in Tasmania (to 3,500 ft in some localities); introduced before 1880. This is certainly one of the hardiest species, but in view of its wide range, both in latitude and altitude, some variability in frost resistance is to be expected. There is a good specimen in the Edinburgh Botanic Garden, growing in a rather exposed position near Inverleith House, planted around 1939; it measures 45 × 4½ ft with a spread of about 30 ft (1965).

var. NANA Blakely WOLGAN SNOW GUM.—A dwarf, mallee-like form reported to flower and fruit when only 6 ft high and further differing from the type in the narrower leaves ; in the short-stalked or almost sessile umbels; and the top-shaped fruits. Found in one locality in New South Wales at 3,500 ft.

E. NIPHOPHILA Maiden & Blakely E. *coriacea* var. *alpina* F. v. Muell. SNOW GUM.—An alpine species confined to high altitudes in the mountains of Victoria and New South Wales (where it ascends to 6,500 ft on Mt Kosciusko). In this respect it differs from E. *pauciflora*, which, though reaching as high as 5,500 ft, has its main distribution at lower altitudes. From that species E. *niphophila* is also distinguished by the green juvenile leaves and by the silvery bloom that covers the young stems.

E. *niphophila* was first described in 1929; previous to that it had been regarded as part of E. *pauciflora* and only in recent years has it come into prominence. By any standard it is one of the most beautiful of the eucalypts that can be grown in this country and perhaps the hardiest; in very few gardens did it suffer any damage in the winters of 1961–3. 'E. *niphophila* . . . is the gem in my collection of eucalypts. The glossy leaves reflect sunlight like small mirrors: the branchlets in winter are glossy dark red to orange-red; when growth starts in the spring they turn bluish-white with a glaucous bloom which may be rubbed off by branch movement in gales but is renewed by exudation during the growing season: branches which have not yet started bark-shed are also covered with the same glaucous bloom much of which persists through the winter: naked buds and leaf petioles are orange, newly opened leaves mahogany red to light brown . . .' (R. C. Barnard, *Journ. R.H.S.*, Vol. 91, p. 296). Mr Barnard adds that this species grows rather slowly for two years but thereafter at 3 to 4 ft annually. The seed germinates poorly unless given cold, moist stratification for four to six weeks.

The ultimate height of this species in cultivation is uncertain, but it will almost certainly exceed the 20 ft given as the maximum attained in its natural habitat.

E. MITCHELLIANA Cambage WEEPING SALLY.—A very rare species in the wild state, found only on Mt Buffalo in Victoria at about 4,000 ft. It is a tree to about 50 ft high, with a smooth, white bark; the young branches are drooping, hence the popular name. Adult leaves 3 to 6 in. long, scarcely ½ in. wide, green. Buds cylindrical or tapered at both ends. Fruit globular to barrel-shaped.

E. STELLULATA Sieber BLACK SALLY.—A species closely allied to the preceding but not so elegant; and differing in the broader and shorter leaves, which are elliptical to broadly lanceolate, up to 3 in. long and 1 in. wide. It is a native of Victoria and New South Wales.

Both these species are in cultivation. E. *mitchelliana* is an ornamental eucalypt of great promise, which is growing well at Glendoick in E. Perthshire and suffered no damage there in the winters of 1961–3.

E. URNIGERA Hook. f.   URN GUM

A tree usually not more than 50 ft in height, though considerably taller in favoured situations; bark peeling, white to red or brown. Young shoots of juvenile trees warted; leaves orbicular, often notched or with a small mucro at the apex; 1 to 1¾ in. wide; adult leaves ovate to lanceolate, 2 to 4 in. long, ¾ to 2 in. wide; tapered or rounded at the base. Flowers three together on a main-stalk up to 1 in. long, the stalk of the individual flowers also distinctly developed and ¼ to ⅓ in. long. Calyx-tube urn-shaped, ¼ in. long. Fruit urn-shaped, with the valves deeply enclosed. *Bot. Mag.*, n.s., t. 536.

EUCALYPTUS URNIGERA

Native of the mountains of Tasmania at 2,000 to 3,500 ft; introduced before 1860. It is a variable species in the colour of the leaves, which may be green or glaucous. There is also some variability in hardiness, but it is certainly to be reckoned as one of the hardiest species. There were two fine specimens at Crarae Lodge, Argyll, planted in 1907, the taller of which measured 96 × 10 ft. Both were blown down early in 1968. There are also some forty or fifty younger trees in the collection with conspicuously glaucous foliage raised (Sir Ilay Campbell tells us) from two batches of seed collected near Lake Fenton by Dr Martin of Hobart. Plants from this provenance have been distributed from Crarae to many Scottish gardens.

In Ireland the following specimens were recorded in 1966: Mount Usher, Co. Wicklow, Eire, 100 × 8 ft; and in Northern Ireland: Rowallane, Co. Down, 95 × 7¼ ft; Castlewellan, Co. Down, 105 × 9 and 102 × 8½ ft.

This species has been confused with *E. gunnii* to which it is closely allied but from which it is well distinguished by the stalked, urn-shaped fruits on a long common-stalk.

E. VIMINALIS Labill.   RIBBON GUM
E. angustifolia Desf.

A tree to 120 ft high, sometimes taller; bark becoming rough and persistent near the base of the trunk but shed in long ribbons on the upper part and yellowish or white when first exposed; young stems dark red and warted. Juvenile leaves opposite, ovate to lanceolate, 2 to 4 in. long, $\frac{1}{2}$ to 1 in. wide, tapered at the apex, sessile and sometimes stem-clasping at the base; dark green, often with a crimson midrib. Adult leaves alternate, lanceolate or sickle-shaped, 4 to 7 in. long and up to 1 in. wide. Umbels three-flowered; buds more or less sessile, ovoid to cylindrical. Fruit globular to top-shaped; disk prominent; valves exserted.

Native of Tasmania, South Australia, Victoria and New South Wales, from sea-level to about 4,500 ft; introduced before 1885. It is tender, and of the many trees planted in the late nineteenth and early twentieth century most succumbed to frost. Notable exceptions are the three specimens at Mount Usher, Co. Wicklow, Eire, probably planted in 1904 and measuring 105 × 9½, 105 × 13¾ and 95 × 12 ft (1966). There is also a smaller specimen in the garden, pl. 1945, which is already 72 × 4½ ft (1966). There are other examples at Kilmacurragh in the same county and at Fota and on Garinish Island, Co. Cork.

In its adult foliage, flowers and fruit, E. viminalis bears a close resemblance to E. dalrympleana, but is perfectly distinct in its tapered, dark green juvenile foliage and also differs in its bark, which peels in long, narrow strips, whereas in E. dalrympleana it is shed in irregular flakes. Also, in the wild it exudes a sugary secretion from the bark and is for that reason sometimes known as the manna gum. However, the similarity between the two species is so great that seed of "E. dalrympleana" received from Australia often produces E. viminalis, or a mixture of the two. This has been Mr Barnard's experience; and the plot of E. viminalis at Crarae was raised from seed of "E. dalrvmpleana" (Journ. R.H.S., Vol. 88, p. 333).

EUCOMMIA   EUCOMMIACEAE

This genus, consisting of a single species, was once placed in the Hamamelidaceae, but is now considered to rank as a monotypic family, allied to the Elm family.

E. ULMOIDES Oliver   [PLATE 23

A deciduous tree, not yet found by Europeans in a wild state, but from 30 to 65 ft high, as seen cultivated by the Chinese. It probably attains a larger size. Leaves alternate, ovate or oval, long and slender-pointed, toothed, 3 to 8 in. long, slightly hairy on both surfaces when young, becoming glabrous above. Flowers unisexual, the sexes on separate trees; they are inconspicuous, the males consisting of brown stamens only; female ones of a single pistil. Fruit flat and winged, one-seeded, rather like an enlarged fruit of wych-elm, oval-oblong, 1½ in. long, tapering at the base to a short stalk; apex notched.

Introduced to France from China about 1896, and a few years later to Kew. It was first discovered in China by Henry as a cultivated tree, 20 to 30 ft high, but as its bark is and has for 2,000 years been highly valued by the Chinese for its real or supposed tonic and other medicinal virtues, it is never allowed to reach its full size, but is cut down and stripped of its bark.

The most interesting attribute of the tree is its containing rubber. The rubber is apparently of inferior quality, but the tree is of peculiar interest as the only one hardy in our climate that is known to produce this substance. If a leaf be gently torn in two, strings of rubber are visible. Fossils found in tertiary brown-coal deposits in Germany, and known as 'Monkey's Hair', derive from the leaves of some extinct species of *Eucommia*; they are well enough preserved to burn when a match is put to them, giving off a smell of burning rubber.

At Kew, grown in good loam, it has proved absolutely hardy, and a vigorous grower. There is a good specimen to be seen by the Temple of Bellona, planted 1930 and measuring 42 × 4¾ ft (1967), and another fine specimen (see Plate 23) is in the Duke's Garden. Two others of about the same size grow in the Cambridge Botanic Garden. It can be propagated by cuttings made of half-ripened wood put in gentle heat. Wilson introduced seeds to the Coombe Wood nursery, from which, no doubt, trees of both sexes have been raised, though female trees seem to be rare in gardens.

EUCRYPHIA   EUCRYPHIACEAE

A genus of four or five species—two native of Chile and two of Australasia —and four hybrids, all of great interest and beauty. One of the species is occasionally a tree 80 to 100 ft high, another gets to be 50 ft or more, the others are smallish trees or large shrubs. All are evergreen and each continent has one species with pinnate leaves and one with simple leaves. The leaves are opposite, the flowers axillary and large; sepals and petals four; and the stamens in a brush-like mass. Fruit a woody or leathery capsule, usually requiring more than twelve months to ripen.

E. glutinosa (*pinnatifolia*) is the only species hardy in our average climate, but *E. cordifolia* is a success thirty miles or more south of London. They seem on the whole to prefer a soil pretty free from lime, although *E.* × *nymansensis* grows quite well near Worthing on the chalk at High-down, on the south slope of the South Downs; but *E. glutinosa* is a failure there. So too is *E. cordifolia*, but for climatic reasons: this species is quite tolerant of chalky soils. All the species are admirable in the great rhodo-dendron gardens of the south and south-west. All need plenty of light to flower freely and will tolerate almost full sun if the soil is cool and moist.

E. CORDIFOLIA Cav.　ULMO

An evergreen shrub or tree up to 70 ft high, with downy branchlets and simple, oblong leaves, heart-shaped at the base, 1½ to 3 in. long, dull green; the margins wavy, very downy beneath (in juvenile specimens the leaves are longer, more pointed and strongly toothed). Flowers produced singly in the terminal leaf-axils, white, 2 in. across; petals four. Stamens very numerous; anthers terracotta coloured. *Bot. Mag.*, t. 8209.

Native of the temperate rain-forests of Chile in the provinces of Valdivia, Llanquihue and Chiloe, where it is commonly associated with *Nothofagus dombeyi* and makes (in virgin forest) a broad-crowned tree to 70 ft high; introduced in 1851. More tender than *E. glutinosa*, this species has never attained a good footing in gardens and thrives best in places where the climate is moist and mild. In Sussex, given the protection of woodland, it grows well enough but suffered rather badly in the cold winters of 1961–3, which severely cut the old specimen at Nymans, Sussex, planted in 1906. There are, however, other examples in the collection, which flower well, some of them raised from Comber's seeds. At Grayswood Hill, Surrey, a rather stunted tree, growing in full sun, suffered no damage in those winters. The tallest specimen recorded grows at Tregrehan in Cornwall, which measures 57 × 5 ft (1971). Others of around 40 to 55 ft grow at: Trelowarren, Trewithen, Trengwainton, Penjerrick, and Caerhays Castle, Cornwall; Logan, Wigtown; Castlewellan, Co. Down, N. Ireland; at Mount Usher, Co. Wicklow, and Garinish Island, Co. Cork, Eire. In N.W. England there is a specimen at Muncaster Castle, Cumberland, measuring 50 × 3¼ ft, with a fine bole (1971).

E. cordifolia will grow well on chalky soils, though there must be few chalk gardens with the climate it demands.

E. GLUTINOSA (Poepp. & Endl.) Baill.

Fagus (sic) *glutinosa* Poepp. & Endl.; *E. pinnatifolia* Gay

A deciduous or partially evergreen small tree 10 to 25 ft high, with erect branches, bearing the leaves in a cluster towards the end of each shoot. Leaves opposite, pinnate, composed of three or five leaflets, which are ovate to oval, 1½ to 2½ in. long, regularly toothed, dark shining green. Flowers produced singly or in pairs from the end of the shoot, and from terminal leaf-axils, each one 2½ in. across; petals four, white; stamens numerous, with yellow anthers. Fruit a hard, woody, pear-shaped capsule ½ to ¾ in. long. The young wood, leaf-stalks and leaves are hairy when young. *Bot. Mag.*, t. 7067.

Discovered by Gay,* the Chilean botanist, about 1845, on the rocky banks of the river Biobio; introduced in 1859 by R. Pearce, when collecting in Chile for

---

* Poeppig had collected a flowerless specimen some years earlier, which he and Endlicher considered to represent a new species of southern beech, with pinnate leaves, and described it under the name *Fagus glutinosa*. There is no doubt that Poeppig's plant was the eucryphia and indeed Gay gave *Fagus glutinosa* Poepp. & Endl. as a synonym of his *E. pinnatifolia*. Under the rules of nomenclature the epithet *glutinosa* must be used since it was the first to be published for this species.

Messrs Veitch. It is the finest and best of the eucryphia species, and the only one
hardy near London. Blossoming in July and August, it is then a plant of singular
beauty with its large pure white petals and conspicuous tufts of stamens.
Unfortunately, although hardy, it is not easy to propagate or transplant, consequently it has never become common. In a young state it is apt to die off
without any apparent reason, although when once established it appears to
continue in good health indefinitely. A moist peaty soil is best for it in the

EUCRYPHIA GLUTINOSA

juvenile state, and a little plot of this should be provided for it when planted.
Afterwards when established and strong, its roots will spread into the ordinary
soil around if it is free from lime. The best success with it at Kew has been
obtained by planting it in beds of heaths where its roots are shaded. I think
many premature deaths are due to the sun, on scorching summer days, beating
on naked soil about its roots, in the Lower Thames Valley at any rate. Seeds are
produced in this country, and it can also be increased by layering. Seedlings
should be given peaty soil; they are worth every care. The dying leaves fade off
into orange and red.

In contrast to E. *cordifolia*, which is a regular constituent of the rain forests
of the Chilean lake region, this species is very rare in the natural state. In cultivation it has reached 44 ft in height at Lanarth in Cornwall but the larger specimens
seen in gardens are usually around 15 to 20 ft high.

There is a double-flowered form, not of much value, which often appears
among seedlings.

E. × INTERMEDIA Bausch

A small evergreen tree; young shoots slightly grooved. Leaves simple or
trifoliolate; the former oblong, up to 2½ in. long, slightly toothed and shortly
mucronate; the trifoliolate ones have the middle leaflet of the same size as the
simple leaf with a short stalk; the side leaflets are much smaller, stalkless, up to

1 in. long; all are dark green, rather glaucous beneath, slightly hairy on the stalk and margins. Flowers single or in pairs at the apex of the branches, pure white, 1 to 1¼ in. wide; petals four, widely obovate and overlapping. *Bot. Mag.*, n.s., t. 534.

A hybrid between *E. glutinosa* (*pinnatifolia*) and *E. lucida*, which appeared spontaneously in the grounds at Rostrevor, Co. Down. The clonal name for this, the original form of the cross, is 'ROSTREVOR'. It was shown in flower by Lord Aberconway, 1st September 1936, at Vincent Square, when it was given an Award of Merit. An attractive hybrid and interesting as originating from an Australian species crossed with a Chilean one. It is vigorous, fast-growing, and of the same order of hardiness as *E.* × *nymansensis*.

E. × HILLIERI Ivens (*E. lucida* × *moorei*).—The typical form of this cross, 'WINTON', arose as a self-sown seedling in the Chandlers Ford nursery of Messrs Hillier and Sons. The leaves are pinnate as in *E. moorei*, with two or three pairs of leaflets, which are relatively broader and blunter than in that species. Flowers solitary, about 1 in. across, borne on quite young plants. From *E.* × *intermedia* 'Rostrevor' this hybrid differs in its pinnate (rarely trifoliolate leaves), with entire margins. The same hybrid has arisen at Trengwainton in Cornwall and received the clonal name 'PENWITH'.

E. LUCIDA (Labill.) Baill.

Carpodontos lucida Labill.; *E. billardieri* Spach

An evergreen tree occasionally up to 100 ft high, but usually 20 to 50 ft, of slender habit, the trunk cylindrical, as much as 9 ft in girth; young shoots downy. Leaves opposite, simple, oblong, rounded at the apex, toothless; 1½ to 3 in. long, ⅜ to ⅝ in. wide; deep glossy green above, glaucous beneath; stalk ⅛ in. long. Flowers pure white, 1 to 2 in. across, sweetly scented, solitary and pendulous on a stalk ½ in. long that is produced from the leaf-axils; petals four; stamens numerous, ⅜ in. long, with yellow anthers. Fruit dry, woody, ⅝ in. long, cylindrical, splitting longitudinally when ripe. *Bot. Mag.*, t. 7200.

Native of Tasmania, where it flowers in February; with us it blooms in June or July. It is a very beautiful tree on its native island, growing usually on the banks of rivers. The leaves and young shoots are very resinous. It is a pleasing small tree of slender, columnar habit which makes an admirable specimen for mild, sheltered gardens, growing rapidly when young and ultimately attaining a height of about 20 ft. The flowers are more elegantly fashioned than in either of the Chilean species. Although less hardy than *E. glutinosa* it thrives in many gardens not so far distant from London. There are good specimens in the Savill Gardens; at Nymans in Sussex; and in the Chandlers Ford nursery of Messrs Hillier. Two fine examples on the Terrace Walls at Bodnant are about 25 ft high; they were badly damaged in the winter of 1962–3.

E. MILLIGANII Hook. f. *E. lucida* var. *milliganii* (Hook. f.) Summerhayes— A close ally of *E. lucida* and also confined to Tasmania. It differs in its shrubby habit, shorter leaves, and smaller flowers. On some Tasmanian specimens preserved at Kew many of the leaves are only ⅛ to ¾ in. long. It is treated as a distinct species by Bausch (Kew Bull., 1938) and by Dr Curtis (*The Endemic Flora of Tasmania*, Vol. 1 (1967), p. 62, where both species are beautifully figured). It does not normally exceed 12 ft in height.

E. (*lucida* × *cordifolia*).—This beautiful hybrid between the two simple-leaved species of *Eucryphia* arose at Trengwainton, Cornwall, before the second world war but is still uncommon in gardens. It inclines to the first parent and like it flowers at an early age, but the leaves are larger, wavy-edged, occasionally shallowly toothed above the middle, and recall *E. cordifolia* in their poise.

E. MOOREI F. v. Muell.

An evergreen tree of small or medium size; young shoots and common-stalk of leaf clothed with pale, short, brown hairs. Leaves opposite, pinnate, composed of five to thirteen leaflets. Leaflets scarcely stalked, narrowly oblong, not toothed, oblique at the base, the midrib terminated by a bristle-like mucro; ½ to 3 in. long, ¼ to ⅜ in. wide; glossy dark green and with short, appressed hairs above when young; rather glaucous and downy (chiefly on the midrib and veins) beneath; margins downy. Flowers about 1 in. wide, solitary in the axils of the current year's growth; flower-stalk downy, up to ¾ in. long, with a cup-like bract towards the top. Petals four, pure white, obovate; stamens white, ⅜ in. long, very numerous and forming a brush-like cluster ⅝ in. wide.

Native of New South Wales on wooded hills near the source of the Clyde and Shoalhaven rivers; originally discovered by Chas. Moore about 1860; introduced to Kew in 1915. It most closely resembles the Chilean *E. glutinosa*, having, like it, pinnate leaves and four-petalled flowers, but differs in the more numerous, much narrower leaflets and evergreen habit. It flowered in the Temperate House at Kew in August 1921, but is not so attractive in bloom as the Chilean species, the flowers being so much smaller. The foliage is handsome and the growth elegant. It succeeds in S. Devon, Cornwall, Scilly Isles and similarly favoured spots, and has reached 20 ft at Nymans in Sussex. The finest specimen known grows at Trewithen in Cornwall, which measures 54 × 2¾ ft (1971). There is one almost as large at Mount Usher in Co. Wicklow, Eire.

E. × NYMANSENSIS Bausch [PLATE 24

A hybrid between the two Chilean species, *E. glutinosa* and *E. cordifolia*. It is an evergreen tree of erect handsome shape, its foliage being intermediate between that of its parents in the fact that some of the leaves are compound as in *glutinosa*, whilst others are simple as in *cordifolia*. They are firm, rather leathery in texture and the compound leaves are mostly trifoliolate, the central leaflet being the largest and 1½ to 3½ in. long by 1 to 1½ in. wide; all have regular marginal teeth, a dark shining upper surface, a paler lower one, and a slight down on both. Young shoots ribbed, downy. The flowers open in August and are pure white, 2½ in. wide; petals four, spreading, overlapping, with uneven margins; stamens numerous with yellow anthers; flower-stalk downy.

This famous cross first arose at Nymans, Handcross, Sussex, from seed sown in 1914, shortly before the death of Leonard Messel, the founder of the garden. *E. cordifolia* had first flowered there in 1909 and it is known that seedlings from it were raised in the hope of producing a hardier form. But it may be that in 1914 seed from both the parents was sown and that the cross occurred in both batches. Shortly after the end of the first world war, the late Lt. Col. L. C. R. Messel gave away plants to friends, among them the late Sir Frederick Stern, whose plant, received in 1919, first flowered in September 1922. Others were retained and planted in the garden. Tradition has it that the group in the north-east corner of the garden are some of the original seedlings, their small size being due to the exposed position in which they grow and also, perhaps, to the preponderance of *E. glutinosa* in their make-up.

Of the plants grown on at Nymans, two were selected as outstanding and were designated 'Nymans A' and 'Nymans B'. The first of these was shown at Vincent Square in August 1924 as 'Nymansay', when it received an Award of Merit and two years later a First Class Certificate. The same cross also occurred at Mount Usher, Co. Wicklow, Eire.

E. × *nymansensis* is usually seen as a slender, erect shrub or small tree which may attain 40 to 50 ft in height. It needs a moist soil and a position protected from searing winds. Given those conditions it will tolerate full sun and indeed will prove shy-flowering if grown in too shady a place. It was badly damaged in a few gardens in the severe winters of 1961-3 but can be considered as hardy and satisfactory except in the more continental parts of eastern and south-eastern England. Fortunately, like *E. cordifolia*, it has no aversion to limy soils. It sets fertile seed, but the seedlings will of course be variable and perhaps slower to flower than plants raised by cuttings or layers from selected parents.

EUODIA   RUTACEAE

A genus of unarmed trees and shrubs widely spread over E. Asia, and extending to Australia and Madagascar. Of about fifty species, the only hardy species in cultivation are a few deciduous ones which were intro-duced from China by Wilson, and one from Korea. They are small trees of the same type as *Phellodendron*, sometimes aromatic. Young shoots very pithy, marked with lenticels, axillary buds exposed. Leaves opposite, pinnate. Flowers borne in broad flattish corymbs terminating the shoots of the year, often unisexual, small; sepals, petals, and stamens four or five in number. Fruit a capsule of four or five carpels which split from the top, revealing shining black seeds the size of gun-shot.

Among cultivated trees these euodias most closely resemble *Phello-dendron*, but they are very readily distinguished from that genus by the buds in the leaf-axils being exposed. (In *Phellodendron* the buds are quite hidden in the base of the leaf-stalk.)

The Forsters, father and son, who founded this genus in 1776, spelt the name 'Euodia', but convention once demanded that the Greek prefix 'eu-', when occurring before a vowel, should be written 'ev-' —hence 'Evodia', the established spelling. This rendering is, however, contrary to present-day rules of nomenclature and the original spelling can therefore be restored (cf. 'Euonymus', once commonly spelt 'Evonymus').

E. DANIELLII (Benn.) Hemsl.   [PLATE 25

Xanthoxylum daniellii Benn.

A small tree to about 50 ft high; branchlets downy when young, becoming reddish brown and glabrous. Leaves 9 to 15 in. long; leaflets five to eleven, ovate to ovate oblong, broadly wedge-shaped to slightly heart-shaped at the base, narrowed at the apex to a slender point, 2 to 5 in. long; glabrous above, downy on the midrib and in the vein-axils beneath. Flowers small, white, borne in corymbs 4 to 6 in. wide. Fruit capsules with a short, usually hooked beak.

Native of N. China and Korea; described from a specimen collected by William Daniell, a surgeon with the British forces stationed at Tientsin in 1860–2; introduced to Kew in 1907 from the Arnold Arboretum, which received seed in 1905 from Korea and in 1907 from Shantung province. The trees at Kew are now 40 to 45 ft in height and very handsome in late summer when few other trees are in bloom and later, too, when bearing their large clusters of purplish fruits.

E. HUPEHENSIS Dode—This species is closely allied to the preceding and may be its geographical expression in Shensi and Hupeh, from which province it was introduced by Wilson during his 1907–8 expedition. It is said to differ in its longer-stalked leaflets and the longer beak of the fruit, but these criteria are not reliable. Two notable specimens are: Glendoick, Perths., *pl.* 1923, 62 × 7¾ ft (1970); and Greenwich Park, London, 55 × 7½ ft (1968).

E. GLAUCA Miq.

A small dioecious, deciduous tree with a smooth bark and rather stout, downy branchlets. Leaves 6 to 10 in. long; leaflets five to fifteen, oval-lanceolate to narrowly lanceolate, 1½ to 4 in. long, ½ to 1½ in. wide; distinctly unequal at the base, tapering at the apex gradually to a slender point; indistinctly notched and ciliate on the margin, glabrous and dark green above, vividly glaucous beneath, and furnished with white down at the base; stalk, midrib, and main-stalk red. Flowers in dense, rounded corymbs.

Native of China and Japan; introduced by Wilson in 1907 from W. Hupeh, where it is very common. As represented at Kew, its leaflets are the narrowest in the hardy euodias, and are distinct also in their very glaucous under-surface and red leaf-stalks.

E. VELUTINA Rehd. & Wils.

A deciduous tree 40 ft or more high; young shoots clothed with a velvety down. Leaves up to 10 in. long, composed of seven to eleven leaflets, which are

T S—F

very shortly stalked, oblong-lanceolate with a long tapered point, obliquely rounded at the base, entire, 2 to 4 in. long, 1 to 1½ in. wide, dull green and downy above, paler and clothed beneath with a soft velvety down, especially on the midrib and the nine to thirteen pairs of veins. Flowers small and very numerous, yellowish white, produced in August in a cluster of compound umbels from the end of the current year's shoots and from the uppermost leaf-axils. These flower clusters are 6 to 7 in. wide and high, the stalks velvety like the young shoots. The individual flower is about ⅛ in. wide; petals narrow oblong; calyx, ovary, and the very short thick stalk downy. Fruit purplish brown, hairy, ⅕ in. wide, with a minute beak. Seeds shining black.

Native of W. Szechwan, China; discovered and introduced in 1908 by Wilson (No. 994). It is very distinct in the soft velvety down of the various parts. So far as I know, it first flowered with the late C. J. Lucas of Warnham Court, Sussex, who gave me a flowering shoot in August 1918. It is quite hardy at Kew.

E. HENRYI Dode—Leaves 6 to 12 in. long. Leaflets five to nine, ovate to ovate-lanceolate, slender-pointed, tapered or rounded at the base, shallowly notched on the margin; 2 to 4 in. long, about half as wide, becoming quite glabrous on both sides, pale and rather glaucous beneath; stalk about ¼ in. long. Introduced from Hupeh in 1908 by Wilson (No. 324). It is allied to *E. velutina* but distinguished by the beaked fruit, the almost glabrous leaves and the small pyramidal inflorescence.

EUONYMUS   SPINDLE-TREE   CELASTRACEAE

Few, if any, species of *Euonymus* have any beauty of flower. Their value in the garden dwells in the beauty of their fruits, in the autumnal colours of the foliage of some species, and in the rich evergreen foliage of others. They are evergreen or deciduous trees, shrubs, or creeping plants, with the young shoots often four-angled. The leaves are always opposite and toothed in the cultivated species, except *E. nanus*. The arrangement of the flowers is very characteristic in this genus; they are borne from May to June in cymes from the lower joints of the current season's growth. There is first a slender main-stalk usually about 1 in. long, which terminates in a single flower flanked by one at each side. This three-flowered cyme is seen in *E. europaeus* and others; but often the main-stem, instead of producing two side flowers, forks into two parts, each with its terminal flower and two side ones. The inflorescence is then seven-flowered. Sometimes these secondary stems branch again and the inflorescence becomes fifteen-flowered.

The flowers are usually from ⅙ to ⅓ in. across, greenish, yellowish, or white, rarely purple. The parts of the flower (sepals, petals, stamens, and lobes of the fruit) are in fours or fives, which sometimes afford a convenient means of distinction. The fruits are pendulous and highly coloured, and are composed of three to five one-seeded cells or lobes—the lobes often angled, sometimes winged. The seed is partially covered with an outer coat known as the aril, which is usually brilliantly coloured—scarlet, orange, etc., and adds much to the effect of the fruit when the cells burst.

The only other genus of hardy shrubs with which *Euonymus* can be confused is *Celastrus*, which has a similar fruit, but is well distinguished by its alternate leaves.

These plants are easily cultivated in a good, well-drained loam. Some of the species, e.g. *E. atropurpureus* and *americanus*, like a position shaded during the hottest hours of the day, and all the evergreen sorts grow, if they do not bear fruit well, in permanent, if not too dense, shade. Propagation of the deciduous species is best effected by seeds. Failing this method, cuttings or layers may be used; cuttings of the evergreen species and varieties take root very readily, and may be struck at almost any season if a little bottom heat is given.

Several species, notable *E. europaeus* and *japonicus*, are frequently badly attacked by a caterpillar at the flowering season, which swarms on the branches in cobwebby masses, feeding on the leaves and preventing the formation of a crop of fruit. A quick and effective remedy is to spray with some modern contact insectide.

E. ALATUS (Thunb.) Sieb.
Celastrus alatus Thunb.

A deciduous shrub of open but stiff habit 6 to 8 ft high, and more in diameter, free from down in all its parts; young branches at first square, two or four of the angles afterwards developing conspicuous thin, corky wings $\frac{1}{4}$ to $\frac{1}{2}$ in. broad. Leaves narrowly oval or obovate, 1 to 3 in. long, $\frac{1}{2}$ to $1\frac{1}{4}$ in. wide, tapered at both ends, finely toothed, dark green, glabrous or somewhat downy beneath; stalk $\frac{1}{12}$ in. long. Flowers not more than three on a cyme, greenish yellow to pale green, about $\frac{1}{4}$ in. across. Fruit purplish, composed normally of four ovoid lobes or pods, united only at the base, $\frac{1}{4}$ to $\frac{1}{3}$ in. long; frequently the number of pods is reduced to two or one, through the barrenness and non-development of the others; aril scarlet. *Bot. Mag.*, t. 8823.

Native of China and Japan. This is one of the most distinct in the genus through the curious corky wings that develop on the branches, and through the divided purplish segments of the fruit. As a garden shrub it is valuable for the rich rosy scarlet of its decaying leaves. At Westonbirt, where there is a large group by the entrance to the Acer Glade, this species has assumed a flat-topped habit.

var. APTERUS Reg. *E. subtriflorus* Blume—This variety has no corky wings to the branches; as seen in cultivation, it also has thinner and usually longer leaves and a laxer habit.

cv. 'COMPACTUS'.—A low-growing variety of dense habit, in cultivation in the USA.

E. AMERICANUS L.   STRAWBERRY BUSH

A deciduous shrub up to 6 or 8 ft high, of upright or straggling habit, not downy in any part; twigs four-angled. Leaves of firm texture, glossy, narrowly oval to lanceolate, long-pointed, wedge-shaped at the base, shallowly toothed; 1 to 4 in. long, $\frac{1}{8}$ to $1\frac{1}{4}$ in. wide; stalks $\frac{1}{12}$ in. long. Flowers $\frac{1}{3}$ in. diameter, greenish purple, with five rounded, distinctly clawed petals; produced about midsummer singly or in threes on a slender stalk $\frac{1}{2}$ to $\frac{3}{4}$ in. long. Fruits $\frac{1}{2}$ to $\frac{3}{4}$ in. diameter, red, three- to five-lobed, covered outside with prickly warts; aril scarlet.

Native of the eastern United States; cultivated in 1683, according to Aiton, but rarely seen. In my experience it rarely bears fruit in this country. It is distinguished among euonymuses by its spiny-warted fruits, and by having the parts of its flower in fives. The only other cultivated species uniting these two characters is E. *obovatus*, a prostrate plant with thin, dull green, obovate, short-pointed leaves.

var. ANGUSTIFOLIUS (Pursh) Wood—Leaves narrow-lanceolate, one-fourth to one-fifth as wide as long.

E. ATROPURPUREUS Jacq.   BURNING BUSH

A deciduous shrub 6 to 12 ft high, or a small tree; young shoots glabrous. Leaves oval or narrowly obovate, tapered at both ends, 2 to 5$\frac{1}{2}$ in. long, $\frac{3}{4}$ to 2$\frac{1}{4}$ in. wide, finely toothed, dark green and nearly glabrous above, downy beneath; stalk $\frac{1}{3}$ to $\frac{2}{3}$ in. long. Flowers seven to fifteen, in twice or thrice branched cymes 1 to 2 in. long, expanding in July; each flower $\frac{1}{3}$ in. across, of a dark purple; the parts in fours. Fruit glabrous, four-lobed, crimson on pendent stalks; aril scarlet.

Native of the eastern and central United States; introduced in 1756. In some parts of its native habitat it attains the dimensions of a tree 20 to 25 ft high, with a trunk 1 to 1$\frac{1}{2}$ ft in girth. It has no special merit in this country.

E. BUNGEANUS Maxim.

A deciduous shrub or small tree, ultimately 15 to 30 ft high, of erect, rather thin habit, making long, slender, graceful, round branchlets, not downy in any part. Leaves oval or ovate, 1$\frac{1}{2}$ to 4 in. long, $\frac{3}{4}$ to 1$\frac{3}{4}$ in. wide; broadly wedge-shaped at the base, long and slender-pointed, the margins set with small incurved teeth; pale green and glabrous; stalk slender, $\frac{1}{3}$ to 1 in. long. Flowers yellowish white, $\frac{1}{4}$ in. across, the parts in fours, anthers purple; produced in cymes 1 to 2 in. long. Fruit four-lobed, glabrous, $\frac{1}{2}$ in. across, yellowish white tinged with pink, indented at the top, often unequal-sided through the non-development of the seed in one or more lobes; lobes angle-edged when barren, quite rounded when fertile. Aril orange-coloured. *Bot. Mag.*, t. 8656.

Native of N. China, Manchuria, etc. Seeds were sent to Kew by Dr Bret-schneider from N. China in 1883, which represent, so far as I am aware, its first introduction. In sunnier climates than ours it bears fruit abundantly and regularly.

With us it grows well and flowers freely, but a fine crop of fruit is rather exceptional. On such an occasion, however, the shrub is extremely effective. The
autumn colouring of the leaves is usually soft lemon-yellow, tinged with pink,
and develops rather early.

var. SEMIPERSISTENS (Rehd.) Schneid. *E. hamiltonianus* var. *semipersistens*
Rehd.—Leaves semi-persistent, remaining green well into the winter. Late-
fruiting. There is an example about 20 ft high in the R.H.S. Garden, Wisley, on
a short trunk.

E. EUROPAEUS L.   COMMON SPINDLE-TREE

A deciduous shrub or small tree from 10 to 25 ft high, forming a spreading,
bushy head, often naked towards the ground, not downy in any part. Leaves
narrowly oval, sometimes inclined to ovate or obovate, 1 to 3½ in. long, ⅓ to
1¼ in. wide, slender-pointed, tapered at the base, minutely toothed; stalk ¼ to
½ in. long. Cymes slender-stalked, 1 to 1½ in. long, usually three- or five-
flowered (sometimes more); flowers yellowish green, ½ in. across; petals and
stamens four. Fruit red, four-lobed, ½ to ¾ in. across; aril orange-coloured.

Native of Europe, including the British Isles. There is no more beautiful or
striking object in autumn than a fine spindle-tree well laden with fruit. It has a
number of varieties, some distinguished by the fruit, others by the foliage. One
may frequently see it in gardens as a small tree with a well-formed single trunk,
and Loudon records trees 25 to 35 ft high in Scotland. The wood is hard, and
was in earlier times much favoured for making spindles, hence the popular name.

f. ALBUS (West.) Rehd.—Fruits white. Although this does not produce the
rich effect of the type, it is very striking in contrast with it.

cv. 'ALDENHAMENSIS'.—Fine form of the spindle-tree which appeared in
the Hon. Vicary Gibbs' garden at Aldenham, Herts. It is distinguished by the
brilliant pink and larger size of the fruits, which are also, on account of the
longer stalks, more pendulous than in the type. It received an Award of Merit
on 17th October 1922.

var. ANGUSTIFOLIUS Reichb.—Leaves narrow-lanceolate.

cv. 'ATROPURPUREUS'.—Young shoots and leaves suffused with purple;
autumn colour crimson.

cv. 'AUCUBIFOLIUS'.—Leaves blotched with yellow; rather unsightly.

var. INTERMEDIUS Gaud. *E. europaeus* var. *macrophyllus* Reichb.—Described
by Gaudin in *Flora Helvetica*, in the year 1828, this, perhaps the finest of all the
forms of *E. europaeus*, has not spread in cultivation anything like so much as its
merits entitle it to have done. It was brought into notice in the autumn of 1919,
when Sydney Morris of Earlham Hall, Norwich, exhibited it in full fruit at a
show in Norwich, and again in 1920, when, on 5th October, he obtained from
the Royal Horticultural Society an Award of Merit for it as a beautiful fruit-
bearing shrub. It is distinguished chiefly by the large ovate leaves, sometimes
rounded at the base, which in a figure in Reichenbach's *Icones Florae Germanicae*,
t. 309, are shown as much as 3¾ in. long and 1¾ in. wide; they are even longer
and broader on specimens in Kew Herbarium collected in Italy. Mr Morris's

plant was also remarkable for the enormous crops of fruits it habitually produced and for their bright red colour and large size. In Switzerland this variety is found in Valais and Tessino, intermingled with the type, with which it is said to intergrade.

cv. 'RED CASCADE'.—A free-fruiting form raised by Messrs Jackman and given an Award of Merit in 1949.

E. FORTUNEI (Turcz.) Hand.-Mazz.

Elaeodendron fortunei Turcz.; *E. japonicus* var. *acutus* Rehd.;
E. radicans var. *acutus* (Rehd.) Rehd.

This species, closely allied to *E. japonicus*, is chiefly represented in cultivation by the Japanese variety described below. *E. fortunei*, in its typical state, is confined to the mainland of E. Asia and differs from the Japanese var. *radicans* in its leaves, which are elliptic to elliptic-ovate, 1 to 2½ in. long, with the veins prominent beneath and also rather thicker in texture than in var. *radicans* and not so strongly toothed.

var. RADICANS (Miq.) Rehd. *E. japonicus* var. *radicans* Miq.; *E. radicans* Sieb.; *E. repens* Carr.—A creeping, evergreen, glabrous shrub, rooting as it spreads over the ground, but when trained up house-fronts and such-like places reaching 20 ft or more high; branches minutely warty. Leaves oval or somewhat ovate, ordinarily ½ to 1¼ in. long, ¼ to ⅝ in. wide; tapering about equally to the base and to the blunt apex, shallowly round-toothed, dark green and glabrous; stalk $\frac{1}{12}$ in. long, warty. Flowers and fruits as in *E. japonicus*, but somewhat smaller.

Native of Japan. So far as I have observed, this euonymus never bears flowers or fruit in what we regard as its typical climbing or trailing condition. It appears to be like the ivy, and when it has arrived at the adult or flowering state alters the character of its growth, and instead of the shoots being slender and trailing they become erect and bushy, and bear flowers and fruit of the same character as those of *E. japonicus*; the leaves also become larger. As a garden shrub it is extremely useful; it thrives almost as well as the ivy in deep shade, and makes an admirable ground covering in sunny positions also. It may be used as an edging for paths, being of less trouble, although not so neat, as box-edging. It can be increased with great rapidity and ease by simply pulling old plants apart into small pieces and replanting; every bit will grow. In the New England States, where ivy is not hardy, this plant is used for covering the fronts of dwelling-houses.

f. CARRIEREI (Vauvel) Rehd.—This is the adult state of var. *radicans*, taken off and rooted as so-called 'tree' ivies are. It is a low, spreading shrub with no inclination to climb; leaves 1 to 2 in. long, ⅝ in. to 1 in. wide, glossy. Flowers greenish, four-parted, five or more crowded at the end of a slender stalk; fruit orange-shaped, greenish white or tinged with red, ⅓ in. across; seed with an orange-yellow coat (*Rev. Hort.*, 1881, p. 373, and ibid., 1885, p. 295, with figures).

cv. 'COLORATA'.—Leaves turning crimson-purple in the autumn and remaining so throughout the winter.

cv. 'KEWENSIS'.—This curious little plant—a var. *radicans* in miniature—was introduced from Japan by Prof. Sargent, and sent by him to Kew in 1893. Leaves dull green, with the veins picked out in a paler shade; ¼ to ⅜ in. long, ⅛ to about ¼ in. diameter; ovate, rounded at the base, blunt at the apex, margin slightly decurved and with a few shallow teeth; distinctly, but very shortly stalked. The whole plant, but especially the young shoots, is densely covered with minute warts. In a young state this plant forms low patches an inch or two high. Afterwards, if near a shrub, it will climb up its stems. When support of this kind is lacking it will form a little pyramid of its own branches, growing erect and clinging together. About 1938, Mr Ernest Brown (father of Mr George Brown, Assistant Curator at Kew) planted a piece of 'Kewensis' against the trunk of an oak and found that as it grew upwards it gradually developed into the ordinary juvenile state of *E. fortunei* var. *radicans* and pushed branches outwards and above the supporting trunk. But at the base of the trunk the plant was still of the original 'Kewensis' form (*Gard. Chron.*, Vol. 108, 1940, p. 146). Eventually, in 1958, the aerial branches flowered. Material from Mr Brown's plant, showing all stages of development, is preserved in the Kew Herbarium.

cv. 'MINIMUS'.—Similar to 'Kewensis' but with somewhat larger leaves.

cv. 'SILVER QUEEN'.—This is perhaps the best of the shrubby 'tree' forms. The largest leaves are 2½ in. long and more than 1 in. wide, handsomely variegated in white. It is a little uncertain whether 'Silver Queen' is invariably bushy. Certainly some of the plants in commerce under the name will climb vigorously but quickly produce aerial stems with leaves up to 2½ in. long. It has not been possible to ascertain who first published the name 'Silver Queen', but 'SILVER GEM' was put into commerce by Messrs Veitch in 1885. This is less bushy when grown in the open, with smaller leaves which, in the plant at Kew, have the silver margins stained with red. On a wall it climbs vigorously.

cv. 'VARIEGATUS'.—Leaves are rather larger than in ordinary *radicans*, with a broad marginal band of white, the centre greyish. Introduced from Japan about 1860. When this variety reaches the adult state, the flowering portion assumes a shrubby character and the leaves become larger. As Carrière put it, 'Variegatus' is a "larval stage" which gradually develops towards the adult state and many slightly differing forms may be obtained from the same individual (he claimed to have raised six, though two of these were reversions to the green form). It cannot therefore be regarded as a fixed clone. The red staining often seen on the margins of the leaves is also perhaps a fluctuating character, though plants showing this character were known under such epithets as *roseo-marginatus* or *roseo-variegatus*. It should be added that the cultivar name 'Variegatus' is adopted here because it is the one which seems to have been most used in Britain. On the continent mainly, the names 'Argenteo-marginata' or 'Gracilis' are in use.

var. VEGETUS (Rehd.) Rehd.—This appears to be no more than a minor geographical variant, described from a specimen collected in the North Island of Japan near Sapporo and introduced to the Arnold Arboretum from the same area in 1876. It fruits freely and its adult leaves are broad-elliptic to roundish. What is usually seen under this name is the adult, bushy state, which can be made, however, to cover a fence or low wall if trained.

E. FRIGIDUS Wall.

An evergreen or semi-evergreen shrub to about 15 ft high, glabrous in all its parts. Young growths green, four-angled; buds large, pointed, to $\frac{2}{5}$ in. long. Leaves opposite, oblong to lanceolate, more or less long-acuminate at the apex, up to $5\frac{1}{2}$ in. long, lustrous dark green, with the venation prominent on both sides; margins finely saw-toothed. Flowers borne seven to fifteen together in lax, slender-stalked cymes; petals four, greenish yellow or purple, sometimes

EUONYMUS CORNUTUS

whitish at the margin. Fruits pendulous; capsule with four wings attached near the base; seeds white, almost enclosed by the orange-red aril. *Bot. Mag.*, n.s., t. 161.

Native of the E. Himalaya, Upper Burma and Yunnan; described in 1824 but apparently not introduced until 1931, when Kingdon Ward sent seed under his KW 10124 from the border between Burma and Assam, where it grows at around 9,000 ft altitude. The material for the figure in the *Botanical Magazine* was taken from plants growing at Trewithen in Cornwall, where the species is quite hardy.

E. CORNUTUS Hemsl.—An ally of the preceding. The points of difference are: leaves linear-lanceolate, with veins making an angle of less than 45° with the midrib; cymes usually three-flowered; fruits with four very prominent wings (to $\frac{1}{2}$ in. long) attached near the middle of the capsule and produced outwards as a horn-like prolongation. The fruits are five-horned in var. QUINQUECORNUTUS (Comber) Blakelock.

This species has a wide distribution in W. and S.W. China; introduced by Wilson in 1908 and later by Forrest. An elegant foliage plant remarkable for its large, ridged and horned fruits. It varies in the degree of persistence of its leaves and, as seen in cultivation, is usually more or less deciduous.

E. GRANDIFLORUS Wall.

This species is represented in cultivation by the following form, which seems to differ from the type only in its narrower leaves:

f. SALICIFOLIUS Stapf & F. Ballard—A semi-evergreen tree 25 ft or more high, or a shrub; young shoots slender, glabrous, slightly ribbed. Leaves lanceolate to narrrowly oval, slender-pointed, wedge-shaped at the base, finely toothed; 2 to 4½ in. long, ⅝ to 1¼ in. wide, dark bright green, glabrous on both sides; stalk ½ in. or less long. Flowers greenish or yellowish white, three to nine on a cymose inflorescence, the main-stalk of which is 1 to 2 in. long; the individual flower 1 in. wide on a stalk ⅓ to ½ in. long. Petals four, wrinkled, roundish, ⅓ in. wide; calyx-lobes shallow, reflexed (especially on the fruit); disk large. Fruit four-lobed, ⅝ in. wide, four-ribbed, pale pink; seeds black. *Bot. Mag.*, t. 9183.

Native of N. India (Nepal, Khasia, Bhutan) and of W. China. It was cultivated at Kew in 1867 but was afterwards apparently lost to cultivation until reintroduced from Bhutan by Cooper about 1914, under his number 3562. Plants raised from his seed succeeded very well with the late Sir Chas. Cave at Sidbury Manor, Sidmouth, from whom I had handsome fruit-bearing branches in November 1925. Plants of the same origin have proved quite hardy at Kew and Glasnevin, very healthy, of spreading habit and free growth. It also grows well on chalk at Highdown in Sussex, where two plants have made a clump 20 ft across. It was given an Award of Merit when shown from there in 1953. Plants have also been raised from seeds collected by Forrest in Yunnan in 1922, and from seeds sent home by his collectors in 1933, also from Yunnan.

Judging by specimens in Kew Herbarium from both India and China, *E. grandiflorus* is variable in leaf, the majority having obovate leaves much shorter and broader than in Cooper's plant and with rounded ends; the fruits, however, seem to be fairly uniform in size and shape.

The broad-leaved, more typical form of the species grows at Wakehurst Place in Sussex. This has the leaves up to 4¾ in. long, 2½ in. wide (narrower on the spurs). They are noticeably thicker and glossier than in the narrow-leaved form growing nearby, and turn purple or bronze in the autumn.

E. HAMILTONIANUS Wall.

E. lanceifolius Loes.; *E. europaeus* var. *hamiltonianus* (Wall.) Maxim.;
E. hamiltonianus var. *australis* Komar.

This species, widely distributed in the Himalaya and the Far East, is closely related to the common spindleberry, differing in having the anthers purplish or reddish purple instead of yellow. It is a deciduous or semi-evergreen shrub or a small tree up to 30 ft high. Leaves variable, in size, shape, and relative width, broadest at or slightly below the middle, but sometimes oblanceolate to obovate, 2½ to 6 in. long, ¾ to 2½ in. or slightly more wide, shortly toothed, glabrous on both sides or downy on the veins beneath. Capsules pink, four-lobed; aril orange to blood-red, sometimes split and exposing the seed.

E. hamiltonianus is a taxonomically difficult group, in need of detailed study. It does not subdivide neatly, but plants from the north-eastern corner of its range are distinct in their slender leaves (see var. *maackii*). Plants from Japan,

S. Korea, and Sakhalin have been separated from *E. hamiltonianus* as *E. sieboldianus*, but all the characters given by Rehder to distinguish this species can be found in Himalayan plants. Komarov placed *E. sieboldianus* under *E. hamiltonianus* as a variety and gave as the difference that in var. *sieboldianus* the flowers are heterostylous: those with long styles have stamens with short filaments and *vice versa*, whereas in typical *E. hamiltonianus* the tendency is for flowers with long styles to have long filaments and *vice versa* (C. Jeffrey, *Bot. Mag.*, n.s., t. 548). It is possible that there are also statistical differences in size and shape of leaves and fruits, etc. The Japanese plants, like those of China and the Himalaya, are variable, and Koehne's three "species"—*E. yedoensis*, *E. semiexsertus*, and *E. hians*—represent slightly differing forms and were described from cultivated plants. See further below, under var. *sieboldianus*.

Typical *E. hamiltonianus* is represented in cultivation by plants known by the synonymous name *E. lanceifolius*; these were probably all raised from Wilson's No. 1105, collected in W. China during his expedition for the Arnold Arboretum. They are semi-evergreen, vigorous large shrubs or small trees up to 30 ft high, but do not fruit freely. Wilson also sent seeds from W. China when collecting for Veitch (W. 1202), and the material figured in *Bot. Mag.*, n.s., t. 181, came from a plant at Kew raised from this number.

var. MAACKII (Rupr.) Komar. *E. maackii* Rupr.; *E. europaea* var. *maackii* (Rupr.) Reg.—Leaves narrow-elliptic to lanceolate, mostly 2¼ to 4 in. long, ¾ to 1 in. wide (smaller on the flowering twigs), tapered at both ends, the apex acute, acuminate or even caudate, dark green above, paler beneath, edged with fine incurved teeth; leaf-stalk ¼ to ¾ in. long. Flowers and fruits as in typical *E. hamiltonianus*, but the inflorescences are perhaps fewer-flowered on the average. Native of the Russian Far East, Korea, and N.E. China; described (as a species) in 1857 from specimens collected by Richard Maack on the Amur River; introduced to Kew before 1880.

var. SIEBOLDIANUS (Bl.) Komar. *E. sieboldianus* Bl.; *E. hamiltonianus* subsp. *sieboldianus* (Bl.) Hara; *E. yedoensis* Koehne; *E. hians* Koehne; *E. semiexsertus* Koehne; *E. nikoensis* Nakai; varieties based by Blakelock on the preceding four species; *E. vidalii* Fr. & Sav.—This variety is mainly represented in gardens by the plants called "*E. yedoensis*", with obovate or elliptic leaves up to 5 in. long and 3 in. wide, pink capsules and seeds with an orange almost closed aril. Plants were in commerce under this name before Koehne formally described the "species" in 1904, and are believed to have been introduced from Japan by the American nurseryman Parsons about 1865. In autumn the leaves turn to various shades of rose and red and make a lovely combination with the pink fruits. But the autumn colour varies, either because it depends on soil and situation, or because there is more than one clone in the trade. Another form of the Japanese spindleberry was named *E. semiexsertus* by Koehne. In this the aril is open on one side, exposing the true seed-coat.

E. JAPONICUS Thunb.

An evergreen shrub or small tree of densely leafy, bushy habit 10 to 15, sometimes 25 ft high, free from down in all its parts. Leaves obovate to narrowly oval, 1 to 3 in. long, ¾ to 1¾ in. wide; leathery, dark polished green, tapered at the base, usually blunt or rounded at the apex, obscurely round-toothed; stalk ¼ to ½ in. long. Flowers ⅓ in. across, four-parted, greenish white, five to twelve in stoutly stalked cymes. Fruit glabrous, globose, ⅓ in. across, pinkish; aril pale orange.

Native of Japan; introduced in 1804. Although tender in cold districts, this species is hardy over the south of England, only occasionally being injured. It is a handsome and cheerful evergreen much used in south coast watering-places for hedges, where the sea air seems to suit it.

cv. 'ALBOMARGINATUS'.—Leaves with a thin margin of white.

cv. 'AUREUS'.—Centre of leaf bright yellow with only a marginal line of dark green. Like many shrubs with this type of variegation, it is very apt to revert to the green type.

cv. 'DUC d'ANJOU'.—Leaves dark green, marked with yellowish and greyish green.

cv. 'LATIFOLIUS ALBOMARGINATUS'.—Leaves broadly oval with a wide margin of white. Also known as 'Latifolius Variegatus' and 'Macrophyllus Albus'.

cv. 'MACROPHYLLUS'.—Leaves green, larger than in the type. Introduced from Japan by Siebold and thence to this country by Henderson's nursery, St John's Wood. 'LATIFOLIUS', introduced by Veitch's nursery, is similar.

cv. 'MICROPHYLLUS'.—A very distinct, dwarf, small-leaved form, 1 to 3 ft high, with quite erect branches; leaves dark green, oval-lanceolate, ½ to 1 in. long, ¼ to ⅓ in. wide. More tender than the type. Introduced by Siebold.

cv. 'MICROPHYLLUS PULCHELLUS'.—Leaves very small, variegated with gold.

cv. 'OVATUS AUREUS'.—Perhaps the best of the golden variegated forms; Leaves oval or ovate, with a broad, irregular margin of rich yellow, which suffuses into the green centre.

There are numerous other forms slightly different from the above. *E. japonicus* and all its varieties need a soil of moderate richness only; they are all easily rooted from cuttings.

E. KIAUTSCHOVICUS Loes.
E. patens Rehd.

An evergreen or semi-deciduous shrub up to 9 or 10 ft high, of spreading habit, not downy in any part. Leaves oval or obovate, 2 to 3 in. long, ¾ to 1¾ in. wide; tapered at the base, pointed or bluntish at the apex, round-toothed, of firm texture, and bright green; stalk ¼ in. or less long. Flowers greenish white, ⅓ in. across, four-parted, numerous, on loose erect cymes 1½ to 4 in. wide, on a main-stalk 1 to 1½ in. long. Fruit nearly ½ in. across, pink, glabrous and not lobed; aril orange-red.

A native of China, whence it was introduced into the United States, about 1860, by Dr G. R. Hall. Small plants were sent to Kew in 1905, but it may have been in cultivation before as *E. japonicus*. To that species it is very closely akin, but is probably hardier. It has a wider inflorescence, and its habit is laxer than in *E. japonicus*, the lower branches often taking root. The leaves are thinner, more pointed, and more finely toothed. It fruits late in the autumn, November 28 being the date on which it received an Award of Merit when shown from Regent's Park in 1961.

E. LATIFOLIUS (L.) Mill.   [PLATE 26

E. europaeus var. *latifolius* L.

A deciduous shrub or small tree 10 ft or more high, with a spreading, loose head of branches, glabrous in all its parts; young shoots angled, winter buds elongated. Leaves oval, oblong or obovate, 3 to 5 in. long, 1½ to 2¼ in. wide, rounded or wedge-shaped at the base, pointed, very finely and evenly toothed; stalk about ¼ in. long. Flowers greenish, about ⅜ in. across, the parts normally in fives, produced in early May, seven to fifteen together, on very slender-stalked cymes 2 to 3 ins. long. Fruits pendulous, ¾ in. across before bursting, rich rosy red with five, sometimes four, winged lobes; aril orange-coloured. *Bot. Mag.*, t. 2384.

Native of Europe; introduced in 1730. Excepting the native *E. europaeus*, this is the most ornamental of all the genus in our gardens; its individual fruit is much larger and more effective than that of the common spindle-tree but is not borne in such profusion. Grown as a small tree in rich deep soil, it will reach 20 ft in height, and such a specimen, hung with its long-stalked fruit in September, is one of the most beautiful objects of autumn.

E. LUCIDUS D. Don

E. pendulus Wall., nom. prov.; *E. fimbriatus* Hort., not Wall.

A small evergreen tree; young shoots not downy, but covered with a pale waxy substance. Leaves opposite, narrowly oval to lanceolate, slender-pointed, tapered more abruptly to the base, the margins regularly set with fine, simple, even teeth; 2 to 5 in. long, ¾ to 1½ in. wide; of firm leathery texture; of a rich shining red when young, becoming dark shining green with age; stalk ¼ to ½ in. long. Flowers numerous, produced in May in cymes about 1½ in. long; small, greenish and of no beauty. Fruit ½ in. wide, four-lobed; wings thin; aril orange.

Native of the Himalaya, where it is said to occur locally from Hazara to Assam, but to be nowhere common; introduced about 1850. It is not hardy near London, but succeeds well to the south and west, nowhere perhaps better than in the Channel Islands. A correspondent in Jersey writes: 'Mine is quite a tall tree, lovely in the spring, when the whole of it is covered with blood-red young leaves.' It is also common in Cornish gardens and has attained a height of 46 ft at Tregothnan.

This euonymus has been confused with E. FIMBRIATUS Wall., a quite distinct species with deciduous leaves jaggedly or doubly toothed, and larger fruits 1 in. wide. *E. pendulus* Wall., under which *E. lucidus* appeared in previous editions, is a provisional name and has no standing under nomenclatural rules. The name *E. lucidus* was published in *Prodr. Fl. Nepal.*, p. 191 (1825).

E. MACROPTERUS Rupr.
E. ussuriensis Maxim.

A deciduous shrub 10 ft or more high, of spreading habit, glabrous in all its parts; winter buds spindle-shaped, ¼ in. long. Leaves obovate or oval, mostly slender-pointed, wedge-shaped at the base, finely toothed; 2½ to 4 in. long, 1 to 1½ in. wide; dark glossy green; veins in four or five pairs; stalk ¼ to ⅓ in. long. Flowers small, numerous, green, copiously produced in May on slender-stalked cymes 1 to 2 in. long. Fruits ⅞ in. wide, pink, four-winged; wings ¼ in. long, thin, narrowing to a rounded end; aril deep red.

Native of Pacific Russia, Korea, Manchuria, and Japan; introduced in 1905 by Messrs Veitch, who distributed it under the name "*E. sachalinensis*". It is a very hardy shrub and grows vigorously at Kew. A fine plant, 14 ft in diameter and 10 ft high, with long arching branches, is in the collection there which bears fruit regularly.

E. MYRIANTHUS Hemsl.
E. sargentianus Loes. & Rehd.

A quite glabrous, evergreen shrub up to 12 or 15 ft high, of rounded, bushy shape. Leaves oval-lanceolate to oblong-ovate, 2 to 4½ in. long, ¾ to 1¾ in. wide, edged with very shallow, spine-tipped teeth. Flowers greenish yellow, in dense, rounded, three or four times divided, terminal clusters 2 or 3 in. across. Fruit ⅝ in. long, somewhat square-sided and four-lobed, ½ in. wide at the flat top, tapering thence to the stalk. The fruits are yellow, but their full beauty is only attained when they ripen and split and expose the seeds which become orange-scarlet in December; the tapering stalk is 1 in. or more long. *Bot. Mag.*, n.s., t. 64.

Native of W. China, discovered by Henry and introduced by Wilson in 1908. It flowered with P. D. Williams at Lanarth in 1929 and in several gardens since. It is quite hardy at Kew and a bush there is 10 ft. high and wide and very attractive in early winter. At Wisley it is 12 ft high and fruits regularly.

E. NANUS Bieb.

A low, deciduous or partially evergreen shrub of thin, spreading or procumbent habit, growing 1 to 3 ft high; its young branches long and slender, glabrous, angled. Leaves alternate or opposite, or in a terminal whorl, ¾ to 1½ in. long, 1/12 to 3/16 in. wide, tapered at the base, linear to narrow-oblong, blunt or pointed at the apex, the margins obscurely toothed or entire, glabrous; stalk ½ in. long. Flowers inconspicuous, brown-purple, ⅙ in. across, four-parted, one to three on a very slender stalk ½ to 1¼ in. long. Fruits four-lobed, pink with the outer coat (aril) of the seed orange-coloured; they are about ½ in. long, scarcely as wide. *Bot. Mag.*, t. 9308.

Native of the Caucasus, eastward to China; introduced in 1830. This species, so distinct from all others in cultivation in its narrow, rosemary-like, often alternate leaves, is an interesting shrub but of no great merit in most districts as it does not bear its fruit regularly or freely.

var. TURKESTANICA (Dieck) Krishtofovich   *E. nanus* var. *koopmannii* Koehne—Of sturdier, more erect growth and broader leaves not decurved at the margin. Found by Koopmann on the Thian-Shan and Altai mountains.

E. OBOVATUS Nutt.

A deciduous shrub of usually trailing habit, rarely more than 1 ft above the ground, not downy in any part. Leaves dull green, obovate, tapered at the base, bluntish at the apex; 1 to 2½ in. long, ½ to 1⅓ in. wide; finely or obscurely toothed; stalk ⅛ in. or less long. Flowers ¼ in. wide, greenish purple, with five rounded petals; they are produced during May and June singly, or in threes, on slender stalks ½ to 1¼ in. long. Fruit usually three-lobed, ½ to ¾ in. across, crimson, covered with prickly warts; covering of the seeds scarlet.

Native of eastern N. America; introduced in 1820. This is one of the few warty-fruited species in cultivation, and is closely allied to *E. americanus* (q.v.). Its prostrate habit enables it to take root as it spreads, and thus it may be used where an interesting low ground cover is desired. It thrives better under cultivation than *E. americanus*, and bears fruit occasionally, but is never showy. In a wild state it inhabits damp spots.

E. ORESBIUS W. W. Sm.

A deciduous shrub 5 or 6 ft high; young shoots distinctly square and four-angled, not downy. Leaves linear to oblanceolate, rounded at the end, tapered at the base, margins indistinctly toothed or entire; ½ to ⅞ in. long, ¹⁄₁₆ to ⅛ in. wide; rather pale green and quite glabrous; stalk ¹⁄₁₆ in. long. Flowers borne in June on slender-stalked short cymes, one to three together, green. Fruit four-lobed, scarcely ½ in. wide, four-winged, rich rosy red, eventually showing the scarlet-coated seeds. The fruits are pendulous and usually solitary on a slender stalk ¼ to ½ in. long.

Native of Yunnan, China; discovered by Forrest in 1913 and introduced by him. It is undoubtedly one of the most distinct species in cultivation on account of its small narrow leaves, resembling in this respect *E. nanus*; that species, however, is quite different in its low, prostrate mode of growth. Seen in October with its richly coloured fruits hanging thickly from the underside of its branchlets, *E. oresbius* is very charming. There is a specimen in the Royal Horticultural Society's Garden at Wisley some 9 ft in height, which is the parent of the plants now at Kew.

E. OXYPHYLLUS Miq.

A deciduous small tree up to 25 ft high, with a trunk 3 ft in girth, or a shrub; young shoots glabrous; terminal winter buds pointed, up to ½ in. long. Leaves

EUONYMUS

ovate or ovate-oblong, toothed, tapered towards each end; $1\frac{1}{2}$ to $3\frac{1}{2}$ in. long, 1 to $1\frac{3}{4}$ in. wide; dull green above, pale beneath, glabrous on both sides; stalk $\frac{1}{6}$ in. long. Inflorescence a twice- or thrice-branched cyme; flowers $\frac{3}{8}$ in. wide; petals rounded, greenish purple. Fruit nearly globose, pendulous on long slender stalks, slightly ribbed, rich carmine, $\frac{1}{2}$ in. wide before bursting; afterwards, when the five, sometimes only four, lobes separate, it is 1 in. wide, revealing the scarlet-coated seeds within. *Bot. Mag.*, t. 8639.

Native of Japan and Korea; introduced to this country in 1895. It is very similar in general appearance to E. *latifolius*, but is easily recognised in fruit by the capsules being without the prominent wings characteristic of that species and having only slightly raised lines. A perhaps nearer ally is E. *planipes*, but that is distinguished by its smaller, more distinctly angled fruits. When freely furnished with its richly coloured fruits hanging on their long slender stalks, usually in September, E. *oxyphyllus* is very handsome. At Westonbirt in mid-October there are few more beautiful shrubs than this. The autumn colour of the leaves is a dusky purplish red which, with the bright orange of the arils and the rich maroon of the capsules, creates a most striking display. The bushes there are some 6 to 8 ft in height, of an elegant wine-glass shape.

E. PENDULUS *see* E. LUCIDUS

E. PHELLOMANUS Loes.

A deciduous shrub 6 to 10 ft high, of vigorous spreading habit; young shoots glabrous, furnished with four conspicuous corky wings, which give them a square shape. Leaves oval to obovate, slender-pointed, tapered to almost rounded at the base, finely and bluntly toothed; 2 to $4\frac{1}{2}$ in. long, 1 to 2 in. wide; dullish green above, strongly veined beneath, glabrous on both sides; veins in seven to eleven pairs; stalk $\frac{1}{4}$ to $\frac{1}{2}$ in. long. Flowers three to seven on a cyme less than 1 in. long; anthers purple. Fruits four-lobed, four-angled, $\frac{1}{2}$ in. wide, rich rosy red; aril deep red.

Native of Kansu and Shensi, China; collected in the latter province by Giraldi in 1894. The plants in cultivation were introduced by Farrer under his number 392. At Highdown, near Worthing, there is a large bush raised from this seed. E. *phellomanus* is quite hardy at Kew and has borne fruit there. Its most conspicuous feature is the corky-winged young shoots, and on that account it can only be confused with E. *alatus*. But it is quite distinct from *alatus* in the larger, longer-stalked, conspicuously net-veined leaves. The deeply divided (almost separate) egg-shaped lobes of the fruit of E. *alatus* are also very distinctive.

E. PLANIPES (Koehne) Koehne

E. *latifolius* var. *planipes* Koehne; E. *sachalinensis* (Fr. Schmidt) Maxim., in part, not E. *latifolius* var. *sachalinensis* Fr. Schmidt

A deciduous shrub or small tree, closely akin to E. *latifolius*, and of similar habit and dimensions and with the same long, pointed winter buds. The leaves are like those of that species in most respects, but are coarsely toothed, and the stalk is not channelled on the upper side. The fruit is four- or five-lobed, as in E. *latifolius*, but differs in having the top conical; nor are the wings of each lobe flattened and knife-like as in E. *latifolius*. Except in these respects the two differ but little.

Native of Japan, Korea, the Russian Far East, and N.E. China; introduced to Kew from the Arnold Arboretum in 1895. It is quite as handsome a species as E. *latifolius*, both for its fruit and its red autumn colour, but only in recent years have its merits come to be at all widely appreciated.

E. SACHALINENSIS (Fr. Schmidt) Maxim. E. *latifolius* var. *sachalinensis* Fr. Schmidt—Although closely related to E. *planipes*, this species is well distinguished by its purple or dark red flowers and its small, few-flowered inflorescences. Native of Sakhalin; probably not in cultivation. The species is typified by the plant of Sakhalin which Schmidt described originally as a variety of E. *latifolius*. Maximowicz later raised this variety to the specific level, and at the same time published a new description which, as is clear from the description itself and from the specimens he cites, includes plants which are really E. *planipes*.

In Japan, E. *sachalinensis* is represented by var. TRICARPUS (Koidz.) Kudo, distinguished by the fruits being three-lobed against five-lobed in the type.

E. SANGUINEUS Loes.

A deciduous shrub up to 20 ft high, devoid of down in all its parts; young shoots reddish; winter buds elongated. Leaves ovate, oval, or obovate, 1½ to 4½ in. long, ¾ to 2¼ in. wide; margins set with fine incurved teeth, the base broadly wedge-shaped or rounded, the apex slenderly pointed; dull green; chief veins in four to seven pairs. Flowers yellow, produced in thin, forked cymes, 3 or 4 in. wide and long. Fruit composed of four (rarely five) parts, each part furnished with a wing ⅓ in. long, the whole fruit nearly 1 in. wide, red, showing when split the yellow-coated seed.

Native of central and western China, introduced by Wilson in 1900. It appears to be closely allied to E. *latifolius*, which is, however, distinct in its larger, thinner leaves, more often five-parted flowers, larger fruits with shorter wings, and longer winter buds. A plant in the Mitchell Drive at Westonbirt is attractive even before the autumn colour sets in, on account of the purplish red tinge of the leathery leaves.

E. SEMENOWII Reg. & Herd.

A deciduous shrub up to 10 ft high; young shoots indistinctly four-angled, glabrous. Leaves linear-lanceolate to lanceolate, gradually tapered to the pointed apex, more abruptly so towards the base, very finely toothed; 1 to 2 in. long, ¼ to ½ in. wide; quite glabrous. Flowers produced during May and June generally in threes at the end of a slender, thread-like stalk 1 to 1½ in. long. They are about ¼ in. wide and Wilson gives their colour as 'dark red', Forrest as 'dull greenish crimson'. The fruit is four-lobed, not winged, about ½ in. wide before splitting, seed-coat orange.

Originally named in 1866 from material collected in Turkestan. What is considered to be this species was also found by Wilson in Szechwan in 1908 and by Forrest in the same province in 1922. I saw a healthy plant in the Arboretum of the Edinburgh Botanic Garden, blooming very freely in June 1931 (flowers green), but I learn it has never borne fruit there. Its leaves were then linear and about 1 in. long, borne on gracefully arching branches. The whole shrub struck me as attractive, even without fruit. This plant is now (1966) 8 ft high and 10 ft across. It has never fruited.

E. TINGENS Wall.

An evergreen shrub up to 20 or 25 ft high, devoid of down in all its parts; of bushy habit; young shoots angled; young bark grey. Leaves narrowly oval to lanceolate, tapered towards both ends, finely toothed; 1½ to 3 in. long, ⅜ to 1¼ in. wide; dark glossy green, pale beneath; stalk ¼ in. or less long. Flowers ½ in. wide, 'creamy-white marbled or veined with deep purple' (Forrest), produced in May and June in once- or twice-branched cymes 1 to 1½ in. wide. Fruit ½ to ⅝ in. wide, four- or five-angled, described as flesh-coloured; aril scarlet.

Native of the Himalaya, where it is found up to 10,000 ft altitude, also of Yunnan and Szechwan, China. Originally described by Wallich in 1824, it was cultivated by Jackson of Kingston, Surrey, in the middle of last century, having probably been introduced by Joseph Hooker from India between 1847 and 1851. Forrest collected it several times in W. China. A healthy bush once grew in the rock garden in Edinburgh Botanic Garden, which in June 1931 was 5 ft high and 6 ft wide. A distinctive feature of the species appears to be the purple veins on the petals, which are specially noted by both Wallich and Forrest.

E. VERRUCOSUS Scop.

A deciduous shrub of dense-branched, rounded habit 6 to 10 ft high; bark of the younger branches covered densely with conspicuous warts. Leaves ovate, ovate-lanceolate, or oval; 1 to 2½ in. long, ½ to 1 in. wide; finely toothed, slender-pointed, rounded or wedge-shaped at the base; stalk 1/12 in. long. Cymes with very slender stalks about 1 in. long, usually three- sometimes seven-flowered. Flowers purplish brown, ¼ in. across, four-parted. Fruit yellowish or red, ½ in. across; seed black, with an outer coat of orange.

Native of E. Europe and W. Asia; introduced from Austria in 1763. This species is readily recognised among all cultivated spindle-trees by the remarkably warted bark. It bears fruit very sparingly with us, and has little to recommend it as an ornamental shrub.

E. WILSONII Sprague

An evergreen shrub up to 20 ft high, of lax or scandent habit, quite free from down in leaf and twig; young shoots slender. Leaves 3 to 6 in. long, 1 to 1¾ in.

wide, lanceolate, wedge-shaped at the base, gradually tapered at the apex to a long slender point; shallowly and rather distinctly toothed; conspicuously veined beneath; stalk $\frac{1}{4}$ to $\frac{1}{2}$ in. long. Fruits four-lobed, borne on a main-stalk $1\frac{1}{2}$ in. long; they are clothed with conspicuous, awl-shaped spines $\frac{1}{5}$ in. long, and are altogether about $\frac{3}{4}$ in. across; aril yellow.

Introduced from Mt Omei in W. China by Wilson in 1904, and now growing vigorously in the collection at Kew. It is distinct from cultivated spindle-trees in the remarkable hedgehog-like fruits.

EUPATORIUM COMPOSITAE

A large genus of herbs and shrubs, mostly in Central and S. America but also represented in the Old World. The herbaceous *E. cannabinum*, the hemp agrimony, is a British native.

E. LIGUSTRINUM DC.

E. micranthum Lessing; *E. weinmannianum* Reg. & Koern.; *Ageratina ligustrina* (DC.) R. M. King & H. Robinson

An evergreen bush of dense growth and hemispherical shape, as much as 9 ft high and wide, the whole of the plant free from down except the flower-stalk and the scales of the involucre. Young shoots slender, slightly angular, often purplish on the sunny side. Leaves opposite, elliptical to elliptical-lanceolate, sometimes inclined to obovate, mostly pointed, tapered at the base, shallowly or indistinctly toothed on the terminal half, 2 to 4 in. long, $\frac{3}{4}$ to $1\frac{1}{2}$ in. wide, pale bright green; stalk $\frac{1}{4}$ to $\frac{5}{8}$ in. long. Inflorescence a branching, flattish, rounded cluster of corymbs up to 8 in. wide. Flower-heads $\frac{1}{4}$ in. wide, each composed of six to ten florets surrounded at the base by an involucre of linear, downy scales. Florets tubular, $\frac{1}{4}$ in. long, creamy-white, sometimes slightly rose-tinted, charmingly fragrant, the bi-lobed stigmas much exposed.

Native of E. Mexico from Tamaulipas to Chiapas; and of Guatemala and Costa Rica. In gardens, where it is better known under one or other of the synonyms given above, it is most commonly grown as a pot plant, with greenhouse protection except during the summer. It is, however, hardy enough to be grown outdoors in the mildest parts; a plant at Logan in Wigtownshire has attained a height of 8 ft and a spread of 12 ft. A 6 ft plant at Belhaven House, E. Lothian, flowers throughout the winter and stood 12° of frost.

EUPHORBIA EUPHORBIACEAE

A large genus of herbs, succulents, shrubs and small trees, but of the species that can be counted as woody few are hardy in our climate. Indeed, the species treated below, with the exception of E. *mellifera* and E. *dendroides*, scarcely qualify as shrubs and might more properly be regarded as perennial-stemmed herbs. The apparent flower of *Euphorbia* is a condensed inflorescence known as a cyathium. The single pistillate flower is stalked and lacks both petals and calyx; male flowers numerous, each reduced to a single stamen; the whole surrounded by a calyx-like involucre, with glands between the lobes. The most conspicuous part of the total inflorescence is (in the species described) the pair of opposite bracts that subtends each cyathium.

E. WULFENII Hoppe ex Koch

E. *veneta* Willd., nom. confus; E. *sibthorpii* Boiss.; E. *characias* subsp. *wulfenii*
(Koch) A. R. Smith

A sub-shrubby evergreen plant 3 to 5 ft high and forming a dense thicket of erect unbranched stems of more herbaceous than woody character; increasing in size by new growths from below ground. Stems, leaves and flower-stalks covered with down. Stems ⅓ to ⅝ in. in thickness, round, the lower naked portion thickly marked with the scars of fallen leaves, the terminal portion so thickly set with leaves as to be hidden. Leaves linear, stalkless, not toothed, pointed, 1½ to 5 in. long, ¼ to ⅜ in. wide, blue-green. Inflorescence a terminal panicle as much as 8 to 12 in. high and 3 to 5 in. wide, but usually smaller. The most conspicuous feature of the panicle is provided by the pairs of bracts, which are united into an almost circular leaf-like structure; the final pairs in each subdivision are coloured bright greenish yellow and form a cup-shaped apparent involucre round each cyathium. Glands of the cyathium yellowish brown. *Bot. Mag.*, n.s., t. 482.

Native of Istria, Dalmatia and Greece; introduced some time previous to 1837, in which year it flowered in the Horticultural Society's Garden at Chiswick. The inflorescence opens in spring and remains in good colour for two or three months. The plant is quite hardy and can be propagated by division in spring. As the centre of old plants is liable to become worn out and to decay, a periodical division is advisable. On an April day some years ago I saw this euphorbia giving a wonderful display on some hills bordering the fine mountain road between Cattaro (Kotor) and Cetinje. So abundant were the plants that in places they gave quite a yellowish tinge to the hillsides. It is certainly one of the most ornamental hardy species in the large genus to which it belongs. Like all the spurges the younger parts exude a milky sap when cut or broken.

E. CHARACIAS L.—This closely related species is also in cultivation. It is easily distinguished from E. *wulfenii* by the conspicuous, purplish-brown glands of the cyathia. It has a much wider distribution in the Mediterranean than E. *wulfenii* (N. Africa and from Spain to Greece) and usually (both in the wild and in cultivation) makes a short-stemmed plant to about 3 ft high. The very robust plants sometimes seen in gardens are perhaps the result of chance crossing with E. *wulfenii*. Indeed, the distinction between the two species seems to have become blurred so far as the garden plants are concerned. Furthermore, the two species are so closely allied that it would not be surprising if they hybridised in the wild state where they come into contact, as they certainly do in Greece.

E. MELLIFERA Ait.—A native of Madeira and the Canary Islands, with brown, honey-scented flowers, opening in May. It is too tender for all but the mildest gardens. In the Ludgvan Rectory garden, Penzance, it was 8 ft high and 10 ft through in 1930 and Thurston mentions it as being 15 ft high at Pendrea in the same part of Cornwall. It is allied to E. DENDROIDES L., a native of the Mediterranean in dry, rocky places near the sea.

E. ROBBIAE Turrill—This new species was described by the late Dr Turrill in the *Botanical Magazine* under t. 208 (1953). It is an evergreen plant with stems perennial through several seasons, growing to about 2 ft high and spreading rapidly by underground runners and of great value as ground-cover in rougher places. Introduced by Mrs Robb from Asia Minor between the wars or perhaps earlier. It is allied to E. *amygdaloides* L., a widespread species native to Britain, from which it differs in its glabrous leathery leaves and larger seeds and seed-capsules.

EUPTELEA EUPTELEACEAE

A genus of two species—from N. India, Burma, China, and Japan. They are trees with conspicuously toothed, long-stalked leaves, and remarkable flowers of no beauty; they have no sepals or petals. Stamens numerous; pistils stalked, six to eighteen in number, each developing into a curious flat samara, rather resembling that of the elm, but wedge-shaped, and tapering gradually from a rounded apex to a slender stalk. The Japanese species, and the Chinese form of E. *pleiosperma*, are both quite hardy, of graceful form, and give good colour effects in autumn. Increased by layers or seed.

The eupteleas are of considerable botanical interest in belonging to an anomalous group including *Cercidiphyllum*, *Eucommia*, *Tetracentron*, and *Trochodendron*, whose true place in the vegetable kingdom is variously estimated. The view followed here is that it should rank as a monotypic family (Nast and Bailey, *Journ. Arn. Arb.*, Vol. 27, pp. 186–192, and Smith, ibid., pp. 175–185). Dr Hutchinson places *Euptelea* in the family Trochodendraceae.

E. PLEIOSPERMA Hook. f. & Thoms.

E. davidiana Baill.; *E. delavayi* Van Tiegh.; *E. franchetii* Van Tiegh.

A deciduous tree 20 to 40 ft high. Leaves broadly ovate, wedge-shaped at the base, the apex drawn out into a long narrow point, 2 to 4 in. long and often three-fourths as much wide, the margins irregularly toothed, but not so markedly

so as in E. *polyandra*, green or grey beneath; stalk half to two-thirds as long as the
blade. Flowers as in E. *polyandra* (q.v.). Fruit flat, narrowly wedge-shaped,
notched on one side, borne on a slender stalk ½ in. long, one- to three-seeded.

A native of the E. Himalaya, Upper Burma, S.W. and W. China; discovered
by Griffith in the Mishmi Hills and described in 1864. Three species were later
described from China, all from specimens collected by French missionaries, and
these have been variously treated by botanists. Hemsley considered that all the
Chinese material belonged to one species—E. *davidiana*—allied to but distinct
from E. *pleiosperma*, but his knowledge of the latter species was based on incom-

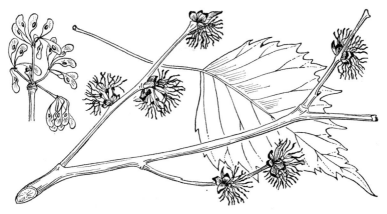

E u p t e l e a   p o l y a n d r a

plete material and the characters by which he distinguished it from the Chinese
trees do not hold good. The view of Rehder and Wilson was that E. *davidiana*
and E. *delavayi* both belonged to the synonymy of E. *pleiosperma*. But E. *franchetii* was maintained by them as a distinct species occupying an area of China
to the east of E. *pleiosperma* and differing from it in having the leaves green
beneath, not glaucous and papillose as in E. *pleiosperma*. This distinction hardly
holds good, however. The leaves of E. *pleiosperma* are covered beneath with
densely packed white cells; those of E. *franchetii* are essentially the same but the
cells are less dense and give more of a honeycomb effect. Furthermore, A. C.
Smith (*Journ. Arn. Arb.*, Vol. 27) has pointed out that this difference, such as it
is, is not so well correlated with geographical distribution as Rehder and Wilson
thought. His view, followed here, is that there is only one species on the mainland of E. Asia, namely E. *pleiosperma*.

E. *pleiosperma* was probably not introduced to Britain until 1900, when
Wilson sent seed from Hupeh (the plants raised from it have generally been
known as E. *franchetii*). There was an earlier introduction to France by Père
Farges and a tree from this seed flowered at Les Barres in 1900.

E. *pleiosperma* is closely allied to the Japanese E. *polyandra*, but differs in the
more regularly toothed leaves and in the fruits containing usually more than one
seed. The foliage of the Wilson introduction dies off a pretty red in the autumn.

E. POLYANDRA Sieb. & Zucc.

A deciduous tree 20 to 30 ft high, with a slender, straight trunk. Leaves broadly ovate to almost orbicular, 3 to 6 in. long and almost as much in width; often cut off straight or heart-shaped at the base, narrowing abruptly at the apex to a long drawn-out point, the margin is irregularly toothed, almost ragged; the leaf-stalk is often two-thirds as long as the blade. Flowers bisexual, borne in clusters, before the leaves; petals and calyx absent; stamens numerous, with red anthers; pistils stalked, six to eighteen in number, with sessile stigmas that are receptive only after the stamens in the same flower and cluster have fallen. Fruit an oblanceolate, obliquely notched samara, containing one seed.

Native of the forests of Central and S. Japan. This tree has some value in the garden, and although it has no beauty of flower its habit is good; its leaves are handsome and distinct in form, and they turn red and yellow before falling.

EUROTIA   CHENOPODIACEAE

A small genus distributed mostly in the more arid parts of the northern hemisphere.

E. CERATIOIDES (L.) C. A. Meyer.

Axyris ceratioides L.; *Diotis ceratioides* (L.) Willd.

A deciduous shrub of spreading habit 3 to 4 ft high, and twice or thrice as wide; branches long, slender, whitish, stellately downy. Leaves alternate, grey-white at first, becoming green, lance-shaped, pointed, ¾ to 2 in. long, ¼ to ½ in. wide, stellately downy especially beneath, and with three longitudinal veins. Flowers produced in July, densely packed in spikes ½ to 1½ in. long, and furnished with linear woolly bracts standing out beyond the flower; these spikes are terminal on short side twigs from the uppermost 1 or 2 feet of the year's shoot, the whole forming a slender panicle of that length. The upper part of each spike is composed of male flowers, grey and very woolly, with the yellow anthers protruding through the wool; below them, and situated in the leaf-axils, are one or two female flowers without sepals or petals, and so small as to be scarcely visible. The seed-vessel becomes covered with silky white hairs, ¼ in. long.

Native of the Caucasus and Asia Minor, eastward to China; introduced in 1780. Over this wide area it shows some variation in shape and size of the leaf, and in the amount of down upon it. In drying for the herbarium the leaves and fruits turn brown. The shrub has considerable botanical interest, but its only garden value is in providing a mass of grey-white foliage in summer. It is perfectly hardy, does not need a rich soil, and is easily increased by cuttings.

E. LANATA (Pursh) Moquin *Diotis lanata* Pursh—A species from western N. America, is also in cultivation. It is a grey-white shrub a yard high, clothed with starry down. Leaves linear, $\frac{1}{2}$ to $1\frac{1}{2}$ in. long, like those of lavender. Flowers in slender panicles 4 to 9 in. long, 1 to 2 in. wide. It inhabits dry regions, and is known as "white sage". Not apparently so good for gardens as *E. ceratioides*, from which it is distinguished by the more recurved margins of the leaves.

EURYA THEACEAE

A genus closely related to *Cleyera*, but distinguished by the smaller, dioecious flowers. There are some fifty species in S.E. Asia and a few in the Pacific.

E. JAPONICA Thunb.
E. pusilla Sieb.

A dwarf evergreen shrub, with alternate, dark, glossy green leaves, which are $1\frac{1}{2}$ to 3 in. long, oval or obovate, toothed, blunt at the apex, quite glabrous (like the twigs), shortly stalked. Flowers unisexual, very small and inconspicuous, white, produced singly or in twos or threes from the axils of the leaves; each flower $\frac{1}{8}$ in. across on a stalk about as long. Fruit black, and as large as a peppercorn. *Bot. Mag.*, n.s., t. 588.

At Kew this little shrub is hardy when once thoroughly established, but is sometimes injured by severe frost when young. It is easily increased by cuttings. What is considered by botanists to be the same species is found not only in China and Japan but in the mountains of N. and S. India, Ceylon, the Malay Archipelago, even as far east as Fiji. In these places, even in Japan, it sometimes becomes a small tree 30 ft high, but the form cultivated in Britain is quite a dwarf and slow-growing bush, and is perhaps the most northerly and hardiest form. It is evidently the plant distinguished as *E. pusilla* by Siebold, who gave several forms of this eurya specific rank. It is an interesting ally of the tea plant, and a neat little evergreen.

EURYOPS COMPOSITAE

A genus of about 100 species of evergreen shrubs, natives of Africa, with conspicuous yellow flower-heads borne singly on leafless stalks. Only the species described here is widely cultivated, but others, such as *E. pectinatus* and *E. virgineus*, are sometimes cultivated outdoors in the mildest parts. The standard work on the genus is: B. Nordenstam, 'The Genus *Euryops*', in *Opera Botanica* (Lund), No. 20 (1968).

E. ACRAEUS M. D. Henderson
E. *evansii* Hort., not Schlechter

A compact evergreen shrub growing to about 3 ft high, spreading by underground stems. Leaves silvery grey, borne in dense clusters near the ends of the branches, linear, three-toothed at the apex, stem-clasping at the base; veins parallel and impressed on the upper surface; margins involute; in cultivated specimens they are up to 1 in. long and ⅜ in. wide. Flower-heads canary-yellow, about 1 in. wide, with numerous ray-florets, produced in May from the axils of the uppermost leaves on scapes 1 to 2 in. long. Achenes woolly.

Native of the Drakensberg Mountains of Natal and Basutoland, discovered in the Cleft Peak area at 9,800 ft and first described in 1961; it had been introduced earlier by R. B. Purves of Evesham, Worcestershire, and was given an Award of Merit when shown by him at Chelsea on 20th May 1952. This plant was at first considered to be *E. evansii* Schlechter.

This delightful shrublet has proved quite hardy and easy to establish so long as it is given a sunny position in a gritty, well-drained soil. A Cultural Commendation was given to Miss Finnis of the Waterperry Horticultural School, Oxfordshire, for a plant lifted from the open ground and shown at Chelsea in 1959. It was replanted a week later and continued to thrive. This plant is figured in colour in *Journ. R.H.S.*, Vol. 89, Oct. 1964, fig. 163.

The true E. EVANSII Schlechter is found in the same region as *E. acraeus* and is closely allied to it, but makes a more robust plant often with much larger leaves.

EUSCAPHIS   STAPHYLEACEAE

A monotypic genus which bears much resemblance to *Staphylea*. It differs in the larger number of leaflets, in the smaller individual flowers and in the smaller, differently shaped fruits.

E. JAPONICA (Thunb.) Kanitz
Sambucus japonica Thunb.; *E. staphyleoides* Sieb. & Zucc.

A deciduous bush up to 12 ft high, with stout, pithy branchlets and prominent buds; twigs glabrous. Leaves 6 to 10 in. long, opposite, consisting usually of seven or nine leaflets. Leaflets opposite, ovate, 2½ to 4 in. long, long-pointed, shallowly toothed, glabrous except for a little down near the base of the midrib. Panicle terminal, branching, 4 to 9 in. long, carrying numerous yellowish white flowers, each about ¼ in. across. Fruit consisting of three somewhat boat-shaped, spreading, rosy pink pods, ½ in. long; seeds black.

Native of China, Korea, and Japan. It is not very hardy, and can be grown outside permanently only in the mildest localities.

EVODIA *see* EUODIA

EXOCHORDA   ROSACEAE

A genus of about four species of deciduous shrubs found in N. Asia. The three species cultivated are all beautiful white-flowered shrubs, allied to *Spiraea*, but differing in the larger flowers, and larger, bony fruits. They like a fairly rich soil and a sunny position. Propagation may be effected by means of cuttings made of rather soft wood and placed in brisk heat, but they do not root with certainty. The best way to raise young plants is from seed. Sucker growths sometimes appear at the base of *E. racemosa*, which can be separated with a piece of root attached, potted, and established in a little bottom heat. So far as is known, all thrive on chalky soils except *E. racemosa*.

EXOCHORDA GIRALDII

E. GIRALDII Hesse

A vigorous shrub of spreading habit with pinkish young shoots. Leaves as in *E. racemosa*, but the petioles and veins usually pinkish and remaining so through the summer. Flowers six to eight in a terminal raceme, those near the apex almost sessile, the lower ones short-stalked; calyx with a red margin; petals pure white, obovate, 1 in. long and ½ in. wide, tapered into the claw; stamens twenty to thirty (cf. *E. racemosa*, in which the stamens number fifteen to twenty-five and the petals are almost orbicular, abruptly narrowed at the base into a short claw).

Native of N.W. China; introduced by the missionary Giraldi and first distributed by Hesse's nurseries at Weener near Hanover; introduced to England in 1909. This exochorda is closely allied to *E. racemosa* but is, perhaps, a better garden shrub.

var. WILSONII (Rehd.) Rehd. *E. racemosa* var. *wilsonii* Rehd.—Habit more erect; leaf-stalks shorter, green. Stamens twenty to twenty-five. Introduced by Wilson in 1907. 'IRISH PEARL', raised at the Glasnevin Botanic Garden, is a hybrid between this variety and *E. racemosa*.

E. SERRATIFOLIA S. Moore—This species may be distinguished from *E. giraldii* by the leaves, which are sharply serrate above the middle and up to 2 in. wide. Petals narrow oblong-obovate, notched at the apex. Native of Korea and Manchuria. Rare in cultivation.

E. KOROLKOWII Lav.

E. albertii Reg.

A deciduous shrub of sturdy, erect habit up to 12 or 15 ft high, with erect branches; branchlets glabrous. Leaves obovate, glabrous, those of the sterile shoots 1½ to 3½ in. long, ¾ to 1½ in. wide, toothed towards the apex, which is pointed, the base tapering to a short stalk, occasionally with two deep, narrow lobes there; leaves of the flowering twigs much smaller, ½ to ¾ in. wide, not toothed. Flowers pure white, about 1½ in. across, in erect racemes 3 to 4 in. long; stamens in five groups of five each. Fruit composed of five flattened, two-edged divisions, each ½ to ¾ in. long, arranged starwise. Flowers in May.

Native of Turkestan, where it was discovered in the eastern part of Bokhara by Albert Regel, at altitudes of 4,000 to 6,000 ft. It is very hardy, and more robust in habit than *E. racemosa*, from which it differs in the greater number of stamens, in the smaller flowers, and larger fruits. The plant became generally known in cultivation in 1886 through Prof. Regel of St Petersburg, but it had previously been grown as *E. korolkowii* at the Segrez Arboretum in France by Lavallée, who sent it to Kew in 1881 under that name.

E. × MACRANTHA (Lemoine) Schneid. [PLATE 27

E. albertii macrantha Lemoine

A hybrid raised about 1900 by Messrs Lemoine of Nancy from *E. korolkowii* fertilised with pollen of *E. racemosa*. It is a shrub of great beauty, producing a raceme of flowers from every bud of the previous year's growth. The raceme terminates a short leafy twig, and is 3 or 4 in. long, carrying six to ten snowy-white flowers, each 1¼ in. across. In the grouping of the stamens it is intermediate between the two parents, the groups consisting of threes, fours, or fives. It blossoms in April and May.

EXOCHORDA × MACRANTHA

E. RACEMOSA (Lindl.) Rehd.

Amelanchier racemosa Lindl.; *Spiraea grandiflora* Hook., not Sweet; *E. grandiflora* (Hook.) Lindl.

A deciduous shrub of rounded, bushy form up to 10 ft high, with glabrous branchlets. Leaves narrowly obovate, 1½ to 3 in. long, about one-third as wide, short-pointed or rounded at the apex, tapering at the base, quite glabrous, the margin entire, or toothed towards the apex. Flowers pure white, 1¼ to 1½ in. across, produced on erect racemes 3 to 4 in. long; petals five, obovate; calyx ½ in. across, with five rounded lobes. Stamens fifteen or twenty-five, in five groups of three or five each. Fruit composed of five flattened, two-edged, bony divisions, each ⅓ in. long, arranged starwise. *Bot. Mag.*, t. 4795.

Native of N. China; introduced by Fortune about 1849. It flowers in May, and even at that season is one of the most strikingly beautiful of shrubs. The white racemes are produced at the end of short lateral twigs from the branches of the previous year, and thus transform each branch into one huge snow-white inflorescence, sometimes 12 to 18 in. long and 8 to 10 in. wide. In order to obtain these fine sprays the shrubs, as soon as they have flowered, should be thinned out; the young shoots should be much reduced in number by weeding out all the weaker ones, especially where they are likely to be overcrowded.

FABIANA   SOLANACEAE

A genus of some twenty-five species of heath-like shrubs, all natives of South America, mostly in temperate parts. It was named in honour of Francisco Fabian y Fuero of Valencia, a patron of botanists, who died in 1801. The genus is allied to *Cestrum* and *Nicotiana* and is characterised by the solitary tubular flowers with five equal included stamens, all of them fertile, and the capsular fruits. Its nearest relative, however, is the interesting but little-known genus *Benthamiella*, with fifteen species of mat- or cushion-plants found in Argentina in the southern Andes and in the Patagonian steppe.

F. IMBRICATA Ruiz & Pavon   [PLATE 29

An evergreen shrub of heath-like appearance, erect in habit when young, ultimately spreading and reaching 6 to 8 ft in height and as much in diameter; it is, however, of variable habit in the wild, becoming lower or even ground-hugging at high altitudes or in dry or exposed situations. Branches downy, long, and tapered, densely furnished with short, slender twigs, from $\frac{1}{2}$ to 2 in. long. These twigs are themselves completely covered with tiny, pointed, three-angled leaves, $\frac{1}{12}$ in. long, and, in June, are each terminated by a solitary pure white flower. Corolla $\frac{5}{8}$ to $\frac{3}{4}$ in. long, tubular, but narrowing towards the base, with the rounded shallow lobes at the apex reflexed; calyx bell-shaped, $\frac{1}{12}$ in. long. Capsules $\frac{1}{4}$ in. long splitting downwards into two halves from the top to the calyx persisting at the base.

Native of the Andes of Bolivia, Argentina, and Chile; introduced in 1838. This beautiful shrub is unfortunately rather tender, and at Kew, although it occasionally survives the winter, has never been a success fully in the open. In milder and more upland localities it is a shrub of great beauty, flowering freely and transforming each branch into a slender raceme of blossom. It likes a light soil, and can be increased easily by late summer cuttings in gentle heat.

f. VIOLACEA Hort. *F. violacea* Hort.—Flowers in some shade of bluish mauve, but not differing from the white-flowered form in any other respect.

The first mention of the name *F. violacea* is in *The Floricultural Cabinet* for

1854, p. 211, where there occurs the following note: 'As hardy as the pretty, hardy F. imbricata, which has tube-shaped heath-like white flowers, very neat and pretty. The new plant is like the old one excepting the flowers being of a *violet* colour; very handsome.'

This variant seems to have been lost to cultivation until reintroduced by H. F. Comber during his Andean expedition 1925–7, when he sent seeds under field number C.247, collected in the Valle Escondido near Zapala, in a dry region of the Argentine Andes. Comber's introduction was shown by Lord Swaythling in 1932, when it received a First Class Certificate. From the form of *F. imbricata* previously cultivated this is very distinct in habit and leaf as well as in flower-colour. It may at once be distinguished by its much more spreading habit, due to the branches springing at almost right angles from older ones. Plants 2 or 3 ft high will be quite as wide as they are tall. In the commonly cultivated form of *F. imbricata*, on the other hand, the branches are attached at an angle of 45° or less, and the plant is erect and slender. The leaves of Comber's plant also are only half the length of those of the other and are more closely appressed. In his field note, Comber described the colour of the flowers as harebell blue but as seen on cultivated plants they are pale mauve. Clarence Elliott, who found and introduced a tall-growing form of f. *violacea* from Bulnes in S. Chile, described the flowers as a good blue-lilac. Both at Kew and in other gardens, Comber's introduction has proved hardier and freer-growing than the old *F. imbricata*. The garden clone 'PROSTRATA' probably derives from it.

Although the name f. *violacea* is maintained here, it really has no botanical significance. In wild populations the colour of the flowers varies from white to lavender-blue and neither colour is more typical than the other. The species is also variable in its foliage, but the type of foliage shown by Comber's plants appears to be more characteristic of the species than the longer more spreading leaves of the original introduction of *F. imbricata* and is certainly not confined to plants with coloured flowers. Plants from Atacama province, in the very dry northern part of Chile, have waxy leaves smelling of beeswax and the dried specimens in the Kew Herbarium are still strongly redolent of honey.

FAGUS BEECH FAGACEAE

The beeches are confined to the northern hemisphere, where they are found on all three continents (for their relatives in the southern hemisphere see NOTHOFAGUS). They form a very homogeneous group of trees with smooth, grey trunks. About ten species are usually recognised. Of these *F. orientalis* from E. Europe and Asia Minor and *F. crenata* from Japan are very near *F. sylvatica*, both being distinguished from it by leaflike appendages at the base of the husk. *F. orientalis* is further distinguished by large, more or less obovate leaves.

They are deciduous, with large, flat, alternate, parallel-ribbed leaves. Flowers unisexual, the two sexes borne on the same tree. Male flowers crowded and numerous in slender-stalked globose heads; stamens eight to sixteen, surrounded by a four- to seven-lobed calyx. Female inflorescence of two flowers, surrounded by numerous bracts united below into a four-parted involucre; styles three. Fruit an ovoid-triangular nut, one or two nuts wholly or partly enclosed in a woody, four-valved involucre (cupule), known colloquially as the husk. The involucre is covered on the outside with appendages which may be prickly or bract-like or (in *F. japonica* and *F. lucida*) short and deltoid.

All the beeches are quite hardy and thrive in a light or medium soil. They should be increased by seeds, but the cultivars of the common beech have to be grafted in spring.

F. CRENATA Blume   JAPANESE BEECH

F. sylvatica var. *sieboldii* (A.DC.) Maxim.; *F. sieboldii* A.DC.; *F. sylvatica* var. *asiatica* A.DC., in part

A tree up to about 100 ft high. Leaves ovate to rhomboidal, the base tapered rounded or slightly heart-shaped, the apex pointed, 2 to 4 in. long, 1 to 2¼ in. wide, silky hairy on the veins beneath, margins wavy, edged with fine hairs, veins in seven to eleven pairs; leaf-stalk ¼ to ⅜ in. long. Husks about ⅝ in. long, furnished with long bristles, those near the base enlarged into linear or spathulate appendages; peduncles stout, thick, somewhat downy, about ½ in. long.

Native of Japan, where it forms considerable forests. The tree itself and its timber are similar in most respects to the common beech. Botanically it differs chiefly in the leaflike appendages attached to the base of the husk; the latter is also more truncate at the base than in *F. sylvatica*. *F. crenata* is also closely allied to *F. orientalis* (q.v. for the marks of difference).

F. crenata is not common in cultivation but two trees at Kew are referred to it. One, *pl.* 1910, is 34 × 2½ ft and the other, *pl.* 1921, 30 × 2 ft (1969).

F. ENGLERANA Seemen

F. sylvatica var. *chinensis* Franch.

A deciduous tree usually 20 to 50 (rarely 70) ft high, nearly always in the wild divided near the base into many stems; young shoots glabrous. Leaves ovate to oval, usually widest below the middle, rounded or broadly wedge-shaped at the base, pointed, the margins wavy, 2 to 4 in. long, 1 to 2 in. wide, rather glaucous when quite young, at first silky-hairy beneath, otherwise glabrous, veins in ten to fourteen pairs; stalk slender, ¼ to ½ in. long. Husks ½ to ⅝ in. long, covered with downy, often spathulate bracts; the stalk slender, glabrous, 1½ to 2½ in. long. Nuts about as long as the husk.

Native of Central China; discovered by Henry, introduced by Wilson to the Arnold Arboretum in 1907 and thence to Kew in 1911 (No. 703). It is quite hardy and grows satisfactorily, if not very quickly, in this country. Its distinctive characters are the long slender stalk of the husk, combined with the glabrous leaves (except when young). *F. japonica*, its nearest ally, is well distinguished by the nuts being twice as long as the husk and consequently exposed. Wilson observed of F. *englerana* that, as seen in China, its many stems diverge somewhat and never attain to any great thickness.

In cultivation F. *englerana* makes a handsome small specimen which in habit agrees well with the wild trees, but it is far from common. The following have been recorded: Westonbirt, Glos., in Silkwood, *pl.* 1928 43 × 2½ ft (1967); Borde Hill, Sussex, in Lulling's Ghyll, 38 × 3½ ft (1967); Benenden Grange, Kent, a fine specimen, 32 × 3¾ ft at 3 ft (1967); Mount Usher, Co. Wicklow, Eire, 35 × 2¾ ft (1966); Birr Castle, Co. Offaly, Eire, *pl.* 1927, 22 × 1¾ ft (1966).

F. GRANDIFOLIA Ehrh.   AMERICAN BEECH
F. americana Sweet; F. ferruginea Ait.

A deciduous tree 70 to 80 ft high, occasionally more, with a thin, smooth, grey bark; spreading by means of root suckers, so that one tree will form of itself a colony of stems; young shoots at first clothed with long hairs, which soon fall away, Leaves ovate or oval, 2 to 5 in. long, ¾ to 2½ in. wide, taper-pointed, usually wedge-shaped at the base, coarsely toothed, at first clothed with silky hairs, but soon dark green and quite glabrous above except along the midrib, paler below, and with tufts of hairs in the vein-axils and along the midrib; stalk ¼ in. or rather more long; veins usually eleven to fifteen pairs. Fruits about ¾ in. long; the three-angled nuts enclosed by a downy, prickly husk, the prickles much recurved.

Native of eastern N. America; introduced in 1766. The American beech, like so many other trees of its region, has never been much of a success in Britain and the only example recorded is a rather shrubby tree at Eastnor Castle, Heref., measuring 35 × 6¼ ft at 2 ft (1970). It is easily distinguished from F. *sylvatica* by the suckering habit, the narrower, more pointed, regularly toothed leaves, with more numerous veins.

f. PUBESCENS Fern. & Rehd.—Leaf-blades permanently downy beneath.

var. CAROLINIANA (Loud.) Fern. & Rehd. F. *ferruginea* var. *caroliniana* Loud.—Leaves more shallowly toothed and more slenderly pointed than in the typical variety and the prickles on the husk shorter. This variety has a more southern distribution than the typical variety. The leaf-blades are occasionally downy beneath (f. MOLLIS Fern. & Rehd.).

F. JAPONICA Maxim.

A tree up to 70 or 80 ft high; young shoots furnished with silky hairs when quite young, soon glabrous. Leaves oval to ovate, sometimes rather diamond-shaped, tapered at both ends, but more abruptly towards the base, 2 to 4½ in. long, 1 to 1¼ in. wide, clad with silky hairs on both sides when young, glaucous and more or less persistently hairy beneath, veins in ten to fourteen pairs; stalks ½ to ⅝ in. long. Nuts ½ in. long; involucre little more than half the length of the nut, covered with short, stiff, deltoid appendages; fruit-stalks 1 to 1½ in. long, glabrous.

Native of Japan, where it is less abundant than *F. crenata* and does not extend into the northern island of Japan (Hokkaido); it is to *F. crenata* that the colloquial name 'Japanese beech' should be applied. *F. japonica* was introduced in 1907 when it was sent to Kew by Prof. Sargent of the Arnold Arboretum. Its most distinctive characters are: the rather glaucous undersides of the leaves; the long, slender and glabrous fruit-stalk; and the relative shortness of the husk (involucre) compared to the nut.

F. LONGIPETIOLATA Seemen
F. sylvatica var. *longipes* Oliver; *F. sinensis* Oliver

A deciduous tree up to 80 ft high, with pale grey bark and glabrous young shoots. Leaves ovate (sometimes narrowly so) broadly wedge-shaped, rarely rounded at the base, gradually tapered to a point, sharply but shallowly toothed or merely wavy at the margin, 2½ to 5½ in. long, 1½ to 2¾ in. wide, dark bright green above, rather glaucous and covered with fine down beneath, veins in nine to thirteen pairs; leaf-stalk ½ to 1⅛ in. long. Husks up to 1 in. long, covered with slender, curled bristles; stalk 1½ to 2 in. long, downy near the husk only.

Native of Central and W. China; discovered by Henry; introduced in 1911. Wilson observes that, whilst at its best it is a stately tree which resembles *F. crenata* in general appearance, it is usually rather small. Its leaves in size and shape resemble those of the American *F. grandifolia*, but the leaf-stalk is much longer. This length of leaf-stalk combined with the closely downy undersurface of the leaves, their ovate shape, and the long slender stalk of the husk make the species very distinct.

F. LUCIDA Rehd. & Wils., was discovered in Hupeh, China, by Henry about 1887 and twenty years later by Wilson; plants introduced by the latter in 1911 are in cultivation. He found it a tree from 20 to 30 ft high, with a 'broad, flattened or rounded crown'. The leaves are very distinct. They are ovate, 2 to 4 in. long, 1 to 2¼ in. wide, glossy green on both surfaces, the veins running out from the undulated margins to form small but distinct teeth. Husks covered with short, appressed, deltoid appendages. A tree at Nymans in Sussex appears to be *F. lucida*; it measures 39 × 2¼ ft (1970).

F. ORIENTALIS Lipsky
F. sylvatica var. *asiatica* A.DC., in part; *F. sylvatica* var. *macrophylla* Hohenacker; *F. hohenackerana* Palib.

A deciduous tree sometimes 100 ft or more high in the wild; young shoots silky-hairy. Leaves obovate or rather rhomboidal in outline, usually broadest above the middle, mostly broadly wedge-shaped at the base, acuminate at the apex, margins wavy, rarely toothed, 2½ to 4½ in. long, half as much wide, silky-hairy on the veins and midrib beneath; veins in seven to twelve, sometimes to fourteen pairs; leaf-stalk ¼ to ½ in. long, silky-hairy. Husks about ⅞ in. long, obovoid, downy, the appendages at the base green, linear-oblong or narrowly spathulate, the upper ones bristle-like as in the common beech; stalk up to 3 in. long.

Native of the forests south of the Caspian, the Caucasus, Asia Minor, the Crimea, and the eastern part of the Balkan peninsula, but the western boundary is difficult to define owing to the existence of hybrids and intermediates between it and *F. sylvatica*. It is closely akin to that species, but differs in the larger leaves with more numerous pairs of veins; and the common beech has none of the leafy, spathulate appendages seen on the husks of *F. orientalis*. The latter character is also seen in the Japanese beech, *F. crenata*, to which the oriental beech is as closely allied as it is to the common beech. But in *F. crenata* the leaves are mostly broadest below the middle and the stalks of the involucre are very short; in *F. orientalis* the stalks are at least twice as long as the involucre (and are sometimes remarkably long and slender).

In Thrace, where *F. sylvatica* and *F. orientalis* are in contact, the common beech keeps to the mountains at altitudes of 2,000 to 4,500 ft, where conditions are cool and damp, while the oriental beech prefers lower, more sheltered situations. In the interesting forest discovered by the late Dr Turrill and his Bulgarian companions in the southern Rodopes in 1926, the oriental beech occurs in association with walnut, *Ostrya carpinifolia*, Turkish hazel (*Corylus colurna*), oriental hornbeam, and manna ash: 'We had the impression of being in a Tertiary forest' (W. B. Turrill, *Plant Life of the Balkan Peninsula*, pp. 139–140).

The date of introduction of *F. orientalis* to Britain is not certain, but a grafted tree at Kew, received from Lee's nursery in 1880, as "*F. macrophylla*", agrees better with *F. orientalis* than it does with the common beech. Three trees, received from Fisher, Son, and Sibray in 1911, have been recently identified as *F. orientalis*.

F. ᴛᴀᴜʀɪᴄᴀ Popl.—F. G. Tutin (*Flora Europaea*, Vol. 1, p. 61) considers that this is best regarded as a variant of *F. orientalis*. It has the spathulate appendages on the husks characteristic of that species but in leaf characters it is intermediate between it and the common beech. See also *F. moesiaca*, under *F. sylvatica*.

F. ꜱʏʟᴠᴀᴛɪᴄᴀ L.   Cᴏᴍᴍᴏɴ Bᴇᴇᴄʜ

A deciduous tree up to 100 ft high, occasionally almost 150 ft, with a smooth grey trunk, sometimes of enormous thickness—6 to 8 ft through; young shoots at first silky-hairy, soon becoming glabrous. Leaves with five to nine pairs of veins, oval, inclined to ovate, pointed, unequally rounded at the base, ordinarily 2 to $3\frac{1}{2}$ in. long, $1\frac{1}{2}$ to $2\frac{1}{2}$ in. wide, but as much as 5 in. by 3 in., obscurely toothed or merely unevenly undulated at the margin, midrib and veins hairy, especially beneath; stalk downy, $\frac{1}{4}$ to $\frac{1}{2}$ in. long. Nuts triangular, $\frac{5}{8}$ in. long, usually a pair enclosed in a hard, woody, pear-shaped, four-lobed husk, covered with bristles and $\frac{3}{4}$ to 1 in. long, solitary on an erect downy stalk about as long as itself.

Native of Europe, including most of southern England (planted and naturalised elsewhere in the British Isles). Few trees are more pleasing than a well-grown beech, either in the wide, spreading form it takes when growing in an isolated position, or when, in close association with others of its kind, and drawn up by them, it forms a tall, smooth, column-like trunk. The largest of the former kind

ᴛꜱ—ɢ

in Britain was the famous beech at Newbattle Abbey, 100 ft high, 130 ft in diameter, the trunk 21 ft in girth; of this only a layer now remains. Of the latter the finest was in Ashridge Park, Bucks, known as the 'Queen Beech'—130 to 140 ft high. The young foliage of the beech is one of the most beautiful objects in nature in May—a tender shimmering green of a shade not quite matched by any other tree.

Of the notable trees mentioned by Elwes and Henry, only Pontey's beech at Woburn has been traced. In 1837, according to Loudon, its dimensions were 100 × 12½ ft at 4 ft, with a clear bole of 50 ft; in 1903 it was the same height and 14½ ft in girth (Elwes and Henry measurement); a Forestry Commission measurement for 1956 was 110 × 16¼ ft. The following specimens have been recorded in recent years: Kew, east of Lake, 105 × 14¾ ft, clear bole 20 ft (1965); Kenwood House, Highgate, London, 100 × 18½ ft and 110 × 13¼ ft (1964); Welford Park, Berks, 105 × 17 ft (1966); Wakehurst Place, Sussex, in the Valley, 80 × 16¾ ft, and by the Lake, 100 × 16¼ ft (1965); Handcross Park, Sussex, 95 × 23 ft (pollard) (1961); Beauport Park, Sussex, 91 × 19 ft (1965); Knole Park, Kent, 115 × 18½ ft (1969); Eridge Park, Kent, 80 × 26 ft (pollard) (1958); Bramshill Park, Hants, 90 × 20 ft (1965); Tottenham House, Savernake, Wilts, 110 × 14¾ ft, clear bole 40 ft, and another 100 × 15¼ ft (1967); London Ride, Savernake, 100 × 16 ft and 110 × 16 ft (1967); Wilton House, Wilts, 115 × 19½ ft (1961); Longleat, Wilts, 118 × 20½ ft (1971); Westonbirt House, Glos., 100 × 16¼ ft (1967); Kingscote Wood, Glos., 129 × 16¾ ft (1961); Nettlecombe, Som., 75 × 23½ ft (pollard) (1959); Woolverston Hall, Ipswich, 95 × 20ft (1968); Dunscombe Park, Yorks, 134 × 16½ ft (1956); Bramham Park, Yorks, 100 × 24½ ft (pollard) (1958); Studley Royal, Yorks, 125 × 14¾ ft (1966); Yester House, E. Lothian, 105 × 20¼ ft, clear bole 20 ft (1967); Galloway House, Wigtons., 100 × 18¾ ft (1967); Elioch, Dumfr., 75 × 19¾ ft (1954); Blairquhan, Ayrs., 94 × 17 ft (1954); Canon House, Dingwall, Ross, 95 × 25¼ ft (pollard) (1956); Headfort, Co. Meath, Eire, 125 × 15¼ ft (1966).

The beech has produced many varieties, some of which have first been noticed in gardens, others in the wild. The following is a selection of the more important:

cv. 'ALBOMARGINATA'.—Leaves margined with white (*Gard. Chron.*, Vol. 26 (1899), p. 434). A tree at Kew with narrowish, white-margined leaves has largely reverted. There are other variants with leaves blotched and striped with white, for which the collective name is *F. s. f. albo-variegata* (West.) Domin.

cv. 'ANSORGEI'.—A shrubby variety with brownish purple, lanceolate, almost entire leaves ⅜ to ¾ in. wide. It is a hybrid between a purple beech and some form of cut-leaved beech, which according to Schwerin was *F. s. comptoniifolia* (see under 'Asplenifolia'). Raised by Ansorge at the Flottbeck nurseries, Hamburg.

cv. 'ASPLENIFOLIA'. FERN-LEAVED BEECH.— Of all the forms of beech marked by differences in shape of leaf, this is the handsomest. In this variety the leaf assumes various shapes; sometimes it is long and narrow (4 in. long by ¼ in. wide), sometimes deeply and pinnately lobed, some of the lobes penetrating to the midrib; between these two, numerous intermediate shapes occur, often on the same branch. Unlike many of the varieties of beech with curious foliage, this makes a fine shapely tree, and it is a distinct ornament to any garden.

The common fern-leaved beech of British gardens is very consistent in its characters and may well represent a single clone. Two further features of this tree are the sprays of linear leaves produced at the ends of most of the season's growths; and the twiggy bunches of shoots that sprout from the branches inside the crown. It tends to revert here and there but it is on the whole stable. It is almost certainly the same as the *F. sylvatica asplenifolia* of Loddiges' nursery, who listed it in their catalogue for 1804. A tree in the Knap Hill nursery, believed to have come from France in 1826, belongs to this variety. This tree measures 54 × 11½ ft (1961); the largest trees in Britain, although probably younger, are taller than this (up to 80 ft or slightly more high) and some are larger in girth (up to 13 ft). [PLATE 30

In Britain, the fern-leaved beech has usually been known as *F. sylvatica heterophylla*, but Loudon, who published this name, placed under it, in addition to *asplenifolia*, another beech listed by Loddiges as *F. s. laciniata*. So it seems preferable to revert to the original name, which is, after all, the Latin equivalent of the common name, and the one used by continental authorities. Rehder included the fern-leaved beech in f. *laciniata* (q.v.) but it is very distinct from the beech originally described under that name.

Other variants are known which bear some resemblance to the common fern-leaved beech. In *Arboretum Muscaviense* (1864), Kirchner mentions *F. sylvatica* 'COMPTONIIFOLIA', with finer foliage than in 'Asplenifolia'. There are two specimens in the Kew Herbarium which answer to this description in that they have a greater proportion of linear leaves and the lobed leaves are very slender.

f. ATROPUNICEA. See f. *purpurea*.

cv. 'AUREA PENDULA'.—Leaves yellow when young, the colouring best developed in a shady situation. It is a sport from the slender, erect growing form of weeping beech, and was raised by J. G. van der Bom at Oudenbosch, Holland, shortly before 1900.

cv. 'AUREA VARIEGATA'.—Leaves margined with golden yellow (*Gard. Chron.*, Vol. 26 (1899) p. 434). A beech under this name was listed earlier by the Lawson Company, Edinburgh. William Paul of Waltham Cross had a gold, margined beech which he called *F. s. foliis aureis* and claimed to be the best of the variegated beeches. It may be the same as 'Paul's Gold-margined', which received an Award of Merit in 1902 (*Gard. Chron.* (1867), p. 237; *Journ. R.H.S.*, Vol. 27, xcii). The name for gold-variegated beeches in general is *F. s. f. luteo-variegata* (West.) Domin.

cv. 'BORNYENSIS'.—A small tree with very pendulous branches reaching to the ground and forming a densely-leaved cone. The original tree grew in a garden near the church at Borny in France and is believed to have come from a neighbouring forest; it was 35 ft in 1910. It was propagated by Simon-Louis Frères, and the largest example at Kew came from that firm in 1900.

cv. 'COCHLEATA'.—Leaves concave beneath, broadest above the middle tapering to an acute base; margins with small, pointed, slightly toothed lobules best developed near the apex. It was in commerce by 1842 (Loudon, *Encyclopaedia of Trees and Shrubs*, p. 1118). A similar beech was distributed by Simon-Louis Frères as *F. s. undulata*.

cv. 'CRISTATA'.—Leaves bunched, very shortly stalked, coarsely triangular-toothed, crumpled, the apex decurved. In commerce by 1836; also known as *F. s. crispa*. The largest specimen of this variety on record grows at Chiddingly, Horsted Keynes, Sussex; it measures 80 × 6¾ ft (1967). There are other examples of a good size at Wakehurst Place, Sussex; Hergest Croft, Heref.; and Capenoch, Dumfries.

cv. 'CUPREA'. See under f. *purpurea*.

cv. 'DAWYCK'.—The original tree of this well-known fastigiate variety grows in the garden of Lt-Col. A. Balfour at Dawyck, Peeblesshire, and now measures 82 × 8 ft (1966). It is believed to have originated in the woods there and to have been moved to its present position by the house around the middle of the last century, at which time the property belonged to the Nasmyth family. The tree first came to notice early this century when F. R. S. Balfour, the new owner of Dawyck, distributed scions to Kew and other gardens, around 1907. Scions were also given to Herr Hesse, of Weener, Hanover, and it was he who first described the Dawyck beech in 1912 and his firm that first distributed it commercially.

The Dawyck beech is usually known as 'Fastigiata', but this name belongs to some fastigiate beech cultivated by Simon-Louis Frères and mentioned by Koch in his *Dendrologie* (Vol. 2, part 2 (1873), p. 17).

cv. 'FASTIGIATA'. See cv. 'Dawyck'.

cv. 'FOLIIS VARIEGATIS'.—According to Loudon, the beech distributed by Loddiges under this name had 'the leaves variegated with white and yellow, interspersed with some streaks of red and purple'.

cv. 'GRANDIDENTATA'.—Leaves coarsely but regularly toothed, cuneate at the base, slightly concave beneath. Perhaps a branch-sport from a fern-leaved beech. The fine specimen at Kew came from James Booth's nurseries at Flottbeck near Hamburg in 1872 and almost certainly represents the true clone.

var. HETEROPHYLLA Loud. See cv. 'Asplenifolia'.

f. LACINIATA (Pers.) Domin *F. s.* var. *laciniata* Vignet ex Pers.; *F. laciniata* F. W. Schmidt, *nom. event.; F. s.* f. *quercifolia* Schneid; *F. s.* var. *heterophylla* Loud., in part; *F. s. quercoides* Kirchn., not Pers.—Leaves ovate-lanceolate, cuneate at the base, slenderly tapered at the apex, deeply and regularly serrated, the serrations seven to nine on each side, acute, the sinuses extending about one-third of the way to the midrib. This variant was noticed around 1792 as a branch-sport on a hedging beech, growing on the Tetschen estate in the mountains between Bohemia and Saxony. It was described by Vignet in 1795 (in F. W. Schmidt's *Samml. Phys.-Oekon. Aufs.*, Vol. 1, pp. 175–83) and the above description is made from the excellent figure accompanying the article. Vignet did not actually name this variety but Persoon did so in 1800 (*Trans. Linn. Soc. Lond.*, Vol. 5, p. 232). Whether this sport was ever propagated and distributed cannot be ascertained, though Vignet evidently expected that it would be, and F. W. Schmidt, the Bohemian botanist, added a footnote saying that this beech, which he too had seen, would no doubt shortly be appearing in nursery catalogues under the name *F. laciniata*. The cultivar-name for the original clone would be 'Laciniata'.

A tree at Kew, received in 1930 under the name *F. s. quercifolia*, agrees very well with Vignet's figure. So too does a beech grown under the same name in the Trompenburg Arboretum, Rotterdam, judging from a specimen of the leaves kindly sent by Mr Hoey-Smith. There are three other beeches at Kew, also received as *F. s. quercifolia*, which should probably be referred to the f. *laciniata*, though they have leaves rather more deeply incised than in the type and occasionally produce a few narrow, undivided leaves at the tips of the shoots, in these respects inclining towards 'Asplenifolia' (q.v.).

f. LATIFOLIA Kirchn. *F. sylvatica* var. *macrophylla* Dipp., nct Hohenacker— This appears to be the correct designation for trees which bear larger leaves than normal but in other characters resemble the common beech. In 1898, the King of Denmark's gardener sent to Kew a variety that has been called 'PRINCE GEORGE OF CRETE'. When young these trees had leaves up to 7 in. long, 5½ in. wide, but they are now somewhat smaller, though still strikingly large. The possibility has been considered that this variety is a hybrid with *F. orientalis*, but judging from its fruits this is not the case.

   cv. 'MILTONENSIS'.—This weeping beech was described in a letter to Loudon from the Rev. M. J. Berkeley, dated June 2, 1837, informing him that in 'one of the plantations bordering Milton Park, the seat of Earl Fitzwilliam, in Northamptonshire, there is a beautiful accidental variety of the beech. . . . The branches are beautifully pendent, and even the last six feet of the top bend down. Mr Henderson, the very intelligent gardener, has propagated it by grafts' (Loudon, *Arb. et Frut. Brit.*, Vol. 3, p. 1953, and Vol. 8, plate LXX B). A grafted tree, probably one of the original propagations, still grows in the Pleasure Grounds at Milton Hall and is portrayed in *Qtly. Journ. For.*, Vol. 65 (1971), p. 176. In the accompanying letter Mr S. Egar gives the height of the tree as 45 ft from base to bend of leaders, and the girth 7¾ ft at breast-height. The tree is branched to the ground and has layered itself.

   Loudon expressed the hope that 'so splendid a variety will . . . soon find its way into the public nurseries'. It may have done so, but the three grafted trees at Kew received from James Booth of Hamburg in 1872 and 1876 are not the Milton variety, though they came as *F. s. miltonensis*. One has gracefully drooping branches, but is not truly pendulous; one scarcely differs from any common beech; the third is intermediate. All have roundish, smooth-edged leaves and a distinctive bark, in which the normal grey bark is broken into small angular patches by a network of raised ridges. Judging from Jouin's description, the Milton variety distributed by Simon-Louis was also not the true clone but more probably the common pendulous beech of British collections.

   cv. 'PAGNYENSIS'.—This variety was found near Pagny in the department of Meurthe-et-Moselle, France, where it was known as the *tordu-fou* ('twisted beech', *fou* being a dialect name for beech). Like so many of the interesting wild variants of beech found in France it was propagated by Simon-Louis Frères and according to Jouin, manager of their tree nursery, it had a wide umbrella-shaped crown and did not rise much above the ground if grafted low. 'RETRO-FLEXA', distributed by the same firm, was said to be similar.

   f. PENDULA [Loud.] Schelle *F. s.* var. *pendula* Lodd. ex Loud.— There are several types of weeping beech. The one best known under the name *pendula* is not a high tree, but sends out its great arms in a horizontal or drooping direction;

from these the smaller branches depend almost vertically, the whole making a tent-like mass. There are examples at Kew near the Broad Walk and in the Beech collection. This form of weeping beech is almost certainly the one distributed by Loddiges early last century and therefore the one for which the cultivar name 'Pendula' should be used. But there is another pendulous beech, also known as F. s. pendula, which is perhaps commoner on the continent than here. It is quite distinct from the tent-like clone, being slender in habit with the main branches pendent. This seems to be the F. s. pendula of Kirchner, of which there were already old trees in Germany when he described it in 1864 (in Arboretum Muscaviense). Two trees at Westonbirt facing the main gate to Westonbirt School are of this type. In addition there is the famous weeping beech at the Knap Hill nurseries, which is believed to have come from France in 1826. This tree, which has formed a small copse by self-layering, is certainly not the same as our tent-like pendula, but it is hard to judge its true character, for it grows in a soil and climate unfavourable to the best development of beech. Grown in better conditions it might prove to be the same as the pendula of Kirchner. [PLATE 28

cv. 'PRINCE GEORGE OF CRETE'. See under f. latifolia.

f. PURPUREA (Ait.) Schneid. F. s. var. purpurea Ait.; F. s. f. atropurpurea Kirchn. PURPLE BEECH.—Leaves deep purple when mature; of a beautiful pale red in spring. This is by far the most popular of the varieties of beech. It is not of garden origin, but appears to have been observed growing naturally in at least three places, viz.: in the Hanleiter Forest, near Sonderhausen, in Thuringia; in the Darney Forest in the Vosges; and in the village of Buchs, in the canton of Zurich, Switzerland. The last is the oldest recorded site of the purple beech, three trees there being mentioned in a work dated 1680. They were the survivors of a group originally of five, which, according to legend, had sprung up on the spot where five brothers had killed each other. Most of the trees in cultivation are considered to have sprung from the Hanleiter tree.

The date of introduction of the purple beech to Britain is uncertain. It appears to have been in cultivation here around 1760, and certainly by 1777, when Loddiges listed it in their catalogue. Whether the beech described by Weston as F. s. var. atropunicea in 1770 was really the purple beech, as Rehder assumed, is by no means certain. Possibly it was, but the fact remains that Weston called his var. atropunicea the 'American purple-leaved beech', and Humphrey Marshall, an American nurseryman and collector who was certainly acquainted with Weston's book, actually adopted the name F. sylvatica var. atropunicea for the American beech (Arbustum Americanum (1780), p. 46).

The only old purple beech of which the planting date is known grows at the Knap Hill nurseries, Surrey. It measures 65 × 14¼ ft (1961) and was planted in 1826. Trees with girths in excess of this are: Linton Park, Kent, 90 × 19½ ft (1965); Cobham Hall, Kent, 85 × 18¼ ft (1965); Mote Park, Maidstone, Kent, 72 × 16 ft (1965); Corsham Court, Wilts, 92 × 17½ ft (1965); Wilton House, Wilts, 95 × 16¾ ft (1961); The Lodge, Wateringbury, Kent, 75 × 20¼ ft (1962).

The purple beech comes partially true from seed but the majority of the seedlings are either the ordinary green type or but faintly coloured. The name F. sylvatica CUPREA or copper beech is used for trees with leaves paler than in the true purple beech. Various clones of the purple beech have received names.

'SWAT MAGRET', raised in Germany by Timms and Co., has very dark purple leaves, which are said to retain their colouring until late in the summer. 'BROCK-LESBY' has leaves rather larger than normal, deep purple. It may have originated at Brocklesby Park, Lincs, where there are many fine purple beeches, but curiously enough no reference to it in British literature can be found; the example at Kew, too crowded in to show its characters well, came from Späth's nursery, Berlin. The well-known 'RIVERSII' was raised and distributed originally by Messrs Rivers of Sawbridgeworth, who listed it in their trade catalogues in the 1870s as a very fine form of purple beech. They themselves did not give it a distinguishing name, but it became known as *F. sylvatica purpurea Riversii* in the trade.

cv. 'PURPUREA TRICOLOR'.—Leaves purplish, narrower than normal, edged and striped with rose and pinkish white. This is very pretty when the leaves are young. The tree at Kew, seen from a distance, has the aspect of a small-leaved and slender copper beech. This variety is said to have come to notice almost simultaneously in France and Holland, and to have been first propagated in quantity by Transon's nursery, Orleans, who first exhibited it in 1885 (*Rev. Hort. Belg.*, Vol. 12, p. 145; *Rev. Hort.* (1885), p. 311). A similar or perhaps identical beech was exhibited by Messrs Cripps in 1888 as *F. s. roseomarginata* and was awarded a First Class Certificate.

cv. 'PURPUREA PENDULA'.—The tree commonly grown under this name in Britain (and also seen in continental collections) is slow-growing and makes a small, mushroom-shaped bush; leaves rich purple. It is possible that the correct name for this variant should be 'Purpurea Pendula Nana'.

f. QUERCIFOLIA Schneid. See f. *laciniata*.

f. QUERCOIDES (Pers.) Domin *F. s.* var. *quercoides* Pers.—Bark oak-like. The tree on which Persoon based the name grew at Göttingen in Germany and was thought there to be a hybrid between the oak and the beech (*Trans. Linn. Soc. Lond.*, Vol. 5 (1800), p. 233). This variant occurs occasionally in the wild.

cv. 'REMILLYENSIS'.—An umbrella-shaped tree, with tortuous branches. It was first distributed by Simon-Louis Frères and presumably came from the Remilly stand mentioned under f. *tortuosa*. The specimen at Kew came from Lee's nursery in 1873 and measures 36 × 5¼ ft (1967). It is grafted at 4 ft.

cv. 'ROHANII'.—Leaves brownish purple, cut about as deeply as in the original *laciniata* (q.v.), but with the serrations more irregular and themselves often edged with shallow, roundish teeth. This beech was raised on the estate of Prince Camille de Rohan at Sychrov, in what is now Czechoslovakia, from seeds sown in 1888. The parents are believed to be two trees still growing in the collection—one the purple beech 'Brocklesby', the other a cut-leaved beech called *F. s. quercifolia*, which appears to be similar to the trees grown under that name at Kew (see under f. *laciniata*). After the death of the Prince the garden superintendent V. Mašek set up his own nursery at Turnov nearby, and his son K. Mašek put 'Rohanii' into commerce in 1908, though it seems at the time to have attracted little attention and only recently has become widely known and planted. There is a good specimen in the Winkworth Arboretum, Surrey.

cv. 'ROSEOMARGINATA'. See under 'Purpurea Tricolor'.

cv. 'ROTUNDIFOLIA'.—Perhaps the daintiest of beech varieties; leaves round, ½ to 1¼ in. in diameter, very closely set on the branches. It originated near St Johns, Woking, and was known by 1872, in which year Major McNair of Brookwood sent a specimen to Kew. It was propagated by Messrs Jackman of Woking and received a First Class Certificate when shown by them in 1894. It was figured in the same year in *Gardener's Magazine*, p. 339. The tree at Kew, which came from Späth's nursery in 1900, has larger leaves (1½ in. wide), than in the dried specimen from McNair, but this is probably of no significance. The number of pairs of veins is the same in both—usually four. The Kew tree is of slender, erect habit; there is also a large specimen at Wakehurst Place, Sussex, with a more spreading crown.

f. TORTUOSA (Pepin) Hegi *F. s.* var. *tortuosa* Pepin—A rather heterogeneous group of abnormally branched beeches which often occur in colonies and have been reported from France, Germany, Denmark, and Sweden. The branches are tortuous or zigzagged, sometimes forming 'horse-collars' by the self-grafting of branchlets onto the parent stem. These beeches may form trees of a fair size or large, spreading shrubs; often the branchlets of the tree-like plants are pendulous. The typical trees are known as 'Les Faux de St Basles' and grow in the Forest of Verzy near Nancy (*fau, fou*, are dialect names for beech). They were described by Pépin in *Rev. Hort.* (1861), p. 84, and are now under state protection. Another French stand, described by Carrière in *Rev. Hort.* (1877), p. 374, was situated near Remilly, S.E. of Metz. See further under 'Remillyensis'.

In Germany a famous colony of the spreading sub-form grows in the Süntel Highlands between Cologne and Hanover. One of these was removed to the Berggarten at Hanover, where it still grows. Tortuous beeches in S. Sweden, of which there are many, are described by John Kraft in *Lustgarden* (1966–7), pp. 25–59 (with 40 photographs by Tor Lundgren).

cv. 'TRICOLOR'.—This variety was cultivated by Simon-Louis Frères of Metz. According to Jouin, the manager of their tree and shrub nursery, it was not vigorous and had small leaves that burnt in the sun and were rose-edged when young, the margin later becoming white. He seems to have had no high opinion of it and cautioned that it should not be confused with *F. s. purpurea tricolor* (as in fact it has been). His description will be found in his notes on the variants of the beech sold by his firm, published in *Le Jardin*, Vol. 13.

cv. 'ZLATIA'.—Leaves yellow when young but not of a shade deep enough to be called golden; when mature they scarcely differ from those of the ordinary beech. It was discovered near Vranje in Serbia and put into commerce by Späth, who received scions from Prof. Dragašević in 1890. The name derives from the Serbian word for gold (*zlato*).

In the Balkans and eastern Central Europe beeches occur which are intermediate in foliage between the oriental and the common, but lack the leafy processes seen on the cupules of the former. These have been named F. MOESIACA (Maly) Czeczot. According to P. Fukarek (*Int. Dendr. Soc. Ybk.* (1968), p. 37) the leaves of intermediates found in Jugoslavia are narrower than in the common beech, with a cuneate base and more numerous lateral nerves, and the cupules bear longer and softer processes.

FALLUGIA   ROSACEAE

A monotypic genus of the sub-family Rosoideae, allied to *Cowania*, from which it differs in the larger flowers, an inch or more across; in the more numerous pistils (up to twelve only in *Cowania*); and in having a whorl of bractlets at the base of the flower, alternating with the sepals.

F. PARADOXA (D. Don) Endl.
Sieversia paradoxa D. Don

A slender deciduous shrub 4 to 8 ft high, much branched below, more thinly above; branchlets white, covered with down. Leaves produced in clusters closely and alternately along the twigs, ½ to ⅔ in. long, ⅓ in. wide, cut usually into three or five (occasionally seven) narrow-linear lobes, recurved at the edges and

FALLUGIA PARADOXA

$\frac{1}{12}$ in. wide, dark green above, paler below, and covered all over with pale down. Flowers produced either singly or a few together on a raceme 1¼ to 4 in. long, from the end of the shoot or from the leaf-axis near the end. Each flower is 1 to 1¼ in. across, petals white; calyx ¼ in. diameter, downy, with five ovate, pointed lobes; and five small bracts alternating with them. The heads of fruits are very handsome, each carpel being terminated by a slender style 1 in. to 1½ in. long, clothed with silky hairs, the whole forming a dense feathery mass, 1½ in. across. Flowers in July. *Bot. Mag.*, t. 6660.

Native of S.E. California, New Mexico, Utah, and Nevada; introduced in 1877. This interesting and beautiful shrub is very rare in cultivation, and likely to remain so. Coming from the dry, sun-baked hills of the south-western United States, it finds in the English climate conditions almost the opposite of its native surroundings. It would probably be best suited on a warm slope in the drier parts of England. Elsewhere it will thrive best in well-drained soil at the base of a sunny wall.

× FATSHEDERA   ARALIACEAE

Fatshedera is the generic name given to the plant described below, which is believed to be an intergeneric hybrid between *Fatsia* and *Hedera*.

× F. LIZEI Guillaum.

An evergreen shrub of loose free growth, with stout young shoots that are ⅜ in. or more in diameter, downy at first and thickly furnished with warts. Leaves from 4 to 10 in. across, scarcely so much long, of leathery texture, dark glittering green, five lobed in palmate fashion, the lobes reaching one-third or half-way to the base; stalk terete, about as long as the blade, often purplish. Flowers produced in October and November in a terminal panicle, 8 to 10 in. long and 4 in. wide, made up of numerous hemispherical umbels. Each umbel is 1 in. in diameter and carries from one dozen to three dozen flowers which, individually, are ¼ in. wide; petals five, ovate, pale green finally much decurved; stamens five, sterile. The centre of the flower is occupied by a large green disk, in the centre of which the ovary is set. Flower-stalks thinly covered with loose branching down. Fruit not borne. *Bot. Mag.*, t. 9402.

This interesting plant is a hybrid raised in 1910 by Messrs Lizé Frères, nurserymen, of Nantes, by crossing *Fatsia japonica* 'Moseri' with the pollen of Irish ivy (*Hedera helix* 'Hibernica'). Some doubt has been expressed as to the authenticity of this origin, but Guillaumin states (*Rev. Hort.* (1924), p. 180) that 'Messrs Lizé's plant, showing morphological and anatomical characters of both *Hedera* and *Fatsia* also intermediate ones, appears to be truly a hybrid between the two genera. The constant sterility of the stamens supports this opinion.' Its general appearance certainly suggests this parentage, as also does its mode of growth for although *Fatsia japonica* is a very sturdy shrub, this hybrid has inherited enough of the scandent nature of the ivy to render the support of a stake necessary to keep it upright. For a further discussion see the article accompanying the plate in the *Botanical Magazine*, where the question of the parentage of this plant is left open.

× *F lizei* is a handsome evergreen, grows vigorously and, judging by its parentage, should prove useful for shady situations and for town gardens.

It has been cultivated at Kew for many years and has never suffered from cold; both its parents are indeed very hardy. The flowers, however, come so late in the season that often they do not open. It is very easily increased by cuttings and useful for furnishing very shady places where flowering shrubs will not succeed. Repeated pruning in its young state would probably give it a bushy shape. There are white-variegated forms in commerce.

FATSIA ARALIACEAE

A genus of probably only one species, belonging to the tribe Schefflereae, to which the ivies (*Hedera*) also belong. It is distinguished from *Aralia* by its valvate corollas. The species described by Sir William Hooker as *Aralia papyrifera* was transferred to *Fatsia* by Bentham and Hooker, but properly belongs to the genus *Tetrapanax* as *T. papyriferus* (Hook.) K. Koch. It is tender and not treated in this work. The Formosan species described by Hayata under the name *Fatsia polycarpa* was later removed by Nakai to the monotypic genus *Diplofatsia* and this genus is recognised by Dr Hutchinson in *The Genera of Flowering Plants*, Vol. 2 (1967). The Formosan species is not in cultivation so far as is known, but might prove moderately hardy.

F. JAPONICA (Thunb.) Decne. & Planch. [PLATE 31
Aralia japonica Thunb.

An evergreen shrub or small tree, usually seen as a spreading bush from 6 to 15 ft high. Stems very thick, not much branched, unarmed, marked with large scars left by fallen leaves. Leaves leathery, varying in size according to the size and vigour of the plant, ordinarily 12 to 16 in. across, palmate, with a broad heart-shaped base and usually nine lobes, the lobes reaching more than half-way to the base, ovate, coarsely and bluntly toothed except towards the base, where the opening between the lobes is wide and rounded, upper surface dark shining green, the lower one paler, both quite glabrous; stalk round, stout, smooth, often 1 ft or more long. Flowers milky white, produced in the autumn on large branching panicles of globose heads, each head 2 to 3 in. wide; stalks white like the flowers. Fruits black, pea-shaped. *Bot. Mag.*, t. 8638.

Native of Japan; introduced in 1838. This very handsome shrub, which bears about the largest leaves of any hardy evergreen, is well known as a plant grown in pots for house decoration. It is not so well known that it succeeds very well out-of-doors, and often makes a striking display in October, provided it is given a sheltered, semi-shaded spot. It is well worth growing for its bold and striking foliage. Propagated by cuttings put singly in pots, and plunged in mild bottom heat any time after the wood is fairly firm. 'VARIEGATA' has large blotches of white towards the end of the lobes; 'AUREA' has golden-variegated leaves; 'MOSERI', referred to above as one parent of × *Fatshedera lizei*, is more compact in habit, with larger leaves.

FEIJOA   MYRTACEAE

A genus of two species, natives of central S. America, closely allied to the guavas (*Psidium*). The name commemorates Don Feijo, a botanist of San Sebastian.

F. SELLOWIANA (Berg) Berg

Orthostemon sellowianus Berg

A evergreen shrub or small tree of bushy habit; young shoots, buds and under-surface of the leaves clothed with a whitish felt. Leaves opposite, oval or ovate, toothless, blunt at the apex, tapered or rounded at the base, 1 to 3 in. long, ¾ to 1½ in. wide, dark lustrous green and glabrous above except when quite young, whitish, felted and conspicuously veined beneath; stalk ¼ in., or less, long, felted. Flowers, solitary, produced in July from the lowermost leaf-axils of the current year's shoots, usually two or four of them on each shoot; each flower is 1¼ to 1¾ in. wide and borne on a felted stalk 1 to 1½ in. long. Sepals four, roundish-oblong, ⅜ in. long, felted outside, reflexed. Petals four, broadly oval, concave, finally reflexed, red in the centre, whitish at the margin. Stamens very numerous, erect, ¾ to 1 in. long, rich crimson. Fruit an egg-shaped berry up to 2 in. long, with the remains of the calyx at the top, with a pleasant, rich, aromatic flavour. *Bot. Mag.*, t. 7620.

Native of S. Brazil and Uruguay; discovered in 1819 by a German collector named Sellow, after whom it was named. This shrub is not hardy in the open at Kew, but grows and flowers well on a south wall there. With this protection it has been grown for many years in the R.H.S. Garden at Wisley and succeeded even in Norfolk, at Little Hadden Hall. At Wisley it seldom flowers, however. The flowers are beautiful and richly coloured, especially the brush of long, erect, crimson stamens which constitute the conspicuous feature of the blossom. It grows well in light loamy soil and should have full sunlight. It can be increased by cuttings placed in heat in July or August. Considering the length of time it has been known, this fine shrub has been rather surprisingly neglected in British gardens. It is 18 ft high at Trewidden in Cornwall.

This species very rarely sets fruits in this country even in the milder parts, but the reason for this may be that it is self-sterile. Messrs Duncan and Davies, the New Zealand nurserymen, recommend that to ensure cross-pollination at least two plants should be grown; these would, of course, have to be seedlings, or belong to different clones, for the cross-pollination to be effective.

FENDLERA PHILADELPHACEAE

A genus of four species in the south-western United States and Mexico, allied to *Jamesia* but differing in its entire leaves and tetramerous flowers (the sepals, petals and styles are each four in number, the stamens eight).

F. RUPICOLA A. Gray

This species is represented in cultivation by the following variety:

var. WRIGHTII A. Gr. *F. wrightii* (A. Gr.) Heller—A deciduous shrub 3 to 6 ft high, of somewhat thin, straggling habit under cultivation, and with ribbed, downy young shoots. Leaves opposite, lanceolate on the sterile branches, ½ to 1¼ in. long, ¼ to ½ in. wide, prominently three-nerved, rough with stiff, short bristles above, hairy beneath, almost without stalks; on the flowering twigs the leaves are much smaller, linear, up to ⅜ in. long, ¼ in. wide, clustered on short twigs. Flowers white or faintly rose-tinted, ¾ to 1¼ in. across, usually solitary, sometimes in threes, produced during May and June on short twigs sparingly from the wood of the previous year; petals four, contracted at the base into a distinct claw, hairy outside; calyx downy, with four narrow, ovate lobes; stamens eight. Seed-vessel conical, ½ in. long, with the calyx persisting at the base. *Bot. Mag.*, t. 7924.

Native of the south-western United States, extending into N. Mexico; introduced to Europe about 1879. This shrub—one of the most beautiful of its own region—is too much of a sun-lover to be seen at its best in our climate. It comes from sunburnt slopes in the mountains, where it is a sturdy, rigid-branched shrub, and produces a great wealth of rosy-tinted flowers, which are said to give it the appearance of a peach-tree, although the four petals and opposite leaves, of course, proclaim a different affinity. E. A. Bowles was very successful with it at Myddleton House, Enfield, on the northern outskirts of London, and it would no doubt flower best in the drier parts of eastern England. Elsewhere, and perhaps even there, it needs the sunniest position that can be given it, against a wall. It is propagated by cuttings of rather soft wood in gentle heat.

In the typical variety of *F. rupicola* the leaves are glabrous, or almost so, beneath, and larger (up to 1¼ in. long on the flowering shoots). But it should be added that the cultivated plants have the leaves less hairy beneath than in wild specimens of the var. *wrightii*.

FICUS FIG MORACEAE

A large genus of evergreen trees, shrubs and climbers (some epiphytic), mainly confined to tropical and subtropical rain-forests. The most characteristic feature of the genus is the peculiar inflorescence, which consists of a concave receptacle almost closed at the mouth and containing numerous unisexual flowers. The fertile fruits consist of the enlarged and fleshy receptacle, containing numerous achenes (the 'true' fruits).

F. CARICA L.   COMMON FIG

A deciduous tree, forming in the south of Europe and in the East a short, rugged trunk 2 to 3 ft in diameter, and a low, spreading head of branches; in Britain it is mostly a shrub. Leaves alternate, three- or five-lobed, 4 to 8 in. or even more in length and width, heart-shaped at the base, varying much in the depth of the lobes, which themselves are blunt or rounded at the end, and usually scalloped into broad rounded teeth, both surfaces, but especially the upper one, rough to the touch, with short stiff hairs; stalk 1 to 4 in. long. Flowers produced on the inner surface of a roundish, pear-shaped receptacle, nearly closed at the top, which afterwards develops into the succulent sweet fruit we know as the fig. The leaves have a very characteristic odour.

Native of W. Asia, and the eastern Mediterranean region, cultivated in the south and west of Europe, even in Britain, from early times. The cultivation of the fig in this country for its fruits does not come within the province of this book. Except in the mild parts of the south and west, where its fruits ripen in the open air, it needs more or less the protection of glass, or at least of a south wall. In the open at Kew the fig gets to be a shrub 6 to 10 ft high, according to the mildness or otherwise of successive winters. The severest frosts cut it to the ground, whence strong young shoots spring up the following summer. At the present time (1971) there is no open-ground plant at Kew worthy of mention, but good specimens can be seen in St James's Park, London. On the whole, unless wall protection can be given, the fig is not worth growing in our average climate except for its interest and associations.

The plants cultivated in gardens are exclusively females, which have the power, like the cucumber, to develop fruit without being fertilised. The fertilisation of the wild fig, through the agency of two generations yearly of an insect (*Blastophaga*), is one of the most remarkable instances known of the interrelation of insect and plant life for their mutual benefit. The Smyrna race, widely cultivated in the Mediterranean region for the production of dried figs, also depends on the fig-wasp for fertilisation. This is achieved by growing a certain number of so-called caprifigs (goat-figs) in each plantation, to serve as 'nurseries' for the winter brood of the wasp and as a source of pollen. Dried figs owe their nutty flavour to the fertile seeds they contain. For an account of the life-cycle of the fig-wasp and its role in pollination, see Maclean and Cook, *A Textbook of Theoretical Botany*, Vol. 2, pp. 1327–9.

F. PUMILA L.

F. repens Hort.

An evergreen climber clinging to trees, etc., in the same way as ivy; juvenile shoots thin, wiry, bristly, sending out aerial roots from the joints. Leaves of the juvenile (better known) state alternate, closely set in two opposite rows, obliquely heart-shaped, pointed, ¾ to 1¼ in. long, two-thirds as wide, dull green, usually glabrous; stalk very short. Leaves of the adult or fruit-bearing state remarkably different; they are more leathery, ovate, with a heart-shaped base, pointed, 1½ to 3½ in. long, half as much wide, rich dark green above, paler and beautifully net-veined (especially as seen through a lens) beneath; stalk hairy, about ½ in. long. Fruits of the ordinary fig shape, although more tapered at the end than in the common fig, 2½ in. long, 1½ in. wide at the terminal part, tapering thence to the stalk which is ½ in. long; in colour they are at first green, then bright orange, ultimately tinged with reddish purple and quite decorative. *Bot. Mag.*, t. 6657.

Native of China, Formosa, and Japan; in cultivation 1759. This fig is well known in its juvenile state as a climber in conservatories and cool greenhouses, whose walls it will closely cover with its abundant leafage. The adult stage is reached as a rule only after the plant has grown 10 or 12 ft high and got beyond its support. It then develops thick, non-clinging young shoots bearing the very different leaves described above. *F. repens* is usually seen under glass but its hardiness is shown by a plant (mentioned in previous editions) which has grown on the south wall of Knepp Castle, West Grinstead, Sussex, for about seventy years. Sir Walter Burrell tells us that it is about 30 ft high, despite having been cut in severe winters. The other plant mentioned in previous editions still climbs on St Matthew's Church, Chelston, near Torquay.

cv. 'MINIMA'.—A garden variety which has very small leaves in the juvenile state.

FIRMIANA   STERCULIACEAE

A genus of a few species of trees and shrubs, mainly confined to S. Asia, but also represented in Africa. Leaves large, palmately veined and usually lobed. Flowers apetalous, in panicles or sometimes racemes. Stamens and ovary borne on a short gynandrophore. Filaments of stamens united into a tube. Ovary single-styled, with five carpels each opening and becoming leaflike soon after flowering; seeds about the size of a pea around the edges near the base. The generic name honours an Austrian governor of Lombardy in the 18th century, K. J. von Firmian.

F. SIMPLEX (L.) W. F. Wight
Hibiscus simplex L.; *Sterculia platanifolia* L.f.; *Firmiana platanifolia* (L.f.) Marsigli

A tree up to 60 ft high, with noble foliage and a trunk smooth even in age. Leaves variable in size, but averaging 6 to 8 in. long and as much or more wide; on vigorous young plants they are over 1 ft long. Ordinarily, the leaves have three rather shallow, pointed lobes towards the end, but often they are five-lobed, with the general outline of a maple-leaf, the base heart-shaped; they are either furnished with stellate down beneath, especially in the vein-axils, or are glabrous. The leaf-stalk is two-thirds to quite the length of the blade. Flowers small, yellow, produced on a branching panicle as much as 18 in. long, and 9 in. wide. For fruits see introduction above.

Native of S. China, Formosa, and the Ryukyus, but introduced in 1757 from Japan, where it is much cultivated. It was long treated as a greenhouse plant, and is, indeed, better suited in Cornwall and such-like localities than in the London districts, where, to be safe, it needs wall protection. Its beauty, however, is only fully shown in a spot where it can develop freely on all sides. It is very fine on the Riviera, especially in the Casino Gardens at Monte Carlo.

FITZROYA   CUPRESSACEAE

A monotypic genus of conifers, native to a restricted area of temperate S. America, named after Captain Fitzroy, commander of the surveying voyage of the *Adventure* and *Beagle*, who brought back specimens and gave an interesting account of the tree. Its distinguishing characters are the short, dark green, spreading leaves, arranged in whorls of three; and its cones with nine scales arranged in three whorls, the lowermost sterile, the upper and sometimes the middle one fertile. In *Libocedrus uvifera* (*Pilgerodendron uviferum*), with which it occurs in the wild, and with which it has been confused, the leaves are arranged in four ranks and the cones have only four scales. A related genus, not further treated in this work, is DISELMA, which has been included in *Fitzroya* by some botanists. It contains only one species—D. ARCHERI Hook. f.—a native of Tasmania. It is a shrub or small tree with closely appressed leaves and cones with four scales.

F. CUPRESSOIDES (Mol.) I. M. Johnston
Pinus cupressoides Mol.; *F. patagonica* Lindl.

An evergreen tree attaining 160 ft in height in the wild, with a slender crown, but forming in cultivation a small bushy tree; bark reddish, shed in longitudinal strips. Leaves arranged in whorls of three, oblong or   slightly obovate, ⅛ in. long (longer in young trees), decurrent at the base, the upper part spreading, often thickened and keeled beneath, dark green, with two bands of stomata on each surface. Cones globose, ⅛ in. wide. (see further in the introductory note). *Bot. Mag.*, t. 4616.

Native of Chile and bordering parts of Argentina from just south of Valdivia to the Island of Chiloe and in the main cordillera (where the finest remaining stands are to be found) from Lake Todos los Santos to about 43° S. It occurs above the beech forests at 2,500 to 3,000 ft, where the climate is cool, cloudy and excessively rainy; sea-level stands once existed near Puerto Montt but these were felled in the early days of settlement. It was introduced by William Lobb in 1849, when collecting for Messrs Veitch.

In nature, *F. cupressoides* makes a tall tree, living to an age of 3,000 years and yielding a valuable timber similar to that of the redwood. In this country, although much hardier than was once supposed, it has grown slowly, as the following records show (earlier measurements are added, where available): Killerton, Devon, *pl.* 1864, 34½ × 3¼ ft (1911), now 60 × 6¼ ft at 4 ft (1970); Woodhouse, Devon, 39 × 4¼ ft (1970); Bicton, Devon, 35 ft (1911), now 48 × 4¾ ft (1968); Pencarrow, Cornwall, *pl.* 1882, 21 ft (1902), now 30 × 3½ ft at 4 ft (1957); Scorrier, Cornwall, *pl.* 1868, 50 × 5¼ ft (1959); Borde Hill, Sussex, *pl. c.* 1930, 33 × 1¾ ft (1961); Leonardslee, Sussex, 34 × 2¼ ft (1962); Strone, Cairndow, Argyll, 58 × 6½ ft, branching into three stems at 5½ ft (1969). In Eire there are many specimens of about the same size as the largest English ones, of which the most noteworthy are: Powerscourt, Co. Wicklow, *pl.* 1869, 44 × 5¾ ft (1967); Mount Usher, Co. Wicklow, 41 × 7½ ft (1967); Kilmacurragh, Co. Wicklow, 42 × 7¼ ft (1967).

It is easily propagated by cuttings taken in late summer.

FOKIENIA   CUPRESSACEAE

This interesting genus was first described by Prof. Augustine Henry and H. H. Thomas in the *Gardeners' Chronicle* for February 4, 1911. As was there pointed out, it is intermediate in its characters between *Chamaecyparis* and *Libocedrus*. The cones resemble *Chamaecyparis* and *Cupressus* in having table-shaped scales, but it resembles *Libocedrus* in the unequal wings of the seeds and in foliage. To *Libocedrus* (*Calocedrus*) *macrolepis* especially it is closely alike in foliage. It is a monotypic genus and a native of China.

F. HODGINSII (Dunn) Henry & Thomas
Cupressus hodginsii Dunn

An evergreen tree ultimately 40 to 50 ft high, with a trunk up to 3 ft in girth, without down in all its parts. The ultimate branchlets are arranged in one plane to form tripinnate, frond-like sprays. The leaves are in fours but amalgamated and flattened (as in *Libocedrus*), with only the four points free; the two side ones are longest and have slender points and a white streak of stomata at the back; the back and front ones are shorter and more abruptly pointed. Each quartet of leaves is ⅛ in. long on young trees, becoming shorter on older ones until, on flowering shoots, they become only $\frac{1}{10}$ in. long and quite blunt. Cones ripening the second year, globose, about 1 in. long, with twelve to sixteen scales which are wedged-shaped or club-shaped, with a small boss in the sunken centre of the top. Seeds (two to each scale) have two very unequal wings.

Native of China in the provinces of Fukien, Chekiang, and Kweichow; discovered by Captain A. Hodgins about 1904 and introduced to cultivation by Admiral Clinton-Baker, who sent two plants to his brother's collection at

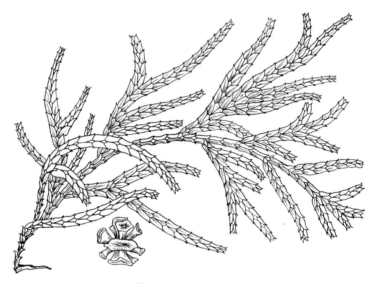

FOKIENIA HODGINSII

Bayfordbury, Herts, in 1909. It is very rare and unlikely to reach any size even in the mildest parts. It is certainly tender, but a plant has survived for more than thirty years at Borde Hill, Sussex, in light woodland, and is about 4 ft high (1968); there is another of about the same size at Leonardslee in the same county and one of 6 ft at Exbury, Hants. That it is lack of summer-heat as much as winter-cold which inhibits the growth of this species is shown by the specimen on Garinish Island, Co. Cork, which is about the same size as the English ones.

FONTANESIA   OLEACEAE

A genus named in honour of R. L. Desfontaines, 1750–1833, director for many years of the Botanic Garden of the Paris Museum and author of *Flora Atlantica* (1798–9), one of the earliest accounts of the flora of N. Africa. It is composed of two deciduous shrubs, or as some authorities hold, but one, closely allied to the ashes, but with simple, opposite leaves. Flowers numerous, small and greenish; petals four; stamens two. Fruit a thin, flat capsule whose two cells are surrounded by a wing. These shrubs have about the same value in gardens as the privet, being easily cultivated in any soil of moderate quality, and readily propagated by late summer cuttings.

F. FORTUNEI Carr.
F. *phillyreoides* var. *sinensis* Debeaux

A deciduous shrub 10 to 15 ft high in gardens, but said to become a tree 30 to 40 ft high in China; young branchlets angular, glabrous. Leaves lanceolate, long-pointed, 1 to 4½ in. long, ⅓ to 1 in. wide, entire, bright green, and quite glabrous. Flowers greenish white, produced in terminal, slender panicles 1 to 2 in. long, and in axillary shorter ones; each flower ⅙ in. long. Fruit a flat oblong disk, ⅜ in. long, with winged margins, notched at the apex.

Native of China; found by Fortune in 1845, and later by several other collectors, near Shanghai. It is very closely allied to the following better known species from Asia Minor; some authors consider it to be merely a variety of this. The most obvious distinctions are the larger more uniformly lance-shaped leaves (often oval or oblong in the other), and the more slender, elongated panicles. In a note by Commander W. Perry preserved in the Kew Herbarium, it is stated that the Chinese make fences round their compounds with branches of this tree interlaced. These take root and form a graceful hedge.

F. PHILLYREOIDES Labill.

A privet-like, deciduous shrub up to 20 ft high, forming a great number of slender twigs, angular and glabrous when young. Leaves greyish green, ovate-lanceolate, oval, or oblong, ½ to 2½ in. long, ¼ to ⅝ in. wide, usually with a tapering point, entire, glabrous. Flowers about ⅛ in. long, greenish white, very numerous on terminal panicles ½ to 1 in. long, supplemented by smaller clusters in the leaf-axils, produced during June on leafy twigs. A prominent feature of the flower is the protruded stamens. Fruit a flat disk, roundish or oblong, ¼ to ⅜ in. long, surrounded by a membranous wing.

Native of the Near East (Cilicia, Syria, etc.); introduced in 1787. This shrub retains its leaves long in the autumn. It is perfectly hardy and flowers copiously, and has about the same decorative value as the privet. It has been stated that the margins of the leaves in this species are rough to the touch and that this character helps to distinguish it from *F. fortunei*. But this character is dubious, and not apparent on most of the specimens in the Kew Herbarium.

cv. 'NANA'.—A form of more compact habit and slower growth.

FORESTIERA   OLEACEAE

A group of New World shrubs, of which three species are occasionally cultivated in botanical collections. They have some affinity with the olive. Leaves deciduous, opposite; flowers small, greenish, without petals, unisexual; the sexes often on separate plants. The fruit, which is oblong or egg-shaped and pulpy, I have never seen produced in this country, and the flowers but rarely. Even in their absence the first two species described below are easily distinguished from each other by the short-stalked, downy leaves of *F. ligustrina*; and the long, narrow, much tapered, smooth leaves of *F. acuminata*. They grow in any ordinary soil, and are easily propagated by late summer cuttings. The genus has also been known as *Adelia*. The name here adopted was given in honour of Charles Le-Forestier, a French physician and naturalist.

F. ACUMINATA (Michx.) Poir.
Adelia acuminata Michx.; *Borya acuminata* (Michx.) Willd.

A deciduous shrub, usually 4 to 8 ft high, or a small tree, sometimes 20 to 30 ft high in the wild, of spreading habit; branches slender, the short ones occasionally spine-tipped. Leaves lanceolate or oval-lanceolate, $1\frac{1}{2}$ to $2\frac{1}{2}$ in. long, $\frac{1}{2}$ to $\frac{3}{4}$ in. wide at the middle, tapering gradually to both ends, shallowly toothed from the middle to the apex; stalk $\frac{1}{4}$ to $\frac{1}{2}$ in. long. Male flowers clustered in small stalkless tufts; female ones on branched stalks; both minute, greenish, and of no beauty. Fruits cylindrical, pointed, $\frac{1}{2}$ in. long, purple.

Native of the S.E. United States; introduced in 1812. A shrub of botanical interest only, and privet-like appearance.

F. LIGUSTRINA (Michx.) Poir.
Adelia ligustrina Michx.; *Borya ligustrina* (Michx.) Willd.

A deciduous shrub up to 10 ft in height, forming a wide bush with slender branches, downy when young, often becoming spine-tipped. Leaves oval or slightly obovate, $\frac{3}{4}$ to $1\frac{3}{4}$ in. long, $\frac{1}{4}$ to $\frac{3}{4}$ in. wide, tapered at both ends, shallowly toothed all round except near the base, dull green and glabrous above, paler and downy beneath; stalks $\frac{1}{4}$ in. or less long. Flowers green, inconspicuous, produced from the twigs of the preceding year; the males in dense stalkless clusters; females fewer, on short spurs. Fruits $\frac{1}{4}$ in. long, egg-shaped, blue-black.

Native of the S.E. United States; introduced in 1812. Of no garden value.

F. NEO-MEXICANA A. Gray
Adelia neo-mexicana (A. Gray) O. Kuntze

A deciduous shrub 6 to 9 ft high, of spreading habit; young shoots glabrous. Leaves opposite, obovate, oval, or oblanceolate, faintly toothed or entire, mostly rounded or bluntish at the apex, tapered at the base; $\frac{1}{2}$ to $1\frac{3}{4}$ in. long, $\frac{1}{4}$ to 1 in. wide, quite glabrous; stalk $\frac{1}{8}$ to $\frac{1}{4}$ in long. Flowers unisexual, clustered at the joints, small and inconspicuous. Fruits black, covered with blue bloom, egg-shaped, scarcely $\frac{1}{4}$ in. long, each on a slender stalk $\frac{1}{8}$ to $\frac{1}{4}$ in long.

Native of the S.W. United States; introduced to Kew in 1925, but known to American botanists long before. *F. acuminata* is easily distinguished from *F. neo-mexicana* by its slenderly pointed, longer leaves and larger cylindrical fruits. The latter species is quite hardy and grows well in this country, but its chief attraction is in the fruits, for whose copious development our climate probably is not sunny enough.

FORSYTHIA* OLEACEAE

This genus, consisting of five or six species of deciduous shrubs, com-memorates William Forsyth, once superintendent of the Royal Gardens at Kensington (1737–1804). They are allied to the lilacs and jasmines, and have opposite, simple or sometimes trifoliate leaves and yellow flowers produced before the leaves on short stalks from single or clustered many-scaled buds borne at the joints of the previous year's wood, each bud producing one, two, or occasionally up to four or five flowers. Calyx four-lobed, green. Corolla also four-lobed, the lobes united at the base into a short tube. Stamens two. Style one, either long or short; both long-styled and short-styled plants occur in each species and cross-pollination between them is usually necessary for the production of fruits. For this reason the fruits, which are many-seeded capsules, are rarely borne in this country except on some tetraploids of garden origin but are mentioned in the account that follows in order to complete the description. One species is a native of S.E. Europe; the others are from E. Asia.

With one exception, all the species of *Forsythia* have lamellate pith, i.e., the stems, cut lengthways, are seen to be filled with transverse plates of pith. But in *F. suspensa* the internodes are hollow, the pith being confined to the nodes. In *F.* × *intermedia* the internodes are mostly irregularly lamellate or hollow.

The forsythias are very easily cultivated and have no objection to lime, but are gross feeders and prefer a good garden soil. They are propagated very easily by cuttings made of half-ripened shoots. The hybrid 'Specta-bilis', and no doubt many other sorts, can be increased by cuttings of ripened wood about 1 ft long, placed in light soil in the open ground at any time between October and January. There is no need for annual pruning, but once the plant is well established a few of the oldest stems should be cut out each year. Plants grown on walls, or in other positions where growth has to be restricted, should be trimmed after flowering.

* Revised with the assistance of Mr P. S. Green of the Kew Herbarium.

The finest display of flowers comes from plants that have been sited where they can grow freely yet are not so remote from the comings and goings of daily life that the birds can destroy their flower-buds undisturbed.

F. EUROPAEA Deg. & Bald.

A deciduous shrub of erect habit from 3 to 10 ft high; young wood not downy, but dotted with lenticels; pith lamellate. Leaves ovate, 2 to 3 in. long, ¾ to 1½ in. wide, of firm texture, glabrous, sometimes sharply and unequally toothed, but usually entire, pointed at the apex, rounded at the base; stalk ⅛ to ⅓ in. long. Flowers yellow, produced in March, mostly singly, occasionally in pairs. Calyx-lobes broadly ovate, green, shorter than the corolla-tube. Corolla 1¼ in. wide, with four narrow-oblong divisions. Fruits smooth, ovoid, with a long beak. *Bot. Mag.*, t. 8039.

A very rare relict species, confined to a small area in northern Albania and bordering parts of Yugoslavia; discovered by Dr Baldacci in 1897 and introduced by him to this country by means of seeds sent to Kew in 1899. Some doubt has been expressed as to its being truly native in Europe, as its fellow species are found only in the Far East; but from the wild nature of the country in which it is found, and the fact that several cases of analogous distribution in other genera exist, this doubt is not justified. It is allied to *F. viridissima*, but differs in the ovate leaves and by a lanky habit which makes it more ungainly. It is the least ornamental of forsythias and the last to flower, but is of phytogeographical interest.

F. GIRALDIANA Lingelsh.

A deciduous shrub up to 15 ft high, branches gracefully spreading; young shoots slender, soon glabrous, black-purple on the upper side; pith lamellate. Leaves 2 to 4 in. long, ¾ to 1¾ in. wide, narrowly ovate-lanceolate, entire, rarely with a few serrations, tapered to rounded at the base, tapered at the apex to a long slender point, glabrous above, slightly hairy on the veins beneath; stalk ⅙ to ½ in. long, slightly hairy. Flowers solitary, soft yellow corolla 1 to 1½ in. wide with a short tube and four oblong-lanceolate, pointed lobes; stamens yellow. Fruits smooth, ovoid, with a short beak. *Bot. Mag.*, t. 9662.

Native of China in the provinces of Kansu, Shensi, and Hupeh; described from material collected in 1897 by the missionary after whom it is named, subsequently found in Hupeh in 1907 by Silvestri and introduced in 1914 by Reginald Farrer, who collected the seeds in Kansu. Farrer's introduction was at first erroneously thought to be *F. suspensa* var. *atrocaulis* (q.v.), and was distributed under that name.

Like all the forsythias it is handsome in flower and of easy cultivation and, although not the best of its kind, it is of value for coming into bloom in late February or the first week of March, usually somewhat earlier than *F. ovata*. Its distinguishing marks—in combination—are its lamellate pith, its entire leaves, and its early flowering.

F. × INTERMEDIA Zab.

An important group of hybrids between *F. suspensa* and *F. viridissima*, of which the first to be observed and described arose shortly before 1885 in the Göttingen Botanic Garden, Germany. The same cross had been made deliberately by Meehan in America before 1868, but whether plants were raised from it is not known. They are shrubs 6 to 8 ft high with erect or arching stems; pith usually irregularly lamellate. Leaves ovate or lanceolate, toothed at least in the upper half, sometimes three-parted on vigorous shoots. Flowers borne in twos and threes from each leaf-scar but singly in some clones. Calyx more than half as long as the corolla-tube, or equalling it in some clones. Corolla-lobes 1¼ to 1½ in. long, usually spreading and often revolute and twisted.

Numerous cultivars of *F. × intermedia* have been raised, and descriptions of the earliest of these will be found in the article by Koehne in *Gartenflora*, Vol. 55 (1906), pp. 226–230. The following are the best known, but of the old clones only 'Spectabilis' is common in commerce:

'ARNOLD GIANT' and 'BEATRIX FARRAND'. See under POLYPLOID DERIVATIVES below.

'DENSIFLORA'.—Flowers crowded, light yellow, usually borne singly; calyx as long as corolla-tube. Corolla-lobes about 1¼ in. long, spreading, not markedly revolute. Long-styled. Raised by Späth and put into commerce 1899.

'KARL SAX'. See under POLYPLOID DERIVATIVES below.

'LYNWOOD'.—A bud-sport of 'Spectabilis', which arose in the garden of Miss Adair of Cookstown, Co. Tyrone, and was put into commerce by the Slieve Donard Nursery Co. in 1935. Leaves less toothed than in 'Spectabilis'. Flowers borne freely all along the branches. Corolla-lobes not so spreading, with the edges less recurved. Considered by many to be superior to the parent.

'PRIMULINA'.—Superseded by 'Spring Glory', q.v.

'SPECTABILIS'.—A vigorous shrub ultimately 10 ft high and as much across. Leaves ovate-lanceolate, 3 to 4½ in. long. Flowers bright, rich yellow, densely and profusely borne. Calyx slightly shorter than corolla-tube. Corolla-lobes usually four in number, as is normal in *Forsythia*, but sometimes five or six, 1½ in. long, about $\frac{5}{16}$ in. wide, widely spreading, margins recurved, tips twisted. Short-styled. This, the best known of the forsythias and deservedly one of the commonest and most loved of garden shrubs, was raised by Späth and put into commerce shortly before 1906.   [PLATE 35

'SPRING GLORY'.—A very free-flowering variety with light brown wood attaining a height of about 6 ft. Flowers bright sulphur-yellow, about 1½ in. wide; corolla-lobes spreading, slightly recurved. Calyx as long as corolla-tube. Short-styled. It is a sport of 'Primulina', raised in the USA (the parent, which it supersedes, was raised in the Arnold Arboretum and described in 1912).

'VITELLINA'.—Flowers about 1½ in. wide, rather deep yellow, tending to be clustered at the base of the previous season's growth; calyx almost as long as the corolla-tube; corolla-lobes not or scarcely revolute; long-styled. Of erect habit. Put into commerce by Späth in 1899.

POLYPLOID DERIVATIVES OF F. × INTERMEDIA.—In 1939 a colchicine-induced tetraploid was raised at the Arnold Arboretum from *F.* × *intermedia* 'Spectabilis' and received the name 'ARNOLD GIANT'. Being difficult to propagate and sparse-flowering, this forsythia has not been widely planted. But in 1944 it was back-crossed to *F.* × *intermedia* 'Spectabilis' by Professor Karl Sax of the Arnold Arboretum, and a number of seedlings were raised. One of these proved to be triploid, but others that have been examined are tetraploid. At least one tetraploid clone was distributed to the trade by the Arnold Arboretum under the name 'Beatrix Farrand', but it appears that this name properly belongs to a triploid which is now extinct. The forsythia introduced to Britain under the name 'Beatrix Farrand' came from the Gulf Stream Nurseries, Virginia, USA, and a plant of this provenance received an Award of Merit when shown from the Savill Gardens, Windsor Great Park, in 1961. This was believed to be the true 'Beatrix Farrand', but investigations by G. E. Marks and K. A. Beckett showed that it, and others from the same source, were in fact all tetraploid (*Journ. R.H.S.*, Vol. 88 (1963), pp. 351–352; see further in Vol. 91 (1966), pp. 307–308). Thus, through no fault of commercial growers, the tetraploid plant grown as 'Beatrix Farrand' is wrongly named and at the moment lacks a name.

A plant received from a nursery under the name 'Beatrix Farrand' has the following characters: it is of very vigorous, erect habit, producing stems from the base that grow up to 8 ft high in a single season. Leaves dull bluish green, very coarsely triangular-toothed. Flowers soft yellow, more or less nodding, the lobes oblong, truncate, almost plane, $\frac{3}{4}$ to 1 in. long, $\frac{3}{8}$ in. or slightly more wide; throat deeper yellow than the lobes, striated. They are short-styled, but in some flowers the style reaches up to the base of the stamens and pushes them apart. Fruits borne abundantly, ovoid with a short beak, producing fertile seeds. It is quite handsome in flower, but the foliage is ugly and the habit gaunt.

Another of Professor Sax's seedlings has been named 'KARL SAX', and was described in *Arnoldia*, Vol. 20 (1960), pp. 49–50. This is of bushier habit than the forsythia called 'Beatrix Farrand' and less tall-growing. The corollas are a shade darker yellow, and being held more or less horizontally they show their deep yellow throats, which enrich the colour of the flowers seen *en masse*. 'Karl Sax' is also tetraploid and bears fruits.

F. OVATA Nakai   KOREAN FORSYTHIA

A deciduous shrub normally not more than 5 ft in height; young shoots glabrous, terete, pale greyish brown, sprinkled with small dark lenticels; pith lamellate. Leaves roundish ovate, with a short slender point and a rounded or slightly heart-shaped base, coarsely toothed to nearly entire, $1\frac{1}{2}$ to $3\frac{1}{2}$ in. long, $1\frac{1}{4}$ to $2\frac{1}{2}$ in. wide, glabrous on both surfaces; stalk $\frac{1}{4}$ to $\frac{1}{2}$ in. long. Flowers opening in March, bright yellow, $\frac{5}{8}$ to $\frac{3}{4}$ in. wide; calyx-lobes broadly ovate, shorter than or equalling the corolla-tube. The flowers are usually solitary, two at each joint. Fruits $\frac{1}{2}$ in. long, ovoid, but drawn out to a slender apex before splitting into two parts. *Bot. Mag.*, t. 9437.

Native of Korea; introduced by Wilson in 1918 under his number 10456. It is usually in bloom in early March if the weather is mild, and is quite an attractive shrub, although scarcely equal to the later-flowering kinds in beauty, its flowers being smaller and not making such a display. Its habit is dwarf and compact; an old plant at Kew has made a densely and intricately branched dome 7 ft in diameter and 4½ ft high, with a few shoots rising up to 1 ft above the general top. Some plants distributed in Britain in the 1950s under the name *F. ovata* bore no resemblance to this species; they were perhaps the same as the "*F. ovata robusta*" of continental nurseries.

The clone 'TETRAGOLD' is a colchicine-induced tetraploid of *F. ovata* raised in Holland and distributed to the trade in 1963 (*Dendroflora*, Vol. 1, pp. 35, 38).

F. JAPONICA Mak.—A spreading shrub with glabrous, terete branchlets; pith lamellate. Leaves ovate or broadly ovate, 3 to 4¾ in. long, short acuminate at the apex, toothed or more usually entire, glabrous above, downy on the veins beneath; leaf-stalk downy. Flowers bright yellow, solitary, about 1 in. across. Calyx about half as long as corolla-tube. Lobes of corolla narrow-oblong. Native of Japan, rare in the wild and not common in gardens. It is very closely allied to *F. ovata*, and it is doubtful whether the two are specifically distinct. The chief difference is that in *F. japonica* the leaves and leaf-stalks are downy beneath, but glabrous in *F. ovata* (and the corolla-lobes are slightly longer and narrower). It flowers about four weeks later. The following variety of *F. japonica* is even closer to *F. ovata*:

var. SAXATILIS Nakai *F. saxatilis* (Nakai) Nakai—Described as only 8 in. high in the wild, but reaching about 3 ft in cultivation. It is more likely to be confused with *F. ovata* than with typical *F. japonica*. It differs from the former in its smaller leaves, ⅞ to 2½ in. long, $\frac{7}{16}$ to $1\frac{3}{16}$ in. wide with finely and minutely saw-toothed margins and with down in the axils of the veins beneath and on the leaf-stalks. On the plant at Kew, received from the Arnold Arboretum, the leaves are larger than on wild plants (3¼ to 4 in. long, 1¾ to 2 in. wide) and sparsely downy to almost glabrous on the midrib below. The var. *saxatilis* is a native of Korea.

If *F. japonica* and *F. ovata* were to be united, as they probably should be, the correct name for the species would be *F. japonica*.

F. 'ARNOLD DWARF'.—A hybrid between some form of *F.* × *intermedia* and *F. japonica* var. *saxatilis*, raised in the Arnold Arboretum in 1941. It makes a low, self-layering shrub of indefinite width, with ovate, bright green leaves 1 to 2 in. long, strongly toothed. It rarely produces its pale yellow flowers but has some value as ground cover.

F. SUSPENSA (Thunb.) Vahl   GOLDEN BELL
Syringa suspensa Thunb.

A deciduous shrub of rambling habit, which if trained on a wall will grow 30 ft high, but in the open, and unsupported, forms a mass of interlacing often pendulous branches, 8 or 10 ft high; young branches glabrous, hollow except at the nodes. Leaves mostly simple, 2 to 4 in. long, 1 to 2 in. wide, but occasionally on strong shoots trifoliolate, three-lobed, or two-lobed, coarsely toothed, pointed, the simple leaves rounded or broadly wedge-shaped at the base, the leaflets wedge-shaped at the base; stalk about ½ in. long. Flowers golden yellow, produced one to as many as six in a cluster from the buds of last year's wood in late March and early April, lasting a month in beauty; each flower 1 to 1¼ in. across. Calyx-lobes oblong-lanceolate, ¼ in. long. Fruits narrow-ovoid, beaked.

Native of China, long cultivated in Japan. It is usual to recognise two varieties:

var. SIEBOLDII Zab.—This is the variety described above. Shoots slender, pendent, rooting where they touch the ground. Leaves rather broad-ovate, usually unlobed. Flowers long-stalked (stalks about twice as long as the buds); petals not so recurved and spreading as in var. *fortunei*. Possibly a Japanese garden variety. According to Siebold *F. suspensa* was introduced to Europe by Verkerk Pistorius in 1833, but whether in the pendent-branched form or the erect-branched (also cultivated in Japan) he did not say. To Britain it was introduced shortly before 1857, in which year what is clearly the var. *sieboldii* was figured in *Bot. Mag.*, t. 4995. According to Rehder, the var. *sieboldii* was represented in European gardens by short-styled plants (*Gartenfl.* (1891), pp. 395–400). It was probably a plant similar to the var. *sieboldii* at least in habit, and probably in its long-stalked flowers, that Thunberg took as the type of his *Syringa suspensa*.

var. FORTUNEI (Lindl.) Rehd. *F. fortunei* Lindl.—A shrub of stiffer growth, with erect or arching (not so pendulous) shoots. Leaves usually three-lobed or parted on strong shoots, more narrowly ovate than in var. *sieboldii*. Flower-stalk not much longer than the bud; petals spreading, slightly recurved. Introduced by Fortune from China to Standish's nursery in 1862. An erect-branched form was also cultivated in Japanese gardens.

The differences between the two varieties given above refer to the plants originally grown in Europe. There are plants now in cultivation that it is difficult to assign to one or the other. *F. suspensa* var. *sieboldii* in its characteristic form is, however, still very common in cultivation. It is useful for covering a steep slope, and for using as a climber on house-walls, arbours, etc. It will flower well on a north-facing wall, and assumes a semi-climbing habit if planted near a tree or tall shrub.

f. ATROCAULIS Rehd.—Young shoots and unfolding leaves of a dark purplish hue; older wood rich brown. Introduced by Wilson from W. Hupeh under W.637, when collecting for the Arnold Arboretum. The plants raised from these seeds seem to have varied somewhat in habit and size of flower (but some so-called inferior forms of *atrocaulis* may be *F. giraldiana*, q.v.). The 'NYMANS VARIETY' is a very beautiful forsythia with soft yellow, nodding flowers about 1¼ in. across, with flat, spreading lobes about ½ in. wide at the base. It is of erect habit and one of the last forsythias to flower. There are, however, unnamed clones very similar to this.

Two garden varieties of *F. suspensa*, neither of much value and now scarce, are 'DECIPIENS' and 'PALLIDA', both raised by Späth.

F. VIRIDISSIMA Lindl.

A deciduous or partially evergreen shrub 5 to 8 ft high, with stiff, erect, somewhat four-angled branches with a greenish colouration even in the second year; pith lamellate. Leaves lance-shaped, 3 to 6 in. long, ¾ to 1½ in. wide, tapering at both ends, but more slenderly towards the pointed apex, toothed in

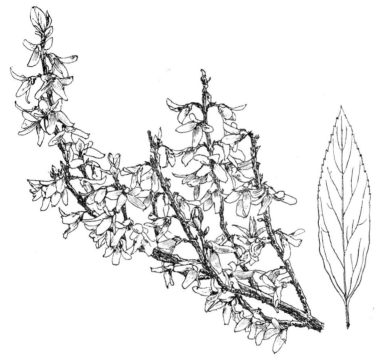

FORSYTHIA VIRIDISSIMA

the upper half or quite entire; stalk ¼ to ½ in. long. Flowers bright yellow, 1¼ in. across, the four corolla-lobed narrow-oblong, ½ in. long. Calyx-lobed ovate, about half to three-quarters as long as the corolla-tube. Fruits broadly ovoid, beaked. *Bot. Mag.*, t. 4587.

Native of China: introduced by Fortune in 1845, by means of a plant sent to the Horticultural Society, in whose garden it first flowered in 1847. It is not so fine a garden shrub as *F. suspensa* or the hybrids between it and that species (*F.* × *intermedia*) and is not so common as it was in the 19th century. It flowers one or two weeks later than *F. suspensa*, usually in April, and is sturdy enough to hold its branches erect. Its distinguishing characters are: the lamellate pith of the branches, the dark green lanceolate to oblong leaves toothed in the upper half and almost invariably undivided; and the short calyx, which is half as long as the corolla-tube.

F. viridissima was for long represented in cultivation by a clone with long-styled flowers. The garden clones of *F. suspensa*, on the other hand, were mainly short-styled. From this the false conclusion was drawn that these were specific characters. In fact, as Darwin surmised, the forsythias, like the common primrose, are heterostylous, some individuals of a species bearing only long-styled and others only short-styled flowers. But a clone, being descended vegetatively from a single individual, bears flowers of one kind only.

cv. 'BRONXENSIS'.—A dwarf compact plant 8 to 12 in. high. Leaves ovate, ¾ to 1¾ in. long, closely set on the stem. Flowers primrose-yellow. Award of Merit April 9, 1958. It was raised in the Boyce Thompson Arboretum from seeds received in 1928 from the Botanic Garden of the Imperial University of Tokyo, under the name *F. viridissima* var. *koreana*. Of three plants raised, two belonged to this variety. The third was a pygmy, of which propagating material was given to the New York Botanic Garden in the Bronx. It was named var. *bronxensis* in 1947 by T. H. Everett, the Curator, who at that time was unaware of the origin of the plant. Its history, as later ascertained by him, is given in *Gard. Chron.*, Vol. 18 (1949), p. 90.

Many gardeners in Britain have found this variety shy-flowering, but it flowers well at the foot of a sunny wall in the Director's garden at Kew, where its soft yellow flowers assort well with the slate-blue ones of *Ceanothus rigidus*.

var. KOREANA Rehd. *F. koreana* (Rehd.) Nakai—Leaves oblong-ovate or lanceolate, 2 to 4¾ in. long, toothed in the upper half or almost entire. Flowers slightly larger than in the typical state of the species and brighter yellow. Calyx more than half as long as the corolla-tube. Introduced from Korea to the Arnold Arboretum by Wilson in 1917 and to Kew in 1925. At Kew, the leaves do not colour in the autumn, as they are said to do in the USA.

FORTUNEARIA   HAMAMELIDACEAE

A monotypic genus, named in honour of Robert Fortune, the famous plant collector. From other hardy genera of the Hamamelidaceae it is distinguished by the following combination of characters: leaves deciduous, pinnately-veined; petals very short and narrow but longer than the sepals; fruit a two-valved, two-seeded capsule. The allied *Sinowilsonia*, another monotypic genus from China, is distinguished from *Fortunearia* by its apetalous flowers.

F. SINENSIS Rehd. & Wils.

A monoecious, deciduous shrub of strong spreading growth, ultimately 20 to 25 ft high; young shoots, leaf-stalks and flower-stalks covered with starry down. Leaves obovate, tapered more abruptly towards the apex than the often rounded or slightly heart-shaped base, unevenly toothed, 3 to 6 in. long, about half as much wide, dullish green and glabrous above, downy on the midrib and veins beneath; stalk $\frac{1}{8}$ to $\frac{1}{4}$ in. long. Flowers green, borne in terminal racemes either entirely male or entirely bisexual; the former are catkin-like, up to $\frac{3}{4}$ in. long, with the small flowers very densely packed; the latter are 1 to 2 in. long with flowers $\frac{1}{6}$ in. across. Capsules $\frac{1}{2}$ in. long.

Native of W. China; discovered and introduced by Wilson to the Arnold Arboretum in 1907, thence to Kew in 1910, where it is very hardy and vigorous. Apart from its botanical interest there is little to recommend it. The flowers, which at Kew appear in February, are inconspicuous, and as regards foliage it has about the same ornamental value as the hazel.

FOTHERGILLA HAMAMELIDACEAE

A genus of two species of deciduous shrubs from eastern N. America, which commemorates Dr John Fothergill, who in the 18th century cultivated in his garden at Stratford-le-Bow, in Essex, one of the earliest and most extensive collections of American plants. They are allies of the witch-hazels, and their flowers appear before the leaves in bottle-brush like spikes terminating short branches. Their sole beauty is in the numerous long stamens. There are no petals, and the seed-vessel is a downy, hard-shelled capsule, opening at the top and containing two seeds.

The fothergillas give beautiful autumn colour and are chiefly grown for that, but are not suitable for limy soils and prefer one that is light and peaty. They colour best if grown in a sunny position. Propagation is by layers; or by cuttings, taken in June or July and rooted in bottom heat.

F. GARDENII Murr.

F. alnifolia L.f.; *F. carolina* Britton

A deciduous shrub of thin habit, rarely more than 2 or 3 ft high, with slender, crooked, often rather weak and spreading branches; young twigs covered with white, stellate hairs. Leaves oval or obovate, 1 to 2½ in. long, ¾ to 1¾ in. wide, heart-shaped, rounded or tapering at the base, with several large unequal teeth above the middle, downy, and green or whitish beneath; stalk ¼ in. long, downy. Flowers in cylindrical terminal spikes, consisting chiefly of a mass, 1 to 1½ in. long, and about 1 in. through, of white stamens with yellow anthers; petals none. *Bot. Mag.*, t. 1341.

Native of the south-eastern United States; first discovered by Dr Garden of Charlestown, USA, and introduced in 1765. It flowers on the naked branches in April and May, and is then very pretty and fragrant. Although hardy, this shrub is not robust. It does not like a heavy soil so much as one of peat and sandy loam combined. The leaf is variable in shape, on account of which attempts have been made to differentiate two or three varieties such as var. OBTUSA (*Bot. Mag.*, t. 1341), with obovate bluntish leaves; and var. ACUTA, with ovate, pointed leaves. The foliage often turns a beautiful crimson before falling. This species differs from the following in its much smaller stature, in the smaller leaves, and in the flowers being borne before the leaves unfold.

F. MAJOR Lodd. [PLATE 32

F. alnifolia var. *major* Sims; *F. monticola* Ashe

A deciduous shrub, ultimately 6 to 10 ft high, forming a rounded bush with mostly erect stems; young branchlets covered with stellate, whitish hairs. Leaves roundish oval or broadly ovate, 2 to 4 in. long, and from two-thirds to nearly as wide, with a few teeth above the middle, or almost entire, upper surface dark glossy green becoming almost or quite glabrous, lower one glaucous, with stellate hairs, especially on the midrib and veins; stalk downy, about $\frac{1}{4}$ in. long. Flowers numerous, in an erect spike, 1 to 2 in. long, terminating short lateral twigs; the inflorescence owes its beauty to the numerous clustered stamens, which have pinkish white stalks $\frac{3}{4}$ in. long, and yellow anthers; petals none. Capsules $\frac{1}{2}$ in. long, splitting at the top. *Bot. Mag.*, t. 1342.

Native of the Allegheny Mountains from Virginia to S. Carolina; grown in English gardens in 1780, but apparently long lost to cultivation until reintroduced to Kew from the Arnold Arboretum in 1902. It is a most charming shrub, especially to those who love out-of-the-way species. It succeeds extremely well in a mixture of peat and sandy loam, producing its fragrant spikes profusely in May. The leaves turn yellow, orange-yellow, or red before falling. It strikes root freely from cuttings of fairly firm wood in gentle heat, and is quite hardy. Certainly it is in every way superior to the commoner *F. gardenii*, and it is strange that it was so long lost to gardens.

The botanical description given in the first paragraph is of the plant that is considered to represent the typical state of *F. major*. More glabrous plants have been given specific rank as *F. monticola* but this species has never been generally recognised by botanists and there seems to be no justification for maintaining it any longer. Differences in habit and autumn colour between *F. major* and "*F. monticola*" have been adduced, but these are really clonal differences which are bound to occur where a variable species is propagated vegetatively. Furthermore, some plants in commerce as *F. monticola* answer to catalogue descriptions in having orange and red autumn colour and being of low, spreading habit; but botanically they would be referable to *F. major* even if *F. monticola* were to be recognised as a distinct species.

FRANKLINIA THEACEAE

A monotypic genus, consisting of the one species described below, which was discovered by John Bartram and his son William Bartram in Georgia,

USA, around 1765 and is now almost certainly extinct in the wild. It is allied to *Gordonia*, from which it differs in the deciduous leaves, almost sessile flowers, and in the curious zigzag dehiscence of the seed-capsule, which splits into ten segments attached alternately to the base and apex of the persistent central axis (or, in Bartram's words, 'opening at each end oppositely by five alternate fissures'). Although many authorities have included this species in *Gordonia*, the modern view is that William Bartram was correct in giving it the rank of a separate genus, which he named in honour of the American statesman, philosopher, and scientist Benjamin Franklin (1706–1790).

F. ALATAMAHA Marsh.

Gordonia alatamaha (Marsh.) Sarg.; *G. pubescens* L'Hérit.

Franklinia alatamaha was first described by Humphrey Marshall in *Arbustum Americanum* (1785) from a plant cultivated in Philadelphia and under the name chosen by William Bartram. The following description, by William Bartram himself, was published a few years later in his classic *Travels* (1791):

'It is a flowering tree, of the first order for beauty and fragrance of blossoms: the tree grows fifteen or twenty feet high, branching alternately; the leaves are oblong, broadest towards their extremities, and terminate with an acute point, which is generally a little reflexed; they are lightly serrated, attenuate downwards, and sessile, or have very short petioles; they are placed in alternate order, and towards the extremities of the twigs are crouded together, but stand more sparsedly below; the flowers are very large, expand themselves perfectly, are of a snow white colour, and ornamented with a crown or tassel of gold coloured refulgent staminae in their centre, the inferior petal or segment of the corolla is hollow, formed like a cap or helmet, and entirely includes the other four, until the moment of expansion; its exterior surface is covered with a short silky hair; the borders of the petals are crisped or plicated: these large white flowers stand single and sessile in the bosom of the leaves, and being near together towards the extremities of the twigs, and usually many expanded at the same time, make a gay appearance: the fruit is a large, round, woody apple or pericarp, opening at each end oppositely by five alternate fissures, containing ten cells, each replete with dry woody cuneiform seed.' To this it is only necessary to add that the leaves are deciduous, 5 to 6 in. long, downy below, and the flowers up to 3 in. across, borne in late summer and early autumn. The fruits, although splitting into ten segments, are five-celled, not ten-celled as Bartram states, and the flowers are very short-stalked, not sessile.

This species was discovered by John Bartram on the Altamaha river, Georgia, where it was confined to an area of two or three acres, and was introduced to cultivation by his son, who visited the stand in 1778 and found ripe seeds. The species was last seen in the wild in 1790 and is probably now extinct in the wild state. The cultivated plants all descend, it is believed, from those raised in the Bartrams' garden in Philadelphia, one of which survived into the 20th century.

Although not really tender in southern England, this species needs warmer and longer summers than ours to grow and flower freely. But even in this country the leaves turn a fine scarlet before falling.

FRAXINUS   ASH   OLEACEAE

A group of some 60 species of deciduous trees and a few shrubs, all except three found in the temperate latitudes of the northern hemisphere. They have normally opposite, equally pinnate leaves, but in some species and varieties the leaflets are reduced to one, and the leaves are sometimes in whorls of three, and on odd shoots not infrequently alternate. The inflorescences vary considerably in beauty in different species. In the most ornamental group, the 'flowering' ashes, both corolla and calyx are present, and the flowers are borne very numerously in panicles from the end of the young shoot and from the axils of the terminal pair of leaves. This is the section *Ornus* (manna ash group). In *F. chinensis* and its Japanese ally the flowers are borne as in the manna ash, but they lack petals (section *Ornus*, subsection *Ornaster*). In the second and larger section of the genus —section *Fraxinus* (*Fraxinaster*)—the flowers are produced before the leaves from lateral leafless buds on the previous season's shoots, and are without petals (except in the anomalous *F. dipetala*). In the subsection *Bumelioides*, to which our common ash (*F. excelsior*) belongs, the calyx, too, is lacking.

The flowers are sometimes perfect, sometimes unisexual; and perfect male and female flowers may be found either altogether or separately on one tree. It is said that the flowers of a tree may sometimes be all or mostly one sex one year, and the other sex the next. Stamens usually two. Fruit one- or two-celled, one- or two-seeded, developing at the end a long, flattened wing or membrane, usually from $\frac{3}{4}$ to $1\frac{1}{2}$ in. long and $\frac{1}{4}$ to $\frac{1}{3}$ in. wide. Many of the species hereinafter described do not flower in this country, and even those that do, like the common ash, do not carry crops of fruit every year. From all its allies in gardens, except *Jasminum* and one species of *Syringa*, *Fraxinus* is distinguished by its pinnate leaves.

In gardens and parks, the ashes are welcome for their stately form and fine pinnate foliage. Some of them, like *F. excelsior* and *F. americana*, yield an admirable timber. They are frequently found in nature on a limestone formation, and should be especially noted by those whose ground is so situated. For the rest, they are gross feeders, and like a good soil and abundant moisture. They should always, if possible, be raised from seeds, which may be sown in cold frames or shallow boxes, and thinly covered with soil. Grafting for the weeping, coloured, and other garden varieties has, perforce, to be resorted to, but the stock should always be of the species to which the variety belongs. The ashes produce a very fibrous and extensive root system, which renders their transplanting safe and easy. The only species at all unsatisfactory in cultivation are those like *F. nigra* and *F. mandshurica*, which, being excited into growth by un-seasonable warmth early in the year, are almost invariably cut back by later frost. Some species, like *F. dipetala*, need rather more warmth than our climate affords. But given a good soil, and not too exposed a position, the ashes generally are satisfactory.

The following is a selection of the more desirable species:
F. angustifolia; *F. americana*; *F. excelsior diversifolia*, 'Jaspidea' and 'Pendula'; *F. latifolia (oregona)*; *F. mariesii*; *F. oxycarpa; F. pennsylvanica*; *F.* 'Raywood'; *F. spaethiana*; *F. velutina*.

The only important modern work on the ashes is Gertrude N. Miller's study of the North American species (Cornell Univ. Agric. Exp. Stn. Mem. 334, February 1955).

F. AMERICANA L.   WHITE ASH
F. alba Marsh.; *F. acuminata* Lam.; *F. juglandifolia* Lam.

A fine timber tree up to 120 ft high in the wild, with a trunk 5 to 6 ft thick; bark grey, furrowed, with narrow interlacing ridges; twigs glabrous, dark polished green or purplish brown, becoming grey the second year; terminal buds ovoid or conical, blunt at the apex. Leaves 8 to 15 in. long; leaflets seven or nine (sometimes five), oblong-lanceolate or oval, stalked, ordinarily 4 to 6 in. long (on vigorous young trees 7 or 8 in.), 1 to 3 in. wide, acute to acuminate at the apex, rounded or tapered at the base, entire, or edged near the apex or throughout with distant teeth, dark green and glabrous above, undersides glabrous or sometimes downy, especially on the main veins, covered with microscopic waxy protuberances (papillae) which are usually dense enough to render them whitish to the eye, but sometimes sparser, the undersides then appearing green; stalks of lateral leaflets about ⅛ in. long, of the terminal one ½ to 1 in. long; common stalk yellowish white, glabrous, round, with a scarcely perceptible groove on the upper side. Flowers unisexual, male and female borne on different trees; calyx minute, campanulate; corolla absent. Fruits 1 to 2 in. long, ¼ in. wide; body rounded in cross-section; wing extending about one-third of the way down the body.

Native of eastern N. America; introduced in 1724. This handsome and striking ash is one of the best of American deciduous trees in this country, being quick-growing and producing timber of similar quality to that of our native ash and used for similar purposes in its native country. It is the only exotic ash that shows promise as a plantation tree in the British Isles, under conditions too dry or too frosty for the native species (Streets, R. J., *Exotic Trees in the British Commonwealth*, p. 394).

F. americana is somewhat variable in the number, shape, texture, toothing, and indumentum of the leaflets, but the variations are not well correlated with each other or with geographical location except that the leaflets are said to be generally greener beneath in the northern part of the area than in the south. It is also variable in its autumn colouring and, in Britain, not reliable in this respect. At Kew, the tree in the Ash Collection colours well, the pair in Pagoda Avenue do not colour at all.

T S—H

It is not always easy to differentiate between the white ash and the red or green ash (*F. pennsylvanica*). The presence of papillae on the undersides of the leaves of the white ash, and their absence in the red ash group is, according to Miss Miller, the most reliable mark of difference, but it may not always be evident to the naked eye. Useful identification points given by her are that the terminal buds of the white ash are usually ovoid and blunt (pointed and conical in the red ash); leaf-scars on old twigs concave at the upper margin, truncate in the red ash (G. N. Miller, op. cit, pp. 12–16).

The dimensions of the trees at Kew are: Pagoda Vista, 88 × 7¾ ft, 70 × 6¾ ft and 63 × 7¾ ft; Ash Collection 74 × 7½ ft (1967). Other notable specimens measured recently are: Syon House, Middlesex, 70 × 5½ ft (1967); Kensington Gardens, London, 58 × 5 ft (1967); Westonbirt, Glos., in Broad Drive, 65 × 6¼ ft (1967); Batsford Park, Glos., 73 × 4¾ ft (1963).

var. MICROCARPA A. Gray—A very handsome specimen in the Ash collection at Kew is grown under this name. It is grafted and measures 68 × 5¾ ft (1969).

F. ANGUSTIFOLIA Vahl   NARROW-LEAVED ASH   [PLATE 33

F. oxycarpa var. *angustifolia* (Vahl) Lingelsh.; *F. tamariscifolia* Vahl

A tree 60 to 80 ft, occasionally 90 ft high; young shoots and leaves perfectly glabrous. Leaves 6 to 10 in. long; leaflets seven to thirteen, lanceolate, glabrous, 1 to 3 in. long, ⅓ to ¾ in. wide, sharply and rather coarsely or even jaggedly toothed except towards the narrowly tapered base, apex long-pointed. The terminal leaflet is the only one that has a stalk (¼ to ⅓ in. long); main-stalk with two wings on the upper side forming a groove that is open from the base to the lowest pair of leaflets, but beyond them closed, except where the leaflets are attached. Flowers produced from the joints of the previous year's wood, and with neither calyx nor corolla. Fruits 1 to 1¼ in. long.

Native of the W. Mediterranean region and N. Africa. It is an elegant tree, allied botanically to the common ash but distinguished by its more furrowed bark, brown buds, and quite glabrous leaflets.

var. LENTISCIFOLIA Henry—Leaflets more spreading (in the typical form they point forwards) and set further apart on the main-stalk, making the leaf sometimes 10 in. or more long, and the tree very graceful.

The following cultivated trees belong either to *F. angustifolia* or to the var. *lentiscifolia*: Kew, 75 × 8¾ ft and 68 × 7¾ ft (1968); Chiswick House, London, 85 × 10 ft (1964) (this tree was 75 × 7½ ft in 1903); Syon House, London, 70 × 7¼ ft (1959); University Botanic Garden, Cambridge, 85 × 6½ ft (1969); Hardwick, Suffolk, 99 × 6¼ ft (1952, measurement by Maynard Greville; this tree is grafted, and was 72 × 7¾ ft above the graft in c. 1905 and 5¼ ft below it); Tortworth, Glos., 80 × 7½ ft (1964); Glasnevin Botanic Garden, Dublin, Eire, 70 × 5½ ft.

F. OXYCARPA Willd. *F. angustifolia* subsp. *oxycarpa* (Willd.) Franco & Rocha Alfonso; *F. excelsior* subsp. *oxycarpa* (Willd.) Wesm.; *F. oxyphylla* Bieb.—This species is closely allied to *F. angustifolia*, of which it is now treated as a

subspecies in *Flora Europaea* (*Bot. Journ. Linn. Soc.*, Vol. 64 (1971), p. 377).
Buds brown. Leaves often in whorls of three. Leaflets mostly three to seven,
lanceolate or narrow-elliptic, usually 1½ to 2½ in. long, tapered to an acute or
acuminate apex, usually cuneate or long-cuneate at the base, sessile or nearly so,
finely to coarsely serrated. The chief distinction from *F. angustifolia* is that the
undersurface of the leaves has a band of hairs each side of the midrib near the base.

F. *oxycarpa* has a more eastern distribution than *F. angustifolia* (E. Mediterranean, parts of S.E. Europe, lower Danube, Asia Minor, Caucasus, etc.). It is
not common in cultivation, and seems to make a smaller less vigorous tree
than *F. angustifolia*, with a smoother bark.

F. *oxycarpa* is mainly represented in British gardens by the cultivar 'RAY-
WOOD', which was raised in Australia and put into commerce in Britain by
Messrs Notcutt of Woodbridge, Suffolk, who received bud-wood around 1925.
It is an elegant tree, of narrow habit when young, but opening up with age.
The leaves are borne mostly in whorls of three (or in fours under the terminal
bud) and have seven or nine slender, sharply serrated leaflets. The feature for
which 'Raywood' is chiefly grown is that they usually turn plum-purple in
autumn, but in some gardens they drop without colouring. It needs a sunny
position and is perhaps best suited in the drier parts of the country.

The oldest tree at Woodbridge, planted soon after 1925, grows on Kyson
Hill above the River Deben, on land presented to the National Trust by the
late Mr R. C. Notcutt in 1930. This is about 5 ft in girth and perhaps 80 ft
high, with an open crown. Another large specimen grows at Talbot Manor,
King's Lynn, Norfolk; this measures 48 × 3¾ ft (1970).

Messrs Notcutt put this ash into commerce as *F. excelsior raywoodii*, but a tree
presented by them to Kew in 1928 came under the name *F. excelsior wollastonii*.
This tree is certainly *F. oxycarpa* and seems to be the same as 'Raywood'.

F. ANOMALA Torr.   UTAH ASH

A tree 18 to 20 ft high, with glabrous, square, slightly winged, slender young
shoots. Leaves simple (rarely with two or three leaflets), ovate, sometimes
roundish or obovate, tapered at the base, bluntish or pointed at the apex,
inconspicuously toothed, 1 to 2½ in. long, ¾ to 1¾ in. wide, grey-green, glabrous
on both surfaces; stalk ½ to 1 in. long. It flowers on the previous year's growths,
and the fruits are ⅔ in. long, obovate or oval.

Native of Colorado, Utah, and Nevada; said by Sargent to be not rare.
Introduced in 1893 to Kew, where it formed a lax-branched, small tree, quite
distinct from every other cultivated ash in the combination of square stems
and simple leaves, but only worth growing as a curiosity. It is no longer in the
Kew collection.

F. BILTMOREANA Beadle
F. *americana* var. *biltmoreana* (Beadle) J. Wright

The status of the Biltmore ash is controversial. By some botanists it has been
considered to be no more than a downy form of *F. americana*, but Miss Miller

in her monograph accepts it as a species and suggests that it may be the result of hybridisation between *F. americana* and *F. pennsylvanica* (op. cit., pp. 22–24 and 41–43). The tree at Kew described under *F. biltmoreana* in previous editions no longer exists, but there is another in the Ash collection, received from the Arnold Arboretum in 1902. This is a very slender-crowned tree, measuring 70 × 5 ft (1969). It has the following characters, which agree well with those of the Biltmore ash as defined by Miss Miller: young twigs grey-brown, downy; terminal buds ovoid with apiculate tips; leaves with seven to nine stalked, entire leaflets, downy and very white beneath; rachis downy. Fruits not seen and probably not borne by this tree. They are described as having terminal wings (i.e., the wing not extending as a rim along the body of the fruits).

F. BUNGEANA DC.

A shrub or small tree up to 15 ft high; twigs minutely downy. Leaves of thin texture, 4 to 6 in. long; leaflets five or seven, stalked, unequal-sided, oval and obovate, 1 to 2 in. long, $\frac{1}{2}$ to 1 in. wide, tapered at the base, with abrupt slender points, round-toothed except towards the base, quite glabrous. Main leaf-stalk minutely downy, with a narrow groove on the upper side; stalk of leaflets $\frac{1}{8}$ to $\frac{1}{4}$ in. long, minutely downy. Flowers (with petals) produced in terminal panicles. Fruits a little over 1 in. long, $\frac{1}{5}$ in. wide.

Native of N. China; introduced in 1881 to the Arnold Arboretum, USA. The true plant is little known in Britain, although many ashes under the name have been introduced, which have turned out to be *F. chinensis* or other species. It belongs to the *Ornus* section, and is very distinct from the only other shrubby ashes in cultivation—the tiny leaved *F. dimorpha* and *xanthoxyloides*. Bunge's ash is one of the few whose twigs and leaf-stalks are downy, whilst the leaf-blades are glabrous.

F. DIPPELIANA Lingelsh., as once sold by Späth of Berlin, is only a form of *F. bungeana*, or very closely allied to it, the leaves perhaps broader (up to $1\frac{1}{2}$ in. wide) and shorter pointed.

F. CAROLINIANA Mill.

A tree rarely more than 40 ft high; young shoots glabrous, brown. Leaves 5 to 12 in. long; leaflets five or seven, stalked, oval, 2 to 4 in. long, $1\frac{1}{4}$ to 2 in. wide (terminal one larger and up to 6 in. long, sometimes obovate), mostly tapered, sometimes rounded at the base, pointed, sharply toothed, dark green and glabrous above, pale duller green beneath, with white hairs along the sides of the midrib and lower veins. Main leaf-stalk round, with a slight groove on the upper side; stalks of side leaflets up to $\frac{1}{2}$ in. long, that of terminal one up to 1 in. long. Flowers without petals, produced in short panicles on the shoots of the preceding year. Fruits elliptical or obovate, up to 2 in. long, frequently three-winged, $\frac{1}{2}$ to $\frac{3}{4}$ in. wide; the body is short, flattened, and completely surrounded by the wing.

Native of the south-eastern United States; introduced in 1783, but extremely rare. Trees which in vegetative characters appear to be true, and which were received from the United States as *F. caroliniana*, were once in the collection at Kew; but one would scarcely expect the tree to be hardy in this country, as it comes from the coastal regions of the Atlantic and Gulf States, and reaches even to Cuba.

F. CHINENSIS Roxb.

It is doubtful whether this species, in its typical state, is in cultivation in the British Isles, but the following variety is sometimes met with in gardens:

var. RHYNCOPHYLLA (Hance) Hemsl. *F. rhyncophylla* Hance; *F. bungeana* Hance, not DC.—A deciduous tree up to 80 ft high in the wild; young shoots glabrous, yellowish. Leaves mostly 6 to 12 in. long, with five leaflets which are

FRAXINUS CHINENSIS VAR. RHYNCOPHYLLA

oblong, ovate, or obovate, shortly and slenderly pointed, wedge-shaped or rounded at the base, coarsely round-toothed, terminal leaflet 3 to 7 in. long, 1 to 3 in. wide, with a stalk up to 1 in. long, the other two pairs successively smaller and very shortly-stalked, dark green and glabrous above, with a fringe of down on the midrib and lower veins beneath; main-stalk slightly grooved, with tufts of down where the leaflets are attached. Flowers produced at the end of leafy shoots in June on panicles 3 to 6 in. long; they have a calyx but no petals. Fruits oblanceolate, $1\frac{1}{2}$ in. long, $\frac{3}{16}$ in. wide.

Native of Korea and China; introduced from Peking to the Arnold Arboretum in 1881. It is quite hardy and grows well in this country, being notable amongst the ashes for the large size of its leaflets, the terminal one especially. It is one of the *Ornus* section but belongs to the subsection *Ornaster*, the flowers of which have a calyx but no corolla.

In *F. chinensis* var. ACUMINATA Lingelsh., the leaflets are more slenderly acuminate at the apex, lanceolate rather than ovate, and saw-toothed. In the Edinburgh Botanic Garden there is an example of this variety measuring 24 × ft 2 (1967) raised from seeds collected by Forrest in Yunnan under his F.21244.

F. CUSPIDATA Torr.

F. macropetala Eastw.

Although perhaps not in cultivation in Britain at the present time, this ash deserves mention as the only American representative of the section *Ornus*. Leaflets five to nine, lanceolate to ovate, 1½ to 2¼ in. long, up to 1 in. wide, acute or acuminately tapered at the apex, glabrous, distinctly stalked. Flowers in glabrous panicles. Petals four, linear, ½ in. or slightly more long, united at the base into a short tube. It is a shrub or small tree, native to the south-western USA and N. Mexico.

F. DIPETALA Hook. & Arn.

A shrub 10 to 12 ft high, or occasionally a small tree; young shoots four-sided and four-winged, slightly warted, not downy. Leaves 2 to 5 in. long; leaflets commonly five, but varying from three to nine, obovate or oval, tapered at the base, rounded or hardly pointed at the apex, ½ to 1¼ in. long, toothed except at the lowest third (sometimes quite entire), glabrous on both surfaces; main leaf-stalk grooved above; the terminal leaflet rather long-stalked, the uppermost pair stalkless, those below more or less stalked. Flowers produced from the joints of the previous year's wood in panicles 2 to 4 in. long. Petals two, broad-elliptic to roundish, about ¼ in. long. Fruits about 1 in. long, ¼ in. wide, with a notched tip.

Native mainly of California, where it was discovered by David Douglas, but found occasionally farther inland and extending southward into the Mexican State of Baja California. It was not introduced until 1879, when Prof. Sargent sent it to Kew. The small tree there did not flower and was sometimes injured at the tips by frost. This plant no longer exists, and a replacement has proved to be wrongly named.

F. dipetala appears to be one of the most ornamental of the ashes in flower, but would perhaps thrive better in eastern England than at Kew. Although it bears flowers with petals, it is not a member of the section *Ornus*, from which it is clearly distinguished by its inflorescences, which are produced from leafless axillary buds as in section *Fraxinus* (*Fraxinaster*), to which it belongs as the only member of the subsection *Dipetalae*.

F. ELONZA Kirchn.

A small, elegant tree with glabrous, grey-green young shoots furnished with whitish warts; buds dark brown, scurfy. Leaves up to 10 or 11 in. long, with nine to thirteen leaflets, which are ovate, oval or lance-shaped, broadly tapered at the base, shortly pointed, sharply toothed, 1 to 3 in. long, $\frac{1}{2}$ to 1 in. wide, stalkless, dark dull green, and glabrous above, with brownish down densely tufted near the base of the midrib beneath; the main leaf-stalk is whitish beneath, downy in places, winged on the upper side, the wings erect and forming a narrow groove. Flowers and fruit not seen. This ash is of uncertain origin, and is supposed to be a hybrid, probably with *F. oxycarpa* as one parent.

There is an example at Kew, in the Ash collection, *pl.* 1900, measuring 73 × 3¾ ft (1967).

F. EXCELSIOR L. COMMON ASH

One of the largest of European deciduous trees, reaching in favoured sites from 100 to 140 ft in height; bark of the trunk pale, fissured; young wood grey, glabrous; buds black. Leaves 10 to 12 in. long; leaflets most frequently nine or eleven, sometimes less or more, oblong lance-shaped, tapered at the base, slender-pointed, toothed, 2 to 4½ in. long, 1 to 1⅓ in. wide, dark green and glabrous above, paler beneath, and with fluffy brown down at the sides of the lower part of the midrib. Main leaf-stalk usually more or less downy, the wings on the upper side meeting and forming a sharp angle. The terminal leaflet is stalked, the lateral ones scarcely so. Flowers produced from the joints of the previous year's wood in short, dense panicles in April. Fruits (commonly called 'keys') pendent in large bunches, each fruit about 1½ in. long, ¼ to ⅓ in. wide.

Native of Europe, including Britain and the Caucasus. It is one of the most valuable of all our timber trees, yielding a whitish wood of great toughness and durability. Elwes considered it the most economically valuable of British timber trees. For some purposes, especially in coachbuilding and implement-making, it has no rival either native or foreign. An isolated ash of goodly size makes a tree of great beauty and dignity, forming a shapely, oval, or rounded head of branches. It likes a deep, moist, loamy soil, and thrives well on calcareous formations. In some parts of the north of England, on the east side of the Plain of York for instance, it is a common hedgerow tree. In such positions, especially where the adjoining fields are arable, it is not an unmixed blessing, being one of the grossest of feeders.

The following specimens of the common ash have been measured recently, notable for height, girth, or both: Cudham Church, Kent, 70 × 14½ ft (1965); Warnham Court, Sussex, 95 × 15 ft (1961); Longleat, Wilts, 115 × 15 ft, with a clear bole of 33 ft (1971); Westonbirt, Glos., in Main Drive, 80 × 13 ft (1966); Williamstrip Park, Glos., 75 × 16¾ ft (1963); Cowley Place, Exeter, Devon, 85 × 15¾ ft (1967); Powderham Castle, Devon, 105 × 9¼ ft, with a clear bole of 60 ft (1963); Enys, Cornwall, 105 × 13¾ ft (1962); Holywell Hall, Lincs, *c.* 90 ft × 19½ ft (1965); Masham, West Riding, Yorks, 80 × 19¼ ft (1965); Duncombe Park, North Riding, Yorks, 148 × 10½ ft (1956); Oakley Park, Shrops., 111 × 10¾ ft (1971); Llanfyllin, Denbighs., 70 × 17½ ft (1960); Kilmacurragh, Co. Wicklow, Eire, 105 × 14¼ ft (1966).

f. ANGUSTIFOLIA Hort.—The name *F. excelsior angustifolia* has been used in gardens for narrow-leaved variants of the common ash. These are apt to be confused with *F. oxycarpa* but the black buds and the longer leaf-stalk of the terminal leaf should distinguish them.

cv. 'ASPLENIFOLIA'.—Leaflets only $\frac{1}{8}$ to $\frac{1}{4}$ in. wide—a monstrosity merely.

cv. 'AUREA'.—Young shoots yellow; older bark yellowish, especially noticeable in winter. Leaves becoming buff-yellow in late summer, deep yellow in autumn. Slow-growing. See also 'Jaspidea'.

cv. 'AUREA PENDULA'.—Young shoots yellow, branches weeping and forming a flat, umbrella-like head. Said to be weak-growing. The golden weeping ash once grown under the name *F. e. jaspidea pendula* may have been distinct from this and more vigorous.

cv. 'CONCAVIFOLIA'.—Leaflets small, boat-shaped.

cv. 'CRISPA'.—This 'has the leaves dark green, crumpled and curled. The darkness of the green of the leaves is remarkable; and this and their crumpled appearance, combined with the rigid stunted character of the whole plant, render it a striking object' (Loudon, *Arb. et Frut. Brit.*, Vol. 2, p. 1217). An old cultivar raised in France and introduced to Britain by Lee and Kennedy toward the end of the 18th century (syns. *F. crispa* Bosc; *F. atrovirens* Desf.).

cv. 'CUCULLATA'.—Leaflets concave and hooded. Raised by Baltet of Troyes, France, and put into commerce in Britain by Lee of Hammersmith in 1867.

f. DIVERSIFOLIA (Ait.) Lingelsh. *F. e.* var. *diversifolia* Ait.; *F. heterophylla* Vahl; *F. e.* var. *heterophylla* Wesm.; *F. monophylla* Desf.; *F. e.* var. *monophylla* (Desf.) Gren. & Godr; *F. e.* var. *simplicifolia* Pers. ONE-LEAVED ASH.—In this remarkable variety the terminal leaflet only, or occasionally one or two more, is developed. In other respects it is the same as the common ash. Its one leaflet is oval or ovate, long-stalked, toothed, and variable in size, usually 3 to 6 in. long, $1\frac{1}{4}$ to $2\frac{1}{2}$ in. wide, but often proportionately broader or shorter—as much as 8 in. long and 5 in. wide. This variety has arisen independently in many places, both cultivated and wild, and varies considerably. 'HESSEI' is a selection of horizontal habit put into commerce by Messrs Hesse of Germany in 1937 (*Dendroflora*, No. 3 (1966), p. 32). There is also a cut-leaved variant of the one-leaved ash ('DIVERSIFOLIA LACINIATA'), and a pendulous one ('DIVERSIFOLIA PENDULA'). The latter was first distributed by Späth's nurseries and is represented at Kew.

cv. 'ELEGANTISSIMA'.—A tree at Kew, received from Simon-Louis Frères of Metz in 1902 as *F. e. elegantissima*, seems to be *F. angustifolia* or near it. It is not a variety of the common ash.

cv. 'GLOBOSA'.—A dwarf rounded bush, densely branched, with small leaves. The plants known as *F. e. nana* and *polemoniifolia* are similar.

cv. 'GLOMERATA'.—Leaflets as many as fifteen closely set on the common stalk, comparatively short and broad; some of them 3 in. long and 2 in. broad, stout in texture, basal pair of leaflets close to the branch; all somewhat hooded and puckered. Very distinct.

This ash is no longer at Kew. It was received from Simon-Louis Frères. Judging from the above description it was similar to 'Crispa' and may perhaps be in cultivation under that name.

cv. 'JASPIDEA'.—This is considered by H. J. Grootendorst (*Dendroflora*, No. 3 (1966), p. 32), to be the correct name for an ash resembling 'Aurea' but of much taller, freer growth. It is described as having leaves yellow when young, becoming tinged with yellow again in September and wholly yellow by October; winter-wood yellow. The tall-growing golden ashes cultivated in Britain may belong here and certainly the name is not new to British gardens, though not in use recently. An ash under the name *F. e. jaspidea aurea* was distributed by Veitch's Coombe Wood nursery, and there is also reference in *Gard. Chron.* (1873), p. 1432, to *F. e. jaspidea pendula*, which is perhaps not the same as the old 'Aurea Pendula' (q.v.).

cv. 'MONSTROSA'.—Branchlets often fasciated; leaves often alternate.

cv. 'PENDULA'.—Branches all weeping, forming a spreading umbrella-like head. There is little doubt that this ash descends by grafting from a tree discovered in the parish of Gamlingay in Cambridgeshire in the middle of the 18th century. It was once much used for making arbours and unless trained does not rise much in height above the point of grafting. Tall specimens were made, as Loudon had advised, by grafting high on specimens of the common ash. For example, the tree in the Glasnevin Botanic Garden, mentioned by Loudon, must have been grafted at about 30 ft, judging from the figure in Niven, *Companion to the Botanic Garden* (1838), reproduced in *Quarterly Journal of Forestry*, Vol. 63, p. 245. What is probably the same tree now measures 50 × 7½ ft (1966). The tree at Castlewellan in Co. Down, measuring 40 × 7 ft, is grafted at 30 ft. There are specimens 45 to 52 ft in height and 5¾ to 6½ ft in girth at Morden Hall, Surrey; Copped Hall, Essex; Arley Castle, Worcs.; Tottenham House, Wilts. But the most remarkable of these high-grafted trees grew at Elvaston Castle, Derbyshire; in this the scions were inserted at the top of an ash about 90 ft high by a worker from Barron's nurseries at Derby in 1848 (*Garden* (Dec. 23, 1905), p. 400, with photograph; Elwes and Henry, *Tr. Gt. Brit.*, Vol. 4, p. 868 and plate 238). Mr Constable, Director of Parks, Derby, informs us that the tree which served as the stock still exists, though the streamers have all disappeared.

cv. 'PENDULA WENTWORTHII'.—Trunk and leading shoots erect but branches very pendulous. An example in the Ash collection at Kew measures 64 × 5¼ ft (1969). It is of rather indeterminate shape, with the lower branches pendulous, the upper ones horizontal or even ascending, but with pendulous ends.

cv. 'SCOLOPENDRIFOLIA'.—Leaflets narrow, often curled and deformed, narrower than in the type. There is an example at Kew in the Ash collection, about 70 ft high, received from Späth's nurseries in 1900. A similar ash was named *F. e. erosa* by Willdenow.

cv. 'TRANSONII'.—This was described in previous editions as having yellow leaves. Unfortunately the tree at Kew no longer exists and it has not been possible to discover any further information about this variety, which was presumably raised or distributed by Transon's nursery in France.

cv. 'VERTICILLATA'.—Leaves occasionally in threes instead of the normal pairs, but in this, as in some other abnormal forms of common ash, the leaves are frequently alternate.

F. FLORIBUNDA Wall.   HIMALAYAN MANNA ASH

A tree reaching a height of 80 to 120 ft in the Himalaya; bark grey, smooth at first but becoming furrowed on old trees; buds dark, usually slightly hairy; branchlets glabrous, slightly compressed. Leaves 10 to 15 in. long; leaflets usually seven or nine, oblong (terminal one obovate), long-acuminate at the apex, 3 to 6 in. long, 1 to 2½ in. wide, sharply toothed, dark green and glabrous above, midrib and main veins prominent and downy beneath; stalks of leaflets ¼ to ½ in. long, but the uppermost pair almost sessile; rachis grooved. Flowers white in terminal panicles up to 12 in. long; petals oblong, ⅛ to $\frac{3}{16}$ in. long. Fruits narrow-oblong to spathulate.

A native of the Himalaya from Kashmir eastward, at 5,000 to 11,000 ft; described from Nepal, whence it was introduced in 1822, but the plants raised were killed by the winter of 1836–7. In 1876 Sir George King, then Director of the Calcutta Botanic Garden, sent seeds of this fine ash to Kew. Of the trees raised one survived until 1915 after being cut to the ground in the winter of 1880–1. A replacement also died and the species is not now (1970) represented in the Kew collection. Indeed, it seems to be very rare in the British Isles, for no specimen has been recorded in recent years. In the natural state this species has, however, such a wide altitudinal and geographical range, and has always been so uncommon in gardens, that it is impossible to make any generalisation about its hardiness or rate of growth in our climate.

F. *floribunda* resembles some of the big-leaved forms of F. *ornus*, but the leaflets are usually much larger, more prominently ribbed beneath, and longer pointed.

F. GRIFFITHII C. B. Clarke
F. *bracteata* Hemsl.

A tree of the *Ornus* group; young shoots glabrous, four-angled, bright green. Leaves variable in size; on young trees 6 to 12 in. long. Leaflets five to eleven, ovate, wedge-shaped or rounded at the base, tapered at the apex to a bluntish point, very variable in size, ordinarily 1 to 3 in. long (but sometimes 5 in.), about half as wide, not toothed, deep polished green, perfectly glabrous, and with impressed veins above, paler and glabrous beneath. The main leaf-stalk has an even, well-defined groove above; terminal leaflet long-stalked, the others shortly so. Panicles terminal, also borne in the upper leaf-axils; downy, pyramidal, 3 to 6 in. long, with a pair of small oblong bracts at the base of each subdivision. Fruits 1 to 1¼ in. long, $\frac{1}{12}$ in. wide.

This species was described from a specimen collected by Dr Griffith in the Mishmi Hills of Assam, and is also a native of Upper Burma and the warmer parts of W. and S. China; the same species, or closely allied species, occur in Formosa, the Philippines, and Malaysia. It was introduced by Wilson from W. Hupeh in 1900, when collecting for Messrs Veitch, but it is doubtful if any of the trees raised from these seeds have survived. This ash is very distinct in its square branchlets and glabrous, shining, entire leaflets, the largest of which resemble the leaf of *Ligustrum lucidum*.

F. HOLOTRICHA Koehne

A tree at present about 70 ft high at Kew; young shoots with a close covering of very short erect hairs (velutinous). Leaves with mostly eleven leaflets, but here and there with five to nine or thirteen leaflets; petiole and rachis spreading, pubescent; leaflets elliptic or oblong-elliptic to lanceolate or sometimes broad elliptic, acuminate at the apex and long cuneate at the base, mostly distinctly stalked (petiolulate), with the stalks up to $\frac{1}{8}$ in. long, but sometimes almost sessile; the leaflets are mostly $1\frac{3}{8}$ to $2\frac{3}{4}$ in. long and $\frac{1}{2}$ to $\frac{3}{4}$ in. wide and widely serrulate to serrate, but sometimes up to 3 by $1\frac{1}{4}$ in. and coarsely serrate, sparsely pubescent above, more closely so on the lower surface, mostly on the veins and markedly so on the midrib, which is more or less densely spreading pubescent. According to Koehne the flowers have hairy ovaries, a most unusual feature among the ashes. Fruits not seen.

F. *holotricha* was described in 1906 from a plant first noticed in Späth's arboretum though others were afterwards found in the Berlin and Dresden Botanic Gardens, all under the name F. *potamophila* (a synonym of F. *sogdiana*, q.v.). The above description was made from a tree at Kew which was received from Späth in April 1909 and now measures 72 × 4½ ft (1969). The native home of this species was not well known when Koehne described it, but specimens in the Kew Herbarium from Ilfov, Rumania, agree with it.

F. PALLISIAE Wilmott F. *holotricha sensu* Borza, not Koehne—This species much resembles F. *holotricha* in the hairiness of all its parts, including the ovary. It differs in being even more hairy and in the leaflets being sessile or almost so. The stems are notably spreading pubescent in addition to having a covering of fine short hairs; the leaves have usually nine to thirteen leaflets, sometimes five to seven, the petiole and rachis are densely spreading-pubescent; leaflets rounded or obtuse to wide cuneate at the base and sessile or almost so, though the cuneate base may sometimes be extended into a short petiolule, upper and lower surfaces hairy as in F. *holotricha* but more densely so with rather longer hairs, so that the lower surface especially can be described as pubescent-villous.

F. *pallisiae* was described in 1916 from material collected in the Danube Delta by Marietta Pallis, and is found in Great Thrace, Rumania, Bulgaria, and parts of eastern Yugoslavia. It is frequently associated in the wild with F. *oxycarpa*. In the *Botanical Magazine*, n.s., in the article accompanying t. 370, the late Dr Turrill suggested that the variability of F. *pallisiae* was due to the introgression of genes from F. *oxycarpa*. For a further discussion see *Kew Bulletin* (1935), pp. 132–141 and *New Phytologist*, Vol. 37 (1938), pp. 160–172.

F. *pallisiae* is represented in the Ash collection at Kew by several trees raised from seeds collected by B. Stefanoff in the Strandja Planina region of E. Bulgaria in 1932. The most notable of these is No. 364 near the end of the Lake, which now measures 42 × 3¼ ft (1969). The material for the figure in the *Botanical Magazine* was, however, taken from a tree in the Experimental Ground at Kew, raised from seeds collected in western Thrace, in 1935.

F. LATIFOLIA Benth.   OREGON ASH

F. oregona Nutt.; *F. americana* subsp. *oregona* (Nutt.) Wesmael; *F. pennsylvanica* subsp. *oregona* (Wesmael) G. N. Miller

A tree up to 80 ft high; young shoots reddish brown, rough with minute warts, more or less downy, sometimes densely so. Leaves 6 in. to over 1 ft long; leaflets five, seven or nine, oval or oblong, 2 to 5 in. long, 1 to 2 in. broad, tapered or sometimes rounded at the base, contracted at the apex to a short or slender point, margins entire or obscurely toothed, dark green and with thin down above, pale and densely downy beneath; main-stalk very pale, downy, grooved above; stalk of the terminal leaflets up to 1 in. long; lateral leaflets very shortly or not at all stalked. Flowers without petals, produced on the previous year's shoots. Fruits 1¼ to 2 in. long, ⅓ in. wide towards the apex; wing extending almost to base of body.

Native of western N. America, where it is a valuable timber tree. It was discovered by Douglas in 1825, but does not seem to have been introduced until many years after. There are two specimens of *F. latifolia* in the Ash collection at Kew, one *pl.* 1914, 76 × 5¾ ft, and the other, probably some forty years older, 80 × 7¾ ft (1969).

F. latifolia is allied to *F. pennsylvanica*, of which it is treated as a subspecies by Miss Miller in her monograph on the American ashes, but is easily distinguished by the stalkless lateral leaflets. The same character can usually be relied on to distinguish the Oregon ash from the velvet ash (*F. velutina*), but hybrids and intermediates between the two occur south of the 37th parallel (G. N. Miller, op. cit., pp. 19–21 and 41, and see also Munz & Laudermilk, *El Aliso*, Vol. 2, pp. 49–62).

F. MANDSHURICA Rupr.   MANCHURIAN ASH

A fine tree often 100 ft high; young shoots glabrous, greyish. Leaves 8 to 15 in. long; leaflets stalkless, or nearly so, usually nine or eleven, sometimes seven or thirteen, oval or oblong-lanceolate, 2 to 4½ in. long, 1 to 2 in. wide, tapered to the base, slender-pointed, sharply (occasionally doubly) toothed, dull green and with scattered bristles above, paler beneath, and more conspicuously bristly, especially on the midrib and veins; main leaf-stalk winged above, the two wings forming a deep groove with tufts of brown down where the leaflets join.

Native of Japan and the adjacent parts of the Asiatic mainland; introduced to Kew from St Petersburg in 1882. It is one of the greatest failures among ashes on account of its suspectibility to injury by spring frost. Its broadly winged fruits, which Sargent says are borne on the previous year's wood in great clusters, have not been produced in Britain. It is a valuable tree in the Far East, and attains to noble dimensions there. The leaf is distinct in the conspicuous sunken veins above, correspondingly prominent beneath. Closely allied to *F. nigra*.

F. MARIESII Hook. f.

A small tree, forming a rounded, bushy head of branches, and apparently unlikely to be more than 15 to 20 ft high; branchlets and buds greyish, downy. Leaves 3 to 7 in. long, with three or five leaflets attached to the upper third of the main leaf-stalk, which is scurfy and purplish on the upper side, and has a swollen, dark purple base, leaflets oval or ovate, 1 to $3\frac{1}{2}$ in. long, $\frac{1}{2}$ to $1\frac{3}{4}$ in. wide, the apex abruptly tapered, the base rounded or wedged-shaped; shallowly toothed

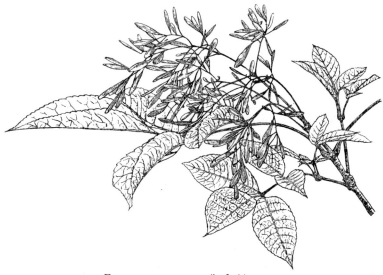

FRAXINUS MARIESII (in fruit)

or almost entire, dull green, glabrous; stalks of side leaflets $\frac{1}{10}$ to $\frac{1}{4}$ in. long, that of the terminal leaflet up to $\frac{3}{4}$ in. long; all purple at the base. Flowers creamy white, in axillary and terminal panicles 3 to 6 in. long; produced in June. Fruits $\frac{1}{2}$ to $1\frac{1}{4}$ in. long, $\frac{1}{8}$ to $\frac{1}{4}$ in. wide; very handsome in July, when they become deep purple.

Native of Central China; introduced by Maries for Messrs Veitch in 1878. Of the flowering ashes (section *Ornus*) this is the most ornamental, being very pretty both in flower and fruit. Being of slow growth and never of large size it is admirable for small gardens. It received an Award of Merit in 1962, when shown by Maurice Mason of Talbot Manor, King's Lynn, Norfolk.

F. NIGRA Marsh.   BLACK ASH
F. *sambucifolia* Lam.

A native of eastern N. America, whence it was introduced to England in 1800, this ash has never been a success, and appears to be unworthy of cultivation.

It is a tree 80 to 90 ft high in the wild, and grows in damp situations; young shoots glabrous. Leaflets seven to eleven, oblong or oblong lance-shaped, slender-pointed, 3 to 5 in. long, 1 to 2 in. wide, glabrous on both surfaces except for reddish down along the side of the midrib and veins, beneath which it is densest towards the base, and extends round the main-stalk. All the leaflets except the terminal ones are stalkless—even more distinctly so than in *F. mandshurica*. In many of its characters the black ash is similar to *F. mandshurica*; the leaflets, however, are much less tapered at the base or may even be rounded, and the marginal teeth are shallow and quite inconspicuous. It has little interest or value in gardens.

F. OBLIQUA Tausch

F. willdenowiana Koehne *fide* Lingelsh.; *F. parvifolia sens.* Willd., in part, not Lam.
F. rotundifolia Hort., in part

A small tree free from down in all parts, forming a rounded, dense head of branches; young shoots with small white warts. Leaves often in threes, 9 to 12 in. long; leaflets usually nine or eleven, sometimes seven, scarcely stalked, ovate-lanceolate, 2 to 3½ in. long, ¾ to 1 in. wide, obliquely tapered at the base, long-pointed, rather coarsely triangular-toothed; the terminal one is up to 5 in. long and 1½ in. wide, the others decreasing in size successively towards the base. The main-stalk has a continuous groove on the upper side, which, with the large terminal leaflet, distinguishes this from the other ashes with perfectly glabrous shoots and leaves. Fruits 1 in. long, ⅓ in. wide, pointed.

This ash was named *F. obliqua* by Tausch in 1834 at which time it was in cultivation as *F. rotundifolia*, a name which clung to it for over seventy years. According to Lingelsheim, a monographer of the ashes, it is a native of the eastern Mediterranean region and W. Asia, but a curious uncertainty as to its origin has always prevailed. Tausch thought it came from North America.

NOTE. The ash described above, which is still in the Kew collection, was received under the name *F. rotundifolia*. It agrees with *F. willdenowiana* Koehne, under which name it is treated in Elwes and Henry, *Tr. Gt. Brit. & Irel.*, Vol. 4, p. 884. Its identification with the *F. obliqua* of Tausch rests on the authority of Lingelsheim. There is also in the Kew collection an ash received under the name *F. excelsior* var. *obliqua*, which is quite distinct from the tree described above and appears to be a variant of *F. excelsior*.

F. ORNUS L.   MANNA ASH   [PLATE 34
Ornus europaea Pers.

A deciduous, very leafy tree, from 50 to 65 ft high, forming a dense rounded head of branches; buds rough, grey; young shoots ordinarily without down. Leaves 5 or 8 in. long, with five to nine leaflets which are ovate or oblong (the terminal one obovate), 2 to 4 in. long, ¾ to 1¾ in. wide, more or less tapered at the base, abruptly pointed at the apex, shallowly round-toothed, dull green and glabrous above, the base of the midrib beneath and the stalk downy; main-stalk grooved above, furnished with brownish down where the leaflets are attached.

Flowers whitish, very abundantly produced in May in terminal and axillary panicles 3 or 4 in. long, along with the leaves of the new shoots; petals linear, ¼ in. long. Fruits about 1 in. long, narrow-oblong.

Native of S. Europe and Asia Minor; cultivated since early in the 18th century, if not before; now one of the best known of exotic trees. It is a handsome tree with very luxuriant leafage, and decidedly ornamental in flower, although the blossom has a faint, not agreeable odour. Manna sugar is obtained from the stems by incision.

The manna ash is somewhat variable in the wild, mainly in the shape and size of its leaflets, which may be relatively broader or longer acuminate at the apex, than in the tree described above, but it is doubtful if these fluctuations are worthy of taxonomic recognition. A more distinct geographical variant is:

var. ROTUNDIFOLIA (Lam.) Ten. *F. rotundifolia* Lam.—Of dwarfer habit than the type with the leaflets about 1 in. long and broadly rhombic-elliptic. Found in Calabria, the Balkans, etc.

How effective the manna ash can be as a specimen is well shown by the group at the east end of the Lake at Kew. The largest here is 45 × 7½ ft (1964). There are two manna ashes in Hyde Park, London, measuring 66 × 7¼ ft and 57 × 7½ ft, and another in Kensington Gardens of 75 × 6¾ ft (all 1967). Others of note are: Beauport, Sussex, 50 × 9½ ft (1965); Frogmore, Berks, 45 × 8¾ ft (1967); Whiteknights, Berks, 62 × 5 ft (1962); Melbury, Dorset, 45 × 8 ft (1967).

F. OXYCARPA *see under* F. ANGUSTIFOLIA

F. PAXIANA Lingelsh.

F. densiflora Lingelsh.; *F. suaveolens* W. W. Sm.

A tree 40 to 60 ft high, with a trunk 3 to 4 ft in girth; terminal winter buds very large, covered with brown down; young shoots glabrous. Leaves pinnate, 10 to 13 in. long, consisting of seven or nine leaflets which are lanceolate, broadly wedge-shaped or rounded at the base, slenderly pointed, toothed, 3½ to 6 in. long, 1 to 2 in. wide, glabrous on both surfaces; stalk absent or up to ¼ in. long. Flowers white, produced during May and June in panicles 8 to 10 in. wide, not so much long, at the end of leafy shoots; flower-stalks glabrous; petals oblong, rounded at the end, ⅛ in. long; calyx 1/16 in. long, bell-shaped, toothed. Wings of the fruit truncheon-shaped in outline, 1 to 1¼ in. long, 3/16 in. wide, rounded at the end. *Bot Mag.*, t. 9024.

Native of the Himalaya from the Simla district and the Jumna River eastward, Assam (Khasia Hills), and W. China; introduced by Wilson in 1901. In a young state it is distinct in its stiff young shoots and especially for its large, downy winter-buds, clasped at the base by two thick scales. It belongs to the *Ornus* section of ashes. The base of the leaf-stalk is sometimes much enlarged after the fashion of F. *spaethiana* and F. *platypoda*. It is hardy at Kew, but cannot be included amongst the best ashes there owing to its liability to injury by spring frosts. In localities where it escapes these it promises to be a handsome flowering ash, as it is, indeed, at Headfort in Co. Meath. It has ripened seed there. This tree, which provided the material for the figure in the *Botanical Magazine*, measures 30 × 5¼ ft (1966).

var. SIKKIMENSIS Lingelsh.—Rachis of the leaves rusty-tomentose, at least at the base of the leaflets. Described from specimens collected by J. D. Hooker in Sikkim but occurring elsewhere in the range of the species. Contrary to what is stated in the *Botanical Magazine* (loc. cit.) this variety was validly published.

F. PENNSYLVANICA Marsh.   RED ASH, GREEN ASH
F. pubescens Lam.; *F. michauxii* Britt.

A tree 40 to 60 ft, sometimes more, high; bark as in the white ash, but less deeply furrowed; young shoots clothed more or less densely with a pale down. Leaves up to 1 ft long; leaflets seven or nine (occasionally five), oblong-lanceolate or narrowly oval, 3 to 6 in. long, 1 to 2 in. wide, broadly tapered at the base, long and slenderly pointed, rather obscurely toothed, or entire, especially at the lower half, dull green on both surfaces, and nearly or quite glabrous above, except along the sunken midrib which sometimes is downy, covered beneath with a pale down. The leaflets, especially the lower ones, are stalked, the stalks grooved and downy, as is also the common stalk. Male and female flowers occur on separate trees, and are produced on the old wood just below the new shoot. Fruits 1 to 2 in. long, rather variable in shape; wing extending half-way or more down the cylindrical body.

American foresters and many botanists no longer make a distinction between the red ash (i.e., typical *F. pennsylvanica*) and the following variety:

var. SUBINTEGERRIMA (Vahl) Fern.   *F. lanceolata* Borkh.; *F. pennsylvanica* var. *lanceolata* (Borkh.) Sarg.—Branchlets glabrous; leaves glabrous except for some down on the veins beneath. According to Sargent this tree, as seen in the east, is distinct enough from typical *F. pennsylvanica*, 'but trees occur over the area which it inhabits, but more often westward, with slightly pubescent leaves and branchlets which may be referred as well to one tree as to the other'. This glabrous extreme of *F. pennsylvanica* was once distinguished as the 'green ash', but this name is now used by American foresters for the species as a whole.

F. pennsylvanica (including the above variety) has a wide range in N. America from the Atlantic to the Rockies and is usually found on wetter soils than the white ash (*F. americana*). As common in gardens as that species, it is not so effective and large a tree, although it grows quickly when young. A tree in the Oxford Botanic Garden, which was 50 × 3 ft when H. J. Elwes measured it early this century, is now 78 × 8 ft (1962). There is another at Hergest Croft, Heref., 65 × 5½ (1961). At Kew the var. *subintegerrima* is represented by two trees, the larger, *pl.* 1897, 50 × 5½ ft (1969).

F. pennsylvanica in its typical state is easily enough distinguished from *F. americana* by its downy shoots, but the glabrous forms are easily confounded with that species. See further under *F. americana*.

cv. 'AUCUBIFOLIA'.—Leaflets mottled with yellow. This garden variety in some of its characters is intermediate between the typical state of *F. pennsylvanica* and the var. *subintegerrima*; the leaves are far from being as downy as in the former, but the shoots are quite downy. A handsome variegated tree.

F. BERLANDIERANA DC.—This ash was described by De Candolle from specimens collected by Berlandier in Texas, and also occurs in Mexico. It is closely allied to *F. pennsylvanica* var. *subintegerrima*, differing in its smaller stature, thicker bark and smaller leaves with usually only five leaflets. As seen at Kew it was a pleasing small tree of free growth, with glossy, deep green leaflets, but is not now in the collection.

F. PLATYPODA Oliver

A deciduous tree ultimately 60 to 70 ft high; young shoots glabrous. Leaves 6 to 10 in. long, made up of seven to eleven leaflets which are oval-oblong or lanceolate, finely toothed, slender-pointed, tapered at the base, 2 to 4 in. long, ½ to 1¼ in. wide, greyish green and glabrous above, papillose beneath, with conspicuous down towards the base of the midrib; stalk of leaflets very short and downy except that of the terminal one which is up to ½ in. long; main-stalk conspicuously dilated at the base and downy there. Panicles 4 to 6 in. long. Fruits oblong but tapered towards each end, especially towards the slender point, about 2 in. long, ⅜ in. wide.

F. *platypoda* was described from a specimen collected by Henry in Hupeh about 1887 and is said to occur in other parts of W. China. Although the type specimen preserved at Kew bears fruits only, there seems to be little doubt that the species belongs to the section *Fraxinus* and not (as Dr Stapf suggested) to the section *Ornus*. The chief distinguishing character of this ash is the enlarged base of the leaf-stalk. This peculiarity is also shown by *F. spaethiana* (until recently erroneously placed in the section *Ornus*) but that species is more glabrous, with the leaflets vividly green above and not papillose beneath. The swollen base of the leaf-stalk is also shown by *F. paxiana* but that species definitely belongs to the section *Ornus*.

F. PUBINERVIS Blume

A tree 45 ft or more high; young shoots glabrous. Leaves up to 1 ft or more long, with the main-stalk grooved on the upper side and made up of five to eleven leaflets which are narrowly ovate to oblong, long-pointed, broadly wedge-shaped or almost rounded at the base, toothed, 2 to 5 in. long, 1 to 2 in. wide, dark green and glabrous above, hairy close along the midrib and base of the chief veins beneath, shortly stalked. Fruits oblanceolate, tapering from near the end (which is often notched) to the base, 1¼ to 1¾ in. long, $\frac{3}{16}$ to $\frac{5}{16}$ in. wide.

Native of Japan. It is a member of the section *Ornus* and is usually stated to belong to the typical subsection, in which the flowers have petals. There is no material at Kew which throws light on this matter, but it should be noted that Franchet and Savatier (*Enum. Pl. Jap.*, Vol. 2, p. 435) stated that in all their specimens the flowers lacked petals and merely suggested, without adducing any proof, that the absence of the petals was due to their having dropped soon after

the flower expanded. Furthermore, this ash is almost certainly the same as the
species treated by Ohwi (*Fl. Japan*, 1965) under the name *F. japonica* Bl., and this
is said to have flowers without petals. It should be added that, despite the eluci-
dation of the true nature of *F. spaethiana*, the nomenclature of the Japanese ashes
of the *Ornus* section remains problematic, owing to the existence of so many
names of uncertain application. The ash described above is generally supposed
to be the one that Blume called *F. pubinervis*, but in Ohwi's work this name
appears with a query among the synonyms of *F. longicuspis* var. *latifolia* Nakai.

There is a grafted tree at Kew received from Späth's nurseries under the name
F. pubinervis but it has not been seen in flower and its identity is uncertain.

F. QUADRANGULATA Michx. BLUE ASH

A tree 60 to 70, occasionally over 100 ft high; branchlets square and distinctly
four-winged, not downy; bark of the trunk covered with loose plates. Leaves
7 to 14 in. long, with five to eleven leaflets, which are ovate to lanceolate, 3 to
5 in. long, 1 to 2 in. wide, rounded or broadly wedge-shaped and unequal at the
base, tapering at the apex to a long, slender point, sharply toothed, yellowish
green and glabrous above, paler and downy beneath, especially about the midrib
and veins. Common stalk minutely downy, and grooved on the upper side;
stalks of leaflets $\frac{1}{8}$ to $\frac{1}{4}$ in. long. Flowers in short panicles from the previous
year's wood, calyx minute, soon deciduous. Fruit, $1\frac{1}{2}$ in. long, $\frac{5}{16}$ in. wide,
oblong, with a notch at the apex.

Native of the south-eastern and central United States; introduced in 1823. It
produces a valuable timber in the United States, but does not seem to have ever
attained any great size in this country. There is a small specimen in the Ash
collection at Kew. It is readily distinguished from all ashes with the same
number of leaflets by its square, winged branchlets, except *F. griffithii*, and
that has untoothed leaflets, and belongs to the *Ornus* section.

F. ROTUNDIFOLIA Mill.

In his *Gardener's Dictionary* (ed. 1768), Philip Miller published the name
F. rotundifolia for a plant with ovate-lanceolate serrate leaflets and coloured
flowers, which 'come out of the side of the branches . . . before the leaves
come out. This tree is of humble growth, seldom rising more than fifteen or
sixteen feet in England.' He said the tree was a native of Calabria, which produced
the manna, and identified it with the *Fraxinus rotundiore folio* of Bauhin. The
ash so named had been described and figured by the pre-Linnean botanist Jean
Bauhin in 1650, from a specimen brought by his brother Caspar from Italy as
Ornus n. 3. Most probably this was the true manna ash *F. ornus*. On the other hand
the cultivated tree described by Miller seems to have belonged to the section
Fraxinaster, and could have been *F. oxycarpa* or some variant of *F. excelsior*.
Unfortunately there is no specimen of Miller's plant in the Herbarium of the
British Museum (where many of his types are preserved), so it is impossible to
be certain about the identity of the plant.

This problem is mentioned here because *F. rotundifolia* Mill. has been used in some works as the name for *F. parvifolia* or even for *F. oxycarpa*. It is better regarded as a name of uncertain application. See further below.

F. PARVIFOLIA Lam. *F. rotundifolia sens.* Rehd. and other authors—The French botanist Lamarck saw that Miller had confused two distinct ashes (see above). He restricted the name *F. rotundifolia* to Bauhin's plant, which he accepted as being the true manna ash, and published the name *F. parvifolia* for an ash growing in the royal garden at Paris, which he evidently considered to be the same as the tree of English gardens described by Miller (*Encl. Meth.*, Vol. 2 (1786), p. 546).

Lamarck's *F. parvifolia* has been recognised by many later botanists as a distinct species, though usually under the name *F. rotundifolia* Mill., with *F. parvifolia* Lam. as a synonym. It seems to be closely allied to *F. oxycarpa*, differing in its relatively wider leaflets and its narrow, parallel-sided fruits. If the two species were to be combined, it would be under the name *F. parvifolia* Lam., which has many years' priority over *F. oxycarpa*.

A tree at Kew received from Späth's nursery in 1894 as *F. parvifolia* seems to be *F. oxycarpa*, but judging from a specimen taken from it in 1911 the leaflets on some of the leaves were relatively broader when the tree was young than they are now. There is also in cultivation at Kew a small, gnarled, burry tree which was listed in early editions of the Kew *Hand-list* as *F. parvifolia* var. *nana*, with *F. lentiscifolia nana* Hort. and *F. tamariscifolia* var. *nana* Dippel as synonyms. Later this tree was transferred to *F. rotundifolia*. Its identity is uncertain, but it could well be a dwarf form of *F. oxycarpa*.

F. SIEBOLDIANA Blume

F. longicuspis var. *sieboldiana* (Bl.) Lingelsh.; *F. longicuspis sensu* Lingelsh., in part, not (?) Sieb. & Zucc.

A slender tree 20 to 30, sometimes 50 ft high in Japan, belonging to the *Ornus* section; young shoots soon glabrous, grey. Leaves ordinarily 4 to 6 in. long; leaflets usually five (rarely seven), which are $1\frac{1}{2}$ to 4 in. long, $\frac{3}{4}$ to $1\frac{1}{2}$ in. wide, ovate to obovate, tapered at the base, the apex abruptly contracted into a slender point, toothed or almost entire, glabrous above, downy only at the sides of the midrib near the base beneath or sometimes quite glabrous beneath. The terminal leaflet, which is the largest, has a stalk $\frac{1}{2}$ to $\frac{3}{4}$ in. long, the uppermost pair are stalkless, the lower pair or pairs shortly stalked; common stalk grooved on the upper side. Flowers white, in terminal and axillary panicles 3 to 5 in. long, produced in June. Petals four, about $\frac{1}{4}$ in. long. It is the Japanese representative of *F. ornus*, differing most obviously in the few leaflets.

This ash is usually called *F. longicuspis*, but according to Ohwi's *Flora of Japan* (1965) the species so named by Siebold and Zuccarini has flowers without petals and differs in other respects also from the plant described above. This conclusion is no doubt based on an examinaton of the type specimen.

F. LANUGINOSA Koidz.—This is said to be very near to *F. sieboldiana*, differing in having the young stems, petioles, and inflorescences either quite glabrous or clad with short, spreading, rather bristly hairs.

F. SOGDIANA Bunge

F. potamophila Herder; *F. regelii* Dipp.

A small tree up to 30 or 35 ft high, with green shoots, free from down in all its parts. Leaves 4 to 12 in. long; leaflets stalked, usually nine or eleven, sometimes seven or thirteen, 1 to 3 in. long, ¾ to 1½ in. wide, tapered at the base, triangular toothed, pointed, dull green; rachis whitish beneath, with a broad, shallow groove above; stalks of the leaflets ¼ to ½ in. long, except the terminal one, which is ¾ to 1 in. long. Flowers as in the common ash and its allies. Fruits narrow-lanceolate, 1¼ to 2 in. long.

Native of Turkestan and other parts of W. Asia; introduced to Kew by way of the St Petersburg Botanic Garden in 1891. It is an elegant small tree, very rare in cultivation, but quite distinct among ashes with the same number of leaflets in these being conspicuously stalked, and, together with the young shoots, quite glabrous. The true species is not at present in the Kew collection (1971).

F. sogdiana varies in the size and shape of its leaflets. The plants called *F. potamophila* have the leaflets relatively broader than in *F. sogdiana* in the strict sense, but judging from material in the Kew Herbarium only one species is involved and *F. potamophila* is accordingly placed under *F. sogdiana* in synonymy, as it is in *Flora SSSR*.

F. SPAETHIANA Lingelsh.

F. serratifolia Hort., not Michx.; *F. sieboldiana* of some authors, not Bl.; *F. platypoda sensu* Dallim. in Kew *Hand-list* 1902, not Oliver; *F. stenocarpa sensu* Rehd., not Koidz

A tall tree in Japan but so far not over 40 ft high in Britain; young shoots shining, grey or yellowish brown. Leaves up to 1½ ft long, with seven or nine (sometimes five) leaflets, which are rather leathery in texture, vivid green and glabrous above, paler and with a few scattered hairs beneath, rather coarsely irregularly round-toothed, shortly acuminate at the apex; the terminal leaflet is narrowly obovate, usually 6 to 6½ in. long (but occasionally up to 8 in. long), 2¼ in. wide, the upper lateral leaflets almost as long, but narrower, forward-pointing, the lowermost pair always much shorter than the others; petiole slightly grooved, very much swollen at the base. Flowers in glabrous panicles from the scars of the previous year's leaves; petals absent; calyx cup-shaped. Fruits broadly lanceolate, 1⅝ in. long, usually narrowed at both ends.

Native of Japan; in cultivation at Kew in 1880 as "*F. serratifolia*", but the trees now in the collection came from Späth's nursery, one in 1896 as "*F. serratifolia*" and two in 1908 under their correct name; these trees are all grafted and undoubtedly derive from the tree in Späth's nurseries from which Lingelsheim described the species in 1907. It is said to make a tall tree in its native habitat but the oldest tree at Kew, although more than seventy years planted, measures only 36 × 4 ft (1969). The species is very rare in cultivation but represented at East Bergholt Manor, Suffolk; Borde Hill, Sussex; and Lanarth, Cornwall. Few ashes have more handsome foliage than this, or of a more vivid green. The enlarged bases of the leaf-stalks are also seen in *F. paxiana*, but that species belongs to the section *Ornus*, in which the flowers are borne at the ends of leafy shoots of the current season's growth. Before its flowers had been seen *F. spaethiana* was also erroneously placed in this section; in fact it belongs to section *Fraxinus* subsection *Melioides*, and is one of the few members of this sub-section found in E. Asia. It appears to be allied to *F. platypoda*.

F. SYRIACA Boiss.

F. sogdiana Dipp., not Bl.; *F. turkestanica* Carr.; *F. oxyphylla* var. *oligophylla* Boiss.; *F. oxycarpa* var. *oligophylla* (Boiss.) Wenzig

A deciduous tree, small in cultivation, and of slow growth; young branches without down, those of a year or two old usually packed closely with protuberances, which are the seats of the fallen leaves and buds. Leaves quite glabrous, normally in whorls of three, and densely crowded, but on free-growing shoots often alternate and well apart. Leaflets one to five (usually three), lance-shaped, tapered at the base, 1 to 4 in. long, ⅓ to 1¼ in. wide, coarsely and sharply toothed, glossy dark green. The whole leaf is from 4 to 8 in. long, the main-stalk and midribs whitish beneath, the former grooved above. Flowers produced in short racemes on the wood of the previous year. Fruits narrowly obovate, 1 to 1½ in. long, ⅓ in. wide.

Native of south-west and central Asia. It is of little value as an ornamental, but is very distinct in the remarkably crowded leaves, and in the conspicuous protuberances on the younger branches. It is allied to *F. oxycarpa* but differs in the glabrous leaflets. *F. angustifolia* resembles *F. syriaca* in its glabrous, slender leaflets, but its leaves are not borne in whorls of three, are not so crowded, and have more numerous leaflets; it also grows taller.

F. TEXENSIS (A. Gray) Sarg.

F. americana var. *texensis* Gray; *F. a.* subsp. *texensis* (Gray) G. N. Miller; *F. a.* var. *albicans* (Buckl.) Lingels., in part; *F. albicans* Buckl., in part

A tree rarely 50 ft high in nature; young shoots finely downy at first, soon glabrous, light brown by the autumn, darkening to deep brown. Leaflets usually five, sometimes seven, 1 to 3 in. long, ¾ to 2 in. wide, oval or ovate, the terminal one sometimes obovate, rounded or acute, sometimes abruptly acuminate at the apex, tapered or rounded at the base, coarsely but shallowly toothed, thick, dark green and glabrous above, pale and downy in the axils of the veins beneath; stalks of the lateral leaflets ¼ to ½ in. long, that of the terminal one up to 1 in. long. Fruits as in *F. americana*, but not much exceeding 1 in. in length.

Native of limestone districts in Texas; discovered by Dr Bigelow in 1852. It is closely allied to *F. americana*, but has thicker, broader leaflets, mostly rounded or acute at the apex and usually five to each leaf; the fruits are also smaller. The remarkable thickness of the leaves of this species is well shown by the specimen in the Ash collection at Kew.

Miss Miller (op. cit., p. 36) has pointed out that there has been a confusion between this ash and *F. americana* var. *microcarpa* (q.v.) and that the *F. albicans* Buckl. and the *F. americana* var. *albicans* (Buckl.) Lingelsh. are a mixture of the two.

F. TOMENTOSA Michx. f. PUMPKIN ASH

F. profunda (Bush) Bush; *F. americana* var. *profunda* Bush

A tree 50 to occasionally well over 100 ft high; young shoots, leaf-stalks and flower-stalks conspicuously downy. Leaves 10 to 18 in. long, composed of usually seven, sometimes nine, leaflets which are oblong-lanceolate or ovate, rounded or broadly wedge-shaped at the base, slender-pointed, inconspicuously or not at all toothed, 3 to 9 in. long, $1\frac{1}{2}$ to $3\frac{1}{2}$ in. wide, nearly glabrous above but softly downy beneath, especially near the midrib and veins; stalk of lower leaflets up to $\frac{1}{4}$ in. long; main-stalk round, not winged. Flowers produced during April on slender axillary panicles up to 5 in. long, the most noticeable feature of which are the cup-shaped calyces, $\frac{1}{8}$ in. long and unusually large for an ash; petals absent. Fruits $2\frac{1}{2}$ in. long, $\frac{3}{8}$ in. wide, often notched at the end.

Native of the E. United States from New York to Florida; introduced to Kew from the Arnold Arboretum in 1912. This fine tree is most closely akin to the red ash, but it has larger keys and leaflets, is more conspicuously downy, and the calyx, as noted above, is larger. The popular name of pumpkin ash is said to have been given to the tree because it is 'swell-butted', which means, presumably, that adult trees show pumpkin-shaped swellings near the base of the trunk.

The taxonomic status of this ash is uncertain. It is reported to be hexaploid (2n = 138) and is perhaps a true-breeding derivative from a cross between *F. pennsylvanica* (2n = 46) and a tetraploid form of *F. americana* (2n = 92). There are other possibilities, but there seems little doubt that the characteristics of the pumpkin ash are attributable to polyploidy, whether or not hybridity is also involved (*Sylvics of Forest Trees of the United States*, p. 188; G. N. Miller, op. cit., p. 21).

F. 'VELTHEIMII'

F. veltheimii Dieck; *F. angustifolia* var. *monophylla* Henry

A tree very similar in form and arrangement of leaf to the one-leaved form of common ash, but easily distinguished from it by the leaves being quite glabrous beneath, and narrower. Leaflets usually solitary, sometimes in twos or threes, in which case the terminal one is always much larger than the lateral ones, lanceolate, 2 to 5 in. long, $\frac{3}{4}$ to $1\frac{1}{2}$ in. wide, tapered towards both ends, the margins set with coarse, sharp, outstanding teeth; dark lustrous green above, quite glabrous on both surfaces. Lateral leaflets, when present, $\frac{3}{4}$ to $2\frac{1}{2}$ in. long, $\frac{1}{4}$ to $\frac{3}{4}$ in. wide. Stalk 1 to $2\frac{1}{2}$ in. long.

Some authorities consider that this ash is a 'one-leaved' form of *F. angustifolia* but the two examples at Kew have very dark brown, almost black buds and a bark very unlike that of *F. angustifolia*. They were received from Dieck's nursery in 1889 and one measures 70 × $5\frac{1}{2}$ ft (1969). Although Henry discounted the theory that these trees are of hybrid origin, it seems to be quite likely. It is puzzling that another one-leaved ash at Kew, at present under the name *F. e.* 'Veltheimii', has a deeply ridged bark as in *F. angustifolia* (No. 80 in the Ash collection). This also came from Dieck in 1889, but as *F. excelsior monophylla laciniata*, a name usually given as a synonym of *F. excelsior* f. *diversifolia*. In Kensington Gardens, London, Alan Mitchell has measured three one-leaved ashes which have the strongly ridged bark of *F. angustifolia* and in this respect are in marked contrast to two examples of the one-leaved common ash growing nearby. These trees resemble the No. 80 from Dieck at Kew, but are probably older, the largest measuring 67 × 7¼ ft (1967).

F. VELUTINA Torr.   ARIZONA ASH

F. pennsylvanica subsp. *velutina* (Torr.) G. N. Miller; *F. coriacea* S. Wats.; *F. velutina* var. *coriacea* (S. Wats.) Rehd.; *F. velutina* var. *glabra* Rehd.; *F. velutina* var. *toumeyi* Rehd.

A tree 25 to 40 ft (rarely 50 ft) high, with a slender trunk; bark with broad, scaly ridges; young stems covered in their first season with a more or less dense covering of fine woolly hairs. Leaves rather thick, 4 to 6 in. long; leaflets three or five (occasionally seven), lanceolate, ovate, elliptic or rhombic-elliptic, acute or acuminate at the apex, ¾ to 3 in. long, the upper part edged with small blunt teeth, upper surface pale green, velvety to glabrous, undersides conspicuously net-veined, usually permanently downy but sometimes becoming almost glabrous, lateral leaflets distinctly stalked to almost sessile, stalk of the terminal one about ½ in. long. Flower panicles downy. Fruits ½ to ¾ in. long with an oblong-obovate to elliptic wing which is shorter than the cylindrical body.

Native of the S.W. United States and Mexico, described from Nevada; introduced to Kew in 1901. It is a variable species, allied to *F. pennsylvanica*, but is a smaller tree with usually thicker leaflets five more rarely seven in number and with the wings of the fruits shorter in relation to the body. No varieties are recognised by Miss Miller, but she notes that the narrow-lanceolate type of leaflet is usually longer-stalked than the ovate or elliptic type. Trees with the former type of leaflet have been distinguished as var. *toumeyi* (Britt.) Rehd., and judging from the examples at Kew near the Lake, are very ornamental. They are of grey-green aspect, with leaflets velvety to the touch on the upper surface even in late summer. The tallest of these, *pl.* 1924, measures 50 × 3½ ft (1969). The tree received as *F. velutina* var. *coriacea*, growing nearby, has much darker green, more glabrous leaflets. *F. velutina* should be more widely planted in the drier parts of eastern and south-eastern England.

F. XANTHOXYLOIDES [G. Don] DC.

Ornus xanthoxyloides G. Don; *F. moorcroftiana* Brandis

A shrub or small tree attaining 25 ft in height in the wild. Young branches, leaf-petioles, rachis, and midrib of leaflets beneath downy or glabrous. Leaves with mostly seven to nine leaflets but occasionally three or up to thirteen; rachis winged. Leaflets variable in size even on the same plant, usually lanceolate or narrow-elliptic, 1¼ to 2¼ in. long, ¼ to ½ in. wide, sometimes broad-elliptic or ovate and up to 4 in. wide, bluntly toothed, scarcely stalked. Flowers in short, dense panicles borne at the leaf-scars of the previous year's growths;

petals absent; calyx cup-shaped. Fruits linear-oblong or spathulate, often retuse at the apex, with the calyx persisting at the base.

A native of the N.W. Himalaya from Garwhal westward, and of Afghanistan, mainly confined to the dry, inner valleys. Farther to the west, in Algeria and Morocco, plants occur which scarcely differ from those of the Asiatic region but are more glabrous and have somewhat smaller leaflets. These have been named var. DIMORPHA (Coss. & Dur.) Wenz. (syn. *F. dimorpha* Coss. & Dur.), but it is doubtful if the distinction is worth maintaining. In his monograph on the ashes, Lingelsheim in effect included the African plants in the typical part of *F. xanthoxyloides*, since his var. *dimorpha* was simply intended to distinguish the larger-leaved plants of the species as a whole from the dwarfer var. *dumosa* (see below).

F. xanthoxyloides is not common in cultivation, but there is a grafted tree at Syon House, London, measuring 43 × 6 ft (1967) and smaller plants at Kew, Edinburgh, and Westonbirt. It is of botanical interest, being more closely allied to various shrubby species of the south-western USA and Mexico than to any Old World species. Also remarkable is its wide but disjunct distribution, which, as Lingelsheim remarks, is not unlike that of the genus *Cedrus*.

var. DUMOSA Carr. *F. xanthoxyloides* f. *dumosa* (Carr.) Rehd.—A purely shrubby variety, forming a dense rounded bush with interlacing branches. Leaves uniformly smaller than in the type, and only ¼ to ⅝ in. long. Described by Carrière from a cultivated plant which was, however, raised from seeds collected in the wild, where similar plants occur. According to Henry, in dry places the branches are very rigid and almost spiny.

FREMONTODENDRON   STERCULIACEAE

The genus *Fremontodendron* contains two species (up to five in some interpretations), natives of California and bordering parts of Arizona and Mexico. The most conspicuous feature of the flower is the bright yellow or orange-yellow calyx; there are no petals. The calyx is five-lobed almost to the base and at the base of each lobe is a nectar-secreting pit. The five stamens are united into a short column, divided at the top into five radiating arms. Ovary conical, with a slender style, developing into a bristly capsule, containing eight to fifteen black or dark-coloured seeds. The genus is named in honour of Captain, later General, J. C. Frémont, who discovered *F. californica* in 1846 during his explorations of the West. The genus has been monographed by M. A. Harvey in *Madroño*, Vol. 7 (1943), pp. 100–110. See also the note by Lord Talbot de Malahide and C. D. Brickell in *Journ. R.H.S.*, Vol. 92 (Nov. 1967), pp. 485–488.

The closest ally of *Fremontia* is the extraordinary handflower tree of Mexico (*Chiranthodendron pentadactylon*), in which the most conspicuous part of the flower is the staminal column and its five branches, which are all bright red and resemble a hand with outstretched fingers.

Regrettably, the cumbrous name *Fremontodendron* must take the place of the more familiar *Fremontia*. Torrey first used the generic name *Fremontia* (in 1843) for a west American plant of the Chenopodiaceae. He later found that this plant was referable to the genus *Sarcobatus*, which antedated his *Fremontia* by two years. Thus *Fremontia* Torrey (1843) became a synonym of *Sarcobatus* Née (1841). Evidently Torrey believed he was free to use the generic name *Fremontia* for another and different genus, and in 1853 he applied it to the one here described. But this is contrary to the rules of botanical nomenclature, and in 1893 Coville renamed the genus, calling it *Fremontodendron*. The generic name *Fremontia* Torrey (1853) was subsequently proposed for conservation but this proposal was rejected and the name here used is therefore the correct one.

F. CALIFORNICUM (Torr.) Cov.

Fremontia californica Torr.; *Chiranthodendron californicum* (Torr.) Baill.

An evergreen or partly deciduous shrub or small tree 5 to 30 ft high, with very downy twigs. Leaves alternate, mostly borne on short spurs, 2 to 4 in. long and 1½ to 3 in. wide on plants cultivated in Britain but smaller on wild ones, roundish to elliptic-ovate in general outline, with one or three main veins springing from the base and usually with three rather shallow, blunt lobes, but sometimes almost entire, upper surface dull green, specked with star-shaped hairs when young, lower surface felted with similar but pale brown hairs; leaf-stalk generally shorter than, occasionally about as long as blades. Flowers solitary, short-stalked, borne on leafy spurs; calyx golden yellow, widely cup-shaped at first, becoming almost flat; lobes roundish, densely downy outside, each with a pit on the inside at the base which is usually hairy with long white cottony hairs, though sometimes only slightly so. Capsules ovoid, 1 to 1½ in. long, acute at the apex. Seeds dull dark brown, downy, each with a conspicuous protuberance (caruncle) at one end. *Bot Mag.*, t. 5591.

Native of California, found on the lower western slopes of the Sierra Nevada from Shasta Co. southward and in various parts of the coastal ranges; also in Arizona. It was discovered in 1846 and introduced soon after to the garden of the Horticultural Society at Chiswick, where it flowered in 1854. About five years later this plant was sold to Henderson's nursery for the sum of £40 but died shortly after the move. In the meantime William Lobb, collecting for Messrs Veitch, had reintroduced it (1853) and since then it has been continually in cultivation.

It is not hardy in the open at Kew but has been grown successfully in a bay on the Temperate House Terrace. It is not long-lived, and although plants occasionally survive twenty or twenty-five years, growing and flowering admirably to the very last season, they are always liable to sudden collapse and death, possibly as a result of excessive wet. This species needs a light, well-drained, poorish soil and it might well be that a dressing of sulphate of potash soon after midsummer might help to keep it hard, especially if the summer is excessively rainy. Usually the plant is given a place on a wall, but this should not be necessary in the mildest parts. It flowers from May to July.

This fremontia produces plenty of its black seeds, which furnish the best and simplest means of increase. So averse is it to root disturbance that young plants should be grown in pots until planted in their permanent places.

F. (*californicum* × *mexicanum*) 'CALIFORNIA GLORY'.—A very vigorous and free-flowering hybrid, raised from seed (sown 1952) of a fine but anomalous form of *F. californicum* that grew in the company of *F. mexicanum* on the old site of the Rancho Santa Ana Botanic Garden in Orange Co., California. The leaves resemble those of *F. californicum* but are five-veined from the base. Flowers shallowly cup-shaped, 1¾ to 2½ in. across, lemon-yellow, becoming slightly red on the outside as they age; nectar-pits downy, as in *F. mexicanum* but with a few of the long hairs characteristic of the nectar-pits of *F. californicum*. Seeds black. For this information we are indebted to the original description by Percy Everett in *Lasca Leaves*, Vol. 12 (Jan. 1962), pp. 2–4. According to Mr Everett vegetative propagation of the fremontias is not easy but 'California Glory' has been increased with fair success under mist by means of tip-cuttings taken late-May to July with a slightly hardened base.

F. NAPENSE (Eastw.) R. Lloyd *Fremontia napensis* Eastw.; *F. californicum* subsp. *napense* (Eastw.) Munz—This minor species or subspecies occurs in Napa and Lake Counties, California. It is described as having slender twigs; leaves ⅜ to 1 in. long, ¼ to ⅝ in. wide, entire to three- or five-lobed, dull almost glabrous above, covered beneath with white down ageing to rust-coloured. Flowers 1¼ to 1⅜ in. wide, yellow sometimes tinged with rose. It is perhaps not yet in cultivation but is said to be attractive (*Calif. Hort. Soc. Journ.*, Vol. 10, pp. 143–144). For other minor species (or subspecies) of *F. californicum* see the monograph by M. A. Harvey cited above. A species described more recently is F. DECUMBENS R. Lloyd (syn. *F. californicum* subsp. *decumbens* (Lloyd) Munz), a decumbent shrub up to 4 ft high and considerably more in spread, with pale orange or brownish flowers 1⅛ to 1⅜ in. wide. It is restricted to a few localities in Eldorado Co.

F. MEXICANUM Davidson

Fremontia mexicana (Davidson) MacBride; *Fremontia californica* var. *mexicana* (Davidson) Jeps.

An evergreen or partially evergreen shrub or small tree 10 to 20 ft high; young shoots densely covered with pale brown, stellate down. Leaves usually roundish in general outline, 1 to 3 in. wide in wild plants, larger in cultivated ones, with five or seven main veins springing from the base and shallowly five- or seven-lobed, cordate at the base, with much the same indumentum as in *F. californicum*; leaf-stalk as long as the blade or shorter. Flowers borne on the main branchlets (not on short side-spurs). Calyx 2½ to 4 in. across, shallowly bell-shaped, orange-yellow, often stained red on the outside near the base; as in *F. californicum* there is a pit at the base of each calyx-lobe, but it is not hairy with long cottony hairs as in that species, though it is downy. Capsules conical, acuminate at the apex. Seeds black, glossy, without conspicuous caruncles. *Bot. Mag.*, t. 9269.

A native of the Mexican State of Baja California (Lower California) but extending across the boundary with the USA into San Diego Co.; described in 1917 from a specimen cultivated by Miss K. O. Sessions. It was introduced to Britain by Tom Hay, Superintendent of Hyde Park, who obtained seeds from Los Angeles in 1926, which he distributed to several gardens, including Kew.

FREMONTODENDRON MEXICANUM

Plants raised from these seeds were not hardy at Kew, even against a south wall, being killed in the winters of 1927–8 and 1928–9. But the seedlings flowered when a few months old and reached 5 to 6 ft in one season, continuing to flower from the leaf-axils from July to September. *F. mexicanum* is said to be more valued by California gardeners than *F. californicum*, its flowers being of a deeper yellow and borne over a longer period. It has never been widely enough grown in Britain for its relative merits to be assessed, but it certainly appears to be more tender than *F. californicum*. It is perhaps worth further trial in the mildest parts, especially if seeds can be obtained.

FREYLINIA   SCROPHULARIACEAE

A genus of five (perhaps fewer) species of glabrous evergreen shrubs, natives of southern Africa. Leaves entire. Flowers in axillary cymes, forming a terminal panicle or more rarely a raceme. Calyx five-lobed. Corolla tubular with spreading lobes; fertile stamens four, included. Fruit a capsule; seeds disk-like.

F. LANCEOLATA (L. f.) G. Don

Caprarial anceolata L. f.; *F. cestroides* Colla

An evergreen shrub of dense, very leafy habit, 12 ft or more high; young shoots slightly hairy, angled. Leaves opposite, linear, tapering towards both ends, slender-pointed, 2 to 5 in. long, $\frac{1}{8}$ to $\frac{3}{8}$ in. wide; dark rather bright green on both surfaces, perfectly glabrous, midrib prominent beneath; scarcely stalked. Flowers sweetly scented, produced in a slender terminal panicle 2 to 4 in. long, also from the axils of the terminal leaves, the whole forming at its best a compound pyramidal panicle 10 to 12 in. high. Corolla $\frac{1}{2}$ in. long, tubular, $\frac{1}{8}$ to $\frac{1}{4}$ in. wide, with five small rounded lobes; yellow or creamy-white outside, richer yellow within and hairy in the throat; lobes often tipped with pink. Calyx $\frac{1}{12}$ in. long, deeply five-lobed. Stamens normally four, occasionally five, included in the corolla, to the inside of which they are attached.

Native of S. Africa; introduced in 1774. Usually grown in greenhouses and too tender for our average climate, this is hardy in the Isle of Wight and in the southern maritime counties. The flowers are richly fragrant and the shrub is elegant in growth. It is evidently a lover of heat and sunshine, which probably explains its flowering after the hot summer of 1921. It blossoms wonderfully in Algiers. The best place for it with us would be against a warm south wall.

FUCHSIA   ONAGRACEAE

A genus of about 100 species of shrubs, some climbing and a few attaining the dimensions of small trees in the wild. They are natives mainly of C. and S. America, but four occur in New Zealand and one in Tahiti. Leaves opposite or whorled, rarely alternate. Flowers epigynous, usually axillary and pendulous but in some species crowded in a terminal cluster. Calyx-tube (hypanthium) bell-shaped, funnel-shaped, or more commonly tubular, with four spreading sepals (calyx-lobes) which are usually free but united at the base in F. regia. Petals four, inserted in the mouth of the calyx-tube, erect, spreading or reflexed, but in some species the petals are inconspicuous or even absent (section Skinnera). Stamens eight, usually exserted and often of unequal length. Style exserted. Some species of Fuchsia are dioecious, i.e., the flowers are unisexual and borne on different plants; in others unisexual flowers may occur as well as perfect ones. The fruit in Fuchsia is a berry, usually with many seeds.

The genus Fuchsia was revised by P. A. Munz in Proc. Calif. Acad. Sci., Vol. 25 (1943), pp. 1–138. Modern horticultural works are: T. Thorne, Fuchsias for all Purposes (1959); S. J. Wilson, Fuchsias (2nd ed. 1969); W. P. Wood, A Fuchsia Survey (2nd ed. 1956). The British Fuchsia Society was founded in 1938 and publishes a yearbook.

The fuchsias can be increased with the greatest ease by means of soft-wooded cuttings, but ripe wood will also strike. For the private gardener the best procedure is to take soft-cuttings about August; these will root without artificial heat but must be overwintered in a frost-free frame or greenhouse.

For the garden hybrids of fuchsia see the separate section starting on page 243.

F. COCCINEA Dryander

F. montana Cambess.; *F. pubescens* Cambess.; *F. elegans* Salisb.; *F. pendula* Salisb.

A small shrub, or sometimes a semi-climber throwing up lax stems 10 ft or more long; young growths reddish, covered with a fine down, sometimes with longer hairs intermixed. Leaves opposite or in threes, narrow-ovate or ovate, up to 2 in. long, rounded or cordate at the base, tapered at the apex, to a fine point, downy on both sides and with longer hairs on the main veins beneath, notably towards the base of the midrib. Flowers much resembling those of *F. magellanica* but with the calyx-tube not exceeding ¼ in. in length. *Bot. Mag.*, t. 97 and t. 5740.

The native country of this fuchsia was for long uncertain. It was described by Dryander in 1789 from a plant growing at Kew, to which it had been introduced the previous year by a Captain Firth. Dryander erroneously identified Firth's plant with the fuchsia seen in Chile earlier in the century by the French traveller Feuillée and figured in his 'Itinerary' (*Journ. Obs. Phys. Math.*, Vol. 3, p. 64, t. 47). Hence Dryander's statement in his original description that *F. coccinea* was a native of Chile. In fact the plant figured by Feuillée was *F. magellanica* and it was partly due to Dryander's error that the two species came to be confused. Eighty years after the introduction of *F. coccinea*, Sir Joseph Hooker pointed out (*Bot. Mag.*, t. 5740) that there were specimens of *F. coccinea* in the British Museum and at the Linnaean Society which had been received from Kew in the year the species was introduced and that these were not *F. magellanica* but agreed best with a Brazilian species. Recently, P. A. Munz in his monograph has adopted the name *F. coccinea* for the Brazilian species previously known as *F. montana* Cambess.

It is interesting that Sir James Edward Smith, author of the article on *Fuchsia* in Rees' *Cyclopaedia* (Vol. 15, published 1819), gives what is probably the true history of the introduction of *F. coccinea* to Kew: 'A plant of this species, apparently in a dead state, was brought by Capt. Firth to Kew Garden, from Lisbon, and it was said to have come from the Brazils. As the spring advanced, it began to sprout, and soon put forth its exquisitely beautiful flowers, to the admiration of all who beheld it.'

With regard to the fuchsia figured in the *Botanical Magazine* in 1789 as *F. coccinea* (t. 97), there is little doubt that it is the true *F. coccinea* of Brazil and not a form of *F. magellanica*. In the article accompanying the plate it was said that the species was introduced by the nurseryman Lee of Hammersmith. According to tradition, Lee obtained his plant from a sailor's wife in Wapping; it is not unlikely that her husband came by it in the same way as Captain Firth had done, and at about the same time.

The true *F. coccinea* was almost extinct in gardens by 1867, in which year two plants were found growing in the greenhouses at the Oxford Botanical Garden and it was from one of these, presented to Kew, that the figure in the *Botanical Magazine* (t. 5740) was made. Unfortunately it is not in cultivation at Kew at the present time (1971) and seems to have become rare again. But the species is of considerable interest, since there is little doubt that it has played an important and largely unacknowledged role in the formation of the fuchsia hybrids. See further under *F.* 'Globosa' (p. 245).

F. EXCORTICATA (J. R. & G. Forst.) L. f.

Skinnera excorticata J. R. & G. Forst.

A deciduous shrub or small tree up to 40 ft high in the wild, the trunk 6 to 18 in. in diameter, with a thin, loose, peeling bark; young shoots glabrous. Leaves alternate, ovate, ovate-lanceolate or oval, tapered or rounded at the base, pointed, slightly or not at all toothed, $1\frac{1}{2}$ to 4 in. long, $\frac{1}{2}$ to $1\frac{1}{2}$ in. wide, dark green and glabrous above, very pale or whitish beneath and downy along the midrib; stalk $\frac{1}{3}$ to 1 in. long. Flowers of the ordinary fuchsia shape, pendulous, solitary in the leaf-axils, $\frac{3}{4}$ to $1\frac{1}{4}$ in. long. Calyx-tube swollen at the base, then, after forming a neck, developing a funnel-shaped tube, finally dividing into four spreading wide-lanceolate, acute lobes $\frac{1}{3}$ in. long, the colour greenish, greenish-purple, or dull red. Petals four, small, showing their pointed purplish tips between the lobes of the calyx. Stamens eight, very variable in length. Fruits $\frac{1}{2}$ in. long, purplish black, juicy.

Native of New Zealand; introduced about 1820. It is very distinct among fuchsias by reason of its alternate leaves and by the globular swelling at the base of the calyx-tube. It cannot be compared with the S. American species in beauty of blossom, but it is interesting in its peeling bark. It grows to a large size in the milder parts of the country.

F. COLENSOI Hook. f.—A very variable species, allied to the preceding. It is usually a low rambling shrub with long straggling procumbent branches. Leaves very variable in shape and size but usually much smaller than in *F. excorticata* and more or less ovate. Flowers very like those of *F. excorticata*.

F. MAGELLANICA Lam.

A shrub usually under 8 ft high but sometimes almost twice as high in shady, sheltered positions; young stems reddish, glabrous or slightly downy; older branches brown, with a peeling bark. Leaves opposite or in threes (often in fours on strong shoots), narrowly ovate to elliptic-ovate, up to 2 in. long, acute or acuminate at the apex, usually wedge-shaped at the base, irregularly edged with small, sharp, forward-pointing teeth, medium to dark green above, paler beneath, glabrous, or slightly downy on the veins beneath; leaf-stalks reddish, slender, $\frac{1}{4}$ to $\frac{3}{8}$ in. long, glabrous or downy. Flowers borne singly or two together in the leaf-axils on slender slightly downy stalks up to 2 in. long. Tube bright red, $\frac{3}{8}$ to $\frac{1}{2}$ in. long, more or less cylindric, but narrowed abruptly at the base where it joins the ovary and often gradually narrowing upwards towards the base of the sepals; sepals coloured like the tube, narrow-lanceolate, acuminately tapered at the apex, $\frac{3}{4}$ to 1 in. long. Petals about half as long as the sepals, purple or blue-violet, obovate, convolute. Stamens exserted beyond the mouth of the corolla and, with the still longer style, forming a conspicuous feature of the flower. Fruits oblong, up to $\frac{7}{8}$ in. long.

Native of Chile and bordering parts of Argentina from the latitude of Valparaiso southward to Tierra del Fuego; described by Lamarck from a specimen collected in December 1767, by the French naturalist Commerson in the region

of the Straits of Magellan, but known earlier from Feuillée's 'Itinerary', in which
it is figured as 'thilco', a rendering of its native name. The date of introduction
is often given as 1788 but it is probable that the fuchsias introduced around that
date were really the Brazilian *F. coccinea* (q.v.). There is no sound evidence of the
introduction of *F. magellanica* to Britain before the early 1820s.

F. magellanica is a moisture-loving plant which in the wild forms thickets along
streamsides or in marshy places. Often its companion is *Berberis darwinii*,
though that species is less demanding of moisture and occurs also in other
associations. Its north–south range in Chile is about 1,500 miles and it is found
from the coast to moderate elevations in the Andes. It varies not only in size of
leaf and length of flower-stalk but also in such characters as leaf-shape, habit,
length of internodes, degree of downiness, and, perhaps most significantly, in
the shape and relative size of the parts of the flower. Apart from the white-
flowered var. *molinae* (see below) Munz (op. cit.) recognises only two varieties:

var. MACROSTEMA (Ruiz & Pavon) Munz *F. macrostema* Ruiz & Pavon—
Leaves 1 to 2 in. long. Flower-stalks 1⅝ to 2¼ in. long. Leaves also more membranous than in the typical variety and flowers somewhat larger.

var. MAGELLANICA *F. magellanica* var. *typica* Munz—This is the typical
variety with leaves up to 1 in. long and flower-stalks ⅞ to 1¼ in. long.

However, Munz points out that the two varieties are linked by intermediates.
The var. *macrostema* has a more northern distribution but there is considerable
overlap. Owing to the indistinctness of these two varieties the description in
the first paragraph comprises both. Some other more marked varieties are
described below, together with some of garden origin:

var. CHONOTICA (F. Phil.) Reiche *F. chonotica* F. Phil.—Leaves crowded,
1⅛ in. long, ⅝ in. wide, on stalks about ¼ in. long. Flowers on rather thick, only
slightly pendulous pedicels, which are only ⅝ to ¾ in. long. Calyx-tube 7/16 in. long;
sepals about twice as long as the tube. Native of Chile, described from the
Guaitecas Islands (part of the Chonos Archipelago) but also reported from
Chiloe Island and adjacent parts of the mainland. Philippi also named a *F.
araucana* but never published a description. From the short account given by his
father, R. A. Philippi (*Bot. Zeit.*, Jahrg. 34 (1876), p. 577, t. 9B, Fig. 6), this
fuchsia resembled the var. *chonotica* in its short calyx-tube, but the flower-stalks
were even shorter than in that variety and the leaves broad-ovate. The type
specimen came from Toltén, on the Chilean coast north of Valdivia.

var. CONICA (Lindl.) Bailey *F. conica* Lindl.; *F. macrostema* var. *conica*
(Lindl.) G. Don—In describing this fuchsia (as a species) Lindley remarked that
a distinctive feature of the flower was 'the figure of the tube of the calyx, which
has a conical form, being much broader at the base than the apex, in consequence
of which it appears divided from the ovarium by a strong contraction'. But a
more significant character was the relative shortness of the sepals, which were
scarcely longer than the petals. Leaves rather broadly ovate. Lindley's description was made from a plant grown in the Horticultural Society's garden at
Chiswick, raised from seeds sent from Chile to Francis Place in 1824. This variety
is one of the parents of 'Globosa' (q.v.). It is doubtful whether this variety is
still in cultivation.

var. DISCOLOR (Lindl.) Bailey *F. discolor* Lindl.—This fuchsia, once known as the 'Port Famine' fuchsia, was introduced to cultivation by means of seeds collected during Captain King's Surveying Voyage to the Magellan region (1826–30) and first put into commerce by Lowe's nursery, Clapton. Port Famine, no longer on the maps, was an anchorage on the Straits of Magellan near to what is now Fuerte Bulnes; it is not, as Lindley erroneously stated, in the Falkland Islands. From the original figure and description (*Bot. Mag.*, t. 1805 (1836)), the typical plant was of dwarf, dense habit, with deep purple branches. Leaves long-stalked, small with undulated margins. The flowers do not show any particularly distinctive character. It was stated to be very hardy and is of interest as the first representative of the wide-ranging *F. magellanica* to come from near the extreme southern end of the area of the species. It was from this remote region that Commerson collected the type of *F. magellanica* and *F. magellanica* var. *discolor* should probably be regarded as a synonym of the typical variety. It is mentioned here because of its historical interest.

cv. 'GLOBOSA'. See *F.* 'Globosa' under hybrids (p. 245).

var. GRACILIS (Lindl.) Bailey *F. gracilis* Lindl.; *F. macrostema* var. *gracilis*, (Lindl.) D. Don; *F. decussata* Graham, not Ruiz & Pavon—A graceful shrub with slender, arching branches which are usually downy and sometimes densely so. Leaves up to 1½ in. long and variable in width from narrow-lanceolate to ovate; stalks about ½ in. long. Flowers on slender stalks 1½ to 2 in. long; they have the normal colouring of the species but are very distinct in their slender, long-tapered sepals which are often more than twice as long as the corolla. This variety was introduced from Chile by Alexander Cruckshanks, who sent seeds to Francis Place in 1822. Lindley's statement that the seeds came from Mexico is certainly incorrect, and the plate he published (*Bot. Reg.*, t. 847) is a poor one. It is, however, of no relevance to the typification of this variety, since Lindley's *F. gracilis* is simply a renaming of *F. decussata* Graham, figured in *Bot. Mag.*, t. 2507.

var. MOLINAE Espinoza—Leaves pale green. Flower-stalks and ovaries green. Sepals almost white. Corolla pale lilac rose. This albino variant was first validly named and described in 1929, the type being a plant found on the island of Chiloe. But the same or a similar form had been introduced to cultivation in Britain by Clarence Elliott in 1926 and is still generally known as *F. magellanica alba*. In this the sepals spread horizontally; the style is pure white and a beautiful feature of the flower. It is interesting to note how this mutation has deprived all parts of the plant of the red or purple pigmentation that characterises the species; even the bark is paler. Unfortunately the cultivated plant is shy-flowering but worth growing, especially in milder parts, where it makes an elegant shrub with a fawn-coloured peeling bark. There is a fine example at Tresco Abbey in the Isles of Scilly and another in the Walled Garden at Nymans in Sussex. A.M. 1932.

cv. 'PUMILA'. See *F.* 'Pumila' under hybrids, p. 246.

cv. 'RICCARTONII'. See *F.* 'Riccartonii' under hybrids, p. 246.

cv. 'THOMPSONII'.—An old garden variety, raised before 1838 and almost certainly derived from the var. *gracilis*. It is bushier and leafier than the common form of that variety; the leaves are shorter and relatively narrower; the flowers are smaller but borne in great profusion from July to autumn. It is still one of the best of the hardy fuchsias, but does not assort well with the larger-flowered kinds.

cv. 'VARIEGATA'.—Leaves fairly regularly margined with creamy-white. A sport from the var. *gracilis*.

cv. 'VERSICOLOR'.—Leaves silvery grey, some of them partly margined with creamy white strips; young leaves flushed crimson-purple, the variegated parts of these bright red. A very attractive fuchsia, best grown in a fairly sunny position to bring out its full colouring. It is sometimes called *F. magellanica* 'Tricolor' and very often wrongly named *F. magellanica* 'Variegata'. Like the true 'Variegata' (see above) it is a sport from *F. magellanica* var. *gracilis*.

F. magellanica was reintroduced from the Andes by the late Harold Comber in 1927 under field number 1031. A plant from these seeds grows against the wall of the Temperate House at Kew.

F. MICROPHYLLA H.B.K.

A shrub 1 to 6 ft high in the wild, occasionally taller; young stems reddish, with curled white hairs. Leaves narrow-elliptic to oblanceolate, $\frac{3}{16}$ to $\frac{3}{4}$ in. long, $\frac{1}{8}$ to $\frac{3}{8}$ in. wide, cuneate at the base, coarsely toothed in the upper half or two-thirds, margins ciliate, otherwise almost glabrous, glossy above, of leathery texture; leaf-stalk up to $\frac{1}{4}$ in. long. Flowers on slender hairy stalks $\frac{1}{4}$ to $\frac{1}{2}$ in. long. Tube dull pale red, cylindric or very slightly widening upward, about $\frac{5}{16}$ in. long, glabrous or almost so; sepals coloured like the tube, about $\frac{3}{16}$ in. long, acute, spreading or slightly reflexed. Petals deep rosy pink, broad-obovate, about as long as the sepals, retuse and pleated at the apex. Ovary slightly hairy. Stamens eight, the four opposite the sepals slightly exserted. Style exserted with four white, linear spreading lobes, arranged in the form of a cross. Fruits black, globose.

A native of Central America. It is a variable species, in which five subspecies are recognised by D. E. Breedlove in *Systematics of Fuchsia section Encliandra* (1969). The above description is of the typical subspecies, which is common in Mexico at high altitudes, often in association with *Abies religiosa*, and was introduced in 1828. The description is made from a cultivated plant known to derive from wild seeds. In other forms of this subspecies the stems may be almost glabrous or the hairs brown, not white, and there is some variation in the colour of the flowers. Also, the species is gynodioecious, some plants bearing perfect flowers as described above, others female flowers only. The true *F. microphylla* has been so little cultivated until recently that nothing useful can be said about its hardiness, though it should survive most winters in a sheltered place.

subsp. HIDALGENSIS (Munz) Breedlove *F. minimiflora* var. *hidalgensis* Munz —Flowers white, with reflexed sepals. Branchlets clad with golden-brown hairs. In cultivation under the name *F. minimiflora*.

F. PROCUMBENS A. Cunn.

F. *kirkii* Hook. f.

A prostrate, creeping shrub (sometimes scrambling through low bushes) with very slender wiry stems and alternate, roundish ovate, or almost orbicular leaves, mostly heart-shaped at the base, sometimes obscurely toothed, $\frac{1}{4}$ to $\frac{3}{4}$ in. long. Flowers erect, solitary in the leaf-axils, $\frac{1}{2}$ to $\frac{3}{4}$ in. long, without petals, opening from July onwards. Calyx-tube pale orange yellow, the four ovate

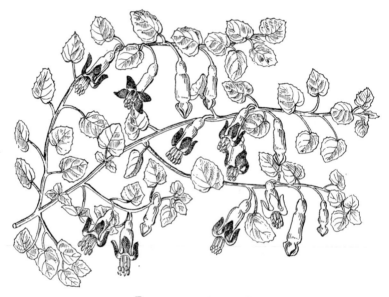

FUCHSIA PROCUMBENS

lobes $\frac{1}{4}$ in. long, at first spreading then reflexed back to the tube, mostly purple but green at the base; anthers blue. Fruits flesh pink, $\frac{3}{4}$ in. long, oval. *Bot. Mag.*, t. 6139.

A native of the North Island of New Zealand, where it is found in rocky, sandy, or gravelly places near the coast. It was discovered in 1834 and introduced about twenty years later. In the wild this species is said to be trioecious—the individual plant may bear bisexual flowers or flowers that are either all male or all female. The cultivated form fruits freely, however, and makes a charming basket plant. It is fairly hardy.

F. THYMIFOLIA H.B.K.

It is uncertain whether this species is in cultivation in Britain at the present time, but the fuchsia 'Reflexa', described below under F. × *bacillaris*, is very near to it. F. *thymifolia* is a native of Mexico and N. Guatemala, allied to F.

microphylla and occupying similar habitats. It has been confused with that species but differs in the following leading characters: Leaves thin, ovate or elliptic, relatively much wider than in *F. microphylla,* and entire or slightly serrated. Tube of flower definitely funnel-shaped (obconic), not cylindric as in *F. microphylla,* greenish white or pale pink; sepals coloured like the tube, slenderly pointed, reflexed, their tips free in the bud-stage. Petals pink at first but deepening to maroon-crimson as the flower ages. A further distinction given by Breedlove in his monograph on the section *Encliandra* is that in this species the nectary is eight-lobed (entire and disk-like in *F. microphylla*).

F. thymifolia was introduced in 1824 and again in 1831, but seems to have given way in gardens to hybrids between it and *F. microphylla* (see *F.* × *bacillaris*).

F. × **BACILLARIS** Lindl. *F. cinnabarina* McClintock; *F. reflexa* Hort., in part—The fuchsia described by Lindley as *F. bacillaris* in 1832 was raised from seeds collected in Mexico. Long considered to be a species, it has recently been identified by D. E. Breedlove (op. cit., pp. 59–60) as a hybrid between *F. microphylla* subsp. *microphylla* and *F. thymifolia* subsp. *thymifolia.* Such hybrids occur in the wild and could have arisen spontaneously in British gardens, or been raised deliberately, at any time from the late 1820s onward. There are at least three cultivated fuchsias of the section *Encliandra* in commerce which appear to be hybrids of this parentage. They are:

1. A fuchsia which seems to agree closely with a plant of California gardens that was recently given botanical status by Miss McClintock under the name *F. cinnabarina.* It has thin leaves, shaped as in *F. thymifolia,* but curiously undulated, as if the plant was affected by a virus-disease, though it seems healthy enough. The flowers have a funnel-shaped tube as in *F. thymifolia* and reflexed sepals, but they are larger (tube up to ¼ in. long) and differently coloured: at first the petals are Mandarin Red and the tube similarly though less intensely coloured, but later the whole flower darkens to varying shades of vermilion. This fuchsia is in commerce as *F. bacillaris,* but also (wrongly) as *F. parviflora.* In Scotland it is grown as "*F. aurantiaca*".

2. A plant seen under the horticultural name *F. cottinghamii* has leaves shaped as in *F. thymifolia* but very leathery and glossy. The flowers are brilliant red, resembling those of *F. microphylla* in their cylindrical tube and spreading (not reflexed) sepals. This could also belong to *F.* × *bacillaris.* It is very vigorous and floriferous under glass.

3. The third fuchsia in this group is very near to *F. thymifolia,* and shows beautifully the darkening of flower-colour with age characteristic of that species. But the flowers are somewhat larger than in wild plants of *F. thymifolia* and more deeply coloured when young. It is cultivated under the erroneous name *F. parviflora* and also as *F.* 'Reflexa'.

Fuchsia Hybrids

The genus *Fuchsia* is mainly represented in gardens by hybrids deriving from *F. magellanica, F. coccinea,* and various species of Central America. Many of these are hardy in their wood in milder parts. In colder, more northerly, and inland localities, the hardier sorts may still be grown in the open air, although they can scarcely be termed shrubs, seeing that most of them are killed to the ground almost invariably. Yet even at Kew, groups of several sorts of these hybrids make very pleasing displays of colour from July onwards. Shoots spring up freely from the old stools, continuing to flower as they lengthen until the frosts come. The flower-buds add much to the beauty of the plants. These hybrids need a rich, deep soil, and plenty of moisture during the growing season. All grow well on chalky soils.

The following selection of the hardier hybrids could have been greatly extended, had space permitted. It will at least serve to emphasise that this genus contains many valuable ornamental plants which are not nearly enough used as permanent features in gardens. For further details see the chapter on fuchsia hedges in the book by S. J. Wilson referred to on page 236. For some small-flowered hybrids see *F.* × *bacillaris* on page 243.

'ALICE HOFFMAN'.—Leaves dark mat-green, purple-tinged when young, $\frac{3}{4}$ to 1 in. long, *c.* $\frac{1}{2}$ in. wide. Tube $\frac{5}{16}$ in. long. Sepals pinkish scarlet, $\frac{3}{4}$ in. long. Corolla white, $\frac{5}{8}$ in. long. Dwarf.

'CALEDONIA'.—Leaves bright green, corrugated. Tube and sepals salmon pink; tube 1 in. or slightly more long; sepals narrow, tapered, forward-pointing, about 1 in. long. Petals pale magenta.

'CHILLERTON BEAUTY'.—Leaves ovate, acute, rather thick, pale sea-green in colour; petiole purplish. Tube about $\frac{5}{8}$ in. long. Sepals *c.* $1\frac{1}{4}$ in. long, pale rose flushed deeper rose. Corolla violet-purple. A beautifully soft-coloured variety of uncertain origin. It is of spreading habit and eventually 4 ft high in milder parts.

'CORALLINA'.—Stems arching to procumbent, reddish when young. Leaves in pairs, threes or fours, mostly ovate or oblong-ovate, up to 3 in. long, folded upwards along the purplish midrib; undersides tinged purple, especially on the veins. Tube and sepals scarlet; tube *c.* $\frac{5}{8}$ in. long; sepals $1\frac{1}{4}$ in. or slightly more long, $\frac{3}{8}$ in. wide, acuminate, forward pointing. Petals reddish purple, *c.* $\frac{3}{4}$ in. long. This famous fuchsia, one of the oldest of those now cultivated, was raised by Lucombe and Pince around 1844. It was not at that time highly regarded by fuchsia fanciers, the sepals not being reflexed as fashion then demanded, and the petals too infused with red, but it was found to be a vigorous climber and at one time was commonly grown against house-walls on the coasts of the south-western counties and in North Wales, where it sometimes developed a stout trunk and attained eave-height. In colder parts it is herbaceous but very effective in late summer with its brilliant flowers, graceful habit, and bronzy green leaves.

The parentage of 'Corallina' is not known. Porcher suggested it was not a hybrid but a form merely of the Brazilian *F. radicans* (*F. regia* var. *integrifolia*) and although this assertion is incorrect it is not unlikely that 'Corallina' is a hybrid from this variety or from some other Brazilian relative of *F. magellanica*.

'Corallina' is sometimes wrongly called *F.* 'Exoniensis' or *F.* × *exoniensis*. The source of this error is an article by W. B. Hemsley in *Gard. Chron.* (Nov. 3, 1883), p. 560, in which a specimen of 'Corallina' received from R. I. Lynch,

Curator of the University Botanic Garden, Cambridge, is discussed under the name *F. exoniensis*, and is figured as such on p. 565 of the same issue. In the interesting correspondence that followed, Hemsley's error was pointed out by several gardeners, and in a letter on p. 728 he retracted. The true 'Exoniensis', raised by Lucombe and Pince in 1841, is probably no longer in cultivation. It had the sepals fairly strongly reflexed and petals of a much bluer shade of purple.

'DR FOSTER'.—Leaves ovate to broadly so; stems and petioles reddish. Tube and sepals scarlet; tube stout, $\frac{1}{2}$ in. long, $\frac{3}{8}$ in. wide; sepals *c.* $1\frac{1}{2}$ in. long, almost $\frac{3}{4}$ in. wide, spreading, slightly reflexed at tips. Corolla violet-mauve, $1\frac{3}{8}$ in. long, 1 in. wide. The flowers are remarkably large for a hardy fuchsia. Of erect habit.

'GLOBOSA'.—A dwarf, spreading shrub with glabrous, strongly toothed leaves 1 to $1\frac{1}{2}$ in. long, rounded or subcordate at the base. Flower-buds globular; half-expanded flowers balloon-shaped owing to the cohering tips of the sepals. Tube and sepals crimson, the former very short (*c.* $\frac{3}{16}$ in. long) and subglobose. Petals violet, about half as long as sepals. Raised by Bunney of Stratford before 1832. It is said to have been a seedling of *F. magellanica* var. *conica* but is certainly a hybrid, the other parent being in all probability the Brazilian *F. coccinea*, the influence of which is strongly suggested by the very short tube. If so, it was the first cross between *F. magellanica* and *F. coccinea* to be named and validly described (by Lindley in *Bot. Reg.*, under t. 1556). It was much used by the early breeders and a probable parent of 'Riccartonii'. Whether the true 'Globosa' is still in cultivation cannot be said.

'HOWLETT'S HARDY'.—Of low, spreading habit. Tube and sepals soft-scarlet; tube $\frac{1}{2}$ in. long; sepals $1\frac{1}{4}$ to $1\frac{3}{4}$ in. long, spreading at first, eventually strongly reflexed. Corolla violet-blue and about half as long as the sepals, but much enlarging as the flower ages and becoming magenta-pink.

'LENA'.—Of low, rather lax habit. Tube and sepals white tinged with pink; tube $\frac{5}{8}$ in. long; sepals very fleshy, green-tipped, spreading, 1 in. or slightly more long. Corolla semi-double, mauve with white flares at the base, about 1 in. long and wide. Said to be very hardy.

'MADAME CORNELISSEN'.—A strong-growing variety up to 3 ft high, or more in mild gardens. Leaves dark green, long-tapered at the apex to an acute point. Tube and sepals soft scarlet; tube $\frac{3}{4}$ in. long; sepals lanceolate, long-tapered, gracefully reflexed, $1\frac{1}{2}$ in. long, thick. Corolla with a few extra, reduced petals, white. The flowers of this variety are beautifully formed and set off by the unusually elegant foliage.

'MARGARET'.—A very vigorous freely branching variety of vase-shaped habit, eventually 4 or 5 ft high. Leaves light green. Tube and sepals scarlet; tube $\frac{1}{4}$ in. long; sepals $1\frac{1}{2}$ in. long, soon strongly reflexed. Corolla semi-double, petals bluish violet with white flares at the base, spreading. A very showy fuchsia raised by the late W. P. Wood from 'Heritage' crossed with the white-flowered form of *F. magellanica*.

'MRS POPPLE'.—A vigorous variety eventually 4 ft high and wide, very bushy. Leaves mostly ovate, folded upward along the midrib as in 'Corallina'. Tube and sepals soft crimson-scarlet; tube about $\frac{1}{2}$ in. long; sepals 1 in. long, gracefully recurved towards the apex. Corolla violet-blue, ageing to crimson-purple. Free-flowering and one of the best of the hardier sorts. It shows the influence of 'Corallina', especially in its foliage. A.M. 1934.

'MRS W. P. WOOD'.—This fuchsia resembles the white-flowered form of *F. magellanica* but the flowers are pinker, larger and with a shorter, wider tube. It is less hardy. A seedling of 'Margaret', selfed, and like the parent (q.v.) raised by W. P. Wood.

'PHYLLIS'.—Said to be hardy and vigorous. Tube stout, $\frac{5}{8}$ in. long, $\frac{3}{8}$ in. wide. Sepals pale pinkish scarlet, about 1 in. long. Corolla semi-double, slightly deeper coloured than the sepals.

'PIXIE'.—Of upright, bushy habit when established. Leaves lanceolate, light green, with impressed veins. Tube and sepals pinkish scarlet. Corolla lavender, with red veins. A sport of 'Graf Witte' raised by Messrs Russell.

'PUMILA'.—A true dwarf, 6 to 9 in. high and eventually 18 in. across. Leaves lanceolate, mostly about $\frac{1}{4}$ in. wide and under 1 in. long. Tube and sepals glossy crimson-scarlet; tube very short, $\frac{1}{8}$ to $\frac{3}{16}$ in. long; sepals about $\frac{1}{2}$ in. long. Corolla about three-quarters as long as the sepals, deep violet-blue. An old variety, sometimes called 'Tom Thumb' but quite distinct from the fuchsia for which 'Tom Thumb' is now the established name (q.v.). It is sometimes wrongly placed under *F. magellanica*, from which it differs in the very short tube.

'RICCARTONII'.—An almost hardy deciduous shrub 5 to 6 ft high and as much across, but larger in the mildest and rainiest parts of the country. Young stems and petioles reddish on the exposed side. Leaves opposite or in threes, lanceolate, acute, 1 to $1\frac{3}{4}$ in. long, $\frac{3}{8}$ to $\frac{5}{8}$ in. wide, dark, mat green above, edged with well-developed callous teeth; petiole $\frac{1}{8}$ to $\frac{1}{4}$ in. long. Flowers on slender glabrous pedicels $1\frac{3}{8}$ to $1\frac{3}{4}$ in. long. Tube and sepals scarlet; tube $\frac{1}{4}$ in. or very slightly more long, broadest just below the midpoint and hence spindle-shaped; sepals broad-lanceolate to almost elliptic, short-acuminate, $\frac{3}{4}$ to $\frac{7}{8}$ in. long, $\frac{5}{16}$ in. wide. Corolla violet, about $\frac{3}{8}$ in. long.

The origin of 'Riccartonii' is not known for certain but it is believed to have been raised at Riccarton, Scotland, by Young, the gardener there, around 1830. As a greenhouse fuchsia it was soon superseded by more elaborate, larger-flowered confections, but by the end of the 1830s its hardiness had been discovered and from then on it must have become increasingly common in gardens as an open-ground plant (see *Gard. Chron.* 1841 and 1842 *passim*, and the interesting note in the volume for 1846, p. 579).

The oldest specimen in the Kew Herbarium was received from J. McNab of the Edinburgh Botanic Garden in August 1876. In his accompanying letter to Sir Joseph Hooker he wrote: 'The enclosed specimens of Fuchsia Riccartonii were taken off plants which have been growing in a clump about 36 ft round, and which have been standing undisturbed these 22 or more years. The F. Riccartonii when grown on a wall and well manured has a much finer appearance. It certainly is the finest Fuchsia we have, and is much finer than the old F. discolor, which it resembles (except in its compact habit). The true F. discolor I have not seen for years.'

McNab's reference to *F. discolor* is interesting, for there seems to have been a confusion at one time between this, the Port Famine fuchsia (see under *F. magellanica*), and *F.* 'Riccartonii'. For example, Tillery wrote in 1871 (*Florist and Pomologist*, p. 218): 'Some thirty-six years ago, I introduced the Fuchsia Riccartonii, then named the Port Famine Fuchsia, to the Isle of Aran.' In fact, 'Riccartonii' is certainly of garden origin and quite distinct from the Port Famine fuchsia or any other form of *F. magellanica* in the short tube of the flowers. The parentage of 'Riccartonii' is not known for certain, but it was said to be a seedling of 'Globosa' (q.v.) and this seems very likely.

'TOM THUMB'.—Leaves medium green, ovate to lanceolate, mostly ¾ to 1⅛ in. long, slightly toothed. Tube and sepals carmine-pink; tube ¼ to ⅜ in. long, broadest near the middle; sepals elliptic, spreading, about ⅞ in. long. Corolla soft violet-purple, slightly more than half as long as the sepals. A charming softly coloured fuchsia of dwarf compact habit, very free-flowering. The name 'Tomb Thumb' has also been used for 'Pumila' (q.v.). A.M. 1938.

'W. P. WOOD'.—Leaves broad-ovate, strongly toothed, with a raised rim. Tube and sepals dark scarlet; tube stout, ½ in. long; sepals elliptic, about 1 in. long. Corolla reddish purple shading to scarlet at the base. Of erect, dwarf habit.

GARRYA   GARRYACEAE

A genus of about twelve species of dioecious evergreen trees and shrubs, natives of western N. America, Mexico, and Guatemala, and the West Indies. Leaves simple, opposite, without stipules. Flowers apetalous, borne in pendulous catkin-like racemes; staminate flowers consisting of four sepals and four stamens. Pistillate flowers with an inferior ovary bearing (in some species) a few small calyx-lobes near the apex; styles two. Fruit a berry, with one or two seeds. The family Garryaceae, of which this genus is the only member, is allied to the Cornaceae, and more particularly to *Griselinia* and *Aucuba*.

With the exception of *G. elliptica* the garryas have not much value in gardens, being more or less tender and with little flower beauty. In the coldest parts of the British Isles all the species treated here will need wall protection, but in the south of Britain *G. elliptica* and *G.* × *thuretii* are hardy, in sheltered positions in the open ground. Propagation is by cuttings of half-woody twigs in gentle heat.

The genus was named by Douglas, in honour of Nicholas Garry of the Hudson Bay Company, who helped him in his plant-collecting expeditions in western North America.

G. ELLIPTICA Lindl.   [PLATE 38

An evergreen shrub, or even a small tree, of vigorous, rapid growth and bushy habit, growing 6 to 12 ft high in this country (16 ft in the milder parts and higher still on a wall); young wood downy. Leaves oval to roundish, 1½ to

3 in. long, half, or more than half, as wide; more or less rounded at each end, the
apex terminating in a short, abrupt tip, dark shining green above, grey-woolly
beneath, with curly hairs, margins wavy, but not toothed; stalk stout, woolly,
¼ in. long. Flowers densely crowded on slender pendent catkins 3 to 6 in. long
in cold districts, but 1 ft or more long in warm ones, produced in a cluster
towards the end of the shoot and in the leaf-axils near. Bracts silky in the male
plant, cup-shaped, enclosing the base of the stamens; in the female plant longer
and narrower. Fruits globular-ovoid, silky, with a thin brittle shell, enclosing
two seeds embedded in a dark red juice. *Bot. Mag.*,, n.s., t. 220.

   Native of California and Oregon; introduced by Douglas in 1828. For
Garrya elliptica to be seen at its best, one must visit the gardens of Cornwall,
Devon, and similar places. It becomes there 16 ft high, and as much through,
and bears male catkins up to 12 in. long. It is at its best from November to
February, and at that season no evergreen shrub, perhaps, is more attractive
than is this when laden with a great crop of silvery grey catkins. Near London,
although not so satisfactory as in the south-west, it is an excellent evergreen
if a suitable spot be chosen. It does not need a rich soil nor abundant moisture,
and the best possible position for it is a sunny, rather dry bank sloping south
or west, and protected by other vegetation on the north and east sides. At the
University Botanic Garden, Cambridge, it has lived and flourished in the open
for more than seventy years. It is a bad shrub to transplant, and should be grown
in a pot until given a permanent place. The male plant is much the more ornamental, the catkins of the female being only 1½ to 4 in. long. Cuttings of both
strike root freely if taken in late summer and given a little heat. In very cold
districts this garrya will need wall protection.

   cv. 'JAMES ROOF'.—The original plant of this clone (a male) grew in a
group of seedlings at the Regional Parks Botanic Garden near Berkeley, California, and was selected for its remarkably long catkins—up to 14 in. It was
named in honour of the Garden Director (*Calif. Hort. Soc. Journ.*, Vol. 23,
pp. 80–82). It has recently been introduced to commerce.

   G. ELLIPTICA × G. FREMONTII.—This cross occurred in the garden of
Mrs P. Murray of Issequh, Seattle, USA, around 1960. A female plant of *G.
elliptica* growing in her garden set fruit and, there being no male of this species
in the vicinity, Mrs Murray concluded that the pollen must have come from a
nearby male plant of *G. fremontii*. Seeds were distributed by the University of
Washington Arboretum in 1961, and from his share Lord Talbot de Malahide
raised some eighteen seedlings of both sexes. A selection from these, named
'PAT BALLARD', received an Award of Merit when shown by him in February
1971. The leaves resemble those of *G. elliptica* in shape, but are greener and
the margins less undulate; as in *G. fremontii* the undersurface is glabrous except
for a few long, straight, appressed hairs. The named plant is male, with catkins
5 to 6¾ in. long.

G. FREMONTII Torr.

   An evergreen shrub up to 12 ft in height. Leaves leathery, dark glossy green,
obovate or oval, 1½ to 3 in. long, tapering at both ends, with appressed hairs

on both surfaces when young, afterwards glabrous. Catkins in a terminal
cluster, each catkin 2 to 4 in. long, with grey woolly bracts. Fruits globose, at
first hairy, ultimately glabrous, ¼ in. wide.

Native of California, Oregon, etc. A flowering spray is figured in *Gard.
Chron.* (2 April 1881), p. 431, taken from a plant grown in the gardens of
Gordon Castle, Moray. From the accompanying note it appears to have proved
hardier there than *G. elliptica*, both species being grown on the same wall. Some
years ago I saw it in Messrs Dickson's nursery at Chester, but it is very rare in
cultivation. It has not the fine qualities of *G. elliptica*, from which it may be
distinguished by its differently shaped leaves and the ultimate smoothness of its
foliage and fruit.

G. LAURIFOLIA Benth.

This species is represented in cultivation by the following variety, which
perhaps represents no more than the upper part of a range of variation in size
and shape of leaf, but is worth recognising in gardens:

var. MACROPHYLLA (Benth.) Wanger. *G. macrophylla* Benth.—A very robust
evergreen shrub, forming naturally a small tree; young wood covered with
a grey tomentum. Leaves on wild plants 2 to 6¼ in. long, 1³⁄₁₆ to 2¼ in. wide,
broad elliptic, obtuse to rounded and apiculate at the apex, wedge-shaped to
rounded at the base, dark green and glabrous above, felted beneath with a grey
tomentum; on cultivated plants the leaves are mostly 6 to 7⅝ in. long, 2¼ to 3⅛
in. wide, and may be obovate but in other respects are like those of wild ones;
stalk ½ to 1 in. long. Male catkins 1 to 3 in. long, axillary, often branched; female
flowers produced in the axils of leaflike bracts on lateral shoots 3 to 5 in. long.

Introduced from Mexico in 1846. This species can be grown on a wall near
London, but in Guernsey it makes a small tree of very striking aspect. It is one
of the largest leaved evergreens that can be grown in the open air. Flowers in
May and June, but has no attractions apart from its striking foliage. This shrub
is frequently met with as *G. fadyeni*, which is a quite different species with much
smaller leaves, found in the West Indies, and not hardy.

G. × THURETII Carr.

A quick-growing, robust evergreen up to 15 ft high; branchlets stout,
downy. Leaves narrow-oblong, 2½ to 4 in. long, 1 to 1¼ in. wide, tapering
equally to both ends, the apex ending in a short, abrupt tip; upper surface
becoming glabrous and glossy, lower one covered with a greyish down; stalk
½ in. long. Catkins more or less erect, greyish, terminal and axillary, 1½ to 3
in. long, with the bracts in pairs at ⅓ in. apart, ovate-lanceolate, pointed, and
very hairy.

A hybrid raised about 1862 at Antibes by Gustave Thuret, who crossed
G. fadyeni with the pollen of *G. elliptica*. This shrub is interesting but of little
ornament. At Kew it is 12 ft high, and as hardy as the pollen parent. Where the
winters are not severe it forms a large, vigorous bush, but is disfigured by
exceptionally severe frost. It blossoms in June.

× GAULNETTYA   ERICACEAE

A genus of hybrids between *Gaultheria* and *Pernettya*. The plant described here—'Wisley Pearl'—arose in cultivation and is of interest in that it unites a Californian species of *Gaultheria* with a very dissimilar species of *Pernettya* from South America. Hybrids between the two genera also occur in the wild. Dr Philipson records (Philipson and Hearn, *Rock Garden Plants of the Southern Alps*, p. 80) how he discovered a colony of such hybrids in the Southern Alps of New Zealand: 'I paused to look at one plant [of *Gaultheria depressa*] that seemed different and saw that its berries instead of being spherical were all shaped like five-pointed stars. Between the spreading fleshy rays was set a globular centre-piece. The whole looked like a flower fashioned in wax, and its beauty was heightened by the delicate shell pink flush that deepened on the broad points of the star.' The other parent of this gaulnettya was *Pernettya nana*. Among the other crosses recorded in New Zealand are *G. depressa* × *P. macrostigma* and *G. antipoda* × *P. macrostigma*. Gaulnettyas have also been found in Central and South America.

It should be noted that the correct name for this hybrid genus is × *Gaulnettya* Marchant (*Choice Trees, Shrubs*, 1937). The name was there published with a statement of the parent genera and that is sufficient under the rules of botanical nomenclature (*Code*, 1966, Art. 40); it has priority over *Gaulthettia* Camp (1939). But the name × *G. wisleyensis* has never been validated by a Latin description.

× G. 'WISLEY PEARL'

× *Gaulnettya wisleyensis* Marchant; × *Gaulthettia wisleyensis* (Marchant) Rehd.

A bushy evergreen shrub 3 ft or more high, spreading by suckers. Leaves mostly elliptic or elliptic-oblong and 1 to 1½ in. long (somewhat longer on sterile shoots), pointed at the apex, wedge-shaped or rounded at the base, of firm, leathery texture, almost glabrous, medium green above, paler beneath, strongly net-veined on both surfaces. Flowers pearl-white, borne in downy, glandular clusters of terminal and axillary racemes near the end of the shoots, each 1½ to 2½ in. long, carrying six to fifteen flowers and opening in May and June. Fruits dark purplish red, fleshy, oblate-globose, about ¼ in. across, clasped at the base by the enlarged fleshy calyx.

The hybrid described above was noticed in 1929 in the garden of the Royal Horticultural Society at Wisley, where it grew on a mound in the Wild Garden in the company of other ericaceous plants, including *Gaultheria shallon* and *Pernettya mucronata*. There can be little doubt that it is a hybrid between these two species, showing the influence of the former in its net-veined foliage and in the enlarged fleshy calyx seen at the base of the fruits; and of the pernettya parent in its inflorescence and fleshy fruits. For an illustrated note on this hybrid by B. O. Mulligan see *Journ. R.H.S.*, Vol. 64 (1939), pp. 125–127.

This shrub, now common in cultivation, makes a neat evergreen and is attractive in flower and fruit. It was given an Award of Merit at Vincent Square on 20 June 1939. It is propagated by half-ripe cuttings or by division.

The name 'Wisley Pearl', published by Mr Mulligan in the note referred to above, should be regarded as a clonal name for the descendants by vegetative propagation of the original plant.

GAULTHERIA   ERICACEAE

A genus of over 200 species of evergreen shrubs, most abundant in the Americas but found also in the Himalaya, S. India, E. and S.E. Asia and Australasia. Leaves usually alternate. Corolla pitcher-shaped or bell-shaped, five-lobed (rarely four-lobed). Calyx five-lobed (the lobes sometimes small and tooth-like). Stamens usually ten. Ovary superior, five-celled, developing into a many-seeded capsule which, with a few exceptions, is enclosed by the enlarged, fleshy calyx. Seeds very small.

In outward appearance *Gaultheria* is often very similar to *Vaccinium*, especially in leaf. There is no easily discernible character to distinguish them in that respect. In flower, however, they are easily distinguished by the relative positions of corolla and ovary. In *Vaccinium* the calyx and corolla are uppermost, and the remnants of the calyx are usually present on the top of the fruit; in *Gaultheria* the ovary is uppermost and (with the exception of two or three species from New Zealand) the fruit becomes enclosed by the calyx-lobes which enlarge upwards and become fleshy. In *Pernettya* the calyx does not usually enlarge in fruit, but the ovary instead of developing into a dry capsule as in *Gaultheria*, becomes fleshy. But it is doubtful whether this difference is really of sufficient weight to justify the continued recognition of *Pernettya* as a genus distinct from *Gaultheria*.

At the beginning of this century only two gaultherias were at all widely cultivated, namely *G. shallon* and *G. procumbens*, both North American, and despite the introduction since then of so many East Asiatic species these two remain among the best and hardiest of the genus. Others of equal merit to these for general planting on suitable soils are *G. cuneata* and *G. miqueliana*. All are peat- and moisture-loving shrubs and most prefer sheltered positions and some shade. Small-leaved alpine and subalpine species such as *G. thibetica* and *G. sinensis* are, however, best grown in fairly light, open positions, provided the soil can be kept permanently moist.

The gaultherias can be propagated by seeds in the same way as rhododendrons, by half-woody cuttings, or in some cases by means of small off-sets, which should be grown on in pots or frames before planting out.

The generic name commemorates Dr Gaulthier, an 18th-century botanist and physician of Canada.

G. ADENOTHRIX (Miq.) Maxim.

Andromeda adenothrix Miq.

A dwarf shrub to about 1 ft high, spreading by underground runners; young stems zigzagged, reddish brown, clothed with gland-tipped hairs. Leaves leathery, dark green, conspicuously net-veined, broadly ovate, ⅜ to 1¼ in. long, ⅜ to ¾ in. wide, acute or shortly acuminate at the apex, margins slightly saw-toothed towards the apex and edged with a few gland-tipped hairs. Flowers solitary in the upper leaf-axils, borne in May on wiry, pendulous peduncles, which are furnished with numerous bracteoles and clad, like the red-tinged calyces, with gland-tipped hairs. Corollas pure white, glabrous within, $\frac{5}{16}$ in. long. Filaments of stamens glabrous; anthers without awns. Fruits globular, red, about ¼ in. wide, the swollen calyx hairy.

Native of Japan in coniferous forests and open places near the tree-line; introduced in 1915. Botanically, it is quite distinct from any other Asiatic gaultheria and most closely allied to *G. ovatifolia* and *G. humifusa* of western N. America. It grows well at the Sunningdale Nurseries, in light shade.

G. ANTIPODA Forst. f.

An evergreen erect shrub 2 to 4 ft high; young shoots usually bristly and downy. Leaves oval, orbicular or obovate, toothed, ⅓ to ⅔ in. long, thick and leathery, more or less undulate, strongly veined, glabrous, apple-green; stalk very short, bristly. Flowers solitary in the terminal leaf-axils. Corolla white, ⅛ in. long, cylindrical, borne on a downy flower-stalk about as long as itself. Calyx-lobes ovate-oblong, pointed, usually enlarging at the fruiting stage and becoming fleshy and enclosing the seed-vessel, the whole a white or red berry-like fruit about ½ in. across.

Native of New Zealand in the North and South Islands from sea-level to 4,000 ft altitude; introduced in 1820. It is a variable shrub, especially in habit and size of leaf; the latter, on young plants raised from seed, remain for some years about ¼ in. or less in length. Sometimes the upper leaves of the flower-bearing shoots are much reduced, so that the inflorescence becomes racemose at the top. It is perhaps the hardiest of the New Zealand gaultherias.

G. DEPRESSA Hook. f.   *G. antipoda* var. *depressa* (Hook. f.) Hook. f.—A dwarf shrub with creeping and rooting stems. Leaves elliptical to rounded, faintly toothed, the teeth bristle-tipped, at least when the leaves are young. Fruits larger than in *G. antipoda*, being up to ⅔ in. wide, globular, white or red. A native of New Zealand, extending to about 6,000 ft; and of Tasmania, where it is less common, however. It should be hardy, but is said to be difficult and short-lived in cultivation.

G. CODONANTHA Airy Shaw

A large, bushy, evergreen shrub up to 8 ft high, with long graceful shoots, bristly when young. Leaves alternate, distichous, ovate to ovate-lanceolate, acuminate, cordate at the base, from $2\frac{1}{2}$ to 7 in. long, 1 to 5 in. wide, with two thin marginal veins and two stouter ones running out with the midrib to the point; beautifully net-veined between and covered with short brown hairs beneath; stalk very short. Flowers in very short-stalked axillary clusters; pedicels with two bracteoles at the base. Corolla white, often banded with red when fully open, cup-shaped, $\frac{3}{4}$ in. across, glabrous within; filaments glabrous. Fruits purplish black, $\frac{3}{4}$ in. wide. *Bot. Mag.*, t. 9456.

Native of the Assam Himalaya; found by Kingdon Ward in the Delei Valley in 1928 at 5,000 to 7,000 ft and introduced by him under his number 8024. It flowered at Exbury in November 1933 and was given an Award of Merit when shown at Vincent Square the same month. A very striking and handsome shrub, which is only hardy in the mildest counties. The flowers are unusually large for the genus.

G. CUNEATA (Rehd. & Wils.) Bean   [PLATE 36
G. pyroloides var. *cuneata* Rehd. & Wills.

A low evergreen shrub 1 to $1\frac{1}{2}$ ft high, of close compact habit; young shoots very downy. Leaves of firm, leathery texture, obovate, oblanceolate, or narrowly oval, pointed, wedge-shaped at the base, shallowly toothed, $\frac{1}{2}$ to $1\frac{1}{8}$ in. long, $\frac{1}{4}$ to $\frac{1}{2}$ in. wide, dark glossy green and glabrous above, paler and dotted with dark glands beneath; stalk $\frac{1}{16}$ in. long. Flowers produced from June onwards in a cluster of axillary racemes, each 1 to $1\frac{1}{2}$ in. long, near the end of the twigs; main flower-stalk minutely downy. Corolla white, nodding, urn-shaped, $\frac{1}{4}$ in. long, with five small recurved lobes. Stamens ten, enclosed within the corolla, their stalks downy. Calyx whitish, five-lobed, the lobes triangular, $\frac{1}{12}$ in. long, ciliate; ovary silky. Fruits snow-white, globose, and $\frac{3}{8}$ in. wide. Seeds numerous, shining, brown. *Bot. Mag.*, t. 8829.

Native of W. Szechwan, China; introduced in 1909 by Wilson, who found it 'quite common on humus-clad rocks in moist woods'. It differs from *G. miqueliana* (q.v.) and *pyroloides* in the silky ovary and downy fruit; the latter, however, is hidden by the white fleshy calyx. The white 'berries' are ripe from August onwards and give the plant an interesting appearance. It is very hardy and makes a pretty, dwarf ground cover.

G. ITOANA Hayata *G. merrilliana* Hort.—This species, a native of Formosa, is closely allied to *G. cuneata* but is most easily distinguished by its narrow leaves, $\frac{3}{8}$ to $\frac{5}{8}$ in. long, $\frac{1}{8}$ to $\frac{1}{4}$ in. wide. It was introduced from Formosa shortly before 1936 by K. Yashiroda, under his number 149, and was at first erroneously known in gardens as *G. merrilliana*, possibly because one of Yashiroda's specimens of this gaultheria had been identified as *Vaccinium merrillianum*, a gaultheria-like species also found in Formosa. It has about the same garden value as *G. cuneata* but is dwarfer. If the two species were to be united it would be under the name *G. itoana*, which has priority.

G. ERIOPHYLLA (Pers.) Sleumer

Andromeda eriophylla Pers.; *G. willisiana* R. C. Davie

A dwarf shrub growing to about 3 ft high; branchlets buff-pink when young and clad with a dense covering of curly brown hairs. Leaves oblong-ovate to broadly elliptic, with a mucronate tip, up to 2¼ in. long and 1½ in. wide but decreasing in size towards the ends of the stems and the region of the inflorescences, covered on both sides with woolly hairs when young but later more or less glabrous above. Flowers borne in axillary racemes which are sometimes clustered at the ends of the shoots, forming apparently terminal panicles; the whole inflorescence, including the calyx and corolla, is reddish pink and clad with brown hairs; the individual flower-stalks are subtended by large bracts, and on each there are two alternate bracteoles near the base. Corollas urn-shaped, about ¼ in. long, furnished with white hairs within; style glabrous; anther-cells each with two awns. Fruits black, about 3/16 in. wide. *Bot. Mag.*, n.s., t. 254.

Native of S.E. Brazil, in the Organ Mountains and other ranges near the coast; introduced by Dr Sleumer in 1949 by means of seeds collected by him near Therezopolis, and distributed to gardens as *G. willisiana*. The reasons for referring these plants to *G. eriophylla* is explained by B. L. Burtt in the note accompanying the figure in the *Botanical Magazine*, to which we are indebted for most of the information given here.

G. FORRESTII Diels

An evergreen shrub 1 to 5 ft high; young shoots furnished with scattered bristles pointing forwards. Leaves leathery, oblong, narrowly oval or oblanceolate, pointed, tapered at the base, shallowly toothed, 1½ to 3 in. long, ½ to 1½ in. wide, dark bright green above, paler beneath and at first sprinkled with bristles, which fall and leave dark brown spots; stalk about ¼ in. long. Racemes slender, 1 to 2 in. long, produced from the axils of the leaves in spring over the whole length of the previous season's shoots; main flower-stalk angular, downy, white. Corolla rather globose, ⅕ in. wide, waxy white; calyx-lobes ovate, minutely ciliate. Fruits egg-shaped to globose, ¼ to ⅜ in. long, the colour described by Forrest as 'light China to Prussian blue', each on its stalk about ⅛ in. long.

Native of Yunnan, China; discovered by Forrest in 1906 at altitudes of 10,000 to 12,000 ft on the eastern flank of the Tali Range. The flowers are fragrant and the whiteness of the main and secondary flower-stalks adds to the beauty of the plant. It is in cultivation, seems to be fairly hardy, and should make an attractive addition to peat-loving evergreens, but chiefly in regard to its flowers. The late Francis Hanger of the R.H.S. gardens at Wisley considered it the best of the gaultherias in that respect, but poor (in this country) in regard to its fruits.

G. forrestii received an Award of Merit when shown from Trewithen, Cornwall, in 1937 and it still flourishes there. The plant that was given this award ten years earlier proved later not to be the true species, but probably a form of *G. tetramera*.

G. CAUDATA Stapf—This species is allied to *G. forrestii* and was discovered by Forrest at the same time and in the same locality. It differs in its more finely tapered, less closely toothed leaves, which are not markedly paler green beneath than above. The bracteoles on the flower-stalks are not situated near the calyx as in *G. forrestii*, but lower down. The plant figured in *Bot. Mag.*, t. 9228, was grown by E. J. P. Magor of Lamellen, Cornwall, raised from seeds sent home by Forrest, but under what number is not known.

G. FRAGRANTISSIMA Wall.
G. ovalifolia Wall.

A large evergreen shrub or small tree; young shoots angled (even triangular), not downy. Leaves leathery, ovate narrowly oval, pointed, tapered at the base, toothed, 1½ to 4 in. long, ¾ to 2 in. wide, glabrous or nearly so, bright green above, freely sprinkled with dark brown dots beneath (the remnants of bristles); stalk $\frac{1}{12}$ to $\frac{1}{6}$ in. long. Racemes 1 to 3 in. long, produced from the leaf-axils in April from the shoots made the previous year; main-stalk angled, downy. Flowers drooping, fragrant, closely packed on the raceme; bracts very small. Corolla ovoid to bell-shaped, scarcely ¼ in. long, greenish yellow or whitish, glabrous or nearly so outside; calyx five-lobed to half its depth. Fruits surrounded as they usually are in this genus, by the enlarged fleshy calyx which is a beautiful dark blue (sometimes pale blue); each one is borne on a stalk $\frac{1}{12}$ to $\frac{1}{6}$ in. long and downy like the main-stalk. *Bot. Mag.*, t. 5984.

Native of the mountains of India, where it is widely spread; also of Ceylon; introduced about 1850, but described originally by Wallich in *Asiatic Researches* in 1818. It succeeds well in the open air in Cornwall and similar places, and survives out-of-doors at Kew, but it really needs greenhouse treatment in many parts of the country. It is most nearly related to *G. forrestii* but is a much more vigorous plant.

G. HISPIDA R. Br.

An evergreen shrub 2 to 3 ft, occasionally 6 to 7 ft high; young shoots furnished with spreading reddish bristles, sometimes downy also. Leaves leathery, oblong or narrowly elliptic-lanceolate, very shortly stalked, minutely toothed, tapered at both ends, the apex with a short mucro, 1 to 2¼ in. long, ¼ to ¾ in. wide, dull dark green and eventually glabrous above, downy or bristly on the midrib beneath. Inflorescenses terminal on young shoots and short axillary branchlets, forming in effect a panicle; they are noticeably bracteate, the lower bracts sterile and imbricated, the upper ones separated and each subtending a flower. Corolla broadly urn-shaped, $\frac{1}{6}$ in. long, white. Calyx-lobes triangular-ovate, enlarging and becoming succulent and snow-white, enclosing the seed-vessel and forming a flattened, globose, berry-like fruit ⅜ to ½ in. wide.

Native of Tasmania up to 4,000 ft. Although it has survived even hardish winters at Kew and passed through mild ones uninjured, it really requires a warmer locality to do itself justice. The first Lord Wakehurst showed a charming

plant from his garden in Sussex at Westminster in August 1927, and the species
still grows there in the Heath Garden.

G. APPRESSA A. W. Hill—This species is closely allied to *G. hispida* and
takes its place on the Australian mainland, in Victoria and New South Wales.
Chiefly it differs in the hairs on the stems and the midribs of the leaves being
appressed, not spreading. The leaves are a trifle broader in relation to their
length, elliptic-oblong to elliptic, obtuse at the apex, which is sharply contracted
to an apiculate point.

G. HOOKERI C. B. Clarke
G. veitchiana Craib

A low evergreen shrub forming a dense, rounded tuft, and spreading by
underground stems but sometimes erect and up to 6 ft high; branchlets clothed
with minute down, with which are intermixed long bristles. Leaves of hard
texture, 1½ to 3½ in. long, half as wide, oblong or slightly obovate, rounded or
broadly tapered at the base, abruptly narrowed at the apex to a short glandular
tip, shallowly toothed, the teeth often bristle-tipped, upper surface much wrinkled, dark glossy green, conspicuously net-veined, without down, lower surface
at first furnished with bristles which partially fall away, leaving it harsh to the
touch; stalk 1/12 to ⅛ in. long. Flowers densely packed in axillary racemes, 1 in.
or more long, white. Corolla ⅙ in. long, nodding, narrowed from the base to the
mouth; calyx-lobes lanceolate to ovate, usually acute or acuminate; main-stalk
downy, each flower produced in the axil of an ovate, membranous more or less
ciliated bract ¼ in. long; the short glabrous flower-stalk is also furnished with
bracts partially hiding the flower. Fruits indigo-blue, about the size of a small
pea. *Bot. Mag.*, t. 9174.

The type of *G. hookeri* comes from Sikkim, but the species, as now understood,
has a wide range, through the eastern Himalaya to W. China. The first recorded
introduction was by Wilson in 1907 from W. Szechwan. The plants of this origin
have the low, tufted habit as described above and are quite hardy. They were
long known as *G. veitchiana*, but the characters used to separate this species from
G. hookeri are not constant. The species may also be in cultivation from Kingdon
Ward's No. 7552, collected in Upper Burma in 1926.

G. STAPFIANA Airy Shaw—A close ally of *G. hookeri*, differing in the
absence or virtual absence of the long bristles which are such a prominent
feature of the young branches of *G. hookeri*. If bristles are present they are short
and sparse and more or less appressed. But, as in *G. hookeri*, the floral bracts are
large (up to ¼ in. long) and form a prominent feature of the inflorescence. This
character serves to distinguish *G. stapfiana* from *G. fragrantissima* and *G.
forrestii*, in both of which the floral bracts are small. This species is in cultivation
at Wakehurst Place, Sussex, where it is liable to be cut in winter. It is probably
to be found in other collections, raised from Forrest 14997 or 18501 (though the
latter number is incorrect, the corresponding herbarium specimen being
Vaccinium forrestii).

G. MIQUELIANA Takeda
G. pyroloides Miq., in part

An evergreen shrub 8 to 12 in. high; young shoots at first downy becoming glabrous. Leaves oval, toothed, tapered about equally at both ends, ½ to 1¼ in. long, ⅝ to ¾ in. wide, glabrous, distinctly net-veined beneath, dark green above. Flowers drooping, solitary to as many as six on racemes 1 to 2 in. long; main flower-stalk downy. Corolla rather globose, ¼ in. wide, white, with small triangular teeth at the mouth; ovary glabrous. Calyx-lobes triangular at first, ciliate, afterwards enlarging and enclosing the seed-vessel, forming a berry-like fruit ⅜ in. wide, globose, white or pink, edible. *Bot. Mag.*, t. 9629.

Native of Japan and a handsome small evergreen both as regards flowers and fruits. It is quite hardy and flowers in June. It is most nearly related to the *G. cuneata*—a white-fruited Chinese species but with a downy ovary and narrower obovate leaves. It received an Award of Merit in 1948.

It may be noted that the names *G. pyroloides* and *G. pyrolifolia* are much confused. The species described by Miquel in 1863 under the name *G. pyroloides* comprised two distinct gaultherias. One was the white-fruited species of Japan just described. The other was a Himalayan blue-fruited gaultheria of which Miquel had received a dried flowering specimen from Kew, collected in the wild by Hooker. Unaware of Miquel's earlier name, C. B. Clarke in 1882 published the name *G. pyrolifolia* for Hooker's Himalayan species and this was widely used until quite recently. The confusion was later cleared up by Takeda, who restricted the name *G. pyroloides* Miq. to the Himalayan plant, and published a new name—*G. miqueliana*—for the plant of Japan.

G. miqueliana is distinguished from *G. pyroloides* by its rather globose flowers, its four-awned anthers (two-awned in *G. pyroloides*) and by its white or pinkish fruits.

G. NUMMULARIOIDES D. Don

A dwarf evergreen shrub 4 to 6 in. high, forming dense tufts, and spreading by underground shoots; stems slender and wiry, covered with bristles, and bearing over their whole length leaves ¼ in. apart in two opposite rows. Leaves leathery, heart-shaped, becoming smaller towards the tip of the shoot, ¼ to ⅝ in. long, about the same wide; the lower surface and the margins are bristly, the upper side dark dull green and wrinkled, the lower one very pale polished green; stalk ⅛ in. or less long. Flowers produced singly in the leaf-axils from the underside during August; corolla egg-shaped, white or tinged with pink, scarcely ¼ in. long. Fruits bluish black, rarely borne on cultivated plants.

Native of the Himalaya and thence north-east to W. China and south-east to Java and Sumatra; introduced from the Himalaya in the 19th century and later, by Forrest and other collectors, from China. Its roundish leaves, closely and regularly set in two rows, and gradually decreasing in size towards the end of the shoot, with the slender, conspicuously bristly stems, render it quite distinct from any other plant in cultivation except *Vaccinium nummularia*. It makes charming tufts of foliage and stems, but needs some shelter.

G. *nummularioides* is somewhat variable, and the above description is of a representative specimen and not of the species in its totality. In var. ELLIPTICA Rehd. & Wils., found by Wilson in W. Szechwan, the leaves are elliptic, cuneate at the base. In a form introduced by Forrest the stems are very slender and quite prostrate, the leaves very small; it was distributed under the horticultural epithet *minuta*.

G. OPPOSITIFOLIA Hook. f.

A very leafy evergreen shrub of sturdy, bushy, much-branched habit, up to 8 ft high in the wild; young shoots mostly glabrous, but with scattered bristles sometimes. Leaves thick, opposite, stalkless, ovate-oblong to ovate, heart-shaped to somewhat truncate at the base, toothed, the base often overlapping the stem, 1 to 2 in. long, ¾ to 1½ in. wide, dark glossy green and glabrous above, pale, strongly net-veined and occasionally with scattered bristles beneath. Flowers borne very numerously in terminal panicles as much as 4 in. wide and long; flower-stalks glabrous. Corolla bell-shaped, white, about ⅛ in. long; calyx-lobes narrow triangular, glabrous, dry, and never apparently becoming fleshy and enlarged, as is usual in this genus.

Native of New Zealand in the mountains of the North Island up to 3,000 ft. It flowers with us in May and June. The species is very distinct among cultivated gaultherias in its opposite leaves, though at the upper part of the branches towards the flower-panicle there are sometimes three in a whorl. It is the most ornamental of the gaultherias in New Zealand in regard to its flowers and comparable in this respect with the better Chinese and Himalayan species. Although generally considered to be tender, it has grown in the Heath Garden at Wakehurst Place, Sussex, for over forty years.

G. FAGIFOLIA Hook. f. is near the above, having its white flowers in racemes up to 2 in. long. The leaves, however, are alternate and usually ½ to 1 in. long. The calyx-lobes do not enlarge nor become succulent. New Zealand. It is a hybrid between *G. oppositifolia* and *G. antipoda*. Hooker described this gaultheria from specimens collected by Colenso at Motukino, near Lake Taupa. In other forms of the cross, fruits with the succulent calyces of *G. antipoda* and the dry ones of *G. oppositifolia* are found on the same plant.

G. OVATIFOLIA A. Gray

A low evergreen shrub of spreading or trailing habit from 8 to 12 in. high, the branches erect, sparingly furnished with comparatively long hairs. Leaves broadly ovate, pointed at the apex, rounded or slightly heart-shaped at the base, very shallowly toothed of hard rather leathery texture and arranged regularly on the shoots about ¼ in. apart, ¾ to 1¼ in. long, ½ to 1¼ in. wide, dark glossy green and wrinkled above, margins of young leaves hairy; stalk $\frac{1}{16}$ to $\frac{1}{12}$ in. long, hairy. Flowers solitary in the leaf-axils, each on a stalk $\frac{1}{12}$ in. long, furnished with numerous bracteoles. Calyx five-lobed, bristly, the lobes about half as long as the tubular part. Corolla white or pinkish, bell-shaped, ⅕ in.

long, with five small teeth at the mouth. Anthers not awned. Fruits scarlet, $\frac{1}{4}$ in. wide, globose, described as very spicy and delicious.

Native of western North America from the northernmost part of California through Oregon to southern British Columbia, including Vancouver Island. It is not common in cultivation and reputed to be difficult.

G. HUMIFUSA (Graham) Rydb. *Vaccinium humifusum* Graham; *G. myrsinites* Hook.—This species is nearly akin to *G. ovatifolia* but is of neater, closer, more tufted habit and about 4 in. high. The leaves are about half the size and the calyx is glabrous. There is no constant difference in the size of the fruits. It is quite hardy and suitable for the rock garden. Native of western N. America.

G. PROCUMBENS L.   CREEPING WINTERGREEN

A low, tufted evergreen shrub growing 2 to 6 in. high, spreading by creeping roots, from which it sends up slender stems naked except at the top, where they carry a cluster of about four leaves; stems at first downy, afterwards glabrous

GAULTHERIA PROCUMBENS

and glossy. Leaves dark glossy green, thick and leathery, quite glabrous, obovate or oval, $\frac{3}{4}$ to $1\frac{1}{2}$ in. long, $\frac{1}{2}$ to $\frac{7}{8}$ in. wide, faintly toothed, the teeth often bristle-tipped; they have a strong aromatic odour and taste like that of birch, and turn reddish as winter approaches; stalk $\frac{1}{6}$ in. long. Flowers produced in July and

August, singly in the leaf-axils, and at the top of the stem. Corolla ovoid-cylindrical, $\frac{1}{4}$ in. long, nodding, pinkish white; calyx-lobes broadly ovate, edged with tiny hairs; flower-stalk downy, $\frac{1}{4}$ in. long, decurved. Fruits bright red, globose, $\frac{1}{3}$ in. wide, with a pleasant, rather insipid taste. *Bot. Mag.*, t. 1966.

Native of eastern N. America; introduced in 1762. It has there a variety of popular names such as 'box-berry', 'creeping wintergreen', and, because of the fondness of partridges for the berries, 'partridge-berry'. An oil is extracted from it which possesses stimulating and tonic properties, but the main source of this is now *Betula lenta*. As a garden plant it is very pleasing for the cheerful dark green of its lustrous leaves, forming neat close tufts. It makes a pleasing undergrowth or furnishing beneath thin deciduous shrubs. Owing to the leaves in a great measure hiding the drooping flowers and fruit, its attractiveness is almost wholly in the habit and foliage.

G. PYROLOIDES Miq., emend. Takeda
G. pyrolifolia C. B. Clarke

An evergreen shrub of close tufted habit 4 to 8 in. high; young shoots slightly downy. Leaves clustered towards the end of the twig, obovate to roundish, wedge-shaped at the base, rounded or blunt at the apex, toothed except towards the base $\frac{5}{8}$ to $1\frac{1}{2}$ in. long, $\frac{3}{8}$ to 1 in. wide, glabrous except for scattered bristles beneath; stalk $\frac{1}{12}$ in. or less long. Flowers produced in May and June, two to five on a downy raceme up to 1 in. long; corolla egg-shaped, $\frac{1}{5}$ in. long, white or pink, with small teeth at the orifice; calyx-lobes small triangular; ovary glabrous. Fruits $\frac{1}{4}$ in. wide, globose-ovoid, blue-black.

Native of the Himalaya; found by Hooker in Sikkim in 1849. In 1922 it was collected during the Mt Everest expedition at 13,500 ft altitude. In places it forms a dense ground cover in the way of the North American *G. procumbens*. It is related to *G. cuneata* which is, however, well distinguished by its white fruits, its downy ovary, and by the oval or narrowly obovate leaves which are distributed all along the downy young shoots. (See also *G. miqueliana*.)

G. pyroloides is also in cultivation from seed collected by Ludlow, Sherriff, and Hicks in Bhutan under LSH 21153.

G. RUPESTRIS (L. f.) D. Don
Andromeda rupestris L. f.

A shrub 1 to 2 ft high, with erect or spreading branches; stems more or less bristly. Leaves leathery, shortly stalked, dull green above, paler beneath, elliptic to elliptic-oblong or lanceolate-oblong, apiculate at apex, $\frac{4}{5}$ in. to $1\frac{2}{5}$ long (occasionally to almost 2 in.), margins finely saw-toothed (sometimes coarsely so). Flowers in racemes up to about 3 in. long, borne at the apex of the shoots and in the uppermost of leaf-axils, the racemes sometimes branched; inflorescence-axis and pedicels downy. Calyx deeply lobed, the lobes ovate, acute, minutely toothed, Corolla urn-shaped, white and waxy, about $\frac{1}{6}$ in. long. Fruit a capsule, surrounded by the persistent but dry calyx.

A native of the mountains of the South Island of New Zealand, but descending to near sea-level in the southern end of its range. It has never been common in British gardens but is striking in flower and should be hardy if introduced from a high altitude. There is a fine photograph of this species in Philipson and Hearn, *Rock Garden Plants of the Southern Alps*, Plate 55.

The following species, closely allied to *G. rupestris*, and included in it by other authorities, are recognised by Allan in *Flora of New Zealand* (1966). In all of them the calyx remains dry in the fruiting stage.

G. COLENSOI Hook. f.   *G. rupestris* var. *colensoi* (Hook. f.) Hook. f.; *G. rupestris sensu* Cheesem., in part—A native of the North Island of New Zealand, differing from *G. rupestris* mainly in its low-growing habit and its downy not bristly stems.

G. CRASSA Allan   *G. rupestris* var. *parvifolia* Hook. f.—This species occurs in both islands of New Zealand and differs from *G. rupestris* in its stiffly leathery, smaller leaves, up to about ¾ in. long at the most. In cultivation at Wakehurst Place, Sussex.

G. SUBCORYMBOSA Col.   *G. rupestris* var. *subcorymbosa* (Col.) Burtt and Hill; *G. rupestris sensu* Cheesem., in part—Corolla glabrous within. Leaves usually less than 1 in. long. The inflorescences are sometimes branched. A native of the North Island of New Zealand and of the Aorere Valley in South Island (Nelson).

G. SHALLON Pursh   SALAL, SHALLON

An evergreen shrub 2 to 6 ft high, forming a dense thicket of stems, and spreading by means of underground stems; young branches reddish and bristly, becoming rough with age. Leaves leathery, broadly ovate, the base rounded or heart-shaped, the apex always sharply pointed, evenly and finely bristle-toothed, 1½ to 4 in. long, ¾ to 2½ in. wide; stalk reddish, hairy, ⅛ to ¼ in. long. Flowers produced during May and June in viscid, glandular racemes 1½ to 5 in. long, at the end of the previous year's shoots, and in the axils of several terminal leaves; each flower produced from the axil of a hooded, ovate bract, ¼ in. long. Corolla pinkish white, egg-shaped, downy, ⅜ in. long, five-toothed at the mouth; calyx white, its lobes triangular, downy, pressed to the corolla. Fruit a juicy, top-shaped hairy berry, dark purple, ⅜ in. wide, carrying many tiny seeds, and pleasantly flavoured; the bracts adhere at the base. *Bot. Mag.*, t. 2843.

Native of western N. America; introduced by Douglas in 1826. This useful and handsome shrub is one of the best we have for forming a dense evergreen thicket in moist, shady spots. It can be propagated by seeds, which it ripens in great numbers, also by division of the old plants, but to do the latter with success it is necessary to plant the pieces in a few inches of sandy soil on a hotbed. Broken up and planted in the open ground the pieces take long to recover. It may be recommended as cover for game.

G. TETRAMERA W. W. Sm.

An evergreen shrub 2 ft and upwards high, usually more in width; young shoots bristly. Leaves leathery, obovate to oblanceolate and roundish, 1 to

2 in. long, about half as wide, rounded to pointed at the apex, rounded to cuneate at the base, shallowly toothed, glabrous above, sparsely bristly below; stalk short. Flowers fragrant, crowded in axillary racemes about 1 in. long; corolla greenish white, ovoid, nearly closed at the mouth where are four or five tiny revolute lobes. Fruits brilliant violet-blue or china blue, globose, ¼ in. wide. *Bot. Mag.*, t. 9618.

Native of S.W. China, discovered and collected several times by Forrest in 1912, in one instance at 13,000 ft altitude. It should, therefore, be fairly hardy but will, no doubt, succeed best in the south and west. I have for instance seen it very attractively in fruit at Exbury on the Solent.

G. tetramera was given an Award of Merit when shown by Messrs Hillier at Vincent Square in September 1950. For a note on this species by the late Francis Hanger see *Journ. R.H.S.*, Vol. 68, p. 109.

G. SEMI-INFERA (C. B. Clarke) Airy Shaw *Diplycosia semi-infera* C. B. Clarke—This species is closely allied to *G. tetramera* but differs consistently from it and from all other members of the section *Leucothoïdes* in having only five stamens to the flower instead of the usual ten. Other characters distinguishing it from *G. tetramera* are its taller stature (to about 6 ft high) and the more or less elliptic leaves. Native of the region from the Sikkim Himalaya eastward through N. Burma to S.W. China. It was given an Award of Merit when shown by N. G. Hadden of West Porlock, Somerset, in September 1950, and the figure in *Bot. Mag.*, n.s., t. 197, is made from his plant.

The date of introduction of *G. semi-infera* is uncertain, but Forrest probably sent seeds on more than one occasion and it was reintroduced from Bhutan in 1949.

G. TRICHOPHYLLA Royle

A low shrub of densely tufted habit 3 to 6 in. high, spreading by means of underground shoots; stems wiry and slender, clad with spreading bristly hairs and furnished with twelve or more leaves to the inch. Leaves stalkless, elliptic-oblong or elliptic-lanceolate, ¼ to ½ in. long, ⅛ to ¼ in. wide, glabrous on both surfaces, but bristly on the margins, glossy dark green above, paler beneath. Flowers solitary in the leaf-axils; corollas pink, ⅙ in. long and wide, bell-shaped; anther-cells each with one awn. Fruits blue, occasionally purplish red, broadly ovoid, ⅜ to ½ in. long. *Bot. Mag.*, t. 7635.

Native of the Himalaya from Kashmir eastward, S.E. Tibet, Upper Burma, S.W. and W. China, ascending in the Himalaya to 13,000 ft. It was introduced to Kew in 1897, but there have been numerous reintroductions since then from various parts of its range. The lovely blue fruits have been likened to thrushes' eggs, but in many gardens they are produced sparsely or not at all.

The following are closely allied to *G. trichophylla:*

G. SINENSIS Anthony—Leaves elliptic-oblong or oblong-obovate, ½ in. or slightly more long and about one-third as wide, mostly acute at the apex, glossy and of leathery texture, hairy on the midrib beneath, margins glabrous. Flowers urn-shaped. Fruits blue-pink or white, globular or fig-shaped. This species was found by Forrest in Yunnan and extends westward to the Assam Himalaya. The date of first introduction is not known but probably most of the plants in cultivation derive from seeds collected by Kingdon Ward on the frontier between Burma and Assam under KW 8562. The herbarium specimen under this number is referred to G. HYPOCHLORA Airy Shaw, which is part of G. *sinensis* as understood by Anthony, but differs from the type of that species in the less leathery, relatively wider leaves (about half as wide as long), rounded at the apex. This is also true of at least some of the cultivated plants raised from KW 8562 but it is preferable to leave them under G. *sinensis* until the taxonomy of this group is better understood.

G. THYMIFOLIA Stapf ex Airy Shaw G. *thibetica* Hort.—Leaves shorter than in G. *trichophylla*, mostly less than ¾ in. long, and narrower, linear-oblong or widest in the upper half and tapered to the base, with almost glabrous margins. Fruits violet-blue, rosy-red, or white. This species was described from a flowering specimen collected by Forrest on the Yunnan–Burma border and came into cultivation in the 1930s under the unpublished name G. *thibetica*, probably raised from seeds collected by Kingdon Ward in 1926 under KW 6849. The field number KW 6845 under which the plants were distributed is certainly incorrect. Seeds of a white-fruited form were sent by the same collector under KW 9639.

G. WARDII Marquand & Shaw

An evergreen shrub of low spreading growth 3 or 4 ft high; young shoots covered with pale brown hairs. Leaves almost stalkless, of hard leathery texture, elliptic-lanceolate, slenderly pointed, rounded at the base, margins recurved, 1 to 3½ in. long, ½ to 1¼ in. wide, at first bristly, finally glabrous above and with conspicuously sunken, netted veins; thickly covered beneath with long brown hairs. Racemes produced from the axils of the terminal leaves of the previous season's growths, about ½ in. long, with the six to ten flowers closely packed. Calyx deeply five-lobed, the lobes ovate-lanceolate, ⅙ in. long, hairy outside; corolla white, ⅕ in. wide, only slightly exceeding the calyx-lobes, pitcher-shaped; ovary downy. The floral bracts (which are narrowly obovate) and the flower-stalks are downy and bristly. Fruits purplish, with a white bloom. *Bot. Mag.*, t. 9516.

This species was discovered by Kingdon Ward in S.E. Tibet in 1924, growing on 'pine-clad slopes amongst bracken, etc.', and also occurs in the Assam Himalaya and Upper Burma. He introduced it under KW 7134, for which he supplied the following field note: 'Flowers snow-white, in masses. Berries blue with white bloom; undershrub growing on sunny boulders, in thickets.' He sent seeds again under his numbers 8725 and 10409.

The most marked characters of G. *wardii* are its general hairiness, the deeply sunken veins of the leaf, and the very short racemes of flowers. It is not reliably hardy and does not really succeed except in the milder parts of the country.

G. YUNNANENSIS (Franch.) Rehd.

Vaccinium yunnanense Franch.; *G. laxiflora* Diels

An evergreen shrub 3 to 6 ft high; young shoots and leaves not downy. Leaves ovate-lanceolate, rounded or slightly heart-shaped at the base, tapered to a very slender, slightly curved apex, finely and regularly toothed, 2 to 4½ in. long, ½ to 1¾ in. wide, dark glossy green, prominently net-veined, of stiff, rather hard texture; stalk ⅛ to ¼ in. long. Flowers produced in slender axillary racemes 2 to 3 in. long, carrying twelve to twenty or more blossoms, white or yellowish, the broadly bell-shaped corolla ⅛ in. long; anthers yellow; ovary shaggy. Fruits globose, ¼ in. wide, purplish black, ripe in August.

Native of S.W. China. Cultivated at Edinburgh and raised there, no doubt, from seeds collected by Forrest, who describes the bark, foliage, and all parts of the plant as strongly aromatic with a pungent pleasant odour, and the flowers as being fragrant. It makes graceful shoots 1 to 2 ft long in a season and the racemes spring from the leaf-axils of the terminal half during the following May.

For a detailed account of this species see *Journ. R.H.S.*, Vol. 65, pp. 319–320.

G. yunnanensis and the species described below are the northernmost representatives of the mainly Malaysian section *Gymnobotrys*, which extends as far as New Guinea.

G. CUMINGIANA Vidal—This species bears some resemblance to *G. yunnanensis*, but the leaves are smaller and more slenderly pointed, the stems sparsely clad when young with long, spreading hairs, and the inflorescences shorter. The mature fruits are purplish black. It was introduced from Formosa but is of wide distribution in S.E. Asia. In *Flora Malesiana*, it is reduced to *G. leucocarpa* Blume f. *cumingiana* (Vidal) Sleumer.

GAYLUSSACIA   HUCKLEBERRY   ERICACEAE

This genus contains some forty to fifty species which belong exclusively to the New World, the greater proportion being found in S. America. About half a dozen species are in cultivation, all from eastern N. America, and, with the exception of *G. brachycera*, deciduous shrubs. The leaves are alternate, not toothed except in *G. brachycera*, and often resin-dotted. The corolla resembles that of *Vaccinium*, to which genus *Gaylussacia* is closely allied. The fruit is berry-like, outwardly similar to that of *Vaccinium*, but markedly different in containing ten cells and ten nutlets, instead of the four or five cells and numerous minute seeds of *Vaccinium*. The genus commemorates J. L. Gay-Lussac, the French chemist (1778–1850). Cultivation the same as for *Vaccinium*; but these shrubs have obtained little attention in gardens. Some of the species yield in the wild large crops of edible fruits in N. America, but have no value in that respect with us.

G. BACCATA (Wangenh.) K. Koch   BLACK HUCKLEBERRY

Andromeda baccata Wangenh.; *G. resinosa* (Ait.) Torr. & Gr.; *Vaccinium resinosum* Ait.

A deciduous, much-branched shrub 1 to 3 ft high, the young wood minutely downy and viscid. Leaves obovate or oval, mostly bluntish at the apex, 1 to $2\frac{1}{4}$ in. long, $\frac{1}{2}$ to $\frac{3}{4}$ in. wide, deep green above, paler yellowish beneath with resin-dots on both surfaces. Flowers produced in May in drooping racemes 1 in. or less long, carrying six to eight flowers, each on a thin stalk $\frac{1}{8}$ to $\frac{1}{4}$ in. long. Corolla conical, $\frac{1}{5}$ in. long, narrowed towards the mouth, dull red. Fruits $\frac{1}{4}$ to $\frac{1}{3}$ in. diameter, globose, shining black, without bloom.

Native of eastern N. America; introduced in 1772. In the United States it is considered the best of the huckleberries for eating, although said to vary very much in quality in different localities. It is distinguishable from the other deciduous huckleberries by the abundant resinous secretion on twig, leaf, flower-stalk, etc., in combination with the short, dense racemes and glabrous fruits.

f. LEUCOCARPA (Porter) Fern.—Fruits whitish.

f. GLAUCOCARPA (Robins.) Mackenzie—Fruits glaucous.

G. BRACHYCERA (Michx.) A. Gray   BOX HUCKLEBERRY

Vaccinium brachycerum Michx.; *Vaccinium buxifolium* Salisb.

A dwarf evergreen shrub 6 to 12 in. high; young stems angled, glabrous or minutely downy. Leaves thick, leathery, oval to ovate, toothed, $\frac{1}{3}$ to 1 in. long, about half as wide, dark glossy green above, paler below, glabrous, very shortly stalked. Flowers produced in May and June in short axillary racemes near the end of the shoot, each flower on a very short stalk. Corolla cylindrical, but contracted at the mouth, $\frac{1}{4}$ in. long, white, faintly striped with red. Fruits blue.

Native of the eastern United States, on the mountains and hills from Kentucky, Tennessee, and Virginia northwards to New Jersey; originally introduced in 1796. It was subsequently quite lost to cultivation but through the agency of the Arnold Arboretum was restored to gardens. It is not common in cultivation, but one of the daintiest of evergreens, forming low, neat patches, resembling to some extent *Vaccinium vitis-idaea* var. *minus*. Award of Merit, 1940, when shown by Messrs Marchant.

G. DUMOSA (Andr.) Torr. & Gr.   DWARF HUCKLEBERRY

Vaccinium dumosum Andr.

A deciduous shrub 1 to 2 ft, or sometimes twice as much high, spreading by underground stems, the young twigs furnished with gland-tipped hairs. Leaves narrowly oval or obovate, pointed, $\frac{3}{4}$ to $1\frac{1}{2}$ in. long, $\frac{1}{4}$ to $\frac{5}{8}$ in. wide, deep shining green, more or less glandular downy on both surfaces and at the edges, not toothed; stalk very short. Flowers produced in June on short downy racemes furnished with oval, persistent, leaflike bracts $\frac{1}{4}$ in. or more long, from the axils of which the flowers spring. Corolla bell-shaped, $\frac{1}{3}$ in. long and wide, pure waxy white, nodding; calyx with downy triangular lobes. Fruits globose, black, ¼ to ⅓ in. wide, downy; not much valued for eating. *Bot. Mag.*, t. 1106.

Native of eastern N. America from Newfoundland to Florida, never far

GAYLUSSACIA DUMOSA

from the coast, and said to prefer sandy soil; introduced in 1774. It is a handsome shrub both in flower and fruit, and differs from the other deciduous species in cultivation by the large, white, open bell-shaped flowers and the downy inflorescences with persistent, leaflike bracts.

G. FRONDOSA (L.) Torr. & Gr.   DANGLEBERRY
Vaccinium frondosum L.; *V. venustum* Ait.

A deciduous shrub 3 to 6 ft high, with slender, divergent branches; young wood glabrous or nearly so. Leaves obovate or oval, rounded or notched at the apex, 1 to 2½ in. long, ½ to 1¼ in. wide, bright green and glabrous above, rather glaucous, downy, and sprinkled with resin-dots beneath. Flowers produced in June and July on loose, slender racemes 1½ to 3 in. long, each flower on a threadlike, pendulous stalk ⅓ to 1 in. long. Corolla roundish bell-shaped, scarcely ⅕ in. long, purplish green; calyx-lobes glabrous, triangular. Fruits blue, ⅓ in. or more wide, globose, glabrous, very palatable.

Native of the eastern United States; introduced in 1761. This is one of the handsomest of the gaylussacias, and is distinct in the long-stalked flowers and lax racemes, and the bluntish leaves. The popular name refers to the loosely hanging fruits; they are not freely developed in this country.

G. URSINA (M. A. Curtis) Torr. & Gr.

Vaccinium ursinum M. A. Curtis

A deciduous shrub of loose branching habit 2 to 5 ft high; young twigs slightly downy. Leaves obovate or oval, pointed, tapering or rounded at the base, 1½ to 4 in. long, ¾ to 1½ in. wide, green and more or less downy on both sides, thin. Flowers produced during June in racemes 1 to 2 in. long, each of the six to ten flowers being borne on a slender stalk about ½ in. long. Corolla roundish, bell-shaped, dull white or reddish, ⅕ in. long, lobes recurved. Fruits shining black, globose, ⅓ to ½ in. across.

Native of the south-eastern United States, and especially on the mountains of N. Carolina, whence it was introduced to Kew in 1891. It is most nearly allied to *G. frondosa*, differing in the pointed, thinner leaves, green on both sides, and in having a black fruit, but resembling that species in the loose sparsely flowered racemes. The fruit is described as insipid. The foliage usually colours well in the autumn.

GENISTA   BROOM   LEGUMINOSAE

A large genus of shrubs, mostly deciduous, but sometimes acquiring the character of an evergreen from the colour of the young branches. They vary from dwarf and prostrate plants a few inches high to tall ones with a stature of over 20 ft. In a wild state they are found almost exclusively in Europe, but a few reach the western borders of Asia and the southern shores of the Mediterranean. With but one exception among cultivated hardy species (*G. monosperma*, with white flowers), the blossom is of some shade of yellow, and all have the pea-flower (or papilionaceous) form. The leaves are simple or trifoliolate, often so small and few as to be negligible; in these cases the work usually done by leaves devolves upon the green branches.

As garden shrubs some of the genistas, such as *G. aetnensis, hispanica, pilosa*, and *tenera*, are in the very front rank, and are all worth growing. They are easily accommodated and do not require a rich or manured soil. A sunny position (for most of them are essentially sun-lovers) and a well-drained, light loam suits them best. Whenever possible, genistas should be raised from seed, as plants so obtained are usually healthier and longer-lived than cuttings. Still cuttings are frequently employed. They are taken in late July or August, and dibbled in very sandy soil in frames, usually pushing roots the following spring. The taller species are all improved by shortening back several times in the young state to induce a bushy habit. They transplant badly after a few years, and should be given permanent quarters early, or else grown in pots. (See also CYTISUS.)

A considerable number of tender or half-hardy species have been, and continue to be, introduced from the south of Europe and the islands of the Mediterranean. Many of them can be cultivated in the Scilly Isles, but they are of no use for the ordinary climate of Great Britain. The species dealt with in the following pages include all in cultivation that are really hardy.

Genista and *Cytisus* are closely allied, and many species have been assigned to one or the other genus according to which differential character is given most weight. The majority of the species concerned conform to the following distinctions: *Cytisus* has the upper lip of the calyx shortly toothed and the seeds are strophiolate, i.e. there is a wart-like swelling at the base of the seed, known as the strophiole or elaiosome; in *Genista* the upper lip of the calyx is deeply cut into two lobes and the seeds lack a strophiole. However, there are a number of species which are in one or more respects either anomalous or controversial, and the modern tendency is to remove these to separate genera, so making it possible to draw a sharper line between *Genista* and *Cytisus*. Thus *C. monspessulanus* and its allies (a group most numerously represented in Madeira and the Canary Islands) have certain 'Genista' characters such as a deeply divided upper calyx-lip, and are on that account sometimes placed in the segregate genus *Teline*. In *C. nigrescens* the seeds have a very small strophiole and in this respect the species inclines towards *Genista*; but it would be out of place in that genus and has been treated as a separate genus—*Lembotropis*. Both these genera are recognised in *Flora Europaea*. It should be added that commonly the leaves in *Genista* consist of a single leaflet, whereas in *Cytisus* they are usually trifoliolate. Unfortunately there are so many exceptions, as well as many species that are virtually leafless, that this difference is of little value as a spotting character, though it holds good for the species most frequent in gardens.

The species treated below are mostly retained in *Genista* in *Flora Europaea*. But the anomalous *G. horrida* (and allied species not treated here) are removed to the genus *Echinospartum*, in which the branches are opposite as in *G. radiata* and its allies, but the calyx is inflated, as in *Erinacea*. Two other segregate genera recognised in *Flora Europaea*, but here included in *Genista*, are *Lygos* (syn. *Retama*) and *Chamaespartium*. In the former, in which *G. monosperma*, *G. sphaerocarpa*, and *G. raetam* would belong, the pods are inflated and split tardily or not at all. To *Chamaespartium* would belong *G. sagittalis* and the closely allied *G. delphinensis*, of which the distinctive character is the flattened and winged stems.

G. AETNENSIS (Bivona) DC.   [PLATE 40
Spartium aetnense Bivona

A tall shrub up to 15 or 20 ft high, occasionally even more, with a main stem 6 to 12 in. thick, and assuming the form of a small tree of erect, sparse habit, with very little foliage, but numerous slender, bright green, rushlike branches, which are pendulous when young. Leaves very few and scarcely noticeable, being narrow, linear, and ¼ to ½ in. long. Flowers produced in great profusion in July, scattered singly on the shoots of the year towards the end, each ½ in. or so across, the petals golden yellow, the calyx green, angular-toothed, bell-shaped. Seed-pods ½ in. long, ending in a sharp, decurved point and carrying two or three seeds.

Native of Sardinia and Sicily, and found on the slopes of Mt Etna at altitudes of 3,000 to 6,000 ft. It flowers during July and early August, when few hardy shrubs are in bloom; being of great beauty then, this broom is one of the most valuable of all its kind. Its tall habit makes it useful for planting at the back of shrubberies, where it can overtop without unduly shading other things. Although practically devoid of foliage, the bright green young branchlets give the plant almost the quality of an evergreen. It always makes a conspicuous feature in the grounds at Kew in July. It is a very hardy shrub. There is a fine specimen about 30 ft high in a private garden on Kew Green.

G. ANGLICA L.   NEEDLE FURZE, PETTY WHIN

A deciduous, more or less prostrate shrub 1 to 2 ft high; branches slender, interlaced, downy or glabrous, very spiny; spines numerous ¼ to ¾ in. long. Leaves simple, glabrous, ovate-lanceolate, pointed, about ¼ in. long. Flowers yellow, ½ in. long, crowded on short racemes terminating leafy twigs; bracts conspicuous; flower-stalks each with two bracteoles. Pods about ½ in. long, glabrous, inflated, obliquely narrowed at both ends.

Widely distributed over western Europe and frequent on moors and heaths in Great Britain, though uncommon in Scotland. Although pretty when in flower, it is not one of the most attractive of genistas. The spines are really modified branches, and may often be seen bearing leaves.

G. germanica (q.v.) is allied to this species, but is distinguished by the following characters: leaves hairy; bracts subtending the flower-stalks small and inconspicuous; flower-stalks without bracteoles.

var. SUBINERMIS (Legrand) Rouy—This name is available for plants almost or wholly without spines. They are found throughout the range of the species.

G. CINEREA (Vill.) DC.
Spartium cinereum Vill.

A deciduous shrub 8 to 10 ft high, with long, slender, scourge-like branches, grooved and clothed with fine silky hairs when young. Leaves grey-green, simple, stalkless, narrowly lanceolate, pointed, ⅛ to ½ in. long, covered with silky hairs beneath. Flowers in short clusters, usually two to four in each, bright yellow, ½ in. long; standard petal roundish with a notch at the top, about ½ in. long. Calyx ⅙ in. long, silky. Pods very silky, ½ to ⅔ in. long, containing two to five seeds. Blossoms June and July. *Bot. Mag.*, t. 8086.

Native of S.W. Europe, especially of Spain, where it grows on the Sierra Nevada up to an altitude of 6,000 ft. It is one of the showiest and most desirable of genistas, and although cultivated at Kew for over sixty years is still quite rare in gardens. It is useful in flowering after the majority of the brooms are past. Very similar in leaf and flower to *G. tenera* (*virgata*), it may be distinguished by longer, more slender branchlets and less twiggy habit when old, and in its flowers being mostly produced in small lateral clusters (not near the ends of short lateral branchlets as in *G. tenera*). Also the leaves in *G. cinerea* are mostly rather small and inconspicuous, often under ⅕ in. long (but up to ½ in. on extension shoots). For the plant grown in gardens as *G. cinerea* see under *G. tenera*.

G. RAMOSISSIMA Poir.—This North African species is very similar to *G. cinerea* but the flowers (including corolla) are more villous and sessile or very shortly stalked; *G. cinerea* is less hairy and the flowers distinctly pedicellate.

G. DELPHINENSIS Vill.

A prostrate, dwarf, scarcely woody shrub only a few inches high, its young shoots very crooked, zigzagged, winged (like *G. sagittalis* on a small scale), the wings silky-haired beneath. Leaves few and ¼ in. or less long, appressed-silky beneath, ovate, oval. Flowers bright yellow, borne at and near the end of the shoots in June in axillary and terminal clusters of three or more, but often singly or in pairs; calyx silky. Pods ½ to ¾ in. long, $\frac{3}{16}$ in. wide, appressed-silky, abruptly pointed, carrying three to six seeds.

A rare native of the mountains of southern France, said to be confined to the E. Pyrenees and Drôme and found mostly in rocky calcareous sites where it flowers from June to August. A very distinct and interesting as well as pretty dwarf plant for the rock garden or alpine house. The flowers individually are amongst the largest in the genus. It was excellently grown by the late Fred Stoker in Essex. A photograph of it (fig. 29) accompanies the article by him on dwarf brooms in *Journ. R.H.S.*, Vol. 67 (1942), pp. 76–80.

G. delphinensis is closely allied to *G. sagittalis*, of which it was made a subspecies by Fournier in *Quatre Flores de France* (under *Genistella*).

G. EPHEDROIDES DC.

A deciduous shrub of erect habit, much branched, up to 3 or 4 ft high, young shoots very slender, finely grooved, downy at first. Leaves very sparse; each made up of three linear leaflets ¼ in. long, soon dropping, those towards the end of the shoot simple, grey, downy. Flowers yellow, solitary, fragrant, borne alternately on the shoot mostly towards the top, ⅜ in. long; they are of the ordinary broom-flower shape. The calyx has two large triangular teeth and three small ones. Pods $\frac{1}{4}$ to $\frac{1}{3}$ in. long, oval, ending in a curved beak, downy, carrying one to three seeds. Seeds black, shining. Flowers in May and June.

Native of Sardinia, Corsica, and Sicily, often near the sea coast. It bears some resemblance to *Ephedra distachya* in habit and this suggested the specific name. It appears to be nearest to *G. radiata*, but that species has its flowers in a terminal head. It is one of a fair number of brooms that have practically no foliage, the normal functions of which are performed by the green stems. It is a rather tender shrub and needs a sunny, sheltered nook. It is allied to *G. aetnensis* but differs in its smaller stature and its trifoliolate, not simple, leaves.

G. FALCATA Brot.

A very spiny, gorse-like shrub, the young shoots very stiff, more or less hairy, ribbed, the spines mostly three-pronged or branched, $\frac{1}{2}$ to 2 in. long, downy. Leaves quite small, narrowly obovate to oval, stalkless, $\frac{1}{6}$ to $\frac{1}{2}$ in. long, $\frac{1}{12}$ to $\frac{1}{4}$ in. wide, ciliate. Flowers yellow, $\frac{1}{8}$ to $\frac{1}{4}$ in. long, solitary in the axils of the spines or a few in short clusters, very copiously produced and sometimes collectively forming very handsome, woody, columnar panicles over 1 ft. long; bracts and bracteoles minute or absent; calyx glabrous or thinly downy. Pods inflated, glabrous, sickle-shaped, up to $\frac{1}{2}$ in. long.

Native of W. Spain and W. Portugal, on acid soils. It flowers in late April and early May.

G. BERBERIDEA Lange—This species is closely allied to *G. falcata*, but differs in its densely hairy calyx and in the presence of conspicuous bracteoles on the flower-stalks. Native of the north-western parts of the Iberian peninsula.

Both the above species are allied to *G. anglica*, but that species is distinguished by its usually low and spreading habit and by the combination of a glabrous calyx and the inflorescence with conspicuous bracts and bracteoles.

G. FLORIDA L.

G. leptoclada Spach; *G. polygalifolia* DC.; *G. florida* var. *maroccana* Ball; *G. florida* var. *atlantica* E. K. Balls, *nom. ined.*

A shrub up to 8 ft high in the wild; shoots erect, distinctly grooved, downy. Leaves simple, shortly stalked, elliptic to oblanceolate or linear, mostly $\frac{5}{8}$ to $\frac{7}{8}$ in. long, rarely to 1 in., and $\frac{1}{8}$ to $\frac{1}{4}$ in. wide, but in some plants only $\frac{1}{24}$ to $\frac{1}{12}$ in. wide, silky-hairy on both sides, but especially beneath. Flowers yellow, $\frac{1}{2}$ in. long, borne towards the top of the shoots, making racemes or leafy panicles 1 to 3 in. long; standard petal broadly ovate with at most a few scattered silky hairs. Pods narrowly oblong, silky, with three to eight seeds.

Native of Spain, Portugal, and Morocco. This species seems to be little known in cultivation, but the Moroccan plants are said to be very beautiful, with silvery leaves and fragrant flowers (*Journ. R.H.S.*, Vol. 69, p. 358, and Vol. 90, p. 386). But judging from the material from Morocco in the Kew Herbarium the plants there fit into the normal range of variation of the species.

G. GERMANICA L.

A deciduous shrub about 2 ft high, with spiny, hairy shoots; spines mostly branched, $\frac{1}{2}$ to $\frac{3}{4}$ in. long. Leaves ovate-lanceolate, $\frac{1}{2}$ to $\frac{3}{4}$ in. long, $\frac{1}{8}$ to $\frac{1}{4}$ in. wide, hairy especially about the margins, dark green. Racemes 1 to 2 in. long, terminating leafy, spineless shoots. Flowers yellow, $\frac{1}{3}$ to $\frac{1}{2}$ in. long; standard petal reflexed. Pods $\frac{1}{2}$ in. long, hairy. Blossoms in June.

This species is fairly widely distributed, from S.W. France through central Europe to western central Russia and as far south-east as Bulgaria. Its nearest ally is *G. anglica* (q.v. for the marks of difference). It is apt to grow rank, and become rather ragged in rich garden soil; a sunny, rather dry position suits it best.

G. HISPANICA L.   SPANISH GORSE

G. hispanica subsp. *occidentalis* Rouy

A deciduous shrub usually from 1 to $1\frac{1}{2}$ ft (sometimes $2\frac{1}{2}$ ft) high, forming dense, cushion-like masses; branches interlacing, spiny and hairy, the spines much branched, $\frac{3}{4}$ to 1 in. long, each subdivision needle-pointed. Leaves confined to the flowering twigs, linear-lanceolate, about $\frac{1}{8}$ in. long, $\frac{1}{16}$ to $\frac{1}{8}$ in. wide, hairy beneath. Flowers as many as twelve in a rounded head or cluster 1 in. or so across, terminating short, erect, leafy, hairy shoots; each flower is $\frac{1}{3}$ in. long, rich golden yellow. Pods flattish oval, carrying one to four seeds. *Bot. Mag.*, t. 8528.

Native of S.W. Europe; introduced in 1759. It flowers in the latter half of May and in June, and produces at that time a more gorgeous display of golden yellow blossom than probably any other dwarf shrub. Healthy plants are completely covered with bloom, and when they have been planted to cover a breadth of 10 ft or so, produce a most brilliant colour effect. On shelves or small plateaux of the rock garden single plants are very charming. Although its leaves are deciduous, this shrub gives an evergreen effect through the deep green of its crowded twigs and spines. As with others of the spiny group of genistas, it is not advisable to give it rich or manured soil, otherwise it is apt to grow rank and soft, and during winter the younger parts are apt to die in patches and spoil the next crop of flowers. A soil of moderate quality, and especially a well-drained, sunny position, suits it best. It can be propagated by seeds and by August cuttings. One of the most indispensable shrubs in the south of England.

In *Flora Europaea* two subspecies are recognised, namely the typical one with the hairs on the stems and leaves spreading and the standard petals of the corollas $\frac{1}{4}$ to $\frac{3}{8}$ in. long; and subsp. *occidentalis* Rouy, said to be confined to the W. Pyrenees and N. Spain, in which the hairs are appressed and the standard longer—$\frac{3}{8}$ to $\frac{7}{16}$ in. long. If this distinction were to be recognised, cultivated plants would belong to the latter. But the two variants are not clearly distinguishable in wild material and certainly do not merit the rank of subspecies. The description given above is made from a cultivated plant.

GENISTA HISPANICA

G. HORRIDA (Vahl) DC.

Spartium horridum Vahl; *Echinospartium horridum* (Vahl) Rothm.; *Cytisanthus horridus* (Vahl) Gams

A dwarf, flat-topped, very spiny shrub of close, tufted habit; stems grooved, opposite, rigid, ending in a sharp spine, and clothed with short silky hairs at first, later glabrous. Leaves opposite, small, trifoliolate, composed of three linear leaflets $\frac{1}{4}$ to $\frac{3}{8}$ in. long, covered with silky hairs. Flowers $\frac{3}{8}$ to $\frac{1}{2}$ in. long, produced in small terminal heads, three to eight together, standing just clear of the branches; yellow. Calyx, flower-stalk, and pod hairy. Calyx inflated.

Native of the Pyrenees; introduced in 1821. Although hardy enough, it does not always flower freely, and is not much grown. Our climate apparently is not sunny enough to develop its full beauty. It is one of the interesting groups of

T S—K

genistas with opposite leaves and branches, and does not appear likely to become more than 1½ to 2½ ft high. The whole plant has a silvery grey hue, and forms a dense, cushion-like mass. A specimen in the Kew Herbarium collected in Spain by the late N. Y. Sandwith on 13 July 1957, is annotated: 'The arid, eroded mountainsides of the Spanish Pyrenees are golden with the flowers of this species in July.'

### G. JANUENSIS Viv.	GENOA BROOM

G. genuensis Pers.; *G. triangularis* Willd.; *G. scariosa* Viv.; *G. triquetra* Waldst. & Kit., not L'Hérit.

A low, procumbent, deciduous shrub a few inches high, but sometimes erect, the triangular stems without down, but with thin transparent wings. From the stems arise erect flowering twigs 1 to 3 in. long, bearing a single flower in each of the four to ten terminal leaf-axils. Leaves linear-lanceolate to narrowly ovate, glabrous, pointed or bluntish, ¼ to 1 in. long, $\frac{1}{16}$ to $\frac{3}{16}$ in. wide, dark green with thin transparent margins. Flowers clear bright yellow; standard petal, roundish ovate, ¼ in. wide; keel and wing petals about as long. Pods 1 in. long, $\frac{3}{16}$ in. wide, glabrous, containing four to seven seeds. *Bot. Mag.*, t. 9574.

Native of northern and central Italy eastward and south-eastward to Slovenia, W. Rumania, and the Balkan Peninsula; introduced long ago and cultivated at Kew in 1850. It went out of cultivation, but at the Chelsea Show of May 1932 a group of young plants in a pan were shown by G. P. Baker of Sevenoaks, charmingly in flower, under the name "*G. triquetra*". It was originally named in 1802 from a plant found on the island of Palmaria, near Spezia in Italy, but it is also widely spread on the mainland. It is essentially a plant for a ledge in the rock garden, where it will spread 2 to 3 ft wide. The distinctive characters are (in combination) its prostrate habit, triangular stems, simple leaves, axillary blossoms, and its entirely glabrous parts. It is allied to *G. lydia* (q.v.).

The name *G. triquetra* was given to this broom by Waldstein and Kitaibel in 1805, but it had already been used by L'Héritier in 1784 for quite a different shrub with trifoliolate leaves and therefore has no standing. The true G. TRI-QUETRA L' Hérit. is figured in *Bot. Mag.*, t. 314, and is said by Aiton to have been cultivated in England by a Mr Ord as long ago as 1770. It does not appear to exist in the wild and could be a hybrid between *Cytisus monspessulanus* and *Genista tinctoria*.

G. LOBELII DC.

A deciduous dwarf or prostrate shrub reaching when old 6 to 10 in. in height, usually dwarfer; young shoots downy, distinctly grooved, becoming spine-tipped with age. Leaves alternate, simple, very tiny (about ¼ in. long), linear, hairy, soon falling. Flowers ⅜ in. long, pale yellow, solitary in the terminal leaf-axils or in clusters of two to four, each on a downy stalk ⅛ to ¼ in. long. Corolla of the normal broom-flower shape. Calyx downy, $\frac{3}{16}$ in. long, with narrowly triangular lobes. Pod ⅜ in. long, ⅛ in. wide, pointed, downy. Blossoms in June.

Native of S. France and S. Spain. This interesting dwarf shrub is charming for a sunny spot in the rock garden. A plant grew at Kew for many years and proved perfectly hardy there. Planted above a stone, it had draped itself over it and formed a pendulous mass of spine-tipped twigs 18 in. in diameter and about 3 in. in thickness. It needs the sunniest possible position. *G. horrida* has similar spine-tipped twigs, but its leaves are opposite, and *Erinacea anthyllis*, similarly spiny, has purplish-blue flowers.

G. lobelii is one of a number of very closely allied genistas of the Mediterranean region which are exceedingly difficult to discriminate, varying as they do in their basic differential characters. Of these, G. SALZMANNII DC., native of Corsica, Sardinia, etc., differs chiefly in habit. For in *G. lobelii* the branches are short and sinuous, and bear numerous short, spine-tipped branchlets crowded into a tuft or dome, while in *G. salzmannii* the branches are straighter, with the branchlets and flowers arranged all along them. In both species the flowers may be solitary or clustered. The genista of S. Spain known by the illegitimate name *G. baetica* Spach is also closely allied to *G. lobelii*. These three species are scarcely separable from G. ASPALATHOIDES Lam., described from Tunisia.

G. LYDIA Boiss. [PLATE 42]
G. spathulata Spach

A deciduous shrub about 2 ft high, of lax, pendulous growth; young shoots slender, four- or five-angled, glabrous, green. Leaves linear, pointed, glabrous or almost so, ⅜ in. long, $\frac{1}{16}$ in. wide, set about half an inch apart. Flowers produced three or four together towards the end of short lateral twigs in May and June, bright yellow, ⅜ in. long, standard petal ¼ in. wide; calyx glabrous, $\frac{1}{12}$ in. long, tubular, with five narrowly triangular, pointed, erect lobes. Pods about 1 in. long with a short bristle at the end, containing one to five seeds. *Bot. Mag.*, n.s., t. 292.

A native of the E. Balkans and western Asia Minor; introduced in 1926 by the late Dr Turrill by means of seeds collected by him in the Rodopi massif in Bulgaria, on limestone rocks above Bačkovo. The merits of this beautiful shrub were soon appreciated and since World War II it has become common in gardens. In a sunny, well-drained position it is quite hardy in the sense that it will withstand low winter temperatures. The sudden death of branches or whole plants may be the belated effect of hard early winter frosts after a rainy mild autumn, or of late spring frosts. It is best suited to a ledge in a large rock garden or the top of a dry wall, where its graceful habit can show to best advantage. But more compact plants can be obtained by light pruning as soon as the flowers are over.

G. lydia is allied to *G. januensis*, but that species (q.v.) differs in its broader leaves and triangular stems. Also, *G. januensis* has a more northern and western distribution, though intermediates may occur.

G. MONOSPERMA (L.) Lam.

Spartium monospermum L.; *Retama monosperma* (L.) Boiss.; *Lygos monosperma* (L.) Heywood

A straggling, unarmed shrub 2 to 4 ft high in this country, but more than twice as high in its native state; branches very slender, pendent, and rush-like, grooved, covered with short, silky hairs when young. Leaves few and inconspicuous, ¼ to ¾ in. long, linear. Racemes short, silky, distributed along the branches, ½ to 1½ in. long, carrying from five to fifteen blossoms. Flowers milky white and delightfully fragrant, ½ in. long; the petals covered with silky hairs, the calyx dark, and contrasting with the petals; keel of corolla cuspidate at the apex. Pods wrinkled, obovoid, mucronate at the apex, about ½ in. long, containing one (sometimes two) black-brown seeds.

Native of S. Portugal, S.W. Spain, and N. Africa, mostly on coastal sands. It has always been rare because of its tenderness. In the Scilly Isles it thrives admirably, but near London it needs the protection of a sunny, sheltered wall, such as that outside a hothouse. The soil must be lightish and well drained. In its native country the thin flexible branches are used for tying—in the same way as willows are here.

G. NYSSANA Petrović   NISH BROOM

A deciduous, erect shrub of sparse habit, thickly covered with soft hairs in all its parts—branches, leaves, flowers, and pods. Branches leafy, but little forked, slender, erect, slightly furrowed. Leaves trifoliolate; leaflets linear, pointed, ½ to ¾ in. long, ⅛ in. or less wide, margins slightly decurved. Flowers yellow, ½ in. long, in slender terminal racemes 4 to 6 in. long, each flower produced in the axil of a trifoliolate, leaflike bract, which becomes smaller towards the apex of the inflorescence. The growth of the year, including branch and raceme, will measure from 12 to 18 in. long. Pods short, thick, ovate, pointed, carrying one or two seeds.

Native of southern Yugoslavia around Niš; introduced to Kew in 1899. It has proved quite hardy, and is most distinct in its dense covering of short soft hairs.

This species is closely allied to G. SESSILIFOLIA DC., a species of wider distribution in S. Yugoslavia and extending into Bulgaria. It is not so densely hairy as *G. nyssana* and the leaflets are narrower.

G. PILOSA L.

A deciduous shrub growing 1 to 1½ ft high, procumbent when young, after-wards forming a low, tangled mass of slender, twiggy shoots. Leaves distributed along the branchlets of the year, but gathered in clusters on the year-old shoots; they are simple, ¼ to ½ in. long, narrowly obovate, the margins folded upwards, and the lower surface covered with closely pressed, silvery hairs. Flowers bright yellow, produced singly or in pairs (but each on its own short stalk) from the leaf-axils, the whole forming a crowded raceme 2 to 6 in. long; bracteoles on flower-stalks absent. Standard petal and keel both silky-hairy, wings glabrous. Pods ¾ to 1 in. long, narrow, silky, two- to six-seeded.

A native of much of Europe as far east as Poland and the northern Balkans, and north to S.W. Scandinavia; rare and local in the British Isles on sandy and gravelly heaths. This pretty broom is valuable for forming a dense covering for the ground, even for plots planted with groups of taller shrubs or trees, provided of course it is not unduly shaded. It is also useful for the rock garden, and for covering dry, sunny banks. When in blossom the whole plant becomes a mass of bright yellow.

cv. 'PROCUMBENS'.—Stems quite prostrate.

G. RADIATA (L.) Scop.

Spartium radiatum L.; *Cytisus radiatus* (L.) K. Koch; *Enantiosparton radiatum* (L.) K. Koch; *Cytisanthus radiatus* (L.) Lang

A rounded bushy shrub 3 ft high, with deciduous leaves, but evergreen from the green colour of the shoots. Branches opposite, distinctly grooved, slender, occasionally spine-tipped, very distinctly jointed. Leaves opposite, trifoliolate, stalkless, consisting of three narrowly linear leaflets, ¼ to ½ in. long, silky. They soon fall, but short shoots are produced in their axils which serve as photosynthetic organs. The flowers are in a terminal head of about six blossoms; bracteoles on the flower-stalks shorter than the calyx-tube. Each flower is about ½ in. long, deep yellow; calyx silky; standard petal glabrous or with a line of hairs down the centre. Pods silky, ovate, tapering at the end to a sharp curved point, usually one-seeded.

Native of the southern Alps, extending southward into central Italy and western Yugoslavia, with a few localities farther south and east. The var. SERICOPETALA Bucheg., which differs in its uniformly silky standards and in having the bracteoles on the flower-stalks longer than the calyx-tube, is found mainly in S.E. France and N.W. Italy but is also reported from Greece. More distinct is:

var. NANA Spach G. *holopetala* (Fleischmann) Baldacci; *Cytisus holopetala* Fleischmann ex K. Koch—Of lower, more cushion-like habit. Such plants occur in N.W. Yugoslavia (e.g., on the Velebitska Planina) and are said to differ from the type in certain botanical characters which might be of specific value if well correlated.

G. SAGITTALIS L.

Chamaespartium sagittale (L.) P. Gibbs; *Genistella sagittalis* (L.) Gams

A prostrate shrub under 1 ft in height, and evergreen from the character of its green, foliaceous, winged branches. Stems with a slender, woody core, but edged on each side with a membranous wing, sometimes continuous up the stem, sometimes interrupted at the joints, the stem thus becoming flat and nearly ¼ in. wide. Leaves few and scattered, oval or ovate, ½ to ¾ in. long, hairy. Racemes erect, terminal, cylindrical, 1 to 1½ in. long, hairy. Flowers closely packed, each ½ in. long, yellow, the petals expanding but little; calyx hairy. Pods ¾ in. long, silky, four- to six-seeded. Blossoms in June. *Bot. Mag.*, n.s., t. 332.

Native of central and S.E. Europe, frequently inhabiting upland pastures. It is very hardy, and thrives well in gardens, where it attracts notice for its pretty flowers and unusual stems. It may be used as an edging for borders, or grown in patches in the front of shrubberies.

GENISTA SAGITTALIS

G. SCORPIUS (L.) DC.
Spartium scorpius L.

A shrub 3 to 6 ft high with numerous interlacing, angular, grey stems, armed with stout axillary simple or branched spines. Leaves simple, linear-lanceolate, ⅛ to 7⁄16 in. long, 1⁄16 to 1⁄12 in. wide, slightly hairy beneath; petioles with a pair of short spines near the apex. Flowers yellow, produced in early summer in axillary clusters on the upper part of the stems and along the spines. Lips of calyx equal, shorter than the tube. Standard glabrous, 5⁄16 to ½ in. long; keel glabrous, slightly shorter than the standard. Pods linear-oblong, containing three to seven brownish-green seeds.

Native of southern France and Spain (the same or a very closely related species in Corsica and Sardinia), inhabiting dry places; although Aiton, citing Lobel as his authority, gives 1570 as the earliest known date of cultivation in Britain, it is probable that it was not introduced until the late 18th or early 19th century. It is an interesting strongly armed shrub, almost leafless by midsummer.

G. SERICEA Wulf.

A deciduous shrub of low, tufted growth, usually under 1 ft in height, and consisting of a cluster of short, erect growths; young shoots finely silky-hairy. Leaves simple, linear to narrowly oblong, tapered towards both ends, mostly $\frac{1}{3}$ to $\frac{3}{4}$ in. long, about $\frac{1}{8}$ in. wide, glabrous above, clothed beneath with silky hairs. Flowers yellow, about $\frac{1}{2}$ in. long, borne in terminal clusters of three to five, opening in late May or June; they are of the typical broom-flower shape. Petals, calyx, and seed-pod silky-hairy; pods about $\frac{3}{4}$ in. long.

Native of Dalmatia, Istria, Tyrol, etc., found in calcareous soil often on stony mountainous sites. It is common on Monte Spaccato, near Trieste. Though known to botanists since the 18th century, it has been little cultivated and I had not seen it alive until 1925, when it was obtained for Kew from Trieste. It is essentially a plant for a sunny ledge in the rock garden, a spot for which its low, tufted, compact habit fits it admirably.

G. SPHAEROCARPA (L.) Lam.

Spartium sphaerocarpon L.; *Lygos sphaerocarpa* (L.) Heywood; *Retama sphaerocarpa* (L.) Boiss.

A deciduous shrub 3 to 4 ft high (or more in cultivation); stems erect, slender, ribbed, mostly glabrous, pale green. Leaves simple, stalkless, very small and downy beneath, only present on young plants and soon falling, leaving the plant leafless for the greater part of its career. Flowers yellow, $\frac{1}{8}$ to $\frac{1}{6}$ in. long, crowded and set alternately in two rows on axillary racemes $\frac{1}{2}$ to $1\frac{1}{2}$ in. long, borne mostly singly or in pairs; calyx and corolla glabrous; pods globose, $\frac{1}{4}$ in. wide, carrying usually one kidney-shaped seed.

Native of N. Africa and Spain, cultivated in the Jardin du Roi, Paris, in 1780. Interesting for its very numerous tiny blossoms open in May and June and its curious, globose pods.

G. SYLVESTRIS Scop.

G. dalmatica Bartl.; *G. sylvestris* var. *pungens* (Vis.) Rehd.; *Cytisus sylvestris* var. *pungens* Vis.

A dwarf deciduous shrub, forming a neat dense tuft 4 to 6 in. high, ultimately 1 ft or more through; branches thin, angular, very hairy and spiny. Spines stiff and sharp, being really the terminations of curious pinnately divided branchlets. Leaves simple, mostly confined to the base of the shoot; thin, linear, pointed, about $\frac{1}{3}$ in. long, hairy. Racemes terminal, 1 to $1\frac{1}{2}$ in. long, erect, densely set with golden yellow flowers. Flowers $\frac{1}{3}$ in. long; standard petal broadly ovate; calyx with five slender awl-shaped lobes, hairy. Pod round and flat, $\frac{1}{2}$ in. long, ripening usually but one seed. Blossoms in June and July. The plant in general suggests a miniature G. *hispanica*. *Bot. Mag.*, t. 8075.

Native of Dalmatia, Herzegovina, etc., where it forms part of the underwood of pine forests, and generally affects dry situations. Introduced to Kew in 1893, it has proved a delightful plant. It may be used for furnishing shelves in the rock garden, and it provides a pleasing undergrowth for groups of thinly planted taller shrubs, provided the shade is not too dense. At flowering time the tufts are entirely hidden by the closely packed, golden yellow racemes. The flowering shoots die back considerably during winter, springing up from the base in spring. Propagation is best effected by means of cuttings placed under a bell-glass in an unheated frame in August.

G. *sylvestris* is somewhat variable in habit and spininess. The plant described above could be called var. *pungens* (Vis.) Rehd., to distinguish it from what is considered to be the more typical race, which is less spiny and of laxer habit.

G. TENERA (Jacq.) O. Kuntze

Cytisus tenera Jacq.; G. *virgata* (Ait.) Link, not Lam.; *Spartium virgatum* Ait.;
Genista cinerea Hort., not DC.

A deciduous shrub of bushy habit when old, up to 12 ft high, and as much or more through; young branches grooved. Leaves simple, grey-green, with little or no stalk, about $\frac{1}{2}$ in. long, $\frac{1}{8}$ in. wide, silky beneath, edges slightly decurved. Racemes 1 to 2 in. long, terminating short shoots of the year, very abundant. Flowers bright yellow, $\frac{1}{2}$ in. long, standard petal roundish, about $\frac{1}{2}$ in. across. Calyx clothed with silky hairs. Pods 1 in. long, very silky, carrying three to five seeds. Flowers in June and July, and intermittently until October. *Bot. Mag.*, t. 2265.

Native of Madeira, and one of the few shrubs from that island that are really hardy with us; it also occurs in Teneriffe. It was brought home from Madeira by Francis Masson in 1777, on his return from the Cape of Good Hope, where he had for five years been collecting plants for Kew. It has naturalised itself in several parts of the Kew woods, and is never injured in the least by frost, but until quite recently it was scarcely known in gardens. It flowers in June and July when shrubs generally are going out of flower, and thrives quite well in semi-shaded positions in thin woodland. For these two reasons it is an exceptionally valuable broom, the more so as it grows well in rough grass which gets no more attention than an annual mowing. It resembles G. *cinerea* previously described (q.v.), and the two probably are geographical forms of one species.

In addition to the freely seeding form there is also in cultivation what appears to be a sterile clone of G. *tenera*, which is usually grown under the name "G. *cinerea*". It is of more graceful habit than the fertile form, and the flowers more fragrant.

G. *tenera* is generally known in gardens by its synonymous name—G. *virgata* (Ait.) Link. It should not be confused with G. *virgata* Willd., which is a variety of G. *tinctoria*.

G. TINCTORIA L.   DYER'S GREENWEED

In its modern acceptation, this name may be taken to cover a group of allied forms put under one variable species. Plants have been received at Kew under perhaps a score of different specific names; they differ in certain characters of more or less importance, but still bear a striking resemblance to each other. It has been found impossible to fix on permanent characters that would clearly differentiate them, and they have, in consequence, been all included under *G. tinctoria*. Many are minor forms of the tall, erect dyer's greenweed (var. *virgata*). Others are distinguished by characters defined below.

G. TINCTORIA (type)—A low, often semi-prostrate shrub with creeping roots, usually only a few inches high in the wild, but up to 2 ft under cultivation. Stems more or less grooved, clothed with simple, dark green leaves that are linear-lanceolate, ½ to 1 in. long, hairy on the margins. Racemes erect, terminal, each 1 to 3 in. long, produced on the shoots of the year from June to September. Owing to the branching of the stems near the top under cultivation, a crowd of racemes is often produced, forming one large panicle. Flowers ½ to ¾ in. long, yellow, without hairs; pods ½ to ¾ in. long, glabrous, carrying eight to twelve seeds.

This typical form is common in the British Isles, especially in poor grassland, and dry gravelly soils. It is also spread over Europe, and reaches Siberia. Under cultivation it is a pretty plant and flowers freely, but is not so attractive as its variety 'PLENA', which is also a dwarf, semi-prostrate shrub, but owing to the more numerous petals more brilliant in colour. This is, indeed, one of the best of all dwarf yellow-flowered shrubs. Seeds and cuttings can be employed to increase the typical form, but the double-flowered one, being sterile, can only be propagated by cuttings. In former times this genista was of some value as the source of a yellow dye.

Although known as 'greenweed', the colour derived from it was a bright yellow, and it was only by afterwards dipping the yellow yarn or cloth into a blue solution of woad (*Isatis*) that the green tint was obtained. This was the process by which was obtained the once celebrated 'Kendal green', so-called from the town of Kendal in Westmorland, in the vicinity of which the plant was abundant, and where also the process was first introduced by Flemish emigrants in the reign of Edward III. (*Treasury of Botany*, Vol. I, p. 526.)

The varieties given below comprise most of the main variations of *G. tinctoria* found in Europe, but intermediate forms occur. It is obviously desirable that commercial clones should be given distinctive names, as has been done in the case of 'Royal Gold'. The variations of *G. tinctoria* are discussed by P. E. Gibbs in *Notes R.B.G. Edin.*, Vol. 27, pp. 33-37.

var. ALPESTRIS Bertol.—Of procumbent habit, with small, narrow leaves and unually glabrous pods. Found in the Alps, Italy, etc. Similar plants occur on sea-coasts (var. LITORALIS Corbière).

var. ANXANTICA (Ten.) Fiori—This has a similar habit to typical *G. tinctoria* but is wholly glabrous and the flowers are considerably larger (⅔ in. long). It was described from the region of Lanciano in central Italy. Introduced 1818; suitable for the rock garden.

var. HUMILIOR (Bertol.) Schneid. *G. ovata* var. *humilior* Bertol.; *G. perrey-mondii* Loisel.; *G. mantica* Poll.; *G. lasiocarpa* Spach, *nom. illegit.*; *G. lasiocarpa* var. *perreymondii* (Loisel.) Spach, *comb. illegit.*; *G. t.* var. *lasiocarpa* (Spach) Gren. & Godr.—This group comprises plants of medium height with downy leaves, stems and pods. S. Europe.

var. OVATA (Waldst. & Kit.) F. Schultz *G. ovata* Waldst. & Kit.—A shrub 2 to 4 ft high. Leaves ovate, elliptic or oblong, up to 1 in. or slightly more long and up to ¾ or ⅞ in. wide. Racemes to 3 in. long, flowers densely arranged. Pods hairy. Native mainly of Rumania, N. Yugoslavia, Hungary, and E. Austria. Introduced 1819.

cv. 'PLENA'. See above.

cv. 'ROYAL GOLD'.—Stems erect. Flowers golden yellow in terminal and axillary racemes, forming a narrow panicle. Ultimate height said to be 2 ft.

var. VIRGATA Koch *G. virgata* Willd., not Lam., nor (Ait.) Link; *G. t.* var. *elatior* (Koch) F. Schultz; *G. elatior* Koch—In its morphological characters this resembles ordinary *G. tinctoria*, but is an altogether bigger, stronger-growing shrub. It is of quite erect habit, 3 to 5 ft high, leaves up to 1½ in. or more long, ¼ to ½ in. wide. Flowers individually no larger than in the common form but borne in larger panicles sometimes 12 to 18 in. high. Native of S.E. and east central Europe. It should not be confused with *G. tenera* ("G. virgata" of gardens).

G. patula Bieb., described from Russian Armenia, is included in *G. tinctoria* *sens. lat.* by P. E. Gibbs in *Flora of Turkey*, Vol. 3, p. 25. The plant described in previous editions under this name was collected by E. K. Balls in 1934 near Trabzon (Trebizond), Anatolia, where it inhabits limestone cliffs up to 3,000 ft altitude. This form was distinguished by its very slender, strongly grooved stems, narrow leaves, and hairy pods.

G. VILLARSII Clementi

G. humifusa Vill., not L.; *G. pulchella* Gren. & Godr., not Vis.

In the wild this is often found in arid mountainous places and is there a pigmy bush a few inches high, consisting of a thick, short main-stem and a gnarled, twisted mass of short twigs. In places more favourable to its growth it will make shoots 1 to 3 in. long in a season, but it is always dwarf; young shoots grey, downy, grooved. Leaves linear, hairy on both surfaces, ¼ in. or so long. Flowers yellow, solitary in the terminal leaf-axils of the shoot, ⅓ in. long, of the usual broom-flower shape; calyx very hairy, with triangular pointed lobes; petals hairy. Pods ½ in. long, very hairy.

Native of S.E. France. This is another of the dwarf alpine brooms very suitable for growing on a sunny shelf in the rock garden. It is perfectly hardy at Kew. In its frequently starved, wild condition, the twigs occasionally become rather spine-tipped, but this tendency disappears under the softer conditions of cultivation. Flowers in May.

GEVUINA   PROTEACEAE

A genus of three species, one in Chile, the other two in Queensland and
New Guinea, allied to the tropical genus *Macadamia*, of which *M. ternifolia*
is cultivated on a commercial scale for its edible seeds.

Molina, the author of the generic name, adopted the spelling 'Gevuina',
which is a perfectly adequate rendering, in Latin, of the native name for
G. avellana. The spelling 'Guevina' should not be used; it is of no account
that the native name is spelt 'guevin' in Spanish.

G. AVELLANA Mol.   [PLATE 37

An evergreen tree 30 to 40 ft high or a large shrub, densely and luxuriantly
leafy; young shoots stout, clothed thickly with a soft brown down as are the
leaf-stalks also. Leaves pinnate or doubly pinnate; from 6 to 16 in. long, 4 to
10 in. wide; the primary divisions three to fifteen, each consisting of one to five
leaflets. The number of leaflets on one leaf may vary from three to over thirty
and individually they vary much in size. On young vigorous plants the largest

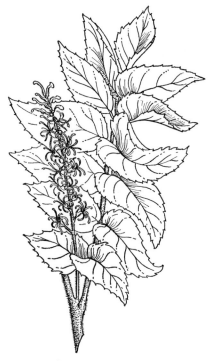

GEVUINA AVELLANA

leaflets are as much as 7½ in. long and 3 in. wide; the smallest less than 1 in. long. They are usually ovate to triangular in outline, sharply toothed, rounded or truncate at the base, pointed at the apex, leathery in texture, and of the richest lustrous green. Racemes produced in the leaf-axils during August, 4 in. long, carrying twenty to twenty-five pairs of usually ivory-white flowers with very narrow recurved sepals, beyond which the stamens project half an inch; style ¼ in. long, curved, hairy at the base. Fruit a hard nut the size of a small acorn, turning red, then purple, finally black. Seeds edible. *Bot. Mag.*, t. 9161.

Native of Chile; introduced in 1826. It is not really hardy at Kew, and although it survives normal winters in a sheltered spot, it is not worth struggling with out-of-doors. But in Devonshire and Cornwall it is very fine. The best tree I have seen is one at Trewidden, near Penzance, which when I saw it in 1930 was 35 ft high and 13 ft in diameter of spread at the base—a pyramidal tree of great beauty. [This tree still exists, and there is another of about the same height in Eire at Fota, Co. Cork, *pl.* 1938.] In regard to foliage alone it would be difficult to find an evergreen of its type more handsome. Ripe fruits have been developed at Rostrevor, Co. Down, and the seeds found to be palatable. The flowers vary in colour from pure white to yellowish or greenish white, occasionally tinged with red.

GINKGO   GINKGOACEAE

A genus of a single species which was at one time regarded as a very distinct member of the Yew family (Taxaceae) but is now separated from the conifers (Coniferales) altogether and placed in an order—the Ginkgoales —of which it is the only living representative. This group was widespread in the Jurassic and Cretaceous periods. In the Tertiary it was overwhelmed by the advance of the conifers and angiosperms, but the fossil species *G. adiantoides* still grew in Europe during the Pliocene, the last epoch before the onset of the Ice Age. This species is scarcely to be differentiated from the living *G. biloba*. In other fossil species of *Ginkgo* the leaves are deeply lobed and the lobes in some species are themselves divided into slender segments.

The generic name *Ginkgo* derives from a Japanese rendering of one of the Chinese names for the tree. Sir James Smith considered the name to be uncouth and attempted to substitute for it the name *Salisburia*, and with some success, as it was widely used throughout the 19th century, although quite invalid.

G. BILOBA L.   MAIDENHAIR TREE   [PLATE 39
Salisburia adiantifolia Sm.

A deciduous tree over 100 ft high, unisexual, not resinous, usually of somewhat pyramidal habit (the male at least); trunk often branching low, and forming several erect main branches; secondary branches spreading, pendulous at the ends. Branchlets of two kinds: (1) short, stout spurs, which increase very slowly in length and bear the leaves at the tip; (2) long, free-growing shoots with the leaves alternate. Trees in a stunted or unhealthy state produce only the first type of shoot, and will remain practically stationary for many years. Leaves long-stalked, fan-shaped, tapering from the irregularly jagged, often notched apex to the wedge-shaped base, up to 3 in. deep, about 2 to 3 in. wide, not downy, yellowish dull green, the veins all running lengthwise, and repeatedly forking as the leaf broadens towards the end; stalk slender, $1\frac{1}{2}$ to $3\frac{1}{2}$ in. long. Flowers borne on the short shoots, the males in cylindrical, short-stalked catkins about 1 in. long, consisting of green stamens only, the females on a stalk $1\frac{1}{2}$ to 2 in. long, ultimately developing a yellowish green plum-like fruit 1 to $1\frac{1}{2}$ in. long, surrounded by a malodorous, fleshy layer.

According to ancient Chinese texts, the original home of the ginkgo lay in what are now the provinces of Anwhei and Kiangsu, and it still occurs apparently wild in part of its original habitat, namely in the mountainous region between Anwhei and Chekiang provinces (see further in Li's fascinating work *The Origin and Cultivation of Shade and Ornamental Trees* (1963), Chap. 4). In other parts of China and beyond it is known only as a cultivated tree. It is certainly not indigenous to Japan, as is often stated, although it was introduced from there to Europe about 1730, and to England twenty-four years later. It is undoubtedly one of the most distinct and beautiful of all deciduous trees, the leaves being quite unlike those of any other. The popular name refers to their similarity in shape to the pinnules of the maidenhair fern (*Adiantum*).

Most of the large trees in the British Isles are males but a few female trees have been recorded (see below). The first fruits to be produced in Europe were obtained by grafting of the famous female tree at Geneva on male trees. Female shoots on the old tree at Kew, grafted to it in 1911, fruited abundantly until accidentally pruned off. The female tree has been supposed to be less erect in habit than the male or even to have pendulous branches, but Wilson, who saw numerous trees during his journeys in China, Korea, and Japan, stated that there is no difference in habit between the two sexes.

Although the fleshy part of the fruit has a rancid, evil odour, the kernel of the nut is well flavoured, and esteemed by the Japanese. The ginkgo is best raised from seed, and it requires a deep good soil; when young it is often extremely slow of growth, and although very hardy, is no doubt better suited in climates with a hotter summer than ours. Good seeds are now produced by S. European trees, and offer the best means of propagation.

Of the famous tree at Kew, planted in 1762, the following measurements are on record (all girths at 3 ft): 56 × 9 ft (1888), 62 × $10\frac{1}{4}$ ft (1904); 72 × $13\frac{1}{2}$ ft (1970). This tree was originally planted against a wall of the 'Old Stove', built in 1761 and demolished about a century later. The ancient wisteria nearby was originally trained on this structure.

The following are some of the more noteworthy specimens measured recently: Chiswick House, London, 75 × $8\frac{1}{2}$ ft (1964); Knap Hill Nurseries, Surrey, *pl.* 1859, 62 × $8\frac{1}{4}$ ft (1961); Farnham Castle, Surrey, 75 × $8\frac{3}{4}$ ft (1961); Lydhurst, Sussex, 75 × 6 ft (1971); Linton Park, Kent, *pl.* 1844, 90 × $8\frac{1}{4}$ ft (1965); Penshurst Place, Kent, 80 × $6\frac{3}{4}$ ft (1954); Panshanger, Herts, *pl. c.* 1770, 78 × $12\frac{1}{4}$ ft

(1969); Peckover, Wisbech, Cambs., *pl.* 1762, 76 × 11½ ft (1962); Sherborne Castle, Dorset, 74 × 9¾ ft (1963); Melbury, Dorset, 79 × 6¾ + 4¾ ft and another 72 × 9 ft (1970); Oxford Botanic Garden, 83 × 8¼ ft (1970); Longleat, Wilts, 69 × 10 ft (1963); Badminton, Glos., two trees, 69 × 7¾ ft and 68 × 10 ft (1966); Whitfield, Heref., *pl.* 1776, 68 × 12½ ft (1963); Blaize Castle, Bristol, *pl. c.* 1762, 68 × 12¼ ft (1969); Bath Botanic Garden, 80 × 4½ ft, a fine slender tree (1962); Bitton Vicarage, Som., 74 × 9¾ ft (1959); Engelfield House, Theale, Som., 80 × 11 ft (1968); Carclew, Cornwall, 80 × 10½ ft (1962); Maerlluch, Radnor, *pl.* 1820, 72 × 13½ ft, with a triple trunk (1962).

The trees listed above are all male or of unknown sex. The female tree at Bath mentioned in previous editions grows at Glanfield, Weston Park, Bath, and measures 50 × 5¼ ft (1962). Other female trees have been located by A. F. Mitchell at West Dean, Sussex; Snowdenham House, Surrey; and The Rookeries, Dorking, Surrey.

cv. 'LACINIATA' ('MACROPHYLLA LACINIATA').—Leaves deeply laciniated, wavy at the margins and (according to the original description) 10 in. in circumference (Carrière in *Rev. Hort.* (1854), p. 412). Raised by Reynier of Avignon in 1840 and put into commerce by Sénéclauze's nursery.

f. PENDULA (Van Geert) Beissn.—The epithet *pendula* has no doubt been applied to many specimens of the ginkgo in which the branches are to a greater or lesser degree pendulous. The cultivar name 'PENDULA' would belong to the clone first distributed by Van Geert's nursery in 1862. It was described by Carrière as being weak-growing with a leaning main-stem and pendulous branches.

cv. 'PRAGENSIS'.—This interesting cultivar is referred to by J. P. Krouman in his article 'The Trees of Prague' in *Gard. Chron.* (Oct. 3, 1969), p. 15. According to Mr Krouman there are two specimens at Prague, one in the Botanical Garden of Charles University and the other in the garden of the Neotitz Palace, both estimated to be 150 years old. The specimen figured has a low, spreading, umbrella-shaped crown and tortuous branches.

f. FASTIGIATA (Henry) Rehd.—Of fastigiate habit. Many named clones with this character are in commerce in the United States.

GLEDITSIA LEGUMINOSAE

A small group of pod-bearing, deciduous trees named in honour of Gottlieb Gleditsch, a German professor of botany, who flourished in the 18th century, and was a friend of Linnaeus. They are natives of eastern N. America, China, Japan, and Persia. The leaves are beautifully subdivided into numerous leaflets, pinnately or bipinnately arranged, and the trunks and branches of most species are more or less formidably armed with simple or branched spines. These characters of leaf and stem combined distinguish *Gleditsia* as a genus from all other hardy trees. No gleditsia has any beauty of blossom, the flowers being small, green, and borne in racemes a few inches long. They are sometimes perfect, sometimes unisexual, and differ from most of the Leguminosae we are familiar with in the open air in the petals being uniform, and with no resemblance to the pea-shaped blossom so characteristic of the family. The seeds are produced in pods, varying in length from 1 to 2 in. (in *G. aquatica*) to 20 in. long (in *G. delavayi*). In all except *G. aquatica*, *G. heterophylla*, and *G.* × *texana* the pods contain pulp and numerous seeds, which, however, they do not release, as most of the family do, by splitting. They often become spirally twisted before falling. The species best worth growing are *G. triacanthos* and *G. caspica*, both striking and ornamental-foliaged trees very interesting on account of their huge spines.

Gleditsias should be raised from seed. They are rather tender when young, owing to the habit of growing late in the season, so that the succulent tips are cut back in winter. After a few years the hardier species lose this defect. The cultivars of *G. triacanthos* are increased by grafting or budding on seedlings of the type. They like a good loamy soil and a sunny position, thriving better in the south of England, where the summers are hotter, than in the north; still better in France and Italy.

G. AQUATICA Marsh.   WATER LOCUST
G. inermis Mill.; *G. monosperma* Walt.

A tree described by Sargent as 50 to 60 ft high, with a trunk 2 to 2½ ft in diameter, but in this country inclined to be shrubby, and to form several stems; spines ultimately about 4 in. long, branched; young shoots not downy, but marked with conspicuous lenticels. Leaves up to 8 in. long, simply or doubly pinnate; leaflets of the pinnate leaf (or of each division of the bipinnate ones) twelve to twenty-four. Each leaflet is lanceolate-oblong, 1 to 1½ in. long, ¼ to ½ in. wide, rounded, bluntish, or somewhat pointed at the apex, margins wavy, glossy and glabrous except for the down on the short stalk of the leaflet, on the upper side of the main-stalk, and scattered hairs on the margins of the leaflets. Flowers borne on slender racemes 3 or 4 in. long. Pods obliquely diamond-shaped, 1¾ in. long, nearly 1 in. wide, not pulpy inside; seeds solitary (rarely two).

Native of the south-eastern United States; introduced in 1723, according to Aiton, but now extremely rare. It is hardy at Kew, but grows slowly. Its small, one-seeded pod well distinguishes it, but so far as is known this has not been borne in cultivation here. The example now at Kew, about 35 ft high and branching at 4 ft, came from the Arnold Arboretum in 1892.

G. CASPICA Desf.   CASPIAN LOCUST

A tree 30 to 40 ft high, its trunk excessively armed with formidable, branching, slightly flattened spines, 6 in. or more long; young shoots smooth. Leaves

6 to 10 in. long, simply or doubly pinnate. Leaflets up to twenty on the pinnate leaves, or on each division of the doubly pinnate ones, ovate to oval, 1 to 2 in. long, ⅜ to ¾ in. wide, rounded and with a minute bristle-like tip at the apex, very shallowly round-toothed. The midribs and main leaf-stalk on the upper side, as well as the very short stalk of the leaflet, are downy; the leaf otherwise is glabrous and shining green. Flowers green, almost stalkless, densely arranged on downy racemes, 2 to 4 in. long. Pods scimitar-shaped, usually about 8 in. long, 1 to 1¼ in. wide.

Native of the region immediately south and south-west of the Caspian Sea; introduced, according to Loudon, in 1822. It is a sturdy tree with much larger leaflets than G. *triacanthos*, and is remarkable for the size and number of spines on the trunk, which is, indeed, the most formidably armed among cultivated trees. The species is well worth growing on that account. The leaflets are not so large in this country as on trees grown on the continent. At Vienna I have seen them as much as 2½ in. long, by over 1 in. wide. It is much confused with, and usually grown as G. *sinensis*, a confusion which apparently existed in Loudon's time. There is an example at Kew measuring 60 × 3¾ ft (1968).

G. JAPONICA Miq.
G. *horrida* (Thunb.) Mak., not Salisb.; *Fagara horrida* Thunb.

A tree 60 to 70 ft high, the trunk and branches very formidably armed with branched, slightly flattened spines; young shoots on plants at Kew dark purplish brown, smooth and shining. Leaves simply or doubly pinnate, 8 to 12 in. long, each leaf or leaf-section carrying fourteen to twenty-four leaflets. Leaflets ovate to lanceolate, often unequal at each side of the midrib, blunt to pointed at the apex, margins entire; main-stalk, midrib, and stalk of leaflets downy. In Japanese fruit-bearing specimens the leaflets are ¾ to 1½ in. long, ¼ to ½ in. wide, but in small cultivated trees they are only ⅓ to ⅝ in. long. Pods 8 to 10 in. long, 1 to 1¼ in. wide, scimitar-shaped, ultimately twisted.

Native of Japan; introduced to Kew in 1894, where young trees raised from seed supplied by Boehmer are quite hardy, although slow-growing. When the plants are young, the small leaflets give them a very different aspect to mature specimens, but they are unsurpassed among hardy trees in their fern-like elegance. The species appears to be allied to G. *caspica*, under which by one authority it has been placed. The pulp in the pods, as in G. *sinensis*, is saponaceous, and is used by the Japanese for washing cloth.

There are five examples of this species at Kew; two, from the 1894 introduction, are rather flat-topped, not very shapely trees, about 30 ft high.

G. DELAVAYI Franch.—This species, which seems to be closely allied to G. *japonica*, was introduced by Wilson to Veitch's Coombe Wood nursery in 1900, during his visit to Yunnan. But according to Elwes and Henry (*Tr. Gt. Brit. & Irel.*, Vol. 6, p. 1513), all the seedlings there were killed in the winter of 1905–6. A dried specimen from a tree once cultivated at Kew under the name G. *delavayi* is not that species but agrees better with G. *heterophylla* Bge, a native of N.E. China, not treated in this work. A tree now in the Kew collection, received as *G. delavayi* from a nursery, is also wrongly named, but of uncertain identity.

G. MACRACANTHA Desf.

A deciduous tree 50 to 60 ft high, the trunk armed with great, branched, terete, very stiff spines; shoots glabrous, ribbed, more or less warted. Leaves simply pinnate; leaflets six to twelve, ovate oblong sometimes inclined to obovate, 1 to 3½ in. long, ½ to 1½ in. wide, shallowly toothed, glabrous except on the main and individual very short stalks. Flowers in downy, stalked, simple, slender racemes 3 to 6 in. long. Pods 6 to 13 in. long, about 1½ in. wide, blackish and long-persistent.

G. macracantha was described in 1800 from a tree growing in the garden of the Paris Museum. It was probably raised from seeds collected in Central China and is usually considered to be a native of that region.

G. FEROX Desf.—This species, like the above, was described by Desfontaines from a tree at Paris probably raised from Chinese seeds. His description is scanty and it seems probable that the tree died without ever producing flower or fruit. Schneider's amplified description (*Handbuch*, Vol. 2, p. 10) was made from a tree grown under the name *G. ferox* in the Simon-Louis nurseries early this century. According to Henry, many of the trees cultivated under this name are *G. caspica*.

G. SINENSIS Lam.   [PLATE 41
G. horrida Willd.

A deciduous tree up to 40 or 45 ft in the wild, armed with often branched, terete spines several inches long; young shoots glabrous or soon becoming so. Leaves pinnate, 5 to 8 in. long, composed of eight to fourteen (sometimes more) leaflets, which are ovate or ovate-lanceolate, blunt or pointed, obliquely tapered at the base, margins slightly wavy, 1¼ to 3 in. long, ⅝ to 1⅛ in. wide, downy on the midrib above, soon glabrous elsewhere, net-veined beneath, stalks and rachis downy. Flowers greenish white, in pendulous downy racemes 2½ to 3½ in. long, each flower ¼ in. wide on a downy stalk about ⅓ in. long. Pods 5 to 10 in. long, ¾ to 1¼ in. wide, scarcely curved, dark purplish brown, flat.

Native of China; described and named by Lamarck in 1786 from a tree growing at Versailles. This honey-locust, according to Henry, occurs wild on the mountains near Peking, but there are plants at Kew raised from Wilson's seeds collected in 1908 in Szechwan (W.1214) and distributed under this name. It would seem, therefore, if this identification be correct, to have a wide distribution in China. The old trees in France and Italy came from eastern China. The flowers of this species have no beauty.

To the above it should be added that the tree at Kew, received from the Arnold Arboretum in 1909 under number Wilson 1214 (see above), certainly seems to belong to *G. sinensis*, judging from a recent examination of its foliage. A tree in the University Botanic Garden, Cambridge, measuring 42 × 2½ ft (1968), is certainly authentic.

G. × TEXANA Sarg.

A deciduous tree up to 120 ft high with smooth, pale bark; young shoots glabrous, branches spineless. Leaves 4 to 8 in. long, the main-stalk at first hairy, pinnate or bipinnate, with six or seven pairs of pinnae, each carrying six to sixteen pairs of leaflets which are oblong-ovate, ½ to 1 in. long, very shallowly toothed, apex rounded, scarcely stalked, dark shining green. Flowers in glabrous racemes 3 or 4 in. long, the males dark orange-yellow. Pod flat, 4 to 5 in. long, 1 to 1¼ in. wide, dark chestnut-brown without pulp.

A natural hybrid between *G. triacanthos* and *G. aquatica*, found only in a grove on the bottom lands near Brazoria in Texas, first noted in 1892; introduced to cultivation in 1900. In foliage it is like *G. triacanthos* but differs in having no spines; from *G. aquatica* it differs by its many-seeded pods.

There is a small specimen at Kew, planted 1900.

G. TRIACANTHOS L.   HONEY LOCUST

A tree reaching in the wild 140 ft in height, with a trunk up to 5 or 6 ft in diameter, both it and the branches more or less armed with stout, sharp spines 3 to 12 in. long, and branched. Young shoots slightly downy at the base only;

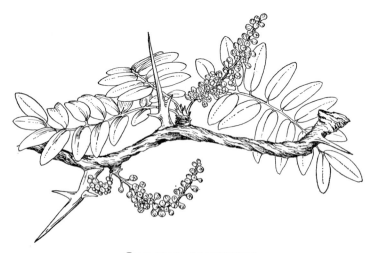

GLEDITSIA TRIACANTHOS

spines when present on them simple or three-forked. Leaves 4 to 8 in. long, either simply or doubly pinnate, the latter confined to vigorous leading shoots; the leaves of the short, flowering twigs are invariably simply pinnate. Leaflets on each pinnate leaf (or section of bipinnate one) fourteen to thirty-two, ½ to 1½ in. long, $\frac{3}{16}$ to $\frac{5}{8}$ in. wide, oblong-lanceolate, mostly rounded at the apex, wavy or shallowly toothed at the margin, glossy dark green; both surfaces at first downy. Male flowers green, crowded on downy, often clustered racemes about 2 in. long; female racemes few-flowered. Fruits more or less scimitar-shaped, 1 to 1½ ft long, 1 to 1½ in. wide, dark shining brown. Native of central N. America; introduced in 1700. The honey locust is the best of the genus in this country, and deserves to be more commonly planted than it is, not only for its interest but for the beautiful fern-like foliage, which turns a clear bright yellow in autumn. The spines are not so formidably developed in this country as on the continent, nor do they develop in woods or shady spots as they do in places fully exposed. It only occasionally bears fruit with us, never with the freedom and regularity seen in more sunny climates, e.g., in the south of France. A tree well laden with dry pods, rattling with every fitful movement of the air, makes rather a weird sound in the dusk. The popular name refers to the likeness of the tree in foliage to the locust (*Robinia*), and to the thick, succulent, sweetish pulp in which the seeds are set.

There are two large specimens of *G. triacanthos* at Kew measuring 60 × 6¼ ft and 60 × 5¼ ft (1965) (see also f. *inermis*). Other examples measured recently are: St James's Park, London, 58 × 5 ft (1963); Syon House, London, 50 × 3¾ ft (1967); Mote Park, Maidstone, Kent, 57 × 5¼ ft (1965); Avington House, Hants, 56 × 5½ ft (1965); Wilton House, Wilts, 68 × 5½ ft (1961); Pampisford, Cambs., 54 × 5¾ ft (1959).

cv. 'BUJOTII' ('PENDULA').—A very elegant, pendulous tree; branches and branchlets very slender; leaflets narrower than in the type, often mottled with white.

cv. 'ELEGANTISSIMA'.—A variety of dense, shrubby habit with elegant foliage, raised by the nurseryman Charles Breton of Orleans around 1880. The original plant attained a height of about 13 ft in twenty-five years; an old plant at Wakehurst Place, Sussex, is about 25 ft high.

f. INERMIS (L.) Zab. *G. inermis* L.—Some trees appear never to bear thorns, and have been distinguished by this name; but unarmed plants are said to occur among batches of seedlings raised from thorn-bearing trees. In the USA, where the honey locust is much used as a street tree, unarmed trees are preferred, for obvious reasons. Many named clones of this nature are in commerce there, the best known being 'MORAINE', patented in 1949. This is sterile, as are some of the others, the absence of pods being another merit so far as street-planting is concerned, in those countries where they are borne.

The following specimens of the unarmed form have been recorded: Kew, 58 × 5½ (1968); University Botanic Garden, Cambridge, 65 × 6½ ft (1969); Pampisford, Cambs., 75 × 6¼ ft (1969).

cv. 'NANA'.—The name *G. t.* var. *nana* was published by Henry in 1907, in reference to a tree growing at Kew. He described it as 'a small, round-headed tree of compact habit with dark green foliage, and leaflets shorter and broader than in the type'. There are in fact three trees at Kew under this name. One, received from Simon-Louis Frères in 1888, is now (1970) 45 ft high; this may be the plant that Henry had in mind. The other two, of unknown provenance, are 43 and 52 ft high respectively. Henry suggested that this variant might be the same as the *G. sinensis* var. *nana* of Loudon.

cv. 'Sunburst'.—Leaves golden yellow in spring, becoming green later; unarmed. Raised in the United States and patented in 1954. One of the most striking of golden-leaved trees.

GLOBULARIA   GLOBULARIACEAE

A genus of about twenty-eight species, natives of the Canary and Cape Verde Islands, southern and central Europe, and Asia Minor. Flowers bisexual, united into a globular head, surrounded at the base by a many-bracted involucre. Calyx five-lobed. Corolla two-lipped, the upper lip short, two-lobed, the lower three-lobed. Stamens four, inserted on the corolla-tube. Ovary superior, with a single style. Fruit a one-seeded nut-let, surrounded by the persistent calyx. The only other genus in the family is confined to Somaliland and Socotra.

G. CORDIFOLIA L.   [PLATE 43

An evergreen prostrate shrub forming tufts or mats 2 to 4 in. high, the root-stock and lower parts woody; young shoots glabrous, purplish, often creeping. Leaves alternate, wedge-shaped, once or twice notched at the broad rounded apex, tapered gradually to the base, ¾ to 1½ in. long (including the long, slender stalk), ⅛ to ⅜ in. wide, margins towards the apex often wavy or faintly crenulate. Flowers blue, closely packed in a hemispherical head ½ to ¾ in. wide, borne at the top of an erect glabrous stalk 1½ to 4 in. high. Corolla two-lipped, the upper lip two-lobed, the lower one three-lobed, all the lobes linear. Calyx five-lobed, hairy, the lobes awl-shaped. Stamens four, conspicuously exposed.

Native of the Alps, Tyrol, and mountains of S. Europe, usually in rocky places and in limestone districts; cultivated in England in 1633, according to Aiton. It flowers in July and August and is worth a place in the rock garden for its neat close habit and its pretty heads of blue flowers with prominently outstanding stamens. Increased by division or by cuttings.

GLYPTOSTROBUS   TAXODIACEAE

A monotypic genus allied to *Taxodium*, from which it differs in the stalked cones, broadest near the apex, and in the winged seeds.

G. LINEATUS (Poir.) Druce

Thuja lineata Poir.; *G. pensilis* (Staunton) K. Koch; *Thuja pensilis* Staunton

The Chinese swamp cypress is a small deciduous tree with glabrous young shoots. As in the nearly related *Taxodium distichum* the young shoots are of two kinds: 1) persistent and bearing axillary buds; 2) deciduous and without any buds. The former, which are usually terminal, bear the leaves spirally round the twig; the latter bear the leaves distichously (that is, arranged in two opposite rows) and they fall off in autumn, carrying the leaves with them. The leaves also are of two kinds: those on the budless, deciduous twigs are linear, $\frac{1}{4}$ to $\frac{1}{2}$ in. long, $\frac{1}{20}$ in. wide, pointed or bluntish; those on cone-bearing twigs short, scale-like, $\frac{1}{12}$ to $\frac{1}{8}$ in. long. There are also others of intermediate size. Cones obovoid or pear-shaped, $\frac{3}{4}$ to 1 in. long, $\frac{3}{8}$ to $\frac{1}{2}$ in. wide towards the top.

Native of S. China, in damp places, known mainly as a cultivated tree; there are specimens in the Kew Herbarium from Kwantung, Fukien, and Chekiang provinces. The twigs and leaf arrangement very much resemble those of the American swamp cypress. It is not hardy at Kew, but plants grown in pots under glass are very charming for many weeks in autumn and early winter for the soft glowing red of the fading leaves. According to Henry, the Chinese peasants plant it on the north side of their villages to bring luck to the home, and amongst the rice fields to increase the crop.

This species is very rare in British gardens. There is an example at Nymans, Sussex, about seventy years old, measuring 12 × 1 ft (1968), and a smaller one grows against a wall at Leonardslee in the same county. The plant at Exbury mentioned in previous editions died recently.

GORDONIA THEACEAE

A genus of some forty species of trees and shrubs, all save one (the American *G. lasianthus*) natives of E. Asia, allied to *Camellia* and *Stuartia*. The name commemorates James Gordon (*d.* 1781), who had a celebrated nursery at Mile End, London, and is best known as the introducer of the maidenhair tree, *Ginkgo biloba*.

G. AXILLARIS (Roxb.) D. Dietr.   [PLATE 44

Camellia axillaris Roxb. ex Ker; *G. anomala* Spreng.; *Polyspora axillaris* (Roxb.) Sweet

An evergreen shrub or small tree; young shoots smooth, grey. Leaves shortly stalked, stout, very leathery, oblanceolate to oblong, tapered more gradually towards the base than to the often blunt apex, shallowly toothed towards the end only, 2½ to 7½ in. long, ¾ to 2½ in. wide, glabrous and dark glossy green. Flowers creamy white, 3 to 6 in. wide, solitary on very short stalks produced from the terminal part of the shoot. Petals five or six, 1½ in. wide, deeply notched; stamens very numerous; anthers yellow. Fruits erect, oblong, 1¼ to 1½ in. long, ⅝ in. wide, hard and woody, the hardened sepals persisting below. *Bot. Mag.*, t. 4019.

Native of China and Formosa; first named *"Camellia axillaris"* by Roxburgh, whose description was published by Ker in 1818, and figured under that name in the *Botanical Magazine*, t. 2047, the following year. So poor was this figure that another plate in the same periodical was allotted to the species in 1843. It has been cultivated in a cool greenhouse at Kew for many years, but in Cornwall and other places is grown in the open air. In flower it resembles a single white camellia and at its best is very beautiful. Both Wilson and Forrest found it plentifully in western China. It likes a soil free from calcareous matter. Its flowering season is an intermittent one extending from November to May and the flower-buds are frequently killed by frost.

G. CHRYSANDRA Cowan—This species was discovered by Forrest in 1912 west of Tengyueh near the frontier between Yunnan and Burma; he appears to have introduced it in 1917 under F.15559, collected at 9,000 ft on the western flank of the Tali range, where it makes a large shrub 20 to 30 ft high. First described in 1931, this species differs from *G. axillaris* chiefly in its smaller leaves (up to about 4 in. long) and smaller flowers (about 2 in. or slightly more wide). It has been so little tried out-of-doors that it would not be possible to state whether or not it is less tender than *G. axillaris*; it is likely, in any case, to be bud-tender. In the Edinburgh Botanic Garden it is grown under glass and has never survived when planted outside. There was a specimen in the old Temperate House at Wisley which flowered well in January and February. Propagation is by cuttings of nearly ripened wood. *Bot. Mag.*, n.s., t. 285.

G. LASIANTHUS (L.) Ellis *Hypericum lasianthum* L. LOBLOLLY BAY.—This American species scarcely merits more than a short mention, since not only is it tender but, like the related *Franklinia alatamaha*, it needs considerable summer heat. It is an evergreen tree growing to about 70 ft high, found in the coastal parts of the south-eastern USA from southern Virginia to Florida and Louisiana. The white flowers, measuring 2½ in. across, are borne on stalks about 3 in. long —a character which serves to distinguish it from *G. axillaris*, in which the flowers are very shortly stalked. *Bot. Mag.*, t. 668.

GRABOWSKIA   SOLANACEAE

A genus of about twelve species in S. America, allied to *Lycium*. It was named in honour of Dr Grabowski, a Silesian botanist of the 18th century.

G. BOERHAAVIFOLIA (L.) Schlecht.

Lycium boerhaavifolium L.

A deciduous shrub 6 to 10 ft high, of loose, spreading habit; young branches glabrous, armed with sharp spines which are ¼ in. long the first year, but grow longer. Leaves alternate, grey, fleshy, roundish, widely ovate or obovate, 1 to 1½ in. long, ¾ to 1¼ in. wide, wavy at the margin, tapering at the base, glabrous; stalk ¼ in. or less long. Flowers ⅖ in. long and wide, produced in May, sometimes singly on a short stalk in the leaf-axils, sometimes in terminal or axillary racemes 1 in. long; corolla pale blue, tubular at the base, spreading to five reflexed lobes; calyx ⅙ in. long, bell-shaped, with five angular teeth.

Native of Brazil and Peru; introduced in 1807, but rarely seen. Near London it requires the protection of a south wall. The foliage resembles that of *Atriplex halimus*, and the flowers are like those of *Lycium chinense*. It has little more than botanical interest.

GREVILLEA   PROTEACEAE

The remarkable family Proteaceae, which is almost wholly confined to the southern hemisphere, contains but few species that can be cultivated out-of-doors in the British Isles with any chance of survival, and many of these belong to *Grevillea*. This genus is most abundantly represented in the Australian subcontinent but extends to New Caledonia and the Celebes. The species described here show well the characteristic flower structure of the family. The floral envelope is not differentiated into calyx and corolla but consists of a perianth ('calyx-tube') made up of four valvate segments which are more or less united in the bud stage but separate as the flowers develop. The four stamens are placed opposite the perianth segments, and in *Grevillea* they are united to them, the anthers being sessile and inserted in the concave ends of the segments. The fruits in *Grevillea* are pod-like and contain one or two seeds.

Propagation is by means of half-ripened shoots taken about July, and placed in a frame with a little bottom heat. They enjoy a proportion of peat in the soil and are not suitable for limy soils.

The genus was named by Robert Brown in honour of Charles Francis Greville (1749–1809), once a Vice-President of the Royal Society, to whom the botanists of his period were 'indebted for the introduction and cultivation of many rare and interesting plants'.

G. ACANTHIFOLIA A. Cunn.

An evergreen plant 4 to 6 ft high; young shoots slightly angular and glabrous except for a few whitish hairs at first. Leaves 2 to 3 in. long, 1 to 1¼ in. wide, bipinnately lobed, the five or six primary lobes $\frac{1}{2}$ to $\frac{3}{4}$ in. long, reaching nearly to the midrib, again cut into three triangular lobes, each lobe ending in a stiff spine, dark dull green and glabrous except for a few pale hairs when young similar to those on the shoot; stalk $\frac{1}{4}$ to $\frac{1}{2}$ in. long. Inflorescence terminal or axillary, $1\frac{1}{2}$ to 3 in. long, with the closely packed flowers all on one side. Flowers dull pink, each about $\frac{1}{2}$ in. long except for the long, strongly curved, glabrous style so characteristic of the grevilleas, which stands out $\frac{5}{8}$ in. beyond the rest of the flower; they have no petals and the calyx is four-lobed, rather bellied below, the lobed part strongly curved. A feature of the inflorescence is the dense furnishing of silky white hairs that cover the flower-stalk, ovary, and calyx. *Bot. Mag.*, t. 2807.

Native of the Blue Mountains, New South Wales, where it was found by Allan Cunningham in 1817; it was introduced soon after. It is evidently hardier than is generally supposed for it was grown out-of-doors at Nymans, near Handcross in Sussex, for a good many years until it perished in the winter of 1928–9. It flowers in May, and whilst the blossom is more curious than attractive, the much-divided, stiff, prickly foliage makes it a distinct and handsome evergreen.

G. ALPINA Lindl.

G. alpestris Meissn.

An evergreen shrub usually dwarf and under 2 ft high in gardens, of bushy rounded shape; young shoots clothed with spreading hairs. Leaves set on the twigs several to the inch, narrowly oblong or oval, blunt-ended, $\frac{1}{3}$ to 1 in. long, $\frac{1}{12}$ to $\frac{1}{4}$ in. wide, but made narrower by their recurved margins; dark green, downy, minutely warted above; silky-hairy beneath, stalkless. Flowers produced about five together in terminal clusters, the perianth (calyx) about $\frac{1}{2}$ in. long, curved, swollen at the base, red at the lower part, yellow upwards, downy. A conspicuous part of the flower is the stout downy style with its knob-like stigma standing out $\frac{1}{4}$ in. beyond the calyx and of a similar colour. *Bot. Mag.*, t. 5007.

Native of South Australia in mountainous districts; first flowered in this country apparently by Messrs Rollisson of Tooting in May 1857. It is very frequently shown in spring at the Royal Horticultural Society's meetings grown in pots. Although in a climate like that of Kew its tenure as an outdoor shrub is insecure and often short, it is about as hardy as *G. sulphurea*, and (say) thirty miles south of London, is well worth growing in a sunny sheltered spot in the rock garden. It blooms freely and over a long season, but the red of the flowers is not particularly bright.

G. ROSMARINIFOLIA A. Cunn.

An evergreen shrub of loose, graceful habit 6 or 7 ft high, with slender, downy branches. Leaves alternate, closely set on the branches, very like those of rosemary, 1 to 2 in. long, averaging $\frac{1}{8}$ in. wide, stalkless, pointed, dark grey-green and rough above, covered beneath with closely pressed silvery hairs. Flowers deep rosy-red, densely arranged in terminal racemes, each flower 1 in. or less long, on a glabrous stalk ¼ in. long. Perianth silky inside, glabrous outside, scarcely ½ in. long. with hooked divisions, two long and two short, in the apex of each of which is enclosed an anther; styles about ¾ in. long, red. *Bot. Mag.*, t. 5971.

Native of New South Wales; discovered by Allan Cunningham in 1822. Near London this shrub will only survive mild winters but has succeeded and flowered well at Grayswood Hill, Haslemere. In Cornwall it is quite at home, and makes fine bushes 6 or 7 ft high, and twice or thrice as much wide.

G. SULPHUREA A. Cunn.

G. *juniperina* var. *sulphurea* (A. Cunn.) Benth.

An evergreen bush of sturdy habit, probably 6 ft high ultimately; young shoots very downy. Leaves linear or needle-like, ½ to 1 in. long, $\frac{1}{16}$ to $\frac{1}{12}$ in. wide, made narrower by the curling back of the margins, prickly pointed, pale beneath, glabrous except for a few appressed hairs beneath when young, produced in alternate .closely set tufts. Flowers pale yellow, produced during May

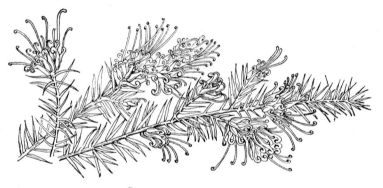

GREVILLEA SULPHUREA

and June at the end of short lateral twigs in a short raceme (almost an umbel) of a dozen or more blossoms. The perianth is a slender tube ½ in. long, covered on the outside with silky hairs, and slit deeply on one side; the inch-long style protrudes through the slit, and the concave, dilated ends of the four divisions of the calyx are curled back, each enclosing a stalkless anther. Seed-vessel a dry, spindle-shaped pod ½ in. long, with the erect style still attached at the end.

Native of New South Wales. This interesting and pretty shrub is the hardiest of grevilleas. It is not really hardy except against a warm, sheltered wall in south-eastern England but with this protection grows and flowers well. It is admirably adapted for Cornwall and other mild counties.

GREWIA   TILIACEAE

The genus was named by Linnaeus in honour of Dr Nehemiah Grew, who wrote works on the anatomy of plants, and died in London in 1712. It is allied to the limes, but is confined to Asia and Africa, containing numerous species. The inner bark has the tough fibrous nature characteristic of the family.

G. BILOBA G. Don

G. parviflora var. *glabrescens* Rehd. & Wils.

This species is mainly represented in cultivation by the following variety:

var. PARVIFLORA (Bge.) Hand.-Mazz.   *G. parviflora* Bge.—A deciduous shrub 6 to 8 ft high, with the young shoots and leaves furnished with starlike down. Leaves alternate, ovate, or sometimes three-lobed, rounded, slightly heart-shaped, or tapered at the base, pointed at the apex, 2 to 5 in. long, half to two-thirds as wide, rough to the touch above, downy beneath. Flowers creamy yellow, with numerous yellow stamens; about ½ in. across; produced during July and August, in small axillary umbels of about six flowers on the shoots of the year. Fruits roundish, orange or red, ¼ in. wide.

Native of N. China and Korea; introduced in 1888. It is of little value in gardens, and not very hardy with us, probably needing a hotter summer than ours. The finest specimen I have seen in Europe was in the collection of the late Mr de Vilmorin, at Les Barres in France. When I saw it, it was 7 ft high and 10 ft through, flowering freely in July. It flowers a month later in England.

G. biloba in its typical state is a native of E. China and Formosa. It differs from the above variety in its longer and relatively narrower leaves, which are glabrous above and less downy beneath, but the distinction is not very well marked and intermediate states occur.

G. OPTIVA Drummond ex Burret   *G. oppositifolia* Buch.-Ham. ex D. Don, not DC.—This species is sometimes seen in cultivation but is not so hardy as *G. biloba*. It is widely cultivated along the foothills of the Himalaya, in the Salt Range of the Punjab and farther west, the foliage being stacked for winter fodder, the drupes eaten and the wood used in carpentry. It is believed to be wild in Garwhal and Kumaon and perhaps also in Nepal. It is very distinct from *G. biloba* in bearing the flowers in a short inflorescence on the opposite side of the shoot to that where the leaf-stalk is attached. Flowers yellowish; fruits black.

GRINDELIA   COMPOSITAE

A genus of about sixty species, natives of western N. America and S. America. Most are perennial and several are sub-shrubs. The generic name commemorates David H. Grindel, a Russian botanist of German origin, 1776–1836.

G. CHILOENSIS (Cornelissen) Cabrera

Hoorebekia chiloensis Cornelissen; *Grindelia speciosa* Hook. & Arn.

An evergreen shrub of bushy shape 2 to 3 ft high and as much or more wide, with thick stems woody at the base which produce annually stout, erect, semi-herbaceous shoots, sticky to the touch, scurfy, and densely clothed with leaves over their whole length. Leaves linear-oblong to oblanceolate, pointed, tapering at the base, the margins usually more or less toothed, often coarsely, shortly or not at all stalked, 2 to 4½ in. long, ⅓ to ¾ in. wide, grey-green, sticky when young, ultimately thickly sprinkled with small circular patches of dried gum. Flower-heads produced during the summer singly from the end of the shoot on a stout erect stalk up to 12 or 15 in. long; they are about 3 in. wide, both the ray- and the disk-florets of a rich bright yellow; ray-florets pointed, about 1 in. long, ⅛ to 3/16 in. wide. Bracts of the involucre awl-shaped to narrowly triangular, ⅜ to ½ in. long. *Bot. Mag.*, t. 9471.

A native of Argentina in dry places from about 30° to 50° S., and probably also occurring in bordering parts of Chile. It was first described from a plant growing in the Ghent Botanic Garden, said to have been raised from seeds received from Chile, though the epithet *chiloensis*, which implies that it came from the island of Chiloe off the Pacific coast of Chile, may have been given in error, since it is unlikely to occur so far west.

It seems originally to have been introduced to Britain by H. Wooler of Upper Tulse Hill, about 1850, seeds having been sent to him by his son, who found it just above high-water mark at a place called New Bay on the coast of Patagonia. In 1911 it was flowered at The Elms, Yalding, Kent, by Captain S. G. Reid. The plants at present in cultivation were raised from seed collected in 1925–6 by H. F. Comber. It is grown at Kew, and in many of the gardens in the south of England, in all places hardy but more truly shrubby in the warmer places. Wooler, its first cultivator, was quite successful with it over ninety years ago. According to Lindley and Paxton, who figure it in their *Flower Garden*, iii, p. 119, he had thirty to forty flower-heads open on his plant at one time. An interesting character of the plant is the coating of pale gum which covers the top of the flower-head whilst it is in the bud state. The flowers are not very agreeably scented but the young shoots have a pleasant and slightly aromatic fragrance.

GRISELINIA   CORNACAEAE

A genus of six species of trees and shrubs, natives of New Zealand, Chile, and S.E. Brazil. Two species are found in the former country, both of which are cultivated out-of-doors in the milder parts of the British Isles.

They are somewhat tender, especially *G. lucida*, but where they thrive make handsome evergreens. Male and female flowers are produced on different plants; they are quite small, dull coloured, and of no ornament. The attractions of both species are in their shapely habit and shining foliage (though in some forms of *G. littoralis* the leaves are dull green). In both species the male flowers have five minute, tooth-like sepals, five spreading petals, and five stamens. The female flowers consist of an inferior ovary surmounted by three short spreading styles; in *G. lucida* they have minute sepals but no petals, while in *G. littoralis* petals are present but the sepals are lacking or scarcely visible.

G. LITTORALIS (Raoul) Raoul

Pukateria littoralis Raoul

A large evergreen shrub or small tree up to 60 ft in the wild; trunk furrowed, young stems greenish yellow. Leaves leathery, oval or ovate, 1 to 4½ in. long; half to two-thirds as wide (occasionally almost as broad as long), usually glossy above medium green or yellowish green, glabrous, the apex blunt, the base slightly unequal-sided but often more or less symmetrical; stalk yellowish, ½ to ¾ in. long. Flowers yellowish green, small, produced during May in axillary racemes or panicles 1 to 3 in. long. Fruits oblong, ¼ in. long.

Native of New Zealand up to 3,500 ft altitude; cultivated at Kew since the middle of the last century, but only hardy there in mild winters or with the protection of a wall. Perhaps the climate of the Thames Valley does not suit it, for there are many inland gardens in the southern and western parts of the country where it is hardy. It may be too that some clones are more tender than others, as might be expected in a species with such a wide range, both in latitude and altitude. In the western and south-western parts of the country it makes an excellent shelter plant against the Atlantic winds. It has no objection to chalky soils.

Being completely dioecious and usually represented in any one garden by a single clone, *G. littoralis* is not often seen in fruit. But at Inverewe in north-western Scotland both sexes are grown and self-sown seedlings appear in abundance.

In previous editions a tree at Kilmacurragh in Co. Wicklow was mentioned, then 20 ft high. This is now 45 ft high and 11 ft in girth at 1 ft (1966). In other western gardens, and at Wakehurst Place in Sussex, it is almost as high though of smaller girth.

G. littoralis is variable in the relative width of its leaves. The more common form, of which there are both male and female clones, has leaves on the average slightly over half as broad as long and not markedly oblique at the base. But some cultivated plants have relatively broader leaves (often almost as broad as long), more lop-sided at the base. It is likely that some plants of this character have been wrongly called *G. lucida*. These broad-leaved plants, like the commoner form, also occur in both sexes: those at Exbury are male, but the similar tree at Tresco Abbey in the Isles of Scilly is female. In both gardens the leaves are dull green.

G. littoralis strikes very readily from cuttings of half-ripened wood in gentle heat, or of somewhat harder wood under handlights.

cv. 'VARIEGATA'.—Leaves with a whitish marginal variegation which is very irregular in width and often interrupted; centre grey-green, splashed with dark glossy green. On young leaves the marginal variegation is golden and the centre bright green. This striking variety evidently derives from a broad-leaved form of the species, but from one with dark, glossy leaves. Perhaps the oldest and largest plant in the British Isles grows at Tresco Abbey in the Isles of Scilly; a handsome pair, probably propagated from it, can be seen by one of the gates of the Morrab Gardens, Penzance. A peculiarity of this variety is that it frequently produces a branch sport in which the variegation is at the centre of the leaf instead of at the margin; this can be perpetuated by cuttings.

G. LUCIDA (J. R. & G. Forst.) Forst. f.

Scopolia lucida J. R. & G. Forst.; *G. lucida* var. *macrophylla* Hook. f.

An evergreen species of variable habit in the wild, sometimes a small tree rarely more than 30 ft high and 3 ft in girth, sometimes a small shrub found growing on rocks or the branches of trees. Leaves leathery, thick, glossy as if varnished, rich green, oblong or broadly ovate, 4 to 7 in. long, 2 to 5 in. wide, glabrous on both sides, markedly unequal at the base; stalk 1 to 1½ in. long. Flowers small, green, in axillary panicles almost as long as the leaves (3 to 6 in. long); female ones without petals. Fruits ⅓ in. long, purple.

Native of New Zealand at low altitudes, and only hardy in Cornwall and similar localities. At Kew it will not survive permanently even against a wall. The true species is grown at Tresco Abbey in the Isles of Scilly and no doubt in other gardens in the milder parts. But some plants under its name may be large-leaved forms of *G. littoralis*.

Being tender, *G. lucida* is not so useful a shrub as *G. littoralis*, although from the larger size of its leaves it is more striking. Propagated by grafting on *G. littoralis*.

GYMNOCLADUS   LEGUMINOSAE

A genus consisting of four deciduous, pod-bearing trees, one native of N. America, the others of E. Asia, and most nearly related among hardy trees to *Gleditsia*. They have doubly pinnate leaves, flowers in racemes or panicles, and large thick pods; the flowers are regular, being composed of five equal-sized petals, and a tubular, five-lobed calyx, with no indication of the pea-flower shape so common in this family.

G. DIOICA (L.) K. Koch   KENTUCKY COFFEE-TREE

Guilandina dioica L.; *G. canadensis* Lam.

A deciduous tree up to 110 ft high, with a trunk 6 to 10 ft in girth, usually branching low down, and forming a narrow, rounded head. Branchlets downy when young, light grey, marked by numerous small scars. Leaves up to 3 ft long and 2 ft wide, bipinnate, the two lowest pairs of pinnae being simple leaflets, but the upper ones composed of four to seven pairs of leaflets; the leaflets are ovate, 1½ to 2½ in. long (the two lowest pairs considerably larger), grey-green and hairy beneath, principally on the veins and midrib. The tree is dioecious, the panicles of the female tree being 8 to 12 in. long, 3 to 4 in. wide, narrowly pyramidal; flowers downy, ¾ to 1 in. long; petals greenish white, calyx not quite so long as the petals, tubular at the base, with five linear teeth. In the male tree the inflorescence is about one-third the length of the females. Pods 6 to 10 in. long, 1½ to 2 in. wide.

Native of the eastern and central United States; cultivated in England before the middle of the 18th century. In its foliage it is perhaps the most beautiful of all hardy trees. It is perfectly hardy in the south of England, but grows extremely slowly, and rarely flowers. It evidently needs more summer heat than it gets here, for there are fine specimens both in France and Germany suggesting in their leafless state the habit and branching of the horse chestnut. In autumn a curious effect is produced by the leaflets falling off and leaving the naked common stalk on the branches for some time. In winter, young trees have a very distinct and rather gaunt appearance, the branches being few, thick, and rough. It likes a deep rich soil and is propagated by imported seeds. The common name is said to have originated through the people of Kentucky and Tennessee at one time roasting and grinding the seeds to make a beverage like coffee.

The largest specimens in Britain so far recorded are all in the south-eastern part of the country. They are: Nymans, Sussex, 55 × 5 ft (1966); Kew 47 × 4¾ ft and 37 × 3 ft (1964–6); Dulwich College Road, London, 45 × 2 ft (1957); Linton Park, Kent, 47 × 2¾ ft (1965). There is an old tree in the Oxford Botanic Garden which is dying back; it measures 49 × 4¾ ft (1970). The best specimen in the country was at Claremont, Surrey; it attained 60 × 7 ft and flowered regularly, but no longer exists. In Eire there is one at Ashbourne House, Co. Cork, measuring 46 × 4½ ft (1966). There is a white-variegated form, of no beauty.

G. CHINENSIS Baill.—A tree up to 40 ft high, with leaves 1 to 3 ft long, each of the pinnae consisting of twenty to twenty-four oblong leaflets, ¾ to 1½ in. long, silky beneath. Flowers lilac-purple, both perfect and unisexual, borne on the same tree, in downy racemes. Pods 4 in. long, 1½ in. wide. Native of China, and said by Henry to be rather rare. Introduced to Kew in 1888, but not hardy there.

HAKEA proteaceae

A genus of about 100 species of shrubs and small trees, endemic to Australia (including Tasmania, with about nine species). The genus is most numerously represented in western Australia and there the most beautiful species are found, none of them likely to be satisfactory even in the mildest parts.

Hakea is allied to *Grevillea*, but differs in its axillary inflorescences, woody fruits, and samara-like seeds. Some species make useful hedging plants in Australia, California, etc. Several, notably *H. gibbosa* Cav., have become noxious weeds in South Africa, usurping the place of the native flora where it has been weakened by fire-damage. Perhaps the most ornamental species of *Hakea*, and the best-known, is H. laurina R. Br., cultivated on the French and Italian Rivieras. Known in Australia as the sea-urchin or pincushion hakea, it has red flowers with long-exserted yellow styles, arranged in dense clusters. It is in cultivation at Tresco Abbey in the Isles of Scilly but does not thrive even there.

H. lissosperma R. Br.

H. acicularis var. *lissosperma* (R. Br.) Benth.; *H. sericea* var. *lissosperma* (R. Br.)
Maiden & Betche

In cultivation this species makes an erect-branched shrub 8 to 10 ft high, but in the wild may be tree-like and up to 20 ft high; branches stout. Young shoots, leaves, and flower-stalks covered at first with silky hairs, later glabrous. Leaves simple, erect, 1½ to 5 in. long, circular in cross-section, very rigid, pungently pointed at the apex, narrowed at the base. Flowers white or creamy white, in axillary almost sessile clusters of six or more. Individual flower-buds tubular, bent and swollen at the apex. Perianth-segments narrowly lanceolate, free to the base when the flower is fully expanded. Fruits about 1 in. long, roundish, woody, wrinkled or warted, shortly beaked or unbeaked. Seeds smooth on both sides.

Native of Tasmania, where it ascends to an altitude of 4,000 ft, and of Victoria and New South Wales. Probably the plants now in cultivation derive from the seeds collected by H. F. Comber during his expedition to Tasmania in 1929–30. It is an interesting shrub, much resembling a conifer when seen from a distance, but the flowers make little display. It is hardy from mid-Sussex westward in a sunny sheltered position and occasionally fruits. There is a fine group at Nymans in Sussex, growing in an exposed position; they are seedlings of the plants raised originally from the seeds sent by Comber.

H. sericea Schrad. & J. Wendl. (1797) *Banksia tenuifolia* Salisb. (1796); *Hakea tenuifolia* Dum.-Cours. (*nom. nov.*, 1805); *Hakea tenuifolia* (Salisb.) Britten (1916); *Hakea acicularis* (Sm. ex Vent.) Knight (1809); *Conchium aciculare* Sm. ex Vent. (1803)—Resembling the preceding but with more slender, shorter leaves (1 to 3 in. long), more spreading, not narrowed at the base, and having fruits with a pronounced beak. *Bot. Mag.*, n.s., t. 229 (as *H. tenuifolia*). Native of

Tasmania, Victoria, and New South Wales. It was introduced before 1796 but
has probably not been in cultivation continuously since then. The material for
the plate in the *Botanical Magazine* came from a plant growing in a cool greenhouse in the Oxford Botanic Garden. It flowers there in December and January and produces fertile seeds. In the milder parts it would probably be hardy
and attain a height of 8 to 10 ft. The flowers are tinged with pink in some forms.

It should be noted that although *H. acicularis* is a synonym of *H. sericea*
some of the plants grown under that name may be *H. lissosperma*.

H. MICROCARPA R. Br.—A shrub 2 to 8 ft high. Leaves terete, spine-
pointed, 1 to 3½ in. long, erect or slightly spreading. Flowers white or cream-
coloured in small axillary clusters. Fruits flattish, obliquely obovate, beaked,

HAKEA MICROCARPA

⅜ to ½ in. long, with smooth rather thin valves. Native of E. Australia and Tasmania. Raised from seeds collected by Lord Talbot de Malahide in Tasmania, it
has proved quite hardy at Jermyns House, Romsey, and fruits freely there.

HALESIA   SILVER BELL OR SNOWDROP TREE
STYRACACEAE

In British gardens the snowdrop trees are almost exclusively represented
by the beautiful *H. carolina* and the still finer but much more recently

introduced *H. monticola*. A third species, *H. diptera*, is sometimes seen. A fourth species, *H.* PARVIFLORA Michx., a native of S. Georgia and Florida, is not known in cultivation in the British Isles and appears to be inferior to the above in ornamental value. It is not further treated in this work. All these species are from the south-eastern USA. There is also one species in China.

The leading characters of the genus are the pendulous snowdrop-like flowers, produced in clusters on the previous year's wood; the inferior ovary; and the winged fruits. The family Styracaceae is also represented in gardens by species of *Pterostyrax*, *Rehderodendron*, *Sinojackia*, and *Styrax*, but from all of these *Halesia* is distinguished by the combination of characters given above.

The halesias like a moist, well-drained soil, and thrive best in a sheltered, sunny position. Propagation is by seeds and layers.

The genus was named in honour of Dr Stephen Hales, the pioneer physiologist, who was born at Bekesbourne, in Kent, in 1671, and died at Teddington in 1761.

H. CAROLINA L.

H. tetraptera Ellis; *H. parviflora* Lindl., not Michx.; *H. carolina* var. *glabrescens* Perkins; *H. stenocarpa* K. Koch; *H. carolina* var. *stenocarpa* (Koch) Bean

A deciduous tree 20 to 30 ft high in this country; said to be occasionally twice as high in its native places, with a trunk 3 ft in thickness. With us it is of spreading habit, often a shrub; young shoots at first clothed with stellate down. Leaves ovate, ovate-oblong, or elliptic, acute or acuminate at the apex, wedge-shaped or rounded at the base, 2 to 5 in. long, minutely toothed, downy or glabrous above, covered beneath with grey stellate down, densely so in var. *mollis* (see below); stalk ¼ to ⅔ in. long, downy. Flowers produced in May on slender, downy, pendulous stalks ½ to 1 in. long, in clusters of three to five from the joints of the naked, year-old wood. Corolla white, bell-shaped, ½ to ¾ in. long and wide, shallowly four-lobed. Fruits somewhat pear-shaped, but with four prominent wings running lengthwise and an awl-shaped termination; altogether about 1½ in. long. *Bot. Mag.*, t. 910.

Native of the south-eastern United States; introduced by J. E. Ellis in 1756. It is undoubtedly one of the most beautiful flowering trees introduced to this country from N. America: yet it is by no means abundantly planted. There is a fine example at Kew on the north-west side of the Broad Walk, about 16 ft high and more than twice that in spread (1970).

A distinction is usually made between what is said to be the typical state of the species, in which the leaves are relatively narrow and their indumentum thin, and var. MOLLIS (Lange) Perkins, in which the leaves are broader and the indumentum denser. According to Sargent, the two states occur together, with var. *mollis* predominating in Florida. The distinction is hardly worth making in gardens and the above description comprises both.

f. DIALYPETALA (Rehd.) Schneid. *H. tetraptera* f. *dialypetala* Rehd.— Corolla divided almost to the base.

T S—L

HALESIA CAROLINA

cv. 'MEEHANII'.—This was raised from seed in Meehan's nursery, German-town, Philadelphia. It differs from ordinary *H. carolina* in its smaller, shorter-stalked flowers; the corolla is more cup-shaped; leaves thicker and more coarsely wrinkled. May be a hybrid.

NOTE

H. stenocarpa K. Koch (*H. carolina* var. *stenocarpa* (Koch) Bean) was the name given to a plant with narrow, elongated-elliptic fruits attenuated to base and apex. In the Elwes and Henry herbarium preserved at Kew there is a specimen from a tree at Syon Park, collected August 1910, with such fruits. No doubt it represents the plant des-cribed in their *Trees of Great Britain and Ireland*, Vol. 6, p. 1602, as *H. stenocarpa*. Accord-ing to Henry, it has the corolla divided nearly to the base and hairy filaments as in *H. diptera*, but the foliage and four-winged fruits of *H. carolina*, and hence Henry thought it might be a hybrid between the two species as Koch had suggested. But Koch described the corolla as four-lobed (as in *H. carolina*). Rehder follows Perkins, the monographer of the genus, in sinking *H. stenocarpa* in *H. carolina*, while recognising the plants with corolla divided almost to the base as a *forma* (see above).

H. DIPTERA Ellis

A deciduous shrub 8 to 15 ft high (occasionally a small tree twice as high in the wild); young branches stellately downy at first. Leaves elliptic or obovate, 3 to 5½ in. long, 1½ to 3 in. wide, minutely and rather distantly toothed, abruptly pointed, wedge-shaped or rounded at the base, downy on both sides on first opening, but soon almost glabrous except on the midrib and veins beneath; stalk ½ to ¾ in. long. Flowers pendulous, produced in May in clusters or short racemes from the joints of the year-old wood; stalks ½ to ¾ in. long, slender, downy. Corolla bell-shaped, ¾ in. long, deeply four-lobed, white; calyx very downy; stamens hairy. Fruits oblong, 1½ to 2 in. long, ¾ in. wide, with two longitudinal wings ¼ to ⅜ in. wide, ending in a short spike.

Native of the south-eastern United States; introduced in 1758. This is far from being as good a garden plant as *H. carolina* or *monticola*; it is less hardy and is shy-flowering. It grows well, and is over 12 ft high at Kew, but never flowers as it does in France, especially south of Paris. Easily distinguished from *H. carolina* by the two-winged fruits.

The tree at Kew mentioned above was 20 ft high in 1946 but died a few years later, when about fifty years old. It bore flowers about ¾ in. long, as described above, which seems to be about the upper limit for the normal state of *H. diptera*.

This species received an Award of Merit when shown from Borde Hill, Sussex, in 1948. This plant still exists, but does not thrive and rarely flowers. It was raised from seeds collected from cultivated trees on the Vanderbilt Estate at Biltmore, N. Carolina, by the New York Botanical Garden Expedition to the Appalachians (1933) under field number NY 157. The trees there were said to be variable in size of flower.

var. MAGNIFLORA Godfrey—This is distinguished from the typical variety by its larger flowers, ¾ to 1¼ in. long, and by its different habitat—upland woodland in contrast to the flood-plain woodland where the typical variety is found (Kurz and Godfrey, *Trees of Northern Florida*, pp. 263, 265 and fig. 168; and see also the discussion by R. de Belder in *Journ. R.H.S.*, Vol. 94 (1969), pp. 90–91). M. de Belder states that a floriferous tree in the Kalmthout Arboretum, Belgium, belongs to this variety and also refers to it the tree in M. de Vilmorin's collection at Verrières, suggesting that it is this tree that Mr Bean had in mind when he said that *H. diptera* flowered well in France 'especially south of Paris', which is almost certainly the case. It is possible that the variety *magniflora* would prove a greater success in Britain than typical *H. diptera*, coming as it does from upland locations.

H. MONTICOLA (Rehd.) Sarg.   MOUNTAIN SNOWDROP TREE
H. carolina var. *monticola* Rehd.   [PLATE 45

A deciduous tree often 80 to 100 ft high in the wild, with a trunk 3 ft in diameter and free of branches for more than half its height. It grows at altitudes of not less than 3,000 ft on the mountains of the S.E. United States where, according to Sargent, it is an important timber tree. Botanically it is evidently very nearly related to the well-known snowdrop tree, *H. carolina*, differing in its larger flowers, larger fruit, and of course in size, for *H. carolina* rarely attains more than one-third its stature and is indeed more usually a shrub with us than even a small tree. *H. monticola* is distinct also in its bark, which separates from the trunk in large, loose, plate-like scales, whereas the main stem of *H. carolina* has a close bark with only small appressed scales. The leaves scarcely differ from those of *H. carolina* in shape or size. When unfolding they are downy above and beneath, but once unfolded they are glabrous above and the undersides too become glabrous apart from scattered hairs on the midrib and main veins. The flowers are ¾ to 1 in. long and up to 1 in. or even slightly more wide at the mouth. Fruits 1¾ to 2 in. long, 1 in. wide.

The distribution of *H. monticola* is given by Sargent as western North Carolina, eastern Tennessee, and western Georgia. It gives way westward to var. VESTITA Sarg., which is distributed from North Carolina to Arkansas and eastern Oklahoma. In this variety young leaves are densely coated beneath with white wool and remain downy beneath even at maturity. The flowers in this variety are sometimes flushed with rose (f. ROSEA Sarg.).

H. monticola was first separated from *H. carolina* as late as 1913, and then only as a variety. It was given specific rank by Sargent in 1922.

This beautiful tree is fast-growing and flowers when young. Some specimens are of conical habit with well-developed single or double leaders, but others have made bushy crowns and are unlikely ever to become tall trees.

So far as is known there are no grounds for the belief that the var. *vestita* has larger flowers than the typical variety, the difference between them being only in the indumentum of the leaves, which is really of no horticultural significance. The tree that received an Award of Merit in 1958 when shown by the Crown Commissioners is referable to the var. *vestita* and has large flowers. But there are glabrous-leaved trees just as fine, and some examples of the var. *vestita* have rather small flowers, both varieties being variable in this respect.

× HALIMIOCISTUS   CISTACEAE

A genus of hybrids between *Cistus* and *Halimium*, which occur occasionally in the wild. Of those described below, only × *H. wintonensis* is of garden origin.

× H. 'INGWERSENII'

× *H. ingwersenii* E. F. Warb., *nom. inedit.*

A low procumbent shrub 1 to 1½ ft high; stems and inflorescence axes clad with long erect hairs intermixed with much shorter ones. Leaves linear-lanceolate, ¾ to 1⅜ in. long, ⅛ to 3/16 in. wide, with revolute margins, three-veined, sessile, upper surface dark green with scattered stellate hairs and shorter simple hairs, densely stellate-tomentose beneath. Flowering branches slender, produced from the axils of the leaves or of leaf-like bracts, bearing a terminal umbel-like cyme subtended by a pair of boat-shaped acuminate bracts; lower bract-pairs sterile or subtending solitary flowers. Sepals four (on specimen examined, but probably varying from three to five), furnished with long spreading hairs, the outer pair ovate. Flowers 1 in. or slightly more across, with white petals. Style very short.

A natural hybrid, probably between *Halimium umbellatum* and *Cistus psilosepalus* (*hirsutus*), discovered by W. E. Th. Ingwersen in Portugal around 1929 and introduced by him. The name given to it by E. F. Warburg appears in the Kew *Hand-list* of 1934 but has never been validated by a Latin description. × *H.* 'Ingwersenii' is a pretty shrub of low, mounded habit, bearing its white flowers over a long period (May–July). It is hardy.

× H. REVOLII (Coste & Soulié) Dansereau
Cistus revolii Coste & Soulié

A dwarf densely branched shrub 1 to 2 ft high; stems densely covered with white, spreading hairs. Leaves elliptic to broadly so, obtuse to rounded at the apex, cuneate at the base, $\frac{1}{4}$ to $\frac{3}{4}$ in. long, $\frac{1}{8}$ to $\frac{1}{4}$ in. wide, the lower ones green above and short-stalked, the upper ones sessile, grey-hairy above, all leaves hairy beneath; venation pinnate, prominent beneath. Flowers in terminal cymes. Sepals mostly five, silky-hairy on the outside. Petals white, yellow at the base (or pale yellow with a deeper yellow base). Ovary glabrous; stigma sessile.

A natural hybrid between *Halimium alyssoides* and *Cistus salviifolius*, described from a plant found in 1914 in the Cevennes, France, on the borders between the departments of Ardèche and Gard; introduced by Sir Oscar Warburg and his son E. F. Warburg and first shown by the former from his garden at Epsom in 1936. It is a pretty, moderately hardy shrub, flowering June and July. The flowers remain open until late afternoon.

× H. SAHUCII (Coste & Soulié) Janchen   [PLATE 46
Cistus sahucii Coste & Soulié

A natural bigeneric hybrid between *Halimium umbellatum* and *Cistus salviifolius* found wild in France. It was introduced and cultivated first by Sir Oscar Warburg in his garden at Boidier near Epsom about 1929. Being very attractive and satisfactorily hardy, it has become pretty well known in gardens. It is an evergreen shrub, 15 to 18 in. high, of spreading but close growth, with linear to linear-oblanceolate leaves, $\frac{1}{3}$ to $1\frac{1}{2}$ in. long and $\frac{1}{12}$ to $\frac{3}{16}$ in. wide, hairy especially beneath. Flowers white, up to $1\frac{1}{8}$ in. across, opening in June and borne in abundance.

× H. WINTONENSIS O. & E. F. Warb.

This is a hybrid raised in Messrs Hillier's nursery at Winchester and it originated from *Halimium lasianthum* or *ocymoides* crossed with *Cistus salviifolius*. It is an evergreen shrub of bushy, rather spreading habit and $1\frac{1}{2}$ to 2 ft high. The young shoots are covered with a soft white wool as are also the leaves, both becoming a dull green later. Leaves elliptic-lanceolate, pointed, tapered at the base rather prominently three-nerved, ¾ to 2 in. long, scarcely stalked. Flowers 2 in. wide, the five petals white, broadly wedge-shaped, each having a crimson-maroon blotch towards the base, which gives the flower a striking zone of colour, the actual base being marked with a bright yellow, triangular patch. These successive zones of white, crimson, and yellow give the blossom a beauty as unusual as it is conspicuous. It is admirable for a sunny, rather dry spot in the rock garden or elsewhere, but has not a very strong constitution. The flowers often keep open well on in the afternoon. It is scarcely hardy enough to withstand a severe winter except in the milder counties, but survives our ordinary winters near London. It flowers in May and June.

HALIMIUM   CISTACEAE

A genus of about seven species closely related to *Helianthemum*, to which they have been united. They differ from that genus in having a very short, straight style and three or five sepals, whereas *Helianthemum* has an elongated style, curved or bent at the base, and always five sepals. They require the same cultural conditions, and have no objection to chalky soils.

The genus *Halimium*, as here understood, is confined to the Old World, and has its centre of distribution in the Iberian peninsula, but ranges as far east as Syria and into France and N. Africa. Allied species in N. America, included in *Halimium* by Grosser, and earlier placed in the genus *Crocanthemum*, are not treated in this work.

H. ALYSSOIDES (Lam.) K. Koch

Cistus alyssoides Lam.; *Helianthemum alyssoides* (Lam.) Vent.; *Cistus scabrosus* Ait.; *Helianthemum scabrosum* (Ait.) Pers.

A shrub about 2 ft high, but twice as much in diameter, forming a low mound of tangled, slender, spreading branches, densely clothed with grey, partly starry down. Leaves narrowly obovate or oblong to ovate-lanceolate, mostly tapered at the base, rounded or blunt at the apex, ⅓ to 1¼ in. long, ⅛ to ½ in. wide, grey with a dense down. Flowers in a branched, terminal hairy corymb; each flower 1½ to 1¾ in. diameter, bright yellow, unblotched. Sepals three, ovate, pointed, densely but shortly hairy, ⅓ in. long; flower-stalk thickening upwards.

Native of the north-western part of the Iberian peninsula, and also of western and central France, where it extends east as far as the Massif Central and north to the region of Le Mans and Orleans; in cultivation 1775. It is allied to *H. lasianthum* but differs in having shorter hairs on the sepals and pedicels, in the absence of purplish bristles on the calyx, and in the always unspotted petals. The low, spreading form described above is not reliably hardy, but the species has such a wide north–south range that it is likely to vary in hardiness, as it certainly does in habit, some wild plants being erect-branched and up to 3 ft high. Also, the plant described above, having the leaves grey and hairy above, probably came from the southern part of the area of the species. More commonly, *H. alyssoides* has the leaves green above.

H. ATRIPLICIFOLIUM (Lam.) Spach

Cistus atriplicifolius Lam.; *Helianthemum atriplicifolium* (Lam.) Willd.

A shrub 4 to 6 ft high in the wild; young stems clad with short hairs and with a more persistent coating of whitish scales. Leaves scaly and silvery on both sides, those on the non-flowering shoots stalked, pinnately veined, elliptic to broadly so, ¾ to 2 in. long; leaves immediately below the flowering stems sessile, oblong, cordate at the base, with three or five more or less parallel veins. Flowering stems leafless, rigid, up to 8 in. or more long, with conspicuous, long, spreading, often purplish hairs and a dense coating of short, whitish, matted hairs; cymes rather sparsely arranged, with two to eight flowers, which are 1½ to 1¾ in. across; petals bright yellow, unmarked or with a brown spot at the base; sepals three, hairy, not scaly.

A native of central and south Spain and of Morocco. The date of introduction is not certain, but the plant cultivated by Philip Miller and described by him under the name *Cistus halimifolius* sounds more like *H. atriplicifolium* than *H. halimifolium* (*Gard. Dict.* (1768), under 'The seventeenth sort'). According to Loudon there was an introduction in 1826, but Sweet could not find a plant and the species is consequently not figured in his *Cistineae* (1830). Although the finest of the halimiums it is also the most tender and the rarest in gardens. It is only likely to be confused with *H. halimifolium*, but in that species the flowering stems are scaly and lack the spreading hairs seen in *H. atriplicifolium*; also, its calyx is scaly and has two linear outer sepals, lacking in *H. atriplicifolium*. Some authorities state that this species always has the petals spotted at the base, but there is an excellent flowering specimen in the Kew Herbarium in which the petals are unmarked, and another, from the Ronda–Marbella road, which, according to the field-note, had pure yellow petals.

H. HALIMIFOLIUM (L.) Willk. & Lange

Cistus halimifolius L.; *Helianthemum halimifolium* (L.) Willd.

A densely branched shrub attaining a height of 6 ft in the wild; branches erect, scaly, downy and white when young. Leaves narrowly obovate or elliptic, rounded or acute at the apex, tapered at the base, the lower ones shortly stalked, the upper sessile, ¾ to 1¾ in. long, ¼ to ¾ in. wide, white and tomentose on both sides when young, becoming dull grey-green with age, with a permanent coating of scales and stellate hairs. Flowering stems scaly. Cymes sometimes densely arranged in a short panicle-like inflorescence, sometimes more widely spaced along the main axis. Flowers about 1½ in. across; petals yellow, wedge-shaped or inversely heart-shaped, with or without a dark spot on the base; sepals five, the outer two much narrower and shorter than the inner three, scaly and sometimes with simple or stellate hairs also.

H. halimifolium is the most widely distributed of the yellow-flowered species, ranging from Spain and Portugal through Corsica and Sardinia to S.E. Italy and from Morocco to Algeria; it is absent from the mainland of France. The above description covers all the main variations of the species, of which two subspecies are recognised in *Flora Europaea:*

subsp. HALIMIFOLIUM.—The typical subspecies with the flower-bearing laterals rather widely spaced; sepals scaly but not hairy; petals wedge-shaped. Found throughout the range of the species.

subsp. MULTIFLORUM (Dun.) Maire *H. multiflorum* Dun.; *H. halimifolium* f. *multiflorum* (Dun.) Grosser—Not so tall-growing as the typical subspecies. Cymes more densely arranged. Sepals with stellate hairs as well as scales. Petals inversely heart-shaped. Portugal, S.W. Spain, and Morocco.

Grosser also recognises f. LASIOCALYCINUM (Boiss. & Reut.) Grosser, which seems to belong to the typical subspecies, but has simple hairs on the calyx as well as the usual scales. Described from Morocco.

H. halimifolium is believed to be the species listed in the catalogue of Tradescant's garden as *Cistus halimi folio.* If so, it would have been in cultivation in the middle of the 17th century. It is not hardy and seems always to have been less common in gardens than the dwarfer species. The subspecies *multiflorum*, being of more compact habit, would receive more protection from snow and might be hardier than the taller forms.

H. LASIANTHUM (Lam.) Spach   [PLATE 47

Cistus lasianthus Lam.; *Helianthemum lasianthum* (Lam.) Pers.

H. lasianthum is mainly represented in cultivation by the following subspecies (and by a form with unblotched flowers mentioned below):

subsp. FORMOSUM (Curt.) Heywood *Cistus formosus* Curt.; *Helianthemum formosum* (Curt.) Dun.; *Helianthemum lasianthum* subsp. *formosum* (Curt.) Coutinho—A low shrub with wide-spreading branches, growing 2 to 3 ft high, but more in width, the young shoots erect, the whole plant grey with short down intermixed with which are numerous whitish, stellate or long simple hairs. Leaves oblong, oval or obovate, ½ to 1½ in. long, ¼ to ½ in. wide, three-nerved at the narrowed base, the apex rounded or abruptly pointed. Flowers borne at the end of short side twigs, clustered, but appearing successively; each flower 1½ in. in diameter, bright rich yellow, each petal with a conspicuous brownish purple blotch near, but not reaching to the base. Sepals three, ovate, taper-pointed, with long, silky hairs and often with purplish bristles.

Native of S. Portugal; introduced in 1780; perhaps the most beautiful of all the sun roses we cultivate. It is perfectly hardy, and I have never seen it permanently injured by frost—even 30° to 32°. It is admirable for covering a dry sunny bank, and remains well furnished with foliage through the winter. It starts to flower in May.

In the typical state of *H. lasianthum* the flowers are smaller and the petals are unblotched or have a small blotch right at the base.

HALIMIUM LASIANTHUM

The unblotched form of *H. lasianthum* (f. CONCOLOR Hort.) has been in cultivation since early in this century and perhaps longer. But some of the plants of this form now in gardens descend from a seedling collected by Hugh Farmar in 1948 in the foothills of the Sierra de Estrela, Portugal, which was propagated and distributed by Messrs Notcutt (*Journ. R.H.S.*, Vol. 88 (1963), p. 262). This clone has proved very hardy.

H. OCYMOIDES (Lam.) Willk. & Lange

Cistus ocymoides Lam.; *Helianthemum ocymoides* (Lam.) Pers.; *Helianthemum algarvense* (Sims) Dun.; *Cistus algarvensis* Sims

An erect shrub 2 to 3 ft high, more rarely procumbent (see below); young shoots clothed with a dense white down, with which are mixed long silky hairs. Leaves three-nerved, those on sterile axillary shoots obovate, up to $\frac{5}{8}$ in. long and $\frac{3}{16}$ in. wide, covered with a close, white down, shortly stalked; those on the flowering shoots larger, being up to $1\frac{3}{16}$ in. long and $\frac{5}{16}$ in. wide, obovate to oblanceolate, sessile, green, deciduous. Panicles erect, but loose and comparatively few-flowered, 3 to 9 in. high, sparsely hairy; flower-stalks slender. Flowers rich yellow, 1 to $1\frac{1}{4}$ in. across, petals triangular, with a black and purple blotch at the base of each. Sepals three, oval-lanceolate, sparsely hairy, or glabrous and glossy.

Native of Portugal and Spain; introduced shortly before 1800. It is a very pretty species, noteworthy for the golden yellow of its flowers and the deeply coloured blotch. It is hardy except in severe winters. It most resembles *H. alyssoides* and *H. halimifolium*, but from the former differs in the blotched petals, and glabrous or nearly glabrous sepals. It is never scaly, as in *H. halimifolium*, and the petal blotch is much deeper.

The first introduction of this species was of prostrate habit and was grown under the name *Helianthemum algarvense*. It is figured in *Bot. Mag.*, t. 627.

H. UMBELLATUM (L.) Spach

Cistus umbellatus L.; *Helianthemum umbellatum* (L.) Mill.

An evergreen bush of erect, open habit about 18 in. high, with the general aspect of a small rosemary; young branches viscid and downy. Leaves linear, viscid when young; stalkless, $\frac{1}{2}$ to $1\frac{1}{4}$ in. long, $\frac{1}{12}$ to $\frac{1}{8}$ in. wide; dark glossy green above, white with down beneath. Racemes erect, 4 to 6 in. high, with the flowers arranged at intervals in whorls, and terminating in a six- or eight-flowered umbel at the top. Flowers white, $\frac{3}{4}$ in. across, the petals inversely heart-shaped, with a yellow stain near the base. Sepals three, ovate, more or less hairy. *Bot. Mag.*, t. 9141.

Native of the Mediterranean region; introduced in 1731. This is a distinct and very pretty shrub.

H. umbellatum is a somewhat variable species but cannot be subdivided into clear-cut categories. The inflorescence may consist of several whorls as in the plant described above, or of a single terminal cyme which is sometimes accompanied by two opposite flowers or reduced cymes in the upper leaf-axils. There is also variation in habit from spreading to erect, and in the degree of viscidness of the stems and leaves. *H. viscosum* (Willk.) Silva and *H. verticillatum* (Brot.) Sennen are both part of *H. umbellatum* in the broad sense.

A halimium found in Syria and Palestine, named *H. syriacum* by Boissier, is of procumbent habit with tortuous whitish or greyish branches marked by black, densely set, annular leaf scars. This belongs to *H. umbellatum* and is scarcely worthy of recognition even as a variety. Similar plants occur in France.

H. COMMUTATUM Pau *H. libanotis* Lange, in part; *Helianthemum libanotis* Willd., in part; not *Cistus libanotis* L.—A low-growing shrub usually under 2 ft high. Leaves linear, with revolute margins, $\frac{1}{2}$ to $1\frac{1}{2}$ in. long, $\frac{1}{16}$ to $\frac{3}{16}$ in. wide, glabrous above, white-hairy beneath. Flowers solitary or in few-flowered cymes, yellow, about 1 in. wide; sepals three, glabrous. Native of Portugal, W. Morocco, and S. Spain. It is a pretty, free-flowering shrub, but not reliably hardy.

HALIMODENDRON LEGUMINOSEAE

A genus of a single species, allied to *Caragana*, differing in the purplish flowers and the stalked, oblong or obovate, very inflated pods.

H. HALODENDRON (Pall.) Schneid. SALT TREE

Robinia halodendron Pall.; *Halimodendron argenteum* (Lam.) DC.; *Caragana argentea* Lam.

A deciduous shrub, naturally 4 to 6 ft high, with very spiny, spreading, somewhat angular branches, greyish, and covered with a fine down when young. Leaves pinnate, composed usually of two pairs of leaflets, the common stalk

ending in a stiff spine, which remains after the fall of the leaflets. The latter are
¾ to 1½ in. long, ⅛ to ¼ in. wide, oblanceolate, stalkless, tapering to the base, and
covered with a minute, grey down. Flowers two to four together on racemes
2 in. long, produced from short leafy spurs on the old wood; each flower ⅝ in.
long, with pale purplish pink petals and a bell-shaped, five-toothed, downy
calyx. Pods ½ to 1 in. long, ¼ to ½ in. wide, inflated, produced on a stalk protruding beyond the persistent calyx. *Bot. Mag.*, t. 1016.

Native mainly of Russian central Asia, but extending into Mongolia, the
region south and south-west of the Caspian Sea and the steppe region north of
the Black Sea. In central Asia it is a characteristic member of the interesting
'tugai' vegetation which grows on moist, salt-rich soil in the flood-plains of the
rivers that flow from the Tian Shan into the Aral Sea and Lake Balkash. It was
introduced by Dr William Pitcairn in 1779. It is best grafted on *Caragana
arborescens*, to which it is near allied, but laburnum has also been used as the
stock. Standards 4 to 5 ft high should be chosen so as to display the very graceful
habit of the plant. In this way it forms a small round-headed tree whose lower
branches are pendent. It flowers in June and July, and very freely on well-
ripened wood. At such times its elegance of growth, its abundant flowers, and
its handsome grey foliage render it very attractive.

It is said that this species can also be grown satisfactorily on its own roots,
raised from seed or (according to Loudon) from root-cuttings.

cv. 'Purpureum'.—This has deeper rosy-purple flowers. Propagated by
grafting.

HAMAMELIS   Witch-Hazel   HAMAMELIDACEAE

A remarkable and beautiful genus of small trees and shrubs, consisting
of four or five species. They are distinguished very readily from all other
hardy shrubs by the thin, narrow, yellow petals, sometimes ¾ in. long,
and only $\frac{1}{16}$ to $\frac{1}{12}$ in. wide. The leaves are alternate, and much resemble
those of our native hazel. This resemblance led the early settlers in N.
America to use branches of *H. virginiana* as divining-rods—as hazel twigs
were (and still are) at home; to its supposed magic property it owes its
popular name. The parts of the flower are in four.

The witch-hazels like a good, but not very heavy soil, and are benefited
in a young or not well-rooted state if peat and leaf-soil are added. When
established this is not necessary. The quaint habit of the species is one of
their charms, but without interfering with this it is worth while to train
up a leading shoot to obtain height, especially if the plants, as they often
do, assume and retain a low, sprawling mode of growth. The Asiatic
species graft easily on *H. virginiana*. It is best to establish a quantity of
seedlings of the latter in pots, and put on the scions about the beginning
of April, they should then be placed in gentle heat. Seeds, it must be
remembered, frequently take two years to germinate.

An excellent account of the species and cultivars of *Hamamelis* by Roy Lancaster was published in *Gardeners' Chronicle*, Vol. 167 (1970), Nos. 21–24 (May 22–June 12). There is also much useful information in H. J. Grootendorst's *Hamamelis*, published in *Dendroflora*, No. 2 (1965). To both of these works we are indebted for some of the information about the newer cultivars given here.

H. × INTERMEDIA Rehd.

H. japollis Lange

A group of hybrids between *H. japonica* and *H. mollis*, originally described by Rehder in 1945 from plants growing in the Arnold Arboretum, the seed parent of which was *H. mollis* (the Wilson introduction), and the pollen parent a yellow-flowered *H. japonica*. The foliage of these hybrids was described by Rehder as being intermediate between those of the parents in shape and indumentum. It is very likely that some of the seedlings of *H. mollis* raised and distributed over the past half-century belong to *H.* × *intermedia*. At any rate, plants under the name *H. mollis* have been noted which differ from that species in having the leaves narrower at the base, darker green above, more sparsely downy beneath and with longer and more slender stalks.

Some of the best known witch-hazel hybrids were raised at Kalmthout in Belgium, where as early as 1902 the nurseryman Kort had a collection of the species and cultivars then known (*Rev. Hort. Belg.*, Vol. 28 (1902), p. 61). Later he must certainly have added the newer introductions, including *H. mollis* and *H. japonica* var. *flavopurpurascens*. In the late 1920s this nursery fell into decay, but after the second world war part of the site was purchased by MM. Georges and Robert de Belder, who have carried on the work started by Kort. In a lecture to the Royal Horticultural Society Robert de Belder said of these Kalmthout hybrids: 'I am still doubtful about the origin of our plants. I presume that they were originally seedlings of a plant labelled *H. japonica* var. *flavopurpurascens*. There are two possibilities: either the plant that we grow at Kalmthout under that name is a hybrid already or the plant, being a form of *japonica*, has been pollinated by *mollis* and, subsequently, by intermediate forms. Either way, the large *intermedia* plants that we grow show hybrid vigour and are very fertile. This enables us to raise thousands of seedlings for selection. Flower colour varies from pale to dark yellow, orange, red and dark red' (*Journ. R.H.S.*, Vol. 94 (1969), p. 85).

Varieties of *H.* × *intermedia* have also been raised in Britain, Denmark, Germany and Japan. The following is only a selection, and further information can be found in the works cited in the introductory note to *Hamamelis*.

'ARNOLD PROMISE'.—A selection from the typical plants of *H.* × *intermedia* raised at the Arnold Arboretum, named in 1963. The original plant there, thirty-five years old, is 18 ft high, 20 ft across and colours reddish in the autumn (Wyman, *Shrubs and Vines for American Gardens*, 1969). It is as yet scarcely known in Britain.

'HILTINGBURY'.—A seedling of *H. japonica* var. *flavopurpurascens* raised by

Messrs Hillier before 1945. It is inferior in flower to the newer hybrids but the leaves colour well in the autumn.

'JELENA'.—Flowers bright copper-orange when seen from a distance in sunshine, but the petals are really bi-coloured, described as Jasper Red at the base, passing to Yellow Ochre. Free-flowering and vigorous. A.M. 1955. It was raised at Kalmthout by Kort but first named by MM. de Belder after they took over the property.

'FEUERZAUBER' ('Fire Charm', 'Magic Fire').—Flowers copper-red, fragrant, the petals about ⅝ in. long. Raised by Messrs Hesse of Weener. Said to be an improvement on the older 'RUBY GLOW' (syn. 'Adonis'), which was raised by Kort at Kalmthout in 1935 and originally distributed as *H. japonica flavopurpurascens superba*.

'ORANGE BEAUTY'.—Flowers deep yellow verging on orange-yellow, fragrant and freely borne. A seedling from *H. mollis*, pollinated by *H. japonica*, raised by Heinrich Bruns in Germany and originally distributed under the name 'Orange'. A variety from Japan, named 'WINTER BEAUTY', is said to be similar but with longer petals, brownish red at the base (Grootendorst, *Dendroflora*, op. cit., pp. 16 and 17).

H. JAPONICA Sieb. & Zucc.   JAPANESE WITCH-HAZEL

A deciduous, spreading shrub or small tree, often sparsely branched; the quite young twigs furnished with stellate hairs. Leaves oval, ovate or obovate, 2 to 3½ in. long, 1¼ to 2½ in. wide, with wavy margins, base unequal and sometimes slightly heart-shaped; the five to eight pairs of parallel veins run forward at an acute angle from the midrib; lower surface densely covered when young with down which mostly falls away by autumn; stalk ¼ to ¾ in. long, downy. Flowers yellow, slightly scented, produced a few together in globose heads during January and February on the then leafless twigs made the previous summer; petals ⅔ in. long, very narrow, strap-shaped, and much crumpled; calyx-lobes, downy outside, red, reddish-brown or greenish inside.

Native of Japan. This is one of the most beautiful of winter or early spring-flowering shrubs. It flowers freely, and its thin wrinkled petals make a very pretty picture at the inclement season when they appear, especially if the shrub has a dark background of evergreens. The species is a somewhat variable one, the shrub grown in gardens as *H. japonica* is a flattish, widespreading shrub.

var. ARBOREA (Mast.) Gumbleton *H. arborea* Ottolander ex Mast.; *H. japonica* var. *rubra* Kache—This is not a very well-marked variety. Masters, describing *H. arborea* (*Gard. Chron.* (Feb. 7, 1874), p. 187), said it was being offered under that name by the nurseryman Ottolander of Boskoop (who received his stock from Siebold) and also by Cripps's nursery, Tunbridge Wells. The flowers were described as rich primrose, with the calyx of a deep claret colour. A few years later (in 1881) Veitch's nursery received a First Class Certificate for a hamamelis under the name *H. arborea* in which the leaves were narrower than in the plant described by Masters, the petals less crumpled, and golden yellow. This is the plant figured in *Bot. Mag.*, t. 6659, and was probably introduced by Veitch directly from Japan. No doubt many other slightly differing forms have been raised. The plants cultivated under the name *H. japonica* var. *arborea* grow taller than what is considered to be typical *H. japonica* and have a deeper coloured calyx, but it is doubtful if the distinction is worth maintaining or even valid. The plants originally distributed as *H. japonica* are no more typical than those called var. *arborea*.

var. FLAVOPURPURASCENS (Mak.) Rehd. *H. obtusata* f. *flavopurpurascens* Mak.; *H. incarnata* Mak.; *H. obtusata* Mak. (*nom. illegit.*); *H. japonica* var. *obtusata* (Mak.) Ohwi; *H. japonica* var. *rubra* Hort. ex Bean, not Kache—This witch-hazel was shown in flower as "*H. japonica rubra*" at one of the early spring shows of the Royal Horticultural Society in 1919, which was the first time I had seen it. It differs from ordinary *H. japonica* in the petals being suffused with dull red, giving them a rather indeterminate hue; the calyx is dark purple inside. It appears to be wild in several provinces of Japan: Oshima, Musashi, Mutsu, etc., having been collected in the last-named as long ago as 1880. To my taste, the red suffusion in the petals rather spoils, than improves, the clear yellow of the type. It was described as a new species by Mr Makino in the *Tokyo Botanical Magazine* for 1913, under the name *H. incarnata*. Whilst it does not seem likely that the world contains another hamamelis that would be as distinct from *mollis* and *japonica* as they are from each other, probably slightly varying forms of *H. japonica* will continue to appear.

To the above, which is taken unchanged from previous editions, it should be added that the plant shown in 1919 as *H. japonica rubra* may be the same as the variety distributed by Chenault of Orleans before 1915, as *H. zuccariniana rubra*. The name *H. japonica rubra* was given by Kache in 1919 to a plant with yellow petals and a deep red calyx.

cv. 'SULPHUREA'.—Petals pale yellow, about ⅔ in. long, very crumpled. Calyx red on the inside. A.M. Jan. 21, 1958. Raised by Messrs Russell of Windlesham.

cv. 'ZUCCARINIANA'.—The plants cultivated under the name *H. japonica zuccariniana* are probably all of a single clone, characterised by the pale lemon-yellow flowers borne towards the end of the witch-hazel season (late February and March) and the greenish inside of the calyx. It is of erect habit when young, broadening later, and attains about 15 ft in height. The flowering branch depicted in *Bot. Mag.*, n.s., t. 420, came from one of several plants growing in Windsor Great Park.

H. MOLLIS Oliver   CHINESE WITCH-HAZEL [PLATE 48

A deciduous shrub or small tree, with stout, zigzag, spreading branches, very downy when young. Leaves roundish or very broadly obovate, shortly and abruptly pointed, heart-shaped, but unequal-sided at the base, 3 to 5 in. long, three-fourths as broad, widely and shallowly toothed, covered beneath with clustered (stellate) hairs; stalk ¼ in. long, stout and downy. Flowers rich golden yellow, very fragrant, produced in stalkless, crowded clusters from December to February on the twigs of the previous summer's growth; petals strap-shaped, about ⅝ in. long, not wavy as in *H. japonica*; calyx-lobes rich red-brown, hairy outside, glabrous within. Seeds jet black. *Bot. Mag.*, t. 7884.

A native of western and western central China; described in 1888 from specimens collected by Augustine Henry near Patung, in Hupeh province. Some years earlier—in 1879—Charles Maries had sent seeds of this species to Messrs Veitch from the district of Kiu-kiang near the Yangtze River, but the one plant raised from these seeds grew unrecognised in the Coombe Wood nursery for almost twenty years, thought to be a superior form of *H. japonica*. This plant was identified by George Nicholson, the Curator of Kew, around 1898, and only then, it seems, did Messrs Veitch start to propagate it. A few years later, Wilson collected specimens of *H. mollis* during his Veitch expedition to China, but whether he also sent seeds is not known (neither of the specimens from this expedition in the Kew Herbarium are in ripe fruit). He certainly reintroduced the species in 1907–8 when collecting for the Arnold Arboretum, by means of both seeds and living plants.

H. mollis is undoubtedly the finest of all the species, both as regards flower and foliage; and because of the early date at which it flowers (it is often in full bloom on Christmas Day), it has made a very precious addition to the garden flora. It received a First Class Certificate in 1918 when shown by Messrs Robert Veitch of Exeter and an Award of Garden Merit four years later.

For many years *H. mollis* was rare in gardens and probably represented mainly or wholly by the Maries clone, which makes a bush of spreading habit. A recent introduction to commerce is *H. mollis* 'GOLDCREST', which was raised at Bodnant, probably from seeds collected by Wilson. It makes a large sparsely branched shrub with ascending branches and flowers unusually late, usually from mid-February to mid-March or later. The petals are deep golden yellow, suffused with crimson at the base. A.M. 1961.

The following clones are usually placed under *H. mollis* but are probably of hybrid origin:

H. 'BREVIPETALA'.—Petals rather short, about ⅜ in. long, coloured 'Butter Yellow'. Calyx greenish brown or brownish red on the inside. Put into commerce by Chenault's nurseries around 1935 but of uncertain origin. A.M. 1960. The leaves agree with those of *H. mollis* in shape, but on the Kew plants the indumentum of the undersides is unusually thin, and Roy Lancaster has further noted that they are glaucous beneath when young.

H. 'PALLIDA'.—Petals soft sulphur-yellow, about ¾ in. long. The flowers are very profusely borne in January and February (or even earlier) and thanks to their pale yet vivid colouring the bush shines out on even the dullest day. 'Pallida' was raised in the Garden of the Royal Horticultural Society from seeds which, according to the records, came from a neglected nursery in Holland. Robert de Belder (*Journ. R.H.S.*, Vol. 94 (1969), p. 85) suggests that this nursery may have been Kort's Kalmthout nursery (see under *H. × intermedia*), which is in Belgium but near the Dutch frontier. 'Pallida' received an Award of Merit as long ago as 1932 but was little known until the early fifties.

The leaves of 'Pallida' do not resemble those of *H. mollis*. They are somewhat lustrous above, thinly clad with stellate hairs beneath, mostly narrower at the base and less cordate, and longer stalked.

H. VERNALIS Sarg.

Professor Sargent (*Trees and Shrubs*, Vol. 2, p. 137, t. 156) figured and described this as a new species in 1913. It is closely allied to *H. virginiana*, but is a native of Missouri, Arkansas, and Louisiana, and resembles the Asiatic species in flowering on the leafless wood from January to March. It differs from *H. virginiana* also in the following respects: the inner surface of the calyx-lobes is red, and it has the habit of spreading by suckers or underground stems. The leaves are of a paler duller green. It grows naturally on gravelly, often inundated banks of streams, and was collected by Engelmann in Missouri as long ago as 1845. The flowers have a pungent, not very agreeable odour. *Bot. Mag.*, t. 8573.

H. vernalis was introduced to Kew in 1910 but has never been common in British gardens. According to Dr Wyman (*Shrubs and Vines for American Gardens* (ed. 1969), p. 237) the flowers 'have the interesting quality of opening fully on warm sunny days, and closing or rolling their petals together on cold days, and so remain effectively in bloom for several weeks'. The petals vary in colour in the wild from yellow to reddish, or may be red at the base and yellow at the ends. The leaves are permanently stellate-downy beneath in f. TOMENTELLA Rehd. Although plants that grow naturally in wet habitats do not necessarily need or even tolerate such conditions in our climate, *H. vernalis*, on its own roots, is perhaps worthy of trial for decorating the edges of reservoirs.

cv. 'SANDRA'.—Young leaves flushed with plum-purple. Autumn colour orange, scarlet, and red. Raised by Messrs Hillier (Lancaster, op. cit., pt 4, p. 27).

H. VIRGINIANA L.   VIRGINIAN WITCH-HAZEL

A small deciduous tree 20 or even 30 ft high in the wild, often a shrub of bushy habit, with a short thick trunk and crooked, wide-spreading branches; young shoots at first downy. Leaves broadly ovate to obovate, 3 to 5 in. long, 2 to 3½ in. wide; unequal at the base, unevenly and coarsely round-toothed, especially on the upper part; glabrous or nearly so above, downy with stellate hairs on the midrib and veins beneath; stalk downy, ¼ to ½ in. long. Flowers golden yellow, opening in September and continuing until November, produced two to four together in a cluster at the end of a stalk ¼ in. long; petals ½ to ⅔ in. long, narrowly strap-shaped, crumpled; calyx with four short, broadly ovate, hairy lobes, yellowish brown inside. *Bot. Mag.*, t. 6884.

Native of eastern N. America from Nova Scotia to the mountains of the Carolinas and Tennessee; introduced in 1736. This interesting shrub or tree, although so long an inhabitant of our gardens, is not very common nowadays, being eclipsed by the newer, winter-flowering, Asiatic species. The beauty of this witch-hazel is sometimes decreased by its being in full leaf at flowering time, so that the blossoms, closely tucked to the twigs, have little chance to show themselves, especially as the leaves turn yellow also before falling. The fruits—woody, nutlike bodies ½ in. long, bursting at the top—do not ripen and discharge their seeds until twelve months after the time of flowering. Various popular remedies are made from extracts and decoctions of the bark and leaves.

To the above it should be added that seedlings of *H. virginiana* have been raised in the Arboretum de Kalmthout, Belgium, which flower after the leaves have fallen (*Journ. R.H.S.*, Vol. 94 (1969), p. 85).

HAPLOPAPPUS   COMPOSITAE

A genus of about 150 species of herbs and shrubs, confined to the New World and found mainly in California, Mexico, and Chile.

H. ERICOIDES (Lessing) Hook. & Arn.
Diplopappus ericoides Lessing

An evergreen shrub 3 to 5 ft high, with erect branchlets, slightly downy and glutinous when young. Leaves very small, numerous, and heath-like, from ⅛ to ⅓ in. long, of the thickness of stout thread; dark green, stalkless, produced in clusters at each joint. Flower-heads in corymbs borne on long slender stems, the whole forming a crowded mass of yellow blossom at the end of the shoots of the year; at their best in August and September. Each flower-head is ⅓ in. in diameter, with five ray-florets.

Native of California, and not hardy at Kew except on a wall. On the south coast it thrives well, especially at Worthing; it succeeded also in the Vicarage garden at Bitton, near Bristol. Like some other shrubby composites it is apt to wear out under cultivation, and should be occasionally renewed by means of cuttings, which root freely if put in a propagating frame with gentle heat in July. It is a pretty and interesting plant, quite distinct from all other introduced shrubby composites, especially in its deep green, heath-like foliage.

HEBE   SHRUBBY VERONICA   SCROPHULARIACEAE

A genus of about 100 species of evergreen shrubs or small trees, the great majority of them confined to New Zealand. Two species—*H. elliptica* and *H. salicifolia*—occur in southern S. America as well as in New Zealand, and the former is also native in the Falkland Islands. About seven Australian species have also been referred to *Hebe*. Leaves opposite, usually stout or leathery, usually superposed in four vertical rows, but in a few species the leaves are tiny and scale-like and often also closely imbricated. The older parts of the stems are conspicuously ringed with the scars of fallen leaves. No specialised resting bud is formed, but in most of the larger-leaved species the uppermost visible pair of leaves, whether the plant is in growth or not, is held erect and encloses the younger leaves. These two leaves are pressed tightly together, and in some species their margins are in contact right to the junction with the stem. But in others the margins diverge from each other at the base, forming a LEAF-BUD SINUS of characteristic shape—a window, as it were, through which the stem can be seen. Much use is made of the presence or absence of this leaf-bud sinus in the treatment of *Hebe* in *Flora of New Zealand*, Vol. 1 (1961), and the excellent key in that work cannot be used without an understanding of this character.

The flowers in *Hebe* are arranged in simple or branched racemes or spikes which are axillary in most species but truly terminal in the 'whipcord' group and in *H. hulkeana* and its allies; in some species terminal spikes may be formed in addition to the axillary ones. The calyx is four-lobed. The corolla consists of a tubular base expanding at the mouth into four more or less spreading lobes. Stamens two, their filaments attached to the top of the corolla-tube. Seed-vessel a capsule which in most species is dorsally compressed, i.e., flattened as if by pressure acting from the subtending bract towards the stem. But in *H. macrantha*, *H. cuppressoides*, and in the 'semi-whipcords' (*H. tetrasticha* and its allies) it is laterally compressed.

The genus *Hebe* is closely allied to *Veronica*, a genus of herbs mainly confined to the northern hemisphere and, though long included in it, is treated as distinct in all modern works. A few New Zealand species, of which the best known are *V. cattaractae* and *V. lyallii*, were retained in *Veronica* even by botanists who recognised the genus *Hebe*. This group has now been separated from both genera under the name *Parahebe* (q.v.).

In his *Manual of the Flora of New Zealand* (ed. 1, p. 491) Cheeseman wrote as follows about the difficulties with which this genus confronts the taxonomist: 'Many of the species are singularly protean in habit, foliage, and inflorescence. . . . Intermediate forms are numerous, connecting species that would otherwise appear most distinct, and in not a few cases these intermediates blend so freely into one another that an apparently continuous series of forms is produced, while several species hybridise so readily in cultivation that the supposition at once arises that natural hybrids may also occur.' It is now generally agreed that the occurrence of hybrid swarms in large measure explains the amazing polymorphy of the New Zealand hebes, and it is scarcely surprising that many garden plants grown under this or that specific name do not really fit well under any described species.

There is no monographic study of the genus, but an excellent, critical treatment by Lucy Moore and Margot Ashwin will be found in Allan's *Flora of New Zealand*, Vol. 1 (1961). This has been of great assistance in preparing the much revised account of the species in this edition.

The New Zealand hebes are of the easiest cultivation, provided the climate is not too severe for them. They can be very readily increased by means of young-wood cuttings, and thrive best in a light, well-drained soil, and will probably prove hardier in one which is on the poor side. None has any dislike for chalky soil, so far as is known. For the garden hybrids, see the special section starting on p. 348.

H. AMPLEXICAULIS (J. B. Armstr.) Ckn. & Allan
Veronica amplexicaulis J. B. Armstr.

A shrub 1 to 3 ft high, with the branches erect or ultimately prostrate. Leaves glaucous, ½ to 1 in. long, ⅓ to ⅔ in. broad, broadly oblong or oval, cupped, superposed in four vertical rows and closely set together, rounded at the apex, the bases overlapping, heart-shaped, not stalked, but partially clasping the stem. Flowers white, ¼ in. across, stalkless, borne from leaf-axils near the end of the shoot in simple or branched spikes 1 to 1½ in. long, the main-stalk of which is minutely downy; bracts long, concealing the calyx-lobes. Ovary downy near apex. Capsules rounded. *Bot. Mag.*, t. 7370.

Native of the South Island of New Zealand in the Canterbury province; discovered by Armstrong about 1880 and soon after introduced. It is allied to, and about as hardy as *H. carnosula* and *H. pinguifolia*. From the former it is distinguished by its downy ovary and round-tipped seed-vessel, and from both by its stem-clasping leaves, heart-shaped at the base, and in the longer, sometimes branched inflorescence.

H. ALBICANS (Petrie) Ckn. *Veronica albicans* Petrie—This species, which is very near to *H. amplexicaulis*, is given provisional recognition in *Flora of New Zealand* (Vol. 1, p. 919), where it is stated that 'the best contrasting characters are probably the glabrous subacute capsules, smaller bracts and obvious pedicels of lower flowers'. Petrie's description appears to have been based, at least partly, on a plant introduced by F. W. Gibbs from Mount Cobb in Nelson province and, according to Cockayne and Allan, this clone, which they considered to be of hybrid origin, was the sole representative of *H. albicans* in New Zealand gardens (*Tr. N.Z. Inst.*, Vol. 57 (1927), p. 35; ibid., Vol. 60 (1929), p. 468). In Britain, plants agreeing essentially with *H. albicans* are variable in size and relative width of leaf, but the leaves are always of the oblong order, not or scarcely narrowed at the base. They are usually of horizontal habit, 1 to 2 ft high; but much more in width.

A very distinct hebe cultivated by Messrs Jackman of Woking is near to *H. albicans* but makes a dense rounded bush and has leaves relatively narrower than in that species, narrowed to branchlet width at the base.

H. ANOMALA (J. F. Armstr.) Ckn.
Veronica anomala J. F. Armstr.

A shrub 3 to 5 ft high, with slender branches, minutely downy in a strip above each leaf-axil when young. Leaves ⅓ to ¾ in. long, oval-lanceolate or narrow-oblong, pointed, entire, tapering at the base to a very short, broad stalk (leaf-bud sinus elliptical), somewhat keeled, dark shining green and quite glabrous. Flowers white or pale pink, produced in June and July in a cluster of spikes at the end of the shoot, and thus forming a panicle, or several panicles, each 1 to 1½ in. long, and nearly as wide. Corolla ¼ to ⅓ in. across, with a slender tube about twice the length of the calyx. Anthers blue. Seed-vessel ovate-oblong, glabrous. *Bot. Mag.*, t. 7360.

This species (if such it be) is best known as a garden plant and very few matching specimens have been found since the type was first collected. The peculiarity to which it owes the epithet *anomala* is that the calyx in the type plant was three-lobed through fusion of the two posterior lobes, but this is not a constant character. Doubts have been expressed whether this hebe is really separable from *H. odora* (q.v. under *H. buxifolia*), but the garden plant is distinct enough in its narrower, more pointed leaves and narrow-elliptic leaf-bud sinus.

In previous editions *H. anomala* was described as being of erect, narrow habit, but the hardy clone now so common in gardens is bushy and grows to about 3 ft high and more in width. This form is also characterised by the pale leaf-margins and young stems. In the original introduction to Kew the young stems were tinged with red, and the same character is noted by J. B. Armstrong in his redescription of the species (*Tr. N.Z. Inst.*, Vol. 13, p. 355).

H. ARMSTRONGII. *See under* H. OCHRACEA

H. BRACHYSIPHON Summerhayes

Veronica brachysiphon (Summerhayes) Bean; *V. traversii* Hort., not Hook. f.

An evergreen shrub up to 6 ft high, or more, forming a wide-spreading, rounded bush of dense habit; branches erect, at first minutely downy, soon becoming quite glabrous. Leaf-bud with a narrow sinus. Leaves densely arranged on the shoot (ten or twelve to the inch), superposed in four vertical rows; narrowly oval or oblong, sometimes slightly obovate, ½ to 1 in. long, ⅛ to ¼ in. wide, pointed, tapered at the base to a short, broad, hinged stalk, dark, rather dull green. Racemes produced in July from the leaf-axils near the end of the shoot, usually about ¾ in. long, 3 in. wide, the main-stalk minutely downy. Flowers ¼ to ⅓ in. in diameter, white. Sepals ovate with minute hairs at the edges. Corolla-tube broad, about twice as long as calyx. Anthers purple-brown. Seed-vessel ⅙ in. long, much compressed, about twice as long as the sepals. *Bot. Mag.*, t. 6390.

Native of New Zealand; introduced about 1868. This has proved the most hardy, and on the whole the most ornamental of New Zealand veronicas in gardens. The only time I have seen it killed by cold was in February 1895. It makes a handsome and shapely evergreen, worth growing on that account alone, but it has the additional attraction of flowering freely and regularly after mid-summer, when shrubs in flower cease to be abundant. It is pleasing as an isolated specimen on a lawn.

H. TRAVERSII (Hook. f.) Ckn. & Allan *V. traversii* Hook. f.—*H. brachysiphon* was long cultivated in gardens as *Veronica* or *Hebe traversii*. The true species, which has certainly been in cultivation, is easily distinguishable from

H. brachysiphon by its very slender corolla-tubes and, in fruit, by its capsules being about four times as long as the calyx-lobes. The inflorescences are of the same length as in *H. brachysiphon*, the leaves of similar dimensions but more oblong.

H. VENUSTULA (Col.) L. B. Moore *V. venustula* Col.; *V. laevis* Benth., not Lam.; *H. laevis* (Benth.) Ckn. & Allan—This species is allied to *H. brachysiphon*. Plants at Kew probably belonging to this species have the leaves more densely set on the shoot than in *H. brachysiphon*. They are oblong-oblanceolate, $\frac{1}{2}$ to $\frac{5}{8}$ in. long, about $\frac{3}{16}$ in. wide, blunt at the apex, slightly concave, medium, mat green above; leaf-bud without sinus. Flowers white in dense racemes about $1\frac{1}{4}$ in. long, some of them branched; peduncles hairy, shorter than the subtending leaf; bracts equalling or slightly shorter than the pedicels. Native of the mountains of North Island.

H. BUCHANANII (Hook. f.) Ckn. & Allan
Veronica buchananii Hook. f.

A dwarf, much-branched shrub up to 12 in. high, compact in habit; branchlets with two lines of fine down. Leaves $\frac{1}{8}$ to $\frac{1}{4}$ in. long, closely set together on the stems, spreading, broadly elliptic, broadly ovate or almost rounded, obtuse to almost acute at the apex, sessile (leaf-bud without sinus), slightly concave, green or somewhat glaucous, glabrous, often keeled beneath, especially near the tip. Flowers white, about $\frac{3}{16}$ in. wide, stalkless, produced in June and July in a cluster of three or four spikes near the end of the shoot, each spike $\frac{1}{2}$ to $\frac{3}{4}$ in. long, with a very downy main-stalk. Seed-capsule downy.

Native of the mountains of the South Island of New Zealand in Canterbury and Otago provinces, up to 6,000 ft. A rock garden shrub and quite hardy. Cheeseman in his *Manual* said that this species, in its larger-leaved forms, was scarcely to be distinguished from *H. pinguifolia*. But in its typical state *H. buchananii* is distinct enough in its smaller leaves. It is also of dwarfer, denser habit, the leaves are leathery rather than fleshy, the main-stalk of the inflorescence is more hairy and the bracts and calyx-lobes are more markedly ciliate. Apparent intermediates between the two species may well be hybrids. *H. buxifolia* may occasionally have leaves as small as in the larger-leaved forms of *H. buchananii*, and is sometimes of dense habit. But the leaves of *H. buxifolia* are abruptly narrowed at the base to a short petiole, and the leaf-bud consequently has a pronounced sinus; also, it has glabrous seed-capsules.

The diminutive plant called *H. buchananii* 'MINOR' represents the extreme of the species in smallness of leaf and dwarfness.

H. BUXIFOLIA (Benth.) Ckn. & Allan
Veronica buxifolia Benth.

A neat shrub 2 to 5 ft high, with erect branches; young shoots pale green, glabrous, except for a thin strip of down reaching from the axil of one leaf to the opening between the pair next above it; leaf-bud with a pronounced sinus.

Leaves in four superposed rows, $\frac{1}{3}$ to $\frac{1}{2}$ in. long, $\frac{3}{16}$ to $\frac{1}{4}$ in. wide, oblong inclined to obovate, pointed, rounded at the base, dark glossy green, perfectly glabrous, covered with minute dots beneath; stalk about $\frac{1}{12}$ in. long, dilated where it joins the stem and slightly hairy there. Flowers white, $\frac{1}{4}$ to $\frac{1}{3}$ in. across, produced in June and July at and near the apex of the shoots in closely packed clusters, $\frac{1}{2}$ to 1 in. long, which are often branched and collectively form a corymb, 1 to 2 in. across, the stalks minutely downy. Sepals narrow oblong, rounded at the end, edged with minute hairs; seed-vessel about twice as long, glabrous.

Native of the North and South Islands of New Zealand. The plant in cultivation under this name and described above is very distinct in general appearance from native grown specimens, which have the leaves much more densely arranged on the stem, and less distinctly stalked. But in all essential particulars they appear to be the same. Probably the differences are due to the different environment of cultivated plants. It reaches up to 4,000 ft altitude in New Zealand, and is one of the hardiest members of this group. It flowers annually, but not freely.

H. buxifolia is very closely allied to, and perhaps not specifically different from:

H. ODORA (Hook. f.) Ckn. *Veronica odora* Hook. f.—This species, which owes its specific epithet to its jasmine-like scent, was described by the younger Hooker from specimens collected in the Auckland Islands, which lie between the South Island of New Zealand and Antarctica. Bentham, who described *Hebe buxifolia* from specimens collected in the North Island of New Zealand, was evidently aware that it was closely allied to Hooker's species, and according to Dr Lucy Moore there is no reliable difference by which they can be separated except perhaps that in *H. odora* the margins are 'minutely crenulated', not entire as in *H. buxifolia*. If the two species were to be united, it would be under the name *H. odora*.

For another member of this complex, see *H. anomala*.

H. CANTERBURIENSIS (J. B. Armstr.) L. B. Moore

Veronica canterburiensis J. B. Armstr.; *H. vernicosa* var. *canterburiensis* (J. B. Armstr.) Ckn. & Allan

A low, spreading shrub 1 to 3 ft high; shoots furnished with extremely minute down. Leaves densely packed on the stem, $\frac{1}{4}$ to $\frac{1}{2}$ in. long, $\frac{1}{8}$ to $\frac{3}{16}$ in. wide, oval to obovate, pointed, tapered at the base to a short stalk, dark glossy green, glabrous except for minute hairs on the margins and stalks; on the spreading branches the stalks of the lower leaves are often twisted so as to bring the faces of all the leaves to pretty much the same plane. Racemes in pairs towards the ends of the shoots, $\frac{1}{2}$ to 1 in. long, four- to eight-flowered; stalks downy. Flowers white, $\frac{1}{4}$ to $\frac{1}{3}$ in. in diameter; corolla-tube slightly longer than the calyx or about the same length. Seed-vessel dark brown, about twice the length of the calyx. *Bot. Mag.*, n.s., t. 136.

Native mainly of the South Island of New Zealand, described from specimens collected on Arthur's Pass at 3,000–4,000 ft; introduced to the Edinburgh

Botanic Garden in 1910 by means of seeds sent by the famous New Zealand botanist Dr L. Cockayne. This is one of the daintiest of the hebes and flowers freely.

H. VERNICOSA (Hook. f.) Ckn. & Allan *Veronica vernicosa* Hook. f.—This species, a native of the South Island of New Zealand, is allied to *H. canterburiensis* and has the same 'varnished' foliage. It differs in its longer racemes (up to 2 in. long) with more numerous, smaller flowers; corolla-tubes shorter than the calyx; seed-vessels pale brown, about three times as long as the calyx.

H. CARNOSULA (Hook. f.) Ckn.

Veronica laevis var. *carnosula* Hook. f.; *Veronica carnosula* (Hook. f.) Hook. f.

A shrub usually more or less prostrate, and rarely more than 1 ft high with us, occasionally 3 ft high in New Zealand, young shoots with a vertical strip of down above each leaf-axil. Leaf-buds with a pronounced sinus. Leaves glaucous green, scoop-shaped, obovate, pointed, ⅓ to ¾ in. long, ¼ to ⅔ in. wide; narrowing to a stalkless base, closely superposed in four rows. Flowers densely crowded in spikes near the end of the shoot, the whole forming a dense terminal cluster; flower-stalks very downy. Flowers ¼ in. across, white; sepals erect, as long or rather longer than the corolla-tube, edged with minute hairs. Ovary, style and seed-vessel free from down, the last pointed.

Native of the South Island of New Zealand, where it is said to be rare. In describing this hebe Hooker said it really differed from *H. pinguifolia* only in having glabrous, acute capsules. But Dr Moore has pointed out that Hooker's type specimen 'differs in other ways also, particularly in the distinct sinus in the leaf-bud'. Garden plants under the name *H. carnosula* also show this character and are well distinguished from the common run of *H. pinguifolia*, and resemble Hooker's type, in their large, fleshy, semi-erect leaves and glabrous capsules.

H. carnosula is a very pleasing little evergreen, making low densely leafy tufts of a striking glaucous hue, and of neat appearance. It is also one of the hardiest of the group and grows well on the rock garden in the University Botanic Garden, Cambridge.

H. COLENSOI (Hook. f.) Ckn.

Veronica colensoi Hook f.

An evergreen shrub of bushy habit 1 to 2 ft high; young shoots carrying leaves eight to twelve to the inch. Leaves obovate-oblong, abruptly pointed, scarcely stalked, ¾ to 1¼ in. long, ⅛ to ½ in. wide, rather glaucous when young, becoming dark green, quite glabrous. They appear to be mostly entire but are sometimes sparsely toothed. Flowers white, ¼ in. wide, produced densely in racemes about 1 in. long from the terminal leaf-axils during July and August. Corolla-tube shorter than the calyx.

Native of the North Island of New Zealand, collected first on the Ruahine Mountains by W. Colenso, whose original specimens have some distinctly toothed leaves. The plant figured as *V. colensoi* in the *Botanical Magazine*, t. 7296, is not the true plant, nor are some of the plants going by this name in cultivation or under the name *H. colensoi* 'Glauca'.

var. HILLII (Col.) L. B. Moore *V. hillii* Col.—Leaves elliptic, about 1¼ in. long, ⅜ in. wide, with numerous marginal incisions; in exposed places the leaves are linear-oblong, ¾ in. long, ¼ in. wide, with fewer incisions or none (*Fl. N.Z.*, Vol. 1, p. 895).

H. CUPRESSOIDES (Hook. f.) Ckn. & Allan
Veronica cupressoides Hook. .

A shrub usually seen 2 to 4 ft high in this country, but sometimes taller (to 6 or even 8 ft). It has a rounded, dense habit, much like that of a dwarf cypress or juniper, the branches being very much forked and subdivided, and final ramifications very slender and short (½ to 1 in. long). Branchlets about $\frac{1}{32}$ in. thick, often minutely downy. Leaves on adult plants scale-like, about $\frac{1}{16}$ in.

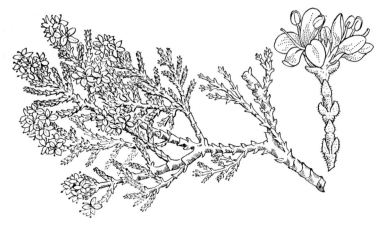

HEBE CUPRESSOIDES

long, dusty green or somewhat glaucous, glabrous except for minute hairs on the margin, rounded at the apex; they do not, as in *H. hectoris* and *lycopodioides*, completely hide the stem, although usually appressed to it; the bases of each pair are united and clasp the stem. In young plants (occasionally on odd branches of older ones), the leaves are as much as ¼ in. long, narrowly oblong, ovate or somewhat obovate, and vary from entire to irregularly or pinnately lobed, pointed and distinctly stalked. Flowers pale blue, ⅛ in. diameter, produced three to eight together at the ends of the branches in a small head about midsummer. *Bot. Mag.*, t. 7348.

Native of the South Island of New Zealand; long cultivated. It is fairly hardy, and during some seasons blossoms quite freely in June and July. It is worth growing for its neat appearance and remarkable cypress-like growth.

H. DECUMBENS (J. B. Armstr.) Ckn. & Allan
Veronica decumbens J. B. Armstr.

An evergreen decumbent plant 1 to 3 ft high, with purplish black shoots that have two opposite vertical strips of down proceeding upwards from each pair of leaf-axils. Leaves usually closely set on the branches, mostly oval or inclined to oblong or obovate, ½ to ¾ in. long, about half as much wide, of thick, rather fleshy texture, quite glabrous, dark green, red on the margins. Flowers densely packed in two or four racemes near the end of the shoot, each ½ to ¾ in. long; main flower-stalk downy; bracts and flower-stalks very short. Corolla white, ¼ in. wide, four-lobed, lobes oblong and blunt, the tube twice as long as the calyx; calyx-lobes edged with minute down.

Native of the South Island of New Zealand, up to 4,500 ft. Cheeseman, the New Zealand botanist, described it as a very beautiful plant well distinguished from its allies by the polished purplish black young shoots, red margins to the leaves, shortly stalked flowers and long corolla-tube. It is one of the hardiest species and flowers during July and August.

H. DIEFFENBACHII (Benth.) Ckn. & Allan
Veronica dieffenbachii Benth.

A shrub of wide-spreading habit 3 to 4 ft high. Leaves narrow-oblong, 2 to 4 in. long, ½ to 1 in. wide, pointed, thick in texture, rather pale green, the base stalkless and partially clasping the stem. Racemes showy, produced in pairs a little below the apex of the shoot in the leaf-axils, 3 or 4 in. long, ¾ to 1 in. wide, densely crowded with blossom. Flowers ¼ in. diameter, purplish lilac or white. Bot. Mag., t. 7656.

Native of the Chatham Islands, where it was discovered in 1841 by Dieffenbach. It is closely allied, and bears a considerable resemblance to H. speciosa, from which it differs in its generally narrower, paler green sessile leaves, its round, not angled stems, and in the seed-vessel being about thrice (instead of twice) the length of the calyx. It is tender.

H. DIOSMIFOLIA (A. Cunn.) Ckn. & Allan
Veronica diosmifolia A. Cunn.; V. diosm. var. trisepala T. Kirk; V. jasminoides Hort.

A much-branched evergreen shrub 2 to 5 ft high in cultivation but up to 20 ft in the wild; young shoots often minutely downy. Leaves closely arranged in the usual four superposed rows, narrowly oblong, tapered about equally to both ends, finely pointed, margins slit or entire, ½ to 1 in. long, $\frac{1}{10}$ to ⅛ in. wide, dark bright green above, paler beneath, midrib prominent beneath, but with no visible veins; stalk very short. Flowers produced near the ends of the shoots in June in usually one or three rounded, corymbose clusters ¾ to 1 in. wide. Corolla pale lavender-blue to white, ¼ to ⅓ in. wide, with a short funnel-shaped tube and four lobes, the rearmost (or inner) lobe the largest; corolla-tube as long as calyx. Calyx usually three-lobed, the anterior lobe broader than the others or more or less deeply notched. Flower-stalks minutely downy. Native of the North Island, New Zealand, discovered by Richard Cunningham in 1834 in the Bay of Islands. Its distinguishing characters are the downy shoots and flower-stalks, the corymbose inflorescence, the usually three-lobed (rarely four-lobed) calyx. It is a neat and pleasing shrub and has been successfully cultivated in the Edinburgh Botanic Garden for over half a century. At Kew it is killed or injured in severe winters. The so-called variety *"trisepala"* has no proper standing, being based merely on the absence of a bilobing of one calyx segment, thereby making the calyx three-lobed, which is its normal condition in this species.

H. MENZIESII (Benth.) Ckn. & Allan—This species was described by Bentham from specimens collected by Menzies at Dusky Bay, Fiordland, South Island, in 1791, but no plants agreeing with these specimens have been found there since. Dr Moore considers that the plants usually placed under *H. menziesii* should be referred to H. DIVARICATA (Cheesem.) Ckn. & Allan, which differs from *H. diosmifolia* in the following characters: leaves entire; anterior calyx-lobes free for most of their length; corolla-tube longer than calyx.

H. ELLIPTICA (Forst. f.) Pennell

Veronica elliptica Forst. f.; *Hebe magellanica* Gmel.; *Veronica decussata* Ait.

A tree up to 20 ft high, or a shrub a few feet high, in the wild; branches round, with a downy strip above each leaf-axil, or wholly downy. Leaves oval or obovate, narrowed abruptly at the apex to a short point; $\frac{1}{2}$ to $1\frac{1}{4}$ in. long, $\frac{1}{4}$ to $\frac{1}{2}$ in. wide, standing out at right angles from the stem, the base rounded and distinctly but shortly stalked, the stalk flattened to the stem; pale green and glabrous except that the margin is downy. Racemes crowded near the ends of the branches, 1 to $1\frac{1}{2}$ in. long, erect, not or slightly downy. Flowers almost the largest in the genus, being sometimes $\frac{2}{3}$ in. diameter, white or bluish, fragrant, four to twelve of them appearing on a raceme. Seed-vessel twice the length of the sepals.

Native of New Zealand, Chile, Tierra del Fuego, and the Falkland Islands, whence it was, according to Aiton, introduced by Dr Fothergill in 1776. It is one of numerous instances showing the close affinity of the flora of New Zealand with that of southern S. America. Reintroduced from the Falkland Islands by the late Clarence Elliott.

The true species is rare in gardens, most of the plants grown under its name being forms of *H. × franciscana*, its hybrid with *H. speciosa*.

H. EPACRIDEA (Hook. f.) Ckn. & Allan

Veronica epacridea Hook. f.

A low or prostrate evergreen shrub, the young stems completely clothed with leaves arranged in opposite, overlapping pairs on the stem. Leaves about $\frac{3}{16}$ in. long, ovate, pointed, united at the base, distinctly recurved, V-shaped in cross section, glabrous except for a streak of down where the leaves join at the base, dark dull green with pale margins; they persist on the stems for several years. Flowers fragrant, closely packed in compact, egg-shaped, terminal heads, $\frac{1}{2}$ to $1\frac{1}{4}$ in. long by $\frac{3}{4}$ in. wide. Each flower is about $\frac{1}{8}$ to $\frac{3}{16}$ in. wide, white, the tube of the corolla slender. Calyx deeply four-lobed, the lobes narrow oblong, as long as the corolla tube, margined with fine hairs.

Native of the South Island of New Zealand; discovered by Dr Sinclair, in 1860, at Tarndale, a few miles from the Wairau Gorge, Nelson. It is a species distinct in the very stiff, thick, rigid leaves, dense compact head of flowers and long slender corolla-tube. It occurs wild at elevations of 3,000 to 5,000 ft and is quite hardy. Suitable for the rock garden. Flowers in July.

H. HAASTII (Hook. f.) Ckn. & Allan V. *haastii* Hook. f.—This species is related to H. *epacridea* but does not have its keeled leaves. Its variations are treated in *Fl. N.Z.*, Vol. 1, pp. 939–40. Both species are figured in Philipson and Hearn, *Rock Garden Plants*, plates 48 and 46 respectively.

H. × FRANCISCANA (Eastw.) Souster

Veronica franciscana Eastw.; *V. lobelioides* Anderson-Henry, *nom. inedit.*; *V. decussata* Hort., in part, not Ait.; *V. elliptica* Hort., in part, not Forst f.; *V. speciosa* Hort., in part, not A. Cunn.

A group of garden-raised hybrids between H. *elliptica* and H. *speciosa*. They are shrubs of dense habit, usually under 4 ft in height. Stems rather stout, glossy, with two bands of down on each internode. Leaves rather formally arranged in four rows at right-angles, obovate to almost elliptic, obtuse and usually apiculate at the apex, distinctly stalked, palish green, slightly fleshy in texture. Flowers very large (up to $\frac{1}{2}$ in. wide across the lobes), violet-blue, pinkish purple or sometimes white, arranged in simple axillary racemes 2 to 3 in. long; tube broad, about as long as the calyx.

Although long known in gardens, this hybrid was first validly described by Miss Alice Eastwood in 1943, from a plant cultivated in the Golden Gate Park, San Francisco, under the name "*V. decussata*". The first recorded cross between H. *elliptica* and H. *speciosa* was made before 1859, in which year a gardener signing himself 'Devonian' sent a specimen to the editor of the *Gardeners' Chronicle* from a hybrid between these species which he had made. The original plant was then 4 ft high and 22 ft in circumference and bore violet-blue flowers (*Gard. Chron.* (1859), p. 563). In the same year and in 1860 the Royal Horticultural Society distributed some seventy plants to its members under the name "*V. decussata devoniana*" and it seems almost beyond doubt that these were the hybrid raised by 'Devonian'. The same cross was also made by Isaac Anderson-Henry of Edinburgh before 1862 and named by him *V. lobelioides*. The variety 'BLUE GEM' was raised in 1868 by H. W. Warren, a nurseryman of Salisbury, who found it growing as a self-sown seedling in the root-ball of a potted azalea. When noticed it bore only its first pair of leaves, yet so rapidly was the plant multiplied that by the autumn of the following year 'Blue Gem' had received five First Class Certificates. Warren sold the stock to Messrs Cripps of Tunbridge Wells, who put it into commerce (*Journ. of Hort.* (Nov. 30, 1876), p. 472).

H. × *franciscana* is common in coastal gardens of the Atlantic zone, but is not reliably hardy inland. Young vigorously growing plants are very vulnerable to frost but may become hardier if they can be brought through the first winter. It is one of the most wind- and spray-resistant of shrubs and much used for hedging in the Isles of Scilly, where it is known as the 'hedge veronica'.

In *H.* × *franciscana* 'VARIEGATA' the leaves are margined with creamy white.

H. GIBBSII (T. Kirk) Ckn. & Allan
Veronica gibbsii T. Kirk

An evergreen shrub of thin habit, 9 to 18 in. high; young shoots completely hidden by the closely packed leaves twelve to sixteen to the inch. Leaves ovate, mostly pointed, stalkless, overlapping at the base, ½ to ¾ in. long, ⅓ to ½ in. wide, glaucous, often tinged with purplish red, of stout texture, glabrous except for the margins which are conspicuously fringed with pale hairs. Flowers white, ⅕ in. wide, produced during July and August in two or four clusters about 1 in. long near the end of the branches. The bracts, flower-stalks, and margins of the long and narrow calyx-lobes all furnished with white hairs.

Native of the South Island, New Zealand, up to 4,000 ft. It is a native of the Nelson Provincial District and appears to have a restricted distribution, having been found on two peaks only of the Dun Mountain Range—Mt Rintoul and Ben Nevis. If all the New Zealand hebes were as distinct as this, their study would be simple. The hairy margins of the leaves distinguish it from any other. Coming from such a lofty altitude it is quite hardy, but it is still uncommon in cultivation although one of the best of the glaucous-leaved species.

H. GIGANTEA (Ckn.) Ckn. & Allan
Veronica gigantea Ckn.; *V. salicifolia* var. *gigantea* (Ckn.) Cheesem.

A native of the Chatham Islands, where it makes, according to Cockayne, a tree 15 to 30 ft high with a close, rounded crown. Leaves rather thick, dull green, 3 to 4 in. long, ⅓ to ½ in. wide, ciliate, the blades downy on one or both sides when young, sessile. Flowers white, in racemes usually shorter than the leaves. This species, Cockayne observed, is remarkable for going through a juvenile phase in which the stems are densely downy and the leaves deeply and coarsely toothed. He likened it to a gigantic form of *H. salicifolia* but it is quite distinct from that species in its completely sessile leaves, shorter racemes, and corollas with a tube equal in length to the calyx.

There is a picture of a tree growing in the Chatham Islands in the *Kew Bulletin* for 1910, taken by Captain Dorrien-Smith in December 1909. The species was introduced by him to his garden at Tresco Abbey in the Isles of Scilly at the same time. One of the original trees is about 15 ft high with a trunk 2½ ft in diameter at the base.

H. BARKERI (Ckn.) Ckn. *V. barkeri* Ckn.—The type of this species is a garden plant, and Cockayne, who first described it in 1899, later refused to recognise it as a natural species. But the type almost certainly came from the Chatham Islands and Dr Moore (*Fl. N.Z.*, Vol. 1, p. 910) considers that this and *H. gigantea* are probably one and the same species, for which *H. barkeri*, having priority, would be the correct name.

H. GLAUCOPHYLLA (Ckn.) Ckn.
Veronica glaucophylla Ckn.; *V. darwiniana sensu* Cheesem., in part

A shrub to about 3 ft high; branches slender, with a strip of down above each leaf-axil running up to the base of the leaf above, or occasionally finely downy all over. Leaf-bud without sinus. Leaves spreading, lanceolate, ½ to ⅝ in. long, about 3/16 in. wide, tapered at the apex to a fairly acute point, usually glaucous above, glabrous except for the minutely ciliate margin. Inflorescence from the upper leaf-axils, two to three times as long as the subtending leaf; inflorescence axis downy; bracts shorter than the pedicels. Calyx-lobes ciliate, with a pale membranous border. Corollas white; tube about as long as the calyx, the corolla-lobes rounded, longer than the tube. Ovary and base of style downy. Capsules downy, rather pointed, more than twice as long as the calyx.

A native of the South Island of New Zealand. This species is part of the *Veronica* (*Hebe*) *darwiniana* aggregate as understood by Cheeseman, but the plant so named by Colenso is different, notably in having glabrous capsules (see further below). There is no wild material of *H. glaucophylla* in the Kew Herbarium, nor has any cultivated plant been seen which could unequivocally be referred to this species. The above description is therefore based on that given in *Flora of New Zealand* (Vol. 1 (1961), p. 917). A plant at Kew on the Temperate House terrace, which bore the label *H. glaucophylla*, disagrees with that species in a number of characters, notably in having glabrous capsules. A commercial plant seen under this name is *H. albicans* or near it. On the other hand the hebe known as *H. darwiniana* 'Variegata' is tolerably near to *H. glaucophylla* and so too are some plants in commerce as *H. darwiniana*. Both have slender, acute leaves.

H. DARWINIANA (Col.) Ckn. *Veronica darwiniana* Col.—This species is considered by Dr Lucy Moore (*Fl. N.Z.*, Vol. 1, p. 946) to be of uncertain status. Colenso described it from specimens that he collected in North Island, in the hills behind Hawke's Bay, but they have not been matched by any later collection. The specimens Colenso sent to Kew show that the species is very near to the later-named *H. glaucophylla* of South Island, but has glabrous ovaries and capsules. Whether the true *H. darwiniana* was ever introduced is not known, but Colenso certainly sent fruits and seeds to Sir Joseph Hooker, from which plants may have been raised. The plants grown in gardens as *H. darwiniana* 'Variegata' or as *H. darwiniana* are near to *H. glaucophylla* (see above); but one commercial plant so named was *H. pinguifolia*.

H. TOPIARIA L. B. Moore—This species, first described in 1961 but known earlier, is perhaps not in cultivation in Britain at present (1971) but is in commerce in New Zealand. It is described as a low-growing, much-branched shrub, assuming in the open 'a globular form as if clipped to shape'. Branchlets with two lines of rather coarse down. Leaf-buds without sinus. Leaves glaucous, spreading-erect, broad-elliptic or slightly obovate, about $\frac{1}{2}$ in. long, $\frac{1}{4}$ in. wide, almost glabrous. Inflorescences lateral, simple, very short; bracts almost as long as pedicels. Calyx-lobes rather broad, with a narrow membranous border, finely ciliate. Corolla white, tube broad, longer than calyx, the corolla-lobes rounded, as long as the tube. Capsules glabrous, about twice as long as the calyx. Native of Nelson Province (South Island).

H. GRACILLIMA (Kirk) Ckn. & Allan
Veronica ligustrifolia var. *gracillima* Kirk; *V. gracillima* (Kirk) Cheesem.

This species, as interpreted in *Flora of New Zealand*, has the following distinguishing characters: Branchlets finely downy. Leaves of rather spongy texture, narrow-lanceolate, about $1\frac{1}{2}$ in. long, $\frac{1}{4}$ in. wide; leaf-bud sinus present, though sometimes very small. Racemes longer than leaves, sometimes very much longer; pedicels long, bracts small and narrow. Corolla white or pale coloured; tube not much longer than calyx. Capsules glabrous, about twice as long as calyx.

Native of the South Island of New Zealand, mainly west of the divide, found in damp places and attaining about 6 ft in height. A plant at Kew on the Temperate House Terrace is of compact habit and bears in July a profusion of racemes up to 6 in. long—a remarkable length considering that the leaves are only $1\frac{1}{4}$ in. or slightly more long.

Although *H. gracillima* is recognised as a species in *Flora of New Zealand*, similar plants might arise from the crossing (in the wild or in cultivation) of *H. salicifolia* with certain species with shortish leaves. It has even been suggested that it might be a hybrid between *H. salicifolia* and *H. ligustrifolia*, though the latter species is confined to the northern part of North Island.

H. × DIVERGENS (Cheesem.) Ckn.—A shrub 2 to 5 ft high; young branchlets finely downy. Leaves $\frac{3}{4}$ to $1\frac{1}{4}$ in. long, up to $\frac{1}{2}$ in. wide, narrow-oblong or elliptic-oblong, flat, glabrous, midrib raised beneath. Racemes densely flowered, up to 3 in. long (sometimes longer); bracts about equal to the pedicels. Flowers white; corolla-tube rather broad, about as long as the calyx and shorter than the corolla-lobes. A hybrid described from Nelson province, South Island. It is suggested in *Flora of New Zealand* that the parentage might be *H. gracillima* × *H. elliptica*.

H. HECTORIS (Hook. f.) Ckn. & Allan
Veronica hectori Hook. f.

A shrub 6 in. to 2 ft high, with stiffly erect, much-branched, round stems, almost completely hidden by closely appressed, scale-like leaves; shoots of the year, with their covering of leaves, $\frac{1}{12}$ to $\frac{1}{8}$ in. thick, the lateral ones springing from the stem at a narrowly acute angle. Leaves broadly deltoid, $\frac{1}{10}$ to $\frac{1}{6}$ in. long, each pair united by their margins at the base, thick, roundly convex on the exposed side, obtuse at the apex, the margins ciliate. Flowers $\frac{1}{4}$ in. wide, white or pinkish, crowded in a small terminal head. Sepals narrowly oblong, about as long as the corolla-tube. *Bot. Mag.*, t. 7415.

Native of the South Island of New Zealand. It is one of the very hardiest of the New Zealand hebes and makes an interesting small evergreen, but is rather shy-flowering. *H. lycopodioides* has equally stout stems, but they are distinctly four-angled, not terete as in *H. hectoris*.

H. HULKEANA (F. v. Muell.) Ckn. & Allan   NEW ZEALAND LILAC

Veronica hulkeana F. v. Muell.

A loose-habited, straggling shrub, occasionally reaching a height of 4 to 6 ft, or even more when grown against a wall—as it usually is in this country. Leaves in pairs somewhat far apart on the branches, broadly ovate, 1 to 2 in. long, ½ to 1¼ in. wide, broadly wedge-shaped or rounded at the base, coarsely toothed, the teeth and apex either blunt or sharp, dark glossy green; stalk ¼ to ½ in. long. Flowers ¼ to ⅓ in. diameter, of a delicate lavender or lilac shade, produced in May and June in huge branching panicles which terminate the shoots. These panicles are sometimes 18 in. long, with side branches 3 to 7 in. long. The flowers themselves are without stalks, but the ramifications of the panicle are downy. *Bot. Mag.*, t. 5484.

This species, of remarkable beauty and distinction, is a native of the north-eastern part of the South Island of New Zealand, where it inhabits dry rocky cliffs and bluffs, often in association with *Pachystegia insignis*; introduced about 1860. It received a First Class Certificate in 1882 as a plant for the greenhouse, and until recently was reckoned to be a very tender species. But in southern England it survived the testing winters of 1961-3 in some gardens, and at Belhaven House in East Lothian it has lived out-of-doors for forty years and seeds itself into the crumbling mortar of garden walls. Possibly there are two or more strains in cultivation, of differing hardiness (in the wild it ranges from sea-level to 3,000 ft). Or it may be that its reputation for tenderness is partly the result of giving the plants too rich a soil or too cool a position. It is most likely to succeed if planted against a sunny wall, in a well-drained rubbly soil. Plants raised from autumn cuttings will flower well in their second summer, so this lovely species could become a feature of any garden where there is a frost-free greenhouse or frame for overwintering the young plants. It is advisable to remove the panicles as soon as the flowers fade, for these are produced so abundantly that seed-setting may weaken the plant.

H. 'FAIRFIELDII'. – A shrub of dwarfer, sturdier habit with leaves ½ to 1 in. long and shorter, broader flower panicles. It first appeared in the Fairfield nursery, near Dunedin, N.Z., and was described by Hooker, and figured, in *Bot. Mag.*, t. 7323. Hooker suggested that it might be a hybrid between *H. hulkeana* and *H. lavaudiana* (see below).

H. LAVAUDIANA (Raoul) Ckn. & Allan *V. lavaudiana* Raoul—This species is closely allied to *H. hulkeana*, but is a dwarfer shrub with smaller leaves, and with white or mauvish pink flowers in denser and shorter inflorescences (*Bot. Mag.*, t. 7210). Its main home is in the Banks Peninsula, South Island, where it grows in volcanic rock. See further in *Journ. R.H.S.*, Vol. 97, pp. 31, 461-2.

H. RAOULII (Hook. f.) Ckn. & Allan *V. raoulii* Hook. f.—This species, un-common in cultivation, is allied to *H. hulkeana* and *H. lavaudiana*. It is a dwarf shrub with erect or procumbent stems. Leaves smaller and narrower than in its allies, oblong-spathulate, ¼ to 1 in. long, ⅛ to ⅜ in. wide, long-tapered at the base, with serrated and usually reddish margins. Flowers white or pale lavender, in dense, short panicles (sometimes reduced to a single terminal spike). It is a rock-plant, confined to dry places in Canterbury province. Two varieties are described in *Flora of New Zealand*, Vol. 1.

H. LEIOPHYLLA (Cheesem.) Ckn. & Allan
Veronica leiophylla Cheesem.; *V. parviflora* var. *phillyreaefolia* Hook. f.

For reasons explained in *Flora of New Zealand*, Vol. 1, p. 947, the correct application of the name *H. leiophylla* is uncertain. Plants in cultivation under this name in Britain do, however, agree moderately well with Cheeseman's description and also with the type material of *V. parviflora* var. *phillyreaefolia* Hook. f., which Cheeseman cited as a synonym of his *V. leiophylla*. Since the cultivated plants cannot be identified with any species recognised in *Flora of New Zealand*, it seems reasonable to retain the name *H. leiophylla* for them, at least until the difficult group to which they belong has been further studied.

These cultivated plants in many respects resemble *H. gracillima*, notably in bearing racemes that are disproportionately long in comparison with the leaves (5 to 6 in. long with peduncle, leaves about 1¼ in. long). But the corolla-tube greatly exceeds the calyx in length, whereas in *H. gracillima* it is only slightly longer.

H. LIGUSTRIFOLIA (A. Cunn.) Ckn. & Allan
Veronica ligustrifolia A. Cunn.

An evergreen shrub up to 3 ft high, of lax habit; young shoots glabrous; leaf-buds without sinus. Leaves ¼ to over 1 in. apart on the branchlets, scarcely or not stalked, narrowly oblong to narrowly lanceolate, 1 to 2¼ in. long, ¼ to ½ in. wide. Flowers produced in slender cylindrical racemes 2 to 3 in. long from the terminal leaf-axils. Corolla white, small, scarcely ¼ in. wide, with a funnel-shaped tube shorter than the calyx and four spreading pointed lobes. Calyx deeply divided into four lobes of ovate-lanceolate shape, pointed and often minutely downy on the margins. Blossoms in July and August.

Native of the North Island of New Zealand. Related to *H. salicifolia* which has leaf-buds with a distinct sinus, much larger, more slenderly pointed leaves, racemes much longer, the corolla-tube longer than the calyx, and is altogether a stronger, bigger shrub.

H. LOGANIOIDES (J. F. Armstr.) Wall
Veronica loganioides J. F. Armstr.

A dwarf, conifer-like shrub, usually well under 1 ft in height; often only 4 to 6 in. Stems erect, becoming decumbent with age; when young, furnished with soft, pale hairs. Leaves $\frac{1}{8}$ to $\frac{1}{6}$ in. long, ovate or lanceolate, tapering from a broad stalkless base to a bluntish point, sometimes entire, sometimes with one or two comparatively large teeth at each side, erect or spreading, keeled at the back, dull green, glabrous. Flowers pure white (sometimes pink-veined), $\frac{1}{4}$ to $\frac{1}{3}$ in. across, produced in June and July in a terminal, single or three-branched inflorescence, on which the flowers open successively for some weeks. Sepals ovate-oblong, pointed, with hairy margins; corolla-tube short, scarcely so long as the sepals. Main and secondary flower-stalks hairy. *Bot. Mag.*, t. 7404.

H. loganioides is a pleasing dwarf evergreen distinct among this group in its hairy stems and racemes; its small, closely set, spreading, frequently toothed leaves; and in the flattish seed-vessel splitting across the narrowest diameter.

The taxonomic status of this hebe is uncertain. Most probably all the cultivated plants descend by cuttings from the original one discovered by J. F. Armstrong in the Upper Rangitata in 1869. It is possibly a hybrid between a whip-cord hebe and *Parahebe lyallii*. See further in *Flora of New Zealand*, Vol. 1, p. 950.

H. LYCOPODIOIDES (Hook. f.) Ckn. & Allan
Veronica lycopodioides Hook. f.

A shrub 1 to 2 ft high, with stiff, erect branches densely clothed with over-lapping scale-like leaves and much resembling a lycopod. The branchlets, as clothed with leaves, are four-sided, each face about $\frac{1}{8}$ in. wide. Leaves on adult plants about $\frac{1}{10}$ in. long, rather more wide, triangular, flattened to the branches and strongly keeled at the back (it is the prominent keel that gives the quadrangular form to the branchlets), abruptly narrowed at the apex to a blunt, thick cusp or spine, each pair united at the base. On young plants, and on occasional 'reverted' branches of older ones, the leaves are twice as long, not pressed to the branches, awl-shaped with a broad base, and often more or less linear-lobed. Flowers produced about midsummer in a small head $\frac{1}{2}$ in. across at the end of the branches; the corolla $\frac{1}{4}$ in. diameter, white, against which the large blue anthers are in effective contrast. *Bot. Mag.*, t. 7338.

Native of the South Island of New Zealand up to 5,500 ft. It is about as hardy as *H. cupressoides* and is equally shy-flowering in this country. From that species it is easily distinguished by the much less dense habit, the final subdivisions of the branches being longer, thicker, and more open; and by the much more closely imbricated leaves (see also *H. hectoris*).

H. MACRANTHA (Hook. f.) Ckn. & Allan
Veronica macrantha Hook. f.

An evergreen shrub of sparse, rather ungainly habit, 1 to 2 ft high, with the leaves about eight to the inch on the young shoots. Leaves obovate, often narrowly so, pointed or rounded at the apex, tapered at the base, conspicuously toothed at the upper half, $\frac{1}{3}$ to 1 in. long, $\frac{1}{4}$ to $\frac{1}{2}$ in. wide, of thick fleshy texture, thickened at the margins, glabrous bright green; stalk short and thick. Flowers

T S—M

pure white, ¾ in. wide, produced from the terminal leaf-axils in clusters of three to eight. *Bot. Mag.*, n.s., t. 177.

A native of the Southern Alps of New Zealand up to 5,000 ft. Although described in 1864, it is of quite recent introduction to Britain (the plate in the *Botanical Magazine* was painted in June 1949 and the sprays figured came from

HEBE MACRANTHA

a plant cultivated in the grounds of the Department of Botany, University of Aberdeen). It is remarkably distinct in the leathery, toothed leaves, but more especially in the flowers being ¾ in. wide and the largest borne by any shrubby New Zealand species. As it occurs up to 5,000 ft altitude on the South Island it should be one of the hardiest. Cheeseman observes that in growth it is by no means so attractive as many other species, but that when in flower few have a more charming appearance: 'The sight of a rocky slope covered with multitudes of the pure white flowers is a spectacle not easily paralleled.'

H. MACROCARPA (Vahl) Ckn. & Allan
Veronica macrocarpa Vahl

A shrub 4 to 8 ft high with stout glabrous branches; leaf-bud without sinus. Leaves 2½ to 6 in. long, ½ to 1¼ in. wide, elliptic, oblong-elliptic, or oblong lanceolate, acute at the apex, dark green, almost glabrous, rather leathery in texture. Flowers white in simple racemes 3 to 6 in. long; bracts small, shorter than the pedicels. Calyx-lobes broad-oblong, obtuse or acute in the same flower. Corolla ¼ in. or slightly more wide at the mouth; tube broad, twice as long as the calyx; corolla-lobes rounded at the apex, longer than the tube. Capsules glabrous, ¼ to almost ½ in. long, much longer than the calyx.

Native of the North Island of New Zealand. A very striking species but also very tender.

var. LATISEPALA (Kirk) Ckn. & Allan *V. latisepala* Kirk—Flowers bluish purple or deep violet. Calyx-lobes short and broad. Racemes usually shorter than the leaves. The material figured in the *Botanical Magazine*, n.s., t. 358, was taken from a plant in the Temperate House at Kew, propagated from one at Tresco Abbey in the Isles of Scilly. In this the flowers are of a deepish lavender-colour.

var. BREVIFOLIA (Cheesem.) L. B. Moore *V. speciosa* var. *brevifolia* Cheesem. —A distinct variety confined to one locality at the northern end of North Island. Flowers reddish purple or violet-purple. Leaves 1 to 2½ in. long, ½ to ¾ in. wide, oblong-obovate to narrow-oblong. Racemes about as long as the leaves. The tender garden variety *H.* 'HEADFORTII', raised at Headfort, Eire, from New Zealand seeds, seems to be very near to this variety in its botanical characters. It has oblong-elliptic leaves about 1⅜ in. long; inflorescences borne in great numbers from the upper leaf-axils; flowers violet with a white throat. The flowering season is spring and early summer.

H. MATTHEWSII (Cheesem.) Ckn.

Veronica matthewsii Cheesem.

An evergreen shrub up to 4 ft high, with quite glabrous, often purplish red young shoots. Leaves closely set on the branches, of thick, leathery texture, stalkless, oblong or oval, rounded at the apex and base, ¾ to 1½ in. long. Racemes slenderly cylindrical, produced in June and July from the leaf-axils towards the tips of the branches, 2 to 4 in. long, ⅓ to ⅝ in. wide; the main-stalk downy, naked at the base for about an inch. Flowers white or purplish, ¼ to ⅓ in. wide; corolla spreading, four-lobed, the lobes rounded at the end; calyx deeply four-lobed, the lobes blunt, with the margins edged with down and often purplish; flower-stalks downy. Capsules egg-shaped, slightly downy.

According to Cockayne and Allan the cultivated plants all derive from the type collection (by H. J. Matthews in the Humboldt Mountains of South Island) and they doubted whether *H. matthewsii* was a good species. It is, how-ever, retained in *Flora of New Zealand* (vol. 1, p. 920). Although not common in commerce, it is one of the most handsome of the hardy species, being of neat habit and bearing racemes unusually long in proportion to the size of the plant.

H. OCHRACEA M. B. Ashwin

H. armstrongii Hort., in part, not (J. B. Armstr.) Ckn. & Allan; *Veronica armstrongii* Hort., in part, not J. B. Armstr.

A low, openly branched shrub usually under 2 ft high, with stout, blackish, spreading main stems, the laterals arching, and the ultimate branchlets of mature plants confined to the upper side of the laterals. It is a member of the whipcord group, the leaves closely appressed, about $\frac{1}{16}$ in. long, deltoid, narrowed to a keeled, slightly incurved, blunt tip, olive-green, but strongly tinged with ochre-yellow at the tip and to a lesser degree along the margins, connate for about one-third of their length; on the ultimate branchlets the tip of each leaf usually reaches to the junction of the leaf-pair above, so that the internodes are exposed only below the leaf-insertions, but on the extension growths the leaf-pairs are somewhat more widely spaced. Flowers white, in short terminal spikes; anterior calyx-lobes united; corolla-tube as broad as wide, equalling or longer than the calyx. Capsules ovoid, longer than the calyx.

Native of the South Island of New Zealand, where it is confined to Nelson province. Although discovered towards the end of the last century, it was first described in 1961, having been previously confused with *H. armstrongii* and other species. The date of introduction to Britain is not certain, but it seems to have become widely available in commerce quite recently (for an older introduction grown under the name *H. armstrongii* see below).

H. ochracea is remarkable for the brown coloration of the whole plant, which derives mainly from the growing points of the ultimate branchlets, where the ochre-coloured tips of the leaves are concentrated. If a potted plant is turned on its side, the colour appears to change to olive-green.

There is another whipcord hebe grown under the name *H. armstrongii* which is not *H. ochracea* and does not agree well with the true *H. armstrongii*. It is of denser habit than *H. ochracea* and is golden green in colour, not coppery brown. The ultimate branchlets are shorter than in *H. ochracea*, slightly four-angled, and the leaves are sharply keeled from tip to base and end in a cuspidate point. This hebe seems to be rare in commerce and no mature plants have been seen. But it appears to be the same as one cultivated in the Edinburgh Botanic Garden at the end of the last century (as *V. armstrongii*) and figured (from a plant grown by Lindsay of Murrayfield, Edinburgh) in *Gard. Chron.*, Vol. 26 (1899), p. 137. But in *Flora of New Zealand* it is remarked that the plant figured in the *Gardeners' Chronicle* 'does not well match Armstrong's type'; not does it agree well with the authentic specimen of *H. armstrongii* in the Kew Herbarium.

The true H. ARMSTRONGII was described by J. B. Armstrong in 1879 from a plant collected by his father in the Upper Rangitata, Canterbury province, ten years earlier. It has dull, yellowish green leaves, which are thin, not keeled, rounded or truncate at the apex and abruptly narrowed to an acute tip; ultimate branches terete. Whether the true species is in cultivation in Britain is not known; there are no garden specimens in the Kew Herbarium that agree with it.

H. PARVIFLORA (Vahl) Ckn. & Allan
Veronica parviflora Vahl

H. parviflora is represented in cultivation mainly by the following variety:

var. ANGUSTIFOLIA (Hook. f.) L. B. Moore *V. parviflora* var. *angustifolia* Hook. f.; *H. angustifolia* (A. Rich.) Ckn. & Allan; *V. angustifolia* A. Rich., not Fisch. & Link; *V. squalida* Kirk—A shrub 3 to 5 ft high, occasionally more, of rather thin, loose habit; branches slender, erect, glabrous and shining, turning dark brown towards the end of the season. Leaves stalkless (leaf-buds without sinus), linear, $1\frac{1}{2}$ to $3\frac{1}{2}$ in. long, $\frac{1}{8}$ to $\frac{1}{4}$ in. wide, tapering to a point, perfectly glabrous, often pointing downwards. Racemes in pairs from the leaf-axils near the summit of the shoot, 2 to 5 in. long, $\frac{3}{4}$ in. wide; the basal flowers opening long before the terminal ones. Flowers white, tinged more or less with lilac, $\frac{1}{6}$ to $\frac{1}{4}$ in. diameter; tube of corolla slender, twice or thrice as long as the sepals, which are erect, oblong, edged with minute hairs. Individual flower-stalk slender, $\frac{1}{8}$ to $\frac{1}{4}$ in. long, and, like the main-stalk of the raceme, minutely downy. *Bot. Mag.*, t. 5965.

Native of the South Island of New Zealand and probably also of North Island; introduced about 1868, perhaps before. It is very distinct in its narrow leaves and purple-brown stems, and has considerable merit as a flowering shrub, producing its graceful racemes from July until November in successive pairs near the top of the growing shoot. It succumbs in severe winters.

var. ARBOREA (Buchan.) L. B. Moore   *V. arborea* Buchan.; *V. parviflora* var. *arborea* (Buchan.) Kirk—A diffusely branched, evergreen shrub 6 ft and upwards high, but described as being sometimes in the wild a tree 20 to 25 ft high with a trunk 6 ft in girth near the base; young shoots slender, bearing the leaf-pairs from $\frac{1}{8}$ to $\frac{1}{2}$ in. apart. Leaves linear or linear-lanceolate, pointed, stalkless, 1 to $2\frac{1}{2}$ in. long, $\frac{1}{6}$ to $\frac{1}{4}$ in. wide, with minutely downy margins, otherwise glabrous. Flowers white with a tinge of lilac, $\frac{1}{6}$ in. wide, densely produced during July and August on slender racemes up to 3 in. long from near the end of the branchlets; main flower-stalks downy. Calyx-lobes oblong, round-ended, margined with minute hairs; corolla-tube one and a half times the length of the calyx.

Native chiefly of the North Island, New Zealand, up to 2,000 ft altitude, but occurring also near Queen Charlotte Sound at the north of the South Island. It appears to be the largest of all the New Zealand hebes and a tree 28 ft high with a trunk 2 ft in diameter is recorded. This hebe is not common in cultivation and probably tender, but there are specimens in the Kew Herbarium from gardens at Lewes (1948) and Stockbridge, Hants (1961).

It should be noted that the description given above covers a wider range of plants than the original *Veronica arborea* of Buchanan. This was described from plants growing wild near Wellington which are 'perfectly dome-shaped' when young and have leaves 1 to $1\frac{1}{2}$ in. long, $\frac{1}{6}$ in. wide and inflorescences scarcely longer than the leaves; leaves fascicled near the ends of the twigs (*Fl. N.Z.*, Vol. 1, p. 913).

H. PIMELEOIDES (Hook. f.) Ckn. & Allan

Veronica pimeleoides Hook f.; *V. glaucocaerulea*, Hort.; *H. pimeleoides* var. *glaucocaerulea* Hort.

A prostrate or partially erect shrub with downy (sometimes very downy) and often dark-coloured young branches. Leaves closely set in four vertical rows, ovate, oval or obovate, $\frac{3}{16}$ to $\frac{3}{8}$ in. long, tapered towards both ends, concave, more or less glaucous, sometimes edged with red, stalkless and without leaf-bud sinus. Flowers purplish blue, $\frac{1}{4}$ to $\frac{1}{3}$ in. diameter, stalkless, produced during June, July, and August in solitary or branched, cylindrical spikes $\frac{3}{4}$ to 2 in.

long, the main-stalk of the spike very hairy. Corolla-tube very short. Capsules pointed, downy or glabrous. *Bot. Mag.*, t. 8967.

Native of the South Island of New Zealand in dry places. It is a well-marked species but somewhat variable in the size and shape of the leaves and the degree of their glaucousness. In exposed habitats dwarf plants are found with leaves shorter and narrower than described above. The variety *H. pimeleoides* var. *glaucocaerulea* (J. B. Armstr.) Ckn. & Allan is probably only a part of the normal variation of the species, and plants grown under this name do not, in any case, agree with Armstrong's specimens as described in *Flora of New Zealand* (Vol. 1, p. 923). The botanist N. E. Brown remarked eighty years ago that a plant he had seen in cultivation as *V. glaucocaerulea* differed in no way from Hooker's type of *H. pimeleoides* (*Gard. Chron.*, Vol. 8 (1890), p. 69).

H. pimeleoides is a very pleasing dwarf shrub, the purplish blue flowers contrasting admirably with the glaucous leaves. A charming combination of leaf-colour, habit, and shade of flower can be achieved by planting it with the hybrid 'Carl Teschner'. It seems to dislike excessive wet and should be given a sunny position in light, well-drained gritty soil.

H. PINGUIFOLIA (Hook. f.) Ckn. & Allan

Veronica pinguifolia Hook f.

A shrub 1 to 3 ft high, branches at first erect, often ultimately prostrate; minutely downy when young, stained with purple beneath each pair of leaves. Leaves closely superposed in four rows, obovate, blunt at the apex, tapered to a broad stalkless vase, ½ to ¾ in. long, ¼ to ⅜ in. wide, quite entire, concave or scoop-shaped, dull glaucous green. Flowers white, ¼ to ⅓ in. diameter, stalkless, crowded on spikes ¾ to 1 in. long which are borne in the terminal leaf-axils, rachis of spike downy. Calyx with four minutely downy, oblong, blunt divisions. Corolla-tube scarcely as long as the calyx; ovary and style downy. Seed-vessel oblong or obovate, rounded at the apex, downy, nearly twice as long as the calyx. *Bot. Mag.*, t. 6147 and 6587.

Native of the South Island of New Zealand; introduced about 1868. It is killed by very severe frosts, but survives most of the winters in the South of England, flowering about midsummer, although not abundantly nor regularly. It is very similar to, and much confused with *H. carnosula*, under which name it was figured in the *Bot. Mag.*, t. 6587. The differences between the two are in the often comparatively broader leaves of *H. carnosula*, its glabrous ovary and style, and its ovate, pointed, glabrous seed-vessel.

cv. 'PAGEI'.—A low shrub making a clump about 1 ft high and 2 to 3 ft across. Young stems plum-coloured. Leaves very glaucous, oblong-elliptic or slightly obovate, ½ in. or slightly more long. Flowers white, in short clusters, borne in May or even earlier in a mild spring and often again in late summer. A.M. 1958. For a note on the history and botany of this cultivar by J. Souster, see *Journ. R.H.S.*, Vol. 88 (1963), pp. 301–4. It is very beautiful when well grown and needs a sunny position and a well-drained soil.

H. propinqua (Cheesem.) Ckn. & Allan

Veronica propinqua Cheesem.; *V. cupressoides* var. *variabilis* N. E. Brown; *V. salicornoides* Hort., not Hook. f.

This is very closely related to the well-known *H. cupressoides*, having the same small, scale-like leaves and bearing considerable resemblance in leaf and twig to a cypress. The leaves, however, are more closely set on the twigs, blunter and thicker; the plant is dwarfer (1 to 3 ft high), the seed-vessel is $\frac{1}{8}$ in. long ($\frac{1}{12}$ in. in *cupressoides*) and of ovoid instead of obovoid shape. The flowers are white (pale blue in *cupressoides*), about $\frac{1}{4}$ in. wide, produced in small clusters of four to eight near the end of the twigs.

Native of the South Island of New Zealand; cultivated in this country since about 1870, but was at first thought to be the *H. salicornoides* (see below). It was also confused with *H. cupressoides*.

H. salicornoides (Hook. f.) Ckn. & Allan *Veronica salicornoides* Hook. f.

—A sparsely branched erect shrub with rather fleshy stems. Leaves thin, closely appressed to the stem, very short (about $\frac{1}{24}$ in. long), broadly rounded at the apex, the opposite pairs united for about half their length but not overlapping the pair above; the leaves appear to be decurrent onto the stems and hence to be much longer than they really are but the true node is marked by a faint horizontal line.

A native of the South Island of New Zealand. One of its habitats is the Wairau Gorge near Dunedin, and the figure in N. E. Brown's article in *Gard. Chron.*, Vol. 3 (1888), pp. 20–1, fig. 3, was made from a herbarium specimen (preserved at Kew), collected in that locality by Travers in 1861. It is not known to be in cultivation. The plant sometimes seen in gardens under the name *H. salicornoides aurea* does not belong to this species and is near *H. propinqua*.

H. rakaiensis (J. B. Armstr.) Ckn.

Veronica rakaiensis J. B. Armstr.; *H. scott-thomsonii* Allan; *H. subalpina* Hort., not (Ckn.) Ckn. & Allan; *V. subalpina* Hort., not Ckn.

A shrub of dense habit, usually 2 to 3 ft high in cultivation, more in spread branchlets with two lines of down on each internode. Leaf-bud without sinus. Leaves spreading, elliptic, oblong-elliptic or slightly oblanceolate, $\frac{1}{2}$ to $\frac{3}{4}$ in. long, $\frac{1}{4}$ in. or slightly less wide, soft, slightly glossy green above, mat green beneath, glabrous except for the minutely ciliate margins. Flowers white in simple racemes about 2 in. long, including peduncle slightly shorter than the subtending leaf; bracts shorter than the pedicels. Calyx-lobes with a membranous margin. Corolla-tube rather broad, as long as the calyx or slightly shorter; corolla-lobes much longer than the tube. Capsules downy, pointed.

Native of the South Island of New Zealand from mid-Canterbury southwards, on the eastern side of the divide. This species is very common in cultivation but at present (1971) it is almost always seen under the name *H. (V.) subalpina*. It is a hardy evergreen of neat habit and foliage of a cheerful green.

H. subalpina (Ckn.) Ckn. & Allan *Veronica subalpina* Ckn.; *V. montana*

J. B. Armstr., not L.; *V. monticola* J. B. Armstr., not Trautv.—It is not certain if this species is in cultivation; the plants commonly seen under its name are clearly *H. rakaiensis*. The true *H. subalpina* differs from that species in its glabrous capsules and has longer leaves, about 1 in. long. It is also of taller growth, and inhabits the western side of the Dividing Range of South Island. If the two species were to be united, which is not likely, the name *H. rakaiensis* would have priority.

H. RECURVA Simpson & Thomson
Hebe or *Veronica aoira* Hort.

A shrub of low, spreading habit; young stems with short, erect hairs, mostly 1½ in. long, ¼ in. wide on cultivated plants but up to 2 in. long and ⅜ in. wide on wild ones, narrowly lanceolate, tapered fairly evenly from the broad base to the sharp apex, sessile, rather thin, glabrous, glaucous grey, midrib conspicuous. Racemes unbranched, about 2 in. long, downy; bracts from one-half to almost as long as the flower-stalks. Flowers white, on downy stalks which are about ⅛ in. long. Calyx-lobes narrow, fringed with down. Lobes of corolla rounded, tube almost twice the length of the calyx. Capsules glabrous, narrow-ovoid, about twice the length of the calyx-lobes.

Native of N.W. Nelson in the South Island of New Zealand, where it is confined, in its typical state, to one locality on the Aorere River near Bainham. It was described in 1940 but some seventeen years earlier Messrs Hillier had received a plant from Aldenham as 'a species from Mt Aoira' and it was as 'Aoira' (obviously a mistake for Aorere), or under the specific name "*Veronica aoira*" that this hebe spread into gardens (J. Souster, 'Notes on some Cultivated Veronicas: "Aoira" ', *Journ. R.H.S.*, Vol. 88 (Aug. 1963), pp. 357–8).

H. recurva has the aspect of a hybrid but is reported to come more or less true from seed and is accepted as a species in *Flora of New Zealand*. Mr Souster has suggested that the cultivar name 'Aoira' should be maintained for the Aldenham clone, which is probably the one commonest in commerce. *H. recurva* is one of the most attractive of the low-growing hebes, producing an abundance of snowy white flowers in late July and early August. It is not completely hardy but should come through all but the hardest winters. One plant at Kew is about 5 ft wide.

H. SALICIFOLIA (Forst. f.) Pennel
Veronica salicifolia Forst. f.

A shrub 12 to 15 ft high with green, glabrous branchlets. Leaves lanceolate or oblong-lanceolate, 2 to 6 in. long, ½ to 1 in. wide, narrowed at the apex into a long acuminate tip, narrowed at the base into a short, broad petiole (leaf-buds with a distinct sinus), rather thin, glabrous except for minute down on the midrib. Racemes slenderly cylindrical, 4 to 6, sometimes almost 10 in. long, ¾ in. wide, very thickly crowded with blossom; peduncle 1 to 2 in. long. Flowers small, ¼ in. long, shortly stalked, white or white tinged with lilac; corolla-tube rather wide, not much longer than the calyx; corolla-lobes narrow, not spreading; calyx-lobes narrow, pointed, fringed with down. Seed-capsules rounded, glabrous, less than twice as long as the calyx, pointing backward towards the base of the raceme when ripe.

Native of the South Island of New Zealand, where it ranges from sea-level to subalpine elevations, and of south Chile, where it appears to be confined to the coast; discovered at Dusky Bay, Fiordland, New Zealand, during Cook's second voyage. As now represented in cultivation, and as now defined, *H. salicifolia* is quite hardy, but Cheeseman included in *H. salicifolia* as varieties the tender *H. gigantea* and also *H. stricta*. This latter species (q.v.) is in the main confined to North Island and might well have tender forms. The distinguishing characters of *H. salicifolia* are the long, lanceolate leaves acuminately tapered at the apex and abruptly narrowed at the base to a short petiole (leaf-buds with distinct sinus) and the backward-pointing seed-capsules.

H. × AMABILIS (Cheesem.) Ckn. & Allan *V. amabilis* Cheesem.; *V. salicifolia* var. *gracilis* Kirk—This hybrid is believed to be *H. elliptica* × *H. salicifolia*. The type was collected near The Bluff, south of Invercargill in Otago province, and is well figured in Kirk's *Forest Flora of New Zealand*, t. 120. A shrub 6 to 15 ft high. Leaves oblong-elliptic or elliptic-lanceolate, 2 to 4 in. long, ¾ to 1 in. wide, glabrous, flowers white, large, ⅜ in. across at the mouth, with a short broad tube not much longer than the calyx. Capsules about twice as long as calyx. This very robust form of the cross was likened by Kirk to *H. macrocarpa* but that species has the leaf-buds without sinus, whereas the sinus would be well marked in any cross between *H. salicifolia* and *H. elliptica*. And in *H. macrocarpa* (q.v.) the capsules are very large.

Cheeseman also described *H.* × *amabilis* var. BLANDA (*H.* × *blanda* (Cheesem.) Pennell) which is of the same parentage and is perhaps commoner than the typical form in New Zealand; it also occurs in Chile. According to Cheeseman the variety has smaller leaves, up to 2½ in. long, ½ to ¾ in. wide, more closely set, and shorter, relatively broad racemes. Flowers white, ¼ to ⅜ in. across.

H. × KIRKII (J. B. Armstr.) Ckn. & Allan *V. kirkii* J. B. Armstr.; *V. salicifolia* var. *kirkii* (J. B. Armstr.) Cheesem.—A tall shrub with polished dark brown young stems. Leaves lanceolate, 1 to 1½ in. long, ⅜ in. wide, acute, sessile on a broad base (leaf-bud without sinus), midrib prominent beneath. Flowers white in slender racemes 4 to 8 in. long; pedicels short; bracts lanceolate. Calyx-lobes acuminate. Tube of corolla about ⅕ in. long. Capsules downy or glabrous. A probable hybrid between *H. salicifolia* and *H. rakaiensis* described from a colony discovered in the Upper Rangitata in 1868 and introduced to Britain soon after.

H. × LEWISII (J. B. Armstr.) Ckn. & Allan *V. lewisii* J. B. Armstr.—This probable hybrid was described by Armstrong from specimens collected on dunes near the sea in Canterbury province, some near Timaru. It is a densely branched shrub to 6 ft high with downy stems. Leaves pale green, 1½ to 2½ in. long, ¾ to 1 in. wide, oblong or elliptic-oblong, obtuse to acute at the apex, distinctly ciliate. Flowers, according to Armstrong, white, pale purple or blue

and up to ½ in. wide across the limb. They are densely arranged in racemes up
to 2½ in. long and 1½ in. wide.

Armstrong thought this hebe was *H. elliptica* × *speciosa*, but the latter species
does not extend nearly so far south as Canterbury province, and in *Flora of New
Zealand* it is suggested that the hybrid is of the same parentage as *H.* × *amabilis*.
If this is the case, *H.* × *lewisii* would be the correct name for the cross *H.
elliptica* × *salicifolia*.

H. × *lewisii* has certainly been in cultivation in Cornwall and might still be
found there or in other west coast gardens.

H. SPECIOSA (A. Cunn.) Ckn. & Allan
Veronica speciosa A. Cunn.

A shrub up to 5 ft high; branches spreading, very stout even when young,
glabrous, two-edged at first. Leaf-bud with a distinct sinus. Leaves 2 to 4 in.
long, ¾ to 1¾ in. wide, obovate, rounded or bluntish at the apex, tapered at the
base to a very short stalk, dark shining green, leathery, glabrous except that the
midrib above and the margins near the base are minutely downy. Racemes produced in the uppermost leaf-axils, 1½ to 3 in. long, 1 to 1½ in. thick. Flowers
dark reddish purple, ⅓ in. diameter. *Bot. Mag.*, t. 4057.

Native of the North Island of New Zealand, where it was discovered in
December 1833, by Richard Cunningham, at the south head of Hokianga
Harbour. It occurs also in the South Island, but is very rare and confined to
small areas, always on cliffs near the sea. The typical plant is rare in cultivation,
but it is very striking in the great width of its round-ended or broadly tapered
leaves. It has, however, by hybridisation with other species given birth to a
very valuable series of evergreen flowering shrubs, in which its influence is
seen in the purple, violet, or reddish flowers.

H. STRICTA (Benth.) L. B. Moore
Veronica stricta Benth., *H. salicifolia* var. *stricta* (Benth.) Ckn. & Allan;
V. salicifolia var. *stricta* (Benth.) Hook. f.

A shrub of variable habit growing to 10 ft high in the wild, occasionally
taller; leaf-bud without sinus; stems glabrous or finely downy. Leaves linear-
lanceolate or lanceolate, 2 to 5 in. long, ⅓ to ¾ in. wide, tapered to an acute or
acuminate tip, entire or with a few remote small teeth, not glossy, glabrous
except for fine down along the margins and midrib. Flowers white or pale lilac
in simple racemes longer than the leaves; bracts and calyx-lobes downy all over
their surface; corolla about 3/16 in. long, the tube slender, longer than the calyx,
lobes rounded, shorter than the tube. Style and top of ovary downy. Capsules
about twice as long as calyx.

A native of the North Island of New Zealand. It is part of *H. salicifolia* as
understood until recently, but differs in the absence of a leaf-bud sinus and
in the longer, more slender corolla-tubes. Also, in the typical variety described
above the bracts and calyx-lobes are downy all over (only ciliate in *H. salicifolia*),

but this distinction does not hold good for the varieties described below, both of which have probably been introduced:

var. ATKINSONII (Ckn.) L. B. Moore *V. salicifolia* var. *atkinsonii* Ckn.—A shrub up to 6 ft or slightly more high. Leaves narrow-elliptic or linear-lanceolate, 2 to 4 in. long, acute at the apex, not glossy. Bracts and calyx-lobes downy only on the margins. According to Cockayne this variety rapidly colonises cuttings in the vicinity of Wellington, and also occurs in the northern part of South Island.

var. EGMONTIANA L. B. Moore *H. salicifolia* var. *egmontiana* (Ckn.) Ckn. & Allan, *nom. inedit.*—A compact shrub to 10 ft high with linear-lanceolate leaves 2¼ to 2¾ in. long and about ⅓ in. wide, tapered to an acute point. According to Cockayne it forms pure stands on Mt Egmont at about 3,500 ft. In this and the preceding variety the bracts and calyx-lobes are downy only on the margins and the capsule is glabrous.

H. MACROURA (Benth.) Ckn. & Allan *Veronica macroura* Benth.; *H. stricta* var. *macroura* (Benth.) L. B. Moore—A small densely branched shrub. Leaves obovate-oblong to oblanceolate, 1 to 3 in. long, ½ to 1¼ in. wide, glabrous except for the sometimes downy margins. Leaf-bud without sinus. Flowers white or tinged with blue, densely arranged in racemes 2 to 4 in. long. Calyx-lobes oblong, ciliate and sometimes downy on the surface. Capsules pendulous, i.e., pointing towards the base of the inflorescence. Native of the North Island of New Zealand. It is distinguished from *H. stricta* by the relatively shorter and broader leaves, but hybrids between the two are said to occur in the wild. The foliage and the absence of a leaf-bud sinus distinguish it from *H. salicifolia*.

Plants cultivated in Britain under the name *H. cookiana* seem to belong to *H. macroura*. They probably came here originally as *V. macroura* var. *cookiana* (Col.) Cheesem. and agree with that variety in having racemes about 6 in. long. They are said to be fairly hardy. The habit is low and spreading and the leaves are irregularly waved and puckered, 1⅞ to 2½ in. long, ¾ to 1¼ in. wide, ciliate. Bracts and calyx-lobes downy all over the surface.

H. TETRASTICHA (Hook. f.) Ckn. & Allan
Veronica tetrasticha Hook. f.

An evergreen, small, freely branching shrub 3 to 6 in. high, forming tufts up to 1 ft across; shoots decumbent below, upper ones erect, hollowed on four sides and thus making them sharply tetragonous. Leaves very densely-set, 1/12 to 1/10 in. wide, narrowly spathulate, ciliate, imbricated in four vertical rows, each pair joining at the base to clasp the stem. Flowers white, ⅛ to ⅙ in. wide, borne in short two- to four-flowered spikes near the tips of the branches, stalks downy. Seed-vessels laterally compressed.

Native of the South Island of New Zealand at altitudes of 3,000 to 6,000 ft and quite hardy. This distinct and interesting dwarf shrub belongs to a small group of rock-dwelling species which have the whipcord foliage of *H. cupressoides* and its allies but differ in their laterally compressed seed-capsules and functionally unisexual flowers. For this group see *Fl. N.Z.*, Vol. 1 (1961), pp. 944–946. *H. tetrasticha* is figured in Philipson and Hearn, *Rock Garden Plants*, plate 52.

GARDEN HYBRIDS

Of the many hybrids of garden origin available in commerce, only a selection can be treated below. The hybrids of *H. speciosa* are particularly valuable for seaside gardens, not only because they enjoy the greater mildness and dampness of the climatic conditions there, but because many of them are not injured even by salt spray. See also *H.* × *franciscana*, which being a validly named botanical group is treated in alphabetical order among the species.

'ALICIA AMHERST'.—A robust shrub 3 to 4 ft high. Leaves elliptic or elliptic-ovate, mostly acuminately narrowed at the apex to a blunt point, 3 to 3½ in. long, 1 to 1½ in. wide, darkish green, leathery. Flowers very large, deep violet, crowded in racemes 3 in. or more long; corolla-tube broad, not much longer than the calyx and about equal in length to the lobes. A handsome hebe, near to *H. speciosa* but hardier, flowering from August. It is often grown as 'Veitchii', but this cultivar, raised by Messrs Veitch of Exeter and shown by them in 1911, is not the same as the plant described above, judging from the specimen in the Kew Herbarium.

'ANDERSONII'.—Flowers bluish purple fading to white, in racemes 4 to 5 in. long. Corolla-tube about ⅛ in. wide at the mouth, the lobes acute, slightly longer than the tube. Calyx about half as long as the corolla-tube or slightly longer, with ovate, acute lobes. Leaves elliptic or oblanceolate, obtuse at the apex, 3 to 4 in. long, of softly leathery texture. A hybrid of *H. speciosa*, raised by Isaac Anderson-Henry shortly before 1849. The other parent, said to be *H. salicifolia*, was in fact a plant named *Veronica lindleyana*, which had been raised from seeds sent to Scotland from New Zealand in 1843. There must be some doubt whether this plant could have been the true *H. salicifolia* as defined in Allan's *Flora of New Zealand*.

'Andersonii' was once commonly used for greenhouse decoration in early winter. It is now uncommon, but can easily be obtained by propagating reversion shoots from its beautiful variegated sport 'ANDERSONII VARIEGATA', with leaves margined ivory-white, the centre grey-green splashed with the normal darker green. This is tender and commoner as a bedding-plant than as a mature bush. It arose before 1856.

'AUTUMN GLORY'.—An erect, sparsely branched shrub about 2 ft high, with dark stems. Leaves broad-elliptic to obovate, 1 to 1¼ in. long, edged with red when young, glossy green with a slight glaucous tinge. Flowers deep purplish blue, in broad, dense, often compound racemes 1½ to 1¾ in. long; tube white. It flowers more or less continuously from midsummer onwards and is fairly hardy in a well-drained not too rich soil. It is a seedling of 'TOBARCORRANENSIS' and was raised at Smith's Daisy Hill Nursery at Newry, Co. Down, around 1900. The parent, which is perhaps no longer in cultivation, occurred as a self-sown seedling in the garden of Gen. Bland at White Abbey, Tobarcorran, near Belfast (*Gard. Chron.*, Vol. 92, p. 22). Mr Smith believed that the parentage of Gen. Bland's plant was *H. vernicosa* × *H. pime-*

leoides, both of which grew at White Abbey. But this parentage, which is the one suggested for 'Balfouriana', does not seem quite right for 'Tobarcorranensis', judging from herbarium specimens, and is certainly not right for 'Autumn Glory'. But there can be little doubt that 'Autumn Glory' derives partly from *H. pimeleoides*, the influence of which is shown in the habit, the red-edged leaves, the large bracts and the downy ovary and style. The other parent could be *H.* × *franciscana*.   [PLATE 50

'BALFOURIANA'.—This hybrid, of uncertain parentage, was raised in the Edinburgh Botanic Garden from New Zealand seeds and is figured in *Bot. Mag.*, t. 7556 (1897). It is a shrub about 3 ft high with erect purplish stems. Leaves $\frac{1}{3}$ to $\frac{3}{4}$ in. long, $\frac{1}{6}$ to $\frac{1}{4}$ in. wide, oval to obovate, purple-edged when young. Flowers pale purplish blue, produced about midsummer in racemes 2 to 3 in. long; bracts as long as pedicels or slightly longer; calyx-lobes acute, about as long as corolla-tube. This hybrid was at first grown as *H. vernicosa* and is considered by Cockayne and Allan to be a hybrid between that species and *H. pimeleoides*.

It should be added that the name *Veronica balfouriana*, used by Hooker for this hybrid, properly belongs to a cross between two true veronicas, raised by Isaac Anderson-Henry and named in 1867. The parentage was given by him as *V. saxatalis* crossed with *V. fruticulosa*.

'BOWLES'S HYBRID'.—Leaves pale green, slightly glossy, narrow-elliptic or oblong-elliptic, up to 1 in. long. Inflorescences usually compound, made up of two to five racemes, 3 to 4 in. long, including main peduncle. Flowers widely spaced; corolla-tube rather broad, the lobes pale lavender-purple, shorter than the tube.

A charming dwarf shrub, usually under 2 ft high, producing its graceful panicles continuously from July until early winter. It was not raised by Bowles, and is very probably the plant mentioned by him in *My Garden in Summer* (p. 140), which came from the Warham Rectory. It is also known as *H. parviflora* 'Bowles's Variety', as *H. diosmifolia* 'Bowles's Variety' or even as "*H. diosmifolia*". It might be a hybrid between these two species, but there are other possibilities.

The hebe known as 'EVERSLEY SEEDLING' seems to be in every respect the same as 'Bowles's Hybrid', but differences in habit, hardiness, etc., might emerge if the two were grown together over a period of years.

'CARL TESCHNER'.—A procumbent shrub building up to 9 in. or more high in the centre and 3 ft, perhaps more, across. Stems very dark, almost black. Leaves dark green, elliptic, acute about $\frac{3}{8}$ in. long. Flowers violet, borne in July in racemes $1\frac{1}{4}$ to $1\frac{1}{2}$ in. long including peduncle *c.* $\frac{1}{2}$ in. long. A.M. 1964. Said to be *H. elliptica* × *pimeleoides*. Moderately hardy, with strikingly dark stems and richly coloured flowers.

'CARNEA'.—Leaves oblong-elliptic, acute at the apex, $1\frac{1}{4}$ m. or slightly more long, $\frac{1}{4}$ to $\frac{1}{3}$ in. wide, glossy above, with red-tinged margins. Flowers white overlaid with pink, fading to pure white, in racemes 3 to 5 in. long. Corolla-tube much longer than the calyx. Calyx-lobes with a broad membranous margin which is coloured bright red. A very beautiful hebe, which received an Award of Merit in 1925. Judging from the detailed description he gave, it is very similar to a plant which J. B. Armstrong named *Veronica carnea* in 1881, but the racemes are longer and there are other differences. At that time the plant was common in New Zealand gardens and said to have been found originally in the wild, though it has never been rediscovered there.

'E. A. Bowles'. See under 'Mrs Winder'.

'Edinensis'.—Leaves densely set on the shoot, loosely appressed at the base, then arching outwards, narrowly oblong-ovate, up to ¼ in. long, glossy above, keeled beneath. Internodes with two lines of white wool. A hybrid of dwarf habit, raised shortly before 1910 by R. Lindsay of Edinburgh from a plant grown by him under the name *V. hectori*, but a specimen from the actual plant, preserved in the Kew Herbarium, shows that it was not that species and perhaps itself a hybrid. The pollen-parent was said by Lindsay to be *V. pimeleoides* but, as he himself noted, its influence is not apparent. 'Cassinioides', of wild origin, is similar but more robust and upright, and does not have woolly internodes. It is believed to be *H. lycopodioides* × *H. buxifolia*.

'Ettrick Shepherd'.—Flowers magenta-purple at first, fading to pure white, slender-stalked, densely packed in racemes 3 to 4 in. long. Leaves oblanceolate, mat-green, purple beneath when young. July. The flowers fade so abruptly and are so closely set that the inflorescence is distinctly bi-coloured. A very striking hebe, cultivated at Kew and available in commerce. Ultimate height probably 3 to 4 ft.

'Gauntlettii'.—Flowers salmon-pink with a purplish tube, in racemes 6 in. long. Leaves 2¾ to 3¼ in. long. August–October. Tender, near to *H. speciosa*.

'Great Orme'.—Similar to 'Carnea' in habit, foliage and botanical characters, but with pinker flowers.

'Headfortii'. See under *H. macrocarpa*.

'Highdownensis'.—Leaves fairly glossy, bright green, oblong, up to 2¾ in. long. Flowers blue-violet with white tubes, about $\frac{3}{16}$ in. wide at the mouth, in racemes 5 in. long. An erect shrub up to 6 ft high, flowering in July and again in autumn (and well into the winter if the weather is mild).

'La Seduisante'.—Flowers deep magenta-purple, in racemes about 4 in. long, borne July to October. Leaves elliptic, purple beneath when young, 2 to 3 in. long. Near to *H. speciosa*. A.M. 1897. Tender.

'Lindsayi'.—Leaves broadly oblong-elliptic, about ¾ in. long, rounded to almost truncate at the apex, medium green and slightly concave above, with a paler margin. Stems erect, purplish brown. Flowers pale pink, in short dense racemes. A hybrid between *H. amplexicaulis* and (probably) *H. pimeleoides*, raised by R. Lindsay late in the 19th century. It has quite pretty shell-like foliage and was used by the famous gardener E. A. Bowles as a foil to choice ferns.

'Margery Fish'.—A compact shrub 2 to 3 ft high. Leaves oblong-elliptic to oblong-lanceolate, ¾ to 1¼ in. long, rather wavy, margins and often the midrib beneath tinged with red; youngest leaves tufted and bronzy in winter. Flowers violet-blue with white tubes borne in summer and often in autumn in dense racemes 3 to 4 in. long. A delightful hebe of dense habit, fairly hardy. 'Primley Gem' raised at the Paignton Zoo, is similar.

'Marjorie'.—A low spreading shrub 2 to 3 ft high, more across. Leaves resembling those of the Andersonii group but shorter, usually toothed on young plants. Flowers of a clear light blue, in short racemes. Said to be very hardy.

'MᴄEᴡᴀɴɪɪ'.—A dwarf erect shrub with glaucous, acute leaves $\frac{5}{8}$ to $\frac{7}{16}$ in. long, $\frac{1}{8}$ to $\frac{3}{16}$ in. wide. Flowers slightly tinged with blue, in short racemes. Probably a hybrid between *H. colensoi* and *H. pimeleoides*.

'Mɪᴅsᴜᴍᴍᴇʀ Bᴇᴀᴜᴛʏ'.—A hybrid of *H. salicifolia* with elliptic or oblong, acuminate leaves about 4 in. long, strongly tinged with reddish purple beneath when young. Flowers borne from July until early winter in fairly dense racemes about 5 in. long; corollas lavender-purple, the tube only slightly paler than the lobes. It is moderately hardy, very floriferous, growing to about 4 ft in height and more in width. It was put into commerce by Messrs Cheal and received an Award of Merit in 1960. There are many other hybrids similar to this, deriving their hardiness from *H. salicifolia* and the colouring of their flowers from some hybrid of *H. speciosa*. Two known to be very hardy are the old 'Mᴀᴜᴠᴇɴᴀ', raised before 1911, and the newer 'Mɪss E. Fɪᴛᴛᴀʟʟ'. These are described in the article by J. Souster in *Journ. R.H.S.*, Vol. 87 (1962), pp. 37–8.

'Mʀs Wɪɴᴅᴇʀ'.—A shrub of fairly dense habit, 3 to 4 ft high and more in width. Stems dark reddish brown, glabrous. Leaves narrowly oblong-elliptic, 1 to 1¼ in. long, *c.* ¼ in. wide, transversely wrinkled at first, red-rimmed, midrib prominent beneath, tinged with red at the base. Racemes 2½ to 3 in. long including peduncle ¾ in. long; bracts lanceolate or narrow-elliptic, acute, equalling or longer than the pedicels. Tube of corolla white, fairly slender; corolla-lobes violet, obtuse, shorter than the tube. This pretty and free-flowering variety seems to be the commonest in catalogues of a group of hybrids with dark stems, acute leaves usually margined with red when young and flowers with white tubes and violet lobes. 'E. A. Bᴏᴡʟᴇs' and 'Wᴀʀʟᴇʏᴇɴsɪs' (of Messrs Toynbee), bear a very close resemblance to each other and both are similar to 'Mrs Winder', but it is impossible to make valid comparisons unless the plants are grown side by side. Another hybrid in this group is 'Wᴀɪᴋɪᴋɪ', which is well distinguished by its low, spreading habit.

'Sɪᴍᴏɴ Dᴇʟᴀᴜx'.—Flowers in racemes about 5 in. long, the lobes crimson, concave, obtuse, the tube and anthers purplish. Leaves ovate, purple-edged, about 2 in. long. Tender. A hybrid of *H. speciosa*.

'Sᴘᴇɴᴅᴇʀ's Sᴇᴇᴅʟɪɴɢ'.—Flowers white, slender-stalked, in narrow racemes up to 6 in. long; peduncle short. Calyx deeply segmented into long, acute lobes, equalling the corolla-tube. Leaves thin, narrowly elliptic, up to 3 in. long, $\frac{5}{16}$ in. wide. A beautiful hybrid, near to *H. gracillima*, of low spreading habit, bearing its racemes in July in great profusion from the upper leaf-axils. This description is drawn up from a plant in the Hebe collection at Kew. A commercial plant under the name 'Spender's Seedling' is different. Its white flowers have very slender tubes more than twice as long as the calyx and their pedicels are always longer than the bracts (shorter than the bracts or equalling them in the Kew plant). The leaves are narrowly lanceolate, tapered evenly to an acute falcate tip and up to about 2½ in. long, ¼ in. wide. This plant appears to be tall-growing, and judging from identical plants seen (without label) in a Sussex garden, it should attain 6 ft and be perfectly hardy. It is possibly a hybrid between *H. parviflora* var. *angustifolia* and *H. stricta*.

'Tricolor'.—Leaves elliptic, 2 to 3 in. long, centre pale grey-green, darker along the veins, margins yellowish white, the whole blade flushed with purple when young. Flowers magenta-purple, in racemes longer than the leaves.

'Veitchii'. See 'Alicia Amherst'.

'Viceroy'.—Flowers pale blue, short stalked, densely arranged in racemes about 3 in. long. Leaves elliptic or slightly obovate, about 1¾ in. long, ¾ in. wide, three-veined at base, pinnately veined towards apex. Hardy. June–July. Raised by Messrs Burkwood and Skipwith, and of interest as the result of a deliberate cross between *H. salicifolia* and 'Autumn Glory'.

'Waikiki'. See under 'Mrs Winder'.

'White Gem'.—This hybrid is usually listed as a variety of *H. brachysiphon*, differing in its earlier flowering and dwarfer habit. It does not belong to that species, from which it differs in a number of characters, notably its downy style and ovary. It is possibly a hybrid between *H. brachysiphon* and *H. pinguifolia*. It is hardy, very floriferous and makes a useful weed-smotherer if massed. The flowering time is early June. A similar, perhaps identical hebe was once grown under the name "*Veronica traversii praecox*".

HEDERA   Ivy   araliaceae

A small group of evergreen climbers, the number of species in which is a matter of taxonomic judgement. Here five are recognised but of these one—*H. canariensis*—is treated as a subspecies of *H. helix* in *Flora Europaea*. On the other hand, Poyarkova, in *Flora SSSR*, recognises six species in the Soviet Union alone. The genus ranges from the Canary Islands and Madeira through Europe, Asia Minor, the Caucasus, the Himalaya, and thence to southern and Central China, Formosa, and Japan. It is absent from the New World in the wild (the *Hedera quinquefolia* of Linnaeus is the true Virginia Creeper, *Parthenocissus quinquefolia* (L.) Planch.). Some species of New Guinea and Queensland once placed in *Hedera* are now referred to the genus *Kissodendron*.

All the ivies resemble the common one in going through a more or less prolonged juvenile (non-fruiting) stage during which the stems climb or creep by holdfast roots and the leaves are arranged in one plane, forming a mosaic. At length the plant normally produces non-climbing fertile branches, on which the leaves are markedly different in shape from those of the sterile shoots, being unlobed or scarcely lobed, and are arranged spirally round the stem (as they are on seedling plants). A characteristic of the genus is the presence on the young growths and in the inflorescence of stellate hairs or of scales (or both together). The hairs consist of a short 'stalk' from the apex of which a number of branches radiate. The scales are essentially similar in structure, but are appressed to the surface that bears them, and the rays are partly or wholly fused. The flowers in *Hedera* are bisexual, arranged in umbels which are solitary or grouped into panicles. Fruit a drupe. For propagation, see *H. helix*.

The most valuable and up-to-date work on the genus is: G. H. M. Lawrence and A. E. Schulze, 'The Cultivated Hederas', in *Gentes Herbarum*, Vol. 6 (1942), pp. 105–73. Tobler's work *Die Gattung Hedera* (1912) is still of interest. For Shirley Hibberd's *The Ivy*, see under *H. helix*.

H. CANARIENSIS Willd.

H. helix var. *canariensis* (Willd.) DC; *H. h.* subsp. *canariensis* (Willd.) Coutinho; *H. maderensis* K. Koch; *H. algeriensis* Hibberd; *H. grandifolia* Hibberd, in part

Stems green or dark purplish red. Leaves large, leathery, somewhat shallowly three- or five-lobed in the juvenile state, 2 to 6 or even 8 in. across, heart-shaped at the base. On the fertile branches they are entire and rounded or tapered at the base.

Native of the Canary Islands, Madeira, the Azores, Portugal, and of N.W. Africa as far east as Algeria; date of introduction uncertain. It is closely allied to the common ivy but the hairs bear more numerous rays (usually twelve to sixteen) and the rays are united for about a quarter of their length. It has been confused with the Irish ivy (*H. helix* 'Hibernica'), which in the 19th century was very commonly offered under the name *H. canariensis* while the true species was known as "*H. algeriensis*" or "*H. canariensis nova*". Hibberd's name *H. grandifolia* was intended as a substitute for *H. canariensis* and under it he also included the Irish ivy.

H. canariensis is mainly represented in cultivation by the following cultivars:

cv. 'AZORICA'.—A vigorous variety, with leaves 3 to 6 in. across, vivid green, five- or seven-lobed; lobes ovate, blunt-pointed. The quite young wood and leaves are covered with a thick tawny felt. Introduced from St Michael, in the Azores, by Osborn of Fulham.

cv. 'GLOIRE DE MARENGO' ('VARIEGATA').—Leaves mostly ovate, irregularly margined with creamy white passing into a grey-green zone, the normal green occurring in irregular splashes along the chief veins. Stems purplish crimson. Although better known as a house-plant, this cultivar is hardy on a sheltered wall and very handsome.

H. COLCHICA (K. Koch) K. Koch

H. helix var. *colchica* K. Koch; *H. regeneriana* Hibb.; *H. coriacea* Hibb.; *H. helix* var. *raegneriana* Nichols.

Leaves on the juvenile stems ovate or heart-shaped, dark green and leathery, 3 to 7 in. across and as much as 10 in. long, entire or slightly lobed, and sometimes with a few small, sharp teeth; leaves on flowering shoots much resembling those of the juvenile state, but less lobed and narrower. Young shoots and inflorescence parts covered with a yellowish scurf of scales with fifteen to twenty-five rays, which are free from each other only at the tips. Fruits black.

Native of the region south of the Caspian and thence westward through the

Caucasus to the Pontic ranges of Asiatic Turkey. In the Caucasian forests it reaches huge dimensions but is also found in dry, open places. Of all the ivies it is the most distinct in foliage from the common one, the leaves often being of very large size and strongly cordate at the base.

H. *colchica* appears to have reached Britain in the 1840s, and certainly by 1851, from the Odessa Botanic Garden; it was generally known at first as "*H. roegneriana*" (variously misspelt)—a name which, according to Lawrence and Schulze, commemorates Roegner, who was Director of that garden. This introduction is said to have had very leathery, dark green, entire leaves, and plants are still to be seen in gardens which may well descend vegetatively from this introduction.

cv. 'AMURENSIS'.—Leaves up to 1 ft long, sometimes strongly lobed but normally entire except for fine mucronate teeth. It does not cling well and usually needs to be tied to its support. Its origin is unknown and it certainly does not come from the Amur region of Russia. It was put into commerce by Bull's nursery, Chelsea. In *Gardeners' Magazine* (March 5, 1887), p. 136, there is a note by Hibberd on this ivy, where the name used for it is *H. amurensis*, but either later or earlier he called it *H. acuta*.

cv. 'DENTATA'.—This was described by Hibberd as a garden variety of "*H. coriacea*" (i.e., *H. colchica*). Leaves paler and less glossy than in the Roegner introduction, with margins set with small, distant, sharpish teeth. Common in cultivation.

cv. 'DENTATA VARIEGATA' ('DENTATA AUREA').—Leaves as in 'Dentata', but with a creamy-yellow margin and an intermediate zone of grey-green. A.M. 1907, when shown by Messrs L. R. Russell, then of Richmond. A fine and vigorous variegated foliage plant, quite hardy.

Plants with a central variegation of yellow and pale green are in cultivation under various names, such as 'Gold Leaf', 'Paddy's Pride' and 'Sulphur Heart'. These may be of independent origin, but whether they are distinct enough to warrant separate naming can only be decided by comparative trial.

H. HELIX L.   COMMON IVY

An evergreen climber, with a strong, rather acrid odour when crushed, attaching itself to trees, buildings, etc., by means of rootlike growths from the stem, or, where such support is absent, creeping over the ground; young shoots clothed with minute stellate hairs. Leaves alternate, thick, leathery, very dark glossy green, broadly ovate or somewhat triangular, those of the climbing shoots with three or five deep or shallow lobes and stalks of varying length. The starry hairs have five to eight rays. The ivy never flowers on the creeping or climbing shoots, but produces bushy branches, mostly when it has reached the top of its support; these have no aerial roots, and their leaves are never lobed, but are wavy in outline or entire at the margin, and more narrowly ovate. Flowers produced in October, in a terminal cluster of globose umbels, yellowish green. Berries dull inky black, globose, about ¼ in. across, containing two to five seeds.

Native of Europe north as far as southern Scandinavia and east to western

Russia, but in the south extending farther to the east through the rainier parts of Anatolia to the Caucasus. It is found almost everywhere in Britain, especially in shady spots, its natural habitat being the forest, where it can climb trees. The ivy, however, is very adaptable, and can be grown in almost any situation. No introduced evergreen climber can rival it for covering old trees, buildings, etc. Many think that serious damage is done to trees by allowing ivy to climb over them, but this only occurs when the ivy has reached the leafy shoots; so long as the ivy is confined to the trunk and larger branches no harm is done. An ivy-laden tree is one of the most beautiful objects of the winter landscape. On houses ivy is rather beneficial than otherwise, keeping them dry and warm.

Ivy is propagated with the greatest ease by means of cuttings which may be given gentle heat if it is desirable to get them to root quickly, or dibbled thickly under handlights or even in the open air. The more delicate highly coloured varieties are sometimes grafted on the common ivy, but need constant watching to prevent the stock over-running the scion. One of the most useful purposes to which ivy can be put is as a ground-covering under trees where no grass will grow. It is also very useful for covering iron-rail fencing, or posts and chains. As regards its use on buildings it is capable of attaining at least 100 ft in height. Leaves of ivy are eaten by horses, cattle, and sheep apparently with relish and without evil results.

There is no work that deals comprehensively with the garden varieties of the common ivy. Hibberd's book *The Ivy* (1872), with its elegant descriptions and numerous illustrations, is still of some value as a source of information about the older sorts. Unfortunately, Hibberd took it upon himself to rename many of the garden varieties, on the grounds that the nomenclature, especially of the variegated kinds, was confused, or simply because he disliked the established name. In some cases the name he attempted to abolish is known and can be revived, but often this is not possible. There is no doubt that he could have ascertained the correct name for many of the variegated ivies treated in his work, had he troubled to make the attempt. Nowhere in his book is there any reference to William Paul, one of the greatest plantsmen of his generation, who had a large collection of ivies and indeed may have raised some of the varieties treated by Hibberd.

The garden varieties described below are only a selection of those now available, and are in the main confined to those sold as suitable for growing out-of-doors:

cv. 'ADAM'.—Leaves small, shallowly three-lobed or three-angled, with a regular margin of white; centre grey and grey-green. It is self-branching, i.e., the main stems produce side-branches without the need for stopping. A charming ivy, usually seen as a pot-plant, but said to be hardy. The leaves become much larger on open-ground plants.

cv. 'ATROPURPUREA'.—Leaves with a long central lobe and two short laterals, but many almost entire and ovate, blackish green, darkening still further in winter and often then becoming bronze-coloured, with bright green veins (*Journ. R.H.S.*, Vol. 12 (1890), p. 390; *Garden*, Vol. 25 (1884), p. 141). A very handsome ivy at Kew, received under the name *H. helix purpurea*, probably belongs to this variety.

cv. 'BUTTERCUP'.—Leaves with prominent veins, bluntly three- or five-lobed, deeply cordate, golden throughout the summer. It is sometimes sold as "Angularis Aurea", a name which belongs properly to an older form of golden ivy, with scarcely lobed leaves.

cv. 'CAVENDISHII'.—Leaves mostly 1 to 1½ in. long, rather indistinctly lobed, with a broad margin of creamy white, slightly flushed with pink at the edge during autumn and winter. In cultivation by 1863. It is part of the *H. helix marginata minor* of Hibberd.

cv. 'CONGLOMERATA'.—A dwarfed, very slow-growing form, the leaves small and crowded, much crinkled and undulate. Stems stout, procumbent, slightly flattened when young.

HEDERA HELIX 'CONGLOMERATA'

cv. 'CONGLOMERATA ERECTA'.—Like the preceding, this is a non-climbing ivy, but with erect or spreading stems, much flattened at first, with the young bract-like leaves arranged in two rows on the sharp edges. Mature leaves variously lobed, often folded upwards along the midrib. It is also known as *H. helix minima* but unfortunately Hibberd used that name in 1872 for the ivy 'Donerailensis', thus rendering it invalid.

cv. 'DELTOIDEA'.—Leaves very distinct in shape, triangular in main outline, with rounded corners and two deep basal lobes, the inner edges of which overlap. Of stiff habit assuming a bronzy tint in autumn.

cv. 'DIGITATA'.—The ivy distributed by Loddiges's nursery early in the 19th century as *H. helix digitata* is probably the same as the so-called sharp-leaved Irish ivy, which the Irish nurseryman Thomas Hodgins found growing wild near his nursery at Dunganstown, then in Co. Wicklow, and put into commerce around 1825 or earlier. Leaves with five sharp, forward-pointing lobes, separated by narrow sinuses. This ivy has hairs with more numerous rays than is normal in *H. helix*, and was on that account considered by Seemann to belong to *H. canariensis* (*Journ. of Bot.*, Vol. 3, (1865), pp. 201–3).

cv. 'DISCOLOR'. See 'Marmorata Minor'.

cv. 'DONERAILENSIS'.—Leaves small, usually three-lobed, the central lobe narrowly triangular, the lateral lobes usually similar in shape to the central one, margins wavy. The leaves turn brownish purple in winter. This clone only retains its character if grown as a pot-plant, with its roots constricted. Allowed to grow freely on a wall the leaves eventually become much larger and very like those of 'Pedata' (q.v.). The origin of this clone is not known but it was in cultivation in 1854 and may have originated at Doneraile, Co. Cork. Hibberd in *The Ivy* (1872) p. 76, renamed this ivy *H. helix minima*, in accordance with his usual practice of rejecting all epithets derived from placenames or personal names.

cv. 'EMERALD GEM'. See under var. *poetica*.

cv. 'GLACIER'.—Leaves shallowly and bluntly three-lobed, mostly truncate to shallowly cordate at the base, edged with a narrow discontinuous margin of white; centre of leaf green and grey-green.

cv. 'GLYMII'.—Hibberd altered the name of this ivy to *H. helix tortuosa* and describes it as follows: 'The growth is scarcely robust, and rather wiry; the leaves vary in form from regular ovate to long wedge-shaped, many of them obscurely three-lobed. The colour is a deep dull green, overspread with blotches of blackish bronze. The form and colour of the leaves are characteristic features, but they are moreover peculiarly glossy, and every one is more or less curled and twisted, the twisting increasing during cold weather.'

cv. 'GOLDHEART'.—Leaves dark green, glossy, with an irregular, more or less central blotch of rich yellow; stems red when young. A very striking ivy, much more handsome when grown out-of-doors than as a pot-plant. It is also known as 'Golden Jubilee' and, wrongly, as 'Jubilee' (according to Tobler the latter name belongs to an ivy with white-edged leaves put into commerce by Messrs Hesse in 1912). A 'tree-ivy' with similar variegation has been raised from its adult shoots.

cv. 'GRACILIS'.—Hibberd's description reads: 'A light elegant plant with wiry stems of a warm purple colour, and leaves usually three-lobed, placed rather far apart, rendering the wiry stems conspicuous; the colour rather light dull green, richly bronzed in the autumn; the principal veins rise slightly in relief. The veins curl slightly, and are seldom sharply lobed. A very pretty wall-ivy or to clothe a tree-stump.' (*The Ivy*, p. 67, figured on p. 66.)

cv. 'GREEN RIPPLE'.—The plant in commerce as a pot-plant under this name has the following characters: leaves dark mat-green, slenderly stalked, central lobe very slenderly tapered, the main lateral pair similar, forward pointing, basal lobes, when present, shorter and usually blunter; base of leaf usually rounded or cuneate. It is a very elegant ivy, said to be hardy.

cv. 'HELFORD RIVER'.—A large-leaved ivy found growing wild near the Helford Estuary by George Nicholson, Curator of Kew, in 1890, and introduced by him to the collection, where it still grows. The leaves are conspicuously white-veined, variable in shape but mostly with a long central lobe and two backward-spreading laterals.

cv. 'HIBERNICA'. IRISH IVY.—A tetraploid variant of the common ivy with dull green leaves 3 to 6 in. across, with usually five triangular lobes, the terminal one the largest (H. hibernica Hort. ex DC.; H. helix hibernica Hort. ex Kirchn.; H. canariensis Hort., in part, not Willd.; H. grandifolia Hibberd, in part). See also H. canariensis.

The Irish ivy is believed to descend from a plant that was found growing wild in Ireland, but it is not a native of that country in the sense of occurring wild there in significant numbers. It was already well established in cultivation by 1838, and was probably introduced some thirty years before that. It is a strong-growing ivy, useful for ground-cover beneath trees, etc.

cv. 'HIBERNICA AUREA'.—Young leaves variegated with gold, some half or three-quarters golden, becoming paler by midsummer (or wholly green on vigorous plants). Paul called this ivy H. canariensis foliis aureis.

cv. 'HIBERNICA MACULATA'.—Leaves blotched and streaked with creamy white (H. canariensis latifolia maculata Paul).

cv. 'LOBATA MAJOR'.—Very much resembling the Irish ivy but with a longer central lobe, separated from the two lateral lobes by narrower and sharper sinuses. Hibberd remarks: 'In the woods of the Vale of Conway, North Wales, this form may be frequently met with', but the cultivated plants are probably all of one clone.

cv. 'MARGINATA ELEGANTISSIMA'.—Leaves small, scarcely lobed, more or less truncate at the base, with a broad margin of silver. The specimen in the Kew Herbarium is from William Paul. There is an ivy still in commerce as 'Elegantissima' or 'Tricolor' which agrees with this and has leaves which become margined with pink in the autumn (Paul remarked that several silver ivies show this coloration in autumn, adding that it 'is hardly prominent enough . . . to be admitted in the descriptions from the pictorial point of view'—Gard. Chron. (1867), p. 1270).

cv. 'MARGINATA MAJOR'. See under 'Marginata Robusta'.

cv. 'MARGINATA ROBUSTA'.—Leaves large, some of almost adult form, bluish green, with a broad margin of white (Paul, Gard. Chron. (1867), p. 1215; Hibberd, op. cit., p. 78, as H. h. marginata grandis). Plants agreeing with this are still in cultivation. 'Marginata Major' is similar, but the margins are yellowish white.

cv. 'MARMORATA MINOR'.—Leaves speckled and blotched with white, some mainly white, with green markings (H. h. discolor Hibberd).

cv. 'MINIMA'.—An ambiguous and confusing name. The H. h. minima of Hibberd is 'Donerailensis'. The same name is also used for 'Conglomerata Erecta'.

cv. 'OVATA'.—A very distinct ivy, the leaves ovate, pointed rounded at the base, rich green and entire, or very slightly lobed even in the climbing state.

cv. 'PALMATA'.—Leaves strongly five-lobed, mostly truncate at the base; veins prominent beneath (Hibberd, op. cit., p. 77).

cv. 'PEDATA'. BIRD'S FOOT IVY.—Leaves dark green, white-veined, the central lobe disproportionately long, narrowed at the base, often slightly lobulate; lateral lobes spreading; basal lobes, when present, backward pointing. This ivy appears to have been sold by William Paul as *H. helix digitata*, and it is under this erroneous name that Nicholson figured it in *Dict. Gard.*, Vol. 2 (1886), p. 121. 'CAENWOODIANA' is very similar and is perhaps part of 'Pedata' as understood by Hibberd.

var. POETICA West. *H. poetarum* Bertol.; *H. chrysocarpa* Walsh; *H. helix* var. *chrysocarpa* Ten.; *H. helix* subsp. *poetarum* Nyman POET'S IVY.—Juvenile leaves brighter green than in the common ivy, triangular or broadly ovate with a heart-shaped base, shallowly lobed and sometimes more or less entire. Fruits yellow, slightly larger than in the common ivy. Native of the S. Balkans, Asia Minor, and W. Caucasus; naturalised in parts of Italy, probably since Roman times. The garden variety 'EMERALD GEM' probably belongs here.

cv. 'RUSSELL GOLD'.—Leaves greenish gold when young.

cv. 'SAGITTIFOLIA'.—Central lobe acute, triangular (i.e., broadest at the base and not narrowed at the base as in 'Pedata'); lateral lobes spreading more or less horizontally, basal lobes swept backward (Hibberd, op. cit., pp. 68–9). The very common house-plant grown at the present time under this name is not the same clone as Hibberd's plant. The general shape of the leaf is the same, but the lobes are more taper-pointed.

cv. 'SHEEN SILVER'.—Leaves slightly lobed, broadly margined with white; centre blue-green and grey-green.

var. TAURICA (Tobler) Rehd. *H. poetica* (?) var. *taurica* Tobler; *H. taurica* *sensu* Poyark.—This ivy, found wild in the Crimea, is said to differ from the typical state in the leaves on the sterile shoots being predominantly sagittate in shape and (according to Poyarkova) of a light glossy green. The fruits are of the normal colour, not yellow as Tobler surmised.

H. NEPALENSIS K. Koch

H. cinerea (Hibb.) Bean; *H. helix* var. *cinerea* Hibb.; *H. himalaica* Tobler; *H. helix* var. *chrysocarpa* DC.

Leaves triangular-ovate to ovate-lanceolate, taper-pointed, 2 to 4½ in. long, 1 to 2½ in. wide, often with two blunt lobes near the base and with bluntish, lobulate teeth on the upper part of the leaf, greyish green and the veins still paler grey. In the fruiting state the leaves are entire, ovate-lanceolate, half to two-thirds as wide as they are long, tapered at the base. Fruits yellow or orange. The young stems, petioles, and inflorescence parts are scaly, the scales yellowish brown, twelve- to fifteen-rayed.

Native of the Himalaya. The early Himalayan botanists did not separate this

species from *H. helix*, but it is distinct enough in its foliage, in its scaly indumentum and yellow fruits. It was also confused with the poet's ivy, *H. helix*
var. *poetica*, which it resembles only in its yellow fruits. It is rather more tender
than the common ivy, but does well on a wall.

var. SINENSIS (Tobler) Rehd. *H. himalaica* var. *sinensis* Tobler; *H. sinensis*
(Tobler) Hand.-Mazz.—This variety, which is perhaps not in cultivation, has
the juvenile leaves entire or three-lobed near the base and hence lacking the
lobules in the upper part of the leaf so characteristic of the Himalayan ivy.
Native of China.

H. RHOMBEA (Miq.) Bean

H. helix var. *rhombea* Miq.; *H. japonica* W. Paul, not Junghuhn; *H. tobleri* Nakai

Leaves triangular to ovate, often heart-shaped at the base, usually slightly
three-lobed, very dark green. Leaves on adult branches mostly angular ovate,
rounded or broadly cuneate at the base. Fruits black. The indumentum of the
young shoots, etc., consists of scales made up of fifteen to twenty rays.

Native of Japan and Korea (but a closely related ivy grows in Formosa and is
now regarded as a subspecies of *H. rhombea*). It is of rather delicate growth, but
quite hardy.

cv. 'VARIEGATA'.—Leaves with a narrow margin of creamy white (*H. helix*
submarginata Hibb.). In cultivation 1867.

HEDYSARUM   LEGUMINOSAE

A genus of about 150 species of annual and perennial plants, the latter
mostly herbaceous, natives of the temperate regions of the northern
hemisphere. Leaves imparipinnate; flowers in axillary racemes; pods
flat, subdivided into segments, each with one seed (often reduced to a
single segment in the species described here).

H. MULTIJUGUM Maxim.

This species is represented in cultivation by the following variety:

var. APICULATUM Sprague—A deciduous shrub 3 to 5 ft high, of somewhat
sparse, gaunt habit; young branches erect, zigzag in growth, covered with fine
down. Leaves 4 to 6 in. long, alternate, imparipinnate. Leaflets seventeen to
twenty-seven, ¼ to ¾ in. long, ⅛ to ⅓ in. wide, ovate, oblong, oval or obovate,
with an apiculate point, glabrous above, minutely downy beneath. Racemes
axillary, erect, long-stalked, 6 to 12 in. long, produced from the axil of each leaf
as the shoot develops. Flowers pea-shaped, rosy magenta, ¾ in. long, arranged

on the upper two-thirds of the raceme on very short stalks; standard petal ½ in. or a little more across, with a patch of yellow at the base; calyx ¼ in. long, split either above or below. Pods flat, almost circular, rough, containing usually one seed. *Bot. Mag.*, t. 8091.

Origin uncertain. It thrives very well in a sunny position planted in sandy loam, and flowers on the shoots of the year from June to September. Seeds are produced in sunny seasons, but they are uncertain. It is usually propagated by layering, also by cuttings. To correct the rather ungainly habit of this shrub after a few years, it is a good plan to peg down the branches; this causes them to break into new growth at the base. The magenta shade in the flower is objectionable to some people, but the shrub is useful in being late flowering and showy.

H. multijugum, in its typical state, has leaves with twenty-one to forty-one leaflets, which are blunt or retuse at the apex and hairy on the upper surface. It is a native of W. Mongolia, Kansu, and E. Tibet, in dry, hot places. It was described from specimens collected by the Russian traveller Przewalski in 1872, 1879, and 1880. It is very likely that the cultivated plant named var. *apiculatum* by Sprague derived from seeds collected by him in W. Kansu; at any rate, the plant figured in *Gartenflora*, 1883, t. 1122, was raised from these seeds in the St Petersburg Botanic Garden, and belongs to the var. *apiculatum*.

HEIMIA   LYTHRACEAE

A genus of two or three species, ranging from W. Texas through Mexico and the Caribbean to Argentina and Uruguay, though over much of this area only the species described below is found.

H. MYRTIFOLIA Cham. & Schlecht.

H. salicifolia Hort., in part, not (H.B.K.) Link

A deciduous shrub, said to grow to a height of 5 or 6 ft, but usually shorter than that in this country, where, in the open ground, its stems are frequently cut back to the ground in winter, springing up 2 to 4 ft high the following summer. Stems erect, leafy, much-branched, quite glabrous. Leaves linear and willow-like, opposite on the lower portion of the stem, alternate towards the top, 1 to 2 in. long, ⅛ to ¼ in. wide, quite glabrous. Flowers yellow, ⅓ to ½ in. across, very shortly stalked, produced singly in the leaf-axils of the current year's growth from July to September; petals five to seven; stamens ten to eighteen.

Native of Brazil and Uruguay; introduced in 1821 as "*H. salicifolia*" and again under its correct name in 1826. Although it will live in the open ground at Kew, and flowers there, its stems do not become more than half woody, and do not survive the winter. But plants on the Temperate House terrace at Kew have become true shrubs.

H. SALICIFOLIA (H.B.K.) Link   *H. salicifolia* var. *grandiflora* Lindl.; *H. grandiflora* (Lindl.) Hook.; *Nesaea salicifolia* H.B.K.—This species can easily be distinguished from *H. myrtifolia* by its larger flowers, the calyx (receptacle and sepals) being $\frac{3}{16}$ to almost $\frac{1}{4}$ in. long (about $\frac{1}{8}$ in. long in *H. myrtifolia*) and the petals $\frac{3}{8}$ to $\frac{5}{8}$ in. long (only half as long or less in *H. myrtifolia*). Other more technical differences have also been adduced. There is no constant difference between the two in their foliage, both being variable in the size and shape of their leaves.

H. *salicifolia* has a wide range, from Central America to Argentina; and was introduced in 1839. It flowers well outside the greenhouses at the University Botanic Garden, Cambridge.

Both species can be propagated by cuttings in late summer.

HELIANTHEMUM   SUN ROSE   CISTACEAE

A genus of about 100 species, most of which are low, evergreen shrubs or sub-shrubs, though a few are herbaceous (these mostly annual). They are natives of Europe, northern Africa and of western and central Asia; the greatest concentration of species is in the Mediterranean region. Some botanists include in *Helianthemum* a group of about thirty New World species. There are four species of *Helianthemum* in the British flora, of which one is an annual; of the other three—*H. nummularium, appeninum,* and *canum*—only the first is widely distributed.

The leading characters of the genus are: Leaves entire and usually opposite. Flowers of wild plants commonly yellow, more rarely white or pink, arranged in terminal cymes which are usually elongated and raceme-like (compound in a few species). Sepals five, the outer two smaller and usually narrower than the inner three. Petals five. Stamens numerous. Style (in the woody species) long and slender (in the related *Halimium* it is short or absent). Fruit a capsule opening by three valves (and herein lies the chief distinction from *Cistus*, which has a capsule with five, six, or ten valves).

Helianthemums need above all things a sunny spot. They are best on some slope fully exposed to the south. Essentially sun-lovers, their flowers open sluggishly or not at all in dull weather, and their time of greatest beauty is in the forenoon. The flowers never last longer than a day; and in *H. nummularium*, its allies and hybrids, they mostly close up at noon. The flowers appear in extraordinary profusion, but each day's crop is succeeded by an entirely different one the next. They flower from May onwards. Any soil of an open, loamy nature suits them; in nature they often occur on limestone. All are of easy propagation by cuttings. If a mild bottom heat is available, it is preferable to take cuttings in quite a soft condition; but if they are to be rooted under a handlight they must be left to get moderately firm, and put in about August.

For the garden hybrids see p. 367.

H. APENNINUM (L.) Mill.

Cistus apenninus L.; *H. polifolium* Mill.; *Cistus polifolius* Huds.

A low, spreading, much-branched shrub up to 18 in. high, the stems and leaves thickly clothed above and below with a close, white, stellate down, giving the whole plant a mealy appearance. Leaves linear-oblong or linear, the margins much recurved, ½ to 1 in. long, ⅛ to ⅕ in. wide, bluntish or pointed; stipules linear. Cymes terminal, producing numerous flowers in succession. Flowers pure white, 1 in. or rather more across, nodding in the bud state, but becoming erect at expansion. Petals obovate, slightly toothed at the end. Sepals five, the two outer ones linear, very small; the three inner ones ovate, twice as long as the others, all white with down.

Native of S. and W. Europe (and of N. Africa), but absent from the Alps proper and not extending far eastward into Germany. It is a rare native of Britain, found always on limestone, on Brean Down in Somerset and Berry Head in Devon. It was introduced to gardens before 1768, at which time Miller had plants from various sources, though not from the English stands, of which he was probably unaware. *H. appeninum* is slightly variable in its foliage, the leaves being sometimes green above, or more or less plane. But in the allied *H. nummularium* the leaves are invariably green above and never more than slightly revolute; and the flowers commonly yellow or orange-yellow. The key-character by which botanists distinguish the two species is: stipules linear in *H. appeninum*, equalling or slightly longer than the petioles; stipules lanceolate or linear-lanceolate, leaflike and always longer than the petioles in *H. nummularium*.

H. appeninum (and its var. *roseum*) is one of the parents of the garden hybrids.

var. ROSEUM (Jacq.) Schneid. *Cistus roseus* Jacq.; *H. rhodanthum* Dun.; *H. appeninum* var. *rhodanthum* (Dun.) Bean; *H. rhodanthum* var. *carneum* Dun.—Flowers pink. Leaves green and almost glabrous above. Found wild in N.W. Italy (Liguria and Piemonte) and in the Balearic Islands. The garden variety called 'Rhodanthe Carneum' is a hybrid and not, as might be supposed from the synonym given above, a form of *H. appeninum* var. *roseum*.

H. × SULPHUREUM Willd.—Here belong hybrids between *H. appeninum* and *H. nummularium*, which occur quite commonly where the two species are in contact. Flowers pale yellow. Leaves narrow-lanceolate, green and stellate-hairy above. In gardens, hybrids between *H. appeninum* var. *roseum* and *H. nummularium* were in cultivation early in the 19th century, and of the plants figured by Sweet in his *Cistineae* two are considered to be of this parentage (t. 51 as *H. canescens* and t. 66 as *H. cupreum*).

H. CANUM (L.) Baumgarten

Cistus canus L.; *H. vineale* Pers.

A dwarf shrub, forming a compact tuft rarely more than 6 in. high, but 1 ft or more in diameter; young stems and leaves covered with a short down and a few hairs. Leaves without stipules, hairy and green above, grey beneath with stellate down, ovate-oblong, $\frac{1}{4}$ to $\frac{3}{4}$ in. long. Flowers in terminal cymes, sometimes a panicle, usually of three to six blooms, each $\frac{1}{2}$ in. across, bright yellow, unblotched. Sepals five, hairy, the two outer ones very small. Seed-vessel thickly hairy.

Native of Europe, Asia Minor, and the Caucasus, found in a few stations in the British Isles, mostly on limestone (Yorkshire, Cumberland, Westmorland, N. Wales, Glamorgan; and Galway and N. Clare in Ireland). It is hardy, and makes a pleasing little tuft for the rock garden when covered with its brightly coloured flowers. From the other British species, except the herbaceous *H. guttatum* (*Tuberaria guttata*), it differs in having no stipules. With the non-native species cultivated in gardens it is only likely to be confused with *H. alpestre*, which also has no stipules, but whose leaves are green on both surfaces. Botanists also rely on the longer, oval and pointed flower-buds of *H. alpestre*, in contrast to the globose ones of the present species.

H. canum is a rather variable species, with local variants that differ somewhat in indumentum, leaf-shape, or inflorescence from the plant described above, which belongs to the typical subspecies. Six others are described in *Flora Europaea*.

H. CROCEUM (Desf.) Pers.

Cistus croceus Desf. (1800); *C. glaucus* Cav. (1794), not Pourr. (1788); *H. glaucum* Pers. (1807)

A small tufted shrub growing to about 1 ft high. Leaves on the upper part of the shoots linear-lanceolate to ovate-lanceolate or elliptic-oblong, often revolute, the lower ones more rounded, covered on both sides with a dense down of stellate hairs, but the upper sides sometimes also with long unbranched hairs, and the undersides almost glabrous in some forms. Stipules large and leaflike. Flowers yellow or orange, rarely white, up to fifteen in each raceme-like cyme. Sepals with stellate down, at least on the midribs and sometimes throughout.

Native of the W. Mediterranean, including N. Africa; introduced in 1815. This species is closely allied to *C. nummularium*, but is very distinct in summer with its almost white foliage, with which the rich yellow flowers are in admirable contrast. Many of the garden varieties of *Helianthemum* are hybrids of this species, more especially those that are whitish on the upper surface of the leaves.

H. LUNULATUM (All.) DC.

Cistus lunulatus All.

A dwarf, cushion-like, evergreen sub-shrub 4 to 8 in. high; young shoots covered with a close down and sprinkled with hairs. Leaves elliptic-oblong to obovate, tapered at the base, rounded or obtuse at the apex, $\frac{1}{3}$ to $\frac{5}{8}$ in. long, $\frac{1}{8}$ to $\frac{3}{16}$ in. wide, dull green and glabrous above, furnished beneath with starry hairs and long simple ones; margins hairy; stalk $\frac{1}{12}$ in. or less long. Flowers $\frac{1}{2}$ in. wide, opening during June and July, usually singly, at the end of the young shoots; petals bright yellow, roundish, with a crescent-shaped stain at the base; flower-stalk ½ to 1 in. long, downy like the young shoots.

A very local species, found only in the Italian part of the Maritime Alps from the Col di Tenda to Monte Corno, South of Valdieri. It is a neat little plant, forming a gay patch of colour in midsummer. Suitable for a sunny spot in the rock garden. Easily propagated by soft cuttings in gentle heat.

H. NUMMULARIUM (L.) Mill.

Cistus nummularius L.; *H. chamaecistus* Mill.; *H. vulgare* Gaertn.

A low semi-shrubby plant, covering ground over 2 or 3 ft across, but scarcely rising more than 1 ft above it; the older stems prostrate, the young flowering ones erect, somewhat hairy. Leaves flat, variable in size and shape, usually oblong, sometimes approaching ovate or lanceolate, ¼ to 1 in. long, ⅛ to ¼ in.

HELIANTHEMUM NUMMULARIUM

wide, green and more or less hairy above, grey or white with stellate hairs beneath; stalk ⅛ to $\frac{3}{16}$ in. long; stipules lance-shaped, longer than the leaf-stalk. Cymes terminal, with many but successively developed flowers. Flower-stalks decurved, erect only when the flower is expanded. Flowers yellow, about 1 in. across. Sepals five, the two outer ones small, fringed with hairs; three inner ones ovate, with three or four prominent hairy ribs, the rest of the surface hairy or glabrous.

H. nummularium, in the typical state described above, is a native of much of Europe (including Great Britain), and of Asia Minor and the Caucasus, and has long been cultivated. The specific epithet *nummularium*, implying that the leaves are coin-shaped as in *Lysimachia nummularia*, is not at all apt, but it happened that the type, collected near Montpelier in the 17th century, had the lower leaves roundish, as is sometimes the case in this species.

In southern and central Europe and the Near East the species is much more variable than with us, and the numerous races have been grouped into sub-species, some of which are not very clearly demarcated.

cv. 'AMY BARING'.—A mat-forming plant only a few inches high but eventually two or more feet across. Leaves oblong-elliptic or oblong-lanceolate, mostly ⅝ to ⅞ in. long, whitish and hairy beneath. Flowers deep yellow, darkening to orange-yellow at the centre, about 1 in. wide. This charming variety descends from a plant collected by Mrs Amy Doncaster (*née* Baring) while staying at Gavarnie in the Pyrenees. She gave it to A. K. Bulley, the well-known grower and collector of alpines, who was staying at the same hotel, and it was he who named and first propagated it.

subsp. GLABRUM (K. Koch) Wilczek *H. vulgare* var. *glabrum* K. Koch; *H. grandiflorum* var. *glabrum* (K. Koch) Rehd.—Flowers as in subsp. *grandiflorum*. Leaves glabrous except for scattered hairs on the margins and midrib. Alps and Appenines to the Caucasus.

subsp. GRANDIFLORUM (Scop.) Schinz & Thellung *Cistus grandiflorus* Scop.; *H. grandiflorum* (Scop.) DC.—Leaves green and sparsely hairy beneath. Flowers up to 1½ in. across, golden- or orange-yellow, usually rather few in each cyme. Sepals downy on the ribs, otherwise more or less glabrous. This has a more 'alpine' distribution than the typical subspecies, occurring at high elevations in the mountains of S. and C. Europe from the Pyrenees to the Carpathians; also in the Caucasus. Introduced in 1800.

subsp. OBSCURUM (Čelak.) J. Holub *H. nummularium* subsp. *ovatum* (Viv.) Schinz & Thellung; *Cistus ovatus* Viv.; *H. obscurum* Pers.—Leaves more hairy than in subsp. *grandiflorum* but still green on both sides. Flowers up to about 1 in. across only. Sepals usually hairy between the ribs, downy on them. Common in C. Europe and extending north to Sweden and east to Asia Minor.

subsp. PYRENAICUM (Janchen) Schinz & Thellung *H. pyrenaicum* Janchen; *H. nummularium* var. *roseum* (Willk.) Schneid.; *H. vulgare* var. *roseum* Willk.—In foliage this does not differ much from the typical subspecies, but the flowers are pink. Native mainly of the Pyrenees and one of the parents of the garden hybrids. Two other pink-flowered subspecies occur in the Maritime Alps and the Appenines.

f. SURREIANUM (L.) *Cistus surrejanus* L.; *H. surrejanum* (L.) Mill.; *H. chamaecistus* subsp. *surrejanum* (L.) Gross.—This curious variety is said to have first been found near Croydon in Surrey. It is distinguished from the type by the narrow petals being deeply notched at the end; they are linear-lanceolate, about ⅛ in. wide, ⅜ in. long, yellow. This variety has little beauty and is really a deformity. Similar plants have been observed growing wild in the Tyrol.

Linnaeus took the description of this plant from the *Hortus Elthamensis* of J. J. Dillenius, a work published in London in 1732.

subsp. TOMENTOSUM (Scop.) Schinz & Thellung *Cistus tomentosus* Scop., not Sm.; *H. nummularium* var. *scopolii* (Willk.) Schneid.—This is very near to the typical subspecies, but is more robust, with larger leaves, ¾ to 1¾ in. long, ¼ to ⅝ in. wide, and flowers up to 1¼ in. across. It was originally described from the S. Tyrol and is said to be common there and in the Italian Dolomites, but also occurs farther east.

Certain garden varieties figured by Sweet in *Cistineae* (1825–30) are near to *H. nummularium* and may derive from it without intermixture of any other species.

H. OELANDICUM (L.) DC.

Cistus oelandicus L.

As interpreted in *Flora Europaea*, *H. oelandicum* is a polymorphic species, subdivided into five subspecies, of which the typical one (subsp. *oelandicum*) is confined to Öland, off the south-east coast of Sweden, and Spitzbergen. The first of the two subspecies described here is certainly in cultivation and the second may be:

subsp. ALPESTRE (Jacq.) Breitst. *Cistus alpestris* Jacq.; *H. italicum* subsp. *alpestre* (Jacq.) Beger—A dainty little shrub 3 to 5 in. high, forming a tuft of dense spreading branches covered thickly with pale, minute hairs. Leaves without stipules, green on both sides, oblong-elliptic, elliptic-lanceolate, or narrow-oblong, tapered at the base, ¼ to ½ in. long, up to ⅛ or slightly more wide, furnished with a few comparatively long hairs, especially at the margins. Flowers produced in June and July, three to six (rarely more) in a terminal raceme-like cyme, each flower ½ to ¾ in. wide, bright yellow, unblotched, borne on a slender downy stalk. Sepals five, hairy, the three inner ones oval and about half as long as the petals.

Native of the mountains of C. and S. Europe, usually on limestone, extending high into the alpine zone (to 8,000 ft or more); introduced in 1818. It is quite hardy and admirable for the rock garden.

subsp. ITALICUM (L.) Font Quer & Rothm. *Cistus italicus* L.; *H. italicum* (L.) Pers.; *H. penicillatum* Thibault ex Dun.—This subspecies is mainly confined to the Mediterranean region, but is also found in the S. Tyrol. From subsp. *alpestre* it differs mainly in its laxer habit, its inflorescences with up to twenty flowers and sometimes branched, and in the flowers being much smaller, up to ½ in. wide. The stems are often reddish, though this may not be a constant character. It is sometimes of procumbent habit.

The typical subspecies of *H. oelandicum* has almost glabrous leaves and very small flowers, with petals scarcely exceeding the sepals in length. The type came from the limestone island of Öland, where it was collected by Linnaeus in 1741.

GARDEN HYBRIDS

The genus *Helianthemum* is mainly represented in cultivation by plants of garden origin, deriving for the most part from intercrossing between *H. appeninum*, *H. croceum*, and *H. nummularium*, though some other species may have been involved. Many of these are near to *H. nummularium*, which they resemble in their flat leaves, green and sparsely hairy above; and it is possible that some of these may be the result of sporting and intercrossing within that species. But many, perhaps the majority, clearly cannot belong to *H. nummularium* since their leaves are covered more or less densely on the upper surface with whitish hairs, rendering them grey-green or even silvery.

A number of hybrids between the above-mentioned species were already in cultivation when Sweet published his *Cistineae* (1825–30), but the present garden stock is of more recent origin. The famous 'Ben' group, named after Scottish mountains, was raised by John Nicoll of Monifieth near Dundee, who died in 1926.

The following is only a selection from the large number of hybrids now in commerce. All flower from late May until end June, with a few flowers later. For cultivation and propagation see the introductory note to *Helianthemum*. The plants, especially those that are of open habit, should be trimmed after flowering.

'AFFLICK'.—Bright deep orange, centre brownish orange. Foliage medium green, fairly glossy.

'ALICE HOWORTH'.—Deep mulberry-crimson, semi-double. Foliage deep green, glossy.

'AMY BARING'. See under *H. nummularium*.

'BEN ATTOW'.—Pale primrose with deeper centre.

'BEN AVON'.—Bright Tyrian-rose, base tinged orange. Foliage medium green.

'BEN FHADA'.—Bright saturated yellow with contrasting orange eye. One of the most popular of the 'Ben' group.

'BENGAL ROSE'.—Rose-red. Grey-green foliage.

'BEN HOPE'.—Carmine-red. Foliage grey-green.

'BEN LEDI'.—Deep Tyrian-rose. Foliage dark green.

'BEN LUI'.—Bright crimson, tinged orange at the centre. Foliage dark green. A.M. 1925.

'BEN MORE'.—Flame-orange. Foliage glossy.

'BEN NEVIS'.—Orange-yellow with a bronzy crimson centre. Dark leaves. Compact habit. A.M. 1924.

'BEN VENUE'.—Bright scarlet orange, centre darker. Foliage dark green. A.M. 1924.

'CERISE QUEEN'.—Rose-pink, double. Said to be an improvement on 'Rose of Leeswood'.

'FIREBALL'.—Bright bronzy orange, centre orange. Foliage dark green. A.M. 1925.

'FIRE DRAGON'.—Bright orange-scarlet. Foliage grey-green.

'HENFIELD BRILLIANT'.—Bright brick-red. Grey foliage.

'JUBILEE'.—Primrose-yellow, double. Dark green foliage. A.M. 1970.

'MRS C. W. EARLE'.—Scarlet, double, the petals yellow at the base. Dark green foliage.

'MRS CLAY'.—Orange-red with a darker centre. Foliage grey-green. A.M. 1970.

'RHODANTHE CARNEUM'.—See 'Wisley Pink'.

'ST JOHN'S COLLEGE YELLOW'.—Bright golden yellow with orange centre. Grey-green foliage. A.M. 1925.

'SUDBURY GEM'.—Flowers deep pink, with a flame centre. Foliage greyish.

'THE BRIDE'.—What is believed to be the true variety is of low, compact habit, with grey rather short leaves; flowers white with a small yellow blotch. It was sent to the recent trials at Wisley and is also grown at Kew.

'TIGRINUM PLENUM'.—Tawny orange, double. A.M. 1970.

'WATERGATE ROSE'.—Rosy-crimson tinged with orange at the centre. Foliage grey-green. A.M. 1932.

'WISLEY PINK'.—Pale pink with an orange centre. Grey foliage. Very beautiful but of rather sparse habit and dropping its petals early in the afternoon. In the report on the Trials held at Wisley 1924–5 this was bracketed with 'Rhodanthe Carneum' and the two were said to be very alike.

'WISLEY PRIMROSE'.—Flowers bright primrose-yellow. Foliage grey-green. Compact, very vigorous. A.M. 1970.

HELICHRYSUM* COMPOSITAE

A large Old World genus of herbs and a few shrubs, mostly in Africa and Australia, popularly known as 'everlastings'. Involucral bracts dry, papery, often brightly coloured; flower-heads with outer female and inner bisexual florets; receptacle without scales.

In addition to the African species described below there are in cultivation a number of perennial helichrysums from the Mediterranean region, grown for their grey or silvery foliage, but these are scarcely shrubby enough to fall within the scope of this work. Many of these belong to the variable H. ITALICUM (Roth) G. Don.

The shrubby section *Ozothamnus* of Australia and New Zealand is here treated as a distinct genus, for which see *Ozothamnus* in Vol. III.

H. SPLENDIDUM (Thunb.) Less.
Gnaphalium splendidum Thunb.; *Helichrysum trilineatum* Hort., not DC.; *H. alveolatum* Hort., not DC.

An evergreen, white-woolly shrub up to 6 ft tall in the wild; stems ascending, rigid, not angled, rather densely leafy. Leaves sessile, linear-oblong, up to 1½ in. long, ¼ in. wide, white-woolly on both surfaces, often revolute at the margins, with three more or less parallel main veins springing from the base. Flower-heads bright yellow, about ¼ in. wide, borne at the tips of the shoots throughout the growing season in globose or hemispherical cymose clusters.

Native of the mountains of Africa from Ethiopia to the Cape; discovered by C. P. Thunberg, a pupil of Linnaeus, during his visit to the Cape 1772–5 and described by him in 1800. The date of first introduction is not known, but the present stock probably derives from seeds collected by Mrs Milford in the Drakensburg Mountains between the wars. In recent years *H. splendidum* has become common in gardens, grown for its silvery foliage rather than for its flowers, which have no ornamental value. It is remarkably hardy, and will in time grow to 3 ft in height and twice that in width, though it is more decorative if kept compact and well furnished with foliage by regular pruning. Mrs

* Revised with the assistance of Mr C. Jeffrey of the Kew Herbarium.

Underwood recommends that the plants should be pruned hard in April and trimmed in early July (*Grey and Silver Plants* (1971), p. 116). Propagation is by cuttings.

HELWINGIA   ARALIACEAE

A genus of probably only three species of deciduous shrubs ranging from the E. Himalaya to Japan and Formosa. It is in certain respects intermediate between the Araliaceae and Cornaceae and by some botanists is separated as a distinct monotypic family—the Helwingiaceae.

The genus was named in honour of G. A. Helwing (1666–1748), author of works on the botany of Prussia.

H. JAPONICA (Thunb.) F. Dietr.
Osyris japonica Thunb.

A deciduous dioecious shrub 3 to 5 ft high, with glabrous twigs. Leaves simple, alternate, ovate, tapering at both ends, long-pointed, 1½ to 3 in. long, ½ to 1¼ in. wide, with fine, rather bristle-like teeth on the margins, quite glabrous and bright green on both surfaces; stalk ½ to 1 in. long; stipules hair-like. Flowers unisexual, very small, pale green or greenish white; females produced singly or in threes on the midrib about the centre of the upper surface of the leaf; males more numerous; they are stalkless, and of no beauty. Fruit a black drupe ¼ in. long, roundish oval.

Native of Japan, S. and W. China, and probably of Formosa; introduced to Europe by Siebold in 1830. It has not the least merit as an ornamental shrub, although the foliage in a milder climate is larger and perhaps more striking than as here described; but it is a plant of singular botanical interest. The morphological explanation of the anomalous position of the flowers in the middle of the leaf (for no true leaf ever produces flowers) is that the flower-stalk in reality originates in the axil of the leaf, but is united from end to end with the stalk and midrib. This shrub is hardy at Kew, and is propagated by cuttings of young wood.

HEMIPTELEA   ULMACEAE

A monotypic genus from China and Korea, allied to *Zelkova*, from which it differs in its thorny branches and winged fruits.

H. DAVIDII (Hance) Planch.

Planera davidii Hance; *Zelkova davidii* (Hance) Hemsl.

A small deciduous tree, armed with stout thorns; young shoots hairy. Leaves oval, $\frac{3}{4}$ to $2\frac{1}{4}$ in. long, $\frac{1}{2}$ to 1 in. wide, pointed, slightly heart-shaped at the base, with seven to fifteen teeth along each side; upper surface dark green and at first beset with pale, scattered hairs, each springing from a curious circular depression which, after the hair falls away, turns dark; lower surface glabrous except for a few scattered hairs on the midrib and chief veins at first. Fruits conical, $\frac{1}{4}$ in. long, scarcely so wide, two-edged, slightly winged, shortly but distinctly stalked; stalk $\frac{1}{12}$ in. long.

Native of N.E. and Central China, Manchuria, E. Mongolia, and Korea; introduced to France by Maurice de Vilmorin, and from his garden at Les Barres to Kew in 1908. The thorns in wild trees are very formidable, sometimes 4 or 5 in. long, but they become much less so on our cultivated trees.

HIBISCUS   MALVACEAE

A genus of some 200 species of trees, shrubs, and herbs, inhabitants mainly of the tropics and subtropics. It belongs to a group of the Mallow family in which the carpels of the ovary are completely united and the fruit a capsule.

H. SYRIACUS L.

Althaea frutex Hort.

A deciduous shrub, with rather erect branches but bushy habit, up to 10 ft and more high. Leaves variable in size, ordinarily from 2 to 4 in. long, of ovate outline, more or less distinctly three-lobed and coarsely toothed, glabrous except for an occasional bristle on the veins, stalk $\frac{1}{4}$ to 1 in. long. Flowers produced singly on short stalks from the leaf-axils towards the end of the branch. Each flower is from $2\frac{1}{2}$ to 4 in. across, with five free petals forming a trumpet mouth. The colour is exceedingly variable in the numerous forms of this shrub, some being white, others red, violet, purple, or striped; others again have double or semi-double flowers. Calyx unequally five-lobed, with an involucre of linear bractlets scarcely $\frac{1}{12}$ in. wide and shorter than the calyx.

The date of the introduction of this shrub to Britain is not known, but as it was included by Gerard among the garden shrubs of his time, it has been cultivated here for probably 350 years. In early times it was known as the 'Syrian Ketmie', and in the specific name Linnaeus suggested that it was from Syria, but it has never been found truly wild except in India and China. In Syria, as in more western countries, it exists as a cultivated plant only. It is perfectly hardy in most parts of Britain, but owing to its late-flowering habit, it is often necessary in the north to treat it as a wall plant in order that its flowers may develop under more favourable conditions. In the south, where the cold rains do not come so early, it can be grown quite in the open, and there is no shrub more beautiful during September, especially if that month be hot and sunny. In selecting a place for it, shady and ill-drained spots should be avoided. Any soil of moderate or good quality suits it. It can be propagated by cuttings or by layers, and rare sorts may be grafted on common ones. Plants growing too large for their places may be pruned back in early April. One of the common features of the gardens at Versailles are large bushes of this hibiscus, cut hard back annually into formal shape. Both in France and in Italy it flowers with greater profusion and regularity than under our uncertain skies. A great number of varieties have been raised and named, and the following list must only be regarded as a selection of a representative few of approved merit. On the whole, single-flowered ones are to be preferred.

Flowers Single

'Blue Bird'.—Flowers large, opening widely, rich mauvish blue with a deeper centre. A.M. 1965. Raised in France and originally named 'Oiseau Bleu'.

'Coelestis'.—A reliable old variety similar to the newer 'Blue Bird' but with slightly smaller flowers. A.M. 1897.

'Dorothy Crane'. See under 'Monstrosus'.

'Hamabo'.—Flowers white, blush-tinted, with conspicuous bronzy markings in the throat. A.M. 1935. Not to be confused with the species H. hamabo Sieb. & Zucc. Raised in Japan.

'Mauve Queen'.—Flowers mauve with a crimson throat. Raised by Messrs Notcutt.

'Monstrosus'.—This old variety with white, crimson-centred flowers is superseded by two new introductions—'Dorothy Crane', raised by Messrs Notcutt; and 'Red Heart', of French origin.

'Rubis'. See under 'Woodbridge'.

'Totus Albus'.—Flowers pure white.   [plate 52

'Woodbridge'.—Flowers very large, deep rosy crimson with a darker throat. This fine variety was raised by Messrs Notcutt and received the Award of Merit in 1935. It derives from 'Rubis', which has smaller flowers of a similar shade.

'W. R. Smith'.—Flowers pure white, larger than in 'Totus Albus', with crimped petals. Raised in the USA.

Flowers Double or Semi-double

'Admiral Dewey'.—Flowers white, double. Raised in the USA at the end of the 19th century.

'Duc de Brabant'.—Flowers very double, deep crimson-pink, maroon in bud

'ELEGANTISSIMUS'. See under 'Lady Stanley'.

'LADY STANLEY'.—Flowers semi-double; petals white, shaded with rose and blotched with crimson at the base. An old variety, listed by Barron's Nurseries, Elvaston, near Derby, in 1875 and perhaps raised by them. There appears to be confusion between this variety and 'ELEGANTISSIMUS', which, according to the American authority Dr Donald Wyman, has semi-double flowers of a pale purplish pink, with deep pink blotches and red streaks reaching three-quarters of the way to the ends of the petals (*Arnoldia*, Vol. 18 (1958), p. 48 and pl. xi).

'VIOLET CLAIR DOUBLE'.—Flowers blue-purple, large, semi-double. Also known as 'Violaceus Plenus'.

H. SINOSYRIACUS L. H. Bailey—This species, described in 1922, is allied to *H. syriacus*. The leaves are relatively broader, 2¼ to 4 in. long and about as wide, with three short, triangular lobes; the toothing of the leaves is finer than it is in *H. syriacus*. A further point of distinction is that the involucral bracts outside the calyx are as long as the calyx or even longer and ⅛ to ⅜ in. wide. Flowers resembling those of *H. syriacus*, lilac-coloured, 3¼ to 4 in. wide at the mouth, blotched with crimson at the base. See further in *Baileya*, Vol. 13 (1965), p. 106.

Native of China in the provinces of Kweichow, Hunan, Kansu, and Shensi; introduced to Britain by Messrs Hillier, who received seeds from the Lushan Botanic Garden in 1936. They have named three clones and we are indebted to them for the following descriptions:

'AUTUMN SURPRISE'.—Petals white, with attractively feathered cerise base.

'LILAC QUEEN'.—Petals flushed lilac, with garnet-red base.

'RUBY GLOW'.—Petals white, with cerise base.

Their flowers do not open so widely as those of *H. syriacus*, but they are more handsome in foliage.

HIPPOPHAË   ELAEAGNACEAE

Two species of deciduous, dioecious willow-like trees and shrubs found in Europe and temperate Asia. Leaves alternate. Flowers inconspicuous and of no beauty; the male with two sepals and four stamens; the female with a single one-styled ovary surrounded by a receptable which in the fruiting stage becomes fleshy, enclosing a one-seeded stone. In both sexes the flowers are borne at the base of lateral shoots but often the axis of the shoot does not develop beyond the flowers, or is converted (in female plants) into a spine. The genus is allied to *Elaeagnus* and *Shepherdia*; the former differs in its bisexual flowers and scaly, silvery fruits; the latter has opposite leaves. For cultivation, see *H. rhamnoides*.

H. RHAMNOIDES L.   SEA BUCKTHORN

A deciduous shrub, sometimes a tree 30 to 40 ft high, the whole of the younger parts of the plant covered with silvery grey scales; twigs stiff, frequently spine-tipped. Leaves scarcely stalked, linear, 1 to 3 in. long, $\frac{1}{8}$ to $\frac{1}{4}$ in. wide, tapered at both ends, upper surface dark greyish green, and not so scaly

HIPPOPHAË RHAMNOIDES

as the silvery grey undersurface. Flowers very small, produced in April in short clusters; each flower solitary in the axil of a deciduous bract. Fruits orange-coloured, between globose and egg-shaped, $\frac{1}{4}$ to $\frac{3}{8}$ in. long, shortly stalked; in colour by September.

Native of Europe (including Britain) and temperate Asia. With its narrow, silvery leaves and brightly coloured berries clustered thickly on the branches from autumn until February, the sea buckthorn stands out remarkably distinct from all others in our gardens. Its beauty is so striking that it ought to be indispensable to every garden where winter effects are desired. Whilst it is, as the popular name suggests, frequently found on sea-shores, it thrives perfectly well in inland districts. At Kew it succeeds admirably at the margin of water, and in the ordinary soil of the gardens. It is not generally known that the plants are unisexual, so that the female one alone bears fruit, and then only if a male plant be growing near enough for the flowers to become pollinated. It is best grown in groups of about six females to one male. The pollen is carried by wind. Solitary female plants can be fertilised by hand, which is best done by waiting until the pollen of the male plant is ripe—shown by the little shower of yellow dust when the branch is tapped—and then cutting off a branch and shaking it over the female plant. Perhaps no other fruiting shrub is so attractive as this for so long a time. However pressed by hunger, birds will not eat the berries, which are filled with an intensely acid, yellowish juice.

Propagation may be effected by seeds or by layers. The latter is the simpler way of obtaining plants whose sex is known. There appears to be no way of distinguishing seedlings until they flower. In winter, the sex of flowering plants can be ascertained from the buds, which on male plants are conical and conspicuous, while those of the females are smaller and rounded.

Although the sea buckthorn is coastal in distribution in north-west Europe, farther south it is found on rivers and extends to about 6,000 ft in the Alps; the centre of its distribution is in the steppe regions of central Asia. In W. Szechwan, Wilson found plants up to 60 ft high, which differed from the typical state of the species in having the leaves stellate-tomentose above at first, and the twigs covered with villous hairs. These were given varietal status as var. PROCERA Rehd. Typical *H. rhamnoides* is found in the same area.

H. SALICIFOLIA D. Don

A deciduous, somewhat spiny tree 30 to 40 ft high, with a coarse bark cut into longitudinal flakes; young shoots covered with brownish down as well as scales. Leaves linear-oblong, 1 to 3 in. long, ¼ to ½ in. wide, dull green (not silvery) above, the lower surface covered with a greyish white felt; midrib brown; stalk ⅛ to ¼ in. long. Flowers as in *H. rhamnoides*. Fruits pale yellow.

Native of the Himalaya up to 10,000 ft altitude, and perfectly hardy at Kew, where there are three trees in the borders north of the Temperate House, the largest measuring 27 × 4¾ ft (1970). This species is inferior to *H. rhamnoides* in beauty. It is easily distinguished from it by its broader, not silvery leaves, felted rather than scaly beneath, and by the paler, less brilliantly coloured fruit. Introduced in 1822.

HOHERIA   MALVACEAE

A genus of five species of deciduous or evergreen trees and shrubs, endemic to New Zealand. Leaves simple, varying in shape according to the age of the plant. Flowers white, usually in axillary cymes (more rarely the cymes are terminal, and sometimes the flowers are solitary in the leaf-axils). Stamens arranged in usually five bundles. Pistil of five to fifteen one-ovuled carpels, which are often winged and each of which develops into a dry, indehiscent, one-seeded capsule. Styles as many as there are carpels, united at the base; stigma capitate. The generic name derives from the Maori word for *H. populnea*—*houhere*.

The following account is based largely on the revision of the genus by the late Dr Allan in *Flora of New Zealand* (1961).

H. LYALLII Hook. f.

Plagianthus lyallii (Hook. f.) Hook. f.; *Gaya lyallii* (Hook. f.) Baker; *G. lyallii* var. *ribifolia* T. Kirk

A deciduous shrub or small tree growing to about 20 ft high in the wild; branchlets densely covered with stellate down. Leaves on adult plants 2 to $4\frac{1}{2}$ in. long, $1\frac{1}{2}$ to 2 in. wide, ovate, heart-shaped to truncate at the base, downy

HOHERIA LYALLII

on both sides but usually more so beneath than above, margins deeply double- or triple-too hed, the principal teeth often lobe-like; stalks half to fully as long as the blade. Plants grown from seed go through a juvenile phase in which the leaves are broadly ovate to almost orbicular and deeply lobed, the lobes crenately toothed. Flowers white, 1 to $1\frac{1}{2}$ in. across, borne two to five together in cymose clusters in the leaf-axils of the current season's growth (sometimes solitary), each flower on a slender drooping stalk 1 to $1\frac{1}{4}$ in. long. Petals overlapping; almost translucent, usually five in number. Anthers purple. Styles ten to fifteen; stigma set obliquely on the filament and often adnate to its upper part (decurrent). Carpels ten to fifteen, downy, slightly winged.

Native of the South Island of New Zealand, found in the mountains east of the divide, where the climate is more 'continental' than on the rainier west side. This species is discussed below together with its ally *H. glabrata*. Here it should be pointed out that the latter species was only separated from *H. lyallii* in 1926, so that references to *Hoheria* or *Plagianthus lyallii* in garden and botanical literature before that date refer to one or the other species and more frequently to *H. glabrata* so far as garden plants are concerned, for that was and still is the commoner species in cultivation.

H. GLABRATA Sprague & Summerhayes *Hoheria lyallii* var. β Hook. f.; *Plagianthus lyallii* Hook. f. in *Bot. Mag.* under t. 5935; *Gaya lyallii* T. Kirk and other authors; *H. lyallii* var. *glabrata* (S. & S.) E. H. M. Cox—In the *Kew Bulletin* for 1926, pp. 214–20, Sprague and Summerhayes show that the material originally described as *Hoheria lyallii* by J. D. Hooker in 1852 actually comprises two species. One is the true *H. lyallii*, as described above. The other, which they named *H. glabrata*, differs from *H. lyallii* in the following characters: stems and leaves glabrous or almost so when mature; margins coarsely toothed but not lobulate and the toothing simpler; apex of leaves usually acuminate and sometimes drawn out into a 'drip-tip'; stigma capitate or only slightly decurrent; carpels scarcely or not at all winged.

H. glabrata, like *H. lyallii*, is confined to the South Island of New Zealand but is found west of the divide, where the climate is rainier and somewhat more equable than on the eastern side of the divide, where *H. lyallii* has its home. It was introduced before 1871 and is figured in *Bot. Mag.*, t. 5935.

Both species are beautiful. Perhaps *H. lyallii*, with its grey leaves and its more tree-like habit, is the finer species, though it seems to be less common in commerce. *H. glabrata* is more of a shrub and faster growing, but perhaps softer-wooded and hence more subject to die-back. But a form of *H. lyallii* distributed in the 1930s under the name *H. lyallii* var. *ribifolia* seems to have been tender or at least difficult to cultivate. There is a fine specimen of *H. lyallii* at Wakehurst Place, Sussex, at the top of the Slips.

H. POPULNEA A. Cunn.

An evergreen tree up to 45 ft high in the wild, glabrous in all its parts except for some stellate down on the young leaves and inflorescences. Adult leaves broad ovate to ovate-lanceolate or elliptic, 3 to 6½ in. long, usually acute at the apex (more rarely acute, obtuse or rounded), rounded to truncate or slightly heart-shaped at the base, margins coarsely double-toothed; leaf-stalks about ⅘ in. long. Juvenile plants may resemble the adult ones in foliage and branching, or they may form a mass of slender, tangled stems with small leaves of very variable shape, but such plants would not be seen in cultivation unless the species were raised from seeds. Flowers white, about 1 in. across, borne singly in the leaf-axils or in five- to ten-flowered cymose clusters. Calyx campanulate, with triangular teeth. Styles five, rarely six; stigmas capitate. Carpels five, rarely six, with broad wings.

Native of the North Island of New Zealand, at low elevations. It is a very variable species, occurring here and there in forms that depart markedly from the above description in their leaves. *H. populnea* is certainly tender, and not common in Britain.

cv. 'ALBA VARIEGATA'.—Leaves with a broad margin of white. Raised by Messrs Duncan and Davies of New Plymouth, New Zealand. To the catalogues of this firm we are indebted also for the following descriptions.

cv. 'OSBORNEI'.—Leaves purplish beneath. Flowers with purplish blue stamens. In cultivation at Garnish Island, Co. Cork, Eire.

cv. 'PURPUREA'.—Veins and undersurface of leaves copper-coloured.

cv. 'VARIEGATA'.—Leaves variegated creamy yellow.

H. ANGUSTIFOLIA Raoul *H. populnea* var. *angustifolia* (Raoul) Hook. f.— This species is allied to *H. populnea* but the leaves are only $\frac{7}{8}$ to $1\frac{1}{4}$ in. long and relatively narrower, set with large, distant, spine-like teeth. The flowers are mostly borne singly in the leaf-axils, more rarely in clusters, and measure about $\frac{3}{4}$ in. across. Styles and carpels five.

A plant at Borde Hill, in Sussex, grown against a garden wall, appears to belong to this species. The clone derived from it has been named 'BORDE HILL' and is in commerce. Award of Merit 1967.

H. SEXSTYLOSA Col.

H. populnea var. *lanceolata* Hook. f.; *H. lanceolata* Hort.

A densely branched evergreen shrub or small tree, usually of rather fastigiate habit, growing to about 25 ft in height. Branchlets covered with stellate down, especially when young. Leaves glossy, light green, variable in shape, but usually lanceolate, tapered at the apex to a sharp point, or acuminate, usually cuneate at the base, $2\frac{1}{2}$ to 3 in. long, deeply and jaggedly toothed. Juvenile plants form tangled shrublets with small usually roundish leaves. Flowers white, $\frac{3}{4}$ in. wide, borne in August two to five together in cymose clusters (sometimes singly). Calyx campanulate, with triangular teeth, downy. Styles pinkish, usually six to seven in number, very rarely five; stigmas capitate. Carpels the same in number as the styles, broadly winged.

Native of New Zealand, in openings of lowland and mountain forests. In North Island it ranges from 36° 30' southward; in South Island it is found as far south as Canterbury. It has been confused with *H. populnea* but in that species the flowers are larger and more numerous in each cyme (usually five to ten) and the styles and carpels usually number five only (rarely six). The shape of the leaves is less diagnostic (see var. *ovata* below) but in *H. sexstylosa* in its typical state they are relatively narrower than they are in *H. populnea*. The third evergreen species—*H. angustifolia*—has only five styles and carpels, small, oblong, rather spinily toothed leaves.

H. sexstylosa is the commonest evergreen hoheria in gardens. It is fast growing, and handsome at all times with its neat, glossy leaves, but especially in

July and August when covered with its innumerable small white flowers. It is fairly hardy in the southern counties from Sussex westwards, and in the western counties. Elsewhere it needs the protection of a wall. It is defoliated in cold winters, but quickly recovers.

var. OVATA (Simpson and Thomson) Allan *H. ovata* Simpson and Thomson— Leaves resembling those of *H. populnea*, being ovate to broadly so, but smaller (2 to 3 in. long at the most). Styles and carpels five to eight in number. Native of the South Island of New Zealand (Nelson and northern Westland).

H. 'GLORY OF AMLWCH'.—Leaves about 3½ in. long, ovate, pale green, serrated, slender-pointed. Flowers about 1½ in. wide, in clusters of three to eight. A free-flowering small tree keeping its leaves in all but the severest winters. Award of Merit July 12, 1960, when shown by the late Sir Frederick Stern from Highdown, Sussex, where it grows on chalk (*Journ. R.H.S.*, Vol. 85, p. 528). It was raised by Dr Jones of Amlwch, Anglesey, and is thought to be a hybrid between *H. glabrata* and *H. sexstylosa* (Arnold-Forster, *Shrubs for the Milder Counties* (1948), p. 139). It was put into commerce by the Slieve Donard Nursery Company. Similar hybrids have arisen in other gardens.

[PLATE 49

HOLBOELLIA   LARDIZABALACEAE

A genus of five species of evergreen climbers native of China and the Himalaya named after F. L. Holboell, once superintendent of the Botanic Garden at Copenhagen.

As in many other members of the family, the apparent petals are really sepals, the true petals being reduced to nectaries. In the male flowers there are six stamens and a rudimentary ovary. The female flowers have small non-functional stamens (staminodes) and three carpels, each developing into a fleshy 'pod'. The stamens are free from each other and the sepals fleshy, whereas in the related genus *Stauntonia* (q.v.) the stamens are united and the sepals thin.

H. CORIACEA Diels

A vigorous evergreen climber growing, according to Wilson, 20 ft high in the wild, but apparently capable of becoming much taller under cultivation; young shoots twining, ribbed, purplish, and, like the leaves and flower-stalks, quite glabrous. Leaves composed of three leaflets borne on a common stalk 1½ to 3½ in. long, each leaflet having its own stalk ¼ to 1 in. long. Leaflets 2½ to 6 in. long, 1 to 3 in. wide, the middle one the largest and longest-stalked, oval or oblong inclined to obovate and usually widest towards the pointed apex, rounded at the base, side leaflets ovate to lanceolate, all three dark glossy green, leathery, and conspicuously veined beneath. Male flowers scarcely $\frac{1}{2}$ in. long; sepals erect, white, oblong, $\frac{1}{8}$ in. wide, stamens with pale purple stalks scarcely longer than the anthers. The male flowers are produced in a group of corymbs at the end of the previous year's growth or in the leaf-axils, the whole making a cluster of blossom 3 in. long and 4 in. wide. Female flowers produced

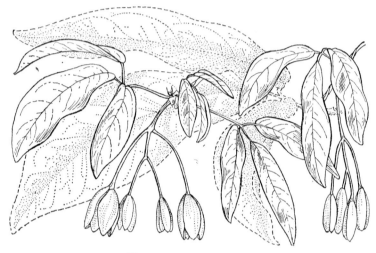

HOLBOELLIA CORIACEA

in corymbs of usually three or four blooms from the axils of the lower leaves of the young shoots. They are rather larger than the males and appear on a main-stalk up to 5 or 6 in. long; sepals fleshy, much paler than the males, greenish white tinged with purple; styles three, erect, cylindrical $\frac{1}{4}$ in. long. The fleshy fruits are purple, $1\frac{3}{4}$ to $2\frac{1}{4}$ in. or even more long, nearly 1 in. wide. Seeds jet black. *Bot. Mag.*, n.s., t. 447.

Native of Hupeh, China; introduced by Wilson in 1907. It is quite hardy and is vigorous enough to climb into and over a small tree. The description given above was made from a plant which first flowered at Kew in April and May 1921. There is a fine plant on the south facing wall of the General Museum.

H. LATIFOLIA Wall.—This species, a native of the Himalaya, was introduced in 1840. It is a luxuriant climber, which thrives exceedingly well in the south-western counties, but is not reliably hardly nor so vigorous in colder parts. The flowers are exquisitely fragrant. This species is so closely allied to *H. coriacea* that it is difficult to find any reliable character by which they may be distin-guished botanically, except that in *H. coriacea* the leaflets appear to be constantly three in number again up to seven, but often only three, in *H. latifolia*. If the two were to be united, it would be under the name. *H. latifolia*, which has long priority.

Neither species fruits freely in this country but might do so more freely if the female flowers were hand-pollinated. The plant of *H. latifolia* at Dartington Hall, Devon, occasionally bears fruits.

HOLODISCUS   ROSACEAE

A genus of eight species, natives of the New World from western N. America through Mexico to Colombia. It belongs to the subfamily Spiraeoides and within this group is distinguished by the combination of the following characters: leaves simple (not pinnate as in *Sorbaria*), without stipules; flowers small, borne in panicles; fruits composed of five achenes.

H. DISCOLOR (Pursh) Maxim.
Spiraea discolor Pursh; *S. ariaefolia* Sm.

A large deciduous shrub, usually 8 to 12 ft high, considerably more in width. Stems erect at the base, but branching and gracefully arching or pendulous at the top; young branches downy and slightly ridged. Leaves ovate, with a straight or broadly wedge-shaped base, 2 to 3½ in. long, 1½ to 3 in. wide on the barren stems, smaller on the flowering branches, each margin cut up into four to eight lobes which are themselves sharply toothed, upper surface slightly hairy, lower one covered with a grey felt; stalk ¼ to ⅜ in. long. Flowers creamy white, small, produced during July in pendulous, plume-like panicles 4 to 12 in. long; flower-stalks and calyx downy. Fruit an achene, non-splitting, woolly.

Native of western N. America; introduced by Douglas in 1827. It was once known in gardens as *Spiraea ariaefolia*—an appropriate name, recalling the resemblance of its leaves to some of the Aria group of *Sorbus*. It produces an extraordinary profusion of blossom, and is exceedingly graceful in habit. Many fine plants are scattered over the south of England. This shrub is seen to best advantage as an isolated specimen with a dark green background, say of holly. In thin woodland it also thrives admirably.

H. DUMOSUS (Nutt.) Heller *Spiraea dumosa* Nutt.; *H. discolor* var. *dumosus* (Nutt.) Coult.—A spreading shrub attaining a height of 10 ft in the wild, but often much lower. Leaves obovate, mostly ¾ to 1½ in. long, cuneate at the base and tapered gradually into the stalk, grey-green above, woolly beneath, with three to six teeth on each side. Panicles erect. Native of western N. America from Wyoming to Texas and Arizona, and of N. Mexico. It is rare in gardens.

HOVENIA   RHAMNACEAE

A genus of probably only one species, with the characters given below. As in all members of the Rhamnaceae the stamens are placed opposite the petals. In the absence of fruits the leaves, three-veined from the base, distinguish it from any species of *Rhamnus*.

H. DULCIS Thunb.
H. acerba Lindl.

A deciduous tree 30 ft high (much more in the wild); twigs downy when young. Leaves alternate, oval or heart-shaped, three-veined from the base, from 4 to 7 in. long, 3 to 6 in. wide, taper-pointed, coarsely and unequally toothed, downy beneath, especially on the veins. Flowers in terminal and axillary forked clusters 2 to 3 in. across; the individual flower ¼ in. or so wide, yellow. Flower-stalks swelling unevenly after the decay of the flower into a fleshy, contorted mass, red, and sweet to the taste. They are chewed by the Japanese and Chinese. Fruit about the size of a pea, containing three seeds, and often partially embedded in the fleshy stalks. *Bot. Mag.*, t. 2360.

This species, described from Japan, is recorded as a wild plant from Japan, Korea, and China, but is so widely cultivated throughout eastern Asia that its exact distribution in the truly wild state is uncertain. In the Himalayan region it is grown from Hazara in the west to Bhutan in the east; it is thought by some to be native here and there in those parts, notably Nepal and Kumaon, though Buchanan in 1802 reported the tradition that it had originally come to Nepal from China 'or some country subject to it'. In 1939 the Japanese botanist Kitamura revived the name *H. acerba* Lindl. for the Chinese plants, but the distinction he gives between this species (actually described from a plant of Himalayan origin) and *H. dulcis* do not hold good over all the material in the Kew Herbarium and it seems that only one variable species is involved.

This curious tree is fairly hardy at Kew though the growths may be cut back in winter if not fully ripened. The tree mentioned in previous editions died in 1954 when 33 ft high. The present example, raised from seeds received from Les Barres in 1948, is about 12 ft high (1970).

HUDSONIA   CISTACEAE

A genus of three species exclusively North American, and allied to *Cistus* and *Helianthemum*, which it resembles in the fleeting nature of its blossom. Its yellow flowers and three-valved seed-vessel distinguishes it from *Cistus*, and from both it differs markedly in the heath-like habit. Named in honour of William Hudson, an English botanist of the 18th century.

H. ERICOIDES L.   FALSE HEATHER

A low, bushy, evergreen shrub of heath-like aspect, rarely more than 6 or 8 in. high. Leaves grey-green, awl-shaped, ¼ to ⅓ in. long, erect and overlapping but not pressed to the stem, hairy. Flowers bright yellow, ⅓ in. across, produced during May singly on very slender, silky stalks about ½ in. long, crowded at the upper parts of the branches; petals five, soon falling; sepals three, silky.

Native of eastern N. America, in dry sandy soil near the coast, from Newfoundland to N. Carolina; introduced in 1805, but always rare owing to the difficulty in cultivation. The late Sir John Ross of Bladensburg, who, so far as I know, is the only one who has had any success with it, told me that it did best planted in a made bed consisting of peat at the bottom, and about 6 in. of sand at the top. So far as winter cold is concerned, it must be hardy anywhere in Britain, considering the high latitudes it reaches in a wild state. But even in American gardens it is not easy to establish. It may be recommended to those knight-errants in gardening who delight in mastering difficult subjects. It probably needs a sandy, well-drained, slightly saline soil, with full sunshine.

A closely related species—H. MONTANA Nutt.—is found in the mountains of N. Carolina.

H. TOMENTOSA Nutt. BEACH HEATHER.—This species is very distinct from *H. ericoides* in its smaller leaves, which are closely appressed to the stem and almost concealed by the dense, woolly down. Native of north-eastern N. America in sandy places on the coast, around the Great Lakes, and in the prairies.

Forms intermediate between the two species are found where they grow together, as on the sand-barrens of New Jersey. These may be hybrids but curiously enough they also occur in parts of E. Canada where *H. ericoides* is absent (Gray's *Manual of Botany*, Ed. 8 (1950), p. 1018; M'Nab in *Edin. New Phil. Journ.*, No. 35 (1835)).

HYDRANGEA   HYDRANGEACEAE

A small genus of shrubs, small trees, and climbers, represented in cultivation almost wholly by species of the typical section (section *Hydrangea*), which is confined to N. America, E. Asia, and the Philippines. In this group the leaves are deciduous and the inflorescence is not enclosed by bracts in the bud-stage (except in *H. involucrata*). In the section *Cornidia*, with twelve species in Central and S. America, the Philippines, and Formosa, the leaves are evergreen and the inflorescence is enclosed in the bud-stage by large ovate bracts. Of the hydrangeas grown outside in this country only *H. serratifolia* (*integerrima*) belongs to this section. In both sections the leaves are opposite. The inflorescence is corymbose (but paniculate in *H. paniculata* and *H. quercifolia*), composed of numerous fertile flowers and, in the majority of species, of a few showy sterile flowers (also known as ray-flowers). In the fertile flowers the sepals are very small and inconspicuous; the petals are four or five in number, white, blue, or pink; stamens normally eight or ten. Ovary partly or wholly enclosed in the receptacle, with usually two to four styles. The sterile flowers are usually arranged around the outside of the inflorescence and their most conspicuous feature is the large calyx, with three to five petal-like sepals. Normally the other parts of these sterile flowers do not develop, and even if petals, stamens, and ovary are formed (as is often the case among the hortensias), they rarely if ever produce seeds. In some species mutants occur in which the majority or at least a large proportion of the flowers are of the sterile type (see *H. arborescens, H. paniculata*, and *H. macrophylla*).

All the species need a good garden soil and resent dryness at the root. in areas of low rainfall hydrangeas are best planted where they are shaded from the hottest sun. The late Sir Frederick Stern found that in the dry chalky soil of his garden at Highdown the species that thrive best are *H. aspera (villosa)* and *H. involucrata* 'Hortensis'. Most of the hydrangeas are easily increased by cuttings made of moderately ripe summer wood, but layering is often used for large-leaved species such as *H. aspera, H. sargentiana, and H. quercifolia*, and also for the climbing *H. petiolaris*. *H. paniculata* and *H. arborescens* (and its subspecies) may be lightly pruned in spring (but see further under *H. paniculata* 'Grandiflora').

The standard botanical treatment of the genus is: Elizabeth McClintock, *A Monograph of the Genus Hydrangea* (1957). In this excellent work a number of species familiar in gardens are reduced to the level of subspecies or sunk altogether. In the treatment that follows some species reduced by Miss McClintock have been maintained, but only where there is taxonomically some room for manœuvre. For example, it is arguable that *H. petiolaris* and *H. sargentiana* are distinct enough from *H. anomala* and *H. aspera* respectively to merit specific rank, and they are retained here, though in truth more for the convenience of gardeners and nurserymen than from any conviction that Miss McClintock's decision to reduce them to the rank of subspecies is wrong. On the other hand, it would be preposterous to attempt to maintain the specific identity of *H. cinerea* and *H. radiata*, which are barely more than states of the variable *H. arborescens*.

The standard horticultural work on the genus is: M. Haworth-Booth, *The Hydrangeas* (Ed. 2, 1955). His taxonomic and nomenclatural treatment of *H. macrophylla* and *H. serrata* is highly controversial and is not followed here. Nevertheless, Mr Haworth-Booth has done much to popularise in gardens many beautiful hydrangeas which were largely unknown or ignored until he brought them to notice.

H. ANOMALA D. Don

H. altissima Wall.

A deciduous climber up to 40 ft or more high, attaching itself to tree trunks by aerial roots in the wild; young shoots either hairy or glabrous; the bark of

the older branches peeling off in large, thin, brown flakes. Leaves ovate of
oval, 3 to 5 in. long (more in mild climates), half to three-fourths as wide,
rounded at the base, pointed, regularly triangular- or roundish-toothed,
glabrous on both sides except for tufts of down in the vein-axils beneath; stalk
at first hairy, 1 to 3 in. long. Corymbs 6 to 8 in. across, with a few white sterile
flowers at the margins, each ⅜ to 1½ in. in diameter; the small fertile flowers are
yellowish white; stamens nine to fifteen. Blossoms in June.

Native of the Himalaya and China; introduced in 1839. It is nearly allied to
H. petiolaris, but differs in having fewer stamens, not so flat an inflorescence,
and usually more coarsely toothed leaves. It is not so hardy probably as *H. petiolaris*, although it grows well outside on a wall at Kew. Both these species are
distinguished by the petals of the fertile flowers cohering into, and falling away
in, one cap-like piece.

H. ARBORESCENS L.

A deciduous shrub of somewhat loose habit 4 to 10 ft high; young shoots
rather downy at first, becoming glabrous. Leaves broadly ovate, oval or
roundish, 3 to 7 in. long, 2 to 6 in. wide, pointed at the apex, rounded or heart-
shaped at the base, coarsely toothed, upper surface bright dark green, lower one
paler, both glabrous, or with down only on the veins or in the vein-axils
beneath; stalk 1 to 3 in. long. Corymbs flattish, much branched, usually 4 to
6 in. across, with few or no large sterile flowers. Fertile flowers dull white, very
small and crowded; flower-stalks downy. Seed-vessels eight-ribbed, with calyx
adhering at the top.

Native of the eastern United States, from the State of New York southwards;
introduced by Peter Collinson in 1736. A vigorous and hardy species, which
flowers freely in July and August, but is not particularly attractive.

cv. 'GRANDIFLORA'.—A very beautiful form, in which all the flowers are
of the large sterile type and pure white. It is a clone descended from a plant
found growing wild in Ohio late in the 19th century and was introduced to
Britain in 1907. It is quite hardy, and showy enough to be regarded as an admirable substitute for the hortensias in the colder parts of the country. It blooms
from July to September, and is probably the best hydrangea to cultivate out-
of-doors near London and in places with a similar climate. Its one defect is
that its flower-heads are often so heavy that the stalk is not stout enough to
hold them upright.

var. OBLONGA Torr. & Gr.—Leaves rounded or tapered at the base, narrow-
ovate to elliptic-oblong. There is a form of this—f. STERILIS (Torr. & Gr.)
St John—in which all the flowers are sterile. It was originally described by
Torrey and Gray in 1840 from a plant found wild in Pennsylvania, but so far
as is known the original plant was never propagated.

In previous editions, two allies of *H. arborescens* were described under the
names *H. cinerea* and *H. radiata*, but these are really only part of the variation of
H. arborescens and cannot reasonably be maintained as distinct species. Following
Miss McClintock, they are treated here as subspecies:

subsp. DISCOLOR (Ser.) McClintock *H. arborescens* var. *discolor* Ser.; *H. cinerea*

Small—Undersides of leaves sparsely downy, or with a continuous but thin greyish indumentum; hairs covered with numerous microscopic 'warts' (tubercles). This subspecies is mainly represented in cultivation by the cultivar 'STERILIS', in which all or most of the flowers are of the sterile type. The hydrangea named *H. canescens* by Kirchner (*Arb. Muscav.* (1864), p. 198) is near to subsp. *discolor* but according to Rehder the hairs lack the characteristic tubercles.

subsp. RADIATA (Walt.) McClintock *H. radiata* Walt.; *H. nivea* Michx.— Upper surface of leaves dark green, the lower covered with a close snow-white felt. Native of the southern Appalachians; introduced in 1786. The vividly white undersurface of the leaf distinguishes this hydrangea from all others in cultivation and gives it a peculiar interest.

H. ASPERA D. Don

H. villosa Rehd.; *H. aspera* var. *velutina* Rehd.; *H. aspera* var. *strigosior* Diels;
H. rehderana Schneid.; *H. fulvescens* Rehd.; *H. kawakamii* Hayata

A deciduous shrub up to 12 ft high in cultivation, more in width, occasionally a small tree in the wild; young stems clad with short appressed hairs and/or longer more spreading hairs. Leaves mostly lanceolate to narrow-ovate, 4 to 10 in. long, 1 to 4 in. wide, acute or acuminate at the apex, cuneate to rounded at the base, sparsely hairy above, lower surface densely coated with soft, whitish, erect or spreading hairs, the midrib beneath sometimes with longer, brownish hairs, margins edged with forward-pointing or spreading teeth, which are sometimes reduced to threadlike projections; petioles 1 to 4 in. long, with hairs similar to those of the branchlets. Inflorescence a flat-topped or slightly convex cymose corymb up to 10 in. across, borne terminally on the season's shoots but often supplemented by subsidiary clusters from the uppermost leaf-axils; inflorescence-axes with hairs similar to those of the branchlets. Receptacles of fertile flowers truncate at the apex, enclosing the ovary, usually purplish pink but sometimes uncoloured. Calyx very small. Petals five, coloured like the receptacle, soon falling. Stamens ten, blue. Styles two to four, blue. Ray-flowers variable in number, up to 1 in. across (occasionally wider); sepals mostly four, roundish, toothed or entire, varying in colour from white through pale pink to purple, the veins often more deeply coloured than the rest of the surface. Capsules hemispheric, $\frac{1}{10}$ to $\frac{1}{8}$ in. wide. Seeds tailed.

H. aspera was described in 1825 from a specimen collected in Nepal and ranges from there eastward to western and central China and Formosa; it also occurs in Java and Sumatra.

H. aspera varies somewhat in the size, shape, and toothing of its leaves, in the indumentum of the leaf-undersides, branchlets, etc., and in the colour of the flowers, though the variation is not so great as the large number of synonymous names might suggest. Mainly the species is represented in gardens by plants called *H. villosa*, which derive from seeds collected by Wilson during his two expeditions to western China for the Arnold Arboretum (some, perhaps, from seeds sent later by Forrest from Yunnan). The origin of the plants distributed as *H. aspera* or *H. aspera* var. *macrophylla* is not certain, but these too appear to be Chinese forms of the species.

In its best forms, *H. aspera* is a very beautiful species and all the more valuable for flowering after midsummer. It is, moreover, one of the few hydrangeas that really thrives in chalky soil; how well it does so is proved by the fine specimen in the chalkpit at Highdown in Sussex, which has produced numerous self-sown seedlings in its time. *H. aspera* is not, however, an easy plant to suit and is subject to damage by late spring frosts. It is said to succeed best in a

HYDRANGEA ASPERA

dryish soil and should never be planted where the soil lies excessively wet in winter. Like many other hydrangeas, it is tender when young and should be given some protection during its first few winters.

H. aspera varies in its garden characters as well as botanically. Some plants agree with the type of *H. villosa* in having the ray-flowers bluish purple but they may be pink or white with pink veins There is also variation in flowering time, so that two or three selected plants could provide colour from July until September. A particularly fine form of *H. aspera* is grown at Westonbirt in Gloucestershire, with bold foliage and flower-heads 10 in. or more across. This clone appears to be sterile and it has been suggested that the original plant might have been a hybrid with *H. sargentiana*, though there is no sign of the influence of the latter species in the specimen seen. Similar plants are grown under the erroneous names *H. aspera macrophylla* or *H. strigosa macrophylla* (see further below under subsp. *strigosa*). On the other hand, some plants distributed under the name *H. aspera* are a poor form of the species, and it has been suggested that for this reason it would cause confusion if *H. villosa* were to be sunk in *H. aspera*. But this poor form, although still to be seen in collections, is probably not in commerce. Furthermore, the plants raised from the seeds collected by Wilson and grown under the name *H. villosa* are also very variable in ornamental value.

subsp. STRIGOSA (Rehd.) McClintock *H. strigosa* Rehd.; *H. aspera* var. *macrophylla* Hemsl.; *H. strigosa* var. *macrophylla* (Hemsl.) Rehd.—This subspecies differs from the typical subspecies described above only in having the undersurface of the leaves covered with short, stiff, appressed hairs. It was introduced by Wilson when collecting for the Arnold Arboretum, and, from the details given in *Plantae Wilsonianae*, it would seem that the seeds were collected at a comparatively low altitude, which may explain why some of the plants in cultivation are not very hardy and tend to flower late in the season. One clone that has been distributed commercially develops its inflorescences so late that it has never flowered in Michael Haworth-Booth's collection, except under glass. In the *Gardeners' Chronicle* for October 19, 1935, Besant mentions a plant raised from Wilson 757 that regularly flowered in that month at the Glasnevin Botanic Garden, Dublin, and there is a plant at Rowallane in Northern Ireland which is also October-flowering and certainly belongs to the subsp. *strigosa*, judging from the specimen in the Wisley herbarium. However, this late flowering is certainly not a character of the subsp. *strigosa* as a whole. In the Kew Herbarium there are flowering specimens from garden plants taken in almost every month from June to October. A poor form of the subsp. *trigosa*, distributed under the erroneous name "*H. longipes*", flowers in August.

The plant at Wakehurst Place, Sussex, from which a flowering branch is figured in *Bot. Mag.*, t. 9324, was raised originally by H. J. Elwes from a stray in a packet of seeds of *Decumaria sinensis*, collected by Wilson during his second expedition for the Arnold Arboretum.

The subsp. *strigosa* is, or was, also in cultivation from Kingdon Ward's No. 20940.

A specimen collected by Henry in China, and named *H. aspera* var. *macrophylla* by Hemsley, has the leaves strigose beneath and the variety was accordingly transferred to *H. strigosa* by Rehder. No doubt for this reason some garden plants called *H. aspera macrophylla* have been renamed *H. strigosa macrophylla*, although these plants, at least those examined, do not belong to the subsp. *strigosa* but to the typical subspecies. They are, in other words, *H. aspera macrophylla* of gardens, but not of Hemsley.

For *H. aspera* subsp. *robusta* see *H. longipes*; for *H. aspera* subsp. *sargentiana* see *H. sargentiana*.

H. HETEROMALLA D. Don

H. vestita Wall.; *H. khasiana* Hook. f. & Thoms.; *H. dumicola* W. W. Sm.; *H. xanthoneura* Diels; *H. hypoglauca* Rehd.; *H. mandarinorum* Diels (for a fuller list of synonyms see McClintock, op. cit., p. 215)

A deciduous shrub or small tree; young branchlets clad with short erect or appressed hairs, lenticellate; second-year stems with a close bark (but see cv. 'Bretschneideri'). Leaves variable in shape, mostly ovate to broad-ovate, cuneate to rounded or sometimes cordate at the base, 3½ to 8 in. long, 1¼ to 5½ in. wide, serrate, glabrous or with scattered hairs above, the underside usually more or less densely coated with appressed or spreading hairs, but sometimes glabrous except for hairs on the veins; petiole ½ to 1¼ in. long. Inflorescence corymbose. Fertile flowers white, numerous, with usually ten stamens; ovary semi-inferior, i.e., its upper part projecting above the rim of the receptacle, which bears five triangular calyx-lobes about 1/10 in. long; styles two to four. Ray-flowers always present, white, 1 to 2 in. across. Capsules surmounted by the thickened bases of the styles and with the rim of the receptacle persisting at or slightly above the middle.

H. heteromalla ranges from the Himalayan region of Kumaon eastward and northward to western, west central and northern China. It was described from Nepal and introduced in 1821, though the present garden stock is wholly or for the most part of much more recent origin. It varies in leaf-shape and indumentum and numerous species have been made out of these variations, none of which is recognised by Miss McClintock—hence the long list of synonyms.

Before the publication of Miss McClintock's monograph the name *H. heteromalla* was used in a narrower sense for a hydrangea fairly common in collections, with leaves 3 to 8 in. long, 1½ to 3 in. wide, covered with a close tomentum beneath, with reddish petioles. It is of erect habit, flowers in July and August, and attains a height of 20 ft or more in the milder parts. It is quite hardy south of London and often produces self-sown offspring in great abundance. Other forms of the species were introduced from China by Wilson and by Forrest, but none of these are on the average any better than the more typical form of the species.

cv. 'BRETSCHNEIDERI'.—A shrub 8 to 10 ft high, forming a sturdy bush; second-year stems chestnut-brown, peeling. Leaves oblong to ovate, 3 to 5 in. long, 1 to 2¼ in. wide, sparsely hairy beneath. Corymbs flattened, 4 to 6 in. wide (*H. bretschneideri* Dipp.; *H. pekinensis* Hort.).

This hydrangea was very properly included by Miss McClintock in *H. heteromalla* without distinction, but it seems reasonable to maintain the name at the level of cultivar, on the grounds that all the plants under the name *H. bretschneideri* descend from seeds collected by Dr. Bretschneider in the mountains near Peking and probably represent a clone or at least a group of similar clones. The type of the species was one of these plants. 'Bretschneideri' is easy to distinguish from other forms of *H. heteromalla* by its peeling second-year bark, and is probably the most suitable for general cultivation, being completely hardy and of moderate size.

H. INVOLUCRATA Sieb.

H. longifolia Hayata

A deciduous, semi-shrubby plant often less than 1½ ft high, but much higher in milder climates; young shoots, leaves, flower-stalks, and ovary covered with bristly, pale down. Leaves ovate-oblong, rounded or tapered at the base, slender-pointed, margined with numerous fine, bristle-like teeth, 3 to 6 in. long, 1 to 2½ in. wide, roughened, especially above; stalk ¼ to 1 in. long. Corymb 3 to 5 in. across, enclosed in the bud state by about six large broadly ovate bracts, the largest about 1 in. long, covered with a felt of appressed whitish down. Sterile flowers at the margin of the corymb, ¾ to 1 in. across, the three to five sepals white or blue-white, slightly downy. Small fertile flowers blue. Blossoms from August to October.

Native of Japan and Formosa. The distinguishing feature of this species is the whorl of bracts (involucre) at the base of the inflorescence, which persists through the flowering. It is very pretty when in bloom, the blue (sometimes rosy-lilac) fertile flowers making an effective contrast with the large sterile whitish ones. Unfortunately it is not very hardy, and is often killed back more or less in winter, the flowers being borne on the new shoots which spring from the base. It thrives well in the west country.

In floral characters and foliage *H. involucrata* is near to *H. aspera* but it differs from all the other species of the section *Hydrangea* (the 'true' hydrangeas) in having the inflorescence enclosed in the bud-stage by an involucre, as in the section *Cornidia*.

cv. 'HORTENSIS'.—Sterile flowers double and also more numerous than in the wild form, coloured an attractive shade of buff-pink (but almost white on plants grown in shade). Of Japanese garden origin, described in 1867 but not introduced to Britain until 1906. It is not completely hardy but has lived for many years in the gardens of the Royal Horticultural Society at Wisley, in a sheltered border.

H. LONGIPES Franch.

H. aspera subsp. *robusta* (Hook. f. &. Thoms.) McClintock, in part

A shrub of speading habit 6 to 8 ft high; young shoots more or less covered at first with loose down. Leaves rough to the touch, roundish ovate, with a heart-shaped or rounded base, and an abrupt, slender point, 3 to 7 in. long, one-half as much or more wide, sharply and prominently toothed, both surfaces, but especially the lower one, covered with short bristles; stalks slender, bristly when young, and from half to fully as long as the blade. Corymbs flattish, 4 to 6 in. across, the sterile flowers ¾ to 1¾ in. across, white. Fertile flowers small, white; flower-stalks bristly. Seed-vessels roundish, glabrous, with the calyx at the top.

Native of Central and W. China; introduced by Wilson, for Messrs Veitch in 1901. It is a lax-habited shrub, with remarkably long-stalked leaves like those of *H. petiolaris*. It was first described by Franchet in 1885, and by a curious coincidence Hemsley described it again as a new species two years later, adopting the same name. It is rare in cultivation, but has long been grown at Borde Hill in Sussex, where it is hardy.

H. ROBUSTA Hook. f. & Thoms. *H. rosthornii* Diels; *H. aspera* subsp. *robusta* (Hook. f. & Thoms.) McClintock—This species is closely allied to *H. longipes* but has larger and thicker leaves more densely strigose beneath. It ranges from the Himalaya to western China, whence Wilson sent seeds during his expedition for the Arnold Arboretum. Whether the species is still in cultivation is not known. Plants seen under the synonymous name *H. rosthornii* are a fine form of *H. aspera* (*villosa*); a hydrangea distributed under the name *H. robusta* has proved to belong to *H. heteromalla*; and the garden plant figured in *Bot. Mag.*, t. 5038, which has been confused with *H. robusta*, is *H. stylosa*, a species not treated in this work.

H. MACROPHYLLA (Thunb.) Ser.

Viburnum macrophyllum Thunb.; *Hydrangea hortensis* Sm.; *Hortensia opuloides* Lam.; *Hydrangea opuloides* (Lam.) Hort. ex Savi; *Hydrangea hortensia* Sieb.

The mop-headed 'Hortensia' hydrangeas of gardens descend from plants with normal inflorescences that grow wild in a small area on the east coast of Japan. It was a garden plant of the hortensia kind, known as 'Otaksa', from which Thunberg described the species and it is usual to treat the normal wild plants as a variety of this, namely:

var. NORMALIS Wils. *H. macrophylla* f. *normalis* (Wils.) Hara; *H. mariti m* Haworth-Booth—An almost glabrous shrub 3 to 10 ft high in the wild; young growths stout, pale green. Leaves broad-ovate to broad-obovate, 4 to 8 in. long, about two-thirds as wide, abruptly narrowed at the apex to an acute or acuminate apex, coarsely saw-toothed, lustrous above, greasy to the touch and of rather fleshy texture; stalks ¾ to 2 in. long. Inflorescence a broad, flat-topped cymose corymb, much branched, with a few ray-flowers round the outside, its branches covered with loosely appressed hairs. Fertile flowers usually blue or pink. Calyx-tube usually tapered at the base into the pedicel, bearing five short, triangular calyx-lobes. Petals narrow-ovate. Stamens ten. Ovary completely enclosed in the calyx-tube when the flowers first expand but later thickening at the apex and projecting above the rim of the calyx-tube. Styles usually three. Capsules ¼ to $\frac{5}{16}$ in. long, including styles. Ray-flowers pink or bluish, entire or toothed, up to 2 in. or slightly more across.

A native of Japan, found near the coast on the Chiba peninsula south-east of Tokyo and on the islands south of Tokyo as far as Hachijo. The existence of this wild progenitor of the hortensias appears to have been unknown to western botanists until Wilson called attention to it. He introduced it from Oshima (de Vries Island) in 1917, but whether plants raised from these seeds are still in cultivation in this country is not known. A reintroduction by Michael Haworth-Booth has proved tender and has not yet flowered (1971). Of the established garden varieties the nearest to the wild maritime hydrangea is probably 'SEA FOAM', which is a sport from the mop-headed hydrangea 'Sir Joseph Banks' (see below). This is moderately hardy and flowers quite freely against a house-wall provided the terminal buds are not frosted. The ray-flowers are bluish pink, about 2 in. across, the fertile flowers blue except for the pinkish calyx-tube. The handsome, thick, vivid green leaves persist unchanged on the plant until killed by the first hard frost.

As stated above, the type of *H. macrophylla* is not the wild ancestral plant, but a garden variety, known as 'OTAKSA'. Thunberg saw and collected this hydrangea during his stay in Japan on Deshima Island and, mistaking it for a viburnum, described it as *Viburnum macrophyllum* in his *Flora Japonica* (1784). *Hydrangea* 'Otaksa' was later described more fully, and figured, in Siebold and Zuccarini, *Flora Japonica* (1845), p. 105 and t. 52. It had been imported from China, where the Japanese maritime hydrangea had long been cultivated, and was still rare in Japanese gardens when Siebold and Zuccarini published their account. It was introduced to Europe soon after, but has become scarce.

Hydrangea 'Otaksa' was, however, not the first variety of *H. macrophylla* to be introduced to Europe. Around 1788 Sir Joseph Banks procured from China and presented to Kew a mop-headed plant which Sir James Smith identified as a member of the genus *Hydrangea* and described in 1792 under the name *H. hortensis*. By 1800, it had become quite frequent in gardens, and less than forty years later there were huge specimens in the milder parts of the British Isles, one 'as big as a large haycock' (Loudon, *Arb. et Frut. Brit.*, Vol. 2 (1838), p. 997). This hydrangea, recently renamed 'SIR JOSEPH BANKS', is still common in milder maritime localities.

To end this historical account, something must be said about the synonymous name *Hortensia opuloides* Lam. This was given by Lamarck in 1789 to a specimen sent to Paris some years earlier by the French naturalist Commerson, who had gathered it from a plant growing on the island of Mauritius. Here the French naturalist and explorer Pierre Poivre (1719–86) had made a famous garden which contained several Chinese species, including this hydrangea, which he may have acquired during his visit to Canton (Bretschneider, *Botanical Discoveries*, Vol. 1, pp. 117–20). The generic name *Hortensia*, proposed by Commerson, is botanically no more than a synonym of *Hydrangea*, but it persisted among French growers and has now become a horticultural name for the mop-headed derivatives of *H. macrophylla*. It is believed to commemorate some lady with the Christian name Hortense, and her identity has been the subject of much speculation. She was not, as some have said, Commerson's mistress, who accompanied him on Bougainville's expedition round the world, disguised as his manservant. The name of that remarkable woman was Jeanne Baret. Nor, as was pointed out in previous editions, was she Queen Hortense, who was born several years after Commerson's death. Most authorities have followed Duhamel in stating that the name commemorates Mme Lepaute, a brilliant mathematician and wife of a famous maker of clocks and scientific instruments. Unfortunately for that theory, her Christian name was Nicole-Reine, not Hortense. According to Ebel, in *Hydrangea et Hortensia*, the generic name was proposed in honour of the daughter of the Prince of Nassau-Siegen, who (the Prince) took part in Bougainville's expedition and accompanied Commerson on his botanical explorations.

Garden Varieties

H. macrophylla has given rise to many hundreds of garden varieties, most of which are not really suitable for cultivation outdoors. They were bred as pot-plants and, grown in the open, are either sparse-flowering or produce excessively large and heavy heads, or fail to flower if their terminal buds are killed by spring frosts. However, there is now available in commerce a fairly wide choice of free-flowering varieties, mostly of recent origin some of which have the additional merit of producing inflorescences from axillary buds if the terminal buds are killed. There are, too, a number of varieties which have the normal inflorescences of wild plants, with a centre of fertile flowers and comparatively few ray-flowers round the circumference. These varieties, of which 'Blue Wave' is the best known, are useful for natural plantings, where the mop-headed hortensias would be put out of place. To distinguish them from the hortensias, these varieties are now widely known in Britain as lacecaps.

The hortensias and lacecaps (except the white-flowered sorts) have the peculiarity that the colouring of the flowers, especially of the ray-flowers, is governed by the concentration of aluminium ions in the soil-water. This depends in turn on the acidity of the soil, being highest on very acid soils and lowest where the soil is alkaline. The colour range depends on the variety, but the bluest shades are always produced on the most acid soils. For example, 'Vibraye' will be pure blue on a very acid soil, but an indifferent shade of pink or bluish pink on slightly acid or neutral soils. Crimson varieties develop their characteristic colouring where the soil is near to neutral and often become violet-coloured on good 'blueing soils'. Where the soil is neutral or slightly acid it is possible to induce or intensify the blueness of the flowers by top-dressing the plants with alum, or watering them with a solution of that substance, or by using a proprietary hydrangea colourant. For a practical discussion of this matter see M. Haworth-Booth, *The Hydrangeas*, pp. 135–42.

It is very probable that many of the modern hortensias and lacecaps are not unmixed derivatives of *H. macrophylla* but rather hybrids between it and the woodland hydrangea (*H. serrata*). Wilson considered and rejected this possibility, but when he wrote his study of this group (*Journ. Arn. Arb.*, Vol. 4 (1923), pp. 233–46) the varieties that show the influence of the woodland hydrangea most clearly were still very new or had still to be raised. This hypothesis, even if proved, would present no nomenclatural difficulties if modern authorities were followed in placing the woodland hydrangea under *H. macrophylla* as a variety or subspecies, since the hybridity would then be 'within the species'. In practice, however, it is not a matter of much horticultural importance, either way, since it is perfectly legitimate to put the cultivar name directly after the generic name, e.g., *H.* 'Ami Pasquier' or, more formally, to write *H.* (Hortensia) 'Ami Pasquier'.

For the following notes and descriptions we are indebted to Michael Haworth-Booth.

Hortensias

The following, with flower-heads forming a globose corymb, are a selection of the hardier sorts suitable for outdoor growing. With most, the protection afforded by the north or west wall of an occupied house will be found to be necessary for reliable freedom of flower. On the other hand, 'Generale Vicomtesse de Vibraye' (shortened in practice to 'Vibraye') and 'Altona' are usually hardy and are satisfactorily grown in the open in most parts of the British Isles.

'ALTONA'.—Dense, large heads of cherry-pink or mid-blue of very firm texture on strong stems, lasting well and turning green and then red in autumn. The most effective sort for foundation plantings at the foot of north or west house walls. 3 ft. A.M. 1957.

'AMETHYST'.—Double, frilled pale pink or mauve flowers. Perpetual flowering. 2½ ft.

'AMI PASQUIER'.—Crimson or purplish flowers, less vivid than 'Westfalen'. 2 ft. A.M. 1953.

'AYESHA'.—Concave lilac-like mauve flowers, not free-flowering. Branch-sport. 3 ft.

'BOUQUET ROSE'.—Like 'Vibraye' but inferior on all points. Considered hardier than 'Vibraye' in Holland. 5 ft.

'DOMOTOI'.—Double frilled flowers, weak growth. Branch-sport. 2½ ft.

'EUROPA'.—Pink or clear blue, open head. Like a less compact and bluer 'Altona'. 3 ft.

'FISHER'S SILVERBLUE'.—Very free-flowering. Ice-blue or pale pink. Compact grower. 2½ ft.

'FRILLIBET'.—Deckle-edged frilly flowers, pale pink or Cambridge blue. Very pretty and effective. 2½ ft.

'GENERALE VICOMTESSE DE VIBRAYE' ('Vibraye').—Hortensia pink or clear blue flowers; hardier and freer flowering than others but stems rather weak. Fine outdoor bushes are now to be found in every county of Britain. 5 ft. A.M. 2947.

'GENTIAN DOME' ('Enziandom').—Intense vivid deep blue durable flowers. The most colourful deep blue but needs the protection of the wall of an occupied house. 3 ft.

'KLUIS SUPERBA'.—Deep pink or blue. Very sensitive to any trace element deficiency. 3 ft.

'MARECHAL FOCH'.—Early, free-flowering, deep pink or deep blue. Rather delicate. 3 ft. A.M. 1923.

'MME A. RIVERAIN'.—Like 'Vibraye' but less reliable in colour. Distinguishable by the coloured leaf-stalks. 5 ft.

'MME E. MOUILLÈRE'.—The best white, perpetual flowering, needs a north house-wall. The flowers blush-pink in sunlight, though the rare fertile flowers stay blue. 6 ft. A.M. 1910.

'MISS BELGIUM'.—Rosy crimson flowers. 2½ ft.

'NIEDERSACHSEN'.—Late-flowering, pale pink or pale blue. This would be a valuable sort to succeed 'Vibraye' but it is slightly less hardy and needs settled weather for the flowers to last well. 4 ft. A.M. 1968.

'NIGRA' ('Mandshurica').—Remarkable only for its almost black stems.

'OTAKSA'—Important Chinese foundation variety from Japan; deep blue, red leaf-stalks, weak stems, rather tender. This interesting sort is now rare. The flower stalk bends down with the weight of a wet flower-head. 3 ft.

'PARSIFAL'.—Crimson-pink or deep blue, serrated sepals. The flowers show many strange colour mixtures in heterogeneous soil. 3 ft. A.M. 1922.

'PIA'.—A tiny branch-sport, 6 in. high with pink flowers in an irregular small corymb. Requires care.

'PRINCESS BEATRIX'.—Pink flowers seldom blue; very free-flowering. 2½ ft.

'ROSEA'.—Important Japanese foundation cultivar imported by C. Maries, 1880. Similar to 'Vibraye' but weaker in colour and deportment. Still widely grown in Japan. The flower-heads are smaller and tighter than 'Vibraye' and of a less pure blue in a given soil pH. 4 ft.

'VIOLETTA'.—Unusually vivid violet flowers in compact head. 3 ft.

'WESTFALEN'.—The richest colour of all; pure vivid crimson or deep purple-blue. Free and perpetual flowering. 2½ ft.

LACECAPS

As noted above, this group consists of varieties in which the flower-head, instead of being globose and almost wholly composed of sterile flowers, has a form similar to that of the wild prototype. Those described below are the only varieties widely available in commerce at present. See also *H. serrata*.

'BLUE WAVE'.—Ray-flowers with four wavy-edged sepals, rich blue on very acid soils, otherwise pink or lilac. July–August. A vigorous shrub 6 ft high and as much through, with bold foliage, growing best in light shade. It is a seedling of 'Mariesii' raised by Messrs Lemoine and originally distributed by them under the name *H. mariesii perfecta*. A.M. 1956. F.C.C. 1965.

'LANARTH WHITE'.—Ray-flowers pure white, fertile flowers blue or pink. Early July–August. Compact and fairly dwarf (to 3 ft high and wide) if grown in sun, which it tolerates. The present stock comes from Lanarth in Cornwall, but where the variety originated is not known. It may be a sport from 'Thomas Hogg' (a white hortensia introduced from Japan by the American gardener Thomas Hogg in the 1860s).

'LILACINA'.—Ray-flowers with four serrated pink or blue sepals. August–September. A vigorous variety 5 ft high, more in width, raised by Lemoine early this century.

'MARIESII'.—This variety differs from other lacecaps in having a few sterile flowers scattered among the fertile ones but similar in shape to the normal ray-flowers that edge the inflorescence. Sepals of ray-flowers roundish, entire, nearly always pink or mauve-pink (pale blue on very acid soils only). July–August. Leaves rather narrow and evenly tapered. It grows to 4 or 5 ft high. Introduced from Japan by Charles Maries in 1879. Award of Garden Merit 1938.

'QUADRICOLOR'.—Leaves unusually variegated, showing vivid yellow, cream, pale green, and deep green colourings. Flowers pale pink or blue. 4 ft.

'SEA FOAM'. See p. 391.

'VEITCHII'.—Ray-flowers white with three or four large, entire sepals. Fertile flowers blue. July–August. A very beautiful hydrangea of rather lax habit, up to 5 ft high, needing light shade. It was first shown in 1903 by Messrs Robert Veitch of Exeter, who probably imported it from Japan. They described it in their catalogue for 1905 and in 1915 it was mentioned by Rehder in Bailey's *Cyclopaedia* under the name *Hydrangea opuloides veitchii*. Unfortunately, Wilson later published the name *H. macrophylla* f. *veitchii* for the hortensia 'Rosea', thus causing confusion.

'WHITE WAVE'.—Another beautiful white-flowered lacecap, differing from 'Veitchii' in having the sepals of the ray-flowers toothed and always four in number. It is very free-flowering in an open situation. It was raised by Messrs Lemoine from 'Mariesii' and distributed by them under the name *H. mariesii grandiflora*. A.M. 1948.

H. PANICULATA Sieb.

A deciduous shrub, sometimes tree-like, and 12 to 20 ft high; young shoots at first downy, becoming glabrous. Leaves often in threes, oval or ovate, tapered at both ends, or rounded at the base, toothed; 3 to 6 in. long, 1½ to 3 in. wide, with scattered, flat, bristly hairs above, and pale bristles on the veins beneath; stalk ½ to 1 in. long. Panicles pyramidal, varying in size according to the strength of the shoot, usually 6 to 8 in. long, two-thirds as wide at the base. A few of the outermost flowers sterile, ¾ to 1¼ in. wide, white changing to purple-pink; the small fertile flowers yellowish white; flower-stalks downy.

Native of Japan, Sakhalin, and of eastern and southern China. It was introduced in 1861, but the normal wild form, in which the inflorescences are sparsely furnished with ray-flowers, has never been common in cultivation. The flowering branch figured in the *Botanical Magazine* is from a plant growing in Captain Collingwood Ingram's garden at Benenden, Kent, originally collected by him as a seedling on Aso-san, a volcano in Kyushu. This specimen was received at Kew in July and it appears to be in this month and in August that it normally flowers in cultivation. The species appears to be variable in habit in the wild. Sargent saw it as a tree 25 to 30 ft high in central Hokkaido, but Siebold described it as a lax shrub up to 6 ft high. It is also variable in foliage; the leaves on the Benenden plant are glabrous and glossy above and long-acuminate at the apex—hence very different in appearance from those of the cultivars.

cv. 'FLORIBUNDA'.—Ray-flowers more numerous than in the normal form, but not so numerous as to conceal the fertile flowers. Sepals of ray-flowers ⅜ to ¾ in. long, mostly broad-elliptic to rounded, four or five in number, overlapping. A beautiful hydrangea, flowering end July into September. Award of Merit 1953. It agrees well with the plant described by Regel under the name *H. p.* var. *floribunda* and figured in *Gartenflora*, Vol. 16 (1867), t. 530. The hydrangea figured in *Gardeners' Chronicle*, Dec. 5, 1925, facing page 448, as *H. paniculata* simply, appears to be 'Floribunda'. [PLATE 54

cv. 'GRANDIFLORA'.—A form introduced from Japan about 1870, in which all, or nearly all, the flowers are sterile and large, forming a closely packed pyramid of blossom at first white then purplish pink, finally brown

This variety is undoubtedly the most showy of hydrangeas in localities where the hortensias cannot be grown. To obtain it at its best, it should be planted in good loamy soil, rich, but not too stiff. The shoots should be pruned back in spring before growth recommences, and after the young shoots are a few inches long the weakest should be removed. If very large panicles are desired the shoots may be reduced to six or ten on plants 1 to 2 ft high—more for larger plants. A mulching of rotted manure should be given when growth is well started. Such treatment will produce panicles 18 in. high, and 12 in. through at the base. The typical form may be treated in the same way. To many people's taste these monstrous panicles may be objectionable, and to my mind a bush moderately thinned, or not at all, is more elegant and pleasing. Hard pruning and thinning tends to shorten the life of these plants.

cv. 'PRAECOX'.—A vigorous erect shrub growing quickly to about 8 ft or more in height. Inflorescences with a few ray-flowers at the base, the upper part much congested and bearing only fertile flowers; they also tend to be asymmetrically flattened. Sepals of ray-flowers four, about 1 in. long, elliptic to ovate, subacute, scarcely overlapping. This cultivar starts to flower about mid-July or even slightly earlier, i.e., about six weeks before 'Grandiflora'. Award of Merit July 17, 1956. It was raised at the Arnold Arboretum from seeds collected by Prof. Sargent in the northern island of Japan (Hokkaido) in 1893.

cv. 'TARDIVA'.—The plant received by M. Haworth-Booth from Chenault's nurseries under the name *H. p. tardiva* is distinguished by its very late flowering (September or even early October). It bears some resemblance to 'Floribunda' but the ray-flowers are less numerous and smaller, the sepals being ½ to ¾ in. long and mostly four in number (commonly five in 'Floribunda').

H. PETIOLARIS Sieb. & Zucc.   [PLATE 53

H. anomala subsp. *petiolaris* (Sieb. & Zucc.) McClintock; *H. scandens* Maxim.

A deciduous climber, reaching in Japan to the tops of trees 60 to 80 ft high, and attaching itself closely to the trunks and limbs by means of aerial roots; young stems glabrous or hairy, older ones with peeling brown bark. Leaves roundish ovate, straight or heart-shaped at the base, and with short, tapered points; regularly, sharply, and finely toothed, 1½ to 4½ in. long, two-thirds to nearly as wide, dark vivid green and glabrous above, paler and often with tufts of down in the vein-axils beneath; stalk varying in length from ¼ to 4 in. Corymbs expanding in June, flat, from 6 to 10 in. across, with large white sterile flowers on the margins, 1 to 1¾ in. across, and on stalks 1 to 1½ in. long; the small fertile ones with which the centre is filled being a duller white; stamens fifteen to twenty-two; flower-stalks downy. *Bot. Mag.*, t. 6788.

Native of Japan, Sakhalin, Quelpaert Island (Korea), and Formosa; introduced in 1878. This climber ascends trees, walls, or whatever support it has, in much the same way as ivy does. It grows vigorously, and flowers well on a wall, but a more effective way of growing it is as a bush in the open, for it is very hardy. A few plants may be put round the base of an upturned tree-stump, boulder, or even a mound, which they will soon climb over and cover. After that, the mass assumes a low, spreading, bushlike form, light and elegant in appearance, and very striking when in flower. This hydrangea is in gardens often called "*Schizophragma hydrangeoides*", a name that belongs to an allied but quite distinct climber. In place of the three- to six-parted sterile blossom of the present species, the sterile flower of *Schizophragma* consists of a single ovate sepal, 1 to 1½ in. long.

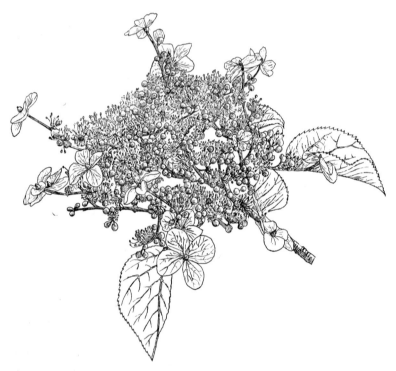

HYDRANGEA PETIOLARIS

H. QUERCIFOLIA Bartr.   OAK-LEAVED HYDRANGEA
H. platanifolia Hort.

A deciduous shrub up to 6 ft or more high in the wild, rarely seen more than half as high in this country; young shoots thick and stout, woolly. Leaves broadly oval or broadly ovate, sometimes roundish in general outline, but five- or seven-lobed, after the fashion of the large-leaved American red oaks like *Quercus rubra*; minutely toothed, 3 to 8 in. long, two-thirds to fully as wide, dark dull green and glabrous above, downy beneath; stalk 1 to 2½ in. long. Panicle erect, 4 to 10 in. high, round-topped, pyramidal. Outer flowers sterile, 1 to 1½ in. diameter, white, changing with age to a purplish shade. Fertile flowers very numerous, crowded, ⅛ in. diameter; petals five, oblong. Flower-stalks furnished with loose hairs. Blossoms from June to September. *Bot. Mag.*, t. 975.

Native of the south-eastern United States; introduced in 1803. From all the cultivated hydrangeas this is readily distinguished by its large scalloped leaves. It is very handsome both in foliage and flower, but has the reputation of being slightly tender. Young plants may be so, but become hardy once a woody framework has been built up. This hydrangea needs a moist, fairly rich soil and should be given a sheltered and not too shaded position. Indeed, provided it is kept well mulched with leaf-mould it might thrive best in full sun; unless the wood is well ripened, the terminal buds may be lost during the winter, and no flower will then be produced. In favourable seasons the leaves turn crimson, orange, or purple in the autumn. Propagation is by layers, suckers, or cuttings taken soon after midsummer and rooted in bottom-heat.

In previous editions it was stated that a broader-leaved and superior form was sometimes distinguished as "*H. platanifolia*". Such plants are not now in commerce in Britain, so far as is known—at least not under that name, the origin of which cannot be traced. It is interesting, however, to note that a plant in the Berlin Botanic Garden, figured in Krussmann's *Handbuch der Laubgeholze* (Vol. 2, pl. 3), bears some leaves that are distinctly plane-like.

H. SARGENTIANA Rehd.
H. aspera subsp. *sargentiana* (Rehd.) McClintock

A shrub up to 10 ft high; young shoots very stout, ribbed, and thickly clothed with stiff transparent bristles and small erect hairs, giving the shoot a remarkable, somewhat mossy aspect. Leaves ovate, with a rounded base, 4 to 5 in. long, 2 to 3 in. wide on the flowering shoots; but broadly ovate, with a heart-shaped base, 6 to 10 in. long by 4 to 7 in. wide on the sterile shoots, deep dull green, and covered with minute hairs above; pale, bristly, and prominently net-veined beneath; stalk 1 to 4½ in. long, bristly and downy. Flowers produced in July and August in a flattish corymb 6 to 9 in. across, with sterile flowers, 1¼ in. across, pinkish white, confined to the outside; fertile flowers deep rosy-lilac; flower-stalks downy, the main ones bristly also. *Bot. Mag.*, t. 8447.

A native of W. Hupeh, China; introduced by Wilson in 1908, while collecting for the Arnold Aboretum. Well grown, this is a magnificent shrub, but it is not often seen in good condition. It is too frequently given a position in shady woodland where it suffers from the competition of tree-roots and becomes an ugly gaunt single-stemmed plant, deserving the condemnation or qualified praise that is often accorded it. The ideal conditions for this species are a rich soil and a position where it has abundant light but some protection from the midday sun. Grown thus, it will become as noble in habit as it is in leaf, clothed to the ground with foliage and becoming ever wider thanks to the abundantly produced suckers. It is perfectly hardy in its wood and recovers remarkably quickly from damage suffered by spring frosts. Mid-May frosts may kill every leaf but the damage simply stimulates the young shoots (which are more resistant) to produce a second flush of growth and within a space of less than a month the whole plant is again furnished with leaves. Earlier frosts may be more damaging, but even from these it quickly recovers. But like so many other hydrangeas, it is vulnerable when very young and still semi-herbaceous.

H. SCANDENS (L. f.) Ser.

Viburnum scandens L. f.; *H. virens* (Thunb.) Sieb.; *Viburnum virens* Thunb.

A small shrub with slender pendulous or prostrate branches; stems glabrous or downy. Leaves oblong-ovate or lanceolate, mostly 2 to 3½ in. long, shortly toothed, bright green above, paler and usually slightly downy on the veins beneath; leaf-stalks less than ½ in. long. Corymbs up to 3 in. across, borne terminally on short, leafy axillary shoots. Ray-flowers few, ¾ to 1½ in. wide, with white or blue saw-toothed sepals; fertile flowers with obovate clawed petals. Capsules half-enclosed in the calyx-tube. Seeds not tailed.

Native of southern Japan. This species is scarcely known in this country and nothing can be said about its garden value, though it would seem to be worthy of introduction. According to previous editions of this work it was cultivated at Rostrevor in Co. Down by Sir John Ross of Bladensburg.

A curious form of *H. scandens* has been described by the Japanese botanist Koidzumi under the name H. LUTEOVENOSA. It is distinguished by its very small leaves (mostly 1 to 1⅜ in. long, ⅜ to ¾ in. wide), which are blotched or veined with yellow. It apparently occurs wild in Japan and is not a cultivar. It has been identified by Miss McClintock with *H. liukiuensis* Nakai from the Ryukyu Islands, described earlier and treated by her as a subspecies of *H. scandens*.

subsp. CHINENSIS (Maxim.) McClintock *H. chinensis* Maxim.; *H. davidii* Franch.; *H. umbellata* Rehd.—This subspecies has a wide range in E. Asia outside Japan. It differs from the typical subspecies described above in its taller growth, its larger and more leathery leaves 2 to 6 in. long, ½ to 2¼ in. wide (against 1⅜ to 3 in. by ⅝ to 1¼ in. in typical *H. scandens*) and its larger inflorescences, which are 3 to (mostly) 4 to 6 in. wide (against 1¾ to 3 in.). The leaves may be downy on the veins beneath or almost glabrous. This hydrangea was at one time in cultivation from seeds sent by Wilson from W. China in 1908 and grown under the name *H. davidii*. This introduction flowered in June and July and had the fertile flowers blue and the sterile ones white.

H. SERRATA (Thunb.) Ser.

Viburnum serratum Thunb.; *H. macrophylla* subsp. *serrata* (Thunb.) Mak. in part; *H. macrophylla* var. *acuminata* (Sieb. & Zucc.) Mak.; *H. serrata* f. *acuminata* (Sieb. & Zucc.) Wils.; *H. acuminata* Sieb. & Zucc.; *H. japonica* Sieb., at least in part

A small deciduous shrub with slender branches; young stems glabrous or appressed-downy. Leaves rather thin, lanceolate, ovate elliptic, acute, acuminate or caudate at the apex, 2 to 6 in. long, 1 to 2½ in. wide, finely to coarsely serrate, usually glabrous above, veins beneath often covered with short appressed or curled hairs. Flowers in flat-topped corymbs; ray-flowers present, with variously shaped pink or bluish toothed or entire sepals. Capsules as in *H. macrophylla* but smaller, *c.* ⅛ in. long (including styles).

Native of the mountains of Japan and of S. Korea (Quelpaert Island); introduced in 1843. It is allied to *H. macrophylla*, in which it is included as a subspecies or variety by some botanists. It is a less robust shrub, with more slender stems, thinner, relatively narrower leaves and smaller flowers and seed-capsules. It is also mainly a plant of montane woodlands, whereas *H. macrophylla* occurs at low altitudes and never far from the coast. This no doubt serves to explain its greater hardiness (see further below).

H. serrata is represented in cultivation mainly by cultivars, discussed below. First the following variety must be described:

var. THUNBERGII (Sieb.) *H. macrophylla* var. *thunbergii* (Sieb.) Mak.—As represented in gardens it is a small, neat, deciduous shrub, usually 2 to 3 ft in height, the young stems smooth and very dark, ultimately almost black. Leaves oval or ovate-oblong, tapered about equally towards both ends, toothed at the terminal part only, 1½ to 3½ in. long, ⅝ to 1½ in. wide, dull green and with appressed hairs above, paler and glabrous beneath except for occasional tufts of down in the vein-axils. Corymbs 2 to 4 in. across, the sterile flowers ½ to ¾ in. across, the sepals overlapping, broader than long, blue or pink, often with a shallow notch at the apex; flower-stalks downy. Hardier than the hortensias, but liable to be injured in hard winters. A dainty shrub, flowering in July and August. Similar plants occur wild in S. Japan. A tea is made from the dried leaves of this variety.

The following cultivars are usually placed under *H. serrata* and appear to belong to it:

'BLUEBIRD'.—Ray-flowers pale pink or pale blue, entire. Early flowering. A vigorous and hardy variety unusually resistant to drought. 5 ft. A.M. 1960. *Journ. R.H.S.*, Vol. 74 (1949), fig. 191; *The Hydrangeas*, plate V.

'DIADEM'.—Ray-flowers serrated, clear blue or pink; inflorescences on side-shoots all the way up the stems, opening in June. The foliage is purple in an open position. Compact habit. 2½ ft. A.M. 1963.

'GRAYSWOOD'.—Ray-flowers about nine in each corymb, white at first, ageing to pink and eventually, in sun, to bright red; sepals coarsely toothed towards the apex, the outermost longer than the other three. 5 ft. A.M. 1948. *Journ. R.H.S.*, Vol. 65 (1940), fig. 105; *The Hydrangeas*, plate XIX.

'PREZIOSA'.—This variety is unusual in having an inflorescence of the hortensia type, though smaller. Ray-flowers at first pink, shaded deeper at the edge, later clear crimson, blotched with deeper shades of the same colour. Young stems reddish brown. Very hardy and flowering well in sun or half-shade. About 4 ft. F.C.C. 1964.

'ROSALBA'.—Leaves yellowish dull green. Ray-flowers six or seven in each corymb, white at first, becoming heavily blotched with pure crimson; sepals serrated. Of upright habit, to about 4 ft, usually somewhat less. This variety has long been grown in British gardens, indeed the first introduction of *H. serrata*, figured in *Bot. Reg.* (1844), t. 61, as *H. japonica* Sieb., closely resembles the present-day clone. A very similar plant is grown in Japanese gardens under

T S—O

the name Benikaku and is figured in Siebold and Zuccarini, *Fl. Japonica* (1840), t. 53 (as *H. japonica*). 'Rosalba' is the 'type' of a group of garden varieties of *H. serrata* with ray-flowers that never 'blue' even in acid soils. Here belong 'Grayswood' and 'Preziosa', described above, and also the hydrangeas known as 'Intermedia' and 'Macrosepala' (not described here).

A number of Japanese garden forms of *H. serrata* with multisepalous ray-flowers and often with double or proliferous fertile flowers have been grouped under the name *H. serrata* f. PROLIFERA (Reg.) Wils. Such plants have been introduced to this country but none has been traced by Mr Haworth-Booth. The plant figured in *Fl. Japonica*, t. 59 (I), as *H. stellata*, belongs here.

H. SERRATIFOLIA (Hook. & Arn.) Phil. f.

Cornidia serratifolia Hook. & Arn.; *H. integerrima* (Hook. & Arn.) Engler; *Cornidia integerrima* Hook. & Arn.; *H. scandens* Poepp., not Ser., nor Maxim.

An evergreen climbing shrub growing wild on tall trees and on rocks; young shoots clad with starry down and in the climbing state adhering by aerial roots. Leaves entire, stout and leathery, elliptic or slightly obovate in the adult state, pointed, tapered to cordate at the base, 2 to 6 in. long and 1 to 3 in. wide, distinctly net-veined, dark green and glabrous; stalk from ¼ to 1¾ in. long. Curious small pits often occur in the vein-axils beneath. In the juvenile plants in cultivation the leaves are less than 2 in. long, heart-shaped at the base, and with stalks ¼ in. or less long. Inflorescence terminal and axillary, sometimes a columnar panicle as much as 6 in. long and 3½ in. wide, sometimes smaller and more rounded, but always made up of numerous small corymbs, each of which is enclosed during the bud-stage in four papery bracts, and in that state are globose and ½ in. or more wide. Normally all the flowers are of the small, fertile type, their most conspicuous feature being the stamens, which are up to ¼ in. long; only very rarely are sterile ray-flowers produced. Seed-capsules vase-shaped, ⅛ in. wide, with the styles persisting at the hollowed apex. *Bot. Mag.*, n.s., t. 153.

Native of Chile from Aconcagua to Aysen provinces, and of bordering parts of Argentina, from sea-level to about 5,000 ft. It was first described in 1830 under the invalid name *H. scandens*, but was probably not cultivated in Britain until H. F. Comber sent home seeds from Chile during his journey in that country and Argentina in 1925–7. It has proved quite hardy on walls sheltered from cold, drying winds. Captain Collingwood Ingram has a plant on the stables cottage at Benenden Grange, Kent, which has reached the top of the chimney and flowers freely. Exhibited by him, the species received an Award of Merit in 1952. It is also hardy at Nymans in Sussex. The flowering shoot figured in the *Botanical Magazine* was from a plant cultivated at Crarae, Argyll.

As in *H. petiolaris* the climbing shoots with aerial roots are sterile, flowers being produced only on growths of a bushy nature. In the wild it climbs to a great height; the late Clarence Elliott saw it 50 ft high, and in the southern part of its range in Chile, where the climate is very humid, it is said to attain 100 ft.

Although inferior to *H. petiolaris* as an ornamental, *H. serratifolia* is of interest as the only member of the section *Cornidia* that is hardy in the British climate.

Note: The leaves in this species are normally entire or very slightly denticulate—a character expressed in the name *H. integerrima*, by which the species has been generally known. In the type of *H. serratifolia* (Cuming 34 from Chiloe) the leaves are serrate towards the apex, but there seems to be no doubt that only one species is involved. The two species were published (in the genus *Cornidia*) in the same work and on the same page, but unfortunately, in *Hydrangea*, the combination *H. serratifolia* (Hook. & Arn.) Phil. has ten years' priority over *H. integerrima* (Hook. & Arn.) Engler, and must be accepted as the correct name of the species, inappropriate though it is.

HYMENANTHERA   VIOLACEAE

A genus of some four or five species of shrubs or small trees, evergreen or nearly so. Leaves alternate, small; flowers also small, with the sepals and petals in fives; stamens also five, cohering to form a tube; fruit a berry.

H. ANGUSTIFOLIA DC.

An evergreen (or, at Kew, partly deciduous) shrub of erect, slender shape; young shoots finely downy, afterwards warted. Leaves quite glabrous, linearoblanceolate, $\frac{1}{12}$ to $\frac{1}{6}$ in. wide, $\frac{1}{2}$ to $1\frac{1}{4}$ in. long; usually quite toothless, dark green, turning purplish in winter. Flowers yellowish, $\frac{1}{4}$ in. wide, the five petals recurved, solitary or in pairs, produced from the leaf-axils. Anthers five, almost stalkless, arranged on the inner wall of a staminal tube, which narrows towards, and is fringed at, the top. Calyx $\frac{1}{12}$ in. long, with five ovate lobes, green. Fruit a fleshy berry, globose, $\frac{1}{8}$ in. long, white with purple markings.

Native of Tasmania, South Australia, Victoria, New South Wales, and of New Zealand. In Tasmania it grows on the summits of the Western Mountains at 3,000 to 4,000 ft altitude. In New Zealand it occurs in both islands at comparatively low elevations in river beds and along forest margins, its place being taken at high altitudes by *H. alpina*. The flowers in New Zealand plants are said to be unisexual, though male and female may occur on the same plant; in Tasmania they are more commonly hermaphrodite (Allan, *Fl. N.Z.*, p. 196, and Curtis, *St. Fl. Tasm.*, part 1, p. 53). It is quite hardy at Kew, where there are two plants in the Berberis Dell.

H. DENTATA DC.—This species, of which *H. angustifolia* has been considered a variety, differs in its much larger conspicuously toothed leaves. Native of Victoria and New South Wales.

H. ALPINA (Kirk) W. R. B. Oliver *H. dentata* var. *alpina* Kirk—In its typical state this species differs markedly from *H. angustifolia* by its dwarf habit and thick, rigid branchlets, which are often spine-tipped, but intermediates between it and *H. angustifolia* are said to occur. It is found in open rocky places in the mountains.

H. CRASSIFOLIA Hook. f.

A low, semi-evergreen shrub of dense, rounded habit, 3 to 6 ft high, twice as much in diameter in this country, with stiff, flat-growing branches, covered when young with a short pubescence. Leaves obovate, entire, rounded or slightly notched at the apex, ½ to 1 in. long, glabrous, firm, and thick in texture

HYMENANTHERA CRASSIFOLIA

densely crowded and alternate on the branches. Flowers almost stalkless, very small (⅛ in. wide), borne in leaf-axils, with five brownish, reflexed petals of no beauty, and five stamens. Berry almost globular, about ¼ in. diameter, white often stained with purple. *Bot. Mag.*, t. 9426.

Native of New Zealand; first seen in this country about 1875. It is a shrub of great botanical interest in being related to the violet and pansy, and although with not the least beauty of flower, is very attractive in autumn when laden with its abundant pure white berries. It is quite hardy at Kew. One of the finest specimens in the British Isles is in the Glasnevin Botanic Garden, 6 ft high and 12 to 15 ft diameter. It retains some of its leaves through the winter, but can scarcely be called evergreen. Propagated by cuttings or by seeds.

H. OBOVATA Kirk—A close ally of the preceding and not very clearly demarcated from it. The leaves are usually more than 1 in. long and the habit commonly more erect. It is found in both islands of New Zealand. A plant considered to belong to this species was 6 ft high at Wakehurst Place, Sussex, in 1933.

HYPERICUM   HYPERICACEAE

A large and well-marked genus, composed mainly of herbaceous plants, but comprising also a good number of shrubby and sub-shrubby species, hardy in this country and of considerable beauty. The leading characters of these species are invariably opposite or whorled leaves, often dotted with pellucid glands; the five, rarely four, sepals and petals; the numerous stamens, often grouped into three or five bundles; the three or five, rarely two or four, styles; the capsular, usually more or less cone-shaped, fruits (which are, however, fleshy in *H. androsaemum* and in some species not in cultivation, and somewhat fleshy at first in *H.* × *inodorum*); and the cylindrical seeds. *Hypericum* is the largest genus in the small family Hypericaceae, which is by some botanists included in the Garcinia family (Guttiferae).

The hypericums rarely grow more than 4 or 5 ft high in this country, and most of them retain more or less foliage in mild winters; in severe ones they are deciduous. The stems of some of the species here described are only half woody, and naturally die back some distance every winter. Although the flowers are always yellow in these shrubby species, there is considerable variety among them either in size or depth of shade. The plants themselves vary much in foliage and general aspect.

In gardens, perhaps the chief value of the hypericums is in their habit of flowering during late summer and autumn, when comparatively few shrubs remain in bloom. Planted in groups, as the hardier species should always be, they also give during a large part of the year healthy masses of deep green or blue-green foliage. They are of the simplest culture, and all of them like a well-drained loamy soil and abundant moisture. All, except perhaps the American species, will grow on chalky soils. Many of them produce seeds, and none, so far as I am aware, will not increase easily by cuttings. These should be taken off in August, dibbled in pots of sandy soil, and placed in gentle heat. Species like *H. calycinum* and *xylosteifolium*, that produce creeping root-stocks, are very easily increased by division.

The revised treatment of *Hypericum* that follows owes much to the work of Dr N. K. B. Robson of the British Museum (Natural History), and we are further indebted to him for reading and commenting on the manuscript. The treatment of the species of the section *Ascyreia* is based on his notes published in *Journ. R.H.S.*, Vol. 95 (1970), pp. 482–97. The nomenclature of the European and Anatolian species follows that adopted by the same author in *Flora Europaea*, Vol. 2 (1968), and *Flora of Turkey*, Vol. 2 (1967).

H. ACMOSEPALUM N. Robson

H. patulum var. *henryi* Hort., in part, not Bean; *H. kouytchense* Hort., in part, not Lévl.; *H. oblongifolium* Hort., in part

A semi-evergreen shrub 4 or 5 ft high, with arching branches; young stems reddish, flattened and four-angled beneath the flower clusters. Leaves very short-stalked, $\frac{3}{4}$ to $2\frac{1}{4}$ in. long, $\frac{1}{4}$ to $\frac{3}{4}$ in. wide, elliptic, oblong-elliptic, or oblanceolate, blunt or rounded at the apex, sometimes shortly apiculate, wedge-shaped at the base, dark green above, pale and slightly glaucous beneath, with the veins, except the marginal loops, scarcely visible. Flowers $1\frac{1}{2}$ to $1\frac{7}{8}$ in. across, borne singly or in cymose clusters of two or three (occasionally up to six); buds ovoid, pointed at the apex. Sepals triangular-ovate to lanceolate or linear-lanceolate, tapered at the apex to a slender point, spreading in the bud-stage and after flowering. Petals golden yellow, spreading. Stamens about three-quarters as long as the petals, in five bundles. Styles free to the base, slightly shorter than the ovary.

Native of Yunnan, China; introduced by George Forrest, who also collected the type material under his number F.19448. This specimen was originally referred to H. patulum var. henryi and the cultivated plants have been grown under this name or as H. kouytchense or H. oblongifolium. The late Dr Stapf recognised that it was a distinct species but it was first described as such by Dr N. K. B. Robson in 1970 (Journ. R.H.S., Vol. 95, p. 494).

This is a very distinct and pretty hypericum, with unusually narrow leaves that colour red in the autumn. As will be seen from the coloured plates accompanying Dr Robson's article (op. cit., fig. 238 and 240) the flowers resemble those of H. kouytchense in their shape and long stamens, but they are of a deeper yellow and the petal apiculus is not so sharp as in H. kouytchense and its immediate allies. It also grows taller than that species.

The following two species, both at present uncommon in gardens, are placed by Dr Robson in the same group as H. acmosepalum:

H. BEANII N. Robson H. patulum var. henryi Bean—This species was described in 1905 (as H. patulum var. henryi) from a plant growing at Kew, raised from seeds sent from southern Yunnan, China, by Augustine Henry seven years earlier. It was distributed by Messrs R. Veitch of Exeter and no doubt by other nurserymen, but was soon superseded by other species that have wrongly been called H. patulum var. henryi in gardens (see H. pseudohenryi below, and H. forrestii). The characters that, in combination, serve to distinguish it from its allies (and from other species with which it might be confused) are: stems slightly flattened and four-lined near the ends and under the flowers; leaves obtuse at the apex, not mucronate; sepals ovate or narrowly so, acute or acuminate at the apex; stamens from one half to almost three-quarters as long as the petals; styles about two-thirds as long as the ovary.

The cultivar 'GOLD CUP' is near to H. beanii but its leaves are lanceolate, the flower-buds are almost twice as long as wide (not barely longer than wide as in H. beanii and its allies) and the stamens and styles are rather shorter than is usually the case in H. beanii. It is a beautiful variety growing 3 to 5 ft high, with bright yellow cup-shaped flowers shading to paler yellow at the edges of the petals. The leaves turn pale red in the autumn.

H. PSEUDOHENRYI N. Robson H. patulum var. henryi sensu Rehd., in part, not Bean—This species, a native of W. China, was introduced by Wilson from the neighbourhood of Tatsien-lu (Kangting) in 1908 (W.1355). It was identified by Rehder as H. patulum var. henryi and at one time was common in gardens under that name but seems to have become rather rare (most of the plants grown under that name are *H. forrestii*, q.v.). Its distinguishing characters, in combination, are: branchlets much flattened and four-lined at first, then two-lined, finally terete; sepals ovate or oblong, appressed to the buds and fruits; stamens about three-quarters as long as the petals or slightly longer; styles slightly longer than the ovary. In its long stamens it recalls *H. kouytchense*, but the petal apiculus is not hooked as in that species (q.v.).

H. AEGYPTICUM L.

A dwarf, evergreen shrub 1 ft or more high, with round stems. Leaves crowded, ovate or obovate, pointed, ⅛ to ⅓ in. long, greyish green. Flowers solitary at the end of short twigs, pale golden yellow; petals erect rather than spreading, ¼ in. long; sepals oblong, erect, half as long as the petals. Stamens in three bundles, united for about half their length, alternating with three fleshy staminodes. *Bot. Mag.*, t. 6481.

Native of the Mediterranean coasts and islands, but not of Egypt; said to have been introduced in 1787, but now rarely seen. The reason of this, no doubt, is its tenderness; it can only be grown permanently either in our mildest districts or with winter protection. This is unfortunate, for it is one of the daintiest and prettiest of its genus. It flowers in August.

H. ANDROSAEMUM L.   TUTSAN
Androsaemum officinale All.

A half-woody shrub of vigorous bushy habit 2 to 3 ft high, with angled or slightly winged stems branching towards the top, and bearing flowers on each branchlet. Leaves slightly aromatic, the largest among hardy hypericums, and sometimes 3½ to 4 in. long, 2 to 2¼ in. wide ovate, blunt at the apex, cordate at the base, and stalkless. Flowers three to nine together in cymose clusters at the end of the main-stalk and lateral branches; each flower about ¾ in. across, light yellow; stamens in five bundles, united only at the base; styles three; sepals nearly as long as the petals. Fruit a three-celled, berry-like capsule, nearly globose, and about the size of a pea, turning first purple, finally almost black, filled when ripe with a wine-coloured juice.

Native of W. Europe, N. Africa, N.W. Yugoslavia, and of the forest region south and east of the Black Sea and south of the Caspian. It is widely distributed but local in Britain in the wild, but naturalised in many gardens in shrub borders, shady dry-walls, etc. Although of no great beauty in regard to flower, this species is handsome in its healthy, robust appearance, fine big leaves, and dark fruits. The name 'Tutsan' is a corruption of *toute-saine* (heal-all), and refers to the many curative properties the plant was once supposed to possess. It is one of the best things for furnishing rather shaded places, and flowers from June until September.

H. AUGUSTINII N. Robson

H. leschenaultii Hort., in part, not Choisy

A shrub to about 3 ft high with arching branches; upper internodes of stems distinctly four-lined to slightly four-angled. Leaves sessile, ovate to broad-ovate, mostly 1½ to 2⅝ in. long, 1 to 1⅞ in. wide, obtuse to subacute and sometimes apiculate at the apex, broad-cuneate to rounded at the base, the leaves immediately below the inflorescence stem-clasping and slightly cordate at the base. Inflorescence much branched and corymb-like, with up to nineteen flowers. Buds ovoid, obtuse, ¾ to ⅞ in. long. Flowers clear yellow, about 2¼ in. across. Sepals erect or slightly spreading, rather unequal in length and width, oblong or elliptic. Stamens in five bundles, about as long as the petals to almost three-quarters as long. Styles about as long as the ovary or slightly longer.

This striking hypericum, described by Dr Robson in 1970 (*Journ. R.H.S.*, Vol. 95 (1970), p. 495), was found by Augustine Henry in S. Yunnan, China, in 1898, but when or how it reached cultivation is not known. It has already turned up in a number of gardens, usually grown under the erroneous name "*H. leschenaultii*", but it is not yet possible to assess its hardiness. From all other cultivated species it is distinguished by the large, stem-clasping leaves of the upper part of the stem.

H. BALEARICUM L.

A remarkably distinct species of close, shrubby habit and about 2 ft high, the stems winged and more or less warted. Leaves ¼ to ½ in. long, ovate or oblong, rounded at the tip, the lower side covered with curious wart-like lumps with a corresponding depression on the upper side; the margin entire, but very wavy or wrinkled. Flowers yellow, terminal and solitary, 1½ in. wide, fragrant; petals narrow and fragile; stamens ½ in. long. *Bot. Mag.*, t. 137.

Native of the Balearic Isles; introduced to Britain from Majorca in 1714. This curious plant, quite different in its warted leaves from all other cultivated hypericums, is, unfortunately, not hardy except in the warmer parts of the country. It flowers from June to September.

H. BELLUM Li

A semi-evergreen densely branched dwarf shrub, about 2 ft high in the R.H.S. Garden at Wisley; branchlets reddish, slightly flattened below the flowers but not lined. Leaves short-stalked, broadly ovate to almost orbicular, ½ to 1⅜ in. long, ¾ to 1⅛ in. wide, obtuse at the apex, rounded to slightly cordate at the base, medium green above, paler beneath. Flowers golden yellow, cup-shaped, about 1½ in. wide, borne singly or in two- or three-flowered cymes. Sepals ovate or elliptic, obtuse and sometimes apiculate at the apex. Stamens about one-third as long as the petals, in five bundles; styles free, slightly shorter than the ovary.

A native of the Assam Himalaya, S.E. Tibet, N. Upper Burma, and bordering parts of S.W. China. It was introduced early this century by Père Monbeig, who sent seeds to M. Vilmorin's collection at Les Barres. Kew received plants from there in 1911 and 1914, but those now cultivated in British gardens were probably all raised from seeds sent by Ludlow, Sherriff and Elliot (LSE 13235

HYPERICUM BELLUM

and 15737), collected in S.E. Tibet in 1946–7. The species was first described in 1944 but Dr Stapf of Kew had recognised its distinctness earlier and had proposed for it the unpublished name *H. monbeigii*.

H. bellum is a charming species, allied to *H. forrestii* but well distinguished by its dwarfer habit, rounded leaves, and smaller flowers. As in that species, the older leaves turn colour in later summer and the ripening capsules are bronzy red. It would make a pretty ground-cover, but being in nature an inhabitant of open scrub it would probably need a fairly sunny position. It is as yet scarcely available in commerce.

H. BUCKLEYI M. A. Curtis

A dwarf, deciduous, semi-woody plant forming a dense rounded tuft of slender, angled stems, 6 to 12 in. high. Leaves ¼ to 1 in. long, oblong or obovate, rounded at the apex, tapered at the base. Flowers one or three at the end of the shoot, bright yellow, ½ to 1 in. diameter. Petals narrowly obovate. Sepals about half as long as the petals, spreading in the fruiting stage. Styles three, united.

This charming little shrub is one of the rarest of N. American plants, being confined in the wild to a few mountain tops in N. Carolina and Georgia. It was introduced to Kew in 1893, but had been discovered fifty years before. Of too fragile and delicate a nature to hold its own in an ordinary shrubbery, it is on the other hand admirably adapted for some nook of the rock garden, where it makes gay patches in July. It produces abundant seed. Under cultivation its leaves and flowers are considerably larger than in wild examples, and its dainty character is apt to be spoilt by too rich a soil.

H. CALYCINUM L.   ROSE OF SHARON, AARON'S BEARD

A low, nearly evergreen shrub, with a creeping root-stalk and erect, obscurely angled, unbranched stems, 12 to 18 in. high. Leaves rich bright green, ovate oblong, 2 to 3 in. long, slightly odorous, with little or no stalk. Flowers solitary, rarely in pairs, at the top of the stem, 3 to 4 in. across, bright yellow; petals obovate; sepals green, roundish, ¾ in. long; stamens in five bundles, yellow, ¾ to 1 in. long, very numerous; styles five. *Bot. Mag.*, t. 146.

Native of S.E. Bulgaria, European Turkey, and N. Anatolia. Introduced by Sir George Wheeler in 1676, this has proved so well adapted to our climate as to have become naturalised in some parts of the country. On the whole, it is the most useful and not far from the most beautiful of hypericums, admirable for making a dense carpet on the ground in half-shaded places beneath trees, etc., where most shrubs would not thrive, flowering from the end of June to September. In hard winters it loses much of its foliage, and in any case, if a clean level growth is desired, it is best to cut the old stems down to the ground just as the new growths are pushing from the base in spring. Propagated with the greatest ease by dividing up the plants.

H. OBLONGIFOLIUM Choisy   *H. cernuum* D. Don—This species, a native of the Himalaya from W. Pakistan to Nepal, is perhaps not in cultivation at the present time. It is placed by Dr Robson in the same group as *H. calycinum*. For a description see *Flora Iranica* (1968), Guttiferae, p. 4.

The *H. oblongifolium* of Wallich and the *H. patulum* var. *oblongifolium* of Koehne are not this species but *H. hookeranum*. The *H. oblongifolium* of *Bot. Mag.*, t. 4949, is *H. lobbii*.

H. CERASTOIDES (Spach) N. Robson

Campylopus cerastoides Spach; *H. rhodoppeum* Frivaldsky

An evergreen sub-shrub of tufted habit, producing dense rounded clusters, 12 in. or more across, with erect or procumbent, slender, hairy, terete stems 3 to 6 in. long, springing from a woody root-stock. Leaves in decussate pairs, rather crowded, stalkless, ¼ to ⅝ in. long, oval, apex rounded, hairy on both surfaces. Flowers bright yellow, 1 to 1½ in. across, springing from the terminal leaf-axils in clusters of three or four; petals oblong, ⅛ to ¼ in. wide; stamens very numerous, about ¼ in. long.

Native of the south-eastern parts of the Balkan peninsula and of north-west Turkey. It is profuse flowering and attractive in May. Suitable for the rock garden.

H. CHINENSE *see* H. MONOGYNUM

H. coris L.

An evergreen, semi-shrubby plant, erect and 6 to 15 in. high, or sometimes procumbent; stems round, very slender and clustered, glabrous. Leaves in whorls of four, rarely three, linear, ⅓ to 1 in. long, ¹⁄₁₆ in. or less wide, stalkless, revolute, blunt; midrib prominent beneath. Flowers borne in axillary clusters of three to five, forming terminal panicles 2 to 5 in. long. Corolla ¾ in. wide, glowing yellow; petals ovate-oblong; sepals linear-oblong, about ⅕ in. long, margined with dark, stalked or stalkless glands; stamens in three bundles. Blossoms in June and July. *Bot. Mag.*, t. 6563.

Native mainly of the northern Appenines, Maritime Alps and southern Alps; cultivated in 1640. It is related to *H. empetrifolium*, which has angled stems and fewer, usually three, leaves in a whorl, and petals which fall before the fruits are ripe. *H. coris* is a lime-loving plant and needs a sunny position, in well-drained soil.

H. densiflorum Pursh

An evergreen shrub 2 to 4 ft high (6 ft in the wild); branches erect, two-angled. Leaves 1 to 2 in. long, usually less than ¼ in. wide, linear-lanceolate, recurved at the edges. Flowers very numerous, in compact cymose panicles; each flower ½ in. across. Fruits three-celled, slender, ¼ in. long, subtended by the five oval-oblong, spreading sepals.

Native of the pine-barrens from New Jersey to Florida, and from Kentucky west to Arkansas and Texas. It is a near ally of the commoner *H. prolificum*, but is smaller in flower and narrower in leaf; its fruit also is more slender.

H. lobocarpum Gattinger *H. densiflorum* var. *lobocarpum* (Gattinger) Svenson—Capsule deeply lobed, four- or five-celled; styles four or five. N. Carolina to Louisiana.

H. empetrifolium Willd.

A dwarf evergreen shrub up to 12 or 15 in. high, with slender, erect, angled branches. Leaves produced occasionally in pairs, but usually three at each joint; ¼ to ½ in. long, linear, with the margins curled under; stalkless. Flowers in an erect panicle, producing three cymes in each tier; each flower ½ to ⅔ in. across, pale golden yellow; sepals small, oblong, with black glands on the margin. Fruit a three-celled capsule ¼ in. long, with the spreading sepals attached at the base. *Bot. Mag.*, t. 6764.

Native of Greece and the islands of the Grecian Archipelago; introduced to the Hammersmith nursery of Messrs Lee in 1788. It is a rather tender plant, and will survive only our mildest winters without protection. But for the warmer counties few more charming dwarf shrubs could be found. Even in cooler districts it is well worth the little protection it requires. Flowers from late July to September.

var. oliganthum Rech. f. *H. e.* var. *tortuosum* Rech. f.; *H. e.* var. *prostratum* Hort.—Habit procumbent. Inflorescences fewer-flowered than in the typical state of the species. It occurs in the mountains of Crete. An almost prostrate example of this variety, with the flowers mostly borne singly at the ends of the shoots, is figured in *New Flora and Sylva*, Vol. 10, facing p. 59. It is also figured in Sibthorp and Smith, *Fl. Graeca*, Vol. 8 (1833), t. 774.

H. ericoides L.

A dwarf heath-like sub-shrub forming a woody root-stock from which arise numerous erect wiry stems 3 or 4 in. high. Leaves densely set on the shoot, in whorls of four, linear-lanceolate, about $\frac{1}{12}$ in. long, prolonged at the apex into a mucronate tip, rounded at the base, covered with numerous sunken glands, margins strongly recurved. Flowers yellow, about $\frac{1}{2}$ in. across, borne from May onwards in terminal clusters. Sepals oblong-lanceolate, often edged with stalked, black glands. *Bot. Mag.*, n.s., t. 36.

Native of eastern and south-eastern Spain and of North Africa (Morocco and Tunisia); introduced by Dr Giuseppi in the 1930s from the Sierra de Cazorla, Andalucia; reintroduced in 1948 by P. H. Davis and V. H. Heywood from the Barranco de Gargantas in the same region. It is a rather variable species. The above description is of the form originally introduced, but the plants may be prostrate, and in some forms the leaves and flowers are somewhat larger, or the leaves blunter (Heywood, in *Journ. R.H.S.*, Vol. 75 (1950), pp. 447–8). The North African plants are placed in two subspecies by Maire and Wilczek.

In the natural state this species inhabits crevices in limestone rocks and in cultivation is perhaps best suited to a dry-wall. It is allied to *H. coris* and *H. empetrifolium*, but its dense heath-like foliage distinguishes it.

H. forrestii (Chittenden) N. Robson

H. patulum var. *forrestii* Chittenden; *H. patulum* var. *henryi* Hort., in part, not Bean; *H. patulum* f. *forrestii* (Chittenden) Rehd.; *H. calcaratum* Hort.

An almost deciduous shrub 5 to 6 ft high, with erect main stems and horizontal or drooping branchlets, which are slightly flattened at the ends and under the flowers but not lined or edged. Leaves short-stalked, lanceolate or ovate, $\frac{7}{8}$ to $1\frac{3}{4}$ in. long, $\frac{1}{2}$ to $\frac{3}{4}$ in. wide, obtuse and mucronate at the apex, rounded to cuneate at the base. Flowers golden yellow, saucer-shaped, $1\frac{1}{2}$ to $2\frac{1}{2}$ in. across, borne singly or in three- or five-flowered cymes; flower-buds broadly ovoid. Sepals broad-ovate or broad-elliptic, usually entire, rounded or broadly obtuse and rarely shortly mucronate at the apex. Stamens in five bundles, about half as long as the petals. Styles free, about half as long as the ovary (from two-fifths to three-fifths as long).

Native of China in Yunnan and W. Szechwan, of the Assam Himalaya and of upper Burma; introduced by Forrest about 1906 and again in greater quantity in 1917–19. It was originally described by Chittenden as *H. patulum* var. *forrestii* but was raised to specific rank by Dr Robson in 1970. It is sometimes seen in gardens under the name *H. patulum* var. *henryi*, but the hypericum of S. Yunnan described by Bean under that name (see *H. beanii*, p. 406) differs in its narrower sepals which are acute or acuminate at the apex and in its longer styles and stamens.

Although not so much planted in gardens, nor so common in the trade, as it was before the coming of 'Hidcote', *H. forrestii* is still worthy of cultivation. It does not have such a long flowering season as 'Hidcote', but the bronzy red young fruits are attractive and the older leaves colour orange and red as autumn approaches. It makes an elegant small specimen.

H. 'HIDCOTE'.—An almost evergreen shrub up to 5 ft high and 8 ft across. Leaves lanceolate, dark green above, pale and fairly conspicuously net-veined beneath. Flowers shallowly saucer-shaped, golden yellow, up to 3 in. wide, borne continuously from midsummer to October in few-flowered cymes. Sepals as in *H. forrestii*. Stamens about one-third as long as the petals, with orange anthers. Styles as long as the ovary or slightly longer. Fruits rarely or never set.

This famous hypericum first came to notice in the garden at Hidcote Manor created by Major Lawrence Johnston. It is possible that it was raised from seeds collected by him during his visit to China in the 1920s. But according to the late Sir Frederick Stern (*A Chalk Garden* (1960), p. 127) the Hidcote plants were raised from cuttings received from W. Miller-Christy of Watergate near Chichester. If this is so, the likelihood of 'Hidcote' being of wild origin is much lessened. Dr Robson considers that it is very possibly a hybrid of garden origin between *H. forrestii* and *H. calycinum* (*Journ. R.H.S.*, Vol. 95, p. 487).

'Hidcote' is quite hardy, though the younger wood may be cut by frost.

H. FRONDOSUM Michx.

H. aureum Bartr., not Lour.

A deciduous, much-branched shrub of rounded habit, about 4 ft high, often rising on a single stem from which the lower branches have fallen, thus giving it the aspect of a miniature tree; the older branches covered with a greyish brown, peeling bark; young shoots two-winged. Leaves blue-green, oblong, 1 to 2 in. long, with a minute, abrupt point, and numerous transparent glands. Flowers in clusters terminating the shoot and its upper branches, orange-yellow, 1½ in. across, the stamens forming a dense brush ¾ in. across. The fruit is a three-celled, broad-based cone ½ in. high, with the very large, leaflike, unequal sepals at the base. *Bot. Mag.*, t. 8498.

Discovered by Bartram in 1776 'upon the steep dry banks of the Patse-Lega Creek, a branch of the Flint River', Georgia, this hypericum, despite its great beauty, does not appear to have reached this country until late in the 19th century. Healthy plants flower and set their fruit in extraordinary abundance, and it is wise to remove the latter except such as may be required for seed. It appears to prefer rocky places in its native home, and is often found on the cliffs of river-courses where it gets some shade. It is wild in several of the south-eastern United States, and is the handsomest of all the American species in cultivation here.

H. GALIOIDES Lam.

An evergreen bush 2 to 3 ft high, of broad, compact habit, and with round stems, much branched towards the top. Leaves from ¾ to 2 in. long, ⅙ in. or less wide, dark green dotted with pellucid glands, margins recurved. Flowers ½ to ¾ in. across, yellow, borne in cymes both terminal and axillary on the many branchlets, and thus transforming the end of each branch into a large panicle of flowers 6 to 10 in. long and 3 to 4 in. wide; sepals and petals narrow. Styles and cells of seed-vessel three; calyx linear, as long as the fruit.

Native of the eastern United States from Delaware to Florida; introduced to the Jardin des Plantes at Paris about 1790, but almost lost sight of until 1897, when it was reintroduced to Kew from the Arnold Arboretum. It begins to flower in July and continues until October. Its very narrow leaves and terete stems distinguish it among allied species.

H. HIRCINUM L.

An almost evergreen, semi-woody plant, usually 2 to 3 ft, sometimes 5 ft high, with erect, two-angled stems much branched towards the top. Leaves with a goat-like odour when crushed, ovate, stalkless, 1 to 2½ in. long. Cymes terminating the stem and its numerous branches; on strong shoots borne in the leaf-axils also. Flowers 1½ in. across, bright yellow; sepals lanceolate to ovate-lanceolate, deciduous; stamens ¾ to 1¼ in. long; styles three, rather shorter than the stamens. Fruits three-celled, ¼ in. long, tapered.

Native of the middle and southern latitudes of Europe and the Mediterranean region; introduced in 1640. It is now established in some parts of Britain, an escape from gardens. The only hypericum with which it is likely to be confused is H. × inodorum, but besides its distinctive odour H. hircinum has longer stamens and styles, smaller leaves, later flowers, and the sepals fall away from the fruit. It flowers from early August to October. A very hardy, handsome plant.

var. MINUS Ait. H. hircinum var. pumilum Wats.; H. h. var. minor Lav.—Of dwarf, compact habit, with smaller leaves. This variety has been cultivated in Britain since 1732 or earlier, and may be a clone. Plants with similar foliage are found in the Balearic Islands and are said to grow 15 to 24 in. high there.

H. HOOKERANUM Wight & Arn.

H. oblongifolium sensu Wall, not Choisy; H. patulum var. oblongifolium Koehne; H. garrettii Craib

An evergreen or semi-evergreen shrub 2 to 5 ft high in the wild; stems four, lined or four-angled under the inflorescence. Leaves shortly stalked, lanceolate to narrow-ovate, 1¼ to 2½ in. long, ½ to 1 in. wide (rarely to 3 in. long, 1¾ in. wide), tapered at the apex to a blunt point, but sometimes acuminately pointed or obtuse. Inflorescences with mostly one to seven flowers (occasionally up to eleven). Flowers varying in colour from deep golden yellow to pale yellow-cup-shaped, 1½ to 2 in. wide. Sepals broadly spathulate-obovate to almost circular or oblate, always rounded at the apex. Stamens in five bundles, one-quarter to one-third as long as the petals. Styles one-fifth to one-half as long as the ovary.

H. *hookeranum* was described from a specimen collected in the Nilghiri Hills of southern India, but is also found in the Himalaya from Nepal eastwards, and in Burma and Thailand. The date of first introduction is not certain, but it has probably been in cultivation off and on since early in the 19th century, and had certainly been introduced from Sikkim by 1911. In recent years seeds have been sent from the Himalaya and bordering regions, two of the most recent introductions being by the late Frank Kingdon Ward from the Triangle, Burma, and by Cox and Hutchison from the Assam Himalaya. The hypericum described in previous editions under the name H. *hookeranum* is H. *lobbii*, and the date of introduction, given as 'shortly before 1857' in some works of reference, is of that species.

Judging from herbarium specimens, H. *hookeranum* is variable in habit, in size and shape of leaf, in the number of flowers in each inflorescence, and in their size. The finest Himalayan forms have still to be introduced, but might not prove hardy.

Despite its variability, H. *hookeranum* is a well-marked species, at once recognisable by the short styles and stamens in combination with the sepals smoothly rounded at the apex.

cv. 'ROGERSII'.—This superior form of H. *hookeranum*, with deep-yellow flowers, was raised in the garden of Sir John Ross of Bladensburg at Rostrevor House, Co. Down, from seeds collected in the mountains of Burma shortly before 1921 by an officer of the Indian Forestry Service. It reached commerce in the 1930s but has been displaced by its hybrid 'Rowallane'. The true plant is now rare. Plants seen in two gardens in 1970 under the name 'Rogersii' proved to be 'Rowallane'.

H. (*hookeranum* 'Rogersii' × *leschenaultii*) 'ROWALLANE'.—This beautiful hybrid arose as a self-sown seedling in the garden of H. Armytage-Moore at Rowallane, Co. Down. The flowers are bowl-shaped and deep yellow as in the first-named parent, but the influence of H. *leschenaultii* shows in their large size —up to 3 in. wide. From both parents it differs in the shape of the sepals, which are rounded at the apex, not acute or subacute as in H. *leschenaultii*; and whereas the sepals of H. *hookeranum* are smoothly rounded at the apex and obovate-cuneate or almost circular, those of 'Rowallane' are more or less apiculate, and the roundish upper part is usually rather abruptly narrowed to a claw.

'Rowallane' is not quite hardy south of London, but if severely cut by frost will usually break again from the base and flower late in the same season, while slight frost-damage is of no account, some pruning in spring being always desirable. In the milder parts it will attain a height of 6 ft.   [PLATE 51

H. × INODORUM Mill.

H. *elatum* Ait.; H. *persistens* F. Schneider; H. *multiflorum* Hort.

A sub-evergreen shrub up to 5 ft high, with slightly angled, branching stems. Leaves slightly to strongly aromatic when crushed, deep green, 1½ to 3 in. long, ovate, blunt or rounded at the tip, sessile. Flowers borne in abundant cymes at the ends of the shoots, and in the axils of the terminal leaves, one to three flowers in each final subdivision of the inflorescence; they are yellow, 1 in. across; sepals narrowly to broadly ovate, persistent at least until the fruit ripens; petals longer than the sepals, which are ovate, reflexed in fruit; styles three, about twice as long as the ovary or slightly longer. Fruits dark brown or reddish, not quite so persistently fleshy as in *H. androsaemum*, and longer and more tapered at the top.

A variable hybrid between *H. androsaemum* and *H. hircinum* which occurs in the wild where the two species are in contact and has also arisen in gardens, no doubt at many times and in many places. It was in cultivation and in commerce by the mid-18th century and has become naturalised in some of the rainier parts of the British Isles, e.g., in Cornwall, Argyll, Perthshire, and Co. Down. It is also found in apparently wild conditions in Madeira.

H. × *inodorum* is sometimes confounded with *H. androsaemum*, but is distinguished by its flowers, which have sepals shorter than the petals, stamens longer than the petals and styles twice or slightly more the length of the ovary; it is also of somewhat taller growth. But it resembles *H. androsaemum* and differs from *H. hircinum* in its persistent sepals; also, its leaves lack the goat-like smell of *H. hircinum*, though they are often aromatic. *H.* × *inodorum* is mainly represented in cultivation by the cultivar 'ELSTEAD', raised by W. Ladhams of Elstead, which received an Award of Merit in 1933. This is of dwarf habit and the ripening fruits are soft orange-scarlet. It is this variety that is figured in *Botanical Magazine*, n.s., t. 376. Unfortunately it is subject to a rust disease which discolours the leaves and weakens the plant.

H. KALMIANUM L.

An evergreen bush 2 to 3 ft high, with four-angled branches. Leaves glaucous green, 1 to 2 in. long, $\frac{1}{8}$ to $\frac{1}{3}$ in. wide, narrow-oblong or oblanceolate, dotted with transparent glands. Flowers produced in small cymes at the end of the branch and in the axils of the terminal leaves, $\frac{3}{4}$ to 1 in. across, bright yellow; sepals $\frac{1}{4}$ to $\frac{1}{3}$ in. long. Fruits ovate, five-, rarely four-celled. *Bot. Mag.*, t. 8491.

Native of eastern N. America, where it is confined to the cliffs of rivers and lakes from the Falls of Niagara northwards; said now to have become rather rare. It is named after Peter Kalm, the famous Swedish naturalist and traveller who discovered it in 1750. Nine years later it was introduced to England, but appears to have disappeared from cultivation for a long period, the plants so-called being always *H. prolificum*. In 1911, John Dunbar of the Parks Department, Rochester, N.Y., sent seeds of the true plant to Kew. *H. prolificum* has narrower petals and not so handsome a flower.

H. × NOTHUM Rehd.—A hybrid between *H. kalmianum* and *H. densiflorum*, raised from seeds of the latter at the Arnold Arboretum in 1903. It is a low densely branched shrub to about 1½ ft high with narrow, dark green leaves and oblong-linear sepals. The number of cells of the ovary varies from three, as in *H. densiflorum*, to five (as in *H. kalmianum*). The flowers are about $\frac{3}{4}$ in. across.

H. KOUYTCHENSE Lévl.

H. patulum var. *grandiflorum* Hort.; *H.* × *penduliflorum* Hort.; *H. patulum* var. *forrestii* Hort., in part, not Chittenden; *H. patulum* 'Sungold'

A semi-evergreen, laxly branched shrub 2 to 4 ft high; stems beneath the inflorescence flattened. Leaves ovate to narrow-ovate, 1½ to 2¼ in. long, ⅝ to ⅞ in. wide, acute at the apex, medium green above, pale beneath, shortly stalked. Flower-buds narrowly ovoid to almost conical, acute, slightly more than twice as long as wide. Flowers light golden yellow, about 2½ in. wide. Sepals lanceolate to ovate-lanceolate, rather spreading, with slender acuminate tips. Petals spreading or reflexed, with a hooked acute apiculus at the apex of the inner margin (i.e. the longer, thicker margin). Stamens a very prominent feature of the flower, about three-quarters as long as the petals, in five bundles. Styles free, as long as the ovary or slightly longer.

Native of Kweichow, China, whence it was introduced to Maurice de Vilmorin's collection at Les Barres around the turn of the century by one of the French missionaries. It appeared in Britain under the name *H. patulum grandiflorum*, but its provenance was uncertain and its long, prominent stamens gave rise to the theory that it might be a hybrid of garden origin, with *H. stellatum* (*H. "dyeri"* of gardens), or *H. calycinum*, as one parent. But Dr Robson has found that this hypericum agrees well with the type-specimen of *H. kouytchense*, now preserved at Edinburgh, and that the hypericum introduced by Wilson under W.256, which Rehder had identified as *H. kouytchense*, represented a distinct, hitherto undescribed species (see *H. wilsonii*). It should be added, however, that some plants distributed commercially as *H. kouytchense* before 1970 are not *H. wilsonii* but *H. acmosepalum*.

H. kouytchense is a very hardy and decorative species, flowering from midsummer until September. Its characters are well shown in the drawing by Graham Thomas in *Gard. Chron.* (April 16, 1960), p. 255 (as *H. penduliflorum*). The ripening capsules turn bright red soon after the petals drop.

H. LESCHENAULTII Choisy

H. triflorum Bl.

A shrub, evergreen in mild climates, lax in growth, ordinarily 4 to 8 ft high; branches slender, reddish brown. Leaves more or less shortly stalked, ovate-oblong, bluntish at the end, rounded at the base, 1½ to 2½ in. long, ¾ to 1¼ in. wide, dark, slightly glaucous green above, more definitely glaucous and thickly sprinkled with translucent dots. Flowers rich yellow, 2½ to 3 in. wide, produced singly or in threes (sometimes in sevens) at the end of the shoot. Petals 1 in. wide, rather concave, roundish obovate, slightly overlapping. Sepals ⅜ to ⅝ in. long, narrowly oblong or narrowly elliptic to oblanceolate, acute at the apex. Stamens less than half as long as the petals, very numerous, arranged in five bundles. Ovary conical, tapering upward to the five recurved styles, which are half as long as the ovary, or even shorter. *Bot. Mag.*, t. 9160.

Native of Java and other parts of Malaysia; discovered on the Javan mountains by Leschenault about 1805. The date of its introduction is not definitely known, but it was flowering in Mr Riall's garden at Old Conna Hill, Co. Wicklow, Eire, in July 1882. It is, in combined size and richness of colouring, the finest flowered of all hypericum species. It is not quite hardy at Kew, where it has been grown in a practically unheated house, making shoots half to fully a yard long in a season, attaining a height of 12 ft or more and flowering during the summer and autumn months. In the milder parts it is hardy in the open ground, but even there it is better on a wall, owing to its rather lank habit.

It belongs to the same group as *H. patulum* (section *Ascyreia*) and is quite closely allied to *H. hookeranum*, which it resembles in its short stamens and styles, but is distinguished by its 'very variable but always herbaceous and spreading calyces with their acute or acuminate, often unequal sepals and the rather large, long-tapering, conical capsules' (Stapf in *Bot. Mag.*, loc. cit.).

At the present time (1971) some plants grown as *H. leschenaultii* are really *H. augustinii* (q.v.).

H. LOBBII N. Robson

H. oblongifolium sensu Hook. f.; *H. hookeranum* Hort., in part

A tall, erect species 3 to 5 ft in cultivation, evergreen or partly deciduous according to the locality and winter; branchlets not angled. Leaves 1 to 2 in. long, ½ to 1½ in. wide, ovate or triangular-ovate, round or pointed at the tip, truncate at the base, glaucous beneath, distinctly though shortly stalked. Inflorescence a terminal cymose cluster with up to fifteen or sixteen flowers (occasionally more), each flower about 2 in. across, rather cup-shaped owing to the concave shape of the full, broad, overlapping petals. Sepals erect or slightly spreading, ovate-oblong to broad-elliptic, rounded and irregularly toothed at the apex and often with a small apicule near the tip. Petals strongly toothed along the inner margin (i.e., the margin overlapped on the outside by the neighbouring petal). Stamens in five bundles, slightly more than half as long as the petals to about three-quarters as long. Styles slightly longer than the ovary. *Bot. Mag.*, t. 4949, as *H. oblongifolium*.

This hypericum was introduced by Thomas Lobb from near Mufflong, Assam, while collecting for Messrs Veitch of Exeter. It was at first identified as *H. oblongifolium*, though it is quite distinct from the species so named by Choisy (for which see under *H. calycinum*). It also came to be known as *H. hookeranum* (q.v.) and was featured under that name in previous editions of this work. Dr Robson, however, has recognised it as a distinct species, which he named and described in 1970 (*Journ. R.H.S.*, Vol. 95 (1970), p. 496).

H. lobbii is moderately hardy, but needs a sheltered place. It flowers from early August to October. It is apt to become gaunt in habit and naked at the base with age, and should be renewed when that condition arrives. It was fairly common in gardens when the first edition of this work was published but seems to have almost dropped out of cultivation since the coming of the Forrest and Wilson introductions from China and, more recently, of such garden varieties as 'Hidcote' and 'Rowallane'. It has, however, survived in the University Botanic Garden, Cambridge, and will shortly be available in commerce once again.

H. MONOGYNUM L.

H. chinense L.

A woody species growing about 2 ft high; stems round. It has evergreen, narrow-oblong leaves, stalkless, 1½ to 3½ in. long, ½ to 1 in. wide. Flowers either solitary or in terminal cymes of three to seven, bright yellow, 1½ to 2½ in. across; stamens in five bundles, some as long as the petals; styles united to form

HYPERICUM MONOGYNUM

one slender tapering column ½ to ¾ in. long, divided at the top into five radiating stigmas. *Bot. Mag.*, t. 334.

Native of China and Formosa; introduced by the Earl of Northumberland who received seeds from China in 1753, from which plants were raised in 'his Lordship's curious garden at Stanwick' (Miller). It was at one time grown in greenhouses, where it flowered most of the year, but Miller grew it in the open air at Chelsea, keeping reserve plants in pots in case the outdoor ones were killed. The species may be tender in some forms, but at Grayswood Hill near Haslemere it has thrived in the open air at the foot of a south-facing terrace-wall for over half a century and the offspring of these plants have proved hardy in other and colder gardens (see the note by Frank Knight in *Journ. R.H.S.*, Vol. 96 (1971), p. 38). It flowers from July until autumn.

It is unfortunate that the familiar name *H. chinense* has had to be altered to *H. monogynum*. The reason for this nomenclatural change will be explained by Dr Robson in a forthcoming paper.

H. × MOSERANUM André

A hybrid between *H. patulum* and *H. calycinum*, raised in Moser's nursery at Versailles about 1887. It is a dwarf plant of tufted habit, sending up arching, reddish shoots each year 1 to 1½ ft long. Leaves intermediate between those of the parents and up to 2 in. long, ovate, rather glaucous beneath. Flowers from one to five in a cluster at the end of the shoot, but not more than one of each cluster is open at any one time; each flower 2 to 2½ in. across, with broad, overlapping, golden yellow petals. Stamens in five bundles with pinkish-purple anthers.

This is one of the most attractive of the hypericums, whose only fault is that it is frequently killed back in winter, and when planted in a group, leaves the ground bare until the young growths push again, which is not until May. It is hardier than *H. patulum*, although it has inherited the cymose inflorescence of that species, and thus a great flower beauty. A bed at Kew stood unchanged for twenty years, only protected by dry leaves during hard frost. It flowers from July up to October.

cv. 'TRICOLOR'.—Leaves edged with rose-colour and white; flowers small. A charming plant, perhaps slightly less hardy than the green-leaved form.

H. NUDIFLORUM Michx.

A deciduous shrub or sub-shrub up to 3 or 4 ft, stems square, glabrous, slender, erect. Leaves oval-oblong, 1 to 2¼ in. long, ¼ to ¾ in. wide, apex rounded, base tapered, thin in texture, glabrous, scarcely stalked. Flowers bright yellow, ½ to ¾ in. wide, borne dichotomously on terminal and axillary cymes 4 or 5 in. across; sepals ⅛ in. long, oval-oblong; fruits conical, ¼ in. long, pointed. Blossoms in July and August.

Native of the S.E. United States from N. Carolina to Florida and quite hardy. The inflorescence usually stands out leafless and clearly above the foliage and is interesting for its successive branching into two below each flower. It has become rare in cultivation.

H. OLYMPICUM L.

H. repens Hort., not L.; *H. fragile* Hort., in part, not Boiss.

A deciduous, glabrous sub-shrub with a procumbent root-stock, sending up shoots 6 to 15 in. high, or tufted; stems mostly unbranched, slightly two-edged. Leaves narrowly oval or oblong, ⅓ to 1¼ in. long, 1/12 to ¼ in. wide, pointed, stalkless, grey-green. Flowers bright yellow, 1½ to 2 in. across, borne in terminal clusters of up to five, ovate to obovate, ½ to ⅝ in. wide, opening from mid-summer onwards. Sepals large, pointed, persistent in fruit, without glands or with at the most a few scattered black glands on the surface. Stamens in three bundles.

Native of the Balkan peninsula and Anatolia; introduced by Sir George Wheeler by means of seeds which he collected on the Bithynian Olympus (Uln

Dagh), south of the Turkish town of Bursa, in the autumn of 1676 and sent to the Oxford Botanic Garden. From there it was introduced to Clifford's garden at Amsterdam, and it was from a plant growing in the garden that Linnaeus described the species.

H. *olympicum* is variable, being erect in some forms, in others decumbent, and varies also in size of flower and shape of leaf. It was at one time spread in gardens under the name H. *fragile*, under which it received an Award of Garden Merit in 1930. The true H. FRAGILE Boiss., which is endemic to eastern Greece, is a smaller plant with rather rounded, glandular leaves up to ¼ in. long. Its sepals are fringed with black, stalked glands, and the yellow flowers are usually tinged with red (*Fl. Europaea*, Vol. 2, p. 265).

H. *olympicum* 'CITRINUM' is a beautiful dwarf shrub with flowers of a pale lemon-yellow.

H. POLYPHYLLUM Boiss. & Bal.—This species, a native of Anatolia, is closely allied to H. *olympicum* and not easily distinguished from it. The most valid mark of difference, according to the key in *Flora of Turkey*, Vol. 2, p. 364, is that in H. *polyphyllum* the leaves are more glandular, with a regular row of glands near the margins and sometimes with scattered glands all over the leaf-surface, whereas in H. *olympicum* there is never more than an irregular row of glands near the margin. Also, in H. *polyphyllum* the sepals and petals are usually dotted all over with black glands; in H. *olympicum* they are nearly or wholly undotted; and, finally, in H. *polyphyllum* the sepals are apiculate or acute to rounded, whereas in H. *olympicum* they are more or less long-acuminate. H. *polyphyllum* is probably not in cultivation at the present time.

H. PATULUM Thunb.

An evergreen or semi-evergreen shrub to about 3 ft high; uppermost inter-nodes (i.e., those immediately under the flowers or at the ends of vegetative shoots) strongly flattened and two- or four-lined, the adjacent (older) ones four-angled, mature stems terete. Leaves short-stalked, ovate, ovate-oblong or lanceolate oblong, 1 to 2½ in. long, obtuse and usually apiculate at the apex, dark green above, rather glaucous beneath. Flowers golden yellow about 2 in. wide, cup-shaped, borne singly or in few-flowered cymes. Sepals erect, broadly ovate to almost orbicular, finely toothed, usually mucronate at the apex. Stamens about half as long as the petals, in five bundles. Styles almost as long as the ovary, free.

Native of S.W. China; cultivated and naturalised in Japan; described by Thunberg in 1784 from a Nagasaki garden; introduced from Japan by Oldham in 1862. It is now very rare in gardens. In previous editions it was said to be not quite hardy but to produce stems 1 to 2 ft long if cut to the ground by frost, bearing their flowers from July to October.

H. URALUM D. Don H. *patulum* var. *uralum* (D. Don) Koehne—This species is closely allied to H. *patulum* but has smaller leaves and flowers, and entire sepals. It is quite a pretty and fairly hardy shrub, flowering in August and September; introduced 1820. Native of the central and eastern Himalaya, and of Indochina and Sumatra. The epithet *uralum* derives from the native name for the species (*urala swa*).

H. PROLIFICUM L.

A stout, erect-growing evergreen bush 3 to 5 ft high, the growths of the year but little branched, two-edged especially towards the top. Leaves dark, shining green, narrow-oblong, tapering to a short stalk, 1½ to 2½ in. long, ¼ to ½ in. wide, dotted with numerous transparent glands. Flowers in terminal clusters and in the leaf-axils near the end of the shoot; each flower about 1 in. across, bright yellow. Fruits three-celled.

Native of the eastern and central United States; introduced about the middle of the 18th century. Under cultivation it is the healthiest and most vigorous of the American species, although not so handsome in flower as *H. frondosum* or *kalmianum*. It bears enormous crops of fruit. Allied to *H. densiflorum*, it differs in its larger leaves and flowers and more elongated inflorescence; and from *H. kalmianum* its three-celled fruits distinguish it. Starting to flower in July, it continues for six or eight weeks.

H. REPTANS Hook. f. & Thoms.

A low, prostrate, self-rooting shrub a few inches high, often tufted; stems very slender, almost threadlike, two-edged, glabrous. Leaves ¼ to ½ in. long, oval-oblong, apex blunt, usually crowded ⅛ to ⅓ in. apart on the stem. Flowers terminal, solitary, golden yellow, 1¼ in. across; petals obovate; sepals about ½ in. long, oval, blunt; capsule globose, ½ in. wide.

Native of the Himalaya at from 9,000 to 11,000 ft.; in cultivation 1881. It is not completely hardy but should survive most winters if grown in a sheltered position in the rock garden, in a well-drained soil.

H. STELLATUM N. Robson

H. lysimachioides Hort., not Wall. ex Dyer; *H. dyeri* Hort., not Rehd.

An evergreen or semi-evergreen shrub up to 3 or 4 ft high, with arching branches; branchlets two- or four-angled near the ends. Leaves shortly stalked, ovate to lanceolate or oblong-lanceolate, ¾ to 1½ in. long, acute or obtuse and mucronate at the apex, pale but not glaucous beneath. Flowers bright golden yellow, 1 to 1¾ in. across, borne in corymbose clusters. Petals obovate, about twice as long as wide, with an acute apiculus at one side near the apex. Sepals linear-lanceolate, spreading in the bud-stage and after flowering. Stamens in five bundles, about two-thirds as long as the petals. Styles slightly longer than the ovary to one and a half times as long.

Native of Yunnan, W. Szechwan, and bordering parts of S.E. Tibet; introduced to cultivation about 1893 by means of seeds sent by one of the French missionaries to Maurice de Vilmorin, in whose collection at Les Barres it first flowered in 1897. It was identified there by Bois as *H. lysimachioides* Wall. ex

Dyer, and under this name it was introduced to Kew in 1904. Later it was also grown as *H. dyeri*, which is simply a renaming of *H. lysimachioides* Dyer. Dr Robson, however, has recently pointed out this Chinese hypericum differs from the W. Himalayan *H. dyeri* in several respects and has described it as a new species—*H. stellatum* (*Journ. R.H.S.*, Vol. 95 (1970), p. 493).

H. DYERI Rehd. *H. lysimachioides* Wall. ex Dyer, not Boiss. & Noë—This species, a native of W. Himalaya as far east as Nepal, is perhaps not in cultivation. From *H. stellatum* (see above) it differs, according to Dr Robson, in the following particulars: leaves whitish beneath, with the reticulations fairly conspicuous; petals narrower (about three times as long as wide); ovary subglobose (not ovoid); styles longer, one and a half to twice as long as ovary.

H. WILSONII N. Robson

H. kouytchense sensu Rehd. and of *Bot. Mag.*, t. 9345, not Lévl.

A low almost deciduous shrub with spreading branches; stems flattened and four-lined under the flower-clusters, the next internodes two-lined, the lower ones terete. Leaves short-stalked, mostly narrow-ovate, obtuse at the apex, 1 to 1½ in. or slightly more long, ½ to ⅝ in. wide, greyish green beneath. Flower-buds slender, conical. Flowers 1¼ to 1¾ in. wide, cup-shaped, soft yellow, usually borne singly or in three-flowered cymes. Petals with an acute, hooked apiculus at the apex of the inner margin (as in *H. kouytchense*). Sepals ovate-oblong or oblong-lanceolate, with slender, acuminate tips. Stamens about half as long as the petals, in five bundles. Styles free, about as long as the ovary or slightly longer. *Bot. Mag.*, t. 9345.

A native of W. China; introduced by Wilson in 1907–8 under W.256. Wilson sent no specimens of the wild plants from which the seeds were taken and it was not until 1924 that a garden plant raised from W.256 was identified by Rehder. He considered it to be *H. kouytchense* but this hypericum is in fact an allied but quite distinct species, which Dr Robson has described under the name *H. wilsonii* (*Journ. R.H.S.*, Vol. 95 (1970), p. 492). The true *H. kouytchense* (q.v.) is a much stronger growing species, with longer, very prominent stamens.

H. wilsonii is not common in gardens but is in cultivation in the R.H.S. Garden at Wisley, where it is hardy. The plants there bear soft-yellow flowers, but they are shown as golden yellow in the plate in the *Botanical Magazine*.

H. XYLOSTEIFOLIUM (Spach) N. Robson

Androsaemum xylosteifolium Spach; *H. inodorum* Willd., not Mill.

An elegant shrub 3 to 4 ft high, evergreen, with long, slender, usually unbranched stems compressed or slightly two-winged towards the top, and luxuriantly leafy (the leaf-pairs from ¼ to 1 in. apart). Leaves oblong or ovate, 1 to 2 in. long, dull dark green, rounded at the apex, inodorous. Flowers small compared with the size of the plant, and wanting in beauty, often solitary at the end of the shoot, but on strong shoots produced in small terminal clusters, they are ¾ or 1 in. across, with narrow, fragile petals, linear sepals, and three styles. Stamens longer than petals.

Native of north-east Turkey and south-west Georgia. In its graceful arching habit and strong vigorous growth this species is attractive, but it is one of the most disappointing in its flowers, which appear a few at a time from July to September. It has a creeping root stock, and eventually forms a large dense thicket; it is thus easily increased by division.

HYSSOPUS   LABIATAE

A small genus of shrubs and sub-shrubs, ranging from S. Europe to C. Asia. Only the species described here is native to Europe. Of allied genera treated in this work, *Perowskia* is distinguished by its toothed leaves and flowers with only two fertile stamens and *Thymus* by always having much smaller leaves. In *Satureia* the stamens are included under the upper lip of the corolla, not exserted and conspicuous as in *Hyssopus*.

H. OFFICINALIS L.   HYSSOP

A low, partially evergreen, aromatic bush, quite woody at the base, 1½ to 2 ft high; shoots erect, green, square, covered when young with minute down. Leaves opposite, linear or narrowly oval, ⅓ to 1½ in. long, 1/16 to ¼ in. wide, tapered at both ends, very minutely toothed, or roughened at the edges, rich green, glandular-punctate on both surfaces. Flowers produced in close, axillary whorls on the shoots of the year, forming a terminal panicle, and starting to open about midsummer and continuing until September. From six to twelve or more flowers appear in each whorl, and they of a bluish purple shade in the type, about ½ in. long, two-lipped. Stamens exserted. As in all the labiates the fruit consists of four nutlets. The leaves and young shoots have a pleasant mint-like scent. *Bot. Mag.*, t. 2299.

Native of S. Europe, in the Mediterranean region, and W. Asia. Cultivated as a medicinal herb in England since 1548, probably long before. An infusion of hyssop is an old-fashioned remedy for removing phlegm. It is an easily cultivated plant requiring a warm, light soil, and is easily increased by cuttings during the summer and autumn. There is a white-flowered form, f. ALBUS (West.) Schneid., and one with red flowers, f. RUBER (West.) Hegi, both known in the wild and both in cultivation since at least the 18th century.

H. officinalis is a variable species. A race found in the central and eastern Pyrenees was named H. ARISTATUS by Godron but has been treated as a subspecies by later authorities. The distinguishing characters given are: leaves of a cheerful green, glabrous, scarcely glandular-punctate beneath; flowers in dense spikes; bracts and calyx-teeth terminated by fine, long, aristate tips. Cultivated plants are of dense rather fastigiate habit, 1¼ to 1½ ft high.

IBERIS CRUCIFERAE

The majority of the species in this well-known genus are herbaceous, often annuals, but the following species are perennial and sufficiently woody to claim notice here. The most characteristic features of the genus are, firstly, the inflorescence, which is a flattish raceme often elongated by the time the seed is formed, and, secondly, the petals; of these there are (as always in this Family) four to each flower, the two outermost of which are distinctly larger than the two inner ones, especially on the flowers at the edge of the inflorescence. They like a sunny position, a well-drained soil, and are easily propagated by late summer cuttings.

I. GIBRALTARICA L.   GIBRALTAR CANDYTUFT

An evergreen, flat-topped, half-woody plant up to 12 in. high or sometimes more, and in favourable localities as much as 2 or 3 ft in diameter. Leaves linear-obovate, ¾ to 2 in. long, ¼ to ½ in. wide, rounded at the apex and usually although often inconspicuously toothed on the terminal half, gradually tapered towards the base, glabrous. On the flower-stems the leaves decrease in size, finally becoming linear and about ⅛ in. wide. Flower-stems 6 to 8 in. long, often branched towards the top. Flowers crowded in flattish umbel-like clusters 2 to 3 in. wide; white or reddish lilac, or both, with the paler ones in the centre. The two outer petals are much larger than the two inner ones and those of the outermost flowers may be ½ to ¾ in. long. The flat seed-pod is about ⅜ in. long, notched at the top. *Bot. Mag.*, t. 124.

Native of S. Spain and Morocco, its best-known habitat being the Rock of Gibraltar, from which it takes its specific name; introduced in 1732. It grows in crevices and holes in the face of the cliffs, where to all appearance there is no soil. The true plant is not common, although other species often may be seen under this name. It is very suitable for sunny gardens on the south coast, planted in full sun in a light soil with which stones or rubble have been freely mixed. In colder parts it survives only mild or moderately severe winters. It blossoms from May to July. From the other species it can be distinguished by its usually branched flower-stems, usually toothed leaves, and more highly coloured flowers.

I. SEMPERFLORENS L.

An evergreen shrub up to 2 ft high of bushy shape, free from down. Leaves narrowly obovate, rounded at the apex, tapered to the base, ¾ to 2½ in. long, ¼ to ½ in. wide, dark dull green, not toothed. Flowers white or tinged with pink, fragrant, produced in crowded, flattish racemes 1 to 2 in. long and wide. Seed-pod ⅜ in. wide, ¼ in. long, very slightly notched at the apex.

Native of S. Italy and Sicily, often in calcareous soil; introduced in 1679. In shape and size of leaf it resembles *I. gibraltarica*, but the latter is well distinguished by its toothed foliage, also by the more distinctly notched seed-pod.

I. semperflorens is the tenderest of these shrubby candytufts. Suitable for sunny places on the south coast. Its flowering season is from November to April.

I. SEMPERVIRENS L.

An evergreen sub-shrub 6 to 12 in. high, of spreading habit, free from down; stems slender, thickly furnished with linear or oblanceolate leaves which are $\frac{1}{2}$ to 2 in. long, $\frac{1}{8}$ to $\frac{3}{16}$ in. wide, blunt or rounded at the apex, not toothed. Flowers white, produced from April to June in racemes at first flattish and 1 to 1$\frac{1}{2}$ in. wide, but elongating later; main flower-stalk 2 to 4 in. long with the flowers at the terminal half. Seed-pod roundish or obcordate, $\frac{1}{4}$ in. wide, notched at the top.

Native of S. Europe and W. Asia; introduced in 1731 and for very many years a favourite in gardens and the commonest of these sub-shrubby candytufts. It is very hardy and covers itself every spring with a sheet of white flowers. It is well distinguished from the two preceding species by its narrow leaves.

var. GARREXIANA (All.) Cesati *I. garrexiana* All.—Of dwarfer more compact habit than typical *I. sempervirens*, with somewhat narrower leaves, sometimes pointed at the apex. Described from the Maritime Alps, where it grows near Garessio and on the Col di Tenda; also found in the Pyrenees.

cv. 'LITTLE GEM' ('WEISSER ZWERG').—A dwarf, dense shrublet with short narrow pointed leaves. Flowers pure white, rather small, in narrow trusses. Raised in Germany.

cv. 'SNOWFLAKE'.—A compact shrub up to 1 ft high and 2 ft across. Leaves dark green, oblong. Flowers in trusses about 2 in. wide which elongate before all the flowers are expanded.

I. SAXATILIS L. *I. vermiculata* Willd.—A dwarf plant 3 to 5 in. high with hairy shoots. Leaves linear, $\frac{3}{8}$ to 1 in. long, fleshy, almost cylindrical in cross-section, blunt or sharply pointed at the apex and usually ending in a short mucro, ciliate or quite glabrous. The inflorescences elongate in the fruiting stage as in *I. sempervirens* but the two species are easily distinguished by their foliage. Native of the mountains of S. Europe from Spain to the Crimea. Admirable for the rock garden.

I. CORIFOLIA (Sims) Sweet *I. saxatilis* var. *corifolia* Sims—The identity of the plant figured in the *Botanical Magazine* (1826), t. 1642, as *I. saxatilis* var. *corifolia*, is uncertain, the plate being a poor one and the description scanty. The iberis that Farrer knew as *I. corifolia* was a form of *I. saxatilis* but was not the plant of the *Botanical Magazine*. Many of the plants once grown as "*I. corifolia*" were really the hybrid *I.* 'Correifolia' (see below).

I. 'CORREIFOLIA'.—A vigorous hybrid raised by H. Turner in the Botanic Garden, Bury St Edmunds, before 1857. Leaves spathulate, dark glossy green, up to 1$\frac{1}{2}$ in. long. Flowers borne towards the end of May in corymbs which gradually elongate into rounded heads about 3 in. long. It grows 8 in. to 1 ft high and up to two yards across. One parent was almost certainly *I. semper-*

virens; the other perhaps *I. tenoreana*. It seems to be now rare in gardens but was much grown in the 19th century, often as "*I. corifolia*".

IDESIA   FLACOURTIACEAE

An E. Asiatic genus consisting, so far as is known, of the one species described below. The generic name commemorates E. I. Ides, a Dutchman who travelled in China in the 18th century.

I. POLYCARPA Maxim.

Polycarpa maximowiczii Lind.

A deciduous, dioecious tree 40 to 50 ft high. The branches usually grow out from the trunk horizontally, and the younger ones have a large core of pith. Leaves dark green and quite glabrous above, glaucous beneath, and hairy at the base where the main veins join the stalk, heart-shaped, contracted at the apex to a short point, rather distantly toothed, and ordinarily about 6 in. long by 5 in. wide, but occasionally half as large again; leaf-stalk usually three-fourths as long as the leaf, furnished with a pair of oblong glands near the apex. Flowers fragrant, yellow-green, without petals, in terminal panicles; unisexual, and produced on different trees. Male panicles 5 or 6 in. long, each flower ⅓ in. across, the usually five sepals covered, like the flower-stalks, with a short brownish down; stamens numerous. Female flowers smaller, and in a longer, looser panicle than the males, with similar but smaller sepals, and a prominent globular ovary. Fruits hanging like a bunch of small grapes, each berry about the size of a pea, globular, containing numerous seeds lying in pulp; at first green, the berries become dark brown, finally a deep red. *Bot. Mag.*, t. 6794.

This interesting tree was first made known to Europeans by R. Oldham, the Kew collector, who found it in Japan in 1862–3; it is a native also of China. Soon after, it was introduced to Europe by way of St Petersburg, and was already in the famous arboretum at Segrez in 1869. It was later reintroduced from China by Wilson and by Forrest and probably most of the trees now cultivated derive from these sendings.

In general appearance it suggests a catalpa, but the leaves are thicker and not so large. It grows very well in a loamy soil, and is hardy at Kew, where it flowers in June and July and produces fruit annually. As a flowering tree it has no claims to notice, but the fruits make it interesting, and, if the autumn be fine enough to enable them to reach their final stage of colouring, distinct and handsome. A fine crop of berries was produced at Wakehurst Place, Sussex, in the warm dry summer of 1934, and specimens grown in the garden there were given an Award of Merit by the Royal Horticultural Society on November 6, 1934. Fruits are, however, only produced by this species if trees of both

sexes are grown. At Kew, the tree at the south end of the Rhododendron Dell
occasionally produces good crops, although the male is several hundred yards
distant.

Seeds are usually available in commerce and afford a better means of increase
than cuttings, though vegetative propagation is, of course, essential if plants
of known sex are to be produced.

var. VESTITA Diels—Differs from the type chiefly by the undersurface of
the leaves being densely downy. Wilson found it in Western Szechwan, China

IDESIA POLYCARPA in fruit

at elevations of over 8,000 ft as a tree 20 to 50 ft high with a trunk 1 ft in
diameter and introduced it in 1908. The flowers are yellow as in the type; fruit
described as brick red. The species varies considerably in the size and shape of
its leaves, but this variety is well distinguished by its downy leaves which are
almost felted when young. Forrest sent home seeds of it and of the typical
variety as well. The late Sir Frederick Stern raised the var. *vestita* from Farrer's
seeds sent from Kansu, but only one was planted and this was male (*The Chalk
Garden*, pp. 147–8). Farrer described it as 'a beautiful and graceful tree, with
abundant long and loose panicles of rich scarlet berries'.

ILEX HOLLY AQUIFOLIACEAE

A very large genus of deciduous and evergreen trees and shrubs found in almost all parts of the habitable globe except western N. America and Australasia. In gardens they are best known by the evergreen group, especially by *I. aquifolium* and its numerous forms and hybrids. They have very frequently angular young shoots; leaves alternate, stalked. Flowers of little or no beauty, small, often dull white, produced in the leaf-axils, the males and females usually on separate plants. Petals and stamens four to six. Fruit although commonly called a berry, really a drupe, usually red or black, with a thin, fleshy outer layer, surrounding one of several nutlets—generally termed seeds.

The most valuable hollies are undoubtedly those with evergreen foliage, but the deciduous ones, especially those earlier known under the generic name of *Prinos*, are sometimes handsome in fruit. Owing to the frequently unisexual character of the plants, these often fail to appear if both sexes are not grown. All the species like a moist, loamy soil. (For propagation, see under *I. aquifolium*.)

The standard work on *Ilex* is: T. Loesener, 'Monographia Aquifoliacearum', *Nov. Act. Acad. Caes. Leop.-Carol. Nat. Cur.*, Vol. 78 (1901), pp. 8–500, and Vol. 89 (1908), pp. 20–312. For the species of China, this is superseded by: S.-Y. Hu, 'The Genus *Ilex* in China', *Journ. Arn. Arb.*, Vol. 30 (1949), pp. 283–344 and pp. 348–387, and Vol. 31 (1950), pp. 39–80, 214–40 and 242–63.

I. × ALTACLARENSIS [Loud.] Dallim.

I. aquifolium var. *altaclerense* Loud.; *I. perado* Hort., not Ait.; *I. maderensis* Hort., not Lam.

A group of hybrids between *I. aquifolium* and *I. perado* (or its var. *platyphylla*), to which belong some of the finest of hardy evergreen small trees and shrubs. The early history of the group is not known for certain, but *I. perado* was originally grown in greenhouses for its decorative fruits, and the first-generation hybrids were probably raised from these female plants, fertilised deliberately or accidentally by pollen of the common holly. The fact that some of the early hybrids were named as varieties of *I. perado* or *I. maderensis* (a synonym of *I. perado*) suggests that this species was the seed-parent of the original crosses. Once these first-generation hybrids, which are hardy, had become established in gardens, back-crosses would have been raised from females such as 'Hendersonii', pollinated by the common holly, and certainly some of the hybrids are the result of deliberate crossing. In this way a diverse assemblage of hollies has arisen, and the boundary between *I. × altaclarensis* and *I. aquifolium* has become rather blurred. But the majority of the group are easily enough distinguished from the common holly by their larger leaves, flowers, and fruits, and by their great vigour and robustness.

'ALTACLARENSIS'.—This cultivar name, or 'Highclere', would belong to the holly, assumed to be a hybrid, that was distributed by Loddiges' nursery and described by Loudon as having 'Leaves broad, thin and flat' (*Arb. et Frut. Brit.* (1838), Vol. 2, p. 507). Whether this clone is still in cultivation it is impossible to say. The holly described by Dallimore under the name *I. altaclarense* was said by him to be a male similar to 'Hodginsii', and the tree at Kew which is believed to be the one he had in mind is scarcely distinguishable from 'Hodginsii', if at all.

"BALEARICA".—Some of the hollies once in the trade as *I. aq. balearica* appear to have been hybrids similar to "Maderensis", but the specimens which Moore put under this name are not uniform, and one, received from the Lawson Company as *I. aq. hodginsii*, is clearly 'Hendersonii'. The old clone to which the name *I. aq. balearica* originally belonged may have been a hybrid, but it was accepted by Loesener as a variant of the true Balearic holly and is further discussed under *I. aq.* var. *balearica*.

'BELGICA AUREA'.—Leaves quite flat, ovate-lanceolate to almost elliptic, 3¼ to 4 in. long, 1½ to 1¾ in. wide, edged with pale yellow; centre rich green shading to grey-green; margins with a variable number of slender spine-teeth, some leaves entire. Female. A very handsome holly raised in Holland by Koster and Son and first shown by them in 1908. It was originally distributed under the erroneous name "*I. perado aurea*" (*Dendroflora*, No. 8, p. 30).

'CAMELLIIFOLIA'.—Young wood, petioles, and base of midrib beneath purplish. Leaves dark burnished green, oblong, the largest 5 in. long, 2 in. wide, mostly without spines but a few with one to eight spines. Female, with rather large, dark red berries. It makes a fine specimen. In 'MARNOCKII' the leaves are of similar outline and toothing, but curiously twisted just above the middle. Also female.

'GOLDEN KING'.—A sport from 'Hendersonii' having the leaves margined with rich gold. Like the parent it is female, and has leaves of similar shape. The sport occurred at the Bangholm nursery of the Lawson Company shortly before 1876. At the dissolution sale of that famous Scottish nursery, which took place in 1888, the entire stock including the mother plant was bought by Little and Ballantyne, and it was they who named it 'Golden King'. The Lawson Company was one of the many nurseries who used the name *I. aquifolium hodginsii* for what is now called 'Hendersonii' and they originally named the sport *I. aq. hodginsii aurea*. 'Golden King' appears to be the same as the holly which Dallimore called 'King Edward VII'.

'HENDERSONII'.—Leaves mostly oblong-elliptic, with a well-marked 'shoulder', rather dull green above, with the lateral veins impressed, the margins entire or with a few scattered spines. A female, with large fruits, not very freely borne. This holly was raised by Thomas Hodgins, nurseryman of Dunganstown, Ireland, early in the 19th century. The Lawson Company of Edinburgh appear to have received scions direct from Hodgins and distributed this holly, as did some other nurserymen, under the name *I. aquifolium hodginsii*, but the cultivar-name 'Hodginsii' (q.v.) is now used for another quite different hybrid holly also raised by Hodgins. The now established name 'Hendersonii' starts in the catalogue of the Handsworth nursery of Fisher and Holmes (later Fisher, Son, and Sibray), who received propagating material from Shepherd, Curator of the Liverpool Botanic Garden, and named their stock after a friend of Shepherd (Elwes and Henry, *Tr. Gt. Brit. & Irel.*, Vol. 7, p. 1714). The fact that Hodgins raised two hybrid hollies, both of which were named after him by one or another nurseryman, has been the cause of much confusion, though William Paul called attention to it as early as 1863.

'Hendersonii' is a vigorous holly of which there is a large specimen at Kew with a stout trunk and about 40 ft high. But in its foliage it is inferior to many other members of the *Altaclarensis* group. Its chief claim to fame is that it is the parent by sporting of 'Lawsoniana' and 'Golden King'.

'HODGINSII'.—Young stems purplish. Leaves broad-ovate or broad-elliptic, 3 to 4 in. long, 2¼ in. wide, broadly cuneate, rounded or truncate at the base, deep sea-green, with large, rather distant, triangular teeth; on old plants the teeth are mainly confined to the apical part of the leaf, and some leaves are entire. Male. This holly was raised by the nurseryman Thomas Hodgins of Dunganstown, Ireland, who, some time before 1836, sent it to Shepherd, curator of the Liverpool Botanic Garden. The Handsworth nursery of Fisher and Holmes received propagating material from there and distributed this holly as *I. aquifolium shepherdii*. But other nurserymen called it after its raiser, and 'Hodginsii' is now the established name for it (Elwes and Henry, *Tr. Gt. Br. & Irel.*, Vol. 7, p. 1713). See further under 'Hendersonii'.

'Hodginsii' soon became common in the industrial Midlands because of its ability to withstand a heavily polluted atmosphere. But even under normal conditions it is a valuable evergreen, making a fine pyramidal specimen up to 50 ft high.

'LAWSONIANA'.—Leaves dull dark green at the edge, with a central variegation of gold and brighter green. A sport from 'Hendersonii', raised by the Lawson Company, Edinburgh, shortly before 1869. Unfortunately it is very apt to sport back to the green-leaved parent.

"MADERENSIS".—*I. maderensis* Lamarck is a synonym of *I. perado*, the Madeira holly, but in gardens the name came to be used for hybrids, probably seedlings of the true *I. perado*. Moore's description is based on specimens from a number of nurseries and judging by the leaves from these preserved at Kew, they may have represented a single clone. Leaves plane, ovate or ovate-oblong, short-acuminate 3 to 3½ in. long, about 1¾ in. wide, fairly regularly edged with slender spines lying in the plane of the leaf and pointing forward. According to Dallimore, this variety is male. In 'MADERENSIS VARIEGATA' the leaves have a central variegation of gold and bright green.

'MUNDYI'.—Largest leaves 4 in. by 2½ in., dullish green, oval or roundish oval, the margins set regularly with slender spines, the surface rugose. Male. Another hybrid holly of similar character, also male, is 'ATKINSONII'. This has larger, very rugose leaves of a deeper green, up to 4½ in. long, 2¼ in. wide, with somewhat larger spines. Both are in the Kew collection.

'NIGRESCENS'.—Stems purplish green. Leaves not undulate, ovate to broad elliptic, 3 in. long, 2¼ to 2½ in. wide, entire or occasionally with regular, forward-pointing teeth. There is a fine specimen at Kew about 35 ft high with a stout trunk. This, like other similar specimens in the collection, is male, but there is reason to believe that the original 'Nigrescens' was female.

'NOBILIS'.—According to Moore's description and specimen this is very similar to 'Hodginsii', but with the leaves more strongly toothed. The two varieties may have become confused, for the firm William Barron and Son of Derby said in their catalogue for 1875 that their *I. aq. nobilis* was the same as what other nurserymen were selling as *hodginsii*. There are male plants at Westonbirt, Glos., which may belong to this variety; the leaves are darker than in 'Hodginsii'.

"PLATYPHYLLA".—The epithet *platyphylla* seems to have been applied to various hybrid hollies of the *altaclarensis* group, some male, some female. They have been confused with the Canary Island holly *I. perado* var. *platyphylla*, of which they may have been seedlings. This confusion, remarked on by Goeppert well over a century ago, still persists. These hybrids are probably first-generation crosses, with flattish, broad-ovate or broad-elliptic, shortly spine-toothed leaves.

'SHEPHERDII'.—The holly distributed by the Handsworth nursery under the name *I. aq. shepherdii* is 'Hodginsii' (q.v.). The holly sold by the Knap Hill nursery under the same name was quite different. Judging from Moore's description it was similar to 'Maderensis', but with longer spines. It is no longer grown at Knap Hill.

'WILSONII'.—Branchlets green. Leaves broad-elliptic or obovate, up to 5¼ in. long, 3 in. wide, rich fairly glossy green and slightly concave above, with conspicuous lighter green veins which are raised on the underside, margins slightly wavy or flat, with scattered forward-pointing teeth. Female. A very handsome holly, attaining a height of 30 ft or more, raised at the Handsworth nursery. F.C.C. 1899. On old trees some of the leaves are quite entire. Henry suggests that this is a renaming of the variety which the Handsworth nursery originally called *I. aq. princeps*, of which the parentage was given as *I. a. nigrescens* pollinated by a male seedling from *balearica*, which seems very probable (*Tr. Gt. Brit. & Irel.*, Vol. 7, p. 1713; *Gard. Chron.*, Vol. 13 (2nd series), p. 45). The name is believed to commemorate G. F. Wilson, who presented the Wisley property to The Royal Horticultural Society.

'W. J. BEAN'.—A slow-growing female variety, free-fruiting, which inclines to the common holly in its rather small, strongly undulated and spiny leaves. It was raised by the Handsworth nurseries and the plant at Kew was received from them in 1929.

I. AQUIFOLIUM L.   COMMON HOLLY

An evergreen tree up to 80 ft high, of very leafy, much-branched habit, forming naturally a dense pyramidal mass; branchlets often clothed more or less with minute dark down. Leaves glossy dark green, 1 to 3 in. long, ¾ to 2½ in. wide, very variable in size, outline, and toothing. Ordinary seed-raised young trees have very wavy leaves with large, triangular, outstanding teeth ½ in. long; but as they increase in height the leaves of the upper branches become less spiny, until finally the tops of good-sized trees will be found almost wholly furnished with quite entire leaves. Flowers small, dull white, short-stalked, fragrant; produced during May and June, clustered in the leaf-axils. Berries round, red, $\frac{1}{4}$ in. diameter, containing two to four nutlets. The common holly may be either male, female, or bisexual.

Native of Europe (including Britain, where it is found wild in all parts except the north-east of Scotland) and W. Asia. The common holly is on the whole the most useful of evergreen trees and shrubs. For providing shelter nothing else equals it, because of its habit of keeping dense near the ground; and during the dark months a holly tree well laden with its bright red fruit is one of the handsomest and most cheerful objects our winter landscape provides. It makes the best of all evergreen hedges. [PLATE 56

The holly does not transplant well, and unless it be removed with a considerable amount of soil attached to its roots, this operation can only be done safely either about the end of September or in May, when root-activity has commenced. If the roots have been injured in transplanting, it is a good plan to reduce proportionately the top growth by as much as one-half (see chapter on Transplanting in Vol. I). The common holly should be raised from seed. Being slow of germination it is advisable, as with *Crataegus*, to mix the berries with sand or fine earth in a heap, which should be exposed for a year to all weathers and turned occasionally. This rots the outer covering and allows the two to four nuts or seeds each fruit contains to separate. They are then sown (soil and seed together) shallowly. The varieties do not come true from seed, and have to be propagated by cuttings or by grafting. Cuttings are best made of thin side twigs about 4 in. long, with a heel attached, and placed in mild heat. They will also take root under a handlight out-of-doors, but are slower. Grafting is done in spring on the seedlings of the type.

Cultivated, as it has been, for hundreds of years in Britain, the common holly has sported into an enormous number of varieties, most of them handsome, some curious, and a few worthless. An unfortunate practice, started long ago when they were few in number, has obtained of giving them cumbersome Latin names when colloquial ones would have served quite as well. In the 18th century many variegated hollies were grown under such pleasant names as Eale's Holly, The British Holly, Glory of the East Holly, Fine Phyllis Holly, Painted Lady Holly. These and many other sorts were described shortly by Miller in the early editions of his *Dictionary*. Most were still in the trade later in the 18th century but the old names were discarded when Latin epithets became the fashion.

The most authoritative work on holly cultivars is: 'The Common Holly and its Varieties' by Thomas Moore, published in fourteen parts in *Gardeners' Chronicle*, 1874–6. Dallimore's treatment in *Holly, Yew and Box* (1908) is, with acknowledgement, largely based on Moore's work. The following selection is mainly confined to varieties in commerce or represented in the Kew collection, but many others, not treated, may still be found in old collections.

It may be remarked that all variegated hollies whose variegation is in the centre of the leaf have a strong tendency to 'run out', that is, to revert to the green sorts from which they originally sprang, and it is necessary to cut out the green twigs as they appear. The marginally variegated ones do not show such a tendency.

cv. 'AMBER'.—Berries bronzy yellow. Raised by Messrs Hillier.

cv. 'ANGUSTIFOLIA'.—It is clear from Moore's account that the name

T S—P

I. a. angustifolia was in use for three similar hollies, all of narrow habit. The one he considered to be the true variety has lanceolate leaves 1½ in. long, ½ in. wide, with a longish entire point and five to seven narrow, rather weak spines lying in the plane of the leaf. In 'Myrtifolia' the spines are broader and the apex less elongated, while in 'Serratifolia' the apex is elongated as in 'Angustifolia' but the blade concavely folded and the spines divaricating. But all three hollies were sent out as *I. a. angustifolia* by one nurseryman or another.

cv. 'ARGENTEA LONGIFOLIA'.—Young wood purplish. Leaves elliptic or elliptic-ovate, 2½ to 3 in. long, strongly armed, with an irregular mostly rather narrow band of creamy white. In the Kew collection.

cv. 'ARGENTEA MARGINATA'.—Young wood green. Leaves broadly ovate, up to 3 in. long, 2 in. wide, dark green in the centre, with a silver edge. Female. Common in cultivation.

cv. 'ARGENTEA MEDIO-PICTA'. SILVER MILKMAID HOLLY.—Young bark green. Leaves ovate, cuneate at base, up to 2 in. long, margins very wavy and strongly toothed, blades dark green with a blotch of creamy white which is often confined to the base of the leaf. Apt to revert. Moore described two other white-blotched hollies, both differing from this in having entire or few-spined leaves. They were 'ARGENTEA PICTA' and 'LACTEA PICTA', the latter characterised by reddish-brown young wood.

cv. 'ARGENTEA PENDULA'. PERRY'S WEEPING.—Branches pendulous; young stems purplish. Leaves 2½ to 3 in. long, green mottled with grey-green at the centre, with a broad margin of creamy white. Female. Moore also described 'PERRYANA MAJOR', in which the principal branches were erect, the sprays pendulous.

cv. 'ARGENTEA REGINA'. See 'Silver Queen'.

cv. 'AUREA MARGINATA'.—The designation *aurea marginata* or *marginata aurea* has probably been used for many hollies with gold-edged leaves. The one described by Moore had leaves up to 3 in. long, stoutly and unevenly spined, with a narrow edge of gold best developed near the tips. It was female, but not free fruiting, and inferior to 'Golden Queen' (q.v.).

cv. 'AUREA MARGINATA OVATA'.—Leaves roundish ovate, with large regular spines and a broad edge of pale yellow.

cv. 'AUREA MEDIO-PICTA'. GOLDEN MILKMAID.—The holly described by Moore under this name had small leaves with a central blotch of yellow, strongly developed spines and a very pronounced spiny tip. It was sold by the Knap Hill nurseries as 'Gold Milkmaid' and by others as *I. a. aurea picta*. A very similar one, included in 'Aurea Medio-picta' by Dallimore, was sold by the Handsworth nurseries of Fisher and Holmes. In 'AUREA PICTA LATIFOLIA' the leaves were broadly ovate and the spines mostly confined to the upper half of the leaf. But there are numerous other hollies with gold-blotched leaves, usually known as Golden Milkmaid hollies, but without distinctive names.

cv. 'AUREA PENDULA'.—A pendulous variety with purple bark, the dark green centre of the leaf surrounded by a margin of gold.

cv. 'AUREA REGINA'. See 'Golden Queen'.

f. BACCIFLAVA (West.) Rehd. *I. a. fructu-luteo* Dallim.—Fruits yellow.

var. BALEARICA (Desf.) Loes. *I. balearica* Desf.—The Balearic or Minorca holly, as it is called, is said to differ from the common holly only in having plane, entire or sparsely toothed leaves. The name *I. a. balearica* was, however, used in gardens in Loudon's time and later for a female holly, propagated by grafting, which had yellowish green, rather thick leaves, the margins sparsely spine-toothed, not undulate but with the blade rather obliquely concave above and with the reticulations prominent beneath. Loesener accepted this holly as belonging to var. *balearica*, while remarking on its reticulated leaves. This holly was used in breeding the hybrid called 'Princeps' (see under *I. altaclarensis* 'Wilsonii') and similarly shaped leaves occur in other of the hybrids. The name *I. a. balearica* has also been used for hollies which are not the same as the old *balearica* and may be hybrids of the *Altaclarensis* group.

var. CHINENSIS Loes. *I. centrochinensis* Hu—This variety, perhaps better treated as a species, differs from the European holly in having the branches of the male inflorescences one-flowered instead of three-flowered, in the very short fruit-stalks, and in the differently sculptured nutlets. It has a local distribution on the borders between Hupeh and Szechwan and was described from a specimen collected by Henry near the Ichang Gorge. Said to have been introduced by Wilson in 1901.

cv. 'CILIATA'.—Leaves ovate to lanceolate, 1½ to 2 in. long, with long, slender rather soft spines. Some leaves entire. Of rather narrowly pyramidal habit (*I. aquifolium pyramidalis* Nichols.).

cv. 'CILIATA MAJOR'.—Leaves ovate-elliptic with slender spines pointing forward in the plane of the leaf; some leaves entire. Female.

cv. 'CRASSIFOLIA'. LEATHER-LEAF HOLLY.—An extraordinary variety, with thick, purple young branches. Leaves 1½ to 2 in. long, ¾ to ⅞ in. wide, very thick and leathery, the triangular spines ⅛ to ¼ in. long. It has no beauty, but is remarkably curious. Female.

cv. 'CRISPA'.—Bark purple. Leaves spirally twisted and contorted, some having several spines, but mostly with few or none. One of the least ornamental. 'CRISPA PICTA' is a form of it, blotched with yellow in the centre. Male.

cv. 'DONNINGTONENSIS'.—An elegant variety with purple bark, glossy, dark purplish green narrow-oblong leaves, with a lance-shaped apex, 2 in. long, ½ to ¾ in. wide, with a few large spines or none. Male.

cv. 'ELEGANTISSIMA'.—Leaves oblong or elliptic, 2 to 2½ in. long, with divaricate spines. Margins creamy white; centre grey-green and dark green. Young wood green. Also known as *I. a. argentea marginata elegantissima*.

cv. 'FEROX'. HEDGEHOG HOLLY.—Bark purple. Leaves small, and besides having the usual marginal spines, armed with curious clusters or bands of them on the surface. Male. 'FEROX ARGENTEA' is similar, but the spines and margin are white. 'FEROX AUREA', leaves with the spines and margin green, the centre yellow.   [PLATE 55

cv. 'FISHERI'.—Leaves dark green, leathery, up to 4 in. long and 2¾ in. wide, formidably armed with large spines. Male. Raised by the Handsworth nurseries.

cv. 'FLAVESCENS'. MOONLIGHT HOLLY.—Leaves as in the common holly, but suffused with yellow, especially when young. 'AURANTIACA', also known as the bronze holly, is similar but with the leaves flushed golden bronze.

cv. 'GOLDEN QUEEN'.—This holly, also known as 'Aurea Regina', is the commonest of the golden-margined sorts. Young wood green. Leaves broad-ovate, up to 3½ in. long and 2 in. wide, strongly spined, with a regular margin of gold; some leaves golden in one half or completely so. Male. In 'AUREA REGINA NIGRA' the young wood is purple and the golden margin narrower. 'AUREA MARGINATA LATIFOLIA' is similar to this. Both these varieties are female.

cv. 'GRANDIS'.—Leaves up to 3 by 2 in., strongly spined but fairly flat, with a broad margin of creamy white; centre of leaf green splashed grey-green. On some leaves the ends are mainly cream and grey. Young wood blackish purple. A very handsome holly.

cv. 'HANDSWORTHENSIS'.—Leaves ovate, about 1½ in. long and half as wide, with large regular forward-pointing spines, margin slightly undulate. Of compact habit.

cv. 'HANDSWORTH NEW SILVER'.—One of the best of the white-margined hollies. Bark purple. Leaves elliptic-oblong, up to 3½ in. long, very dark green, the margin clear white, armed with large spines mostly lying in the plane of the leaf. Female.

cv. 'HASTATA'.—A curious green-leaved variety of no beauty. Bark purple. Leaves ½ to 1½ in. long, narrow, the basal part armed with disproportionately large spines. Loesener named it *I. aq.* var. *kewensis* in his monograph on *Ilex*.

f. HETEROPHYLLA (Ait.) Loes.—Leaves entire or sparsely toothed. There are several clones of this nature, of both sexes. A free-fruiting selection has been named 'PYRAMIDALIS'.

cv. 'J. C. VAN THOL'.—Leaves dark, rather dull green, oblong-ovate or oblong-elliptic, 1¾ to 2¼ in. long, sparsely toothed or entire, slightly bullate owing to the impressing of the lateral veins. Fruits large, bright red, freely borne. Raised in Holland at the end of the last century and often known as *I. a. polycarpa laevigata.* In 'GOLDEN VAN THOL' the leaves are margined with yellow; it is a sport from the normal green form.

cv. 'LATISPINA'.—Bark purple. Leaves green, ovate, 2 to 3 in. long, marked by a long, slender, deflexed point, and one or more irregularly placed, slender spines on the margin, ¼ to ¾ in. long; very distinct.

cv. 'LAURIFOLIA'.—A tall-growing sort with dark, glossy leaves which are mostly unarmed but occasionally with a few spines, 2 to 3 in. long and 1 to 1½ in. wide. Male. In 'LAURIFOLIA AUREA' the leaves are similar, but edged with yellow.

cv. 'LICHTENTHALII'.—Leaves narrow-oblong, almost three times as long as wide, dark glossy green but pale green along the midrib and margins.

cv. 'MADAME BRIOT'.—A continental variety already in commerce in Britain in the 1870s. Young stems purple. Leaves narrow-ovate, up to 3 in. long, 1½ in. wide, strongly armed, with a margin of gold and a centre mottled with gold and light green. Female.

cv. 'MONSTROSA'.—Resembling 'Latispina', with the apex and spines of the same character, but with more of the latter—often four or five down each side.

cv. 'MURICATA'.—Leaves ovate or oblong-ovate, up to 2½ in. long, not much undulated, margined with a rather bilious shade of yellowish green.

cv. 'MYRTIFOLIA'.—Leaves small, mostly about 1½ in. long by ½ to ⅝ in. wide, well armed with slender spines mostly lying in the plane of the leaf; some leaves larger and less spiny. Male. 'MYRTIFOLIA AUREA' has similar leaves, but with a fairly well-marked margin of gold; its young bark is purple. In 'MYRTIFOLIA AUREOMACULATA' the leaves have an irregular central variegation of yellow; young bark purple.

cv. 'OVATA'.—A very distinct and pleasing sort; bark purple. Leaves especially thick and leathery, dark glossy green, 1½ to 2½ in. long, ovate, very regularly armed on the margin with short outstanding spines. Male. There is an attractive variant of this—'OVATA AUREA'—whose leaves are narrowly margined with gold.

f. PENDULA (Loud.) Rehd.—The pendulous holly described by Loudon in 1842 was found in a garden in Derby and propagated by William Barron, who had a nursery at Elvaston Castle. But other pendulous trees have been recorded. The pendulous green-leaved hollies at Kew are female and make dense specimens of conical outline.

cv. 'PYRAMIDALIS'. See under f. *heterophylla*.

cv. 'RECURVA'.—A dwarf kind with small, very spiny leaves, dark green, ovate, 1 to 1¾ in. long, the midrib much decurved, the blade also twisted. Male.

cv. 'SCOTICA'.—A very distinct sort, with lustrous deep green oval leaves up to 3 in. long, remarkable for the entire absence of marginal spines; the apex is sometimes spine-tipped, usually blunt. Female. In 'SCOTICA AUREA' the leaves are margined with gold. 'SCOTICA AUREOPICTA', a sport raised by Paul of Cheshunt, has a central blotch of yellow.

cv. 'SILVER QUEEN'.—Young wood purplish, the variegation clear and broad. Male. Also known as 'ARGENTEA REGINA'.

cv. 'SMITHII'.—Of the same type as 'Donningtonensis', but without the intense purple bark and purple tinge in the leaves of that variety. Male.

cv. 'WATERERANA'.—A compact kind, usually wider than high when young but at length developing a leader and becoming of conical habit, with a broad base. Leaves often quite without marginal spines or with only a few, dark green with a rich yellow border. Male. There is a fine example at Kew near the Stone Pine, and another in the Knap Hill nursery, where it was raised.

I. CASSINE L.   DAHOON

I. caroliniana Mill.

A small evergreen tree to about 40 ft high in the wild; twigs slender, glabrous. Leaves leathery, 2 to 4 in. long, oblong or oblanceolate, rarely obovate, acute or sometimes rounded at the apex, cuneate at the base, almost glabrous on both surfaces when mature, the upper glossy, margins entire or with a few sharp mucronate teeth near the apex; stalk to $\frac{1}{2}$ in. long, stout. Flowers borne in stalked clusters in the axils of the current season's growth (occasionally on that of the previous year), the male and female on different trees; peduncles up to $\frac{3}{4}$ in. long, those of female plants bearing one to three flowers. Fruits about $\frac{1}{4}$ in. wide, red to almost yellow. Nutlets ribbed.

A native of the south-eastern USA in swamps and by rivers, north to Virginia, west to Texas; also of Cuba. Although introduced in 1726 (by Mark Catesby) it has never been common in Britain, most of the plants grown under the name being *I. vomitoria* (*I. cassine* Walt., not L.). Nothing useful can be said about either its hardiness or its garden value in Britain.

I. MYRTIFOLIA Walt. *I. cassine* var. *myrtifolia* (Walt.) Sarg.—This species is closely allied to the preceding but differs in its smaller leaves $\frac{3}{8}$ to 1 in. long (rarely more), $\frac{3}{8}$ to $\frac{3}{4}$ in. wide, with the midrib very prominent beneath, and by its usually solitary fruits. It is said to have a more coastal distribution than *I. cassine*.

I. CILIOSPINOSA Loes.

I. bioritsensis var. *ciliospinosa* (Loes.) Comber

An evergreen shrub up to 12 or 15 ft high; young shoots covered with short down. Leaves leathery, ovate to oval, slender-pointed, spine-tipped, rounded to wedge-shaped at the base, spiny toothed, 1 to 2 in. long, $\frac{1}{2}$ to 1 in. wide, dark dull green above, pale below, quite glabrous. Berries egg-shaped, $\frac{1}{4}$ in. long, red, containing two stones; the berry is usually solitary in the axil of the leaves on a stalk $\frac{1}{8}$ in. long.

Native of W. Szechwan, China; discovered by Wilson in 1904, introduced in 1908. This is a neat, small-leaved holly, erect and slender when small, and appears to be quite hardy at Kew. The specific name refers to the rather numerous, slender, forward-pointing teeth of the leaves, which are not particularly distinctive in this respect. It is considered to be related to *I. dipyrena* but is well distinguished by its much smaller stature, smaller, darker green leaves and round (not angular), more downy shoots.

It is hardy at Kew, where there is a multi-stemmed plant in the bed of *I. verticillata*, about 16 ft high.

I. CORALLINA Franch.

An evergreen tree to about 35 ft high in the wild, glabrous in all its parts. Leaves leathery, glossy above, dull beneath, ovate-lanceolate to elliptic, 2 to 6 in. long, $\frac{5}{8}$ to 2 in. wide, rounded or broadly wedge-shaped at the base, acute or shortly acuminate at the apex, margins bluntly toothed (but spiny on young plants); petioles $\frac{3}{16}$ to $\frac{3}{8}$ in. long. Male and female inflorescences both consisting of dense axillary clusters. Fruits red, about $\frac{1}{8}$ in. wide, but numerous in each cluster; nutlets four, wrinkled and faintly ribbed.

Native of W. and S.W. China; introduced by Wilson from Hupeh around 1900, when collecting for Veitch's nursery (seed number 781), and later reintroduced by Forrest from Yunnan. There is an example at Trewithen in Cornwall, 30 ft high (1971).

I. FORRESTII Comber—This species was described by H. F. Comber in 1933 from material collected by Forrest, some of which had previously been placed under *I. corallina*. It somewhat resembles that species in foliage, but the leaves are mostly broadest above the middle, with a more pronounced acuminate tip, and are usually toothed only in the upper part. The fruits are small as in *I. corallina*, but the nutlets are smooth and five to seven in number. Also the flowers usually have five or six petals and sepals, against four in *I. corallina*.

I. CORNUTA Lindl.   HORNED HOLLY

An evergreen shrub 8 to 10 ft, perhaps more high, of bushy, dense, rounded habit, and usually wider than high; young shoots glabrous, pale, and somewhat angular the first year. Leaves leathery, dark, glossy green, 1½ to 4 in. long, 1 to 3 in. wide, of variable shape, but usually more or less rectangular, with four large spines at the corners; there is, in addition, always a terminal spine usually much decurved, and frequently one or two pairs of smaller spines at the sides. The number of spines therefore varies from five to nine, and they are rigid and needle-pointed; but on the upper branches of old specimens the spines are fewer or absent, as in the common holly; stalk ⅛ in. or less long. Flowers small, dull white, produced in axillary clusters in April. Fruits round, red, larger than in common holly, borne on a stalk ⅓ to ⅝ in. long. *Bot. Mag.*, t. 5059.

Native of China and Korea; found by Fortune near Shanghai, and sent to him to Standish of Bagshot in 1846. It is still a rather uncommon plant, although quite hardy in the London district. Of comparatively slow growth, and of neat compact habit, it is suitable for positions where many evergreens would soon become too large. Its distinct and handsome foliage also makes it interesting, but it bears fruit only shyly.

There is a pair of specimens at Kew, one on either side of the Australian House, the larger 7 ft high and 12 ft across; in the garden of the Wood Museum there is a plant 10 ft high and 12 ft wide.

cv. 'BURFORDII'.—Leaves with a terminal spine, otherwise entire or almost so. Free-fruiting. A handsome evergreen raised in the USA.

var. FORTUNEI (Lindl.) Hu *I. fortunei* Lindl.—According to Dr S.-Y. Hu, in her monograph on Chinese hollies, the essential difference between this variety and the type is that the branches of the male inflorescence each bear three flowers and that the fruit-stalks are longer (½ to ¾ in. long). Introduced by Fortune to Glendinning's nursery, Turnham Green, in 1853, but possibly also in cultivation from seeds collected by Wilson in W. Hupeh. This variety is as variable in leaf as the type. According to Lindley the plants from Fortune's seeds had the appearance of 'a very broad-leaved, entire-leaved European Holly', but in the plants found by Wilson the leaves were spinose (Hu in *Journ. Arn. Arb.*, Vol. 30 (1949), pp. 356–7; Lindley in *Gard. Chron.* (1857), p. 868).

The following hybrids of *I. cornuta* were raised in the USA and are available in commerce in Britain:

I. (*cornuta* × *pernyi*).—Here belong 'JOHN T. MORRIS', of dense vigorous habit with leaves intermediate between those of the parents; and 'LYDIA MORRIS', of more open habit, nearer to *I. pernyi*.

I. (*aquifolium* × *cornuta*) 'NELLIE STEVENS'.—Leaves bullate, slightly glossy, with two or three teeth on each side. Free-fruiting.

I. CRENATA Thunb. [PLATE 58

An evergreen shrub usually 5 to 9 ft high, or a small tree of very dense, rigid, compact habit; young shoots angular, and covered with minute dark down. Leaves crowded, elliptic to oblong-lanceolate or obovate, ½ to ¾ in. long, ⅛ to ¼ in. wide, tapered at the base to a short stalk, sharply pointed and with a few incurved teeth at the margins, glossy green, and of hard texture, dotted beneath with pellucid glands. Male flowers in cymose clusters, female solitary, borne in the leaf-axils of the current season's shoots, dull white. Fruits black.

Native of Japan and Korea; introduced to Europe about 1864. It is not easy to ascertain what is the typical form of this holly, but the one above described is what is commonly regarded as such—very distinct in its close habit and small leaves, and rarely more than 3 or 4 ft high.

cv. 'CONVEXA'.—A clone of Japanese origin making a dense bush broader than high. Leaves elliptic, glossy, about ½ in. long, convex above, concave beneath, somewhat bullate.

cv. 'GOLDEN GEM'.—Leaves golden. Habit low and spreading. The colouring is best developed in a sunny position.

cv. 'HELLERI'.—A low, dense, spreading bush. Leaves dark green, elliptic, up to about ¼ in. long, with a few teeth on either side. Raised in the USA.

f. LATIFOLIA (Goldring) Rehd. *I. crenata* var. *latifolia* Goldring—A small tree occasionally 20 ft high, with box-like oval leaves ½ to 1¼ in. long, ¼ to ⅝ in. wide, minutely round-toothed. Fruits round, ¼ in. wide, on stalks ¼ in. or less long. It was introduced by Fortune and is probably of garden origin.

f. LONGIFOLIA (Goldring) Rehd. *I. crenata* var. *longifolia* Goldring—Leaves narrowly lanceolate.

cv. 'MARIESII'.—A very stiff-habited, extraordinarily dwarf holly, with stunted twigs hidden by orbicular or broadly ovate leaves about ¼ in. wide, sometimes entire, sometimes with a pair of shallow teeth near the apex. Fruits black, on stalks 1/12 in. long. Interesting for the rock garden as a pigmy. Introduced for Messrs Veitch by Maries about 1879. It only grows part of an inch a year. (*I. nummularioides* Franch. & Sav.; *I. crenata* var. *nummularioides* (Franch. & Sav.) Yatabe.)

var. PALUDOSA (Nakai) Hara *I. radicans* Nakai; *I. radicans* var. *paludosa* Nakai—Of prostrate habit. Found wild in swampy situations.

cv. 'STOKES'.—Of low, dense, rounded habit.

cv. 'VARIEGATA' ('Aureovariegata').—Leaves of the same shape and size as the normal form, but spotted or blotched with yellow, sometimes wholly of that colour.

I. crenata is a popular shrub in Japan. It is used largely for clipping into fantastic shapes, also as a dwarf hedge. So dense and hard are some of these flat-topped hedges that a man can walk along the top of them. It is also much grown in the United States, and for a full account of the garden varieties cultivated there see the article by D. Wyman in *Arnoldia*, Vol. 20 (1960), pp. 41–6.

I. MUTCHAGARA Mak. *I. crenata* var. *mutchagara* (Mak.) Ohwi—Branchlets angled. Leaves rather thin, up to 2 in. long, broadly lanceolate to obovate-oblong, bluntly pointed. A close ally of *I. crenata*, described from the Ryukyu Archipelago.

I. CYRTURA Merrill

An evergreen tree already about 50 feet high in cultivation; bark almost smooth, grey; branchlets pendulous at the tip, glabrous. Leaves leathery oblong- or elliptic-lanceolate or oblanceolate to broadly oblanceolate, $3\frac{1}{2}$ to $6\frac{1}{2}$ in. long, $1\frac{3}{8}$ to $2\frac{1}{4}$ in. wide, acuminately tapered at the apex to a slender, often falcate tip, broadly cuneate at the base, margins serrate throughout; main lateral veins seven to eleven, making an angle of 50° to 70° with the midrib; leaf-stalk $\frac{3}{8}$ to $\frac{3}{4}$ in. long. Male inflorescence umbel-like or paniculate, the axis stout, $\frac{1}{12}$ to $\frac{3}{8}$ in. long, the branchlets often three-flowered; flowers on stalks, $\frac{1}{8}$ in. or very slightly more long; petals four, oblong, about $\frac{1}{8}$ in. long, united at the base. Female inflorescence of similar form to the male, but the axis elongating in the fruiting stage to a length of about $\frac{3}{4}$ in. and the branchlets usually one-flowered; petals of female flowers broadly oblong, about $\frac{1}{12}$ in. long, free; ovary globose-ovoid, with a four-lobed, disk-like stigma. Fruits red, globose, about $\frac{3}{16}$ in. wide, with four nutlets, lined and grooved on the back.

I. cyrtura is now considered to be the correct name for a puzzling holly cultivated at Trewithen in Cornwall, where there is a group of seven trees of which one measures $51 \times 3\frac{1}{2}$ ft (1971), the others being of about the same size as this. There can be little doubt that they were raised from seeds collected by Forrest in Yunnan or some adjacent area, but there is some doubt concerning the field-number under which the seeds were sent. They were originally grown under the name "*I. forrestii*" but are not the holly described by Comber under that name; they have also been incorrectly identified as *I. ficoidea*. In many respects they agree with *I. melanotricha* (q.v.), but that species has leaves narrower in proportion to their length, the base more narrowly cuneate, the margins less conspicuously toothed or almost entire, and the main lateral veins making a narrower angle with the midrib (about 45°).

Recently, however, material from Trewithen was examined by Dr Hu of the Arnold Arboretum, who identified it as *I. cyrtura*, a species described by Dr Merrill from a single specimen with female flowers collected by Kingdon Ward in the Adung Valley, Upper Burma. This is outside the area covered by Forrest's botanical explorations, but *I. subodorata* Hu, a species very closely allied to

I. cyrtura, and described in 1950, was found by him on the frontier between Burma and China in an area lying about 200 miles distant from the type-locality of *I. cyrtura.*

The Trewithen holly, as it might appropriately be called, has attained a greater height than any other exotic holly so far measured in British gardens, but is unlikely to thrive so well outside the milder and rainier parts of the country. A holly at Caerhays Castle, Cornwall, also probably belongs to *I. cyrtura.*

The above account is based on information kindly provided by Mr David Hunt of the Kew Herbarium, who concurs with Dr Hu's identification. The description is a shortened version of one made by him from material collected off the trees at Trewithen and from his personal observations.

I. DECIDUA Walt.
I. prinoides Ait.

A deciduous shrub usually 5 to 10 ft high, occasionally a small tree up to 30 ft in the southern parts of its habitat; shoots glabrous and covered with a grey bark. Leaves oval or narrowly obovate, tapered at both ends, often blunt at the apex, shallowly round-toothed, 1 to 2½ in. long, ⅓ to ¾ in. wide, of firm texture, glabrous except along the midrib; stalk downy, ⅛ to ⅓ in. long. The leaves are often crowded on short lateral spurs. Male flowers on slender stalks ½ in. long; females on shorter ones, clustered. Fruits round, orange to scarlet, ¼ in. in diameter; nutlets ribbed.

Native of the south-eastern and central United States; introduced in 1760. It occasionally bears a good crop of its berries, which are very persistent on the branches. The branches do not break into leaf until May, and the fruits formed the previous autumn are then still remaining. From the red-fruited *I. verticillata* and *I. laevigata,* this differs in having the nutlets many-ribbed; in the others they are smooth. Its habit of producing short spurs crowded with leaves and flowers also gives it a distinct aspect.

I. AMELANCHIER M. A. Curtis *I. dubia* Britton, Sterns and Poggenburg, not Weber—A rare species allied to the above, differing in its oblong leaves rugose beneath, solitary female flowers and dull red berries. It grows to about 6 ft high.

I. DIPYRENA Wall.   HIMALAYAN HOLLY

An evergreen tree ultimately 40 ft or more high, the angular young shoots and winter buds minutely downy. Leaves oblong or narrowly oval, tapered at the base, slenderly pointed and spine-tipped, 2 to 5 in. long, ⅝ to 1½ in. wide, dull, opaque green, leathery; stalk ¼ in. or less long. Like the common holly it is very spiny on the margins when young, but as the plant attains maturity the spines become fewer and finer, and ultimately the leaves of the upper branches become entire. Flowers very numerous, in dense round clusters in the leaf-axils. Fruits oval, red, large for a holly, commonly two-seeded.

Native of the Himalaya, Assam, Upper Burma, and Yunnan. Whilst inferior to the common holly as an ornamental evergreen, both in the lack of lustre on the foliage, and as rarely bearing fruit, this species is interesting and worth growing for its distinctness. It is perfectly hardy at Kew, where there is a handsome specimen in the Holly Avenue. The largest recorded in Britain grows at Linton Park, Kent; this measures 48 × 5¼ ft (1970). There are slightly

ILEX BEANII

smaller trees at Leonardslee and Wakehurst Place in Sussex. At Caerhays, Cornwall, there are two trees raised from seeds collected by Forrest in Yunnan (F.25362 and F.25424).

I. dipyrena varies in its leaves, which may sometimes be sparsely toothed or entire. The var. *paucispinosa* Loes., and var. *connexiva* W. W. Sm. are founded on such variations, but neither variety is recognised by Dr Hu in her monograph.

I. × BEANII Rehd. *I. elliptica* (Dallim.) Bean, not H. B. K.; *I. dipyrena* var. *elliptica* Dallim.—A hybrid between *I. dipyrena* and the common holly. It resembles the former in general appearance, the leaves being dull green, although shorter and comparatively broader.

I. FARGESII Franch.

An evergreen small tree up to 15 or 20 ft high, quite devoid of down in all its parts. Leaves narrow-oblong or narrowly oblanceolate, 2 to 5 in. long,

⅜ to 1⅛ in. wide, slenderly tapered and entire towards the base, more abruptly tapered towards the apex, where are a few incurved teeth, dull green; stalk ⅓ to ½ in. long, reddish. Fruits red, globose, often in threes or fours in the leaf-axils, ¼ in. diameter; stalk ⅛ in. long, reddish. *Bot. Mag.*, t. 9670.

Native of W. China, in the province of Szechwan; introduced by Wilson for Messrs Veitch in 1900. It is very distinct in its long, narrow, opaque leaves. In a sheltered situation it is quite hardy as far east as Sussex and is 26 ft high, 2 ft in girth at Caerhays, Cornwall (1966). A.M. 1926.

It is allied to *I. franchetiana*, which scarcely differs except in its shorter relatively broader leaves, and also to *I. melanotricha* and to *I. hookeri*. For these species see under *I. melanotricha*.

I. GENICULATA Maxim.

A deciduous shrub 5 to 8 ft high; young shoots angular, free from down. Leaves ovate to oval-lanceolate, toothed, with a long slender point and a rounded or broadly wedge-shaped base, 1½ to 2½ in. long, ¾ to 1¼ in. wide, downy only on the midrib and chief veins beneath; stalk ⅛ to ⅜ in. long. Fruits globose, cinnabar-red, ¼ in. wide, usually solitary on a very slender, purple-brown, pendulous, glabrous stalk ¾ to 1½ in. long.

Native of the mountains of Central Japan where, according to Wilson, it is everywhere rare. He writes: 'The first wild bush of this holly I had ever seen was about 6 ft high and as much in diameter, bearing thousands of its brilliantly coloured fruits suspended from slender stalks. I thought I had never seen, in fruit, a shrub so lovely.' It has been growing in the Arnold Arboretum, Mass., since 1894 and succeeds admirably there. It was added to the Kew collection in 1926, but apparently had not previously been in cultivation in this country. It belongs to the *Prinos* or deciduous section of hollies, which includes *I. verticillata* and *I. serrata*, but is distinct from all cultivated species in the length of its fruit-stalks. The specific name refers to a curious joint or 'knee' on the terminal half of these stalks, which marks the place whence abortive flowers have fallen. When these remain on and develop, as they occasionally do, there may be three fruits on a stalk.

I. GLABRA (L.) A. Gray   INKBERRY
Prinos glaber L.

An evergreen shrub 3 to 7 ft high, with erect branches, densely leafy; young shoots angular, minutely downy. Leaves narrowly obovate to oblanceolate, entire, or with a few obscure teeth near the apex, ¾ to 1¾ in. long, ⅓ to ⅝ in, wide, dark green above, paler beneath, glossy and glabrous on both surfaces; stalk ⅛ to ¼ in. long. Male flowers borne three or more together on a slender stalk; females solitary; both very small. Fruits round, black, ¼ in. diameter; nutlets smooth.

Native of eastern N. America; introduced in 1759. Emerson says this shrub is occasionally found 8 or 9 ft high, but it is very slow-growing, and plants

I know to be forty years old are only 3 or 4 ft high. It is a neat-habited ever-green, quite unarmed, but of no particular merit, and rather like a phillyrea.

I. INTEGRA Thunb.

Othera japonica Thunb.

An evergreen tree 30 to 40 ft high in Japan, about half as high at present in this country, pyramidal when young; young shoots angled, glabrous. Leaves obovate or oval, $1\frac{1}{2}$ to 4 in. long, $\frac{3}{4}$ to $1\frac{1}{4}$ in. wide, tapered more gradually, to the stalk and to the blunt apex, margin quite devoid of teeth or spines, dark glossy green; stalk $\frac{1}{4}$ to $\frac{1}{2}$ in. long. Fruits deep red, globose, nearly $\frac{1}{2}$ in. in diameter.

Native of Japan, Korea, and possibly of Formosa; introduced in 1864. This is distinct from the large-leaved hollies in the entire absence of spines on the leaves of either old or young plants. It is a handsome evergreen, slightly tender when raised from seed the first one or two winters, but perfectly hardy after-wards. A form with yellow fruits is cultivated in Japan.

var. LEUCOCLADA Maxim. *I. leucoclada* (Maxim.) Mak.—This variety occurs at higher altitudes than the type and is shrubby. The leaves are larger (up to 6 in. long) and somewhat thinner.

I. INTRICATA Hook. f.

A prostrate evergreen shrub forming wide, dense mats at high altitudes, glabrous in all its parts. Leaves dull green, leathery, densely set on the shoots, obovate to elliptic, rounded at the apex up to $\frac{5}{8}$ in. long and half as wide; stalks very short. Flowers inconspicuous, in small clusters. Fruits bright red, globose, about $\frac{3}{16}$ in. across, borne singly or in clusters of two or three.

Native of the Himalaya from Sikkim eastward, S.E. Tibet, N.E. Upper Burma, and Yunnan; the date of introduction is not certain but seeds were sent home by Kingdon Ward in 1931 from Upper Burma, where he found it growing beneath rhododendron bushes in the upper *Abies* forest and remarked in his field note, 'One of the most fascinating of Alpine hollies.'

I. NOTHOFAGIFOLIA F. K. Ward *I. oblata* (W. E. Evans) Comber; *I. intricata* var. *oblata* W. E. Evans—Although very different in habit, this species is closely allied to *I. intricata*. It makes a horizontally branched shrub or small tree with broadly ovate to orbicular leaves (sometimes broader than long). The young stems are densely warted. Native of N.E. Upper Burma and bordering parts of Yunnan and Assam; discovered by Farrer in 1919. Seeds were probably sent by him and later by Kingdon Ward, and an account of it in the wild will be found in Kingdon Ward's *Plant Hunting on the Edge of the World* (1930), pp. 223–224. It was reintroduced by Cox and Hutchison from the Assam Himalaya in 1963.

I. KINGIANA Cockerell

I. insignis Hook. f., not Heer; *I. nobilis* Gumbleton, *nom. illegit.*

A small evergreen tree without any down; branchlets stout, silvery grey, lustrous. Leaves oblong inclining to elliptic or ovate, 5 to 9 in. long, 2 to 2½ in. wide, slender-pointed, tapered at the base, armed at the edges with small spine-tipped teeth, rarely almost entire, thick and rather rigid, dark green above, midrib pale green, prominent; stalk ¾ to 1 in. long, purplish. Flowers clustered scarcely stalked. Fruits bright red, roundish oval, ⅜ in. long, each containing a single stone made up of four fused nutlets.

Native of the E. Himalaya at 6,000 to 8,000 ft. In a small or seedling state it is quite distinct, the leaf-margins being wavy and formidably armed with numerous spiny teeth ¼ to ⅓ in. long, pointing different ways. It is unfortunate that this splendid holly can only be grown in the milder parts of the British Isles. At Kew it has to be given the protection of a cold greenhouse. There are two examples at Caerhays in Cornwall, and it received an Award of Merit when shown from there on 25 February, 1964.

It is unfortunate that the name *I. insignis* given to this species by the younger Hooker is invalid, having been used earlier by Heer for a fossil species.

I. LAEVIGATA (Pursh) A. Gray

Prinos laevigatus Pursh

A deciduous shrub 6 to 8 ft high; young shoots glabrous. Leaves narrowly oval, obovate or lanceolate, tapered at both ends, 1½ to 2½ in. long, ½ to ¾ in. wide, finely pointed, obscurely toothed, pale green and glossy on both surfaces, and glabrous except sometimes for a little down along the veins beneath; stalk ¼ in. or less long. Male flower on slender stalks ⅓ to ¾ in. long; female ones on very short stalks; calyx glabrous. Fruits orange-red, ⅓ in. in diameter, solitary.

Native of the eastern United States; introduced in 1812. This is not so well known in gardens as *I. verticillata*, nor is it perhaps so ornamental with us. It is closely allied to that species, under the notice of which some distinctions are pointed out. It may be added here that the leaf-stalks are generally shorter and the fruits larger in *I. laevigata*. Both species grow in low, wet situations in the wild.

f. HERVEYI Robins.—Fruits yellow.

I. LATIFOLIA Thunb.   TARAJO

An evergreen tree occasionally 50 to 60 ft high in Japan, rarely more than 20 ft high in this country; young shoots very stout, ⅓ in. in diameter, angular, not downy. Leaves very thick, dark lustrous green, oblong, 4 to 8 in. long, 1½ to 3 in. wide, tapered about equally at both ends, the marginal teeth shallow and not spiny; the undersurface is rather yellow; stalk ½ to 1 in. long. Fruits red, globose, ⅓ in. in diameter, crowded in considerable numbers on short axillary racemes. *Bot. Mag.*, t. 5597.

Native of Japan; introduced to Europe by Siebold in 1840. Although this species is hardy at Kew it does not succeed very well. But a few miles to the south it thrives admirably in favourable situations. Sargent regarded it as the handsomest broad-leaved evergreen of Japan. It received an Award of Merit in 1952 when shown by Lord Bessborough of Stansted Park, Hants.

I. × KOEHNEANA Loes. (*I. aquifolium* × *I. latifolia*).—Leaves almost as long as in *I. latifolia* and similarly shaped, with more strongly spined and often slightly undulate margins.

I. MACROCARPA Oliver

A deciduous tree attaining a height of about 50 ft in the wild and nearing that height in cultivation; young shoots green and glabrous. Leaves papery in texture, elliptic, acuminate at the apex, rounded to broadly wedge-shaped at the base, 3 to 4 in. long, 1¼ to 2 in. wide, shallowly toothed, glabrous. Male flowers in clusters on short axillary spurs. Female flowers borne singly in the leaf-axils on stalks about ⅝ in. long. Fruits black, globose, but flattened top and bottom, about ⅝ in. wide; nutlets seven to nine, strongly ribbed. *Bot. Mag.*, n.s., t. 72.

A native of S. and S.W. China, also reported from Indo-China; discovered by Henry in W. Hupeh; introduced by Wilson in 1907 when collecting for the Arnold Arboretum. It is quite hardy at Kew, where there are three specimens; one is female and bears abundantly the large black fruits which are the most remarkable characteristic of this species. The tallest of these measures 27 × 1¾ ft (1970). There is a specimen in the Main Drive at Westonbirt measuring 40 × 1¾ ft (1967).

I. MELANOTRICHA Merrill

An evergreen shrub or small tree to about 40 ft high, with a striated bark, young stems stout, reddish at first, later dark purplish brown. Leaves thinly leathery, oblong to elliptic, 3 to 4 in. long, 1 to 1½ in. wide, with shallow crenate teeth, glabrous, venation visible on both sides. Male flowers in dense, panicle-like inflorescences which are borne on short spurs in the leaf-axils of the second-year wood; pedicels downy. Fruits red, globose, about ⅜ in. wide, borne in dense clusters on short downy stalks; nutlets four, ribbed. *Bot. Mag.*, n.s., t. 84.

A native of N.W. Yunnan and Upper Burma; described from a specimen collected by Kingdon Ward in the latter region and introduced by Forrest from Yunnan under F.25069 and F.26070. It has been confused with *I. franchetiana* (see below) and was for many years grown under that name (and may still be found so labelled in collections). It is hardy at Exbury on the Solent and fruits freely there. The fruit-clusters are very showy and persist long on the tree.

I. FRANCHETIANA Loes.—This species, a native of W. Szechwan and parts of Hupeh, is closely allied to *I. melanotricha* but differs in its sessile, glabrous male inflorescences and glabrous fruit-stalks. Seeds may have been sent by Wilson, but whether the true species is in cultivation in Britain is not certain. Forrest's introduction from Yunnan under this name is really *I. melanotricha*, see above.

I. HOOKERI King—This is the type species of the group to which the above two species, and also *I. fargesii*, belong. It was described from Sikkim and extends as far east as the Chinese province of Yunnan. It is rare in cultivation.

I. MONTANA A. Gray

I. monticola A. Gray; *I. dubia* var. *monticola* (A. Gray) Loes.

A deciduous shrub (sometimes a tree in the wild), with glabrous young stems. Leaves ovate to oval, with a long, tapering, lanceolate point, and a wedge-shaped base, sharply toothed, 2 to 5 in. long, $\frac{3}{4}$ to $2\frac{1}{4}$ in. wide, pale green, glabrous, or downy only on the midrib and veins; stalk slender, $\frac{1}{4}$ to $\frac{3}{8}$ in. long. Flowers white, the males crowded at the end of short spur-like branches, or in the leaf-axils of the previous year's growth, along with two or three leaves; the females short-stalked, fewer, often solitary. Calyx-lobes ciliate. Fruits globose, bright orange red, $\frac{3}{8}$ in. across, borne on stalks about $\frac{1}{4}$ in. long.

Native of the eastern United States from New York State southwards. It is allied to *I. decidua*, having the fruits red, the seeds many-ribbed at the back, and leaves often clustered on short spurs, but *I. decidua* has round-toothed leaves usually widest above the middle, and blunt at the apex. Introduced to Kew from N. Carolina in 1899, but possibly in cultivation earlier.

I. OPACA Ait.   AMERICAN HOLLY

An evergreen tree sometimes 40 to 50 ft high in the wild, with a trunk 6 to 9 ft in girth, resembling the common holly in habit; young shoots minutely downy. Leaves dull green above, yellow-green beneath, oval, tapered more abruptly at the base than at the spine-tipped apex, $1\frac{1}{2}$ to $3\frac{1}{2}$ in. long, half as wide, the margins armed with broad, spine-tipped teeth, which tend to disappear from the uppermost leaves of adult specimens; stalk grooved, $\frac{1}{4}$ to $\frac{1}{2}$ in. long, minutely downy. Male flowers in three- to nine-flowered, slender-stalked cymes; females usually solitary; all small, dull white; calyx-lobes edged with minute hairs. Fruits red, round, $\frac{1}{4}$ in. diameter, on a stalk about as long.

Native of the eastern and central United States; introduced in 1744. In gardens this species is only likely to be confused with the Himalayan *I. dipyrena*, which has similarly opaque, evergreen foliage, but that species has longer narrow leaves with shorter stalks, and much shorter-stalked, more congested flower-clusters. The fruit also is larger. *I. opaca* sometimes bears fruit very freely in this country, and is then ornamental, but it is never so attractive as our common native species. There is a fine specimen of this species at Kew near the south end of the Holly Avenue.

f. XANTHOCARPA Rehd.—Fruits yellow; has been found wild in Massachusetts. Introduced in 1901.

In the USA, the American holly is a valued ornamental, and numerous cultivars are in commerce there, scarcely known in Europe. Hybrids between it and *I. cassine* are also grown, the most noteworthy being 'EAST PALATKA', a female with almost entire leaves, and the narrow-leaved Foster hybrids. This cross also occurs in the wild, and its botanical name is I. × ATTENUATA Ashe.

I. PEDUNCULOSA Miq.

An evergreen shrub, or a tree up to 20 or 30 ft high; young stems glabrous. Leaves unarmed, ovate or oval, tapering or rounded at the base, slender-pointed, margins entire, 1½ to 3 in. long, ¾ to 1¼ in. wide, dark glossy green and glabrous; stalk ½ to ¾ in. long. Male flowers in clusters; female usually solitary, borne on the current season's shoots. The chief peculiarity of this holly is the length of the fruit-stalk, which is 1 to 1½ in. long, so that the bright red fruits, each ¼ in. across, stand out conspicuously.

Native of Japan and China; introduced by Sargent from Japan in 1893. It is quite hardy. Some of the Chinese plants have somewhat longer leaves than is usual in Japan, whence came Miquel's type. But the difference is not significant except in the case of some Hupeh plants, with leaves 3 to 4 in. long. Such plants were introduced by Wilson in 1901 and 1907 and were distributed from Veitch's Coombe Wood nursery. They may be distinguished as f. CONTINENTALIS Loes. Loesener also noted that the calyx in this form is more clearly ciliolate than in the typical form, but this does not hold good for all Chinese material. The Wilson introduction is perhaps commoner in Britain than Sargent's introduction from Japan.

I. PERADO Ait.   MADEIRA HOLLY

I. maderensis Lam.; *I. perado* var. *maderensis* (Lam.) Loes.

An evergreen tree, hardy in the warmest parts of the British Isles, with deep green leathery leaves of variable shape, oval, obovate or rounded, 2¼ to 4 in. long, 1⅜ to 2¼ in. wide, sometimes entire, sometimes with spine-tipped teeth near the apex, more rarely spiny throughout, apex acuminate and spine-tipped or often blunt or rounded, base wedge-shaped or slightly heart-shaped, decurrent onto the leaf-stalk, venation usually prominent beneath; leaf-stalk winged owing to the decurrence of the blade, grooved beneath, 3/16 to ⅝ in. long. Fruits ellipsoid to globose, red, about ⅜ in. wide.

Native of Madeira, with varieties or subspecies in the Canary Islands and the Azores; cultivated in Britain since 1760. It thrives very well in the Isle of Wight and in Ireland, and no doubt in other mild parts. It has been confounded with *I. aquifolium* and has hybridised with it in gardens (see *I.* × *altaclarensis*). It differs from *I. aquifolium* in the distinctly winged leaf-stalk, at each side of which there is a groove beneath, but this character shows up clearly only on dried specimens. The leaves are mostly entire and the spines, when present, are shorter and usually forward-pointing. Also the venation is usually prominent beneath and the leaves are mostly longer and relatively wider.

var. AZORICA Loes. *I. p.* subsp. *azorica* (Loes.) Tutin—Leaves small, 1 to 2¼ in. long, ovate, elliptic or rounded, entire or with very few forward-pointing spines. Azores.

var. PLATYPHYLLA (Webb & Berth.) Loes. *I. platyphylla* Webb & Berth.; *I. aquifolium* var. *platyphylla* Dallim., in syn., not T. Moore nor Goeppert—Leaves mostly ovate, larger than in the typical state of the species, being 4 to 6 or even 8 in. long, 2¼ to 4½ in. wide, thick and leathery in texture, the margins often entire but sometimes set with short or long spines, pointing forward and irregular in number and size. Fruits deep red, globose, ⅜ in. in diameter.

Native of the Canary Islands mainly but also found on Madeira, where, according to Loesener, it intergrades with typical *I. perado*. Dallimore (*Yew, Holly and Box*, p. 134) treated this holly as a species and placed under it various garden hollies which are almost certainly hybrids of the *I.* × *altaclarensis* group. The holly which Moore described as *I. aquifolium* var. *platyphylla* is not *I. perado* var. *platyphylla* but probably another form of *I.* × *altaclarensis*.

I. perado var. *platyphylla* was described (as a species) in 1842 but may have been in cultivation earlier and, like typical *I. perado*, cultivated as a greenhouse shrub.

For *I. perado aurea* of gardens see *I.* × *altaclarensis* 'Belgica Aurea'.

I. PERNYI Franch.

An evergreen small tree occasionally 20 to 30 ft high in the wild, more often a shrub half as high; branches stiff, densely furnished with leaves, and clothed with a short dense pubescence when young. Leaves squarish at the base, with a

ILEX PERNYI

long triangular apex and two large spines, and often a smaller one, at each side, ⅜ to 2 in. long, ⅜ to 1 in. wide, dark glossy green, leathery; stalk $\frac{1}{12}$ in. long, at first downy like the young shoot. Flowers pale yellow, produced in minute axillary clusters, the sepals roundish and edged with minute hairs. Fruits stalkless or nearly so, red, roundish oblong, ¼ in. in diameter, with two to four stones.

Native of Central and W. China; discovered in 1858 by the Abbé Perny; introduced by Wilson for Messrs Veitch in 1900. It appears to be widely spread and common in certain parts of China. It bears most resemblance to *I. cornuta*, but its smaller leaves, with the apices much more elongated, and its downy shoots distinguish it. Its habit, when young at least, is slenderly pyramidal and very shapely, and altogether it is a charming addition to dwarf, slow-growing evergreens. Paul Perny, after whom it is named, was a courageous French missionary who worked in the province of Kweichow between 1848 and 1862. He was the first naturalist who explored that province, which he is said to have originally entered in the guise of a Chinese beggar.

var. VEITCHII Hort. ex Bean *I. veitchii* Veitch *nom. nud.; I. pernyi* f. *veitchii* (Bean) Rehd.; *I. bioritsensis* var. *ovatifolia* Li—Leaves larger and relatively broader, $1\frac{1}{2}$ to 2 in. long, with three to five spines on each side. A.M. 1930. Material in the Kew Herbarium from Szechwan, Hupeh, Kweichow, and Yunnan is referable to this variety. The var. MANIPURENSIS Loes. is very near to the var. *veitchii* and was described earlier.

The Formosan species I. BIORITSENSIS Hayata is very near to *I. pernyi* and should probably be included in it as a synonym of *I. pernyi* var. *veitchii* or as a separate variety.

I. GEORGII Comber—A shrub up to 30 ft high in the wild. Leaves lanceolate or ovate, $\frac{3}{4}$ to $1\frac{3}{4}$ in. long, up to $\frac{5}{8}$ in. wide, acuminate and spine-tipped at the apex, rounded or cordate at the base, thick and rigid in texture, with up to seven spines on each side. Fruits red, in clusters of five to eight, $\frac{3}{16}$ to $\frac{1}{4}$ in. long, with one or two nutlets. Native mainly of Yunnan and Upper Burma, discovered by George Forrest and cultivated at Caerhays, Cornwall, from seeds collected by him. It is allied to *I. pernyi* var. *veitchii* but has differently shaped leaves and the fruits often contain only one nutlet.

I. ROTUNDA Thunb.

An evergreen tree up to 70 ft high in the wild, glabrous in all its parts. Leaves entire, ovate or elliptic, rounded or cuneate at the base, the apex obtuse or acute and often abruptly narrowed to a short acuminate tip; petiole $\frac{3}{8}$ to $\frac{3}{4}$ in. long. Flowers borne on the current season's growths in axillary umbel-like clusters, on peduncles $\frac{3}{8}$ to $\frac{1}{2}$ in. long; pedicels shorter than the peduncle. Fruits globose or ellipsoid, $\frac{1}{4}$ to $\frac{5}{16}$ in. long, red, three to eight on each peduncle; nutlets five to seven, grooved and lined on the back.

Native of Japan, Formosa, E. China, etc. It is not certain if the typical state of the species is in cultivation, though it should be hardy if introduced from the northern end of its range in Japan, where it is much cultivated for ornament.

var. MICROCARPA (Paxt.) Hu *I. microcarpa* Lindl. ex Paxt.—Leaves mostly oblong-elliptic, shortly acuminate at the apex. Inflorescence axes downy, not glabrous as in the typical state. Fruits globose, mostly $\frac{3}{16}$ in. long. This variety was introduced by Fortune in 1848 from near Ningpo (about 100 miles south of Shanghai) and may not have survived long in gardens. A more recent introduction to the United States is said to be hardy in a sheltered place as far north as Maryland and very fine in fruit. A staminate clone is also available there (*Baileya*, Vol. I (1953), p. 44.)

I. RUGOSA Fr. Schmidt

A low evergreen shrub of spreading, sometimes prostrate habit; young shoots not downy, angled. Leaves narrowly oval or oblong, tapered about equally to each end, blunt or rounded at the apex, shallowly round-toothed, ¾ to 2 in. long, ⅜ to ¾ in. wide, dark bright green and wrinkled above, paler and conspicuously veined beneath, not downy; stalk ⅛ in. long. Flowers shortly stalked; males six or eight, females one or two in the leaf axils. Fruits often solitary, roundish ovoid, about ¼ in. wide, red, ripe in September.

Native of Japan and Sakhalin; originally described and named in 1868; introduced to cultivation in 1895, but very rare in this country. It is very distinct among cultivated hollies in its lax growth (making slender shoots up to 1 ft long in a season) and especially in the wrinkled surface of its leaves. It is very hardy in the Arnold Arboretum and ought to be quite hardy with us, but shrubs from its native regions are often excited into growth too early in spring and suffer from late frosts in consequence.

I. SERRATA Thunb.

A deciduous shrub up to 12 or 15 ft high, with spreading branches; young shoots angled, zigzag, minutely downy. Leaves oval and ovate to somewhat obovate, tapered at both ends, usually more slenderly at the apex, finely toothed, 1 to 3 in. long, ⅓ to 1 in. wide; dull green above, and soft with minute down when young, becoming glabrous later; covered with a more conspicuous, persistent down and prominently veined beneath; stalk ⅛ in. or less long, downy. Flowers inconspicuous in axillary clusters. Fruits red, globose, ⅛ in. diameter; nutlets smooth.

Native of Japan and China; apparently introduced for the first time in 1893 to Kew from Yokohama, but known in the United States since about 1866. It is quite hardy, and bears good crops of fruit. It has very much the aspect of the North American *I. verticillata*, but is not so ornamental, the fruits being smaller and scarcely so bright; its leaves are also more finely toothed. Sargent observes that the leafless branches are sold in immense quantities in Tokyo for house decoration; for this purpose they are admirably suited, as the berries hang on and retain their colour a long time.

f. LEUCOCARPA Beissn.—Fruits white; leaves shorter and broader. Introduced in 1893.

f. XANTHOCARPA (Rehd.) Rehd.—Fruits yellow.

I. VERTICILLATA (L.) A. Gray
Prinos verticillatus L.

A deciduous shrub 6 to 10 ft high, of spreading habit; young shoots glabrous. Leaves oval, obovate, or lanceolate, tapered at both ends, 1½ to 3 in. long ½ to 1 in. wide, shallowly and often doubly toothed, glabrous above, downy beneath, especially on the midrib and veins; stalk ¼ to ½ in. long. Male flowers in clusters of six or more in the leaf-axils; female ones fewer. Calyx edged with small hairs. Fruits often solitary or in pairs, bright red (or, in f. CHRYSOCARPA Robins., yellow), ¼ in. wide, round.

Native of eastern N. America; introduced in 1736. This is the most ornamental of the American deciduous hollies, and is frequently very showy in autumn with the glossy scarlet berries, which are in full colour before the leaves fall. It received an Award of Merit when shown from Kew on 6 November 1962. The only species with which it is likely to be confused is *I. laevigata* (q.v.), a species which also has red berries and is deciduous. That species differs from *I. verticillata* by its glabrous or nearly glabrous leaves; its male flowers being borne on long and slender stalks; its calyx margins not being hairy; and by its solitary fruits. *I. verticillata* is somewhat variable, and American botanists distinguish the following varieties:

var. FASTIGIATA (Bickn.) Fern.—Branches more ascending. Leaves narrowly lanceolate, glabrous or nearly so.

var. PADIFOLIA (Willd.) Torr. & Gr.—Leaves downy all over the lower surface.

var. TENUIFOLIA (Torr.) S. Wats.—Leaves thinner and less downy than in the type. Female flowers more often solitary.

The garden variety 'NANA', raised in the USA, is of dwarf habit and bears large fruits (Wyman, *Shrubs and Vines for American Gardens* (1965), p. 258). 'XMAS CHEER' is a free-fruiting selection.

I. VOMITORIA Ait. YAUPON
I. cassine Walt., not L.

An evergreen shrub, sometimes a small tree, 15 to 20 ft high; young shoots rigid, spreading, covered with a minute down. Leaves glabrous, glossy dark green, narrowly oval or inclined to ovate, tapered at the base, bluntish at the apex, the margin shallowly and remotely toothed, ½ to 1½ in. long, ¼ to ¾ in. wide; stalk ¹⁄₁₂ to ⅛ in. long, downy like the young wood. Flowers produced in axillary clusters on the year-old wood, the males numerous and on stalks ⅛ in. long; females solitary or in pairs. Fruits scarlet, round, ³⁄₁₆ in. in diameter.

Native of the south-eastern United States; introduced before 1700. A neat evergreen shrub something like a phillyrea in appearance, but incapable of withstanding our hardest winters.

The epithet *vomitoria* refers to the use to which the leaves were put by the Indians. At certain times of the year they would forgather on the coast where the holly was abundant and, having made an infusion of the leaves, 'they begin drinking large drafts, which in a very short time vomit them severely; thus they continue drinking and vomiting, for the space of two or three days, until they have sufficiently cleansed themselves; then they gather every one a bundle of the shrub to carry away with them, and retire to their habitations' (Miller, *Gard. Dict.* (1768), under *Cassine paragua*).

I. YUNNANENSIS Franch.

An evergreen shrub ultimately 10 to 12 ft high, with bright green branchlets covered with outstanding down which persists two years. Leaves of a beautiful brownish red when quite young, becoming glossy green with age, ovate, rounded at the base, acutely pointed, widely and shallowly crenulate-serrulate to crenulate, ¾ to 1⅛ in. long, rather more than half as wide. Fruits usually solitary, about ¼ in. wide, red.

Native of W. China and Upper Burma; introduced by Wilson about 1901 for Messrs Veitch (W.2344) and again during his Arnold Arboretum expedition (W.4458); plants from both sendings are or were in cultivation. It is a neat, cheerful-looking evergreen, allied to *I. crenata*, but the leaves are more leathery, not gland-dotted beneath, the branches more downy and the fruits red.

f. GENTILIS Loes.—Leaves more noticeably crenate. The cultivated plants incline to this form, but the difference is really too slight to merit recognition.

I. SUGEROKII Maxim.—This species is closely allied to *I. yunnanensis*, from which it differs in its almost glabrous branchlets (shortly downy when young) and in its leaves being entire in the lower part. Native of Japan.

ILLICIUM   ILLICIACEAE

A genus of about forty species of evergreen trees and shrubs, natives of E. and S.E. Asia, the eastern USA, Mexico, and the West Indies. It is the only genus in the family Illiciaceae, which is allied to the Magnolia family but differs in the carpels being borne in a single whorl round a central axis, developing into a star-shaped fruit, not cone-shaped as in Magnoliaceae. A closer ally is the Winteraceae (*Drimys*, etc.) but in that group the sepals are valvate, not imbricate as in *Illicium*.

Three species are grown out-of-doors in the British Isles, one from the S.E. United States, the other two from China and Japan. All are rather tender. They prefer a partially peaty soil, especially until well-established, and can best be propagated by layers.

I. ANISATUM L.

I. religiosum Sieb. & Zucc.

A shrub or small tree, the young branches of which are glabrous, green spotted with brown. Leaves 2 to 4 in. long, ¾ to 1 in. wide, narrowly oval, blunt at the apex, tapering at the base to a short thick stalk. Flowers borne from March to May, about 1 in. across, shortly stalked, clustered in the leaf-axils, not fragrant. Petals narrow, numerous (up to thirty), pale greenish yellow. *Bot. Mag.*, t. 3965.

Native of China and Japan; introduced in 1790. South of London it is moderately hardy in a sheltered position, growing slowly but steadily to a height of about 6 ft in the open, and flowering freely. In the milder parts it will attain twice that height or even more; at Trewidden in Cornwall it is 20 ft high.

The leaves and wood have a strong and agreeable fragrance. This shrub was long thought to be the 'star anise' of the Japanese and Chinese, but that tree is really quite a different species—I. VERUM Hook. f.

I. HENRYI Diels—A small tree in the wild. Leaves oblanceolate, 4 to 6 in. long, 1 to 2 in. wide, acuminate at the apex, tapered at the base to a stalk ½ to ¾ in. long, fairly glossy above, leathery. Flowers fragrant, varying in colour on wild plants from pink to deep crimson (pink in the cultivated plants), solitary in the leaf-axils on stalks 1 to 1½ in. long. Petals ovate or oblong-ovate, about twenty in number. Carpels eight to thirteen. A native of W. China, discovered by Augustine Henry; it was later collected by Wilson, but the origin of the plants now in cultivation is uncertain. It is hardy in woodland south of London, but slow-growing.

I. FLORIDANUM Ellis

A shrub 6 to 8 ft high, of compact, much-branched habit. Leaves 3 or 4 in. long, lance-shaped to narrowly oval, tapered at both ends, entire, leathery, glabrous. Flowers borne in May and June singly near the end of the shoots

ILLICIUM FLORIDANUM

each one composed of from twenty to thirty strap-shaped, pointed petals, ¾ to 1 in. long, maroon-purple. Fruits a little over 1 in. wide.

Native of the southern United States; first found by Bartram in W. Florida in 1766, and introduced to England five years later. A small specimen lived outside for a long time without protection in the Coombe Wood nursery, Kingston-on-Thames, where it stood on a sunny slope, but as a rule near London it requires the shelter of a wall or some winter covering. It is really best adapted for

Cornwall and places with a similar climate. The whole plant is permeated with an agreeable aromatic fragrance.

INDIGOFERA   LEGUMINOSAE

A large genus of herbs and shrubs, mostly tropical and subtropical, notable in containing the indigo plant (*I. tinctoria*). Of the shrubby species a few may be grown outdoors in Britain, but the shoots in our climate, although woody, are usually only of annual duration, unless given the protection of a wall. The leaves, in the species described here, are odd-pinnate. Flowers usually pink or purple, with the typical shape of the pea family, arranged in axillary racemes; the keel has a swelling or spur on either side. Pods dehiscent, not jointed, but with thin partitions between the seeds. A feature of the indigoferas is that the hairs are attached by their centres, like cleats (medifixed).

The species here included are all handsome plants, requiring a light or medium garden soil and a sunny position. All, so far as is known, will grow on chalky soils. They are increased by cuttings made of half-ripened shoots placed in a close, slightly heated frame. The cuttings should be kept under glass the first winter, remaining in their pots until the spring.

I. AMBLYANTHA Craib

A deciduous shrub 5 or 6 ft high; young shoots furnished with appressed whitish hairs. Leaves pinnate, 4 to 5 in. long, composed of seven to eleven leaflets; leaf-stalk $1\frac{1}{4}$ to $1\frac{1}{2}$ in. long. Leaflets narrowly oval, tapered towards both ends, the apex terminated by a short mucro, $\frac{1}{2}$ to $1\frac{1}{4}$ in. long, $\frac{1}{8}$ to $\frac{2}{3}$ in. wide, the terminal one the largest; there are pale appressed hairs on both surfaces, more abundant beneath; stalks $\frac{1}{16}$ in. long. Racemes 3 to $4\frac{1}{2}$ in. long, slender, erect, produced continuously from the leaf-axils from June until October on very short peduncles. Flowers arranged closely on the raceme (ten or so to the inch) each $\frac{1}{4}$ in. long, varying in colour from pale rose to deep pink. Calyx green, hairy, $\frac{1}{8}$ in. long, with awl-shaped lobes of unequal length; flower-stalk $\frac{1}{6}$ in. long. Pods 1 to $1\frac{3}{4}$ in. long, $\frac{1}{8}$ in. wide, covered with close down.

Native of China. Plants at Kew obtained from Messrs Veitch in 1913 were introduced by Purdom from Kansu. Wilson found it previously in W. Hupeh, where it is abundant, and it was originally named from specimens collected by him in that province in June 1907. It is quite a pretty shrub, flowering over a long period when shrubs in bloom are not plentiful. It seems to be hardier than most of the indigoferas and its stems survive winters of at least moderate severity.

var. PURDOMII Rehd.—Flowers slightly larger than in the type, lilac-pink. Described from plants in the Arnold Arboretum, raised from seeds collected by Purdom.

I. POTANINII Craib—This species is closely allied to *I. amblyantha*, the difference, according to Craib, being that the peduncle of the raceme is about as long as the petiole of the subtending leaf or slightly longer, but much shorter than the petiole in *I amblyantha*. Perhaps a more reliable mark of distinction is that the leaves are shorter than in *I. amblyantha*, $1\frac{3}{4}$ to 2 in. long, on shorter petioles $\frac{1}{2}$ to $\frac{5}{8}$ in. long, and the leaflets smaller, the lateral leaflets being $\frac{7}{16}$ to $\frac{5}{8}$ in. long, $\frac{1}{8}$ to $\frac{1}{4}$ in. wide. In describing this species Craib cited only the type specimen, which was collected by the Russian traveller Potanin in Kansu, but he later placed under it plants raised in the Arnold Arboretum from seeds collected by Purdom in Kansu under No. 539a. But judging from specimens in the Kew Herbarium taken from garden plants raised from Purdom's seeds, it was not *I. potaninii* but *I. amblyantha* that Purdom introduced under No. 539a, and this was also Dr Rehder's view. So it may be that most of the plants grown under the name *I. potaninii* are really Purdom's introduction of *I. amblyantha*, while those grown under the latter, correct, name represent the Wilson introduction from farther south.

With regard to the true *I. potaninii*, the only cultivated specimen in the Kew Herbarium is from a plant in the garden of the late Sir Frederick Stern, at Highdown in Sussex, which was raised from seeds collected by Farrer in Kansu under No. 260.

I. PSEUDOTINCTORIA Matsum.—Leaves up to $2\frac{1}{4}$ in. long, with mostly seven or nine, occasionally eleven leaflets; leaf-petiole up to $\frac{5}{8}$ in. long. Leaflets downy on both sides, the lateral ones $\frac{3}{8}$ to $\frac{5}{8}$ in. long, $\frac{3}{16}$ to $\frac{5}{16}$ in. wide. Flowers small, about $\frac{1}{6}$ in. long, pale red to almost white, densely packed in racemes 2 to 4 in. long; peduncle of raceme very short. According to Craib it can be distinguished from *I. amblyantha* by the shorter leaf-petiole, from *I. potaninii* by the peduncle of the raceme being shorter than the leaf-petiole; the flowers are also much smaller than in *I. potaninii*.

Native of Japan, Formosa, and Central China; described by the Japanese botanist Matsumura in 1902; introduced to Kew by A. Henry in 1897 from Yunnan. Craib referred to this species plants found by Wilson in W. Hupeh, but these were true shrubs up to 8 ft high, while typical *I. pseudotinctoria* is a sub-shrub less than 3 ft high. Whether the true species is now in cultivation it is impossible to say. The plant at Highdown in Sussex, which received an Award of Merit in 1965 under the name *I. pseudotinctoria*, has not been examined, but it does not agree well with this species, judging from the photograph reproduced in *Journ. R.H.S.*, Vol. 90, fig. 180. The Highdown plant flowers early for an indigofera, from end-May.

I. DECORA Lindl.

Hedysarum incanum Thunb. (1784), not *Indigofera incana* Thunb. (1800); *Hedysarum incarnatum* Willd., *nom. illegit.; Indigofera incarnata* (Willd.) Nakai

A low deciduous shrub 1 to 2 ft high, perhaps more in mild districts. Stems reddish brown, slender, bearing pinnate leaves 4 to 6 in. long at intervals of 1 to $1\frac{1}{2}$ in. Leaflets seven to thirteen, 1 to $2\frac{1}{2}$ in. long, $\frac{1}{2}$ to 1 in. wide, ovate-lanceolate to oval, with a short, abrupt, bristle-like tip, glabrous above, furnished beneath with fine hairs. Racemes 6 in. long, produced in the leaf-axils, twenty to forty flowers on each. Flowers ⅝ to ¾ in. long, each borne on a slender stalk ¼ in. long, the oblong standard petal white, lined with pale crimson towards the base; wing-petals pink. Calyx with broadly triangular lobes. *Bot. Mag.,* t. 5063.

Native of China and Japan; introduced about 1845 by Fortune, who found it growing in the gardens of Shanghai. It is a charming dwarf shrub, flowering freely in July and August, its shoots being mostly cut back to the ground in winter. It is not adapted for rough treatment, and should be given a front place in the shrubbery, or even a place in the rock garden.

f. ALBA Sarg. *I. incarnata* f. *alba* (Sarg.) Rehd.—Flowers white.

I. DIELSIANA Craib

A deciduous shrub 3 to 5 ft high, of thin diffuse habit; young shoots angular, thinly furnished at first with pale appressed hairs, afterwards nearly or quite glabrous. Leaves 2½ to 5 in. long, made up of seven to eleven leaflets which are oval-oblong or obovate, rounded or tapered at the base, rounded at the apex, with a minute prolongation of the midrib there, ½ to ⅞ in. long, ¼ to ⅜ in. wide, pale beneath, with appressed hairs on both surfaces. Racemes sub-erect, up to 5 or 6 in. long, slender, densely set with blossom. Flowers of an approximately pea-flower shape, nearly ½ in. long, pale rose; calyx silky, ⅛ in. long, with awl-shaped lobes; petals downy.

Native of Yunnan, China at 7,000 to 8,000 ft altitude; discovered by Forrest on the eastern flank of the Tali Range in 1906. It has succeeded very well at Kew, starting to blossom in June and continuing to September by racemes successively produced in the leaf-axils.

I. HEBEPETALA Benth.

A deciduous shrub, growing about 4 ft high at Kew, but considerably taller where it is not cut back during winter; stems glabrous, except when quite young. Leaves pinnate, 7 to 9 in. long, with usually seven to nine (occasionally eleven) leaflets, which are oblong, broadly oval or slightly ovate, short-stalked, 1 to 2½ in. long, half as much wide, rounded or notched at the apex, glabrous above, with appressed hairs beneath. Racemes 3 to 9 in. long, produced from the leaf-axils of the terminal part of the shoot, and developing in succession as it lengthens. Flowers closely set, twenty to sixty on one raceme, each ½ to ⅝ in. long, the standard petal crimson, wing and keel petals rose-coloured. Pods 1½ to 2 in. long, cylindric, glabrous, carrying eight to ten seeds. *Bot. Mag.,* t. 8208.

Native of the north-western Himalaya, where it is widely spread at altitudes of 6,000 to 8,000 ft. It is strange that so handsome a shrub should be so little known in gardens. The date of its introduction is not recorded, but it has been cultivated at Kew since 1881, when it came with a collection of plants bequeathed by J. C. Joad, a well-known amateur of his time. It produces its richly coloured racemes during August and September. In the open ground its stems rarely

survive the winter, and are generally cut back to the old woody stool, a new
crop springing up in early summer.

I. HETERANTHA Wall. ex Brandis (1874)

I. gerardiana Wall. ex Baker (1876); *I. dosua* Lindl., not D. Don

A deciduous shrub with downy, slightly-ribbed branches. At Kew, where it is
almost invariably cut back to the ground each winter, it sends up a dense thicket
of erect, scarcely branched shoots 2 to 4 ft high, clothed from top to bottom with
leaves. Where the climate is milder the shoots survive, and it then becomes a
much-branched shrub, perhaps 6 or 8 ft high. On a wall at Kew it has reached a
height of 10 ft. Leaves pinnate, 2 to 4 in. long, composed of thirteen to twenty-
one leaflets; leaflets ¾ to ⅝ in. long, obovate or oval, clothed with grey appressed
hairs on both sides, the apex notched or rounded and having a short bristle-like
tip. Racemes produced from the leaf-axils in succession from below upwards, on
the terminal part of the shoot. They are 3 to 5 in. long, bearing short-stalked,
pea-shaped flowers ½ in. long, rosy purple, two dozen or more on each raceme.
Calyx downy, with lance-shaped lobes. Pods deflexed when ripe, 1½ to 2 in.
long, ⅛ in. wide, cylindric, six- to ten-seeded.

Native of the north-western Himalaya. Commencing to blossom about the
end of June, and continuing until the end of September, having also foliage of
great beauty and luxuriance, this is one of the most ornamental of late-flowering
shrubs. It has the disadvantage of starting late into growth, and it is not until
June that the stools become well furnished. For this reason it is not suitable for
planting alone in masses. It likes abundant sunshine, and does not flower so
freely in dull seasons.

This species is better known as *I. gerardiana*. This name, and *I. heterantha*,
appear without description in Wallich's *Catalogue*, and it was the latter that was
first validated.

I. KIRILOWII Palib.

I. macrostachya Bge., not Vent.

A small shrub or sub-shrub, with erect stems, which are slightly hairy when
very young, soon glabrous and somewhat angular. Leaves pinnate, 4 to 6 in.
long, composed of usually seven to eleven leaflets which vary in shape from
roundish to broadly ovate, obovate, or rhomboidal, ½ to 1¼ in. long, wedge-
shaped or rounded at the base, tapered at the apex, and terminated by a fine
bristle-like elongation of the midrib, bright green above, both surfaces furnished
with pale flattened hairs. Racemes erect, about 5 in. long, the flowers crowded on
the upper half; rose-coloured, ¾ in. long; calyx slightly hairy, and with sharp,
unequal, lance-shaped lobes. Pods 1½ to 2 in. long, ⅙ in. wide. *Bot. Mag.*, t. 8580.

Native of N. China, Korea and S. Japan; introduced to Britain before 1914,
by which time there were plants at Kew received from M. de Vilmorin and from
the Arnold Arboretum. Like *I. decora* it is a dwarf shrub, but it is easily distinguished from that species by the shorter, broader leaves, hairy on both sides. If

the stems are killed to the ground in winter a new crop will be produced the following summer, bearing their flowers in June and July.

I. PENDULA Franch.

A deciduous shrub of spreading habit, ultimately 8 to 10 ft high; young shoots furnished with pale hairs flattened to the bark. Leaves pinnate, 8 to 10 in. long. Leaflets nineteen to twenty-seven to each leaf, oblong to oval, rounded at the apex, where is a short prolongation of the midrib, rounded or tapered at the base, ¾ to 1¼ in. long, about ½ in. wide, soon glabrous above, furnished beneath with appressed pale hairs. Racemes quite pendulous and very slender, the largest 1½ ft long, produced during August and September from the leaf-axils of the current year's shoots. Flowers of nearly the common broom shape, very numerous, opening successively from the base onwards, each ⅓ to ½ in. long; petals rosy purple, downy outside; calyx downy, with awl-shaped lobes; flower-stalk very short. Pods 2 in. long. *Bot. Mag.*, t. 8745.

Native of Yunnan, China; discovered by Delavay in 1887; introduced by Forrest in 1914. This species is remarkable for the great length and slenderness of its racemes which develop successively along the shoots. At Kew, hard frosts kill it back to the ground, but it springs up again, and as the flowers come on the leafy shoots of the year its blossom is not lost thereby.

ITEA   ESCALLONIACEAE

A small genus of deciduous shrubs and evergreen small trees or shrubs, one species native of N. America, the others of E. Asia. Leaves alternate. Flowers in terminal racemes. Petals five, valvate, linear. Fruit a five-valved capsule. The generic name derives from a Greek word for willow.

I. ILICIFOLIA Oliver   [PLATE 57

An evergreen shrub of bushy habit, said to attain a height of 18 ft occasionally in the wild, and already 6 to 12 ft high in this country; stems quite glabrous. Leaves holly-like but thinner, broadly oval, 2 to 4 in. long, 1½ to 2¾ in. wide, the apex short-pointed, dark glossy green above, paler below, both surfaces glabrous except for tufts of hair in the axils of the chief veins beneath margins armed with stiff spiny teeth; stalk ¼ to ½ in. long. Racemes pendulous, arching 6 to 12 in. long, ½ in. wide, crowded with greenish-white flowers; petals narrow, ⅙ in. long. Blossoms in August. *Bot. Mag.*, t. 9090.

Native of W. China; discovered by Henry, and first raised from seeds sent by him to the late Lord Kesteven, with whom it flowered at Casewick in 1895. It is not hardy at Kew except against a wall, but is very suitable for the rather warmer parts of the British Isles. At Borde Hill, Sussex, there is a bush about 8 ft high and as much wide, in perfect health. Its foliage is handsome and its racemes elegant. Easily increased by cuttings of moderately ripened shoots.

I. VIRGINICA L. [PLATE 59

A deciduous shrub 3 to 5 ft high, with erect, glabrous clustered stems, branched only towards the top. Leaves narrowly oval or oblong, tapering at both ends, $1\frac{1}{2}$ to $3\frac{1}{2}$ in. long, $\frac{3}{4}$ to $1\frac{1}{4}$ in. wide, bright green and glabrous above, paler and slightly hairy beneath, chiefly on the midrib and veins, margins set with fine, regular teeth; stalk $\frac{1}{8}$ to $\frac{1}{4}$ in. long, downy, grooved on the upper side. Flowers fragrant, creamy white, $\frac{1}{3}$ to $\frac{1}{2}$ in. across, produced very close together on slender, erect, cylindrical, downy racemes 3 to 6 in. long and about $\frac{5}{8}$ in. through, terminating short, leafy twigs; each flower is on a downy stalk, $\frac{1}{8}$ in. long. Petals narrow, $\frac{1}{4}$ in. long; calyx downy, with five linear, pointed lobes half as long as the petals. Seed-vessels brown, dry, $\frac{1}{4}$ in. long, downy. *Bot. Mag.*, t. 2409.

Native of the eastern United States, usually affecting moist places; introduced in 1744. This is a pretty shrub, and useful in flowering during July. The leaves often remain on the plant until December. It sends up its erect, slender stems one summer, which branch copiously near the tip the next, each twig producing a raceme at the end. It may be increased by means of cuttings made of moderately ripened wood in July or August, and given gentle heat; but for ordinary garden purposes division of the old plants is quicker and usually sufficient. Pruning should consist of entirely removing sufficient of the older stems to afford light and space for the young ones, by means of which the plant is continually renewing itself from the base. It loves a good soil and abundant moisture.

I. YUNNANENSIS Franch.

An evergreen shrub 6 to 10 ft high, in general appearance very much resembling *I. ilicifolia* in the holly-like leaves, which are not, on the whole, so strongly and spinily toothed or so frequently of rounded shape; they are 2 to 4 in. long, $1\frac{1}{4}$ to 2 in. wide, spine-tipped, dark glossy green and glabrous; stalks $\frac{1}{4}$ to $\frac{5}{8}$ in. long and on the average longer than in *I. ilicifolia*. Flowers crowded on slender, arching, cylindrical racemes up to 7 in. long, each flower (stalk and all) only $\frac{1}{4}$ in. long with narrowly linear, dull white petals. In the wild it flowers in May and June, later in cultivation.

Native of Yunnan, China; originally discovered by Delavay in 1883; introduced to cultivation by Forrest about 1918. It is closely related to *I. ilicifolia*, but on the average the leaves are narrower in proportion to their length, longer-stalked and less conspicuously toothed. Franchet alludes to the 'included' stamens, but in both species they appear to be about as long as the very narrow petals. It requires to be grown on a south wall at Kew. It does not promise to be any improvement on *I. ilicifolia*, especially as one sees the latter at Borde Hill, Sussex, laden every summer with graceful blossom.

IVA   COMPOSITAE

A genus of about fifteen species of herbaceous or shrubby plants, some of the former annual; natives of N. and C. America and of the West Indies.

I. FRUTESCENS L.

A sub-shrub with stems somewhat fleshy, 3 to 10 ft high, branched at the upper parts; shoots minutely downy. Leaves opposite, nearly stalkless, oblong-lanceolate, pointed, rather strongly toothed, cuneate, 4 to 6 in. long, 1 to 2 in. wide, three-veined, being reduced in size upwards until, in the flowering parts, they become small and linear. Inflorescence terminal, more or less pyramidal; flower-heads greenish white, $\frac{1}{6}$ in. wide, hemispheric, axillary, each consisting of staminate and four to five pistillate flowers and beset by four or five broadly ovate bracts.

A native of the S. United States; introduced in 1711. It is mostly found growing in salt marshes and muddy sea-shores, and although quite hardy has little to recommend it for gardens. Both the typical variety and the following one are in cultivation, as well as intermediates between them.

var. ORARIA (Bartlett) Fern. & Griscom—This differs in being less tall (1½ to 6 ft high), with broader leaves and slightly larger heads (five to six bracts and five to six pistillate flowers).

JAMESIA   PHILADELPHACEAE

A genus of a single species in western North America belonging to the same subdivision of the Philadelphus family as *Carpentaria* and *Fendlera*. It is named after Dr Edwin James, who first found it in 1820; he was then acting as botanist and historian to Major Long's expedition to the Rocky Mountains.

J. AMERICANA Torr. & Gr.   [PLATE 62

A deciduous shrub 4 to 7 ft high, of bushy, rounded habit, and usually more in diameter than it is high; branches stout, stiff, very pithy, covered with a bright brown, downy bark, which afterwards peels off in papery flakes. Leaves opposite, on the barren shoots ovate, 1 to 3 in. long, $\frac{3}{4}$ to 2 in. wide, coarsely and regularly toothed, with scattered, flattened hairs above, downy, almost felted beneath; on the flowering twigs the leaves are much smaller, and often of more oval outline; stalk downy, $\frac{1}{4}$ to $\frac{3}{4}$ in. long. Flowers slightly fragrant, pure white, $\frac{1}{2}$ in. across, produced during May in erect, terminal pyramidal panicles 1 to 2½ in. long and broad. Petals five, oblong. Calyx woolly, with five ovate acute lobes. Stamens ten. Styles three to five, united only at the base. Fruit a capsule. *Bot. Mag.*, t. 6142.

Native of western North America; introduced to Kew in 1862. This interesting and pretty shrub can be propagated by cuttings and, given a sunny position, and an open, not too rich soil, thrives excellently. A plant with pink flowers, found by Purpus in Nevada, has been named f. ROSEA (Rehd.) Rehd.

JASMINUM   JASMINE   OLEACEAE*

Of the large number of species belonging to this genus (about 200) only about a dozen are cultivated permanently in the open air in Britain. They are either climbers or shrubs of loose, spreading habit, and are either evergreen or deciduous; leaves alternate or opposite, simple, trifoliate, or pinnate. Flowers yellow or white, rarely red, usually fragrant; corolla with a slender, tapering tube, expanding at the mouth into normally five (sometimes more) spreading lobes. Stamens two. The berry-like fruits are normally twin, but frequently only one develops.

The species cultivated in North America have been treated by P. S. Green in *Baileya*, Vol. 13 (1965), pp. 137–172, and a revision of the alternate-leaved species by the same author was published in *Notes Roy. Bot. Gard. Edin.*, Vol. 23 (3), pp. 355–384 (1961). Earlier Kobuski treated the Chinese species in *Journ. Arn. Arb.*, (1932), pp. 145–179, with a revised key in the same journal, Vol. 40 (4), pp. 385–390 (1959).

Provided the climatic conditions are suitable, the jasmines are easily cultivated; they like a good garden soil and a sunny position. All are easily increased by cuttings of moderately ripened wood.

The jasmines need no annual pruning but should be periodically thinned. See further under *J. nudiflorum* and *J. officinale*.

J. BEESIANUM Forr. & Diels

A deciduous species of variable habit, being in nature an erect shrub or a climber, or found trailing on the ground and rooting at the nodes; shoots minutely downy when young especially at the joints, slender, grooved. Leaves simple, opposite, ovate to lanceolate, $1\frac{1}{4}$ to 2 in. long, $\frac{1}{3}$ to $\frac{3}{4}$ in. wide, dark green above, greyish green beneath with short down on both sides, at least when young; stalks $\frac{1}{8}$ in. or less long. Flowers usually in threes produced in the terminal leaf-axils of short, leafy twigs. Each flower is $\frac{3}{4}$ to $\frac{1}{2}$ in. wide, rose to carmine (also, according to Wilson, rarely pale rose to white); the corolla is tubular at the base, hairy in the throat, spreading at the mouth into usually six rounded lobes,

* Revised with the assistance of P. S. Green.

fragrant. Fruit a rather flattened, globose berry, black, $\frac{1}{2}$ in. wide. *Bot. Mag.*, t. 9097.

Native of Szechwan and Yunnan, China; introduced by Forrest in 1906 for the firm of Bees Ltd. I have never seen it noticeably attractive in flower, but it produces large crops of shining black berries which give a fine effect and remain on the branches well into winter. The completely red flowers are unique for the genus. It is quite hardy and one of the parents of *J.* × *stephanense*.

J. FLORIDUM Bunge

A nearly evergreen shrub of rambling habit; branches angled, glabrous. Leaves alternate; mostly composed of three leaflets, but occasionally five, never apparently more. Leaflets oval, sometimes obovate or ovate, $\frac{1}{2}$ to $1\frac{1}{2}$ in. long, $\frac{1}{4}$ to $\frac{5}{8}$ in. wide, pointed, glabrous. Flowers yellow, in terminal cymose clusters, usually produced from July onwards; corolla $\frac{1}{2}$ to $\frac{3}{4}$ in long, the lobes five, pointed. Calyx-lobes five, about $\frac{1}{8}$ in. long, awl-shaped. Fruit about the size of a small pea, black. *Bot. Mag.*, t. 6719.

Native of China; cultivated in that country and Japan; introduced by Lord Ilchester about the middle of last century. It was originally discovered in North China, but Henry found it frequently in Central China, about Ichang. It is closely akin to *J. humile*, having alternate leaves and yellow flowers, but differs in the longer, more slender calyx-lobes. It has long been grown on a wall at Kew, but is not so hardy as *J. humile*.

J. FRUTICANS L.

A semi-evergreen shrub producing a dense mass of slender, erect stems from 3 to 5 ft high, but thrice as much against a wall; young shoots angular, glabrous. Leaves alternate, composed of three leaflets on a common stalk about $\frac{1}{8}$ in. long, or of one leaflet only. Leaflets narrow-oblong or linear obovate, $\frac{1}{4}$ to $\frac{3}{4}$ in. long, one-third as much wide, tapering at the base, more rounded at the apex, deep green, glabrous on both surfaces, but edged with minute hairs. On strong sucker shoots, the leaflets are occasionally twice as large. Flowers yellow, produced from June onwards, usually in three or fives at the end of short twigs. Corolla $\frac{5}{8}$ in. long and wide; calyx bell-shaped, with five slender lobes. Fruits globose, shining black, the size of a pea. *Bot. Mag.*, t. 461.

Native of S. Europe, N. Africa, and Asia Minor; cultivated since the middle of the 16th century, perhaps before. On the hills above Hyères, it grows abundantly and is quite handsome in the fall of the year by reason of the crop of shining black berries. There the shrubs are mostly $1\frac{1}{2}$ to 3 ft high. In hot seasons it fruits freely in England.

J. HUMILE L.

This variable species, native to the Sino-Himalayan region, is represented in gardens from several introductions. The earliest type to reach Europe f. *humile*, came in the 17th century and was known in British gardens as the 'Italian Yellow Jasmine', the plants, according to Philip Miller, 'being commonly brought from thence by those who come over with the Orange-trees'. This name served to distinguish it from the common yellow jasmine (*J. fruticans*), on which it was often grafted. It is inferior to the cv. 'Revolutum' as a garden plant, having smaller, less fragrant flowers, but is often hardier.

f. FARRERI (Gilmour) P. S. Green, *comb. & stat. nov. J. farreri* Gilmour in *Bot. Mag.*, 47 (1934), t. 9351.—A wide-spreading shrub, 6 to 8 ft high. Young stems angled; stems, leaves, and inflorescences lightly pubescent. Leaflets three to five, the terminal 1⅓ to 3½ in. long, the lateral 1 to 2 in. long. Flowers bright yellow, not fragrant, seven to twelve per inflorescence, borne in June.

Introduced by Farrer from Upper Burma in 1919, under his No. 867, and at first cultivated under the incorrect name of *J. giraldii* (a synonym of and the pubescent expression of *J. floridum*).

f. HUMILE.—A nearly evergreen, glabrous shrub. Leaves alternate with three to seven, sometimes nine leaflets, the terminal ¾ to 2 in. long, the lateral ½ to 1½ in. long. Flowers yellow, often not fragrant, 5 to 10 borne together. *Bot. Reg.*, t. 350. This is the typical form of the species.

This, the 'Italian Yellow Jasmine', is native from Afghanistan and W. Pakistan to Burma and China (Yunnan and Szechwan). It has been reintroduced in more recent times both from the Himalayas and, as Forrest 18927, from S.E. Tibet.

cv. 'REVOLUTUM' *J. revolutum* Sims; *J. humile* var. *revolutum* (Sims) Stokes— A nearly evergreen, stout, glabrous shrub. Leaves with three to five or seven leaflets, the terminal 1½ to 2½ in. and the lateral 1 to 2 in. long. Flowers yellow, fragrant, six to twelve or more together. Corolla large ¾ to 1 in. diameter; short styled with the acute apices of the two stamens visible in the throat. *Bot. Mag.*, t. 1731, *Bot. Reg.*, t. 178.

The most desirable variant of *J. humile*, it is somewhat less hardy than the other forms and is sometimes cut back in a bad winter. It grows best in a sheltered position or a temperate greenhouse. In the past it has also been known under the names *J. reevesii* and *J. triumphans*.

f. WALLICHIANUM (Lindl.) P. S. Green *J. wallichianum* Lindl.; *J. pubigerum* D. Don var. *glabrum* DC.; *J. humile* var. *glabrum* (DC.) Kobuski—This shrub differs from f. *humile* in the more numerous leaflets (seven to thirteen) with the terminal particularly long-acuminate, and relatively few more or less pendulous flowers. *Bot. Reg.*, t. 1409.

Introduced from Nepal, first about 1812, and, more recently, in the 1950s by the expeditions sponsored by the Royal Horticultual Society. The very pubescent plant known as *J. pubigerum* D. Don is also a form of this species, although not in cultivation.

J. MESNYI Hance   PRIMROSE JASMINE   [PLATE 60
J. primulinum Hemsl.

An evergreen, rambling shrub probably 6 to 10 ft high, forming a dense interlacing mass of branches; young stems four-angled, glabrous. Leaves

T S—Q

opposite, composed of three leaflets borne on a common stalk about $\frac{1}{3}$ in. long; leaflets lance-shaped or narrowly oval, 1 to 3 in. long, $\frac{1}{3}$ to $\frac{3}{4}$ in. wide, short-stalked (the side ones smaller), dark glossy green. Flowers $1\frac{1}{2}$ to $1\frac{3}{4}$ in. diameter, bright yellow, produced in spring and summer, solitary on stalks $\frac{1}{2}$ to $1\frac{1}{2}$ in. long, and furnished with tiny, green, leaflike bracts. Corolla often semi-double, composed of from six to ten divisions, each $\frac{1}{3}$ to $\frac{1}{2}$ in. wide, rounded at the end. Calyx-lobes usually five or six, narrow, pointed, $\frac{1}{4}$ in. long, glabrous or minutely ciliate. *Bot. Mag.*, t. 7981.

Native of W. China; introduced by Wilson for Messrs Veitch in 1900. As the plant had never been found bearing seed, the collector was obliged to send home living plants by an overland route to Hong Kong, and thence to England. This jasmine is certainly the most striking of all those that can be grown out-of-doors anywhere in this country, but it is only likely to thrive in the very mildest spots. At Kew, even against a wall, it succumbs to severe frost. The best method of cultivating it is, apparently, to grow it in pots out-of-doors, exposed to full sunshine and generously treated at the root, then to house it and keep it as dry as possible without losing its foliage during the winter. It then makes a fine display in spring. It appears to have found acceptable conditions in middle and south Italy, where it flowers profusely. It is closely allied to *J. nudiflorum* in all essential characters, but is much larger in all its parts, and flowers later.

J. NUDIFLORUM Lindl.   WINTER JASMINE
J. sieboldianum Bl.

A deciduous shrub of rambling habit, growing 12 to 15 ft high against a wall, with long, slender, pendulous, glabrous, four-angled branchlets. Leaves opposite, composed of three leaflets borne on a common stalk about $\frac{1}{4}$ in. long, one-third to half as wide, tapered at both ends, deep lustrous green, not toothed, but furnished at the margin when young with tiny hairs. Flowers bright yellow, $\frac{3}{4}$ to 1 in. diameter, produced from November to February; they are solitary on stalks $\frac{1}{4}$ in. long, clothed with several small, narrow green bracts. Corolla tubular at the base and nearly 1 in. long, spreading into six divisions. Calyx-lobes six, linear, pointed.

Native of China; introduced by Fortune for the Horticultural Society in 1844. A very hardy plant, of great value in gardens because of its habit of flowering during the very darkest months. No plant does so much to lighten up in midwinter dull suburban streets of London, and the fact that it will thrive in such places adds much to its worth. It blossoms best against a sunny wall, but, after warm summers especially, flowers very freely in the open ground. A pleasing arrangement is to plant it in association with *Mahonia aquifolium*, against whose purplish winter-shade of leaf the leafless flower-laden sprays of this jasmine are peculiarly bright and effective.

J. nudiflorum is not by nature a climber, nor does it produce self-supporting stems. The leading shoots should be fixed to the wall and periodically replaced by younger growths, careful training and spacing being more important than annual pruning. On steep sites, where there are high retaining walls, it should be planted at the top of the wall and allowed to grow downward, as is its natural propensity.

cv. 'AUREUM'.—Leaves blotched with yellow.

J. OFFICINALE L.   COMMON JASMINE

A deciduous, or nearly deciduous, climbing shrub, making shoots 6 ft or more long in one season, and ultimately, if carefully trained, reaching 40 ft in height; young shoots very slender, angled, glabrous or soon becoming so. Leaves opposite, pinnate, composed of five, seven, or nine leaflets, which are ½ to 2½ in. long, ⅛ to 1 in. wide, slightly downy at or about the margin, the terminal one much the largest and stalked, side ones stalkless. Flowers white, deliciously fragrant, produced from June until October in a terminal cluster of cymes, each cyme with three or five blossoms. Corolla ⅞ in. long, and about the same across the four or five spreading lobes. Calyx-lobes almost threadlike, ⅓ in. long; flower-stalk about 1 in. long. Fruits not regularly or freely produced, black, ⅓ in. long, solitary or twin.

Native of the Caucasus, N. Persia, Afghanistan, the Himalaya, and China. The common jasmine has been cultivated from time immemorial in Britain, and its fragrance and beauty have given it a place in English gardens as secure as that of the lilac or lavender. In the north it is hardy only against a wall or on a roof, but in the south it grows well in the open, where if supported in the early stages and pruned back every spring it will make a self-supporting bush. But perhaps its charm is greatest when allowed to form a loose tangle on a house front, as one may often see it in cottage gardens between London and the south coast. Even in winter the tangle of young stems has a cheerful green effect.

f. AFFINE (Lindl.) Rehd. *J. affine* Lindl.; *J. grandiflorum* Hort., not L.; *J. officinale grandiflorum* Hort.—A form with flowers pink on the outside and broader calyx-lobes, raised from seeds sent by Dr Royle from the Himalaya (*Bot. Reg.*, Vol. 31 (1845), t. 26).

cv. 'AUREUM'.—Leaves rather handsomely blotched with yellow; scarcely as hardy as the normal form.

J. PARKERI Dunn

An evergreen shrub from 6 to 12 in. high, young shoots grooved, very minutely downy, becoming glabrous. Leaves alternate, pinnate, ½ to 1 in. long, made up of three or five leaflets. Leaflets oval or ovate, pointed, tapered at the base, not toothed, stalkless, ⅛ to ¾ in. long. Flowers yellow, solitary or two together, terminal or produced from the leaf-axils. Corolla-tube slender, ½ to ¾ in. long, ½ in. across the six spreading lobes. Calyx cup-shaped, scarcely ⅛ in. long, minutely downy, five-ribbed and with five awl-shaped lobes. Fruits ¼ in. wide, two-lobed, globose, greenish white, translucent.

This species was discovered by R. N. Parker in 1919 in the upper basin of the river Ravi, in what was then the Indian State of Chamba, now part of Himachal Pradesh, and was introduced by him in 1923. Parker observed that it flowers in June (as it does also with us) and grows on rocks or hot, dry banks. Except when trailing over a rock it is never more than 12 in. high. It is a curious little jasmine, often forming in the wild a ball of densely packed twigs a few inches wide. Under cultivation, with better soil, it grows more freely, and

JASMINUM PARKERI

makes a charming little shrub for the Alpine garden. Quite hardy at Kew. Its dwarf habit and usually solitary flowers make it very distinct. The plant at Kew, set at the top of a vertical rock-face about 5 ft high, has formed a curtain of pendent leafy growth reaching to the stream at the base of the rock, and about 8 ft wide.

J. POLYANTHUM Franch.   [PLATE 61

An evergreen climber growing 6 to 10 ft high (but up to twice that height in favourable conditions); young shoots slightly warted, not downy. Leaves opposite, 3 to 5 in. long, pinnate, composed mostly of five or seven leaflets, the lowest pair rather near the stem. The side leaflets are ovate, ½ to 1½ in. long, very shortly stalked, the terminal one lanceolate, 1½ to 3 in. long, more slenderly pointed; all are of thin texture, quite glabrous except for a tuft of down at the vein-axils beneath, obliquely rounded or cordate at the base. Panicles axillary, many-flowered, 2 to 4 in. long, glabrous. Flowers very fragrant, white inside, rose-coloured outside in greenhouse plants but deeper-coloured in outdoor ones; the slender tube of the corolla ¾ in. long, spreading at the mouth into five obovate lobes, giving it a diameter of ¾ in. Calyx ⅛ in. long with five erect, awl-shaped teeth nearly as long as the tube. *Bot. Mag.*, t. 9545.

Native of Yunnan, China; discovered in 1883 by Père Delavay. Forrest found it flowering between May and August 1906 in the Tali valley and along the eastern flank of the Tali range up to 8,000 ft altitude, and also sent seeds before

1925, when the species was already cultivated at Kew (*Gard. Chron.* (Jan. 1939), p. 12). It did not become known to British gardeners until the *Botanical Magazine* figured it in 1938 from a spray sent by Captain de la Warre from his garden on the French Riviera. His plant was a gift from Major Lawrence Johnston, who had introduced it to his garden at Mentone in 1931 from Tengyueh in Yunnan, while collecting with Forrest. As the specific name implies, it is free-flowering, and the rosy or red colouring outside the corolla is unusual in the genus. It must have wall protection in a climate like that of Kew and is no doubt better suited for the south and west. Sometimes thirty to forty flowers are borne on a single panicle.

J. polyanthum is one of the finest of climbers for a cool greenhouse. It received an Award of Merit when shown from Kew in 1941 and a First Class Certificate eight years later.

J. × STEPHANENSE Lemoine

A hybrid between *J. beesianum* and *J. officinale*, raised at St-Etienne in France by Thomas Javitt and put into commerce by Messrs Lemoine and Son of Nancy, about 1921. It is a vigorous climber with slender, glabrous, angled young shoots. The leaves vary from the simple ovate-lanceolate ones of *J. beesianum* to the pinnate ones of *J. officinale*, but the leaflets rarely, if ever, number more than five to each leaf, the terminal leaflet the largest; they are dull green above, slightly downy beneath; stalk ¼ to ½ in. long. Flowers borne in terminal clusters, fragrant, soft pale pink. The slender tube of the corolla is about ½ in. long and the flower is about the same in width across the rounded, auricled lobes. The bell-shaped base of the calyx is ⅛ in. long, downy, with erect awl-shaped lobes of about the same length.

At Kew this jasmine flowers in June and July. It is attractive enough to have been given an Award of Merit, July 6, 1937. The same hybrid has also been found in the wild. Père Delavay collected it in 1887 and in 1922 Joseph Rock found it in Yunnan.

JOVELLANA   SCROPHULARIACEAE

A genus of a few species of herbs and sub-shrubs, natives of New Zealand and temperate South America, It is very closely allied to *Calceolaria*, but differs in its corolla, which is divided into almost equal, erect 'lips', with flat or only slightly inrolled margins, and thus not showing the 'pouch' characteristic of the true calceolarias.

The genus was named by Ruiz and Pavon in honour of C. M. de Jovellanes, a student of the flora of Peru.

J. VIOLACEA (Cav.) G. Don
Calceolaria violacea Cav.

A semi-deciduous or, in mild winters, evergreen shrub up to 6 ft high young shoots semi-woody, slender, minutely downy. Leaves opposite, ovate in main outline, but very coarsely and irregularly toothed or even lobed, pointed, ½ to 1¼ in. long, ¼ to ⅜ in. wide, dark dull green and with scattered hairs above, paler, and occasionally with a few hairs on the midrib and chief veins beneath. Flowers produced about midsummer in corymbs 1½ to 3 in. across, that terminate slender, erect, downy flower-stalks. Corolla helmet-shaped, with a deep notch at each side (often described as 'two-lipped'), ½ in. or less long, nearly as wide at the mouth, pale violet, spotted with purple inside and with a blotch of bright yellow in the throat; downy outside and at the margins. Calyx four-lobed, hairy outside and at the margins, the lobes ovate; stamens two, very shortly stalked, situated at the base of the corolla and surrounded with bristles there.

Native of Chile; introduced early in the 19th century. It is not genuinely hardy at Kew, although it has lived and occasionally flowered at the foot of a south wall there. In the warmer counties, if given a sunny spot, it succeeds very well, increasing its area by sucker growth and flowering very prettily.

JUBAEA   PALMEAE

A genus of a single species of palm, endemic to Chile. It is allied to the coconut, *Cocos nucifera*, and has similar though smaller fruits.

J. CHILENSIS (Mol.) Baill.   WINE PALM
Cocos chilensis Mol.; *J. spectabilis* H. B. K.

A tall evergreen tree, with a trunk 40 to 60 ft high and 15 ft in girth, the stem naked to the leaves, but covered with small cracks running lengthwise. Leaves pinnate up to 15 ft long in adult specimens, the upper ones more or less erect, the lower ones horizontal; leaflets ('pinnae') 1 to 2 ft long; the whole forming a dense hemispherical head of foliage. On young plants, of course, the leaves are much smaller and only 3 or 4 ft long and on seedlings the leaves are undivided and remain so for a few seasons; they become larger as the tree grows older, and reach their maximum size just before the trunk commences to form and grow in height.

Native of Chile, where until early in the 19th century it was very plentiful. Darwin, in his *Voyage of the Beagle*, records that on one estate alone it numbered hundreds of thousands. That was early in the 19th century; now it is comparatively rare, having been cut down for the sake of its sugary sap which, when concentrated by boiling, acquires a treacle-like consistency and taste. It seems that the sap can only be acquired by felling the palm and collecting it at the upper end of the trunk, from which it continues to flow for a considerable time. A large tree will in the end yield as much as 90 gallons. The boiled sap was known to the Chileans as 'palm honey' and was much esteemed by them, but the genuine product is now no longer produced in any quantity.

There is a magnificent example of this palm in the Temperate House at Kew, its trunk 10 ft in girth and some 45 ft high, the spread of its foliage 30 ft. Irwin Lynch, who left Kew in 1879, records in the *Journal of the Royal Horticultural Society*, Vol. 38, p. 202, that a fine specimen once existed near the principal entrance to the gardens from Kew Green. It had disappeared before I entered Kew in 1883, and subsequent attempts to grow it in the open air have failed. Magnificent trees may be seen in several gardens on the shores of Lake Como.

In his garden at Torquay, Devon, Mr G. R. Muir has three specimens of *Jubaea chilensis*, of which the most thriving measures 23 × 10 ft (1972). It is believed to have been planted about 1900.

JUGLANS   WALNUT   JUGLANDACEAE

The walnuts, of which eight or nine species are in cultivation, are deciduous trees, or occasionally shrubs, with pinnate leaves aromatically scented. Flowers unisexual, both sexes on the same plant; the male flowers very numerous in slender, pendulous catkins, borne towards the ends of the previous year's shoots; perianth segments adnate to the bracts and bracteoles to form a five- to seven-lobed scale; stamens eight to forty. Female flowers few, in a short spike terminal on a short shoot of the current season; ovary inferior, enclosed in a lobed perianth adnate to the fused bracts and bracteoles; stigma with two spreading branches. Fruit a hard-shelled nut, surrounded by a thin or fleshy husk. The cultivated species are from Europe, N. Asia, and N. America, but two or three species of which little is known are found in S. America. The only other genus of trees with which *Juglans* is likely to be confused is *Carya* (the hickories), but among other differences, *Juglans* is distinguished by the pith of the young shoots being in thin transverse plates, thus dividing the hollow portion of the shoot into a series of chambers, and by the unbranched male catkins. In *Carya* the pith is continuous, and the male catkins three-branched.

In gardens, *Juglans* is seldom represented except by the common walnut, grown for its nuts, and by the black walnut, grown for its stately form and noble foliage. The striking group of Asiatic species—*J. ailantifolia, cathayensis*, etc.—are rare in British gardens. Hopes were once entertained that this group might prove of value for their edible nuts, which they bear, many together, in clusters, but neither they, nor any other species except the common one, is worth growing for the fruit in the British Isles. *J. nigra* and *J. regia* both yield a valuable timber.

Walnuts should always, if possible be grown from seeds, and as they bear transplanting badly, should be given permanent places early. The nuts should be sown as soon as ripe, and not allowed to become dry. All the species like a deep loamy soil. The named varieties of common walnut are propagated by grafting on the type. Some of the species are tender in a young state and apt to be cut by late frost, thus rendering them bushy-topped. It is, in consequence, sometimes necessary to tie up a shoot to form a new leader. The walnut flowers have no colour beauty, and are fertilised by wind; hybrids have been obtained from species growing near to each other.

J. AILANTIFOLIA Carr.   JAPANESE WALNUT
J. sieboldiana Maxim., not Goeppert

A tree over 50 ft high, with stout young shoots clothed, like the common stalk of the leaf, with glandular hairs. Leaves 1½ to 2 (occasionally 3) ft long, composed of eleven to seventeen leaflets, which are oblong, taper-pointed, finely toothed, obliquely rounded or slightly heart-shaped at the base, 3 to 7 in. long, 1½ to 2 in. wide, downy on both surfaces, especially beneath. Male catkins slender, up to 1 ft long. Fruits clustered on long racemes, roundish ovoid, 2 in. long, covered with sticky down; nut about 1¼ in. long, rounded at the base, pointed at the top, nearly glabrous, but with a prominent ridge at the union of the two halves.

Native of Japan and Sakhalin; introduced to Europe about 1860, by Siebold. It is abundant in the forests of Japan, and its nuts are valued as food there. In Britain it gives no promise of bearing fruit to any advantage, and in spite of the considerable period that has elapsed since its introduction, there are few large specimens in the country. It appears to differ from *J. mandshurica* chiefly in the apex of the leaflet being more abruptly tapered and shorter-pointed, and in the prominent ridge and smoother surface of the nut.

The best specimen of the Japanese walnut so far recorded in Britain grows in the Edinburgh Botanic Garden; *pl.* 1906, it measures 55 × 6 ft (1967). There are three examples at Batsford Park, Glos., planted by the first Lord Redesdale. The two largest are both 45 ft high with girths of 6¼ ft at 3 ft and 7 ft at 4 ft respectively (1963). Other examples recorded are: East Bergholt Place, Suffolk, 30 × 4¼ ft (1966); West Hill Nurseries, Winchester, 35 × 3¾ ft (1961); Glasnevin Botanic Garden, Dublin, Eire, 37 × 3¼ ft (1966).

var. CORDIFORMIS (Maxim.) Rehd. *J. cordiformis* Maxim.—Nuts thin-shelled, with a broad, heart-shaped base. This is not known in the wild. An example at Kew, *pl.* 1899, measures 47 × 3½ ft (1956). It flowers freely and the male inflorescences are very striking, being almost yellowish green. The fruits occasionally mature. There is another of 40 × 4 ft in the Edinburgh Botanic Garden (1967).

J. CALIFORNICA S. Wats.

A large shrub or small, round-headed tree whose leaves are made up of eleven to fifteen leaflets each 1 to 2½ in. long, ⅓ to ¾ in. wide, and glabrous. Fruits globose, ⅓ to ¾ in. wide, enclosing a nut deeply grooved lengthwise. Coming from S. California it is not hardy with us.

Very closely related to *J. californica* and perhaps not specifically distinct from it is:

J. HINDSII (Jeps.) R. E. Smith *J. californica* var. *hindsii* Jeps.—A native of Central California and a tree 40 to 70 ft high (occasionally more) with fifteen to nineteen leaflets to each leaf. The entire leaf is 9 to 12 in. long, the leaflets 2 to 4 in. long, ¾ to 1 in. wide, coarsely toothed, downy on the midrib and veins beneath. Young shoots and leaf-stalks very downy. Fruits globose, downy, 1 to 2 in. wide; nut, thick-shelled, shallowly grooved.

J hindsii was introduced to Kew in 1926 and is hardy there. It is related to *J. microcarpa* which differs in having even more (up to twenty-three) leaflets, narrower and more finely toothed. It is much planted in Californian towns as a street tree.

J. CATHAYENSIS Dode

A tree up to 70 ft high, with thick young shoots covered the first year with very viscid, gland-tipped hairs, as are also the main-stalks of the leaves, the fruits, and fruit-stalks. Leaves 2 to 3 ft long, with eleven to seventeen leaflets, which are ovate-oblong, 3 to 6 (occasionally 8) in. long, half as wide, obliquely rounded or heart-shaped at the base, taper-pointed, finely toothed, dark green and downy above, paler and with starry down beneath; midribs with gland-tipped hairs like those of the main leaf-stalk. Male flowers in pendulous, cylindrical catkins 9 to 15 in. long. Fruits clustered at the end of a stout stalk about 6 in. long, egg-shaped, 1½ to 1¾ in. long, pointed; nut of similar shape, sharply pointed, six- to eight-angled, the angles spiny-toothed; rind ⅛ to ⅙ in. thick.

Native of Central and W. China, where it is common. Introduced by Wilson in 1903 to the Coombe Wood nursery, where young trees 8 or 10 ft high bore fruits. Owing to the thickness of the shell, the nuts are of small value for eating, although the kernel is of good flavour. It is a fine-foliaged tree of the same type as *J. mandshurica*; but the present species is a better grower.

The finest specimen of *J. cathayensis* so far recorded in the British Isles grows at Hergest Croft, Heref.; it measures 50 × 4½ ft (1963). In Eire a tree at Birr Castle, Co. Offaly, *pl.* 1941, is now 30 × 1¾ ft (1966), and there is another example in the Glasnevin Botanic Garden, measuring 35 × 4¼ ft (1966).

NOTE. Although the material in the Kew Herbarium is not sufficient to decide the matter, it is doubtful if this species is really separable from *J. mandshurica*. The differences in the fruits adduced by Dode are not correct and there seems to be no difference in the female catkins. The male catkins, however, seem to be longer (up to 10 in. in the material seen, against 3 to 4 in. in *J. mandshurica*). The difference in foliage is not clear-cut but the leaflets of *J. mandshurica* are mostly oblong to oblong-elliptic, tapering-acuminate or long-acute, undersurface faintly downy on the veins to almost glabrous; in *J. cathayensis* they are mostly oval-oblong or ovate, short-acuminate, lower surface persistently hairy, especially on the veins.

J. CINEREA L. BUTTER-NUT

A tree 50 to 60, rarely 100 ft high, usually forming a wide-spreading head of branches; young wood covered with a dense, rusty brown, clammy felt, which partly falls away by the end of the season. Leaves 10 to 20 in. long, composed of seven to nineteen leaflets, which are 2 to 5 in. long, ¾ to 2¼ in. wide, oblong lance-shaped, taper-pointed, obliquely rounded at the base, finely and regularly toothed, upper surface at first hairy, especially on the midrib; lower surface covered with soft, star-shaped hairs; common-stalk thickly furnished with gland-tipped, sticky hairs. Male flowers in catkins 2 to 4 in. long. Fruits three to five in a drooping cluster, each tapering to a point at the top, rounded at the base, 1½ to 2½ in. long, covered with sticky hairs; nut 1 to 1½ in. long, with a short point; kernel sweet, oily.

Native of eastern N. America; introduced early in the 17th century. Although so long cultivated, this tree is comparatively rare in Britain, and is evidently not so well adapted for our climate as the black walnut, rarely bearing fruit. As a small tree it is quite handsome, but grows slowly. From *J. nigra* it differs in its pointed, more numerous fruits, its more downy leaves, and by a transverse tuft of down between the scar left by each fallen leaf and the bud above it.

There are two specimens of *J. cinerea* at Westonbirt, Glos., one in the Acer glade of the Arboretum, measuring 65 × 3½ ft (1967) and another in the grounds of Westonbirt School, *pl.* 1928, now 55 × 2½ ft (1967). Both are graceful straight trees. Two recorded in Scotland are: Edinburgh Botanic Garden, 47 × 3½ ft (1967), and Glendoick, Perths., 46 × 4¼ × 3 ft (1970).

J. × INTERMEDIA Carr.

J. intermedia var. *pyriformis* Carr.; *J. regia* var. *intermedia* C. DC.

This is the collective name for hybrids between the common walnut, *J. regia,* and the black walnut, *J. nigra.* They have arisen in various places, both in Europe and the USA, where the two species grow together. These hybrids, at least in the first generation, have the aspect and bark of the common walnut, but the young shoots are sometimes downy, as in the black walnut. Leaves usually with five or six pairs of leaflets, slightly toothed. Fruits nearer to those of the black walnut. Carrière was not the first to identify this hybrid: a year earlier Casimir de Candolle had described one that grew at Trianon but chose to call it *J. regia* var. *intermedia.*

The most famous specimen of *J. × intermedia* grows in the garden of M. de Vilmorin at Verrières-le-Buisson, near Paris (*J. × intermedia* var. *vilmoreana*). Planted in 1816, this tree measured 80 × 7½ ft in 1863, and 95 × 10 ft in 1905.

J. MANDSHURICA Maxim.

A tree 50 to 70 ft high; young shoots very stout, and like the common stalk of the leaf, clothed with brown, glandular hairs. Leaves $1\frac{1}{2}$ to 2 ft (in vigorous young trees 3 ft) long, composed of eleven to nineteen leaflets, which are oblong, taper-pointed, finely toothed, obliquely rounded or slightly heart-shaped at the base, 3 to 7 in. long, $1\frac{1}{4}$ to $2\frac{1}{2}$ in. wide; when young, both surfaces are furnished, the lower one especially, with starry tufts of down, much of which afterwards falls away from the upper side. Male catkins 4 to 10 in. long, slender, pendulous. Fruits clustered several on a stalk, roundish ovoid, $1\frac{3}{4}$ in. long, covered with sticky down; nut deeply pitted and grooved, $1\frac{1}{2}$ in. long, abruptly pointed at the top.

Native of the Russian Far East, especially in the region of the Amur and Ussuri rivers, and of N. China; first introduced by Maximowicz to the St Petersburg Botanic Garden. As a young tree it is, like *J. ailantifolia*, remarkably striking in the size of its leaves. It is closely allied to that species but does not succeed so well; botanically, the chief difference is in the form of the nuts, and the leaves of *J. mandshurica* are distinctly more slender-pointed.

J. MICROCARPA Berl.   TEXAN WALNUT
J. rupestris Engelm.; *J. nana* Engelm.

A small tree, often semi-shrubby; young shoots covered with short, yellowish down. Leaves 6 to 12 in. long; leaflets thirteen to over twenty, lance-shaped or narrowly ovate, 1 to 3 in. long, $\frac{1}{4}$ to $\frac{3}{4}$ in. wide, long and taper-pointed, finely toothed, obliquely rounded at the base; when young both surfaces are covered with minute down, which mostly falls away except on the midrib and chief veins; common stalk downy like the young shoots. Male catkins slender, 2 to 4 in. long. Fruits globose, $\frac{1}{2}$ to 1 in. in diameter, covered with a thin, smooth husk. Nut deeply grooved.

Native of central and western Texas, western Oklahoma, south-eastern New Mexico, and parts of Arizona; also of northern Mexico; it was discovered by Berlandier in 1835 and described by him under the above name in 1850 (the more familiar name *J. rupestris* was published in 1853). It was sent to Kew by Prof. Sargent in 1881 and again in 1894. It is a handsome bushy tree, quite distinct from all other cultivated walnuts in its small, narrow, thin leaflets.

A very handsome specimen grows in the University Botanic Garden, Cambridge; planted in 1923 it measures 36 × $3\frac{3}{4}$ ft (1969).

var. MAJOR (Torr.) Benson *J. rupestris* var. *major* Torr.; *J. major* (Torr.) Heller—A tree 50 ft high, with larger, fewer leaflets (usually eleven to fifteen). It is also stated that the male flowers have more numerous stamens (thirty to forty) than in *J. microcarpa* (normally twenty). It should perhaps rank as a species, but the name used for it at that level—*J. major* (Torr.) Heller—is illegitimate. Probably its correct name as a species should be *J. torreyi* Dode (the earlier *J. elaeopyron* Dode has been cited as a synonym of *J. major*, but judging from the material of the type-collecting at Kew this species agrees better with *J. microcarpa*).

This walnut has a more western distribution than *J. microcarpa* and is of a coarser, less interesting appearance.

J. NIGRA L. BLACK WALNUT [PLATE 63

A tree 80 to over 100 ft high, with a wide-spreading head and a tall dark trunk, with deeply furrowed bark; young shoots downy. Leaves 1 to 2 ft long, composed of eleven to twenty-three leaflets, the terminal odd one often absent; leaflets fragrant when rubbed, 2 to 5 in. long, ¾ to 2 in. wide, ovate or oblong lance-shaped, obliquely rounded at the base, long and taper-pointed, unevenly toothed, glossy and glabrous above except when quite young, downy beneath; common stalk minutely downy. Male catkins 2 to 4 in. long. Fruits globose or slightly tapered at the base, solitary on the stalk or in pairs, 1½ to 2 in. thick, not downy. Nuts 1 to 1½ in. across, broader than long.

Native of the eastern and central United States; introduced early in the 17th century. Next to the common walnut this is the best known in the genus. Its nuts are of no value as food, but it is a more ornamental tree than *J. regia*, thriving almost as well in the south-eastern parts of this country as in any of its native haunts. As a young tree the black walnut is particularly handsome, with its shapely pyramidal habit and large pinnate leaves. One of the most valuable of the world's timber trees, it is now becoming rare in the wild.

The magnificent tree in Marble Hill Park, Twickenham, mentioned in previous editions, measures 88 × 16¾ ft (1968); when Elwes measured it in 1905 its dimensions were 98 × 14¼ ft. At Mote Park, Maidstone, Kent, he measured a tree of 101 × 12½ ft in the same year; there is still a fine spreading specimen there but its measurements are 74 × 12 ft (1965). The following are some of the other notable specimens recorded recently (the measurements dating from the 1950s were made by the late Maynard Greville): Kew, 72 × 10¼ ft (1967); Syon House, London, 70 × 16¾ ft (taller until recently shortened) (1967), and two others of lesser girth; Albury House, Surrey, 82 × 14½ ft (1968); Much Hadham Rectory, Herts, *pl. c.* 1820, 80×19¾ ft., with a bole of 9 ft (1964); Stansted Hall, Essex, 60 × 16 ft (1951); Hatfield Forest, Takely, Essex, 105 × 14 ft (1952); Hartwell House, Aylesbury, Bucks, 99 × 13½ ft (1957); University Botanic Garden, Cambridge, 75 × 9¾ ft (1969); Pusey House, Oxon, 90 × 15½ ft a superb tree (1968); Oxford Botanic Garden, 88 × 9¾ ft, (1970); Hartwell House, Aylesbury, Bucks, 99 × 13½ ft (1957); Corsham Court, Wilts, 77 × 13¼ ft (1965); Middle Woodford Rectory, Wilts, *pl. c.* 1820, 70 × 14½ ft (1967). A tree at Brahan Castle, Ross and Cromarty, measures 60 × 9¾ ft (1970), a remarkable size for such a northern locality.

cv. 'ALBURYENSIS '.—An interesting variation from the type grows at Albury Park, near Guildford; this bears its fruits in clusters like *J. cinerea*, sometimes as many as six together, and it is also distinct in its pendulous branches. This tree measures 70 × 11½ ft (1966).

J. REGIA L. COMMON WALNUT [PLATE 64

A tree 60 to 100 ft high, with a rounded, spreading head of branches; the bark of the upper branches smooth and ash-coloured; young shoots without down. Leaves somewhat acrid-scented when rubbed, usually 8 to 12 in. long, on vigorous young growths 18 in., composed mostly of five or seven, sometimes nine, rarely eleven or thirteen leaflets. These are oval or ovate, shortly pointed, margins entire; terminal leaflet the largest, 3 to 6 in. long, the basal pair less than half the length and width; both surfaces glabrous except for small tufts of hair in the vein-axils beneath. Male catkins 2 to 4 in. long. Fruits green, glabrous, $1\frac{1}{2}$ to 2 in. across; nuts variously sculptured, with thick or thin shells.

The common walnut has been cultivated for so long and over such a wide area that its natural distribution is uncertain. But it and its subspecies (not treated here) are certainly native in S.E. Europe, in the forests south and east of the Black Sea, in the rain-forests of the Himalaya, N. Burma, and S.W. China, and in the mountains of Central Asia. The date of its introduction is not known, but it has existed in this country for many centuries. As an ornamental tree the common walnut is not so striking as several other species. It is chiefly grown for its nuts and for its soft, unripe fruits, which are made into a pickle. Its timber is a very valuable one, being perhaps the best obtainable for gunstocks. It is also largely used for furniture and veneering.

Because of the value of its timber the common walnut is rarely allowed to attain a venerable age, but there are specimens 60 to 80 ft high and $12\frac{3}{4}$ to $21\frac{1}{2}$ ft in girth in the following places (measurements made 1952–65, mostly by the late Maynard Greville): Little Sampford Hall, Essex; Laverstoke Park, Hants; West Suffolk Hospital, Thetford, Norf.; Grenville College, Stoke, Suff.; Gayhurst, Newport Pagnell, Bucks; Pilton Chase, Northants; Settrington, Malton, Yorks; Gordon Castle, Moray, Scotland.

Numerous variants of the common walnut have sprung up in cultivation and received names of botanical form. Some (especially those distinguished by their fruits) must have occurred regularly among seedlings. None, except 'Laciniata', is of any but historical interest:

cv. 'HETEROPHYLLA'.—Leaflets long, narrow, irregularly lobed. The original tree was noticed in 1827 near Poitiers and propagated by grafting at the Royal Nurseries, Neuilly.

cv. 'LACINIATA'.—Leaflets cut into deep, narrow lobes. A handsome foliage tree, superior to 'Heterophylla'. It arose early in the 19th century but seems to have been always scarce. The specimens recorded in the British Isles are all of much the same girth (4 to $5\frac{1}{4}$ ft) and are 35 to 52 ft in height, but must date from long after the original introduction. Their locations are: Melbury, Dorset; Westonbirt School, Glos.; Hergest Croft, Heref.; Lindon Park, Kent; Chilton Court, Caversham, Berks.

f. MACROCARPA K. Koch *J. regia* var. *maxima* Loud.—Nuts about twice the ordinary size, but not good keepers and with kernels only half the size of the shell. Probably the same as the 'Noyer à bijoux' of the French, so-called because of the large shells being often mounted as jewel boxes. Also known as the Ban-nut or Claw-nut.

f. MONOPHYLLA (C. DC.) Schneid. *J. regia* var. *monophylla* C. DC.—Leaflets reduced in number to a large terminal one and a pair of small ones, the latter often absent.

cv. 'PENDULA'.—This cultivar name belongs to a pendulous variety growing with the nurseryman Armand Gothier of Fontenay-aux-Roses, who brought it from Waterloo in Belgium in 1850 (*Rev. Hort.* (1853), p. 480). A small pendulous tree at Kew came from the nurseryman Lee of Hammersmith shortly before 1880.

f. PREPATURIENS (Pepin) Rehd.—The original plant was raised around 1830 by the French nurseryman Chatenay, of Doué, Maine-et-Loire, who found it bearing fruit in a bed of three-year-old seedlings. Its offspring by seed were said to be more or less true to type and bear fruit when less than 3 ft high (*Rev. Hort.* (1882), p. 419; *Fl. d. S.*, Vol. 4, p. 367).

f. RACEMOSA (C. DC.) Schneid. *J. r.* var. *racemosa* C. DC.—Fruits in clusters of ten to fifteen. Known in orchards as Cluster or 'Noyer à grappe'.

f. RUBRA Hort.—Flesh of the kernel red, the skin blood-red; found wild in Styria and said to come true from seed. The name first appears in *Wien. Ill. Gart. Zeit.* (1897), p. 209 (an article by 'A.C.R.', probably A. C. Rosenthal).

f. TENERA (Loud.) *J. r.* var. *tenera* Loud.—A curious variant known as the Thinshelled Walnut or Titmouse Walnut—the 'Noyer à Coq tendre' or 'Noyer Mésange' of French gardens. The shells are so thin that they are easily pierced by birds.

The varieties cultivated for the qualities of their fruit are beyond the scope of this work.

J. STENOCARPA Maxim.

Little is known of this walnut, but it is akin to *J. mandshurica* and *ailantifolia* differing, however, in the following respects: the terminal leaflet is obovate, and thus very distinct in shape from the side leaflets, which are oblong; there is no patch of down above the scar left by the fallen leaf, as in the *J. mandshurica* group. The species was discovered in Manchuria by Maximowicz, who described the nuts as cylindrical or oblong-oval, with a long tapering apex. *J. stenocarpa* has been grown on the continent as *J. macrophylla*, an appropriate name, for I have a leaf 2 ft 8 in. long, with only eleven leaflets, the terminal one 8 in. long by 5 in. wide; the largest side ones 7½ in. long by 3 in. wide.

JUNIPERUS   JUNIPER   CUPRESSACEAE

The junipers are spread widely over the temperate and subtropical regions of the northern hemisphere, the hardy species coming from China and Japan, N. America, Europe, and N. Africa. The only species native of the British Isles is *J. communis*, which is not uncommon on chalk hills. They are evergreen, and range from trees up to 100 ft high down to low, spreading, or prostrate shrubs. The bark is usually thin, and often peels off in long strips. Leaves of two types: (1) awl-shaped, and from ⅛ to

$\frac{7}{8}$ in. long, borne in whorls of threes or in pairs; (2) small, scale-like, and rarely more than $\frac{1}{16}$ in. long, arranged oppositely in pairs and closely appressed to the branchlet. The first kind is found on the juvenile plants of all species; and several species, notably those of the communis group, retain it permanently. But other species, namely, those of the *Sabina* section, including *J. virginiana* and *chinensis*, as they get older develop more and more of the minute scale-like type of leaf which is essentially characteristic of the adult plant. A number of species, long after they have reached the fruit-bearing stage, continue to produce the juvenile as well as the adult type. This peculiarity is, however, apparently more characteristic of cultivated than of wild specimens. The flowers are unisexual, and most frequently the two sexes occur on separate trees, sometimes on one. The male flowers are small, erect, columnar or egg-shaped bodies, composed of ovate or shield-like scales, overlapping each other and each carrying anthers at the base. The fruit is composed of usually three to six coalescent, fleshy scales, forming a 'berry' that carries one to six seeds. It is this fruit that distinguishes the scale-leaved junipers from *Cupressus*, which they much resemble in foliage. Without fruit, the junipers can usually be recognised by a peculiar, aromatic, somewhat pungent odour, especially strongly developed in the savin.

Junipers like a well-drained soil, and most of them are lime-tolerant. This gives the genus a special value in chalky districts, where the impossibility of growing satisfactorily most of the heath family somewhat limits the number of evergreens available. Many of the species take two years to ripen their fruit, and the seeds will often lie dormant a year. Their germination may sometimes be hastened by plunging them in boiling water from three to six seconds, but this should only be regarded as an experiment, and tried with a portion of the seeds. All junipers can be increased by cuttings, a method especially suitable for the shrubby sorts.

J. CHINENSIS L.

J. sphaerica Lindl.; *J. sheppardii* (Veitch) Van Melle; *J.* × *media* Van Melle

A tree up to 60 ft high or a shrub; young shoots terete. Leaves of two types that are nearly always found on the same tree, viz., juvenile awl-shaped ones, and small, scale-like, adult ones. The former are $\frac{1}{4}$ to $\frac{1}{3}$ in. long, sharply and stiffly pointed, arranged either in threes or oppositely in pairs, with two glaucous lines on the upper surface, green elsewhere. Scale-like leaves usually in pairs, rarely in threes, closely flattened to the branchlet, $\frac{1}{16}$ in. long, blunt at the apex. The plants are usually unisexual, and the male flowers, very freely borne in early spring, are yellow and pretty. Fruits about $\frac{1}{4}$ in. in diameter, roundish or rather top-shaped, whitish with bloom when ripe; seeds two or three, occasionally more.

Native of Japan, Mongolia, and China; introduced to Kew in 1804 by W. Kerr. This juniper and *J. virginiana* are the commonest of tree-like junipers in gardens. It is perfectly hardy. From *J. virginiana* it differs in its blunt, scale-like leaves, and in the awl-shaped ones being frequently in whorls of threes. As a rule both juvenile and adult leaves occur on the same tree, but occasionally specimens of good age have nothing but juvenile foliage. There are male trees at Kew which bear flowers in the axils of leaves of the awl-shaped, juvenile type. Although *J. chinensis* is commonly dioecious, plants with flowers of both sexes occasionally occur.

Van Melle's controversial treatment of *J. chinensis* is set out in his book *Review of Juniperus chinensis et al.*, published by the New York Botanical Garden in 1947.

A. F. Mitchell has found that few trees survive of those that were mentioned by Elwes and Henry early this century or even of those listed in the returns to the R.H.S. Conifer Conference of 1933. The largest existing specimens are mostly of poor habit and 50 to 60 ft in height and 3½ to 6 ft in girth.

cv. 'AUREA'. YOUNG'S GOLDEN JUNIPER.—The whole of the young parts of this plant are golden yellow, very striking in summer. Raised in Young's nursery at Milford, in Surrey; of rather dense, slender form. The colouring of this variety comes mainly from the adult foliage, which predominates; the juvenile leaves are paler.

cv. 'BLAAUW'—Resembling 'Plumosa' but more erect and with bluish grey foliage. Introduced from Japan by J. Blaauw & Co. of Holland *c.* 1924 (Den Ouden and Boom, *Man. Cult. Conif.* (1965), p. 149). 'GLOBOSA CINEREA', distributed by Messrs Wallace as "J. virginalis globosa, grey form", and re-named by Hornibrook, is very similar; it was also imported from Japan, before 1916.

cv. 'COLUMNARIS'.—Of slender columnar habit. Leaves mostly awl-shaped, deep green. A selection from plants raised from seeds collected by F. N. Meyer in Hupeh, China, in 1905. 'COLUMNARIS GLAUCA' is similar but with glaucous foliage (Den Ouden and Boom, *Man. Cult. Conif.* (1965), p. 150).

cv. 'FEMINA'.—A small tree with rather lax branches. Leaves scale-like, closely appressed. Fruits small, with a vivid blue bloom. The plants grown under this name are probably a clone descended from the plant introduced from China in 1839 by J. R. Reeves as *J. flagelliformis* and also known as *J. reevesiana*.

cv. 'JAPONICA'.—This has become the established name for what is probably a clone, characterised by very stiff, sharp, glaucous juvenile leaves; such leaves predominate, but on old plants the terminal branchlets bear some adult, scale-like foliage. It grows to a few feet high. This juniper is probably the same as the one described by Carrière in 1855 as *J. japonica* and said by him to have been introduced to Europe in 1840. But the epithet *japonica* has been used for other forms of *J. chinensis* imported from Japan. See 'Plumosa'.

cv. 'KAIZUKA'.—Main stem and branches slanting; branchlets clustered. Leaves scale-like, vivid green. Female. A very picturesque large shrub (or an irregularly branched tree if the leader is trained). It is also known as *J. chinensis* var. *torulosa* Bailey (*J. sheppardii* var *torulosa* (Bailey) Van Melle).

cv. 'KETELEERI'.—Of columnar habit. Leaves scale-like, very pointed. Free-fruiting. It is sometimes placed under *J. virginiana*. Van Melle refers it to *J. sphaerica* and notes it is well matched by a specimen collected by Henry in northern Hupeh.

cv. 'PFITZERANA'.—A medium-sized shrub with arching branches spreading at an angle of about 45° to the horizontal, eventually becoming about 8 ft high and flat-topped. Taller specimens can be obtained by training and pruning when the plant is young. Leaves mainly appressed and sharply pointed (not at all like the true adult leaves of *J. chinensis*); others acicular and spreading, both kinds occurring together in the same spray. This juniper is now much valued as an architectural plant, but was little known before the second world war. It was put into commerce by Späth's nurseries in 1899 but he had received the original plant as *J. chinensis* var. *pendula* many years earlier.

Van Melle considers that this juniper is *J. chinensis* × *sabina* (*J.* × *media* Van Melle). He states that similar plants have been found recently in the Ho Lang Shan range of Mongolia and suggests that 'Pfitzerana' may have originally been introduced from there by the French missionary David around 1866. It should be added that 'Pfitzerana' is a tetraploid (*Journ. Arn. Arb.*, Vol. 14 (1933), p. 369).

Clones resembling 'Pfitzerana' in botanical characters are: 'PFITZERANA AUREA', with golden sprays; 'OLD GOLD', denser and more golden than the preceding; 'HETZII', a vigorous shrub with glaucous foliage.

cv. 'PLUMOSA'.—Branches spreading; branchlets short, with dense, drooping sprays. Leaves mostly scale-like. This cultivar was at one time distributed as *J. japonica* or *J. chinensis* var. *japonica*, but it is not the *J. japonica* of Carrière (see 'Japonica'). It attains a height of about 3 ft, but more in spread. 'PLUMOSA AUREA' is somewhat more erect and has the foliage green-gold at first, later bronze-gold. There are two variegated cultivars in this group—'PLUMOSA ALBOVARIEGATA' and 'PLUMOSA AUREOVARIEGATA'.

var. SARGENTII Henry *J. sargentii* (Henry) Takeda; *J. procumbens* Sarg., not Sieb.—A prostrate plant producing long creeping stems. Leaves on adult plants all scale-like. Henry described this variety from a specimen collected by Professor Sargent on the coast of the North Island of Japan (Hokkaido) in 1892; it was introduced by him to the Arnold Arboretum at the same time. According to Ohwi's *Flora of Japan* this variety is found on sea-shores throughout Japan and also on rocky cliffs in the mountains. It is also a native of Korea, Sakhalin, and the Kuriles.

cv. 'VARIEGATA'.—A well-marked form in which a considerable portion of the younger growth is wholly creamy white, the rest wholly green. Introduced from Japan by Fortune, one of whose original plants used to grow in the Knap Hill nursery. This variety is of sturdier habit and dwarfer than the type.

J. DAHURICA Pall.—A procumbent shrub with prostrate or at least horizontally spreading very stout main branches and erect secondary branches. Leaves mainly awl-shaped and spreading, but often scale-like, especially at the ends of the shoots, the scale-leaves rhombic, sharply pointed. Fruits about $\frac{3}{16}$ in. wide, globular, dark brown with a greyish bloom. Seeds two to four. A native of the Russian Far East, from Transbaikalia eastward to the Ussuri region, in rocky places in the mountains, and of N. Mongolia; closely allied to *J. chinensis*. It was introduced to Britain in 1791 but probably all the plants now cultivated in Europe and America descend from a later introduction by Parsons' nurseries, Flushing, USA. These show well the very stout main branches mentioned by

Pallas in his original description, but according to Van Melle (op. cit., p. 37) it differs from the 'type' in its fruits; he suggests that it may have been raised from seeds collected in Korea. The Parsons juniper is generally known as *J. chinensis* var. *parsonsii* Hornibr. (*J. dahurica* var. *parsonsii* (Hornibr.) Van Melle), or as *J. chinensis* 'Expansa'.

J. COMMUNIS L.   COMMON JUNIPER

A shrub of spreading habit, sometimes a small tree, usually 6 to 12 ft high (occasionally 20 to 40 ft); prostrate forms also occur. Young shoots three-cornered, bearing the leaves in whorls of three. Leaves spreading, $\frac{1}{4}$ to $\frac{5}{8}$ in. long, $\frac{1}{16}$ in. wide; always awl-shaped and terminated by a needle-like point, concave on the upper surface, with one comparatively broad glaucous band of stomata up the centre, divided sometimes by a green line towards the base; beneath, the leaf is green and keeled. Fruits globose or rather oval, about $\frac{1}{4}$ in. in diameter, black covered with a blue bloom, and containing two or three seeds embedded in resinous mealy pulp, ripening the second or third year.

The juniper of the chalk downlands and limestone hills of Britain belongs to the typical part of a species which extends, with many variations, throughout the temperate parts of the northern hemisphere; no other coniferous species has so wide a range. In elevated gardens on calcareous soils it is, with its garden varieties, one of the most satisfactory and pleasing of evergreens, but it will thrive equally well where the soil is neutral or slightly acid. In the mountains of Europe and towards the Arctic Circle it gives way to the dwarf juniper (subsp. *nana*, described below). The berries of both were once used as a diuretic in medicine and are still used to flavour gin. In Norway a kind of beer is made from them.

The common juniper as described above is the typical subspecies (*J. communis* subsp. *communis*), but three others are recognised by J. Amaral Franco in *Boll. Soc. Broteriana*, Vol. 36 (1962), pp. 101–120, and his classification is followed in the present revision. There are also many garden varieties, of which only a few can be mentioned.

cv. 'AUREA'.—Young shoots and young leaves yellow; otherwise resembling the typical common juniper.

cv. 'COLUMNARIS'.—Taller than 'Compressa' and of freer growth.

cv. 'COMPRESSA'. NOAH'S ARK JUNIPER.—A slender, cone-shaped shrub of minute dimensions, with branches and leaves so dense as to form a rigid mass, the leaves very short. This remarkable shrub is the daintiest of conifers, and probably the slowest growing of them. Plants twenty years of age will often not have reached $1\frac{1}{2}$ ft in height but may in time become almost twice as high. '. . . this dwarf form seems undoubtedly less hardy than the type; it frequently gets 'browned' by cold, cutting winds or severe frosts, and seems to resent very exposed situations—the finest specimens I have seen were in rather heavy soil and somewhat moist conditions' (Murray Hornibrook, *Dwarf and Slow-growing Conifers*, 2nd ed., p. 115).

subsp. DEPRESSA (Pursh) Franco *J. communis* var. *depressa* Pursh; *J. c.* var. *canadensis* Loud.—How, if at all, the North American representatives of the common juniper are to be differentiated from the Old World forms has never been quite clear. Franco states that the only reliable difference is that in the American plants the stomatal band on the upper surface of the leaves is very narrow—scarcely as wide as each green margin. In this subspecies, found in both the United States and Canada, the plant is usually prostrate, but not invariably so.

It should be noted that the clone commonly cultivated under the name *J. communis* var. *depressa* must be wrongly named, if the character given by Franco is valid, since the leaves have a glaucous band much wider than each green margin. In this clone the exposed side of the leaves becomes tinged pale brown in winter.

cv. 'DEPRESSA AUREA'.—A prostrate plant with the young leaves golden yellow.

cv. 'ECHINIFORMIS'. HEDGEHOG JUNIPER.—Of dwarf, globose habit. Leaves opposite, rather thick. Award of Merit, 25 April 1961 (*Bull. A.G.S.*, Vol. 30, p. 68 and p. 176 (plate)).

subsp. HEMISPHAERICA (J. & C. Presl) Nyman *J. hemisphaerica* J. & C. Presl; *J. depressa* Stev.; *J. communis* var. *depressa* (Stev.) Boiss., not Pursh— Leaves oblong-linear, densely set on the shoots, mostly under ½ in. in length but occasionally longer (up to ¾ in.), $\frac{1}{16}$ to $\frac{1}{12}$ in. wide, rather thick, upper surface with a broad stomatal band and covered with a waxy coat. In habit this juniper is variable; it may be erect and up to 8 ft high, prostrate (as in the Caucasian and Crimean plants), or take the form of a hemispherical cushion (as in the type from Mt Etna and the Monti Nebrodi in Sicily). A native of N. Africa, S. Europe, and the Near East.

cv. 'HIBERNICA' ('Stricta').—A narrowly conical tree of silvery grey aspect and dense habit; outside twigs erect, not drooping as in cultivated plants of f. *suecica*. It is very striking when in good health and effective in formal arrangements. See further under f. *suecica*. It is known as the Irish juniper and may be the same as the plant listed by Loddiges (1836 catalogue) as *J. hibernica* but this is not certain, and it may not even be of Irish origin.

cv. 'HORNIBROOKII'.—'This is a form which I found in Co. Galway, in the West of Ireland, among the normal bushy forms which the common juniper assumes in that country. It was a perfectly prostrate mat, flowing down over rocks and absolutely following their contours—it was then about a yard across and not more than 4 to 5 in. in height. I found it easy to propagate from cuttings, and it soon strayed into cultivation' (M. Hornibrook, *Dwarf and Slow-growing Conifers*, 2nd ed., p. 111). Although the subsp. *nana* (q.v.) has been reported from W. Ireland, Hornibrook's juniper does not belong to it, as has been erroneously stated (though not by Hornibrook himself), and is probably one of the many intermediates that occur between this and the typical subspecies.

subsp. NANA Syme *J. communis* var. *montana* Ait.; *J. sibirica* Burgsdf.; *J. communis* var. *saxatilis* Pall., *nom. inedit.*; *J. nana* Willd.—A prostrate or procumbent shrub with stout, rigid branchlets. Leaves mostly under ½ in. long, about $\frac{1}{16}$ in. wide, obtuse or acute and shortly mucronate at the apex, densely set on the shoot and pointing forward along it, often incurved, stomatal band on upper surface twice to three times as wide as each green margin.

Native of Eurasia in high latitudes and in mountains farther south. This juniper has been confused with prostrate forms of the common juniper but is quite distinct in the shape and posture of its leaves. Intermediate forms occur where the two subspecies are in contact.

cv. 'OBLONGA PENDULA'.—Branches horizontal, drooping at the tips; branchlets pendulous. The epithet *oblonga* might suggest that this is a pendulous variety of *J. communis* var. *oblonga* (Bieb.) Parl., a native of the E. Caucasus and Armenia. But that variety is described as having brownish fruits, whereas 'Oblonga Pendula', as seen in gardens, has the fruits of typical *J. communis*.

f. SUECICA (Mill.) Beissn. *J. communis* var. *suecica* (Mill.) Ait.; *J. suecica* Mill.; *J. communis* var. *fastigiata* Parl., in part. SWEDISH JUNIPER.—Of fastigiate habit but variable in shape and size; leaves said to be shorter than in the normal shrubby form. Found wild in N.E. Germany, Denmark, Sweden, and Norway. The Swedish juniper was first formally described by Miller in 1768, from a plant grown by him, but he mentions it in earlier (pre-Linnaean) editions of his *Dictionary* under the name *J. vulgaris arbor*. Plants (and seeds) were available in commerce in Britain by 1775, and have been in cultivation ever since, though it is very unlikely that they were all of one clone. At the present time there are at least two clones in commerce in Germany and Holland under the illegitimate cultivar name 'Suecica'. One is very distinct from 'Hibernica' in its broader and looser habit and its drooping twigs. The correct name for this is 'PYRAMIDALIS' (Van Ouden and Boom, *Man. Cult. Conif.*, p. 169; F. J. Grootendorst in *Dendroflora*, No. 5, p. 31 and fig. on p. 32). The other, which was recently highly rated after trial at Boskoop, is a slender tree tapered at the apex, with slightly drooping outer twigs and needles soft to the touch (Grootendorst, op. cit., p. 30). This is likely to be an improvement on 'Hibernica' but at the moment appears to lack a distinguishing name.

J. CONFERTA Parl.
J. litoralis Maxim.

An evergreen prostrate shrub with angular young shoots densely clothed with leaves. Leaves in whorls of three, awl-shaped, ¼ to ⅜ in. long, 1/16 in. or less wide; very sharply pointed, pale glossy green and keeled beneath, grooved above with one broad glaucous line of stomata along the middle. Fruits globose, ¼ to ⅓ in. wide, black covered with glaucous bloom and containing three ovoid, triangular seeds.

Native of the sea-coasts of Japan, especially on the sand dunes of Hakodate Bay in Hokkaido, where it was found by Maximowicz in 1861. Introduced by Wilson in 1914. It should be a useful plant for growing near the sea and certainly makes an excellent low ground cover. Botanically it is most closely allied to *J. rigida*, especially in the grooved leaves with one stomatic stripe above and in the three-seeded fruit, but that species is a small tree with much more thinly disposed leaves. In habit *J. conferta* more resembles *J. procumbens*, a species well distinguished by the green midrib dividing the stomatic upper surface into two stripes. *J. procumbens* has been grown erroneously under the name of "*J. litora-*

lis". which is really a synonym of *J. conferta*. Young plants of *J. conferta* have their leaves much less densely set on the branchlets than adult ones.

J. DEPPEANA Steud.   CEDRO

This species is represented in cultivation by the following variety:

var. PACHYPHLAEA (Torr.) Martinez *J. pachyphlaea* Torr. ALLIGATOR JUNIPER.—A tree 50 to 60 ft high, with a very distinct bark that cracks up into curious small squares. Leaves of two kinds, awl-shaped and scale-like, with intermediate states; the former $\frac{1}{8}$ to $\frac{1}{4}$ in. long, very sharply pointed, mostly in threes, whitish on the upper side, glaucous beneath; the scale-like ones in pairs or in threes, closely flattened to the branchlet, $\frac{1}{16}$ in. long, ovate, pointed, with the points incurved. Under a strongish lens minute teeth can be seen on the margin, and there is a resin-gland on the back. Fruits ripening the second year, globose or slightly longer than broad, $\frac{1}{2}$ in. long, covered with blue bloom.

Native of dry mountain-sides in the south-western United States. It was introduced to Kew about 1873 but our climate is scarcely sunny and hot enough for it. Two trees in the National Pinetum at Bedgebury, planted in 1926, are about 20 ft high and just under 1 ft in girth (1970). A tree at Kew did not thrive and died in 1958; it showed, however, the curious chequered bark which is the most distinctive feature of this juniper. It is very pretty in the silvery young growth of the juvenile form.

J. deppeana in its typical state is a native of Mexico, where it is widespread. It differs from the above variety in the absence of active resin-glands on the backs of the leaves.

J. DRUPACEA Labill.

Arceuthos drupacea (Labill.) Ant. & Kotschy

A dioecious tree of pyramidal or columnar shape, 30 to 50 ft high in cultivation, 60 ft high in nature; young shoots three-cornered, and bearing the leaves in spreading whorls of three. Leaves uniformly awl-shaped, sharply and stiffly pointed, $\frac{1}{2}$ to $\frac{7}{8}$ in. long, $\frac{1}{12}$ to $\frac{1}{8}$ in. wide at the base, upper surface slightly concave, marked with two dull glaucous bands of stomata separated by a narrow green midrib, margins also green. The undersurface is wholly green, and has the midrib rather prominent. Fruits globose, $\frac{3}{4}$ to 1 in. wide, brown with a glaucous covering.

Native of the mountains of Greece, Asia Minor, and Syria; introduced about the middle of last century. Although not now in the collection, it throve better than most junipers at Kew, and from its beauty and the distinctness of its shape, is well worth cultivation. It is easily distinguished by the size of its leaves, which (like the fruits) are the largest found among junipers. It differs from other species in the leaf-bases being attached to the stem, and extending downward to the next whorl (decurrent). Some other specimens recorded recently are: Wakehurst Place, Sussex, 42 × 2¼ ft (1964); Leonardslee, Sussex, 43 × 1½ ft (1961); Batsford Park, Glos., 47 × 5½ ft at 1 ft (1963).

J. EXCELSA M. Bieb.

J. macropoda Boiss.; *J. seravshanica* Komar.

A monoecious or dioecious tree 50 to 70 ft high in the wild; bark brown peeling off in strips; branchlets very slender. Leaves of both adult and juvenile form, the latter awl-shaped, in pairs or in threes, $\frac{1}{8}$ to $\frac{1}{4}$ in. long, sharply pointed. Adult leaves scale-like, in pairs, closely appressed to the branchlets, ovate, $\frac{1}{24}$ in. long, thickened towards the pointed apex, which is incurved; there is a glandular hollow towards the base. Male and female flowers usually on the same plant. Fruits globose, about $\frac{3}{8}$ in. diameter, dark purplish brown, covered with a blue bloom, containing usually four to six seeds.

J. excelsa ranges from the southern Balkans eastward through Asia Minor to Pakistan and Central Asia. It belongs to the same group as *J. virginiana* and *J. chinensis* but has more seeds in each fruit. The fruits are purplish brown, not bluish as in *J. virginiana*, and the juvenile leaves are usually in opposite pairs, whereas in *J. chinensis* they are commonly in threes. Juvenile foliage is rarely seen in adult plants.

According to H. Riedl in *Flora Iranica* (Cupressaceae, 1968), the species is variable in the wild in colour of bark, thickness of branchlets, form and length of leaves, and in colour and size of the fruits. The above description, however, only covers the cultivated form.

J. excelsa is an elegant, narrowly pyramidal tree in cultivation, and thrives very well. The typical form loses its juvenile foliage, but in the handsomer 'PERKINSII', well marked by its glaucous hue, the leaves are wholly of a semi-juvenile or intermediate type, half or less than half of the length of the true juvenile ones, but quite distinct from the true adult scale-like leaves. They are from $\frac{1}{16}$ to $\frac{1}{8}$ in. long, in pairs or in threes, awl-shaped and spreading. 'STRICTA' has the same type of foliage as 'Perkinsii' but is not so glaucous.

J. FOETIDISSIMA Willd. *J. sabinoides* Griseb.—This species, a native of the Balkan Peninsula and the Near East, is allied to *J. excelsa* but differs in its quadrangular branchlets and in the tips of the leaves being free, not appressed. The fruits are brown or dark grey, and contain only one to three seeds. It grows to a height of 50 to 60 ft in the wild.

J. FLACCIDA Schlecht.   MEXICAN JUNIPER

A tree of distinct habit, producing long, weeping, graceful branches; young shoots very thin and slender. Adult leaves in opposite, decussate pairs, narrowly lanceolate, appressed to the twigs at the base, slightly spreading at the end, sharply pointed, $\frac{1}{12}$ to $\frac{1}{10}$ in. long. Juvenile leaves often in threes, sometimes in pairs, awl-shaped, $\frac{1}{4}$ in. long, spine-tipped. Fruits up to $\frac{1}{2}$ in. wide, angular-globose, reddish brown, covered at first with glaucous bloom, carrying six to twelve seeds.

A native mainly of Mexico, whence it was introduced by Hartweg in 1838. It is found throughout the country, except the extreme south-east, and is one of its most beautiful and distinctive trees. At the northern end of its range it extends into the Chisos mountains of Texas. The most notable specimen in the

British Isles, at Bicton in Devon, was blown down in 1967; in 1959 it measured 39 × 4¼ ft. There are two small trees at Westonbirt, Glos.

J. FORMOSANA Hayata
J. taxifolia Parl., not Hook. & Arn.

A shrubby tree under 40 ft in height, dividing near the base into three or more stems; branches erect to spreading; branchlets pendulous, triangular; bark fibrous, peeling in thin, narrow strips. Leaves in threes, awl-shaped, ½ to ⅜ in. long, about 1/16 in. wide, jointed at the base, green and keeled beneath, upper surface with two bands of stomata separated by the raised midrib. Fruits orange-red to reddish brown, globular or ovoid.

Native of China, where it is widespread, and of Formosa. Although known since at least the middle of the 19th century, it was confused with *J. taxifolia* and first distinguished 1908. There is an example 15 ft high in the National Pinetum at Bedgebury, Kent.

J. HORIZONTALIS Moench   [PLATE 66
J. prostrata Pers.; *J. sabina* var. *procumbens* Pursh; *J. sabina* var. *prostrata* Loud.;
J. sabina var. *hudsonica* Knight and Perry

A shrub with procumbent or trailing main branches and erect, spreading or horizontal branchlets, often forming wide, low mats and rarely more than 2 ft high. Leaves green or glaucous, the adult ones scale-like, appressed, four-ranked, ovate or oblong, acute and usually sharply apiculate at the apex, with a conspicuous resin-gland on the back; juvenile leaves in opposite pairs, slightly spreading. Fruits blue, with a glaucous bloom, on recurved stalks, with two or three seeds.

A native of North America, with a wide range of habitats, from the coasts of New England to the dunes of the Great Lakes and dry slopes in the Rocky Mountains; introduced early in the 19th century. It is allied to *J. sabina*, *J. virginiana*, and *J. scopulorum*, and hybridises with the two latter species where it is in contact with them in the wild.

cv. 'ALPINA'.—Branches erect at first, becoming horizontal; branchlets erect, up to 2 ft high. Leaves awl-shaped, slightly glaucous. Rehder described this juniper from a plant received from the American nursery of Ellwanger and Barry. It may be the same as the *J. sabina* var. *alpina* of Loudon, described from a plant sold by Loddiges' nurseries.

cv. 'BAR HARBOR'.—This name seems to have been used in a collective sense for plants found wild near Bar Harbor on the north-eastern side of Mt Desert Island, Maine. These grow 'in crevices on the rocky coast and may frequently be found well within the reach of salt spray'; they are steel-blue in colour and of prostrate habit (H. Teuscher, in *New Flora and Sylva*, Vol. 8 (1936), p. 194).

cv. 'DOUGLASII'. WAUKEGAN JUNIPER.—Main branches prostrate, branchlets spreading. Foliage glaucous, scale-like or intermediate, becoming plum-purple in winter. Sprays densely set, pointing forward and upward. It makes a wide, dense mat and is a useful ground cover. The original plant grew near Douglas's nursery at Waukegan, Illinois, on Lake Michigan. Similar plants are found wild in sand-dunes on the shores of that lake. 'To see this Juniper as it grows naturally is a revelation. Its main branches are entirely buried in the sand, only the branchlets coming above the surface, where they form a dense, soft carpet which follows in every detail the outline of the dune.' (H. Teuscher, loc. cit., p. 195).

cv. 'GLAUCA'.—This variety was selected by Prof. Sargent of the Arnold Arboretum as the best-coloured form of *J. horizontalis* and sent by him to Murray Hornibrook, who named it, and described it as having 'extremely blue—practically steel-blue—whipcord-like foliage, with a very flat habit' (*Dwarf and Slow-growing Conifers*, 2nd ed., p. 120).

cv. 'PLUMOSA'.—A wide-spreading, flat-topped shrub with prostrate main branches and spreading branchlets, ultimately 2 ft high. Leaves grey-green, awl-shaped, purplish in winter. It was found growing wild on the coast of Maine and distributed by the Andorra nursery, Philadelphia (Rehder, *Journ. Arn. Arb.*, Vol. 6, p. 204). It is sometimes known misleadingly as the Andorra juniper.

cv. 'WILTONII'. ('Blue Rug').—Of completely prostrate habit. Ultimate branchlets slender, with small, closely appressed, bluish-grey leaves. The colouring is retained throughout the winter. The original plant was found in 1914 by J. C. van Heiningen of the South Wilton nurseries, Connecticut, growing on Vinalhaven Island, Maine (Den Ouden and Boom, *Man. Cult. Conif.* (1965), p. 179).

J. OCCIDENTALIS Hook.   WESTERN JUNIPER
J. pyriformis A. Murr.

A round-headed tree up to 45 ft (rarely 60 ft) high, or a shrub; its trunk occasionally 2 to 3 ft in diameter. Young shoots $\frac{1}{16}$ to $\frac{1}{12}$ in. thick with the scale-like, grey-green, overlapping leaves closely pressed to the stem, and arranged in threes; the exposed part is diamond-shaped, $\frac{1}{16}$ in. long, bluntish, with a conspicuous gland on the back. The leaves on juvenile shoots are awl-shaped, sharply pointed, keeled at the back, $\frac{1}{8}$ in. long, sometimes in pairs. Fruits subglobose to egg-shaped, $\frac{1}{4}$ to $\frac{1}{3}$ in. long, covered with a glaucous bloom, carrying two or three seeds.

Native of N.W. America from the State of Washington and British Columbia to California; first collected by Douglas about 1829. It has always been very rare in cultivation although as it has been found up to elevations of 10,000 ft it should be hardy enough. Douglas found trees 50 to 60 ft high with clean erect trunks.

J. OXYCEDRUS L.   PRICKLY JUNIPER

A dioecious shrub or small tree with a reddish-grey bark. Leaves in whorls of three, spreading, awl-shaped, $\frac{1}{2}$ to $\frac{3}{4}$ in. long, about $\frac{1}{12}$ in. wide, swollen and jointed at the base, tapered at the apex to a prickly point, green and sharply keeled beneath, upper surface with two glaucous bands of stomata, separated by the raised green midrib. Fruits dark red or purplish, about ½ in. wide.

Native of S. Europe eastward to the Caucasus and Iraq. It is rare in cultivation, needing a warmer and drier climate than ours to thrive well. The only specimen of any size recorded recently grows in the National Pinetum at Bedgebury, Kent; it measures 27 × 1½ ft (1967).

subsp. MACROCARPA (Sibth. & Sm.) Ball *J. macrocarpa* Sibth. & Sm.—This differs from the typical subspecies described above only in its slightly larger

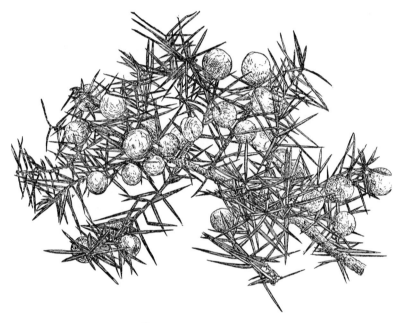

JUNIPERUS OXYCEDRUS

fruits and slightly wider leaves (about ¹⁄₁₀ in. wide). It occurs almost throughout the range of the species, usually in rocky or sandy places near the sea, while typical *J. oxycedrus* is an inhabitant of hills and lower mountain slopes.

J. oxycedrus is related to *J. communis* but is easily distinguished by its leaves with two glaucous bands above, separated by the raised midrib.

J. CEDRUS Webb & Berth.—A native of the Canary Islands, closely allied to *J. oxycedrus*, from which it differs in its larger size and more rigid needles. Of this interesting tree very few specimens are said now to remain in the wild, mostly in almost inaccessible places. Dr Perez of Orotava did much to revive an interest in this remarkable juniper, some specimens of which he said have trunks a yard or more in diameter. The wood of this tree is very pleasantly perfumed and was valued by the Guanches of Tenerife for making mummy cases.

Unfortunately it is only hardy in the milder parts and the only large specimen known grows at Castlewallan in Co. Down; this measures 33 × 2½ + 2 ft (1966).

J. PHOENICEA L.

Although trees and shrubs bearing this name are occasionally to be met with in gardens, it would seem that the true plant is now rare, and only to be found in the warmer parts of the country. It is a native of S. Europe, N. Africa, and the Canary Islands, and according to Aiton was introduced in 1683. The adult leaves are in pairs or in threes, scale-like, $\frac{1}{25}$ in. long, very closely arranged and appressed to the branchlet; the juvenile leaves (few or absent in old trees) are needle-like and in whorls of threes. Fruits variable, but mostly globose, about $\frac{1}{3}$ in. in diameter, dark reddish or yellowish brown, without bloom, containing three to nine seeds.

var. TURBINATA Parl.—Fruits egg-shaped, sometimes top-shaped, as compared with the usually spherical ones of the type.

J. PROCUMBENS Sieb. ex Miq.
J. chinensis var. *procumbens* Endl.

A low, spreading shrub of sturdy habit, 1½ to 2 ft high, densely furnished with stiff branchlets which turn upwards at the ends. Leaves ¼ to ⅓ in. long, always awl-shaped and in threes, ending in a sharp, stiff point, concave on the upper surface and glaucous, but with a distinct green midrib and margins, lower surface blue-green, speckled with white, with a groove near the base, and with two white marks at the base from which two glaucous lines run down a ridge which is really the lower part of the leaf adherent to the stem. Fruits not seen on cultivated plants but said to be about $\frac{3}{16}$ in. across, with two to three seeds.

A native of Japanese gardens and apparently little known in the wild state, but said by Ohwi (*Flora of Japan*, 1965) to occur wild on the coasts of Kyushu. It was named by Siebold in 1844 and introduced by him, but the name was first validly published by Miquel in 1870, in the posthumous part of Siebold and Zuccarini's *Flora Japonica*. Siebold listed this species in his 1856 catalogue but it seems to have been uncommon in European gardens until Japanese nurserymen began to export it around the turn of the century.

There was a fine example of this juniper in the Vicarage Garden at Bitton, 4 or 5 yards across and about 18 in. high. No dwarf juniper is handsomer than this, or makes a more striking low, dense covering for the ground. It never appears to have borne fruit in cultivation, but strikes root readily from cuttings.

J. RECURVA D. Don   HIMALAYAN JUNIPER
[PLATE 65

A tree 30 to 40 ft high, or a shrub, usually broadly pyramidal in shape, and clothed to the ground with branches, which are curved downwards at the ends;

bark brown, peeling off in thin flakes. Leaves in whorls of threes, $\frac{1}{8}$ to $\frac{1}{4}$ in. long, uniformly awl-shaped, all pointing forwards and rather appressed to the branchlet which they completely hide, upper (inner) surface very concave and glaucous, outer surface dull green changing to brown before the leaf falls, grooved along the middle. Fruits egg-shaped, $\frac{3}{4}$ in. long, brown the first year, ripening to a dark purple the second; one-seeded.

Native of the E. Himalaya, N. Burma, and W. Yunnan; introduced in 1830. A graceful tree and distinct, its value in gardens is decreased by the dull colour of the foliage, giving very frequently the impression of bad health. Male and female flowers occur on the same tree. It has lived out-of-doors at Kew for many years, but requires the moister conditions of the northern and western parts of the British Isles to be seen at its best.

The most notable specimens recorded recently are: Scorrier, Cornwall, 46 × 5 ft at 3 ft (1959); Mamhead, Devon, 49 × 4 ft (1963); Bicton, Devon, 43 × 2$\frac{3}{4}$ ft (1959); Hafordunas, Denbighs., 46 × 4$\frac{3}{4}$ ft (1960); Cortachy Castle, Angus, 51 × 5$\frac{1}{4}$ ft (1962); Abercairney, Perths., 44 × 3 ft (1962). At Castlewellan in Northern Ireland there is a tree 49 ft high with the main stem 3$\frac{1}{2}$ ft in girth and another with pendulous branches, 39 × 5$\frac{3}{4}$ ft at 1 ft. In Eire there are specimens of comparable size to the above at Birr Castle, Co. Offaly, and Mount Usher, Co. Wicklow.

cv. 'CASTLEWELLAN'.—This name has been given to the clone descended from the beautiful pendulously branched tree at Castlewellan, mentioned above.

var. COXII (A. B. Jacks.) Melville *J. coxii* A. B. Jacks.—The following three paragraphs are taken unchanged from previous editions, where this juniper was given the rank of species. But it is now generally agreed that it should rank as a variety of *J. recurva*:

This fine juniper was found by Messrs E. H. M. Cox and R. Farrer in Upper Burma in 1920 and was introduced by them, but it had been discovered some six years previously by Kingdon Ward. It is an evergreen tree 80 to 100 ft high with a single erect stem and graceful weeping branches, and Mr Cox estimates that the girth of the largest tree is 30 ft or more. The habit is narrowly pyramidal, the branchlets slender and rich dark green; the leaves are $\frac{1}{4}$ to $\frac{1}{2}$ in. long, $\frac{1}{16}$ in. or less wide, borne in threes, prickly pointed, with the two longitudinal strips of stomata on the upper side yellowish rather than glaucous and divided by a green median line. Fruits egg-shaped, $\frac{3}{8}$ in. long, dark purplish brown, and each contains one seed only.

Up to the publication of Mr Jackson's name in the *New Flora and Silva*, Vol. 5, p. 31, in October 1932, there was a disposition amongst botanists to regard this tree as a variety of *J. recurva*. But I think its enormous size and single stem (*J. recurva* is always more or less branched at the base), its very pendulous habit, and its longer, more outstanding leaves set further apart, amply justify its ranking as a species.

Farrer describes this tree as growing always at altitudes of over 10,000 ft in a region 'where the summer is wet and sunless, the winters of Alpine cold, and the springs late, ungenial and chilly'. This species is quite hardy at Kew, but it succeeds better in the warmer, softer counties of the south and west. In the woods at Exbury, near the Solent, it is growing extremely well and has borne fruit there. There seems to be no reason why it should not develop in such places not only into the finest of all junipers (which it is naturally) but into one of the most beautiful of all conifers. According to Farrer the wood is 'close and fine in grain, immortal, and of the most delicious fragrance, either fresh or burned'. It is probably to its 'immortal' quality that is due the love of the Chinese for this wood for coffin-making. The prices they are willing to pay for it make it one of the most costly of timbers.

The specimen at Exbury mentioned above now measures 41 × 2½ + 1¾ ft (1970). Others are: Hergest Croft, Heref., 34 × 2 ft and 32 × 2¼ ft (1969); Haldon Grange, Exeter, 26 × 1¼ ft (1967); Mount Usher, Co. Wicklow, Eire, 24 × 2½ ft and 24 × 2¼ ft (1966).

cv. 'EMBLEY PARK'.—Leaves bright green; young stems yellowish green. Propagated from a plant at Embley Park, Hants, which was probably raised from seeds collected by Forrest in Yunnan. The three plants there have also been referred to under the name *J. recurva* var. *viridis* (H. G. Hillier, *Dwarf Conifers* (1964), p. 39; H. J. Welch, *Dwarf Conifers* (1966), p. 201).

J. RIGIDA Sieb. & Zucc.

A tree sometimes 20 ft or more high, of elegant form, the branches being pendulous at the ends; young shoots glabrous, triangular. Leaves triangular in section, always needle-like and very slender, ⅓ to ¾ in. long, and produced in spreading whorls of threes, very sharply pointed. The upper surface is deeply grooved and has one glaucous band of stomatic lines along the middle; elsewhere the leaf is bright green. Fruits ¼ in. or more wide, at first broadly conical, then globose, dark brown, ripening the second year. Seeds one to three in each berry.

Native of Japan; introduced by John Gould Veitch in 1861. It thrives very well in the southern counties of England, making a small, broadly pyramidal shrub or small tree, but is not very common. Most closely allied to *J. communis* it is still very distinct in its narrower, longer leaves grooved along the upper side, and thinner, more elegant habit.

The finest specimen of *J. rigida* so far recorded in the British Isles grows at Tongs Wood, Hawkhurst, Kent; this measures 39 × 4½ ft (1970). Others measured recently are: Leonardslee, Sussex, 37 × 2½ ft (1970); Borde Hill, Sussex, 40 × 2 ft (1958); Smeaton Hepburn, E. Lothian, 34 × 2¼ ft (1966); Headfort, Co. Meath, Eire, 30 × 3¼ ft (1966).

subsp. NIPPONICA (Maxim.) Franco *J. nipponica* Maxim.; *J. communis* var. *nipponica* (Maxim.) Wils.—A prostrate shrub found high in the mountains of Japan (Hokkaido and the northern part of the main island). This juniper is usually placed under *J. communis* but Franco points out (*Boll. Soc. Broteriana*, Vol. 36 (1962), p. 119) that it is really much nearer to *J. rigida* which it resembles in the grooved upper surface of the leaves.

JUNIPERUS RIGIDA

J. SABINA L.   COMMON SAVIN
J. sabina var. *cupressifolia* Ait.

A shrub reaching in certain conditions 10 to 15 ft in height, but usually less than half as high; the whole plant emitting a strong, aromatic odour when bruised. The habit is usually stiff and spreading. Leaves of two types: the juvenile awl-shaped, and the adult scale-like. Juvenile leaves in opposite pairs, spine-tipped, $\frac{1}{8}$ to $\frac{1}{6}$ in. long, the concave upper side glaucous, except on the margins. The scale-like, genuinely adult leaves are on very slender branchlets, and about $\frac{1}{20}$ in. long, green, bluntish at the apex, thickened and rounded at the outside, which is marked about the centre with a sunken gland. As in other junipers with dimorphic foliage, there is an intermediate state in which the leaves are larger and more pointed than the fully adult ones. Plants either uni- or bi-sexual. Fruits globose or broadly top-shaped, $\frac{1}{5}$ to $\frac{1}{4}$ in. diameter, dark brown, ultimately covered with a blue bloom, and containing usually two seeds.

Native of the mountains of Central and S. Europe, where it is chiefly, but not invariably, found on limestone; also of W. Russia as far east as the Altai. It was cultivated in England in the first half of the 16th century. It is one of the handsomest and most useful of dwarf evergreens, especially for elevated and chalky districts. It is easily increased by cuttings.

Although *J. sabina* var. *cupressifolia* Ait. is clearly a synonym of *J. sabina* L., the plants cultivated under the name are usually dwarf; the example in the Nisbet collection in the R.H.S. Garden at Wisley fruits freely.

cv. 'MUSGRAVE'.—Of low, spreading habit. Leaves glaucous, some juvenile but loosely appressed, others adult. It arose in C. Musgrave's garden at Hascombe, Surrey.

cv. 'KNAP HILL'.—Resembling the Pfitzer juniper in habit but lower and denser. Foliage fine, adult. Raised at the Knap Hill nurseries in the early 1920s. It has been wrongly considered to be synonymous with the Pfitzer juniper.

var. TAMARISCIFOLIA Ait.—A low spreading shrub with most of the leaves of the juvenile type, borne in opposite pairs or in threes, bright green. The form often seen in gardens makes a fine architectural plant with closely tiered branches. It is not a geographical variety, but is occasionally met with in the wild.

cv. 'VARIEGATA'.—A dwarf shrub with close branches whose younger parts are tipped with creamy white.

J. SALTUARIA Rehd. & Wils.

This juniper is very rare in cultivation. It was discovered by Wilson in N.W. Szechwan, China, in 1904, and found again by Purdom in Kansu seven years later. Wilson described it as a shapely tree 10 to 48 ft high, of pyramidal shape and dense erect branching. Leaves scale-like, closely pressed to the stem, 'clear deep green', about $\frac{1}{12}$ in. long, the exposed portion diamond-shaped, incurved at the bluntish tip and with a gland at the base. The tree is bi-sexual, its egg-shaped or nearly globose fruits about $\frac{1}{5}$ in. long, black, shining and one-seeded. It appears to be most nearly related to *J. wallichiana*, which has berries twice as long. Wilson records that there are extensive woods of this juniper in the neighbourhood of Sungpan and that most of the houses in this city are built of it.

J. SCOPULORUM Sarg.

J. virginiana var. *scopulorum* (Sarg.) Lemm.

A tree up to 40 ft high, forming a round-topped head of branches, its trunk often dividing near the ground; bark reddish brown; young shoots slender. Leaves scale-like, closely pressed to the stem, overlapping, arranged in pairs and altogether very like those of *J. virginiana*. There is on the back of each leaf a usually well-defined gland. Fruits globose, ¼ in. wide, covered with a bright blue bloom, ripening the second year, carrying one or two seeds.

Native of the western United States, where it represents the *J. virginiana* of the eastern States. That species is closely akin to it but is well distinguished by ripening its seeds the first season. *J. scopulorum*, too, has only six stamens to each male flower, whilst *J. virginiana* has ten to twelve. The former, which was made a species by Sargent in 1897, is quite hardy, but owing to its similarity with *J. virginiana* has not obtained much notice from cultivators, and although it was introduced in 1839, is quite uncommon today. Numerous cultivars have been named in the United States, some of them dwarf.

J. SQUAMATA D. Don

J. densa Gord.

A low shrub with the main branches spreading over the ground, and the branchlets rising about 2 ft above them. Leaves always awl-shaped (never scale-like), and arranged in threes; they are pointed forwards, but not appressed to the stem, ⅛ to ¼ in. long, terminated by a slender fine point; margins green on the upper side and incurved, the concave centre uniformly glaucous or with two glaucous bands; lower side of leaf wholly green, and with a central groove. Fruits egg-shaped, about ⅓ in. long, reddish brown the first year, ripening and changing to purplish black the second, each carrying one seed.

Native of the Himalaya and China; introduced from Nepal about 1836, or perhaps earlier. It is allied to *J. recurva*, which it resembles in its uniform foliage, and the purple-black, one-seeded berries. The leaves, however, are broader, shorter, and more conspicuously glaucous, and the habit and general aspect very different. There was a good specimen at Bayfordbury from which the above description was made, which made a handsome low shrub, very dense and leafy in growth

var. FARGESII (Komar.) Rehd. & Wils. *J. fargesii* Komar.; *J. lemeean*, Lévl. & Blin—A very distinct variety, introduced by Wilson from Szechwan W. China, in 1908. It varies in habit from a small, even quite prostrate, shrub to a tree 15 to 40 ft high. Occasionally it is found even taller—in *The Garden* for 8 March 1924, Wilson figured a tree 85 ft high which he saw in China. This variety differs from the type in the spreading branches, in the leaves being longer (¼ to ⅓ in.) and narrower; also in the smaller fruits ¼ in. or less long. As in the type, the berry carries one seed. It seems on the whole distinct enough to rank as a species.

Handel-Mazzetti, who observed this juniper at first hand in N.W. Yunnan, remarked that it retains its distinctness from *J. squamata* even where it is found as a prostrate shrub at high altitudes—in other words that it is not simply a more arborescent form of *J. squamata*. He discussed it under the name *J. lemeeana*, which would be the correct name for this juniper as a species (*Symb. Sin.*, Part VII, p. 7).

cv. 'LODERI'.—Of dense, conical habit. Raised at Leonardslee from seeds received under the label "*J. wallichiana*" (*Gard. Chron.* (19 January 1929), p. 50).

cv. 'MEYERI'.—A variety of Chinese gardens, not known in the wild, which is believed to have originated in the horticultural centre of Lungchuan in N. Honan. It is a clone, which the Chinese propagated by grafting on *Thuja orientalis*, and was used by them as a pot-plant. Introduced by F. N. Meyer to the USA in 1910 and now common in gardens (*Journ. Arn. Arb.*, Vol. 3, p. 20, and Vol. 4, p. 127). It is, at least when young, one of the most beautiful of the junipers. The leaves point forward along the shoots, exposing the glaucous undersides, which give to the whole plant a steel-blue colouring. Main branches (including the leader) arching outwards; branchlets short, pendulous at the tips. It will grow to 15 or even 20 ft high but is at its most attractive as a young plant. [PLATE 67

f. WILSONII Rehd.—A shrub up to 6 ft high of very dense habit, the shoots recurved at the tips and crowded with leaves that are about $\frac{1}{6}$ in. long and broader than in the type. Discovered and introduced by Wilson in 1909. According to Rehder, this is an ecological form linked by intermediates to the prostrate forms found in the same area. Wilson's seed number 985 was taken from both kinds. The original plant of the clone 'PROSTRATA' was raised by Hornibrook from this seed number and further propagated by cuttings. *J. squamata* f. *wilsonii* also occurs in Yunnan, where it was collected by Forrest.

J. MORRISONICOLA Hayata *J. squamata* var. *morrisonicola* (Hayata) Li & Keng—The taxonomic status of this juniper, a native of Formosa, remains to be decided, but it is certainly very close to *J. squamata* var. *fargesii*. The cultivated plants, which are probably from seeds collected by Wilson in the mountains of Formosa, differ from this in having the branchlets more erect, so that the glaucous upper sides of the leaves are more exposed. This difference gives a distinctive colouring to young plants. The oldest plants in cultivation in Britain are no more than about 8 ft in height.

J. THURIFERA L.   SPANISH JUNIPER

A tree 30 to 40 ft high in the wild; narrowly pyramidal in cultivation. Leaves of two sorts, viz., awl-shaped and scale-like; the former sharply pointed, $\frac{1}{8}$ to $\frac{1}{6}$ in. long, arranged in opposite pairs in four superposed rows, the upper surface having two glaucous lines separated by a green one; scale-like leaves $\frac{1}{20}$ to $\frac{1}{16}$ in. long, pointed, and with a hollow at the back. Intermediate forms occur. Fruits $\frac{1}{4}$ to $\frac{1}{3}$ in. diameter, roundish, covered with glaucous bloom when ripe.

Native of Spain, S.E. France, and N. Africa; long introduced, but rare. It is fairly hardy at Kew, and is now about 30 ft high, most of its foliage being of the juvenile or intermediate kind. Its young shoots are nevertheless occasionally much cut by severe winters, as they were in that of 1908–9. The trees are unisexual.

This juniper is not common in cultivation, but the following examples have been recorded: Sheffield Park, Sussex, 45 × 3 ft (1960); Leonardslee, Sussex, 33 × 2¼ at 3 ft (1962). There is a smaller one at Westonbirt, Glos.

The French stands of this juniper are of great interest, being far removed from the main area of the species; the best known is the Genévraie de St Crepin in the upper valley of the Durance, where the climate is abnormally dry.

J. VIRGINIANA L.   EASTERN REDCEDAR

A tree usually 40 to 50, occasionally 60 to 100 ft high; the bark peeling off in long loose strips. It is pyramidal when young, becoming more round-topped with age. Leaves of both awl-shaped (juvenile) and scale-like (adult) forms on the same tree. The former, arranged in pairs, are ⅛ to ¼ in. long, pointed, concave inside and glaucous except on the margins, grey-green and convex outside, pointing forward. Scale-leaves 1/16 in. long, ovate, pointed (sometimes slenderly), thickened and convex outside, overlapping. Young specimens have none other than the awl-shaped type of leaf; as they grow older, branches of scale-like leaves appear until, in the adult state, the tree bears scarcely any other, and it is on these that the fruits are borne; fruits, however, are sometimes to be seen on branches bearing an intermediate type of leaf. Male and female flowers are usually separated on different trees, but occasionally appear on the same. Fruits roundish, ¼ in. long, scarcely so wide, covered with a blue glaucous bloom, carrying one or two seeds.

Native of the eastern and central United States and eastern Canada; introduced about the middle of the 17th century. This juniper is by far the commonest and largest of the arborescent species cultivated in gardens. It likes a well-drained soil, is perfectly hardy, and altogether one of the best thriving of eastern N. American trees in this country, especially on chalky soils. From the next most common of tree-like junipers, *J. chinensis*, this in all its forms is best distinguished by its awl-shaped leaves being nearly always in pairs, and by its scale-like leaves being always pointed. Small plants are like *J. sabina*, but that to be distinguished by its peculiar rank smell when crushed.

J. virginiana is a variable species in the wild and it is believed that this variability may be due in part to crossing with neighbouring species.

Cultivars of this species are greatly to be preferred to seedlings and unselected plants, which usually become of ugly habit with age. The oldest specimens of these latter are about 35 to 60 ft in height and 5¼ to 10¼ ft in girth. The number of named cultivars is large, but the following are the best known and are available in commerce:

'BURKII'.—Habit fastigiate, dense. Foliage blue-grey, slightly purplish in winter. It has attained a height of 20 ft at the R.H.S. Garden, Wisley.

'CANAERTII'.—Habit columnar. Leaves rich green. Free-fruiting. An example in the National Pinetum at Bedgebury, Kent, *pl.* 1926, is 34 ft high (1969).

T S—R

'ELEGANTISSIMA'.—Sprays golden at the tips.

'GLAUCA'.—Under this cultivar name Van Ouden and Boom (*Man. Cult. Conif.*, p. 200) describe a tree of narrow, columnar habit with thin, round, blue-bloomy branchlets and small glaucous appressed leaves (some leaves inside the plant acicular). But not all the plants that are or have been known by the name *J. virginiana glauca* belong to this clone.

'GREY OWL'.—A spreading shrub 3 to 4 ft high and more in width, with silvery grey leaves and slender sprays. Very elegant. It is possibly a hybrid, with *J. chinensis* 'Pfitzerana' as the pollen-parent.

'HILLII'.—Habit columnar, dense. Leaves glaucous, purplish in winter. Also known as *J. v.* 'Pyramidiformis Hillii' and *J. v.* 'Dundee'.

'SCHOTTII'.—A columnar tree with bright green scale-like foliage.

'SKY ROCKET'.—A very slender fastigiate variety with glaucous scale-like foliage. Some authorities consider that it belongs to *J. scopulorum*.

'TRIPARTITA'.—A shrub of low, spreading habit. Leaves mostly acicular, ascending to spreading, their exposed upper sides giving a glaucous cast to the whole plant; lower sides rich green.

J. WALLICHIANA Parl.　　BLACK JUNIPER
J. pseudosabina Hook. f., not Fisch. & Mey.

A tree 60 ft high in Sikkim, according to Brandis, with spreading branches. Leaves of two types: (1) juvenile, in whorls of threes, ⅛ to ¼ in. long, sharply pointed, pointing forwards, concave and very glaucous above, green and keeled below, all very closely set upon the branchlet, with the stalk extending down and attached to it (decurrent); and (2) adult leaves 1/16 in. long, scale-like, arranged in opposite pairs overlapping each other and appressed to the branchlet, pointed with the points incurved, grooved outside, bright green. Male and female flowers on separate trees. Fruits egg-shaped, tapered at the top, ¼ to ½ in. long, at first dark brown, blue when ripe, one-seeded.

Native of the Himalaya, up to 15,000 ft elevation; introduced by Sir Joseph Hooker to Kew in 1849, but no longer represented in the collection. It is rare in cultivation, and the trees considered to belong to it are 20 to 35 ft high and up to 2 ft in girth. There are specimens in this range of size at Wakehurst, Leonardslee, and Borde Hill, Sussex; National Pinetum, Bedgebury, Kent; Bodnant, Denbighs; East Bergholt, Suffolk; and Castlewellan, Co. Down.

J. PSEUDOSABINA Fisch. & Mey.—This allied species has been confused with *J. wallichiana* but is shrubby and has the scale-like leaves blunt or rounded at the end; the fruits are like those of *J. wallichiana* in being one-seeded, but are more globose and smaller. Native of Siberia and parts of central Asia.

KADSURA   SCHISANDRACEAE

A small genus of twining evergreen shrubs, natives of E. Asia and W. Malaysia. It is allied to *Schisandra*, but differs in having the fruits arranged in a globose head instead of an elongated spike.

K. JAPONICA (Thunb.) Dun.
Uvaria japonica Thunb.

A climbing, evergreen shrub up to 12 ft, with slender, twining branches. Leaves oval or lanceolate, slender-pointed, dark green, 2 to 4 in. long, 1¼ to 1¾ in. wide, quite glabrous and remotely toothed. Flower solitary on a slender stalk 1 to 1½ in. long, and borne singly in the leaf-axils of the current season's growth from June until autumn; the corolla yellowish white, ¾ in. across, composed of six to nine fleshy petals. Berries scarlet, clustered in a globose head 1 to 1¼ in. wide.

Native of Japan, China, and Formosa; introduced in 1860. This interesting and uncommon twiner is not particularly hardy in the open, and should be given the shelter of a wall. It can be increased by cuttings of half-ripened wood put in gentle heat.

cv. 'VARIEGATA'.—Leaves with an irregular border of creamy white.

KALMIA   ERICACEAE

A small group of shrubs, mostly evergreen, native of N. America, and named by Linnaeus in honour of Peter Kalm, one of his pupils, and the author of a famous 18th-century book of North American travel. They are all handsome plants, especially *K. latifolia* and *K. polifolia*, with the leaves in some species alternate, in others opposite or in threes. Flowers five-parted, flattish, open, and produced in showy clusters. They show an interesting mechanism to secure fertilisation. There are ten stamens, which on first expanding are bent back so that the anthers are held in little cavities in the corolla. The 'knee' formed by the stalk of the stamen is sensitive, and when the pollen is ripe, if it be touched, the anther is released with a jerk, sending a little dust of pollen in the direction of the stigma, or over the insect whose movements set it in motion. The fruit is a globose capsule, five-celled and many-seeded. The foliage of kalmias is mostly considered poisonous to animals that graze on it. *K. angustifolia* is on this account known as 'lamb-kill' in the United States.

Kalmias like a peaty soil and cool, permanently moist conditions at the root. They are best propagated by seed, which should be sown as advised for rhododendrons, and afterwards pricked off in boxes. *K. poli-folia* may be increased by cuttings of moderately ripened growths in July and August.

K. ANGUSTIFOLIA L.   SHEEP LAUREL

An evergreen shrub, varying considerably in height and habit. The largest form is 2 to 4 ft high, and of thin, open growth, the smallest a dwarf, tufted plant 6 in. or so high; young wood slightly downy. Leaves in pairs or in threes, oval or ovate, ¾ to 2 in. long, ¼ to ¾ in. wide, glabrous and bright green above, paler or semi-glaucous beneath; stalk ⅙ to ⅓ in. long. Flowers produced in June, densely packed in rounded clusters 2 in. across at the termination of the previous year's growth. Corolla saucer-shaped, ⅓ in. across, deep rosy-red; lobes five, shallowly triangular. Calyx and flower-stalks downy and glandular. *Bot. Mag.*, t. 331

Native of eastern N. America; introduced in 1736. It spreads by sucker growths at the base, and the dwarfer forms are dainty shrubs. Propagated by seed or by pulling old plants apart in spring.

f. CANDIDA Fern.—Flowers white.

var. OVATA Pursh—Leaves ovate, broader.

f. RUBRA (Lodd.) Zab.—Flowers deeper red.

K. CAROLINA Small *K. angustifolia* var. *carolina* (Small) Fern.—Leaves coated beneath with a fine, greyish, velvety down. Calyx not glandular. Introduced 1906. It may also be in cultivation from seeds collected in 1933 by the New York Botanic Garden Expedition to the Appallachians, under No. 63. These came from Flat Rock, N. Carolina, which is the type-locality of the species, and the plants were described in the field notes as 2 ft high, with bluish foliage and flowers rather larger than in those of *K. angustifolia*, and of clearer pink.

K. CUNEATA Michx.

A deciduous, sometimes partially evergreen shrub 3 to 4 ft high, of thin, erect, gaunt habit; young shoots reddish, glandular-hairy. Leaves alternate, nearly or quite stalkless, obovate or narrowly oval, ¾ to 2 in. long, ⅕ to ½ in. wide, always narrowed towards the base, but pointed or rounded at the apex, glabrous and dark green above, paler and with scattered gland-tipped hairs beneath. Flowers produced in June and July at the end of the previous year's growth in a series of clusters (fascicles), each consisting of two to six blossoms. Corolla white, ½ to ⅝ in. across, cup-shaped; lobes shallow, rounded. Calyx-lobes ⅛ in. long, ovate, green, glabrous; flower-stalks threadlike, ¾ to 1¼ in. long, beset with a few scattered hairs. *Bot. Mag.*, t. 8319.

Native of the Carolinas, south-eastern United States; discovered by Michaux, and introduced to Britain in 1820, but for many years quite lost to cultivation, until reintroduced to Kew in 1904. It is a distinct species, but has a somewhat inelegant habit owing to its sparse branching. It loses all or nearly all its leaves in severe weather, and is, perhaps, seen to best advantage planted thinly with an undergrowth of some dwarf peat-loving evergreen like *Leiophyllum* or *Bruckenthalia*.

K. HIRSUTA Walt.

This, the 'hairy kalmia', is an evergreen shrub 1 to 2 ft high, with very bristly slender young shoots. Leaves alternate, very shortly stalked, oval or oblong, pointed, tapered at the base, $\frac{1}{4}$ to $\frac{1}{2}$ in. long, $\frac{1}{12}$ to $\frac{1}{4}$ in. wide, bright green, bristly like the young shoots. Flowers solitary in the leaf-axils, $\frac{1}{2}$ in. wide, each borne on a slender bristly stalk; corolla pink, flattish, saucer-shaped; sepals linear-lanceolate, pointed, $\frac{1}{4}$ in. long, bristly, persisting after the corolla has fallen. *Bot. Mag.*, t. 138.

Native of the S.E. United States from Virginia to Florida, where it flowers in June; introduced from Carolina in 1790 by Watson, 'nurseryman of Islington'. It was figured during the following year in the *Botanical Magazine*, but has never secured a firm footing in English gardens, being too tender for all but our mildest counties. It is very distinct in its bristliness, and in habit and size of leaf rather resembles *Daboecia cantabrica*. I have not seen it in flower, but pictures show that it has considerable beauty. The corolla has the typical flat, round shape, and it has, like the other species, little pockets towards which the stamens are bent back and in which the anthers are retained. It would be interesting to try this species again in some of the warm south coast gardens.

K. LATIFOLIA L.   CALICO BUSH, MOUNTAIN LAUREL
K. *lucida* Hort.   [PLATE 69

A large, robust, evergreen shrub with rather the aspect of a rhododendron when not in flower, a single plant sometimes forming a dense thicket 10 ft high, and 15 ft through; young shoots slightly downy. Leaves alternate, leathery, glabrous, rich glossy green, oval, 2 to 5 in. long, $\frac{3}{4}$ to $1\frac{1}{2}$ in. wide, tapering at both ends, often in a cluster at the end of the twig; stalk $\frac{1}{4}$ to 1 in. long. Flowers crowded in several flattish or rounded clusters, terminating the growth of the previous year, and collectively 3 or 4 in. across. Corolla saucer-shaped, $\frac{3}{4}$ to 1 in. across, varying in colour from white or pale blush to deep rose, with five triangular blunt lobes. Stamens white, with brown anthers. Calyx-lobes ovate $\frac{1}{10}$ in. long, covered with viscous hairs like the flower-stalk, which is slender, and $\frac{3}{4}$ to $1\frac{1}{4}$ in. long. The flowers vary much in depth of shade, size, and density in the truss. *Bot. Mag.*, t. 175.

Native of eastern N. America; introduced in 1734, and probably the most beautiful evergreen shrub obtained from that region. There are bushes of the dimensions given above in the south of England, but generally the species has not been planted so extensively as it deserves. It is said sometimes to be over 30 ft high in the wild. A great breadth of it in the Arnold Arboretum, near

Boston, USA, 200 to 300 yards long, provides every June one of the public flower feasts of that city. I have also seen it wild on the New Hampshire Hills, where it grows in woods, but is seen at its best on grass- and juniper-covered hills sprinkled in groups, or as isolated bushes, generally 4 to 6 ft high.

f. MYRTIFOLIA (Jäger) K. Koch—A dwarf bush, usually 2 to 4 ft high, the largest leaves about 2 in. long. It is a pretty, neat bush, useful in places where the type is too large. It is usually propagated by seeds, and very variable in habit and size of leaf.

f. POLYPETALIA (Nichols.) Rehd.—A form in which the corolla-lobes are divided almost to the base. It was found near South Deerfield, Mass., and is merely a curiosity of no merit.

f. RUBRA K. Koch—Flowers deep pink.

K. *latifolia* is not an easy plant to please in the British climate and may be a failure even where rhododendrons thrive. The explanation is perhaps partly that it needs more 'continental' conditions than most members of the Ericaceae. Also, it is evidently a variable species and, being difficult to propagate vegetatively, it has been commonly raised from seeds, which yield plants of unequal merit, some of which are reluctant to flower. At Sheffield Park in Sussex, A. G. Soames selected many fine seedlings, of which one—'CLEMENTINE CHURCHILL'—received an Award of Merit in 1952. This has been successfully propagated by cuttings and will eventually become available in commerce. The Sheffield Park strain derives from selected plants raised in the Knap Hill nursery and from one sent by Prof. Sargent from the Arnold Arboretum (*Journ. R.H.S.* Vol. 59 (1934), pp. 98–100). Provided it is kept mulched, it is best grown in almost full sun and preferably in groups, away from other shrubs.

K. POLIFOLIA Wangenh.

K. glauca Ait.; *K. glauca* var. *rosmarinifolia* Pursh; *K. polifolia* var. *rosmarinifolia* (Pursh) Rehd.

An evergreen shrub 1 to 2 ft high, of rather thin, erect, bifurcating habit, but bushy; young shoots two-edged, covered with a fine down at first. Leaves opposite or in threes, narrowly oblong or ovate, ¾ to 1½ in. long, ⅛ to ⅜ in. wide, plane or recurved at the margins, tapered at both ends, dark lustrous green above and glabrous except on the midrib, lower surface glaucous white. Flowers in a terminal, flattish cluster 1 to 1½ in. across, produced late in April; flower-stalks glabrous, very slender. Calyx-lobes ovate-oblong. Corolla saucer-shaped, about ½ in. across, with five broad, shallow lobes, of a beautiful pale purplish rose. Stamens of the same colour, but with brown anthers. *Bot. Mag.*, t. 177.

Native of both eastern and western N. America; introduced in 1767. Naturally a plant of bogs and other wet places, it likes a cool, moist soil. Under the drier conditions usually given it in cultivation it is a sturdier more erect shrub than it appears to be in nature, where it is said to be straggling. It is very hardy and one of the brightest of spring-flowering shrubs of its colour.

var. MICROPHYLLA (Hook.) Rehd. *K. glauca* var. *microphylla* Hook.; *K.*

microphylla (Hook.) Heller—A dwarf, spreading shrub usually less than 6 in. high. Leaves ⅜ to ¾ in. long, half or less wide. Flowers about ⅜ in. wide, usually rose-purple. An alpine variety of the species ranging from Alaska to California and Colorado. For a photograph of this variety taken in Colorado see *New Fl. & Sylv.*, Vol. 8, fig. lvii.

KALMIOPSIS   ERICACEAE

A genus of a single species, discovered in Oregon, USA, in 1930 and described two years later. It is most closely allied to *Rhodothamnus* and perhaps not separable from it; from that genus it differs only in its scaly (lepidote) leaves and its campanulate rather than rotate corolla. It also bears some resemblance to *Kalmia*, particularly to *K. polifolia*, but the anthers are not contained in pockets as they are in *Kalmia*, and the lepidote leaves also serve to distinguish it from that genus.

KALMIOPSIS LEACHIANA

K. LEACHIANA (Henderson) Rehd.

Rhododendron leachiana Henderson; *Rhodothamnus leachianus* (Henderson) Copeland

An evergreen shrub 6 to 12 in. high, of compact, tufted habit; young shoots minutely downy. Leaves ¼ to ¾ in. long, about half as wide, oval or slightly obovate, pointed, cuneate at the base, dark green and densely dotted with glistening, sunken glandular scales beneath. Flowers axillary and terminal, each on a slender, glandular, hairy stalk ½ to ¾ in. long, forming erect clusters of about ten, 1 to 2 in. long. Corolla open bell-shaped, ½ to ⅝ in. wide, rosy-red tinged purple, five-lobed; calyx also five-lobed, the lobes ⅛ in. long, pointed, rosy; stamens ten, packed in the mouth of the corolla, the base of each fringed with hairs.

K. *leachiana* is a rare species in the wild, occurring in a few scattered localities in the mountains of Oregon, USA. It was discovered by Mr and Mrs Leach in 1930 in the Siskiyous, and introduced to Britain a few years later. The late Mrs Anley showed it at the R.H.S. Hall on 23 March 1937, when it received an Award of Merit. Later the species was found again by M. le Piniec in the upper reaches of the Rogue River in S. Oregon. There are plants in the R.H.S. Garden at Wisley raised from seeds collected in another new locality by Brian Mulligan, Director of the Washington Arboretum, and others from wild seeds collected by Carl English Jun. Mr Mulligan tells us that, in the wild, this species is often found on bare, sunny slopes.

KALOPANAX   ARALIACEAE

An E. Asiatic genus comprising the one species described below. It is allied to *Acanthopanax*, but in that genus the leaves are compound.

K. PICTUS (Thunb.) Nakai

Acer pictum Thunb.; *Acer septemlobum* Thunb.; *Kalopanax septemlobus* (Thunb.) Koidz.; *Acanthopanax ricinifolium* (Sieb. & Zucc.) Seem.; *Kalopanax ricinifolius* (Sieb. & Zucc.) Miq.; *Panax ricinifolium* Sieb. & Zucc.

A large, deciduous tree 80 to 90 ft high in the wild, with a trunk as much as 4 ft in diameter. In cultivation it is a very elegant tree, the branches armed with stout, broad-based, yellowish prickles. Leaves palmate, measuring in young plants as much as 14 in. in width, scarcely so much in length, deeply five- or seven-lobed, becoming smaller as the trees increase in age, and then from 7 to 10 in. wide, the shallow lobes ovate-triangular, long-pointed, toothed, reaching about one-third or less towards the centre; upper surface dark shining green, lower one paler and covered with grey down when young, which falls away afterwards except from the vein-axils. Flowers small and white, and produced in numerous umbels forming a large flattish inflorescence up to 2 ft across.

Native of Japan, where it attains a large size in the forests of Hokkaido and is also found on the other islands. It is also native to Sakhalin, the Russian Far

East, Korea, and China. It is said to have been introduced by Maximowicz in 1865, though some of the seeds he sent may have yielded the var. *maximowiczii* (see below). It is one of the most remarkable of cool temperate trees, for its foliage is of a type very sparsely represented in the open air, though common enough in greenhouses and stoves. It is quite hardy, though the shoots may decay back if not fully ripened.

The species is variable in foliage. In western China the lobing is often very shallow, as shown on trees at Kew raised from seeds sent by Wilson, in which the lateral lobes are reduced to cusps. At the other extreme is var. MAXI-MOWICZII (Van Houtte) Li, which in its typical state has lanceolate lobes reaching two-thirds of the way or more towards the middle of the leaf. The type plant of this variety was raised by Van Houtte from a stray seed sent from St Petersburg and was figured in 1874 in *Flore des Serres*, t. 2067. It may have represented a juvenile phase of the species, subsequently perpetuated by vegetative propagation. On the other hand, Nakai (*Journ. Arn. Arb.*, Vol. 5, pp. 11–14) recognises the var. *maximowiczii* as a wild-occurring variety and points out that trees with the deeply lobed leaves of this variety may bear flowers. Certainly the specimen at Nymans in Sussex, sixty or slightly more years old, bears leaves as deeply cut as in the seedling plant from which the var. *maximowiczii* was first described, but flowers and bears fruits. The following specimens are not differentiated into 'type' and var. *maximowiczii* as the degree of lobing has not been noted in every case: Kew 40 × 3¼ ft and 45 × 3 ft (1967); Lythe Hill, Haslemere, Surrey, 48 × 3¼ ft (1969); Nymans, Sussex, 36 × 5 ft (1966); Wakehurst Place, Sussex, 40 × 5 ft (1964) and 45 × 4½ ft (1965); Exbury, Hants, 46 × 6 ft at 3 ft (1970); Hergest Croft, Heref., 35 × 5¾ ft (1969); Endsleigh, Devon, 45 × 5½ ft (1957); Dawyck, Peebl., 50 × 4 ft (1966); Kelburn, Ayrs., 49 × 3¼ ft (1970).

KERRIA ROSACEAE

A genus of a single species, allied to *Rhodotypos*, but differing in its yellow, five-petalled flowers and one-seeded carpels. It is named in honour of William Kerr, who introduced the double-flowered form of the species. He was a young Kew gardener who was sent to China in 1803 to obtain plants for the Royal Gardens. He was at Canton for some time, visited Java and the Philippines and returned to Canton, whence in 1804 he sent a collection of plants to Kew. He was appointed Superintendent of the Ceylon Botanic Garden in 1812 and died in Ceylon in 1814.

K. JAPONICA (L.) DC.
Rubus japonicus L.; *Corchorus japonicus* Thunb.

A deciduous shrub of bushy form 4 to 6 ft high, branches and twigs slender, supple, quite glabrous and glossy, forming a dense interlacing mass. Leaves alternate, $1\frac{1}{2}$ to 4 in. long, ovate-lanceolate, parallel-veined, the base rounded, the point long and tapering, glabrous above, hairy (especially on the veins) beneath, the margins doubly toothed. The leaves are much larger on the barren shoots of the year than on the flowering twigs. Flowers yellow, solitary at the end of short leafy twigs springing from the previous year's shoots, $1\frac{1}{4}$ to $1\frac{3}{4}$ in. across. Petals normally five, obovate. Calyx green, $\frac{1}{2}$ in. across, with five oblong lobes. Stamens numerous, yellow. Fruits not often produced in this country, but as seen on wild specimens, is a cluster of two or three nutlike bodies about the size of peppercorns, enveloped in the persistent calyx. Flowers in April and May.

cv. 'PLENIFLORA'.—A double-flowered variety much commoner in gardens than the type, and remarkably distinct in growth, the branches being stouter, more erect, and the shrub of a gaunt and rather lanky habit, showing none of the dense twiggy character of the type. The flower is a rounded mass of bright yellow petals, $1\frac{1}{2}$ to 2 in. across. It is as hardy as the type, but is often given wall protection. In the vicarage garden at Bitton it was 12 ft high.

The kerria has long been cultivated in Japan, and its existence there was known as long ago as 1700, but the double-flowered form (the first introduced) did not reach England until 1804, when it was introduced to Kew by William Kerr, a plant collector sent out from that establishment the previous year to China. As the reproductive parts were wanting, its botanical affinities could only be surmised, and it was called "*Corchorus japonicus*". *Corchorus* is a genus allied to the lindens. When the single-flowered typical plant was introduced in 1834 by Reeves, and blossomed two or three years later, it was seen to belong to the rose family, and was then named *Kerria* by De Candolle. This species is a native of China, and is only naturalised or cultivated in Japan. It was collected in flower and fruit by Wilson in W. Hupeh, China, in 1900, and earlier by Henry. Wilson also collected it in W. Szechwan, and Giraldi in N. Shensi.

The typical kerria is a beautiful shrub when in flower, and quite hardy, thriving in good loamy soil. It is easily increased by moderately soft cuttings placed in brisk bottom heat. All the kerrias are benefited by an occasional thinning out of old stems.

In addition to the well-known double-flowered form, the following is also cultivated:

cv. 'VARIEGATA'.—Like the type in habit, but scarcely so vigorous; its leaves are deeply and irregularly margined with white. It flowers more or less during the whole summer, but is scarcely so hardy as the type (*K. japonica picta* Sieb.). A cultivar with yellow-margined leaves is also known.

KETELEERIA PINACEAE

A genus of a few species in China, named in honour of J.-B. Keteleer, a French nurseryman of Belgian birth, partner in the firm of Thibaud and Keteleer. It is allied to *Abies*, differing from it most markedly in the cones, which fall in one piece, whereas in *Abies* they break up on the tree. The male catkins are borne in umbels. The leaves on young plants are unlike those of any species of *Abies*, being tapered into a sharp point. The buds consist of numerous scales, which persist at the base of the shoot.

K. FORTUNEI (A. Murr.) Carr.
Abies fortunei A. Murr.

An evergreen tree probably 100 ft high, with horizontal branches; young shoots furnished with scurf which soon falls away leaving them smooth; winter-buds small, the basal scales with long, free, linear points. Leaves linear, 1 to 1½ in. long, $\frac{1}{12}$ to $\frac{1}{5}$ in. wide, flat, pointed, broadest near the base, where they are abruptly narrowed to a short stalk, shining green on both sides, with twelve to sixteen stomatic lines beneath, forming a pale, faintly defined band each side the midrib, which is quite prominent on both surfaces. The leaves are arranged like those of many silver firs, being attached spirally, but twisted at the base so as to bring them into two opposite spreading sets; they persist five or more years. Cones erect, cylindrical, 4 to 6 in. long, stalked, purple when young, pale brown when ripe.

Native of China; introduced by Fortune in 1844, and extremely rare in cultivation. The finest tree in Europe was in Messrs Rovelli's nursery at Pallanza, in Italy. I saw this tree in May 1912, when Mr Rovelli told me it was 85 ft high: its trunk was 2 ft 9 in. in diameter; many old cones were scattered beneath. Fortune described the wild trees as having the appearance of a cedar of Lebanon; the Pallanza tree, comparatively young, had very much the aspect of a silver fir.

The failure of *K. fortunei* to thrive in the British Isles is perhaps due to insufficient summer-heat rather than to any lack of hardiness. The largest specimens recorded are: Leonardslee, Sussex, 37 × 2 ft (1962); Wakehurst Place, Sussex, 39 × 2¾ ft and 30 × 1¾ ft (1971).

K. DAVIDIANA [Bertrand] Beissn. is another species native of W. China. It was introduced to Kew by Henry in 1889, and Wilson found it and introduced it again in 1908. The young shoots differ from those of *K. fortunei* in remaining downy for two years or more. According to Wilson's specimens of adult plants, the leaves of cone-bearing or adult branches differ from those of *K. fortunei* in becoming blunt and conspicuously notched at the apex, and in having the midrib sunken above. The cone-scales are also more reflexed at the margin. Wilson found cones 8 in. long.

KOELREUTERIA   SAPINDACEAE

A genus of a few species of deciduous trees, natives of eastern Asia and the Fiji Islands. They have alternate, pinnate or bipinnate leaves, and flowers in large terminal panicles; calyx unequally five-lobed; petals four; fruits bladder-like. Named after J. G. Koelreuter, a professor of botany at Karlsruhe, 1733–1806.

K. PANICULATA Laxm.   [PLATE 68

A deciduous tree up to 30 to 60 ft high, with soft, pithy wood and rather gaunt habit when young, becoming more compact with age; young shoots minutely downy. Leaves alternate, pinnate, sometimes partially bipinnate; the nine to fifteen leaflets ovate, short-stalked or stalkless, coarsely and irregularly toothed, downy beneath. The whole leaf is from 6 to 18 in., or even more, in length, and the separate leaflets from 1 to 4 in. long, the larger ones often pinnately lobed at the base. Flowers in a large, terminal pyramidal panicle, sometimes over 12 in. long, made up of a series of elongated, slender racemes, carrying numerous short-stalked, yellow flowers, each about $\frac{1}{2}$ in. wide; petals four; sepals ovate or ovate-oblong, acute; stamens eight, downy. Fruit a conical, inflated, three-valved capsule, $1\frac{1}{2}$ to 2 in. long; valves acute or acuminate. Seeds about the size of peas, dark brown.

Native of China; introduced to England in 1763, and said to have first been cultivated at Croome, in Worcestershire. It is quite hardy and very handsome, flowering in July and August. When seen at its best the tree is a mass of deep yellow flowers, and these are succeeded by the striking bladder-like fruits. It loves the sun, and I have never seen it quite so fine in this country as it is in central France. Its handsome leaves turn bright yellow in autumn. It likes a good loamy soil. The seeds afford the best means of propagation, and are sometimes set in this country. Failing them, root-cuttings may be used. The tree is probably not long-lived, and is rather subject to the attacks of coral-spot fungus.

There are several specimens at Kew, none of great age, 30 to 40 ft in height and $1\frac{3}{4}$ to 4 ft in girth. An example near the Pinetum, planted 1934, measures 40 × $2\frac{3}{4}$ ft. Others recorded are: Syon House, London, 45 × 3 ft (1967); Oxford Botanic Garden, 49 × $3\frac{1}{2}$ ft (1970); Hergest Croft, Heref., 40 × $3\frac{1}{2}$ ft (1961); Victoria Gardens, Bath, 30 × 5 ft (1962).

var. APICULATA (Rehd. & Wils.) Rehd.—This variety differs from the typical state of the species in having usually bipinnate leaves, broadly ovate or roundish sepals and the valves of the fruits rounded or obtuse at the apex, with a short, sharp point. It has a more westerly distribution than typical K. paniculata, to which it is linked by intermediate forms.

This variety was introduced by Wilson from W. Szechwan in 1904. It first flowered at Kew in 1921 and has ripened seeds from which young plants have been raised. Wilson described it as a low tree with a spreading head and relatively thick trunk, inhabiting hot, dry river valleys. The specimen now at Kew measures 33 × $2\frac{1}{4}$ ft (1967). Others are: Savill Gardens, Windsor, 30 × $2\frac{3}{4}$ ft (1967); University Botanic Garden, Cambridge, 30 × 2 ft (1969).

cv. 'FASTIGIATA'.—Of narrowly fastigiate habit. The original tree was raised at Kew from seeds sent by Miss Corner in 1888 from Shanghai, and still grows in the Sapindaceae collection near the Ruined Arch.

K. BIPINNATA Franch.—This species, also from China, is not hardy here nor in Paris, although it has been tried several times. It differs from *K. paniculata* in its leaves being invariably doubly, sometimes trebly, pinnate, in its more regularly and less coarsely toothed leaflets, and the rounder, broader valves of the fruit. Some trees at Kew received under the name *K. bipinnata* have proved to be *K. paniculata*.

KOLKWITZIA   CAPRIFOLIACEAE

The flowers of *Kolkwitzia* resemble those of the closely allied *Abelia* but are borne in pairs and the fruits are very distinct, being bristly and prolonged at the apex into a narrow beak, so that the persistent sepals, which are also bristly, appear to be borne on a stalk. The sepals do not, however, enlarge in fruit as they do in *Abelia*. The genus contains the single species described below and is named in honour of Richard Kolkwitz, a German professor of botany.

K. AMABILIS Graebn.

A deciduous bush up to 12 feet high, of twiggy habit; young shoots at first hairy, then rough. Leaves opposite, broadly ovate, long-pointed, rounded at the base, shallowly and remotely toothed, 1 to 3 in. long, ¾ to 2 in. wide, dark dull green and sparsely hairy above, paler, prominently net-veined and bristly on the veins beneath, ciliate, chief veins three or four each side the midrib; stalk bristly, $\frac{1}{12}$ to $\frac{1}{8}$ in. long. Flowers twin, produced during May and June in corymbs 2 to 3 in. across, terminating short lateral twigs. Corolla bell-shaped, ⅝ in. long and the same in width at the mouth, where are five roundish, spreading lobes, pink with yellow in the throat, hairy. Calyx ½ in. across, with five or six very narrow, radiating lobes, hairy; flower-stalk ¼ to ⅜ in. long, slender, hairy. Stamens four. Fruits egg-shaped, ¼ in. long, covered with brown bristles ⅛ in. long. A curious feature is the persistent elongated calyx standing out beyond the fruit. *Bot. Mag.*, t. 8563.

Native of the province of Hupeh, China, on the watershed of the Han and Yangtse rivers, where it occurs among rocks at 9,000 to 10,000 ft; introduced by Wilson for Messrs Veitch in 1901, and cultivated in the nursery at Coombe Wood, where it first flowered in June 1910. It received an Award of Merit when shown from Nymans, Sussex, in 1923, but for many years it was more prized in the United States than in Britain, where it did not become widely available in commerce until after the second world war. Even now this lovely species is not really common in gardens. One reason for this is perhaps that inferior seedlings have been distributed, with small, poorly coloured flowers. However there are now named clones available such as 'ROSEA', raised in

Holland, and 'PINK CLOUD', raised at the R.H.S. Garden, Wisley, in 1946 from seeds received from the Morton Arboretum. Both have clear pink flowers of a good size and are very floriferous.

K. *amabilis* will grow on any soil and delights in chalk, but must be given a sunny position. It is easily propagated by cuttings of half-ripened wood, placed in gentle bottom-heat, or even by taking the suckers which it produces freely. It needs no regular pruning but once it is established a few of the older stems should be removed from the base each year. Vigorous young stems produced from the base of the plant are very thick and heavy; it is advisable to give these some support, to prevent their being snapped off by wind or heavy rain.

+ LABURNOCYTISUS   LEGUMINOSAE

A genus of graft hybrids between *Laburnum* and *Cytisus*, in which only this one described here has been authenticated.

+ L. ADAMII (Poiteau) Schneid.

Cytisus adamii Poiteau; *Laburnum adamii* (Poiteau) Kirchn.

A deciduous tree with the habit and aspect of *L. anagyroides*, up to 25 ft high. Leaflets oval or obovate, 1½ to 2½ in. long. Racemes 5 to 7 in. long; flowers yellowish suffused with purple, of the same shape and character as those of *L. anagyroides*, but, like the leaflets, smaller. The leaves and young shoots differ in being nearly or quite glabrous.

Although much inferior to either of the common laburnums in beauty, there is no more interesting tree in our gardens than this. It appeared in the nursery of Jean Louis Adam, at Vitry, near Paris, in 1825. According to Adam's account, he had grafted the dwarf purple broom (*Cytisus purpureus*) on a common laburnum, and on the grafted plant a branch appeared with purplish-yellow flowers intermediate in hue between those of scion and stock—+*L. adamii*, in fact, as we know it today. A few years after +*L. adamii* had been put into commerce, a further remarkable phenomenon was observed in connection with this tree. It was found that it had a tendency to 'sport' back more or less to both the parent types. This character it has maintained ever since, and today almost every specimen of +*Laburnocytisus adamii* shows on its branches, not only the hybrid itself but pieces of pure *L. anagyroides* and pure *Cytisus purpureus* that have sprung spontaneously from its tissues. All three flower together, the curious tufts of the cytisus suggesting witches' brooms. Many authorities have in times past doubted the possibility of a hybrid being produced by grafting, but the correctness of Adam's account was proved by Prof. Winkler of Tübingen, who produced graft hybrids between the tomato and black nightshade. Further, a similar instance has been brought to light of graft hybrids between medlar and hawthorn (see + *Crataegomespilus*). These graft hybrids have been termed 'chimaeras', because there seems to be a mixture of the parents in their tissues, rather than a genuine and entire fusion. The outer tissues are often found under the microscope to resemble those of one parent, the inner ones those of the other.

LABURNUM   LEGUMINOSAE

A genus consisting of three species, two of them small trees, one shrubby, together with some hybrids and numerous varieties. *Laburnum* is very closely related to *Cytisus*, differing chiefly in the structure of the seed. The leaves are composed of three leaflets, and the flowers are produced in pendent racemes on the arborescent species, and in erect ones on the shrubby one (*L. caramanicum*).

Few trees of a similar character are so beautiful as the two common laburnums. When fully in flower, and laden with streaming racemes of golden colour, as they usually are in late May and June, nothing can surpass them in effectiveness. The German popular name, 'Golden Rain' (*Goldregen*) is peculiarly appropriate. They look their best in a group of three to six trees, with a dark evergreen mass, like holly or holm oak, behind them. Of very easy culture and raised readily from seed, no special directions are needed for their treatment. The garden varieties and hybrids are propagated by grafting or budding. They thrive in any soil that is not waterlogged. It is often advisable to remove the seed-pods as soon as the flowers are past. In some seasons the trees develop and ripen enormous crops of pods, and this, besides being of no value or beauty, is apt to induce a stunted condition of growth and reduce succeeding crops of blossom. Laburnums are not particularly long-lived, and attention to this matter will be repaid, especially in the case of valued or fine specimens, by increased longevity. They should be firmly staked after planting.

The seeds contain a poisonous alkaloid, and children have been known to die from eating them when green. The heart-wood of the trunk is of a dark colour and very hard; it is sometimes used as a substitute for ebony, occasionally also for furniture making. Many trees and shrubs of the Leguminosae can be grafted on laburnum, and the abundance of its seed and easy cultivation have made it very much used as a stock for many of its allies.

A monograph on *Laburnum* by Wettstein was published in *Oester. Bot. Zeitschr.*, Vol. 40 (1890), pp. 395–399, 435–439; Vol. 41 (1891), pp. 127–130, 169–173, 261–265.

L. ALPINUM (Mill.) Bercht. & Presl   SCOTCH LABURNUM
Cytisus alpinus Mill.   [PLATE 70

A deciduous tree 20 ft (rarely 30 ft) high, with usually a short, sturdy trunk. Young stems green, with a few spreading hairs at first, later glabrous. Leaves trifoliolate, with a stalk 1 to 2 in. long; leaflets oval or obovate, 2 to 4 in. long, deep green, not so downy beneath as in *L. anagyroides*. Racemes pendulous, slender, 10 to 15 in. long, carrying numerous golden-yellow flowers, each ¾ in. long on a thin stalk ¼ to ½ in. long; both the flower-stalks and the main-stalk of the raceme are glabrous or thinly downy. Seed-pods 2 to 3 in. long, flat, with the upper seam (suture) distinctly winged and forming a knife-like edge, glabrous.

Native mainly of the southern Alps, but also occurring wild in the northern Apennines, N.W. Yugoslavia, and southern Czechoslovakia. It is found in damper places than the common laburnum and is not confined to limestone soils. It has been cultivated in the British Isles for at least 350 years but is not a native. It was long confused with the common laburnum until its distinctness was noted by Miller in his *Dictionary*. It differs in the following characters: young stems glabrous except when quite young; leaflets larger and less hairy; racemes longer and denser, opening their flowers two to three weeks later (early June); upper seam of pod flattened out into a thin edge in place of the thickened one of *L. anagyroides*. *L. alpinum* is undoubtedly the superior species for gardens.

A botanical distinction has been made between f. MACROSTACHYS (Endl.) Koehne, with long racemes and large leaflets, said to be commoner in the west; and f. MICROSTACHYS (Wettst.) Koehne, with shorter racemes, said to be commoner at the eastern end of the range of the species, in sunny places. But the former is really synonymous with the type. Other variants are:

cv. 'PENDULUM'.—Branches pendulous. Described by Loudon, who figured a specimen growing in Loddiges's nursery (*Arb. et Frut. Brit.*, Vol. 5, t. 70a).

var. PILOSUM (Wettst.) Koehne—Underside of leaflets with scattered hairs. Said to be common in the S. Tyrol and the Tessino.

An old variety known as 'Latest and Longest' was mentioned in previous editions as still one of the best laburnums.

L. ANAGYROIDES Med.   COMMON LABURNUM
L. vulgare Bercht. & Presl; *Cytisus laburnum* L.

A deciduous tree 20 to 30 ft (rarely more) high, often branching close to the ground and forming a wide-spreading, bushy tree. Leaves trifoliolate, with a stalk 2 to 3 in. long; leaflets oval or slightly obovate, 1½ to 3 in. long, downy beneath. Racemes pendulous, cylindrical, 6 to 10 in. long, downy. Flowers golden yellow, ¾ in. long, each borne on a thin, downy stalk ¼ to ½ in. long. Seed-pods 2 to 3 in. long, the upper seam or suture thickened and keeled, but not winged as in *L. alpinum*. It blooms from the third week of May into June.

Native of Central and S. Europe, long cultivated in, but not a native of

Britain. It was probably one of the earliest ornamental plants introduced to this country, as its great beauty would attract early travellers, and the seed could be easily obtained and transported. No foreign tree is better adapted to our climate. The differences between it and *L. alpinum* are indicated under that species.

var. ALSCHINGERI (Vis.) Schneid.—A wild variety which differs chiefly from the type in the calyx being distinctly two-lipped, the lower lip the longer; the leaflets are more silky-hairy and grey-blue beneath.

cv. 'AUREUM'.—Leaves golden yellow; one of the prettiest of golden-leaved trees. It affords one of the commonest instances showing the influence of scion on stock, for on grafted trees yellow-leaved shoots frequently appear considerably beneath the point of union. This variety was in commerce in Britain by 1874, but where it was raised cannot be ascertained. It was figured in *Fl. d. Serres*, Vol. 21 (1875), tt. 2242–3.

cv. 'CARLIERI'.—There seems to be some confusion over the correct use of this name. Kirchner's original description, from a plant growing in the Muskau Arboretum, states that the variety had very small grey-green leaves and was free-flowering, with long densely flowered racemes. Many of the trees at Muskau were supplied by James Booth and Sons of Hamburg, and there is a specimen in the Kew Herbarium from a tree received from that firm in 1872, which agrees well with Kirchner's description. The leaflets are remarkably small, $\frac{3}{8}$ to 1 in. long, $\frac{1}{8}$ to $\frac{3}{16}$ in. wide, and the racemes 5 to 10 in. long. Another specimen, obviously of the same variety, was taken from a tree received at Kew from Späth in 1903. But the laburnum described by Schneider as *L. anagyroides* var. *carlieri* sounds quite different, having very short, almost erect racemes (*Handbuch*, Vol. 2, p. 38).

cv. 'INVOLUTUM'.—Leaves curled. A curiosity merely. Listed by James Booth of Hamburg in 1838. A variant described in France in 1847 as *Cytisus laburnum* var. *bullatum* may be the same (*L. anagyroides* f. *bullatum* (Jacques) Schneid.).

cv. 'PENDULUM'.—Branchlets slender and weeping; very graceful in habit.

cv. 'QUERCIFOLIUM'.—Leaflets curiously lobed after the fashion of an oak leaf, the main leaf-stalk being sometimes winged. The leaf is occasionally five-parted (quinquefoliolate). A very distinct and rather handsome form.

cv. 'SESSILIFOLIUM'.—Leaves crowded, almost stalkless, their bases thus being brought close to the branchlet. A curiosity of no garden value, the branches having a stiff, stunted appearance; not free-flowering.

In addition, garden varieties were once in commerce under such epithets as *autumnale*, *biferum* and *semperflorens*; which flower again in autumn or more or less continuously throughout the summer.

L. CARAMANICUM (Boiss.) Benth. & Hook. f.

Podocytisus caramanicus Boiss.

Although described as a small tree in its native country, this species is usually seen in Great Britain as a shrub 3 to 6 ft high. It is deciduous, and has a thin habit, making long, straight, erect shoots, which towards the end of the summer produce near the top a number of short, stiff twigs, each terminated by an erect raceme of flowers. Leaves grey-green, trifoliolate, short-stalked; leaflets almost stalkless, obovate, with a short abrupt point, from ¼ to ¾ in. long, the side ones the smaller. Racemes terminal, erect, 3 to 7 in. long. Flowers golden yellow, ¾ in. long; the stalk slender, ¼ in. long, with a small bracteole about the middle. Standard petal roundish, ½ in. in diameter. Seed-pods 2 to 3 in. long, ½ in. wide, flat, the upper seam, distinctly winged, developing one to four seeds. *Bot. Mag.*, t. 7898.

Native of the southern Balkans and Asia Minor; introduced about 1879, but still very uncommon. It has lived outside at Kew for a good many years, but the shoots are cut back severely every winter. Owing to its flowering late in the season on the shoots of the year, this does not affect its blossoming, although the plants increase slowly in size. To be seen at its best, no doubt, it needs a hotter, sunnier climate than ours. It flowers too late to ripen seed with certainty, but they do occasionally ripen. Cuttings taken in August will strike root in gentle heat.

L. × WATERERI (Wettst.) Dipp.

L. vulgare watereri Kirchn.; *Cytisus × watereri* Wettst.

Hybrids between *L. alpinum* and *L. anagyroides* have arisen on several occasions in gardens and have also been found in the wild. The group-name for such hybrids, wild and cultivated, is *L. × watereri*, the type being the laburnum raised at the Knap Hill nurseries at some unknown date before 1864, and distributed as *L. vulgare watereri*. The distinguishing characters of the Knap Hill laburnum are: Young stems glabrous as in *L. alpinum*. Leaflets thinly appressed-hairy beneath and hence intermediate in indumentum between the parents. Inflorescences dense as in *L. alpinum* but with flowers almost as large as in the other parent. Pods intermediate, being less hairy than in *L. anagyroides* and neither winged nor much thickened at the suture.

cv. 'PARKESII'.—The Knap Hill laburnum, although the typical form of the cross, was not, however, the first of the group to be put into commerce. In 1842, J. D. Parkes, a nurseryman of Dartford, advertised in the *Gardeners' Chronicle* (p. 705) a new laburnum which became known in gardens as *L. parkesii* or *L. vulgare parkesii*. These names have been given as synonyms of *L. × watereri* with the result that the Parkes and the Knap Hill forms became confused. They seem in fact to have been very similar, but according to Nicholson (*The Garden*, Vol. 27 (1884), p. 519) the Knap Hill form was the finer of the two, and, according to Parkes, his form had 'pendent' branches.

cv. 'VOSSII'.—This beautiful hybrid, raised in Holland late in the 19th century, is now the commonest laburnum in gardens and has superseded the older forms of *L. × watereri*. The racemes are up to 2 ft in length and the young stems are appressed-hairy, not glabrous as in the typical form of the cross.

LAGERSTROEMIA LYTHRACEAE

A genus of about fifty species in E. and S.E. Asia and Australia. It was named by Linnaeus after his friend Magnus von Lageström of Gothenburg (1696–1759).

L. INDICA L.   CRAPE MYRTLE

A deciduous tree 20 to 30 ft high, or a shrub, the bark of the trunk and older branches grey and smooth; young shoots glabrous, four-angled. Leaves opposite, alternate or in whorls of three, privet-like, mostly obovate, not toothed, glabrous, 1 to 2½ in. long, ¾ to 1½ in. wide, very shortly stalked. Flowers produced from July to September in panicles terminating the current year's growths, and 6 to 8 in. long by 3 to 5 in. wide. Each flower is 1 to 1½ in. wide and the colour varies from pink to deep red on different plants; there is also a white-flowered form. Petals six, obovate, curiously crinkled, contracted at the base to a slender claw. Calyx bell-shaped, ⅓ to ½ in. long, green, glabrous, with six triangular pointed lobes, persisting during the fruiting stage. Stamens numerous, the slender style standing out beyond them. *Bot. Mag.*, t. 405.

Native of China and Korea; introduced to Kew in 1759; figured in the *Botanical Magazine* in 1798. Wilson found it in open grassy places and on cliffs at low altitudes from Central to W. China. It is a common garden shrub in lands with warm temperate climates. In the British Isles it is best known as a shrub for the cool greenhouse, where potted plants, cut hard back in spring, will bloom profusely on the young wood. Grown out-of-doors in a very sunny position it is hardy in the south of England, but blooms only when the summer has been consistently warm. A specimen at Borde Hill in Sussex, about 10 ft high, has lived in its present position for over sixty years and the following note on it by the owner is quoted from *Borde Hill Trees* (1935): It 'grows in front of a wall about 3 ft high, consequently more than half the shrub is without protection. It flowered freely in 1911. Sir Edmund Loder told me that a plant produced flowers the same year at Leonardslee which had not bloomed for twenty years previously. The plant at Borde Hill next flowered in 1933. Its autumn colouring is invariably good and its leaves are retained for several days after assuming their rich tints.' This plant flowered again after the hot summer of 1959; in 1969, perhaps owing to the late spring, flower-buds were set but failed to open.

Although the crape myrtle cannot be relied on to flower regularly in our climate it is worthy of further trial in southern and south-eastern England, as it grows quickly and flowers even when quite young. It is propagated by leafy cuttings placed in bottom-heat, or by imported seeds. Seedlings will flower in their second year.

LAPAGERIA PHILESIACEAE

A genus of a single species, native mainly of Chile, named by Ruiz and Pavon in honour of the Empress Josephine of France, first wife of Napoleon Bonaparte, whose maiden name was de la Pagerie. It is a member of a very distinct family of monocotyledons to which also belong *Luzuriaga* and *Philesia*, both treated in this work. The family Philesiaceae is confined to the southern hemisphere.

L. ROSEA Ruiz & Pavon   CHILEAN BELLFLOWER, COPIHUE

An evergreen climber 10 to 15 ft high, with glabrous, slender, stiff, hard shoots which attach themselves to their supports by twining round them. Leaves alternate, stiff and leathery in texture, the larger ones heart-shaped and five-nerved, the smaller ones ovate and three-nerved, always pointed, 1¼ to 4 in long, ¾ to 3 in. wide, dark glossy green, stalk ¼ to ⅜ in. long. Flowers solitary, or two or three together, produced from the ends of the shoots, or in the

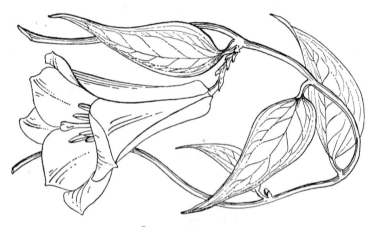

LAPAGERIA ROSEA

terminal leaf-axils. Each flower is 3 in. long, 2 in. wide, pendulous, composed of six fleshy segments, the three inner ones much the larger, rich crimson, faintly spotted with rose, the whole forming a flower of long bell-like shape. Stamens six, white, 2 in. long; anthers yellow, ¼ in. long. Flower-stalk ½ in. long, mostly covered with clasping bracts. Fruit an ovoid-oblong berry, rather three-sided, 2 in. long, 1 in. wide, tapering towards the apex, with numerous seeds embedded in its pulp. *Bot. Mag.*, t. 4447.

Native of Chile and Argentina; introduced to Kew in 1847, ever since which date it has been prized as one of the most beautiful-flowered of greenhouse climbers. In later times it has been much grown on shady walls in Cornwall,

Devon, and similar climates. It has also been successfully grown and flowered in the Edinburgh Botanic Garden on a south wall shaded by a high building. It is one of the remarkable woody climbers belonging to the lily family, and has a rambling root system from which it sends up new shoots. The whole plant at maturity is curiously stiff in texture and apart from the flowers, in no way attractive. Although it does not like fierce sunshine, the lapageria is a warmth-loving species, and in the wild does not extend farther south in Chile than latitude 41° S. It needs abundant moisture and a deep open-textured soil. It flowers over most of the summer and autumn months. Propagated by seeds or layers.

The flowers vary in size, marking, and depth of colouring. According to Dr C. Muñoz Pizarro (*Flores Silvestres de Chile* (1966), p. 32), the deepest coloured and perhaps also the largest flowers are to be seen in the region of Concepcion. An exquisitely beautiful white-flowered form (var. ALBIFLORA Hook., *Bot. Mag.*; *L. alba* Gay) was introduced to the British Isles by Richard Pearce in 1860. Such plants, according to Dr Muñoz, are rare in the wild but occasionally to be seen in Cautin province. Dr Wilfrid Fox, when travelling in Chile in 1932, found a form of lapageria growing wild whose flowers were striped lengthways with crimson. Many colour variants are cultivated in Chile, where the copihue is the national flower (see further in *Calif. Hort. Soc. Journ.*, Vol. 25, pp. 62–69). Of those raised in Britain the finest is perhaps 'NASH COURT', with soft-pink, slightly marbled flowers. It received a First Class Certificate in 1884 and is still available in commerce.

LARDIZABALA   LARDIZABALACEAE

A genus of one or two species of climbing shrubs, the one described here confined to Chile. The leading characters are: Flowers functionally unisexual with six fleshy sepals, in two series of three, the much reduced petals (honey-leaves) opposite the sepals; functionally male flowers with six stamens united by their filaments into a short tube, enclosing three rudimentary carpels; functionally female flowers with three, sometimes six, erect carpels, each comprising a subcylindrical ovary surmounted by a conical papillose stigma, and with six free sterile stamens; fruit a sausage-shaped, many-seeded berry developed from one carpel.

L. BITERNATA Ruiz & Pavon

A vigorous evergreen climber, with ternate, biternate, and triternate leaves. The three, six, or nine leaflets are of hard texture, each 2 to 4 in. long, the middle one of each trio the largest. They vary much in outline, but are mostly ovate, the lateral ones more or less oblique, and often sessile, margins shallowly crenate, with here and there a sharply pointed tooth; leaf-stalks covered with short brown hairs. Flowers functionally unisexual; males ¾ in. across, produced in drooping spikes 3 to 4 in. long from the leaf axils; the sepals form the most effective part of the flower, being broadly ovate, fleshy and dark chocolate purple; petals small, narrow, white and mealy. Female flowers of slender stalks 1 in. long, solitary in the leaf-axils, rather larger than the male. Fruits sausage-shaped, 2 to 3 in. long; seeds flattened and about the size of small peas. *Bot. Mag.*, t. 4501.

Native of Chile; introduced in 1844, it flowered in the Exeter nursery of Messrs Veitch five years later. Seen in flower, it is very striking. The fruit is sweet, pulpy, and edible, and is said to be sold in the markets of Chile. This climber is essentially one for the milder parts of the kingdom. It is too tender to be satisfactory even on a wall at Kew.

LARIX   Larch   pinaceae

Amongst the comparatively few deciduous conifers, the larches stand out as peculiarly well marked and distinct. They are all trees of timber-producing size, forming an erect, tapering trunk, carrying usually a cone-shaped head of horizontal branches upturned at the ends, the branchlets pendulous. As in the cedars, the branchlets are of two kinds: (1) elongated slender ones, growing from a few inches to 2 ft or more yearly, and bearing the leaves singly and spirally; and (2) short, spur-like ones which lengthen a minute fraction of an inch annually, and bear numerous (20 to 40) leaves crowded in a terminal tuft. Leaves linear or needle-like, falling in autumn. Flowers unisexual, both sexes appearing on the one tree. Males globose to cylindrical, made up of numerous yellow-anthered, short-stalked stamens. Females erect, globose, usually red, developing into a cone composed of thin, concave, rounded, very persistent, woody scales; bracts either protruded or included. Seeds in pairs on each scale, winged, ripening and falling the first autumn. Of its nearest allies, with a similar leaf arrangement, *Pseudolarix* differs in the much larger, more woody cone-scales falling away early from the central axis; *Cedrus* is, of course, evergreen, and its cones much larger.

The larches are widely spread over the cool parts of the northern hemisphere, often in mountainous regions. They like a fairly good loamy soil, and an abundant rainfall. One species, *L. laricina*, succeeds in damp spots, but the rest like a well-drained site. They should always, if possible, be raised from seeds, which should be sown evenly and thinly, and slightly covered with soil—the common larch out-of-doors, usually in raised beds not more than 4 ft wide to facilitate weeding, the rarer ones in unheated frames for better protection. They may be planted out permanently at 1½ ft high and upwards. Rarer sorts can be grafted in spring on seedlings of the common larch.

L. DECIDUA Mill. COMMON OR EUROPEAN LARCH
L. europaea DC.

A tree reaching 100 to 140 ft in height in this country, with an erect, tapering trunk, 2 to 5 ft thick, clothed with fissured, scaling bark; branchlets pale yellowish grey, not downy. Leaves light green, ¾ to 1½ in. long, linear, with the midrib raised beneath, and with two to four lines of stomata at each side of it. Female flowers red, ½ in. long, egg-shaped. Cones reddish when young, 1 to 1½ in. long, ¾ to 1 in. wide at the base, tapering slightly towards the top; scales rounded, downy at the base outside bracts slightly exserted.

The main home of the common larch lies in the mountains of central Europe from S.E. France through the main chain of the Alps eastward to the neighbourhood of Vienna. In this region it forms beautiful forests, often in association with *Pinus cembra*, wherever the climate is 'continental' enough to give it the bright summers and moderate rainfall that it demands. In the more 'oceanic' parts of the Alps it is displaced by spruce. Beyond the Danube, the larch, as a wild tree, occurs only in a few localities in the mountains between Czechoslovakia and Poland, but var. *polonica* (see below) carries the distribution of the species into the hills of southern and central Poland and a few probably wild stands occur in the Carpathians of Rumania. The wild races most valued by foresters as a source of seed come from these isolated outposts, notably the Sudetan larch from the mountains around Jesenice and Vrbno in Czechoslovakia (about 120 miles east of Prague) and the Tatra larch, which occurs farther east in the High and Low Tatras.

The common larch was introduced early in the 17th century, but first brought into notice as a forest tree in the British Isles by the third and fourth Dukes of Atholl, 100 to 150 years later. Two of the oldest in the British Isles are standing near the old cathedral at Dunkeld, planted there in 1738.   [PLATE 72

As a garden tree the larch has much to recommend it; in habit it is singularly beautiful when grown as an isolated specimen, the horizontal or upwardly curved branches being furnished with pendulous branchlets. It attains to an imposing height; its trunk is handsomely coloured, and no tree exceeds it in the beauty and soft tenderness of the young green foliage.

The common larch is not suitable for exposed positions, nor for low-lying sites subject to spring frost. It grows best in deep, moist soils and does not thrive on very chalky nor on peaty soils. Once the most widely planted of all exotic conifers, it is now little used in afforestation, partly because it is unsuited to many of the areas now being converted to forest, partly because it is less productive than some other exotic conifers even in the soils and situations most favourable to it. The total area devoted to common larch in 1965 was 129,000 acres, against 875,000 acres under spruce and 233,000 acres under Japanese larch. It remains a useful tree for small-scale planting on estates and the bulk of its acreage is privately owned. The chief disease of this species is larch canker, but research has shown that the plantations most ravaged by this disease in the earlier decades of this century were raised from seed procured from high elevations in the Alps. Trees of Sudetan and Tatran provenance are less subject to it, and some of the old plantations in Scotland are held to be the equal of the wild Carpathian stands as a source of seed for forestry.

The following is no more than a short selection of the outstanding European larches growing in the British Isles: Dunkeld Cathedral, Perths., *pl.* 1738, 105 × 16¾ ft (1970); Lee Park, Lanarks., *pl.* 1685, 80 × 13 ft (1971); Monzie Castle, Perths., *pl.* 1738, 111 × 18½ ft (1962); Gordon Castle, Moray, 98 × 17¼ ft (1970); Dawyck, Peebl., *pl.* 1725, 70 × 13½ ft (1966); Ardvorlich, Perths., *pl.* 1789, 139 × 8¾ ft (1961); Ombersley Court, Worcs., 72 × 17¾ ft (1964); Parkhatch, Dunsfold, Surrey, *pl.* 1855, 142 × 9½ ft (1970).

f. PENDULA (Laws.) R. E. Fries *L. europaea pendula* Laws.—The epithet *pendula* has been attached to many different trees of more or less pendulous habit. For a discussion see Elwes and Henry, *Tr. Gt. Brit. & Irel.*, Vol. 2, p. 350, but it should be noted that the Henham Hall tree mentioned there belongs to *L.* × *pendula*, not to the common larch—an error later corrected by Henry.

var. POLONICA (Raciborski) Ostenfeld & Syrach-Larsen *L. polonica* Raciborski. POLISH LARCH.—The common larch is subdivided into numerous races, differing in their climatic preferences and in various other ways of significance to foresters, but more or less identical in their botanical characters. The Polish larch, which is really only one of these races, is, however, usually recognised as a distinct species, subspecies, or variety, since it differs from the larch of the Alps in its smaller cones with more concave scales. It is perhaps intermediate botanically, as it certainly is geographically, between the European larch and the West Siberian larch (*L. sibirica*). Even in quite recent times it was widespread in Poland but is now almost extinct in the wild, the main concentration being in the Little Poland Highlands, south of Warsaw.

There is a specimen of this variety in the National Pinetum at Bedgebury, *pl.* 1926, 72 × 4½ ft (1965). Its shoots are pendulous, and paler than in the typical common larch.

L. SIBIRICA Ledeb. *L. russica* (Endl.) Trautv.; *Pinus larix* var. *russica* Endl. SIBERIAN LARCH.—Although closely related to the common larch, this may be distinguished by the earlier growth in spring, the longer, more slender leaves, and in the downy, more concave scales of the cone. Native of N.E. European Russia and W. Siberia, also of N. Mongolia and parts of the Tianshan. It appears to have no value in this country. Its early growth renders it very subject to injury by late spring frosts.

L. × EUROLEPIS A. Henry   DUNKELD OR HYBRID LARCH

L. henryana Rehd.   [PLATE 71

A hybrid between *L. decidua*, the common larch, and *L. kaempferi*, the Japanese one, first raised about 1900 at Dunkeld in Perthshire, where considerable plantations of it are growing. The year-old shoots resemble those of common larch in their yellowish colour but show the influence of *L. kaempferi* in being sometimes slightly downy; also the bracts of the young cones are reflexed, this character being one of the best distinctive features of the Japanese species. The adult cones take after common larch in being conical, in having yellowish stalks, and in the bracts being occasionally exposed. I have seen plantations at Dunkeld and Blair-Atholl which are notable for their vigour and cleanliness. Hybrid seedlings have repeatedly been obtained from ten trees of *L. kaempferi* at Dunkeld that were raised from Japanese seed sown in 1884. They are evidently fertilised by pollen wafted on to them when in flower from numerous common larches growing near.

For the first half-century after it first arose at Dunkeld, *L.* × *eurolepis* was little planted outside Scotland, owing to the scarcity of seed. This is now being raised in quantity in special plots, where selected strains of the two parent species are grown intermingled. Vigour is at its maximum in trees from this 'first-cross' seed, and falls off in later generations (H. L. Edlin, *Qtly. Journ. For.*, Vol. 57, p. 112).

The following examples of the Dunkeld larch have been recorded recently: National Pinetum, Bedgebury, Kent, *pl.* 1925, 70 × 5 ft (1968); Warnham Court, Sussex, 73 × 5¾ ft (1971); Colesborne, Glos., 92 × 6¼ ft (1971); Killerton, Devon, 79 × 6 ft (1970); Blair Atholl, Perths., *pl.* 1905 (original), 84 × 8¾ ft (1970); Dunkeld, Perths., 97 × 7¼ ft (1970); Murthly Castle, Perths., 98 × 6½ ft (1970); Crarae, Argyll, *pl.* 1918, 74 × 6 ft (1969). The rapid growth when young is shown by a tree growing in the garden of Alan Mitchell, who has provided virtually all the tree-measurements given in this revised edition. Planted in 1963, it measured 27 × 1½ ft in 1969.

L. GMELINII (Rupr.) Kuzeneva DAHURIAN LARCH
Abies gmelinii Rupr.; *Larix dahurica* Turcz.

A tree attaining 100 ft in the wild, but dwarfed or even prostrate in unfavourable situations; branchlets usually glabrous, yellowish when young. Leaves ⅝ to 1⅛ in. long, their upper surface flat, the undersurface keeled and with numerous stomata. Cones ¾ to 1 in. long, ovoid or cylindric, opening widely when ripe; scales ten to sixteen in number, occasionally more numerous, glabrous, light brown and rather glossy, truncate or shallowly notched at the apex, flat or slightly concave, not reflexed at the apex; bracts dark brown, concealed by the scales.

In its typical state, *L. gmelinii* is a native mainly of Russia, from the Pacific coast to a south-western limit around Lake Baikal and a north-western one near the lower reaches of the River Yenisei. On the south it extends into Korea and Manchuria. It was introduced, according to Loudon, in 1827. Coming from a region of cold or very cold winters and hot summers, *L. gmelinii* in its typical state does not really thrive in this country. The following examples have been recorded: Wakehurst Place, Sussex, 49 × 4½ ft (1966); National Pinetum, Bedgebury, Kent, *pl.* 1930, 62 × 2½ ft (1969) and another in the Plots, *pl.* 1949, 48 × 3 ft (1970); Hergest Croft, Heref., 60 × 2¾ ft (1969).

var. JAPONICA (Reg.) Pilger *L. japonica* Reg.; *L. kurilensis* Mayr; *L. kamtschatica* (Rupr.) Carr.; *Abies kamtschatica* Rupr.—Branchlets yellowish grey or dark brown, more or less densely covered with brown hairs and often pruinose. Leaves about 1 in. long, broad in proportion to their length. Cones about ¾ in. long with about fifteen glabrous scales. Native of the Kuriles, S. Sakhalin, and the coast of mainland Russia from Valentin Bay to Vladimir Bay, attaining a height of over 100 ft in sheltered places; described from a tree cultivated in Japan, but not native there. It was introduced to Kew from Japan in 1897 but is not now in the collection. This variety does not thrive in Britain but is cultivated in the National Pinetum at Bedgebury and a few other places. *Bot. Mag.* n.s., t. 159.

var. OLGENSIS (Henry) Ostenfeld & Syrach-Larsen *L. olgensis* Henry— This larch was originally described in *Gardeners' Chronicle*, Vol. 57 (1915), p. 109. It is chiefly remarkable for its stunted habit, for the dense covering of reddish hairs that clothe the young twigs, and the downy outer surface of the cone-scales. The cones are ¾ to 1 in. long, the scales entire, rounded at the apex. It was collected in 1860 on the shores of Olga Bay, 120 miles to the north-east of Vladivostok, and is confined to that area (Korean trees referred to this variety by Ostenfeld and Syrach-Larsen are probably typical *L. gmelinii*).

Seeds of this variety were introduced in 1911, but the young plants that once grew at Kew and Bedgebury did not thrive. Another, planted at Borde Hill in Sussex in 1927, died after attaining a height of 4 ft in about twenty years.

var. PRINCIPIS-RUPRECHTII (Mayr) Pilger *L. principis-ruprechtii* Mayr; *L. dahurica* var. *principis-ruprechtii* (Mayr) Rehd. & Wils.—A tree 80 to 100 ft high, found by H. Mayr in 1903 at Wutai in the province of Shansi, N. China. Forests of it were afterwards found by Purdom and the American collector Meyer on the slopes of Wutai mountain. It appears to be a geographical race, differing from typical *L. gmelinii* chiefly in the larger cones (up to 1¾ in. long) with more numerous scales (thirty to forty). Rehder and Wilson (*Pl. Wils.*, Vol. 2, p. 21) remarked that it is connected to the typical state of *L. gmelinii* by a chain of intermediates stretching from N.W. China through Manchuria to Korea. Some of the specimens collected by Wilson in Korea in 1918 agree with the var. *principis-ruprechtii*, but others approach the typical variety in their smaller cones and should perhaps be referred to it. Some trees at Kew, received from the Arnold Arboretum in 1916, also bore cones smaller than in Mayr's type. The last of this set blew down in 1965.

L. GRIFFITHII Hook. f.   SIKKIM LARCH
L. griffithiana Carr.

A tree up to 60 ft high in the wild, resembling the common larch in habit but with more markedly pendulous branches; young shoots downy. Leaves 1 to 1¼ in. long, light green. From other larches *L. griffithii* is well distinguished by the large size of its purplish cones, which are 2½ to 3 in. long, 1 to 1¼ in. in diameter, cylindrical, slightly tapering towards the top; scales roundish obovate, straight cut across the top, downy outside; bracts yellowish, longer than the scales, the awl-like apex much reflexed, at least when young. *Bot. Mag.*, t. 8181.

Native of the E. Himalaya at 8,000 to 13,000 ft; discovered by Dr Griffith during his botanical explorations of Sikkim and Bhutan. Sir Joseph Hooker sent seeds to Kew in 1848 from E. Nepal and from these plants were raised and widely distributed, but most succumbed to frost or to larch aphis. One survivor from this sending still grows at Strete Ralegh, Devon, and measures 62 × 7¼ ft

(1964); another old tree at Coldrenick, Cornwall, mentioned in previous editions, is 71 × 6 ft (1957). A seedling of the Strete Ralegh tree, planted at Hergest Croft, Heref., in 1920, measures 62 × 3 ft (1963).

L. KAEMPFERI (Lamb.) Carr.   JAPANESE LARCH

Pinus kaempferi Lamb.; *Larix leptolepis* (Sieb. & Zucc.) Gord.; *Abies leptolepis* Sieb. & Zucc.

A tree 80 to 100 ft high, with a trunk 3 to 4 ft thick, and (in the open) a wide-spreading head of branches; bark scaling, showing a pale grey-brown surface beneath; young shoots glabrous to downy, rich reddish brown the first winter. Leaves 1¼ to 1⅝ in. long, 1/16 to 1/12 in. wide, rather glaucous, flat above, ridged beneath, and with two bands of stomatic lines there. Cones somewhat globose, and broader in proportion to their length than those of any other larch, being about 1 in. wide and long; also very distinct in the thin, rounded scales being markedly curved back when ripe.

Native of Japan; introduced by John Gould Veitch in 1861. It is very distinct

LARIX KAEMPFERI

from the common larch in the reddish-brown colouring of the ripened shoots, in the broader rather glaucous or grey-green leaves, and the broader cones with spreading scales.

It is now widely planted in Britain as a forest tree, especially in the western parts of the country. It is more susceptible to drought than the common larch but more tolerant of shallow, acid soils and more resistant to canker. It does not thrive on chalky soils.

Seeds of the Japanese larch were brought from Japan by J. G. Veitch in 1861, and a tree at Kew, *pl.* 1868, probably derives from these. It measures 63 × 4¼ ft (1971). Apart from this tree and a grafted tree in Inverary planted in 1876 (90 × 8¼ ft in 1969), the oldest trees of known planting date were raised from an introduction of seeds to Scotland in 1883. The dimensions of those that remain from this batch are: Dunkeld, Perths., 102 × 9¾ ft; Blair Atholl, Perths., 121 × 9 ft; Munches, Kircudb., 88 × 9¼ ft; Kirkennan, Kirkcudb., 79 × 7¾ ft (all measurements 1970). Other old trees in Scotland are: Glamis Castle, Angus, *pl.* 1894, 108 × 7¼ ft and 105 × 7¼ ft (1970); Blairquhan, Ayrs., *pl.* 1900,

105 × 6½ ft (1970); Langholm, Dumfr., *pl.* 1900, 106 × 6¾ ft (1969); Drum-
lanrig, Dumfr., *pl.* 1916, 93 × 8¼ ft (1957); Glen House, Peebl., *pl.* 1906,
90 × 8¾ ft (1966); Brahan Castle, Ross and Cromarty, *pl.* 1901, 104 × 6¼ ft
(1970).

Outside Scotland few large trees have been recorded. There is one at Fonthill
Abbey, Wilts, *pl.* 1906, 120 × 4½ ft (1965), and another at Stourhead, Wilts,
102 × 7¾ ft (1970).

L. LARICINA (Du Roi) K. Koch   AMERICAN LARCH,
TAMARACK

Pinus laricina Du Roi; *Larix americana* Michx.; *L. microcarpa* (Lamb.) Desf.;
Pinus microcarpa Lamb.

A tree usually 50 to 80 ft high (up to 100 ft in favourable situations), with a
trunk sometimes nearly 2 ft in diameter; bark reddish, dividing into small,
roundish, closely appressed scales; young shoots often glaucous, turning
yellowish brown, not or only very slightly downy. Leaves three-sided, ¾ to 1¼ in.
long, very slender, bluntish. Cones egg-shaped, ⅓ to ⅔ in. long, ¼ to ½ in. wide,
with fifteen to twenty scales; bracts very small, enclosed by the scales.

Native of N. America from Newfoundland and Labrador west across the
continent to Alaska and extending into the United States as far as N. Pennsylvania
and the Lake States; introduced, according to Aiton before 1760 (this refers to
the tree planted at Hounslow by the Duke of Argyll, but it is very likely that the
tree which Peter Collinson had at Peckham as early as 1739 was also *L. laricina*).
The tamarack has never been much cultivated, owing, no doubt, to the greater
beauty and economic value of the European larch. From other larches it is
easily distinguished by the reddish, scaly bark and very small cones. For trees
cultivated in the British Isles the curling shoot-systems are another useful field
character.

In the course of his researches in British tree collections, Alan Mitchell has
found none of the trees mentioned earlier this century by Elwes and Henry,
which suggests that this larch is short-lived in our climate. He has recorded the
following, nearly all comparatively young: National Pinetum, Bedgebury,
Kent, *pl.* 1925, 54 × 5¼ ft. (1968); Sutton Place, Guildford, 63 × 6 ft (1966);
Wakehurst Place, Sussex, 60 × 3½ ft (1968); Leonardslee, Sussex, 53 × 5 ft
(1962); Nymans, Sussex, 75 × 3¼ ft (1970); Borde Hill, Sussex, 65 × 3¾ ft
(1957); Leighton Hall, Montg., 66 × 3¼ ft (1968).

L. OCCIDENTALIS Nutt.   WEST AMERICAN LARCH
[PLATE 73

A tree 100 to 200 ft high, with a narrow, pyramidal head, and a trunk sometimes 6 to 8 ft in diameter; bark scaling. On some of the young trees at Kew the
young shoots are glabrous, on others downy. Leaves 1¼ to 1¾ in. long, scarcely
distinguishable from those of common larch. Cones oblong to egg-shaped,
about 1½ in. long, ¾ in. wide; the scales thin, rounded, slightly reflexed at the

margin. The cone is rendered very distinct by the conspicuous tongue-like apex of the bracts protruding horizontally ¼ in. or more beyond the scales. *Bot. Mag.*, t. 8253.

Native of western N. America, from British Columbia southwards. In N. Montana, in the neighbourhood of Flat Head Lake, it is, according to Sargent, sometimes 250 ft high. It is, therefore, the most magnificent of all larches, and produces a fine timber. It was introduced to Kew in 1881 by Prof. Sargent, and trees are now over 60 ft high, with shapely trunks and short branches, in general appearance very like the common larches close by, except for the prominent bracts of the cones alluded to above and the more slender habit. For many years these were the only trees in the country, but a considerable quantity of seed was later imported from which thousands of thriving young trees were raised. It is, however, no longer planted in the British Isles as a timber tree, being of slower growth than the common and Japanese larches.

There is a specimen at Kew from the original introduction of 1881 referred to above which was planted in 1889 and now measures 72 × 4¼ ft (1971) and another, *pl.* 1903, of 75 × 5 ft (1971). Other examples are: National Pinetum, Bedgebury, *pl.* 1924, 70 × 7¾ ft (1965); Woburn, Beds, *pl.* 1929, 75 × 3¾ ft (1970); Bayfordbury, Herts, 85 × 4¾ ft (1968); Edinburgh Botanic Garden, two trees *pl.* 1909, 62 × 4 ft and 60 × 5½ ft (1967).

Inhabiting the same geographical region as *L. occidentalis* is:

L. LYALII Parl.—This is a tree 40 to 50, occasionally 80 ft in height. Its cones resemble those of *L. occidentalis* in having conspicuously protruded bracts, but it is quite distinct in other respects. The young wood is densely woolly, almost felted, the leaves four-sided, cones up to 2 in. long, with the scales distinctly fringed, pink when young. A few small plants have been introduced, but they have a miserable appearance, and the species does not give any promise of succeeding in the British Isles. It occupies a small area in the Cascade and northern Rocky Mountains, at subalpine elevations.

L. × PENDULA (Soland.) Salisb.

Pinus pendula Soland.; *Larix americana* var. *pendula* (Soland.) Loud.

A tree so far up to 90 ft in cultivation. Young shoots glabrous, pinkish by the end of the first season, brown in the second year. Leaves as in *L. decidua* but somewhat blunter at the apex. Cones ¾ to 1¼ in. long, ovoid; scales twenty to thirty, downy on the outside at the base; bracts concealed.

L. × pendula was described (as *Pinus pendula*) by Solander in 1789, from a tree growing at Ridgway House, Mill Hill, formerly the property of Peter Collinson, who had died twenty years earlier. Solander said it was a native of North America and that Collinson had it in cultivation in 1739, citing Miller's *Dictionary* as the authority for the date and origin. Miller's account, under *Larix*, reads: 'There is a particular Sort of this Tree, which was brought from *America*, which is growing in the garden of Mr. Peter Collinson at Peckham in *Surry*, which differs from the *European* Kind, in having darker Shoots. This Kind I do not find mentioned by the Botanists nor has it long been known in *Europe*, tho' it grows plentifully in some of the Northern parts of *America*. This doth not promise to make so large Trees as the *European* kind . . . It may be propagated by Seeds, after the same manner as hath been directed for the *European* Kind . . . and being a Native of cold Countries, will endure the severest Cold of this Climate' (*The Gardeners Dictionary*, abridged edition, 1740).

At the time when Miller wrote this account Collinson lived at Peckham, but around 1737 he had started to plant in his father-in-law's garden at Ridgway House, Mill Hill, which he inherited in 1749, living there for the rest of his life (N. Brett-James, *Life of Peter Collinson*, p. 48). It is usually assumed that Collinson transplanted the Peckham larch to Mill Hill, and that it was this very same tree that provided the type specimen of *Larix pendula*. If that is indeed so, we must conclude either that *L. pendula* is or was a native of North America; or, alternatively, if *L. pendula* is a hybrid between the European and American larch, the latter must have been introduced to Britain well before 1739, in order to have produced the Peckham tree of 1739. With regard to the first possibility, it can only be said that there is no evidence that *L. pendula* exists or ever has existed in North America in the wild. The second possibility, however, cannot be rejected out of hand. According to Aiton's *Hortus Kewensis*, the American larch was cultivated by the Duke of Argyll before 1760. The Duke, who was a friend of Collinson, had started planting at Whitton near Hounslow around 1724, and received a share of many of the seeds that Collinson imported from America. Nor can it be ruled out that there had been some earlier, unrecorded introduction of the American larch. So there is no insuperable objection to the theory that the Peckham tree of 1739 was a garden hybrid, provided we are prepared to assume that Miller's statement about its origin was incorrect.

There is, however, a third possibility that really accords best with common sense and is not contradicted by any known fact. It is that the Peckham larch mentioned by Miller was the American larch and that the tree at Ridgway house, from which Solander described *L. pendula*, was not physically the same tree as the one that grew at Peckham, but a seedling of it. If *L. pendula* is, as is now generally accepted, a hybrid between the American and European larch, the cross could have taken place in either of Collinson's two gardens. Solander himself never said that the tree at Ridgway House from which he described *L. pendula* was the very same tree that grew at Peckham, and if he had not seen that tree he would naturally have assumed that it belonged to the same species as its seedling. It is not even certain if the Peckham tree was ever moved to Ridgway House. Loudon states that it was moved, but he was writing three-quarters of a century after Collinson's death.

The tree at Ridgway House, Mill Hill, was cut down about 1800 'to make a rail'. Nothing seems to be known of its size or habit, but Sir James Smith, who must certainly have seen it, refers to it as 'one of the treasures of the Mill Hill garden'. The famous tree at Woburn, figured in 'Elwes and Henry' (as *L. dahurica*) also no longer exists. Recent records are: Kew, 62 × 5 ft (1970); Warnham Court, Sussex, 90 × 4½ ft (1969); National Pinetum, Bedgebury, Kent, *pl.* 1925, 72 × 4¾ ft (1970); Hergest Croft, Heref., *pl.* 1859, 60 × 6 ft (1969).

cv. 'REPENS'.—In his *Encyclopaedia* (1842), p. 1054, and in *Gard. Mag.*, Vol. 15, p. 626, Loudon describes a remarkable tree at Henham Hall, Suffolk, planted about 1800, which 'at the height of 8 ft sends out its branches horizon-tally, and these, being supported, extended north and south over a covered way more than 80 ft in length and 16 ft in width'. This larch, which still exists, cer-tainly belongs to *L.* × *pendula*. A photograph of it was published in the *East Anglian Daily Times*, 31 December 1963; it is 9 ft high with a spread of 120 by 40 ft, and at one time had 100 posts to support its branches.

L. POTANINII Batal.

L. thibetica Franch.; *L. chinensis* Beissn.

A tree 60 to 70, sometimes 100 ft high; young shoots brown and slightly downy. Leaves 1 in. long, pointed, somewhat four-sided through the prominence of the midrib above and below. Cones egg-shaped, about $1\frac{1}{2}$ in. long, $\frac{3}{4}$ to 1 in. wide, rounded at the top; scales rounded, downy outside; bracts protruded. *Bot. Mag.*, t. 9338.

Native of W. China; introduced for Messrs Veitch by Wilson from the neigh-bourhood of Kangting (Tatsien-lu) in 1904. The leaves have a strong aromatic and distinctive odour when crushed. Wilson described it as a symmetrical tree, with rather short, horizontal branches and pendulous branchlets of a shining orange-brown or purple-brown colour, becoming grey in the second or third year.

The Tibetan larch is closely allied to the Himalayan—*L. griffithii*—and the taxonomic and geographical boundaries between them are not as yet clear. A specimen considered to be the true species grows at Wakehurst Place, Sussex. Planted in 1913 it measures 50 × $2\frac{1}{2}$ ft (1971). A tree at Borde Hill, raised from seeds collected by Forrest in Yunnan, and planted as *L. potanii*, measures 48 × $2\frac{1}{4}$ ft (1957); this tree has still to be examined scientifically.

LAURELIA   ATHEROSPERMATACEAE

A genus of three evergreen trees, two in Chile and Argentina, the third in New Zealand. Flowers mostly unisexual. Male flowers with numerous stamens and a campanulate many-lobed calyx-tube. Female and perfect flowers with a spindle-shaped to ovoid or globular calyx-tube; carpels numerous and distinct, each developing into a feathered achene.

Laurelia, with *Atherosperma* (q.v.), constitutes the small family Athero-spermataceae, which is closely allied to the Monimiaceae and included by some botanists as a subfamily. In Chile the Monimiaceae proper are represented by the genus PEUMUS, whose sole species, *P. boldus* Mol., has aromatic leaves from which the Chileans make a digestive tea, much used after meals in place of coffee. It is too tender for a fuller description in this work.

L. SERRATA Bertero

L. philippiana Looser; *L. aromatica* Mast., not Poir.

An evergreen tree with four-angled downy young stems, often of very slender habit in the wild. Leaves leathery, opposite, narrowly elliptical, 2½ to 5 in. long, 1 to 2½ in. wide, tapered at both ends, saw-toothed, dark glossy green and glabrous above, midrib beneath furnished with yellowish, centrally attached hairs; stalk ¼ in. long, downy. When crushed the leaf has a pleasant, spicy fragrance, similar to that of the bay laurel. Flowers borne in the leaf-axils in clusters of three to nine; pedicels about ⅛ in. long. Calyx-tube (receptacle) cup-shaped, with eight equal lobes (perianth segments). Stamens of male flowers four in number; filaments glabrous, shorter than the anthers. Receptacle globose in the fruiting stage; achenes furnished with a tuft of long, fine, brown hairs, which enable them to travel long distances on the wind. *Bot. Mag.*, t. 8279.

Native of Chile and bordering parts of Argentina. This interesting tree is quite hardy in Sussex if well sheltered from cold winds but grows best near the Atlantic seaboard. A tree at Penjerrick in Cornwall measured 47 × 3¼ ft in 1911; it is now about as high and 6½ ft in girth, but dying at the top (1966). Others in the same county are: Tregothnan, 46 × 4½ ft (1971) and Caerhays, 42 × 3¼ ft (1971). The plate in the *Botanical Magazine* was drawn from material from the fine specimen at Kilmacurragh in Co. Wicklow, Eire. Planted about 1868 this measures 51 × 7¼ ft (1966). This tree bears flowers of both sexes and produces fertile seeds.

L. SEMPERVIRENS (Ruiz & Pavon) Tulasne *Pavonia sempervirens* Ruiz & Pavon; *L. aromatica* Poir.—This species has a more northern distribution than *L. serrata* and yields a superior timber, but is now rather rare, owing to over-exploitation and to the felling or burning of the forests of *Nothofagus obliqua* which were its main habitat. It is closely allied to *L. serrata* but can be distinguished by the following characters: leaves with rather shallow, appressed teeth and a glabrous midrib; flowers on pedicels ⅜ to ¾ in. long; filaments of stamens downy and as long as the anthers. Also, according to Dr Muñoz Pizarro (*Sinopsis de la Flora Chilena*, p. 244) the bark of *L. sempervirens* is aromatic and the wood odourless, whereas in *L. serrata* the bark is odourless and the wood has an unpleasant smell.

There is a fine specimen of *L. sempervirens* at Nymans in Sussex, near the glasshouses, raised from seeds collected by H. F. Comber in Chile in 1926 under No. 592.

LAURUS   LAURACEAE

Two species of evergreen trees or shrubs with entire, glabrous leaves, aromatic when crushed. Flowers with the sexes on different plants and borne in small, axillary, almost stalkless clusters; sepals four; stamens usually twelve; anthers opening by valves. Fruit a black berry. The name is an old Latin one.

L. AZORICA (Seub.) J. Franco
L. canariensis Webb & Berthelot, not Willd.; *Persea azorica* Seub.

An evergreen tree up to 60 ft high in the wild, with a trunk 2 to 3 ft in diameter; young shoots dark purplish brown, downy, giving off a pleasant aromatic fragrance like that of the common bay laurel when crushed. Leaves similarly aromatic, alternate, firm and leathery, ovate or oval, abruptly pointed or with a short slender point, wedge-shaped to rounded at the base, 2½ to 5 in. long, 2 to 3 in. wide, lustrous dark green and glabrous above, pale, dull, conspicuously veined and more or less hairy especially on the midrib beneath; stalk ¼ to ½ in. long. Flowers ⅜ in. wide, pale greenish yellow, produced in April on short, downy-stalked umbels in the axils of the leaves of the previous summer. The perianth has four segments with down on the back; stamens usually sixteen to twenty. Fruits egg-shaped, ½ in. long, each borne on a stout stalk ¼ in. long.

Native of the Canary Islands and the Azores. This fine evergreen is hardy in the southern and western maritime counties and in localities with a similar climate. It is cultivated at Lanarth and Caerhays in Cornwall and at Abbotsbury in Dorset. The tree is unisexual, the male flowers with their numerous stamens being the more ornamental. On large old trees the leaves appear to be comparatively narrow, longer and more lanceolate in outline than in the younger cultivated ones. This species differs from *L. nobilis*, a much hardier one, in its leaves being much larger and in its twigs being downy.

The two examples at Caerhays are 50 ft high, and the single-stemmed plant has a girth of 5½ ft (1971).

L. NOBILIS L.   BAY LAUREL

An evergreen, aromatic tree or shrub, 20 to 40 ft, sometimes 60 ft high, usually of dense pyramidal shape, and formed of a cluster of erect, much-branched stems; young shoots and leaves glabrous. Leaves alternate, narrowly oval or ovate, 1½ to 4 in. long, ½ to 1½ in. wide, usually about equally tapered to each end, of firm texture, dark glossy green, often with wavy margins; stalk ⅛ to ⅓ in. long. Flowers greenish yellow, small, very shortly stalked, produced in small umbels in the uppermost leaf-axils; the sexes on different trees. Fruits globose or slightly oval, shining, black, ½ in. long.

Native of the Mediterranean region; cultivated in Britain since the 16th century, probably before. It is quite hardy at Kew, although occasionally browned by hard winters. This is the true 'laurel' of the ancients, and the one whose leaves were used to make crowns for triumphant heroes, and the fruiting sprays to make wreaths for distinguished poets (poets laureate). It is interesting to note in the latter connection that the term 'bachelor' as applied to the recipient of degrees, has been derived through the French *bachelier* from 'bacca-laureus', i.e., laurel-berry. Nowadays the leaves are put to a more prosaic use,

T S—S

and are commonly used for flavouring stews, soups, and sauces. It has no relationship with common or cherry laurel (see *Prunus laurocerasus*), or with the
Alexandrian laurel (see *Danaë racemosa*).

The bay laurel bears clipping well, and is very largely grown in tubs and pots
on the continent as formal standards or pyramids for the decoration of entrances
to mansions, hotels, etc. At Opatija, on the East Istrian coast, and at Rijeka
across the Bay of Quarnero, there are, or were, beautiful woods of primeval
bay laurel; in these places, growing on rocky sites, they form thickets of slender
stems 50 ft. high.

f. ANGUSTIFOLIA (Nees) Markgraf—The species shows some variation in
shape of leaf; of several forms this is the most distinct. The leaves are 1½ to
3½ in. long, but only ¼ to ⅞ in. wide.

f. CRISPA (Nees) Markgraf *L. nobilis* var. *undulata* Meissn.—Leaf-margins
conspicuously wavy.

LAVANDULA   LAVENDER   LABIATAE

A genus of aromatic shrubs and herbs in which twenty-five species are
recognised by Miss D. A. Chaytor in her monograph in *Journ. Linn. Soc.*,
Vol. 51 (1937–8), pp. 153–204. Inflorescence a distinctly stalked terminal
spike. Fruits dividing into four nutlets. The species treated here belong
to the sections *Spica* and *Stoechas* in both of which the spikes are cylindrical, with bracts arranged in opposite pairs, the fertile ones each subtending a condensed cyme with two to seven flowers; calyx and corolla
tubular, the upper tooth of the calyx much enlarged. In this section *Spica*
the bracts are uniform, all subtending flowers, and the corolla is markedly
two-lipped and longer than the calyx. In the section *Stoechas* the uppermost
bracts are sterile and form a conspicuous tuft known as the 'coma'; the
corolla-lobes are more or less equal; and the corolla-tube is not much
longer than the calyx.

The genus ranges from the Atlantic islands through the Mediterranean
to the Near East, India, and N.E. tropical Africa.

L. ANGUSTIFOLIA Mill.   COMMON LAVENDER
L. spica L., in part; *L. officinalis* Chaix; *L. vera* DC. (but not of gardens); *L. spica*
var. *angustifolia* L. f.

A sub-shrub with a well-developed woody base, growing to a height of about
2 ft, occasionally more. Leaves of two kinds: the principal leaves linear, narrow-
elliptic or narrow-oblanceolate, not much broader at the apex than at the middle,
mostly 1 to 1¾ in. long, occasionally longer, up to $\frac{3}{16}$ in. wide, slightly revolute
or plane, greyish at first, later more or less green; leaves on the axillary shoots

narrower than the primary leaves, more revolute and more persistently grey above. Inflorescences spike-like, terminal on slender four-angled stems. Flowers almost sessile, produced in whorls, each of which consists of a pair of opposite, much condensed cymes; the whorls may be densely arranged or, especially towards the base of the spike, more or less widely spaced, the lowermost whorl usually at some distance from the others. Bracts papery, brown, prominently veined, ovate to broadly oblate-ovate or obovate in outline, acuminate at the apex; bracteoles small, brownish, sometimes absent. Calyx about $\frac{3}{16}$ in. long, with thirteen longitudinal ribs, tinged with purple and usually densely coated with a woolly tomentum. Corolla lavender-purple, the upper lip two-lobed, the lower with three narrower lobes; exposed part of corolla-tube slightly shorter than the calyx.

A native of the west Mediterranean region, but extending some way inland, and up to 6,000 ft altitude; naturalised in parts of central Europe, especially in the wine-growing areas. It is said to have been cultivated in Britain since the early 16th century, but in all probability the Benedictine monks brought it here much earlier, perhaps even before the Conquest. *L. angustifolia* is the source of the true oil of lavender, which was once esteemed as a medicine for innumerable ills and also, according to Sir James Smith, for making a spiritous tincture which was 'a popular cordial, very commodious for those who wish to indulge in a dram, under the appearance of an elegant medicine'. In France, which is the main home of the true lavender, the oil was once produced from portable stills which were carried to the wild stands at flowering time. At the present day, much of the annual production comes from artificial 'lavanderaies', in which the true lavender has been partly replaced by more productive plants which are known as 'lavandin' and are considered to be hybrids between the true lavender and the spike lavender (*L. latifolia*). See further under GARDEN LAVENDERS below.

The common lavender varies somewhat in the wild. Some plants are dwarf, with flowering stems 8 to 14 in. long and linear, revolute leaves. At the other extreme is the Dauphiné lavender, which is robust, with flowering stems up to 20 in. long and leaves not or only slightly revolute. This is said to inhabit valleys and to be less fragrant than the dwarfer kind. But these variations may be, at least in part, the result of differences in environment. More distinct is:

subsp. PYRENAICA (DC.) Guinea *L. pyrenaica* DC.—Bracts of inflorescence very large, as long as the calyx and wider than long. Hairs of calyx mostly confined to the ribs. Pyrenees.

GARDEN LAVENDERS.—In her monograph on *Lavandula*, referred to in the introductory note, Miss Chaytor stated that most plants grown in gardens under the names *L. spica* and *L. latifolia* are really hybrids between the true lavender (*L. angustifolia*) and the spike lavender (*L. latifolia*). She deferred consideration of these plants, and her intended study of them was never published. It would be beyond the scope of a general work such as this to attempt such a study, but it would seem to be the case that most commercial varieties show hybrid characters in some degree. The main exceptions are the early-flowering dwarf sorts such as 'Hidcote' and 'Munstead', which show no obvious signs of hybridity. At the other extreme are the robust, late-flowering varieties, some of which are known as "Dutch" lavenders or, quite wrongly, as "*L. vera*". The fact that these varieties flower late (some not starting until the end of July) is itself a probable sign of hybridity, since the spike lavender is decidedly later-flowering in the wild than *L. angustifolia* (see *L. latifolia*). Hybrid characters shown by these plants are elongated bracts, prominent bracteoles, branched inflorescences, sparsely hairy calyces, spatulate, often silvery leaves, and in some cases a camphorous element in the fragrance of the crushed calyx. But a single variety may show only one or two of these characters and in other respects agree with *L. angustifolia*, which seems to be the dominant element in most of these putative hybrids.

So far as garden nomenclature is concerned the problem discussed in the preceding paragraph is perhaps of no great importance, since the majority of the commercial varieties have clonal names, which can with perfect correctness be placed immediately after the generic name *Lavandula*, without the intervention of any specific name. For reasons explained under *L. spica*, that name cannot be used for any species, and still less for any hybrid, while *L. vera* is simply a superfluous name for *L. angustifolia* (though the Dutch lavenders, for which it has been misused, are farther removed from that species, and nearer to *L. latifolia*, than any of the other garden varieties). The following is only a selection of the named varieties, though it includes those most widely available in commerce. They need an open, sunny position and a light, not too rich soil. It is advisable to trim off the flowering stems in late summer and to clip the plants more closely in spring, before growth commences. Propagation is by cuttings, inserted in August or September under a cloche or in a cold frame.

'ALBA'.—Flowering stems about 21 in. long. Spikes 2 to 3 in. long, with one or two distant whorls; secondary spikes well developed. Bracts of main part of spike more or less as in *L. angustifolia* but those subtending the lowermost whorl broadly awl-shaped and greenish, in this respect inclining to those of *L. latifolia*. Calyx grey-green, fairly woolly. Corolla pinkish white. The basal leaves, although tapered to the apex (not spathulate), are much broader than in *L. angustifolia*. Late July.

'FOLGATE'.—Flowering stems about 12 in. long. Spikes rather open, 3 to 4 in. long (excluding lowermost whorl). Bracts broad-ovate; bracteoles not conspicuous. Calyx woolly but not densely so, bluish purple. Corolla purple. A vigorous medium-sized lavender of dense habit, very free-flowering. July, A.M. 1963.

'GRAPPENHALL'.—A vigorous lavender with obvious hybrid characters. Woody base short in proportion to the length of the flowering stems, which are up to 2½ ft long and mostly branched. Spikes rather open, with a very distant whorl at the base. Bracts narrow, with long slender tips; bracteoles well developed, some about as long as the calyx, which is pale bluish purple, thinly woolly. Corolla lavender-purple. Late July. The same or some similar variety has been known by the name 'GIGANTEA'.

'HIDCOTE'.—Flowering stems 10 to 15 in. long. Spikes very dense at the apex, with one or two distant whorls at the base. Bracts broad, short-pointed; bracteoles very small. Calyx rich purple, densely woolly, the hairs almost concealing the ribbing. Corollas purple. A very fine lavender of silvery appearance which first came to notice at Hidcote Manor, Glos. Its history is not known, but Major Johnston, who made the garden, may have brought it from France. It seems to be a form of L. *angustifolia*, not a hybrid and, unlike many garden lavenders, produces a good crop of seeds. It has been stated that 'Hidcote' is the same as the older 'NANA ATROPURPUREA', but a plant at Wisley under the latter name is not the same, though superficially similar. Its calyx is paler and less woolly. Both flower late June–July. A.M. 1950, FCC. 1963.

'HIDCOTE GIANT'.—A rather coarse but very fragrant lavender with flowering stems about 2 ft long, some of them branched. Spikes dense, 2 to 3 in. long, with mostly one distant whorl. Calyx bluish purple at the apex, woolly. Flowers lavender-purple, very numerous in each cyme. Bracts ovate, long-pointed; bracteoles well developed. July. This bears a strong resemblance to the lavender from Mitcham mentioned below.

'HIDCOTE PINK'.—Similar to 'Hidcote', but with a pinkish-white corolla and a greenish calyx.

'MUNSTEAD'.—Flowering stems about 12 in. long. Spikes short, rather open, with one or two lower, distant whorls. Bracts broad-ovate, fairly long-pointed; bracteoles present. Calyx purplish, paler at the base, thinly woolly. Corolla bluish purple. Late June–early July. A.M. 1955.

'NANA ALBA'.—A dwarf with flowering stems 3 to 4 in. long. Spikes dense at the apex, with one or two lower, distant whorls. Bracts broad, short-pointed; bracteoles small. Calyx pale green, fairly densely coated with straight hairs.

'TWICKEL PURPLE'.—Flowering stems about 15 in. or slightly more long, rather spreading. Spikes open, about 4 in. long (excluding the basal whorl). Calyx woolly, purple almost to the base. Corolla purple. July. A.M. 1961.

Of the so called Dutch lavenders (L. *vera* Hort., not DC.) there are a number of clones, flowering late in the season (from the end of July), with spatulate basal leaves, very silvery in one commercial variety. The origin of the common name is not known for certain, but it was probably used by the producers of lavender oil for varieties which they judged inferior either because they yielded low-quality oil or because they were slow to flower. There are many examples in the English language of 'dutch' being used in a derogatory sense.

Lavender was once grown extensively at Mitcham in Surrey, but it is impossible to say whether there is a single variety entitled to be called the Mitcham lavender. Mr H. P. Boddington, Director of Parks at Merton, kindly sent a specimen from an old plant 5 ft high and as much across, found growing on an allotment where the lavender fields were once situated. This plant is very fragrant and bears very dense spikes with numerously-flowered cymes—an important attibute in an oil-producing variety, since the essence is mainly contained in the calyces.

L. DENTATA L.
Stoechas dentata (L.) Mill.

An evergreen well-branched shrub 1½ to 3 ft high; young shoots four-angled, downy. Leaves dark green, opposite, 1 to 1½ in. long, ⅛ to ¼ in. wide linear in main outline, but regularly cut on each side into round-ended teeth halfway or more to the midrib, dull green and downy beneath. Main flower-stem 3 to 12 in. long, slender, square in cross-section, downy, bearing at the top of a spike, 1½ to 2½ in. long, of densely packed flowers. A conspicuous and ornamental feature of the head of flowers is the lavender-blue bracts which are ovate or diamond-shaped, often three-lobed, pointed, strongly veined and downy. The base of the flowers themselves is hidden by these bracts, the exposed part of the corolla being about ¼ in. wide, five-lobed, pale lavender-blue; they are lavender scented but not very strongly so. *Bot. Mag.*, t. 400.

Native of Spain and the Mediterranean region, often in arid situations; also of the Atlantic islands, Abyssinia, Arabia, etc. It occurs on the Rock of Gibraltar. It was cultivated in Gerard's time (1597); he writes of it and *L. stoechas*: 'We have them in our gardens and keep them with great diligence from the injury of our cold climate, covered in winter or grown in pots and carried into houses.' It prefers a climate like that of the Scilly Isles; in cooler parts elsewhere a sheltered sunny corner is needed for it, giving it protection in frosty weather. Even then it succumbs in hard winters. It is easily distinguished from other lavenders by its narrow much-toothed leaves which give it a charming appearance. It belongs to the section *Stoechas* but the sterile bracts of the 'coma' are shorter than in *L. stoechas* and *L. pedunculata* and not so markedly different from the fertile bracts (i.e., those subtending the flowers). The foliage has a pleasant aromatic scent only faintly suggestive of lavender. Blooms from July onwards.

L. LANATA Boiss.

An evergreen shrub 1½ to 2 ft high; young shoots and leaves covered with a whitish wool. Leaves opposite, stalkless, linear or oblanceolate, tapered at the base, rounded or blunt at the end, 1 to 2 in. long, ¼ in. or less wide. Flower-spikes 1 to 2 ft high, four-angled, slender, not so woolly as the leaves, with the flowers crowded in a group (1½ to 3 in. long) of whorls at the top. Flowers ⅓ in. long, bright violet and ⅛ in. wide at the mouth, downy outside. Calyx tubular, eight-ribbed, ¼ in. long, downy, toothed, with one tooth much enlarged.

Native of Spain, where it was discovered by Boissier in 1837, in calcareous mountainous regions, especially on the Sierra Nevada. It is very distinct from *L. angustifolia* and *L. latifolia* in the longer, much more thickly woolly leaves, but the habit is the same and the flowers are similarly arranged at the top of a long slender stalk. Those species differ from it in the (up to) thirteen ribs of the calyx. Boissier observes that in Spain, where it flowers in July and August, it is 'infinitely more fragrant, very much esteemed by the mountaineers for its medicinal virtues, and occupies a region more elevated than [*L. latifolia*]'.

L. LATIFOLIA (L. f.) Med.   SPIKE LAVENDER
L. spica var. *latifolia* L. f.; *L. spica* L., in part; *L. spica sensu* DC., Mill. and many other authors

This species is related to the true lavender (*L. angustifolia*) but quite distinct from it. It is more of a sub-shrub, developing a shorter wood base, though producing annual stems as long as or longer than in its ally. The leaves are relatively broader (from four to six times as long as wide), plane, oblong or spathulate, long-tapered to the base, those on the flowering stems eventually green as in the true lavender but the lower ones permanently silvery and densely clustered. The flowering stems are usually branched, i.e., secondary flowering spikes are produced on each side of the principal one. The most marked difference, however, is to be found in the inflorescence. Whereas in the true lavender the bracts subtending the flower-clusters are ovate in outline, brown and numerously veined, those of the spike lavender are green and awl-shaped and only the central vein is conspicuous; the bracteoles are always well developed and similar to the bract, though shorter. The calyx is covered with rather short hairs and is never woolly as in the true lavender and the corollas are somethat smaller. The spike is usually more slender, and the flowering time is, at least in France, two or three weeks later than that of the true lavender.

L. *latifolia* is a native of the western Mediterranean region. It is more warmth-loving than the true lavender, not ascending in France to more than 2,000 ft. The oil it yields (*oleum spicae*, in France called '*essence d'aspic*') is inferior to that of the true lavender and of a different chemical composition, but is used in perfumery. The fragrance of the crushed calyx is pleasant, resembling that of the true lavender but with an intermixture of camphor.

The true spike lavender is rare in gardens but was known to Philip Miller, who said it was cultivated in a few gardens in his time but 'does not often produce flowers'. It is one parent of the so-called Dutch lavenders, and perhaps of other garden varieties. See further under L. *angustifolia*.

L. PEDUNCULATA Cav.

An evergreen shrub 1½ to 2½ ft high; the leaves, stems, and flower-stalks covered with a fine grey down. Leaves linear, ½ to 1½ in. long, 1/16 to ⅛ in. wide, margins recurved. Main flower-stalk 4 to 12 in. long, four-angled, bearing the flowers at the top in a dense spike ½ to 1¼ in. long and ½ to ⅝ in. wide. Bracts violet-purple, broadly wedge-shaped, ¾ in. wide, downy, margined with hairs; they constitute the most attractive part of the inflorescence. Of the flower itself only the deep purple corolla shows and it is only ⅛ in. or a little more across. The spike is surmounted by a tuft of violet-purple, linear-oblong, leaflike bracts which are up to 1½ in. long and ¼ in. wide.

L. *pedunculata* is a variable species distributed from the Atlantic Islands through Spain and Portugal and N. Africa to the S. Balkans and Asia Minor; but in its typical state, as described above, it is mainly confined to Spain. It is closely related to L. *stoechas* (with which it was associated as a variety by Linnaeus and other botanists), but its spike of clustered flowers is shorter, comparatively broader, and borne on a much longer main-stalk; the terminal tuft of bracts also is longer, and the bracts composing it are narrower. In general aspect the two plants are much the same. On the whole this appears to be the handsomest of the lavenders, but unfortunately is not really hardy with us. It grows wild up to elevations of 4,800 ft in Spain, often in arid calcareous localities. Probably its tenderness with us is due as much to lack of summer sunshine as to winter cold. It should be grown at the foot of a sunny wall where it can conveniently be covered with a mat in times of severe frost. It flowers from June to August.

L. VIRIDIS L'Hérit.—Leaves and stems covered with rough, greenish hairs. Flowers white, bracts white or greenish white. S. Portugal and Madeira. It is intermediate botanically between L. *pedunculata* and L. *stoechas*.

L. SPICA L., *nomen ambiguum*

Under the name L. *spica*, still commonly used in gardens, Linnaeus described two lavenders that almost all other botanists, before and since his time, have regarded as quite distinct species. These are the narrow-leaved, broad-bracted lavender L. *angustifolia* Mill. (the 'true' lavender), and the broad-leaved, narrow-bracted lavender L. *latifolia* (L. f.) Med., commonly known as 'spike'. This was not an unusual situation, and no confusion would have resulted had there been agreement among botanists as to which of the two species should retain the name L. *spica*. Unfortunately, Linnaeus had chosen a misleading epithet for his compound species. At the time when he described it in his *Species Plantarum* (1753), the epithet *spica* was in use for both the lavenders concerned or at least was not yet of fixed meaning (Miller used it first for L. *angustifolia*, later for L. *latifolia*). But by the end of the century it seems to have become restricted to the broad-leaved lavender, whose oil was known as '*oleum spicae*'. So it is not surprising that many botanists, in the absence of any other clues as to the identity of the typical L. *spica*, used this name for the spike lavender. The 'other' lavender therefore needed a new name and in the event it received three—L. *angustifolia* Mill., L. *officinalis* Chaix, and L. *vera* DC. Other botanists of repute, however, considered that the typical L. *spica* was the narrow-leaved 'true' lavender, which Linnaeus described first, immediately under the heading. According to this interpretation it was the broad-leaved lavender ('spike') that had to be separated from L. *spica*, and for it the pre-Linnaean name L. *latifolia* was taken up.

Thus it came about that one name—L. *spica*—was used almost equally by botanists for two distinct species. In 1932, Miss M. L. Green proposed that L. *spica* should be discarded as a *nomen ambiguum*, in accordance with the rule that a name must be rejected if it has become a persistent source of confusion, and in the *International Code of Botanical Nomenclature* (ed. 1966), Art. 69, L. *spica* is actually cited as an example of such a name. The two species involved in the confusion will be found in the present work under the names L. *angustifolia* and L. *latifolia*.

In gardens, the name L. *spica* has been used for horticultural varieties some of which are near to L. *angustifolia* (syn. L. *spica* of some botanists; L. *officinalis* Chaix; L. *vera* DC.), while others are clearly hybrids between L. *angustifolia* and L. *latifolia* (L. *spica sensu* de Candolle, Bentham *et al*). See further under these species.

The misuse of the name L. *vera* in gardens seems to be a result of the ambiguity of the name L. *spica*. It is often used at the present time for the so-called Dutch lavenders, which are near to L. *latifolia* and therefore far removed from L. **vera**

DC. It is easy to see that this mistake could have arisen through wrongly equat-
ing *L. spica* Hort. with *L. spica sensu* DC., thus bringing de Candolle's other
species, *L. vera*, into equivalence with *L. latifolia* or hybrids near to it.

L. STOECHAS L.   FRENCH LAVENDER

An evergreen shrub 2 to 3 ft high, all of whose vegetative parts are covered
with a fine grey down. Leaves stalkless, not toothed, linear, $\frac{1}{3}$ to $1\frac{1}{4}$ in. long,
$\frac{1}{16}$ to $\frac{1}{8}$ in. wide, the margins recurved. Main flower-stem from $\frac{1}{2}$ to $1\frac{1}{2}$ in.
long, carrying at the top a spike of closely set blossom 1 to 2 in. long, $\frac{1}{2}$ in.
wide. The variously shaped bracts constitute the most conspicuous and beautiful

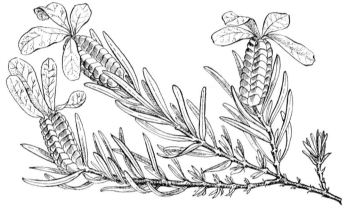

LAVANDULA STOECHAS

part of the inflorescence, being purple, ovate or rhomboidal, $\frac{1}{4}$ to $\frac{3}{4}$ in. wide,
downy, strongly veined. Flowers deeply purple, the small exposed part of the
corolla $\frac{1}{8}$ in. wide. The inflorescence has at the top a few enlarged leaflike
purple bracts of obovate outline and $\frac{1}{2}$ to 1 in. long.

Native of S.W. Europe, extending eastwards along the Mediterranean region
to Greece; also of N. Africa. It flowers in its native haunts from April onwards,
but commences later with us. It was in cultivation in the middle 16th century
and is mentioned by Turner and Gerard in their Herbals as 'French lavende'.
Its hardiness is about the same as that of *L. dentata* (q.v.). It is easily distinguished
by its very short main flower-stalk and stout spike of flowers crowned with a
tuft of large foliaceous bracts (but see also *L. pedunculata*). The shoots and leaves
have a curious somewhat pine-like odour when crushed. It succeeds well on
the chalk at Highdown, near Worthing.

var. LEUCANTHA Gingins de Lassaraz *L. s.* var. *albiflora* Bean—A white-
flowered variety both as regards bracts and corolla. Messrs Ellman and Sandwith, in June 1925, found a plant growing near Villefranche, in the Eastern
Pyrenees, bearing both white and typical purple bracts and flowers.

The name 'stoechas', once applied generically to this species and to *L. pedunculata*, is derived from the Stoechades of the ancients (now the Iles d'Hyères). Plants growing there were most highly esteemed for their medicinal virtues.

LAVATERA   MALVACEAE

A genus of about twenty-five species of herbs and soft-wooded shrubs natives mainly of Europe, W. Asia, and the Canary Islands, but one species is indigenous in California. Leaves lobed or angled. Flowers axillary, solitary, in pairs or in clusters. Involucre (epicalyx) present, with two or three segments united at the base, at least in the bud-stage (free in *Malva*). Fruits splitting into numerous segments (mericarps), each containing one seed.

The genus is named in honour of the brothers Lavater, naturalists of Zürich.

L. ARBOREA L.   TREE MALLOW

A shrub up to 6 or 8 ft high, with stout, erect, woody, annual or biennial stems, 1 to 2 in. thick, and resembling a small tree in form. Leaves long-stalked, very variable in size, from 3 to 9 in. long, and as much broad, they are five- to seven-lobed, the lobes unequally round-toothed at the margins, the base heart-shaped; both surfaces are densely covered with soft hairs. Flowers borne very abundantly; covering as much as 1½ to 2 ft of the terminal part of the branches, some on short leafy racemes, some clustered in leaf-axils. Each flower is 1½ in. across, enclosed at first by a large, woolly, three-lobed involucre or epicalyx. Calyx five-cleft. Petals five, broadly wedge-shaped, pale purple-red, marked at the base with a patch of dark purple veins.

Native of S. Europe and the Atlantic coasts, this handsome plant is also found wild in Great Britain. It inhabits maritime situations on the south and west coasts from Hampshire to the Isle of Man, and occurs either naturalised or wild on Ailsa Craig, the Bass Rock, and other places on the coasts of Scotland. It is worth cultivating in the warmer parts of the kingdom, especially near the sea, its abundant seed making it easy to increase. It is chiefly known in inland gardens by 'VARIEGATA', whose leaves are handsomely marked with white. This form must be propagated by cuttings.

L. ASSURGENTIFLORA Kell.

A shrub 3 to 8 ft high, occasionally twice as high in the wild, with downy or glabrous stems. Leaves 3 to 6 in. long and about as wide, palmately five- or seven-lobed, the lobes acute, coarsely toothed, green and slightly downy above, white and downy beneath; stalk 2½ to 5½ in. long. Flowers in axillary two- to four-flowered clusters; stalks 1⅜ to 1¾ in. long, curving upwards at the ends (hence the specific epithet); involucre with usually three, lanceolate lobes. Calyx densely white-downy, with triangular sepals. Petals cerise with deeper veins, 1 to 1¾ in. long. *Bot. Mag.*, t. 9450.

Native of Santa Barbara Islands and Santa Catalina off the coast of California, but widely cultivated on the mainland and sometimes escaping. It is not common in British gardens but has been successfully grown at Highdown near Worthing, Sussex, and in Cornwall. It is resistant to salt-laden winds and is used in California as a windbreak. There it blooms all the year, but most abundantly in the summer.

L. MARITIMA Gouan

An evergreen shrub 2 to 5 ft high; young stems densely covered at first with a white, woolly indumentum, later glabrous. Leaves roundish in general outline, 2½ to 4 in. long and wide, shallowly five-lobed, covered with white stellate down on both surfaces but occasionally only thinly so on the upper surface; stalk up to 1¼ in. long (rarely longer). Flowers borne singly or in pairs in the leaf-axils on scurfy stalks much longer than the leaf-stalks. Involucre much shorter than the calyx, which has triangular-ovate sepals, becoming united in the fruiting stage. Petals pale pink, with a crimson blotch at the base, obcordate, ⅞ to 1⅛ in. long. Segments of fruits black when ripe, flat or slightly concave on the back. It flowers in cultivation from May until autumn. *Bot. Mag.*, t. 8997. Native of the W. Mediterranean, including N.W. Africa; date of introduction uncertain.

subsp. BICOLOR Rouy *L. bicolor* (Rouy) Stapf—This is perhaps no more than an extreme state of the species, with leaves of above average size and flowers 2¼ to 2½ in. across. It was described from a plant found at Pont St Louis near Mentone, but, curiously enough, specimens in the Kew Herbarium collected near the type locality are ordinary *L. maritima* and so too are all other specimens from the French coast. Those that best match subsp. *bicolor* are one from Ventimiglia and two from Oran in Tunisia. It was in cultivation at Kew and in the garden of the Bitton vicarage early this century and Lord Talbot has a fine specimen growing against a sunny garden wall at Malahide Castle, near Dublin.

L. OLBIA L.

A soft-stemmed shrub 5 to 6 ft high, branching from the base; stems and leaves covered with white stellate hairs when young. Leaves up to 6 in. long, the lower ones three- to five-lobed, cordate at the base, the upper ones lanceolate or oblong-lanceolate, slightly three-lobed or almost unlobed. Flowers short-stalked, borne singly or in pairs in the leaf-axils. Segments of the involucre almost equal in length to the calyx. Sepals of calyx triangular-ovate. Petals obovate, ⅝ to 1⅛ in. long, purplish red. Segments of fruits hairy, yellowish when ripe, with rounded angles. It flowers from midsummer until autumn.

A native of the coasts of the W. Mediterranean, introduced before 1570. Although usually seen in herbaceous borders it is really more of a shrub than a herbaceous plant and is not out of place when planted with other sun-loving shrubs from the Mediterranean. It will grow in any soil that is not too wet or sour but is most at home on chalk. One of the localities in which it grows wild is the Iles d'Hyères off the coast of France, known in Roman times as Olbia Gallo-provincialis.

cv. 'ROSEA'.—Flowers rose-coloured. Preferable to the wild form.

LEDUM   ERICACEAE

A small genus of aromatic evergreen shrubs, with alternate, short-stalked, leaves, and white flowers produced in terminal roundish clusters. Calyx teeth five; corolla of five distinct, spreading petals; stamens from five to ten, with the anthers opening by two apertures at the top. Seed-vessel a capsule, with five divisions which separate from the base upwards.

L. *groenlandicum* and L. *palustre* inhabit moors and swampy districts in high northern latitudes and like a peaty soil or sandy loam free from lime. They can be propagated by seeds, treated as recommended for heaths, also by layers and cuttings.

L. GLANDULOSUM Nutt.

An evergreen bush, said to become as much as 6 ft high in its native home. Leaves oval or ovate, ½ to 2 in. long, ¼ to ¾ in. wide, dark green above, whitish and smooth beneath except for a covering of minute glistening scales, stalk ⅙ to ¼ in. long. Flowers white, ½ in. across, produced during May in a terminal cluster about 2 in. across. Petals cupped, obovate, spreading; sepals minute, rounded, hairy on the margin; stalks ½ to 1 in. long, and, like the calyx and ovary, covered with tiny, scale-like glands. Capsules globose. *Bot. Mag.*, t. 7610.

Native of western N. America; originally discovered by Douglas in 1826. A batch of plants was raised at Kew in 1894 from native seed, which grew and flowered very well a few years later. For some indiscernible reason the plants died one by one until none was left. It was, however, later reintroduced and sucessfully cultivated by Messrs Marchant of Wimborne, Dorset.

It is easily distinguished from the two following species by its smooth stems and leaves.

L. COLUMBIANUM Piper L. *glandulosum* subsp. *columbianum* (Piper) C. L. Hitchcock—Leaves up to 3 in. long and relatively narrower than in L. *glandulosum*, with revolute margins. Inflorescence dense and rounded. Capsules oblong-ovoid. British Columbia to Santa Cruz County, California.

LEDUM

L. GROENLANDICUM Oeder   LABRADOR TEA

[PLATE 75

L. latifolium Jacq.; *L. palustre* subsp. *groenlandicum* (Oeder) Hulten; *L. pacificum* Small

An evergreen shrub 2 to 3 ft high and as much in diameter; branches erect, clothed when young with more or less rust-coloured wool. Leaves aromatically fragrant when bruised, narrowly oblong or oval, ½ to 2 in. long, ¼ to ½ in. wide, the margins much recurved, the base tapering or slightly heart-shaped, dark green with a few loose hairs above, covered beneath with a thick rust-coloured felt. Flowers in rounded terminal clusters 2 in. across, consisting of one or more corymbs; each flower ½ to ¾ in. across, white, borne on a slender, downy stalk ½ to 1 in. long. Calyx edged with very minute teeth; petals oblong; stamens five to eight, sometimes more; seed-vessel somewhat cylindrical in shape.

Native of N. America, also of Greenland; introduced in 1763. A very hardy and pretty shrub, the commonest of the ledums in gardens and the most useful. It flowers from the end of April to June. From *L. palustre* it is distinguished by its leaves being twice as wide. It has been said that it further differs in its fewer stamens (five to eight against seven to eleven in *L. palustre*), but according to Hulten (*Fl. Alaska and Yukon* (1948), p. 1219) this character is not reliable. He considers that *L. groenlandicum* should rank as a subspecies of *L. palustre* but it seems preferable to retain it as a species until this complex has been studied in detail throughout its vast geographical range. It also varies to some extent in stature and shape of leaf.

cv. 'COMPACTUM'.—Of dwarf habit, with short branches, very woolly stems, short broad leaves, and small flower clusters.

L. PALUSTRE L.   MARSH LEDUM

A dwarf evergreen shrub of thin habit, 1 to 4 ft high; young shoots clothed with rust-coloured wool. Leaves linear, ½ to 1¼ in. long, 1/12 to ¼ in. wide, the margins much recurved and thus reducing their width, dark dull green above, covered with rust-coloured wool beneath. Flowers white, ½ in. across, produced during April and May in terminal clusters; calyx minutely toothed; stamens more numerous than in *L. groenlandicum*, usually seven to eleven; seed-vessel egg-shaped.

L. palustre (including its varieties) is distributed throughout the arctic and subarctic regions of the northern hemisphere; in Europe it extends southward into central Germany, Austria, and the Carpathians, and may be truly native in one locality in Scotland; it also ranges southward in the mountains of western N. America and in N.E. Asia. According to Aiton it was introduced to Britain in 1762, but as a garden shrub it is inferior to *L. groenlandicum* and much less common. The differences between them are pointed out under that species.

f. DECUMBENS (Ait.) O. Fedtsch. *L. palustre* var. *decumbens* Ait.; *L. p.* subsp. *decumbens* (Ait.) Hulten; *L. decumbens* (Ait.) Lodd.—A decumbent shrub to 8 in. high with linear revolute leaves less than ⅛ in. wide and usually less than ¾ in long. It was originally described from a plant said to have been introduced from Hudson Bay but is of fairly wide distribution within the range of the species.

f. DILATATUM (Wahlenb.) O. Fedtsch. *L. palustre* var. *dilatatum* Wahlenb.—
This has broader, oval-oblong leaves but is otherwise like the typical state of
the species. It was described from material from Lapland, but similar plants
occur here and there throughout the range of the species. Some plants from
Japan and other parts of N.E. Asia, and also from western North America, have
been referred to var. *dilatatum* but are better placed in the complex described
below.

var. HYPOLEUCUM Bean—This well-marked variant was described in the
first edition of this work (Vol. 2 (1914), p. 11) from a plant at Kew raised from
Japanese seeds received from Prof. Sargent of the Arnold Arboretum on 4 January 1893. It has short, relatively broad leaves, with only the margins revolute,
so that nearly all the undersurface is visible, and this is strikingly white from a
dense covering of crisped white hairs, except on the yellowish midrib, which
bears a few dark or rusty hairs, some of which may occur elsewhere on the
surface. If some closely matching Japanese specimens are taken into account,
the dimensions of leaf-blade in this variety are $\frac{5}{8}$ to $1\frac{3}{8}$ in. long, $\frac{1}{6}$ to $\frac{1}{2}$ in. wide.
In 1916 the famous Russian botanist V. L. Komarov described *L. hypoleucum*
(as a new species) from specimens collected on the coast of the Russian Far
East and on Sakhalin. This differs from *L. palustre* var. *hypoleucum* Bean only
in its larger leaves (up to $2\frac{3}{4}$ in. long, $\frac{11}{16}$ in. wide, *fide* Komarov). Other specimens
from N.E. Asia agree in size of leaf with either var. *hypoleucum* Bean or *L.*
hypoleucum Komar., but have the crisped white tomentum overlaid with a more
or less dense covering of rusty wool, such as is characteristic of typical *L.*
palustre. It was Japanese material of this nature that Nakai named *L. palustre*
var. *diversipilosum*. Finally, specimens from Sakhalin and the Amur region with
the rusty wool almost completely hiding the white hairs, or the latter absent,
have been described as *L. macrophyllum* Tolmatchev.

Some of the material discussed above has been erroneously included in *L.*
palustre var. *dilatatum*. The Alaskan plants named *L. pacificum* by Small have also
been referred to this variety but seem better placed under *L. groenlandicum*.

LEIOPHYLLUM   ERICACEAE

A genus of a single species in the eastern United States. It resembles
Ledum and, as in that genus, the petals are quite free, but is easily distinguishable from any species of that genus by the small, quite glabrous,
short-stalked to almost sessile leaves. The capsules open from the top
downward (the reverse in *Ledum*) and the pollen escapes from a slit
running the whole length of each anther (in *Ledum* it is released through a
small aperture).

L. BUXIFOLIUM (Berg.) Ell.   SAND MYRTLE

Ledum buxifolium Berg.; *L. thymifolium* Lam.; *Leiophyllum thymifolium* (Lam.)
Eaton; *L. serpyllifolium* DC.

A small evergreen shrub variable habit in the wild, being erect and up to 3 ft
high, or prostrate or decumbent, according to situation and altitude; usually
seen in cultivation as a dense bush up to $1\frac{1}{2}$ ft high. Leaves alternate or opposite,
oblong, oval, ovate to almost orbicular, $\frac{3}{16}$ to $\frac{1}{2}$ in. long, $\frac{1}{16}$ to $\frac{3}{16}$ in. wide
(occasionally wider), glabrous, glossy, dark green, very shortly stalked. Flowers

LEIOPHYLLUM BUXIFOLIUM

rosy in the bud, opening in May and June, in crowded terminal clusters $\frac{3}{4}$ to 1 in.
across, each flower $\frac{1}{4}$ in. in diameter. Petals five, white tipped with pink, oval,
spreading almost to the full extent; sepals narrow lance-shaped, about half as long
as the petals. Stamens ten, spreading, on slender filaments; anthers reddish
brown, opening down the side. Flower-stalks slender, glabrous or clad with
stalked glands intermixed with short down. Seed-vessel a two- to five-celled
capsule, many-seeded.

A native of eastern North America from New Jersey southward, westward
into the mountains of the Carolinas, Tennessee, and E. Kentucky. The above is
an overall description of the species, which is usually subdivided into three not
very well marked varieties:

var. BUXIFOLIUM.—This, the typical variety, is mainly confined to the pine-
barrens of the coastal plain of New Jersey, but has been recorded from farther
south. It has mostly alternate leaves about $\frac{1}{4}$ in. long, occasionally longer, and
the flower-stalks are glabrous or finely downy, not glandular.

var. HUGERI (Small) Schneid. *Dendrium hugeri* Small—This variety occurs in New Jersey with the typical variety. Its main distribution, however, lies farther south, in the coastal plain mainly but extending west into the mountains. The lowland plants differ from the typical variety only in having the flower-stalks glandular, but the type of this variety (i.e., the type of *Dendrium hugeri* Small) came from the high mountains of the Carolinas and seems to have been near to the var. *prostratum*, except in having alternate, not opposite leaves. In habit this variety may be erect or decumbent.

var. PROSTRATUM (Loud.) A. Gray *Ammyrsine prostrata* Loud.—This variety appears to be confined to the mountains of the south-eastern states and despite its name it is variable in habit, being erect or prostrate according to situation. It resembles the var. *hugeri* and differs from the typical variety, in having glandular flower-stalks, but its leaves are mostly opposite, not alternate as in var. *hugeri* and var. *buxifolium*. Also the leaves are generally larger, $\frac{5}{16}$ to $\frac{1}{2}$ in. long, $\frac{1}{8}$ to almost $\frac{1}{4}$ in. wide. The plant figured in *Bot. Mag.*, t. 6752 (1884), appears to belong to this variety, judging from the specimen preserved in the Kew Herbarium, and not to the var. *hugeri*, as Rehder states in the *Manual*.

Other characters have been used to distinguish the varieties, but they do not hold good constantly.

L. buxifolium was introduced by Peter Collinson in 1736, though in which variety is not known. The plants now cultivated probably all belong to the var. *hugeri* or *prostratum*, but it is doubtful whether there is any point in recognising these varietal names in gardens. As normally seen, *L. buxifolium* is a charming little shrub of neat aspect, and is at its prettiest just before the flowers expand, when the buds are very rosy. It blossoms very freely, the flowers almost hiding the foliage. The best method of propagating it is by cuttings made of shoots 1 to $1\frac{1}{2}$ in. long in July or August, dibbled in sandy peat, and placed in gentle bottom heat; they should be covered with a bell-glass until rooted.

LEITNERIA   LEITNERIACEAE

The species described below is of botanical interest as the sole member of the family Leitneriaceae, the taxonomic position of which is controversial. In most classifications it is given the rank of an Order—the Leitneriales—which is placed near to the Salicales (*Populus* and *Salix*) and the Myricales (*Myrica*). The staminate catkins consist of numerous bracts, each of which subtends a cluster of three to twelve stamens; corolla and calyx absent. In the pistillate catkins most of the bracts subtend a female 'flower' (perhaps a reduced inflorescence) consisting of a pistil surrounded by secondary bracts and bract-like sepals and surmounted by a single style. Fruit a leathery drupe.

L. FLORIDANA Chapm.   CORKWOOD

A deciduous shrub or small tree usually 5 to 10, sometimes 20 ft high, with a stem 3 to 5 in. in diameter; young shoots downy. Leaves alternate, entire, narrowly oval, tapered at both ends, 3 to 7 in. long, 1½ to 3 in. wide, covered with short hairs at first above, grey-felted beneath; stalk downy, 1 to 1½ in. long. Flowers unisexual, the sexes on separate trees. Males in erect, axillary catkins, 1½ in. long, each flower consisting of three to twelve stamens borne on a hairy bract, calyx and corolla absent. Female catkins smaller and more slender than the males; all of a greyish hue and of little beauty. Fruit an oval, flat, dry drupe, ¾ in. long, ¼ in. wide.

Native of Missouri, Florida, etc., inhabiting swamps; discovered about 1835; introduced to Kew in 1910. I saw this interesting tree in 1910 thriving quite well in the Arnold Arboretum, Mass., in Highlands Park, Rochester, N.Y., and in the New York Botanic Garden. It seemed to grow as well in ordinarily moist as in damp spots. All these places have considerably greater extremes than we have of heat and cold, and its capability of permanently supporting our duller climate has yet to be ascertained. Plants have so far succeeded fairly well. According to Prof. Trelease it often grows in rich soil, mostly covered with 6 in. or more of water. But many American trees found in such places succeed better here under drier conditions. Still, a site moderately moist should be given it. Its wood is remarkably light, having a specific gravity less than that of cork; but it is still much heavier than balsa wood, from which the Kontiki raft was made.

LEPTODERMIS   RUBIACEAE

A genus of about thirty species of deciduous shrubs native of the Himalaya, Japan, and China. They belong to the madder family, which is very meagrely represented in the open with us (save by the native bedstraws and woodruffs, etc.). They have opposite, entire leaves with persistent stipules. The flowers are borne in clusters on the growing shoots, each enclosed at the base in an involucre made up of two united bracteoles. The corolla is tubular or slenderly funnel-shaped, with usually five lobes. Stamens borne in the throat of the corolla, equal in the number to the lobes. The ovary is inferior, bearing a single style, dividing at the top into five linear arms. Fruit a capsule, splitting into five valves, but the inner wall of the valves remaining closed and enveloping each seed in a loose or appressed fibrous coat. The flowers in *Leptodermis* are usually dimorphic, the functionally female flowers having the style exserted and the stamens included in the corolla-tube, while in the functionally male flowers the style is included and the anthers exserted.

The cultivated species are sun-lovers, being often found wild in dry stony places. Propagation is by cuttings.

L. KUMAONENSIS Parker [PLATE 77

A shrub 3 to 6 ft high in the wild, with slender, glabrous, dull purplish young branchlets, the older wood with a brown or grey peeling bark. Leaves opposite, with six or seven pairs of veins, narrow- to broad-elliptic, $1\frac{3}{8}$ to $2\frac{1}{2}$ in. long, $\frac{7}{16}$ to $1\frac{1}{4}$ in. wide, tapered at both ends, dark green and downy above, paler and downy on the midrib and main veins beneath; stalk up to $\frac{3}{16}$ in. long, downy. Flowers sessile, three or five in a cluster, borne in the axils of the uppermost leaves or terminally on very short shoots from the axils of the next one or two pairs of leaves. Corolla white or pale pink, becoming purplish with age, narrowly funnel-shaped, about $\frac{1}{2}$ in. long, widening gradually upward to the five spreading rounded, acuminate lobes, finely downy inside and out. Seeds not seen on a cultivated plant but described as ovoid with a loose fibrous covering.

Native of the central Himalaya (Garwhal, Kumaon, and Nepal) at 8,000 to 10,000 ft. It is reported to grow as undergrowth in silver fir forest or dry oak forest, but also in open positions. A. D. Schilling found it growing in full sun on the summit of Phulchoke mountain south of Katmandu, at 9,000 ft, where it is locally frequent and forms an untidy gnarled shrub.

L. *kumaonensis* was discovered in Kumaon by Duthie in 1886, but his specimens, and others collected later, were identified at first as L. *lanceolata* Wall., and later as L. *parkeri* Dunn. It was recognised as a distinct species by R. N. Parker, a botanist of the Indian Forestry Service, who described in it 1922, and introduced it to cultivation from Kumaon in the following year. It was reintroduced by Stainton, Sykes, and Williams in 1954 under their numbers 9101 and 9081.

The species is not completely hardy at Kew and is no longer in the collection. It needs full sun, and a sheltered position.

L. *kumaonensis* is most closely related to L. LANCEOLATA Wall., which differs in its leaves with eight to ten pairs of veins, flowers in loose terminal panicles, and glabrous corolla; it is widely distributed in the Himalaya. Another ally is L. PARKERI Dunn, which has leaves with fewer pairs of veins (three to six), white or pinkish flowers that do not turn purplish with age, and also differs in its ovoid seeds with a closely adherent fibrous covering. This species is reported to be common on the Dhaula Dhar river and in the Upper Ravi valley, in northern Himachal Pradesh (Chamba). It was discovered in this region by R. N. Parker, whose name is also commemorated in *Jasminum parkeri*, found by him at the same time and described by Dunn in the same issue of the *Kew Bulletin*.

L. OBLONGA Bunge

Hamiltonia oblonga (Bge.) Franch.

A deciduous twiggy shrub 3 or 4 ft high; young shoots purplish, downy. Leaves opposite, ovate to oblong, entire, pointed, tapered at the base, $\frac{1}{2}$ to 1 in. long, $\frac{1}{8}$ to $\frac{1}{3}$ in. wide, roughish above, slightly downy beneath; stalk $\frac{1}{10}$ in. or less long. Flowers produced from July to September in stalkless axillary clusters, a few together. Corolla violet-purple, $\frac{1}{2}$ to $\frac{3}{4}$ in. long, tubular, with five oblong lobes, downy outside and in the throat.

Native of N. China, where it has been collected by Purdom and others. The plants in cultivation now in England were probably all raised from seed sent home by Farrer (No. 259). He calls it 'a sturdy little bush with panicles of Persian lilac-like flowers in July.' According to *The Plant Introductions of Reginald Farrer* it flowered at Highdown, Sussex, but died in the winter of 1928/9.

L. PILOSA Diels

Hamiltonia pilosa Franch. in MS

A deciduous shrub 6 to 10 ft high; young shoots downy. Leaves opposite, grey-green, ovate, pointed, wedge-shaped at the base, entire, ½ to 1¼ in. long, ⅓ to ⅜ in. wide, hairy on both sides; stalk ¼ in. or less long. Flowers fragrant, borne in axillary clusters towards the end of the current season's shoots and forming there a panicle several inches long. Corolla lavender-coloured, downy outside, ½ in. long, slenderly funnel-shaped at the base, spreading at the mouth into five ovate lobes and measuring there ¼ in. wide.

Native of Yunnan, China; discovered by the Abbé Delavay in 1887; introduced by Forrest in 1904 from the Lichiang Valley. In the milder parts of the country it can be grown in the open, but in colder places like Edinburgh it needs the protection of a wall, one preferably with a southern exposure. It starts to flower in July and keeps on until the early frosts. The daphne-like fragrance of the pleasingly coloured blossom and the long period over which the flowering continues appear to make this shrub well worth its place in gardens.

L. PURDOMII Hutch.

A deciduous shrub up to 5 ft high, with long very slender, wiry young shoots, covered with a close down at first. Leaves opposite, borne in clusters at the joints, linear, ¼ to ½ in. long, 1/10 to ⅛ in. wide, glabrous, margins recurved. Flowers produced towards the end of the current season's growth in August and September in a slender panicle several inches long. Corolla slenderly tubular, ½ in. long, five-lobed, pink.

Native of N. China; discovered by Purdom; introduced by Farrer in 1914 (No. 260). It was, I believe, first distributed as *L. virgata*, a Himalayan shrub of similar habit, but Dr Hutchinson made it a new species in 1916, distinguishing it by its long slender branchlets which become quite glabrous (not covered in short coarse hairs as in *L. virgata*) and by its shorter and broader stipules. Farrer described it as a 'shrub of inimitable grace with its delicate stems bowed down beneath long and lilac-like panicles that open in August'. It flowered at Highdown near Worthing, in 1921. The thin, wiry shoots and small, narrow, glabrous leaves amply distinguish it from the preceding species.

LEPTOSPERMUM   MYRTACEAE

A genus of some thirty species of evergreen, small trees or shrubs mostly natives of Australia but found also in New Zealand, New Caledonia, and the Malay Archipelago. The leaves are small, alternate, entire. Flowers solitary or in pairs or threes; petals five, spreading; stamens numerous; seed-vessel woody. Provided they are grown in a climate sufficiently mild, they are of easy cultivation, but none is genuinely hardy in the average climate of Britain. *Leptospermum* is from the Greek and refers to the small seeds.

L. FLAVESCENS Sm.

A tall evergreen shrub of which Bentham in his *Flora Australiensis* makes five varieties; of these the one I know as a shrub of the open air in this country is the var. OBOVATUM. There is a fine bush of this in the garden at Sheffield Park, Sussex, which grows outside and was 10 ft high when I saw it in 1928. The leaves are ¼ to ⅜ in. long, ⅛ to ¼ in. wide, almost uniformly obovate, except that some are rather wider in proportion to their length than others and they are very frequently notched at the apex, the base wedge-shaped. Flowers scarcely stalked, white, ⅜ in. wide, opening in July, solitary on short twigs or in the leaf-axils; calyx glabrous. It was figured by Sweet in his *Flora Australasica*, t. 36, published in 1828, as '*L. obovatum*'. He mentions that the plant figured was raised in the nursery of Messrs Whitley, Brames & Milne at Fulham, from seed sent by a Mr C. Frazer from New South Wales. Sweet observes that the plant will 'without doubt stand our winters very well in the open air with a slight covering in severe frost'. Its distinguishing characters are its five-celled ovary, its glabrous calyx-tube, and its notch-ended leaves. Besides New South Wales, this shrub is also wild in Victoria, Queensland, and Tasmania.

L. flavescens is allied to *L. lanigerum* but in that species the leaves and stems are hairy, and the receptacles and sepals densely woolly-tomentose or villose. It is represented at Wakehurst Place, Sussex, by a plant in the Heath Garden about 15 ft high (1971). This has smallish leaves and is nearest to var. *microphyllum* Benth.

L. HUMIFUSUM Schauer   [PLATE 74

L. rupestre Hook. f.; *L. scoparium* var. *prostratum* of some gardens, not of Hook. f.

A low shrub with prostrate or rock-hugging main stems and erect or spreading branchlets, usually 6 to 9 in. high. Leaves glabrous, plane or slightly concave on the lower side, ¼ to ⅜ in. long, elliptical to obovate, rounded at the apex, dark glossy green. Flowers about ½ in. across, white, borne singly in the leaf-axils. Capsules about ⅕ in. wide.

Native of Tasmania at high altitudes; introduced by H. F. Comber in 1930. It is very hardy in a position sheltered from cold winds: though the leaves may be scorched in hard winters, the wood is rarely damaged. It will quickly drape a dry-wall or boulder. Usually seen in gardens under the name "*L. scoparium prostratum*", it is quite distinct from any form of *L. scoparium* in its leaves, which lack the prickly tip characteristic of that species. There are some remarkable plants in the Heath Garden at Wakehurst Place which appear to be draped over rocks but are in fact free-standing, on short trunks.

L. LANIGERUM (Ait.) Sm.

Philadelphus laniger Ait.; *L. pubescens* Lam.; *L. cunninghamii* Schauer

An evergreen shrub or small tree of erect habit, the slender twigs clothed with outstanding pale hairs. Leaves alternate, set about ten or twelve to the inch, obovate-oblong or oval, abruptly pointed, variable in size but usually ⅓ to ½ in. (occasionally ¾ in.) long, about ⅛ in. wide or more less silky, especially beneath, but sometimes glabrous and glossy green above. Flowers white, borne along or at the ends of leafy side growths; they are about ½ in. wide, the centre filled with a cluster of twenty to thirty stamens. Receptacle (calyx-tube) and sepals densely white-villous, the hairs appressed or spreading; sepals long-triangular and pointed or rounded-acuminate. Seed-vessel woody, nearly globose, ¼ to ⅓ in. wide.

Native of Australia and Tasmania; introduced in 1774. This species seems to be hardier than the commoner *L. scoparium*. It was grown on a south wall at Kew and the winter of 1928–29, which very much injured *L. scoparium*, left it unaffected; it succumbed, however, during the hard winter of 1946–47. As long ago as 1879, a writer in the *Gardeners' Chronicle* remarked on its hardiness against a wall in Lancashire. It is quite an attractive, very leafy evergreen, flowering from June onwards. It is variable in the size and silkiness of its leaves, also in the size of its flowers, which in Loddiges' *Cabinet*, t. 1192, are depicted as 1 in. wide.

There are at least two forms of this variable species in general cultivation. The first is represented by plants at Wakehurst Place, Sussex, which derive from one given to Lord Wakehurst by Canon Boscawen of Ludgvan Rectory, Cornwall, about 1930 (*Journ. R.H.S.*, Vol. 88, p. 163). It was received as *L. cunninghamii* and agrees quite well with it, but this species is now included without differentiation in *L. lanigerum*. In this form (which has been widely distributed under the name *L. cunninghamii*) the young growths are pinkish brown, the leaves grey, small (up to ½ in. long at the most and usually shorter), from narrowly to broadly obovate; the calyx-tube has rather short silky hairs. The flowering time of this form is usually late July or early August. It is fairly hardy (though it may lose most of its leaves in winter) and fruits abundantly, even excessively.

The second form has longer, relatively narrower leaves, up to ¾ in. long, glossy and tinged with purple when young. The hairs on the calyx-tube are much longer than in the Ludgvan (Wakehurst) form, and the sepals are longer, concealing the petals even in the late bud-stage. It is also earlier flowering by two or three weeks. This is in cultivation as typical *L. lanigerum*. It is difficult for the non-botanist to believe that these two leptospermums belong to the same species.

Lord Talbot de Malahide has in his garden three further examples of *L.*

lanigerum from Tasmania, collected in the wild. One, representing the form commonly met with there, resembles the Wakehurst clone but the leaves are narrower, oblong or narrow-obovate. The second, collected near Hobart by Mr Jackson, is of pendulous habit but similar in foliage to the preceding. The third is very distinct in having the leaves dark green and almost glabrous above; this is of fastigiate habit.

L. LIVERSIDGEI R. T. Baker & H. S. Smith

An evergreen shrub 6 to 12 ft high, of graceful habit and with drooping branches, devoid of down in all its parts; young twigs very slender with over twenty leaves to the inch. Leaves ⅛ to ¼ in. long, linear-oblong to obovate, specked very freely with oil-glands. Flowers solitary, very shortly stalked, coming from the leaf-axils, ¼ to ⅓ in. in diameter, white. Petals orbicular, clawed. Seed-vessel circular, much flattened. Blossoms in June.

Native of New South Wales; first described in 1905. Port Macquarie appears to be one of its chief habitats. It is very distinct species on account of the smallness of its leaves and flowers, also in the slender, virgate character of the branches. It was finely grown at Ludgvan Rectory, near Penzance, and lived and flowered on the west side of a sheltered wall at Kew for a good many years, but the latter plant was killed by the severe weather during the winter of 1946-7. In the winter of 1928-9 it was cut to the ground but sprang up again freely afterwards. The leaves when crushed have a lemon-like odour and from them can be obtained a fragrant oil. The species is known in Australia as the 'lemon-scented tea-tree'. In our cultivated plants the odour is rather faint, possibly owing to lack of sunshine.

L. NITIDUM Hook. f.

An evergreen shrub 3 to 20 ft high, bark peeling; young shoots hairy, erect, densely leafy. Leaves oval-lanceolate to oblong, sharply pointed, tapered to the base, ⅓ to ¾ in. long, ⅛ to ¼ in. wide, shining green and glabrous above, more or less hairy beneath and on the margins; both surfaces are covered with minute oil-glands; stalks very short. Flowers white, reddish inside, ½ to ¾ in. wide, short-stalked and closely packed in the terminal leaf-axils of short shoots. Sepals and calyx-tube silky hairy. Fruits scaly.

Native of Tasmania, where it was discovered in flower as far back as February 1845. H. F. Comber collected it on his Tasmanian journey and described his No. 2128 as 'a very beautiful dwarf late-flowering shrub 1 to 2 ft high'. His 2139 he recorded as 10 to 20 ft high and his 2153 as 8 to 12 ft. It was exhibited in flower from Nymans at Vincent Square, 16 June 1934.

L. RODWAYANUM Summerhayes & Comber

An evergreen shrub 10 ft high, of spreading habit, young shoots covered with fine grey down. Leaves grey-green, obovate to narrowly oval, ⅓ to 1 in. long,

$\frac{1}{8}$ to $\frac{3}{8}$ in. wide, tapered to a very short stalk, pointed or rounded at the apex, at first with minute white hairs beneath and pitted with tiny dark glands. Flowers solitary, terminal on short lateral twigs, pure white, scarcely stalked, $1\frac{1}{4}$ in. wide, the mainly orbicular petals contracted to a short stalk. Receptacle obconical, densely white-pubescent; sepals ovate, covered with fine white down, and with membranous margins. Fruits woody, persisting many years, broadly top-shaped $\frac{3}{8}$ to $\frac{1}{2}$ in. wide, scaly on the flatly rounded summit.

Native of Tasmania; introduced by Comber in 1930. Plants were raised from his seeds at Nymans, Handcross, Sussex, and flowering shoots were shown by Colonel Messel at Vincent Square on 5 August 1936.

There seems to be some confusion between this species and *L. grandiflorum* Lodd. The plant so named by Loddiges (*Bot. Cab.*, t. 723) almost certainly belongs to *L. flavescens*, under which Bentham placed it as a variety—*L. flavescens* var. *grandiflorum* (Lodd.) Benth. The confusion may arise from the fact that a specimen in the Kew Herbarium with receptacle and sepals glabrous has been named *L. rodwayanum* though it would seem to belong to *L. flavescens*. In *L. rodwayanum* the receptacle is densely appressed white pubescent and the sepals slightly pubescent.

L. SCOPARIUM J. R. & G. Forst.   MANUKA

A compact evergreen bush of rounded, very twiggy habit, occasionally attaining the dimensions of a small tree in the wild; young wood sparsely hairy. or almost glabrous. Leaves alternate, linear-oblong to linear lanceolate or ovate lanceolate, $\frac{1}{3}$ to $\frac{1}{2}$ in. long $\frac{1}{12}$ to $\frac{1}{6}$ in. wide; sharply pointed, fragrant when bruised, dotted with transparent oil-glands. Flowers white, $\frac{1}{2}$ in. in diameter, produced singly from the leaf axils in spring; petals round, set well apart from each other, the triangular calyx-lobes showing between them. Fruit woody, globose, the size of a pea, many-seeded.

Native of Australia and New Zealand. It thrives outside in the south-western counties where there are bushes 15 to 20 ft high. In the woods at Tresco Abbey in the Isles of Scilly there are beautiful groves of self-sown seedlings, some with pink flowers. At Kew it has to be grown against a wall, and even there is apt to be killed in severe weather. Easily increased by cuttings.

cv. 'BOSCAWENII'.—Flowers white, 1 in. across, with a bright rose centres buds rosy-pink. Award of Merit when shown by the Rev. A. T. Boscawen on 22 May 1912. He raised it from seed received from New Zealand in 1909.

cv. 'CHAPMANII'.—Flowers deep rosy-red; foliage bronze-coloured. The first of the coloured forms to be cultivated, 'Chapmanii' was found by Justice Chapman in 1890 near Dunedin, Otago. It is hardier than the more famous 'Nichollsii' and produced self-sown seedlings in the late N. G. Hadden's garden at West Porlock, Somerset.

var. EXIMIUM Burtt—Leaves broadly ovate to almost orbicular. Flowers about $\frac{3}{4}$ in. across, pure white. Habit robust. A native of S. and S.E. Tasmania, near the coast. Introduced by Comber from near Port Arthur under C.1508 and recommended for an Award of Merit when shown from Exbury in May 1938 (award confirmed 1940). *Bot. Mag.*, t. 9582.

var. INCANUM Ckn.—Flowers large, tinged with pink. Leaves lanceolate or linear-lanceolate, silky-hairy beneath when young. Common in North Auckland, New Zealand. 'Keatleyi' (q.v.) may belong here.

cv. 'KEATLEYI'.—Flowers soft pink, paler at the edge, about 1 in. across. Foliage grey-green. Found by Capt. Keatley in the North Island of New Zealand. It is tender and was given an award of Merit as a shrub for the cool greenhouse when shown by P. M. Synge on 25 April 1961.

cv. 'LEONARD WILSON'.— Flowers double, pure white. Found by L. H. Wilson growing on his own property at Port Levy in the Banks Peninsula.

LEPTOSPERMUM SCOPARIUM

Another double-flowered white was discovered at Torrent Bay in Nelson and distributed by Messrs Nairn (Cockayne, *Trans. N.Z. Inst.*, Vol. 50, p. 179).

cv. 'NANUM'.—A dense dwarf shrublet growing to about 12 in. high with dark bronzy-green leaves. Flowers pale pink, with crimson centres. It is not reliably hardy, but will come through average winters in a sheltered position. Raised by Messrs Duncan and Davies of New Zealand, and given an Award of Merit when shown by Messrs Ingwersen on 10 June 1952.

cv. 'NICHOLLSII'.—The original plant of this well-known crimson manuka grew wild on a sheep-run north of Christchurch. The man whom the name commemorates, a wool-buyer, did not discover it but procured a branch with ripe capsules which he gave to Messrs Nairn around 1904. From these, 107 seedlings were raised, of which seven had crimson flowers, and of these the best was named 'Nichollsii'. It was introduced to Britain in 1908, when a plant was received at Tresco. In 1912 it was shown by the Rev. A. T. Boscawen at the International Horticultural Exhibition at Chelsea, when it received a First Class Certificate and a cup for the finest plant exhibited.

The flowers of 'Nichollsii' are crimson with a deeper centre and about ⅝ in.

across. Leaves linear-lanceolate, rather small, deep bronzy-purple on open-ground plants.

cv. 'NICHOLLSII NANUM'.—Flowers deep crimson pink with a darker eye. Foliage deep bronzy-purple. Habit dwarf. Raised by J. Hope, head gardener to A. T. Bulley and later to Miss Bulley at Mickwell Brow, The Wirral, Cheshire (now the Botanic Garden of the University of Liverpool). It received an Award of Merit when shown by Mr Hope in 1953.

var. PROSTRATUM Hook. f.—Described by Hooker (*Fl. Nov. Zel.*, Vol. 1, p. 70) as a prostrate shrub with ascending branchlets and broad-ovate to orbicular leaves. Prostrate plants are quite common in the wild and some may retain their habit when brought into cultivation. They would not, however, necessarily have leaves as in Hooker's type specimen. Most of the plants grown in gardens as *L. scoparium prostratum* are really the Tasmanian *L. humifusum*.

cv. 'RED DAMASK'.—See below.

cv. 'ROSEUM'.—Flowers about 1 in. across, pale pink with a crimson centre. Raised by Canon Boscawen at the Ludgvan Rectory. Award of Merit 1928 and First Class Certificate 1937.

cv. 'RUBY GLOW'.—See below.

In 1939 Dr W. E. Lammerts of the University of California crossed 'Nichollsii' (seed-parent) with a manuka with double rose-coloured flowers. The seven plants raised all had single flowers. Seed from these was sown in the autumn of 1943 and about 1,000 seedlings were raised of which 830 were planted out in 1944. Many of these had double flowers (*Journ. Calif. Hort. Soc.*, Vol. 6, pp. 250–257). One of the first to be named and distributed (1946) was 'RUBY GLOW', with deep-red, fully double flowers about ½ in. across, red stems and bronzy foliage. But the best-known of these crosses, named and distributed a little later, is 'RED DAMASK', which received an Award of Merit when shown by the Slieve Donard Nursery Company on 28 June 1955. Flowers fully double, slightly over ½ in. across, deep cherry-red. It is of dense habit, grows to about 6 ft high and is exceptionally free-flowering.

LESPEDEZA   BUSH CLOVER   LEGUMINOSAE

Of the fifty or more species belonging to this genus, not more than half a dozen are cultivated in gardens. Many are really semi-herbaceous, dying back to ground-level every winter, but sending up in spring from a woody root-stock a crowd of shoots which flower during late summer and autumn. Leaves trifoliolate; flowers pea-shaped; pods roundish, flat, one-seeded, and thus very distinct from the long, narrow, jointed several-seeded pods of desmodiums with which some lespedezas have been confounded, and which they resemble in mode of growth. The species mentioned in the following notes succeed in ordinary loamy soil in an open position. Where seeds are not available, the most woody ones may be increased by cuttings; others by division. (See under *L. thunbergii*.)

L. BICOLOR Turcz.

A deciduous shrub becoming in some climates a bush 8 or 10 ft high, although at Kew its stems are only annual and grow from 3 to 7 ft high during the season, dying down to ground-level every winter. Leaves trifoliolate, slender-stalked; leaflets varying in size from ¾ to 2 in. in length by about two-thirds as much wide, broadly oval or obovate, the midrib enlongated into a small terminal bristle, the middle leaflet is larger and longer stalked than the others, all being dark green above, pale beneath, and clothed sparsely on both sides with appressed hairs or glabrous above. Racemes slender stalked, 2 to 5 in. long, produced in the leaf-axils from the uppermost 2 ft of the stem. Flowers rosy-purple, less than ½ in. long, confined to the terminal part of the raceme. Calyx ⅛ in. long, hairy, the teeth not so slender and sharp-pointed as in *L. thunbergii*. Pods ovate, downy, ⅛ in. long, one-seeded.

Native of Manchuria, N. China, and Japan; introduced to Europe by Maximowicz, the Russian botanist, in 1856. It is not so handsome and desirable a plant as *L. thunbergii*, with which it has been much confounded. In countries with a hotter summer than ours, the stems made each year do not die back more than half their length, and the plant thus increases gradually in height. In the Arnold Arboretum, Mass., it forms a bush comparable with a colutea. Flowers in August and September.

L. CYRTOBOTRYA Miq.

A small deciduous shrub, which in this country sends up from the base every summer a number of erect, woody stems 2 to 3 ft high, that do not survive the winter, but die back to ground-level; bark downy. Leaves trifoliolate, 3 to 5 in. long; leaflets 1 to 1¾ in. long, ½ to ¾ in. wide, oval or obovate, covered beneath with a fine down especially early in the season, apex rounded or slightly notched, the midrib ending in a short bristle; base tapered. Flowers crowded in umbel-like racemes 1½ in. long, which spring from the axils of the upper leaves of the shoot, rosy-purple, ½ to ⅝ in. long. Calyx-teeth spine-tipped. Pods ovate, ¼ in. long, one-seeded.

Native of Japan and Korea; introduced to Kew in 1899. It is a pretty plant scarcely known in cultivation, and blossoms in August.

L. JUNCEA Pers.

A semi-woody plant in this country, sending up annually from a woody root-stock a crowd of slender, grooved stems 2 to 3 ft high, clad with whitish hairs. Leaves trifoliolate, with a slender main-stalk ¼ to ½ in. long; leaflets oblanceolate, ⅓ to ¾ in. long, broadest near the apex, where they are $\frac{1}{12}$ to ⅛ in. wide and short-pointed, tapering thence to a short stalk, covered beneath with fine grey hairs. Flowers in very short-stalked, two- to six-flowered umbels, produced from the leaf-axils; each flower $\frac{1}{4}$ to $\frac{1}{3}$ in. long, white or partly blue; the calyx half as long, hairy, with slender, linear lobes.

Native of the Himalaya, China, Japan, and Siberia; introduced to Kew in 1895. It is not a showy plant, but distinct and striking for its long slender stems of rather broom-like appearance, very densely clothed with the erect, rather appressed leaves. It flowers in September.

L. SERICEA (Thunb.) Miq., not L. *sericea* (Wall.) Benth., *nom. nud. Hedysarum sericeum* Thunb.; *L. cuneata* (Dum.-Cours.) G. Don; *Anthyllis cuneata* Dum.-Cours.; *L. juncea* var. *cuneata* (Dum.-Cours.) Bean—Leaflets narrowly oblanceolate, $\frac{3}{8}$ to $\frac{7}{8}$ in. long, truncate or retuse at the apex. Flowers whitish. Of no decorative value, but used as a fodder plant in the warmer parts of the world.

L. THUNBERGII (DC.) Nakai

Desmodium thunbergii DC.; *L. sieboldii* Miq.; *Desmodium penduliflorum* Oudemans

A semi-woody plant, producing stout, pithy, rather herbaceous, grooved stems 4 to 8 ft high, from a woody root-stock; they die back to ground-level during the winter, and are replaced by a fresh crop the following year. Leaves trifoliolate; leaflets $1\frac{1}{2}$ to 2 in. long, one-third as much wide, becoming smaller towards the upper part of the stem, the centre one longer-stalked than the side ones, oval or oval-lanceolate, coated beneath, especially on the midrib, with appressed greyish hairs. Racemes numerous, up to 6 in. long, produced from the leaf-axils of the upper part and at the end of the shoot, the whole constituting a loose panicle 2 to $2\frac{1}{2}$ ft in length. Each flower is $\frac{1}{2}$ to $\frac{5}{8}$ in. long, pea-shaped, rosy-purple. Calyx $\frac{1}{4}$ in. long, covered with greyish hairs, and divided half-way down into five awl-shaped teeth. Pods ovate, flat, silky, $\frac{1}{3}$ in. long. *Bot. Mag.*, t. 6602.

Native of N. China and Japan; introduced to Europe about 1837, by Siebold. Although strictly speaking it is scarcely a shrub, it is shrub-like. It is a plant with a luxuriant annual growth of great elegance and beauty, although, flowering late in the season, it does not always reach its best before the frost comes. This is more especially the case after dull wet summers. It starts to flower in September. A single fully grown plant will form a mass 10 ft or more across, the outer stems arching outwards. It is not suitable for planting by itself in large groups in conspicuous places, as it starts into growth late in the season and is still bare of leaf when most other shrubs are in their full spring greenery. The old dead stems must be cut away in spring. Propagated by pulling or chopping the root-stock into the smaller pieces about April. Pieces small enough, with root attached, may be potted and placed in a house where there is bottom-heat.

L. JAPONICA Bailey *L. bicolor* var. *alba* Bean; *L. bicolor* var. *intermedia* f. *albiflora* Matsum.—Closely allied to *L. thunbergii* but with white flowers and leaves with appressed silky hairs on the upper surface. Not known in the wild and considered by Ohwi (*Flora of Japan*, 1965) to be a cultivar of *L. thunbergii*— cv. 'Albiflora'.

LEUCOPOGON   EPACRIDACEAE

A genus of over 100 species, mainly Australian, but a few in Malaysia and New Zealand. The genus is closely allied to *Cyathodes*, and the species described here was recently transferred to it by Dr Allan (*Fl. N.Z.*, Vol. 1, pp. 513 and 517), together with the other New Zealand species included in *Leucopogon* in earlier works. The greater part of the material in the Kew Herbarium under these two genera conforms to the following characters: In *Leucopogon* the flowers are generally small, in slender, often dense, sometimes interrupted spicate inflorescences, each flower subtended by a bract and having two bracteoles close to the calyx (but towards the base of the pedicel in two species). The corolla-lobes in *Leucopogon* are conspicuously white-bearded. In *Cyathodes* the flowers are generally solitary in the axil of foliage leaves; the pedicel is covered with a series of overlapping scale-like "bracts", increasing in size upward and the uppermost around the base of the calyx. The corolla-lobes in *Cyathodes* are glabrous or, if hairy, then not conspicuously so.

There are, however, variations which tend to blur these distinctions. It would be too much of a digression to discuss these in detail, since the species mainly concerned are not in cultivation. But it should be remarked that in *Leucopogon* some species have the inflorescences much reduced, sometimes to a single flower, but the flowers retain the bract and two bracteoles characteristic of the genus. If *Leucopogon* is to be retained as a genus distinct from *Cyathodes*, then *L. fraseri*, described here, would belong to it. But it should be added that the position of *Cyathodes colensoi*, described in Vol. I, is debatable. It was described by Hooker in *Leucopogon* and later transferred by him to *Cyathodes*, but his earlier judgement was perhaps more correct.

L. FRASERI A. Cunn.

Cyathodes fraseri (A. Cunn.) H. H. Allan

A dwarf evergreen shrub 3 to 6 in. high, of close compact growth, forming a dense mat and spreading by underground stems. Branchlets more or less erect, very slender, minutely downy when young, almost entirely hidden by the foliage. Leaves stalkless, alternate, overlapping each other, obovate-oblong, abruptly tapered at the apex to a slender, bristle-like tip, $\frac{1}{8}$ to $\frac{3}{16}$ in. long, $\frac{1}{16}$ to $\frac{1}{12}$ in. wide, dull green, the longitudinal veins distinct beneath, margins fringed with tiny hairs. Flowers sweetly scented, solitary in the leaf-axils. Corolla a slender tube $\frac{3}{8}$ in. long, pinkish white, divided at the mouth into five short triangular lobes which are downy on the underside; inside of tube hairy. The four brown anthers are fixed near the top of the corolla tube and have very short stalks. Style slender, downy. Fruit an oblong drupe, $\frac{1}{3}$ in. long, yellowish orange, sweet and edible.

Native of New Zealand up to 4,500 ft altitude, where it was found by C. Fraser in 1820; also of Tasmania and Australia. I do not know when this interesting little shrub was originally introduced, but I first saw it in Messrs Cunningham and Fraser's nursery at Comely Bank, Edinburgh, in 1911, and obtained it for Kew, where it has proved hardy. It does not flower freely enough to render it very noticeable, but it makes a neat tuft a few inches high very suitable for the rock garden, and its flowers, borne in May and June, have a hay-like fragrance.

LEUCOTHOË   ERICACEAE

A genus of about forty-five species of evergreen or deciduous shrubs, natives mainly of Northern, Central, and South America, but with a few species in E. Asia. Leaves alternate. Flowers in axillary or terminal racemes. Calyx of five nearly free lobes, which are imbricate (i.e., overlapping) in the bud. Corolla urn-shaped or cylindrical. Stamens ten, included within the corolla; anthers with or without awns and always without spurs at the base. Seed-vessel a round, flattened, loculicidal capsule.

Some species of *Gaultheria* closely resemble *Leucothoë* but can always be distinguished by their fruits. *Lyonia* differs in having the sepals valvate in the bud (i.e. not or just touching but not overlapping). *Pieris* also has valvate sepals.

The chief cultural need of the leucothoës is a moist, peaty soil or a sandy lime-free loam with leaf-mould added; they prefer semi-shaded positions. Propagation is by cuttings of half-ripened shoots.

L. AXILLARIS (Lam.) D. Don

Andromeda axillaris Lam.; *L. catesbaei* (Walt.) A. Gray; *Andromeda catesbaei* Walt.

An evergreen shrub 2 to 4 ft high, with spreading branches zigzagged towards the end, clothed with very short down when young. Leaves leathery, ovate to ovate-oblong, 2 to 4½ in. long, ¾ to 1½ in. wide, usually abruptly and shortly pointed, spine-toothed, mainly in the upper half, dark glossy green and glabrous above, pale and with scattered hairs beneath; stalk ¼ in. or less long. Flowers produced during April and May in axillary racemes 1 to 2½ in. long, crowded, and very shortly stalked. Corolla white, cylindrical or pitcher-shaped, narrowing slightly towards the mouth, where are five ovate teeth; sepals ovate; flower-stalks minutely downy.

Native of the south-eastern United States from Virginia southwards; introduced in 1765. It is not so common in cultivation as *L. fontanesiana*, which it much resembles, and with which it is much confused. Its leaves, however, are comparatively shorter and broader, and abruptly pointed; their stalks are also shorter, and the sepals are broader. Coming from the lowlands of Virginia, Florida, etc., it is much less hardy than *L. fontanesiana*, which inhabits the mountains. Personally, I have only seen one or two plants, and they were not in good health. A dwarf form of *L. fontanesiana* is sometimes offered for it.

var. AMBIGENS Fern.—Leaves lanceolate or narrowly lanceolate, less abruptly pointed.

L. DAVISIAE Torr.

An evergreen shrub 1 to 3 ft high in cultivation, of neat, very sturdy habit; branches erect, stiff, perfectly glabrous. Leaves ovate-oblong, rounded or slightly heart-shaped at the base, short-pointed or blunt at the apex, lustrous dark green, of firm texture, 1¼ to 2½ in. long, ¾ to 1 in. wide, very slightly and evenly toothed stalk ⅛ to ¼ in. long. Flowers produced in mid or late June in a cluster of erect racemes springing from the end of the shoot and its upper leaf-axils, each raceme 2 to 4 in. long, and furnished with short, scattered bristles. Corolla nodding, pitcher-shaped, white, ¼ in. long, five-toothed. Sepals short, ovate, edged with a few glandular teeth; flower-stalk ⅛ in. long. *Bot. Mag.*, t. 6247.

LEUCOTHOË DAVISIAE

Native of the Sierra Nevada, California at 3,000 to 8,000 ft, and of neighbouring parts of Oregon: discovered and introduced in 1853 by William Lobb, for Messrs Veitch, and at first distributed by them as "*Leucothoë lobbii*". Subsequently found by Miss N. J. Davis, after whom it was named. It is, perhaps, the most beautiful in the genus, because its erect, terminal cluster of racemes stands well above the foliage. It thrives very well in the neighbourhood of London.

L. FONTANESIANA (Steud.) Sleum.

L. catesbaei auct., not (Walt.) A. Gray; *L. editorum* Fern. & Schubert; *Andromeda fontanesiana* Steud.

An evergreen shrub 2 to 6 ft high, with slender, arching, zigzagged branches, which when young are reddish, and covered with a very short down. Leaves glabrous and leathery, narrowly lanceolate, 3 to 5 in. long, 1 to 1½ in. wide, with a long tapering point, rounded or shortly tapered at the base, spine-toothed, dark lustrous green above, paler and with scattered hairs beneath; stalk ⅓ to ⅔ in. long. Flowers produced during May, crowded on axillary racemes 1 to 2 in. long, occasionally in panicles 3 in. long. Corolla ¼ in. long, slenderly pitcher-shaped,

LEUCOTHOË FONTANESIANA

white; sepals narrowly ovate, pointed; flower-stalks very short. *Bot. Mag.*, t. 1955.

Native of mountainous regions in the south-eastern United States; introduced in 1793. When fully in blossom, a well-grown plant with its long arching branches, laden for 12 to 18 in. of their length with racemes, is decidedly handsome. But owing to the flowers being all produced on the lower side, the branch often requires elevating for its full beauty to be seen. During the flowering season it is worth while to elevate a few of the branches by means of forked sticks.

cv. 'RAINBOW'.—Leaves irregularly variegated with white; quite striking in early summer, when the young stems and petioles are crimson and the variegation pink. Raised in the USA and also known after its raiser as 'Girard's Rainbow'.

cv. 'Rollissonii'.—A variety with smaller, narrower leaves, 2 to 4 in. long, ½ to ¾ in. wide.

L. grayana Maxim.

L. chlorantha A. Gray, not DC.; *Eubotryoides grayana* (Maxim.) Hara

A deciduous or semi-evergreen shrub up to 3 or 4 ft high, with glabrous, red young shoots. Leaves of hardish texture, very shortly stalked, oval, ovate, oblong, or inclined to obovate, pointed, tapered or roundish at the base, bristly on the margin, 1½ to 3½ in. long, more or less bristly and conspicuously net-veined beneath. Racemes terminal, up to 4 in. long, erect, bearing the flowers at ⅛ to ½ in. apart. Corolla bell-shaped, ivory-white to pinkish, ¼ in. long, hairy inside; calyx-lobes ovate to ovate-lanceolate, membranous. Each flower springs from the axil of a linear or awl-shaped bract. Fruit flattened-globose, ⅕ in. wide.

Native of Japan; erroneously identified with *L. chlorantha* DC. by Asa Gray in 1859; given its present name by Maximowicz in 1873; introduced in 1890, but not very common. It is a gaultheria-like shrub, but dry-fruited. Nakai, the Japanese botanist, includes under it five varieties, *typica*, *glabra*, *glaucina*, *venosa*, and *intermedia*, based mainly on leaf characters, but judging by a long series of specimens in the Kew Herbarium, it will be difficult to differentiate them.

L. grayana is characterised by its terminal racemes, borne on leafy side-shoots of the current season, combined with its awnless anthers and flower-stalks with bracteoles, which are borne at some distance from the calyx. In *L. racemosa* and *L. recurva* the racemes are formed in late summer at the ends of side growths but do not open until the following year and the bracteoles on the flower-stalks are borne immediately under the calyx.

L. grayana flowers in June and July, and is quite hardy. The leaves turn purple or bronzy yellow in the autumn.

As remarked in the second paragraph, *L. grayana* is very variable, and Japanese botanists have recognised at least thirteen varieties and forms. If the species has to be subdivided, then the above description would correspond more or less to the var. *oblongifolia* (Miq.) Ohwi. Typical *L. grayana* has larger and broader leaves and is confined to Hokkaido and the northern part of the main island (Ohwi, *Fl. Jap.* (1965), p. 705).

L. keiskei Miq.

A dwarf evergreen shrub with slender, zigzagged, erect or semi-procumbent stems; young shoots glabrous, red. Leaves leathery, ovate-lanceolate, round at the base, drawn out into a long slender apex, inconspicuously toothed, 1½ to 3½ in. long, ½ to 1½ in. wide, glabrous except for a few appressed bristles beneath; stalk ⅙ to ¼ in. long. Flowers few, borne during July in short racemes at or near the end of the young shoots. Corolla nodding, pure white, cylindrical, ½ to ⅝ in. long, ¼ in. wide, with five small, erect, triangular teeth. Calyx-lobes broadly ovate, minutely ciliate. Stamens hairy. Fruits flattened-globose, ¼ in. wide.

Native of Japan; introduced in 1915 by Wilson. It is hardy, and is rather distinct on account of the size of its flowers, which are the largest in the cultivated species, its shining red young shoots, and leaves which are red when young, deep red in autumn. An attractive shrub.

L. POPULIFOLIA (Lam.) Dipp.

Andromeda populifolia Lam.; *A. acuminata* Ait.; *Leucothoë acuminata* (Ait.) G. Don

An evergreen shrub said to attain a height of 12 ft in the wild, but usually 2 to 4 ft high in cultivation; stems glabrous, hollow except for fine plates of pith. Leaves glabrous, ovate-lanceolate, 1¼ to 4 in. long, slenderly tapered at the apex to an acute point, finely and irregularly serrated or entire, fairly conspicuously net-veined on both sides. Racemes axillary, peduncled, few-flowered; pedicels slender, ¼ to ¾ in. long. Calyx-lobes triangular. Corolla cylindric, white, about ⅜ in. long; filaments of stamens with an S-shaped bend near the apex; anthers not awned.

A native of the S.E. United States; introduced 1765, but not common in gardens. It is the only representative in the USA of the section *Agastia*, whose other members are found in Central America and Brazil. It is an elegant foliage-shrub, hardy in a sheltered place south of London and westwards. Its wood was used by the Indians for making pipe-stems.

L. RACEMOSA (L.) A. Gray

Andromeda racemosa L.; *A. spicata* Wats.; *L. spicata* (Wats.) D. Don; *Eubotrys racemosa* (L.) Nutt.

A deciduous shrub of bushy, erect habit, generally 4 to 6 ft high in cultivation but occasionally twice as high; young shoots usually finely downy. Leaves narrowly oval or inclined to obovate, 1 to 2½ in. long, ½ to 1¼ in. wide; pointed at both ends, shallowly round-toothed, of firm texture, downy on the midrib beneath; stalk ⅛ in. or less long. Flowers produced during June in one-sided racemes 1 to 4 in. long, sometimes branched, usually terminating short twigs of the previous year. Corolla white, cylindrical, ⅓ in. long; sepals triangular-ovate, finely hairy on the margin; flower-stalk very short, glabrous, with two bracteoles close beneath the calyx. Each anther is terminated by four awns, two to each cell.

Native of the eastern United States from Massachusetts southwards; introduced in 1736. This is a perfectly hardy, free-growing shrub which flowers abundantly, and is one of the prettiest of June-flowering shrubs. It requires an occasional thinning out of the older wood. Propagated by cuttings of nearly ripened young shoots. Allied to *L. recurva* (q.v.).

L. RECURVA (Buckl.) A. Gray

Andromeda recurva Buckl.; *Eubotrys recurva* (Buckl.) Britt.

A deciduous shrub usually 3 to 8 ft high, the young shoots slightly downy or glabrous. Leaves narrowly oval or lanceolate, tapering at both ends, thin but

T S—T

firm, toothed, 1½ to 4 in. long, ½ to 1¼ in. wide, downy on the veins and midrib beneath; stalk very short. Flowers produced during May and June in decurved racemes, 2 to 3 in. long, terminating short twigs of the previous year. Corolla white, cylindrical, ¼ in. long; sepals ovate, pointed; flower-stalk very short and stout; anthers terminated by two awns, one to each cell.

Native of the southern Allegheny Mountains from Virginia to Alabama; introduced to England by Prof. Sargent about 1890, but very rare. It is probably not so hardy, nor so good a garden plant, as its near ally, *L. racemosa*, from which it differs chiefly in its more diffuse habit, the recurved racemes, and very distinctly grooved seed-vessel; each pollen bag, too, is surmounted by only one bristle instead of two.

LEYCESTERIA   CAPRIFOLIACEAE

A genus of six deciduous shrubs native of the Himalaya and China and named after William Leycester, Chief Justice in Bengal in the early nineteenth century, who, 'during a long series of years pursued every branch of horticulture with munificence, zeal and success'.

For a revision of the genus see Airy Shaw in *Kew Bulletin* (1932), pp. 161–76.

L. CROCOTHYRSOS Airy Shaw

A shrub apparently 6 to 8 ft high, producing long, slender, hollow young shoots thinly furnished with glandular hairs. Leaves 2 to 6 in. long, 1 to 2¾ in. wide, ovate, slenderly pointed, rounded at the base, sparsely toothed, rich dull green above, rather glaucous, minutely downy and conspicuously net-veined beneath, margins slightly hairy; stalk about ¼ in. long. Each joint of the stem is furnished with a pair of conspicuously large, kidney-shaped, interpetiolar stipules ¼ to ¾ in. wide, each stipule being adnate for a short distance to the petiole on either side. Inflorescence an arching terminal raceme 5 to 7 in. long on which the flowers are closely arranged in whorls of six, the whorls set about 1 in. apart. Corolla rich yellow, ¾ in. long and as much wide, five-lobed, the base tubular, hairy outside. Calyx green, five-lobed, ⅜ in. wide; ovary ovoid, ¼ in. long, covered with sticky glandular hairs. Fruit ⅝ in. long, globose-ovoid, very like a small gooseberry, with the calyx adhering at the top. *Bot. Mag.*, t. 9422.

Native of the Delei Valley, Assam, at 6,000 ft altitude; discovered and introduced by Kingdon Ward in 1928. He describes it as a 'small lax shrub growing on steep sheltered gneiss face, in dense thickets'. Seeds were originally distributed under the name 'Golden Abelia', No. 8180. In Col. Stern's chalk-pit garden at Highdown, near Worthing, a very sunny spot, it flowered abundantly in early June, 1934, but did not prove hardy there. At Kew it was promptly killed the first winter it was put in the open air. Except in the mildest parts it must be treated as a shrub for the cool greenhouse and as such was given an Award of Merit when shown by Maurice Mason on 30 May 1960.

In *Plant Hunting on the Edge of the World*, Kingdon Ward gave the following account of the discovery of *L. crocothyrsos*.

On May 8th we started again up the valley, our object being to camp near the pass, not more than three days' march, as we reckoned it. The river above Watersmeet was a roaring torrent; we were still high above it, but could often see it thundering through the gorge below. As for the path, it was a mere ledge high up on the rock face, with terrifying cliffs where we had to climb down shaky ladders forty or fifty feet high, holding on to roots and creepers. On the cliff, which was overgrown with shrubs, I found the golden Leycesteria, a solitary plant with long hanging racemes of golden-yellow flowers, and large auricled stipules at the base of the leaves.

LEYCESTERIA CROCOTHYRSOS

L. FORMOSA Wall.   [PLATE 76

A half-woody, deciduous plant, with erect, hollow stems, 4 or 5 ft sometimes much more high, covered with glaucous bloom, glabrous, very leafy. Leaves opposite, ovate, heart-shaped at the base, with long tapered points, varying in size according to the vigour of the shoot from 2 to 7 in. long, about half as wide, entire or with small teeth, deep green above, greyish and slightly downy when young beneath; stalk ¼ to 1 in. long. Flower-spikes produced from June to September, either at the end of the shoot or in the uppermost leaf-axils, 1 to 4 in. long. Flowers stalkless, arranged in tiers, each tier supported by handsome claret-coloured bracts of the same shape as the leaves and from ½ to 1½ in. long, which persist until the fruit is ripe. Corolla ¾ in. long and wide, funnel-shaped, five-lobed, purplish, slightly hairy; calyx one-third the length of the corolla, with five erect, awl-shaped, hairy lobes. Berry like a small gooseberry, reddish purple, glandular-downy, about ½ in. long, many-seeded, surmounted by the persistent sepals; ripe in October. *Bot. Mag.*, t. 3699.

Native of the Himalaya in shady forests, and of W. China and E. Tibet; introduced in 1824. This handsome shrub likes a rich soil, and, in spite of its natural habitats, a sunny spot. The bracts and fruits colour better under a full exposure. Birds, especially pheasants, are very fond of the berries, for which reason it is sometimes planted as covert. It should be propagated by seed, which ripens in such abundance and germinates so freely that an enormous stock can soon be raised.

LIBOCEDRUS CUPRESSACEAE

A genus of evergreen coniferous trees which, in the wide sense, consists of thirteen species. Of those treated here three come from the northern hemisphere (*L. decurrens* from western N. America, *L. macrolepis* and *L. formosana* from E. Asia); two are natives of temperate S. America (*L. chilensis* and *L. uvifera*) and two of New Zealand (*L. plumosa* and *L. bidwillii*). The other six species, not cultivated in this country, and certainly not hardy with us, are from New Guinea and New Caledonia.

The leading characters of this group are: Ultimate branches usually flattened (more rarely tetragonous) and arranged in one plane. Leaves scale-like. Cones small, ripening and releasing their seeds in the first season; scales four or six, valvate or imbricate, woody, the lower pair short, sterile; the next pair fertile and much larger, each scale bearing one or two seeds; the upper (innermost) pair, when present, sterile and connate. Seeds unequally two-winged.

It must be admitted that the species treated here do not form a homogeneous group. In 1931 the Swedish botanist Florin remarked that the three species of the northern hemisphere are more closely allied to *Thuja* than to *L. plumosa* (the type-species of *Libocedrus*) and its immediate allies and this was also the view of Li (*Journ. Arn. Arb.*, Vol. 34, 17–36). These three northern species, if treated as a separate genus, would take the name *Calocedrus*.

With the removal of these three species, all characterised by cones with six imbricate scales, the genus *Libocedrus* becomes more uniform, all the remaining species having cones with four valvate scales. But the two S. American species both differ in other respects from *L. plumosa* and its immediate allies. *L. uvifera* (*tetragona*) has uniform, spreading leaves and outwardly bears more resemblance to *Fitzroya* than to any libocedrus. This species was transferred by Florin in 1931 to the new monotypic genus *Pilgerodendron*. The other S. American species—*L. chilensis*—is less distinct, and was allowed to remain in *Libocedrus* until 1954, when it was transferred by Florin and Boutelje to another new monotypic genus—*Austrocedrus*. It differs from *Libocedrus sens. strict.* chiefly in its cones, the scales of which have a short mucro near the tip instead of the long, curved appendage on the back seen in *L. plumosa* and its allies; there are also differences in foliage and in wood anatomy. Finally, it should be added that the three species from New Guinea were transferred by Li in 1953 to the new genus *Papuacedrus*. Thus the genus *Libocedrus*, if the segregate genera are all to be recognised, would become a genus of five species: *L. plumosa* (the type-species) and *L. bidwillii*, both of New Zealand, and three species endemic to New Caledonia.

In this work, the older conception of *Libocedrus* is maintained on practical rather than taxonomic grounds. Only one species of this group —*Libocedrus (Calocedrus) decurrens*—is at all common in cultivation and only one other species—*Libocedrus (Austrocedrus) chilensis* is both hardy and worthy of cultivation. It seems best, therefore, to describe and discuss the group in one place. In the headings to the descriptions given below the correct name of the species in the segregate genus is given in capitals, before the other synonyms.

L. CHILENSIS (D. Don) Endl.

AUSTROCEDRUS CHILENSIS (D. Don) Florin & Boutelje; *Thuja chilensis* D. Don; *Thuja andina* Poepp. & Endl.

A tree 60 to 80 ft high in nature, at present under 50 ft high in cultivation; bark peeling. Young trees have a pyramidal habit, the branches being much divided and leafy at the ends. Leaves in four ranks, arranged in two opposite, very unequal pairs; the top and bottom ones are very small, the lateral ones $\frac{1}{8}$ to $\frac{3}{16}$ in. long. bluntish, dark green on the upper side of the branchlet, with white stomatic bands underneath. Cones with four valvate scales, each with a small boss near the apex. Seeds with two wings, one wing much longer than the other.

Native of Chile and Argentina, with its main development in the transitional zone between the temperate rain forests and the Patagonian steppe; introduced from Chile by T. Bridges, who sent it to Messrs Low, then of Clapton, in 1847. In gardens it is a very pretty small tree, with frondose, laterally spreading sprays, very distinct from the vertical sprays of *L. decurrens*, from which it differs also in the unequal size and length of the leaves and their whiteness underneath. Comber found a variegated form at St Martin de los Andes in the Argentine, in October 1926.

L. chilensis appears to be quite hardy and grows well though rather slowly in the National Pinetum, Bedgebury, Kent. The largest specimens recorded recently in the British Isles are 36 to 46 ft in height and 2 to $4\frac{1}{2}$ ft in girth (1964–8). There are specimens in this range of size at: Wakehurst Place, Sussex; Nymans, Sussex; The Royal Horticultural Society Garden, Wisley, Surrey; and Mount Usher, Co. Wicklow, Eire. The tree at Whiteways, Devon, mentioned in previous editions, no longer exists; according to the measurement given to Elwes it was 47 ft high and $5\frac{1}{2}$ ft in girth in 1907.

L. DECURRENS Torr. [PLATE 78

CALOCEDRUS DECURRENS (Torr.) Florin; *Thuja gigantea* Carr., not Nutt.;
Heyderia decurrens (Torr.) K. Koch

A tree 125 to 150 ft high in the wild, with a trunk occasionally 7 ft in diameter. Numerous trees between 50 and 70 ft high are to be found in this country, all marked by a stiff columnar or narrowly pyramidal habit. The branches are erect, and have their branchlets and leaves set vertically or edgewise instead of horizontally, so that they are equally exposed to the light on both sides, and are uniformly green on both surfaces. Leaves in four rows and in opposite pairs; about ⅛ in. long, free only at the sharp points, the lower part appressed to and completely covering the branchlet, dark glossy green. Cones erect, ¾ in. long ¼ to ⅓ in. wide at the base, tapered. Seeds four, ⅓ in. long, awl-shaped, with a large wing on one side and a small one on the other.

Native of Oregon and California; introduced by Jeffrey for the Oregon Association of Edinburgh in 1853; discovered seven years previously by Col. Frémont. It was frequently called *Thuja gigantea* in gardens, but is quite distinct from the tree to which that name properly belongs, whose horizontally spreading branchlets showing white stomata beneath are quite different (see *Thuja plicata*).

Libocedrus decurrens grows rather slowly, but is perfectly hardy and should be represented in every garden large enough to accommodate it, because of its distinct and formal shape—admirable for a group planted as Lombardy poplars sometimes are. A very fine tree measuring 99 × 15½ ft (1966), and quite columnar, is in the Royal demesne of Frogmore. It is an original from the 1853 introduction and was planted in 1857. The tree at Eastnor Castle of which the dimensions are given below is also of the original introduction and like the Frogmore tree has retained a dense, columnar habit. In Italy the branches are more spreading and the tree more broadly pyramidal than is usual with us, and in this respect they resemble the wild trees, which may be slender-crowned, especially when young, but are never closely fastigiate. Whether environmental or genetic factors are responsible for this difference is not known. Alan Mitchell has noted that trees in Ireland are broader than in England, and broader still in western Ireland. For a discussion on this matter see *Qtly. Journ. For.*, Vol. 56 (1962), pp. 78–80.

In addition to the Frogmore tree mentioned above, the following other notable specimens have been recorded recently:

Tittenhurst Park, Ascot, Berks., 116 × 11½ ft (1963); Lythe Hill, Haslemere, Surrey, 110 × 12½ ft (1963); Westonbirt, Glos., 97 × 10¾ ft (1966); Eastnor Castle, Heref., 100 × 16¼ ft (1961); Broxwood Court, Heref., 111 × 10¼ ft (1957); Oakley Park, Ludlow, Heref., 117 × 9½ ft (1960); Bicton, Devon, from original introduction, 88 × 12¼ ft (1957); Fota, Co. Cork, Eire, from original introduction, 82 × 12¼ ft (1966).

cv. 'AUREO-VARIEGATA'.—Pieces of the shoots entirely yellow. These pieces vary in size from bits of branchlets ½ in. long to pieces 2 to 3 in. across, giving the tree a curious spotted appearance. There are examples at Nymans, Sussex, and Little Hall, Kent.

L. MACROLEPIS (Kurz) Benth. & Hook.

CALOCEDRUS MACROLEPIS Kurz; *Heyderia macrolepis* (Kurz) Li

An evergreen tree up to 100 ft high, of graceful pyramidal shape; the bark of the trunk described by Henry as 'remarkably white'. Branchlets flat and frondose, the ultimate divisions on young trees $\frac{1}{8}$ to $\frac{1}{6}$ in. wide, bright green above, glaucous beneath. Leaves in four rows, very much compressed, the side ones folded lengthwise with their margins joined to the upper and lower ones so that only the short sharp points of all four are free; each set of four leaves is from $\frac{1}{8}$ to $\frac{3}{8}$ in. long, being considerably smaller in mature trees than in juvenile ones. Cones cylindrical, $\frac{5}{8}$ in. long, composed of six scales.

Native of S. Yunnan, China; first described and named *Calocedrus macrolepis* in 1873 from a specimen collected in 1868 by D. J. Anderson; introduced by Wilson in 1899 from Szemao in Yunnan. It was given a First Class Certificate by the Royal Horticultural Society in 1902, which was perhaps rather in excess of its merits, for although it is a quite handsome conifer of the thuja type, it is only hardy in our mildest counties. The free tips of the leaves are not so conspicuous in adult trees as in young ones. It is very rare in cultivation.

L. FORMOSANA Florin—This species, a native of Formosa, is closely allied to *L. macrolepis* and perhaps hardier. Its name in the genus *Calocedrus* is *C. formosana* (Florin) Florin.

L. PLUMOSA (D. Don) Druce

Dacrydium plumosum D. Don; *Thuja doniana* Hook.; *L. doniana* (Hook.) Endl.

An evergreen tree 30 to 70 ft high, with a trunk 6 to 13 ft in girth, the bark falling away in long, thin ribbons. In the young state the ultimate branchlets are flat, arranged in two opposite rows, $\frac{1}{2}$ to 1 in. long, and (with the leaves) about $\frac{1}{4}$ in. wide. Leaves in four rows as in *Thuja*, the side ones $\frac{1}{8}$ to $\frac{1}{5}$ in. long, flattened to form a keel, pointed, overlapping the small upper and lower ones, of which only the quite small triangular tips are exposed. In the adult state (as with many New Zealand conifers), the branchlets and leaves are quite different; the distichous (two-rowed) arrangement of the branches is not so conspicuous and they are narrower, about $\frac{1}{12}$ in. wide, less flattened, with the leaves proportionately smaller, blunter, and more equal in size. Cones egg-shaped, $\frac{1}{2}$ in. long, composed of four scales, each having a pointed curved spine nearly $\frac{1}{4}$ in. long at the back.

Native of New Zealand on both islands, but more frequent on the North, where it is said to be often rare and local; discovered in the Bay of Islands by Robert Cunningham in 1833. Kirk describes it as a noble tree. We know it only in a small state in cultivation, but it is a handsome conifer of the thuja type. There is an example measuring 16 × 1 ft at Wakehurst Place, Sussex (1971).

L. BIDWILLII Hook. f.—This is often confused with *L. plumosa*, but differs in the juvenile state from that species in the branchlets being narrower, and still more in the adult state when they become distinctly four-sided and

$\frac{1}{15}$ to $\frac{1}{12}$ in. wide, with the leaves almost uniform, triangular, pointed, cypress-like, and closely pressed to the stem. Cones as in *L. plumosa*, but only $\frac{1}{4}$ to $\frac{1}{3}$ in. long. It is an evergreen tree, rarely more than 50 ft high. As it reaches altitudes of 3,000 to 4,000 ft in New Zealand it should be hardy with us. There is a healthy plant at Nymans in Sussex, 26 × 2 ft (1970), and another of about the same size at Blackmoor, Hants.

L. UVIFERA (D. Don) Pilger

PILGERODENDRON UVIFERUM (D. Don) Florin; *Juniperus uvifera* D. Don;
Libocedrus tetragona (Hook.) Endl.; *Thuja tetragona* Hook.

A tree up to 70 ft in the wild in sheltered positions away from the sea, but smaller in exposed places; bark reddish, shed in thin plates. Leaves four-ranked, scale-like, appressed to the stem at the base, the free part spreading, tapered to an acute apex. Cones egg-shaped, brown, $\frac{3}{8}$ to $\frac{1}{2}$ in. long, with four scales. Seeds small, unequally winged.

Native of Chile and Argentina, but rare in the latter country and having its main distribution on the Pacific coast south of 42° S. It is common on the Guaitecas Islands and in the Chonos archipelago. At one time this conifer was confused with *Fitzroya cupressoides*, to which it bears some similarity in foliage and with which it sometimes occurs in the wild. But in *L. uvifera* the leaves are four-ranked and tapered to the apex, while in *Fitzroya* they are in threes and broadest above the middle.

Although introduced in 1849, *L. uvifera* is very rare in collections. Mr Hillier tells us he had a small tree at Chandler's Ford, Hants, which produced fertile seed. There is a thriving young plant at Wakehurst Place, Sussex, of rather fastigiate habit.

LIGUSTRUM*   OLEACEAE

There are about sixteen hardy species of *Ligustrum* introduced to this country, all of which are natives of China or Japan, with the exception of the common privet, found in Europe and England. The genus is exclusively Old World, and reaches from China through the Himalaya, etc., to Java, the Philippines, and Australia. Leaves opposite, never toothed. Flowers of some shade of white, borne in terminal panicles. Calyx scarcely or only minutely toothed; corolla tubular, with four spreading lobes. Stamens two, attached to the tube of the corolla. Fruit a berry, usually black, or black with a purplish bloom. The most recent account of the genus is by R. Mansfeld in *Botanische Jahrbücher*, Vol. 59, (1924), Beibl. No. 132, pp. 19–75.

Whilst the privets as a whole are not amongst the most attractive of hardy shrubs, a few of them are either striking or useful. One of their least

* Revised with the assistance of Mr P. S. Green of the Kew Herbarium.

attractive features is the penetrating odour of the flowers—heavy, and to most people objectionable at close quarters. The privets are easily cultivated in any soil that is not very impoverished, and they can be rooted from cuttings about as easily as any shrubs, either with or without a little heat. A selection for the garden would be as follows:

For flower—*L. sinense* and *L. quihoui*; for foliage—*L. japonicum*, *L. lucidum*, *L. l.* 'Tricolor', and *L. ovalifolium* 'Aureum'; for hedges— *L. ovalifolium* and *L. delavayanum*.

L. COMPACTUM Brandis

L. yunnanense L. Henry

A deciduous, sometimes partially evergreen shrub 10 to 15 ft high, of open, vigorous habit; branches spreading or somewhat pendent, slightly warted, and at first clothed with a very minute down, which mostly falls away by the end of the year. Leaves oval lance-shaped, tapering at both ends, 3 to 6 in. long, about one-third as wide; glabrous. Flowers creamy white with an odour like common privet, produced in July in numerous terminal panicles 6 or 7 in. high, and the same or more wide at the base. Fruits ¼ to ⅜ in. long, rounded at the top, covered with purple bloom at first, then black.

Native of the N.W. Himalaya and of Yunnan, China; introduced from the Himalaya in 1874. Plants raised at Paris from seeds sent by the Abbé Delavay in 1888 were named *L. yunnanense* but later proved to be conspecific with *L. compactum*. In its general aspect it is very like *L. lucidum* 'Alivonii' but it flowers before that privet does, and regularly sets its fruit. It is also nearly deciduous.

L. CHENAULTII Hickel—Raised in France from seeds sent from Yunnan by Ducloux in 1908, this privet is very close to *L. compactum* and doubtfully distinct as a species. It is said to differ by its acute winter-buds and by its leaves which, although of the same shape, may be up to 10 in. long.

L. CONFUSUM Decne.

A deciduous or, in warm localities, a more or less evergreen shrub or small tree, said to be sometimes 40 ft high in Sikkim; young shoots clothed with down. Leaves 1½ to 3½ in. long, ½ to 1 in. wide, lanceolate, pale glossy green, quite glabrous; stalk ¼ to ⅜ in. long, grooved on the upper side. Panicles downy like the young shoots, produced in June and July at the end of leafy twigs that spring from the previous year's branches. Flowers white, ⅛ in. wide, scarcely stalked. Calyx cup-shaped, glabrous, with shallow triangular lobes. Stamens white with pink anthers. Fruits black, covered with a plum-like bloom, ½ in. long, ⅛ in. wide.

Native of the Himalaya from E. Nepal to Bhutan, and of the Hills of Khasia; introduced to Kew in 1919 by means of seeds from Calcutta. It is not genuinely hardy in the open at Kew (although it survives) but grows luxuriantly on a south wall. There it flowers very freely, producing its panicles, each 3 or 4 in.

long and 2 or 3 in. wide, numerously in a cluster at the end of the previous year's growth. It is one of the best of the privets in regard to blossom, the corolla being of a purer white than is usual, but it is even more striking when thickly hung with its panicles of black-purple berries. I believe it would make a handsome small tree in the southern and western maritime counties. The specific name refers to its having been confused with *L. robustum* (not described in this work), which has more cylindrical fruits and larger leaves.

L. confusum is at present represented at Kew by a plant 10 ft high in the Ligustrum collection, raised from seeds received from Darjeeling in 1940. It is cut in severe winters.

L. DELAVAYANUM Hariot

L. ionandrum Diels; *L. prattii* Koehne

An evergreen shrub up to 10 ft high, of dense habit; young shoots thickly clothed with short fine down, becoming greyish. Leaves glabrous, of thin texture, ovate, oval or obovate, mucronate or bluntish at the apex, rounded or wedge-shaped at the base, $\frac{1}{2}$ to $1\frac{1}{4}$ in. long, about $\frac{1}{2}$ in. wide, dark bright green above. Flowers white, scented like common privet, densely packed in terminal panicles which are $\frac{3}{4}$ to $1\frac{1}{2}$ in. long, augmented sometimes by axillary racemes. Corolla $\frac{1}{8}$ in. long, anthers violet-coloured; flower-stalks downy. Fruits black, roundish ovoid, $\frac{1}{4}$ in. wide, produced in closely packed clusters. *Bot. Mag.*, n.s., t. 60.

Native of Yunnan and W. Szechwan; introduced by the Abbé Delavay by means of seeds sent to Maurice de Vilmorin at Les Barres in 1890. It flowered there in 1893 and was described as a new species under the above name in 1900, at about which time it was introduced to Kew. Forrest found it in the Lichiang range in 1906 and from the specimen he sent home Diels, in 1912, described a new species—*L. ionandrum*—and when Forrest later sent seeds they were distributed under that name. But there is no doubt that Forrest's privet belongs to *L. delavayanum* and that *L. ionandrum* was therefore a superfluous name. Another introduction was by Wilson from Szechwan, when collecting for the Arnold Arboretum; this was at first known as *L. prattii*, another synonym of *L. delavayanum*.

It is a pity that Forrest cannot be credited with either the discovery or the first introduction of this privet, for he thought highly of it and considered it to be one of the twelve best shrubs that he had introduced. Grown in the open, it makes a dense flat-topped bush about 6 ft high, but becomes taller if drawn up by the shade of trees. It is not completely hardy, but would make an attractive hedge in the milder parts of the country, and is so used at Headfort in Ireland.

L. HENRYI Hemsl. [PLATE 79

An evergreen bush up to 12 ft high, of neat habit especially when young; young shoots very downy. Leaves glabrous, variously shaped, from roundish ovate or almost round to ovate-lanceolate, $\frac{3}{4}$ to $1\frac{1}{2}$ in. long, inconspicuously veined, of an almost black, shining green above. Flowers white, scented, in short-stalked terminal pyramidal panicles 2 to 6 in. long. Corolla ⅓ in. long; calyx and individual flower-stalk glabrous. Fruits oblong, black, ⅓ in. long.

Native of Central China; discovered by Henry; introduced by Wilson in 1901 for Messrs Veitch. As a small shrub it makes a neat and pleasing ever-green, effective because of the black-green lustre of its leaves. Perhaps not absolutely hardy in severe winters.

L. JAPONICUM Thunb.

An evergreen shrub, rarely more than 6 to 12 ft high in this country, of bushy habit; twigs covered when young with minute dark down, becoming quite glabrous. Leaves glabrous, almost black-green, very glossy, ovate, 1½ in.

LIGUSTRUM JAPONICUM

to 4 in. long, ¾ to 2 in. wide, usually rounded, sometimes tapering at the base, taper-pointed at the apex; stalk ¼ to ½ in. long. Flowers white, borne in ter-minal pyramidal panicles 4 to 8 in. high and as much wide; flower-stalks clothed with minute down. In bloom from July to September.

Native of N. China, Korea, Japan; introduced to Europe by Siebold in 1845. It is closely allied to L. *lucidum*, and much confused with it in gardens, but is a less vigorous shrub, its leaves are darker green, shorter, more rounded at the base, and the nerves beneath are raised, whereas in L. *lucidum* they are sunken; the corolla-tube is twice as long as the calyx and equal to the corolla-lobes in L. *japonicum* in contrast to equal to or slightly less than the lobes and the calyx in L. *lucidum*; furthermore the inflorescence is looser, and the young shoots minutely downy. It is a useful and effective evergreen because of the intensely dark shining foliage, but needs a sheltered spot.

cv. 'ROTUNDIFOLIUM' ('Coriaceum').—An exceedingly stiff-habited ever-green shrub 4 to 6 ft or perhaps more high; young shoots short, stunted, covered with very minute dark down the first season. Leaves crowded, 1 to 2½ in. long, from two-thirds to fully as wide, broadly oval or round, very blunt or notched at the apex, dark glossy green, thick and leathery; stalk ⅕ in. long. Flowers white, in erect pyramidal panicles 2 or 3 in. long. Fruits black, globose, about ⅕ in. wide. *Bot. Mag.*, t. 7519. An inhabitant of Japanese gardens, not known in the wild; introduced by Fortune in 1860. A curiosity only, for the flowers have little beauty and it has no elegance of habit or foliage (L. *j.* var. *rotundifolium* Bl.; L. *coriaceum* Carr.; L. *j.* var. *coriaceum* (Carr.) Lav.).

L. LUCIDUM Ait. f.

An evergreen shrub of erect habit, 10 to 18 ft high, or a small tree up to 50 ft; devoid of down in all its parts. Leaves narrowly oval or ovate, from 3 to 6 in. long, 1 to 2½ in. wide, tapering at the base, long-pointed, glossy dark green above; stalk ⅓ to ½ in. long. Flowers white, produced during August and September in erect terminal panicles 6 to 8 in. high and nearly as much wide. Fruits oblong, ⅓ to ½ in. long, blue-black, not frequently produced with us. *Bot. Mag.*, t. 2565.

Native of China; introduced in 1794. Of the truly evergreen privets, this is the handsomest and best. A well-grown plant with the large lustrous leaves and a crowd of erect panicles is one of the most effective of autumn garden pictures. According to Henry, this privet is 20 to 30 ft high, and the com-monest evergreen tree in some parts of Hupeh, China. Wilson, in the Min River Valley, found one example 60 ft high and 10 ft in girth. In China it possesses some economic importance in being the tree on which the 'white-wax' insect deposits its eggs. It is sometimes confused with L. *japonicum* (q.v.).

L. *lucidum* makes a larger tree than was once supposed. By Winchester Cathedral there was a specimen measuring 49 × 6 ft (1961), probably the finest in the country; it was damaged beyond repair by a gale in 1970 and has been felled. The largest example at Kew, near the stone pine, is 42 × 3 ft and about 25 ft wide (1967).

cv. 'ALIVONII'.—Leaves longer, narrower, thinner, and less glossy, often variegated; they are 3 to 7 in. long and 1 to 2 in. wide; young twigs minutely downy. Fruits black, rounded at the top. It is not so handsome as L. *lucidum* and is of uncertain taxonomic status.

cv. 'AUREOVARIEGATUM'.—Leaves variegated with dull yellow; ineffective.

cv. 'EXCELSUM SUPERBUM'.—In the *Manual* of Messrs Hillier this is described as a very striking variegated form, with the leaves margined and mottled deep yellow and creamy white.

cv. 'TRICOLOR'.—Leaves with a broad but irregular border of white, pinkish when young. Very striking when well grown. This variety has reached a height of 35 ft at Winchester in Messrs Hilliers' West Hill nursery, where it is grown without wall protection.

L. OBTUSIFOLIUM Sieb. & Zucc.
L. *ibota* Sieb. (1830), *nom. nud.*, not L. *ibota* Sieb. & Zucc. (1846)

A deciduous shrub, dense with luxuriant leafage but of graceful habit, ultimately 8 to 10 ft high; twigs downy. Leaves oval or slightly obovate, 1 to 2 in. long, ⅓ to 1 in. wide, always tapered at the apex, glabrous except on the midrib beneath, and on the margins when young. Flowers white, produced in July in terminal, nodding clusters 1½ in. long on short side twigs. Calyx bell-shaped, scarcely toothed, usually slightly downy. Corolla ⅓ in. long. Fruits globose, ultimately black, but at first covered with a purplish bloom.

Native of Japan; introduced in 1860. This privet is a strong and vigorous grower, and when well furnished with its short clusters is distinctly ornamental. But it does not make so good a display here as in countries with a hotter summer. I saw it in the Arnold Arboretum in July 1910, and was much struck with its beauty and grace. As a flowering or fruit-bearing shrub it is at Kew inferior to L. *sinense*. It is allied to L. *ovalifolium*, but is distinct in habit and in the downy midrib. Both species have a corolla-tube two or three times as long as the lobes, but *ovalifolium* is nearly devoid of down.

var. REGELIANUM (Koehne) Rehd. L. *regelianum* Koehne—This shrub of dense habit, with branches spreading horizontally, was first described from cultivation as a species but merits no more than varietal rank under the variable L. *obtusifolium*, differing, within this species, by its more pilose stems and leaves. In cultivation it is represented by plants which have been propagated vegetatively and are characterised by their low spreading habit with leaves arranged distichously on more or less horizontal branches.

L. × IBOLIUM Coe ex Rehd. (L. *obtusifolium* × *ovalifolium*).—This hybrid, raised in Connecticut about 1910, is intermediate between the parent species. It is particularly useful as a hedge-plant in regions with severe winter conditions, being hardier than L. *ovalifolium*, which is so commonly used for hedges in Britain.

L. OVALIFOLIUM Hassk.

A semi-evergreen or, in severe winters or in poor soil, a deciduous shrub 10 to 15 ft high, of vigorous growth, forming a dense thicket of erect stems; young shoots usually quite glabrous. Leaves 1 to 2½ in. long, ½ to 1¼ in. wide, oval, wedge-shaped at the base, blunt or pointed at the apex, glossy green and glabrous on both surfaces; stalk ⅛ in. long. Flowers produced during July in a stiff, erect, terminal panicle, 2 to 4 in. high and about the same wide; they are very crowded in the panicle, dull white, and have a heavy, unpleasant odour. Calyx and individual flower-stalk smooth. Corolla ⅓ in. long. Fruits globose, shining, black.

Native of Japan. The oval-leaved privet is a worthy associate of the common one for dark corners or places starved by roots of trees where scarcely anything else will grow. For hedges it is preferable to the common privet because of its more evergreen nature; it has, in fact, almost entirely displaced it for that purpose. It is not worthy of being put to better use, being of stiff, ungainly habit, its flowers dull, and to most people evil-smelling.

cv. 'ARGENTEUM'.—Leaves bordered with creamy white. This pale variegation is not as rich and effective as that of the following.

cv. 'AUREUM'. GOLDEN PRIVET.—Leaves green only in the centre, with a border of varying width of rich golden yellow. This is the most popular of all variegated shrubs, and has been propagated by hundred of thousands for town planting. Although it is the fashion to revile it, it certainly produces a very bright effect and brings colour into many a hemmed-in garden or dull city yard where little of any kind will grow. It is also useful in a small state for town window-boxes. In habit it is less rigid and more graceful than the type and the young shoots, seen under the lens, are thickly but very minutely downy.

L. PRICEI Hayata
L. formosanum Rehd.

An evergreen shrub up to 10 ft high; young shoots purplish, minutely downy. Leaves leathery, broadly ovate or oval, or almost round, finely pointed, broadly wedge-shaped or almost rounded at the base, ½ to 1¼ in. long, ½ to ¾ in. wide; dark green and quite glabrous; stalk 1/12 in. long, purplish. Flowers small, produced in a terminal panicle 1 to 2 in. long, lax and slightly downy.

Native of Formosa; discovered by Henry in 1894, but first described from a specimen collected by Price in 1912 and subsequently introduced by Wilson. The leaves in texture resemble those of L. japonicum, but they are of course much smaller. Rehder compared it also with the Chinese L. henryi, which differs in its thinner leaves rounded at the base, its denser inflorescence, and its more conspicuously downy young twigs. L. pricei is probably not very hardy.

L. QUIHOUI Carr.
L. brachystachyum Decne.

A rounded, deciduous bush of thin, diffuse, but elegant habit, 6 to 10 ft high; branches thin, wiry, rather rigid, covered with a darkish minute down when young. Leaves 1 to 1½ in. long, one-third to half as wide, oval or obovate, tapering to a short stalk at the base, often bluntish at the apex, glabrous on both surfaces, but minutely downy on the stalk. Flowers white, fragrant, produced in September and October in slender downy panicles, 4 to 8 in. long, 1½ to 3 in. in diameter. Fruits ovoid, shining, purplish. *Bot. Mag.*, t. 9209.

Native of China; introduced to France about 1862. The habit of flowering so late in the season gives this species a special value in the garden, for it is one of the prettiest and most elegant of privets in bloom. Its flowers do not always open if September be dull and cold, but it deserves to be more extensively grown. The specific name was given in compliment to M. Quihou, once superintendent of the Jardin d'Acclimatation at Paris.

L. SINENSE Lour.

A deciduous or, in mild winters, nearly evergreen shrub, 12 to 20 ft high, occasionally taking the form of a small tree, of dense habit, rounded or flat-topped; twigs covered with a short, dense, brownish down. Leaves pale green, thin, elliptic, elliptic-oblong, or lanceolate, 1 to 3 in. long, ½ to 1 in. broad, tapering at the base, acute to bluntish at the apex, downy on the midrib beneath; stalk ⅛ to ¼ in. long. Flowers white, produced in July in numerous downy panicles, 3 or 4 in. long, 1½ to 2 in. wide. Fruits globose, black-purple, about ⅙ in. diameter, remaining on the branches until after the New Year.

Native of China; introduced by Fortune about 1852. I consider this the best and most ornamental of deciduous privets. It bears immense feathery masses of blossom in July, and they are usually followed by a wealth of dark purple fruits about the size of large shot, which make the shrub interesting through the winter. It is never seriously injured by cold, although in hard winters the twigs are occasionally cut back. Still, a sheltered position for it is preferable to one bleak and exposed, as it grows and flowers better then. It is now naturalised in parts of Australia and of the USA.

cv. 'MULTIFLORUM'.—This privet was grown by E. A. Bowles at Myddleton House, Enfield, as "*L. ovalifolium multiforum*" under which name he described and figured it in *My Garden in Summer*, pp. 284–285, and in *Gard. Chron.*, Vol. 50 (1911), p. 237 and fig. 109. He received it from the nurseryman George Paul, who found the original plant in France growing in a hedge of *L. ovalifolium* and bought it for ten francs. It seems to have been, in fact, a floriferous form of *L. sinense* with reddish-brown anthers, and appeared in the first edition of this work (1913) as *L. sinense* var. *multiflorum*. It is possibly the same as the *L. sinense floribundum*, for which Paul had received a First Class Certificate in 1885.

var. STAUNTONII (DC.) Rehd. *L. stauntonii* DC.—Leaves oval or ovate, usually blunt at the apex and mostly less than 2 in. long. Panicle broader and less dense. Described by de Candolle from a specimen in Lambert's herbarium, collected during Lord Macartney's Embassy to China in 1793. Wilson later found it in W. Hupeh and W. Szechwan, where it grows 6 to 12 ft high. The privet described by Carrière as *L. chinense* var. *nanum* is probably a dwarf form of this variety.

cv. 'VARIEGATUM'.—Leaves variegated grey-green and white.

L. STRONGYLOPHYLLUM Hemsl.

An evergreen shrub of elegant, loose habit, occasionally a small tree in the wild, sending out long, slender branches each season which, whilst young, are covered with a dense, minute down. Leaves nearly round, broadly oval or ovate, $\frac{1}{3}$ to $\frac{3}{4}$ in. long, often ending in a short abrupt tip, of firm texture, dark glossy green; margins slightly recurved; stalk $\frac{1}{20}$ in. long. Flowers white, $\frac{1}{4}$ in. in diameter, produced during July in a terminal pyramidal panicle, 2 to 4 in. high and as much wide at the base. Corolla-tube $\frac{1}{8}$ in. long; lobes pointed, $\frac{1}{8}$ in. or less long. *Bot. Mag.*, t. 8069.

Native of China; introduced by Maries for Messrs Veitch in 1879. Maries no doubt collected it in the Yangtze Kiang valley, about Ichang, where it was afterwards found by Henry. It is an elegant privet, and its numerous, small, almost round leaves give it a distinct appearance. But it is not very hardy, and at Kew has only flowered satisfactorily on a south wall.

L. VULGARE L.   COMMON PRIVET

A deciduous or more or less evergreen shrub 6 to 10 ft high, of rather lax habit; young shoots covered with minute down. Leaves narrowly oval or lance-shaped, 1 to $2\frac{1}{2}$ in. long, $\frac{1}{4}$ to $\frac{5}{8}$ in. wide, glabrous. Flowers dull white, produced during June and July on erect compact panicles 1 to 2 in. long, terminating the twigs; they have a heavy odour objectionable to most people. Fruits globose or egg-shaped, black.

Native of Europe, including Britain, where it is considered wild from Yorkshire southwards. The common privet may nowadays be regarded almost as the Cinderella among shrubs. It is relegated to dark corners and other damp out-of-the-way places under the drip of trees, where scarcely anything else will grow. But one can scarcely wish it a better fate. With so many beautiful things available the privet is not needed; even in its own genus it is about the least attractive, and for hedges is now superseded by *L. ovalifolium*. Its flowers are under suspicion of producing a kind of hay-fever. The berries are eaten by birds.

cv. 'AUREUM'.—Leaves yellow.

cv. 'BUXIFOLIUM'.—Leaves oval, scarcely 1 in. long; habit dense. Introduced to Kew before 1885.

cv. 'INSULENSE'.—A variant of unknown origin with linear-oblong leaves 2 to $4\frac{1}{2}$ in. long, $\frac{1}{2}$ to 1 in. wide, taper-pointed; young shoots velvety-downy. Flowers in a panicle 3 in. long and broad; fruits roundish oblong, $\frac{1}{3}$ in. long, black (*L. insulense* Decne.; *L. insulare* Decne.; *L. vulgare* var. *insulense* (Decne.) Höfker).

var. ITALICUM (Mill.) Vahl *L. italicum* Mill.; *L. vulgare* var. *sempervirens* Loud.—A more regularly evergreen shrub than the type. This variant was much planted until displaced by the more reliably evergreen *L. ovalifolium*. It is common in the southern part of the range of the species.

cv. 'LODENSE'.—Of dwarf dense habit (hence 'lodense'—low and dense);

leaves narrow, semi-persistent. Raised in the USA (*L. vulgare* f. *nanum* (Kohankie) Rehd.).

cv. 'PYRAMIDALE'.—Of dense, fastigiate habit. Put into commerce by Späth.

Besides the ordinary form with black berries, three others, differing in their fruits, are, or have been, in cultivation: f. CHLOROCARPUM (Loud.) Schelle, green-berried; f. LEUCOCARPUM (Sweet) Schelle, white-berried; and f. XANTHOCARPUM (G. Don) Schelle, yellow-berried.

LINDERA   LAURACEAE

A genus of about eighty species of evergreens or deciduous shrubs or trees, the majority from E. and S. Asia, but a few in eastern North America. Leaves alternate, aromatic. Flowers unisexual, male and female borne on separate plants in dense clusters (or singly in some species not described here). Each cluster is surrounded by an involucre with usually four bracts, which is folded over the flower-cluster in the bud-stage. Petals absent. Sepals usually six in number and petal-like. Anthers two-celled. Fruits (rarely seen in this country) fleshy, or becoming dry and splitting at maturity, containing a single stone.

Sargent remarked that in Japan the linderas make a notable feature in the shrubby growth of the hillsides and on the borders of streams and lakes.

L. BENZOIN (L.) Blume   SPICE BUSH
Laurus benzoin L.; *Benzoin aestivale* Nees

A spicily aromatic, deciduous shrub 6 to 12 ft high, forming a rounded bush as much in diameter; young shoots glabrous or slightly downy. Leaves pinnately veined, obovate, 2 to 5 in. long, 1 to 2½ in. wide, tapered towards both ends, but more gradually towards the stalk, not toothed, thin, glabrous above, glabrous or slightly downy and glaucous beneath, margins ciliate; stalk ¼ to ½ in. long. Flowers greenish yellow, small, and not showy; produced in tiny clusters during April from the joints of last year's naked shoots; the sexes are on separate plants; corolla none; calyx with six lobes. Fruits red, oval, ⅓ in. long, juicy.

Native of the eastern United States; introduced in 1683. When crushed the leaf emits a pungent spicy odour too strong to be quite pleasant. This species is perfectly hardy at Kew, where it makes a neat bush of no particular merit or distinction.

L. MEGAPHYLLA Hemsl.

Benzoin grandifolium Rehd.

An evergreen shrub or tree; young shoots darkish purple, marked with a few pale lenticels; terminal bud woolly. Leaves pinnately veined, oblong to oblanceolate, entire, pointed, tapered to a wedge-shaped or rounded base, 4 to 9 in. long, 1 to 2¼ in. wide, brilliantly glossy and dark green above, dull, pale and glaucous beneath, perfectly glabrous, midrib yellow; stalk ½ to 1 in. long. Flowers produced numerously in short-stalked, axillary umbels about 1 in. wide. Fruits black, egg-shaped, about ¾ in. long.

Native of S. and S.W. China and of Formosa; introduced by Wilson about 1900. The above description is based on the plants raised in the Coombe Wood nursery, where it formed a very handsome evergreen and proved quite hardy, remaining, however, a shrub. The leaves rather suggest, in their sheen and size, those of a cinnamon; they are aromatic when crushed.

To the above account, written when this species was still of very recent introduction, it has only to be added that *L. megaphylla* has never become common in gardens. At Kew there is a specimen about 20 ft high in an open position near the Pagoda. The species is also grown in Sussex at Wakehurst Place and Borde Hill, and in other collections. It seems fairly hardy but may lose its leaves in severe winters and is perhaps tender when young. The Kew specimen was protected during its early life by neighbouring shrubs, which have since been removed.

L. OBTUSILOBA Blume

Benzoin obtusilobum (Blume) Kuntze; *Lindera triloba* Hort., not (Sieb. & Zucc.) Blume

A deciduous shrub or small tree 20 to 30 ft high, the brown branchlets not downy, but marked with pale, narrow lenticels. Leaves three-veined from the base, variable in shape, mostly broadly ovate, sometimes entire, but usually more or less conspicuously three-lobed towards the apex, the lobes pointing forward, base heart-shaped, rounded or abruptly wedge-shaped, 2½ to 5 in. long, 1½ to 4 in. wide, dark shining green and glabrous above, pale and downy on the veins beneath, prominently triple-nerved; stalk ½ to 1 in. long, downy. Flowers yellowish, produced in March and April from the joints of the leafless wood in small dense clusters; each flower is about ⅙ in. across, borne on a stalk ¼ in. long, clothed thickly with silky hairs. Fruits described by Sargent as shining black, globose, ¼ in. across, and as forming a very handsome contrast to the yellow autumn foliage (but these would be produced in cultivation only if trees of both sexes were grown).

Native of China, Japan, and Korea; introduced by Maries in 1880, and grown and flowered in the Coombe Wood nursery. Wilson reintroduced this species from W. China in 1907–8 when collecting for the Arnold Arboretum. He described it as a handsome shrub or small tree, common in the woods of W. Hupeh and in spring 'very conspicuous on account of the brilliant colour of the young leaves'.

Messrs Hillier have pointed out that the lindera which they distributed for some years under the name *L. triloba* is not that species but almost certainly *L. obtusiloba*, and this seems indeed to be the case. The Award of Merit given to "*L. triloba*" in 1952 for its beautiful butter-yellow autumn colouring therefore belongs really to *L. obtusiloba*.

L. CERCIDIFOLIA Hemsl. *Benzoin cercidifolium* (Hemsl.) Rehd.—This species is very closely allied to *L. obtusiloba* but differs in the leaves being almost invariably unlobed and in the longer flower-stalks. *Bot. Mag.*, n.s., t. 492. A native of China, introduced by Wilson in 1907–8 when collecting for the Arnold Arboretum. Wilson described the fruits as dark red. Forrest sent seeds of this species from Yunnan and possibly all the plants grown in Britain are of this provenance. *L. cercidifolia* received an Award of Merit when a flowering branch was shown by W. Bentley of Quarry Wood, Newbury, on 25 March 1952; the plant there was raised from F.29087. The species is also cultivated at Exbury, probably from the same batch of seeds. The figure in the *Botanical Magazine* was made from material taken from the Exbury tree, which was 25 ft high in 1964. The leaves turn yellow in the autumn.   [PLATE 80

L. PRAECOX (Sieb. & Zucc.) Blume

Benzoin praecox Sieb. & Zucc.; *Parabenzoin praecox* (Sieb. & Zucc.) Nakai

A deciduous shrub or bushy tree 15 to 25 ft high, young shoots shining dark brown, not downy, but prominently warted. Leaves thin, ovate or oval, occasionally rotund, 1 to 3½ in. long, ½ to 1½ in. wide, taper-pointed or blunt at the apex, dark green above, pale and glaucous beneath, usually glabrous, pinnately-veined; stalk ¼ to ¾ in. long. Flowers small, greenish yellow, produced in March and April in small short-stalked umbels about ½ in. in diameter. Fruits dry, ¾ in. in diameter, reddish brown, marked with numerous pale dots.

Native of Japan and Korea. This lindera is fairly hardy at Kew, but only flowers well on a wall. It forms its umbels usually in pairs or threes during the summer; in the leaf-axils they remain through autumn and winter as little round knobs, bursting in the first warm days of spring. The leaves die off yellow.

LINNAEA   CAPRIFOLIACEAE

A genus of a single species allied to the honeysuckles, named by Gronovius after the great Linnaeus. In his *Critica Botanica* (1737), pp. 80–81, Linnaeus himself commented: 'Linnaea is a plant of Lapland, lowly, insignificant, disregarded, flowering but for a brief space—from Linnaeus, who resembles it' (Sir Arthur Hort's translation, p. 64, 1938).

L. BOREALIS L.   TWIN-FLOWER   [PLATE 82

A creeping evergreen plant, a few inches high with a woody base; branches long, slender, wire-like, hairy when young. Leaves opposite, obovate, oval or ovate; $\frac{1}{4}$ to $\frac{3}{4}$ in. long, $\frac{1}{8}$ to $\frac{1}{2}$ in. wide, rounded or broadly tapered and coarsely toothed at the apex, wedge-shaped and entire at the base with scattered hairs on the margin, upper surface, and on the midrib below; stalk $\frac{1}{12}$ to $\frac{1}{8}$ in. long. Flowers produced in summer, in a pair at the top of an erect, threadlike stalk, $1\frac{1}{2}$ to 3 in. high, terminating short, erect, lateral twigs; each flower has its own secondary stalk $\frac{1}{2}$ to $\frac{3}{4}$ in. long. Corolla pink or white, $\frac{1}{2}$ in. long, nodding, funnel-shaped, with five rounded lobes, hairy inside; calyx with five linear lobes; stamens four; ovary hairy. Fruits dry, yellow, one-seeded, downy.

This little plant is found in the high latitudes of the northern hemisphere including a few places in the north-east of Britain. It is a dainty plant with pretty, fragrant flowers, best adapted for some shady moist spot in the rock garden in rather sandy soil. It is naturalised under pines and bracken at the Sunningdale Nurseries, Berks. Plants of North American origin are the easiest to grow in this country.

LINUM   LINACEAE

A genus of about 100 species of annuals and perennials (most of these herbaceous), found in the temperate and subtropical regions of both hemispheres, but most numerously represented in S. Europe and the Near East.

L. ARBOREUM L.   TREE FLAX

A low compact evergreen glabrous shrub from 9 in. to 2 ft high, more in hotter countries. Leaves of a conspicuously blue-white colour 1 to 2 in. long, $\frac{1}{8}$ to $\frac{1}{2}$ in. wide, broadest near the apex, tapering thence to the base, with little or no stalk. Panicles erect, terminal, 3 to 6 in. long, continuing to produce flowers as they lengthen from May until July or August. Flowers bright, clear yellow, $1\frac{1}{2}$ in. across when fully expanded, but opening indifferently in dull weather and lasting in good condition but one day. Petals five, each 1 to $1\frac{1}{4}$ in. long, of very fragile texture. Sepals five, green, narrow-lanceolate, fine-pointed, $\frac{1}{3}$ in. long.

This gay little shrub is a native of the eastern Mediterranean region; introduced in the 18th century. It is not so much grown as it deserves, for when it is in flower few plants of its character are so bright. It makes a neat little tuft, and although the flowers are so fugitive, they are borne so freely on fine summer days that the plant is almost hidden by blossom. It is hardy at Kew in all but the severest winters, but is not a long-lived plant in our climate. It is very easily increased by means of cuttings taken whilst the wood is comparatively soft, and placed in brisk heat. Seeds are borne freely, but it helps to prolong the life of the plant if they are not allowed to develop. The soil need not be very rich, but as sunny a spot as possible is desirable. Even out of flower its vividly glaucous foliage is pleasing.

For allied, less woody species, see *Flora Europaea*, Vol. 2, pp. 207–208.

LIQUIDAMBAR   HAMAMELIDACEAE

A small genus of trees with a remarkably scattered distribution in nature; one species being found in Asia Minor, one in eastern N. America, and one or more in China and Formosa. In general appearance they bear most resemblance to the maples (*Acer*), but are easily distinguished by their alternate, not opposite leaves. The flowers have no beauty, being greenish or yellowish, and borne in small globose heads. Male and female flowers are in separate heads, the male flower-heads in short racemes; the female heads solitary. The male flowers consist of stamens only, the females of calyx and carpel only. The best known and most useful of liquidambars is *L. styraciflua*, which, like the rest, should, if possible, be raised from imported seeds. These frequently do not germinate until the second year. Failing them, layering must be resorted to. Young plants are apt to be injured by late spring frosts.

L. FORMOSANA Hance

L. acerifolia Maxim.; *L. formosana* var. *monticola* Rehd. & Wils.

A tree up to 125 ft in the wild; young shoots hairy or glabrous. Leaves palmately three-lobed (occasionally five-lobed through the production of subsidiary lobes at the base), up to 5 in. long, 6 in. wide, cordate to truncate at the base, lobes acute to acuminate or long-acuminate at the apex, finely serrate and sometimes with a few scattered lobules, glabrous above when mature, the undersides always in some degree hairy beneath but occasionally almost glabrous; leaf-stalks 1¾ to 2½ in. long, glabrous or hairy. Fruits in a globular cluster about 1½ in. across; each capsule is beaked, and subtended at the base by awl-shaped scales.

L. formosana was described from Formosa, where it is common in the mountains and extends to 6,500 ft. On the mainland it is widespread in southern and central China from the coast to Szechwan and Hupeh, south to Kwantung province, and also occurs in Indochina. Despite its wide distribution the species exhibits little or no variation of taxonomic significance. The var. *monticola* Rehd. & Wils. was described from specimens collected by Wilson in E. Szechwan and W. Hupeh (W.795). It was said to differ from the type in having the branchlets and leaves glabrous, but the authors admitted that the distinction was most evident on juvenile plants and much less apparent in the adult stage. Judging from the extensive set of specimens in the Kew Herbarium the species varies in the hairiness of the lower surface of the leaves and the nearly glabrous specimens from East Szechwan and West Hupeh are really no more than an extreme of the range of variation.

L. *formosana* was introduced to Kew in 1884, when seeds were received from the British Consul at Hankow; a plant from this sending lived there for many years on a wall. Most of the trees now in British gardens are under the label *L. formosana* var. *monticola*, and presumably derive from Wilson's W.795 (see above) collected between 2,000 and 4,000 ft in W. Hupeh in 1907. These trees have the leaves nearly glabrous beneath when fully expanded, cordate at the base, widely spreading lateral lobes which are rarely lobulate, plum-purple when unfolding, later bronzy crimson, finally dull green, but turn crimson again in the autumn. The colouring of the young foliage is most evident on vigorous young trees, which grow continuously throughout the summer. This variant is quite hardy, but the season's growth may be cut in winter if not fully ripened.

At Borde Hill in Sussex there is another form of the species in cultivation, also hardy, which was received as *L. formosana* simply. In this the leaves are of a much brighter green than in the commoner "var. *monticola*", with more acuminately tapered lobes, which sometimes bear a few jagged lobules in addition to the normal serrations. They are mostly truncate or shallowly cordate at the base. Its provenance is unknown. There is no difference in degree of hairiness between the two trees, both having the leaves glabrous beneath except for some longish hairs at the junction of the midrib with the two lateral veins. *L. formosana* has recently been reintroduced by means of seeds received from Formosa, but these plants are proving to be tender.

L. ORIENTALIS Mill.

L. *imberbe* Ait.

A deciduous tree up to 100 ft high; but rarely one-fourth as high in this country, bushy-headed. It has a rugged trunk covered with small squarish plates of thick bark; young shoots glabrous. Leaves 2½ to 3½ in. wide, scarcely as long, maple-like, five-lobed, the lobes oblong and reaching half or two-thirds of the depth of the blade, coarsely toothed or even lobed again, especially the three upper ones, the margins set with fine glandular teeth, quite glabrous on both surfaces; stalk 1 to 2 in. long. Flowers (rarely or never seen in Britain) greenish, produced in globose heads from the terminal part of the shoot with the young leaves in spring. Seed-vessels woody, in a rounded cluster 1 in. across.

Native of Asia Minor; introduced about 1750. Fine specimens are to be found on the continent, the best I have seen being in the Bologna Botanic Garden—90 to 100 ft high, and 5 ft in diameter of trunk. In Britain it is an interesting small tree, growing very slowly. It is quite hardy, but coming from one of the hottest parts of the Levant it lacks in this country the sunshine necessary for its complete development. From the inner bark of this tree the soft, viscid, balsamic resin known as 'liquid storax' is obtained. This substance has certain medicinal properties of reputed value in bronchial affections, and is said to form part of the popular preparation known as 'friar's balsam'.

There are no specimens of any note to be recorded. A small, bushy tree at Kew was 10 ft high in 1884; twenty-four years later it was 15 ft high; today it measures 25 × 4¾ ft at 6 ft (1965). Others are: Whiteknights, Reading, 13 × 2½ ft (1962) and Westonbirt, Glos., in Morley Drive, 12 × 2 ft (1965), with girths measured at 4 ft. A tree at Woburn Abbey, probably bought from Loddiges' nursery in 1838, is figured in *New Flora and Sylva*, Vol. 1, fig. lii (p. 173).

L. STYRACIFLUA L.   SWEET GUM

A deciduous tree up to 150 ft high in the wild, but not much more than half as high in England. It has a straight, erect trunk, with slender branches forming (as the tree is usually seen in this country) a narrow, pyramidal head. Branchlets glabrous and round at first, but during their second year they turn grey, and often begin to form corky wings after the fashion of the English elm, but in some trees the branchlets remain quite smooth. Leaves maple-like, usually five- sometimes seven-lobed, 5 to 7 in. wide, scarcely as long, heart-shaped at the base, the lobes minutely toothed, ovate-lanceolate; upper surface glabrous and glossy, the lower one with tufts of hair in the axils of the veins; stalk slender, 2½ to 4 in. long. Male flowers in small round heads arranged on a downy spike 2 or 3 in. long; female inflorescence rather larger, ½ in. wide. Seed-vessels in a roundish cluster 1 to 1½ in. across.

Native of the eastern United States, often in swampy ground, and also of Mexico and Guatemala. It was introduced in the 17th century, and has long been valued for its stately form and handsome foliage. It is often mistaken for a maple, but from all maples is, of course, distinguished by the alternate leaves. In autumn its foliage turns to shades of purple, crimson, and orange. The tree produces a fragrant resin, known as 'sweet gum'. The timber, although not of first quality, is largely imported under the name of 'satin walnut', for furniture making. Under cultivation it likes a good deep soil, and a moderately moist but not a swampy position.

The largest tree at Kew, situated in the *Liquidambar* collection, measures 90 × 7 ft (1965) and there is a smaller specimen of 62 × 4¾ ft by the Clematis wall (1967). At Syon House the largest is 93 × 8¾ ft (1967); this was about 75 × 6 ft in 1904. Others near London are: Mote Park, Maidstone, 82 × 5¾ ft, and Linton Park, Maidstone, 85 × 6 ft (1965), both superb trees, the latter with a 45-ft bole; Royal Horticultural Society Garden, Wisley, Surrey, 72 × 6½ ft (1964); Knap Hill nurseries, Surrey, 69 × 8 ft (1962); Lydhurst, Sussex, 69 × 3¾ ft (1965); Stratfield Saye, Hants, 87 × 9 ft (1968). Farther west the most notable specimens are: Escot, Devon; 74 × 9¾ ft and 90 × 7 ft (1965); Arley Castle, Worcs., 72 × 5 ft (1961); Westonbirt, Glos., in The Downs, 67 × 7¼ ft (1967).

cv. 'LEVIS'.—Branches without corky bark. Leaves brilliantly coloured in the autumn. Distributed by Messrs Marchant of Wimborne, Dorset.

cv. 'PENDULA'.—Main stem pendulous at the top; branches pendulous, forming a narrow crown. Described by Rehder from a tree found growing in Arkansas around 1935.

cv. 'VARIEGATA'.—Leaves marked with yellow.

LIRIODENDRON   MAGNOLIACEAE

A genus of two species, one North American, one Chinese. They are deciduous trees closely related to the magnolias, but differing from them in the truncate, never pointed leaves, the differently shaped, terminal winter-bud, and closed seed-vessels. Leaves alternate; flowers solitary at the end of a short branch; sepals three; petals six; carpels densely packed on a spindle-shaped column.

The tulip trees are gross feeders, and will only attain their best in good deep soil. They are impatient of disturbance at the root, and should be given a permanent place early. Like magnolias, they are probably most successfully transplanted in May. Seeds are produced in immense quantities, but comparatively few are fertile. Even in America it is said of the native species that barely 10 per cent can be expected to grow. Still seeds can now be cheaply obtained from American nurserymen, and they afford the best means of increase. The varieties may be grafted on seedlings of L. *tulipifera* in March; given a little heat in a propagating case, they unite very readily.

L. CHINENSE (Hemsl.) Sarg.
L. tulipifera var. *chinense* Hemsl.

Introduced to this country in 1901, this tree is perfectly hardy, and is growing admirably at Kew, where one of the original specimens is about 50 ft high. It was first noticed in China in 1875, in the Lushan Mountains, and was subsequently found by Henry, in Hupeh, at 3,000 to 6,000 ft altitude. Living plants were first introduced by Wilson for Messrs Veitch. It never appears to become so large as L. *tulipifera*. The leaves are of very much the same shape as those of the American species, having the same truncate apex and two lateral lobes; they are, however, narrower waisted, the sinus between the lobes being deeper and the midrib more prolonged. The flowers are smaller, the petals narrower and expanding more widely, and the fruit is more elongated. The apices of the carpels are not so acute, and not recurved as in the American tree. The leaves beneath, seen with a strong lens, are found to be covered with tiny warts (papillae). The trunk is much smoother than on the American tree. It flowered at Borde Hill, Sussex, in July 1927. It is easily grafted on seedlings of L. *tulipifera*.

There are two specimens at Kew, *pl.* 1908, measuring 50 × 3¾ ft and 40 × 3 ft (1967), and two at Borde Hill bought from Veitch's Coombe Wood nursery in 1913, the dimensions of which are 56 × 5½ ft (North Park Garden) and 68 × 4¼ ft (Little Bentley Wood). In Eire there is an example of 62 × 6 ft at Mount Usher, Co. Wicklow (1966).

L. TULIPIFERA L.   TULIP TREE   [PLATE 81

Tulipifera liriodendron Mill.

A tree of the largest size, reaching in its native haunts 150 to 190 ft in height, with a magnificent columnar trunk 8 or 9 ft in diameter. In the British Isles it has attained a stature of over 100 ft. The leaves vary in size, but are usually 3 to 8 in. long, and about one-third more in width, and by their form distinguish this from all other hardy trees except its Chinese ally; they are usually saddle-shaped, the apex being broad, and cut off almost square, or to a very shallow notch, the base truncate, or slightly hollowed, and extended at each side into an acute lobe with occasionally one or two more subsidiary ones. The leaf-stalk is slender, 2 to 4 in. long; the midrib is slightly extended beyond the blade. Flowers produced in June and July, and except for the three deflexed sepals, resemble a tulip in form. Petals oblong, 1½ in. long, greenish white with an orange-coloured spot at the base, erect with their edges overlapping, thus giving the flower its cupped shape. In the centre is the large, pointed pistil surrounded by numerous stamens. The foliage turns rich yellow in autumn.

In a wild state the tulip tree extends from Nova Scotia south to Florida, reaching its finest development in the south Allegheny region. It was one of the earliest introductions from N. America, and is known to have been cultivated by Bishop Compton at Fulham in 1688; but it was probably introduced some time before, because it is on record that a tree at Waltham Abbey, in 1745, was already 96 ft high and 9 ft in girth of trunk. When once it has attained the adult stage, the tree flowers very abundantly in this country, but the colouring of its blossoms is too dull to render them very noticeable. It is for its noble trunk and stately dimensions, its fine and unique foliage, that it is so much prized in gardens. The timber is extensively used in N. America under the name of 'white wood', especially for indoor purposes. It is yellowish, smooth, and fine-grained, and although not strong, does not split easily. The bark o both root and branches has a pleasant, rather pungent scent.

Of the specimens of the tulip tree mentioned by Elwes and Henry many still exist, including all those portrayed (*Tr. Gt. Brit. & Irel.*, Vol. 1, pp. 70–73 and plates 25–7). They are: Woolbeding Rectory, Sussex, 105 × 21 ft (1958); Leonardslee, Sussex, 111 × 13½ ft (1958); Horsham Park, Sussex, 82 × 17¼ ft (1960); Deepdene, Dorking, Surrey, *pl.* 1846, 90 × 17¼ ft (1964); Esher Place, Surrey, reputed to be from the introduction of 1675, 85 × 27¼ ft at 2 ft (1967); Erlestoke, Wilts, girth 15 ft (1966); Killerton, Devon, lopped, girth 17¼ft(1959).

Other specimens of note are: Kew, 100 × 10¾ ft, a fine tree; Kitlands, Leith Hill, Surrey, *pl.* 1860 (?), 108 × 18¼ ft, a superb tree, bole 10 ft (1964); Taplow House, Bucks, 115 × 19 ft. meas. by P. H. Gardner (1962); Hedingham Castle, Essex, 78 × 12 ft (1958); Stanway, Glos., 102 × 15½ ft (1964); Haffield House,

Heref., 102 × 18 ft at 3 ft (1966); Dean Court, Wimborne, Dorset, 85 × 18¼ ft (1967); Stourhead, Wilts, 102 × 18 ft, 98 × 16½ ft, and 82 × 18 ft (1970); Priory Lodge, Bradford-on-Avon, Wilts, 117 × 15 ft, meas. by E. Barnes (1971); Nettlecombe, Som., 98 × 16½ ft (1970); Glendurgan, Cornwall, *pl.* 1832, 80 × 18 ft (1965).

cv. 'AUREOMARGINATUM'.—Leaves margined with yellow. This is the commonest and best of several variegated sorts, and was figured in *Flore des Serres*, Vol. 19 (1873), t. 2025. The following specimens have been recorded: Blackmoor, Hants, 65 × 4¼ ft (1968); Holkham Hall, Norfolk, 62 × 3¾ ft (1968); Melbury, Dorset, 78 × 3¼ ft (1957); Woodhouse, Uplyme, Dorset, 75 × 7 ft (1957); Stourhead, Wilts, 75 × 6 ft (1970). Less common is 'AUREO-PICTUM', in which the centre of the leaf is blotched with yellow.

cv. 'CRISPUM'.—Leaves broader than long, with wavy margins.

cv. 'FASTIGIATUM'.—Of columnar habit. There are two examples at Wakehurst Place, Sussex, measuring 57 × 3 ft and 54 × 3¼ ft (1964).

f. INTEGRIFOLIUM Kirchn.—Leaves without the lateral lobes, and therefore of almost rectangular outline. This is the juvenile condition persisting; the first leaves of all tulip trees are of this form. An example at Kew measures 65 × 7½ ft (1967).

LITHOCARPUS   FAGACEAE

This genus is part of *Quercus* as understood by some botanists but the group is in fact very distinct from the true oaks and indeed is now placed in a different subdivision of the Fagaceae, namely the subfamily Castaneoideae. The botanical characters by which it differs from *Quercus* are: flower-spikes erect (in *Quercus* the male spikes are pendulous); male flowers with a rudimentary ovary and usually twelve stamens (six or less in *Quercus*); anthers minute; female flowers with minute pore-like stigmas. Other characters found in many species of *Lithocarpus* but not in *Quercus* are: flower-spikes often androgynous, i.e., comprising both male and female flowers, the latter usually at the base; shell (pericarp) of acorn sometimes thick, woody and furrowed (as in the type-species *L. javensis*); cup (cupule) sometimes of a bony or woody consistency (e.g., in *L. pachyphyllus*, q.v.).

With the exception of *L. densiflorus* of California all the species (about one hundred in all) are confined to E. and S.E. Asia (two of them in Japan).

The generic name *Pasania*, used in some works, is a synonym of *Lithocarpus*.

L. CLEISTOCARPUS (Seem.) Rehd. & Wils.

Quercus cleistocarpa Seem.; *Q. wilsonii* Seem.

An evergreen tree from 30 to 50 ft high; young shoots glabrous. Leaves oblong or narrowly oval, long and slenderly pointed, tapered at the base, quite toothless, 3 to 8 in. long, 1 to 2½ in. wide, but on vigorous young plants as much as 1 ft long and 3 or 4 in. wide; greyish green, quite glabrous; midrib and veins yellowish, the latter in nine to twelve pairs; stalk ¼ to ¾ in. long. Acorn-cups ¾ to 1 in. wide, densely clustered on a stiff spike 2 to 3 in. long, the acorns almost enclosed.

Native of W. Hupeh and Szechwan, China; introduced for Messrs Veitch by Wilson in 1901. In regard to the individual leaf this is probably the finest of the newer Chinese oaks. But it needs rather warmer conditions than our average climate affords to develop its best qualities. The finest plant in this country grows in the woods at Caerhays, in Cornwall, where it is of erect habit and vigorous growth, a most attractive evergreen. It measures 58 × 5½ ft at 4 ft (1966). It should have shelter from wind. Wilson describes old trees as having a much-branched, wide-spreading, flattened crown.

L. DENSIFLORUS (Hook. & Arn.) Rehd.   TANBARK OAK

Quercus densiflora Hook. & Arn.; *Pasania densiflora* (Hook. & Arn.) Oerst.

An evergreen tree 70 ft or more high, in a young state pyramidal; young shoots clothed with a thick pale wool which persists through the second season. Leaves stiff and leathery, oval or oblong, rounded or broadly tapered at the base, pointed, twelve to fourteen parallel ribs on either side the midrib, each rib ending in a sharp tooth, 2 to 4 (occasionally 6) in. long, ⅞ to 2¼ in. wide; upper surface at first covered with loose, stellate down which falls away by the end of the season, leaving it dark glossy green, lower surface with a thick down, at first pure white, becoming tawny and ultimately falling away, leaving it grey, glaucous, and nearly glabrous; stalk ⅓ to ¾ in. long. The leaves remain on the tree for two or three years. Male flowers in erect, slender spikes, 2 to 4 in. long. Acorns solitary or in pairs, ¾ to 1 in. long; the cup shallow, covered with slender, downy, reflexed scales.

Native of California and Oregon; introduced in 1874 to Kew, where it has proved a perfectly hardy and very striking oak. The milk-white down which covers the young leaves of the new shoots is very effective, and with the strong parallel ribs renders the species quite distinct from all other evergreen oaks. It is becoming rare in the wild through being cut down for its bark, which is exceedingly rich in tannin.

There is an example at Kew in the Oak collection, *pl.* 1923, which measures 29 × 1½ ft (1965). A tree of about the same height grows at Exbury, Hants.

var. ECHINOIDES (R. Br.) Abrams *Q. echinoides* R. Br.—A shrub up to 10 ft high. Leaves elliptic or elliptic-oblong, 1½ to 2¼ in. long. Acorn-cup with slender recurved scales. Mountains of Oregon and California.

L. EDULIS (Mak.) Nakai

Pasania edulis Makino; *Quercus edulis* Mak.; *Q. glabra* var. *sublepidota* Bl.; *Q. glabra* Sieb. & Zucc., not Thunb.; *Q. laevigata* Hort., in part, not Bl.

An evergreen small tree up to 30 ft high, usually a shrub in this country, of spreading habit; young shoots glabrous. Leaves glabrous, narrowly oval or oblanceolate, tapered at both ends, blunt-pointed, entire, of hard, leathery texture, 3½ to 6 in. long, 1 to 2¼ in. wide, glossy yellowish green above, dullish green beneath but with a slight silvery sheen due to the presence of minute scales; veins nine to eleven on each side the midrib; stalk ⅓ to 1 in. long. Acorns produced in triplets on stout woody spikes 2 to 3 in. long, but only an occasional acorn attains to full size, for which it requires two seasons; it is then about 1 in. long, ⅜ in. wide, pointed at the apex, bullet-shaped. The cup is about ¼ in. deep.

Native of Japan; introduced in the first half of the 19th century but still uncommon in gardens. It is a distinct and handsome evergreen bearing a slight resemblance to *Quercus acuta*, which being a true oak has quite different flowers, and leaves of a deeper green, not so tapered at the base and distinctly woolly when young. The confusion between the two species may in part be due to the fact that *L. edulis* has been distributed under the erroneous name *Quercus laevigata*, which is properly a synonym of *Q. acuta*. It is also often wrongly called *Q. glabra* (see below).

L. edulis is quite hardy south of London in a sheltered position and occasionally produces fertile acorns.

L. GLABER (Thunb.) Nakai *Q. glabra* Thunb.; *Pasania glabra* (Thunb.) Oerst.—This species has been confused with *L. edulis*, but is easily distinguished by the dense grey or yellowish down on the young branchlets, and by the leaves, which are silvery below from a close tomentum of very short hairs and have only six to eight pairs of lateral veins. Also the flowering and fruiting spikes are terminal and tomentose in this species, axillary and glabrous in *L. edulis*. Native of Japan and S. China. Probably most of the plants grown as *Quercus glabra* are not *L. glaber* but *L. edulis*. That this confusion should have arisen is understandable, for it is *L. edulis* that is the glabrous species; *L. glaber*, despite its name, is far from glabrous.

L. HENRYI (Seem.) Rehd. & Wils.

Quercus henryi Seem.

An evergreen tree up to 50 ft high, forming a neat, oval, or rounded crown of branches as seen in the wild; leaves and shoots glabrous except for a thin down when quite young. Leaves quite untoothed, narrowly oblong, tapered at both ends, more slenderly to the point, 4 to almost 10 in. long, 1½ to 2 in. wide, leathery, pale green, shining; stalk up to 1 in. long. Acorns closely packed on a stout spike 4 to 8 in. long at or near the end of the shoot; they are globose, flattened at the top, ¾ in. wide. Acorn-cup shallow, thin, ⅛ in. deep.

Native of W. Hupeh and E. Szechwan, China; introduced to the Coombe

Wood nursery by Wilson in 1901. This oak is hardy at Kew but is very slow in growth. Like *L. cleistocarpus*, which it much resembles, it will succeed much better in the warmer counties, and make a handsome evergreen tree with probably larger leaves than those described above. It is quite distinct from that species in the longer spikes of acorns and especially in the shallow thin cup; but in foliage it is not so easy to distinguish the two. *L. henryi* has leaves greener beneath, with more pairs of veins on the average, and longer stalks.

There are two examples of this species at Caerhays, Cornwall. One is 30 × 3 ft; the other, dying, is of the same size (1966).

L. PACHYPHYLLUS (Kurz) Rehd.

Quercus pachyphylla Kurz

An evergreen tree attaining a considerable height in the wild, but occasionally a shrub; stems downy when young. Leaves entire, leathery, elliptic or oblong-lanceolate, mostly 6 to 8 in. long, 1⅞ to 3 in. wide, prolonged at the apex into a slender tail-like point, cuneate at the base, glabrous above, the underside of a beautiful silvery green and covered with a fine felt of stellate hairs; veins in eight to ten pairs; petioles ¼ to ½ in. long. Female flowers sessile in concrescent clusters of three. Fruit-spikes stout, lenticellate, up to 6 in. long. Fruits in threes, sessile, fused together by their cups into a bony mass 1½ in. or more wide, the upper clusters partly united to their neighbours, forming conglomerations of six or nine fruits. Acorn wider than long, almost wholly enclosed in the cup.

A native of the eastern Himalaya. There is an example of this species at Caerhays, Cornwall, measuring 44 × 4½ + 3¼ ft, with a wide spread (1971). This occasionally bears the remarkable fruits, resembling colonies of giant barnacles.

LITHOSPERMUM   BORAGINACEAE

A genus of about fifty species of herbs and sub-shrubs, with a few shrubs. Leaves alternate, entire; calyx five-parted; corolla funnel-shaped or salver-shaped spreading at the mouth into five lobes. The generic name refers to the hard, stone-like seeds. The genus is found in the temperate parts of both hemispheres.

L. DIFFUSUM Lag.

L. prostratum Loisel.; *Lithodora prostrata* (Loisel.) Griseb.; *Lithodora diffusa* (Lag.) I. M. Johnston

A prostrate evergreen shrub, growing from 6 to 12 in. only above the ground, but forming a wide-spreading mass. Shoots semi-herbaceous, slender, trailing, thickly covered with pale, bristly hairs. Leaves alternate, linear-oblong.

½ to ¾ in. long, ⅛ in. wide, stalkless, blunt at the apex, dark dull green, clothed on both surfaces with pale hairs. Flowers stalkless, borne in the axils of leafy bracts on a terminal leafy elongated inflorescence, of a beautiful gentian blue, faintly striped with reddish violet. Corolla ½ in. long, tubular at the base, spreading into five rounded lobes at the mouth, hairy in the throat and externally; calyx with erect, hairy, awl-shaped lobes.

Native of W. France, the Pyrenees, and N.W. Spain, usually on acid soils and often found in association with *Daboecia cantabrica*; introduced in 1825. A singularly beautiful sub-shrubby plant, very effective in the rock garden, or at the top of banks over which its trailing shoots may hang. It also grows well if planted among heaths and allowed to clamber through them. It does not need a rich or wet soil, but one of a light nature, well drained, and neutral or slightly acid. Although not really tender, it detests winter wet, and is a complete failure in gardens where the soil lies soggy and cold in winter. It should be planted in full sun. Increased by cuttings in summer, and kept in pots the first winter. Where the soil and exposure are suitable it makes delightful patches in front of a low shrubbery or border, flowering continuously during May and June, often again later. It should be lightly trimmed after the main flowering is over.

In the 19th century *L. diffusum* was represented in gardens by plants with dark blue flowers, streaked with red. But early in the present century Messrs Perry of Enfield put into commerce 'HEAVENLY BLUE', with larger flowers of a purer and paler blue, which quickly displaced the older forms and long remained without rival. Messrs Perry obtained their stock from E. A. Bowles, who had received his original plant from Dr D. H. Lowe (*Journ. R.H.S.*, Vol. 52, p. 255). But whether it arose as a garden seedling or was collected in the wild is not known. In the 1930s 'GRACE WARD' came into commerce, with larger flowers than in 'Heavenly Blue' and of less spreading habit.

L. FRUTICOSUM L. *Lithodora fruticosa* (L.) Griseb.—Allied to *L. diffusum* but of erect habit and with the corolla glabrous on the outside and in the throat. A native of the W. Mediterranean, found in hotter and drier places than *L. diffusum* and always on limestone soils.

L. OLEIFOLIUM Lapeyr.

An evergreen prostrate shrub 3 ft or more wide, forming a dense mass of branches only 5 or 6 in. high; young shoots clothed with silky hairs. Leaves obovate or oval, rounded or slightly pointed at the apex, tapering to a very short stalk, ½ to ¾ in. long, ¼ to ⅜ in. wide on flowering shoots, sometimes twice as long and wide on barren shoots, dull dark green with appressed silky hairs above, completely covered with whitish silky hairs beneath. Flowers blue, opening successively in May and June on flattish curving racemes 1 in. or more long, of the type common to the borage family, five to seven flowers on each raceme. Corolla ¾ in. long, ⅜ in. wide, hairy outside, glabrous inside, slenderly tubular at the base, more bell-shaped towards the top, with five rounded, slightly notched lobes there. Calyx five-lobed, the lobes narrowly linear, ¼ in. long. Stamens five, hidden in the corolla. Style shorter than the corolla (but see further below).

Native of Spain; discovered on the eastern Pyrenees in 1814, growing in crevices of rocks. No one probably in this country succeeded so well in cultivating this rare and beautiful shrub as Miss Willmott, who grew it in her rock garden at Warley, in Essex, for over thirty years. She recommended for it a dry, well-drained position, with some old mortar rubble about the roots, and that it should be protected from excessive moisture. It can be propagated by cuttings and by division in the absence of seeds.

This species has two types of flower. In one the calyx is as long as the corolla-tube, the stamens are almost sessile at the top of the corolla-tube, and the style is long, exceeding the corolla-tube. In the other type, the calyx is much shorter than the corolla-tube, the anthers are borne above the tube on well-developed filaments, and the style is short and included in the tube. Both types are figured in the *Botanical Magazine*, the long-styled at t. 8994 and the short-styled at t. 9559.

LOISELEURIA   ERICACEAE

A genus of a single species bearing some resemblance to *Leiophyllum* but distinguished by its united petals and by its five (not ten) stamens, included in the corolla. Linnaeus described this species in his genus *Azalea* (now included in *Rhododendron*) but *Loiseleuria* differs from *Rhododendron* in its opposite leaves and in having anthers that open by slits, not pores.

L. PROCUMBENS (L.) Desv.   ALPINE AZALEA

Azalea procumbens L.

A procumbent evergreen shrub, much-branched, forming low tufts 3 to 6 in. high; branches tortuous, very leafy, glabrous, rooting freely along the ground. Leaves opposite, oval or oblong, ⅛ to ⅓ in. long, scarcely half as wide, with the margins so much recurved as almost to hide the undersurface, glabrous and dark glossy green above, glabrous or sometimes with a whitish mealy down beneath; stalk one-fourth to half as long as the blade. Flowers rosy or nearly white, about ¼ in. in diameter, produced in May in short terminal clusters, two to five together. Corolla erect, bell-shaped, with five lobes. Calyx with five deep lobes half as long as the corolla. Stamens five, shorter than the corolla. Seed-vessel a dry capsule, with two or three divisions, many-seeded.

Native of the Alpine summits and sub-arctic regions of the three northern continents, and the only species known. Found on the Scottish highlands. It needs a peaty soil. In the south of England it does not thrive well; the summer is usually too hot and dry for it. Some cool damp spot on the lower part of the rock garden should be selected for it.

LOMATIA   PROTEACEAE

A genus of about a dozen species of evergreen small trees or shrubs with alternate or opposite leaves, the cultivated species of which come from South America and Australia. It is allied to *Embothrium* and has flowers of a similar structure. The generic name is from the Greek and refers to the winged edge of the seeds.

L. FERRUGINEA (Cav.) R. Br.

Embothrium ferrugineum Cav.

An evergreen shrub or a tree up to 30 ft high; branchlets clothed with a rich brownish red, velvety down. Leaves mostly pinnate, with the pinnae (i.e., primary divisions) deeply and pinnately lobed; but some of the smaller leaves have unlobed segments. They vary from 3 to 8 in. in length and in main outline are oblong to ovate; the pinnae are usually up to 2 to 3 in. long, and vary from six to fifteen in number, decreasing in size towards each end; the ultimate segments being of oblong or obovate shape, pointed, about ½ in. long, dull dark green and at first downy above, covered beneath with down which is whitish, becoming tawny with age. The main and secondary leaf-stalks are covered with velvety down like that of the young shoots. Racemes axillary, 1½ to 2 in. long, carrying a dozen or more flowers, each about ½ in. long, tawny yellow and red; there are four perianth-segments, the style is curved and terminated by the large stigma characteristic of the genus; flower-stalks and petals downy. Flowers in July. *Bot. Mag.*, t. 8112.

Native of Chile and bordering parts of Argentina; introduced by William Lobb between 1845 and 1848 for Messrs Veitch; it is frequent on the island of Chiloe. Its foliage is of a fern-like character and in this respect it is one of the handsomest trees that have come from S. America. The flowers, which are not particularly handsome, are of curious structure, the segments of the perianth bearing the stalkless anthers on their recurved tips.

L. ferruginea is incapable of withstanding the winters at Kew but is hardy at Wakehurst, in Sussex, where there are several small specimens. The tree is, however, happiest in the milder and rainier parts of the British Isles and nowhere more so than in Ireland, where the following examples were recorded in 1966 (to mention only those over 30 ft in height): Castlewellan, Co. Down, a five-stemmed bush 49 ft high; Mount Usher, Co. Wicklow, Eire, *pl.* 1928, 39 × 1½ ft; Ashbourne House, Co. Cork, Eire, 39 × 2¼ + 1¾ ft.

The description given above is based on the foliage, etc., as usually seen in this country. In the Chilean rain-forests *L. ferruginea* often occurs as a very sparsely branched shrub or small tree with leaves of enormous size concentrated around the terminal buds. There is a leaf collected on the island of Chiloe and preserved at Kew which is 20 in. long and 10 in. wide. A possible explanation of the difference is that in the very mild and moist conditions of the temperate rain-forests the terminal buds are able to maintain their dominance over the axillary buds, which remain mostly dormant. In cultivated plants, growing

in less favourable conditions, the terminal buds are either killed by frost or
fail to develop. This 'pruning' results in the production of numerous axillary
shoots bearing shorter leaves.

L. HIRSUTA (Lam.) Diels

Embothrium hirsutum Lam.; *L. obliqua* (Ruiz & Pavon) R. Br.; *Embothrium obliquum*
Ruiz & Pavon

An evergreen shrub or small tree 20 to 60 ft high; young stems slightly
downy. Leaves alternate, leathery, ovate, 1½ to 4 in. long, ¾ to 2½ in. wide,
wedge-shaped or rounded at the base, blunt at the apex, coarsely round-
toothed; as they unfold they are covered with tawny down, but afterwards
become perfectly glabrous, and of a deep glossy green; stalk brownish, about
one-fourth the length of the blade. Flowers borne in axillary racemes 2 to
3 in. long, pale greenish yellow, not showy. *Bot. Mag.*, n.s., t. 335.

Native of Chile, Argentina, Peru, and Ecuador; introduced by H. J. Elwes
in 1902. It proved hardy at Kew, planted on an outside border near one of the
plant-houses where it was 9 ft high until the winter of 1946–7, when it was
killed by the severe weather. This species would no doubt be better suited
growing under the same conditions as Embothrium. Probably the best specimen in the country grows in woodland at Nymans in Sussex. Raised from seeds
collected by H. F. Comber on his Andean expedition (1925–7), it is now about
50 ft high.

L. DENTATA R. Br.—Seeds of this, the third Chilean lomatia, were sent
home by H. F. Comber under his number 987 but there is no record of any
garden plant from this source. It was reintroduced in 1963 by means of cuttings
taken from a bush about 8 ft high growing near Lake Pangipulli in Osorno
province. A plant from this sending, raised at Kew, is now growing at Wakehurst Place, Sussex, but has yet to experience a hard winter. *L. dentata* is very
distinct from *L. hirsuta* in its toothed leaves and pure white flowers. It is
unlikely to be as hardy.

L. MYRICOIDES (Gaertn.) Dorrien

Embothrium myricoideum Gaertn.; *Lomatia longifolia* R. Br.

An evergreen shrub 4 to 8 ft high in cultivation but taller and occasionally
tree-like in the wild. Young stems angled, slightly downy. Leaves glabrous,
narrowly lanceolate or oblong-lanceolate, 3 to 6 in. long, ¼ to ½ in. wide,
distantly and coarsely toothed in the upper part or sometimes entire, acute or
obtuse at the apex, tapered at the base, sessile or shortly stalked. Inflorescences
racemose, terminal or from the upper leaf-axils, as long as the leaves or slightly
longer. Flowers creamy white or pale yellow, borne June–July, about ½ in.
wide, on stalks ¼ to ¾ in. long. *Bot. Mag.*, t. 7698.

Native of S.E. Australia; introduced 1816. It is hardy south of London in a
sunny place protected from cold winds. Award of Merit 1955.

T S—U

L. TINCTORIA (Labill.) R. Br.

Embothrium tinctorium Labill.; *L. silaifolia* Hort., in part, not (Sm.) R. Br.

An evergreen, often suckering shrub usually 2 to 3 ft high (occasionally somewhat taller in the wild), glabrous in all its parts or with the young stems, leaf undersides, and inflorescence-axes covered with short appressed hairs. Leaves dark green, occasionally simple but more commonly pinnate or slightly bipinnate, 2 to 3½ in. long, the segments linear, blunt or mucronate at the apex, parallel-sided or slightly contracted at the base. Inflorescences racemose, terminal or from the upper leaf-axils, 4 to 8 in. long, produced July–August. Flowers pale yellow, tipped green in the bud, heliotrope-scented, borne singly or in pairs on stalks about ⅝ in. long. *Bot. Mag.*, t. 4110.

Native of Tasmania, where it is widespread up to 3,000 ft and often forms large colonies in dry places, introduced in 1822. It was once cultivated in greenhouses for its elegant foliage, but is almost hardy and has lived for many years in the heath garden at Wakehurst Place, Sussex. Plants raised from seeds collected by the late Harold Comber during his Tasmanian expedition 1928–9 have survived many hard winters at Nymans and at Borde Hill in the same county. It needs a sunny sheltered position and a well-drained soil.

L. SILAIFOLIA (Sm.) R. Br. *Embothrium silaifolium* Sm.—This species, a native of the coastal parts of S.E. Australia, is allied to *L. tinctoria* and like it is of dwarf habit. But the leaves are larger, more elaborately divided, and the ultimate subdivisions widen towards the base. Some at least of the plants distributed under the name are really *L. tinctoria*.

LONICERA   HONEYSUCKLE   CAPRIFOLIACEAE

A genus of about 180 deciduous or sometimes evergreen species of bushy or climbing shrubs, with usually peeling bark, named by Linnaeus after Lonizer, a German naturalist who flourished in the middle part of the 16th century. The leading generic characters are: Leaves opposite, shortly stalked or stalkless; flowers pentamerous, in axillary pairs on a common stalk, or in whorls, subtended by bracts and usually bractlets; calyx five-toothed (sometimes almost untoothed); corolla tubular or bell-shaped and five-lobed, the lobes sometimes equal, but more frequently forming two 'lips', the upper lip composed of four short lobes, the lower lip of a single strap-shaped lobe ovary inferior. Fruit a fleshy berry. The flowers often change from white to yellow with age.

Lonicera is usually divided into two subgenera. In the larger of the two the flowers are borne in pairs in the axils of leaves; mostly these species are shrubs, but those of the section *Nintooa* are climbers (e.g., *L. japonica*). In the other subgenus, which is smaller but horticulturally more important, the species are mostly twiners and produce their flowers at the ends of the shoots in whorls, which may be distant from each other, forming a spike; or clustered into a terminal head.

The standard work on the genus is 'Synopsis of the Genus Lonicera' by Dr Alfred Rehder, published in *Rep. Missouri Bot. Gard.*, Vol. 14 (1903), pp. 27–232.

Although the value of the genus in gardens is not commensurate with its size, it does contain a number of extremely beautiful species, and of the climbing group, every species that is hardy is worth growing. The free-growing woodbines are best accommodated on pergolas or similar supports, or planted to ramble over small trees or bushes; but some of the less rambling ones may be at first trained up stout posts 4 or 6 ft high, and then allowed to form loose, spreading shrubs, needing no further support. The climbing honeysuckles are very subject to attacks of aphides in summer, especially during hot dry spells; if these are not repelled by applications of some insecticide they sometimes destroy the crop of blossom. All the species like a good loamy soil, and especially cool moist conditions at the root—given these, the attacks of aphides are often naturally overcome.

The bush honeysuckles are in this country somewhat disappointing shrubs. Many of them, especially those of North Asiatic origin, are almost invariably cut by spring frosts and much of their blossom destroyed. Consequently we never see their full beauty of flower or of fruit—and many species are extremely handsome when bearing full crops of red, yellow, black, blue, or white, often translucent, berries. The propagation of those species that do bear fruit is easily effected by seed, but I do not know of any species that cannot be increased by cuttings of firm young shoots, placed in gentle bottom heat about July or August. If heat be not available, cuttings of somewhat harder wood may be dibbled in sandy soil under handlights out-of-doors.

L. ALBERTII Reg.
L. *spinosa* var. *albertii* (Reg.) Rehd.

A deciduous shrub of low, spreading habit, unarmed, becoming about 4 ft high and twice as much in diameter; young shoots glabrous or glandular, slender. Leaves linear-oblong, $\frac{5}{8}$ to $1\frac{1}{4}$ in. long, about $\frac{1}{8}$ in. wide, bluntish at the apex, with often a few teeth near the base, blue-green, glabrous; stalk very short. Flowers rosy-lilac, fragrant, produced in pairs from the leaf-axils, each pair on a stalk about $\frac{1}{4}$ in. long. Corolla-tube $\frac{1}{3}$ to $\frac{1}{2}$ in. long, slender, cylindrical, glabrous outside, downy inside; lobes spreading horizontally, oblong, giving the flower a diameter of about $\frac{3}{4}$ in. Stalk of the stamens twice as long as the anthers. Berries $\frac{1}{3}$ in. in diameter, purplish red, not united. *Bot. Mag.*, t. 7394.

Native of the mountains of Turkestan; introduced by Albert Regel to St Petersburg about 1880 and described by his father Dr Eduard Regel. It is sometimes regarded as a variety of L. SPINOSA (Decne.) Walp., which inhabits the inner, arid ranges of the north-western Himalaya. This differs from L. *albertii* in its sturdier, spiny, sometimes leafless, branches, in the ovate lobes of the corolla, and in the filaments of the stamens being only as long as the anther. *L. albertii* is a pleasing shrub of graceful habit, very distinct from other cultivated honeysuckles in its narrow, bluish foliage.

L. ALPIGENA L.

A deciduous shrub, 4 to 8 ft high, with erect branches; young shoots mostly glabrous; winter-buds with several ovate, bluntly pointed scales. Leaves oval, oblong, or somewhat obovate, usually tapered, sometimes rounded at the base, slender-pointed, 2 to 4 in. long, 1 to 2 in. wide, sometimes glabrous, but usually with hairs on the midrib and veins both above and below when quite young, margins always hairy; stalk ½ in. or less long. Flowers yellow, deeply tinged with red, borne during May in pairs at the end of a stalk 1½ to 2 in. long; corolla ½ in. long, with a short tube protruded on one side near the base, distinctly two-lipped, very hairy inside, the lower part of the stamens hairy. Fruits red, up to ½ in. long, cherry-like, united for at least part of their length.

Native of central and southern Europe, but with varieties or closely allied species in E. Asia; cultivated since the 16th century. The species is very distinct among cultivated bush honeysuckles in its long flower-stalks, large leaves and large fruits, but has no particular garden value.

f. NANA (Carr.) Nichols.—A dwarf form whose leaves have scattered hairs all over the lower surface, more densely on the veins and midrib.

L. ALSEUOSMOIDES Graebn.

A climbing evergreen shrub, with slender, glabrous, young shoots. Leaves narrowly oblong, tapered at both ends, 1¼ to 2 in. long, averaging about ¼ to ⅓ in.

LONICERA ALSEUOSMOIDES

wide, the decurved margins furnished with appressed hairs, otherwise glabrous. Flowers produced from July to October at the apex of the shoot, and in the terminal leaf-axils, the whole forming a short broad panicle. Corolla purple within, yellow outside, funnel-shaped, $\frac{1}{2}$ in. long, glabrous outside, downy within. Fruits globose, $\frac{1}{8}$ to $\frac{1}{4}$ in. in diameter, black covered with purple bloom, borne in a close head.

Native of China; introduced by Wilson for Messrs Veitch about 1904. An interesting and pretty climber, which first flowered at Coombe Wood in 1909. Closely akin to L. *henryi*, which has hairy young shoots and bigger leaves.

L. ALTMANII Reg.

A deciduous shrub 6 to 8 ft high; young shoots purplish hairy; winter-buds with two outer scales. Leaves ovate or oval, $\frac{3}{4}$ to 2 in. long, half to three-fourths as wide, rounded or tapered at the base, mostly pointed, ciliate, more or less hairy; stalk $\frac{1}{8}$ in. or less long. Flowers in pairs, each pair subtended by two hairy bracts $\frac{1}{4}$ in. long; corolla white, $\frac{1}{2}$ in. long, the slender tubular base rather longer than the lobes, and with a protuberance near the base, hairy outside; flower-stalk about $\frac{1}{4}$ in. long. Berries $\frac{1}{3}$ in. wide, orange-red.

Native of Turkestan; introduced from St Petersburg in 1899, but very rare. It belongs to the same group as L. *hispida*, but has comparatively inconspicuous bracts, and the corolla-tube differs in being longer than the lobes. Flowers in April and May.

L. × AMERICANA (Mill.) K. Koch

Periclymenum americanum Mill.; L. *italica* Tausch; L. *grata* Ait.

This interesting and beautiful woodbine is a hybrid between L. *caprifolium* and L. *etrusca*, with both of which it is often confused. It has most resemblance to L. *caprifolium* in growth and foliage; young stems purple, glabrous. The uppermost pairs of leaves unite into a cup, as in L. *caprifolium*, but the lower ones differ in being more pointed. Flowers fragrant, in whorls not confined (as in L. *caprifolium*) to the axils of the connate leaves, but with several other whorls above them springing from the axils of small bracts. Corolla 2 in. long, yellow more or less suffused with reddish purple, the tube slender, usually glandular, downy outside, the two lips giving a diameter of 1 to $1\frac{1}{2}$ in.

The origin of this lovely hybrid is not known, but it existed in the time of Linnaeus, who confused it with L. *caprifolium*. According to Rehder, it is very rare in the wild, but has been found in S. and S.E. Europe, although even there possibly as an escape from cultivation. It is a very effective climber, the terminal part of the shoot often branching and forming a panicle over 1 ft long and 8 in. through. It received an Award of Garden Merit in 1955.

This hybrid was in cultivation in 1730 and reputed to grow wild in N. America. Philip Miller seems to have doubted the correctness of this belief, so it is the more the pity that he should have adopted for it the epithet *americanum*. The fallacy was encouraged by Pursh, who, in his *Flora Americae Septentrionalis* (1814), listed this honeysuckle as an American native. Some European botanists of that time identified it with *L. virginiana* Marsh., which was, in fact, *L. sempervirens.* This explains how Loudon, who grew this hybrid as *L. grata* Ait., could confidently assert that it was an American species that grew wild in Virginia and Carolina.

L. ANGUSTIFOLIA Wall.

A deciduous shrub 8 to 10 ft high, of rounded elegant habit, the outer branches pendulous. Leaves ovate-lanceolate, rounded or tapering at the base, slender pointed, ¾ to 2 in. long, ¼ to ½ in. wide, bright green and glabrous above except at first, paler and slightly downy beneath, especially on the midrib; stalk $\frac{1}{12}$ in. or less long, woolly. Flowers pinkish white, produced in May and June in pairs from the lower leaf-axils of the young branchlets, each pair on a slender drooping stalk ½ to ⅝ in. long. Corolla tubular, the tube ⅛ in. long, the lobes equal, about one-third as long as the tube. Style quite short and hidden. Berries red, edible; each pair united.

Native of the Himalaya; introduced by Sir Joseph Hooker about 1849. If it flowered more freely it would be an attractive shrub, as it is perfectly hardy and of elegant growth; its flowers are fragrant.

It is allied to *L. myrtillus*, but differs in its longer, differently shaped leaves and drooping peduncles.

L. × BROWNII (Reg.) Carr.

L. etrusca var. *brownii* Reg.

A group of hybrids between *L. sempervirens* and *L. hirsuta* with the habit and general aspect of the former species, but somewhat hardier and showing the influence of *L. hirsuta* in their corollas, which are more or less two-lipped (not equally lobed as in *L. sempervirens*) and glandular-downy on the outside. The typical form of the cross arose before 1853 but its origin is unknown. Another form of the cross, very similar to the type, is 'FUCHSIOIDES'. In 'PLANTIER-ENSIS' the flowers are less strongly two-lipped but still show the influence of *L. hirsuta* in being glandular on the outside. A more recent member of this group is 'DROPMORE SCARLET', raised in Canada by F. L. Skinner and awarded a Gold Medal in the Boskoop Trials, 1964. It is said to have a very long flowering season.

L. CAERULEA L.

A deciduous sturdy bush of rounded habit 2 to 4 ft high; branchlets stiff, glabrous, or hairy only when young. Leaves oval, obovate or oblong, rounded at the apex, ½ to 1½ in. long, ¼ to 1 in. wide, more or less (sometimes very) hairy beneath especially on the midrib and veins; stalk hairy, ⅛ in. or less long. Flowers twin, produced from the leaf-axils, yellowish white. Corolla ½ to ¾ in. long, funnel-shaped, hairy outside, with a sac at the base of the tube; bracts awl-shaped, ciliate. Fruits blue. *Bot. Mag.*, t. 1965.

A widespread species inhabiting, in one or other of its numerous forms, the higher altitudes and latitudes of the three northern continents. It has little or no merit for gardens, but has some botanical interest. The single oval berry which constitutes the fruit is not, as was long supposed, the wholly united ovaries of each pair of flowers, but really a pair of free ovaries enclosed by the cupula—an upgrowth of the bractlets.

A variable shrub, the leaves and branches in some forms much more hairy or downy than in others, and the fruit sometimes roundish. They are all distinguished by the curious character mentioned, where two flowers appear to rise from one ovary.

L. CAPRIFOLIUM L.

A deciduous climber up to 20 ft high, not downy on any part except sometimes the outside of the corolla. Leaves obovate or oval, usually tapered at the base, rounded at the apex, 2 to 4 in. long, about half as wide, glaucous, especially beneath. The lower leaves of the shoot are stalked, the higher pairs are sessile; finally, the uppermost one to three pairs are united round the stem, each pair forming a cup, and in their axils the flowers are borne. Flowers in whorls, fragrant, produced from June onwards. Corolla yellowish white, tinged with pink, 1½ to 2 in. long, two-lipped, the tube slender. Fruits orange-coloured.

Native of Europe, naturalised in Britain, possibly wild in the south-east of England; also naturalised in the eastern United States. This beautiful fragrant honeysuckle differs from L. *periclymenum* in the uppermost pairs of leaves (in whose axils the flowers are borne) being united.

cv. 'PAUCIFLORA'.—Flowers tinted with rose on the outside.

L. CAUCASICA Pall.

L. orientalis var. *caucasica* (Pall.) Rehd.

A deciduous shrub of bushy habit up to 8 or 9 ft high, rather more in diameter; winter-buds as in L. *nigra*; shoots quite glabrous. Leaves oval or ovate, broadly wedge-shaped or rounded at the base, pointed, 1½ to 4 in. long, ¼ to 1½ in. wide, green above, greyish beneath, glabrous, or with a few scattered dull hairs beneath; stalk ¼ in. or less long. Flowers borne during May and June in pairs from the leaf-axils of the current year's shoots, pink, slightly fragrant, ½ in. long; corolla two-lipped; tube very short, much swollen on one side, downy within; stamens and style exposed, both downy; flower-stalk ½ to ¾ in. long, glabrous. Fruits black, each pair wholly united by the inner edges.

Native of the Caucasus and Near East; introduced in 1825. It varies somewhat, and the description given above is of a cultivated plant. It is of no particular merit.

L. KESSELRINGII Reg. L. *savranica* Spaeth; L. *kamtschatica* Hort.; L. *orientalis* var. *longifolia* Dipp.—Leaves oblong or oval-lanceolate 1½ to 2½ in. long, rarely more than ¾ in. wide. Flowers pink, smaller than in L. *caucasica*, the corolla-tube only slightly swollen; common stalk ⅜ in. long. Of unknown origin. Introduced 1888.

L. CHAETOCARPA (Batal. ex Rehd.) Rehd.
L. *hispida* var. *chaetocarpa* Batal. ex Rehd.

An upright deciduous shrub 5 to 7 ft high; shoots bristly and glandular. Leaves ovate to oblong, sometimes oval, 1½ to 3 in. long, blunt to pointed at the apex, bristly, especially beneath. Flowers in pairs or solitary, borne on hairy stalks up

LONICERA CHAETOCARPA

to ¾ in. long; corolla tubular, 1¼ in. long, dividing at the mouth to five roundish spreading lobes, primrose yellow, hairy and glandular outside; ovary densely glandular and bristly. Berries bright red. *Bot. Mag.*, t. 8804.

Native of W. China; introduced for Messrs Veitch by Wilson in 1904. It is an attractive shrub of comely habit, closely akin to L. *hispida*, which differs in its more slender corolla-tube and its glabrous or glandular ovary and in being less but more harshly hairy. It is quite hardy and flowers in June.

L. CHRYSANTHA Turcz.

A deciduous shrub up to 12 ft high, with hollow branchlets; young shoots usually rather shaggy at first, but variable in this respect and sometimes nearly glabrous; winter-buds pointed with ciliate scales. Leaves oval to ovate-lanceolate, pointed, broadly tapering or rounded at the base, 2 to 4½ in. long, about half as wide, downy on the midrib above, also beneath especially on the veins; stalk ⅛ to ¼ in. long. Flowers twin, each pair borne on a slender hairy stalk ½ to ¾ in. long, springing from the leaf-axils; they are pale yellow becoming deeper in shade with age, ¾ in. long, slightly downy outside; stamens downy at the lower part; ovaries glandular. Fruits coral-red.

Native of Siberia, N. China, and Japan. It has long been in cultivation and was in the Kew collection in 1880. As a flowering bushy honeysuckle it is one of the most ornamental and very hardy.

var. LATIFOLIA Korshinsky *L. chrysantha* f. *turkestanica* Hort. ex Rehd.—Leaves broader and stouter, less downy beneath. It resembles *L. ruprechtiana* in many respects, but that species has a glabrous ovary.

var. LONGIPES Maxim.—This variety differs from the type only in having the leaves rather more sparsely hairy beneath and slightly longer peduncles.

f. REGELIANA (Kirchn.) Rehd. *L. regeliana* Kirchn.—Flowers smaller, deeper yellow.

L. CILIOSA (Pursh) Poir.

Caprifolium ciliosum Pursh; *C. occidentale* Lindl.; *L. occidentalis* (Lindl.) Hook.; *L. ciliosa* var. *occidentalis* (Lindl.) Rehd.

A twining honeysuckle of the same group as *L. sempervirens*, but differing in having leaves hairy on the margins, but otherwise glabrous; the style also is hairy. Leaves ovate or oval, 2 to 3 in. long, glaucous beneath, the upper pairs united by their bases round the stem. Flowers 1¼ to 1½ in. long, yellow or orange-scarlet, downy outside; they are produced in a terminal stalked spike of one to three whorls. Corolla slightly two-lipped, more so than in *L. sempervirens*. Fruits red.

Native of western N. America from British Columbia south to N. California and east to Montana and Utah; introduced in 1824. Although rare in gardens it is a fine species, which should be more widely cultivated. It received an Award of Merit when shown by Lady Gurney from her garden in Norfolk in 1919, and is said to be perfectly hardy.

L. ARIZONICA Rehd.—Allied to *L. ciliosa*, but differing in its smaller leaves (up to 1¾ in. long), more slender and more strongly two-lipped corollas and glabrous styles. Native of Arizona and New Mexico; introduced to Europe by Purpus in 1900. It was in cultivation at Borde Hill in Sussex in 1933 and according to *Borde Hill Trees* (p. 139) is a very beautiful species and a far better garden plant than *L. sempervirens*.

L. DEFLEXICALYX Batal.

A deciduous shrub of elegant spreading habit; branches often horizontal or drooping, the branchlets in opposite rows, hollow; young shoots purple, downy. Leaves 1½ to 3 in. long, scarcely half as wide, rounded at the base, narrowly ovate, pointed, dull green and downy above, greyish and hairy beneath, especially when young; stalk ⅓ in. long. Flowers in pairs from each axil along the branchlets, all expanding upwards; calyx dry, scarcely lobed, splitting down one side; corolla yellow, ⅝ in. long, downy outside, the lower lip much deflexed, tube shorter than the lobes; stamens hairy at the base; style wholly hairy; stalk ¼ in. long; fruits orange-red. *Bot. Mag.*, t. 8536.

Native of China and Tibet; introduced in 1904. A notably elegant, free-growing shrub, very hardy and floriferous, showing its flowers to good advantage by producing them on the upper side of the long feathered branches. It flowers in May and June, and grows probably 8 ft or so high.

var. XEROCALYX (Diels) Rehd. *L. xerocalyx* Diels—Leaves slightly longer and narrower, somewhat glaucous beneath; ovaries surrounded by a cupula made up of the united bractlets. Introduced by Forrest from Yunnan.

L. DIOICA L.

L. glauca Hill

A spreading or twining deciduous shrub; young stems and leaves quite glabrous. Leaves oval or oblong, tapered at both ends, 1½ to 4 in. long, 1 to 2 in. wide, green above, vividly glaucous beneath. Flowers yellow, tinged with purple, produced during June and July in terminal clusters, two or more pairs of leaves beneath being united. Corolla two-lipped, ¾ in. long, the tube about equal to the lips in length, swollen at the base, glabrous outside. Berries red.

Native of eastern N. America; introduced in 1776. This honeysuckle succeeds very well under cultivation in a good garden soil; if given the support of a stout central stake, it will form a low, spreading, rather elegant bush, and although without any great beauty of flower is striking for the very glaucous undersurface of the leaf.

Nearly allied to the above, and sometimes confused with it, is L. GLAUCESCENS Rydb. This differs chiefly in having the leaves downy beneath and the corolla downy outside; as a rule only the uppermost pair of leaves is united. The style and the base of the stamens are downy; the corolla-tube rather longer than the lips. It has a more western distribution than *L. dioica*.

L. ETRUSCA Santi

A very vigorous half evergreen or deciduous climber, young shoots (in the cultivated form) reddish purple. Leaves oval or obovate, rounded at both ends or broadly tapered at the base, 1½ to 3½ in. long, 1 to 2 in. wide, glaucous and usually somewhat downy beneath. The lower ones are shortly stalked; approaching the top they become stalkless; whilst the uppermost pairs are united at the base (connate). Flowers fragrant, at first yellowish, suffused with red, becoming deeper yellow with age; born from July onwards in terminal and axillary groups of three long-stalked heads. Corolla 1¾ in. long, the tube slender, sometimes glabrous, sometimes glandular, conspicuously two-lipped.

Native of the Mediterranean region; introduced probably two hundred years ago, but not often seen. At its best perhaps it is the most gorgeous of all honeysuckles, but I have not seen it at its best out-of-doors, although no doubt it may reach perfection in the south-western counties. Farther north it is hardy, but not wholly satisfactory out-of-doors; in an unheated greenhouse it is wonderfully beautiful in late summer, the long shoots branching and forming immense bouquets. The species varies very much in the amount of down on the leaves, but the form now cultivated is downy on both sides of the leaf (var. PUBESCENS Dipp.).

cv. 'SUPERBA'.—Very vigorous; panicles larger. *Bot. Mag.*, t. 7977. There are fine specimens of this variety at Bodnant, and at Mount Stewart in N. Ireland. It received an Award of Merit when shown from the Savill Gardens, Windsor Great Park, in 1953.

var. VISCIDULA Boiss.—Leaves very glandular above, less so beneath; young shoots also glandular. Native of Asia Minor; rather tender.

L. FERDINANDII Franch.

A very robust deciduous shrub, of spreading, open habit, becoming in a few years 8 or 9 ft high and more in diameter; buds awl-shaped, at first hairy; young shoots glandular when quite young. Leaves ovate, rounded or heart-shaped at the base, slender-pointed, 1½ to 4 in. long, ¾ to 1¾ in. wide, dull green, hairy on both sides and on the margins. On the vigorous barren shoots the leaf-stalks (each about ¼ in. long) are attached to a pair of stipules, which are united and form a shield-like disk surrounding the stem at each joint. These are not present on the flowering branches. Flowers yellow, produced in pairs during early June from the apex of the shoot, and in the upper leaf-axils. Corolla two-lipped, ¾ in. across, with a bellied tube ⅓ in. long, downy outside. Each pair of flowers is subtended by two leaflike bracts and the ovaries are surrounded at the base by a cupula composed of the united bractlets. Fruits bright red.

Native of Mongolia and China; introduced in 1900. It is a remarkably distinct species, and flowers freely. The shield-like stipules mentioned above persist through the winter and become brown, stiff and brittle the second year.

L. FLAVA Sims

The real *L. flava* is perhaps not now in cultivation, or, if it be, it is extremely rare. It appears to be very local in its distribution, and was originally discovered on the summit of Paris Mountain, in S. Carolina, by John Fraser; introduced early in the 19th century. The plants that went in cultivation under the name were either *L. prolifera* or *L. glaucescens*, both of which are inferior to it. It is about the most beautiful of American honeysuckles. The bright orange-yellow flowers are about 1¼ in. long, the corolla-tube glabrous outside, slenderly tapered downwards, not bellied. The flowers are produced in two or more whorls on a stalked, terminal inflorescence; style glabrous. Leaves rather glaucous beneath, glabrous, the uppermost one to three pairs connate, not glaucous above as they are in *L. prolifera. Bot. Mag.*, t. 1318.

L. FRAGRANTISSIMA Lindl. & Paxt.

An evergreen, partially evergreen, or deciduous bush 6 to 8 ft high, glabrous except for the bristly margins of the young leaves and sometimes the midrib

Leaves oval, rather stiff and leathery, 1 to 2 in. long, two-thirds as wide, broadly wedge-shaped at both ends, but terminated by a short bristle-like tip, and bristly on the margins when young, dark dull green above, rather glaucous beneath; stalk ⅛ in. or less long. Flowers produced from December to March in several pairs at the joints, creamy white, very fragrant, ⅝ in. long; stalk glabrous, ¼ in. long. *Bot. Mag.*, t. 8585.

Native of China; introduced by Fortune in 1845. This is not a showy plant, but is valued in gardens for its early, charmingly fragrant blossoms. It varies from deciduous to evergreen according to the severity of the winter, but is rarely devoid of foliage. Often confused with L. *standishii*, it is, nevertheless, very distinct in the absence of bristles on the young shoots, flower-stalks, and corolla; the leaf, too, is shorter, and the apex is not drawn out as in L. *standishii*. L. *fragrantissima*, which is the superior shrub, starts to grow very early in the year. Both are distinct in their early flowering from all the rest of the honeysuckles.

L. GIRALDII Rehd.

An evergreen climber forming a dense tangle of twining branches, thickly clothed with yellowish erect hairs when young. Leaves narrowly oblong, with a lance-shaped apex and a heart-shaped base, 1½ to 3½ in. long, ½ to 1 in. wide, densely hairy on both sides; stalk ⅓ in. or less long, hairy. Flowers purplish red, borne in a short terminal panicle 1½ in. across; corolla two-lipped, ¾ in. wide, yellowish hairy outside; the tube slender, ½ in. long; the entire flower 1 in. long; bracts inconspicuous. Fruits purplish black. *Bot. Mag.*, t. 8236.

Native of Szechwan, China, whence it was introduced to France in 1899, and first grown by Maurice de Vilmorin. I first saw it growing against a wall in the garden of Phillipe de Vilmorin at Verrières-le-Buisson, near Paris, in June 1908, then in flower. Plants were obtained for Kew the following autumn, and these, so far as I am aware, represent its first introduction to Britain. As I saw it, it was a striking honeysuckle forming a dense thicket, the whole plant having a yellowish tinge, very downy, the rather small flower clusters striking in the contrast of lurid red corolla and yellow stamens. It is hardy in the south and west of England.

It belongs to the same group as L. *japonica* (sect. *Nintooa*).

L. GRIFFITHII Hook. f. & Thoms.

A deciduous twining shrub up to 20 ft high, the older bark peeling off in flakes; young shoots glabrous. Leaves broadly ovate, oblong or roundish in main outline, the terminal pair close to the inflorescence are always roundish and in cultivated plants the lower pairs are often very deeply lobed, 1 to 2 in. long, half to nearly as much wide, glaucous green, quite glabrous; stalk ⅛ to ½ in. long. Inflorescence a terminal, stalked head of flowers closely arranged in two or three tiers opening in May. Corolla rosy-white, of the two-lipped, common honeysuckle shape, 1 in. long, ¾ in. wide, the tube downy and glandular outside, glabrous within; stamens glabrous; style hairy. The main-stalk of the inflorescence is downy and the bracts beneath each tier of flowers are hairy. *Bot. Mag.*, t. 8956.

Native of Afghanistan; discovered in 1840 by Griffith (Superintendent of the Botanic Garden, Calcutta, in the early 19th century). The plants at present in cultivation were obtained by Lt-Col. Mainwaring of Upwey in Dorset, who had seeds sent to him in 1910. Dr Aitchison collected it in 1879 during his notable travels in Afghanistan, and records that he found it in association with *Quercus ilex, Rosa ecae,* and *Populus alba,* all very hardy. It does not appear, nevertheless, to have taken kindly to our climate, although it succeeded at Abbotsbury on the Dorset coast. Coming from a dry region with hot summers and cold winters it might prove to thrive best in eastern England. Only one of the specimens in the Kew Herbarium has the deeply lobed leaves shown in the illustration cited above and in the plant once grown under glass at Wisley (*Journ. R.H.S.,* Vol. 66, p. 369 and figs. 121 and 122). But they seem to have been characteristic of the Mainwaring introduction and are reported to occur occasionally on wild plants. It happens that the one wild specimen with lobed leaves in the Kew Herbarium was collected by Capt. S. M. Toppin, who provided the seeds from which Col. Mainwaring eventually obtained flowering plants, after many years of failure from earlier sending of seeds and cuttings (see *Gard. Chron.,* Vol. 60 (1916), p. 42).

Botanically, the species is closely related to our native *L. periclymenum.* Both Dr Aitchison and Col. Mainwaring found it festooning *Quercus ilex,* and all who have seen it in the wild have been impressed by its beauty.

L. GYNOCHLAMYDEA Hemsl.

A deciduous shrub of erect habit, with glabrous, purplish young shoots. Leaves lanceolate, rounded or broadly tapered at the base, drawn out at the apex to a long slender point, 2 to 4½ in. long, ¾ to 1½ in. wide, downy along the midrib above, with usually a conspicuous strip of down towards the base of the midrib beneath; stalk about ⅓ in. long. Flowers twin, produced in May from the leaf-axils on stalks ⅛ to ¼ in. long, white tinged with pink; corolla ⅓ to ½ in. long, the tube stout, much bellied at the base, downy outside; stamens and style more or less downy. Fruits white or purplish, rather translucent.

Native of Hupeh and Yunnan, China; discovered by Henry, introduced by Wilson in 1901. Henry states that he found it 10 ft high. Although very different in mode of growth, it is botanically akin to *L. pileata,* both having a 'remarkable downward cap-like production of the calyx covering the united bracteoles' (Hemsley).

L. × HECKROTTII Rehd.

A deciduous shrub of loose, spreading, scarcely climbing habit, thought by Rehder to be a hybrid between *L. sempervirens* and *L. americana.* It is a strikingly handsome honeysuckle, its leaves being oblong or oval, glabrous, scarcely stalked, 1½ to 2½ in. long, glaucous beneath. The uppermost pairs are united by their bases (connate). Flowers 1½ in. long, rich pink outside, yellow within; produced in whorls on a rather long-stalked, terminal spike. Corolla-tube not downy outside, slender, slightly hairy inside. Blossoms from June onwards. This hybrid originated or was first noticed in the United States, but its history is unrecorded. It is quite hardy, and one of the best of its type of honeysuckle.

So far as is known there is only one clone of this hybrid. 'Gold Flame' is simply a commercial name for this, not a new cultivar of L. × *beckrottii* (*Arnoldia*, Vol. 22, p. 62).

L. HENRYI Hemsl.

An evergreen or semi-deciduous climber with slender more or less densely strigose shoots. Leaves mostly oblong-lanceolate to oblong-ovate, 1¾ to 4 in. long, ½ to 1⅝ in. wide, abruptly to gradually acuminate at the apex, rounded or cordate at the base, dark green above, paler and rather glossy beneath, downy only on the midrib and margins, sometimes almost glabrous; stalk ⅛ to ½ in. long. Flowers purplish red, produced during June at the end of the shoot in a cluster 2 or 3 in. across, each stalk twin-flowered. Corolla two-lipped, ¾ in. across, the lips much reflexed, the tube ½ to almost ¾ in. long, hairy within, glabrous outside. Stamens slightly downy. Style hairy, protruded ½ in. beyond the corolla. Bracts awl-shaped, about ¼ in. long. Fruits blackish purple. *Bot. Mag.*, t. 8375.

Native of W. China; introduced by Wilson in 1908 and later sent by Forrest. It is closely allied to the more ornamental L. *alseuosmoides*, which has narrower leaves and glabrous stems. At Trewithen in Cornwall a plant from Forrest's seeds has climbed 30 ft into a laurel and would invade neighbouring trees if not continually cut back.

L. *henryi* varies slightly. Plants with larger, less hairy leaves and larger flowers have been named var. SUBCORIACEA Rehd., but this variety is linked by transitions to the typical state and scarcely worth recognition.

L. HILDEBRANDIANA Coll. & Hemsl.

A vigorous evergreen climber (or nearly deciduous in cool places) growing 60 to 80 ft high, without down in all its parts. Leaves broadly ovate, oval or roundish oval, abruptly contracted at the apex to a short point, broadly tapered at the base, 3 to 6 in. long, half to two-thirds as wide, dark green above, paler and with scattered glands beneath; stalk ⅛ to ¾ in. long. Flowers fragrant, produced from the leaf-axils and in a terminal raceme, always in pairs, each pair joined to a short stalk ¼ to ¾ in. long. Corolla 3½ to 6 in. long, creamy white changing to rich orange, the long slender tube dividing at the mouth into two lips, one of which consists of four short lobes, the other of a single narrow lobe much recurved; they give the flower a diameter of 2 to 3 in. Fruits ovoid, 1 to 1¼ in. long. *Bot. Mag.*, t. 7677.

Native of Burma, Siam, and China; discovered by Sir Henry Collet in 1888 on the Shan Hills. Henry found it also in Yunnan, China. The species is of great interest as the largest in size, leaf, flower, and fruit of all the honeysuckles. It is not hardy at Kew, but is grown in the Temperate House, where it climbs to the roof. Shy-flowering in its early years, it starts to flower when of full size if exposed to full sunshine. It is grown out-of-doors in several mild localities. It first blossomed in the British Isles at Glasnevin in August 1898, and it flowered at Kew the following June.

The specific epithet of this species is erroneously spelt *hildebrandtiana* in the *Index Kewensis*. It commemorates a Mr Hildebrand, superintendent of the Southern Shan states, who assisted Sir Henry Collet in his collecting, and not the German botanist Hildebrandt.

L. HIRSUTA Eaton

L. *pubescens* Sweet

A deciduous twiner, with glandular-downy, slender young shoots. Leaves oval, 2 to 3½ in. long, 1¼ to 2 in. wide, dark dull green above, grey beneath, downy on both sides especially beneath, ciliate, uppermost one or two pairs connate, pointed, lower ones stalked. Flowers orange-yellow, about 1 in. long, produced in several whorls on short-stalked spikes at the end of the shoot, and sometimes from the axils of the connate leaves beneath. Corolla two-lipped, the tube slender but slightly swollen towards the base, covered outside with sticky glandular down; hairy within. *Bot. Mag.*, t. 3103.

Native of N.E. America; introduced in 1822. It is now uncommon and *L. glaucescens* has been made to do duty for it in nurseries and gardens, but that species is not glandular on the branchlets or corolla, and its leaves are not downy above. It is one of the parents of *L.* × *brownii* (q.v.).

L. HISPIDA Roem. & Schult.

A deciduous shrub 3 to 5 ft high, with bristly young shoots. Leaves ovate-oblong, rounded or broadly tapered at the base, short-pointed or often blunt at the apex, 1½ to 2½ in. long, about half as wide, hairy on the margins, and more or less so on both surfaces; dark green above, greyish beneath; stalk ⅛ in. long. Flowers produced at the base of the young shoots at the end of May; corolla funnel-shaped, about 1 in. long, ⅝ in. wide at the mouth, yellow or yellowish white, the tube longer than the lobes. Each pair of flowers is subtended by two roundish ovate membranous bracts up to 1 in. long, edged with bristles; stalk ⅛ to ½ in. long, bristly.

Native of Turkestan; introduced early last century. Interesting on account of the large bracts.

var. BRACTEATA (Royle) Rehd. ex Airy Shaw *L. bracteata* Royle—Leaves oblong-lanceolate to oblong, apex drawn out, softly downy. Introduced by Kingdon Ward from S.E. Tibet in 1924. *Bot. Mag.*, t. 9360.

L. SETIFERA Franch.—This species, belonging to the same group as *L. hispida*, was introduced by Kingdon Ward from the Assam Himalaya in 1924 (KW 5688), and is also in cultivation in H. G. Hillier's collection at Jermyns House, Romsey, from seeds collected by Rock in China under field number 13520. Stems bristly. Leaves usually coarsely toothed, oblong-lanceolate, 1¾ to 3 in. long, downy on both sides. Flowers borne before the leaves. Corolla regular, straw-coloured or pinkish, bristly inside and out. Ovary glandular and bristly.

L. IBERICA Bieb.

A deciduous shrub of dense, bushy, rounded habit, up to 10 ft high and 12 ft through; young shoots hairy. Leaves mostly heart-shaped, sometimes roundish, the apex scarcely pointed, dark dull green above, grey beneath, both surfaces

LONICERA IBERICA

downy. On the vigorous barren shoots some of the leaves are 2 in. long and nearly as much wide; on the flowering branchlets they are mostly ½ to 1 in. long; stalk ⅛ to ⅓ in. long. Flowers produced in pairs from the end and upper leaf-axils of short shoots; corolla two-lipped, ¾ in. long and the same wide, pale yellow, not fragrant, downy outside, the tube curved and about as long as the slightly lobed limb. Bracts like the leaves but ovate, and ¼ to ½ in. long; flower-stalk very short.

Native of the Caucasus, Persia, etc.; introduced in 1824. A very robust shrub of neat habit, free-flowering without being showy. Botanically, it is distinguished by the bractlets coalescing into a cup-shaped organ enveloping the two ovaries, which, however, grow out of the cup and develop into bright red berries which are very attractive.

L. IMPLEXA Sol. MINORCA HONEYSUCKLE

An evergreen climber 8 ft or more high, with slender, purplish, usually glabrous young shoots. Leaves oval, ovate or oblong, stalkless, blunt or pointed, ¾ to 2 in. long, ⅓ to 1 in. wide, very glaucous beneath, glabrous. The upper pairs of leaves are united at the base so as to form a kind of cup-shaped bract, in the axils of which the stalkless flowers are produced in a whorl. Corolla 1½ to 2 in. long, yellow suffused with pink outside, white within, changing to yellow. *Bot. Mag.*, t. 640.

Native of the Mediterranean region; introduced in 1772. It is a pretty honeysuckle, but rather tender and slow-growing, and best with the shelter of a west wall. It flowers from June to August. It probably grows much higher in its native haunts.

L. JAPONICA Thunb.

Nintooa japonica (Thunb.) Sweet

An evergreen climber of vigorous habit, growing 20 to 30 ft high; stems hollow, twining, densely covered with spreading hairs when young, green or reddish purple. Leaves variable in shape, from elliptic to broad elliptic or ovate, rounded or truncate or cuneate at the base, apex acute or sometimes rounded and then narrowed abruptly to an acuminate tip, 1¼ to 3¼ in. long, margins ciliate, the blade varying in indumentum from downy or villous above and villous beneath (especially on the veins) to almost glabrous; although normally entire they are not infrequently lobed; leaf-stalk about ⅜ in. long. Flowers fragrant, produced from June onwards in pairs from the leaf-axils on peduncles ½ to ¾ in. long; bracts leaflike, ovate or elliptic, ½ to ¾ in. long. Corolla 1¼ to almost 2 in. long, hairy on the outside, white or purple-tinged, ageing to yellow; limb two-lipped, the upper lip varying from shorter to longer than the tube. Ovary glabrous. Fruits black, not united.

Native of Japan, China, and Korea; for date of introduction see under var. *repens*. It is a variable species and the above description is a generalised one. The plant (probably a cultivated one) from which Thunberg described the species, had flowers purple outside and leaves hairy beneath, but this typical variety is probably not in cultivation here, all the garden plants having the leaves quite or almost glabrous beneath when mature.

cv. 'AUREO-RETICULATA'.—Leaves mostly less than 2 in. long, sometimes pinnately lobed, the veins and midrib picked out in bright yellow. A very effective variegated plant in summer, but often killed back a good deal in winter. It flowers quite freely against a wall. Introduced by Fortune, shortly before 1862.

cv. 'HALLIANA'.—Flowers very fragrant, pure white, ageing to yellow; tube of corolla slightly longer than the upper lip. Leaves slightly hairy on the veins beneath at first, soon glabrous. A vigorous and almost hardy evergreen climber flowering from midsummer until early autumn. It was introduced by Dr George Hall to Parsons' nursery, Flushing, USA, in 1862, but did not reach Britain until the 1880s. It is the commonest representative of the species in gardens, and the most beautiful.

var. REPENS (Sieb.) Rehd. *L. brachypoda* var. *repens* Sieb.; *L. flexuosa* Thunb.; *L. japonica* var. *flexuosa* (Thunb.) Nichols.; *L. brachypoda* DC.; *L. chinensis* Wats.; *L. japonica* var. *chinensis* (Wats.) Baker—Leaves soon glabrous, often heavily tinged with purple beneath (if so, then the stems also reddish-purple). Flowers usually stained purple on the outside, the tube about equal in length to the upper lip or shorter. This variety, which only differs from the type in being less hairy, was introduced from China early in the 19th century in a form with a strong infusion of purple in the stems, leaf-undersides, and flowers, and with a tube of the corolla about equal to or slightly longer than the upper lip. *Bot. Mag.*, t. 3316. This may still be in cultivation, but a commercial plant, while agreeing with this in colouring, has a shorter corolla-tube.

In the eastern USA *L. japonica* has become 'a most pernicious and dangerous weed, overwhelming and strangling the native flora and most difficult to eradicate' (Gray's *Manual of Botany*, 8th ed., p. 1334).

L. CONFUSA DC.—This species is allied to *L. japonica* but is quite distinct in its awl-shaped bracts. Also the inflorescence-axes and ovaries are hairy and the undersurface of the leaves is covered with a close indumentum of short hairs. A native of S. China, naturalised in Jamaica; almost certainly tender. It was originally confused with *L. japonica* under which name it is figured in *Bot. Rep.*, t. 583, and *Bot. Reg.*, t. 70

L. KOROLKOWII Stapf

A deciduous shrub of loose, spreading, graceful habit, 6 to 10 ft high; branchlets hollow; young shoots very downy. Leaves ovate or oval, usually tapered at the base, pointed, ¾ to 1¼ in. long, ½ to ⅞ in. wide, pale glaucous green, downy on both surfaces, especially beneath; stalk up to ¼ in. long. Flowers produced in pairs from the leaf-axils of short lateral branchlets in June, pale rose-coloured. Corolla ⅔ in. long, two-lipped, the tube slender and about as long as the lobes, downy inside; flower-stalk ⅛ in. long, downy. Berries red.

Native of the mountains of Soviet Central Asia and of the bordering parts of Afghanistan and Pakistan; first cultivated by A. Lavallée, of Segrez, France, who received seeds from Col. Korolkow of Moscow, but first distinguished as a species in 1893 from a plant growing in the Arnold Arboretum, received from Lavallée. Its most striking character when in leaf is the pale grey hue of the whole plant. It is a beautiful and graceful shrub, but does not flower so freely in this country as on the continent and in the USA.

var. ZABELII (Rehd.) *L. zabelii* Rehd.—Leaves glabrous on both sides, rounded or slightly narrowed at the base. This should not be confused with the "*L. zabelii*" of the trade, which is a cultivar of *L. tatarica*.

L. LEDEBOURII Eschs.

L. *involucrata* var. *ledebourii* (Eschs.) Zab.

A deciduous shrub of sturdy, erect habit, up to 8 or 9 ft high, and as much through; young shoots stout, four-angled, soon glabrous. Leaves ovate-oblong, rounded or narrowed at the base, pointed, 2 to 4 in. long, 1 to 1¾ in. wide, dull dark green above, bright green and downy beneath, margins downy; stalk ¼ in. long. Flowers deep orange-yellow tinged with red, produced in pairs from the leaf axils in June, each pair on a downy stalk 1 to 1¾ in. long, and subtended by two large, reddish, heart-shaped bracts ⅝ in. wide, and two smaller ones; all glandular. These bracts grow after the flower is fertilised. Corolla downy outside, tubular, ⅝ to ¾ in. long, ³⁄₁₆ in. wide, with a curious sac at the base; the lobes rounded, erect; stamens not longer than the tube, glabrous or nearly so; style longer, also glabrous. Berries black. *Bot. Mag.*, t. 8555.

Native of California in coastal localities; introduced in 1838. A robust species very distinct from all others except *involucrata* (see below). In habit, foliage, and the long flower-stalk it has some resemblance to L. *alpigena*, but the short-tubed, two-lipped corolla with spreading lobes, and the tiny, linear bracts of that species are very different. L. *ledebourii* grows well close to the sea.

L. INVOLUCRATA (Richardson) Spreng. *Xylosteum involucratum* Richardson—L. *ledebourii* is included in this species by many botanists. According to Rehder it differs in the following particulars: smaller habit; leaves thinner, not so downy (sometimes glabrous); corollas yellow, with shorter stamens. Native of Mexico, western North America, S. Canada, and the region of the Great Lakes; introduced in 1824 (according to Loudon, the plants from this introduction grew 2 to 3 ft high). Flowers in May.

f. HUMILIS Koehne—A dwarf form, 1½ to 2 ft high. Leaves ovate or oblong-ovate.

f. SEROTINA Koehne—Differs mainly in its later flowering (July–August). Both these forms were probably introduced from Colorado by Purpus and distributed by Späth's nursery.

L. MAACKII (Rupr.) Maxim.

Xylosteum maackii Rupr.

A deciduous shrub 10 to 15 ft high, with wide-spreading branches, often arranged in a flat, distichous manner; young shoots downy. Leaves oval-lanceolate, with long, slender points, and tapered at the base, 1½ to 3 in. long, ½ to 1½ in. wide, dark green, downy on both surfaces; stalk ⅛ in. or less long. Flowers fragrant, pure white at first, turning yellowish with age, all produced in pairs on the upper side of the branchlets, where they form a dense row; peduncles very short. Corolla two-lipped, the tube ¼ in. long, the narrowly oblong, round-ended lobes ½ in. long, the two outer ones of the upper lip deeper than the middle ones; stamens about twice as long as the corolla-tube, downy at the base; style hairy. Flower-stalk about ⅛ in. long. Fruits dark red.

Introduced to St Petersburg, about 1880, from Manchuria; and from China by

Wilson in 1900. It is one of the most beautiful of bush honeysuckles, especially the Chinese form, which is distinguished as f. PODOCARPA Rehd. 'having the ovaries, together with the bractlets, on a short, stalk-like elongation above the bracts' (Rehder). This seems also to be of freer growth than the Manchurian form, and is remarkable for the abundance and purity of its blossom. *L. maackii* belongs to the same section of the genus as *L. xylosteum* and *L. morrowii*, from both of which it is distinguished by the very short flower-stalks and pure white corolla. It varies in the amount of down on the leaves, and is sometimes almost glabrous.

Of very much the same character as *L. maackii* is L. KOEHNEANA Rehd.; introduced from China by Wilson in 1908. It is a vigorous grower, with softly downy, often rather diamond-shaped leaves up to 3 or 4 in. long, and yellow flowers. From *L. maackii* it is at once distinguishable by the slender, much longer peduncles (up to 1 in. long).

L. MAXIMOWICZII (Rupr.) Maxim.

Xylosteum maximowiczii Rupr.

A deciduous shrub of erect habit up to 10 ft high; winter-buds as in *L. nigra*; young shoots glabrous or slightly bristly. Leaves oval, tapered or rounded at the base, pointed, $1\frac{1}{2}$ to 3 in. long on flowering shoots (up to $4\frac{1}{2}$ in. long on vigorous barren shoots) about half as wide, glabrous, dark green above, furnished more or less with pale down beneath. Flowers deep purplish rose, produced in pairs, each pair on a slender stalk up to 1 in. long. Corolla scarcely $\frac{1}{2}$ in. long, two-lipped, short-tubed, glabrous outside, hairy within; stamens hairy at the base, style hairy the whole length. Fruits ovoid, red, united.

Native of Amurland (Manchuria) and Korea; cultivated in this country since about 1878. The flowers are rather brightly coloured, but the species has no outstanding merit with us, although favourably mentioned in more sunny climates.

var. SACHALINENSIS Fr. Schmidt *L. sachalinensis* (Fr. Schmidt) Nakai— Leaves ovate, $1\frac{1}{2}$ to 3 in. long, $\frac{3}{4}$ to $1\frac{1}{2}$ in. wide, usually glabrous beneath. Flowers deep red. N. Japan, Sakhalin, Korea, and the Ussuri region.

L. MICROPHYLLA Roem. & Schult.

A deciduous shrub of stiff, sturdy habit, up to 3 ft high; branchlets short, glabrous. Leaves oval or obovate, $\frac{1}{2}$ to 1 in. long, $\frac{1}{4}$ to $\frac{1}{2}$ in. wide, dull grey-green, above, glaucous, finely downy, and with well-defined nerves beneath; stalk $\frac{1}{16}$ in. long. Flowers pale yellow, produced in pairs from the leaf-axils, on stalks $\frac{1}{4}$ in. long. Corolla two-lipped, scarcely $\frac{1}{2}$ in. long, the tube about as long as the lips. Berries bright red, united.

Native of the arid parts of the north-west Himalaya, Tibet, Siberia, etc.; introduced in 1818. It is suitable for the rock garden, where, however, its chief attraction would be it low, neat habit and grey aspect, for it bears flowers and fruits very sparingly in our climate.

L. MORROWII A. Gray

A vigorous, deciduous shrub 8 ft or more high, of loose, spreading habit; branchlets hollow; young shoots grey with down. Leaves oval or ovate, 1 to 2½ in. long, half as wide, rounded or tapering at the base, rounded or with a short slender point at the apex, downy and dull green above, greyish and woolly beneath; stalk ⅛ in. long. Flowers creamy white changing to yellow with age, produced in pairs from the middle or upper leaf-axils of short branchlets, in May and June. Corolla downy, two-lipped, with a slender tube ¼ in. long, the deep spoon-shaped lobes ½ in. long, spreading; style hairy; flower-stalk up to ⅗ in. long; bracts hairy on the margins. Fruits dark red, rarely yellow.

Native of Japan; allied to *L. xylosteum*, from which it differs in having a glabrous, not glandular, ovary. It is useful for furnishing semi-wild parts of the garden.

L. × BELLA Zab.—Hybrids between *L. morrowii* and *L. tatarica* raised in the Münden Botanic Garden from seeds of *L. morrowii* received from the St Petersburg Botanic Garden before 1889. They show the influence of *L. tatarica* in their more pointed almost glabrous leaves and larger mostly pink or red flowers. Several of the seedlings were given distinguishing names, including 'CANDIDA' with white flowers and 'ATROROSEA', in which the flowers are dark rose with a lighter edge.

L. MYRTILLUS Hook. f. & Thoms.

A deciduous shrub of dense, compact, rounded habit, 3 or 4 ft high; shoots downy when quite young. Leaves oval or ovate, ⅓ to 1 in. long, about ¼ in. wide, dark green above, rather glaucous beneath, glabrous on both surfaces, margins decurved. Flowers pinkish white, fragrant, borne in very shortly stalked pairs; corolla between tubular and bell-shaped, ¼ in. long, glabrous outside, hairy at the mouth inside; lobes equal, spreading; style much shorter than the tube, glabrous; bracts linear, ⅛ to ¼ in. long. Fruits orange-red, ¼ in. wide.

Native of the Himalaya and Afghanistan. It forms a neat, pleasing bush, but our climate is too dull for it to flower sufficiently freely to produce any effect. It is one of the bush honeysuckles which are distinguished by a very short style and a tubular, regularly lobed corolla, hairy at the mouth inside. From the others of this group here mentioned it is distinguished by its stiff branches and small leaves, and from all except *L. angustifolia* by the two-celled ovary. Blossoms in May.

var. DEPRESSA (Royle) Rehd. *L. depressa* Royle—Differs from the above only by the flower-stalks being twice as long, and the broader, oval bracts.

L. NERVOSA Maxim.

A deciduous shrub up to 8 ft high, with glabrous young shoots and leaves; winter-buds as in *L. nigra*. Leaves oval or inclined to oblong, abruptly pointed tapered to rounded at the base, ¾ to 2 in. long, ½ to 1 in. wide, reddish at first, turning bright green above, the midrib and veins remaining reddish; stalk $\frac{1}{8}$ to $\frac{1}{6}$ in. long. Flowers pale pink, $\frac{2}{5}$ in. long, produced in pairs on a slender stalk of the same length; the pairs are borne on short peduncles in the leaf-axils of very slender leafy shoots in May and June. Fruits black.

Native of China; discovered in Kansu by Przewalski in 1872; introduced from St Petersburg to Kew in 1892. It succeeds well in the Arnold Arboretum, Mass., where it is valued as a graceful bush honeysuckle with handsomely veined leaves and plentiful crops of black berries. The specific name refers to the reddish-veined leaves.

L. NIGRA L.

A deciduous shrub of stiff, rounded habit, 3 to 5 ft high; winter-buds pointed, four-angled, with several lanceolate scales. Leaves mostly oval, 1 to 2 in. long, downy along the midrib beneath, sometimes over the entire surface when quite young. Flowers produced in axillary pairs, each pair on a glabrous or slightly downy, slender stalk $\frac{3}{4}$ to over 1 in. long; corolla pink, about $\frac{1}{3}$ in. long and broad, two-lipped, the tube short and broad. Berries bluish black, united only at the base.

Native of the alpine regions of Middle and S. Europe; introduced in the 16th century, but of little value in gardens. Several forms, varying chiefly in the degree of pubescence on the leaves, flower-stalks, etc., have been distinguished, but are not of sufficient importance to be noticed here. It is best marked by its slender flower-stalks and black fruits.

L. NITIDA Wils.

L. *ligustrina* var. *yunnanensis* Franch.; L. *pileata* f. *yunnanensis* (Franch.) Rehd.

An evergreen shrub 5 to 12 ft high, of densely leafy habit; young shoots slender, erect, purplish, downy, and sparsely bristly. Leaves of stout texture, closely set on the shoot, ovate to roundish, heart-shaped at the base, blunt at the apex, $\frac{1}{4}$ to $\frac{5}{8}$ in. long, dark and glossy above, pale beneath, glabrous except for a few minute bristles which ultimately fall away; stalk $\frac{1}{20}$ in. long, minutely bristly. Flowers produced in axillary, short-stalked pairs, creamy white, fragrant; corolla $\frac{1}{4}$ in. long. Fruits globular, blue-purple, about $\frac{1}{4}$ in. across, transparent. *Bot. Mag.*, t. 9352.

Native of W. Szechwan and Yunnan, China, at altitudes of 4,500 to 7,000 ft; introduced by Wilson in 1908. Seeds were also sent by Forrest from Yunnan, but the plants from this introduction were at first grown as L. *ligustrina* var. *yunnanensis* or L. *pileata* var. *yunnanensis* or even as "L. *yunnanensis*"—the name of a quite different species (q.v.). For the following account of the garden selections of L. *nitida* we are indebted to the article by Dr P. F. Yeo in *Baileya*, Vol. 12, pp. 56–66, and to the descriptions by G. Krüssmann in *Handbuch der Laubgehölze*.

cv. 'ELEGANT'.—Krüssmann (op. cit., Vol. 2, p. 81) proposes this name for the plants distributed by German nurseries under the name "L. *pileata yunnanensis*" and remarks that this clone is quite distinct from the plants offered by

British nurseries under the same name (see 'Yunnan'). According to Krüssmann this shrub grows to about 3 ft high, with horizontal or slightly pendulous branches. Leaves mat green, about $\frac{3}{8}$ in. long, ovate to roundish ovate, blunt at the apex. Yeo suggests this may be a hybrid between L. *nitida* and L. *pileata*.

cv. 'ERNEST WILSON'.—This is the clone of L. *nitida*, probably raised from Wilson 833, that was once widely used as a hedging plant and is still very common. It is inferior to 'Yunnan' for that purpose and began to give way to it shortly before the second world war. Lateral branches drooping. Leaves bright glossy green, mostly lanceolate-ovate or triangular-ovate, less than $\frac{1}{2}$ in. long.

cv. 'FERTILIS'.—Stems arching or erect; lateral branchlets mostly long and arching with rather distant, widely spreading ovate to lanceolate dark green leaves up to slightly more than $\frac{1}{2}$ in. long. It flowers and fruits well and the flowers are slightly scented. Distributed by Messrs Hillier, who received it around 1927 under the name L. *ligustrina* var. *yunnanensis*. It is distinct in its dark green leaves and further differs from 'Ernest Wilson' and 'Yunnan' in the leaves being somewhat larger and slightly tapered to the base.

cv. 'GRAZIOSA'.—A dense, spreading shrub with rather small leaves. It is a seedling of the "L. *pileata* var. *yunnanensis*" of German nurseries (see 'Elegant') raised by the nurseryman Jürgl of Sürth near Cologne (Krüssmann, op. cit., p. 81).

cv. 'YUNNAN'.—This resembles 'Ernest Wilson' but the lateral branchlets are shorter and mostly erect and the slightly larger leaves are usually not arranged in two ranks. It also flowers more freely. 'Yunnan' was distributed before 1939 by R. Tucker and Sons of Farringdon who received plants from the Brookside nurseries, and became widely distributed under the name L. *pileata yunnanensis*. It makes a stiffer hedge than 'Ernest Wilson' (i.e. the old L. *nitida*).

In addition to the above green-leaved selections there is also a variety with golden leaves—'BAGGESEN'S GOLD'. It is of low, spreading habit and was raised by J. H. Baggesen of Pembury, Kent.

L. PERICLYMENUM L.   WOODBINE, HONEYSUCKLE

A twining shrub scrambling in the wild over bushes and hedgerows; stems often over 20 ft long, hollow when young, downy or glabrous. Leaves ovate, oval, or obovate, more or less tapered at the base, mostly pointed, sometimes blunt, $1\frac{1}{2}$ to $2\frac{1}{2}$ in. long. 1 to $1\frac{1}{2}$ in. wide, green above, rather glaucous beneath, slightly downy or glabrous, lower pairs of leaves stalked, uppermost ones almost or quite stalkless, but never united as in L. *caprifolium*. Flowers yellowish white and red in varying proportions, produced in a series of close whorls at the end of the shoot, forming a terminal stalked inflorescence. Corolla $1\frac{1}{2}$ to 2 in. long, two-lipped, the tube slender, tapering, glandular-downy outside. Berries red.

The common woodbine, best known of British species, reaches eastward to Asia Minor, the Caucasus, and W. Asia. No wild plant adds more to the charm of our hedgerows and thickets in July and August than this, especially in the cool dewy morning or evening when the fragrance of its blossoms is richest. Of several varieties, the following are the most noteworthy:

cv. 'BELGICA'. DUTCH HONEYSUCKLE.—Of more bushy habit; stems purplish and, like the leaves, glabrous. Flowers purplish red outside, fading to yellowish; yellow within. This honeysuckle probably originated in the Low Countries, and has been cultivated in Britain since the 17th century (*Periclymenum germanicum* Mill.; *L. periclymenum* var. *belgica* Ait.).

f. QUERCINA (West.) Rehd.—Leaves lobed after the fashion of those of the common oak. Occasionally found in the wild and first recorded in Britain in the 17th century.

LONICERA PERICLYMENUM 'BELGICA

cv. 'SEROTINA'.—The plant known to Philip Miller as the Flemish or Late Red honeysuckle bore its flowers late in the summer in 'close bunches' over a period of not much more than a fortnight, during which time they made a finer display than the Dutch variety (*Gard. Dict.*, abridged edition, Vol. 1 (1741)). He called it 'Caprifolium Germanicum, flore rubello, serotinum' (*Caprifolium* being an old generic name, used for the common woodbine as well as for *L. caprifolium*). The honeysuckle known at the present time as 'Serotina' has the flowers dark purple outside, becoming paler with age, and flowers over a long period in summer. It is, in other words, long- rather than late-flowering, and indeed it has also been known as *L. periclymenum semperflorens*. It is very doubtful whether this is really the true 'Serotina'. It is possibly the same as Miller's 'long blowing' form of the Dutch honeysuckle, which Weston listed as a variety distinct from the Dutch and the late-flowering sort, under the name *Lonicera-Periclymenum longiflorens* (*Flora Anglicana* (1775), p. 21).

L. PILEATA Oliver

An evergreen or partially deciduous shrub of low, spreading, neat habit; branches often horizontal; young shoots purple, very downy. Leaves box-like, ovate-oblong or somewhat lozenge-shaped, tapered at the base, blunt or rounded at the apex, $\frac{1}{2}$ to $1\frac{1}{4}$ in. long, $\frac{1}{8}$ to $\frac{1}{2}$ in. wide, dark lustrous green, nearly glabrous on both surfaces, scarcely stalked. Flowers yellowish white, produced in May in very short-stalked pairs; corolla-tube downy outside, $\frac{1}{4}$ in. long; stamens hairy, one and a half times the length of the corolla. The fruit is a translucent amethyst colour, $\frac{1}{5}$ in. wide, and is invested at the top by a curious outgrowth from the calyx. *Bot. Mag.*, t. 8060.

Native of China; discovered by Henry, and introduced for Messrs Veitch by Wilson in 1900. Although it has but little flower beauty, and is very shy in bearing fruit, its neat habit and dark shining foliage are pleasing. The pairs of leaves are often only from $\frac{1}{4}$ to $\frac{1}{2}$ in. apart on the shoot. Young plants are more inclined to be evergreen than older ones. It thrives well by the sea.

L. PROLIFERA (Kirchn.) Rehd.

Caprifolium proliferum Kirchn.; *L. sullivantii* A. Gray

A deciduous spreading shrub, with stems up to 6 ft long, lax, but scarcely climbing. Leaves oval, obovate or oblong, 2 to 4 in. long, $1\frac{1}{4}$ to $2\frac{1}{2}$ in. wide, glaucous and slightly downy beneath, more glaucous on the upper side, one or more of the upper pairs are united at the base, and form a roundish disk clasping the stem; of thickish substance. Flowers yellow, not fragrant, produced in June at the end of the current season's growth in a terminal stalked spike, composed of two or more whorls, sometimes branched at the base. Corolla two-lipped, about 1 in. long, the tube longer than the lips, slender, slightly swollen on one side; glabrous outside; style slightly hairy. Berries reddish yellow, $\frac{1}{4}$ to $\frac{1}{2}$ in. diameter.

Native of central N. America; long grown in gardens—in early times as "*L. flava*", which is a rarer and more beautiful shrub than *L. prolifera*. The latter is closer to *L. dioica*, a species distinguished by its shorter corolla, the tube of which is about as long as the lips, the leaves and style quite glabrous. *L. prolifera* does not need a support except when quite young and may be grown in the open as an elegant, loose bush.

L. PROSTRATA Rehd.

A deciduous bush of low, rounded habit, forming a hemispherical mass of slender hollow branches; young shoots slightly hairy and purplish. Leaves oval or ovate, tapered at both ends, but more abruptly at the base; $\frac{3}{4}$ to $1\frac{1}{4}$ in. long, $\frac{1}{4}$ to $\frac{1}{2}$ in. wide, ciliate, upper surface downy at first, becoming glabrous, midrib and chief veins sparsely downy beneath; leaf-stalk hairy, $\frac{1}{10}$ in. long. Flowers pale yellow, not fragrant, borne in pairs from the leaf-axils on slightly downy stalks, $\frac{1}{4}$ in. long; corolla $\frac{2}{3}$ in. long, two-lipped, the tube not so long as the lips, hairy within and without; stamens and style hairy at the base; bracts linear, hairy,

$\frac{1}{6}$ in. long; bractlets rounded, ciliate. Berries distinct egg-shaped, reddish, $\frac{1}{4}$ to $\frac{1}{3}$ in. long.

Native of W. China; discovered and introduced by Wilson about 1904. It is not of any special beauty in flower, but its prostrate habit is distinct, and will make it useful for ground cover. It used to thrive in the Coombe Wood nursery, where it flowered about the beginning of June. Akin to *L. trichosantha.*

L. PURPURASCENS Walp.

A sturdy bush 5 to 8 ft high; young shoots stiff, purplish, covered with a soft. fine down. Leaves oblong or somewhat obovate, tapered or bluntish at the apex, rounded or tapered at the base, 1 to 2 in. long, $\frac{1}{2}$ to 1 in. wide, dull green above, grey beneath, downy on both surfaces but especially beneath; stalk $\frac{1}{6}$ to $\frac{1}{4}$ in, long, downy, purplish. Flowers in pairs from the leaf-axils on a slender downy stalk, $\frac{1}{3}$ in. or more long. Corolla $\frac{3}{5}$ in. long, with five short nearly equal lobes, which are purple; the tube paler, hairy, funnel-shaped, and protruded at the base; bracts awl-shaped. Berries more or less united, blue-black.

Native of the Himalaya up to altitudes of 13,000 ft, and very hardy; introduced to Kew in 1884. A neat bush with a purplish cast, but of little merit.

L. × PURPUSII Rehd.

A deciduous shrub of dense, rounded habit, up to 10 ft high, more in diameter; young stems glabrous or almost so. Leaves ovate to oval, 2 to $3\frac{1}{2}$ in. long, 1 to $1\frac{3}{4}$ in. wide, pointed, broadly tapered to rounded at the base, glabrous above, slightly hairy on the midrib and veins beneath, margins bristly. Flowers white, fragrant, in axillary clusters of two to four; corolla $\frac{5}{8}$ in. long, $\frac{1}{2}$ in. wide, the short rounded lobes reflexed; stamens glistening white, anthers bright yellow, conspicuously exposed. *Bot. Mag.*, n.s., t. 323.

A hybrid between *L. fragrantissima* and *L. standishii.* Flowering like them early in February, it makes an attractive addition to early flowering shrubs.

This hybrid resembles *L. fragrantissima* in having the branchlets almost glabrous and the corollas glabrous on the outside; but the leaves are edged with bristly hairs as in *L. standishii.*

L. PYRENAICA L.

A deciduous shrub 2 to 5 ft high, branches erect; free from down in all its parts. Leaves obovate to oblanceolate, tapered to a stalkless base, abruptly pointed, $\frac{3}{4}$ to $1\frac{1}{4}$ in. long, $\frac{1}{4}$ to $\frac{3}{8}$ in. wide, glaucous, especially beneath. Flowers produced during May and June in pairs from the terminal leaf-axils of short branchlets or the lower leaf-axils of stronger ones, each pair subtended by two rather sickle-shaped bracts $\frac{1}{4}$ in. long, and borne on a stalk $\frac{1}{4}$ to $\frac{1}{2}$ in. long. Corolla rosy-tinted white, $\frac{5}{8}$ in. in diameter; the tube scarcely as much long, swollen on one side at the base; the lobes roundish ovate, spreading. Berries red, globose, $\frac{1}{4}$ in. diameter; each pair united only at the base. *Bot. Mag.*, t. 7774.

Native of the eastern Pyrenees and the Balearic Isles; introduced, according to Aiton, in 1739. A very pretty shrub, perhaps the most pleasing in flower of all the dwarf bush honeysuckles. There is a specimen about 5 ft high at Kew on the wall of the North Gallery.

L. *pyrenaica* received an Award of Merit on 22 May 1928, when shown by Messrs Marchant.

LONICERA PYRENAICA

L. QUINQUELOCULARIS Hardwicke
L. *diversifolia* Wall.

A large deciduous shrub 12 to 15 ft high in cultivation, said to be sometimes a small tree where wild; young shoots purplish, very downy. Leaves oval, sometimes inclined to obovate and orbicular, rounded or tapered at the base, mostly short-pointed, but sometimes rounded at the apex, 1 to 2½ in. long, ⅝ to 1½ in. wide, dull green and at first downy above, greyish and more downy beneath. Flowers creamy white changing to yellow, arranged in pairs, produced on a stalk $\frac{1}{12}$ in. long from the leaf-axils in June. Corolla two lipped, ¾ in. across; the upper lip round-toothed; tube ¼ in. long, bellied; stamens about as long as the upper lip, downy at the base. Berries translucent white, round to oval.

Native of the Himalaya and China; long cultivated at Kew. It is a robust and, when in flower, rather handsome shrub, flowering more freely than the majority of bush honeysuckles do with us. It is very distinct on account of its white transparent fruits, which distinguish it from L. *deflexicalyx*, *maackii*, *xylosteum*, and other of its immediate allies.

f. TRANSLUCENS (Carr.) Zab. L. *translucens* Carr.—Leaves longer pointed; more markedly ciliate, and the upper surface rougher than in L. *quinquelocularis* the corolla-tube also is shorter and more protuberant on one side. A sturdy bush 10 ft high, that flowers freely. The epithet '*translucens*', implying as it does that this form has the fruits more transparent than in the type, is misleading. There is no difference between them in this respect.

L. RUPICOLA Hook. f. & Thoms.

A very dense bush forming a rounded mass of interlacing branches 6 to 8 ft high; branchlets slightly downy or glabrous when young; bark peeling off in thin strips the second year. Leaves often in threes, oblong or ovate, rounded or slightly heart-shaped at the base, blunt at the apex, ½ to 1 in. long, about half as wide; dull green and glabrous above, paler and downy beneath, often becoming glabrous; stalk ⅛ in. or less long. Flowers produced in May and June in pairs from the shoots of the current year, often six at one joint, fragrant; corolla pale pink, ½ in. across, the tube ¼ in. long, downy on both sides; lobes rounded-ovate, equal. Calyx-lobes narrow-oblong, downy; style and flower-stalk very short.

Native of the Himalaya; long cultivated at Kew. It is closely allied to L. *thibetica*, but is distinguished by the dull green, blunt-ended leaves not being white-felted beneath. These two species differ from all other cultivated honeysuckles in their globose shape and impenetrable mass of branches. It is an interesting species, but does not blossom freely.

L. RUPRECHTIANA Reg.

A deciduous shrub forming a shapely bush 8 to 10 ft high, branchlets hollow; young shoots downy. Leaves ovate to oblong, pointed (often slenderly so), tapered at the base; 1½ to 4 in. long, ⅝ to 1½ in. wide, dark green and downy only on the sunken midrib above, paler and downy beneath; stalk ¼ in. or less long. Flowers not fragrant, produced during May and June in pairs, each pair on a slender downy stalk ½ to ¾ in. long, borne in the leaf-axils; corolla white at first, changing to yellow, ¾ in. long, glabrous on the outside. Stamens and style hairy. Fruits bright red, ⅓ in. wide, rather transparent.

Native of N.E. Asia; introduced to Kew from St Petersburg in 1880. According to Maximowicz, who discovered it, it is sometimes 20 ft high. As a flowering shrub it is pretty, although in no way outstanding amongst the bush honeysuckles. But as I saw it in the Arnold Arboretum in June 1910, laden with its scarlet fruit, it struck me as one of the best in the fine collection then in full fruit-bearing there. It is very hardy, but is subject to injury with us by late spring frosts.

var. CALVESCENS Rehd.—Leaves shorter and comparatively broader, slightly downy on the veins beneath. Fruits dull red.

cv. 'XANTHOCARPA'.—Fruits yellow; flowers smaller. Raised in the Münden Botanic Garden, Germany.

L. × NOTHA Zab.—A group of hybrids between L. *ruprechtiana* and L. *tatarica*, raised in the Münden Botanic Garden from seeds of the former species received from the St Petersburg Botanic Garden around 1878. They resemble the seed-parent but have the flowers in shades of pink, turning yellow later. The most attractive are 'GRANDIFLORA' with large rose-tinted flowers and 'CARNEO-

ROSEA' with the deepest rose-coloured ones. These are among the best of the numerous hybrid bush-honeysuckles.

L. SEMPERVIRENS L.   TRUMPET HONEYSUCKLE

[PLATE 83

A vigorous, climbing shrub, evergreen in mild localities; young shoots glabrous, glaucous. Leaves oval or somewhat obovate, 1½ to 2¾ in. long, ¾ to 2 in. wide, rich green and glabrous above, bluish and slightly downy beneath; stalk ¼ in. or less long. One or two of the uppermost pairs of leaves are united and form a circular or oblong disk. Flowers unscented, rich orange scarlet outside, yellower within, 1½ to 2 in. long, produced in three or four whorls (each whorl of usually six flowers), forming a terminal stalked spike. Corolla-tube slender, slightly swollen near the base; the four upper lobes are smaller than the lower one, but the corolla is not markedly two-lipped; style glabrous. *Bot. Mag.*, t. 781.

Native of the eastern and southern United States, reaching as far north as Connecticut and westwards to Texas; introduced in 1656. This beautiful honeysuckle thrives best in the milder parts but is hardier than was once supposed and should succeed with the protection of a wall over much of the British Isles. It received an Award of Merit in 1964.

L. sempervirens is a parent of *L.* × *brownii* and *L.* × *heckrottii*.

cv. 'MAGNIFICA'.—Said to have bright red flowers.

var. MINOR Ait.—Described by Aiton in 1789 as a variety with oblong leaves. The plant discussed and figured under this name in *Bot. Mag.*, t. 1753 (1815) was from a reintroduction by Frasers' nursery of Sloane Square, London. It was said to have come from Carolina and to be more delicate, with slenderer flowers, than the plants from Virginia. Philip Miller also made a distinction between the Carolina and Virginia forms: 'The old sort, which came from Virginia, has stronger shoots; the leaves are of a brighter green; the bunches of flowers are larger, and deeper coloured, than the other which came from Carolina' (*Gard. Dict.*, 1768). The distinction seems to have some basis, in that plants answering to the description of var. *minor* have a more southerly distribution than the type, and might be expected to be more tender.

cv. 'SUPERBA'.—Leaves broadly oval. Corollas orange-scarlet on the outside (*Gartenfl.* (1853), p. 3).

f. SULPHUREA (Jacques) Rehd.—Corollas yellow on the outside. Occasional in the wild state.

L. SIMILIS Hemsl.

This species is probably not in cultivation in its typical state, but the following variety has been introduced:

var. DELAVAYI (Franch.) Rehd. *L. delavayi* Franch.—This variety was sent to Kew in 1907 from France by Maurice de Vilmorin, who had received it from W. China in 1901, and with whom it first flowered three years later. It is an evergreen climber of the *L. japonica* group. Its leaves are ovate-lanceolate, rounded or slightly heart-shaped at the base, taper-pointed, 2 to 5 in. long, ¾ to 2 in. wide, glabrous above, grey felted beneath; stalk ⅛ to ¼ in. long. Flowers sweet-scented, in axillary pairs, and at the end of the shoot forming a kind of panicle. The corolla is pale yellow, and has a very slender cylindrical tube 2 in. long, and a two-lipped apex; the larger lip ¾ in. long, with four short lobes, the smaller one linear; calyx-lobes awl-shaped, edged with hairs. It was originally discovered in Yunnan by the Abbé Delavay, in 1888. It flowers in August. *Bot. Mag.*, t. 8800.

L. SPLENDIDA Boiss.

A vigorous evergreen climber allied to *L. periclymenum* and *L. etrusca*, making growths up to 6 ft or more long in a single season. Leaves on the flowering shoots oval to oblong, 1 to 1½ in. long, glabrous and glaucous, all sessile and the upper pairs connate; leaves on the extension growths smaller and stalked. Inflorescences glandular, sessile, with three to five whorls of flowers. Corolla 1 to 1½ in. long, reddish purple and glandular on the outside, yellowish white within. Flowering season June to August. *Bot. Mag.*, t. 9517.

Native of Spain; introduced about 1880. It differs from the common woodbine in having the upper pairs of leaves connate; from *L. etrusca* in having the flowers in a terminal stalkless spike, springing directly from the uppermost pair of leaves; and from both in its glaucous leaves and glandular inflorescences. This beautiful plant, which fully deserves its specific epithet, is not common in gardens but is hardy on a south-facing wall. There is a fine specimen in the National Trust garden at Sissinghurst in Kent.

L. STANDISHII Jacques

A deciduous or partially evergreen bush 6 or 8 ft high in the open, 12 ft or more against a wall; the bark of the stem and older branches peeling; young shoots warted and bristly. Leaves oblong-lanceolate, 2 to 4½ in. long, ¾ to 2 in. wide, rounded or broadly wedge-shaped at the base, slenderly pointed, prominently veined beneath, bristly on the margins and on both sides of the midrib, also more or less over the surface; stalk bristly, ⅛ in. long. Flowers produced from November to March (according to the mildness of the season), often in two pairs at each joint; flower-stalk has downward pointing bristles. The flowers are creamy white, very fragrant, about ½ in. wide, the tube of the corolla bristly outside. Fruits ripe in early June, red, the two ovaries united nearly to the top and forming an inversely heart-shaped berry; stalk ½ in. long, bristly. *Bot. Mag.*, t. 5709.

Native of China; introduced by Fortune in 1845. It is in no way showy, but has always been a favourite because of the early date at which it flowers and for its charming fragrance. Although the first flowers come as early as November, it is usually at its best in February. It is perfectly hardy, and is only grown on walls for the sake of protection for its early flowers.

var. LANCIFOLIA Rehd.—Leaves narrowly lanceolate, usually under 1 in. in width. Introduced by Wilson in 1908, from W. China.

L. SYRINGANTHA Maxim.

A deciduous shrub of graceful, spreading habit, up to 6 ft high; young shoots slender, quite glabrous. Leaves in pairs or threes, oblong or inclined to ovate, the base rounded or slightly heart-shaped, the apex bluntish or broad-pointed, ½ to 1 in. long, ⅜ to ⅝ in. wide, dull rather glaucous green, quite glabrous; stalk 1/12 in. long. Flowers in axillary pairs, produced on a slender stalk ¼ in. long during May and June from the lower and middle joints of the young shoots, soft lilac in colour, lilac-scented. Corolla-tube ½ in. long, slender, cylindrical, glabrous outside, hairy within; the flower is ½ in. across the rounded-ovate lobes. Calyx-lobes lance-shaped, glabrous. Style quite short. Fruits red. *Bot. Mag.*, t. 7989.

Native of China and Tibet; introduced about 1890. A very elegant and pleasing shrub, with delicately coloured and charmingly fragrant flowers, which are not always abundantly borne. It is allied to L. *thibetica* and L. *tomentella*, differing in the quite glabrous leaves.

var. WOLFII Rehd.—Of lower, more spreading habit. Leaves longer and relatively narrower; calyx-teeth ciliate, connate at the base; flowers deeper pink. Described from a plant introduced from Central China by the nursery firm of Kesselring and Regel, late in the 19th century. Some of the plants grown under this name in British gardens scarcely differ from typical L. *syringantha*.

L. TANGUTICA Maxim.

A deciduous spreading bush 4 to 6 ft high, with slender, usually glabrous twigs. Leaves obovate, more gradually tapered towards the base than towards the bluntish apex, ½ to 1½ in. long, ¼ to ¾ in. wide, sprinkled with appressed hairs on both surfaces and on the margins; stalk 1/12 to ⅛ in. long. Flowers twin, yellowish white tinged with pink, about ½ in. long, each pair pendulous from the leaf-axils on a very slender stalk ½ to 1½ in. long; corolla tubular, bellied at the base, glabrous, with almost equal lobes, produced in May and June. Fruits scarlet, united for about half their length.

Native of W. China and S.E. Tibet, discovered by Przewalski in Kansu in 1872. It was introduced in 1890 and later became more common through seeds sent home by Farrer from Kansu. It is distinct on account of its small obovate leaves and the long stalk on which each pair of flowers is borne. It is also one of the most beautiful in its pendulous scarlet fruits. Wilson's specimens from Hupeh and Szechwan have leaves that are larger (up to 2½ in. long) and proportionately narrower than those from Kansu. Forrest's No. 19027 from Tsarong (S.E. Tibet) has downy shoots and some Delavay specimens collected in Yunnan resemble it in this respect.

L. TATARICA L.

A deciduous shrub of vigorous growth and bushy habit, 8 to 10 ft high; branchlets hollow; young shoots glabrous. Leaves oblong-ovate, slightly heart-shaped or rounded at the base, pointed; on vigorous growths they are 1½ to 2½ in. long, 1 to 1½ in. wide; on the flowering branches less than half the size;

green above, rather glaucous beneath, glabrous; stalk ⅛ in. long. Flowers white or pinkish, borne in pairs on a slender stalk, ½ to 1 in. long; corolla two-lipped, glabrous outside, hairy within, ¾ to 1 in. long; tube much shorter than the reflexed oblong lobes. Berries globose, red. *Bot. Mag.*, c. 8677.

In the wild this species reaches from Central Asia to S. Russia. It was introduced in 1752, and is so perfectly adapted to our conditions that it is now the commonest of bush honeysuckles, running semi-wild in some gardens. It is a variable plant so far as the colour of the flowers is concerned, and only the best red forms should be selected. They are often very showy at flowering time, which is May and early June. Many of these red-flowered forms were raised and named in France during the 19th century (*Rev. Hort.*, 1868, pp. 392–3). Modern selections are 'HACK'S RED', raised in Canada, with flowers of a deep purplish red; 'ZABELII', with flowers near Ruby Red; and 'ARNOLD RED', raised at the Arnold Arboretum, said to have even deeper coloured flowers.

L. *tatarica* f. *sibirica* (Pers.) Rehd. is simply a collective name for plants differing from the typical state in having red flowers, and is not a geographical variety. Persoon's original description reads simply 'fl. rubris' (*Syn. Pl.* (1805), Vol. 1, p. 213).

Yellow-fruited forms are known (f. LUTEA (Loud.) Rehd.).

L. TATSIENENSIS Franch.

A deciduous shrub up to 8 ft high; young shoots glabrous. Leaves oval, slightly obovate, or oblong-lanceolate, pointed, wedge-shaped to rounded at the base, entire or wavy margined on flowering shoots, often (by no means always) deeply lobed on virgin shoots, 1 to 2½ in. long, ⅝ to 1 in. wide, sometimes with scattered hairs on both surfaces, sometimes glabrous; stalk ⅛ to ⅓ in. long. Flowers ½ in. long, borne in a pair at the end of slender stalks 1 to 1½ in. long; corolla dark purple, short-tubed; stamens downy at the base. Fruits red, each pair ¾ in. wide. Flowers in May.

Native of Szechwan, China; originally discovered by Père Faurie in the environs of Tatsien-lu; introduced by Wilson in 1910. Like some forms of L. *japonica* and L. *griffithii* (both climbers and very different in other respects) this species is well marked by its frequently deeply lobed leaves. Combined with its large red fruits and purple flowers, this character makes it distinct.

L. × TELLMANNIANA Spaeth

This is a hybrid between L. *tragophylla* and L. *sempervirens* 'Superba' raised in the Royal Hungarian Horticultural School, Budapest, from which institution it was acquired and, in 1927, put into commerce by Messrs Späth of Berlin. It was first seen in flower in London on 16 June 1931, when Sir William Lawrence showed it at Westminster from his garden at Burford, near Dorking. It was then given an Award of Merit. It is one of the most successful results in the hybridisation of honeysuckles that has been achieved, uniting in itself as it does perhaps the showiest of Chinese species and not far from the most beautiful of American ones. It is a deciduous climber with elliptical-ovate leaves 2 to 3½ in. long, the upper pair united by their bases and forming a collar round the stem. The slender-tubed flowers are borne in terminal heads of six to twelve, each bloom about 2 in. long and measuring about 1 in. across the two lips of the corolla, which is of a beautiful yellow, flushed in the bud state and at the tips with bronzy red. In habit it is luxuriant and is hardy, a quality it inherits from *L. tragophylla*. Like all this class of honeysuckle, it likes a good soil and prefers to have its roots and lower branches in the shade.

L. THIBETICA Bur. & Franch.

A deciduous shrub of low, spreading habit when young, forming in the adult state a dense rounded mass of intertwined branches 6 ft high and 10 ft or more through; young shoots purplish, downy, the bark peeling in thin strips

LONICERA THIBETICA

the second year. Leaves often in threes, narrowly oblong, rounded at the base, pointed, ⅓ to 1 in. long, ⅛ to ⅓ in. wide, dark glossy green and glabrous above, covered with a dense white felt beneath; stalk 1/12 in. or less in length. Flowers produced in pairs during May and June from the leaf-axils of the young shoots, often six flowers at each joint, fragrant, ⅓ in. across, lilac-coloured and perfumed like lilac. Corolla-tube ½ in. long, downy within and without; lobes equal, roundish ovate. Calyx-lobes awl-shaped, downy, as long as the style. Berries red, oblong, ¼ in. long.

T S—X

Native of W. China; introduced in 1897. A very pretty and distinct honey-suckle, allied to *L. rupicola*, but easily distinguished by the white-felted under-surface of the leaves, and deeper coloured smaller flowers.

L. syringantha is another close ally, but has leaves quite glabrous beneath and the corolla glabrous on the outside.

L. TOMENTELLA Hook. f. & Thoms.

A deciduous shrub of erect habit, 6 to 10 ft high; branchlets woolly, outer bark splitting and becoming detached the second season. Leaves in pairs, ovate, sometimes inclined to oblong, ¾ to 1½ in. long, ¼ to ⅜ in. wide, rounded or slightly heart-shaped at the base, bluntish or broad-pointed at the apex, dull green and sparsely downy above, grey-woolly beneath; stalk ¹⁄₁₆ in. long. Flowers produced towards the end of June, pendulous, in pairs from the leaf-axils of the young shoots, white with a pinkish tinge. Corolla about ½ in. long, downy; calyx-lobes ovate, very short, pink-tipped; style as long as the corolla-tube. Berries blue-black. *Bot. Mag.*, t. 6486.

Native of Sikkim; introduced by Sir Joseph Hooker in 1849. This species has some affinity with and resemblance to *L. rupicola*, but is more erect; the leaves are in pairs, the style is longer, the calyx-lobes shorter, and the fruits black. The long style and black fruits also serve to distinguish this species from *L. thibetica*.

L. TRAGOPHYLLA Hemsl. [PLATE 85

A deciduous climbing shrub, with glabrous young shoots. Leaves oval, tapering about equally to both ends, 2 to 4½ in. long, ¾ to 2 in. wide, slightly glaucous above, glaucous and slightly downy beneath. The uppermost pair of leaves are wholly united by their bases forming a diamond shape, the next pair lower down is less united, but still clasp the stem, still lower down come short-stalked leaves. Flowers bright yellow, produced in a terminal head of ten to twenty. Corolla-tube 2½ to 3½ in. long, slenderly cylindrical, glabrous outside, downy within; across the two lips the corolla measures 1 in. or more in width. Berries red. *Bot. Mag.*, t. 8064.

Native of the province of Hupeh, China; discovered by Henry and introduced for Messrs Veitch by Wilson in 1900. It flowered for the first time at Coombe Wood in July 1905. *L. caprifolium* is closely related, but differs in its whorled flowers and in the glabrous interior of the corolla-tube.

L. tragophylla is the largest-flowered and most showy of the climbing honey-suckles. Wilson, from his knowledge of the wild plants, recommended it for a semi-shaped position, but in British gardens it is no more shade-loving than the others of its group and is happiest in a good garden soil on a trellis or pergola, placed where its roots and stems are shielded from the hottest sun. It will then make a bushy self-supporting crown, and the leaves will be coloured bronze or bronzy purple until flowering time, when it makes a display equalled by few temperate climbing plants. It would be a pity to reject this beautiful species merely because the flowers are not scented.

L. TRICHOSANTHA Bur. & Franch.
L. ovalis Batal.

A deciduous bush, of vigorous growth and rounded, dense, leafy habit, probably 8 ft or more high, the whole plant with a pale greyish aspect; young shoots at first downy, becoming glabrous later in the season. Leaves oval, often inclined to obovate, rounded or broadly wedge-shaped at the base and short pointed or rounded at the apex, 1 to 2 in. long, ½ to 1¼ in. wide, dull grey-green above, paler beneath, both sides at first downy becoming almost glabrous, especially above; stalk ⅛ to ¼ in. long. Flowers pale yellow, fading to a deeper shade; corolla ½ to ¾ in. long, hairy outside, swollen at the base. Calyx bell-shaped, but split into two parts. Berries dark red.

Native of Szechwan, China; discovered by the Russian traveller Potanin. Introduced in quantity by Wilson about 1908. A robust species of the same class as *L. deflexicalyx* and *L. quinquelocularis*.

L. XYLOSTEUM L.   FLY HONEYSUCKLE

A deciduous shrub up to 10 ft high, more in diameter, very bushy; branchlets hollow; young shoots downy. Leaves oval or obovate, rounded or broadly tapered at the base, mostly with a short abrupt apex, 1¼ to 2½ in. long, half or more than half as wide, downy on both surfaces; stalk ¼ in. long, downy. Flowers not scented, yellowish white, tinged sometimes with red, produced in pairs on downy stalks up to ⅜ in. long. Corolla very downy, conspicuously two-lipped, ⅝ in. across, the tube short and bellied; ovary glandular. Fruits red, often showy in August.

Native of Europe, Asia Minor, and W. Siberia, found wild in parts of S.E. England, where it may be a true native.

f. LUTEA (Veillard) Rehd.—Fruits yellow. There are numerous other varieties varying in the degree of pubescence on the plant, etc., which need not be described further.

cv. 'CLAVEY'S DWARF'.—Of dense, low habit. Raised in the USA.

L. YUNNANENSIS Franch.

A low creeper, with slender, glabrous stems. Leaves oblong or narrowly obovate, 1½ to 3 in. long, about one-third as wide; glabrous above, glaucous and glabrous or slightly downy beneath, very shortly stalked. The upper pair or pairs of leaves are united into a round or oblong disk, in the axils of which the stalkless flowers are borne. Corolla yellow, ¾ to 1 in. long, glabrous outside, hairy within.

Native of Yunnan; discovered by Delavay. It is allied to the American *L. dioica*. Probably not in cultivation.

var. TENUIS Rehd.—A smaller-leaved form found by Henry at Mengtze in Yunnan, inhabiting rocky mountains up to 6,000 to 7,000 ft. Corolla ¾ in.

long, white changing to yellow. It was introduced in 1901 by Wilson to the Coombe Wood nursery.

This species should not be confused with *L. nitida* 'Yunnan', for which the name *L. yunnanensis* has erroneously been used.

LOROPETALUM   HAMAMELIDACEAE

A genus of a single species in E. Asia resembling *Hamamelis* in its narrow, strap-shaped petals and four-parted flowers, but amply distinguished by its evergreen nature and white flowers. There may be two species in this genus if *L. lanceum* Hand.-Mazz., described from a single fruiting specimen, belongs to *Loropetalum* and is distinct from *L. chinense*. A third species—*L. subcordatum* (Benth.) Oliver—is now regarded as generically distinct and takes the name originally given to it by Bentham, namely *Tetrathyrium subcordatum*. It is a native of Hong Kong and has never been introduced to cultivation.

L. CHINENSE (R. Br.) Oliver
Hamamelis chinensis R. Br.; *L. indicum* K. Tong

An evergreen shrub of bushy, very twiggy habit, 5 or 6 ft high; branchlets crooked, wiry, covered thickly with brownish stellate down. Leaves ovate or oval, 1 to 2½ in. long, ¾ to 1¼ in. wide, markedly unequal at the base, pointed at the apex, rough and with scattered hairs above, paler beneath, margin finely toothed; stalk about ⅛ in. long, hairy. Flowers very like those of witch-hazel in appearance, but white; they are produced in February and March, three to six crowded in a head; petals four to each flower, strap-shaped, ¾ in. long, 1/16 in. wide; flower-stalk and outside of calyx clothed with white stellate down. Seed-vessel a woody, ovoid, nut-like capsule.

Native of China and Assam; also found in one locality in Japan; introduced by Maries for Messrs Veitch in 1880. This singular and pretty shrub is too tender to thrive near London without protection, and can only be recommended for trial in the mildest parts of these islands. Grown out-of-doors in summer, and wintered in the coolest conservatory, it makes a very pretty shrub in February when covered with blossom. It likes a proportion of peat in the soil, and is easily increased by cuttings.

In China, this species is mainly or wholly confined to warm regions and low altitudes—hence its tenderness. It might prove hardier if reintroduced from Japan.

LUETKEA   ROSACEAE

A genus of a single species in western N. America, allied to *Spiraea*, but differing in the much-segmented leaves, filaments of stamens united at the base and follicles splitting along both edges. For the derivation of the generic name, see below.

L. PECTINATA (Pursh) Kuntze

Saxifraga pectinata Pursh; *Spiraea pectinata* (Pursh) Torr. & Gr.; *Luetkea sibbaldioides* Bong.; *Eriogynia pectinata* (Pursh) Hook.

An evergreen sub-shrub a few inches high, of tufted habit, spreading by underground suckers; young growths and leaves glabrous. Leaves glossy green, three-lobed, the lobes usually again divided into two or three secondary lobes, so that one leaf may have from three to nine (occasionally more) segments. The entire leaf is $\frac{1}{3}$ to 1 in. long and all its divisions are linear, pointed, $\frac{1}{24}$ to $\frac{1}{16}$ in. wide; the winged leaf-stalk is somewhat wider. Flowers white, $\frac{1}{4}$ to $\frac{1}{3}$ in. wide; produced in May and June in ten- to twenty-flowered racemes 1 to 2 in. long borne at the end of erect leafy branchlets which give the plant when in flower a height of 3 to 6 in.; flower-stalks downy. Calyx of five glabrous, pointed sepals; stamens twenty, united at the base to form a ring round the five carpels, each of which develops into a few-seeded follicle.

Native of western N. America, from Alaska to California. The oldest specimen in the Kew Herbarium, received from St Petersburg in 1835, was collected during the Russian voyage round the world (1826–9) under Admiral Luetke, after whom the plant was named. It was, apparently, long after that before it got into cultivation. In its lower latitudes it occurs at high elevations; on Vancouver Island, for instance, it ascends to altitudes of 5,000 to 6,000 ft. It requires, therefore, cool, moist conditions such as suit the mossy saxifrages. Given these, it makes a charming plant for the rock garden.

LUPINUS   LUPIN   LEGUMINOSAE

A genus of some 300 species, mostly herbs but containing a few shrubs, most abundant in western N. America, but represented also in eastern N. America, Central and South America, and the Mediterranean region.

L. ARBOREUS Sims   TREE LUPIN

An evergreen shrub of remarkably quick and luxuriant growth, becoming 6 to 9 ft high, and nearly as much through, in three or four years when planted in rich soil. Branchlets round, semi-woody, covered with silky hairs. Leaves alternate, digitate, with seven to eleven (usually nine) grey-green leaflets; each ¾ to 2 in. long, varying in size according to the vigour of the plant; they are oblanceolate, pointed, downy beneath, the common leaf-stalk rather longer than the leaflets. Flowers in erect, terminal racemes 6 to 10 in. long, fragrant, sulphur-yellow in the type and in most wild plants, but occasionally blue or purplish. Seed-pods 1½ to 3 in. long, ½ in. wide; covered with a sort of felt, and containing five to twelve blackish seeds.

Native of California in the coast region; of unrecorded introduction. This beautiful, half-woody shrub is apparently quite hardy near London, but is sometimes short-lived, especially if grown in rich soil. Young plants, it has been noticed, will pass through a winter quite unharmed but then, a few years later, will succumb during another winter not any more severe. This is not an unusual characteristic of plants which grow so rapidly and produce seed in such abundance as this does. It points to the advisability of removing all seed-pods that are not required as soon as they are formed, also to the necessity of renewing the stock from seed (or, in the case of special varieties, from cuttings) every few years. For so beautiful a shrub this is trouble well repaid. Cuttings should be made in July and August of short side-shoots with a heel attached, and placed in gentle heat. This lupin likes a good but not close or heavy soil, and it should have a sunny position. It succeeds well on dryish banks, but does not grow so large there. The typical yellow form is very beautiful and so too is 'Snow Queen', which was raised by Ladham's nursery and received an Award of Merit in 1899. It is still in commerce.

The flowers of the tree lupin appear from May to August, but are at their best in June and July.

L. CHAMISSONIS Eschs.

A sub-shrubby plant from 1½ to 3 ft high, woody at the base; young shoots silky-hairy. Leaves digitate, made up of five to seven leaflets, which are lanceolate, abruptly pointed, tapered at the base, ½ to 1¼ in. long, ⅛ to ¼ in. wide, silvery with appressed hairs on both surfaces; main-stalk ½ to 1 in. long. Raceme 3 to 6 in. long, erect, slender, the flowers more or less whorled, each on a silky stalk which is ¼ in. long and bears a silky linear bract at the base of the flower. Corolla ⅝ in. long, the standard petal blue or lilac with a large yellow blotch at the base; wing petals and keel of the same blue or lilac shade, both paling towards the base. Calyx ¼ in. long, two-lipped. Pods 1 to 1¼ in. long, ³⁄₁₆ to ¼ in. wide, silky. *Bot. Mag.*, t. 8657.

Native of California, often on sandy hill-slopes near the shore between San Francisco and San Diego; also of a few places along the coast in Washington. Although originally described in 1826, about which period it was collected by David Douglas, it never appears to have been common in cultivation. Its combination of silvery leaves and blue or lavender-coloured flowers is very charming. As is the case with so many Californian shrubs cultivated in this country, its tenure no doubt is shortened by lack of sunshine. But I do not think the shrubby lupins are ever particularly long-lived in our gardens. *L. chamissonis* should be planted in well-drained soil at the foot of a sunny south wall. It has been confused in gardens with L. *argenteus*, another silver-leaved but more herbaceous species, a native of the inner ranges of western N. America. L. *chamissonis* is distinguished amongst the silvery lupins by the large yellow blotch on the standard petal. It flowers at Kew from June onwards till autumn and ripens seed there.

LUZURIAGA   PHILESIACEAE

A genus of two or three species in temperate S. America and New Zealand, belonging to the same family as *Philesia* and *Lapageria*, both of which it resembles in its net-veined leaves and fleshy fruits. It is, however, easily distinguished from both by the shape of its flowers. The family belongs to the monocotyledons and is closely allied to the Liliaceae, in which it is included by some botanists.

L. RADICANS Ruiz & Pavon

An evergreen plant with perennial stems, creeping over the forest floor or climbing up the trunks of trees to a height of 6 ft or more, attached by roots springing from the joints of the stems. Its young shoots are thin, ribbed, wiry, and like the rest of the plant quite devoid of down. Leaves stalkless, set in two opposite rows, ovate-oblong, or oval to narrowly linear, tapered at both ends, ½ to 2 in. long, ⅛ to ⅜ in. wide, bright green above, rather glaucous beneath, with six to twelve distinct ribs running lengthwise. Flowers fragrant, produced singly or two or three together from the leaf-axils, each drooping on a slender stalk up to 1 in. long; they are white, 1 to 1½ in. across; the six 'petals' ⅛ to ¼ in. wide, pointed; anthers yellow, stalkless, forming a slender cone in the centre of the flower. Berry the size of a pea, brilliant orange or scarlet.

Native of Chile and Argentina; introduced by the middle of the 19th century, since when it has been cultivated at Kew. It is not hardy there, but can be grown out-of-doors in the milder south and south-western districts. It flowers in June in the Temperate House at Kew. Whether grown under glass or out-of-doors it should have a shaded position. It loves a peaty soil and abundant moisture. H. F. Comber, who collected it on his Chilean journey (1925-7), says it bears its flowers and fruits most freely when growing on tree trunks. Other collectors have noted that it *never* flowers freely when growing on the ground. It would probably succeed best out-of-doors in the mildest and rainiest parts of the British Isles, grown against the trunk of a tree or tree-fern. A damp, mossy wall might also be to its liking.

LYCIUM   Box Thorn   solanaceae

A genus of about one hundred species of loose-habited shrubs allied to the deadly nightshade (*Atropa belladonna*), with usually spiny branches. Leaves alternate, often in clusters. Flowers from one to four in the leaf-axils, their parts usually in fives; corolla funnel-shaped or tubular. Fruit a berry, very ornamental.

The lyciums or box thorns are easily cultivated; they do not need a rich soil, flowering and fruiting better in a well-drained one of moderate quality. *L. afrum* needs a wall, but the others here described are perfectly hardy. They are best propagated by seeds when these are obtainable, but cuttings and layers may also be used.

L. afrum L.

A deciduous shrub, much branched, spiny, growing 8 to 10 ft high against a wall; young shoots pale, slightly angled, glabrous. Leaves clustered, $\frac{1}{2}$ to 1 in. long, $\frac{1}{12}$ to $\frac{1}{8}$ in. wide, linear, tapered at the base, grey-green, glabrous. Flowers on stalks $\frac{1}{8}$ in. long, produced in May and June. Corolla tubular, $\frac{1}{4}$ in. wide, $\frac{3}{4}$ to 1 in. long, with five shallow, erect lobes, very dark purple. Calyx bell-shaped, $\frac{1}{4}$ in. long, with five triangular teeth; stamens enclosed within the corolla, each with a tuft of hairs half-way down. Berries red, finally purple-black, egg-shaped, $\frac{1}{8}$ in. long, with the calyx persisting at the base.

Native of South Africa; in cultivation 1712. This species requires a sunny wall for it to be seen at its best. It was highly spoken of by early writers growing in such a position, and it has flowered with great freedom in the garden at Bitton. It is cultivated in N. Africa, about Algiers, etc., but does not appear to be a genuine native of that region. It is cultivated in southern France, in hedges around habitations, and sometimes escapes into waste ground. The records of this species from Spain and Portugal may have the same explanation, as certainly do the Italian records.

L. barbarum L.   Chinese Box Thorn

L. halimifolium Mill.; *L. chinense* Mill.; *L. barbarum* var. *chinense* (Mill.) Ait.; *L. vulgare* Dun.; *L. ovatum* Veillard; *L. rhombifolium* Dipp.; *L. chinense* var. *ovatum* (Veillar.; Schneid.; *L. chinense* var. *rhombifolium* (Dipp.) Bean; *L. megistocarpum* Dun.; *L. lanceolatum* Villard; *L. halimifolium* var. *lanceolatum* (Veillard) Schneid.; *L. subglobosum* Dun. *L. halimifolium* var. *subglobosum* (Dun.) Schneid.; *L. trewianum* Roem. & Schult.; *L. europaeum* Hort., not L.

A deciduous, glabrous, spiny or unarmed shrub with arching, pendulous on prostrate branches. Leaves very variable in shape and size, even on the same plant, narrowly to broadly elliptic, lanceolate, ovate-lanceolate or rhomboid obtuse or acute at the apex, usually wedge-shaped at the base, 1 to $2\frac{1}{2}$ in. long (or shorter at the ends of the shoots), bright green or grey-green, short-stalked.

Flowers axillary, mostly in pairs or threes at each joint, each on a slender stalk $\frac{1}{4}$ to almost 1 in. long, borne from May to July. Calyx persistent in fruit, with five acute or obtuse lobes. Corolla purple, the tube funnel-shaped, about $\frac{1}{2}$ in. long, the five spreading lobes shorter than, or almost as long as, the tube. Filaments of stamens bearded at the base. Berries scarlet or orange, oblong, ellipsoid or egg-shaped, $\frac{2}{3}$ to 1 in. long.

A native of China, long known in gardens and now naturalised in many parts of the world, including Britain. The correct use of the name *L. barbarum* Linnaeus has long been uncertain and it has mainly been used for quite a different species (properly known as *L. shawii* Roem. & Schult.). Recently, however, a flower from the type-specimen at the Linnean Society was dissected and from this it was established that *L. barbarum* L. (1753) is the same species as *L. halimifolium* Mill. (1768) (*Journ. Israel Bot.*, Vol. 12 (1964), pp. 114–123). Miller described his species from a plant raised from seeds sent to him about 1752 by Bernard de Jussieu, which had been collected in China, almost certainly by the Jesuit missionary d'Incarville, near Peking. It is possible that the type-specimen of *L. barbarum* was of the same origin.

Miller also described in his *Dictionary* another lycium—*L. chinense*—'of which the seeds were brought to England a few years past and the plants were raised in several gardens, and by some were thought to be the Thea [the tea-plant]'. *L. chinense* has by most authorities been considered as a good species, differing from *L. halimifolium* in its more scandent habit, less spiny branches, greener and broader leaves and in the corolla-lobes being equal to or longer than the tube (against shorter than the tube in *L. halimifolium*). But an examination of the material in the Kew Herbarium made some years ago showed that the plants in Britain, Europe, and China variously named *L. chinense* and *L. halimifolium* are simply states of one variable species. And, for the reason explained above, the correct name for this species is *L. barbarum*.

This shrub is very common on the cliffs of south-coast towns like Eastbourne and Bournemouth. Few plants are better for seaside planting and when laden with its abundant, pendent, highly coloured fruits it is extremely ornamental. Birds appear to eat the fruits, as plants may frequently be seen growing on the tops of old walls and suchlike places. In villages between London and the south coast, plants may often be seen beautifully in fruit on cottage walls in August and September.

L. barbarum was at one time known erroneously in gardens as *L. europaeum*. The true L. EUROPAEUM L. (*H. mediterraneum* Dun.; *L. salicifolium* Mill.) is misleadingly named, being confined in Europe to the Mediterranean region. It differs from *L. barbarum* in having quite glabrous stamens (not bearded at the base), in the longer-tubed corolla with lobes much shorter than the tube, and its small narrow leaves.

Closely allied to *L. barbarum* is L. RUTHENICUM Murr., a species widely distributed in eastern Eurasia and Central Asia. It is a spiny upright shrub of greyish aspect with linear, slightly fleshy leaves; flowers usually borne singly in the axils, the corolla-lobes longer than half the tube. Berries pea-sized, black. Introduced 1804.

L. CHILENSE Bert.
L. grevilleanum Miers

A deciduous shrub 4 to 6 ft high, forming a dense mass of overlaying branches; young shoots pale, more or less downy or scurfy. Leaves obovate or oblanceolate, ½ to 2 in. long, ⅛ to ½ in. wide, tapered to the base, more abruptly towards the apex, densely arranged, ciliate, rather fleshy. The larger-sized leaves are only on young vigorous sucker-growths; most of the leaves are less than 1 in. long. Flowers solitary or in pairs in the leaf-axils, ½ in. diameter; corolla funnel-shaped, deeply five-lobed (the lobes longer than the tube), purple and yellowish white; calyx bell-shaped, the triangular-pointed lobes ciliate; stamens hairy at the base. Fruits orange-red, globular, ⅓ in. in diameter.

L. *chilense*, in the broad sense, is a variable species found in the drier and warmer parts of Chile and Argentina. The description given is of a comparatively broad-leaved and robust form of the species described under the name L. *grevilleanum*, which proved hardy at Kew.

LYCIUM PALLIDUM

L. PALLIDUM Miers

A deciduous shrub of rather thin, lax, sprawling habit, at present 5 or 6 ft high in cultivation; branches long, tortuous, or semi-pendulous, quite glabrous, but armed with spines which are really arrested branches, often bearing leaves. sometimes flowers. Leaves oval lance-shaped, up to 2 in. long by ⅜ in. wide on the young, non-flowering shoots, but narrowly obovate, 1 in. or less long, and produced in rosettes on the year-old, flowering shoots, quite glabrous, entire, of a glaucous green, tapering at the base to a short stalk. Flowers nodding on stalks ¼ in. long, often solitary or in pairs at each joint. Corolla funnel-shaped, ¾ in. long, ½ in. wide at the mouth, where are five shallow, rounded lobes, pale green veined with darker lines, and tinged with purple. Calyx bell-shaped, about ⅛ in. long, with five pointed lobes. Style much protruded; stamens rather shorter. Fruits scarlet, globose, ⅜ in. long; ripe in August. *Bot. Mag.*, t. 8440.

Native of south-western N. America, originally described by Miers from a specimen collected by Fendler in New Mexico, which has the corolla-tube glabrous inside; the form figured in the *Botanical Magazine* was discovered by Frémont in 1844 on the Rio Virgen, one of the tributaries of the Colorado river, and has the corolla-tube hairy inside below the insertion of the stamens. It was introduced to Kew in 1886. It is a distinct and quite hardy shrub, whose prettily coloured flowers hang in profusion from the underside of the branches, and make it the best of the lyciums in flower. It is also ornamental in fruit, but with us the crop is uncertain. It is best propagated by layering, in the absence of seed. The foliage varies in the intensity of its glaucous hue.

LYONIA ERICACEAE

A genus of about thirty evergreen or deciduous shrubs and small trees, found in E. Asia and the Himalaya, also in N. America, Mexico, and the West Indies. Leaves alternate, usually toothed. Flowers in axillary racemes or clusters on the previous year's wood; flower-stalks with a pair of bractlets at the base. Calyx-lobes valvate in bud. Corollas cylindrical, egg-shaped, urn-shaped, or globular urn-shaped. Stamens usually ten in number; anthers without apical awns (but in some species spur-like appendages occur on the filaments under the anthers). Fruits capsular, the valve-margins paler than the rest of the surface and usually much thickened. See further under *Pieris*, to which genus *Lyonia* is closely allied. For a note on the cultivated species by John Ingram, with key and figures, see *Baileya*, Vol. 11, pp. 29–35.

The genus commemorates John Lyon, a famous collector of North American plants, who died about 1818 during one of his expeditions to the mountains of the United States—the 'savage and romantic mountains which had so often been the theatre of his labours'.

L. LIGUSTRINA (L.) DC.

Vaccinium ligustrinum L.; *L. paniculata* Nutt.; *Xolisma ligustrina* (L.) Britt.

A deciduous shrub 3 to 8 ft high; young shoots either covered with a close soft down or nearly glabrous, and of a rather zigzag growth. Leaves alternate, oval or obovate, 2 to 3 in. long, ½ to 1¼ in. wide, entire or nearly so, pointed, covered with short down and dark green above, more downy beneath and paler, the nerves very prominent; stalk ⅛ in. long. Flowers produced in July and August on the leafless terminal portion of the preceding year's growth, in downy racemes or small panicles 1 to 1½ in. long, the whole forming a compound panicle from 3 to 6 in. long. Corolla downy, dull white, ⅛ to 3/16 in. wide, globose or orange-shaped, with five small, reflexed teeth at the nearly closed mouth. Calyx pale green or white, downy, appressed to the corolla. Seed-vessel a dry, five-celled capsule, with the calyx persisting at the base.

Native of eastern N. America; introduced in 1748. This is not one of the most attractive of the heath family, but is desirable through flowering so late in the season. It grows naturally in moist situations, but in cultivation thrives in ordinary peat or light sandy loam. Propagated by seed or by cuttings taken with a slight heel from the shoots that spring freely from beneath the flower panicle.

This species is very variable and the plant described above represents only one of many phases found in the wild. The following three varieties were all introduced to Britain early in the 19th century:

var. CAPREIFOLIA (Wats.) DC. *L. capreifolia* Wats.—Leaves broad-elliptic or ovate, acuminate. Bracts of inflorescence leafy.

var. PUBESCENS (A. Gray) Bean *Andromeda ligustrina* var. *pubescens* A. Gray; *Lyonia frondosa* (Pursh) Nutt.—Branches grey-hairy. Leaves appressed-hairy above, the whole plant of greyish aspect. Said to range from Virginia to Georgia.

var. SALICIFOLIA (Wats.) DC. *L. salicifolia* Wats.—Leaves lanceolate, slightly glossy.

In addition Fernald recognises var. FOLIOSIFLORA (Michx.) Fern., with the inflorescences leafy-bracted as in var. *capreifolia*, but the leaves narrower and not acuminate.

L. MACROCALYX (Anthony) Airy Shaw

Pieris macrocalyx Anthony

A shrub 3 to 6 ft high; shoots glabrous, greyish brown. Leaves oblong-ovate, varying to lanceolate and ovate, 2 to 4 in. long, about half as wide, rounded at the base or occasionally slightly cordate there, slenderly pointed, entire, glabrous and bright green above, very glaucous and with minute, appressed, reddish down beneath. Flowers fragrant, pendulous in axillary racemes 3 or 4 in. long; corolla white, globose-ovoid, ⅖ in. long, ¾ in. wide, with five minute, triangular lobes at the mouth, slightly red-downy outside, glabrous within; sepals ¼ in. long, erect. Blossoms in July. *Bot. Mag.*, t. 9490.

Native of N.W. Yunnan, China, and of S.E. Tibet; found in 1924 by Forrest and Kingdon Ward, both of whom sent seeds. From these, flowering plants were raised at Trewithen, Cornwall, and at Headfort, Co. Meath.

L. MARIANA (L.) D. Don   STAGGER-BUSH   [PLATE 84

Andromeda mariana L.; *Pieris mariana* (L.) Benth. & Hook.

A deciduous almost glabrous shrub, up to 6 ft high in the wild. Leaves oblong, elliptic or narrowly obovate, mostly rounded or blunt at the apex, ¾ to 3 in. long, glabrous except for down on the veins beneath (occasionally the whole undersurface is downy). Flowers nodding, borne late May to July in umbellate clusters on the leafless ends of the previous year's growths. Calyx often tinged with red. Corolla white or pinkish, ovoid to tubular, not or hardly constricted at the mouth, ¾ to ½ in. long. *Bot. Mag.*, t. 1579.

Native of the eastern and southern USA; introduced by Peter Collinson, before 1736. It is perhaps the most decorative of the American lyonias, since the flowers are better displayed than in the other species and the leaves colour red in the autumn. It is quite hardy.

L. LUCIDA (Lam.) K. Koch   *Andromeda lucida* Lam.; *Pieris nitida* (Bartr.) Benth. & Hook.; *Xolisma lucida* (Lam.) Rehd.; *Lyonia marginata* D. Don; *Andromeda coriacea* Ait.—This evergreen glabrous species of the southeastern USA is rarely cultivated. Branches green, three-angled. Leaves leathery, dark green, glossy, broad-elliptic, oblong, or oblong-ovate, entire; margins with a well-marked peripheral vein. Flowers clustered in the leaf-axils on the shoots of the previous year. Calyx-lobes lanceolate, reddish. Corolla ovoid to conic, about ¼ in. long, white (red in f. *rubra* (Lodd.) Rehd.). Introduced 1765. *Bot. Mag.*, t. 1045.

L. OVALIFOLIA (Wall.) Drude

Andromeda ovalifolia Wall.; *Pieris ovalifolia* (Wall.) D.Don; *Xolisma ovalifolia* (Wall.) Rehd.

A semi-evergreen or deciduous shrub or tree, the tree-forms said to attain a height of 40 ft in the wild; young stems glabrous. Leaves ovate or elliptic or ovate-oblong, 2 to 7 in. long, 1 to 4 in. wide, entire, usually rather leathery, acute or shortly acuminate at the apex, usually rounded at the base, glabrous or downy on the veins beneath. Flowers in axillary, one-sided racemes 2 to 4 in. long, sometimes with leafy bracts at the base, borne on the previous year's wood in May–June. Corollas white or flesh-pink, narrowly egg-shaped, downy on the outside. Sepals triangular-lanceolate or ovate. Capsules about 3/16 in. wide.

A common species in the mountains of E. Asia from Kashmir to China and Formosa, and represented in Japan by the var. *elliptica* (see below); introduced from the Himalaya in 1825 and reintroduced by Forrest from Yunnan in 1930–1 under F.30956. The Himalayan form is rather tender and has always been rare in cultivation, nor is the hardier Forrest form any commoner. The main interest of the species is that it is one of the most characteristic members of oak- and pine-associations in the Sino-Himalayan region, often found in the Himalaya with *Rhododendron arboreum*.

var. LANCEOLATA (Wall.) Hand.-Mazz.   *A. lanceolata* Wall.; *Pieris ovalifolia* var. *lanceolata* (Wall.) C. B. Clarke—Leaves lanceolate, narrowed at the base. Sepals usually longer and narrower. Himalaya, China, and Formosa.

var. ELLIPTICA (Sieb. & Zucc.) Hand.-Mazz. *Andromeda elliptica* Sieb. & Zucc.; *Pieris ovalifolia* var. *elliptica* (Sieb. & Zucc.) Rehd. & Wils.—Leaves thinner, fruits smaller. Native of Japan and also of China.

LYONOTHAMNUS   ROSACEAE

A genus of a single species confined to a few islands off the coast of California. The generic name commemorates W. S. Lyon, who discovered the tree in 1884 on Santa Catalina.

L. FLORIBUNDUS A. Gray

This species is represented in cultivation in Britain by the following variety (for typical *L. floribundus* see the remarks below):

var. ASPLENIFOLIUS (Greene) Brandegee *L. asplenifolius* Greene—An evergreen tree 30 to 50 ft high, of slender form, with a red-brown peeling bark; young shoots glabrous. Leaves opposite, pinnate, 4 to 8 in. long, made up of three to nine leaflets. Leaflets stalkless, 2 to 4½ in. long, ½ to ⅝ in. wide, cut up into hatchet-shaped segments ¼ to ½ in. long by incisions reaching to the midrib, veins set at right angles to the midrib, dark green and glabrous above, paler and downy beneath. Flowers white, ¼ in. across, produced numerously on terminal paniculate corymbs 3 to 6 in. broad; petals five; stamens fifteen. 'Fruit of two woody, glandular, four-seeded parts, splitting on both sides' (Eastwood).

Native of the islands of Santa Catalina, Santa Cruz, etc., off the coast of California; not yet found on the mainland. Although the typical *L. floribundus* differs from this variety only in foliage (its leaves being simple, oblong, lanceolate, and either toothed minutely or not at all) it is far from being so ornamental a tree. But between it and var. ASPLENIFOLIUS there is every intermediate state. So far as I know, the fern-leaved variety is the only one introduced to this country. A tree raised from seed sent to Kew in 1900 grew to be 20 ft high in a corner facing east outside the wall of the Temperate House, where it attracted much admiration for the beauty of its fern-like leaves, its luxuriance and graceful habit. It was so much injured by the cold winter of 1928–9 that it did not recover its health again. A taller specimen at Borde Hill in Sussex was cut in the winter of 1962–3 but later recovered. The arrangement of the leaves opposite each other on the twig and their distinctive shape make this tree easily recognisable in the rose family. So far as is known it has not flowered in Britain.

'On Santa Cruz Island, perhaps the most satisfying of all sights are large stands of Lyonothamnus. It grows high up the canyons and in those protected places is able to attain its full beauty. The foliage is fern-like and very lovely, and the small white flowers borne in broad terminal panicles, overspread the top branches, so that when a colony of the tree, cupped in the hollow of a hill, is seen from a vantage point above, the aspect is of a sea of creamy white upon green' (L. Rowntree).

MAACKIA   LEGUMINOSAE

A genus of six deciduous trees natives of E. Asia and named after Richard Maack, a Russian naturalist who died in 1886. They are nearly akin to *Cladrastis* and have by some authorities been put in that genus. But they are really very distinct in that the wood is not brittle as in *Cladrastis*; the leaf-buds are solitary and not hidden by the base of the leaf-stalk; the leaflets are opposite and the flowers are densely packed in more or less erect racemes. They are very hardy and grow well in good open soil in full sunshine, but they have no very outstanding merits. They flower in July and August and occasionally bear seeds.

M. AMURENSIS (Rupr. & Maxim.) K. Koch
Cladrastis amurensis Rupr. & Maxim.

A small deciduous tree, said to be 40 ft or more high in the wild, with peeling bark, but usually shrubby in cultivation in this country; young shoots minutely downy. Leaves 8 to 12 in. long, pinnate, with seven to eleven leaflets; the main-stalk rather swollen at the base, but leaving the bud quite exposed; leaflets opposite, ovate, blunt at the top, 1½ to 3 in. long, dark green above, paler and glabrous beneath. Flowers borne in July and August, pea-shaped, dull white, closely set on stiff, erect racemes, 4 to 6 in. long, sometimes branched at the base. Each flower is ½ in. long on a short stalk about half its length; calyx bell-shaped, ¼ in. long. Pods 2 to 3 in. long, ⅓ in. wide, flat, with the seam slightly winged.

Native of Manchuria; introduced in 1864. An example at Kew, *pl.* 1922, measures only 15 × 1¼ ft (1968).

var. BUERGERI (Maxim.) Schneid. *Cladrastis amurensis* var. *buergeri* Maxim.—This is a native of Japan and differs chiefly in the leaflets beneath being furnished with appressed hairs, also the calyx.

M. CHINENSIS Takeda
M. hupehensis Takeda

A deciduous flat-headed tree 16 to 50 ft (rarely more) high, the largest trees with a trunk 7 ft in girth; young shoots glabrous by summer. Leaves pinnate,

5 to 8 in. long, composed usually of nine to thirteen leaflets, the lower ovate and about 1 in. long, the others becoming larger and more oblong or oval in outline towards the end of the leaf and 1¾ to 2½ in. long by ¾ in. wide; they are bluntish at the apex, tapered to rounded at the base, silvery grey with down when young, remaining densely covered beneath with velvety appressed down; stalk ⅛ in. long, downy. Flowers opening in July and August on a terminal panicle 6 to 8 in. long and 4 to 5 in. wide, consisting of several cylindrical downy racemes densely crowded with flowers. These are a dull white, ⅜ in. long; calyx bell-shaped, toothed, ⅛ in. long and, like the short flower-stalk, downy.

Native of Hupeh and Szechwan, China; discovered by Wilson and introduced by him in 1908. He observes that it is common in W. Hupeh in moist open country, but that large specimens are rare. It flowered in the Arnold Arboretum, Mass., in 1920, and at Kew four years later. Its chief beauty is in the silvery sheen of the young unfolding leaves; the flowers are of little account. It appears to be closely related to M. amurensis, differing in the smaller shorter leaves and in the narrower more downy leaflets. There is an example about 30 ft high at Wakehurst Place in Sussex. Another at Kew, pl. 1911, measures 15 × 2 ft (1968): this is from Wilson's original introduction of 1908 (W.709).

M. FAUREI (Lévl.) Takeda
Cladrastis faurei Lévl.

A deciduous tree up to 25 ft high, with a trunk 2 ft in girth, but often a bush 6 ft or more high; young shoots glabrous. Leaves pinnate, about 8 in. long; leaflets nine to seventeen, oval or ovate, rounded or broadly wedge-shaped at the base, 1½ to 2 in. long, ⅝ to ⅞ in. wide, rather downy when young, becoming glabrous; stalk of leaflet ⅛ to 3/16 in. long. Flowers white, ⅜ in. long, produced on a panicle made up of slender racemes 2 to 3 in. long, on which they are closely packed; calyx bell-shaped, scarcely toothed, finely downy. Pods 1½ to 1¾ in. long.

Native of Quelpaert Island, Korea; discovered by the Abbé Faurie in 1907 at an altitude of 3,700 ft. E. H. Wilson collected seeds on the island in 1917, which represent its first introduction to cultivation. It flowers there in August at the end of leafy shoots. Introduced to Kew in 1922.

MACLURA   MORACEAE

A genus of one North American species allied to Morus (mulberry), Broussonetia, and Cudrania, but easily distinguished from these by its unlobed and untoothed leaves. Male flowers in dense clusters or more rarely in racemes. Female flowers in dense globose clusters developing

into a compound fruit, which is pitted and covered with a rind. A bigeneric hybrid with *Cudrania* has been recorded.
Named in honour of William Maclure, an American geologist.

M. POMIFERA (Raf.) Schneid.   OSAGE ORANGE
Ioxylon pomiferum Raf.; *M. aurantiaca* Nutt.

A deciduous tree occasionally 40 ft or more high; branches armed with spines
up to 1¼ in. long; young shoots downy, soon becoming glabrous. Leaves
alternate, ovate or oval to oblong-lanceolate, 1½ to 4 in. long, about half as
wide, pointed, mostly rounded at the base, dark green and glabrous above,
paler and downy beneath, especially on the veins and midrib; stalk ½ to 1½ in.
long. Male flowers green, produced in June along with one or two leaves from
the joints of the previous year's wood, numerous in a short-stalked roundish
cluster; they are quite inconspicuous, as are also the female ones, borne of
separate trees. Fruit like an orange in shape, 2 to 4 in. across, yellowish green.
    Native of the South and Central United States; introduced in 1818. This tree
is remarkable for its large, ornamental, but quite inedible fruits, rarely seen in
this country, perhaps because the two sexes are not often associated. They are
full of a milky juice. In the United States this tree is largely used as a hedge
plant, and I have also seen it used for the same purpose in Central Europe.
Propagated by layers or root-cuttings, in the absence of seeds. Where only one
tree is grown, an endeavour should be made to graft the other sex upon it.
    There is an example in the University Botanic Garden, Cambridge, which
colours clear yellow in the autumn.

MAGNOLIA   MAGNOLIACEAE

A genus of deciduous or evergreen trees and shrubs named by Linnaeus
in honour of Pierre Magnol, a professor of botany and medicine at
Montpelier, who died in 1715.
    The genus is most numerously represented in E. and S.E. Asia, as far
south-east as Java. A little over one-quarter of the species are natives of
the New World, from the N.E. United States (one species just extending
into Canada) to northern South America. More than half the species are
tropical; of the temperate species, almost every one has been introduced
to Britain.
    In one respect magnolias are the most splendid of all hardy trees, for
in the size of their individual flowers they are easily first; the evergreen
species, too, have some of the largest leaves of all evergreen trees hardy
with us. The leaves are alternate, simple and entire, with stipules that are
free from the petiole in some species, in other adnate to it. Flowers
bisexual, produced singly at the end of a shoot; peduncles with one or

more spathe-like bracts. Perianth of six or nine (occasionally more) segments known as 'tepals', arranged in whorls. In some species the tepals of the outer whorl are small and sepal-like; in describing these species it is usual to term the outer whorl a calyx and the inner segments petals, but in no species of magnolia is there a complete differentiation of the perianth into calyx and corolla. The stamens are numerous, spirally arranged to the lower part of structure (the torus), the upper part of which bears numerous free carpels, also spirally arranged. In the fruiting stage the torus is much enlarged and the carpels split on their outer side to release one or two red, scarlet, or orange seeds, each of which is attached to the carpel by a silk-like thread.

In most of the species, the bark when crushed emits a pleasant aromatic odour, and some of the American species, as well as the Chinese *M. officinalis*, have medicinal properties.

Perhaps no group of exotic trees gives more distinction to a garden than a comprehensive collection of magnolias. There is not one that is not worthy of cultivation, the early-flowering or Yulan section being especially noteworthy for the brilliant effect they produce in spring.

The only difficulty experienced in cultivating these trees is in establishing some of them after transplanting. The roots are thick and fleshy, and apt to decay if disturbed and lacerated when the trees themselves are at rest. Any planting, therefore, which involves root injury should be done when active growth has commenced, so that the wounds may heal and new roots be formed immediately. May is a suitable month. The more delicate-rooted species like *M. sieboldii* and *stellata* like a proportion of peat in the soil, more especially when they are young. All of them like abundant moisture and where the soil is shallow and poor, holes 18 in. deep and 2 to 4 yards in diameter should be prepared by mixing good loam, and if possible one-fourth peat and decayed leaves with the ordinary soil. The dimensions of the prepared ground should, of course, be proportionate to the vigour of the species. In most gardens the ordinary soil, well trenched and improved by adding decayed leaves, will be found suitable, but for such delightful plants as these a little extra labour and expense at the outset will be repaid.

Magnolias are propagated by seed, layering, and grafting. For the pure species, seeds no doubt are preferable, but their production in this country is uncertain, and it has to be remembered that being of an oily nature they retain their vitality but a short time if kept dry. It is advisable to sow them singly in small pots of light soil under glass. Seeds of magnolias are sometimes very long in germinating. A batch of about two hundred seeds of *M. wilsonii*, ripened at Kew some years ago, remained dormant after sowing for over two years, then germinated simultaneously with scarcely a failure.

Layering is a very useful means of increase and was much used by Messrs Veitch at their Coombe Wood nursery, where there were many old stools, each of which had produced hundreds of young plants. Air-layering is a possibility in gardens, when only a few plants are needed. Where layering is inconvenient or impossible, grafting will have to be employed; *M. acuminata* can be used as the stock for the stronger growing kinds, and *M. kobus* for *M. stellata*, *M. × loebneri* and other smaller growing species and hybrids. But grafting should be the last resort. Some magnolias can be propagated by cuttings, notably *M. grandiflora* and *delavayi*, both evergreen, *M. stellata*, *salicifolia*, and *kobus* (and their hybrids); some success has also been attained in propagating *M. × soulangiana* by this means.

With regard to the attitude of magnolias towards chalky soils, the late Sir Frederick Stern wrote, in his book on the garden at Highdown, near Worthing: 'Few magnolias do well on this hot dry soil. The American magnolias, like so many of the American plants, will not tolerate lime. Some of the Asiatic species do not mind lime, such as *M. delavayi*, *M. kobus*, *M. sinensis*, *M. wilsonii* and *M × highdownensis*. None of the other Asiatic magnolias have ever succeeded here; perhaps the ground and the position of the garden facing south is too hot and dry for them' (*A Chalk Garden* (1960), p. 44). But a wide range of magnolias is grown by Lord Rosse at Birr Castle in central Ireland, where the soil is alkaline but not chalky as it is at Highdown and is also moister (*Journ. R.H.S.*, Vol. 78 (1953), pp. 102–104).

The standard work on the magnolias of temperate E. Asia is: G. H. Johnstone, *Asiatic Magnolias in Cultivation* (1955), with fourteen coloured plates, twenty half-tone figures, and one map. An older work on the whole genus, still of interest, is: J. G. Millais, *Magnolias* (1927). See also: *Camellias and Magnolias*, R.H.S. Conference Report (1950). Information on new cultivars and hybrids not included here will be found in *Bud-grafted Magnolias*, published periodically by Messrs. Treseder of Truro; and in the *Manual* of Messrs Hillier of Winchester. An account of magnolias at Kew, by S. A. Pearce, was published in *Journ. R.H.S.*, Vol. 84 (1959), pp. 418–426; and of tree magnolias in Windsor Great Park, by T. H. Findlay, in *Journ. R.H.S.*, Vol. 77 (1952), pp. 43–46, and Vol. 88 (1963), pp. 461–463.

M. ACUMINATA L.   CUCUMBER TREE

A large deciduous tree 60 to 90 ft high, forming a trunk 6 to 12 ft in girth. Branches at first erect, ultimately arching. Leaves oval to oblong, 5 to 10 in. long, about half as wide, green on both sides, downy beneath; they narrow to a point at the end, the base is rounded. Flowers comparatively inconspicuous, dull greenish yellow; sepals 1 to 1½ in. long; petals erect, 2 to 3 in. long, in two sets of three each. Fruits dark red, columnar, 3 in. long *Bot. Mag.*, t. 2427.

Native of eastern N. America, from New York State southwards, reaching its finest development in the S. Allegheny region. This tree, the noblest of American magnolias in growth and the least effective in blossom, was discovered by John Bartram, and introduced by him to England in 1736. It was raised from seed by Peter Collinson, and flowered with him for the first time 20 May, 1762. The flowers have a slight fragrance. The popular name of 'cucumber tree' refers to the shape and colour of the fruits when quite young. It ripens seed freely, and young plants make perhaps the best stocks for grafting other magnolias upon, especially the stronger-growing species.

A tree at Kew by the Main Gate measures 52 × 7 ft (1967). Others that have been recorded in recent years are: Waterlow Park, Highgate, London, 65 ×7¾ ft (1964); Albury House, Surrey, 85 × 7 ft (1966)—this tree was 75 ft high in 1905; Knap Hill Nurseries, Surrey, 50 × 7½ ft (1961); Frensham Hall, Shottermill, Surrey, *pl.* 1905, 78 × 6 ft (1968); West Dean Arboretum, Sussex, 60 × 9½ ft, with a 15-ft bole (1967); Fairlawne, Kent, 60 × 9 ft (1965); Westonbirt, Glos., in Main Drive, 68 × 5 ft (1965); Leaton Knolls, Shrops., 75 × 7¼ ft (1954); Eastnor Castle, Heref., 52 × 8¼ ft (1969). In Scotland there is an example at Biel, East Lothian, which was 30 × 5 ft in 1911 and now 40 × 6 ft (1967).

Trees under the name var. *maxima* are grown at Kew, but except for a possibly more vigorous growth and larger foliage there is nothing to distinguish them. Sent out by the firm of Loddiges about 1830.

cv. 'VARIEGATA'.—Leaves handsomely blotched with golden yellow.

M. CAMPBELLII Hook. f. & Thoms.   [PLATE 86

A deciduous tree occasionally over 100 ft high in the wild but so far not much over 60 ft in cultivation and then only when grown in woodland conditions; often, both in the wild and in gardens, it is many-stemmed from the base, wide-spreading but of no great height. Bark in cultivated trees pale grey (Hooker in his *Journal* describes the bark of the trees on Sinchul near Darjeeling as almost black, but this colouring may be due to lichens or algae). Leaves usually broadly elliptic, shortly acuminate or apiculate at the apex, rounded, obliquely rounded, or broad-cuneate at the base, 6 to 10 in. long, medium green and glabrous above, covered beneath with appressed hairs at least when young and usually permanently so (the leaves on some wild specimens are more narrowly elliptic and tapered at both ends). Flower-buds ovoid, hairy. Flowers produced in early spring before the leaves on usually glabrous peduncles; they are about 10 in. across with twelve to sixteen tepals which are clear pink, crimson, or white on the outside, paler within when coloured, the outer ones spreading, the inner four upright in the mature flower but forming a cap over the stamens and pistils when the flower first expands. Fruits about 8 in. long. *Bot. Mag.* t. 6793.

Native of the Himalaya from Nepal to Assam, commonest between 8,000 and 10,000 ft—a zone in which the forest is dominated by magnoliaceous species, oaks, and tree-rhododendrons; described in 1855 but known earlier. The first of many introductions was around 1865. *M. campbellii* is believed to have first flowered in the British Isles at Lakelands, Co. Cork, Ireland, in 1885; among the earliest flowerings in England were: Veitch's Exeter nursery (1895), Abbotsbury, Dorset, (*c.* 1900); Leonardslee, Sussex (1907).

This fine tree—perhaps the most magnificent of the magnolias—flowers from February to early April according to the season and its flower-buds are susceptible to damage by frost and chilling winds from the time they first begin to swell. But the many thriving specimens at Kew and in gardens south of London testify to the hardiness of this species, even though the crop of flowers may be lost there more frequently than in south Cornwall and other more favoured regions. Unfortunately, fifteen to twenty or even more years will pass before the tree first produces flowers, by which time it may be 25 ft high.

M. *campbellii* thrives remarkably well at Kew, where there are two specimens —one, by the Victoria Gate, planted in 1904, and another of about the same age in a more open position near the Azalea Garden. The former produced well over 500 flowers of a good pink in 1959 (*Journ. R.H.S.*, Vol. 84, p. 421 and fig. 120); the latter flowered well in 1972. In the woodland gardens of Sussex *M. campbellii*, though it may not flower so frequently as in Cornwall, grows just as well. A specimen at Wakehurst Place measures 60 × 7¼ ft (1969) and the largest at Caerhays in Cornwall is 66 × 7 ft (1971). At Windsor Great Park near London, where the climate is by no means ideal for the Asiatic tree magnolias, *M. campbellii* attained a height of 35 ft and a spread of 18 ft in seventeen years and produced its first flowers when sixteen years old (*Journ. R.H.S.*, Vol. 88 (1963), p. 461).

f. ALBA Hort.—White-flowered trees of *M. campbellii* are said to be common in the wild, but in the gardens of this country they are rare. The largest recorded grows in the Tolls at Borde Hill, Sussex; it was received from Messrs Gill in 1925 as ordinary *M. campbellii*, first flowered about 1949 and is now 62 × 4 ft (1968). The original white-flowered specimen at Caerhays, raised from seeds received from Darjeeling in 1926, was severely cut by frost in 1939 and is only 37 ft high (1966). It received a First Class Certificate when a flowering branch was shown at Vincent Square in 1951. Seedlings from it planted in 1957 have grown with remarkable vigour, the largest of them being 35 × 1¾ ft by 1966. The first of them flowered in that year, only nine years planted (see further in 'The Garden at Caerhays' by Julian Williams, *Journ. R.H.S.*, Vol. 91 (1966), p. 285). In Eire there is a white-flowered example of *M. campbellii* in Garinish Island, Co. Cork, 38 ft high, on two stems (1966).

A tree of *M. campbellii* with flowers of a rich pink grows in the Lloyd Botanic Garden, Darjeeling, India, with flowers of an exceptionally dark pink ('wine-coloured' according to Collingwood Ingram in *A Garden of Memories* (1970), p. 129). A seedling from this, growing in the garden of Sir George Jessel at Goudhurst, Kent, flowers usually late for this species—towards the end of April or even into early May. It received an Award of Merit on April 18, 1972. Graft-wood from the Darjeeling tree was procured recently by Messrs Hillier, who have given their stock the clonal name 'DARJEELING'.

var. MOLLICOMATA (W. W. Sm.) F. K. Ward *M. mollicomata* W. W. Sm.; *M. c.* subsp. *mollicomata* (W. W. Sm.) Johnstone—The magnolias known in gardens as *M. mollicomata* derive from seeds collected by Forrest in 1924 in the Chinese province of Yunnan near the Burma frontier (Shweli–Salween divide) under numbers F.24213, F.24214, and F.24118 (for F.26524 see below under 'Lanarth'). Farrer had sent seeds a few years earlier from the Burma side of the frontier under his number 816, but these failed to germinate.

It is doubtful whether this magnolia is really distinct enough from *M. campbellii* to merit even the rank of subspecies given to it by G. H. Johnstone and it seems better to accord it the rank of variety given by Frank Kingdon Ward (*Gard. Chron.*, Vol. 137 (1955), p. 238). But horticulturally the Forrest intro-duction differs in two respects from the forms of *M. campbellii* introduced from

Sikkim. First, they take only half as long to reach the flowering stage (nine to twelve years from seed); secondly, the flower-colour is usually a mauvy-pink, and never the clear rose-pink of the best forms of *M. campbellii* from Sikkim.

As to the botanical differences between the two varieties, the trees cultivated as *M. mollicomata* are distinguished from cultivated specimens of *M. campbellii* by their downy peduncles, and this character is also mentioned in Sir William Wright Smith's original description of *M. mollicomata*, which was drawn up from specimens collected by Forrest in various parts of Yunnan. But Mr. Johnstone did not consider this character to be of much diagnostic value, since specimens of *M. campbellii* with downy peduncles have been collected from as far west as Bhutan. Another difference, noted by Mr Johnstone, is that if the flower-buds of typical *M. campbellii* and var. *mollicomata* are compared around January, after the outer bud-scales have fallen, those of *M. campbellii* will be seen to be ovoid, those of the var. *mollicomata* oblong in the lower part and tapered at the apex, with a slight constriction between the two parts. But whether this difference holds good constantly for wild plants it is impossible to say.

At Caerhays, Cornwall, there are three specimens of var. *mollicomata* raised from the seeds sent by Forrest and planted about 1926. One of these, from F.24214, measures 33 × 3 ft at 4 ft; the second is about the same size; the third is of fastigiate habit, dividing into several stems at 4 ft and about 40 ft high (1966). At Werrington, Cornwall, there is an example with almost white flowers, raised from F.24118; it is 45 × 4 ft with a bole of 9 ft (1966).

The following clones of var. *mollicomata* have been named:

cv. 'BORDE HILL'.—See under 'Lanarth'.

cv. 'MARY WILLIAMS'.—Flowers decribed as Roseine Purple shading to Orchid Purple. Raised at Caerhays, Cornwall, and given an Award of Merit when shown from there in 1954.

cv. 'LANARTH'.—Flowers deep lilac-purple; leaves mostly rounded at the apex, glabrous beneath, with the veins deeply impressed on the upper surface. First Class Certificate when shown by the late M. P. Williams of Lanarth, Cornwall, in April 1947. The tree at Lanarth is one of only three raised from Forrest 25655, collected in 1924 on the Salween–Kiu-chiang divide. Another is at Werrington Park, Cornwall, where it is now about 50 ft high. The third, raised at Borde Hill, Sussex, died before flowering but a layer from it grows in Mrs Johnstone's garden at Trewithen, Cornwall. This clone has been distributed under the name 'BORDE HILL'. These trees are discussed by G. H. Johnstone in op. cit., pp. 61–64, under the name convar. WILLIAMSIANA; 'Lanarth' is figured there in colour on Plate 5.

M. campbellii var. CAMPBELLII × var. MOLLICOMATA.—This cross was made by the late C. P. Raffill of Kew in 1946, the parents being the specimens of the two varieties that once grew in the Temperate House there. Seedlings were distributed to a number of gardens in 1948–51 and first flowered ten to fourteen years later. Two clones have so far been named:

cv. 'CHARLES RAFFILL'.—Tepals deep purple on the outside, white with pinkish-purple margins on the inner side. Award of Merit when shown by the

Crown Estate Commissioners, Great Windsor Park, on April 18, 1963. This tree was received from Kew when 2 ft high in 1948-9 and flowered in 1959. It is figured in *Journ. R.H.S.*, Vol. 88 (1963), figs. 173 and 174).

cv. 'KEW'S SURPRISE'.—Flowers slightly deeper in colour than in 'Charles Raffill'. First Class Certificate March 14, 1967, Planted at Caerhays in 1951, it first flowered in 1966 and is about 20 ft high (*Journ. R.H.S.*, Vol. 93 (1968), p. 355).

Unnamed forms of the cross were shown by the Royal Botanic Gardens, Kew, at the R.H.S. Show on April 2-3, 1968.

It is very likely that this cross has also occurred spontaneously in gardens.

M. CORDATA Michx.
M. acuminata var. *cordata* (Michx.) Sarg.

A shrub or small bushy tree allied to *M. acuminata* with a dark brown scaly bark that does not become furrowed even on old specimens; young stems densely downy. Leaves smaller and comparatively broader than in *M. acuminata*, 4 to 6 in. long, $2\frac{1}{2}$ to $3\frac{1}{2}$ in. wide, more rounded at the apex, bases mostly rounded or broad cuneate (rarely cordate as the name would imply), of a deeper more lustrous green above and covered beneath with rather long, matted hairs. Flowers resembling those of *M. acuminata* in shape but smaller and with the petals yellow on the inside. *Bot. Mag.*, t. 325.

This species was found by the elder Michaux growing wild 'on open hillsides in upper Carolina and Georgia' and described by him in 1803. He or his son may have introduced the species to France. There were at any rate two introductions to England in 1801—by John Lyon to Loddiges's nursery; and by John Fraser, a plant collector who travelled in the south-eastern USA and had his own nursery in Sloane Square, London.

According to Prof. Sargent, writing in 1891 (*Sylv. N. Am.*, Vol. 1, p. 8), *M. cordata* was at that time no longer known in the wild, though forms approaching it were to be found on the Blue Ridge of Carolina and in central Alabama. But in 1913 the species was rediscovered by Louis Berckmans in Georgia south of Augusta, near the Savannah river, growing in dry oak woodland. Since then it has been found in other localities in Georgia and also in N. Carolina.

Cultivated specimens, deriving from the old introductions, make slow-growing, low, stunted trees, perhaps 30 ft high eventually if they live long enough. At Kew a tree planted in 1906 is only 18 ft high (1959). Others in the collection flowered abundantly when only 4 to 6 ft high. *M. cordata* varies in the colour of its flowers; they are usually of a rather pale yellow, but forms with deeper-coloured flowers are, or have been, in cultivation; the rarity of the latter may be due to their tenderness.

It should be pointed out that the synonym given under the heading represents Sargent's earlier view as to the status of this magnolia. In the second edition of his *Manual* he retained *M. cordata* as a species.

M. CYLINDRICA Wils.

A small deciduous tree said to attain 30 ft in the wild; branchlets reddish brown and silky hairy when young; winter-buds small, fairly densely coated with silky hairs. Leaves (of cultivated plants) narrowly to broadly obovate or elliptic obovate, 4 to 6½ in. long, 1¾ to 3¾ in. wide, obtuse or shortly and bluntly acuminate at the apex, cuneate at the base, dark green, glabrous and conspicuously net-veined above, the undersurface pale grey-green, with a few short appressed silky hairs on the midrib and main veins; leaf-stalks ⅝ to 1¼ in. long. Flowers with six petaloid tepals in two whorls and an outer whorl of small, fugitive, sepal-like segments, borne in April on the naked branches. The petaloid segments are white slightly flushed with pink along the midrib, spathulate-oblong, the inner three about 4 in. long, 1½ in. wide, the outer three slightly shorter and narrower; peduncle silky-hairy and remaining so in the fruiting stage. Stamens with pale pink filaments. Fruits described by Wilson as cylindrical, 2 to 3 in. long, ¾ to 1 in. wide.

M. *cylindrica* was discovered by R. C. Ching on the Wang Shan, Anwhei, China, in 1925, growing in shady ravines at 3,500 to 4,500 ft, and was described from fruiting specimens collected by him. The above description is based mainly (and entirely so far as the flowers are concerned) on material from a plant growing in Mr H. G. Hillier's garden at Jermyns House, Romsey.

According to information kindly provided by Mr Brian Mulligan, the stock cultivated on the west coast of the United States and most probably in this country also, derives from seeds obtained from the Lushan Botanic Garden, China, by the late Mrs Henry of Gladwyne, Penn., USA, and was further distributed by the University of Washington Arboretum, Seattle.

M. *cylindrica* is quite hardy in the south of England and flowers freely when only 3 to 4 ft high. It resembles M. *denudata* in the poise, size and shape of its flowers, but in that species the flowers have nine petal-like segments and no sepaloid whorl. In M. *cylindrica* there are only six petal-like segments, with an outer whorl of small "sepals" as in M. *salicifolia* and M. *kobus*.

M. *cylindrica* received an Award of Merit on 30 April 1963, when shown from Windsor Great Park.

M. DAWSONIANA Rehd. & Wils.

A deciduous tree or large shrub described as 25 to 40 ft in the wild but already taller in cultivation; young shoots glabrous. Leaves obovate to oval, shortly pointed or blunt at the apex, usually tapered at the base, 3½ to 6 in. long, about half as much wide, of firm leathery texture and conspicuously net-veined on both surfaces, dark lustrous green above, paler and rather glaucous beneath, glabrous except for down each side of the midrib; stalk ½ to 1¼ in. long. Flowers borne on the naked wood in March and April; peduncles glabrous. Tepals usually nine in number (occasionally up to twelve), 3 to 5 in. long, 1 to 2 in. wide, white faintly streaked and tinged with purple, hanging downward when the flower is fully expanded. Fruits shortly stalked, cylindrical, 4 in. long, 1½ in. wide; seeds ⅝ in. long, orange-scarlet. *Bot. Mag.*, t. 9678-9.

M. *dawsoniana* was found by Wilson in a remote part of W. Szechwan near

Tatsien-lu (Kangting) in October 1908. He collected seeds again two years later, but never saw it in flower. Like *M. sinensis*, it appears to have reached this country from the nursery of Messrs Chenault of Orleans, in 1919 (according to Millais, these plants were grafted). It first flowered at Lanarth, Cornwall, in March 1937.

M. dawsoniana is a very beautiful magnolia and very hardy in its wood, but like all magnolias flowering in early spring its display may be ruined by frost, and it is slow to reach the flowering stage (fifteen years or more). Being of spreading habit it needs plenty of room and will be shy-flowering if planted in too shady a place. The largest plant at Caerhays, Cornwall, measure 54 × 5½ ft at 3 ft (1971) and there are two at Trewithen in the same county, almost as tall but smaller in girth.

The only magnolia with which *M. dawsoniana* is likely to be confused is the typical form of *M. sargentiana*, which has similar flowers but, as seen in cultivation, is easily distinguished from *M. dawsoniana* by its lighter green leaves and tree-like habit.

The name *M. dawsoniana* commemorates Jackson Dawson, first Superintendent of the Arnold Aboretum, Mass., and Professor Sargent's chief assistant in its foundation.

M. DELAVAYI Franch.

A spreading, flat-topped, evergreen tree up to 30 ft high. Leaves 8 to 14 in. long, 5 to 8 in. wide, greyish dull green above, glaucous and with fine down beneath, the midrib prolonged beyond the blade into a short tip; the stalk one-fourth the length of the blade, stout. The flowers are 7 to 8 in. across, cup-shaped and fragrant; the petals about 4 in. long, half as wide, dull, creamy white. The cone-like fruit is 6 in. long. *Bot. Mag.*, t. 8282.

Native of Yunnan, China; discovered by Père Delavay in 1886 near Lankong; introduced by Wilson from southern Yunnan in 1899. It first flowered at Kew, under glass, in 1908. Judging from Wilson's field notes, and those of other collectors, *M. delavayi* is found in open places, or in scrub dominated by species of *Lithocarpus*, on both sandstone and limestone formations, at 4,000 to 8,000 ft. Evergreen woody plants of the Sino-Himalayan region rarely prove hardy if introduced from altitudes much below 10,000 ft, so it is surprising that *M. delavayi* should thrive so well in the open air in this country, especially as the region where Wilson collected the seeds lies not far north of the tropics.

In the milder parts of the British Isles *M. delavayi* thrives better than the American *M. grandiflora* as a free-standing specimen. The flowers are smaller and more fleeting than they are in that species but 'As one sees it in Cornwall, it is, I think, the finest of all evergreen flowering trees' (W. J. Bean, in *New Flora and Sylva*, Vol. 5, p. 13). Near London it is fairly hardy on a wall protected from the north and east but will be cut in severe winters once it reaches above the coping, unless there is further protection from neighbouring trees or buildings. Unlike *M. grandiflora* it is quite happy on chalky soils.

There are three splendid examples of this species at Caerhays in Cornwall, 40 to 50 ft in height and another of the same size at Lanarth. Nearer London the following wall-specimens are recorded: Highdown, Sussex, on the south wall of the gardener's cottage, *pl.* 1912, 36 × 2 ft (1966); Borde Hill, Sussex, on east side of kitchen garden wall, sheltered on the east by trees, *pl.* 1911 25 × 4¼ ft (1968); Pylewell Park, Hants, 25 × 4¾ ft (1966). There are small but healthy specimens in the R.H.S. Garden at Wisley, on the wall of the Laboratory; and at Kew, on the wall of the Herbaceous Ground.

M. DENUDATA Desrouss.   YULAN   [PLATE 87

M. conspicua Salisb.; *M. yulan* Desf.

A rather low, rounded deciduous tree, much branched, rarely more than 30, but sometimes 45 ft high. Leaves 3 to 6 in. long, 2 to 3½ in. wide; oval to obovate, the apex contracting abruptly to a point, downy beneath. Flower-buds conspicuous all the winter by reason of their large scales being covered with grey, shaggy hairs. Flowers pure white, opening from March to May according to the season; petals 3 in. long, at first erect, afterwards spreading, thick, about nine in number. Fruits spindle-shaped, 5 in. long. *Bot. Mag.*, t. 1621.

Native of China; introduced in 1789. One of the most beautiful and distinctive of all flowering trees, this magnolia is, unfortunately, an occasional victim to the inclemency of an English spring. Its flowers respond quickly to premature warmth in late February or March, only too often to be trapped by succeeding frost. A cold February and March suits it best. It never fails to set an abundance of blossom, and the white flowers gleaming in the sunshine of an early spring day render it the most conspicuous of all trees at that season. It was for long an uncommon tree, the most famous specimens being at Kew, Syon, and Gunnersbury House. It became commoner when Dutch nurseries began to propagate it by grafting on *M.* × *soulangiana*. By the Chinese the yulan has been cultivated for at least thirteen hundred years, and was once commonly planted there near temples and in the Imperial gardens.

M. denudata varies in the shape of its flowers. An Award of Merit was given in 1926 to the form distributed by Messrs R. Veitch of Exeter, known in gardens as Veitch's 'Best Yulan'. In this the tepals are broadly obovate, rounded and abruptly acuminate at the apex, in contrast to other forms in which the tepals are more oblong and tapered at the apex. G. H. Johnstone pointed out that the Veitch form agrees very well with the plate in *Bot. Mag.*, t. 1621 (1814), which almost certainly represents the original introduction of 1789.

Perhaps the oldest example of *M. denudata* in Britain grows in the Goldsworth Nurseries near Woking, Surrey. It was planted in 1815.

var. PURPURASCENS (Maxim.) Rehd. & Wils., in part. *M. conspicua* var. *purpurascens* Maxim.—Tepals rosy-purple on the outside. This variety was described from plants cultivated in Japan but also occurs in China in the wild. It should not be confused with *M. sprengeri*, the pink-flowered forms of which were originally identified as *M. denudata.* var. *purpurascens* by Rehder and Wilson.

M. FRASERI Walt.

M. auriculata Bartr.

A deciduous tree 30 to 40 ft high, of open, spreading habit. Leaves produced in a cluster at the ends of the branches, pale green, of thin texture, glabrous on both sides, obovate, pointed and with two distinct auricles (or lobes) at the base, extending below the point where the stalk joins the blade; the entire blade is from 8 to 15 in. long, about half as wide; the stalk 2 to 4 in. long. Flowers

MAGNOLIA FRASERI

8 in. or more across, strongly and not very agreeably scented—at any rate close at hand; produced on the leafy shoots in May and June. Sepals three, oblong-obovate, greenish, larger than the petals, deflexed. Petals six, at first pale yellow, afterwards milky white, narrowly obovate, 3 to 4 in. long, at first erect, afterwards spreading. Seeds red, produced on a rose-coloured cone 4 or 5 in. long. *Bot. Mag.*, t. 1206.

Native of the south-eastern United States; first discovered in S. Carolina, in 1776, by William Bartram, and introduced to England ten years later. This handsome and distinct tree is distinguished from all other magnolias, except the rare *M. pyramidata* and the much larger-leaved *M. macrophylla*, by the auricles at the base of the leaves. The flowers are rather pale, but blend beautifully with the bronze-tinted young leaves. It is well worth growing as a lawn tree. The specific name commemorates John Fraser, who sent to England many North American plants between 1780 and 1810—including this magnolia.

M. fraseri has attained 68 × 4½ ft at Leonardslee in Sussex, and there is a tree at Killerton in Devon almost as large. At Kew the larger of two examples grows near the Azalea garden, and is about 30 ft high.

M. GLOBOSA Hook. f. & Thoms.

M. tsarongensis W. W. Sm.

A deciduous shrub or small tree 10 to 20 ft high; young shoots usually densely clothed at first with tawny velvety down. Leaves oval, rounded or slightly heart-shaped at the base, shortly pointed at the apex, 4 to 10 in. long, nearly half as wide, dark glossy green above with a little rusty down on the midrib and veins, permanently downy beneath, the down on the veins rust-coloured; veins in about twelve to fifteen pairs; stalk 1½ to 3 in. long. Flowers fragrant, slightly creamy white, rather globose, about 3 in. across, produced in June at the end of a leafy shoot, each on a stout slightly nodding stalk 2 in. or more long, which is covered thickly with a tawny felt. Tepals nine to twelve; stamens numerous, very short, bearing richly tinted anthers ½ in. long. Fruits cylindrical, 2 to 2½ in. long, 1 in. wide, pendulous, crimson. *Bot. Mag.*, t. 9467.

M. globosa has a wide distribution in the natural state, from the Sikkim Himalaya to N.W. Yunnan; introduced by Forrest from the Yunnan–Tibet borderland in 1919. It flowered at Loch Inch, Wigtonshire, in 1931 and in the same year received an Award of Merit when a flowering spray was shown from there by the Earl of Stair on June 16. The species was also introduced from Sikkim by Dr Watt of Aberdeen and flowered in his greenhouse in 1938 (*New Flora and Sylva*, Vol. 10, pp. 272–274 and fig. 92). In the following year, Dr Watt gave this plant to the late G. H. Johnstone of Trewithen, and it is still grown there beside an example of Forrest's introduction from Yunnan. The differences between these two plants are discussed in *Asiatic Magnolias*, pp. 117–118.

M. GRANDIFLORA L.

M. foetida (L.) Sarg.; *M. virginiana* var. *foetida* L.

An evergreen tree 60 to 80 ft high, of dense pyramidal form, but as usually seen with us less than half as high and more rounded. Leaves oval to oblong-obovate, from 6 to 10 in. long, less than half as wide; tapered to both ends, leathery in texture, glossy dark green above, covered beneath, especially when young, with a thick red-brown felt; stalk 1 to 2 in. long. Flowers among the finest in the genus, globular, 8 to 10 in. across, very fragrant with a spicy or fruity odour, produced continuously during the late summer and autumn. Petals thick and concave, creamy white, broadly obovate, and 4 or 5 in. long. *Bot. Mag.*, t. 1952.

Introduced from the southern United States to England early in the 18th century, this still remains the finest flowered of evergreen trees; and until the advent of the Chinese *M. delavayi* it was the only really evergreen hardy magnolia. It never suffers from cold at Kew, but open-ground trees grow slowly, especially in height, and are very different from the magnificent pyramids one sees along the Riviera and in Italy. It is apt to have its branches broken during heavy falls of snow, for which reason it is sometimes wise to brace the main branches together by stout wires. In cold localities it makes an admirable wall tree.

The tree ripens seeds freely in the south of Europe and many forms have been raised and named there. But few of these are distinctive enough to be worth mentioning. It is often claimed that this or that variety flowers at an early age, but it would perhaps be nearer the truth to say that a plant of any variety will produce flowers when quite small provided it was raised from layers or cuttings, whereas seedlings may not bloom until twenty or even more years old.

cv. 'ANGUSTIFOLIA'.—Leaves narrow, tapered at both ends; margins wavy. Introduced from France in 1825.

cv. 'EXMOUTH' ('Exoniensis', 'Lanceolata').—Leaves rather narrower than in the type, lanceolate or oval, slightly rusty coloured beneath; of a rather erect or fastigiate habit. *Bot. Mag.*, t. 1952.

The original tree grew in the garden of Sir John Colliton at Exmouth and in Miller's time (*Gard. Dict.*, 1768) was one of the few sizeable specimens in the country, most of the young plants from the first introduction having been killed in the great frosts of 1739–40. Attempts to reintroduce the species had not been successful, with the result that demand greatly exceeded supply. This may explain how the Exmouth tree came to be rented out to nurserymen, who sold the layers at a price of five guineas each, later falling to half a guinea (Loudon, *Arb. et Frut. Brit.*, Vol. 1, p. 263). The tree was cut down by accident in 1794.

cv. 'FERRUGINEA'.—This form was in commerce in 1804 and according to contemporary descriptions it had broader and blunter leaves than 'Exmouth', densely rusty beneath, and of bushier habit. The plants now in commerce under this name may be a different though similar clone.

cv. 'GLORIOSA'.—A broad-leaved form which bears flowers of great size and substance—one of the finest.

cv. 'GOLIATH'.—Leaves oval, rounded and often abruptly acuminate at the apex, up to 8 in. long, glabrous beneath except for a trace of rust along the midrib. Flowers nearly a foot across when fully expanded. This is now considered to be the finest variety. Award of Merit 1931, First Class Certificate 1951. The origin of this magnolia is uncertain. According to Millais it was first sent out by the Caledonia nursery, Guernsey.

M. HYPOLEUCA Sieb. & Zucc.
M. obovata Thunb., *nom. illegit.*

A deciduous, erect-growing tree 50 to 80, sometimes 100 ft high, with a trunk 6 to 9 ft in girth; young bark dark brown-purple. Leaves in a cluster at the end of the shoot, leathery, obovate, 8 to 18 in. long, half as much wide; tapering at the base to a stalk 1 to 2½ in. long; glaucous green above, blue-white and slightly downy beneath. Flowers produced in June, 8 in. across, strongly scented, tepals creamy white; stamens bright purplish red, forming, with the yellow anthers, a conspicuous circular mass 3 in. across in the centre of the flower. The fruit is brilliant red until mature, cone-shaped, rather pointed, 5 to 8 in. high, 2½ in. wide. *Bot. Mag.*, t. 8077.

MAGNOLIA HYPOLEUCA

Native of Japan; introduced in 1884. It attains apparently its largest size in the forests of Hokkaido, where it is highly valued for its light, soft, easily worked timber. One of the most beautiful of all northern trees both in leaf and flower, this magnolia is also quite hardy. When young its habit is open and sometimes rather gaunt.

There is an example at Kew in the Magnolia collection near the Victoria Gate which came from the Yokohama Nursery Company in 1908. It is slightly over 30 ft high. A tree at Trewidden in Cornwall, *pl. c.* 1893, measures 44 × 6¾ ft (1959); it was flowering freely by 1906. Some trees under the label *M. hypoleuca* or *M. obovata* may be *M. officinalis* (q.v.).

We are grateful to Mr Dandy of the British Museum (Natural History) for pointing out that the name *M. obovata* Thunb. is illegitimate under modern rules of botanical nomenclature. The older generation of gardeners knew the species as *M. hypoleuca*, and this now proves to be the correct name.

M. KOBUS DC.

M. *thurberi* Parsons ex W. Robinson

A deciduous tree, ultimately 30 or 40 ft high, with a trunk 3 ft in girth, of quick growth and pyramidal form when young, but eventually round-headed. Young branches aromatically fragrant when crushed; winter leaf-buds downy. Leaves obovate, 3 to 6 in. long, often contracted at the apex to a short point, tapering at the base to a short stalk. Flowers amongst the smallest in the genus, often under 4 in. in diameter when fully expanded; petals six, pure white,

MAGNOLIA KOBUS

obovate; sepals small, soon falling; flower-stalk downy. Fruits pinkish, seeds bright red. Flowers in April. *Bot. Mag.*, t. 8428.

Native of Japan. Although one of the less attractive of magnolias when young, when it does not flower freely, this species is an interesting addition to cultivated Japanese trees on account of its vigorous constitution. It is much used by Japanese gardeners as a stock on which they graft *M. stellata*, and it blooms profusely when older. It was probably first introduced to England by Maries; there was a fine tree in the Coombe Wood nursery sent home by him in 1879. This tree is said to have first flowered around 1909, when thirty years old, and this no doubt has helped to support the belief that *M. kobus* is slow to flower. But other introductions from Japan have flowered when quite young and the truth may simply be that this species is variable in the time taken to reach the flowering stage. Since it is one of those species that can be propagated quite easily by cuttings, forms that take an unconscionable time to reach flowering age will no doubt disappear from commerce.

var. BOREALIS Sarg.—This appears to be a more robust version of the species, found occasionally up to 80 ft high, with stouter branchlets, leaves 6 to 7 in. long and flowers up to 5 in. wide. Sargent described it from specimens that he had collected near Sapporo, in the north island of Japan (Hokkaido), in 1892 and cited other specimens from that area and from the northern part of the main island. This variety does not, however, entirely replace the type in northern Japan; in other words, a form of M. kobus from Hokkaido or the northern part of the main island is not necessarily var. borealis.

In 1876 the Arnold Arboretum had received seeds of M. kobus from Sapporo, and a tree raised from these, growing in his garden at Boston, was considered by Sargent to belong to his var. borealis. In 1908, when almost thirty years old, this tree was still sparse-flowering, but fifteen years later it was making a fine display and bearing more flowers every year (E. H. Wilson, Gard. Chron., Vol. 73 (1923), p. 301). In 1922 the late Charles Eley of East Bergholt Place, Suffolk, obtained seeds which almost certainly came from this tree and distributed a share of these, and later seedlings, to many gardens. Mr Maxwell Eley tells us that of the seedlings planted at East Bergholt all but two were removed because they were so slow to flower. Of those retained, one first bore flowers when twenty-five years old and to quote Mr Eley's words 'never flowered properly till 1964, when it was so dense with flowers that it looked as if a white sheet had been draped over it'. Since then it has flowered every year but not so well as in 1964. This tree measures 35 × 2¼ ft (1966). The sister tree is smaller and has not yet flowered. In other gardens too the Eley introduction has been slow to flower, but evidently there is still hope for them.

M. LILIIFLORA Desrouss.

M. obovata Willd., not Thunb.; M. purpurea Curtis

A deciduous bush of rather straggling growth, rarely more than 12 ft high in the open (although twice as high on walls); young wood aromatic. Leaves ovate, oblong, or obovate, 3 to 8 in. long, 2 to 5 in. wide, tapering rather abruptly to a point, dark green above, downy beneath. Flowers opening from April to June; petals 3 in. long 1¾ in. wide, erect, obovate, vinous purple and white outside, white within. Bot. Mag., t. 390.

Introduced from Japan in 1790, this handsome shrub is now considered to be a native of China, and as existing in Japan as a cultivated plant only. It varies to a considerable extent in the colour of the flowers when raised from seed, but is always purple or a combination of purple and white outside, and white within. The plant figured in Bot. Mag., t. 390 (1797) (as M. purpurea) apparently had the tepals wholly purple on the outside but more deeply so at the base. The colouring may have been exaggerated, since according to Loudon the flowers of the 1790 introduction were never wholly purple on the outside but 'melt off into white at the upper extremities' (Arb. et Frut. Brit., Vol. 1, pp. 282–283.

MAGNOLIA 657

M. liliiflora is quite hardy near London; it usually requires wall protection in the north. The later flowers are accompanied by full-sized leaves.

cv. 'GRACILIS'.—Of narrower, more fastigiate habit than the original introduction, with more slender branches. Leaves narrower, paler green. Flowers with narrower petals, reflexed at the apex, wholly deep purple on the outside. Introduced from Japan in 1804 (*M. gracilis* Salisb.; *M. liliiflora* var. *gracilis* (Salisb.) Rehd.).

cv. 'NIGRA'.—Flowers larger, with petals 4 or 5 in. long, very dark purple outside, borne mainly in May and early June. It makes a less straggly bush than ordinary *M. liliiflora*. It was introduced by J. G. Veitch from Japan in 1861. Nicholson, considering it to be a hybrid between *M. liliiflora* and *M. denudata*, described it as *M. soulangiana nigra* in 1884. It may be that some plants sent out at one time by continental nurserymen under this name were indeed forms of *M. × soulangiana*, but the Veitchian introduction agrees better with *M. liliiflora*.

M. × LOEBNERI Kache

This hybrid between *M. kobus* and the allied *M. stellata* was described from plants raised from a deliberate cross between the two species made by Max Löbner of Pillnitz, Germany, shortly before World War I. The original plants were sold in 1923 and of these Messrs Kordes of Sparrieshoop acquired five (Wilhelm Kordes in *Die Deutsche Baumschule*, August 1964, p. 242). Herr Kordes states in the article cited that one of the original plants, growing in his garden, is 25 ft high and 28 ft across, and produces flowers in unbelievable profusion about one week before *M. × soulangiana*. He adds that it is easily reproduced by cuttings.

M. × loebneri has typically about twelve petals to the flower and narrowly obovate leaves.

cv. 'LEONARD MESSEL'.—Flowers with twelve petals, purplish pink on the outside, white within. Raised at Nymans, Sussex, and believed to be the result of a chance cross between *M. kobus* and *M. stellata* f. *rosea*. Award of Merit, 3 May 1955.

cv. 'MERRILL'.—Petals almost as numerous as in *M. stellata* but twice as wide. This is the result of a deliberate cross made at the Arnold Arboretum. The original plant, from seed sown in 1939, was 25 ft high in 1956 (*Arnoldia*, Vol. 9, p. 11 and Vol. 15, p. 8).

If *M. stellata* is treated as a variety of *M. kobus*, the plants mentioned above would have to be regarded as cultivars of *M. kobus*, since they would be the results of crossing within that species.

M. MACROPHYLLA Michx. [PLATE 88

A deciduous tree 20 to 50 ft high, with an open, spreading head of branches, and a trunk 1 to 1½ ft in diameter. Leaves the largest of all magnolias, measuring 15 to 25 in., sometimes 3 ft in length, and from 7 to 12 in. wide, oblong-obovate, widest above the middle, bluntish at the apex, broadly heart-shaped or auriculate

T S—Y

at the base, bright green and glabrous above, silvery grey and downy beneath. Flowers on leafy shoots 8 to 10, sometimes 14 in. across, fragrant; petals six, dull creamy white, fleshy, 5 to 7 in. long, half as wide. Fruits roundish, egg-shaped, rose-coloured, 3 in. long. *Bot. Mag.*, t. 2189.

Native of the south-eastern United States, where it is rare, and only occurs in small isolated stations. It was discovered by the elder Michaux in 1759 in the mountains of S. Carolina; introduced to Europe in 1800. In foliage this is the most remarkable of magnolias; and is indeed one of the most interesting of the world's trees; but it is, unfortunately, spring tender in a young state. That it will withstand severer frosts than any we experience is shown by two healthy trees growing in front of the museum of the Arnold Arboretum, Boston, USA. The most famous specimen in England was at Claremont, near Esher, a healthy tree which, in 1912, was 40 ft high, its trunk 3 ft in girth. This no longer exists.

The largest specimens recorded recently are: Savill Gardens, Windsor Great Park, 30 × 1½ ft, (1967); Exbury, Hants, 30 × 2¼ ft (1968); Bodnant, Denbigh, 20 × 2 ft (1966). There are also examples about 25 ft high at Tittenhurst Park, Berks, and Nymans, Sussex.

M. ASHEI Weatherby—This species, which is very closely allied to *M. macrophylla*, was described in 1928 from specimens collected by Ashe in western Florida, where it is reported to make a tree up to 25 ft high, growing in deep sandy soil near streams (*M. macrophylla* occurs in the same area, but in drier situations). The differences between the two species are, according to Weatherby, not very clear cut, the most reliable ones being that in *M. macrophylla* the carpels have a fleshy appendage along the line of suture and the fruit-cones are ovoid to subglobose, while in *M. ashei* the appendages are thin and the fruit-cones ovoid-cylindric. Less constant differences are that in *M. ashei* the hairs on the midrib beneath are sparser and less spreading than in *M. macrophylla* and the flowers on the average smaller (8 to 12 in. across) with more or less acute petals.

M. ashei was introduced to Britain in 1949 and survives in a few gardens. Its chief claim to attention is that it flowers when 3 ft or even less high (see *Journ. R.H.S.*, Vol. 78 (1953), pp. 288–289 and fig. 90). It is much more tender than *M. macrophylla*.

M. NITIDA W. W. Sm.

A widely branched evergreen tree or shrub 20 to 30 (occasionally over 40) ft high; young shoots glabrous. Leaves of leathery texture, oval, oblong of inclined to ovate, shortly pointed, broadly wedge-shaped or sometimes rounded at the base, 2¼ to 4½ in. long, 1 to 2 in. wide, reddish bronze when young, becoming dark shining green above, paler beneath, perfectly glabrous; stalk ½ to 1 in. long. Flowers fragrant, creamy white, 2 to 3 in. wide; tepals nine or twelve, oblanceolate to narrowly obovate, 2 in. long, ½ to ⅝ in. wide; sepals three, narrower. Fruits 2 to 3 in. long, 1¼ in. wide, composed of fifteen to twenty carpels, each containing one or two bright orange-red seeds. *Bot. Mag.*, n.s., t. 16.

Native of Yunnan, China, and S.E. Tibet, at altitudes of 9,000 to 12,000 ft discovered by G. Forrest in 1917; plants raised from seed he collected later are in cultivation at Kew and elsewhere. The leaves are very much smaller than, but have some resemblance to, those of *M. grandiflora*; they do not at all resemble those of *M. delavayi*, the third and only other evergreen species in cultivation. Forrest found *M. nitida* flowering in June and he remarks that it is strongly aromatic when in fruit. Writing after a severe frost at Caerhays in Cornwall, in March 1931, J. C. Williams described its foliage as by far the most brilliant to be seen there and absolutely without a trace of injury. It is not hardy at Kew and is very rare in gardens. There are three examples at Caerhays, Cornwall, the largest 33 × 2¾ ft (1971). Another grows at Trewithen, Cornwall, and it was this tree (raised from F.26509) that provided the flowering spray figured in the *Botanical Magazine*.

With its bronze young growths and its polished leaves, *M. nitida* is, in foliage, the finest magnolia cultivated in Britain; indeed, Mr Johnstone considered it to be in that respect the most beautiful of all evergreen trees known to him. But it must be stressed that it is hardy only in the mildest parts.

M. OBOVATA *see* M. HYPOLEUCA

M. OFFICINALIS Rehd. & Wils.
M. hypoleuca Veitch, not Sieb. & Zucc.

A deciduous tree 20 to 50 ft high, its young shoots at first silky downy, yellowish grey. Leaves obovate, rounded at the apex, tapered at the base; 14 to 21 in. long, 5 to 10 in. wide, glabrous and rather pale green above, glaucous and clothed with pale fine down beneath; lateral veins twenty to thirty, prominent beneath; stalk 1 to 1½ in. long. Flower white, fragrant, cupped, 6 to 8 in. across, produced in early summer at the end of the leafy young growth; flower-stalk thick and downy. Sepals and petals nine to twelve, fleshy, up to 4 in. long and 1½ in. wide; stamens numerous, red. Fruits oblong to egg-shaped, flat at the top, 4 to 5 in. high, 2½ in. wide.

Native of W. Hupeh, China; discovered by Henry about 1885, introduced by Wilson in 1900. At first it was confused with the beautiful *M. hypoleuca*, with which it is almost identical in foliage. It differs in the yellowish-grey young shoots (purplish in *hypoleuca*) and flat-topped fruit. It is not so large a tree although equally beautiful in flower and noble in leaf. It is cultivated in W. China for its bark and flower-buds, which yield a drug valued by the Chinese for the medicinal properties. It is quite hardy. As it was sent out by Messrs Veitch as the "Chinese hypoleuca", it no doubt exists unrecognised in some gardens under that name.

var. BILOBA Rehd. & Wils.—Leaves deeply and conspicuously notched at the apex, otherwise similar to the type. This variety was introduced by Messrs Hillier in 1936, by means of seeds received from the Lushan Botanic Garden. Five plants were raised, of which one now grows in the Valley Gardens, Windsor Great Park. G. H. Johnstone remarked that typical *M. officinalis* often bears notched leaves, but in the Windsor plant almost every leaf is of this character.

M. PYRAMIDATA Bartr.

Originally discovered by William Bartram in Georgia, on the banks of the Altamaha River, and recognised by him as a species, this magnolia was by later botanists confused with *M. fraseri*. Although closely allied, the two are now considered quite distinct. The leaves of the present species are much smaller (usually less than 8 in. long), of thinner texture, narrowing to a waist near the base, the basal lobes spreading. The flowers, too, are smaller, 3 to 5 in. across, and the tree more erect and pyramidal, as is implied by the name. Whilst *M. fraseri* is an inland mountain plant, this species affects low-lying regions of Georgia and the Carolinas. Whether it is at present in cultivation I am not aware. It was introduced early in the 19th century, and grew in Messrs Loddiges's nursery at Hackney about 1837. George Nicholson saw it in the Trianon Gardens in 1887, and quite possibly it survives in some of the old gardens in the warmer parts of the country under the name of *M. fraseri*. It is, no doubt, more tender than *M. fraseri*.

M. ROSTRATA W. W. Sm.

A deciduous tree 40 to 80 ft high, with silvery-grey bark and glabrous purplish young shoots. Leaves obovate, rounded at the end, usually tapered to a narrow or slightly heart-shaped base, the largest over 20 in. long by 12 in. wide, purplish red and clothed with tawny down when quite young, becoming glabrous above, glaucous and thinly furnished with down beneath, the midrib and chief veins (of the latter there are frequently over thirty pairs) often clothed with reddish-brown hairs; stalk 1 to 3 in. long. Flowers creamy white or pink, large, terminal, and solitary on leafy shoots of the current season, opening in June; petals tapered to a point, at first erect enough to give the flower a cupped shape. Fruits cylindric, bright red, 5 or 6 in. long, 1½ in. wide, carpels beaked, seeds small.

Native of Yunnan, S.E. Tibet, and Upper Burma; discovered in Yunnan by Forrest in 1917. There was at one time much confusion between this species and "*M. mollicomata*" (or *campbellii*) which bears its rosy-pink flowers in spring on the leafless shoots of the preceding year. The original description of the flowers by Sir W. W. Smith in *Notes, Royal Botanic Garden, Edinburgh*, Vol. xii, p. 213, really refers to those of *M. mollicomata*. Farrer, who found it in Upper Burma in 1919, also confused the two. Kingdon Ward describes the flowers as white, small, borne immediately above the huge leaves and practically invisible from below, and the tree itself as certainly not the magnificent sight in flower Forrest and Farrer originally believed it to be.

It is tender and needs protection from wind. The tallest specimen known grows at Sidbury Manor, Devon; planted in 1935 it measures 50 × 2 ft (1959). An older tree at Trewithen in Cornwall has attained 41 × 3¼ ft (1971) but would be taller if better sheltered from the wind. At Borde Hill, Sussex, a tree raised from seeds collected by Forrest in 1926 was killed in the winter of 1939–40; another, raised from Kingdon Ward 7628, collected in Upper Burma in 1926, has survived in a protected position.

M. SALICIFOLIA (Sieb. & Zucc.) Maxim.
Buergeria salicifolia Sieb. & Zucc.

A slender deciduous tree 20 to 40 ft high, with a trunk 1 ft in diameter; young shoots very slender, smooth the first year, slightly warted the second; leaf-buds quite glabrous. Leaves narrowly oval to lanceolate, tapered at both ends, blunt or pointed at the apex, 1½ to 4 in. long, ⅝ to 1½ in. wide, dull green and glabrous above, slightly glaucous and covered with minute down beneath; stalk slender, ¼ to ⅜ in. long. Flowers 3 to 4 in. across. Petals six, pure white; the three outer ones 2 in. long, ½ in. wide, oblong, pointed; the three inner ones rather shorter and wider, slightly obovate. Sepals short, lanceolate, very soon falling; flower-stalks quite glabrous; flower-buds hairy. Fruits rosy-pink, 2 to 3 in. long; seeds scarlet. *Bot. Mag.*, t. 8483.

Native of Japan (main island and Kyushu); introduced to Kew from the Yokohama nurseries in 1906 (for the Mt Hakkoda form, introduced earlier, see below).

A very distinct species which makes an elegant tree, perfectly hardy. It blossoms in April on the naked shoots and the display is rarely ruined by frost. The flower is similar to that of *M. kobus*, but otherwise the species is very distinct in its narrow leaves, smooth leaf-buds and flower-stalks. It first flowered at Kew in 1911. The bark when bruised emits a pleasant odour, like that of *Aloysia triphylla* (lemon-scented verbena).

M. salicifolia is variable in habit. The tree in the Azalea Garden at Kew, planted in 1906, was fastigiate at first but has now become open-crowned, with the main branches springing from the trunk at a narrow angle but arching downward at their extremities. It measures 40 × 2¾ ft (1967). Other trees imported to Britain from Japan at the same time had the branches spreading from the start. In a third form, named *fasciata* by Millais, the plant has no central leader but consists of a besom-like cluster of stems; this is much less attractive than the freely branching form.

There is also some variation in size and shape of leaf. Sargent, Director of the Arnold Arboretum, described the leaves of trees seen by him on Mt Hakkoda as up to 5 or 6 in. long and 2 in. wide (in the common and more typical form they are only 1¼ to 1½ in. wide); he also noted that when bruised they exhaled 'the delicate odour of aniseed' (*Forest Flora of Japan*, p. 10). J. H. Veitch accompanied Sargent on his visit to Mt Hakkoda (autumn 1892) and both collected seeds there of *M. salicifolia*. Veitch's share did not germinate but the next year he obtained seeds or seedlings from the Arnold Arboretum and was listing *M. salicifolia* in his 1902 catalogue. The Veitchian broad-leaved form, discussed by G. H. Johnstone (op. cit., pp. 98, 100, 101), is almost certainly from the Mt Hakkoda seeds. One tree, growing in the Coombe Wood nursery, was described as follows in previous editions of the present work: it 'differs from the typical form in its more spreading habit, its stouter branchlets, larger flowers, broader petals (1½ ins.), broader leaves (up to 3 ins. wide), differently scented bark, and in flowering a fortnight or so later'. Dr Sprague of Kew recognised this as the var. *concolor* of Miquel.

M. (*salicifolia* × *kobus*) 'KEWENSIS'.—This hybrid arose at Kew as a self-sown seedling found near the two parents. Bark of young stems smelling strongly of lemon-scented verbena (as in *M. salicifolia*); growth-buds with a few silky hairs. Leaves 3½ to 5 in. long, 1¼ to 2 in. wide, narrowly obovate or elliptic, narrowed at the apex to a blunt tip, cuneate at the base, smooth and rather glossy above, slightly glaucous green beneath. Flowers very fragrant, with six petals about 3 in. long. A.M. 1952. It grows vigorously and plants of a good size can be seen in many magnolia collections. The original plant at Kew grows by King William's Temple.

The name *M.* × *kewensis* has never been validated by a Latin description.

M. × PROCTORIANA Rehd.—A hybrid between *M. salicifolia* and *M. stellata* described by Rehder in 1939. As in 'Kewensis' the leaves are broadest at or slightly above the middle and the growth-buds silky-hairy. Petals six to twelve —hence less numerous than in *M. stellata*; they are also broader.

If *M. stellata* is treated as a variety of *M. kobus*, it would follow that *M.* × *proctoriana* is the collective name for all hybrids between *M. kobus* and *M. salicifolia*. The Kew hybrid described above would then come under it as *M.* × *proctoriana* 'Kewensis'.

M. SARGENTIANA Rehd. & Wils.

A deciduous tree not uncommonly attaining a height of 50 to 70 ft in the wild and a girth of 7 to 9 ft (one exceptional specimen seen by Wilson was 80 ft with a trunk 10 ft in girth at 6 ft above the ground); branchlets glabrous, greenish yellow at first, becoming grey or greyish brown. Leaves obovate or less commonly oblong-obovate, 4 to 7 in. long, 2¼ to 4 in. wide, notched, rounded or acuminate at the apex, obliquely wedge-shaped at the base, dark glossy green and glabrous above, undersides paler and usually densely covered with long greyish hairs except on the more or less glabrous midrib; leaf-stalks slender, glabrous. Flower-buds ovoid, acute, covered with greyish hairs; flower-stalks downy. Flowers about 8 in. across, borne before the leaves in March–April. Tepals ten to thirteen, oblong-obovate or oblong-lanceolate, purplish pink on the outside, paler or white within; in a specimen collected in the wild on Mt Omei in 1939 the tepals were 2¾ to 4 1⁄16 in. long, 1 3⁄16 to 1⅝ in. wide, and are of about the same dimensions in cultivated plants. Fruit-cones cylindrical, 4 to 5 in. long, often twisted owing to the uneven development of the carpels. Seeds usually one in each carpel, orange-scarlet.

A native of W. Szechwan (Wa-shan and Mt Omei) and of N. Yunnan; introduced by Wilson in 1908 during his expedition for the Arnold Arboretum and described from fruiting specimens collected at the same time. Wilson never saw this species in bloom, but a flowering specimen was collected by C. L. Sun in 1939 on Mt Omei, about thirty miles east of the type-locality (*Pl. Omeienses* Vol. 1, p. 1944 and Plate 8).

M. sargentiana first flowered at Nymans, Sussex, in April 1932 and received an F.C.C. when shown from there in 1935. When sending material from this tree to Kew in 1943, James Comber, the garden manager, wrote that it was 'a seedling raised by J. Nix esq. from Wilson's seed, and given to me when visiting Tilgate'. This tree, which still grows in the Walled Garden, must be one of the few in this country raised direct from the wild seed. Most of the older trees, both of the type and the var. *robusta*, came from Chenault of Orleans, who received seedlings from the Arnold Arboretum which he multiplied by grafting.

In cultivation *M. sargentiana* makes a tree which has already (at Caerhays) attained the average height of wild trees, but not yet their girth. Its flowers resembled those of *M. dawsoniana*, and are no less beautiful, but that species can always be distinguished by its shrubby habit and deeper green, veiny leaves. *M. sargentiana* in its typical state is not so widely planted as the var. *robusta* described below, partly because it does not seed freely and partly perhaps because it takes longer than the var. *robusta* to reach the flowering state. A tree at Caerhays, Cornwall, *pl.* 1921, measures 50 × 3¾ ft, with a bole of 11 ft; another, six years younger, is 38 × 3 ft (1966).

var. ROBUSTA Rehd. & Wils.—This variety was described from fruiting specimens collected by Wilson in the area from which came the type-specimens of *M. sargentiana*; seeds were also taken and distributed under field number W.923a. According to the original description it differs in its longer and narrower leaves, which in Wilson's specimens are 5½ to 8½ in. long, 2½ to 3½ in. wide, with larger fruits (4¾ to 7¼ in. long). The grafted plants sent out by Chanault as var. *robusta* agree very well with this description in their elongated leaves and in bearing fruit-cones 7 to 8 in. long. They are also distinct in other respects. They make spreading bushy trees, usually dividing into three or more stems at 3 or 4 ft above the ground; in mature specimens the leaves are mostly broadly notched at the apex; and the flowers are strikingly different from those of typical *M. sargentiana*, being up to 12 in. across, with more numerous and much larger tepals (ten to sixteen, 8 in. long, 3 in. wide). If more herbarium material were available—it is very scanty and incomplete—it might prove that the var. *robusta* is linked by intermediates to the typical state of the species. But cultivated plants raised from the original wild seeds are certainly very distinct. Of the two, the var. *robusta* is much to be preferred, the flowers being of a clearer pink and better displayed. [PLATE 89

M. sargentiana var. *robusta* first flowered in Britain at Caerhays, Cornwall, in April 1931. A flower sent by J. C. Williams to Kew on April 14 of that year is still preserved in the Herbarium and has with it a description drawn up by Dr Stapf while the flower was still fresh. Photographs of the Caerhays plant, taken on the same occasion, are reproduced in *New Flora and Sylva*, Vol. 5, figs. iv and v. In France, the var. *robusta* had flowered earlier, by 1923.

M. (sargentiana var. *robusta* × *sprengeri* var. *diva*) 'CAERHAYS BELLE'.—A hybrid of great promise, raised at Caerhays, Cornwall. See *Journ. R.H.S.*, Vol. 91, p. 285 and fig. 151.

M. SIEBOLDII K. Koch

M. parviflora Sieb. & Zucc., not Blume

A small deciduous tree or large shrub, with slender branches. Leaves oblong or obovate-oblong, 4 to 6 in. long, the apex contracting rather abruptly to a point, rounded at the base, dark green and glabrous above, glaucous and downy beneath, usually with seven to nine pairs of veins; leaf-stalk ¾ to ½ in. long, pubescent when young. Flowers fragrant, at first cup-shaped, borne on a stalk 1 to 2½ in. long; petals pure white, about 2 in. long, obovate, very concave. Stamens numerous, forming a rosy-crimson or maroon-crimson disk 1 in. across. Fruit 2 in. long, carmine; seeds scarlet. *Bot. Mag.* t. 7411.

Native of S. Japan and Korea; probably first introduced to Britain around 1879 by Messrs Veitch (but the plant originally grown at Kew came from Yokohama in 1893). The most distinctive character of the species is the comparatively long flower-stalk; also, the flowers, instead of being fully pendent as in the allied *M. wilsonii* and *M. sinensis*, have a more horizontal poise and 'look you in the face' (as Millais put it). The flowers are not always borne in one crop but appear often a few at a time from May until August on the leafy shoots. The crimson stamens show in attractive contrast to the white tepals.

M. sieboldii varies in the colour of its stamens, from pinkish (in a very poor form sometimes still seen in gardens) to rosy-crimson and maroon-crimson. In the catalogue of the winding-up sale of Veitch's Coombe Wood nursery Lot 895 was described as having the stamens 'deep claret', but whether this was their original form or a newer introduction is not known. The form with the brightest crimson stamens is believed to have been raised from seeds collected by Wilson in Korea in 1918. *M. sieboldii* is generally reckoned to be hardy, though there are reports of plants having been badly damaged or even killed in severe winters; having a wide north–south range it is likely to vary in this respect. It will grow 12 to 15 ft high and as much through (even larger in favourable situations). It is not suitable for chalky soils.

M. (*sieboldii* × *tripetala*) 'CHARLES COATES'.—Three self-sown seedlings were noticed in the Azalea Garden at Kew by C. F. Coates, then foreman-propagator in the Arboretum. These were grown on, and when they flowered in 1958 it was established that they were hybrids of the above parentage. The leaves resemble those of *M. tripetala* in shape but are smaller and have long hairs on the midrib beneath. The flowers resemble those of *M. sieboldii* in shape but are held erect as in *M. tripetala*, and are cream-coloured. They are borne in mid-May and very fragrant. Stamens bright magenta (J. R. Sealy, *Gard. Chron.*, Vol. 152 (1962), p. 77).

M. SINENSIS (Rehd. & Wils.) Stapf   [PLATE 90

M. globosa var. *sinensis* Rehd. & Wils.; *M. nicholsoniana* Hort., not Rehd. & Wils.

A deciduous tree or shrub up to 20 ft high; young shoots clothed at first with pale brown silky hairs; becoming glabrous and greyish the second year. Leaves oval, oval-oblong and obovate to roundish; rounded or abruptly pointed at the apex, wedge-shaped or rounded at the base, 3 to 7 in. long, 2 to 5½ in. wide, glabrous and bright green above, slightly glaucous and at first very velvety beneath; stalk ¾ to 2½ in. long and, like the midrib, densely silky-hairy. Flowers saucer-shaped, white, fragrant, 4 to 5 in. wide, produced at the end of young leafy shoots on a stalk 1 to 2 in. long in June; tepals usually nine, oblong-obovate, 1 to 2 in. wide. Stamens numerous, ⅖ in. long, rosy-crimson. Fruits pendulous, cylindrical, 3 in. long, 1½ in. wide, pink; seeds at first pink, ultimately scarlet.

Native of W. Szechwan, China; discovered and introduced to the Arnold Arboretum in 1908 by Wilson. It was found by him at altitudes of 7,500 to 9,000 ft and is perfectly hardy. Introduced to England through Messrs Chenault's nursery at Orleans in 1920 and distributed under the name "*M. nicholsoniana*". The magnolia to which that name was originally given is now regarded as a form of *M. wilsonii* (q.v.).

M. sinensis is a beautiful magnolia which thrives on chalky soils and is quite hardy (the original grafted plants imported from Chenault's nurseries had the reputation of being difficult and somewhat tender, but this is perhaps accounted for by the use of an unsuitable stock.) Its spreading habit makes it less suitable for small gardens than *M. wilsonii*.

M. × HIGHDOWNENSIS Dandy—A probable hybrid between *M. sinensis* and *M. wilsonii*. Young wood darker than in the former but lacking the purple tinge characteristic of the ripe stems of *M. wilsonii*. Leaves up to 7¾ in. long, 4 in. wide, elliptic or oblong-elliptic, acute or acuminate at the apex, rounded or cuneate at the base (thus they are very distinct from the leaves of *M. sinensis* and more like those of *M. wilsonii*, though somewhat larger and the leaves on the extension growths more perfectly elliptic); they are covered fairly densely beneath with white hairs. Flowers as large as those of *M. sinensis*.

The original plants of *M. highdownensis* were received by the late Sir Frederick Stern in 1927 from J. C. Williams of Caerhays. They were seedlings from a pan whose label had been mislaid, so the seed-parent of the Highdown plants is unknown.

The first description of these hybrids was given by Sir F. Stern in a note in *New Flora and Sylva*, Vol. 10, pp. 105–107, headed '*M. sinensis* × *wilsonii*'. The name *M.* × *highdownensis* was published by J. E. Dandy in *Journ. R.H.S.*, Vol.75, pp. 159–161. Mr Dandy, who is the leading authority on the genus *Magnolia*, gave the following reasons for his belief that the Highdown magnolia is *M. sinensis* × *wilsonii*. First, it is intermediate between the two species. Secondly, the seeds came from a garden (Caerhays) in which both species had flowered. Thirdly, it is not matched by any specimens collected in the wild.

M. × SOULANGIANA Soulange-Bodin   [PLATE 91

A hybrid raised in the garden of Soulange-Bodin at Fromont, near Paris, from seed borne by *M. denudata* fertilised by pollen of *M. liliiflora*. The plant first flowered in 1826, and has since become the most popular of all magnolias in European gardens. In habit it is similar to *M. denudata*, forming a low, spreading, but more shapely tree. It flowers in April, rather later than the yulan, and is usually at its best when the flowers of that species are fading. Leaves 3 to 6 in. long, mostly narrower than those of the yulan, and especially more tapering towards the apex; they are downy beneath. The flowers appear first and make their great display on the naked shoots, but continue to develop until early June, when the tree is full of foliage. Numerous forms of this magnolia have appeared since 1826, raised mostly from its seeds. They are all alike in having the petals white inside and stained more or less with purple on the outside; but they vary in depth and shade of colour, and in the width and shape of the petals. Many forms of the cross have been given distinguishing names, but others have been grown as *M.* × *soulangiana* simply, and these certainly do not represent a single clone. It is unlikely that Soulange-Bodin raised, and gave his name to, a single hybrid seedling.

Some of the better known varieties are described below, but the nomenclature is unfortunately very confused. There are, for example, three Alexandrinas, at least two Alba Superbas and two Norbertiis, and in no case is the original description sufficiently detailed for the proper use of these and other confused names to be decided.

'ALBA'.—An ambiguous name, which has been used for both 'Alba Superba' and 'Amabilis'.

'ALBA SUPERBA'.—The plant grown by Millais under this name was near to *M. denudata* but flowered ten days later and was of more upright habit. Leaves said by him to be very similar to those of *M. denudata*; flowers with nine petaloid tepals 3¾ in. long, 2 in. wide at the broadest part, sometimes with a faint pink tinge along the centre line. A magnolia in commerce under the same name seems to be different, the tepals being narrower and the leaves elliptic or fairly narrowly oblong-obovate. Correctly named or not, the latter is a beautiful magnolia, with very fragrant flowers and of dense, erect habit.

'ALEXANDRINA'.—The original variety was raised or distributed by Cels of Montrouge, before 1831, but the name seems to have been used for several distinct varieties. The plant grown by Millais was of erect habit with tepals 4 × 2 in., heavily flushed rosy-purple and with darker purple lines up to three-quarters of their length, but the colouring more purple and less rosy in some seasons. Flowers produced with the leaves in early April. This is perhaps the same as the 'Alexandrina' of Van Houtte's nursery and of *Rev. Hort. Belg.*, Vol. 26, t. 217. The 'Alexandrina' of the Nantes nurserymen is said to have resembled 'Lennei' but with smaller flowers. The 'Alexandrina' described by Mouillefert (*Tr. Arb. et Arbriss.*, Vol. 1, p. 119) had almost pure white flowers, as does the plant at Kew in the garden of the Wood Museum (Duke's Garden).

'AMABILIS'.—According to Millais this is 'a seedling hybrid sent out by the Dutch and Belgian nurserymen. The general habit and flowers are like *M. denudata*, pure white, fairly large and possessing a chocolate centre' (op. cit., p. 83). This is scarcely the same as the 'Amabilis' known to P. C. Veitch, which had small flowers with very narrow petals (*Journ. R.H.S.*, Vol. 46 (1921), p. 316). According to Pampanini's account, 'Amabilis' was raised in France and has spreading petals tinted violet on the outside (*Boll. Soc. Ort. Tosc.*, Vol. 40, p. 199).

'BROZZONII'.—Flowers up to 10 in. across when fully expanded, white on the outside except for a purple flush at the base. This is one of the last of the group to flower (second half of April). According to Millais, this variety was first sent out by Messrs Barbier of Orleans about 1913, but the plant at Borde Hill in Sussex came from Leroy of Angers in 1908. Where it arose is not known, but Sig. Coggiatti, President of the society Giardino Romano, tells us that Camillo Brozzoni had a garden at Brescia in the middle of the last century, and that *Camellia japonica* 'Angela Cocchi' was raised there by his gardener.

'LENNEI'.—This variety is very different from the average forms of M. × *soulangiana*. The leaves are larger and broader (as much as 8 × 5 in.) and more strongly ribbed; the flowers too are finer and more richly coloured. Petals very fleshy, broadly obovate, often 4 in. long and 4 in. wide, concave like a broad spoon, and of a beautiful shade of rose-purple outside, white within. The flowers start to open in late April, and continue through May, so that they are not often injured by frost. Occasionally a second crop is borne in the autumn.

This remarkable magnolia arose in Italy and was introduced to Germany about 1854 by the nurseryman Topf of Erfurt, who named it after Lenné, at one time director of the Royal Gardens of Prussia. Where in Italy it was raised is not certain. Van Houtte, who figured it in *Flore des Serres*, t. 1693, said it was a gift of the 'charming little bees of Lombardy'. Pampanini (*Boll. Soc. Ort. Tosc.*, Vol. 40, pp. 214–216) favoured the tradition that it was raised by Conte Giuseppe Salvi of Florence, who originally named it 'Maometto' ('Mahomet'). According to another version it was raised at Vicenza, around 1850.

'LENNEI ALBA'.—Flowers pure white, goblet-shaped. Near to M. *denudata* and flowering at the same time or slightly later. Despite its name, it is not a white-flowered form of 'Lennei', though it may be a seedling of it. Raised in Switzerland early this century, it has recently come into prominence as a substitute for M. *denudata*, being easier to propagate than that species.

'NORBERTII'.—This was raised in France and offered by Cels of Montrouge in his 1835 catalogue. Some plants seen under this name are of erect, rather gaunt habit, with flowers heavily stained purple on the outside. But the fine specimen grown under this name at Grayswood Hill, Surrey, which received an Award of Merit in 1960, is very near to the magnolia in commerce as 'Alba Superba'. It is of dense, erect habit, with dark green foliage.

'PICTURE'.—Flowers large, all the tepals heavily stained purplish red on the outside. Tepals long, narrowly oblong spathulate, the outer ones spreading. A very fine variety of recent introduction, distributed by Messrs Wada of Japan. A.M. 1969. It is of erect habit.

'RUSTICA RUBRA'.—Similar to 'Lennei' and probably a seedling of it. It was found in a nursery at Boskoop, Holland, some time before 1893 and first distributed by the Hazerswoude nurseries of Leyden. The tepals are more rose-coloured than in 'Lennei' and proportionately shorter and broader (*Fl. & Sylv.*, Vol. 1, p. 17 and plate facing p. 16). The statement made in previous editions of the present work, that this variety was used as a stock for grafting, perhaps refers to a different magnolia, known as M × *soulangiana rustica* simply.

[PLATE 93]

'SPECIOSA'.—The magnolia described under this name in recent works has large flowers, borne late in the season (at about the same time as 'Brozzonii').

Tepals white, flushed purple at the base, remaining erect but the tepals of the outer whorl bending outward at the midpoint. It is puzzling that this magnolia closely resembles the variety described and figured by Millais as 'Spectabilis'. The name 'Speciosa' starts in *Sertum Botanicum*, Vol. 4 (1832), p. 85, where a plant is figured which does not seem to be the same as the one described above; it is said to have come from Ghent. Other descriptions are given in *Rev. Hort.* (1912), p. 371 and in *Gartfl.* (1894), p. 300. The name *M. speciosa* also appears, without description, in the catalogue of the Paris nurseryman Cels for 1835.

'SUPERBA'.—There is a magnolia at Kew near the Azalea Garden, which was received under this name from Messrs Koster of Holland in 1907. The flowers are almost pure white, vase-shaped, rather small, the tepals of the middle whorl being about 3¼ in. long; outer whorl almost as long as the middle one.

'VERBANICA'.—This very striking variety is rare in Britain. The inner and median whorls of tepals are strap-shaped and usually evenly tinted rose on the outside; outer whorl almost as long as the inner two, also rose on the outside but fading to white at the apex. It flowers late, at about the same time as 'Brozzonii'. In some seasons the colouring of the tepals is concentrated in lines and streaks, instead of being more or less evenly diffused.

M. SPRENGERI Pampan.

A deciduous tree up to 65 ft high, the bark on the old branches and trunk light grey and peeling off in small flakes; young shoots glabrous, yellowish. Leaves oblanceolate or narrow-obovate to broad-obovate, 3 to 6¾ in. long, 1⅜ to 4¾ in. wide, lower surface variable in indumentum from glabrous or almost so to appressed-downy, or villose along the midrib and main nerves. Flowers erect, produced before the leaves on glabrous peduncles. Tepals usually twelve in number, pink, or white stained purple at the base, 3 to 3½ in. long and about 2 in. wide at the broadest part. Fruit-cones slender, about 3 in. long.

A native of Hupeh and E. Szechwan, China, where according to Wilson it is common in moist woods and thickets at 3,300 to 5,700 ft. It seems to have been first found by Augustine Henry in 1885; Wilson made further collections during his expeditions for Messrs Veitch and for the Arnold Arboretum, and sent seeds under W.688, collected autumn 1900 in woods near Chanyang Hsien, south of Ichang (see further under the varieties).

Wilson was convinced that this magnolia was no more than the wild prototype of the yulan, *M. denudata*, and it was under the names *M. denudata* var. *purpurascens* and *M. denudata* var. *elongata* that Wilson's collections were treated in *Plantae Wilsonianae,* Vol. 1 (1913), pp. 401–402. On going into the matter thirteen years later, Dr Stapf of Kew recognised that this magnolia was a distinct species, which he had intended to call *M. diva* until his attention was called to *M. sprengeri*, described by Pampanini in 1915 from specimens collected a few years previously in Hupeh by the Italian missionary Silvestri. Examination of Pampanini's type showed that it matched the Wilson specimens so well in flower that Dr Stapf abandoned his proposed name *M. diva* in favour of *M. sprengeri*. Unfortunately the type-specimen of *M. sprengeri* consists of flower only, so we are left without knowledge of the leaves of the typical variety or even of the flower-colour, which does not show up on the dried specimen. For this reason an overall description of the species is given above. In gardens it is necessary to recognise two varieties:

var. DIVA (Stapf) Johnstone *M. sprengeri diva* Stapf—Leaves broadly obovate, 4 to 6¾ in. long, 2 to 4¾ in. wide, densely villose long the midrib and main nerves beneath. Tepals rosy-pink on the outside, paler and streaked with dark lines within. Filaments of stamens rosy-red. *Bot. Mag.*, t. 9116. All the plants of this variety growing in Britain descend by seeds or grafting from the one tree at Caerhays Castle, Cornwall, which was raised from the seeds sent by Wilson to Messrs Veitch in 1900 under W.688 and purchased by J. C. Williams at the Coombe Wood sale in 1913. All the other plants under this number turned out to be the white-flowered var. *elongata*.

The Caerhays tree was flowering by 1919. It was 30 ft high in 1932 and in 1966 measured 54 × 5¾ ft at 2½ ft, with a spread of 36 × 20 ft. Of the many plants raised from its seeds not all have inherited its beautiful clear rosy-pink colouring and some, Mr Johnstone considered, might be hybrids. The true variety is a very fine magnolia, with flowers almost as well coloured as in the best forms of *M. campbellii*, though smaller and not so beautifully shaped. It flowers a week or so later than that species and, what is more important, its flower-buds seem to be more resistant to frost. The erect poise of the flowers distinguishes it from *M. sargentiana* and *M. dawsoniana*, and from *M. campbellii* it is quite different in its leaves, which are broadest above the middle. The var. *diva* received an Award of Merit in 1924.

cv. 'CLARET CUP'.—This received an Award of Merit when shown from Bodnant in 1963. The tepals are rosy-purple on the outside, paler and fading to white within.

var. ELONGATA (Rehd. & Wils.) Johnstone *M. denudata* var. *elongata* Rehd. & Wils.; *M. sprengeri elongata* (Rehd. & Wils.) Stapf—Leaves mostly lanceolate to narrow-obovate but sometimes fairly broadly obovate, mostly 3¼ to 4¾ in. long, 1⅜ to 2¼ in. wide, but larger on strong shoots, lower surface glabrous or almost so. Flowers creamy white, sometimes flushed purple at the base. According to Wilson, white-flowered plants are found growing in the wild intermixed with the pink form, but are rarer. By an unhappy mischance, however, all the plants raised from his W.688, and sold at the winding-up sale of the Coombe Wood nursery, turned out to be the var. *elongata*, with the exception of the one bought by J. C. Williams (see var. *diva*). As seen in cultivation, the var. *elongata* is not to be compared in beauty with either the var. *diva* or with *M. denudata*, but is very hardy. It flowers at the end of March or early April, before the leaves.

M. STELLATA (Sieb. & Zucc.) Maxim.   [PLATE 92

Buergeria stellata Sieb. & Zucc.; *M. halliana* Parsons; *M. kobus* var. *stellata* (Sieb. & Zucc.) B. C. Blackburn

A much-branched deciduous shrub of rounded, compact habit, 10 to 15 ft high, usually half as much more in diameter; young bark very aromatic, at first silky-hairy; winter-buds shaggy. Leaves 2½ to 4 in. long, narrow oblong or obovate, tapering at the base to a short stalk. Flowers fragrant, pure white at first changing to pink; produced on the naked shoots in March and April. Tepals twelve to eighteen, more numerous than in any other magnolia; 1½ to 2 in. long, narrowly oblong or strap-shaped, at first spreading, then reflexed. Most flowers also bear one to three small, inconspicuous and fugitive sepaloid segments.

Native of Japan, found wild only in the mountains north-east of Nagoya; introduced to Britain about 1877. For small gardens this is the most desirable of all magnolias. Its only defect is that its delicate petals are very susceptible to injury by frost, or even excessive wind and rain. But it flowers most profusely, and the first crop of blossoms if destroyed is succeeded by others. It sets its flowers unfailingly, and flowers even when less than 1 foot high. An attractive picture is made by planting this shrub in a group and growing beneath it, thickly, the grape hyacinth (*Muscari armeniacum*). The two flower together. This magnolia is much benefited by an admixture of peat in the soil, even to the extent of one-third.

There can be no doubt that *M. stellata* is closely allied to *M. kobus*, of which it is considered by Blackburn to be a variety (*Baileya*, Vol. 5 (1957), pp. 9–11; *Amatores Herbarii*, Vol. 17 (1955), p. 1).

cv. 'ROSEA'.—Flowers tinged with rosy-pink as they unfold but ageing to almost pure white. Imported by Messrs Veitch from Japan. A.M. 1893. Some plants seen under this name are not the true clone, from which, and indeed from *M. stellata* itself, they differ in their fewer, broader tepals and a much better developed sepaloid whorl.

cv. 'RUBRA'.—Tepals stained purplish pink. A.M. 1948, when shown by Messrs Notcutt, who received their plant from Messrs Kluis of Holland.

cv. 'WATER LILY'.—Tepals longer and somewhat narrower than in the common clone of *M. stellata*, pink in the bud. Raised in the USA.

M. 'NEIL MCEACHARN'.—A magnolia with flowers resembling those of *M. stellata* but fast-growing and of tree-like habit. It was raised at Windsor Great Park from seeds of *M. stellata* 'Rosea' received from the Villa Taranto, Pallanza, Italy, about 1951, and is named after the creator of the famous garden there. A.M. 1968.

M. × THOMPSONIANA (Loud.) C. de Vos

M. glauca var. *thompsoniana* Loud.; *M. glauca* var. *major* Sims

About the year 1808 a Mr Thompson, then a nurseryman at Mile End, noticed a distinct plant amongst some of his seedlings of *Magnolia virginiana*. He propagated it and ultimately distributed it under the above name. It is now usually regarded as a hybrid between *virginiana* and *tripetala*, although there is much less evidence of *tripetala* than of *virginiana*. It is a shrub of loose, ungainly habit, producing very vigorous unbranched growths of great length in one season. The leaves are 4 to 10 in. long, very glaucous beneath, and otherwise similar to those of *M. virginiana*. The flowers are creamy white, fragrant, much larger and less globular than those of *M. virginiana*, the petals

being from 2 to 3½ in. long. They are borne mainly in June and July. I have
not seen or heard of its producing seeds, but if it did and these were sown, the
question of its hybrid or other origin would probably be settled. *Bot. Mag.*,
t. 2164.

M. × *thompsoniana* received an Award of Merit when shown by Graham
Thomas on 17 June 1958. It is a coarser plant than *M. virginiana*, but faster
growing, and flowering when young.

<h2 style="text-align:center">M. TRIPETALA L.   UMBRELLA TREE</h2>
M. umbrella Desrouss.

A deciduous tree 30 to 40 ft high, with a wide-spreading, open head of
branches. Leaves among the largest in the genus, usually 12 to 20 in. long, and
6 to 10 in. wide (sometimes still larger); broadly oblanceolate, acute, tapered
at both ends, pubescent beneath when young, strongly ribbed; stalk 1 to 2 in.
long. Flowers produced in May and June, heavily and not agreeably scented.
Petals six to nine, creamy white, 4 to 5 in. long, 2 in. wide (inner ones smaller).
Fruits 4 in. long, cone-shaped, of a fine rosy-red; produced freely in this country,
and very handsome; seeds scarlet.

Native of eastern N. America in the Allegheny region, from Pennsylvania
southwards; introduced in 1752, and first flowered with Peter Collinson,
24 May 1760. Once the commonest and best known of American magnolias.
It is called the 'umbrella tree' from the pose of its radiating cluster of large
decurved leaves produced at the apex of the shoots. From the other big-leaved
American species it is distinguished by the tapering base of its leaves. As a
fruit-bearing tree it is the handsomest of all the magnolias in this country.

<h2 style="text-align:center">M. × VEITCHII Bean</h2>

A deciduous tree already over 80 ft high in Cornwall; young wood purplish,
clothed at first with appressed hairs, becoming brown the second year. Leaves
obovate or oblong, mostly rounded at the base, shortly and abruptly pointed;
6 to 12 in. long, 3 to 7 in. wide, dark green when mature but purplish (especially
beneath) when young, midrib and chief veins clothed with grey down; stalk
¾ to 1 in. long, downy. Flowers 6 in. long, blush pink, opening in April on the
naked twigs, each borne on a short thick stalk; sepals and petals nine, 1½ to
2 in. wide, rounded and broadest towards the apex, tapered at the base; stamens
½ in. long.

A hybrid between *M. campbellii* and *M. denudata*, raised by the late Peter
C. M. Veitch of the Royal Nurseries, Exeter, who made the cross in 1907, the
seed-bearer being *M. denudata*. It first flowered in 1917. The hybrid is very
vigorous in growth and has noble foliage; moreover it is quite hardy. I first
saw the blooms in April 1919, and was much impressed by their beauty.

Five plants were raised from the original crossing in 1907, four of which
bore creamy-white flowers. It is the fifth, with pink blossom showing the
influence of the pollen-parent, *M. campbellii*, to which the name *Veitchii* was

given. It was a creditable achievement to have hybridised two such fine magnolias.

To the above account, which has been taken almost unchanged from previous editions, it must be added that *M.* × *veitchii* has grown more vigorously than could have been expected when it was first raised. At Caerhays Castle, Cornwall, there are three specimens, planted in 1920, which measure 85 × 6 ft, 79 × 6½ ft and 64 × 7¾ ft (1971). No other magnolia in the British Isles has attained such dimensions. Other examples are: Trewithen, Cornwall, 64 × 6¼ ft (1971); Lanhydrock, Cornwall, 52 × 4¾ ft (1971); Trewidden, Cornwall, a fine specimen only 33 ft high but 51 ft in spread (*Camellias and Magnolias* (1950), p. 110); West Porlock House, Somerset, *pl.* 1924, 62 × 6¼ ft (*Gard. Chron.* (10 May 1968), p. 6); Bodnant, Denbigh, two trees *pl.* 1916, both 40 × 6¼ ft (1966); Nymans, Sussex, 48 × 6¾ ft (1966). Mature trees flower with amazing profusion in some years.

Under the rules of botanical nomenclature the name *M.* × *veitchii* is applicable to any form of *M. campbellii* × *denudata*, though W. J. Bean meant it only for the pink-flowered seedling and its descendants. It is suggested that this clone should be known in future as 'PETER VEITCH'. The clonal name 'ISCA' has already been given to the best of the white-flowered clones.

M. VIRGINIANA L.   SWEET BAY   [PLATE 94
M. glauca L.

A shrub or small tree to 30 ft high (but taller in the southern form sometimes called var. *australis*). Leaves oval or oblong, sometimes obovate, 2½ to 5 in. long, scarcely half as wide, often blunt at the apex, lustrous green and glabrous above, blue-white and downy beneath, especially when young. Flowers 2 to 3 in. wide, delightfully scented, produced in no great numbers, but continuously, on leafy shoots, from June to September. Petals oblong or slightly obovate, 1½ to 2 in. long, at first creamy white, becoming deeper with age. The fruit develops indifferently in this country, but in the eastern United States the fine red cones produce a bright effect. This magnolia varies in the persistence of its leaves; and of two trees at Kew, growing within a few yards of each other, one retains some of its foliage all the winter, the other is quite deciduous. *Bot. Mag.*, n.s., t. 457.

Native of the eastern United States from Massachusetts to Florida, often in swampy places. It was one of the early introductions from America, and is known to have been cultivated by Bishop Compton at Fulham Palace Gardens before the end of the 17th century. It is a most charming plant, readily distinguished by its comparatively small leaves, vividly glaucous beneath (but see also *M.* × *thompsoniana*). It is, or has been, valued in medicine for its tonic and diaphoretic properties.

In the northern part of its range *M. virginiana* is a small tree, shedding its leaves in early winter but tending to become more evergreen southward. In the Carolinas and Florida it is sometimes more tree-like (up to 75 ft high), more evergreen, and with densely silky-downy young stems and peduncles. This variant is sometimes distinguished as var. AUSTRALIS Sarg., though it is not well demarcated from the typical state.

M. virginiana is a warmth-loving species that thrives well in the southern and eastern parts of England. One of the finest specimens in the country grows in the University Botanic Garden, Cambridge, and is about 30 ft high and 20 ft

MAGNOLIA VIRGINIANA

in spread. There is a group about 20 ft high at Gravetye Manor, East Grinstead, once the home of the famous gardener William Robinson.

The great merit of this species is that it produces its sweetly scented flowers over a long period in late summer. Against this must be set the fact that it does not flower freely as a young plant. It needs a sunny sheltered position and a deep soil that does not dry out in summer. According to Sargent, it grows better when grafted on *M. acuminata* than on its own roots.

M. × WATSONII Hook. f.

A deciduous shrub or small tree of stiff habit. Leaves obovate, 4 to 8 in. long, tapering at the base to a stalk ¼ to 1 in. long, apex blunt, dark green above, rather glaucous and finely downy beneath. Flower 5 to 6 in. across, with a strong aromatic odour. Petals obovate, the inner ones ivory-white, outer ones tinged with rose; stamens crimson, forming a conspicuous mass of rich colour across the centre of the flower. Flower-stalks stout, about 1 in. long. *Bot. Mag.,* t. 7157.

This magnolia is probably a hybrid and *M. hypoleuca* and *M. sieboldii* have been suggested as its parents. It first appeared in Europe at the Paris Exposition of 1889, when it was exhibited in the Japanese Court. Like many imported Japanese plants, those originally introduced were badly grafted, and many of them died;

the shrub thereby got the reputation of being difficult to manage. It thrives admirably when once established, and flowers freely in June and July on leafy shoots. It is quite hardy at Kew. Often confused with *M. sieboldii* this species is readily distinguished by its shorter-stalked, larger flowers, and by the larger, more leathery leaves, with ten to fifteen pairs of nerves.

There is an example of this hybrid at Kew near the Victoria Gate and another at Wakehurst Place, Sussex, now an annexe to the Kew collection. It is also represented in the National Trust Gardens at Nymans, Sussex; Trengwainton, Cornwall; Bodnant, Denbigh; and Rowallane, Co. Down.

For a note on this hybrid by Neil Treseder, see *Journ. R.H.S.*, Vol. 94 (1969), pp. 185–187.

M. WILSONII (Fin. & Gagnep.) Rehd.

M. parviflora var. *wilsonii* Fin. & Gagnep.; *M. nicholsoniana* Rehd. & Wils.; *M. wilsonii* f. *nicholsoniana* (Rehd. & Wils.) Rehd.; *M. taliensis* W. W. Sm.; *M. wilsonii* f. *taliensis* (W. W. Sm.) Rehd., *nom. superfl.*

A deciduous shrub or small tree up to 25 ft high, the slender young shoots clothed at first thickly with pale brown felt; glabrous and purplish brown the second year. Leaves ovate-lanceolate to narrowly oval, pointed at the apex, rounded, tapered, or slightly cordate at the base; 3 to 6 in. long, nearly half as much wide, dull green and soon glabrous above, velvety beneath with a dense coating of pale-brown wool; leaf-stalk ½ to 1½ in. long, woolly, marked midway by a scar. Flowers white, 3 to 4 in. wide, cup-shaped, pendulous, fragrant, developing in May and June with the young foliage, each on a woolly stalk 1 to 1½ in. long. Tepals usually nine, incurved, the largest obovate, rounded at the top, 2½ in. long, 1¾ in. wide. Stamens numerous, ½ in. long, rich red. Fruit cylindric-ovoid, 2 to 3 in. long, 1 in. wide, purplish pink; seeds scarlet-coated.

Native of W. Szechwan and Yunnan, China, at 7,000 to 8,500 ft altitude; discovered by Wilson in 1904, introduced in 1908. This magnolia is one of the most beautiful of Wilson's introductions. The finest example in cultivation is at Caerhays in Cornwall, where I have seen it in flower several times in May. It is there a small tree of open habit over 20 ft high and bears scores of its pure white blossoms, each with its conspicuous ring of crimson stamens. The height of this tree enables one to appreciate the beauty of the pendulous flowers to the full extent from the ground, and it is difficult to imagine one more lovely. It is related to *M. sieboldii* and *M. sinensis*, both of which have more abruptly pointed leaves. At Kew it is hardy, but never seems likely to get beyond the shrubby state, and it is frequently injured there by late spring frosts. It prefers a semi-shaded spot. There appear to be two forms in cultivation, one of broader habit with larger, wider leaves and larger flowers than the other, and they vary also in the amount of pubescence beneath the leaf.

A fine example of the species, raised from seeds received from Caerhays, received a First Class Certificate when shown from Wakehurst Place, Sussex, in 1932 (*Journ. R.H.S.*, Vol. 58, p. xxix). The specimen growing there above The Slips may be the original and certainly represents *M. wilsonii* at its best. This is also true of the plant at Quarry Wood, near Newbury, raised from seeds received from Rowallane, Co. Down, in 1939 (*Journ. R.H.S.*, Vol. 53, p. 266 and fig. 97). The then owner of Quarry Wood, the late Walter Bentley, thought this plant might be a hybrid, but Mr Johnstone accepted it as *M. wilsonii* and indeed the beautiful painting of the species by Anne Webster, reproduced in his book, was made from a flowering branch of the Quarry Wood plant. It should be added

MAGNOLIA × WATSONII

that the form of *M. wilsonii* that received an Award of Merit in 1925 as 'Borde Hill form' was certainly raised from the original wild seeds. This plant, which still exists, helps to confirm the supposition that the large-flowered, more robust forms of *M. wilsonii* are of garden origin, since it is greatly inferior to these garden seedlings, although at the time when it was shown it was judged to be superior to the general run of *M. wilsonii*.

It should be noted that the description of *M. wilsonii* given in the first paragraph covers only the forms of *M. wilsonii* usually seen in cultivation. In the types of *M. taliensis* and *M. nicholsoniana*, both now submerged in *M. wilsonii*, the leaves are more or less glabrous beneath except on the midrib and main veins. Also, in the type of *M. nicholsoniana* the leaves are oblong-obovate, cuneate at the base, the young wood yellowish grey and the flowers with twelve tepals. Wilson collected seeds of this form of *M. wilsonii* under W.838, but there is no record of its having been introduced to Britain. The plants distributed as *M. nicholsoniana* by Chenault proved to be *M. sinensis*.

× MAHOBERBERIS   BERBERIDACEAE

A genus of hybrids between *Mahonia* and *Berberis*, of which four have so far been recorded.

×M. AQUISARGENTII Krüssmann

An erect-branched evergreen shrub; ultimate height uncertain. Its leaves are mostly of two kinds. Leaves on strong shoots sessile, trifoliolate, the terminal leaflet much the longest, $2\frac{3}{4}$ to $3\frac{1}{4}$ in. long, very thick and rigid, glossy above, armed on each side with mostly five or six long, narrowly triangular spine-pointed teeth, apex narrowly acute, also terminated by a spine; lateral leaflets much smaller, with a narrow terminal portion and usually one pair of teeth on each side, but on some leaves the lateral leaflets are replaced each by a simple spine. The leaves of the second kind are borne in the axils of the first kind, from which they differ totally. They are thinner, shortly stalked, oblong-elliptic, $2\frac{1}{2}$ to $3\frac{1}{4}$ in. long, veiny and slightly glossy above, edged on each side with up to forty-five or so fine, closely set, spiny teeth; mostly they are simple, but some carry one or two very small leaflets on their petioles. Leaves of intermediate form also occur, which are more coarsely toothed, more spiny and more glossy above than in the second type. Flowers occasionally borne, but not examined.

This hybrid was raised in Sweden by H. Jensen in 1943. The parentage is believed to be *Mahonia aquifolium* crossed with *Berberis sargentiana*, an evergreen species of W. China.

A very similar hybrid is ×M. MIETHKEANA Melander & Eade, described in *Nat. Hort. Mag.*, Vol. 33 (1957), p. 257. This was found in a seed-bed of *M. aquifolium* at H. O. Miethke's nursery, near Tacoma, Washington, USA. The other parent is believed to be a berberis known in the USA as B. 'Renton' or as "*B. knightii*". The specific identity of this plant is uncertain, but the berberis grown in Britain under the erroneous name "*B. knightii*" is B. *manipurana* Ahrendt, an evergreen species which, like B. *sargentii*, belongs to the section *Wallichianae*. Another mahoberberis raised by Mr Jensen is ×M. AQUI-CANDIDULA Krüssmann. This hybrid, of weak growth, has as the berberis-parent B. *candidula*, another member of the section *Wallichianae*.

×M. *aquisargentii* grows vigorously in Mr Hillier's garden at Jermyns House, Ampfield, and the above description was made from a specimen kindly given by him. It is sparse-flowering, and in this respect differs from the American hybrid (not seen) which is said to flower fairly freely and bear fruits (which are infertile).

× M. NEUBERTII (Baumann) Schneid.

Berberis neubertii Baumann; *M. neubertii* var. *ilicifolia* Schneid.; *Berberis ilicifolia* Hort., not Forst.

An evergreen, or partially evergreen shrub, of loose, open habit, 4 to 6 ft high. Leaves very variable; sometimes simple, obovate, $1\frac{1}{2}$ to 3 in. long, with fine marginal teeth like those of *Berberis vulgaris*; other stiff, hard, and holly-like, with a few large spiny teeth resembling the leaflets of *Mahonia*; others trifoliolate or pinnate. Flowers and fruits not seen.

A hybrid between *Mahonia aquifolium* (the seed-bearer) and *Berberis vulgaris*, which appeared in Baumann's once famous nursery at Bolwyller, in Alsace, about 1850. It has but little to recommend it as a garden plant, being in my experience a sterile, flowerless mule. As a scientific curiosity it is interesting, for it unites two genera, although remarkably distinct from either of its parents. The form with spiny-toothed leaves like holly is often erroneously called *B. ilicifolia*.

MAHONIA   BERBERIDACEAE

A genus of evergreen shrubs very closely related to *Berberis* and often united with it. They are very distinct in their invariably evergreen character, in their simply pinnate foliage and in the absence of spines from their branches. In his monograph on *Berberis* and *Mahonia* Dr Ahrendt pointed out a further distinction: 'that three-quarters of the species of *Mahonia* possess a form of inflorescence never found in the simple-leaved *Berberis*, a fascicle of several dense spike-like racemes. Only a minority share a *Berberis*-like form of inflorescence'. (The exceptions are all American species, in which the inflorescence is a panicle, a simple raceme or a few-flowered umbellate cluster.)

The genus contains some very handsome species, the usually prickly-margined leaves being dark and shining. They are not generally so hardy as the true barberries, but those that are hardy are amongst the handsomest of evergreens. All thrive in a good garden soil. The generic name commemorates Bernard M'Mahon, an American horticulturist who died in 1816. Over 100 species are recognised by Dr Ahrendt in his monograph.

M. ACANTHIFOLIA G. Don

A shrub 20 to 25 ft high. Leaves 2 to 2½ ft long, with seventeen to twenty-seven leaflets, the lowermost pair very small, roundish, inserted about ½ in. above the base of the rachis. Leaflets (except the basal pair) oblong-ovate or oblong-lanceolate, mostly 2 to 4 in. long, 1 to 1⅝ in. wide, the middle pairs the longest, the lowermost pairs the widest, acute at the apex, truncate at the base, leathery in texture, slightly glossy above, three- to five-veined from the base, the veins slightly impressed above and raised beneath, margins sinuately toothed, with three to seven teeth on the lower margin, two to five on the upper. Racemes stout, spreading, terminal, in clusters of three or four, up to 12 in. long, with numerous densely arranged deep yellow flowers. Berries purple, covered with a bluish bloom, ovoid, about ⅜ in. long, crowned by a short, persistent style.

Native of the Himalaya from Kumaon to Assam, and of the Naga Hills.

Although included in *M. napaulensis* by Hooker and Thomson, it is now usually regarded as a distinct species, differing chiefly in the longer leaves with more numerous leaflets. Other differences given by Dr Ahrendt are that the leaves are less glossy than in *M. napaulensis* and that the fruits bear more conspicuous styles. In cultivated plants there is also a difference in flowering time: late autumn and early winter for *M. acanthifolia*, early spring for *M. napaulensis*. In foliage *M. acanthifolia* is the finest of all the species that can be cultivated in the open in the British Isles. It is hardy in the southern and western parts of the country, but needs a sheltered position. It received a First Class Certificate when shown from Windsor Great Park on 25 November 1958. The plant in the Savill Gardens, growing on a wall near the propagating houses, is a cutting from the F.C.C. plant; it has attained a height of 9 ft in twelve years (1971).

M. NAPAULENSIS DC.—The mahonia described in previous editions under this name was really *M. acanthifolia*, which is part of *M. napaulensis* as understood by many botanists until recently. With *M. acanthifolia* separated from it, *M. napaulensis* becomes a species of little garden merit, being less hardy and not so handsome. The leaves have fewer leaflets—up to fifteen—and are therefore shorter than in *M. acanthifolia*. It is reported to be an inhabitant of the mainly evergreen type of forest that occurs in Nepal and Sikkim at 6,000 to 9,000 ft. The cultivated plants flower in early spring, i.e. later than *M. acanthifolia*, but this difference does not hold good for all the wild plants.

M. napaulensis is in cultivation at Wakehurst Place, Sussex, from seeds collected by A. D. Schilling in Nepal, and there is a plant in the Savill Gardens, Windsor, introduced from the same region by Dr Herklots. At Kew there is a plant about 8 ft high in the Temperate House. The cultivar 'MAHARAJAH' is in cultivation at Wakehurst Place and in the Savill Gardens; this descends from a plant once cultivated in Guernsey, and bears flowers of a deep yellow.

M. AQUIFOLIUM (Pursh) Nutt.

Berberis aquifolium Pursh

An evergreen shrub reaching a height of 6 ft, but as commonly seen usually 2 to 3 ft high. Stems spineless, but little branched, spreading by underground suckers; bark grey-brown, glabrous. Leaves 6 to 12 in. long, pinnate, consisting of five to nine leaflets, which are stalkless, or nearly so, of variable shape, but usually broadly and (except the terminal one) obliquely ovate, $1\frac{1}{2}$ to $3\frac{1}{2}$ in. long, glossy dark green, turning purplish in winter, the apex and margin set with slender, spiny teeth. Racemes erect, produced in a crowded group from just beneath the terminal bud, each 2 to 3 in. long, thickly set with golden yellow, slender-stalked flowers. The first flowers begin to open in February, or in mild seasons even earlier, but the great flowering time is April and May. Berries very abundant and ornamental, black, but covered with a fine violet-coloured bloom.

Native of western N. America from Vancouver Island southwards; introduced in 1823. For some time after that date it remained very expensive, costing as much as ten pounds per plant, but in 1837 the price had been reduced to five shillings. Prior to 1914 small plants could be obtained for thirty shillings per thousand. Few evergreen shrubs introduced from abroad have proved so valuable in British gardens as this. It is very hardy; I have seen it thriving on the bleak elevations of the Yorkshire wolds. For forming a low evergreen covering for the ground in moderately shaded positions, such as beneath deciduous trees, there is no evergreen so beautiful and so thriving as this. It is also admirable for planting as a groundwork for flowering shrubs that are leafless when in blossom, like the forsythias and *Jasminum nudiflorum*. It is not particular as to soil. Easily increased by seed, but an abundance of plants can be obtained by dividing the old plants in spring and planting the pieces on a gentle hot-bed.

Raised from seed it varies to a considerable extent, and names have been given to several varieties. The following appear to belong to *M. aquifolium*, without admixture of other species:

cv. 'ATROPURPUREA'.—Leaves dark reddish purple in winter.

cv. 'MOSERI'.—Leaves in their first year pale green and more or less tinted with pink or red, the colouring best developed in plants grown in a sunny place. Raised in France. Dr Ahrendt considered that this is a hybrid with *M. pinnata* (*M.* × *moseri* Ahrendt), on the grounds that the petals are shorter than the inner sepals, but this is not a reliable character.

M. aquifolium appears to have hybridised in gardens with *M. repens*, giving rise to seedling plants with the leaflets dull green above or wider than normal. The mahonia called *M. aquifolium murrayana*, mentioned in previous editions, could be such a hybrid. These mongrels are difficult to treat taxonomically, since the two species intergrade in the wild. See also under *M. repens*. For hybrids with *M. pinnata* see under that species.

M. ARGUTA Hutch.

An evergreen shrub 4 to 5 ft high, glabrous in all its parts; young shoots purplish. Leaves pinnate, up to 1 ft long, made up of from nine to thirteen leaflets, which are lanceolate, pointed, spine-tipped, wedge-shaped at the base, entire or with a few sharp teeth, stalkless or nearly so, 1 to 3½ in. long, ¼ to ¾ in. wide, dark dull green, conspicuously net-veined, of stiff hard texture. Flowers ¾ in. wide, pale yellow, borne in May on the uppermost two-thirds of slender, arching panicles 12 to 16 in. long; two to four flowers are carried by each of the branches of the panicle on which they are thinly disposed. Fruits globose, ¼ to ⅓ in. wide, dark blue. *Bot. Mag.*, t. 8266.

This very distinct mahonia is probably a native of Mexico, but it is only known by a plant growing in the Botanic Gardens, Glasnevin, and its progeny. The history of this plant is not known, but it has been cultivated there (with protection in winter) for over fifty years. It will probably be hardy only in our milder maritime counties. The long slender panicle, with its pale yellow, thinly set flowers, is quite attractive.

M. 'CHARITY'

An erect shrub 8 to 15 ft high and almost as much in width. Leaves with mostly seventeen to twenty-one leaflets, the lowermost pair small, roundish, and inserted at the base of the petiole. Leaflets (other than the basal pair) ovate or ovate-lanceolate, 2½ to 4½ in. long, 1 to 1½ in. wide, acuminately tapered at the apex, rounded to broad cuneate at the base, with two or three spine-teeth on the upper margin, three to four on the lower, rich green and slightly glossy above, yellowish green beneath, the principal veins impressed above, prominent beneath. Racemes terminal, very numerous (up to twenty or so in each cluster), 10 to 14 in. long, erect or spreading, many-flowered, but not densely so; bracts leathery, broad-lanceolate or oblong-lanceolate, obtuse, about ¼ in. long; pedicels ¼ to ⅜ in. long. Flowers lemon-yellow; innermost sepals oblong-oval, rounded at the apex, ₅⁄₁₆ in. or slightly more long; petals six, oval, deeply notched, slightly shorter than the inner sepals. Connective of stamens truncate at the apex.

'Charity' was one of three plants selected by Sir Eric Savill from a line of seedlings of M. lomariifolia growing in the nursery of Messrs L. R. Russell of Windlesham, Surrey. These had been procured in 1950-1 from the Slieve Donard Nursery Company, Newcastle, Co. Down, who at that time had over 1,000 young plants in 2½ in. pots (J. L. Russell in Journ. R.H.S., Vol. 94 (1969), pp. 150–151).

There can be no doubt that the pollen-parent of 'Charity' was M. japonica, to which it is much nearer in its botanical characters than it is to the seed-parent. But the influence of M. lomariifolia shows in the more numerous leaflets, with their greener colouring and impressed veins, and in the erect habit. The flowers are soft yellow, as in M. japonica, but of a more vivid shade.

'Charity' is one of the finest of evergreen shrubs, and all the more valuable for flowering in the dullest season of the year (mainly November and December). The racemes develop in succession, and only those that are fully expanded suffer damage by frost; the plant itself is hardy. 'Charity' received a Preliminary Commendation on 5 November 1957, an Award of Merit on 27 January 1959, and a First Class Certificate on 27 November 1962. The original plant, which grows in the Savill Gardens, Windsor Great Park, is 14 ft high and 12 ft wide (1971).

Seedlings have been raised from 'Charity' in the gardens of Windsor Great Park, of which the most notable is 'HOPE', with flowers of a beautiful soft, bright yellow, densely set on the rachis. This received a First Class Certificate in 1966. Another is 'FAITH', which is nearer to M. lomariifolia in habit and foliage, but with more softly coloured flowers. A third generation has been raised at Windsor, but so far none of these seedlings has been named, though the average quality is high. An interesting feature of these F.2 and F.3 seedlings is that the racemes are frequently branched.

Three other clones in this group must be mentioned. Among the seedlings of M. lomariifolia raised by the Slieve Donard Nursery Company (see above) another hybrid was found, among those retained by the nursery, with more erect racemes than in 'Charity'. This has been named 'WINTER SUN'. The other two are the result of a deliberate cross between M. lomariifolia (seed-parent) and M. japonica, made by Lionel Fortescue of Buckland Monachorum, Devon. Some 200 seedlings were raised from this cross, of which five were retained. Of these five, one proved to be very much better than the others and has been named 'BUCKLAND'. This has an inflorescence up to 27 in. across, composed of thirteen or fourteen main racemes, which are numerously branched as in the Windsor seedlings mentioned above; the flowers have some of the fragrance of *M. japonica*. Another of these hybrid seedlings, given by Mr Fortescue to the Savill Gardens, has proved to be an outstanding mahonia, bearing dense sheaves of erect, much-branched racemes up to 16 in. long, with fragrant flowers. This has been named 'LIONEL FORTESCUE'.

M. × MEDIA.—This name has been proposed as the collective designation for hybrids between *M. japonica* and *M. lomariifolia*, including second-generation seedlings and back-crosses. 'Charity' and the other clones mentioned above would therefore belong to it. This name is due to be validated shortly.

M. FORTUNEI (Lindl.) Fedde
Berberis fortunei Lindl.

An evergreen shrub 5 to 6 ft high, with erect, unbranching stems. Leaves 6 to 8 in. long, pinnate, consisting usually of seven leaflets, which are linear-lanceolate, taper gradually to both ends and are 3 to 4 in. long, and about ½ in. wide, margins except towards the base set with forward-pointing teeth; undersurface marked with prominent, netted veins. Flowers yellow, densely crowded on narrow, cylindrical racemes 2 to 3 in. long, erect. Blossoming in late autumn (October and November), the species rarely develops fruits in this country.

Robert Fortune found this shrub cultivated in a nursery at Shanghai, and introduced it in 1846. It has since been found wild in several parts of China. It is rather tender, and will not thrive in the open ground at Kew. It is distinct from all the other mahonias in the narrow, dull green leaflets, and in the slender racemes, less than ½ in. in diameter; but is one of the least effective.

M. FREMONTII (Torr.) Fedde
Berberis fremontii Torr.

An evergreen shrub 3 to 12 ft high, with pinnate leaves composed of five or seven leaflets of a vividly glaucous colour. Leaflets ¾ to 1¼ in. long, spine-tipped, and with one or more spiny teeth at each side, the terminal leaflet is stalked and ovate to lanceolate, the others sessile and shorter. Flowers yellow, and produced four to eight together towards the end of a raceme 2 to 3 in. in length, each flower on a slender stalk ½ to ¾ in. long. Fruits blue, becoming dry and inflated at maturity, enclosing six to eight seeds.

Native of the hot, dry, south-western United States (Texas, Arizona, etc.). This striking and handsome species may be grown on a south wall, and, wherever cultivated, should be given the sunniest position available. The only species in cultivation likely to be confused with this is *M. trifoliolata*, which has leaflets of the same form and (in var. *glauca*) very glaucous hue, but only three of them to each leaf.

M. HAEMATOCARPA (Wooton) Fedde

Berberis haematocarpa Wooton

An evergreen shrub from 6 to 12 ft high in the wild; young shoots glabrous, eventually grey. Leaves pinnate, 1½ to 4 in. long, made up of three to nine leaflets. Leaflets oval, ovate, or lanceolate, with three to five spine-tipped teeth at each side and a slender spine-tipped apex, ½ to 1¾ in. long, ¼ to ⅝ in. wide, terminal leaflet stalked, longer and relatively narrower than the lateral ones, of a conspicuous glaucous hue and quite glabrous. Flowers pale yellow, ¼ in. wide, produced in slender-stalked racemes 1 to 1½ in. long, carrying about six flowers. Fruits juicy, blood-red, globose, ¼ to ⅓ in. wide.

Native of western N. America in the States of New Mexico, Colorado, W. Texas, and California; introduced to Kew in 1916. In general appearance this species bears a strong resemblance to *M. fremontii*. It is, nevertheless, very distinct from that species in its rich red fruits. As sunny a position as possible should be allotted to it. It seems disinclined to branch and makes slender erect shoots densely furnished with leaves. The fruits are used for making jam in its native country, but our climate is doubtless too dull for it to bear them freely enough to be of any value in that respect here.

M. SWASEYI (Buckland) Fedde, is a species from Texas also with red fruits and closely related to the foregoing. It is distinguished by having broadly ovate bracts up to ⅓ in. long (see also *M. nevinii*).

M. 'HETEROPHYLLA'

Berberis heterophylla Hort., not Juss.; *Mahonia heterophylla* (Hort.) Schneid.; *B. aquifolium* var. *heterophylla* Hort. Thibaud & Keteleer (?); *B. (aquifolium × fortunei ?)* Zab.; *B.* or *M. toluacensis* Hort. ex Bean, not *B. toluacensis* J. J.

A shrub about 3 ft high, taller on a wall; young shoots purplish. Leaves 6 to 12 in. long, composed usually of five or seven leaflets. Leaflets lanceolate or narrowly oblong, often unequal-sided, 1 to 3½ in. long, ¼ to ¾ in. wide, each margin set with one to ten slender teeth or sometimes entire, shining green on both sides, stalk of leaflets slender, up to 1 in. long, but sometimes absent (leaflet sessile). Flowers and fruits not freely borne.

This mahonia has been grown in gardens under the erroneous name *Mahonia* or *Berberis* "*toluacensis*", but it is evidently not the plant described as *B. toluacensis* in 1869 (see below). The leaflets are usually curiously twisted or even curled, and their stalks vary much in length; one leaflet in a pair may be sessile, the other long stalked; or one leaflet of the pair may be missing. Schneider mentions Zabel's suggestion that this mahonia might be a hybrid between *M. aquifolium* and *M. fortunei*, but this does not seem very likely. It is more likely to have been a hybrid seedling of the plant originally called *B. toluacensis* (see below). In the texture and colouring of its leaves it recalls *M.* 'Undulata' (q.v. under *M. pinnata*).

M. TOLUACENSIS J. J. (as *Berberis toluacensis*).—The place of publication of this name is usually given as *Gard. Chron.* (1868), p. 435, where a writer signing himself 'J. J.' asked for information about a plant he had received from a nursery under this name, and believed to be of Mexican origin. It seems to have been overlooked that in the following year the same 'J. J.' published the following description: 'Leaves 6–8 in. long, of 4–6 pairs of leaflets, with an odd one. Leaflets about 2 in. in length by ¾ in. broad, they are ovate-lanceolate, sharp-pointed, sinuated, with 5–6 spiny teeth on each side. The foliage is much like that of B. fascicularis, but not quite so wavy and glaucous. The habit of the plant is more erect, throwing up straight shoots of some length from the base, but in other respects its appearance is such that it might be taken for one of the many garden forms of hybrids which have been raised from "fascicularis". From the appearance of the leaves of this plant there seems to be no probability of its proving hardy.' (*Gard. Chron.* (1869), p. 739.)

The identity of this mahonia can only be guessed at, but it is at least full enough to prove that it cannot be the same as M. 'Heterophylla'. It is conceivable that the plant described by 'J. J.' was really the Mexican form of *M. pinnata* (*M. moranensis*) and that it derived from seeds collected near Toluca, west of Mexico City.

M. JAPONICA (Thunb.) DC.

Ilex japonica Thunb.; *Berberis japonica* (Thunb.) R. Br.

An evergreen shrub with stiff, stout, sparsely branched stems. Leaves 12 to 18 in. long, with thirteen to nineteen leaflets, the lowermost pair inserted near the base of the leaf and much smaller than the others; leaflets leathery and fairly rigid, the lateral ones (except the basal pair) lanceolate-ovate or oblong-ovate, 2 to 4 in. long, acuminate and spine-tipped at the apex, obliquely rounded or rounded-cuneate at the base, slightly falcate, armed on each side with three to six spiny teeth (one or two fewer on the inner than on the outer side), terminal leaflet usually broader and slightly longer than the lateral ones, all lustrous green above, yellowish green beneath. Flowers yellow, fragrant, fairly widely spaced on spreading or pendulous racemes 4 to 8 or even 10 in. long, which are borne in clusters of up to ten at the ends of the previous season's growths; bracts of the individual flowers ovate or lanceolate-ovate, $\frac{3}{16}$ to $\frac{5}{16}$ in. long, about ⅛ in. wide; flowers stalks slender, about ¼ in. long. Fruits ovoid, deep bluish purple, about $\frac{9}{16}$ in. long.

This species is cultivated in Japan but is said not to be found wild there. For its occurrence outside Japan, see below. It has been much confused with the related *M. bealei* and has also hybridised with it in gardens. It therefore seems best to describe this species here and thereafter discuss the two together.

M. BEALEI (Fort.) Carr. *B. bealei* Fort.—This species was discovered by Fortune during his visit to China in 1848–9. The plant he first saw was too big to be lifted, but he eventually procured five smaller ones in the Huychow area of Chekiang which, after a sojourn in the garden of T. C. Beale at Shanghai, were despatched to Standish and Noble's nursery at Sunningdale. Plants raised from these, probably both by seeds and cuttings, were put into commerce by Standish in 1858 (advertisement in *Gardeners' Chronicle* 10 April p. 283, of that year). Fortune named the species, and gave an account of its discovery, in *Gard. Chron.* (1850), p. 212.

   M. bealei differs from *M. japonica* chiefly in its inflorescences and floral bracts. In *M. japonica* the inflorescences are lax, the flowers well spaced and subtended by bracts which are almost as long as the flower-stalks. In *M. bealei* the inflorescences are shorter and stouter, erect or slightly spreading, the flowers are more densely set on the axis and subtended by small scale-like bracts which are about $\frac{1}{12}$ to $\frac{1}{10}$ in. long and only half as long or less than the flower-stalks. There is no constant and reliable difference between the two species in their foliage, but in *M. bealei* the leaflets tend to be relatively broader than in *M. japonica* and often quadrangular-ovate and truncate at the base; the terminal leaflet is usually larger and broader than the lateral ones, but not invariably so.

   The confusion between *M. japonica* and *M. bealei* started in the article in which Fortune first described the latter species. Lindley, the editor of the *Gardeners' Chronicle*, high-handedly entitled the article 'An Account of the Discovery of a Fine New Evergreen Shrub named *Berberis japonica*', although Fortune, in the text, stated expressly that he had considered and rejected the suggestion that his plants were *Berberis japonica* (i.e., the mahonia originally described by Thunberg as "*Ilex japonica*"). Sir William Hooker tentatively sided with Fortune against Lindley, and it was under the names *Berberis bealei* and *B. bealei* var. *planifolia* Hook. that two specimens of Fortune's plants, received from Standish, were figured in 1855 in the *Botanical Magazine* (t. 4852 and t. 4846 respectively). For some unexplained reason, Standish distributed some of the offspring of Fortune's original plants as *B. bealei*, others as *B. japonica*, as is clear from his advertisements, and also from the fact that the specimen described by Hooker as *B. bealei* var. *planifolia* (*Bot. Mag.*, t. 4846) was received from Standish's nursery under the label '*B. japonica*', whereas the plant of t. 4852 was received as *B. bealei* and figured as such. However, it was as *Berberis japonica* that the descendants of Fortune's plants from China were known until recently. When Japanese nurserymen began to export the true *Mahonia* (*Berberis*) *japonica* they added to the confusion by calling it *Berberis bealei*! The confusion was cleared up by Takeda in his study of the Old World Species of Mahonia, published in *Notes Roy. Bot. Gard. Edin.*, Vol. 6 (1911–17), pp. 224–227, 240–242, but it persisted in gardens until very recently.
   The geographical distribution of *M. japonica* is not known for certain. It is usually said to be a native of Formosa, but this assertion rests on the reduction of *M. tikushiensis* Hayata to *M. japonica*, and it is questionable whether these two species are really the same. There is no specimen in the Kew Herbarium from the mainland of China that agrees perfectly with *M. japonica*; one specimen from Hupeh has inflorescences as in that species, though the bracts are smaller. On the other hand, there is material agreeing well with *M. bealei* from Hupeh, Hunan, Szechwan, and Formosa. It is possible that *M. japonica* and *M. bealei* are really states of one variable species.
   Mahonia japonica and *M. bealei* are both magnificent hardy evergreens, which will thrive under a quite heavy tree-canopy and indeed can be used, where space permits, in much the same way as *M. aquifolium*. But they are seen to best advantage as specimens. *M. japonica*, with its spreading or pendulous racemes,

is the finer of the two as a flowering-plant. Both flower in late winter and early spring. In his monograph of *Berberis* and *Mahonia* the late Dr Ahrendt remarked that 'many plants raised from seed are hybrids between these two species' and such intermediates seem to be fairly common in gardens.

M. LOMARIIFOLIA Takeda [PLATE 95

An evergreen shrub 8 to 12 ft high; stems erect. Leaves pinnate, 10 to 24 in. long, carrying 9½ to 18½ pairs of leaflets, each leaflet 1½ to 4 in. long, usually ½ to 1 in. wide, stalkless, linear-lanceolate, oblique at the base, more or less incurved towards the apex, the margins and apex spiny-toothed, stiff, leathery, glabrous. Flowers fragrant, bright yellow, densely crowded on erect cylindrical spikes 4 to 8 in. long by 1 in. wide, which are clustered as many as eighteen or twenty together at the apex of the shoots; petals oblong, about ¼ in. long, the apex rounded and notched. Fruits oval, ⅖ in. long, blue-black. *Bot. Mag.*, t. 9634.

Native of Burma, W. China, and possibly also of Formosa, where several mahonias grow which may be forms of *M. lomariifolia* but have not yet been thoroughly studied. Major Johnston of Hidcote Manor, Gloucestershire, originally introduced the species to cultivation by means of seeds he obtained near Tengyueh, Yunnan, in 1931. He raised plants and distributed them from his garden at Menton. This is probably the handsomest of the mahonias. It is not perfectly hardy except in the maritime counties to the south and west, but hardier than once thought. The late Miss Davenport Jones had a fine specimen in her garden in Kent (*Journ. R.H.S.*, Vol. 85, p. 394 and fig. 125).

Sometimes, as seen wild, it is 30 to 40 ft high, its erect trunk and stems each carrying a tuft of foliage at the summit. Its time of flowering seems to be variable. A plant in bloom was given an Award of Merit at Vincent Square on 24 May 1938, and a First Class Certificate on 24 October 1939.

M. NERVOSA (Pursh) Nutt.

Berberis nervosa Nutt.; *B. glumacea* Spreng.

A low, suckering evergreen shrub, with stems rarely more than 12 or 15 in. high, and handsome pinnate leaves up to 18 in. long, composed of usually eleven to fifteen leaflets. Leaflets stalkless, 1½ to 3 in. long, obliquely ovate, very firm and leathery in texture, prominently three-veined beneath, the margins armed with large, spiny teeth. Racemes erect, 8 in. or even more in length, with short-stalked, yellow flowers. Fruit roundish oblong, ¼ in. diameter, purplish blue. *Bot. Mag.*, t. 3949.

Native of western N. America, especially of the State of Washington; introduced in 1822. It is a handsome and striking barberry, but does not appear to thrive very well in this country generally, though it grows well and fruits at Wakehurst Place in Sussex. It always has been and still remains rare. It can be propagated by suckers. The foliage most nearly resembles that of *M. napaulensis*, but *M. nervosa* is readily distinguished by its dwarf habit, and the greater distance of the lowest pair of leaflets from the base of the common leaf-stalk.

M. NEVINII (A. Gray) Fedde
Berberis nevinii A. Gray

An evergreen shrub up to 7 or 8 ft high; young shoots slender, purplish. Leaves pinnate, 2 to 2½ in. long; leaflets usually five, sometimes three or seven, the lowest pair very close to the stem; they are of hard texture, glaucous,

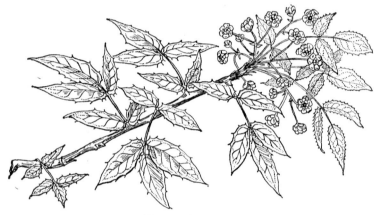

MAHONIA NEVINII

glabrous, pink-tinged when young, ¾ to 1½ in. long, ¼ to ⅜ in. wide, oblong-lanceolate, rounded at the base, tapered to a slender spine-tipped apex; margins set with needle-like spines. Flowers bright yellow, ¼ in. wide, produced about seven together in racemes ¾ to 1½ in. long; stalks slender, glabrous. Fruits egg-shaped, juicy, black, covered with abundant white bloom.

This mahonia was discovered by a Mr Nevin on a sandy plain near Los Angeles, California, and originally named after him in 1895. It is figured in *Garden and Forest*, Vol. ix, p. 415, and is there described as 'exceedingly rare . . . handsome and distinct'. Introduced to this country in 1928, it was first flowered by Mr T. Hay in Hyde Park in March 1931. It is closely related to *M. haematocarpa*, but the red fruits of that species well distinguish it. To the black-fruited *M. fremontii* it is also allied, but that species has leaflets broader in proportion to their length, with marginal teeth larger and fewer, and venation more distinctly marked. *M. nevinii* thrives well at Kew on a wall some yards to the right of the entrance to Cambridge Cottage.

M. PINNATA (Lag.) Fedde

Berberis pinnata Lag.; *M. fascicularis* DC.; *Berberis fascicularis* (DC.) Sims

M. pinnata is possibly not in cultivation in Britain at the present time in its pure state, but some of the finest and most floriferous garden mahonias derive from it by hybridisation with *M. aquifolium* and *M. repens* (see further below). It is allied to *M. aquifolium*, differing in the following characters: leaflets smaller and especially narrower (mostly up to 1 in. wide); lowermost pair of leaflets inserted close to the base of the petiole; inflorescences usually produced from axillary buds as well as terminally; pedicels with two of three bracteoles near the midpoint.

M. pinnata was introduced to the Madrid Botanic Garden by means of seeds (or perhaps plants) collected in September 1791 by the Malaspina expedition. The collection is usually attributed to the chief naturalist Dr Louis Née, but the credit really belongs to his assistant Thaddaeus Haenke, who accompanied the expedition up the coast of western N. America while Née remained behind in Mexico. The Madrid plants were named *Berberis pinnata* by Lagasca in 1803 and thirteen years later he added a description, though this is so short that it scarcely serves to validate the name. In 1821 de Candolle provided a fuller account under the name *Mahonia fascicularis*, based on plants deriving from those at Madrid. Furthermore, around 1818 Lagasca sent seeds of his *Berberis pinnata* to A. B. Lambert of Boyton, Wilts. Two plants raised from these seeds flowered in his greenhouse in February 1823 and a flowering spray from one of them was figured in the *Botanical Register* for the same year (t. 702), with a detailed description by David Don, Lambert's librarian-botanist. The two descriptions agree quite well with each other, and a specimen from one of the Boyton plants, preserved in the Kew Herbarium, in turn agrees with wild specimens collected in the Monterey area of California in later years. *M. pinnata* ranges southward from there in the coastal ranges to San Diego County or slightly beyond. In northern California it is said to intergrade with *M. aquifolium*. In Mexico closely related plants occur which are now usually considered to be a distinct species—M. MORANENSIS (Schult.) I. M. Johnston—but they were included in *M. pinnata* by Fedde in his monograph, and perhaps rightly so.

By 1838 *M. pinnata* was in commerce in Britain, though still rare. It was found to be too tender for the open ground and was usually grown against a wall, where it attained 8 or 10 ft (Loudon, *Arb. et Frut. Brit.*, Vol. 1, p. 309). The first hybrid from it was raised accidentally by Messrs Rivers of Sawbridgeworth around 1840, and was thought by Loudon to be a cross with *M. repens*. In the 1860s and 1870s there are several references in horticultural literature to plants called *Berberis fascicularis hybrida*, thought to be hybrids between *M. aquifolium* and *M. pinnata* (usually referred to in those days as *B. fascicularis*).

At the present time the form of *M. pinnata* originally introduced to Britain is perhaps not in cultivation, having been displaced by the hardier hybrids. Of these there are several, all excellent spring-flowering shrubs, growing 6 ft or even more high. Their great merit is that flower-spikes are borne from the axils of the previous leaves as well as terminally and that most bear additional spikes from short spurs on the older wood, so that, on mature plants, several feet of stem may bear flowers. The following are in cultivation or have been described:

1. A mahonia in the trade as *M. pinnata* has rather short, congested inflorescences, and the flowers are borne on very short stalks, which lack bracteoles. Leaflets dull bluish green where exposed to the sun, but lighter and more glossy on the shaded parts of the plant; lowermost pair very variable in position. Although not the true *M. pinnata*, this is a fine mahonia, very hardy and attaining 10 ft even in far from ideal conditions.

2. A mahonia in the Berberis Dell at Kew, received under the name *B. aquifolium magnifica*, is clearly a hybrid of *M. pinnata* and very floriferous. Indeed no other mahonia in the clump where it grows makes a finer display.

3. A mahonia distributed under the name *Berberis fascicularis* has been seen which is again a hybrid of *M. pinnata*, but the leaflets are permanently papillose and dull beneath, which suggests that *M. repens* may enter into its parentage. The flowers are of a very vivid yellow and the flower-stalks mostly bear bracteoles.

4. Perhaps the finest in this group are the plants called *M. aquifolium undulata*. These have glossy, undulated leaflets and richly coloured, almost orange-yellow flowers. They are near to *M. pinnata*, which they resemble in having bracteoles on the pedicels and the lowermost pair of leaflets inserted near to the base of the petiole (at least on the uppermost leaves of the shoot). The origin of this form is not known, but the plants distributed by Messrs Notcutt derive from cuttings taken at Rowallane in Northern Ireland in 1930. The plants there bore the epithet *undulata nana*, which was scarcely appropriate, considering that even in the dry climate of Suffolk this clone attains 6 ft in height. It is suggested that the plants now called *M. aquifolium undulata* should be provisionally named M. 'UNDULATA', since they do not belong to *M. aquifolium* and may eventually prove to be northern forms of *M. pinnata*.

5. Around 1863 Messrs Simon-Louis Frères of Metz started to propagate a mahonia which they called *M. pinnata* var. *wagneri* and this was shortly described by Jouin, manager of their tree and shrub nursery, in 1910. Rehder considered the Simon-Louis plant to be a hybrid between *M. pinnata* and *M. aquifolium* and published the binomial M. × WAGNERI (Jouin) Rehd. in 1919. This would be the valid collective name for hybrids of this parentage, but these combine the characters of the parents in such diverse ways that the name is of little use in garden nomenclature and would not, in any case, be applicable to plants such as No. 3 above, which has *M. repens* in its ancestry.

M. REPENS (Lindl.) G. Don

Berberis repens Lindl.; *B. nana* Greene; *M. nana* (Greene) Fedde

An evergreen shrub of dwarf, stiff habit, usually less than 1 ft high, spreading by underground stems. Leaves pinnate, consisting of three, five, or seven leaflets, which are ovate, pointed, 1 to 2½ in. long, spine-toothed, of a dull bluish green above, grey and papillose beneath. Racemes 1½ to 3 in. long, produced in a cluster at the end of the branch. Flowers deep yellow, open in April and May. Fruits black, ¼ in. wide, covered with a blue bloom.

Native of western N. America; originally discovered during the famous

expedition under Lewis and Clarke, who crossed the North American continent
for the first time, 1804–6. It ought to be useful in positions where a close evergreen covering is desired, but it has never been extensively grown. It can be
propagated by removing the creeping shoots, but has never adapted itself to our
conditions as *M. aquifolium* has, for instance. From that species it differs markedly
in its dull bluish foliage, which also shows itself in some hybrids between the
two species. It is quite distinct from *M. nervosa* which has glossy foliage, and
twice as many leaflets.

var. ROTUNDIFOLIA Fedde—There are at least two mahonias in cultivation
which bear some resemblance to *M. repens* but are of much robuster habit. Dr
Ahrendt referred to var. *rotundifolia* Fedde the very handsome mahonia in the
R.H.S. garden at Wisley which is about 2 ft or slightly more high and has leaves
with mostly two or three pairs of medium green, roundish ovate, finely toothed
or entire leaflets; flowers rich yellow. There is a similar plant in the Berberis
Dell at Kew, about 5 ft high, which bears rather pale yellow flowers in great
profusion. It was received under the name *M. repens prunifolia*.

M. PUMILA (Greene) Fedde B. *pumila* Greene—A suckering shrub about 1 ft
or slightly more high. Leaves 3 to 5½ in. long; leaflets five to nine, 1 to 2¼ in.
long, ovate or oblong-ovate, dull grey-green and conspicuously net-veined
above, paler and somewhat glaucous beneath with up to ten spine-tipped teeth
on each side. Racemes clustered, 1 to 2 in. long; pedicels with a bracteole at
midpoint. Native of the mountains of California and S. Oregon. This mahonia,
now available in commerce, is very distinct in its grey leaves and dwarf habit
and should make a useful ground cover in a sunny place.

M. 'HERVEI'.—According to the original description, this mahonia is
bushy and compact, with dark green, roundish-oval, plane, almost spineless
leaves; raised by a M. Hervé of Versailles (May, in *Rev. Hort.* (1881), p. 250, as
M. rotundifolia, with *M. hervei* Hort. as a synonym; *M.* × *hervei* Ahrendt
("*herveyi*"), *nom. superfl.*). A plant at Kew, which may have belonged to the true
clone, was said in previous editions to make a low tuft and to have the leaflets
often in threes. This plant cannot be traced. It has been suggested that this
mahonia is a hybrid between *M. repens* and *M. aquifolium*, but other authorities
consider it to be a form of *M. repens* merely. For other possible hybrids between
these two species see under *M. aquifolium*.

M. SCHIEDEANA (Schlecht.) Fedde
Berberis schiedeana Schlecht.

A shrub of variable habit, prostrate at high altitudes but erect and reportedly
up to 15 ft high in favourable situations. Leaflets three to seven, ovate, ¾ to 1¼ in.
long, dull grey-green above, very rigid, margins undulate, with three to six
spine-teeth on each side. Flowers bright yellow, produced on very short racemes
(mostly ½ to 1¼ in. long); pedicels with bracteoles in the lower half. Fruits ovoid,
blue with a pruinose bloom, up to ½ in. long.

A native of Mexico; introduced by E. K. Balls in 1938 under his seed number
T S—Z

4618, collected at 14,000 ft. A specimen taken from the wild plants was identified in an American herbarium as *M. eutriphylla* var. *saxatilis*, but another specimen in the Kew Herbarium, under the same number, is undoubtedly *M. schiedeana*, and so too is the plant at Highdown in Sussex, raised by the late Sir Frederick Stern from seed number 4618. In the true *M. eutriphylla* the leaves have only three leaflets, all springing from the apex of the petiole; in *M. schiedeana* a leaf may have only three leaflets, but then the terminal one is well separated by a length of rachis from the two laterals.

At Highdown *M. schiedeana* is not completely hardy, but has attained a height of 4–5 ft and both flowers and fruits. Plants from the same seed collection grow well in Mr Hillier's collection at Jermyns House near Romsey.

M. TRIFOLIOLATA (Moricand) Fedde
Berberis trifoliolata Moricand

The typical state of this species is confined to S. Texas and bears lustrous green leaves. The following variety is more widely distributed in the wild and is the one commonly seen in cultivation:

var. GLAUCA I. M. Johnston—An erect, rigid shrub 6 or 8 ft high, with only three leaflets to each leaf. Leaflets glaucous or almost white, shaped like a spearhead, 1 to 2 in. long, ¼ to ⅗ in. wide, tapering to a long, spine-tipped point, and bulging at each side into one or two spine-tipped lobes. Flowers yellow, borne in short corymbs. Fruits oval or roundish, black with a blue bloom.

This rare shrub ranges from W. Texas to N. Mexico, and is only hardy against a sunny wall, or in exceptionally mild districts. There was once an old bush, 8 ft high, growing against the house wall at Bayfordbury in Herts.

This variety differs from all the other cultivated mahonias in the glaucous-white leaves with only three leaflets. It was introduced to Britain in 1839 by Hartweg, who collected the seeds in Mexico on the road from Zacatecas to San Luis Potosi.

MALLOTUS   EUPHORBIACEAE

A genus of over 100 species of trees and shrubs, natives of the Old World and mostly tropical. Allied to *Ricinus*.

M. JAPONICUS (Thunb.) Muell.-Arg.
Croton japonicum Thunb.; *Rottlera japonica* (Thunb.) Spreng.

A deciduous shrub 10 or 12 ft high, with very pithy young wood, covered at first with minute specks of white starry down. Leaves like those of a catalpa, ovate, rounded or broadly tapered at the base, gradually tapered at the apex to a long slender point; they vary much in size, the largest being 9 or 10 in. long by 6 in. wide, the smallest less than one-third those dimensions, at first they are clothed with down like that on the shoots, but this soon falls away, leaving them nearly or quite glabrous, the lower surface is specked with minute, transparent glands. Flowers small, crowded on erect, terminal, pyramidal panicles, 3 to 6 in. high; they have little beauty, being small and covered with white down. Males and females occur on separate plants.

Native of Japan and Central China. It is only worth growing for its handsome foliage. It was successfully cultivated at Grayswood Hill, Haslemere, but is uncommon in gardens.

MALUS   CRAB   ROSACEAE

A genus of some twenty-five to thirty deciduous trees, including a few shrubs, distributed over the temperate parts of the northern hemisphere. Leaves simple, occasionally lobed. Flowers usually in umbel-like clusters, white to various shades of pink or purplish. Stamens fifteen to fifty, anthers usually yellow. It differs from *Pyrus*, with which it was long generically united, by the styles being united at the base—free in *Pyrus*. The fruits in most species are crowned with the persistent calyx and vary in shape from rounded to ovoid, but are never truly pear-shaped as in *Pyrus*. In *Pyrus*, moreover, the flesh of the fruit contains stone-cells (grit-cells). In *Malus* these are absent except in a few anomalous species, notably *M. prattii*, *M. yunnanensis*, *M. tschonoskii*, *M. florentina*, and *M. trilobata*.

So far as is known there is no hybrid between *Malus* and *Pyrus*, nor with any other of the genera once included in *Pyrus*, and the fact that it will not readily intergraft with them further shows that *Malus* is more distinct from the other sections of the old genus *Pyrus* than was once imagined. It was the incompatibility of the apple and pear in grafting that chiefly led Philip Miller to maintain the genus *Malus* in defiance of Linnaeus, who had sunk it in *Pyrus*. 'I shall therefore beg leave,' he wrote, 'to continue the separation of the Apple from the Pear, as hath been always practised by the botanists before his time.'

Many of the crabs rank highly as ornamental trees. In all the range of flowering trees and shrubs there is nothing more beautiful and effective than the best of this group, such as *M. spectabilis* and *M. floribunda*. In regard to fruit the genus contains many valuable species and hybrids, such as *M.* × *robusta*, 'John Downie', 'Golden Hornet', 'Red Sentinel' and many others.

The species of *Malus* hybridise with each other, so that with many one cannot rely on seeds to reproduce the parent exactly. Some crabs can be rooted from cuttings made of leafless shoots in early winter, and put in a cold frame, but most of them are increased by grafting on the various stocks used in nurseries for garden apples.

Attention must be called to the fact that the crab apples, like all members of the section Pomoideae of the Rose family, are subject to attack by the devastating disease 'fire-blight', for which see the note in Vol. I, p. 730.

Useful notes on the species and hybrids grown in Britain will be found in the article by H. S. J. Crane in *Journ. R.H.S.*, Vol. 86 (1961), pp. 160–167; and in Hillier's *Manual of Trees and Shrubs*. An assessment by H. J. Grootendorst, based on trials at Boskoop, Holland, was published in *Dendroflora*, Vol. 1 (1964). A valuable American work is: A. F. Den Boer, *Ornamental Crab Apples*, published by the American Association of Nurserymen in 1959. In Dr Donald Wyman's *Trees for American Gardens* (ed. 1965) there is an extensive section devoted to *Malus*.

For the hybrids see the special section starting on p. 714.

M. ANGUSTIFOLIA (Ait.) Michx.
Pyrus angustifolia Ait.

A small tree, semi-evergreen in mild winters, 20 ft or more high; shoots glabrous except when quite young. Leaves oval or oblong, sometimes lanceolate, 1 to 3 in. long, $\frac{1}{2}$ to $1\frac{3}{4}$ in. wide, dark shining green above, paler beneath, and nearly or quite glabrous when fully grown, base usually tapering, margins coarsely toothed, especially towards the apex. On the flowering twigs the leaves are small, 1 to $1\frac{1}{2}$ in. long, oblong, and entire, or with a few teeth only towards the apex. Flowers fragrant like violets, rosy or almost white, 1 to $1\frac{1}{4}$ in. across, produced usually in clusters of four, each flower on a slender stalk, 1 to $1\frac{1}{2}$ in. long; calyx teeth white, woolly inside. Fruits $\frac{3}{4}$ in. across, yellowish green, fragrant, harsh, acid.

Native of eastern N. America; introduced, according to Aiton, in 1750. The true plant was evidently known to Loudon, but it had disappeared from cultivation until about 1900, when it was reintroduced from the United States. It is closely allied to *M. coronaria*, and has been regarded as a variety of it. It has, however, a more southern distribution in the wild, and is quite distinct in the shape of its leaves, which are only about half as wide in proportion to their length, and have wedge-shaped bases.

M. × ARNOLDIANA Sarg.

This beautiful crab originated in the Arnold Arboretum, Mass., where it appeared amongst some seedlings of *M. floribunda* and was first distinguished about 1905. Sargent suggests that it is probably a hybrid between *M. floribunda* and one of the garden forms of *M. baccata*. A plant obtained for Kew in 1912 has proved to be a very charming addition to its group. In habit it is extremely graceful, producing as it does long arching or semi-pendulous shoots which, when young, are redder than those of *M. floribunda*. The foliage is similar but of larger average size. The flowers are more than half as large again and are about 1¼ in. wide. In the bud state the petals are a rich ruby red, paling with age to deep rose outside and pale rose inside. As with *M. floribunda* the beauty of the tree is greatest when half the flowers are still in the bud state. Flower-stalk 1½ to 2 in. long, reddish; lobes of the calyx awl-shaped, ¼ in. long; both are nearly glabrous (downy in *floribunda*). Fruits egg-shaped, ¾ in. long, tapering to the flat apex which is marked with the scars of the fallen calyx, pale yellow, changing finally to dull red. Blooms in April. There are several clones of this hybrid.

M. BACCATA (L.) Borkh.   SIBERIAN CRAB [PLATE 96
Pyrus baccata L.

A tree 20 to 50 ft high, forming a rounded, wide-spreading head of branches, the lower ones arching or pendulous at the extremities; trunk 1 to 2 ft in diameter. Leaves 1½ to 3½ in. long, about half as much wide, oval or ovate, rounded or tapering at the base, acute or acuminate at the apex, finely and shallowly toothed, glabrous and glossy green above, paler and glabrous beneath; leaf-stalk slender, glabrous, about two-thirds the length of the blade. Flowers white, produced during April in umbels, each flower 1½ in. across and borne on a slender stalk 1 to 1½ in. long. Calyx-tube and calyx-lobes glabrous, the lobes longer than the tube, lanceolate. Fruits about ⅜ in. thick, globular, bright red or yellow, slightly hollowed at the base and with a round scar but no calyx-teeth at the top.

Widely spread in nature, this species in its typical state ranges from E. Siberia eastward to the Pacific and southward to Mongolia, N. China, and Korea; but plants from S.W. China and the Himalaya, usually referred to var. *himalaica*, scarcely differ from the type. It is said to have been introduced to Kew in 1784. In fact, plants were being offered in the London nurseries earlier than that, but whether they were the true species is not known. Indeed the true species has never been common in gardens, most of the trees grown as *Malus baccata* until recently being forms of *M.* × *robusta* (see below). It was reintroduced by Farrer from Kansu under numbers 398 and 778 (the latter grown wrongly as *M. theifera*).

cv. 'GRACILIS'.—Habit graceful, with pendent branches. Leaves smaller than normal, but otherwise scarcely differing from the typical variety. Raised from seeds collected by Purdom in Shensi. Dr Wyman considers this variant to be superior to the ordinary Siberian or Manchurian crab as an ornamental.

var. HIMALAICA (Maxim.) Schneid. *Pyrus b.* var. *himalaica* Maxim.—It is very doubtful whether this variety is worth distinguishing; some Himalayan specimens have the coarsely serrate leaves mentioned in the description, others do not. It is also uncertain whether the species is anywhere truly wild in the Himalaya. Plants raised from Forrest's 22188 and 30485, collected in Yunnan, China, and grown as var. *himalaica*, do not differ from the typical variety. A plant cultivated from Ludlow and Sherriff's 17388, collected in Bhutan, differs in having ellipsoid fruits and the name var. *ellipsoidea* was proposed for this variant by Yü, but not published.

cv. 'JACKII'.—A variant of the Siberian crab introduced to the Arnold Arboretum in 1905 by means of scions sent by J. G. Jack from Seoul, Korea. A similar crab was found by Wilson in the Kongo-san, Korea (W.10696). 'Jackii' differs from the var. *mandshurica* in its larger elliptic leaves, up to 4½ in. long,

MALUS BACCATA

2⅝ in. wide, dark green above, glabrous beneath and in its larger flowers and fruits, the latter being about ⅜ in. wide. There is a fine specimen at Borde Hill, Sussex, which came from Vicary-Gibbs's collection at Aldenham. It is very robust, with leaves of a remarkably deep green for a crab.

var. MANDSHURICA (Maxim.) Schneid. *Pyrus baccata* var. *mandshurica* Maxim. MANCHURIAN CRAB.—Leaves with small, distant teeth, or even entire in the lower half, downy beneath when young; petiole usually tomentose. Calyx-tube downy but sometimes only slightly so; calyx-lobes always downy on the inside. Native of the Russian Far East, central and north-west China, Korea, and Japan. This variety was in cultivation at Kew in 1874, in which year it was figured in *Bot. Mag.* 6112 (as *Pyrus baccata*), but had probably been introduced earlier (the figure in Watson's *Dendrologia Britannica* (1825) is considered by Rehder to represent this variety). Wilson reintroduced it from N.W. Hupeh in 1901, when collecting for Messrs Veitch.

The Siberian and Manchurian crabs make sturdy trees which in time attain a fair size. Their foliage is healthy and the ivory-white flowers are borne freely in most years, but the fruits are too small to make much display.

M. CORONARIA (L.) Mill.

Pyrus coronaria L.

A tree 20 to 30 ft high, with a short trunk and a wide-spreading, open head of branches; young shoots downy the first summer. Leaves ovate to three-lobed, 2 to 4½ in. long, sometimes nearly as much wide, but usually 1 to 2½ in. wide, pointed, the base rounded or slightly heart-shaped, sometimes tapering, very soon quite glabrous on both surfaces, margins sharply, deeply, and irregularly toothed; stalk downy, 1 to 1½ in. long. Flowers white, tinged with rose, fragrant like violets, 1½ to 2 in. across, produced in clusters of four to six, each flower on a slender stalk, 1 to 2 in. long. Calyx-tube glabrous. Fruits 1 to 1½ in. across, orange-shaped, yellowish green, very harsh and acid. *Bot. Mag.*, t. 2009.

Native of eastern N. America; introduced in 1724, but not so common as one might expect from the beauty and fragrance of its flowers, which come in May and June—later than any other of the genus, except its two immediate allies. There are two American crabs closely allied to this species: they are *M. angustifolia*, with narrower leaves tapering at the base, and *M. ioensis*, in which the foliage is much more downy (and persistently so) beneath. The larger, broader leaves of *M. coronaria* frequently suggest those of *Sorbus latifolia* in shape.

cv. 'CHARLOTTAE'.—Flowers semi-double, light pink, about 1½ in. across, borne in May. The original plant was found growing wild in 1902 near Waukegan, by Mrs Charlotte de Wolf. Mr H. G. Hillier tells us that in his opinion this is the best of the semi-double American crabs for British gardens, with a much better constitution that *M. ionensis* 'Plena'. The leaves often colour brilliantly in the autumn.

var. DASYCALYX (Rehd.) Fern.—Calyx-tube hairy. This variety has a more western distribution than typical *M. coronaria*.

M. DOMESTICA Borkh.

Malus pumila of many authors, in part, not Mill.; *Pyrus malus* L., in part; *M. communis* Poir., in part; *M. pumila* var. *domestica* (Borkh.) Schneid.; *M. sylvestris* subsp. *mitis* (Wallr.) Mansf.; *Pyrus malus* var. *mitis* Wallr.

M. domestica is the correct name for the orchard apples in general, and for escapes and naturalised trees deriving from them. Superficially, they are remarkably uniform in their essential botanical characters but there is no doubt that they are of hybrid origin. They have in common the following characters: young stems covered with woolly down. Leaves dull green, elliptic-ovate, usually rounded at the base, densely woolly beneath, margins irregularly saw-toothed. Flower-stalks, calyx-tube, and outside of calyx woolly. Fruits indented at the base and usually so at the apex; calyx persistent in fruit.

The domestic apple has evolved, under human influence, from various species found wild in Europe and Asia—all of them belonging to the series *Pumilae*. Those to which it shows the greatest resemblance are M. DASYPHYLLA Borkh. of the Danube basin and N. Balkans; M. PRAECOX (Pallas) Borkh. of European Russia; and M. SIEVERSII (Ledeb.) Roem. of Russian Central Asia (the resemblance to this last is said to be very close). Other species that have made their contribution are *M. sylvestris* and *M. prunifolia*.

The orchard apples do not, of course, come within the scope of this work, but some with flowers of a deeper pink than ordinary have been recommended for garden planting. Such, for example, are the cooker 'ARTHUR TURNER' and the dual-purpose 'UPTON PYNE'.

CRAB APPLES.—The word 'crab' was originally used for the native species (*M. sylvestris*) and for sour-fruited seedlings of the orchard varieties, but was extended later to the various exotic species of *Malus* and today has become in effect the vernacular word of *Malus*, with the exclusion only of the orchard apples. But there is a group of garden varieties for which the term 'crab apple' rather than 'crab' (in the modern sense) could be used. These derive from the orchard apples, many of them (especially the American and Canadian varieties) by deliberate crossing with various "Siberian" crabs, which were probably *M.* × *robusta* and not the true Siberian crab (*M. baccata*). The Astrakhan apples and *M. prunifolia* were also used, the object of North American breeders being to produce apples hardy enough to withstand the harsh winters of the prairie states. A few of these are cultivated as ornamentals for their decorative fruits, notably 'Dartmouth' and 'Hyslop', described in the section on hybrids. In the same section see also 'John Downie', 'Fairy', and 'Veitch's Scarlet', all raised in Britain. Some hybrids, known collectively as the Quarrenden hybrids, were raised in the last century by Philip Fry of Maidstone, Kent, by crossing the dessert apple 'Devonshire Quarrenden' with a "Siberian" crab.

M. × ADSTRINGENS Zab. ex Rehd.—This name is really of no service in horticultural nomenclature but appears in several manuals and must be mentioned. The parentage was originally given by Zabel as *M. dasyphylla* × *M. baccata*, without description. Rehder gave the first parent as *M. pumila* (under which he included the orchard apples) and referred to this group various hybrid crabs raised in the USA from the crossing of orchard apples with "Siberian" crab. See further above.

M. × ASTRACANICA Dum.-Cours. ASTRAKHAN APPLE.—The astrakhan apples appear to be primitive forms of garden apple showing what is probably the influence of *M. prunifolia* in their more deeply toothed leaves, and their longer-stalked and often bloomy fruits. Miller knew the White Astrakhan or Transparent apple, introduced from Russia about the middle of the 18th century. In this the fruits are translucent yellow with a red tinge on one side. In the Red Astrakhan, which is, or was until recently, still cultivated as an orchard variety in the USA, the fruits are a bright red, covered with plum-like bloom, long-stalked. In both the fruits are conical.

M. × ELEYI (Bean) Hesse

Pyrus × *eleyi* Bean; *M.* × *purpurea* f. *eleyi* (Bean) Rehd.

A hybrid crab raised by Charles Eley of East Bergholt, Suffolk, from *M. niedzwetzkyana* crossed with pollen of *M. spectabilis*. It is a small tree, its young shoots downy, both they and the leaves being reddish purple like those of the mother tree, but of a brighter and not so dark a hue. Leaves ovate, with a short, sharply pointed apex, rounded or wedge-shaped at the base, finely toothed, 2 to 4 in. long, 1 to 2½ in. wide, downy beneath especially on the dark purple midrib and veins; stalk dark purple, ½ to 1 in. long; stipules linear to awl-shaped, toothed, ¼ in. long. Flowers in apple-like clusters and of apple-blossom shape, each 1¼ in. wide, of a rich vinous red. Fruits rich purplish red, conical, 1 in. long, ⅝ in. wide at the base, each on a slender stalk 1½ in. long, the apex hollow when the calyx falls away.

The cross between *M. niedzwetzkyana* and *M. spectabilis* was made before the first world war and a large number of seedlings were raised. It was described in 1920 (*Gard. Chron.*, Vol. 68, p. 85) and put into commerce in Britain by Messrs Notcutt shortly after. It received an F.C.C. when shown by them in October 1923 and in May of the same year had been accorded an A.M. for its flowers, when shown by Mr Eley. So far as is known the Eley crab is represented in cultivation by a single clone, descended from the seedling finally selected for naming and propagation. But it is puzzling that in the original description (as in the one reproduced above from previous editions) the fruits are said to be conical, and certainly are so in the fruiting spray figured in Vol. 2, plate 25 of the Seventh Edition. But as usually seen in gardens the fruits are roundish, and not unlike the morello cherries to which they were likened by Mr Eley himself. In both forms the calyx may be persistent or more or less deciduous. The difference in shape of fruit may not be significant, for den Boer has shown conclusively that in the USA, plants of the Eley crab known to be propagated by grafting, from the same individual, may differ strikingly in their fruits according to the locality in which the trees are grown. Plants in the Golden Gate Park, San Francisco, produce small, ovoid fruits on long stems, but grafts from these, grown by Den Boer at Des Moines, Iowa, 'promptly refused to produce the typical "Eleyi" fruit and instead brought forth a fine crop of oblate to round and larger fruit on shorter stems'. Possibly the variation from egg-shaped to cherry-shaped is a fluctuating character. In 'Neville Copeman', which is a seedling from 'Eleyi', there is a marked difference in shape of fruit and in length and thickness of fruit-stalk, even on the same tree.

With regard to the parentage of 'Eleyi', Rehder doubted whether *M. spectabilis* was the pollen-parent, and suggested that it was more likely to have been *M. sieboldii* or some related species or hybrid. He placed it under *M.* × *purpurea*.

According to den Boer, the crab grown in the USA as 'Eleyi' is indistinguishable from 'Jay Darling', which is a renaming of a crab-apple which originally came from France around 1904 and was in commerce in the States at one time under the name *Malus cerasifera atropurpurea*. It is presumably of the same parentage as 'Eleyi'.

M. FLORENTINA (Zuccagni) Schneid.

Crataegus florentina Zuccagni; *Pyrus crataegifolia* Savi; *Eriolobus florentina* (Zuccagni) Stapf

A bush or small tree of rounded habit, with slender, dark brown branches; branchlets woolly when young. Leaves rather hawthorn-like, 1½ to 2½ in. long, ¾ to 1¾ in. wide, broadly ovate in the main, but with the margins always cut up into several lobes which are themselves toothed, base rounded or heart-shaped, dark green above, with scattered hairs when young, paler and downy beneath; stalk downy, reddish, up to 1 in. long. Flowers pure white, about ¾ in. diameter, produced in June five to seven together on lax open corymbs 2 or 3 in. across, each flower on a slender, downy, pinkish stalk 1 to 1¼ in. long; calyx very woolly, the lobes narrow, pointed. Fruits roundish oval, ½ in. long, yellowish changing to red, the calyx fallen away. *Bot. Mag.*, t. 7423.

Native of N. Italy, and very rare both in the wild and in cultivation. There are few more charming small trees than this in June, the long, slender shoots of the previous summer being then clothed with abundant short twigs, each with its cluster of white flowers. The leaves are very similar in form to those of the wild service (*Sorbus torminalis*) only much smaller. Its fruit is not particularly bright, but the foliage often turns a brilliant orange-scarlet before falling. It is very suitably placed as an isolated specimen on a lawn. Plants at Kew were introduced by H. Groves from near Florence in 1886, but the oldest now in the collection by the Palm House Pond, dates from 1892. There is a larger one by the Isleworth Gate, received from the Arnold Arboretum in 1930.

The taxonomy and status of *M. florentina* is discussed by K. Browicz in *Fragmenta Floristica et Geobotanica*, Vol. 16, 1, pp. 61–83 (1970). Browicz upholds the theory, first advanced almost a century ago, that *M. florentina* is a hybrid between *Sorbus torminalis* and *Malus sylvestris* (which, as interpreted by him, includes the orchard apples and their escapes). He publishes the name × *Malosorbus* for this intergeneric hybrid and places *M. florentina* under it as × *M. florentina* (Zuccagni) Browicz.

M. FLORIBUNDA Sieb. ex Van Houtte

M. floribunda Sieb., in cat., *nom. nud.*; *Pyrus floribunda* Kirchn., not Lindl.; *P. pulcherrima* Aschers. & Graebn.

A tree ultimately 20 to 30 ft high, with a spreading tangle of branches forming a rounded head wider than the tree is high; often shrubby; young shoots downy at first, becoming glabrous later. Leaves on the flowering and weaker shoots usually narrowly or broadly ovate, and from 1½ to 3 in. long; rounded or tapering at the base, rather coarsely toothed, on strong shoots they are occasionally three- or five-lobed, 3 to 4½ in. long, and half as wide, upper surface dark dullish green, glabrous; lower one paler and downy; stalk ½ to 1 in. long, downy. Flowers 1 to 1¼ in. across, rosy-red in bud, pale pink when open, produced in clusters of four to seven, each on a stalk 1 to 1½ in. long. Fruits round, ¾ in. in diameter, yellow, with the calyx fallen away.

Introduced from Japan about 1862, and perhaps the most beautiful of all crabs in flower. It blossoms towards the end of April, producing then an amazing profusion of flowers, each branch a garland. Perhaps its beauty is greatest when half the flowers are expanded, the pale pink contrasting with the rich rose of the other half still in bud. This crab is not considered to be a true wild species, but a hybrid from *M. sieboldii* and perhaps *M. baccata* or *prunifolia*. The deeply three- or even five-lobed leaves occasionally seen on strong branches certainly indicate affinity with *M. sieboldii* (q.v.).

M. FUSCA (Raf.) Schneid.   OREGON CRAB

Pyrus fusca Raf.; *Pyrus rivularis* Hook.; *M. rivularis* (Hook.) Roem.

A tree 20 to 40 ft high, often a shrub; branchlets slender, more or less downy. Leaves variously shaped, from broadly ovate to oblong-lanceolate, often three-lobed, the largest 4 in. long, and 2½ in. wide, more often 1 to 3 in. long, and half as wide, the base tapering, rounded or slightly heart-shaped, pointed at the apex, sharply toothed, downy on both sides; stalk downy, 1 to 1½ in. long. Flowers white or rose-tinted, ¾ in. across, produced in clusters of six to twelve. Fruits egg-shaped, ½ to ¾ in. long, red, yellow, or greenish yellow, the calyx teeth fallen away; stalks 1 to 1½ in. long, slender. *Bot. Mag.*, t. 8798.

Native of western N. America; introduced in 1836, according to Loudon, but little known in cultivation now, although it is offered sometimes in tree catalogues of continental firms. It belongs to the same group as *M. sieboldii*, but appears to have no special value for the garden. The fruit has an agreeable sub-acid taste, and the wood, being close and hard, is valued in the western States for uses similar to those of apple- and pear-wood in this country.

M. HALLIANA Koehne

A small tree 12 to 18 ft high; young branches purple, soon quite glabrous. Leaves ovate or oval, 1½ to 3 in. long, half as wide, rounded or tapering at the base, rather long-pointed, slightly toothed, the midrib glandular and slightly hairy above, otherwise the leaf is quite glabrous on both surfaces and of a dark polished green above, often purple-tinted, especially on the midrib; stalk ½ in. or less long. Flowers deep rose, 1 to 1½ in. across, from four to seven in a cluster, each flower on a glabrous, reddish purple stalk 1 to 1½ in. long; petals five to eight; calyx reddish purple and glabrous outside, woolly within; calyx-lobes triangular-ovate, blunt at the apex. Fruits obovoid, purple, the size of a small pea, marked at the top with the scar of the fallen calyx.

A native of Chinese and Japanese gardens, not known in the wild in its typical state. It was first introduced to America from Japan about 1863 by Dr G. R. Hall, after whom it is named. It has some affinity with *M. floribunda* and has been known in gardens as *M. floribunda plena*, the flowers being often semi-double. *M. halliana* is abundantly distinct in habit, in the nearly glabrous character of its parts, and it never appears to have the deeply lobed leaves occasionally seen in *M. floribunda*. Also, in *M. halliana* the leaves are convolute in the bud, not folded as in *M. floribunda*, and dark green.

Wilson collected a specimen in W. Szechwan which was at first identified as *M. halliana* but later proved to be *M. hupehensis*; this error explains the statement made in previous editions that *M. hallinana* occurs wild in W. Szechwan. Although *M. halliana* does not grow wild in Japan in its typical state, a crab closely related to it has been found there. This is:

var. SPONTANEA (Mak.) Koidz. *M. floribunda* var. *spontanea* Mak.—This differs from the typical state in its almost white flowers on shorter stalks (¾ to 1 in. long) and in its elliptic to obovate leaves. It occurs wild on Mt Kirishima, Kyushu.

cv. 'PARKMANII'.—Flowers more double, with about fifteen petals. Introduced from Japan by Hall at the same time as typical *M. halliana* and named after his friend, the historian Francis Parkman, in whose garden it was first grown.

M. × ATROSANGUINEA (Späth) Schneid. *Pyrus floribunda atrosanguinea* Späth; *Malus floribunda* var. *atrosanguinea* Bean—Flowers as in *M. floribunda* but of a richer rose and not fading. Leaves deep glossy green, those on the extension growths slightly lobed. Although usually placed under *M. floribunda*, this crab is botanically near to *M. halliana* which it resembles in having the leaves convolute (rolled) not folded in the bud stage and in the short calyx-lobes. It is probably a hybrid of *M. halliana* with *M. sieboldii*.

M. × HARTWIGII Koehne—A hybrid between *M. halliana* and *M. baccata*, resembling the former in foliage. Flowers red in the bud, opening white flushed with pink, about 1¾ in. wide. Fruits dark red, about ½ in. wide. It is not common in British gardens but is said to be a better grower than *M. halliana*.

M. HUPEHENSIS (Pampan.) Rehd.
Pyrus hupehensis Pampan.; *M. theifera* Rehd.

A deciduous tree up to 40 or even more ft high of stiffish habit; young shoots at first covered with whitish down. Leaves ovate or oval, shortly and slenderly pointed, rounded at the base on virgin shoots but wedge-shaped on flowering ones, finely toothed, 2 to 4 in. long, 1 to 2½ in. wide, dark bright green and glabrous at maturity above, purplish when young, pale beneath and downy on the midrib and chief veins; stalk up to 1⅛ in. long. Flowers white tinged with rose on first opening, fragrant, 1 to 1½ in. wide, produced in April in clusters of three to seven, each on a slender downy stalk 1 in. long; calyx-lobes triangular-ovate, as long as or shorter than the tube and acute or acuminate, downy inside, glabrous and purplish outside; styles usually three. Fruits globose, ⅓ in. wide, greenish yellow tinged on the exposed side with red, with the calyx fallen away from the summit. *Bot. Mag.*, t. 9667.

Native of Central and Western China, where it is widely distributed; introduced by Wilson for Messrs Veitch in 1900, but not named until 1915. It is a beautiful tree when in full bloom with its very profuse white or pink-tinted flowers. Wilson considered it to be the finest deciduous flowering tree he had introduced. It is perfectly hardy. The name *M. theifera* refers to the use of the leaves by the peasants of Central China, who prepare a beverage from them which they call 'red tea'.

M. hupehensis is allied to *M. baccata* and *M. halliana* but in those species the flowers usually have five styles. Also, in *M. baccata* the calyx-lobes are lanceolate, longer than the tube and in *M. halliana* they are blunt at the apex.

f. ROSEA Rehd.—This is simply the botanical name for trees with rosy-pink instead of white flowers; according to Wilson such trees are common in the wild.

M. hupehensis is one of the few species of *Malus* that comes true from seeds even when grown in close proximity to other species. This is because it is a triploid, and produces its seeds apomictically.

M. IOENSIS (Wood) Britt.

Pyrus coronaria var. *ioensis* Wood; *Pyrus ioensis* (Wood) Bailey

A tree of the same character as *M. angustifolia* and *M. coronaria* (q.v.), but differing in the much more downy branches, the down on which persists until the summer of the following year; side branchlets often spine-tipped. Leaves ovate or oval, 3 to 4 in. long, half or a little more than half as wide; persistently woolly beneath, coarsely toothed towards the apex. Flowers 1½ to 2 in. across, white or rosy, four to six in a corymb; stalks 1 to 1½ in. long, covered with white wool; calyx very woolly. Fruits 1¼ to 1½ in. in diameter, dull yellowish green.

As has already been stated under *M. coronaria*, this tree is one of a closely allied group of N. American crabs, but it has a more western habitat than the other two, being found in the Central United States. It differs from both its allies in the much more downy branchlets, leaves, and other young parts of the tree (a frequent characteristic in the most western forms of American trees).

cv. 'PLENA'. BECHTEL CRAB.—In the year 1891, Messrs Bechtel, of Stanton, Illinois, USA, sent out this beautiful double-flowered crab under the name "*M. angustifolia plena*". In the prevailing confusion as to the identity of these three species, it was also called "*M. coronaria plena*". The individual flowers, which on young healthy plants measure 2 to 2½ in. across, are perhaps the finest of the genus, the numerous petals being of a lovely delicate pink. With a delightful odour suggestive of violets, and coming to bloom in early June, this crab would seem to have all the virtues. But unfortunately it is of very poor constitution and evidently not well adapted to the British climate. See also *M. coronaria* 'Charlottae'.

M. × SOULARDII (Bailey) Britt. *Pyrus soulardii* Bailey—This is the name for hybrids between *M. ionensis* and orchard apples (*M. domestica*), which are found occasionally in the wild in the Mississippi basin. Young stems woolly. Leaves broadly ovate or broadly elliptic, often blunt at the apex, coarsely toothed, downy beneath, sometimes slightly lobed. Fruits variable in colour and size (up to 2 in. or even more wide). The clone descended from the type is distinguished by Den Boer as 'SOULARD'.

M. KANSUENSIS (Batal.) Schneid.

Pyrus kansuensis Batal.; *Eriolobus kansuensis* (Batal.) Schneid.

A deciduous shrub or small tree of bushy habit 10 to 25 ft high; young shoots downy. Leaves ovate in main outline, but usually deeply three-lobed at the terminal part, sometimes five-lobed, the smaller leaves scarcely lobed, lobes slenderly pointed, toothed, often curved outwards, the base rounded or slightly heart-shaped, 1 to 3½ in. long, ¾ to 2½ in. wide, slightly downy at first on both surfaces, becoming nearly or quite glabrous; stalk ½ to 1½ in. long. Flowers white, ½ to ¾ in. wide, produced four to ten in May in a terminal corymb 2 to 3 in. wide; main and secondary flower-stalks downy; calyx-lobes awl-shaped, they and the tubular part clothed with pale hairs; stamens about twenty; styles three, united, glabrous or downy at the base only. Fruits scarlet, dotted, egg-shaped, $\frac{1}{3}$ to $\frac{1}{2}$ in. long, the stalks 1 to 2 in. long, the calyx fallen away from the summit.

Native of Kansu, Hupeh, and Szechwan, China; introduced by Wilson in 1910 for the Arnold Arboretum, possibly before for Messrs Veitch. A tree raised from Wilson's number 4115 flowered at St Clere, Kemsing, Sevenoaks, in May 1919, and from a specimen received from there the above description was made—apart from the fruit. It is a handsome species with brightly coloured fruits, very distinct in the three-lobed leaves with three main veins at the base. It is allied to *M. toringoides*, which differs in the more pinnate lobing of the leaf and in having one or two more styles to each flower.

f. CALVA Rehd., differs from the type in having the flower-stalk and calyx devoid of down. Except for some down on the veins beneath, the leaves are also glabrous. One of the trees at St Clere (see above), also raised from W.4115, belongs to this form and from it came the spray figured in *Bot. Mag.*, n.s., t. 251.

M. LANCIFOLIA Rehd.
M. coronaria var. *lancifolia* (Rehd.) Fern.

A deciduous tree up to 25 ft high with frequently spiny branches; young shoots at first woolly, soon glabrous. Leaves ovate or ovate-lanceolate, pointed, usually rounded at the base, those on the barren shoots larger, broader, more strongly toothed than on the flowering shoots, $1\frac{1}{2}$ to $3\frac{1}{2}$ in. long, $1\frac{1}{4}$ to 3 in. wide, woolly beneath when young, soon becoming almost glabrous; stalk $\frac{1}{2}$ to 1 in. long. Flowers $1\frac{1}{4}$ to $1\frac{1}{2}$ in. wide, produced in May in clusters of three to six each on a glabrous, slender stalk 1 to $1\frac{1}{4}$ in. long. Fruits roundish, 1 in. wide, green.

Native of the United States (Missouri, Illinois, etc.); introduced to cultivation in 1912. It belongs to the same group of crabs as *M. coronaria*, *M. angustifolia*, and *M. ioensis*; *M. ioensis* is easily recognised by the often lobed, very downy leaves. From the other two Prof. Bailey notes that *M. lancifolia* is distinguished by its acuminate, less leathery leaves, by the longer calyx-lobes and by the styles being woolly below the middle. Like its allies it is an ornamental flowering tree with larger flowers than is usual amongst crabs in general. The specific name is more applicable to the leaves of the flowering shoots than to those of the barren ones.

M. NIEDZWETZKYANA Dieck
M. pumila var. *niedz.* (Dieck) Schneid.; *Pyrus niedz.* Hemsl.

A small tree of about the size and character of the ordinary apple; young bark reddish purple. Leaves 3 to 5 in. long, 2 to $2\frac{1}{2}$ in. wide, ovate or oval, round-toothed, downy all over the lower surface when young, afterwards on the midrib only; stalk downy, $\frac{3}{4}$ to $1\frac{1}{2}$ in. long. The stalk and midrib are bright red, the blade also is of a decided red tinge when young, becoming purplish later in the season. Flowers in apple-like clusters, deep red-purple, $1\frac{1}{2}$ in. across, flower-stalks $\frac{1}{2}$ to $\frac{3}{4}$ in. long and, like the calyx, covered with whitish wool. Fruits conical, with a few broad grooves running lengthwise, 2 in. long, of a deep vinous red. *Bot. Mag.*, t. 7975.

This apple occurs in the mountains of Russian Central Asia and bordering parts of China. It is recognised as a species in *Fl. SSSR*, near to *M. sieversii*, of which it may only be a colour variant. It has also been suggested that it is really a form of orchard apple (*M. domestica*).

Five seedlings from it were raised at Kew, and of these, three came as green in branch and leaf as the ordinary apple, and the flowers were merely pink—not the beautiful red which makes this one of the most striking of its group. It was introduced to cultivation by Dr Dieck, of Zoeschen, in Germany. The fruit is not of high quality as we know apples, being of rather turnip-like consistency. So completely is the tree permeated with red colouring matter that the young wood, when cut, shows red right through, as does also the fruit. Introduced to England in 1894.

M. niedzwetzkyana is uncommon in gardens, for it does not flower freely and is subject to scab. But many of the garden hybrids owe to it the reddish or purplish colouration of their flowers, fruits and foliage. See *M.* × *purpurea* and the clones cross-referenced there; the Rosybloom group treated below; and also 'Profusion' and 'Liset' (p. 717).

ROSYBLOOM GROUP.—A group of hybrids between the Russian purple crab (*M. niedzwetzkyana*) and various "Siberian crabs" (*M. baccata*, *M. prunifolia*, and their hybrids) raised in Canada and the USA. The original set was raised at the Dominion Experimental Station around 1920 and selected and named by Miss Isabella Preston some ten years later; others were raised and named later by W. R. Leslie in Manitoba. All the original varieties were given the names of Canadian lakes. Other hybrids of similar parentage were produced by W. E. Hansen at the Agricultural Experimental Station in South Dakota, USA. The objective of these breeders was to produce crabs hardy enough to withstand the harsh winters of the Prairie States but the ability to withstand seventy degrees of frost is not a necessary attribute so far as British gardens are concerned. Many of the Rosyblooms have beautiful flowers and nearly all have decorative fruits which are also excellent for making crabapple jelly. The group has not as yet been fully tested in the British climate.

Members of this group described in the section on hybrid clones (pp. 714–717) are: 'Almey', 'Chilko', 'Cowichan', and 'Simcoe', all raised in Canada; and the American 'Hopa'.

M. PRATTII (Hemsl.) Schneid.
Pyrus prattii Hemsl.

A deciduous tree up to 30 ft high; young shoots furnished with whitish hairs when quite young, soon glabrous. Leaves ovate, ovate-lanceolate, or oval, the apex slenderly pointed, the base rounded, sharply and doubly toothed, 2½ to 5½ in. long, 1 to 2¾ in. wide, soon glabrous except for occasional down beneath on the midrib and chief veins; stalk 1 to 1½ in. long. Flowers white, ¾ to 1 in. wide, borne during May in clusters ten or twelve together; styles five, glabrous. Fruits roundish egg-shaped, ½ in. wide, red, specked with tiny white dots, the woolly calyx persisting at the top, flesh gritty; fruit-stalk 1 in. long.

Native of Szechwan, China; discovered by A. E. Pratt, introduced by Wilson for Messrs Veitch in 1904. It bears fruit regularly at Kew and is distinct on account of the largish leaves and handsome, dotted fruits. The foliage often colours well in autumn. Akin to *M. yunnanensis* (q.v.).

M. PRUNIFOLIA (Willd.) Borkh.

Pyrus prunifolia Willd.

A small tree with downy young shoots and ovate or broadly oval leaves, 2 to 4 in. long, half or more than half as wide, unequally toothed, downy beneath. Flowers white, 1½ in. across, fragrant, produced in April in umbels of six to ten; calyx with long, narrow, woolly lobes. Fruits round or slightly ovoid and elongated, 1 in. in diameter, yellowish or red, crowned with the persistent calyx; calyx-lobes on the fruits united at the base into a short fleshy tube, so that the free part of the calyx seems to be inserted on a short pedestal. *Bot. Mag.*, t. 6158.

There is some doubt about the origin of this crab. It was in cultivation in England in 1758 and said to have come from Siberia, though it is not a native of that region; nor indeed has it ever been found wild in its typical state. Closely related trees have, however, long been cultivated in China for their fruits (see var. *rinki* below).

var. RINKI (Koidz.) Rehd. *M. pumila* var. *rinki* Koidz.; *Pyrus ringo* Wenzig; *Malus ringo* Sieb.; *M. asiatica* Nakai—This variety differs from the typical *M. prunifolia* only in being slightly more downy, with shorter flower-stalks and usually pinkish flowers. It is cultivated in China for its fruits, which have an apple-like flavour and are quite pleasant eating. Wilson found it growing apparently wild in western Hupeh. It appears to have been originally introduced to European gardens by Siebold from Japan. In that country it was once widely cultivated for its fruits but has been displaced by varieties of European origin. *Bot. Mag.*, t. 8265.   [PLATE 97

There are red- and yellow-fruited forms of var. *rinki*. The great attraction of the latter is its abundant, gracefully pendent, bright yellow fruits, which hang from the lower side of the branches in long, crowded rows, and make it one of the handsomest of our yellow-fruited hardy trees. But it is perhaps surpassed by 'Golden Hornet', described in the section on hybrids.

Rehder explains that the Japanese names 'rinki' and 'ringo' both derive from the Chinese name for this apple—'linkun'—and that the name 'to-ringo', meaning Chinese apple, is also used in Japan only for this variety. Unfortunately, Siebold used 'toringo' as the specific epithet for the crab now properly known as *M. sieboldii* (*Pl. Wils.*, Vol. 2, pp. 293–294).

M. PUMILA Mill.

Pyrus malus var. *paradisiaca* L.; *P. m.* var. *pumila* (Mill.) Henry; *Malus pumila* var. *paradisiaca* (L.) Schneid.; *M. sylvestris* var. *paradisiaca* (L.) Bailey

In botanical and garden literature the name *M. pumila* Mill. has been used in a very wide sense, to denote the orchard apples, the naturalised trees and escapes deriving from them, and the wild downy-leaved species that they most resemble. Miller himself, as is quite clear from his description, intended *M. pumila* as the botanical name for the French paradise apple, which he believed to be a distinct species 'for it never rises to any height, the branches are weak, scarce able to support themselves, and this difference is permanent when raised from seeds' (*Gard. Dict.*, ed. 1768). The French paradise apple was used in France, in Miller's day and later, as a stock for the production of miniature trees. But in Britain, said Miller, it was not common in gardens, being 'only proper for trees which are kept in pots, by way of curiosity, for these do not continue long'. The French paradise is reputed to have been brought to France in the 16th century from Armenia, where according to an old belief the Garden of Eden had been situated—hence paradise apple. Miller also mentions the less dwarfing stock known as the Dutch paradise apple, but it is clear from the text that he regarded the French variety as the true paradise apple.

The botanical name *M. pumila* derives from the phrase-name published by Caspar Bauhin in his *Pinax* (1623).—'Malus pumila quae potius frutex quam arbor' (the dwarf apple that is rather a shrub than a tree). This phrase was cited by Miller under *M. pumila*, as it had been earlier by Linnaeus under his *Pyrus malus* var. *paradisiaca*.

It is difficult to see how the French paradise apple can be regarded as representative of the orchard apples, which are a complex hybrid race deriving partly from species which are acknowledged to be distinct from *M. pumila* even by those authorities who interpret this species in a wide sense. Miller himself did not place the garden apples under *M. pumila*. Indeed, he did not place them positively under any species but suggested with hesitation that they might belong to *M. sylvestris*—'I have not distinguished the Apples from the Crab, as distinct species, though I have never seen Apples produced from the seeds of Crabs.'

Following the *Flora Europaea*, the name *M. domestica* is used for the orchard apples in this edition. In that work the name *M. pumila* is not used for any wild species, but is given a subordinate position under *M. dasyphylla*.

For *M. pumila* var. *niedzwetzkyana* see *M. niedzwetzkyana*. For various crab apples such as 'John Downie', which are usually placed under *M. pumila*, see the section on hybrid clones starting on p. 714. See the same section for 'Elise Rathke' (*M. pumila pendula*).

M. × PURPUREA (Barbier) Rehd.

Malus floribunda purpurea Barbier; *Pyrus purpurea* Hort.

This beautiful crab was raised by Messrs Barbier of Orleans around 1900 by crossing *M. niedzwetzkyana* with *M.* × *atrosanguinea* (*M. floribunda atrosanguinea*), and was originally distributed as a variety of *M. floribunda*. In habit it is more erect and open than *M. floribunda* and does not develop the same dense thicket of branches. The leaves are larger, sometimes slightly lobed, of a purplish red that is especially pleasing in the delicately tinted early stage. In the bud state the flowers are of a delightful ruby red, becoming paler and more purple on opening fully; they are 1 to 1¼ in. wide, the petals broader and more cupped than in *M. floribunda*; the stamens, calyx, and flower-stalk are also richly coloured. The flowers are in clusters of six or seven and expand in April. Fruits globose, about the size and shape of large cherries, pendulous on stalks about 1 in. long, dark vinous red, the calyx adhering at the end.

It is, of course, from *M. niedzwetzkyana*, the supposed male parent, that the rich colouring of the leaves, flowers, and fruit (also the red colouring that permeates the young wood right through) have been inherited.

The following crabs were treated by Rehder as forms of *M. × purpurea*: 'Aldenhamensis', 'Eleyi', and 'Lemoinei'. These are treated in the section on hybrid clones, starting on p. 714. For *M. × purpurea* f. *pendula* see 'Echtermeyer' in the same section.

M. × ROBUSTA (Carr.) Rehd.
Pyrus microcarpa var. *robusta* Carr.

To this group of hybrids between *M. baccata* and *M. prunifolia* belong many of the plants that have been grown in gardens as Siberian crab or as *Malus* or *Pyrus baccata*. These hybrids differ from *M. baccata* in their larger fruits, which usually, though not invariably, bear persistent calyx-teeth at the top. Those which resemble *M. baccata* in having the fruits without calyx teeth can still be distinguished from that species by the larger size of the fruits and often by the greater downiness of the undersurface of the leaves, leaf-stalk, and calyx-tube.

When the hybrid Siberian crab first came into cultivation in this country is not known, but Bigg's Everlasting crab (also known as the winter crab or *Pyrus borealis*) was, according to Loudon, raised in the Cambridge Botanic Garden from seeds received from Siberia in 1814, and this certainly belongs to *M. × robusta*. Other forms of this hybrid are known as the Cherry crab, the Red Siberian, and the Yellow Siberian, all of which were in cultivation soon after the middle of the last century. All have showy fruits which persist long on the branches.

cv. 'ERECTA'.—Of fastigiate habit. Raised at the Arnold Arboretum from seeds brought by Prof. Sargent from Peking in 1904.

cv. 'PERSICIFOLIA'.—Leaves oblong-lanceolate, resembling those of a peach. The original plant was received by the Arnold Arboretum in 1913 from Veitch's nursery as *Pyrus* species, Purdom 179 (*Journ. Arn. Arb.*, Vol. 2, p. 55).

M. ORTHOCARPA Lav., *nom. nud.*—This name sometimes appears in catalogues, though it has never been validated by a description. According to the German researcher Henning, crabs cultivated in various continental botanic gardens under this name are intermediate between *M. baccata* and *M. prunifolia*. A tree at Kew labelled *M. orthocarpa* was raised from a scion received from the Arnold Arboretum in 1889. It is near to *M. baccata*.

M. SARGENTII Rehd.
Pyrus sargentii (Rehd.) Bean; *M. sieboldii* var. *koringo* f. *sargentii* Koidz.

A shrub of bushy habit 5 to 8 ft high; young shoots downy. Leaves ovate or oval, 2 to 3 in. long, 1 to 2 in. wide, pointed at the apex, rounded or slightly heart-shaped at the base, often three-lobed, sharply toothed, woolly when quite young, becoming nearly glabrous before falling; stalks downy, ⅓ to 1 in. long. Flowers pure white, 1 in. across, produced in clusters of five or six, each on a stalk 1 to 1¼ in. long; calyx glabrous outside, woolly within. Fruits orange-shaped, ⅓ in. wide, bright red, the apex marked by the scar of the fallen calyx. *Bot. Mag.*, t. 8757.

This very attractive species was sent to Kew by Prof. Sargent in 1908. It is distinct among crabs by its purely bushy habit. It was originally discovered by Sargent in 1892 near a brackish marsh, Mororan, Japan, and was named in his honour by Dr Rehder in 1903. The author observes that it is most nearly related to *M. sieboldii*, but differs in its larger, pure white flowers with broad overlapping petals and in its larger fruits. From another ally, *M.* × *zumi*, it is distinguished by 'its broader, often lobed leaves, the shape of the [broader based] petals, the glabrous calyx-tube and the habit'.

It is exceedingly doubtful whether this crab is entitled to rank as a species. Schneider considered it to be a variety of *M. sieboldii* and in Ohwi's *Flora of Japan* (1965) it is treated as synonymous with that species. The fact that *M. sargentii* keeps true to type only when grafted supports this conclusion. The German nursery firm Timms and Co. offer both grafted plants and seedlings, and remark that the latter grow to over 20 ft high.

cv. 'ROSEA'.—Flowers pink in the bud, about 1½ in. across. It grows taller than the true *M. sargentii*. It was raised in the Rochester Parks, New York.

M. × SCHEIDECKERI Zab.

Pyrus spectabilis floribunda scheideckeri Späth; *P. floribunda scheideckeri* Hort.

A tree eventually 20 to 30 ft high, branches somewhat erect on young trees; shoots grey-downy early in the season, becoming glabrous later. Leaves ovate, rounded or tapering at the base, pointed, coarsely and sharply toothed; glabrous and dark shining green above, paler and at first downy beneath, becoming glabrous in autumn except on the midrib; on the flowering twigs the leaves are 2 to 3 in. long and about half as wide, but on vigorous maiden shoots as much as 4½ in. long by 3 in., and sometimes lobed. Flowers often semi-double, 1½ in. across, pale rose, produced in May in umbels of six to ten flowers each on a downy stalk 1 to 1½ in. long; calyx woolly, especially inside. Fruits globose, yellow, ⅝ in. thick, calyx-teeth usually persisting at the top.

A hybrid between *M. floribunda* and *M. prunifolia*, put into commerce by Späth of Berlin in 1888. Through *M. floribunda* it inherits the 'blood' of *M. sieboldii*, as is occasionally evidenced by the lobing of the leaves on vigorous branches. On young trees clean shoots 3 to 4 ft long are made in one season, at every bud of which there appears the following May a cluster of six to ten large blossoms. It is thus possible to cut branches a yard or more long, wreathed from end to end with flowers. Unfortunately, this crab has a poor constitution and has now become rare in the trade. 'Hillieri', described on p. 715, is as fine and a better grower.

M. SIEBOLDII (Reg.) Rehd.

Pyrus sieboldii Reg.; *M. toringo* Sieb. ex Miq.

A small tree, rarely seen more than 10 to 15 ft high, sometimes a low shrub, but said by Sargent to become 30 ft high in the wild; branches arching or pendulous; young shoots downy the first year. Leaves dull green, very variable in shape, and either narrowly oval, ovate, deeply three-lobed, or of some intermediate shape; they are 1 to 2½ in. long, sharply, irregularly, and often coarsely toothed, downy on both sides, but especially beneath, tapering at the base to a downy stalk ¼ to ¾ in. long. Flowers pale pink to deep rose, ⅜ in. in diameter, produced during April in clusters of three to six, each flower on a downy, slender, almost thread-like stalk ¾ to 1 in. long. Fruits globose, the size of a small pea, red or brownish yellow, with no calyx-lobes at the top.

Native of Japan; introduced by Siebold in 1856, and a small tree of very graceful habit, distinct among crabs for its variable, often deeply cut leaves, and its tiny fruits (see also *M. sargentii* and *M.* × *zumi*). It is allied to *M. floribunda*, but is not so valuable a garden tree, its blossoms being shorter lived.

For the epithet 'toringo' used by Siebold, see under *M. prunifolia* var. *rinki*.

M. × SUBLOBATA Rehd. *M. ringo* f. *sublobata* Dipp.—A hybrid between *M. sieboldii* and *M. prunifolia* var. *rinki*, described from a plant raised in the Arnold Arboretum from seeds which Prof. Sargent had brought from Japan, where the first parent is wild and the second cultivated. Something similar, according to Rehder, had been cultivated by Zabel in Germany under the name *Pyrus ringo* var. *sublobata*. Leaves narrowly elliptic or elliptic-oblong, those on the extension growths broader and slightly lobed. Calyx with long hairs. Styles four or five. Fruits with or without a persistent calyx, about ⅝ in. wide, yellow.

M. SIKKIMENSIS (Wenzig) Schneid.

Malus pashia var. *sikkimensis* Wenzig; *Pyrus sikkimensis* Hook. f.

A small tree branching low and of bushy habit, distinct among all other crabs in cultivation through the excessive development of stout, rigid branching spurs on the trunk; young shoots downy. Leaves 2 to 4½ in. long, 1 to 2 in. wide, narrowly oval, tapering or rounded at the base, slender-pointed, very woolly beneath, and more or less so above; stalk downy, ½ to 1½ in. long. Flowers 1 in. across, white (rosy in bud), produced during May in corymbs of four to nine blossoms; calyx downy, with slender-pointed lobes; flower-stalks 1¼ to 1½ in. long, slender. Fruits somewhat pear-shaped, ⅝ in. wide and long, dark red with paler dots, the apex marked with the scar left by the fallen calyx. *Bot. Mag.*, t. 7430.

Native of Himalaya; introduced to Kew more than a century ago by Sir Joseph Hooker, who found it in the interior of Sikkim up to elevations of 10,000 ft. It is strange that so distinct and striking a tree has not spread more in cultivation. The original tree at Kew flowered freely, and annually produced enormous crops of fruits. Brandis observes that this crab is scarcely specifically distinct from *M. baccata*, but as represented at Kew, it is easily distinguished by the low-spreading habit, the excessive development of spurs on the stems, the more woolly leaves and inflorescence, and the smaller pear-shaped fruit. A pleasing lawn tree.

The original tree at Kew no longer exists but the species is still represented in the collection by two trees near the Restaurant.

MALUS SIKKIMENSIS

M. SPECTABILIS (Ait.) Borkh.

Pyrus spectabilis Ait.; *Malus s.* var. *plena* Bean

A tree rarely more than 30 ft high, forming a rounded head of branches often as wide as high; young twigs downy. Leaves oval or obovate to almost round, 2 to 3½ in. long, up to 2 in. in width; toothed, shortly and abruptly pointed, tapering or rounded at the base, glossy green and glabrous above, downy when young beneath, becoming almost or quite glabrous by autumn; stalk ¼ to 1 in. long. Flowers deep rosy-red in the bud state, paling to a blush tint when fully open, and then nearly 2 in. across; they are borne each on a downy stalk ¾ to 1¼ in. long, in umbels six or eight together; petals normally more than five; calyx and flower-stalk downy. Fruits globose, yellow, ¾ to 1 in. wide, bitter and harsh; calyx persisting at the top; base not hollowed.

M. spectabilis has long been cultivated in N. China but is not recorded there in the wild state. The date of its introduction is not known, but it was cultivated by Dr Fothergill in 1780, and had become fairly common in gardens by the end of the century. The form then cultivated, from which Aiton described the species, had semi-double flowers and is figured in *Bot. Mag.*, t. 267 (1794). A single-flowered form was in cultivation by 1825.

M. spectabilis is one of the most beautiful of the genus in its flowers, but has no beauty in its fruits. It flowers almost invariably in great profusion from the middle of April to the second week in May.

cv. 'Riversii'.—Flowers deeper pink, with up to twenty petals; leaves larger and broader. Raised by Rivers' nurseries, Sawbridgeworth, Herts, before 1864 and figured in *Florist and Pomologist* (1872), p. 25, as *Pyrus s. roseo-plena.* The epithet *riversii* was the one under which it was distributed by Booth's nurseries at Flottbeck, near Hamburg, through which many cultivars of British origin passed to continental gardens.

M. × MICROMALUS Mak. *M. spectabilis* var. *kaido* Sieb.; *Pyrus s.* var. *kaido* (Sieb.) Kirchn.; *Pyrus ringo* var. *kaido* (Sieb.) Wenzig—A small erect-branched tree. Leaves elliptic-oblong, narrowly cuneate at the base, glossy above, downy beneath when young, becoming glabrous. Flowers deep red in the bud, when open pale pink at the edge, deeper pink at the centre. Fruits red, about ½ in. across, hollowed at the base and usually without a persistent calyx.

A hybrid of *M. spectabilis*, of which the other parent is thought to be *M. baccata.* It was introduced to Europe by Siebold from Japan before 1856, but according to Makino came originally from China. Its date of introduction to Britain is given by Nicholson as 1874. At Kew it flowers at the end of April and early May.

M. SYLVESTRIS (L.) Mill.   WILD CRAB
Pyrus malus var. *sylvestris* L.; *M. acerba* Merat

A tree up to 30 ft or sometimes more high, or a shrub, with unarmed or more rarely thorny branches and a brown fissured bark; young growths slightly hairy at first, later glabrous. Leaves ovate to elliptic, about 1½ in. long, broadly wedge-shaped to rounded at the base, acuminate at the apex, slightly downy on the veins beneath when young, later glabrous, margins finely but bluntly toothed. Flowers white flushed with pink, 1 to 1½ in. wide, borne on spurs in umbellate clusters. Calyx-tube and inflorescence axes glabrous or almost so. Fruits globose, ¾ to almost 1 in. wide, greenish yellow flushed with red, hard and sour-tasting, with a cavity at both ends and crowned with the persistent calyx-lobes.

A native of Europe, including Britain. This species is really of no importance in gardens except as one of the parents of the orchard apples. It should not be confused with apparently wild seedlings of the orchard apples, which can easily be distinguished from our true wild crab by their downy stems, leaf undersides and calyx-tubes, and by their sweeter fruits. See further under *M. domestica.*

Den Boer considered that the crab called *M. spectabilis* 'Alba Plena' or 'Albiplena' is probably a double-flowered form of *M. sylvestris.* It is little known in this country.

M. TORINGOIDES (Rehd.) Hughes
M. transitoria var. *toringoides* Rehd.; *Pyrus toringoides* (Rehd.) Osborn

A deciduous tree up to 25 ft high, of loose, graceful habit; young shoots long, slender, at first closely covered with grey down, becoming glabrous later. Leaves ovate to lanceolate in main outline, but usually deeply lobed, the pointed or bluntish lobes numbering three to seven, basal leaves of shoot often entire, apex of leaf pointed, sometimes slenderly so, base narrowly wedge-shaped to truncate, 1¼ to 3½ in. long, ¾ to 2 in. wide, both surfaces slightly downy at first, but the upper one becoming quite glabrous, the lower one remaining more or less downy on the midrib and veins, margins slightly toothed; leaf-stalk slender, downy, ¾ to 1½ in. long. Flowers six to eight together in corymbs terminating short leafy spurs, opening in May; each flower is ¾ to 1 in. wide, borne on a slender downy stalk ¾ to 1 in. long; petals creamy white; calyx-tube bell-shaped, the lobes awl-shaped, the whole clothed with grey down. Fruits obovoid to globose, ⅜ to ⅝ in. long, pendulous, yellow, flushed deeply with scarlet on the sunny side, the calyx fallen away from the top. *Bot. Mag.*, t. 8948.

Native of W. Szechwan, China; introduced by Wilson for Messrs Veitch in 1904. This is a very beautiful addition to cultivated crabs, uniting a graceful habit with exquisite colouring of fruit. It is in its highest beauty in September and October. Miss Willmott showed it at Westminster in October 1919, when it was given an Award of Merit.

M. TRANSITORIA (Batal.) Schneid. *Pyrus transitoria* Batal.—This species, under which Rehder originally placed *M. toringoides* as a variety, is also in cultivation. It has more downy, shorter leaves (up to 2 in. or so long) with narrower, deeper lobes, and rarely are the leaves entire. The calyx-lobes are usually shorter and more triangular, and the fruits are smaller (up to about ⅜ in. long). Native of N.W. China; introduced by Purdom from Kansu. It makes a more slender tree than *M. toringoides*.

M. TRILOBATA (Labill.) Schneid.

Crataegus trilobata Labill.; *Eriolobus trilobatus* (Labill.) Roem.

A small tree, perhaps up to 50 ft high, or a shrub, with very downy young twigs. Leaves with three deep main lobes, the terminal one usually three-parted, the side ones two-parted. The leaf thus often becomes seven-parted, but the shape is not uniform, and although the three main lobes are always there, the subsidiary divisions vary in number. Some of the leaves have a maple-like appearance, the blade being 2 to 4 in. wide, scarcely as long, heart-shaped at the base; the stalk ¾ to 2 in. long. The upper surface is glabrous and bright, the lower one downy, more especially on the veins and midrib; margins finely toothed. Flowers white, 1½ in. across, in small terminal corymbs, calyx-lobes long, triangular, with a dense white wool on both sides. Fruits usually reduced to from one to three in a corymb, ⅝ to ¾ in. across, globular or pear-shaped, crowned with the calyx-lobes, red or yellow. *Bot. Mag.*, t. 9305.

Native of Syria, the Lebanon, N. Palestine, and Greek Thrace, but rare both in the wild state and in gardens. There is an example at Kew near the ginkgo measuring 30 × 3¼ ft (1967). It was planted in 1900.

M. trilobata is a very distinct species, and there is much to be said for following those botanists who have treated it as a distinct genus. The distinguishing characters are the combination of lobed leaves, large flowers in a simple umbel, the petals concave, woolly-ciliate at the base, and notably clawed, so that there is a distinct gap between adjacent petals at the base, sepals longer than the densely tomentose receptacle and densely tomentose on both sides, ovary prolonged upwards in the receptacle as a densely hairy cone from which arise five styles united at the base into a densely tomentose column; mature fruit with stone-cells, usually only one cell fertile, with one or two seeds. The fleshy part of the fruit embraces and encloses the conical part of the ovary, leaving only a small depression at the top of the fruit in which is the hairy columnar base of the styles.

M. TSCHONOSKII (Maxim.) Schneid.

Pyrus tschonoskii Maxim.; *Eriolobus tschonoskii* (Maxim.) Rehd.

A tree 30 to 40 ft high, of erect, open, rather pyramidal habit; young branches covered with a greyish down. Leaves broadly ovate, or rounded; 2 to 5 in. long, 1½ to 3 in. wide, pointed, unevenly toothed, the base rounded, covered with loose down above when young, afterwards becoming glabrous, permanently grey-felt beneath, veins in six to ten pairs, parallel; stalk downy, ½ to 1 in. long. Flowers 1 to 1¼ in. across, white, suffused at first with rose, produced four to six together in umbels, each flower on a woolly stalk ½ to ⅝ in. long; calyx covered with white wool. Fruits globose, 1 in. wide, brownish yellow flushed with purple, erect on a stalk 1 to 1½ in. long, crowned with the persistent calyx-teeth.

Native of Japan, where it is rare in the wild; first discovered at the foot of Fujiyama. It was first introduced to cultivation by Prof. Sargent, who, in 1897, sent plants to Kew, raised from seed he had collected five years previously. It does not flower very copiously, and its fruits have no attraction in colour, but the leaves 'assume a wonderful autumnal mixture of colours—bronze, crimson, orange, purple and yellow. The fruits are almost non-existent and it is an ideal tree for roadside planting where the fruit would be a menace. No other crab-apple makes such a valuable contribution of leaf colour in the autumn.' (H. S. J. Crane in *Journ. R.H.S.*, Vol. 86 (1961), p. 162).

M. tschonoskii has attained a height of 45 ft at Westonbirt, Glos., and 38 ft at the Winkworth Arboretum, Surrey (1965–6). In the Knap Hill Nursery there is a specimen about 50 ft high and 30 ft in spread of crown (1971).

M. YUNNANENSIS (Franch.) Schneid.

Pyrus yunnanensis Franch.

A deciduous tree 20 to 40 ft high; young shoots at first felted, afterwards glabrous and reddish brown. Leaves ovate, finely and irregularly toothed, sometimes slightly lobed, pointed, rounded or slightly heart-shaped at the base, 2 to 4½ in. long, 1½ to 3 in. wide, chief veins in six to nine pairs, dull green and ultimately glabrous above, clothed beneath with a pale brown felt; stalk ¾ to 1½ in. long. Flowers white or with a faint pink tinge, ⅝ in. wide, produced during May in flattish clusters 2 to 2½ in. wide at the end of short leafy side twigs. Calyx clothed with white wool at first, its lobes triangular; petals round; stamens twenty with yellow anthers; styles five, glabrous or nearly so. Fruits globose, ½ in. wide, deep red sprinkled with whitish dots, the reflexed calyx-lobes persisting at the top in a cup-shaped depression; flesh gritty, harsh, acid.

Native of Hupeh, Szechwan, and Yunnan, China; discovered by Delavay in Yunnan, introduced by Wilson in 1900. It is more commonly represented in gardens by var. VEITCHII, Rehd., a form with more distinctly lobed leaves but united with the type by intermediates. It was first exhibited and put on the market as *"Pyrus Veitchiana"* and under that name was given an Award of Merit at Westminster on 8 October 1912. The fruit-bearing branches then shown by Messrs Veitch bore a wonderful crop of red crabs and were exceedingly ornamental. I consider this one of the best of Wilson's introductions amongst crabs, for in addition to the beauty of its fruits its leaves turn to scarlet and orange in autumn. It is figured in *Bot. Mag.*, t. 8629. *M. prattii*, a near ally having also gritty, white-dotted, red fruits with a persisting calyx, differs in the leaves soon becoming smooth beneath and in never being lobed. *M. tschonoskii* has somewhat similar but never so distinctly lobed leaves, and larger brownish yellow and purple fruits, without a depression at the apex.

M. × ZUMI (Matsum.) Rehd.

Pyrus zumi Matsum.; *M. sieboldii* var. *zumi* (Matsum.) Asami

A small tree of pyramidal habit; young wood slightly downy. Leaves ovate or oblong; 1½ to 3½ in. long, ¾ to 1½ in. wide, tapering or rounded at the base, glabrous except when quite young; stalks about 1 in. long. Flowers pink in bud, becoming white after opening, 1 to 1¼ in. diameter, produced in clusters of four to seven; calyx-lobes woolly, especially inside, longer than the tube; flower-stalks 1 to 1½ in. long. Styles four or five. Fruits ½ in. in diameter, globose, red.

Native of Japan; introduced to N. America in 1892 by Sargent, and thence to Kew in 1905. It is one of the group of Japanese crabs to which *M. sieboldii* and *M. sargentii* belong, distinguished by small fruits marked at the apex by the scar of the fallen calyx. It is said to be superior to *M. sieboldii* as a garden tree in the Arnold Arboretum, being covered there in May by a mass of flowers, and in autumn by 'attractive bright red fruits'. It differs from both its allies in its oblong leaves being only slightly or not at all lobed, and from *M. sargentii* in its wider flowers and less crowded petals. The fruits are larger than the pea-like ones of *M. sieboldii* and the flowers have four or five styles (three or four in *M. sieboldii*). It occurs wild in Japan, and Ohwi, in *Flora of Japan*, follows Asami in treating it as a variety of *M. sieboldii*. Rehder, however, considered it to be a hybrid between *M. sieboldii* and perhaps *M. baccata* var. *mandshurica*.

cv. 'CALOCARPA'.—This crab arose at the Arnold Arboretum among plants raised from seeds sent from Japan in 1890. It is intermediate between *M. sieboldii* and typical *M. × zumi*, having flowers with three or four styles as in the former and also resembling it in the well-marked lobing of the leaves on the extension growths. But it differs from *M. sieboldii* and resembles *M. × zumi* in its larger fruits, which are bright red, about ½ in. across, and often remain on the tree until Christmas. (*M. sieboldii* var. *calocarpa* Rehd.; *M. × zumi* var. *calocarpa* (Rehd.) Rehd.).

HYBRIDS

In this section are brought together in alphabetical order various hybrid clones which would otherwise have to be scattered through the descriptive text. Most of these bear vernacular names, but some Latin-named hybrids that are usually given botanical status have been brought into this section if they are clones of uncertain parentage.

'ALDENHAMENSIS'.—This crab arose in the garden of the Hon. Vicary Gibbs at Aldenham, Herts. It resembles 'Eleyi' but the fruits differ in being flattened globose, or orange-shaped, instead of conical; they are 1 in. wide, the calyx persists at the top and the stalks are thicker. The leaves are often slightly lobed, and their toothing is coarser and more uneven. The flowers, some of which are semi-double, are borne later than in 'Eleyi', at the end of May. It makes a quite small tree.

'ALMEY'.—Leaves purplish when young, later bronze-green. Flowers about 2 in. across, the petals clear deep pink, but paler at the base, so that the flowers have an almost white, star-shaped centre. Early May. Fruits small, carmine-red but often becoming partly orange when fully ripe. It is a second-generation seedling of the Rosybloom group, named in 1945.

'CHEAL'S CRIMSON'.—Fruits orange with a red cheek, about 1 in. wide. Flowers pink in the bud, opening white. A.M. 1917, as a variety of *M. prunifolia*.

'CHEAL'S GOLDEN GEM'.—Flowers large, pure white. Fruits yellow, about ½ in. wide, ripe in September. Near to *M. prunifolia*. There is an example at Kew near the Cherry Path, planted 1924. A.M. 1919.

'CHILKO'.—Young leaves purplish. Flowers rose-pink, borne in the second half of April. Fruits crimson, glossy, about 1½ in. long, ripe in August. A.M. 1967. It is a member of the Rosybloom group, see p. 703.

'COWICHAN'.—Flowers rose-pink, borne late April. Fruits bright purplish red, about 1½ in. wide (Rosybloom Group, see p. 703).

'CRITTENDEN'.—Flowers pale pink. Fruits deep red on the sunny side, very glossy, ⅝ to almost 1 in. across, roundish but crowned with a fleshy pedestal bearing the persistent calyx. The original tree came from Japan as a seedling in 1921 under the name *"Pyrus malus Toringo"*. A tree grafted from this was acquired by B. P. Tompsett of Crittenden House, Matfield, Kent, and received an Award of Merit when exhibited by him on 24 January 1961. As the date suggests, the fruits remain on the tree almost throughout the winter, and in this respect 'Crittenden' resembles *M.* × *robusta*. It appears to be fairly near to *M. prunifolia* var. *rinki*.

'DARTMOUTH'.—Fruits deep crimson with a purplish bloom, almost 2 in. across. An American variety probably deriving partly from the Red Astrakhan, raised in New Hampshire before 1883.

'DOROTHEA'.—Flowers semi-double, silvery rose, 1½ in. or slightly more across, borne freely even on young plants. Fruits yellow, about ½ in. wide. This hybrid was raised in the Arnold Arboretum and is named after the elder daughter of Dr Donald Wyman, for many years Horticulturalist of that institution. It grows slowly in the R.H.S. Garden at Wisley, but the flowers are certainly very beautiful.

'ECHTERMAYER' ('Oekonomierath Echtermayer').—Branches weeping. Leaves bronzy-purple at first, later green. Flowers light carmine-red. Fruits purplish red, about 1 in. across. This crab was put into commerce by Späth in 1914 and is probably the one mentioned in previous editions (and in Kew Hand-lists) as *Malus* (or *Pyrus*) *purpurea pendula*. It is thought to be a hybrid between the Russian purple crab and 'Excellenz Thiel', the pendulous form of *M.* × *scheideckeri*. Mr Hillier informs us that he has found it to be a plant of poor constitution and very subject to scab.

'ELISE RATHKE'.—An orchard apple with weeping branches and abundant beautiful flowers, followed by handsome yellow fruits of good flavour. Also known as *M. pumila pendula*.

'EXCELLENZ THIEL'.—A hybrid of *M. floribunda* and thought to be of the same parentage as *M.* × *scheideckeri*. It is of very pendulous habit and best grafted on a high stem.

'FAIRY'.—Fruits yellow, flushed and striped with crimson. A seedling of the Red Siberian (i.e., a form of *M.* × *robusta*), raised by Jennings, a nurseryman of Shipston-on-Stour, before 1875.

'GOLDEN HORNET'.—Fruits deep yellow, globose to egg-shaped, ¾ to 1 in. wide, in clusters of three or four, very freely borne every year and remaining long on the tree. This crab, one of the most decorative of those grown for their fruits, was raised by Messrs Waterer, Son and Crisp. It received an Award of Merit in 1949 and a First Class Certificate in 1961. It shows the influence of *M. prunifolia* var. *rinki* in its yellow fruits with a persistent calyx borne on a fleshy pedestal.

'GORGEOUS'.—This crab, raised in New Zealand, is perhaps not in cultivation in Britain at present. It is said to make a small tree, producing large quantities of glossy red, roundish fruits about 1 in. wide, some of them cherry-like, others with a persistent calyx (*Dendroflora*, No. 1, p. 6; Catalogue of Messrs Duncan and Davies (1966), with colour photograph).

'HILLIERI'.—This hybrid, selected by Messrs Hillier in 1928 from a batch of plants received from Holland, is usually considered to belong to *M.* × *scheideckeri*. Flowers semi-double, rose-coloured, deeper in the bud, very freely borne. Foliage (unlike that of *M.* × *scheideckeri*) very healthy. Fruits yellow, flushed with red, soon falling. Mr Hillier recommends that this crab should be grown as a bush as it is not a strong grower. He informs us that some fruit growers have found it to be a good pollinator for 'Cox's Orange'. It is late-flowering.

'HOPA'.—Leaves purplish when young. Flowers not such a clear pink as in 'Almey', but with the same pale, star-shaped centre. Fruits about ¾ in. wide, carmine-red and orange when fully ripe. A vigorous grower, of upright habit when young. It has the same parentage as the Rosybloom crabs (see p. 703), but was raised in the United States by W. E. Hansen. American authorities consider 'PATRICIA' and 'RADIANT' to be improvements on 'Hopa'; both are seedlings from it by open pollination.

'HYSLOP'.—Fruits partly pale yellow, partly crimson with a purplish bloom. An old American variety, which according to Beach was already common by 1869. It is figured in his work *The Apples of New York*.

'JOHN DOWNIE'.—Flowers pink in the bud, opening white, in late May. Fruits conical, 1¼ in. long, 1 in. wide, bright orange and scarlet, slender-stalked, produced in wonderfully profuse clusters. It was raised in 1875 by E. Holmes in his nursery at Whittington near Lichfield and put into commerce in 1885. Award of Merit 1895. John Downie was a Scottish nurseryman and a friend of the raiser, who at one time was partner in the famous Handsworth Nurseries (Fisher and Holmes, later Fisher, Son and Sibray).

'KATHERINE'.—Flowers 2 in. or slightly more across, pale pink, fading to white, double (ten to twenty petals). Leaves dark green. Fruits red, about ¼ in. across. A beautiful crab, but the flowers fade rather quickly; it is also of rather weak growth and best as a bush. It arose in one of the parks at Rochester, New York, and was distributed by the Arnold Arboretum in 1943 (D. Wyman, *Trees for American Gardens*, p. 312). It received an Award of Merit when shown by Messrs Notcutt at the R.H.S. show on 2 May 1967. The parentage is believed to be *M. halliana* × *M. baccata*.

'LADY NORTHCLIFFE'.—Flowers pink in the bud, opening pure white, profusely borne in early May. Fruits brownish, about ½ in. wide; calyx deciduous. A hybrid of uncertain parentage, raised at Aldenham.

'LEMOINEI'.—A hybrid of perhaps the same parentage as *M.* × *purpurea*, raised by Lemoine and put into commerce around 1922. Flowers deep rosy purple, not borne freely on young plants. Leaves dark purple when young, becoming bronzy later. Fruits very dark reddish purple and therefore not showy.

'LISET'. See under 'Profusion'.

'MAGDEBURGENSIS'.—A hybrid of an orchard apple (or possibly of a Paradise apple) raised in Germany at the end of the last century. It has a spreading crown and bears in May dense clusters of flowers with up to twelve petals, each about 1 in. wide, the petals of a lovely deep rose outside, paler towards the base and inside. Fruits subglobose, yellowish, about 1 in. wide. The other parent is usually given as *M. spectabilis* but Den Boer considered that 'Magdeburgensis' shows no trace of the influence of that species and suggested *M. sylvestris* 'Plena' as the other parent. There is an example in the R.H.S. Garden at Wisley at the edge of Seven Acres, near the Restaurant.

'MONTREAL BEAUTY'.—The crab in commerce in Britain under this name has large white flowers and fruits with a yellow to orange ground-colouring overlaid with crimson, almost 2 in. wide. It is perhaps the same as the old Canadian variety 'Montreal', raised before 1833.

'NEVILLE COPEMAN'.—A seedling of 'Eleyi' raised by T. N. S. Copeman at Roydon Hall, Diss, Norfolk, and put into commerce by Messrs Notcutt. A.M. 6 October 1954. It resembles 'Eleyi' in flower, but is of better constitution and more striking in its fruits, which are reddish orange or brilliant crimson. In shape they vary from flattened-globose to broad-ellipsoid.

'PRINCE GEORGE'S'.—Flowers very double, with about fifty petals, light pink and about 2 in. across. Foliage as in *M. ioensis* 'Plena' but narrower. A very striking crab, flowering late May or early June, but rather a weak grower in Britain. According to Dr Wyman it was raised in the USA from seeds collected in the Arnold Arboretum, and is believed to be a hybrid between

M. angustifolia and *M. ioensis* 'Plena'. It was first grown in the Trial Grounds of the Department of Agriculture in Prince George's County, Maryland.

'PROFESSOR SPRENGER'.—Fruits about ½ in. wide, orange-coloured when fully ripe, persisting until December. Raised in Holland.

'PROFUSION'.—Leaves purple at first, later bronze-green, often three-lobed on the extension growths. Flowers deep purplish red, but soon paling, very freely borne. Fruits oxblood-red when fully ripe, about ⅜ in. wide, flattened top and bottom. It makes a small tree, of excellent constitution, and was raised by S. G. A. Doorenbos from a cross between *M. sieboldii* and 'Lemoinei'. A third-generation hybrid from this cross is 'LISET', also raised by Mr Doorenbos. This is as yet little known in Britain but received a higher rating than 'Profusion' in the Boskoop Trials. The flowers are said to hold their colour better than in 'Profusion' and the tree is said to be very resistant to scab. Hybrids of the parentage given above have been named the Moerlandsii Group.

'RED JADE'.—A crab with drooping branches and sharply serrated acuminately tapered leaves, borne on long, slender stalks. Flowers white, borne early May, followed by a profuse crop of small, red, broadly ovoid or globular fruits; calyx deciduous. Raised in the USA.

'RED SENTINEL'.—Flowers white, early May. Fruits deep red, glossy; about 1 in. wide, roundish but flattened top and bottom, slightly ribbed, calyx deciduous or persistent. The fruits remain on the tree through most of the winter. Possibly a form of *M.* × *robusta*.

'RED TIP'.—Leaves reddish when young. Flowers deep purplish pink. Fruits yellowish green and red, almost 2 in. across. A hybrid between the Russian purple crab (*M. niedzwetzkyana*) and either *M. ioensis* or *M. coronaria*, Raised in the USA by Hansen.

'SIMCOE'.—Young foliage copper-tinted. Flowers rose-pink, borne early May; petals incurved at the tips. A member of the Rosybloom group (see p. 703) and perhaps the first to be introduced to Britain. A.M. 1940 (for flower) and 1945 (for fruit), on both occasions being shown by Lady Lawrence from her garden in Surrey.

'VAN ESELTINE'.—A small tree of columnar habit. Flowers double, almost 2 in. across, rosy-pink. It is near to *M. spectabilis* and believed to be a hybrid between it and *M.* × *arnoldiana*. Raised in the USA.

'VEITCH'S SCARLET'.—Flowers white, late May. Fruits scarlet, darkening to crimson on the sunny side, 1¾ in. wide. A hybrid between the orchard apple 'King of the Pippins' and the Red Siberian (a form of *M.* × *robusta*), raised early this century by Messrs Veitch.

'WINTERGOLD'.—Leaves glossy green, some of them three-lobed. Fruits yellow, about ½ in. wide, on long, slender stalks, remaining on the tree until Christmas. A hybrid of *M. sieboldii*, raised in Holland.

MANDEVILLA APOCYNACEAE

A genus of over 100 species of climbers in Central and South America, named in honour of H. J. Mandeville, who introduced the species described below, which is the type-species of the genus. *Mandevilla* belongs to the subfamily Apocynoideae, in which the stamens are united to the head of the style by a viscid substance, and the connective between the anthers is prolonged into a spiny tip. In *Vinca* and *Trachelospermum*, which belong to the subfamily Plumerioideae, this peculiarity is absent.

M. suaveolens Lindl.

M. tweediana Gadeceau & Stapf

A deciduous climbing shrub growing 12 ft or more high; young shoots very slender, glabrous, hollow, exuding milky juice when cut. Leaves opposite, heart-shaped, tapering at the apex to a long fine point, toothless, 2 to 3½ in. long, 1¼ to 2 in. wide, dark dull green and glabrous above, paler beneath, with tufts of white down in the axils of the veins; stalk ½ to 2 in. long. Flowers sweetly scented, produced six to eight together in corymbs from the leaf-axils, from June to September. Corolla white or creamy white, funnel-shaped, 2 in. long, 1½ in. wide, five-lobed, the lobes roundish ovate, spreading, overlapping; glabrous outside, hairy inside the tube. Anthers five, yellow, scarcely stalked, ⅜ in. long, crowded together in a column towards the base of the tube and concealing the stigma. Calyx green, with five awl-shaped lobes ⅜ in. long. Seed-pods (follicles) usually in pairs, each from 12 to 16 in. long, slenderly cylindrical, ¼ in. wide. Seeds bearded. *Bot. Mag.*, t. 3797.

Native of the Argentine; introduced in 1837 by H. J. Mandeville, at that time British Minister at Buenos Ayres, and in compliment to whom the genus was named. Usually grown in greenhouses, where it is valued for the abundant, sweetly scented blossoms, it can, in the milder parts of the country, be grown on a sunny wall, planted in well-drained, light, loamy or peaty soil. It has succeeded well and borne its remarkable seed-pods in the Vicarage Garden at Bitton in Gloucestershire, and at Leonardslee in Sussex. In Cornwall it is even more luxuriant. It is sometimes known as "Chilean jasmine".

M. laxa (Ruiz & Pavon) Woodson *Echites laxa* Ruiz & Pavon—This species, described from Peru, resembles *M. suaveolens* in many respects and is mentioned here because *M. laxa* would be the correct name for the species if the two were united, as they have been by Dr Woodson. But the differences between them are substantial and it seems preferable to retain the name *M. suaveolens* for the plant of Argentina, at least for the time being.

MANGLIETIA MAGNOLIACEAE

This genus is very nearly related to *Magnolia*, and has the same solitary, terminal blossoms, but is distinguished by having often six ovules to each carpel, whereas the magnolias have only two. '*Manglietia*' appears to have been adapted by Blume from the native name in Malaya of the first species of the genus he described.

M. HOOKERI Cubitt & W. W. Sm.

A medium-sized or tall evergreen tree with a conical head of branches; young shoots covered with a close, greyish down. Leaves leathery, oblanceolate to oblong, narrowed at the apex to a short point, tapered at the base; 6 in. to 1 ft long, 1½ to 3½ in. wide, dark glossy green above, paler but also glossy beneath, quite glabrous but finely and distinctly net-veined; stalk ½ to 1⅛ in. long. Flowers solitary, terminal, 4 in. wide; sepals three, oblong, blunt, cream-coloured; petals nine, white. Fruits ovoid or almost globose, 2½ in. long.

Native of Upper Burma at 5,000 to 6,000 ft and of Yunnan at 9,000 ft altitude. It was originally discovered in 1909 by Mr Cubitt in the former country and later by Forrest in Yunnan. The tree is said to yield a timber highly valued by the Burmese. Most or all of the plants in cultivation have been raised from Forrest's seeds, and they are growing vigorously in Cornish gardens, being already handsome and striking evergreens.

There is a specimen at Caerhays, Cornwall, measuring 43 × 4¼ ft at 5½ ft, with a clear bole of 14 ft (1966).

M. INSIGNIS (Wall.) Bl.

Magnolia insignis Wall.

An evergreen tree 40 ft or more high, the young shoots, leaf-stalks, and leaf-buds more or less downy at first, becoming nearly or quite glabrous later; branchlets ringed at the joints. Leaves rather leathery, oblanceolate to narrowly oval, finely pointed, gradually tapered from the middle to the base, 4 to 8 in. long, 2 to 3 in. wide, dark glossy green above, pale and slightly glaucous beneath; stalk ½ to 1 in. long. Flowers magnolia-like, odorous, solitary, terminal, erect, 3 in. wide, opening after the young leaves. The flowers are variously described as 'white or yellowish tinged with pink', 'splendid rose pink', 'richest creamy carmine'; sepals three; petals nine; flower-stalk stout, ¾ to 1 in. long. Fruits ovoid-cylindric, 2 to 4 in. long, 1 to 1½ in. wide, purple. Seeds three or four to each carpel, suspended on a slender filament on becoming free. *Bot. Mag.*, n.s., t. 443.

Native of the Himalaya, where it has long been known; found by Forrest in Yunnan in 1912 and several times since; also by Farrer in Upper Burma; both introduced seeds from which plants have been raised that are now growing in Cornwall and elsewhere. In the garden at Exbury it was 10 ft high in 1931, but had been somewhat injured during the winter of 1928–9. At Kew in a sheltered shrubbery well protected from the north and east, it was 8 ft high in 1932 and perfectly healthy, but has since died.

There is a specimen at Caerhays, Cornwall, which is 28 ft high and 4¾ ft in girth at 3½ ft, dividing into two stems at 4½ ft (1966).

MARGYRICARPUS   ROSACEAE

A genus of a single species in S. America, placed in the tribe Poterieae of the Rose family, with *Acaena*, *Alchemilla*, *Sanguisorba*, and *Poterium*, to name only those genera best known in gardens. The fruit is really an achene, enclosed in the fleshy calyx-tube. The allied genus *Tetraglochin*, also confined to S. America, is included in *Margyricarpus* by some botanists, the combined genus then having about ten species.

M. PINNATUS (Lam.) O. Kuntze   PEARL FRUIT
Empetrum pinnatum Lam.; *Margyricarpus setosus* Ruiz & Pavon

A low, prostrate, evergreen shrub, with glabrous, pale, straw-coloured branches, nearly covered by large, similarly coloured, clasping stipules. Leaves pinnate, about ¾ in. long; leaflets green, finely linear, ⅛ to ⅓ in. long; stipules membranous, furnished at the edges with white, silky hairs. Flowers solitary, stalkless, very inconspicuous, without a corolla; produced singly in the leaf-axils. Fruit a small white berry, about the size of a peppercorn, with a pleasant acid flavour.

Native of the Andes from Colombia to Chile and Argentina, also of Uruguay and S. Brazil. This curious little shrub may be grown by those interested in out-of-the-way plants; but beyond its finely cut leaves it has little to recommend it, although when its pearl-like fruits are borne freely it is distinctive. It appears to be hardy except during the hardest winters. It should have a sunny position on the rock garden, and not a rich soil. I have seen it bearing fruit freely in Notcutt's nursery at Woodbridge, where probably the dry, sunny East Anglian climate suits it. It blooms in July and August but is of no great merit.

MARSDENIA   ASCLEPIADACEAE

After the first volume of this revision had gone to press, it was pointed out to us by Mr A. A. Bullock that the species described below should be segregated from *Marsdenia* as a distinct genus—CIONURA Griseb.—in which its correct name is C. ERECTA (L.) Griseb. Mr Bullock remarks that the species is more closely related to *Dregea* than to *Marsdenia*, from which it differs by the cymes being lateral at the leafy nodes (not in narrow elongated thyrsiform panicles) with much larger flowers which have a very short tube and more or less sinuate spreading lobes (against small flowers which are more or less urceolate-campanulate, with the tube much longer than the lobes).

M. ERECTA (L.) R. Br.

Cynanchum erectum L.; CIONURA ERECTA (L.) Griseb.

A deciduous climber, with slender, twining stems, 20 ft or more high, furnished with a little loose down when young. Leaves opposite, heart-shaped, 1½ to 2½ in. long, from two-thirds to as much wide, with short, abrupt points, pale rather glaucous green, with a little loose down on the midrib and veins beneath; stalk ½ to 1¼ in. long. Corymbs terminal and axillary, the latter often in pairs, but only borne in the axil of one of each pair of leaves, 2 to 4 in. long, erect. Flowers white, ⅓ in. across, sweetly scented, the five segments of the corolla narrow oblong, ¼ in. long, rounded at the end. Calyx-lobes ovate, transparent at the margins. Fruits narrowly cone-shaped or spindle-shaped, 3 in. long, ½ in. wide at the base, tapering to a point; each seed has a brush-like attachment of silky white hairs 1 in. long. Blooms in June and July.

Native of S.E. Europe and Asia Minor; cultivated in England in the 16th century, but long regarded as a greenhouse plant. It is the hardiest member of a large genus, and succeeds very well against a sunny wall, but is liable to be killed in the open. It is not quite so hardy as its ally, *Periploca graeca*. When cut, the stems exude milky juice, which has a blistering effect on the skin, and is very poisonous taken internally.

MAYTENUS   CELASTRACEAE

As once understood, *Maytenus* was a genus confined to the New World, from Florida and S. Texas to the Magellan region, and most numerously represented in the tropics of C. and S. America, and in the West Indies. Recently, however, numerous African species previously placed in *Celastrus* or *Gymnosporia* have been transferred to it. It resembles *Euonymus* and *Celastrus* in having the seeds wholly or partly enclosed in a fleshy aril. The generic name derives from the Indian name for *M. boaria*—'maiten'.

M. BOARIA Mol.   MAITEN

M. chilensis DC.

An evergreen tree up to 70 ft high with slender, drooping branchlets, but sometimes shrubby; glabrous in all its parts. Leaves lanceolate or narrowly ovate

T S—AA

to narrowly elliptic, tapered at both ends, 1 to 2 in. long, ¼ to ¾ in. wide, medium green above, paler beneath, closely and finely saw-toothed; leaf-stalks slender, very short, scarcely differentiated from the narrowed base of the blade. Flowers greenish-white, small and inconspicuous, borne in clusters of commonly two to five in the leaf-axils of the previous year's growth, mostly unisexual but both sexes borne on the same plant. Fruits capsular, the size of a pea, with two seeds, each enclosed in a red aril.

A native of Chile from Coquimbo province to about 42° S.; and of Argentina, where it is perhaps more numerous than in Chile and extends along the eastern side of the Andes from S. Neuquen to Chubut province; also of Peru, Bolivia, and Brazil; introduced in 1829, though the present stock in Britain probably derives from seeds collected in Chile by H. F. Comber and by Clarence Elliott in the mid-1920s. It is rare in cultivation, but there is a specimen measuring 30 × 2½ ft at Wakehurst Place, Sussex (1968), and a smaller one at Highdown, near Worthing, growing on chalk. Bushy plants are quite hardy at Jermyns House, near Romsey, Hants, and bear fruit. At Lanarth in Cornwall it has produced self-sown seedlings.

The maiten is an interesting evergreen and as a tree makes an elegant specimen with an oval crown and drooping branches. It is a beautiful feature of pasture-lands in the lower Andean valley of Central Chile and is a light-loving species, not found in the temperate rain-forest. It has a considerable geographical range and so is likely to vary in hardiness; trees from seeds collected in Argentina might prove hardy even in inland districts.

Cattle have a great liking for the leaves of the maiten, so much so that, accord-ing to Molina, who described the species in 1782, they will look at no other forage when these are within reach. Hence the specific epithet *boaria*, meaning of or for cattle.

M. MAGELLANICA (Lam.) Hook. f. *Cassine magellanica* Lam.—This allied species makes a smaller and more erect tree than *M. boaria*, and has a more southern distribution. The leaves are usually relatively wider, thicker, more strongly toothed, but the most reliable distinction appears to be that the seed is enclosed by the aril only in the lower part. This species was cultivated by Collingwood Ingram at Benenden Grange, Kent, raised from seeds that he collected from a street-tree at Puerto Montt, Chile. In the specimen he sent us, the fruits are mostly borne singly in each leaf-axil, the seed-coat is red and the aril orange-yellow. The leaves are dull above, leathery, mostly 1¼ to 2½ in. long, ½ to ¾ in. wide. This plant died from drought in the autumn of 1971.

The genus is also represented in cultivation by M. CHUBUTENSIS (Speg.) Lourteiz, O'Donell & Sleumer, a dense, dwarf evergreen shrub with thick, broad-elliptic to broad-ovate leaves ⅜ to ½ in. long, ⅛ to 5⁄16 in. wide, covered with short, stiff hairs above, rendering them rough to the touch. Flowers small, reddish, borne singly or in clusters in the leaf-axils. It was introduced by Comber from Neuquen province, Argentina, in 1926 and distributed under the erroneous name *Myginda disticha* Hook. f. He described it in his field notes as a low shrub 1 to 2 ft high, growing with *Nothofagus antarctica* at 3,500 to 4,000 ft. The true *Myginda disticha*, which has been transferred to *Maytenus* as M. DISTICHA (Hook. f.) Urban, is closely allied to *M. chubutensis* and occurs in similar habitats, but has narrower leaves, smooth or softly downy above.

MEDICAGO LEGUMINOSAE

The species described below is chiefly of interest as a woody member of a genus represented in the British flora by five native herbaceous species and by the naturalised *M. sativa* (lucerne). The generic name derives from *'medike'*—the Greek name for lucerne. The genus is remarkable for the many species in which the pods are spirally contorted and frequently prickly. In Hegi's *Flora von Mitteleuropa*, Vol. IV, 3, p. 1249, the capitals of a romanesque church in the Valais, Switzerland, are figured, in which there are carvings of the fruits of various *Medicago* species, mingled with pine cones and bunches of grapes.

M. ARBOREA L.   MOON TREFOIL

This shrub is chiefly interesting as a woody member of a genus represented in the British flora by about half a dozen herbaceous plants known as 'medicks', and including the 'lucerne'. It is not hardy at Kew in the open, but will live against a wall; it is said to have been 11 ft high at one time in the Chelsea Botanic

MEDICAGO ARBOREA

Garden. It is best adapted for the south and south-western counties. A shrub, evergreen where it thrives, usually 6 or 8 ft high; its stems very leafy but little branched, covered with grey down. Leaves trifoliolate, 1 to 1½ in. long; leaflets ¼ to ¾ in. long, wedge-shaped, sometimes toothed, sometimes notched at the apex, silky beneath, glabrous above. Flowers yellow, ½ in. long, crowded at the end of short axillary racemes which continue to appear as the shoot extends, from April well into autumn, but never making a great display at one time. Easily increased by soft cuttings in bottom heat. The leaves are produced in clusters at each joint, and as the joints are usually about ½ in. apart, the stem has a very leafy aspect. The pod is flat, but curled round like a ram's horn. In the south of Europe it makes a pleasing undergrowth in thinnish woodland and at the out-skirts of plantations, especially in maritime districts. Its distribution as a truly wild plant is not precisely known. It is certainly spontaneous in several countries bordering the north shore of the Mediterranean, and in Rhodes and the Cyclades, but may be no more than naturalised in some parts, e.g., S. France.

MELIA   MELIACEAE

A genus of a few species of trees and shrubs, natives of the tropical and subtropical regions of the Old World. The family Meliaceae, to which the mahoganies belong, is scarcely to be met with outdoors in the British Isles, *Cedrela sinensis* being the only hardy representative.

M. AZEDARACH L.   BEAD TREE

A deciduous tree up to 30 or 40 ft high in warm countries; variable in habit. Leaves alternate, doubly pinnate, 12 to 24 in. long, half as much wide; leaflets ovate to oval, slender-pointed, unequally tapered at the base, toothed or lobed, 1½ to 2 in. long, ⅓ to ¾ in. wide, quite glabrous, or sometimes slightly downy on the midrib and main-stalks when young. Flowers fragrant, ¾ in. wide, numerous in clusters of loose axillary panicles 4 to 8 in. long on the young leafy shoots. Calyx five-lobed, the lobes oblong, pointed, downy, ⅛ in. long. Petals five, lilac-coloured, narrow-oblong, ⅛ in. wide, spreading or slightly reflexed. Stamens ten or twelve, their stalks united into a slender, erect, violet-coloured tube about ¼ in. long, the anthers only free. Fruits yellow, roundish egg-shaped, ½ in. long, containing a hard, bony seed.

Native of N. India and of C. and W. China; now cultivated or naturalised in almost every warm temperate or subtropical country, often as a street tree. According to Gerard, it was cultivated by John Parkinson in England at the end of the 16th century. Miller says he flowered it at Chelsea three or four years successively, and that he found it stood cold extremely well in the open ground. I have never heard of its being grown near London in recent years except under glass. So far as I know, Hiatt C. Baker of Oaklands, near Bristol, succeeded as well as anyone with it. He grew it out-of-doors against a wall, where it stood uninjured for over twenty years. He showed a spray gathered from this plant at Westminster in June 1930. I have seen it in flower in S. Italy, in Dalmatia, and on the Riviera, and have always been charmed by the grace and beauty of its foliage and blossom. It is easily raised from imported seed, is of easy cultivation, and flowers at an early age. The name of 'bead-tree' originated through the seeds being strung by monks and others to form rosaries.

var. UMBRACULIFORMIS Berckmans is much grown in the S.W. United States as the 'Texan Umbrella Tree'. It forms a dense, flattened, spreading head of branches, and has narrower leaflets. Said to have appeared originally on the battlefield of San Jacinto, Texas.

MELICYTUS   VIOLACEAE

A genus of six species, all natives of New Zealand (one extending to some of the islands of the S.W. Pacific, the others endemic). It is allied to *Hymenanthera* but differs in its free anthers and almost sessile, three- to eight-lobed stigma (but one species, not treated here, is anomalous and in some respects intermediate between the two genera).

M. RAMIFLORUS J. R. & G. Forst.

A deciduous shrub or small tree up to 30 ft high, with glabrous young shoots and leaves. Leaves alternate, oblong-lanceolate, tapered towards both ends, coarsely toothed, 2 to 6 in. long, $\frac{3}{4}$ to 2 in. wide, bright dark green above; stalk $\frac{1}{3}$ to $\frac{3}{4}$ in. long. Flowers small, produced in June in clusters of three to nine from the joints of the previous season's growth; each flower about $\frac{1}{5}$ in. wide, yellowish green, on a stalk $\frac{1}{5}$ to $\frac{2}{5}$ in. long. Petals five, triangular. Fruit a globose berry, $\frac{1}{5}$ in. wide, violet-blue, very abundant.

Native of New Zealand; long cultivated in the Temperate House at Kew, where a plant flowers but does not bear fruits. As, however, the species is usually, if not always, unisexual, both male and female plants will be necessary to obtain them. The greatest success with it in this country probably has been achieved by the late Canon Boscawen at Ludgvan Rectory, near Penzance, in whose garden it stood ten degrees of frost without injury, and in May 1930 was 20 ft high and wide. He sent to Kew some beautiful sprays covered with fruit in November 1917, which had been gathered from his plants raised ten years before from New Zealand seed.

MELIOSMA   SABIACEAE

A genus of trees and shrubs, with alternate, simple or pinnate leaves, natives of Eastern Asia and America—the hardy ones all from China and Japan, and deciduous. They produce their flowers, which are small and white, in large terminal panicles. Petals five, the three outer ones concave,

orbicular, and larger than the two inner ones. Fruit a drupe containing
one seed, which is remarkable for its twisted radicle. The name refers to
the honey-like fragrance of the flowers of some of the species.

M. BEANIANA Rehd. & Wils.

A deciduous tree ranging from 40 to 80 ft high in the wild, the trunks of the
largest 6 ft in girth; young shoots slightly rusty-downy at first. Leaves pinnate,
6 to 12 in. long, composed of five to thirteen (usually nine) leaflets, which are
oval to ovate, pointed, tapered at the base, the margins remotely and finely
toothed or entire; the lower pairs are the smallest and 1 to 2 in. long, the remainder increasing in size towards the end, where they are 2 to 5 in. long and 1 to
2½ in. wide; upper surface rather rough, dullish green, lower one with tufts of down
in the vein-axils; stalks $\frac{1}{12}$ in. long. Flowers creamy white, borne in axillary, spreading or pendulous panicles up to 8 in. long and 4 in. wide, with rusty-downy
stalks. Individually the flower (as in all meliosmas) is small and about ¼ in. wide.
Fruits globose, black, ¼ in. wide.

Native of Hupeh and Szechwan, China; discovered by Wilson and introduced
in 1907. He praises it highly and describes it as one of the most striking and
handsome of Chinese trees. It flowers in May, when the bloom is so abundant
as to cover the tree. It is often planted near temples and wayside shrines. It differs
from all other pinnate-leaved meliosmas (which have terminal panicles) in the
inflorescence being axillary. It is very hardy. A tree, newly transplanted from
Aldenham, bloomed at Borde Hill, Sussex, May 1933, and again in 1971. There
is no record of its having flowered in the intervening years.

M. CUNEIFOLIA Franch. [PLATE 99

A deciduous shrub, described as up to 20 ft high in the wild; branches erect,
glabrous or nearly so. Leaves simple, 3 to 7 in. long, 1½ to 3 in. wide; obovate
or wedge-shaped, broadest near the apex, where they narrow abruptly to a point,
upper surface rough to the touch, lower one clothed at first with a brownish
down, especially on the midrib and axils of the veins. The veins of the leaf are in
fifteen to over twenty pairs, parallel, and about $\frac{3}{16}$ in. apart; margins set with
bristle-like teeth. Flowers yellowish white at first then almost pure white,
deliciously scented, ⅛ in. across; produced in downy pyramidal panicles terminating the branches, 5 to 9 in. high, and as much through. Fruits globose, about the
size of peppercorns, black. *Bot. Mag.*, t. 8357.

Native of W. China; introduced by Wilson in 1901 for Messrs Veitch, and
first flowered in their nursery at Coombe Wood in July 1909, when I saw it, and
was much attracted by its fine panicles, and especially by the hawthorn-like
fragrance. It was later introduced by Forrest from Yunnan. It is, no doubt, allied
to the older *M. myriantha*, but is a hardier plant, easily distinguished by the shape
of the leaves, the lower two-thirds of which is uniformly and distinctly wedge-
shaped.

M. MYRIANTHA Sieb. & Zucc.

A deciduous shrub or small tree of spreading habit, 20 ft high. Leaves simple, oval-lanceolate, 3 to 8 in. long, 1½ to 3 in. wide, shortly pointed, sharply and regularly toothed, the stalk (½ to 1 in. long) and midrib covered with reddish-brown hairs, veins parallel, as in a sweet chestnut. Panicles terminal, 6 in. or more long, and about the same wide, much branched; the main-stalk and all its ramifications covered with brown hairs. Flowers minute, about ⅛ in. diameter, very numerous, yellowish white, very fragrant. Fruit crowded in a broad panicle, each one about the size of a peppercorn, dark red.

Native of Japan and the Korean Archipelago; introduced from the former to the Coombe Wood nursery in 1879 by Maries. The original plant, now unfortunately no longer at Kew, was a fine spreading bush about 8 ft high and 12 ft through, and flowered with freedom every year in late June and July. It is, nevertheless, a rather tender subject when young; plants unprotected in the open at Kew have often perished. When once a strong woody base has been formed it will probably survive, but until then some winter protection is necessary.

M. PARVIFLORA Lecomte

M. dilatata Diels; M. parvifolia Hort.

A deciduous tree up to 25 ft high in the wild; stems clad with short erect hairs. Leaves obovate, mostly 2½ to 3¾ in. long, 1 to 1½ in. wide, broadly obtuse at the apex with a short acute or acuminate tip, tapered to an often very narrow wedge-shaped base, glabrous on both sides except for short spreading hairs on the veins and in the vein-axils beneath, vein-pairs eight to twelve, the veins mostly branching near the margin and ending in short, hooked, mucronate teeth; petiole about ½ in. long, clad with erect brownish hairs. Flowers very small, white, crowded, borne in August in sparsely branched panicles terminating axillary or leading shoots and 8 to 12 in. long; inflorescence axes rusty-hairy. Fruits red, globose, ³⁄₁₆ in. wide.

A native of Western and Central China; discovered by Wilson in 1903 when collecting for Messrs Veitch, but apparently not introduced until 1936, when seeds were received at Kew from Nanking. There are two examples in the collection: one was recently moved to a new position near the Victoria Gate, where it is now growing well but has never flowered; the other, in a bed between the northern end of the Holly Avenue and the Lake, was flowering, though not strikingly, in August 1971.

Unfortunately this species appears to have been distributed from Kew under the name M. "parvifolia".

M. OLDHAMII Miq.

A deciduous tree up to 60 ft high, but usually much smaller, with stout, very pale grey, glabrous young shoots; terminal winter-buds covered with red-brown down. Leaves pinnate, 7 to 15 in. long, composed of from five to thirteen leaflets. The lowest ones are usually rounded to ovate, about 1 in. long and ¾ in.

wide, the remainder gradually increasing in size and changing in shape to oval and obovate towards the terminal one, which is the largest and from 3 to 5½ in. long by 1¼ to 2½ in. wide; they are pointed and distinctly toothed, the upper surface slightly downy when the leaf is young, the lower one having tufts of down in the vein-axils. Flowers pure white, produced in terminal, erect, much-branched, downy panicles 6 to 12 in. high and wide; each flower is ⅛ to ¼ in. wide.

Native of Korea, where it was discovered in 1863 by Richard Oldham, the Kew collector, and of China, whence it was introduced by Wilson in 1900. It is extremely rare in cultivation, but a tree about 15 ft high at Kew grows freely except when cut by late spring frost. Wilson describes it as a fine tree occurring in the moist woods and thickets of W. Hupeh, but not really common there. It appears to be related to *M. beaniana*, but differs in the terminal inflorescence and in flowering later when the leaves are nearly fully grown. The tree at Kew flowered in July 1942. There is an example measuring 35 × 2½ ft at Talbot Manor, Norfolk (1970). The example at Kew, raised from seeds received from the Lushan Botanic Garden in 1935, measures 27 × 2 ft (1970). It flowers fairly regularly.

M. PENDENS Rehd. & Wils.

A deciduous shrub up to 16 ft high, with graceful branching; young shoots purplish, hairy. Leaves simple, mostly obovate, approaching oval, with usually slender points, but tapering more gradually towards the base, the margin set with distant, bristle-like teeth, 2 to 6 in. long, 1 to 2½ in. wide, dull green above, with short scattered hairs and a bristly midrib, paler beneath and more conspicuously hairy, especially on the midrib and on the twelve to twenty pairs of veins; stalk ¼ to ½ in. long. Panicles terminal, pendulous, many-flowered, 4 to 8 in. long, scarcely as wide. Flowers white, ⅛ in. wide, fragrant; main and secondary flower-stalks downy.

Native of W. Hupeh, China; introduced by Wilson in 1907. A plant obtained from the Coombe Wood nursery flowered at Kew in July 1920. It is evidently near to *M. cuneifolia*, but that species is distinguished by the broader, more erect panicles, also, when out of flower, by the conspicuous tufts of down in the vein-axils beneath the leaves which are absent in *M. pendens*. It is quite hardy but does not grow so freely as *M. cuneifolia*.

M. TENUIS Maxim.

A deciduous shrub, perhaps a small tree in the wild; young shoots purplish, downy when quite young; winter-buds elongated, covered with tawny down. Leaves simple, oval to obovate, abruptly slender-pointed, tapered to the base, toothed, 2 to 5 in. long, half as wide, dark green above and with scattered hairs there, pale beneath with axil-tufts of pale down and hairs on the midrib; veins in ten to fifteen pairs; leaf-stalk ¼ to ⅜ in. long, downy. Flowers produced in loose, slender panicles about 6 in. long, very small, yellowish white. Fruits ³⁄₁₆ in. wide, globose, black, covered at first with a purplish bloom.

Native of Japan; introduced in 1915. This shrub flowered at Wakehurst, Sussex, in August 1930, but it does not promise to be as ornamental as *M. cuneifolia*. It has the same type of small flower as that species but the panicles are not so large nor nearly so thickly packed with blossom. It suffered badly at Kew in the winter of 1928–9 and is apparently best fitted for the milder counties.

M. VEITCHIORUM Hemsl.   [PLATE 98

A deciduous tree 30 to 50 ft high, with very stout, rigid, erect branches. Leaves pinnate, 1½ to 2½ ft long, with about nine or eleven leaflets, which are each 3½ to 7 in. long, about half as much wide, of ovate or oblong outline, occasionally rather heart-shaped at the base, glabrous except on the midrib beneath, margins entire or sparsely toothed. Panicles as much as 18 in. long, and 12 in. wide at the base, more open and less densely furnished with flowers than either of the simple-leaved species before mentioned; flowers creamy white, ¼ in. across. Fruits rich violet, globose, ⅜ in. wide.

Native of W. China at elevations of 5,000 to 7,500 ft, whence it was introduced by Wilson in 1901. It is in cultivation in several places including Kew, and is noteworthy for its fine pinnate foliage with red petioles, and curiously stout, rigid branchlets. It is evidently a perfectly hardy tree and has flowered in several places and borne fruit in recent years. There is an example at Kew near the Ferneries measuring 30 × 2¼ ft (1967). Growing in a damper and more shaded position, this species has attained at Nymans in Sussex the size of 48 × 3½ ft (1968); this fine tree is almost as tall as any that Wilson saw growing wild in China.

MENISPERMUM   MOONSEED   MENISPERMACEAE

Climbing, woody or semi-woody plants, with alternate, long-stalked, peltate leaves, and separate male and female flowers. Sepals six; petals six or nine; stamens nine to twenty-four. The black or purple-black fruit encloses one half-moon or crescent-shaped seed—giving the popular name. The plants spread rapidly by means of underground stems, and are easily increased by division. *Cocculus* is nearly allied, but has the leaf-stalk attached at the margin of the leaf, and only six stamens.

M. CANADENSE L.   CANADA MOONSEED

A deciduous climber, producing a dense tangle of slightly downy, slender, twining shoots 12 or 15 ft high. Leaves 4 to 7 in. wide, ovate to heart-shaped and roundish, with usually three, five, or seven angular lobes, strongly veined and pale beneath, dark green above; leaf-stalk slender, 3 to 4 in. long, attached to the blade near, but not at the base (peltate). Flowers numerous, inconspicuous,

greenish yellow, borne on a slender, long-stalked raceme, one of which is produced a little above each leaf-axil. Fruits in long loose racemes, nearly black when
mature, about the size of a black currant. Each fruit contains one crescent-shaped
seed. *Bot. Mag.*, t. 1910.

　　Native of eastern N. America, where it is widely spread; cultivated in England
since the end of the 17th century. Its stems although truly woody have a herbaceous appearance, and do not live long. The exceptional vigour of the plant and
its habit of spreading rapidly by means of underground suckers render it unsuitable for planting near delicate or slow-growing shrubs, which it is apt to
smother, but it makes a good summer covering for a wall or summer-house, and
is distinctly ornamental when in fruit. It can be pruned back to the ground every
winter.

M. DAURICUM DC.

　　Scarcely different from the American species in stem, leaf, and general aspect,
this can be recognised when in bloom by the flowers being more closely packed
together in a shorter raceme, and by the racemes being produced in pairs a little
above each leaf-axil. In both the leaves have the same three or five lobes, but in
M. dauricum the apex is usually more drawn out, the spaces between the lobes
are more deeply hollowed, and stalk is attached to the blade farther away from its
margin.

　　Native of N.E. Asia from Siberia to China, requiring the same conditions and
treatment as the American species.

MENZIESIA　　ERICACEAE

A genus of deciduous shrubs containing about ten species, three of
which are native of N. America, the rest of N.E. Asia. They have alternate
leaves without teeth and are often clustered at the end of the twig.
Flowers in terminal clusters, the parts in fours or fives; corolla bell-
shaped, urn-shaped, or cylindrical with the stamens enclosed; calyx and
flower-stalks usually bristly. They succeed under the same treatment as
rhododendrons but enjoy more sunshine; a moist, well-drained, lime-free,
loamy or peaty soil suits them. The Japanese species grow slowly and are
quite suitable for the large rock garden.

　　The name commemorates Archibald Menzies, who served as surgeon-
botanist on Vancouver's great expedition of survey, 1790–5, during
which he discovered and introduced many plants—a western North
American species of *Menziesia* among them.

M. CILIICALYX (Miq.) Maxim.

Andromeda ciliicalyx Miq.

A deciduous shrub 2 to 3 ft high, with glabrous, slender young shoots, often produced in tiers. Leaves mostly clustered at the end of the twigs, obovate to oval, tapered towards both ends, usually more abruptly towards the apex, edged with bristle-like hairs and having a few larger bristles on the midrib, otherwise glabrous, $\frac{3}{4}$ to 3 in. long, $\frac{1}{2}$ to $1\frac{1}{4}$ in. wide; stalk $\frac{1}{8}$ in. or less long. Flowers nodding, produced in May in umbel-like clusters at the end of the shoots of the previous year. Corolla between bell-shaped and urn-shaped, $\frac{3}{8}$ in. long, $\frac{1}{4}$ in. wide, with four or five small lobes, yellowish green at the base, purplish at and near the lobes; glabrous outside, downy within. Stamens eight or ten, shorter than the corolla, very downy at the lower part. Calyx slightly lobed, fringed with glandular bristles. Flower-stalk $\frac{1}{2}$ to $1\frac{1}{8}$ in. long, glandular-bristly.

Native of Japan, named by Maximowicz in 1870; introduced about 1914. It is quite a pretty shrub but the var. *purpurea* (see below) is to be preferred.

var. PURPUREA Mak. *M. lasiophylla* Nakai—Flowers purplish pink; some of the hairs on the flower-stalks eglandular. Leaves with long hairs or almost glabrous above. It is probable that most of the plants grown in British gardens as *M. purpurea* belong to this variety and not to the true *M. purpurea* Maxim. In the *Botanical Magazine*, n.s., t. 35, a flowering spray is figured, taken from a plant at Borde Hill, Sussex, in which the flowers are coloured as in var. *purpurea* but the flower-stalks bear eglandular hairs only. This variant was named var. EGLANDULOSA by the late Dr Turrill in his note accompanying the plate, but it is perhaps no more than an extreme state of var. *purpurea*. Commercial plants distributed as "*M. purpurea*" show the same character; they and the Borde Hill plant may well be all of one clone. [PLATE 100

M. ciliicalyx var. *purpurea* is one of the most charming of small ericaceous shrubs. It is quite hardy and flowers unfailingly every year if grown in a not too shady position. The expanding buds are bright blue and almost as decorative as the flowers. In a well-lighted position it makes a bushy plant about 3 ft high.

M. FERRUGINEA Sm.

A deciduous shrub usually 2 to 6 ft high; young shoots with stalked glands and finely downy; afterwards with peeling bark. Leaves narrowly oval or obovate, pointed, tapered at the base, $\frac{3}{4}$ to 2 in. long, $\frac{1}{2}$ to $\frac{3}{4}$ in. wide, bristly hairy above and on the margins, less so beneath. Flowers nodding, in clusters of two to five, each on a glandular stalk $\frac{1}{2}$ to 1 in. long. Corolla cylindrical, $\frac{3}{8}$ in. long, four-lobed, dullish white tinged with pink. Stamens eight, filaments glabrous or downy at the base. Capsule egg-shaped, glandular.

Native of western N. America from Alaska to N. California; in the Cascade Mountains of Oregon it has been found up to 12 ft high. This was the species discovered on the N.W. coast of America by Archibald Menzies during his voyage with Vancouver, 1790–5, and the one on which Sir James Smith founded the genus. Flowers in May but of no great worth in gardens.

M. pilosa of eastern N. America is closely allied, differing in its eglandular stems and in the more rounded, bell-shaped corolla. Also the gland-tipped hairs on the flower-stalks are short, whereas in *M. ferruginea* they are bristle-like and more conspicuous.

M. MULTIFLORA Maxim.

M. ciliicalyx var. *multiflora* (Maxim.) Makino

This species is evidently nearly related to *M. ciliicalyx* described above, and is connected with it by intermediate forms. It was originally described and named by Maximowicz in 1870, and he distinguished it from *M. ciliicalyx* by its shortly racemose instead of umbellate inflorescences, and its obovate rather than oval leaves. His own specimens, however, show little or no difference in shape of leaf. In these specimens the most obvious distinction of *M. multiflora* is in the lobes of the calyx being linear and up to ⅜ in. long. Some authors have relied on the glabrous flower-stalks of *M. multiflora* as distinct from the glandular-bristly ones of *M. ciliicalyx*, but in specimens of the former collected by Wilson in Japan in 1914, whose flowers have very distinctly linear-lobed calyces, the flower-stalks are as glandular-bristly as in *M. ciliicalyx*. The corolla of *M. multiflora* is somewhat shorter and more urn-shaped than that of *M. ciliicalyx*; its colour varies from pale purple to nearly white with deeper coloured lobes.

Native of Japan. It was collected in flower in that country by Veitch's collector, Charles Maries, during August 1880, on Fuji-yama, but if he sent home seeds at that time the plant never became established in gardens.

M. PENTANDRA Maxim.

A deciduous shrub up to 4 ft high, with an often bi- or tri-furcate mode of branching; young shoots slender, bristly. Leaves narrowly oval, tapered at both ends, margined with hairs, bristly above, less so beneath, 1 to 2 in. long, ½ to 1 in. wide; stalk about ⅛ in. long, bristly. Flowers nodding, a few in an umbel, each on a slender, sparsely glandular stalk ½ to 1 in. long. Corolla roundish urn-shaped, ¼ in. long, dull greenish white, five-lobed. Stamens five, glabrous. Calyx five-lobed, ciliate.

Native of Japan and Sakhalin; introduced about 1905, originally named in 1867. It is one of the least attractive of the menziesias, abundantly distinct from the other Asiatic species in having only five stamens, which are glabrous.

M. PILOSA (Michx.) Juss.

Azalea pilosa Michx.; *M. ferruginea* β. Sims; *M. globularis* Salisb.

A deciduous shrub 3 to 6 ft high, rigid and erect in habit, the bark on the older branches hanging in loose shreds; young shoots downy and hairy. Leaves alternate, obovate or narrowly oval, ¾ to 2 in. long, ⅜ to 1 in. wide, tapered at both ends, more or less hairy on the upper surface and on the margins, with a few bristles on the midrib beneath. Flowers yellowish white or greenish and tinged with red, produced together with the young shoots in May in few-flowered clusters terminating the previous year's branches; flower-stalk de-curved, glandular-downy, ¼ to ¾ in. long. Sepals fringed with stalked glands. Corolla bell-shaped, ¼ in. long, usually four-lobed; stamens eight, glabrous.

MENZIESIA PILOSA

Capsules egg-shaped, ¼ in. long, covered with gland-tipped hairs. *Bot. Mag.*, t. 1571.

Native of eastern N. America from Pennsylvania southwards, mostly in mountain woods; introduced in 1806. This is not one of the most attractive of the American Ericaceae, but was commonly grown in the older collections and is still obtainable in nurseries. It likes a peaty soil and should be increased by seeds.

M. GLABELLA A. Gray *M. ferruginea* var. *glabella* (A. Gray) Peck—This species is allied to both *M. pilosa* and *M. ferruginea*, differing from both in having the leaves mostly rounded at the apex, finely downy on both sides. The ovary is downy as well as glandular and the filaments of the stamens downy at the base. Native of north-western N. America from British Columbia to Alberta and Idaho, south to Oregon.

M. PURPUREA Maxim.

A deciduous shrub said to be up to 8 ft high, with glabrous, slender shoots often produced in tiers of three or four. Leaves oval to obovate, tapered at the base, the apex rounded except for a minute tip (mucro), 1 to 1½ in. long, ½ to ⅞ in. wide, with scattered bristles above and some on the midrib beneath; stalk 3/16 in. or less long. Flowers nodding, produced in May and June at the end of the previous year's twigs in umbel-like clusters of four to eight. Corolla red, bell-shaped, ½ in. long, ¼ in. wide, with four shallow, minutely ciliate lobes. Stamens very hairy, in number twice as many as the corolla-lobes. Calyx four- or five-lobed; lobes ovate-oblong, ⅛ in. long, glandular-ciliate. Flower-stalk ½ to ¾ in. long, very slender, glandular-bristly. Ovary with eglandular hairs.

Native of Japan, where, according to Ohwi, it is confined to the Island of Kyushu; named in 1867 by Maximowicz; introduced about 1914. It is the prettiest and brightest coloured of the menziesias, distinguished from all the preceding species by its bell-shaped, bright red corolla, whose lobes are edged with minute hairs, and its round-ended mucronate leaves. But most of the plants distributed as *M. purpurea* are *M. ciliicalyx* var. *purpurea*.

The characters by which Ohwi (*Flora of Japan* (1965), p. 695–696) distinguishes this species from *M. ciliicalyx* are: ovary with eglandular hairs; corolla-lobes four, glandular-ciliate. A further distinction appears to be that in *M. purpurea* the corollas (as shown in Maximowicz's *Rhododendreae Asiae Orientalis*, Plate 1) are not at all constricted at the mouth as they are, though slightly, in *M. ciliicalyx*; they are also, according to Maximowicz's original description, 'thinly membranaceous' in texture.

MESPILUS   ROSACEAE

A genus of a single species, allied to *Crataegus*, *Cotoneaster*, etc., but distinguished by the large solitary flowers and the fruits with always five carpels.

M. GERMANICA L.   MEDLAR   [PLATE 101

A low deciduous tree of crooked, picturesque habit, usually under 20 ft high; young branchlets very hairy, older ones often armed with stiff, straight spines ½ to 1 in. long. Leaves almost without stalks, lanceolate or oval, 2 to 5 in. long, minutely toothed, downy on both surfaces, but more so beneath. Flowers solitary at the end of short leafy branches, 1 to 1½ in. across, white or slightly pink, produced on a very short woolly stalk, in May or early June. Petals five, roundish; sepals covered with grey wool, triangular at the base, drawn out into a long, narrow point standing out beyond the petals. Fruits 1 in. wide, five-celled, apple-shaped, brown, with a broad open eye, surrounded by the persistent calyx, and showing the ends of the bony seed-vessels.

The wild medlar is a native of Europe and Asia Minor, and is found wild in the woods of several counties in the south of England, notably Sussex and Kent, but it is not believed to be truly indigenous. It has long been cultivated for its fruit in English orchards, and several named varieties exist. The cultivated forms are distinguished by thornless or nearly thornless branches, by larger, broader leaves, and by larger fruits up to 1½ or 2 in. across. Although much esteemed by those who have acquired the taste for them, medlars are not a popular fruit. They should be left on the tree until the end of October or later, then stored in a fruit-room until they are 'bletted'—a term given to indicate a state of incipient decay. A jelly made from the fruits meets a more general taste. The medlar is most closely allied to *Crataegus*, differing in the solitary flower, etc. It is very hardy, and not particular as to soil.

METAPLEXIS   ASCLEPIADACEAE

A genus of six species of herbaceous or woody climbers, natives of E. and N.E. Asia.

M. JAPONICA (Thunb.) Makino

Pergularia japonica Thunb.; *M. stauntonii* Schult.; *M. chinensis* (Bunge) Decne.; *Urostelma chinense* Bunge

A deciduous climber, with twining stems covered at first with more or less loose down. Leaves opposite, heart-shaped, tapered to a point at the apex, 2 to 4½ in. long, half to two-thirds as wide near the base, which is deeply notched; somewhat downy on the midrib beneath, dull green; stalk 1 to 3 in. long. Flowers produced from July to September in racemes 3 to 5 in. long, in but one of the axils of each pair of leaves; flower-stalk downy. The flowers are frequently crowded at the end of the inflorescence as in an umbel. Corolla dull rosy-white, about ½ in. diameter, with five reflexed lobes united into a bell-shaped base; the lobes are narrow, curled back at the points, and covered with pale hairs on the upper side. Seed-vessels 4 in. long, spindle-shaped, the seeds furnished at one end with a tuft of beautiful silky hairs 1¼ in. long.

Native of China and Japan; introduced in 1862. It is not often seen in gardens, but it has flowered and borne seed in the vicarage garden at Bitton, near Bristol. It usually dies back to the ground in winter in the open. It is interesting, but not particularly attractive, being allied to *Marsdenia (Cionura) erecta*, which has smaller leaves, sturdier stems, and more rounded petals.

METASEQUOIA   TAXODIACEAE

The genus *Metasequoia* was described by the botanist Miki in 1941 from fossils discovered in Japan in Lower Pliocene strata. Living representatives of this new genus were found growing wild in China in the same year, though specimens were not collected from them until 1944. These living trees were described as *M. glyptostroboides* in 1948.

Metasequoia is allied to *Sequoia* but the leaves, buds, and branchlets are strictly opposite, whereas in *Sequoia* the leaves, though arranged in a single plane on the branchlets, are really alternate and spirally inserted; in *Metasequoia* the primary leaves and the leaf-bearing shoots are deciduous, and the next season's growths and leaf-sprays are produced from buds on the branches, while in *Sequoia* the branchlets with their leaves persist through the winter and bear growth-buds at the apex; in *Metasequoia* the cone-scales are arranged in decussate pairs, spirally in *Sequoia*. In *Taxodium*, another related genus, the bald cypress, *T. distichum*, resembles *Metasequoia* in producing its foliage on deciduous branchlets, but, at least on coning trees, some branchlets bear scale-like leaves and persist through the winter. Also, in all the taxodiums the leaves are spirally inserted, as in *Sequoia*.

For a detailed description see Dallimore and Jackson, revised edition, pp. 317–319, where the more important literature is cited. An account by Prof. Merrill of the discovery of the living species will be found in *Journ. R.H.S.*, Vol. 73 (1948), pp. 211–216 (reprinted with additional material from *Arnoldia*, Vol. 8 (1948), pp. 1–8). There is an interesting chapter on *Metasequoia* in the work by H.-L. Li cited on page 285.

M. GLYPTOSTROBOIDES Hu & Cheng   WATER FIR, SHUI-HSA

[PLATE 102

A tree up to 115 ft high in the wild with a trunk about $6\frac{1}{2}$ to $9\frac{1}{2}$ ft in diameter at the base. Bark fissured, dark grey in colour, peeling off in old trees. Branches opposite, glabrous, green in the young state, turning brown later and becoming brownish grey in the second or third year. Lateral shoots deciduous in winter, glabrous, opposite, up to $2\frac{1}{4}$ in. long, arranged distichously, persistent buds at the base. Winter-buds ovoid or obtuse, $\frac{1}{6}$ in. long, $\frac{1}{8}$ in. wide, glabrous. Bracts decussate, broadly ovate, yellowish brown, paler and thinner on the margins. Leaves deciduous, opposite, arranged in two ranks, linear, $\frac{1}{3}$ to $\frac{1}{2}$ in. long, $\frac{1}{24}$ to $\frac{1}{12}$ in. wide, sessile or nearly sessile, blue-green above, light green below. Flowers monoecious, solitary; staminate flowers axillary and terminal about $\frac{1}{5}$ in. long, in a raceme or panicle; bracts decussate, triangular-ovate or obovate. Pedicels about $\frac{1}{8}$ in. long. Stamens twenty filaments short. Pistillate flowers solitary, about $\frac{1}{3}$ in. long; bracts decussate, both sides glabrous, the lower ones triangular-ovate. Peduncles $\frac{1}{8}$ in. long, leafy. Cones ripening in the first year, pendulous, sub-quadrangular-globose or shortly cylindric, $\frac{3}{4}$ to 1 in. long, $\frac{2}{3}$ to $\frac{9}{10}$ in. wide, dark brown in colour. Seeds five to nine under each scale, winged, compressed, obovate, the apex notched, $\frac{1}{5}$ in. long, $\frac{1}{8}$ in. wide.

The above description is based on that published in the *Bulletin of the Fan Memorial Institute of Biology*, New Series, Vol. i (1948), No. 2, p. 153.

Native of China in a restricted locality on the borders of W. Hupeh and N.E. Szechwan, where it inhabits ravines and the banks of streams. It was first seen by a Chinese botanist in 1941 but specimens were not taken until about three years later; seeds were collected in autumn 1947 and sent to the Arnold Arboretum, whence they were distributed to many gardens in America and Europe in 1948.

In the second volume of the last edition of this work, published in 1951, it was stated that there were small trees at Kew and in the Royal Horticultural Society Garden at Wisley which, in 1949, at the end of their second season, were 3 to 4 ft high. Now, twenty years later, the tallest of the original trees at Kew measures 47 × 3¾ ft (1971) and at Wisley 49 × 2¼ ft (1968). Other trees from the original seed are: Savill Gardens, Windsor Great Park, 51 × 2¾ ft (1967); Ladhams, Goudhurst, Kent, 46 × 3¾ ft (1967); Snowdenham House, Surrey, 40 × 2 ft (1964); Leonardslee, Sussex, 40 × 4 ft, 54 × 2¼ ft and 50 × 2¾ ft (1968); University Botanic Garden, Cambridge, 44 × 3¾ ft (Lake) and 41 × 3 ft (Frameyard) (1969); Emmanuel College, Cambridge, 44 × 3¾ ft (1969); Clare College, Cambridge, 46 × 3¾ ft (1969).

Metasequoia glyptostroboides is perfectly hardy but is subject to damage by late spring frosts. It thrives best in a deep moderately moist soil and on dry sandy soil or shallow chalk it grows slowly. Although it will, perhaps, never make such a fine specimen tree as *Taxodium distichum* it is much faster growing and less demanding. The leaves are a pleasant soft green and turn foxy brown or pinkish brown before falling. It is easily propagated by half-ripe cuttings taken June to mid-August and placed in bottom heat, but hardwood cuttings will root in a cold frame (S. A. Pearce, *Gard. Chron.* (28 July 1956), pp. 86–87). If young plants make multiple leaders, as sometimes happens, the superfluous ones make excellent cutting material. Female cones are borne quite frequently, but there is so far no record of fertile seeds having been produced in Britain or indeed anywhere in the colder parts of Europe. The explanation appears to be that male cones, even if produced, do not ripen, either because the growing season is too short for their complete development, or because they are killed in winter. See further in: D. Wyman, '*Metasequoia* after twenty years in cultivation', *Journ. R.H.S.*, Vol. 95 (1970), pp. 444–451 (reprinted from *Arnoldia*, Vol. 28 (1968), pp. 113–123).

MICHELIA   MAGNOLIACEAE

A genus of about forty-five species, the majority of them confined to the tropical parts of S.E. Asia. It is allied to *Magnolia* but differs in its axillary flowers and stalked gynoecium. Linnaeus named the genus in honour of P. A. Micheli, the Florentine botanist (1679–1737). The type-species, *M. champaca*, is widely grown in the tropics for its handsome foliage and scented flowers.

M. COMPRESSA (Maxim.) Sarg.
Magnolia compressa Maxim.

An evergreen tree, at least 40 ft high, with a trunk 1 ft or more in diameter, and a compact, rounded head of branches. Leaves 3 in. in average length, oblong

MICHELIA

or obovate, tapering at the base to a slender stalk ½ to 1 in. long; glabrous, leathery, and glossy green. Flowers (rarely seen in this country) 1½ to 2 in. across when fully expanded, magnolia-like, fragrant; sepals and petals pale yellow. Fruits on a cone 2 in. long, each containing usually three seeds.

Native of southern Japan and the Ryukyu Islands; introduced in 1894. It was cultivated at Kew for some years and proved hardy though slow-growing. A plant of this rare species grew for some forty years at Borde Hill in Sussex, with the protection of a south-facing wall, but its flowers, though quite freely borne, made little display.

M. DOLTSOPA Buch.-Ham. ex DC.
M. excelsa Blume

A shrub or tree 20 to 40 ft high, or sometimes 50 to 80 ft in the Himalaya; young stems slightly warted, soon glabrous. Leaves of firm texture, oval-oblong, 3 to 7 in. long, 1¼ to 3 in. wide, tapering to an often bluntish apex, rounded to tapered at the base, dark glossy green above, pale beneath; stalk ½ to 1 in. long. Flowers very fragrant, soft pale yellow to white, solitary in the leaf-axils, very shortly stalked, 3 to 4 in. across; petals twelve to sixteen, obovate to oblanceolate, rounded at the apex, ½ to 1 in. wide. The flowers reach the bud state in autumn but do not open until the following spring. Bot. Mag., t. 9645.

Native of W. China, Tibet, and E. Himalaya. Introduced from W. China by Forrest about 1918, first flowered in this country at Caerhays Castle in Cornwall in April 1933. There are five specimens in the collection 42 to 52 ft in height, all branched from the base or near it and with girths below the spring of the branches of 4¼ to 5¾ ft (1966). It is only in the mildest parts that this species is really at home and hardy.

M. FIGO (Lour.) Spreng.
Liriodendron figo Lour.; Michelia fuscata (Andr.) Wall.; Magnolia fuscata Andr.; Liriopsis fuscata (Andr.) Spach

An evergreen shrub ultimately 10 to 20 ft high, of bushy habit; young shoots densely clothed with short brown hairs. Leaves narrowly oval or slightly obovate, tapering towards both ends, the apex blunt, 1½ to 4 in. long, ⅝ to 2 in. wide, furnished with brown down at first, finally nearly glabrous, dark glossy green; stalk ½ in. long, hairy like the shoots. Flowers very fragrant, produced in the leaf-axils, each on a brown, downy stalk ½ in. long; sepals and petals yellowish green stained with dull purple, ¾ to 1 in. long; flower-buds at first enclosed by brown downy bracts. Bot. Mag., t. 1008.

Native of China; introduced according to Aiton in 1789. At Kew this shrub has to be given the protection of a cool greenhouse, but in the mildest parts of our islands it is hardy. It is a cheerful evergreen, not conspicuous for beauty of flower but one of the most fragrant of all shrubs. Two or three blossoms will fill a small greenhouse with their fruity perfume, which strongly recalls that of an old-fashioned sweet known as 'pear-drops'. A succession of flowers is produced from April to summer.

MICROCACHRYS   PODOCARPACEAE

A genus of a single species, distinguished from other members of the Podocarpus family by the following combination of characters: habit prostrate; leaves scale-like, four-ranked; female cones with numerous fertile scales which become fleshy when ripe; seeds partly enclosed in a thin aril.

M. TETRAGONA Hook. f.
Dacrydium tetragonum (Hook. f.) Parl.

An evergreen shrub with slender four-angled branches, growing prostrate on the ground or against rock faces. Leaves scale-like, regularly four-ranked, appressed and overlapping, acute at the apex, about $\frac{1}{16}$ in. long. Cones terminal on short side-shoots. Male cones oblong or ovoid, small. Fruit-cones ovoid or globose, with twenty or more fertile scales which become fleshy, translucent and red-coloured when the fruits are ripe. Each seed partly enclosed in a red aril. *Bot. Mag.*, t. 5576.

Native of the mountains of Tasmania, to which it is endemic; introduced in 1857. It has never been common in gardens, but was at one time grown in conservatories for its colourful fruits and for the graceful habit it assumes if the main stem is trained into an upright position. It is, however, much hardier than was once believed. Mr Will Ingwersen tells us that a plant at the Birch Farm nursery near East Grinstead, Sussex, has lived for at least ten years on a north-facing terrace-bed and was uninjured in the bitter winter of 1962–3.

Most works state that *M. tetragona* is dioecious, but fruits are produced on female plants without pollination and it may be that some individuals bear flowers of both sexes. Mr Ingwersen tells us that some years ago a pot plant growing in an alpine house at his nursery produced fertile seeds from which young plants were raised, although there was no other specimen within one hundred yards of it.

M. tetragona received an Award of Merit when shown by Messrs Ingwersen on 5 January 1971.

MICROGLOSSA   COMPOSITAE

The species described below, although long included in *Microglossa*, really belongs to the genus *Aster*, to which it was transferred by Handel-Mazzetti in 1938. Unfortunately this taxonomic change was overlooked when the previous edition was scrutinised with such intergeneric transfers in mind. The species is treated here under its familiar name, but it should in future be known as *Aster albescens*.

M. ALBESCENS (DC.) C. B. Cl.

ASTER ALBESCENS (DC.) Hand.-Mazz.; *Amphiraphis albescens* DC.; *Aster cabulicus* Lindl.

A plant with semi-woody, erect stems, growing in tufts about 3 ft high, very pithy, and clothed with a grey down. Leaves alternate, lance-shaped, 2 to 5 in. long, ½ to 1 in. wide, tapered to both ends, the margins entire or with minute teeth, grey and downy beneath. Flower-heads ⅓ in. in diameter, produced during July, in compound corymbs 3 to 6 in. across, terminating the current season's growth. Ray-florets about fourteen, narrow, pale lilac-blue or bluish white; disk-flowers yellow.

Native of the Himalaya, up to 12,000 ft; introduced to the Chiswick gardens of the Royal Horticultural Society about 1840. The shoots made during the summer die back considerably during the winter, almost to the ground in severe seasons. The flowers are of a rather indeterminate blue, and the plant has no particular merit except in flowering in late summer. Propagated by cuttings of the young growths in heat, or by dividing old plants.

MIMULUS   SCROPHULARIACEAE

M. aurantiacus is one of a small group of about eight species of woody perennials which are now usually placed in *Mimulus* but have, by some authorities, been treated as a separate genus—*Diplacus*; all the species in this group are natives of western N. America. The genus *Mimulus*, with about 150 species, consists mainly of annuals and herbaceous perennials and is richly represented in western N. America (seventy-six species are treated by Munz in *A California Flora*); it also occurs in S. America, Africa, Asia, and Australia.

The standard work on the *Diplacus* group, is: H. E. McMinn, 'Studies in the Genus Diplacus', *Madroño*, Vol. 11 (1951), pp. 33–128.

M. AURANTIACUS Curt.

M. glutinosus Wendl.; *Diplacus glutinosus* (Wendl.) Nutt.; *D. aurantiacus* (Curt.) Jeps.

An evergreen shrub up to 4 or 6 ft high, of bushy habit; young shoots rather downy and very glutinous. Leaves opposite, narrowly oblong or oblanceolate, shortly pointed, tapered at the base to a short stalk, margins recurved and slightly toothed, 2 to 4 in. long, ⅜ to ¾ in. wide, dark shining green and glabrous above, pale and slightly downy beneath. Flowers produced singly in the leaf-axils of the growing shoots. Corolla trumpet-shaped, the tube 1 to 1¼ in. long, dividing at the mouth into five lobes and there ¾ in. wide; variable in colour but perhaps typically yellow or orange. Calyx tubular, distinctly five-ribbed, nearly as long as the corolla-tube, green, glutinous, with five small, erect, awl-shaped teeth; flower-stalk ¼ to ½ in. long. Seed-vessel ½ to ¾ in. long, slender, ribbed. Native of California; cultivated late in the 18th century and probably introduced by Menzies. It is usually grown in a cool greenhouse, where it is valued for the succession of blossoms borne throughout the summer by the young growing shoots. It does well as a wall plant in the south-west, flowering there in the winter months, and is worth trying in cooler districts on a sunny wall.

The plant known as *M. puniceus* (Nutt.) Steud., figured in *Bot. Mag.*, t. 3655 appears to be no more than a form of *M. aurantiacus*, differing in the redder flowers. It was discovered and introduced to an American nursery by Thomas Nuttall, who also described it. The nursery passed the whole stock to the British firm Messrs Lowe of Clapton in 1837.

MITCHELLA RUBIACEAE

A genus of two species named after John Mitchell, a botanist in Virginia and a correspondent of Linnaeus in the 18th century. They are attractive little plants for the rock garden given a moist, lime-free, well-drained soil and some shade.

M. REPENS L. PARTRIDGE BERRY

An evergreen, creeping, half-woody plant scarcely reaching above the ground; young shoots wiry, squarish, with traces of down when quite young. Leaves opposite, glabrous, dark glossy green, ovate to roundish, rounded at the apex, truncate or slightly heart-shaped at the base, ¼ to ⅝ (sometimes ⅞) in. long and wide; stalk scarcely so long as the blade, downy on the upper side when quite young; stipules minute. Flowers fragrant, opening during June and July at the end of the shoot in scarcely stalked, erect pairs. Corolla up to ½ in. long, tubular at the base, dividing at the top into four spreading ovate lobes which are hairy inside and give the flower a diameter of about ⅜ in., white, often tinged with purple; calyx small, four-toothed; stamens four. Fruits globose, about ¼ in. wide, scarlet, formed by the union of the two ovaries, the two calyces persisting at the top, carrying normally eight seeds.

Native of eastern and central N. America from Nova Scotia to Florida and westwards to Texas; introduced by John Bartram about 1761. It is very hardy, loves some shade, and is suitable for a moist spot in the rock garden. As its prostrate branches root freely as they lie, it is easily increased by division, also by cuttings. A pleasing little plant, perhaps scarcely woody enough to justify inclusion here, very much resembling *Linnaea borealis* in its creeping habit, small leaves, and twin flowers, but the latter belongs to the honeysuckle family, has the parts of its flower in fives, and the blossoms are borne at the top of a thread-like stalk as much as 3 in. long.

f. LEUCOCARPA Bissell has white fruits.

M. UNDULATA Sieb. & Zucc.

M. repens var. undulata (Sieb. & Zucc.) Mak.

An evergreen, sub-shrubby plant with very slender, glabrous stems, self rooting. Leaves opposite, $\frac{1}{4}$ to 1 in. long, heart-shaped to truncate at the base, pointed at the apex, glabrous, margin undulated; stalk about $\frac{1}{8}$ in. long. Flowers terminal, mostly in pairs, very shortly stalked; corolla slenderly cylindrical, $\frac{1}{2}$ in. long, four-lobed and $\frac{1}{4}$ in. wide at the end, pink, becoming darker towards the tips, downy inside; calyx cup-shaped, $\frac{1}{8}$ in. long, four-lobed.

Native of Japan and S. Korea, collected by the late H. J. Elwes in an Arborvitae forest near Aomori in the north, where it was growing in dense shade and flowering in July. Apparently not introduced until 1933, when it reached the late Fred Stoker, who retrieved two plants from some packing material that had come from Japan. It is very hardy and flowers a month later than its American ally, which is distinct also in its more rounded leaves. In *M. undulata* they often approach triangular in shape.

MITRARIA   GESNERIACEAE

A genus of a single species belonging to the same subdivision of the Gesneriaceae as *Asteranthera ovata* (q.v.).

M. COCCINEA Cav.

A slender-stemmed prostrate or climbing evergreen shrub; young shoots densely clothed with short down. Leaves opposite, rather leathery, ovate or oval, pointed, rounded or tapered at the base, toothed, $\frac{1}{2}$ to $\frac{7}{8}$ in. long, $\frac{1}{4}$ to $\frac{3}{8}$ in. wide, dark glossy green and with short hairs above when young; pale, rather glaucous, more or less downy on the midrib beneath; stalk $\frac{1}{16}$ in. long, downy. Flowers solitary on a slender downy stalk 1 to $1\frac{1}{2}$ in. long, produced from the axils of the leaves. Corolla rich scarlet, tubular, 1 to $1\frac{1}{4}$ in. long, $\frac{1}{6}$ to $\frac{1}{4}$ in. wide and rather bellied, downy. Sepals five, of unequal size, lanceolate, clasped on one side by downy bracts. Stamens four, the yellow anthers protruding beyond the corolla. Fruit an ovoid berry $\frac{3}{8}$ in. wide, surmounted at first by the persistent style which is $1\frac{1}{2}$ in. long. *Bot. Mag.*, t. 4462.

A native of Chile, mainly from Maulé province to the region of the Magellan Straits, and of bordering parts of Argentina; in Chile it is also found farther north in the remarkable relict forest of Fray Jorge, in Coquimbo province (30° 30′ to 30° 42′ S.); introduced by William Lobb for Messrs Veitch of Exeter in 1846. The brilliant red flowers of this creeper, with its neat, glossy foliage, are very attractive. It comes into blossom during May and June and continues more or less until autumn. It dislikes drought and hot sunshine. On wild specimens the leaves are often much larger than we are accustomed to see them on cultivated plants, sometimes 1½ in. long and half as much wide.

M. coccinea can be grown out-of-doors south of London in a sheltered, moist position and moderate shade, and will flower quite well in such a position, but

M I T R A R I A   C O C C I N E A

only in the rainier and more equable climate of the Atlantic counties and in Ireland does it really thrive and climb as it does in its native habitat (in the magnificent rain-forests south of Puerto Montt, where it luxuriates, the rainfall exceeds 100 in. per annum). At Rowallane in Co. Down it has reached 18 ft in height and more than that at Rossdohan in Co. Kerry, where it climbs up a fine specimen of *Clethra arborea*.

MOLTKIA   BORAGINACEAE

A genus of some half a dozen species of herbs or sub-shrubs. Leaves alternate, entire; corolla tubular to funnel-shaped, purple, blue, or yellow;

stamens exserted. The genus was named after Count J. G. Moltke, a Danish naturalist who died in 1818.

M. PETRAEA (Tratt.) Griseb.   [PLATE 104

Echium petraeum Tratt.; *Lithospermum petraeum* (Tratt.) DC.

A small semi-evergreen, bushy shrub 1 to 2 ft high; stems erect, and covered with grey hairs pointing upwards. Leaves alternate, narrow-linear, ½ to 1½ in. long, about ⅛ in. wide, covered like the stems with appressed, forward-pointing hairs on both surfaces. Flowers produced during June, in small crowded clusters terminating the young shoots, the whole inflorescence 1 to 1½ in. across. Corolla pinkish purple in bud, becoming violet-blue on opening, tubular, ⅓ in. long, with five short, erect, rounded lobes. Stamens longer than the corolla-lobes. *Bot. Mag.*, t. 5942.

Native of Dalmatia, Albania, etc.; first introduced about 1840, and treated as a cool greenhouse plant. It was afterwards lost to cultivation, but was reintroduced by Messrs Backhouse of York thirty years later. It is not a robust plant and is certainly not adapted for shrubberies, but on a well-drained ledge in the rock garden at Kew it has lived for thirty years. Probably damp is more detrimental to its welfare than cold. Certainly no little shrub of its type deserves better care; it lasts in flower a good while, and no prettier or more dainty plant exists when every twig is crowned by the brilliantly coloured blossoms. The flowers have much the same arrangement as in the common borage; they are closely set, and open successively on the upper side of a stalk which becomes decurved. Summer cuttings take root readily. It needs a light, well-drained soil and a sunny position. Out of flower it has much the appearance of lavender.

M. SUFFRUTICOSA (L.) Brand

Pulmonaria suffruticosa L.; *M. graminifolia* (Viv.) Nyman; *Lithospermum graminifolium* Viv.

A low, semi-evergreen shrub of tufted habit 6 to 18 in. high when in flower; young shoots, leaves, flower-stalks, and calyx all covered with appressed silky grey hairs. Leaves linear, pointed, the basal ones up to 4½ in. long, ⅛ in. or less wide, those of the flowering stems 1 to 2 in. long, silvery beneath. Flowers borne at the top of a leafy stalk 4 to 8 in. high in a branched pendulous cluster 1 to 2½ in. wide; they are blue with a tinge of purple (pink in the bud state), about ½ in. long; calyx-lobes linear, stamens about as long as the corolla or rather shorter. The branches of the inflorescence often curve outwards and have the flowers set on the top, as is common in the borage family. *Bot. Mag.*, n.s., t. 394.

Native of Italy; put into commerce by Messrs Backhouse of York in 1888. H. Correvon in *The Gardener's Chronicle* (2 April 1910), p. 212, writes:

'I was once ascending Monte Summano, near Vicenza, when my eyes were suddenly arrested by a slope covered with a glorious azure of blue flowers. Judge my surprise when I recognized an old friend in Lithospermum graminifolium. It seemed as if the whole mountain were covered with it.'

The plant is essentially one for a sunny place in the rock garden. *M. petraea* is easily distinguished from it by its shorter, comparatively broader leaves and well exposed stamens.

There are hybrids between *M. suffruticosa* and *M. petraea*, for which the correct name is M. ×INTERMEDIA (Froebel) J. Ingram. The typical form of the cross ('Intermedia') inclines to *M. suffruticosa* in its leaves, while in *M.* × *intermedia* 'FROEBELII' the leaves are shorter, more like those of *M. petraea*.

MORUS   MULBERRY   MORACEAE

Of the dozen or so species of mulberry known, four or five can be grown without protection in the south of Britain. These are (with us) small, bushy-headed trees with alternate, deciduous, toothed, and often variously lobed leaves. The flowers are unisexual, the sexes borne on separate spikes, which are small, more or less cylindrical, axillary, and of no beauty. The 'fruit' of the mulberry is really a fruit cluster, composed of closely packed drupes, each enclosed by the persistent, enlarged, succulent sepals.

Mulberry trees like a warm, well-drained, loamy soil, and *M. nigra* especially is worth growing for its luxuriant leafage and picturesque form. It is not much planted now, but nothing gives to a garden fortunate enough to possess it a greater sense of old-world charm and dignity than a rugged old mulberry standing on a lawn. It can be increased by summer cuttings with the greatest ease—the old writers say pieces 8 ft or more long will grow. Branches broken down but not detached will usually take root if they touch the ground. *M. alba* will also root from autumn or winter cuttings.

M. ALBA L.   WHITE MULBERRY

A deciduous tree 30 to 45 ft high, with a rounded head of branches and a trunk 6 ft in girth; young shoots downy at first, becoming more or less glabrous by autumn. Leaves broadly ovate with a heart-shaped base, usually pointed, sometimes rounded at the apex, frequently three-lobed, varying much in size, from 3 to 8 in. long and up to 6 in. wide, coarsely toothed, lightish green and only slightly roughened above, downy near the veins and midrib beneath; stalk ½ to 1 in. long. Flowers produced during May in the leaf-axils and at the base of the new shoots; females on stalked cylindrical spikes ⅓ to ½ in. long; male spikes longer. Fruit-clusters ½ to 1 in. long, white or pinkish, sweet, insipid.

Native of China, and possibly of other parts of temperate Asia; cultivated from time immemorial in many South European and Eastern countries. The white mulberry is the tree on which the silkworm is fed. It succeeds quite well in the south of England, but no success has ever been achieved in establishing the silkworm industry there in spite of several attempts, the first of which was made under the auspices of James I. The climate is considered to be too dull and damp. Nevertheless the tree is quite hardy at Kew; only succulent, over-vigorous shoots are injured by frost. The tree, however, lacks the quaint charm of the common mulberry.

There are three specimens of the white mulberry at Kew; one, near the rock garden, is 45 ft high, on two stems 6½ and 5 ft in girth; and two in the *Morus* collection of 42 × 4½ ft and 47 × 3¾ ft (1967). Others of note are: Shrublands Park, Ipswich, 40 × 7¾ ft at 1 ft (1968); Oxford Botanic Garden, *pl.* 1817, 45 × 6¾ ft (1970).

Many varieties of white mulberry are in cultivation, but those that differ chiefly in their influence on the silk produced by worms that feed on them have little interest to British arboriculturists. The following deserve mention:

cv. 'FEGYVERNEKIANA'.—A pigmy, usually under 3 ft high.

cv. 'LACINIATA'.—Leaves deeply lobed, the lobes narrow, pointed, deeply toothed (*M. alba laciniata* Beissn., not K. Koch; *M. alba* f. *skeletoniana* Schneid.).

cv. 'MACROPHYLLA'.—'This variety produces strong and vigorous shoots, and large leaves, sometimes measuring 8 in. long and 6 in. broad, resembling in form those of *M. nigra*, but smooth, glossy and succulent. The fruit is white' (Loudon, *Arb. et Frut. Brit.*, Vol. 3, p. 1349). The name *M. alba macrophylla* first appears in Loddiges' Catalogue for 1836 and Loudon's description was almost certainly based on a specimen in the Loddiges Arboretum. Under the botanical group name *M. alba* f. *macrophylla* (Loud.) Schneid., Rehder places as a synonym *M. alba* var. *morettiana*, but this mulberry (the Moretti or Dandolo mulberry) was completely distinct from the one offered by Loddiges under the epithet *macrophylla* as is clear from Loudon's account (loc. cit.).

var. MULTICAULIS (Perrotet) Loud. *M. multicaulis* Perrotet; *M. alba* var. *latifolia* Bur.; *M. latifolia* Poir. (?).—A large shrub, many-stemmed from the base and spreading by suckers. Leaves up to more than 1 ft long, concave beneath. Fruits almost black when fully ripe. Widely cultivated in China, whence it was introduced to France via the Philippines in 1821, by Perrotet. According to Loudon, this mulberry was easily raised from cuttings and propagated in large numbers by Italian and French nurseries. The plants cultivated in Europe may therefore be all of one clone. There is a specimen of this mulberry in the Edinburgh Botanic Garden, measuring 35 × 3¼ ft (1967). It was planted in 1906.

cv. 'PENDULA'.—A tree of very weeping habit forming an umbrella-like head. It is of so pendulous a nature that it is necessary to tie up a leading shoot every year to enable a trunk to be formed of the desired height. It should be trained up 20 ft, and will then make one of the most notable of weeping trees. There is an example 20 ft high at Talbot Manor, Norfolk.

cv. 'PYRAMIDALIS'.—Of conical habit.

var. TATARICA [Pall.] Ser. *M. tatarica* Pall.—Leaves smaller, up to 3¼ in. long. Fruits smaller.

f. VENOSA (Delile) Schelle *M. alba* var. *venosa* Delile.—Veins very conspicuous, yellowish. Possibly a clone.

M. AUSTRALIS Poir.

M. indica Roxb., not L.; *M. acidosa* Griff.; *M. stylosa* Ser.; *M. alba* var. *stylosa* (Ser.) Bur.

A deciduous bushy tree up to 25 ft high or, more usually, a shrub up to 10 or 15 ft high; young shoots glabrous. Leaves very variable in size and shape, ordinarily ovate with a truncate or heart-shaped base and toothed, but often very deeply three- or five-lobed, the lobes themselves deeply scalloped, 2 to 6 in. long and from two-thirds to quite as much in width, upper surface dull dark green and covered with minute warts which make it slightly rough to the touch; sparsely downy beneath, soon becoming nearly or quite glabrous; stalk ¾ to 1½ in. long. Male catkins up to 1¼ in. long; female ones one-third as much long, silky-hairy. Fruits dark red, juicy, sweet, ½ in. or rather more long.

Native of China, Japan, Ryukyu Islands, Formosa and Korea; introduced by Wilson in 1907, but cultivated a good many years previously as "*M. alba stylosa*". Griffith (whose name for this mulberry is adopted by Schneider in *Plantae Wilsonianae*, Vol. III, p. 297) found it common in woods near Cheikwar (now spelt 'Saikhoa'), a small town in Upper Assam on the Brahmaputra river. It is quite hardy and grows freely in this country although it is not so large a tree as the white or the common mulberry. It has been confused with *M. alba*, from which it differs in the stigma being borne on a distinct style; in *M. alba* the style is nearly or quite absent. The fruit of *M. australis* has, in consequence, a much more bristly appearance. When not in fruit a good distinction is the absence of tufts of down in the vein-axils of the leaf (present in *M. alba*). The leaves are not used to feed silkworms.

M. CATHAYANA Hemsl.

A tree 10 to 25 ft high, young shoots downy at first, becoming smoother and greyish. Leaves heart-shaped, 3 to 6 in. long on adult plants, three-fourths as wide (considerably larger on young vigorous plants), terminated at the apex by an abrupt slender point, margins roundish-toothed (often three-lobed in young trees); rough with short hairs above, softly downy beneath, primary veins in five or six pairs; stalk about 1 in. long, hairy. Male spikes ¾ in. long, borne on a slender stalk about the same length; female spikes of similar size, but with the flowers more closely packed. Fruits about 1 in. long, white, black, or red.

Native of Central China; first discovered about 1888, by Henry, in Hupeh; introduced twenty years later by Wilson. Young trees have hitherto grown freely, and promise to be quite hardy.

M. KAGAYAMAE Koidz.

A small tree up to 50 ft high, with smooth, polished, glabrous young branchlets. Leaves ovate to wide-ovate, acuminate to caudate at the apex, 1¾ to 3¼ in. long, 1⅜ to 2⅜ in. wide (larger on strong shoots), coarsely and irregularly dentate, sometimes with one or two short lobes on each side, papery in texture, glabrous, upper surface rich deep green, lower surface light green. Female flowers densely crowded in a cylindrical spike about ⅜ in. long, which is bare of flowers along a narrow strip down one side. Fruits said to be black.

A native of Japan in the small islands of Hachijo and Miyake of the Izu-No-Shichito chain, south of the main island. It is closely allied to *M. australis*, but seems distinct enough to rank as a species, differing in the glabrous, coarsely dentate leaves and the peculiarity of the female inflorescence noted above. According to Wilson, who collected it on Hachijo in April 1917 (No. 8373), it grows wild there and is also much cultivated for feeding silkworms. A tree at Kew, whose leaves usually colour bright yellow in the autumn, was almost certainly raised from seeds collected by Wilson.

M. MONGOLICA (Bur.) Schneid.

M. alba var. mongolica Bur.

A deciduous tree up to 25 ft high, or a shrub; young shoots glabrous or soon becoming so. Leaves ovate, with a long, slender, often tail-like apex, heart-shaped at the base, coarsely triangular-toothed, each tooth terminated by a bristle, 3 to 6 in. long, 2 to 3¼ in. wide, nearly glabrous except for axil-tufts beneath when young; stalk 1 to 1⅝ in. long. Male catkins 1 to 1½ in. long, with a bare stalk one-third as long; female ones much shorter. Fruits described by Wilson as 'pale red, sweet, palatable', also as 'black'.

Native of China and Korea; discovered by the Abbé David in 1864; introduced by Wilson in 1907. Originally regarded as a variety of *M. alba*, it was made a species by Schneider in *Plantae Wilsonianae*, Vol. III, p. 296. It is very distinct by reason of the coarse, bristly toothed margins of the leaves. Henry describes it as common on the mountains around Peking and the fruit as 'insipid'. The style is longer than in *M. alba* and in this character the species approaches *M. australis*.

There is an example in the University Botanic Garden, Cambridge, measuring 35 × 2 ft (1969).

var. DIABOLICA Koidz.—Leaves scabrid above, downy beneath and frequently deeply lobed; marginal teeth bristle-tipped.

var. VESTITA Rehd.—Leaves densely hairy beneath and slightly so above, not lobed and up to only 2¾ in. long. Inflorescence hairy.

M. NIGRA L.   COMMON OR BLACK MULBERRY
[PLATE 103

A deciduous tree 20 to 30 ft high, of rugged, picturesque aspect, forming a dense spreading head of branches usually wider than the tree is high, and a short rough trunk; young shoots downy, exuding a milky juice when cut. Leaves broadly ovate or two- to five-lobed, always heart-shaped at the base, and with a short tapered point, coarsely toothed, upper surface rough with short flattened hairs, deep glossy green, lower surface paler and downy. On vigorous barren growths the leaves will be 6 to 9 in. long, and both lobed and unlobed; on fruiting shoots they are 2½ to 5 in. long; stalk 1 in. or less long. Flower-spikes cylindrical, those carrying male flowers about 1 in. long, the females half as long; both on very downy stalks. Fruit clusters oval, ¾ to 1 in. long, dark red, with an agreeable sub-acid flavour.

The black mulberry is, no doubt, a native of one or more Oriental countries, but having been cultivated for thousands of years and naturalised, its original limits have long been obliterated. It is known to have been cultivated in England since the early part of the 16th century, quite possibly long before. It is better

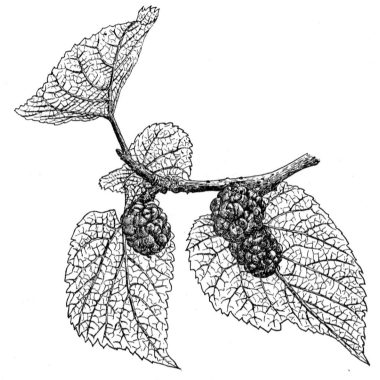

MORUS NIGRA

adapted for the southern part of Britain than the northern, but is always of slow growth. Although not so good for the purpose as *M. alba*, the leaves of common mulberry have been much used to feed silkworms upon. The fruits are sometimes eaten at dessert, and they are also made into various conserves and drinks. So far as I am aware, the common mulberry has never produced any variation from the type—a very unusual circumstance in a tree so long cultivated.

M. RUBRA L. RED MULBERRY

A deciduous tree 40 to over 60 ft high in the wild with a trunk 3 or 4 ft in diameter. Leaves broadly ovate to roundish, heart-shaped at the base, slender-pointed, occasionally two- or three-lobed, toothed, 3 to 5 (occasionally 7 or 8) in.

long, three-fourths to about as much wide, somewhat rough above with scattered stiff hairs, or the remains of them, very downy beneath; stalk ½ to 1 in. long.
Male spikes 1 to 2 in. in length, slender and catkin-like; females 1 in. long; both
downy. Fruit clusters 1 to 1¼ in. long, cylindrical; at first red, then dark purple,
sweet.

Native of the eastern and central United States; introduced in 1629. In my
experience this mulberry thrives the worst of those here mentioned. At Kew it
always has an unhappy appearance, and I do not know of good trees elsewhere.
Probably our climate is as unsuited for it as for several other trees from the same
region. In the United States it produces a light, tough, durable timber, and, according to Sargent, is planted in the southern States for the value of its fruit as
food for poultry and hogs. Several named varieties are also cultivated there for
human use. It is distinguished from *M. alba* and *M. nigra* by the leaves being
much more downy beneath.

M. MICROPHYLLA Buckl.—A small tree or shrub usually under 15 ft high
Leaves ovate, 1½ to 2¼ in. long, often three- or five-lobed, rough above
glabrous or downy beneath. Fruits about ½ in. long, black when fully ripe. A
native of the S.W. United States and N. Mexico, first described from W. Texas,
remarkable for its small leaves.

MUEHLENBECKIA   POLYGONACEAE

A genus of about fifteen species of shrubs or semi-woody climbers,
chiefly Australasian, some South American. Leaves alternate, stalked;
flowers small, greenish or whitish, of little or no ornament, the sexes
sometimes on separate plants. Perianth deeply five-lobed, stamens eight;
fruit a nutlet, three-angled, and enclosed in the perianth, which persists
and sometimes becomes fleshy. The species are so variable that it is
difficult to define their limits, but I believe there to be only two species
commonly grown out-of-doors in this country, viz., *M. axillaris* and
M. complexa.

M. AXILLARIS (Hook. f.) Walp.
Polygonum axillare Hook. f.; *M. nana* Hort.

A tiny, deciduous, creeping shrub 1 or 2 in. high, forming a dense mat upon
the ground of thin wiry branches, and spreading indefinitely by underground
stems. Ultimately it may make a tangled mass of stems 1 foot high. Young shoots
minutely downy. Leaves ovate to round, ⅛ to ⅓ in. long, glabrous, not toothed;
the stalk scarcely so long. Flowers pale green, very tiny, produced singly or in
pairs in the axils of the terminal leaves during July.

Native of the mountainous districts of New Zealand, Tasmania, and Australia.

This little shrub, which is one of the very dwarfest in cultivation, may be recommended to lovers of curiosities. Its flowers are scarcely perceptible, but its thread-like stems, tiny round leaves, and matted growth, make it interesting. It may be grown on some rock garden ledge. Easily increased by division or cuttings.

M. COMPLEXA (A. Cunn.) Meissn.

Polygonum complexum A. Cunn.

A climbing deciduous shrub, forming dense masses of slender, wiry, much interlaced stems; minutely warted when young. Leaves very variable in shape and size, being roundish, heart-shaped, oblong and fiddle-shaped, sometimes on the same plant; they are thin, dull green, quite glabrous, $\frac{1}{8}$ to $\frac{3}{4}$ in. long; stalk rough with minute warts, $\frac{1}{8}$ to $\frac{1}{4}$ in. long. Flowers greenish white, $\frac{1}{8}$ in. long, produced in autumn in small terminal and axillary spikes about $\frac{2}{3}$ in. long; the perianth with its five erect, oblong, blunt-ended lobes persists to the fruiting stage, becoming enlarged and glistening waxy white and enclosing the black shining nutlet.

Native of New Zealand, often found at considerable altitudes. It differs from *M. australis* in its usually smaller leaves and in having its flowers nearly always in short spikes. It makes a dense and interesting cover for old tree-stumps and rubble-heaps; and it is even worth while allowing it to ramble over a common or unimportant shrub 6 to 10 ft high, which it will in time smother by an amazingly thick tangle of dark wiry stems. Hardy in the south and west; killed to ground-level by severe frost at Kew.

var. MICROPHYLLA (Col.) Ckn. *M. microphylla* Col.—A hummock-forming shrub with sparse, very small, roundish leaves. A photograph of this variety in the plant's natural state is reproduced in L. Cockayne, *New Zealand Plants and their Story*, 4th Ed. (1967), fig. 14.

var. TRILOBATA (Col.) Cheesem. *M. trilobata* Col.; *M. varians* Meissn.—Leaves deeply three-lobed.

M. AUSTRALIS (Forst. f.) Meissn. *Coccoloba australis* Forst. f.; *M. adpressa* Hook. f., not Meissn.

—This species, a native of New Zealand, is unlikely to be hardy except in the mildest parts. It is a vigorous, leafy climber with a stout main stem, growing to 30 ft high in the forests, but sometimes seen trailing over rocks. Leaves 1 to 3 in. long, ovate to almost orbicular, cordate to truncate at the base, sometimes lyre-shaped or three-lobed. Inflorescence a much-branched panicle up to 3 in. long.

M. ADPRESSA (Labill.) Meissn. and M. GUNNII (Hook.f.) Walp. (*M. adpressa* var. *hastifolia* Meissn.) are natives of Tasmania and of S. and S.E. Australia, closely allied to *M. australis*.

M. EPHEDROIDES Hook. f.

A deciduous shrub of prostrate sprawling habit, forming a thicket of slender stems which are rush-like the first year, deeply grooved and without down.

Leaves linear to halberd-shaped, $\frac{1}{3}$ to 1 in. long, $\frac{1}{16}$ to $\frac{1}{8}$ in. wide, glabrous, usually inconspicuous or even absent. Flowers small, mostly unisexual, produced from the leaf-axils in short spikes of few-flowered clusters; on the spikes the flowers are predominantly of one sex but often have a few flowers of the other sex mixed with them; they have no beauty. The fruit is black, triangular in cross-section, about $\frac{1}{8}$ in. long, subtended by the persisting, more or less succulent perianth.

Native of the North and South Islands of New Zealand. Perhaps not in cultivation.

var. MURICATULA (Col.) Cheesem. *M. muricatula* Col.—A distinct variety once grown by E. A. Bowles at Myddleton House, Waltham Cross, Herts. It differs from the type in its very slender, almost thread-like young shoots, in the smaller leaves ($\frac{1}{8}$ to $\frac{1}{2}$ in. long) and in the segments of the perianth becoming membranous in fruit. I saw it in July 1932, bearing a large crop of its three-angled seeds rather like miniature beechnuts, but black. Of interest chiefly to botanists and lovers of curiosities. Allan (*Flora of New Zealand*, Vol. 1, p. 224) considers that it is a form of the variable *M. complexa*.

MUSA   BANANA, PLANTAIN   MUSACEAE

A genus of herbaceous monocotyledons attaining, in some species, a giant size and tree-like aspect. The leaves and flower-stalks spring from a rhizome, the apparent aerial stem being made up of the sheathing leaf-bases. For an account of the cultivated bananas (*Musa* and *Ensete*) see *Baileya*, Vol. 5 (1957), pp. 167–194.

M. BASJOO Sieb.

Stems cylindrical, slightly tapering upwards, 6 to 9 ft high, as many or more inches wide at the base, crowned by four to six leaves. Leaves oblong, bright green, the largest 8 or 9 ft long, and 2 ft wide, the smallest, one-third those dimensions, all have the close parallel veins springing at nearly right angles from the midrib that are characteristic of all the musas; stalk 6 to 12 in. long, winged. Flowers borne on a stout arching inflorescence proceeding from the apex of the stem, the main-stalk of which is 1 to $1\frac{1}{2}$ ft long and 2 in. or more in diameter. The flowers (yellowish, cylindrical, of no beauty) open successively over a long season in clusters, each cluster consisting of two rows enclosed in the early stages by a large, concave, leathery bract. Fruit banana-like, 3 or 4 in. long, about 1 in. thick, three-angled, attaining full-size at the base whilst the terminal flower-clusters are still expanding. *Bot. Mag.*, t. 7182.

It is doubtful if this plant has a claim to notice in these pages, for there is nothing woody about it, even at the root. Yet it is tree-like, has a clean stem and persistent evergreen foliage. It is a native of the Ryukyu archipelago, and was cultivated for its fibre in S. Japan, whence it was introduced by Charles Maries about 1881, when collecting for Messrs Veitch, and was first grown out-of-doors in this country at the Coombe Wood nursery in Surrey. It will live in the open air at Kew for a few years but becomes more enfeebled each year and finally succumbs. Dr Wilfrid Fox grew it successfully a few miles south of Godalming, but it is only really at its best in the south-west, where it thrives and often bears fruits (see: E. Thurston, *Trees and Shrubs of Cornwall*, plate XXIV). In general appearance it is a smaller replica of the common banana tree and quite unlike anything else in the open air in this country. It has therefore considerable interest, but otherwise it is not worth its place in the garden except in some out-of-the-way spot. It must be given a sheltered place or the wind will tear the leaves to ribbons. Although with wind protection it may be a handsome and really striking object for a few late summer months, it usually wears a dismal aspect in our climate for the rest of the year with its dead or tattered foliage. Given shelter from wind and a sufficiently mild climate, its only other requirement is a rich soil to grow in. It can be increased by its sucker growths.

MUTISIA*   COMPOSITAE

A genus of evergreen composites notable on account of their mostly climbing habit and showy flower-heads, inhabiting various tropical and temperate parts of S. America, especially Chile, where according to Reiche, the author of a flora of that country, thirty-four species are to be found; altogether about sixty species are known. The leaves are alternate and in one cultivated species, *M. clematis*, they are pinnate; in all the others we grow the leaves are simple, varying from broadly elliptical to linear and from deeply toothed to entire. The midrib is very frequently prolonged into a tendril, sometimes branched. The flowers are crowded in 'heads', as is the case with all composites, and they are terminal, their beauty depending mainly on the ray-florets, which are often beautifully and brilliantly coloured.

Most of this species are only suited for the milder parts of the country and even there are not easily kept in health for a long term of years, although in certain places they go on indefinitely (see note on *M. decurrens*). Some are apt to die off suddenly without any apparent cause. *M. clematis* is an exception and quite amenable to cultivation. Often they grow wild pretty much as the honeysuckle does in our English copses, scrambling over other shrubs. They probably prefer to have their roots and main-stems in the shade, but the younger parts in full sunshine. A perfectly drained light sandy loam, with which stones are freely mixed, is recommended by those who have succeeded best with them.

The genus was named after José Celestino Mutis (1732–1808), who became professor of anatomy at Madrid, and in 1760 accompanied the

* Revised with the assistance of Mr C. Jeffrey of the Kew Herbarium.

T S—BB

Marquis Della Vega to Colombia, where he directed the royal botanical expeditions which explored most of the Spanish territories in the New World. Mutis wrote a flora of Bogota, for which 6,000 folio paintings were made. This was not published in his lifetime, but during the years 1954–63 four sumptuous folio volumes with Mutis's text and coloured plates was issued and more are to follow. The genus was named after him by Linnaeus the younger.

M. CLEMATIS L. f.

A vigorous evergreen climber 30 ft or more high; young stems slender, ribbed, and clothed like the undersurface of the leaves, the flower-stalks, and the outer bracts of the flower head with a thick, soft, whitish wool. Leaves alternate, pinnate, composed of six, eight, or ten leaflets, the woolly main-stalk lengthening out at the end into a slender, forked tendril several inches long, by which the plant supports itself in climbing. Leaflets oblong-ovate, pointed, rounded or widely tapered at the base, entire, $\frac{2}{3}$ to $1\frac{1}{2}$ in. long, $\frac{1}{3}$ to $\frac{1}{2}$ in. wide, woolly on both surfaces at first, the upper one wearing clean; very shortly stalked. Flower-heads solitary, terminal, pendulous, the lower part cylindrical, 2 to $2\frac{1}{2}$ in. long, enclosed in an involucre of four or five series of erect, oblong-lanceolate bracts. Ray-florets nine or ten, brilliant orange-scarlet, spreading horizontally or slightly recurved, giving the flower-head a diameter of 2 to $2\frac{1}{2}$ in. *Bot. Mag.*, t. 8391.

Native of the Andes of Colombia; introduced in 1859. Near London it has to be given cool greenhouse treatment, but it is hardy in the milder counties. A large plant climbed up the Rectory at Ludgvan, near Penzance. A plant formerly grown in the Temperate House at Kew began to flower in May and continued until October; the plant there was pruned back and its weak shoots thinned out before growth commenced in spring. Unlike some of the mutisias this species is very amenable to cultivation and is really so rampant a grower that this annual pruning soon becomes necessary under glass, and desirable out-of-doors. Propagated by cuttings of half-ripened shoots quite easily.

The plants from Ecuador mentioned in the Seventh Edition belong to a related species—M. MICROPHYLLA Willd.—which is distinguished by its smaller leaflets with revolute margins.

M. DECURRENS Cav.

A climbing evergreen shrub, growing 8 to 10 ft high; stems slender, glabrous, but little branched. Leaves narrow-oblong, stalkless; the blade 3 to 5 in. long, $\frac{1}{2}$ to 1 in. wide, the base being extended down each side of the stem as a pair of narrow wings, the apex terminating in a forked tendril which curls round any available support, and thus holds up the stem. Flower-heads 4 to 5 in. across, solitary at the end of the shoot, and borne on a glabrous stalk 3 to 5 in. long. Ray-florets about fifteen, each $\frac{1}{2}$ in. wide, and of a brilliant orange or vermilion colour; disk-florets yellow. The flower-head is supported at the base by a columnar mass of overlapping thin scales tipped with greyish hairs, and has much the aspect of a gazania or single dahlia. *Bot. Mag.*, t. 5273.

Native of Chile and Argentina; introduced for Messrs Veitch in 1859 by Richard Pearce. Except in comparatively few places it has not proved a success in this country, and is now uncommon. One of the greatest successes with it has been obtained in Sir Thomas Acland's garden at Killerton, near Exeter. A plant there is grown against a wall facing south-west, and Mr J. Coutts, who planted it and cultivated it for several years, tells me that it has borne over three hundred flower-heads during one summer. He ascribes his success with it, first to the position and climate; second, to the soil, which is not the ordinary red soil of Devon, but volcanic trap; and lastly, to the practice of placing stones on the ground about the roots. The Killerton plant produces suckers freely, and by them can be propagated; it also ripens seed from which many plants have been raised. This mutisia is capable of withstanding severe cold; soon after it was introduced it experienced 26° of frost at Exeter without injury.

The above account is taken unchanged from previous editions. The plant at Killerton no longer exists and no plant of comparable health and vigour has been traced. There is (1972) a small plant in the Alpine Yard at Kew, raised from a rooted piece collected in Chile below the Termas de Chillán in 1963.

In his article 'The Hardier Mutisias' in *Journ. R.H.S.*, Vol. 74 (1949), pp. 241–245, James Comber emphasised how important it is to protect the suckers of this mutisia: '. . . though flowering stems may last over a considerable period, in time they become effete and are due for replacement. The stem above ground dies and if not replaced by suckers from below, that is the end of the plant.'

There is a note on the propagation of *M. decurrens* by L. B. Stewart in *Notes Roy. Bot. Gard. Edin.*, Vol. 8, pp. 137–138.

var. PATAGONICA (Phil.) Blake differs only in the leaves being white-tomentose beneath.

M. ILICIFOLIA Cav.

(incl. *M. ilicifolia* var. *decandolleana* (Phil.) Cabrera)

A slender-stemmed evergreen climbing plant whose young shoots, as seen on cultivated plants, are furnished with toothed ridges (wings); they are clothed with a whitish or pale brown wool, as are also the leaves beneath and the flower-stalks. Many wild specimens in the Kew Herbarium show that those parts of the plant are often glabrous and the stems merely ribbed. Leaves holly-like, leathery, simple, stalkless, ovate-oblong, deeply heart-shaped at the base, 1 to 2¼ in. long, the margins strongly spiny-toothed, the midrib prolonged 1 to 4 in. so as to form a slender curling tendril, upper-surface dark bright green. Flower-heads solitary, terminal, borne on a stalk usually less than ½ in. long. Ray-florets eight to twelve, of various shades of pink or pale mauve, oblong-lanceolate, pointed, giving the flower-head a diameter of 2 to 3 in. Disk-florets yellow, numerous, forming a circular mass in the centre 1 in. wide. Bracts of the involucre erect, roundish ovate to lanceolate, often constricted at the apex to a short point, but variously shaped. It flowers at almost all seasons. *Bot. Mag.*, t. 6009.

Native of Chile; introduced in 1832. Generally it is regarded as a cool green-house plant, but it is grown as a wall plant in Cornwall and even in the rock garden at Edinburgh Botanic Garden survived twenty winters. The late Clarence Elliott collected it in Chile at 5,000 to 6,000 ft altitude, flowering in November 1927. He notes that it was climbing over and smothering bushes up to 10 and 15 ft high. Easily recognised by its sessile, simple, holly-like leaves and shortly stalked flower-heads, but sometimes found to be difficult to keep in good health.

M. OLIGODON Poepp. & Endl.   [PLATE 105
M. gayana Remy

An evergreen semi-climbing, semi-prostrate shrub with ribbed young shoots covered at first with a loose, pale wool. Leaves 1 to 1½ in. long, ¼ to ⅞ in. wide, oblong, stalkless, the base mostly bi-lobed, the lobes clasping the stem, the midrib prolonged into a slender, curling tendril ½ to 3 in. long, margins coarsely triangularly toothed; dark bright green above, covered with pale wool beneath. Flower-heads solitary, terminal, borne on a slender stalk 1 to 3 in. long; ray-florets six to twelve, elliptical to oblanceolate, roundish or blunt at the end, 1¼ in. long, ⅜ in. wide, of a beautiful silky pink (almost salmon-pink). Bracts of the involucre closely overlapping, roundish-ovate, with down at the margin and a short mucro at the apex. Bot. Mag., t. 9499.

Native of Chile and Argentina at 3,000 to 5,000 ft altitude. Originally described in 1835, and afterwards found by Veitch's collector, Richard Pearce (1859–66), it seems first to have been introduced to cultivation by H. F. Comber during his Andean Expedition, 1925–7. He describes it as covering large areas, spreading by means of underground stems, a single plant often filling a space of 8 to 10 sq. yd. He found it common in rocky places and on hot, dry pastures, growing only 6 in. to 1 ft high (see Journ. R.H.S., Vol. 74 (1949), figs. 86 and 87). It was stated in previous editions that Comber found it up to 8 ft high, but that information came from notes on field specimens which belong to M. spinosa.

James Comber, the collector's father, who was for many years garden manager at Nymans in Sussex, judged this species to be the most successful of the mutisias under ordinary garden conditions. He grew it in light moist loam with the addition of leaf mould and coarse sand, but it might be happier in a rubbly, rock-covered soil. At Borde Hill in Sussex a plant raised from Comber's original seed has lived for over forty years against a low garden wall near a stone path. Fertile seeds are usually produced, and cuttings strike quite readily.

M. SPINOSA Ruiz & Pavon
M. retusa var. glaberrima Phil.

An evergreen climber whose height is given by collectors as 10 to 20 ft. Leaves 1 to 2¼ in. long, half as much wide, stalkless, elliptical or oblong, lobed at the base, notched at the apex, the margins varying from entire to coarsely and tri-angularly toothed down the whole length, but often with the dentation confined to one or two teeth near the apex, dark green and glabrous above, varying from glabrous to loosely woolly beneath; the midrib extended into a tendril up to 3 in.

long. Flower-heads borne on stalks up to 3 in. long: ray-florets about eight, pink, oblanceolate, 1¼ in. long, ¼ to ½ in. wide.

Native of Chile and Argentina. It was collected by Richard Pearce for Veitch's in 1868 and flowered at Kew in 1894. The plants at present in cultivation were introduced by H. F. Comber during his Andean expedition, 1925–7. It succeeds well scrambling through some large shrub in a sunny position, and that is really the best place for it, since the ugly dead leaves of the older stems will then be mostly concealed. It has produced self-sown seedlings at Nymans in Sussex.

This species, as the late Clarence Elliott observed, is not very distinct from *M. ilicifolia* from a gardener's point of view, but the flower-head in *M. ilicifolia* is very shortly stalked as a rule, sometimes almost sessile, and the leaves are harder, more uniformly coarsely toothed and more distinctly net-veined. Mr Elliott considered, from what he saw of the two species in Chile, that *M. ilicifolia* had superior flowers, but *M. spinosa* might be more amenable to cultivation.

There is a variant with white ray-florets, of which Comber sent seeds under his No. 1105.

var. PULCHELLA (Spegazzini) Cabrera *M. retusa* Remy—This has leaves persistently white-tomentose beneath but the species is so variable in the degree of hairiness of the undersides of the leaves that it may be difficult to draw a line between this variety and the typical state.

M. SUBULATA Ruiz & Pavon

An evergreen, slender-stemmed climber reported by collectors as growing 6 to 10 ft high; young shoots grey, ribbed, much zigzagged. Leaves glabrous, linear, 1 to 3 in. long $\frac{1}{16}$ in. or so wide, grey-green, grooved above, the midrib prominent beneath and often prolonged at the apex into a curling tendril. Flower-heads with some eight or ten ray-florets of an orange-scarlet colour, each floret of lanceolate shape, 1½ in. long by ¼ in. wide. Involucre cylindrical, 1½ in. long by ½ in. wide; scales overlapping, ¼ to ⅜ in. wide, broadly ovate, tipped with down. *Bot. Mag.*, t. 9461.

Native of Chile; originally named in 1798 and collected in the wild many times since, but not introduced apparently until 1928, when seeds reached Britain through the agency of G. W. Robinson and the late Clarence Elliott; a living plant brought home by the former flowered in 1930. It is very distinct from the species previously mentioned in its stems which are scarcely thicker than an ordinary strand of worsted. Like other species, it should be planted to grow over a bush or small tree, on which it should eventually form a mass of interlaced branches and flower about midsummer. It is of doubtful hardiness, but would, no doubt, find the south-western counties warm enough.

f. ROSMARINIFOLIA (Poepp. & Endl.) Cabrera *M. linearifolia* Hook., not Cav.; *M. hookeri* Meyen; *M. linariifolia* Remy—This form of *M. subulata* has its dark shining leaves much more crowded on the stem, sometimes, judging by wild specimens, a dozen or more to the inch; they are also shorter, mostly only 1 to 1½ in. long and up to ⅛ in. wide, linear-subulate and pointed; their midribs do not lengthen out into tendrils. Flower-heads described as 'rich and brilliant crimson-scarlet'; involucre bottle-shaped, 1¼ in. long.

The late Clarence Elliott introduced this mutisia from Chile in 1928. He wrote that at 6,000 ft altitude (below which he did not find it) it was a wiry climber trailing over shrubs up to 8 or 10 ft. At 9,000 ft it grew flat upon desolate screes, forming lumps 3 or 4 ft wide, with thick woody root-stocks not rising more than 3 in. above ground level and suggesting when in flower colonies of scarlet gerberas.

It is not certain whether either of the mutisias described above are in cultivation at the present time. Both grow in the Andes of Aconcagua and Coquimbo provinces.

MYRICA   Gale, Bayberry   myricaceae

Deciduous and evergreen shrubs or small trees, with scented alternate leaves and unisexual flowers, the sexes sometimes on the same plant, sometimes separated. Flowers in catkins, and produced in the axils of bracts. There are neither sepals nor petals, the male flower consisting of a varying number of stamens, the female of a one-celled ovary with two stalkless stigmas.

The myricas are not much grown in gardens, but are worth a place for their sweetly scented leaves, and, in the American kinds, their white, wax-coated fruits. They thrive in any ordinary soil. Increased by seed or layering.

M. californica Cham. & Schlecht.   Californian Bayberry

An evergreen shrub usually 10 to 14 ft high, with vigorous shoots, hairy when young. Leaves oblanceolate or somewhat oval, tapered at both ends, regularly and angularly toothed, sometimes almost to the base, 2 to 4 in. long, ½ to ¾ in. wide, dark glossy green, glandular on both surfaces, especially beneath, downy only on the midrib above, slightly fragrant when crushed; stalk ¼ in. or less long. Male catkins borne in the axils of the year-old leaves, about 1 in. long; female catkins usually on the same plant. Fruits globular, ⅛ in. across, purple, but covered with white wax.

Native of California, where it is sometimes a tree 40 ft high. In very hard winters this shrub is cut back to ground-level at Kew, but in ordinary winters survives without injury except to the tips of the young shoots. It is a cheerful, vigorous evergreen, but its leaves are not so strongly scented as those of the other species here mentioned. Very well adapted for the milder parts of the country.

M. CERIFERA L. WAX MYRTLE

M. carolinensis Mill.

A deciduous, or more or less evergreen shrub in this country, but said to be at times a small evergreen tree, 20 to 40 ft high in the wild; young shoots reddish, downy. Leaves narrowly obovate or oblanceolate, very variable in size in different forms, the largest $4\frac{1}{2}$ in. long and 2 in. wide, but normally $1\frac{1}{2}$ to 3 in. long, $\frac{1}{3}$ to $\frac{3}{4}$ in. wide, usually toothed towards the apex, glossy green and glabrous above, dotted with yellowish resin-glands beneath, and downy on the midrib; stalk $\frac{1}{8}$ to $\frac{1}{4}$ in. long. Male catkins $\frac{1}{4}$ to $\frac{1}{2}$ in. long. Fruits globular, $\frac{1}{8}$ in. wide, coated with white glistening wax, stalkless, densely crowded in clusters of two to six on the growths of the previous year.

Native of the south-eastern United States; introduced in 1699. In the early part of the occupation by Europeans of its native region, this shrub was valued by the settlers for the wax yielded by the fruits. This white, waxy coating, which gives so distinctive a character to the plant in autumn, was removed by boiling, and then made into candles. According to Kalm, the Swedish traveller, these candles burnt better and more slowly than ordinary tallow ones, and gave an agreeable smell when extinguished. The species is very variable in leaf, especially in size and toothing.

M. PENSYLVANICA Loisel. *M. carolinensis* of some authors, not Mill.; *M. cerifera* var. *latifolia* Ait. BAYBERRY.—This species is closely allied to *M. cerifera* and perhaps a more northerly form of it. It reaches into Canada, and extends in the wild from Nova Scotia, New Brunswick, and Prince Edward Island south to Florida, etc. It differs in its leaves being more often oblong and oval than obovate, more abruptly tapered at the base, and blunter at the apex than in *M. cerifera*; downy above. Young wood downy. The fruits are coated with white wax, as in the other, but are somewhat larger ($\frac{1}{6}$ in. wide). This species is always shrubby and up to 8 or 9 ft high. It is, no doubt, hardier than the true *cerifera* and probably is grown under that name in many gardens. It is reported to be naturalised in the New Forest.

M. GALE L. SWEET GALE

Gale palustris (Lam.) Chev.; *Myrica palustris* Lam.

A deciduous shrub 2 to 4 ft high, bushy; wood and leaves fragrant when crushed. Leaves oblanceolate, tapering and entire at the base, toothed and broadest near the apex, 1 to $2\frac{1}{2}$ in. long, $\frac{1}{3}$ to $\frac{3}{4}$ in. wide, glossy and dark green above, paler, more or less downy, and with scattered shining glands beneath; stalk $\frac{1}{8}$ in. long. Flowers of the male plant produced during May and June in crowded, stalkless catkins, each catkin $\frac{1}{3}$ to $\frac{5}{8}$ in. long, set with close, overlapping, shining, concave scales. Fruit catkins about as long, but stouter; composed of closely set, resinous nutlets $\frac{1}{12}$ in. wide. The flowers are borne on the naked wood of the previous year; the sexes usually on separate plants.

Native of the higher latitudes of all the northern hemisphere; common in Great Britain, especially in the north, usually in moist peaty places, and on moors. In gardens the sweet gale is sometimes grown for the sake of its pleasant fragrance when handled. On the Yorkshire moors branches were, and perhaps still are, used to flavour a kind of home-made beer known as 'gale beer', considered to be very efficacious for slaking thirst.

var. TOMENTOSA C. DC.—Young wood, both surfaces of the leaf (but especially the lower one), very downy. Siberia, Japan, N. Korea, etc.

MYRICARIA   TAMARICACEAE

A genus of a few species, allied to *Tamarix*, differing from it mainly in the stamens being united at the base and the always pentamerous flowers.

M. GERMANICA Desv.

A deciduous shrub 6 to 8 ft high, glaucous grey, and of rather gaunt habit. Branches erect, plume-like, clothed with flat round-pointed, linear leaves, from $\frac{1}{16}$ to $\frac{3}{16}$ in. long, glabrous and dotted with glands. Flowers densely set in slender racemes 3 to 8 in. long, which terminate the branchlets all over the top of the shrub; each flower is about $\frac{1}{4}$ in. long, produced in the axil of a bract longer than itself; petals five, narrow, pink or pinkish white. Stamens ten; seeds feathery.

Native of Europe, Himalaya, Afghanistan, etc.; cultivated in England since 1582. It inhabits river banks, mountain streams, and other sandy, occasionally inundated places, where it often fills the ground over long distances. It is easily propagated by cuttings made of stout wood of the current year placed in sandy soil in the open ground in October. It flowers from May to August.

MYRSINE   MYRSINACEAE

This genus (if *Rapanea* (*Suttonia*) is included in it) consists of some 200 species of trees and shrubs. The flowers are usually small, or even minute and inconspicuous, often unisexual. Fruit a pea-like drupe, one-seeded and either dry or rather fleshy. The parts of the flower are mostly in fours or fives. The New Zealand species, including two of the following, are sometimes put in a separate genus—RAPANEA.

M. AFRICANA L.

M. retusa Ait.; *M. africana* var. *retusa* (Ait.) A. DC.

An evergreen shrub, usually from 2 to 5 ft high, bushy, and very leafy; young shoots angled, covered with short down. Leaves alternate, about $\frac{1}{8}$ in. apart on the twigs, oval to narrowly obovate, rounded, truncate, or tapering at the apex, always tapered at the base, $\frac{1}{4}$ to $\frac{3}{4}$ in. long, $\frac{3}{16}$ to $\frac{1}{2}$ in. wide, toothed at the terminal half only, glabrous on both surfaces, lustrous dark green above; stalk downy, $\frac{1}{16}$ in. long. Flowers of one sex only on a plant, very tiny, pale brown, produced in stalkless clusters of three to six at the leaf-axils. Berries on the female plant pale blue, orange-shaped, $\frac{1}{4}$ in. or less across, with the persistent calyx at the base, containing a single seed. *Bot. Mag.*, t. 8712.

Native of the Himalaya, China, Azores, and the mountains of eastern and southern Africa. It was introduced from South Africa in the 17th century and again from the Azores in 1778. The plants now in cultivation are mostly of Himalayan or Chinese origin, but Collingwood Ingram has in his garden at Benenden, Kent, a plant introduced by him from the Azores.

This curious little shrub, which is of neat habit and has a general resemblance to *Ilex crenata*, is spread widely over the Old World. It has no flower beauty. Having such a wide range, this species must vary in hardiness, but a plant raised from seed in 1895 grew on the rock garden at Kew unprotected until killed in the winter of 1946–7. This was only 1 ft high. At Nymans in Sussex there is a male plant about 4 ft high and 10 ft across, which is over half-a-century old. The Benenden plant referred to above is also hardy.

The fruiting spray figured in the *Botanical Magazine* came from a female plant at Nymans, which was weaker growing than the male and died some years ago. Fruits have been borne in other gardens also.

M. CHATHAMICA F. v. Muell.

Rapanea chathamica (F. v. Muell.) W. R. B. Oliver; *Suttonia chathamica* (F. v. Muell.) Mez

A small evergreen tree up to 20 ft high; young shoots furnished with short, stiff hairs. Leaves alternate, leathery, obovate, notched at the rounded apex, tapered at the base, not toothed, 1 to $2\frac{1}{2}$ in. long, $\frac{3}{4}$ to $1\frac{1}{2}$ in. wide, glabrous except for down along the midrib beneath, pale green on both surfaces, dotted with glands beneath; stalk $\frac{1}{8}$ in. or so long. Flowers $\frac{1}{10}$ in. wide, unisexual, produced in dense clusters in the leaf-axils and on the lower naked part of the shoot; petals four, ciliate, thickly dotted with reddish glands. Fruits globose, purplish, $\frac{1}{4}$ to $\frac{1}{3}$ in. wide, containing one seed.

Native of the Chatham Islands (New Zealand); introduced by Major A. A. Dorrien-Smith, who visited the islands in December 1909 and found it common there in certain woods. One of its companion trees, then in full bloom, was *Hebe gigantea*, 20 ft high. The myrsine—inconspicuous in its flowers—should succeed where *Olearia semidentata*, perhaps the most beautiful of Chatham Island shrubs, succeeds.

M. NUMMULARIA Hook. f.

Rapanea nummularia (Hook. f.) W. R. B. Oliver; *Suttonia nummularia* (Hook. f.) Mez

A prostrate evergreen shrub only an inch or two high, with very slender, wiry, reddish brown, slightly downy shoots. Leaves alternate, set on the twigs eight to twelve to the inch, rather leathery, broadly obovate to orbicular, tooth-less, often slightly indented at the apex, $\frac{1}{8}$ to $\frac{1}{3}$ in. long and wide, dark green, glabrous, rather wrinkled, dotted beneath with numerous translucent glands; stalk $\frac{1}{16}$ in. long, grooved and downy on the upper side. Flowers unisexual, very small and inconspicuous, produced during May and June singly, in pairs, or in threes in the leaf-axils, very shortly stalked, only $\frac{1}{8}$ in. wide, yellowish white; petals four, edged with tiny hairs, concave; anthers almost as large as the petals. Fruits berry-like, globose, blue-purple, $\frac{1}{5}$ to $\frac{1}{4}$ in. wide, containing one seed.

Native of the North and South Islands of New Zealand, at altitudes of 2,000 to 5,000 ft; also of Stewart Island, where it occurs at sea-level. It is fairly hardy at Kew, also at Edinburgh, where I saw it in flower in June 1931. It is really of more interest than beauty unless the fruits, which I have not seen, are abundant enough to be attractive. In general appearance it suggests one of the dwarf, small-leaved vacciniums or a small *Cotoneaster microphylla*, and is best adapted for the rock garden.

MYRTUS   Myrtle   myrtaceae

Of the species treated in this work under *Myrtus* only one, *M. communis* (the common myrtle), would remain in the genus if all the segregate genera were to be recognised. The genus in the wild sense has been broken up chiefly on seed and embryo characters coupled with geographical distribution. The difficulty is that the so-called generic characters are not very convincing, and, moreover, those derived from seeds and embryos are not known for many species. A further difficulty is the lack of a comprehensive study of the family and the fact that genera have been segregated by botanists working only on a section of the family, or the representatives of it in one geographical area. The last worldwide study of the family was made by George Bentham, whose conclusions are set out in Bentham & Hooker fil., *Genera Plantarum*, Vol. 1 (1865), pp. 690–725, and in *Journ. Linn. Soc.*, Vol. 10 (1869), pp. 101–166. He retained under *Myrtus* the species dealt with here, and until another comprehensive account is available it seems best to follow that meticulous and erudite botanist. Comments on the segregate genera will be found under the species concerned.

The leading characters of the species described here are: evergreen shrubs or trees with opposite, entire, glandular-punctate leaves. Flowers white (sometimes slightly tinged with pink), axillary, solitary or in few-flowered clusters. Sepals and petals four or five. Stamens numerous (except in *M. nummularia*). Ovary enclosed in the calyx-tube, with a single style. Fruits berry-like, crowned by the persistent calyx.

M. BULLATA A. Cunn., not Salisb.

Lophomyrtus bullata (A. Cunn.) Burret

An evergreen shrub 10 to 15 ft high, or a small tree; young shoots downy. Leaves opposite, orbicular or ovate, entire, most usually $\frac{3}{4}$ to $1\frac{1}{4}$ in. long, scarcely as wide (sometimes over 2 in. long), of rather leathery texture, purple and downy when young on both surfaces, changing to reddish brown, the blade conspicuously puckered and blistered between the veins; stalk $\frac{1}{8}$ to $\frac{1}{4}$ in. long, very downy. Flowers $\frac{3}{4}$ in. wide, white, solitary in the leaf-axils, each on a downy stalk $\frac{1}{2}$ to $\frac{5}{8}$ in. long; calyx purple; petals round; stamens numerous, with white stalks and yellow anthers. Fruits a black-red, egg shaped berry $\frac{1}{3}$ in. long. *Bot. Mag.*, t. 4809.

Native of New Zealand; introduced originally to Kew, where it flowered as long ago as June 1854. It is scarcely hardy there, but succeeds well in the south-west, where it has reached nearly or quite 20 ft in height. Its chief feature is the curiously bullate or blistered appearance of the leaves, which makes it quite distinct from any other shrub that, so far as I know, can be grown in the open air in this country. So far as I have seen, it is shy-flowering.

The name *M. bullata* A. Cunn. is invalid, since it is antedated by *M. bullata* Salisb, used forty years earlier for a myrtaceous species of central America—*Calyptranthes bullata* (Salisb.) DC. No alternative name can be found and the established one is therefore retained here. In *Flora of New Zealand*, Vol. 1, pp. 329–330, the two New Zealand species are treated in the genus *Lophomyrtus*, separated from *Myrtus* by Burret in 1941. But the character by which he distinguished this genus is scarcely of generic value.

M. × RALPHII Hook. f. *Lophomyrtus ralphii* (Hook. f.) Burret—Described by J. D. Hooker as a species near to *M. bullata*, this myrtle is now considered to be a variable natural hybrid between that species and *M. obcordata*. Typically the leaves are flat or only slightly bullate, and intermediate between those of the parents in size.

M. CHEQUEN (Mol.) Spreng.

Eugenia chequen Mol.; *E. chekan* DC.; *Myrceugenella chequen* (Mol.) Kausel; *Luma chequen* (Mol.) A. Gray

A densely branched, very leafy shrub (or occasionally a small tree in the wild); young stems brown, finely white-downy. Leaves shortly stalked, broad-elliptic or broad-ovate, acute to obtuse at the apex, rounded or wide-cuneate at the base, on the main shoots mostly $\frac{5}{8}$ to $1\frac{3}{16}$ in. long, $\frac{1}{4}$ to $\frac{3}{4}$ in. wide (but on the short lateral twigs elliptic to obovate, $\frac{1}{4}$ to $\frac{5}{8}$ in. long, $\frac{1}{8}$ to $\frac{5}{16}$ in. wide), entire, leathery, deep green above, light green below, densely gland-dotted on both sides, aromatic. Flowers borne in late summer, singly or in three-flowered cymes in the axils of the uppermost pairs of leaves of the main shoots and of the lateral twigs; peduncles and pedicels $\frac{3}{8}$ in. long, slender; bracteoles two, immediately under the flower; flower-buds globose. Calyx with a very short tube and four or five spreading, rounded or ovate lobes about twice as long as the tube. Petals four (occasionally five), spreading, roundish, $\frac{1}{8}$ to $\frac{3}{16}$ in. wide, white. Stamens numerous, as long or longer than the petals. Style ¼ in. long, with a minute stigma. Fruit a more or less globose berry, black, ³⁄₁₆ to ¼ in. across. Seeds hard and horny; embryo with a stout radicle half encircling the appressed more or less flattened cotyledons. *Bot. Mag.*, t. 5644.

Native of Chile from Coquimbo to Concepcion, usually in wet places; introduced by William Lobb in 1847. It is related to *M. luma* (*apiculata*) but is usually a shrub and lacks the characteristic bark of that species. It is moderately hardy south of London in a sheltered position.

M. COMMUNIS L.   COMMON MYRTLE

An evergreen, very leafy shrub up to 10 or 12 ft high, sometimes a small tree; young wood downy. Leaves opposite, ovate or lanceolate, pointed, 1 to 2 in. long, ⅓ to ¾ in. wide, dark glossy green above, paler beneath, glabrous on both sides, fragrant when crushed, and covered with transparent dots, margins entire, decurved; stalk very short or none. Flowers white, ¾ in. across, fragrant, nearly always solitary on a slender stalk ¾ to 1 in. long. arising from the leaf-axils, the most conspicuous features being the crowded stamens ⅓ in. long, produced in a

MYRTUS COMMUNIS

brush-like cluster, and the five rounded petals; calyx green, with five erect, short, broadly ovate lobes. Fruit a purplish black berry, roundish oblong, ½ in. in length (white in variety LEUCOCARPA DC.).

The common myrtle is now very abundant in S. and E. Europe and the Mediterranean region generally, but is believed to have been introduced there from W. Asia, probably Persia or Afghanistan. It was probably one of the first shrubs introduced to our islands from the Levant, and was well known in the 16th century. One of the favourite plants of the ancients, and held sacred by them to the goddess of Love, a sprig of myrtle still carries its ancient significance in being indispensable in the composition of wedding bouquets. It is not hardy except in the mildest parts of the country, but thrives well upon a south wall. It blossoms usually in July and August.

Of the several varieties of myrtle, which vary in the colour of the fruit (sometimes yellowish white) and in the form of the leaves, the following only need be mentioned here. Most of them pertain rather to the cold greenhouse than the open air.

cv. 'FLORE PLENO'.—Flowers double.

var. TARENTINA L. TARENTUM MYRTLE.—Leaves small, narrowly oval, ½ to ¾ in. long, ⅛ to ¼ in. wide, often alternate; young shoots, leaf-stalks, and base of midrib very downy. This, like the bigger-leaved type, needs wall protection. It bore its whitish fruits at Kew in 1911. Recognisable twigs have been found in Roman tombs of 2,000 years ago. An open well-drained loam suits the myrtles, and cuttings readily take root in gentle heat.

cv. 'VARIEGATA'.—Leaves variegated creamy white.

M. LECHLERANA (Miq.) Sealy

Myrcia lechleriana Miq.; *M. luma* Barnéoud, not Mol.; *Amomyrtus luma* Legrand & Kausel, in part

An evergreen bushy shrub or small tree; bark pale greyish brown when first exposed; young shoots light brown, hairy. Leaves short-stalked, ovate to broad-elliptic, mucronate at the apex, rounded or broad-cuneate at the base, ⅝ to 1 in. long, ¼ to ½ in. wide (larger on sterile shoots), copper-coloured and slightly downy on the margins and midrib beneath when young, becoming dark green, glabrous, and of a stiff, leathery texture. Flowers creamy white, borne in May four to ten together in racemose clusters from the upper leaf-axils; rachis downy, ¼ to ½ in. long; pedicels ¼ to ⅜ in. long. Calyx reddish on the inside, with triangular lobes. Petals five, concave, roundish, about ¼ in. long and wide. Stamens longer than the petals, with yellow anthers. Fruits about ¼ in. wide, red when young, black when ripe; seeds light brown, hard and woody. *Bot. Mag.*, t. 9523.

Native of Chile from 36° to 46° 30′ S.; introduced by H. Comber during his Andean expedition 1925–7 under field number C.1038. The seeds collected by Comber came from plants 4 to 8 ft high, growing at Reyeguaico, in the Andes, about 35 miles S.S.E. of Lake Villarica, but the plants raised from them have grown much taller in cultivation. At Nymans in Sussex there is a four-stemmed specimen in woodland which is about 24 ft high and another, about 18 ft high, in the Walled Garden. At Trewithen in Cornwall there is a beautiful hedge of this myrtle near the house, about 25 ft high.

Flowering as it does in May, when so many trees and shrubs are in bloom, *Myrtus lechlerana* has not been so much planted in the milder parts as *Myrtus luma*, which flowers in late summer and has the additional attraction of a beautifully coloured bark. Also, its flowers are susceptible to damage by spring frosts.

M. LUMA Mol.

Myrceugenia apiculata (DC.) Niedenzu; *Eugenia apiculata* DC.; *Luma apiculata* (DC.) Burret; *Myrceugenella apiculata* (DC.) Kausel

A bush 3 to 20 ft high or a tree up to 60 ft high, with a flaking, cinnamon-coloured bark; young branches brown, downy. Leaves opposite, very shortly stalked, broad-elliptic, cuneate at the base, acute and apiculate at the apex, $\frac{3}{4}$ to 1 in. long, rather more than half as wide, or sometimes slightly longer and more narrowly elliptic, thinly leathery, deep green above, paler below, glabrous except for down on the midrib beneath and on the margins of the basal part of the leaf. Flowers axillary, mostly solitary on pedicels $\frac{3}{8}$ to $\frac{5}{8}$ in. long, bearing two small deciduous bracteoles close to the flower, but sometimes in a three-flowered cyme, with each bracteole subtending a shortly stalked flower. Sepals four, broad-oblong, rounded. Petals white, almost orbicular, about $\frac{1}{2}$ in. long, strongly concave. Stamens very numerous, with yellow anthers, forming a boss in the centre of the flower. Fruits fleshy, globose, $\frac{3}{8}$ in. or slightly less wide, dark purple, three-celled, with one or two seeds in each cell. *Bot. Mag.*, t. 5040.

Native of the temperate forests of Chile and Argentina; introduced by William Lobb in 1844. In Cornwall and in the milder parts of Ireland this beautiful tree has made itself very much at home, growing as happily as in its native country and producing in many gardens innumerable self-sown seedlings. Specimens 30 to 47 ft high, 2 to $4\frac{1}{2}$ ft in girth have been measured recently in Cornwall at Lanarth, Trengwainton, Trelowarren, and at Tresco Abbey in the Isles of Scilly; in Northern Ireland at Castlewellan. And in Eire at Kilmacurragh, Co. Wicklow; Fota, Ardnagashel, and Garinish Island, Co. Cork; Inishtioge, Co. Kilkenny.

This myrtle is perhaps at its most beautiful when drawn up by neighbouring trees, for the bark is then better displayed than on trees grown in the open, which, as at Trengwainton, usually have shorter stems and bushier crowns. There is a fine group of closely planted trees at Tresco Abbey.

In Argentina there is a picturesque stand of gnarled trees near the holiday resort of Bariloche, much frequented by tourists, and others in the same region which are under state protection. The tree yields a dense timber resembling that of the common box (Tortorelli, *Maderas y Bosques Argentinos*, p. 571).

M. luma was placed by Niedenzu in the genus *Myrceugenia*, which is distinguished from *Myrtus* primarily by the seeds having a cartilaginous testa (hard and bony in *Myrtus*) and an embryo with large, foliaceous cotyledons appressed one to the other and much rumpled and folded (in *Myrtus sens. strict.* the cotyledons are small). But *M. luma* does not agree well with the definition of *Myrceugenia*, and, if separated from *Myrtus*, should probably be placed in the genus *Luma*, in which its name would be *Luma apiculata* (DC.) Burret. The differences between *Luma* and *Myrceugenia* are slight, but if the two were to be united it would be under the name *Luma*, which has priority.

M. NUMMULARIA Poir.   [PLATE 106

Myrteola nummularia (Poir.) Berg

An evergreen shrub, usually prostrate and growing into a thick mat only a few inches above the ground; young shoots wiry, glabrous, reddish. Leaves opposite, oval, rounded at both ends, shortly stalked; usually $\frac{1}{8}$ to $\frac{1}{4}$ in. long, half to two-thirds as wide; bright dark green, glabrous on both sides, margins decurved. Flowers white, $\frac{1}{4}$ to $\frac{1}{3}$ in. wide, produced singly from the terminal leaf-axils, each on a very short stout stalk bearing a pair of more or less leafy bracteoles close to the calyx-tube. Calyx four-lobed; corolla of four rounded petals; stamens usually eight or twelve; fruit an oblong pink berry ¼ in. long, crowned with the persisting calyx-lobes.

Native of the southern parts of S. America, especially in the Straits of Magellan and the Falkland Islands. It has long been known, having been described and named in 1796; it was collected originally by Commerson. Charles Darwin gathered it on Tierra del Fuego in 1833 during the voyage of the *Beagle*, and many others have found it since then, but it seems to have been comparatively recently introduced. It is well suited for carpeting moist shelves and stones in the rock garden. It is quite hardy south of London. It flowers during November and December in S. America, equivalent to our May and June. The whole plant is rather suggestive of *Gaultheria trichophylla*.

M. nummularia is one of the six species on which Berg founded the genus *Myrteola* in 1856. The only character by which this group differs significantly from *Myrtus* is that the ovary is imperfectly chambered, the partitions not meeting throughout their length. In face of the close agreement in other characters especially the seed and embryo, this difference is not sufficient to warrant generic status. At the most these species would form a section of *Myrtus*, as was recognised long ago by the famous American botanist Prof. Asa Gray, who referred them to his section *Leandria*.

M. OBCORDATA (Raoul) Hook. f.

Eugenia obcordata Raoul; *Lophomyrtus obcordata* (Raoul) Burret

An evergreen shrub 10 to 15 ft high of dense, very twiggy habit; young shoots downy. Leaves opposite, obcordate (i.e., inversely heart-shaped), conspicuously notched at the apex, tapered to the short downy stalk; otherwise glabrous; usually ⅕ to ½ in. long, ¼ to ⅜ in. wide; dark green above, pale and dotted with oil-glands beneath. Flowers ¼ in. wide, dull white, solitary, produced from the axils of the leaves on a slender downy stalk ⅓ to ½ in. long. Calyx four-lobed, the lobes ovate, the tube downy; petals four, round, ciliate; stamens very numerous and the chief attraction of the flower. Fruit a dark red or violet subglobose berry, ¼ in. wide.

Native of New Zealand; introduced long ago. This pleasing shrub just misses being hardy at Kew, but survives the winters safely thirty or forty miles south of London. In the gardens of the south-west it is quite at home. It rarely blossoms with freedom, and if it did the flowers would not add much to the attractiveness of the plant. This is mainly to be found in its neat habit, slender branching, and in the plenitude of its small, unusually shaped leaves.

M. UGNI Mol.   MURTILLO, UÑI

Ugni molinae Turcz.; *Eugenia ugni* (Mol.) Hook. f.

A shrub usually under 5–6 ft high; young stems hairy. Leaves glabrous, mostly ovate or oblong-ovate, ¾ to 1 in. long, acute and apiculate at the apex, darkish green above, paler beneath. Flowers fragrant, solitary, borne in May on stalks up to 1 in. long from the leaf-axils of the young shoots. Sepals linear, pointed, reflexed. Corolla cup-shaped, with five rose-tinted, rounded, concave petals. Stamens included. Fruits globular, dark reddish brown when ripe, with a mealy flesh.

Native of the forest region of Chile, where it grows in woodland and scrub; introduced by William Lobb in 1844. It is quite hardy in the Atlantic zone, where it is sometimes used for dwarf hedges or grown for its delicious fruits, which taste of wild strawberries. Indeed, it is hardy in the open at least as far east as Furzey in the New Forest and should survive most winters south of London with the protection of a wall. It is easily propagated by cuttings, and flowers and fruits when quite young. There is a white variegated form in commerce.

This is the species on which the Russian botanist Turczaninow founded the genus *Ugni*, which he characterised by the sepals being reflexed in bud, the stamens with strap-shaped filaments which are continuous with the connective, and the embryo like that of *Eugenia*. However, as Asa Gray pointed out, there is some mistake about the last character, for the embryo is in fact that of *Myrtus*, and to that genus he referred *Ugni* as a section. Other characters of the group are the small leathery leaves, the flowers solitary in the leaf-axils on well-developed pedicels, and the two linear bracteoles close to the flower being persistent in fruit.

INDEX

As the general arrangement of this work is alphabetical it has not been considered necessary to index names which appear in their proper sequence. The following is an index of 'popular' or English names; of the more important synonyms which, in accordance with the usual practice, are given in italics; and of a number of trees and shrubs which are not described in their alphabetical order but under related plants.

The attention of the reader is called to the glossary of botanical terms on p. 112, and to the glossary of nursery terms on p. 54 of Vol. I of this edition. The plates are listed on pp. xiii–xvi; the line drawings on pp. ix–x.

Apple. See Malus domestica and M.
  pumila
  Argyle, 130
  'Arthur Turner', 696
  Crab, 696
  Paradise, French and Dutch, 705
  'Upton Pyne', 696
Ash
  Alpine, 131
  Arizona, 231
  Black, 221
  Blue, 226
  Common, 215
  Green, 224
  Himalayan Manna, 218
  Manchurian, 220
  Manna, 222
  Narrow-leaved, 210
  One-leaved, 216
  Oregon, 220
  Pumpkin, 230
  Red, 224
  Utah, 211
  White, 209

Beech
  American, 175
  Common, 177
  Fern-leaved, 178
  Japanese, 174
  Purple, 182
  Southern. See Nothofagus, Vol. III
Broad-leaved Kindling Bark, 130
Broom
  Genoa, 274
  Hedgehog, 112
  Nish, 276
  See also Cytisus, Vol. I

Crab
  Bechtel, 701
  Manchurian, 694
  Rosybloom Group, 703
  Siberian, 693
  Wild, 710
Crowberry
  South American, 88

Daboecia
  polifolia, 1
Daphne
  arbuscula, 19
  buxifolia 17
  cannabina, 8
  collina
    var. *neapolitana, 15*
  dauphinii, 13
  fortuni, 12
  glandulosa, 17
  glomerata, 19
  gnidium, 18
  japonica, 16, 17
  jasminea, 18, 17
  julia, 11
  kamtschatica, 20
  kiusiana, 17
  kosaninii, 18
  laureola
    var. *purpurea, 13*
  longilobata, 7
  × mantensiana, 21
  mazelii, 17
  mezereum
    var. *atropurpurea, 13*
    cv. 'Bowles's White', 15
    cv. 'Paul's White', 15
  papyracea, 8

769